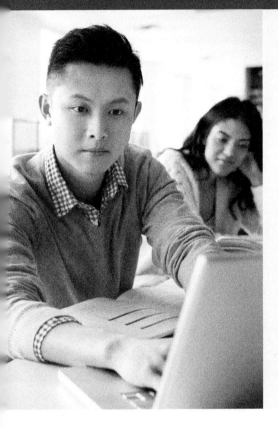

WileyPLUS For Instructors

Save time managing your course

The easy-to-use, intuitive interface saves you time getting started, managing day-to-day class activities, and helping individual students stay on track.

Instructor App
You can modify due dates, monitor assignment submissions, change grades, and communicate with your students all from your phone.

Calendar

SpeedGrader

Gradebook and Analytics

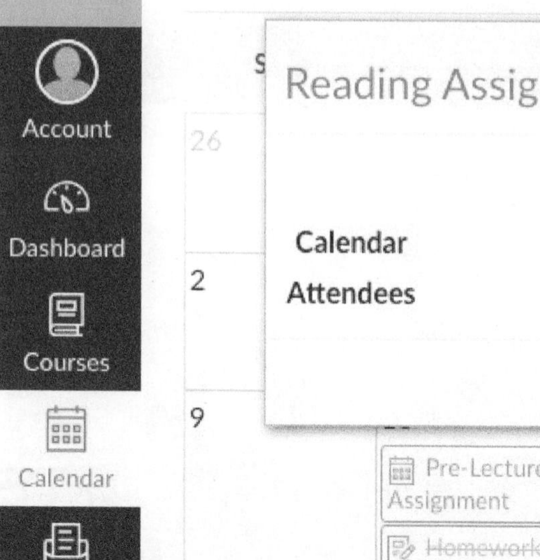

The next generation of WileyPLUS is built on the most modern technology stack. This means that all content, assessments, and platform functionality are hosted by Amazon Web Services, the fastest internet on the planet. With the cloud, there is less reason for downtime or platform maintenance.

It's integrated.

While the next generation of WileyPLUS can be used on its own, Canvas users will have a seamless LMS experience by simply importing their natively built course from Canvas Commons or through a zip file. Blackboard, D2L, and Moodle users will also be able to integrate their WileyPLUS Next Gen courses soon.

It's mobile.

For iOS and Android users, the student, instructor, and eTextbook apps make teaching, learning, and grading possible from anywhere. The eTextbook, videos, animation, and questions are responsive so students can study from any device.

It's accessible.

You can assign and create content without fear of students falling through the cracks. All content and questions have gone through an accessibility audit—and anything that doesn't meet standards is flagged so that you're in control.

Contemporary Business

18th Edition

DAVID L. KURTZ
University of Arkansas

SUSAN BERSTON
City College of San Francisco

WILEY

The 18th edition of *Contemporary Business* is dedicated to my wife, Diane. She is the best thing that ever happened to me.

—Dave Kurtz

To my personal Board of Directors: my son Samuel, as you enter your senior year of college, please know that you are, and will always be, my dream come true, my son, my moon, and my stars; and to my mom and dad, I love you both so much—thanks for never letting me quit. And last, to Sonja.

—Susan Berston

SENIOR VICE PRESIDENT, EDUCATION	Tim Stookesbury
VICE PRESIDENT & DIRECTOR	Michael McDonald
EDITOR	Alden Farrar
PRODUCT DESIGNER	Wendy Ashenberg
SENIOR CONTENT MANAGER	Dorothy Sinclair
PRODUCTION EDITOR	Rachel Conrad
MARKETING MANAGER	Anita Osborne
SENIOR DESIGNER	Wendy Lai
PHOTO RESEARCHER	Jerry Marshall
COVER IMAGE	© Lesik Vitaliy/Shutterstock; © Zlatko Guzmic/Shutterstock

This book was set in Source Sans Pro-Regular 9.5/12.5 by Aptara, Inc. India and printed and bound by Quad/Graphics. The cover was printed by Quad/Graphics.

This book is printed on acid-free paper.

Founded in 1807, John Wiley & Sons, Inc. has been a valued source of knowledge and understanding for more than 200 years, helping people around the world meet their needs and fulfill their aspirations. Our company is built on a foundation of principles that include responsibility to the communities we serve and where we live and work. In 2008, we launched a Corporate Citizenship Initiative, a global effort to address the environmental, social, economic, and ethical challenges we face in our business. Among the issues we are addressing are carbon impact, paper specifications and procurement, ethical conduct within our business and among our vendors, and community and charitable support. For more information, please visit our website: www.wiley.com/go/citizenship.

ISBN-13 978-1-119-49811-7 (Epub)

The inside back cover will contain printing identification and country of origin if omitted from this page. In addition, if the ISBN on the back cover differs from the ISBN on this page, the one on the back cover is correct.

Printed in the United States of America

V10008371_022619

About the Authors

During **DAVE KURTZ'S** high school days, no one in Salisbury, Maryland, would have mistaken him for a scholar. In fact, he was a mediocre student, so bad that his father steered him toward higher education by finding him a succession of back-breaking summer jobs. Thankfully, most of them have been erased from his memory, but a few linger, including picking peaches, loading watermelons on trucks headed for market, and working as a pipefitter's helper. Unfortunately, these jobs had zero impact on his academic standing. Worse yet for Dave's ego, he was no better than average as a high school athlete in football and track.

But four years at Davis & Elkins College in Elkins, West Virginia, turned him around. Excellent instructors helped get Dave on sound academic footing. His grade-point average soared—enough to get him accepted by the graduate business school at the University of Arkansas, where he met Gene Boone. Gene and Dave became longtime co-authors; together they produced more than 50 books. In addition to writing, Dave and Gene were involved in various entrepreneurial ventures.

This decades-long partnership ended with Gene's death in 2005, but *Contemporary Business* will always be the result of the diligent efforts of Boone and Kurtz.

During **SUSAN BERSTON'S** college years as a campus tour guide at the University of California, Berkeley, despite enduring hundreds of crammed elevator rides with visitors eager to reach the Campanile's observation deck 200 feet above, the excitement of being immersed in an academic environment never waned.

After completing an MBA at the University of San Francisco, Susan worked in the corporate banking division of a Japanese bank. Soon bit by the sales bug, she joined the sales force of printer R.R. Donnelley & Sons Company, which is where she realized her passion for satisfying customers, outsmarting competitors, providing creative solutions, and building relationships.

She returned to academia and campus life to eventually become a full-time professor at City College of San Francisco in 2005, where she teaches courses in introduction to business, management, and entrepreneurship—and where her father, also a textbook author, taught business for over five decades. Here Susan feels incredibly lucky mentoring her students, whether as a faculty advisor to various student-led clubs, or as a member of the Academic Senate Executive Council and Board of Directors of the bookstore. For Susan, bringing ideas to life inside and outside of the classroom and creating a personalized and collaborative student experience with the Next Generation of WileyPLUS is simply the icing on the cake.

Proud to continue the legacy of two of the industry's most prolific textbook authors, David L. Kurtz and the late Louis (Gene) Boone, Susan welcomes the opportunity to hear from you with questions, comments, or feedback about the 18th edition of *Contemporary Business* at sberston@ccsf.edu.

Preface

With the advent of artificial intelligence, machine learning, augmented and virtual reality, voice-controlled virtual assistants, Internet of Things, driverless cars, mobile commerce, diversity, inclusion, pay parity, tariff wars, and the sharing economy, businesses need to brace themselves for the biggest transformation—referred to as the "Fourth Industrial Revolution"—seen in the last five decades. Today, digital reality, robotics, cognitive, and block chain are redefining information technology, business, and society at large—and revolutionary growth is being created across businesses and industries. As companies reach market values of a trillion dollars, the impact of the FAANG companies (Facebook, Amazon, Apple, Netflix, and Google) on business, society, and the stock market remains intriguing, to say the least.

The result is exciting new opportunities and growth-oriented career prospects for business students. Now more than ever, business moves at an unimaginable pace. With this edition of *Contemporary Business*, we hope to take you on a journey filled with prospects for your own exciting growth and change.

The first edition of *Contemporary Business*, published in 1976, states, "Contemporary Business is a student's textbook. It is designed to enlighten and enchant the reader as he or she is introduced to the fascinating world of business." We remain committed to enlightening the reader; thus the 18th edition of *Contemporary Business* contains cutting-edge and timely business topics. You'll find this newly revised edition provides context for what today's business environment holds in store for today's students.

A wide variety of global issues, ideas, industries, technologies, and career insights are presented in a straightforward, application-based format. The goal of *Contemporary Business* is to improve a student's ability to evaluate and provide solutions to today's global business challenges and ultimately to thrive in today's fast-paced business environment.

Pedagogical Features

The 18th edition is filled with new pedagogy in each chapter, along with updates and revisions to key features:

- Each chapter begins with **Learning Objectives** that provide students with an overview of the major concepts covered in the chapter. Key terms are highlighted and defined in chapter margins.
- **Changemaker**, the opening vignette for each chapter, highlights business leaders within a variety of industries. Each opener lays the groundwork for discussing chapter topics, with the goal of drawing the student's attention to a professional within a company or organization while highlighting an industry ripe with career opportunities for business majors. Examples include Sundar Pichai of Google; Brian Chesky of Airbnb; Apple's Angela Ahrendts; Nike CEO, Mark Parker; Elon Musk of Tesla and SpaceX; Reshma Saujani of Girls Who Code; and Deloitte CEO, Cathy Engelbert.
- The **Business Model** feature provides students with success stories that focus on traditional and start-up companies, business leaders, and entrepreneurs. Specific topics include digital technologies defining the automobile industry; the use of advertising on NBA jerseys; how startup Casper Mattress keeps the industry awake; the New York Stock Exchange's first female president; and Harley Davidson's efforts to target a younger generation.
- The **Clean & Green Business** feature highlights new and insightful ways companies are conducting business in a sustainable and socially responsible manner in an effort to protect the environment. Specific topics include Cheerio's "No GMO" policy, transforming trash into fashion, and how Starbucks uses crowdsourcing for energy-saving ideas.
- The **Business Technology** feature highlights the intersection between business and technology for companies across many industries. Topics include Nordstrom's technology overhaul, recruiting using cognitive and robotic technology, John Deere's use of Artificial Intelligence to increase yield and kill weeds, how Instagram stories drive sales for brands, and L'Oreal's virtual cosmetic counter.
- **Judgment Call** provides various business scenarios and ethical dilemmas where students are asked to decide what is appropriate. Examples include big pharma persuading the prescribers, soaring drug prices despite falling demand, the rise of activist investors, and the ethics of surge pricing for car sharing services. Each Judgment Call feature includes questions for individual or group discussion.
- The **Job Description** feature describes the responsibilities, requirements (including soft skills), and outlook for certain careers for business majors. Examples include fundraiser/development director, economic analyst, corporate communication specialist, marketing research analyst, accountant and auditor business operations associate, and investment banker.
- **End-of-Chapter Cases** enhance learning and fine-tune decision-making skills. Companies and topics discussed include Shinola, Yelp, SoFi (Social Finance), the Heinz–Kraft merger, and tax implications for the Internet of Things.
- To help understand introductory business concepts, **Video Cases** in 17 of the chapters highlight a range of companies and industries. Examples include Necco, Zipcar, Timberland, and TripAdvisor.

Also New to the 18th Edition

This edition of *Contemporary Business* has been thoroughly revised to reflect the major issues and trends influencing business today. In recent years, nothing has had a greater impact on business than technology, and in some shape or form every business is a technology business. Throughout the textbook, new material, updates, and overviews of new, global business and technology trends have been added. Some of these include:

- Disruptive technologies and trends
- Career readiness, soft skills, and career opportunities in various industries and sectors
- Integration of machines and AI in the workplace
- Updated U.S. merchandise Exports and imports
- Top global franchise companies
- Best industries for starting a small business
- Venture capital investment trends by industry
- Well-known mergers and acquisitions
- A comparison between entrepreneurship and starting a business or staying in school
- The impact of cognitive and robotic technology on human resources (recruitment and selection/employee evaluation)
- Unique and creative employee perks
- The impact of the Me Too movement in the workplace
- An explanation of digital marketing and analytics to quantify and analyze customer behavior through site visits and social media platforms, app downloads, mobile devices, and Twitter tweets
- Analysis of a stock market quote
- Fintech (financial technology) categories and companies

Teaching and Learning Program

With decades of experience teaching introduction to business courses, and an overwhelming amount of student feedback, the authors have updated each chapter of the 18th edition to include relevant, intriguing, and up-to-date examples designed to provide a greater understanding of the content presented. Diverse business sectors are highlighted throughout the chapters, including nonprofits, music, consumer products, hospitality, electronics, health and fitness, e-commerce, apparel, retail, manufacturing, financial services, and automobiles.

Topics, examples, and exercises have been carefully chosen to reflect the diverse range of interests and experiences of students who may be studying in the United States or abroad in a variety of educational settings. Along with those students who may be interested in simply learning more about what "business" really entails, *Contemporary Business* is written to appeal to students interested in or contemplating business as a major.

Designed to engage students and to enliven traditional and online classroom discussion and debate, the 18th edition has been written in a friendly and conversational manner. To further enhance the learning process with WileyPLUS Learning Space, instructors and students receive 24/7 access to adaptive learning and a variety of resources proven to promote positive learning outcomes.

The interactive **Learning Styles Survey**, an especially useful tool, helps students identify how they learn best and provides useful study tips for each type of learner. Resources throughout the learning program have been mapped for learning styles as well.

For Instructors A robust set of resources helps instructors easily navigate a traditional or online classroom learning environment. Designed to provide a "turnkey" solution for instructors working within diverse learning environments, materials engage students who possess different learning styles, and they are designed to aid in comprehension, critical thinking, and application of text concepts. All major teaching materials are contained within the Next Generation of WileyPLUS and include the Instructor's Manual, PowerPoint Presentations, a comprehensive Test Bank, Weekly Updates, and the Wiley Business Video Series. Most resources also can be found on the book's companion site at www.wiley.com/college/boone.

Additional Instructor Resources available with the Next Generation of WileyPLUS *WileyPLUS* provides students with a 24/7 customizable online platform with multiple resources that reinforces goals both inside and outside the classroom. Students have instant access to adaptive learning and feedback on their individual progress, while instructors can quickly analyze class results to assess areas of weakness in which students might need further assistance. The following resources are included and can be used for classroom presentations.

Ready-to-go teaching materials and assessments to help instructors maximize their time:

- Instructor's Manual with teaching suggestions, lecture starters, ideas for classroom exercises, discussions, and questions by chapter.
- Lecture PowerPoint presentations
- Test bank
- Gradebook through *WileyPLUS*
- Wiley *Contemporary Business* Weekly Updates

Additional Student Resources available within the Next Generation of WileyPLUS

- Digital version of the complete textbook
- Interactive flash cards

- Practice exams
- Career-focused student case videos
- Interactive case studies
- Business hot topics (ethics, project management, sustainability, business plan, financial crisis)
- End-of-chapter videos
- Learning styles survey
- Crossword puzzles
- Study guide
- PowerPoint presentations
- Virtual Career Center, including career coaching videos, Career*Shift*, InsideTrack, and ePortfolio assistance

Acknowledgments

Contemporary Business has long benefited from the instructors who have offered their time as reviewers. A special thank you to Amit Shah and Brahm Canzer for their contributions to the ancillaries.

To my many former students who continue to teach and inspire me with their own career, marriage, and family pursuits—William Do, Howard Lee, Marie Seredkina, Peter Dang, Nara Babakhanyan, Jena Mayer, Ian Wu, Luis Reyes, Kiryl Ignatieff, Lena Carew, Joao Possagnoli, Rick Berwick, Vincent Pun, Wes Brown, Anastasia Bogdanova, David Nguyen, Steven Nguyen, Eugene Ma, Hester Loo, Khaled Ramzi, Ethan Dixon, Serena Collins, Alberto Wu, Matthew Ho, Benj Marston, Aaron Estomo, Patrick Ponikvar, Jeff Z. Wu, Katya Lopez, Richard Berwick, Jesse Clayburgh, Kelly Hom, Lori Henderson, and Kirsten Foster.

Contemporary Business has clearly evolved since the first edition was published in 1976—the same year Steve Jobs and Steve Wozniak created a company called Apple, to sell small, easy-to-use computers. The 18th edition would not have been possible without the dedicated team of editorial, production, and marketing professionals from John Wiley and Sons. Many thanks to Alden Farrar, Assistant Editor, who possesses an unparalleled calm; Wendy Ashenberg, Digital Product Designer, whose boundless energy provides fun, insight, and learning; Anita Osborne, marketer extraordinaire who can execute on a dime; Lise Johnson and Jennifer Manias, my previous rock-solid editors and partners in crime who remain steadfastly loyal, and always there for me 24/7 to provide input, intelligence, and ideas; Mike McDonald, Vice President and Director; Rachel Conrad, Senior Production Editor; Jon Boylan, Creative Director; Wendy Lai, Senior Designer; Jerry Marshall, Photo Editor; and Mickey Mankus, Project Manager at Aptara.

The publishing, customer success, learning management, and marketing representatives of John Wiley and Sons deserve our utmost respect and gratitude for their tireless efforts when it comes to traversing the country to differentiate *Contemporary Business* with professors in a competitive marketplace. A debt of gratitude goes out to the the following rock stars who pound the pavement on college campuses throughout this country: Darchelle Leggett, Keli Wherritt, Emily Fox Martin, Margaret Rivera, Ashley Yazbec, Dayna Leaman, Mary Kay Yearin, Jason Whithead, Syd Nicholson, Brenda Brown, Nanette Scholz, Karen Tinley, Sue Fackert, Kathryn Warren (Moreno), Frank Yelenic, Catharine Murray, Taylor Wilkins, Josh Gier, John Swift, Alan Halfen, Claire Filar, Salvatore Spatarella, Will Earman, Jason Dodge, Amanda Wainer, Alison Stanley, Karolina Zarychta, Christine Moore, Nicole Dingley, and Hunter Stark.

Personal Appreciation from Susan Berston: To Dave Kurtz—from the first time I met you, Diane, and the canine kids—Lucy, Molly, and Daisy—I knew right away that I would be humbled and honored to have the opportunity to continue the lasting legacy created by you and Gene. Thank you.

Brief Contents

Contents

4 Competing in World Markets 84

5 Forms of Business Ownership and Organization 114

6 Starting Your Own Business: The Entrepreneurship Alternative 148

9 Top Performance through Empowerment, Teamwork, and Communication 227

10 Production and Operations Management 252

11 Customer-Driven Marketing 279

12 Product and Distribution Strategies 309

13 Promotion and Pricing Strategies 341

Contemporary Business

CHAPTER **1**

The Changing Face of Business

LEARNING OBJECTIVES

1. Define *business*.
2. Identify and describe the factors of production.
3. Describe the private enterprise system.
4. Identify the seven eras in the history of business.
5. Explain current workforce trends in business.
6. Identify the skills and attributes needed for today's manager.
7. Outline the characteristics that make a company admired.

Changemaker

Chesnot/Getty Images

Sundar Pichai, Chief Executive Officer

Company: Google

Industry: Technology/Internet Information Providers

Website(s): www.google.com and https://abc.xyz

Who is Sundar Pichai, and how did he rise through the Google ranks so quickly? Before arriving at Google in 2004, Pichai, who has a formal education in engineering and business, worked in semiconductor manufacturing and management consulting. At Google, he was charged with creating and managing software products, including Gmail, Google Chrome, the Chrome operating system, and cloud file-storage service Google Drive. Pichai oversees tens of thousands of employees and billions in revenue. Over the course of a decade and before being appointed CEO, as Senior Vice President of Products, Pichai oversaw Google's increasingly competitive business offerings and software products such as search, advertising, Android, and YouTube.

Sundar Pichai was named Chief Executive Officer of Google when co-founders Larry Page and Sergey Brin made the decision to dedicate more time to what is referred to inside Google as "moonshot projects," which range from robots that can work alongside humans, smarter homes, self-driving cars, healthcare and disease prevention research, cyber-attack prevention, and solutions to address global issues. Alphabet, Inc., Google's parent company, is led by Larry Page, former Google co-founder and CEO. Alphabet is a collection of companies that separates Google's core businesses of search, maps, and advertising from its other projects. However, Google still generates the majority of Alphabet's revenues and profits.

Pichai, who grew up in Chennai, India, is described as humble, smart, and very low key. With his unassuming management style, he is known for his ability to build strong relationships, which has earned him tremendous respect as a leader. Pichai, in his late 40s, is uniquely positioned to take the lead in furthering product development. Amid strong competition, he has a challenging role to keep up the company's rate of growth. With a vote of confidence from Google's co-founders, Pichai continues to master multi-tasking skills by proving himself well beyond qualified to manage a technology giant that not only dominates search, but also has been forced to manage regulators, tech critics, political issues, and debates over gender inequality.[1]

Overview

Google's CEO, Sundar Pichai leads a company that has gone from clever startup to global technology powerhouse. Innovative companies like Google, and now Alphabet, contribute greatly to the nation's economy. A growing economy, one with increased production of goods and services over time, yields income for its business owners, their employees, and stockholders. A country depends on the wealth its businesses generate, from large enterprises such as the Walt Disney Company to tiny online start-ups, and from respected companies such as jeans maker Levi Strauss & Company to powerhouses such as Google. What all these companies and many others share is a creative approach to meeting society's needs and wants.

Large and small businesses solve our transportation problems by creating innovative ride-sharing options, automobiles, tires, gasoline, and airline tickets. They bring food to our tables by growing, harvesting, processing, packaging, and shipping everything from spring water to cake mix and frozen shrimp. Restaurants buy, prepare, and serve food, and some even provide delivery through mobile ordering or an online app. Construction companies build our schools, homes, and hospitals, while real estate companies bring property buyers and sellers together. Clothing manufacturers design, create, import, and deliver our jeans, sports shoes, work uniforms, and party wear. Entertainment for our leisure hours comes from hundreds of companies that create, produce, and distribute films, television shows, video games, books, and music downloads.

To succeed, companies must first determine what their customers want so that they can supply it quickly and efficiently. That means they often adapt to changes in consumer tastes, such as the growing preference for organic and locally grown produce. But firms can also *lead* in advancing technology and other changes. They have the resources, the know-how, and the financial incentive to bring about new innovations as well as the competition that inevitably follows, as in the case of digital personal assistants by companies such as Amazon and Google.

You'll see throughout this book that businesses require physical inputs such as auto parts, chemicals, sugar, thread, and electricity, as well as the accumulated knowledge and experience of their managers and employees. Yet they also rely heavily on their own ability to adapt to global changes in today's business environment. Flexibility and innovation are key to long-term success—and to growth.

In short, business is at the forefront of our economy—and *Contemporary Business* is right there with it. This book explores the strategies that allow companies to grow and compete in today's interactive and hyper-competitive marketplace, along with the skills that you will need to turn ideas into action for your own success in business. This chapter sets the stage for the entire text by defining business and its role in society. The chapter's discussion illustrates the skills required for success in today's business environment and how the private enterprise system encourages competition and innovation.

1 What Is Business?

Many think of the word *business* as making money or the activity of buying and selling goods and services. Do you think of big corporations like ExxonMobil or The Coca-Cola Company? Or does the local deli or dry cleaner pop into your mind? Maybe you recall your first summer job. *Business* is a broad, all-inclusive term that can be applied to many kinds of enterprises. Businesses provide employment opportunities, as well as the products and services that people enjoy.

business all profit-seeking activities and enterprises that provide goods and services necessary to an economic system.

Business consists of all profit-seeking activities and enterprises that provide goods and services necessary to an economic system. Some businesses produce tangible goods, such as automobiles, breakfast cereals, and smart phones; others provide services such as insurance, hair styling, and entertainment ranging from Disney theme parks and NFL games to concerts.

Business drives the economic pulse of a nation. It provides the means through which its citizens' standard of living improves. At the heart of every business endeavor is an exchange between a buyer and a seller. An example of this exchange is shown in the accompanying photo. A buyer recognizes a need for a good or service and trades money with a seller to obtain that product. The seller participates in the process in hopes of gaining profits. To make a profit, every business requires not only enough customers to whom its products and services can be sold on a consistent basis, but also some form of investment. Businesses can be privately owned, not-for-profit, or state-owned.

A business survives through the exchange between a buyer and a seller.

Courtesy of Samuel Berston

Profits represent rewards earned by businesspeople who take the risks involved in blending people, technology, and information to create and market want-satisfying goods and services. In contrast, accountants think of profits as a positive gain remaining for a business after all costs and expenses have been deducted from total sales. More generally, however, profits serve as incentives for people to start companies, grow them, and provide consistently high-quality competitive goods and services.

The quest for profits is a central focus of business because without profits, a company could not survive. But businesspeople also recognize their social and ethical responsibilities. To succeed in the long run, companies must deal responsibly with employees, customers, suppliers, investors, creditors, competitors, government, and the general public.

profits rewards earned by businesspeople who take the risks involved in blending people, technology, and information to create and market want-satisfying goods and services.

Not-for-Profit Organizations

What do Purdue University's athletic department, the U.S. Postal Service, the American Heart Association, and your local library have in common? They all are classified as **not-for-profit organizations**, businesslike establishments that have primary objectives other than returning profits to their owners. A tax law provision granted to not-for-profits by the Internal Revenue Service is called section 501(c)(3). These organizations play important roles in society by placing humanitarian and environmental needs, for example, above profits, although it is important to understand that these organizations need to raise money so that they can operate and achieve their social goals. Not-for-profit organizations, also called nonprofits, operate in both the private and public sectors. Private-sector not-for-profits include museums, libraries, trade associations, and charitable and religious organizations. Government agencies, political parties, and labor unions, all of which are part of the public sector, are also classified as not-for-profit organizations.

not-for-profit organizations businesslike establishments that have primary objectives other than returning profits to their owners.

Not-for-profit organizations are a substantial part of the U.S. economy, contributing more than $900 billion in a recent year. Currently, more than 1.5 million nonprofit organizations are registered with the Internal Revenue Service in the United States, in categories ranging from arts and culture to science and technology.[2] These organizations use labor and capital in much the same way that for-profit companies do, and employ over 14 million people—more people than the federal government and all 50 state governments combined.[3] In addition, millions of volunteers work for them in unpaid positions. Not-for-profits secure funding from private sources, including individual (tax deductible) donations, and from government sources. They are commonly exempt from federal, state, and local taxes.

Although they focus on goals other than generating profits, managers of not-for-profit organizations face many of the same challenges as executives of profit-seeking businesses. Without funding, they cannot conduct research, hire top talent, market, and promote their cause, or provide services. St. Jude Children's Research Hospital's pediatric treatment and research facility in Memphis treats nearly 7,500 children a year for catastrophic diseases, mainly cancer, immune system problems, and infectious and genetic disorders. Patients come from all 50 states

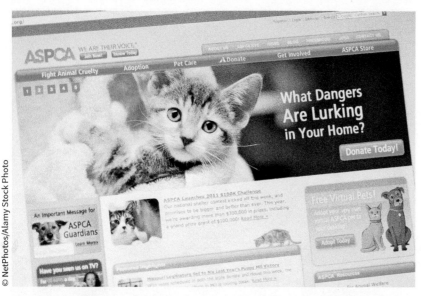

The ASPCA, headquartered in New York City, was the first humane society in North America and 150 years later it is one of the largest privately funded 501(c)(3) not-for-profit corporations in the world.

and all over the world and are accepted without regard to the family's ability to pay. To provide top-quality care and to support its research in gene therapy, chemotherapy, bone marrow transplantation, and the psychological effects of illness, among many other critical areas, St. Jude relies on contributions, with some assistance from federal grants.[4]

The American Society for the Prevention of Cruelty to Animals (ASPCA) was the first humane society in North America. It is a nonprofit national animal welfare organization with the belief that animals are entitled to kind and respectful treatment at the hands of humans and must be protected under the law (see photo).[5]

To subsidize donations and grants, many not-for-profits, such as art museums and national parks, sell merchandise. For example, the Metropolitan Museum of Art in New York sells jewelry, books, calendars, note cards, and posters through both an online store and an on-site bricks-and-mortar gift shop. Founded in 1912, The Girl Scouts of the USA are known for their mouth-watering cookies. The organization has created a cookie empire valued at close to $800 million through sales by local scout troops.[6] Handling merchandising programs like these, as well as launching other fund-raising campaigns, requires managers of not-for-profit organizations to possess effective business skills and experience. Consequently, many of the concepts discussed in this book (such as management, marketing, and finance) apply to not-for-profit organizations as well as to profit-oriented firms.

Assessment Check

1. What activity lies at the center of every business endeavor?
2. What is the primary objective of a not-for-profit organization?

2 Factors of Production

factors of production four basic inputs: land, labor, capital, and entrepreneurship.

An economic system requires certain inputs used in the production of goods and services to make a profit. Economists use the term **factors of production** to refer to the four basic inputs: land, labor, capital, and entrepreneurship. **Table 1.1** identifies each of these inputs and the type of payment or income received by companies and individuals who supply the factor of production.

TABLE 1.1 Factors of Production and Their Factor Payments

Factor of Production	Corresponding Factor Payment
Land	Rent
Labor	Wages
Capital	Interest
Entrepreneurship	Profit

Land, used in the production of a good, includes all production inputs or natural resources that are useful in their natural states such as oil, gas, minerals, and timber. The demand for timber has increased as a result of an improved economy and increased home-building, along with hurricane, tornado, fire, flood, and other recent damages in the United States.[7]

land is used in the production of a good, and includes all production inputs or natural resources that are useful in their natural states such as oil, gas, minerals, and timber.

Labor represents another critical input in every economic system. Labor includes anyone who works, from the chief executive officer (CEO) of a huge corporation to a self-employed writer or editor. This category encompasses both the physical labor and the intellectual inputs contributed by workers. Companies rely on their employees as a valued source of ideas and innovation, as well as physical effort. Some companies solicit employee ideas through online employee feedback or in staff meetings. Others encourage creative thinking during company-sponsored off-site meetings like hiking or rafting trips—or during social gatherings. Effective, well-trained labor provides a significant competitive edge, and companies must look at planning for their workforce in much the same way they do financial or information technology investments.

labor includes anyone who works, including both the physical labor and the intellectual inputs contributed by workers.

Hiring and keeping the right people matters, as we will see later in the case at the end of this chapter. Employees at food and candy maker Mars, Inc. feel they have a great place to work, partly because of the opportunities for advancement and generous pay the company provides.[8]

Capital, another key resource, includes technology, tools, information, and physical facilities. *Technology* is a broad term that refers to such machinery and equipment as computers and software, telecommunications, and inventions designed to improve production. Information, frequently improved by technological innovations, is another critical factor because both managers and operating employees require accurate, timely information for effective performance of their assigned tasks. Technology plays an important role in the success of many businesses. Bill Gates is quoted as saying, "Information technology and business are becoming inextricably interwoven. I don't think anyone can talk meaningfully about one without talking about the other." Technology has led to a transformation when it comes to cars and driving. Waymo, Google's fully self-driving car project, which represents a new way forward in mobility, has recently started driving on public roads without anyone in the driver's seat.[9]

capital includes technology, tools, information, and physical facilities.

Technology often helps a company improve its own products. Netflix, once famous for its subscription-based DVD-by-mail service, offers on-demand Internet streaming media and original content streaming. Netflix has exclusive rights to streaming movies and original TV series, like "Stranger Things."[10]

Retail giant Walmart was recently granted a patent for a system in which drones would shuttle products between different departments inside its stores. The idea is to free customers not only from waiting for a Walmart associate to return with an item from a far-away storeroom, but also from having to walk across its super-sized stores to find what they want.[11]

To remain competitive, a company needs to continually acquire, maintain, and upgrade its capital, which requires funding. A company's funds may come from owner-investments, profits reinvested back into the business, or loans extended by others. Money then goes to work building factories; purchasing raw materials and component parts; and hiring, training, and compensating employees. People and companies that supply capital receive factor payments in the form of interest.

Entrepreneurship is the willingness to take risks to create and operate a business. An entrepreneur is someone with an idea who sees a potentially profitable opportunity and then devises a plan to achieve success in the marketplace. Whitney Wolfe hopes to empower women by changing the antiquated rules of online dating. Her location-based social and dating app, Bumble, referred to by some as "The Feminist Tinder," requires that women make the first move to initiate a conversation.[12]

entrepreneurship willingness to take risks to create and operate a business.

U.S. businesses operate within an economic system called the *private enterprise system*. The next section looks at the private enterprise system, including competition, private property, and the entrepreneurship alternative.

Assessment Check

1. Identify the four basic inputs to an economic system.
2. List four types of capital.

3 The Private Enterprise System

No business operates in a vacuum. All operate within a larger economic system whereby production, resource allocation, and distribution of goods and services are determined. Economic systems must determine what to produce, how to produce and in what quantities, and who receives the output of production. Some economic systems, such as communism, feature strict controls on business ownership, profits, and resources to accomplish government goals.

private enterprise system economic system that rewards companies for their ability to identify and serve the needs and demands of customers.

In the United States, businesses function within the **private enterprise system**, a for-profit system established, owned, and operated by private citizens or individuals. Decisions can be made freely and independent of the government or its agencies, and companies are rewarded for their ability to identify and serve the demands and needs of consumers. Businesses that are adept at satisfying customers gain access to necessary factors of production and earn profits.

capitalism economic system that rewards companies for their ability to perceive and serve the needs and demands of consumers; also called the private enterprise system.

competition a natural force that guides free market capitalism.

Another name for the private enterprise system is **capitalism**. Adam Smith, often identified as the father of capitalism, first described the concept in his book, *The Wealth of Nations*, published in 1776. Smith believed that an economy is best regulated by the "invisible hand" of **competition**, a natural force that guides free market capitalism. Smith thought that competition among companies would lead to consumers' receiving the best possible products and prices because less efficient producers would gradually be driven from the marketplace.

competitive differentiation unique combination of organizational abilities, products, and approaches that sets a company apart from competitors in the minds of customers.

A basic premise of the private enterprise system, the invisible hand concept, also refers to the fact that individuals' efforts to pursue their own interest may benefit society as well. In the United States, competition regulates much of economic life. To compete successfully, each company must find a basis for **competitive differentiation**, the unique combination of organizational abilities, products, and approaches that sets a company apart from competitors in the minds of customers. Under Armour, with the tagline of "I Will," has resonated with football players who have experienced sweat soaked t-shirts that were heavy and uncomfortable. The company has differentiated itself with its signature moisture-wicking t-shirt that stays perpetually dry and fresh. Its tagline speaks to its origin, as the company began in the back of the founder's truck.[13] Companies that fail to adjust to shifts in consumer preferences or ignore the actions of competitors leave themselves open to failure. See the "Business & Technology Intersection" feature to learn more about how Nordstrom sets itself apart from the competition.

Throughout this book, our discussion focuses on the tools and methods that today's businesses apply to compete and differentiate their goods and services. We also discuss many of the ways in which market changes will affect business and the private enterprise system in the future.

Basic Rights in the Private Enterprise System

private property most basic freedom under the private enterprise system; the right to own, use, buy, sell, and bequeath land, buildings, machinery, equipment, patents, individual possessions, and various intangible kinds of property.

For capitalism to operate effectively, people living in a private enterprise system must have certain rights. As shown in **Figure 1.1**, these include the rights to private property, profits, freedom of choice, and competition.

The right to **private property** is the most basic freedom under the private enterprise system. Every participant has the right to own, use, buy, sell, and bequeath most forms of property, including land, buildings, machinery, equipment, patents on inventions, individual possessions, and intangible properties.

Business & Technology

Nordstrom Invests in Technology to Create "Unified Commerce"

Seattle, WA–based Nordstrom, the family-owned high-end fashion retailer, continues to be on a roll as recent annual sales reached a record $14.5 billion. That figure includes sales of $3 billion—growing more than 30% a year over the last decade—for the company's e-commerce site, Nordstrom.com.

Nordstrom has implemented digital selling tools designed to support new ways of serving customers across all brands and channels, which include its physical Nordstrom store, Nordstrom Online, Nordstrom Rack, NordstromRack.com, Hautelook, and Trunk Club (the company's men's-oriented personal shopper brand).

With e-commerce representing 25% of Nordstrom's business, technology spending has accelerated with plans to continue innovating its tech platform, designed to deliver both digital and mobile enhancements. For example, Nordstrom has implemented "unified commerce," whereby, in addition to curbside delivery in all U.S. full-line stores, a customer can buy online, pick up in store (BOPIS). In an effort to bridge its physical and digital businesses, a mobile feature now allows a customer to reserve items online to try on in stores. Perhaps Nordstrom's best-known competitive advantage is its commitment to outstanding customer service, which the company believes must be managed largely in part with technology.

Questions for Critical Thinking

1. Would you want to receive a text message from a sales associate while shopping at your favorite retailer? Why or why not? Research more about how Nordstrom differentiates itself from other clothing retailers by its use of technology.
2. Realizing the changing nature and expectations of customers who prefer to shop in a variety of ways, what are some additional ways Nordstrom can use technology to cultivate customer relationships and compete against online giant, Amazon?

Sources: Company website, "About Us," http://shop.nordstrom.com, accessed February 6, 2018; Micah Solomon, "Modernize Your Customer Experience the New Nordstrom Way," *Forbes*, https://www.forbes.com, accessed February 6, 2018; Lora Kolodny, "Two Ways Nordstrom is Adapting to the Amazon Era," *CNBC*, https://www.cnbc.com, accessed February 6, 2018; Jamie Grill-Goodman, "Nordstrom's Tech Investment Plans for 2017," *RIS (Retail Info Systems)*, https://risnews.com, accessed February 6, 2018.

The private enterprise system also guarantees business owners the right to all profits—after taxes—they earn through their activities. Although a business is not assured of earning a profit, its owner is legally and ethically entitled to any income it generates in excess of costs.

Freedom of choice means that a private enterprise system relies on the potential for citizens to choose their own employment, purchases, and investments. They can change jobs, negotiate wages, join labor unions, and choose among many different brands of goods and services. A private enterprise system maximizes individual prosperity by providing alternatives. Other economic systems sometimes limit freedom of choice to accomplish government goals, such as increasing industrial production of certain products.

The private enterprise system also permits fair competition by allowing the public to set rules for competitive activity. For this reason, the U.S. government has passed fair competition laws to maintain market competition and fairness for consumers by prohibiting anti-competitive practices, which include attempted monopolization, competitor bashing, predatory pricing or price gauging, and deceptive advertising, packaging, and labeling.[14]

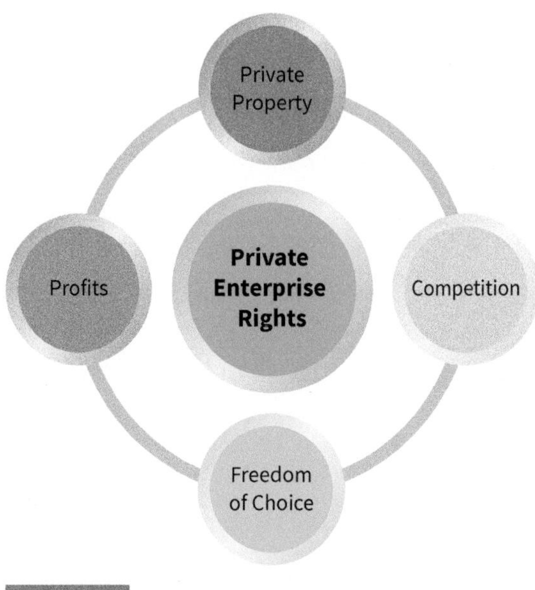

FIGURE 1.1 Basic Rights within a Private Enterprise System

The Entrepreneurship Alternative

The entrepreneurial spirit is a mind-set embodied by individuals who are passionate and fascinated with how things can be improved. An **entrepreneur** is a risk taker in the private enterprise system. You hear about entrepreneurs all the time—two college students creating a mobile app or a new parent who has an innovative idea for a better baby product. Once in a while, the risk leads to rewards that are significant and profitable. However, oftentimes, it takes an entrepreneur repeated attempts, failures, and numerous ideas before achieving success. Individuals who recognize marketplace opportunities are free to use their capital, time, and talents to pursue those opportunities for profit. The willingness of individuals to start new ventures drives

entrepreneur person who seeks a profitable opportunity and takes the necessary risks to set up and operate a business.

economic growth and keeps competitive pressure on existing companies to continue to satisfy customers.

By almost any measure, the entrepreneurial spirit fuels growth in the U.S. economy. Of all the businesses operating in the United States, about one in seven companies started operations during the past year. These newly formed businesses are also the source of many of the nation's new jobs. These companies are a significant source of employment or self-employment. Of the 28 million U.S. small businesses currently in operation, more than 22 million consist of self-employed people without any employees. Almost 8.5 million U.S. employees currently work for a business with fewer than 20 employees.[15] Does starting a business require higher education? Not necessarily, although it certainly helps. Some students choose to launch a business before they finish college. **Table 1.2** lists some of the well-known start-ups that had their humble beginnings in a college dorm room. Today, the venture capital fund DormRoomFund.com provides funding for student entrepreneurs and is run by college students. Entrepreneurs and business startups are discussed in detail in Chapter 6.

Besides creating jobs and selling products, entrepreneurship provides the benefits of innovation. In contrast to more established firms, start-up companies tend to innovate most in fields of technology, making new products available to businesses and consumers. Because small companies are more flexible, they can make changes to products and processes more quickly than larger corporations. Entrepreneurs often find new ways to use natural resources, technology, and other factors of production. Often, they do this because they have to—they may not have enough money to build an expensive prototype or launch a wide-scale promotional campaign.

TABLE 1.2 Dorm Room Entrepreneurs

Company	Founders	Idea	Website
Dropbox	Arash Ferdowski and Drew Houston	Frustrated by the inability to receive and send large files over e-mail, Ferdowski and Houston created an online file storage solution, now the leader in file sharing with millions of users worldwide.	http://www.dropbox.com
Facebook	Mark Zuckerberg, Dustin Moscovitz, Eduardo Saverin, Andrew McCollum, and Chris Hughes	Facebook was created by a group of Harvard students in search of a way to interact with other students. Zuckerberg dropped out of school and continues to run the company today.	http://www.facebook.com
Google	Sergey Brin and Larry Page	Brin and Page began brainstorming while in school about creating the world's largest search engine. They suspended their PhD studies, and both run Alphabet today (see the chapter opening story).	http://www.google.com
Insomnia Cookies	Seth Berkowitz	Insomnia Cookies, now in 70 locations, specializes in feeding the insatiable hunger of college students, companies, and anyone else with warm, delicious cookies delivered right to your door.	http://www.insomniacookies.com
ModCloth	Susan Gregg Koger and Eric Koger	ModCloth offers styles from hundreds of independent designers in a full range of sizes. They also design and sell an exclusive line of their own apparel.	http://www.modcloth.com
SnapChat	Evan Spiegel and Robert Murphy	Approached by a friend who wasn't sure about whether to send a certain photo, Spiegel and Murphy figured out a way to magically send pictures that soon disappear after being viewed by the recipient.	http://www.snapchat.com
Inogen	Alison Perry Bauerlin	While in college, Bauerlin founded Inogen, a lightweight and travel-approved portable oxygen device designed to free patients in need of oxygen from heavy tanks.	http://www.inogen.com

Sources: Rachel Knuttel, "The 12 Coolest Dorm Room Startups," http://thelala.com, accessed February 10, 2018; Ken Yeung, "Mark Zuckerberg on the Real Beginnings of Facebook," *The Next Web,* http://thenextweb.com, accessed February 10, 2018; company website, "About Us," https://insomniacookies.com, accessed February 10, 2018; company website, "About Us," http://modcloth.com, accessed February 10, 2018; company website, www.snapshat.com, accessed February 10, 2018; company website, "Create Your Website for Free," https://wordpress.com, accessed February 10, 2018; Company website, "About Us," accessed February 10, 2018, http://inogen.com.

Sometimes an entrepreneur may innovate by simply tweaking an existing idea. For backcountry campers, hikers, and other outdoor enthusiasts, freeze-dried "just-add-water-and-serve" meals-in-a-pouch are traditionally lightweight with an extensive shelf life. Avid backpacker, chef, and former restaurateur, Jennifer Scism, began experimenting by cooking and dehydrating her own meals prior to heading out on long expeditions. The result is Good To-Go, a Maine-based company that sells gourmet freeze-dried foods free of preservatives and additives. Now in 600 stores nationwide, the gourmet meals in a pouch include herbed mushroom risotto, pad Thai, smoked three-bean chili, and Indian vegetable korma, to name a few.[16]

Entrepreneurship is also important to existing companies in a private enterprise system. More and more, large companies are recognizing the value of entrepreneurial thinking among their employees, hoping to benefit from enhanced flexibility, improved innovation, and new market opportunities. For example, Nike's mobile app called SNKRS uses augmented reality to give "sneakerheads" (people who collect and trade sneakers as a hobby) a one-stop shop for everything Nike, in addition to a heads-up about the release of new models and the ability to purchase new and limited-edition sneakers through the app.[17]

As discussed in the next section, entrepreneurs have played a vital role in the history of U.S. business. As forward-thinking innovators, they have created global companies in new industries, developed successful business methods and processes, and brought about economic wealth, jobs, and opportunities.

Assessment Check

1. What is an alternative term for *private enterprise system*?
2. What is the most basic freedom under the private enterprise system?
3. What is an entrepreneur?

4 Seven Eras in the History of Business

In the more than 500 years since the first European settlements appeared on the North American continent, amazing changes have occurred in the size, focus, and goals of U.S. businesses. As **Figure 1.2** indicates, U.S. business history is divided into seven distinct time periods: (1) the Colonial period, (2) the Industrial Revolution, (3) the age of industrial entrepreneurs, (4) the production era, (5) the marketing era, (6) the relationship era, and (7) the social era. The next sections describe how events in each of these time periods have influenced U.S. business practices.

The Colonial Period

Colonial society emphasized rural and agricultural production. Colonial towns were small compared to European cities, and they functioned as marketplaces for farmers and craftspeople. The economic focus of the nation centered on rural areas, because prosperity depended on the output of farms, orchards, and the like. The success or failure of crops influenced every aspect of the economy.

Colonists depended on England for manufactured items as well as financial backing for their infant industries. Even after the Revolutionary War (1776–1783), the United States maintained close economic ties with England. British investors continued to provide much of the financing for developing the U.S. business system, and this financial influence continued well into the 19th century.

Era	Main Characteristics	Time Period
Colonial	Primarily agricultural	Prior to 1776
Industrial Revolution	Mass production by semiskilled workers, aided by machines	1760–1850
Industrial entrepreneurs	Advances in technology and increased demand for manufactured goods, leading to enormous entrepreneurial opportunities	Late 1800s
Production	Emphasis on producing more goods faster, leading to production innovations such as assembly lines	Through the 1920s
Marketing	Consumer orientation, seeking to understand and satisfy needs and preferences of customer groups	Since 1950s
Relationship	Benefits derived from deep, ongoing links with individual customers, employees, suppliers, and other businesses	Began in 1990s
Social	New ways for businesses and consumers to communicate and share information through the Internet and social media	Since 2000s

FIGURE 1.2 Seven Eras in Business History

The Industrial Revolution

The Industrial Revolution began in England around 1750. It moved business operations from an emphasis on independent, skilled workers who specialized in building products one by one to a factory system that mass-produced items by bringing together large numbers of semiskilled workers. The factories profited from the savings created by large-scale production, bolstered by increasing support from machines over time. As businesses grew, they could often purchase raw materials more cheaply in larger lots than before. Specialization of labor, limiting each worker to a few specific tasks in the production process, also improved production efficiency.

Influenced by these events in England, business in the United States began a time of rapid industrialization. Agriculture became mechanized, and factories sprang up in cities. During the mid-1800s, the pace of the revolution was increased as newly built railroad systems provided fast, economical transportation. In California, for example, the combination of railroad construction and the gold rush fueled a tremendous demand for construction.

The Age of Industrial Entrepreneurs

Building on the opportunities created by the Industrial Revolution, entrepreneurship increased in the United States. Henry Engelhard Steinway of Seesen, Germany, built his first piano by hand in his kitchen in 1825 as a wedding present for his bride. In 1850, the family emigrated to New York, where Henry and his sons opened their first factory in Manhattan in 1853. Over the next 30 years, they developed innovations that led to the modern piano. Through an apprenticeship system, the Steinways transmitted their skills to the following generations. Steinway pianos have long been world famous for their beautiful tone, top-quality materials and workmanship, and durability. Now known as Steinway Musical Instruments, the company still builds its pianos by hand in its factory in Astoria, New York, under the same master-apprentice system that Henry and his sons began. Building each piano takes nearly a year from start to finish (see photo). In response to 21st-century demands, the company has launched Etude, an app for the iPad that displays sheet music the user can play on an on-screen piano keyboard.[18]

Inventors created a virtually endless array of commercially useful products and new production methods. Many of them are famous today:

- Eli Whitney, best known for inventing the cotton gin, introduced the concept of interchangeable parts, an idea that would later facilitate mass production on a previously impossible scale.
- Robert McCormick designed a horse-drawn reaper that reduced the labor involved in harvesting wheat. His son, Cyrus McCormick, saw the commercial potential of the reaper and launched a business to build and sell the machine. By 1902, the company was producing 35% of the nation's farm machinery.
- Cornelius Vanderbilt (railroads), J. P. Morgan (banking), and Andrew Carnegie (steel), among others, took advantage of the enormous opportunities waiting for anyone willing to take the risk of starting a new business.

The entrepreneurial spirit of this golden age in business did much to advance the U.S. business system and raise the country's overall standard of living. That market transformation, in turn, created new demand for manufactured goods.

Fred R. Conrad/The New York Times/Redux Pictures

Steinway has built pianos for home use and for artists from John Lennon to Billy Joel.

The Production Era

As demand for manufactured goods continued to increase through the 1920s, businesses focused even greater attention on the activities involved in producing those goods. Work became increasingly specialized, and huge, labor-intensive factories dominated U.S. business. Assembly lines, introduced by Henry Ford, became commonplace in major industries. Business owners turned over their responsibilities to a new class of managers trained in operating established companies. Their activities emphasized efforts to produce even more goods through quicker methods.

During the production era, business focused attention on internal processes rather than external influences. Marketing was almost an afterthought, designed solely to distribute items generated by production activities. Little attention was paid to consumer wants or needs. Instead, businesses tended to make decisions about what the market would get. If you wanted to buy a Ford Model T automobile, your color choice was black—the only color produced by the company.

The Marketing Era

The Great Depression of the early 1930s changed the shape of U.S. business yet again. As incomes nosedived, businesses could no longer automatically count on selling everything they produced. Managers began to pay more attention to the markets for their goods and services, and sales and advertising took on new importance. During this period, selling was often synonymous with marketing.

Demand for all kinds of consumer goods exploded after World War II. After nearly five years of doing without new automobiles, appliances, and other items, consumers were buying again. At the same time, however, competition also heated up. Soon businesses began to think of marketing as more than just selling; they envisioned a process of determining what consumers wanted and needed and then designing products to satisfy those needs. In short, they developed a **consumer orientation**.

consumer orientation business philosophy that focuses first on determining unmet consumer wants and needs and then designing products to satisfy those needs.

Businesses began to analyze consumer desires before beginning actual production. Consumer choices skyrocketed. Automobiles came in a wide variety of colors and styles, and car

branding process of creating an identity in consumers' minds for a good, service, or company; a major marketing tool in contemporary business.

brand name, term, sign, symbol, design, or some combination that identifies the products of one company and differentiates them from competitors' offerings.

buyers could choose among them. Companies also discovered the need to distinguish their goods and services from those of competitors. **Branding**—the process of creating an identity in consumers' minds for a good, service, or company—is an important marketing tool. A **brand** can be a name, term, sign, symbol, design, or some combination that identifies the products of one company and differentiates them from competitors' offerings.

Branding can go a long way toward creating value for a firm by providing recognition and a positive association between a company and its products. Some of the world's most famous—and enduring—brands include Apple, Google, Microsoft, Coca-Cola, Amazon, and Samsung.[19] There is more in-depth discussion about branding in Chapter 12.

The marketing era has had a tremendous effect on the way business is conducted today. Even the smallest business owners recognize the importance of understanding what customers want and the reasons they buy.

The Relationship Era

transaction management building and promoting products in the hope that enough customers will buy them to cover costs and earn profits.

relationship era business era in which companies seek ways to actively nurture customer loyalty by carefully managing every interaction.

As business continues in the 21st century, a significant change is taking place in the ways companies interact with customers. Since the Industrial Revolution, most businesses have concentrated on building and promoting products in the hope that enough customers will buy them to cover costs and earn acceptable profits, an approach called **transaction management**.

In contrast, in the **relationship era**, businesses are taking a different, longer-term approach to interacting with and creating authentic customer relationships. Companies now seek ways to actively nurture customer loyalty by carefully managing every interaction. They earn enormous paybacks for their efforts. A company that retains customers over the long haul can potentially reduce costs associated with acquiring new customers. Because customer spending tends to accelerate over time, revenues also grow. Companies with long-term customers often can avoid costly reliance on price discounts to attract new business, and they find that many new buyers come from loyal customer referrals.

Business owners gain several advantages by developing ongoing relationships with customers. Because it is much less expensive to serve existing customers than to find new ones, businesses that develop long-term customer relationships can reduce their overall costs. Long-term relationships with customers enable businesses to improve their understanding of what customers want and prefer from the company. As a result, businesses enhance their chances of sustaining real advantages through competitive differentiation.

The relationship era is an age of connections—between businesses and customers, employers and employees, technology and manufacturing, and even separate companies. The global economy is increasingly interconnected, as businesses expand worldwide. In this new environment, techniques for managing networks of people, businesses, information, and technology are critically important to success in today's business environment. See the "Job Descripton" feature to learn more about what it takes to be a business operations associate in a technology company.

The Social Era

social era business era in which companies seek ways to connect and interact with customers using technology.

relationship management collection of activities that build and maintain ongoing, mutually beneficial ties with customers and other parties.

The **social era** of business can be described as a new approach to the way businesses and individuals interact, connect, communicate, share, and exchange information with each other in virtual communities and networks around the world.

The social era, based on the premise that organizations create value through connections with groups or networks of people with similar goals and interests, offers businesses immense opportunities, particularly through the use of technology and **relationship management**—the collection of activities that build and maintain ongoing, mutually beneficial ties with customers and other parties.

Social media tools and technologies come in various shapes and sizes. They include weblogs, blogs, podcasts, and microblogs (such as Twitter); social and professional networks (such as Facebook and LinkedIn); picture-sharing platforms (such as Instagram and Tumblr); and content communities (such as YouTube), to name a few.[20]

Job Description

"BizOps" Associate

Overview The business operations team at a technology company—also called BizOps for short—coordinates and aligns organization-wide operations and strategies. Team members, who gain a holistic view of an organization, are charged with defining and leading strategic, operational, and organizational improvements across a company's product, sales, marketing, and engineering teams.

Responsibilities As a member of a BizOps team, you might work on growth strategies for a variety of goods and services. You might also provide insight to company managers on initiatives for decision making, operations, investments, and acquisitions. In addition, planning and goal setting are integral parts of the daily job activities for a BizOps associate.

Requirements Typically a business degree with an emphasis in finance or management is preferred. Some BizOps professionals also have a few years of experience at management consulting firms where they developed strategies and solutions for clients. Attention to detail, as well as strong organization and communication skills, are essential for a successful career in BizOps. A keen interest in innovation as well as a knack for implementing ideas quickly as part of ongoing business opportunities can be helpful skills.

Outlook Opportunities for BizOps professionals will continue to grow over the next several years, as more technology start-up businesses come on line and other companies expand their operations. Professionals with a proven track record—typically five years of solid BizOps experience–will continue to be in high demand and have significant opportunities at the senior management level. If you like being part of an innovative team that gets involved and executes a technology company's fast-moving strategic priorities, this may be the career for you.

Sources: Tammy Everts, "What Do We Mean When We Talk about BizOps?" *SOASTA*, https://www.soasta.com/, accessed February 7, 2018; Jordan Kong, "Why Your Startup Also Needs a BizOps Team," *Medium*, https://medium.com, accessed February 7, 2018; Dan Yoo, "Why BizOps Is the Hottest Team in Tech," *LinkedIn Pulse*, https://www.linkedin.com, accessed February 7, 2018; company website, "Google Careers—Business Strategy," *www.google.com*, accessed February 7, 2018; Dan Yoo, "How BizOps Adapts to You and Your Company," *LinkedIn Pulse*, https://www.linkedin.com, accessed February 7, 2018.

As consumers continue to log fewer hours on computers and more time on mobile devices, companies have implemented mobile strategies using real-time data and location-based technology. Businesses use mobile social media applications to engage in marketing research, communications, sales promotions, loyalty programs, and other processes. In the social era, businesses tailor specific promotions to specific users in specific locations at specific times to build customer loyalty and long-term relationships. For example, customers who are members of GameStop's PowerUp loyalty program can opt in to receive mobile offers and messages when they are near one of the video game retailer's stores.[21]

Strategic Alliances Businesses are also finding that they must form partnerships with other organizations to take full advantage of available opportunities. One form of partnership between organizations is a **strategic alliance**, a partnership formed to create a competitive advantage for the businesses involved.

strategic alliance partnership formed to create a competitive advantage for the businesses involved; in international business, a business strategy in which a company finds a partner in the country where it wants to do business.

The voice of Amazon's voice-enabled intelligent personal assistant, Alexa, will soon be heard outside the home. In fact, major automobile companies, including Ford, Toyota, Hyundai, and Volkswagen, plan to include Amazon's voice-controlled digital assistant in their cars. This is just one example of how automobile companies are forming strategic alliances with technology companies—all in an effort to make safer cars and to embrace emerging technologies.[22]

Ethan Miller/Getty Images

Automobile maker Ford has included Amazon's voice-controlled digital assistance in their cars.

The Green Advantage Another way of building relationships is to incorporate issues and values into your business that are of concern to your customers. As environmental concerns continue to influence consumers' choices of everything from yogurt to clothing to cars, many observers say the question about "going green" is no longer whether, but how. The need to develop environmentally friendly products and processes continues to be a major focus for businesses today.

Companies in every industry are researching ways to save energy, cut emissions and pollution, reduce waste, and, not incidentally, save money and increase profits as well. King & King Architects of Syracuse, New York, a member of the Green Building Council, recently relocated to a 48,000-square-foot warehouse. A grant from the New York State Energy Research and Development Authority

(NYSERDA) enabled King & King to install energy-improved, high-efficiency windows, heating and cooling, ventilation, and insulation. These and many other improvements will save the company the equivalent amount of electricity consumed by 24 single-family homes per year—and won the company a High Performance Building Plaque from NYSERDA.[23]

Energy remains a significant cost for most companies, and carbon-based fuels such as coal are responsible for most of the additional carbon dioxide in the atmosphere. Many companies have begun to address this issue, none perhaps with more flair than Greensulate, a small business in New York City that insulates rooftops with beautiful meadows of lavender, native grasses, and a hardy plant called sedum. The company's efforts to date have eliminated more than 3,000 pounds of carbon from the atmosphere.[24] Owned by electric vehicle maker Tesla, SolarCity, a California installer of rooftop solar cells, has become a leader in clean energy services for businesses, schools, and not-for-profit organizations.[25]

Each new era in U.S. business history has forced managers to reexamine the tools and techniques they formerly used to compete. Tomorrow's managers will need creativity and vision to stay on top of rapidly changing technology and to manage complex relationships in the global business world of the fast-paced 21st century. As green operations become more cost-effective, and consumers and shareholders demand more transparency from corporations, more companies continue to realize its importance and value.

Assessment Check

1. What was the Industrial Revolution?
2. During which era was the idea of branding developed?
3. What is the difference between transaction management and management in the relationship era?

5 Current Business Workforce Trends

A skilled and knowledgeable workforce is an essential resource for keeping pace with the accelerating rate of change in today's business world. Employers need reliable workers who are dedicated to developing strong ties with customers and partners. To compete in global markets, businesses must be aware of the ongoing transition to a knowledge economy, which involves increased reliance on employees' intellectual capabilities over physical inputs or natural resources. Knowledge-based activities within an organization help accelerate the pace of technical and scientific advances. More recently, the integration of machines and artificial intelligence in the workplace continues to grow as a number of companies in the healthcare and financial sectors have successfully substituted employees with artificial intelligence technologies. See how McDonald's is using intelligent decision making when it comes to packaging in the "Clean & Green Business" feature.[26]

Changes in the Workforce

Companies now face several trends that challenge their skills for managing and developing human resources. Those challenges include aging of the population and a shrinking labor pool, growing diversity of the workforce, the changing nature of work, the need for flexibility and mobility, and the use of collaboration and new models of work such as crowdsourcing and artificial intelligence (intelligence by machines) to innovate and become more efficient.

Aging of the Population and Shrinking Labor Pool There are more than 8.5 million U.S. workers 65 or older in today's workforce, a 60% increase compared to a decade ago.[27] However, today many members of the Baby Boomer generation, the huge number of people born between 1946 and 1964, are still hitting the peaks of their careers. At the same time,

Clean & Green Business

Happy Meal Packaging Not All Happy

After enjoying a Happy Meal at McDonald's, one thought that is probably not at top of mind for kids and parents alike is the impact of the meal's packaging on the planet's forests. In a typical Happy Meal, in addition to the paper cup and napkins, the burger is wrapped in paper, as is the plastic straw; the fries arrive in a paper sleeve; ketchup packets, made from a thin plastic film, are also supplied—and of course, there's the plastic toy. At the world's largest restaurant chain, serving over 69 million people daily, with 37,000 locations in over 100 countries, all of this packaging, made primarily from trees, goes straight into the trash, and subsequently, a landfill.

In an effort to reduce waste, McDonald's is working on improving its sourcing, transportation, and packaging. The company recently announced that by 2025, all packaging, including single-use plastic straws, on customer products will come from "renewable or recycled sources," or sources with a preference for certification by environmental organizations, the Forest Stewardship Council or the Programme for the Endorsement of Forest Certification. Both nonprofit organizations have a goal to protect forests for future generations by setting standards for responsible forest management. Additionally, by 2025, McDonald's has also said that it will make recycling an option at all global locations. To date, only 10% of its 37,000 locations offer recycling. McDonald's customers continue to express concern over the company's green image. The company acknowledges that it has a long road ahead to accomplish its goal of recycling 100% of guest packaging at all of its restaurants. Recycling infrastructure, regulations, and consumer behaviors differ from city to city and country to country. However, the burger giant believes that even small changes can and will make a difference.

Questions for Critical Thinking

1. The average American uses six trees worth of paper each year. In reality, forest products like toilet paper, napkins, tissues, and paper towels are used by people every day. What solutions exist to lessen or prevent clearing the earth's forests to produce such products?
2. McDonald's has also committed to replace recycle bins within its stores and to do away with eco-unfriendly and nearly impossible-to-recycle plastic (polystyrene) foam cups. Research the status and results of its initiatives.

Sources: Organization site, "About Us," https://us.fsc.org/en-us, accessed February 11, 2018; company website, "Thinking Circular with More Sustainable Packaging and Recycling," http://corporate.mcdonalds.com, accessed February 11, 2018; Melissa Locker, "If McDonald's Keeps Its Promise, Your Happy Meal Could Be Green Within Seven Years," *Fast Company*, http://fastcompany.com, accessed February 11, 2018; Robert Reed, *Chicago Tribune*, "McDonald's to Drop Foam Packaging by Year End," http://www.chicagotribune.com, accessed February 11, 2018; Ben Geier, "McDonald's Promises to Become More Eco-friendly," *ABC Action News*, https://www.abcactionnews.com, accessed February 11, 2018.

members of so-called Generation X (born from 1965 to 1981) and Generation Y or Millennials (born from 1982 to 2005) are building their careers, so employers are finding themselves managing a multi-generational workforce with up to five different generations. Other generations include Generation Z, born after Millennials, and the Silent Generation—workers born before 1946. This broad age diversity brings management challenges with it, such as accommodating a variety of work lifestyles, the potential for negative stereotyping changing expectations of work, and varying levels of technological expertise. Still, despite the widening age spectrum of the workforce, some economists predict a labor shortage as Baby Boomers retire.

Continued rapid technological change has intensified the hiring challenge by requiring knowledge workers and workers with even more advanced, often technical, skills. Over 33% of Americans 25 and older have completed a bachelor's degree, an increase from 28% a decade ago. In addition, companies are increasingly seeking—and finding—talent at the extreme ends of the working-age spectrum. Teenagers are entering the workforce sooner, and some seniors are staying longer—or seeking new careers after retiring from their prior careers. Many older workers work part-time or flexible hours. Meanwhile, for those older employees who do retire, employers must administer a variety of retirement planning and disability programs and insurance benefits.

Increasingly Diverse Workforce While the population is aging in much of the developed world, in emerging markets like Brazil, Russia, India, and China, the young population is contributing to a global migration. To gain access to more diverse educational and work opportunities, workers in developing regions have moved to countries like the United States. This pattern has contributed to an increasingly diverse U.S. workforce—beyond simply age, race, and gender differences.

To retain employees, managers must focus on diversity and inclusion in workplace policies—particularly in industries such as technology. Today's U.S. workforce is comprised of more immigrants than ever before, along with highly educated women, military veterans, and people with varying physical and mental abilities. Minority groups will make up approximately 56% of the total population by the year 2060.[28] Aligning diversity initiatives with business goals and objectives might include mentoring and career development opportunities designed to increase diversity in higher-level positions within an organization. In addition, employee retention strategies might include flexible work programs, training to increase technology proficiency, and relevant, meaningful employee perks and benefits.

diversity blending individuals of different genders, ethnic backgrounds, cultures, religions, ages, and physical and mental abilities.

Diversity, blending individuals of different genders, ethnic backgrounds, cultures, religions, ages, and physical and mental abilities, creates far more innovative and creative perspectives. Studies have shown that diverse employee teams and workforces with varied perspectives and experience tend to perform tasks more effectively and develop better solutions to business problems. According to the chief diversity officer for microprocessor maker Intel, the company plans to invest $300 million in its "Diversity in Technology Initiative" to achieve full representation of women and underrepresented minorities.[29]

Outsourcing and the Changing Nature of Work

Not only is the U.S. workforce changing, but so is the very nature of work. Manufacturing used to account for most of the annual output of the United States, but the balance has now shifted to services such as hospitality, retail, healthcare, human services, information technology, financial services, and education. As **Table 1.3** shows, employment by major service industry sectors continues to grow. This means that product firms, for example, with a higher service component, must rely on well-trained employees who have the knowledge, problem-solving and technical skills, and ability to communicate and deal with people as part of their daily work. **Outsourcing** involves the use of outside vendors—contracting work out to another party—for the production of goods or fulfillment of services and functions previously performed in house. Oftentimes, competitive pressures drive a company to reduce costs by outsourcing in order to focus its resources on other components of its business. In addition to cultural and language differences, outsourcing

outsourcing using outside vendors—contracting work out to another party—for the production of goods or fulfillment of services and functions previously performed in house.

TABLE 1.3 Employment by Major Service Industry Sector, 2006, 2016, and Projected 2026

	Thousands of Jobs (000's)			Change	
Industry Sector	**2006**	**2016**	**2026**	**2006–16**	**2016–26**
Services-providing excluding special industries	114,724.2	125,294.1	135,820.6	10,569.9	10,526.5
Utilities	548.5	556.2	559.6	7.7	3.4
Wholesale trade	5,904.6	5,867.0	6,012.8	−37.6	145.8
Retail trade	15,353.2	15,820.4	16,232.7	467.2	412.3
Transportation and warehousing	4,469.6	4,989.1	5,353.4	519.5	364.3
Information	3,037.9	2,772.3	2,824.8	−265.6	52.5
Financial activities	8,366.6	8,284.8	8,764.6	−81.8	479.8
Professional and business services	17,566.2	20,135.6	22,295.3	2,569.4	2,159.7
Educational services	2,900.9	3,559.7	4,066.2	658.8	506.5
Health care and social assistance	15,253.3	19,056.3	23,054.6	3,803.0	3,998.3
Leisure and hospitality	13,109.7	15,620.4	16,939.4	2,510.7	1,319.0
Other services	6,240.5	6,409.4	6,761.4	168.9	352.0
Federal government	2,732.0	2,795.0	2,739.2	63.0	-55.8
State and local government	19,241.2	19,427.9	20,216.6	186.7	788.7

Source: Government website, "Employment by Major Industry Sector," https://www.bls.gov, accessed February 8, 2018.

also creates its own challenges, such as fully understanding the client's business and balancing costs while increasing value to the client.

Offshoring is the relocation of business processes, both production (manufacturing) and services (accounting), to lower-cost locations overseas. In recent years, India ranked as the top offshoring destination worldwide, followed by China and Malaysia.[30] Some U.S. companies are now structured so that entire divisions or functions are developed and staffed overseas. As U.S. firms are becoming increasingly concerned about protecting their intellectual property and keeping jobs in the United States, many have focused on **nearshoring**, outsourcing production or services to locations near a company's home base, or closer to customers.[31]

offshoring relocation of business processes, both production (manufacturing) and services (accounting), to lower-cost locations overseas.

nearshoring outsourcing production or services to locations near a company's home base or closer to customers.

Flexibility and Mobility Millennials, the largest demographic group in today's workforce, tend to care less about money and the work-comes-first lifestyle, and more about training, flexibility, diversity and inclusion, and getting along with co-workers. Millennials expect greater choice and control over their physical space as compared to Baby Boomers, and they also bring a different set of skills to the workplace. Millennials, more open to freelancing or working on contract over traditional full-time employment, expect flexible work hours along with mobility to work at home, a café, or the office. Many prefer to use technology (including their personal smart phones), to collaborate online, where they can share knowledge, a sense of purpose or mission, and a free flow of ideas across any geographical distance or time zone.[32]

To retain valued employees, managers of global workforces need to present exciting work opportunities, build and earn trust, and ensure that employees have a choice over when, where, and how to work. Such managers and their employees need to be flexible and responsive to change while work, technology, and the relationships between them continue to evolve.

Innovation through Collaboration Some observers also see a trend toward more collaborative work in the future, as opposed to individuals working alone. Businesses using teams hope to build a creative environment where all members contribute their knowledge and skills to solve problems or seize opportunities.

Technology continues to break down the physical barriers that once existed in a workplace setting where workers arrived to the office primarily for face-to-face collaboration. To achieve high levels of productivity, employees have become increasingly dependent on technology—including messaging apps, video conferencing for virtual collaboration, and digital devices like smart phones and laptops. Using technology, global teams are able to collaborate from all corners of the world, and physical office presence seems far less important. This has contributed to a new way of working called **crowdsourcing**, enlisting the collective talent of a number of people to get work done. Crowdsourcing allows companies to find workers for a specific task or project in a more efficient and cost-effective way—using online marketplaces to hire global talent beyond their own workforce.[33]

crowdsourcing enlisting the collective talent of a number of people to get work done.

Assessment Check

1. Define *outsourcing, offshoring*, and *nearshoring*.
2. Describe the importance of collaboration and employee partnership.

6 Today's Manager

Ongoing change is causing a radical transformation in today's business environment—where new industries, business models, and technologies are continually developing. Different from the past, the use of data, networks, and artificial intelligence for decision making and communication will impact the way today's managers lead in an environment of hyper-change.

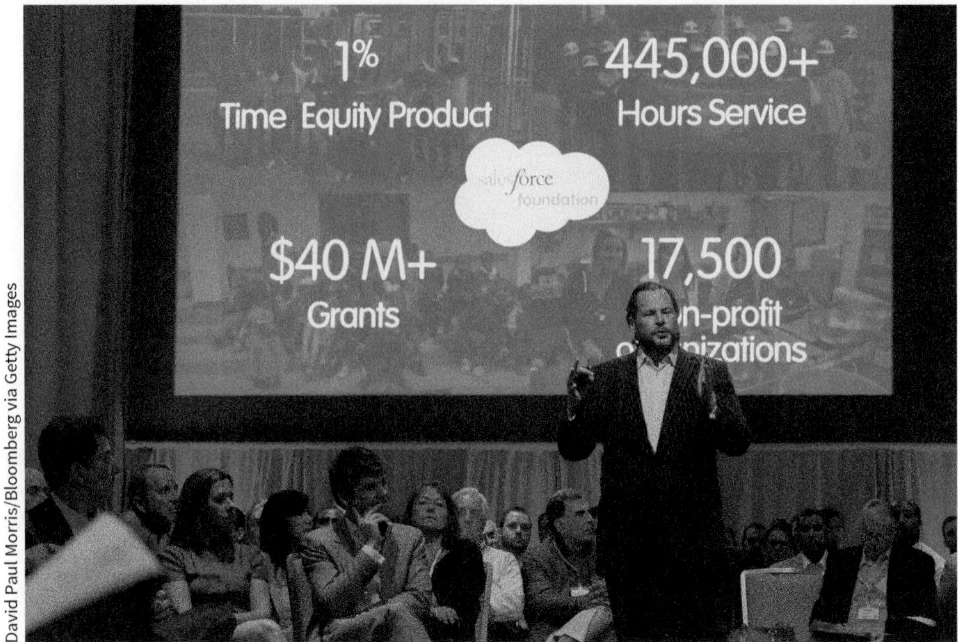

David Paul Morris/Bloomberg via Getty Images

Marc Benioff, CEO of Salesforce.com, is a visionary leader who has disrupted traditional, on-premise enterprise software with customer relationship management (CRM) delivered via the cloud.

Companies now look for highly motivated visionaries and transformational managers and leaders. For today's manager, the ability to communicate and strategically apply critical thinking skills and creativity to both challenges and opportunities will continue to be a top priority.

Importance of Vision

To thrive in the 21st century, businesspeople need **vision**, the ability to perceive marketplace needs and what an organization must do to satisfy them. Marc Benioff, CEO of Salesforce.com (shown in photo), a pioneer of cloud computing, is a visionary leader. Benioff founded Salesforce.com to replace traditional enterprise software—computer programs with business applications—with an on-demand information management service. Because of social and mobile cloud technologies, businesses now have the opportunity to connect with customers, employees, partners, and others in more strategic and effective ways. At a recent conference, Benioff was quoted as saying, "Salesforce.com needs to be for enterprise customers what Steve Jobs has always been to me—to be visionary and paint the future as much as possible."[34] Another leader with a definite vision is Shake Shack's Danny Meyers. See the "Business Model" feature for his story.

Importance of Critical Thinking and Creativity

Critical thinking and creativity are essential characteristics of today's manager. Today's businesspeople need to look at a wide variety of situations, draw connections among disparate information, and develop future-oriented solutions. This need applies not only to top executives but to mid-level managers and entry-level workers as well.

critical thinking ability to analyze and assess information to pinpoint problems or opportunities.

creativity capacity to develop novel solutions to perceived organizational problems.

Critical thinking is the ability to analyze and assess information to pinpoint problems or opportunities. The critical-thinking process includes activities such as determining the authenticity, accuracy, and worth of data, information, knowledge, and arguments. It involves looking beneath the surface for deeper meaning and connections that can help identify critical issues and solutions.

Creativity is the capacity to develop novel solutions to perceived organizational problems. Although most people think of it in relation to writers, artists, musicians, and inventors,

Business Model

Shake Shack Blends Up "Enlightened Hospitality"

If you've been to New York City recently, one of its many tourist attractions is a burger joint which began as a single location in New York's Madison Square Park. Based in New York, Shake Shack is a regional "fast-casual" restaurant known for its high-quality, sustainably sourced food offerings, which include its signature "ShackBurger," hot dogs, crinkle fries, and, of course, milk shakes. The growing "fast-casual" restaurant segment, which includes Chipotle and Panera, is a hybrid of fast food and casual dining. Compared to fast food restaurants, Shake Shack offers healthier, higher quality, and specially prepared food in an upscale setting with top-notch service.

Shake Shack's owner, restaurateur Danny Meyers, is an example of someone who has reaped significant rewards operating within the private enterprise system. By successfully identifying and serving the needs and demands of customers who think nothing of standing in long lines to experience all-natural menu items and great customer service, Meyer has created somewhat of a cult following for his Shake Shack dining experience.

Also coveted for its frozen custard, Shake Shack's core philosophy is based on the simple mantra of "enlightened hospitality," which translates to a warmer, friendlier, and more engaging customer service experience for its burger-loving clientele. Known affectionately as the "Shack Team," employees are expected to embody the "5 tenets of enlightened hospitality": "taking care of each other, our guests, our community, our suppliers, and our stockholders". With its initial public offering (whereby shares are sold to public investors), the Shack Team has more than just a few stockholders to consider and has expanded beyond the Big Apple to locations including Miami, Chicago, Atlanta, and Austin. Globally the company has more than 136 locations throughout the United States, Japan, the Middle East, Russia, Turkey, and the United Kingdom. With a vision of "stand for something good," Meyer's Shack Team seems to be serving up its unique dining experience to an increasing number of satisfied customers.

Questions for Critical Thinking

1. Shake Shack plans to continue its global expansion. Critics are concerned that Shake Shack's regional strength in its New York hub may not translate to a larger potential in other countries. Do you agree? Why or why not?
2. In regard to sustainability, many consumers believe that ethically raised animals are not just better for their diets but also better for the overall community and the global supply chain. Research fast-casual dining and provide examples of how, in addition to using hormone- and antibiotic-free beef, for example, this restaurant sector has gained traction among Millennials.

Sources: Company website, https://www.shakeshack.com, accessed February 10, 2018; Melody Hahm, "Why Shake Shack Won't Be the Next Chipotle," *Yahoo Finance!*, http://finance.yahoo.com, accessed February 10, 2018; Leslie Picker and Craig Giammona, "For Shake Shack and Box, a Harsh Post-IPO Reality Sets In," *Bloomberg Business*, https://www.bloomberg.com, accessed February 10, 2018; Roberto A. Ferdman, "The Chipotle Effect: Why America Is Obsessed with Fast Casual Food," *Washington Post*, http://www.washingtonpost.com, accessed February 10, 2018; Trefis Team, "How the Fast Casual Segment Is Gaining Market Share in the Restaurant Industry," *Forbes*, https://www.forbes.com, accessed February 10, 2018.

that is a very limited definition. In business, creativity refers to the ability to see better and different ways of doing business. A computer engineer who solves a glitch in a software program is executing a creative act.

Reed Hastings, founder and CEO of Netflix, an online provider of digital streaming media, is a manager with vision. In part, his vision for Netflix was to eliminate the fees associated with late video returns at movie rental retailers like now-defunct Blockbuster. Hastings initially developed a better and different way of doing business by allowing consumers a more convenient and less expensive way to watch DVDs at home—by sending them to subscription-based customers through the mail. Next, using broadband technology, Hastings launched a premium and original content streaming service to allow consumers to view movies and TV shows directly from their personal computers, mobile devices, and televisions. With a current subscription base of over 120 million streaming customers, Hastings has creatively transformed his original DVD-by-mail company to an American global on-demand Internet streaming media provider.[35]

With some practice and mental exercise, you can cultivate your own ability to think creatively. Here are some exercises and guidelines:

- In a group, brainstorm by listing ideas as they come to mind. Build on other people's ideas, but don't criticize them. Wait until later to evaluate and organize the ideas.
- Think about how to make familiar concepts unfamiliar. A glue that doesn't stick very well? That's the basis for 3M's popular Post-it notes.
- Plan ways to rearrange your thinking with simple questions such as "What features can we leave out?" or by imagining what it feels like to be the customer.

- Cultivate curiosity, openness, risk, and energy as you meet people and encounter new situations. View these encounters as opportunities to learn.
- Treat failures as additional learning experiences.
- Get regular physical exercise. When you work out, your brain releases endorphins, and these chemicals stimulate creative thinking.

Creativity and critical thinking must go beyond generating new ideas, however. They must lead to action. In addition to creating an environment in which employees can nurture ideas, managers must give them opportunities to take risks in order to innovate and develop new solutions.

Ability to Lead Change

Today's business leaders must guide their employees and organizations through the changes brought about by technology, marketplace demands, and global competition. Managers must be skilled at recognizing employee strengths and motivating people to move toward common goals as members of a team. Throughout this book, real-world examples demonstrate how companies have initiated sweeping change initiatives.

Factors that require organizational change can come from both external and internal sources; successful managers must be aware of both. External forces might include feedback from customers, developments in the global marketplace, economic trends, and new technologies. Internal factors might arise from new company goals, emerging employee needs, labor union demands, or production issues.

Assessment Check

1. Why is vision an important managerial quality?
2. What is the difference between creativity and critical thinking?

7 What Makes a Company Admired?

Who do you admire? Is it someone who has achieved great feats in sports, government, entertainment, business, or as a humanitarian? Why do you admire the person? Does he or she run a company, represent financial success, or give back to the community and society? Every year, business magazines and organizations publish lists of companies that they consider to be "most admired." Companies, like individuals, may be admired for many reasons. Most people would mention profitability, consistent growth, a safe and challenging work environment, high-quality goods and services, and business ethics and social responsibility. *Business ethics* refers to the standards of conduct and moral values involving decisions made in the work environment. *Social responsibility* is a management philosophy that includes contributing resources to the community, preserving the natural environment, and developing or participating in nonprofit programs designed to promote the well-being of the general public. You'll find business ethics and social responsibility examples throughout this book, as well as a deeper exploration of these topics in Chapter 2. For businesses to behave ethically and responsibly, their employees need to have strong moral compasses that guide them. The "Judgment Call" feature describes some of the challenges of defining what is ethical.

As you read this text, you'll be able to decide why companies should—or should not—be admired. *Fortune* publishes two lists of most-admired companies each year, one for U.S.-based firms and one for the world. The list is compiled from surveys and other research conducted by the Hay Group, a global human resources and organizational consulting firm. Criteria for

Judgment Call

Failed Emissions Test: Volkswagen's Costs Mount

Established in 1937, German giant Volkswagen is the second-largest automobile manufacturer in the world behind Toyota, with three cars in the top 10 list of best-selling cars of all time—the Golf, the Beetle, and the Passat. Despite its success as an iconic brand with car models that span multiple revisions and generations, software that turns off emissions controls on 11 million of its vehicles globally has caused the company irreparable damage.

How did this happen? Volkswagen knowingly placed in its cars a device with software that turns emissions control systems on and off. This type of software is commonly referred to as "defeat software," which turns emissions controls off under normal driving conditions and turns them on when the car is undergoing an emissions test. The U.S. Environmental Protection Agency (EPA) first discovered the device (called a defeat device) in diesel engines. Its software detects when engines are being tested—and when Volkswagen's four-cylinder cars weren't hooked up to emissions testing equipment, they did, in fact, emit up to 40 times more pollution than allowed under U.S. standards. When the car recognizes that it is being tested, it communicates with its computer to adjust how the car is running, thereby reducing emissions to legal levels. The result: inaccurate emissions tests on diesel vehicles fitted with the device.

According to the Environmental Protection Agency, using a defeat device in cars to evade clean air standards is illegal and a threat to public health. Fallout from the emissions scandal brings the cost for VW to over $30 billion, which includes a buyback of over 500,000 vehicles, a $4.3 billion settlement with the U.S. Justice Department, $17 billion paid to U.S. consumers and dealers, and a $2.8 billion criminal penalty.

A fine of $400,000 and a seven-year prison sentence have been imposed on a former Michigan-based senior Volkswagen executive in charge of VW's environmental and engineering office. He was found guilty of concealing the software used to evade pollution limits on close to 600,000 diesel vehicles. Although car sales nationwide are declining, VW has still not returned to the sales level achieved prior to the eruption of what some refer to as its worst crisis ever.

Questions for Critical Thinking

1. What impact do you think the emissions scandal will have on the long-term future sales of Volkswagen cars in the United States?
2. Knowing that the company acknowledges its wrongdoing, would you purchase a car from Volkswagen in the near future? Why or why not?

Sources: Karl Russell, Guilbert Gates, Josh Keller, and Derek Watkins, "How Volkswagen Got Away with Diesel Deception," *New York Times*, http://www.nytimes.com, accessed February 8, 2018; Dan Neil, "VW Lost Its Moral Compass in Quest for Growth," *Wall Street Journal*, http://www.wsj.com, accessed February 8, 2018; Alfred Joyner, "VW Emissions Scandal Explained in 60 Seconds," *International Business Times*, http://www.ibtimes.co.uk, accessed February 8, 2018; Bill Chappell, "Volkswagen CEO Resigns, Saying He's Shocked by Emissions Scandal," *National Public Radio*, http://www.npr.org, accessed February 8, 2018; Timothy Gardner and Bernie Woodall, "Volkswagen Could Face $18 Billion Penalties from EPA," *Reuters*, http://in.reuters.com, accessed February 8, 2018; Andrea Murphy, "2015 Global 2000: The World's Biggest Auto Companies," *Forbes*, https://www.forbes.com, accessed February 8, 2018; Eric D. Lawrence, "VW Engineer Gets 40 Months in Prison for Role in Diesel Scandal," *USA Today*, http://usatoday.com, accessed February 8, 2018; Paul A. Eisenstein, "Volkswagen Slapped with Largest Ever Fine for Automakers," *NBC News*, https://www.nbcnews.com, accessed February 9, 2018; Neal E. Boudettenov, "Volkswagen Sales in U.S. Rebound After Diesel Scandal," *New York Times*, https://www.nytimes.com, accessed February 12, 2018.

making the list include innovation, people management, use of corporate assets, social responsibility, quality of management, and quality of products and services.[36] Companies that made the list in a recent year include Apple, Amazon, Alphabet, Berkshire Hathaway, Starbucks, Disney, and Microsoft.

Assessment Check

1. Define *business ethics* and *social responsibility*.
2. Identify three criteria used to judge whether a company might be considered admirable.

What's Ahead

As business continues to evolve at a frenetic pace, new technologies, demographic changes, and fewer global barriers are changing the landscape.

Throughout this book, you'll be exposed to the real-life stories of many businesspeople. You'll learn about the range of business careers available and the daily decisions, tasks, and challenges that they face. By the end of the course, you'll understand how marketing, production, accounting, finance, and management create synergies to provide competitive advantages for companies. This knowledge can help you enhance your career potential while becoming more aware.

Now that this chapter has introduced some basic terms and issues in today's business environment, Chapter 2 takes a detailed look at the ethical and social responsibility issues facing business today. Chapter 3 deals with economic challenges, and Chapter 4 focuses on the challenges and opportunities faced by companies competing in world markets.

Chapter in Review

Summary of Learning Objectives

LEARNING OBJECTIVE 1 Define *business*.

Business consists of all profit-seeking activities that provide goods and services necessary to an economic system. Not-for-profit organizations are business-like establishments whose primary objective is public service over profits.

Assessment Check Answers

1.1 **What activity lies at the center of every business endeavor?** At the heart of every business endeavor is an exchange between a buyer and a seller.

1.2 **What is the primary objective of a not-for-profit organization?** Not-for-profit organizations place public service above profits, although they need to raise money in order to operate and achieve their social goals.

LEARNING OBJECTIVE 2 Identify and describe the factors of production.

The factors of production consist of four basic inputs: land, labor, capital, and entrepreneurship. Land is used in the production of a good, and includes all production inputs or natural resources that are useful in their natural states such as oil, gas, minerals, and timber. Labor includes anyone who works for a company. Capital includes technology, tools, information, and physical facilities. Entrepreneurship is the willingness to take risks to create and operate a business.

Assessment Check Answers

2.1 **Identify the four basic inputs to an economic system.** The four basic inputs are land, labor, capital, and entrepreneurship.

2.2 **List four types of capital.** Four types of capital are technology, tools, information, and physical facilities.

LEARNING OBJECTIVE 3 Describe the private enterprise system.

The private enterprise system is an economic system that rewards companies for their ability to perceive and serve the needs and demands of consumers. Competition in the private enterprise system ensures success for companies that satisfy consumer demands. Citizens in a private enterprise economy enjoy the rights to private property, profits, freedom of choice, and competition. Entrepreneurship drives economic growth.

Assessment Check Answers

3.1 **What is an alternative term for *private enterprise system?*** *Capitalism* is an alternative word for private enterprise system.

3.2 **What is the most basic freedom under the private enterprise system?** The most basic freedom is the right to private property.

3.3 **What is an entrepreneur?** An entrepreneur is a risk taker who is willing to start, own, and operate a business.

LEARNING OBJECTIVE 4 Identify the seven eras in the history of business.

The seven historical eras are the Colonial period, the Industrial Revolution, the age of industrial entrepreneurs, the production era, the marketing era, the relationship era, and the social era. In the Colonial period, businesses were small and rural, emphasizing agricultural production. The Industrial Revolution brought factories and mass production to business. The age of industrial entrepreneurs built on the Industrial Revolution through an expansion in the number and size of companies. The production era focused on the growth of factory operations through assembly lines and other efficient internal processes. During and following the Great Depression, businesses concentrated on finding markets for their products through advertising and selling, giving rise to the marketing era. In the relationship era, businesspeople focused on developing and sustaining long-term relationships with customers and other businesses. In the social era, businesses use technology and relationship management to connect and communicate with consumers and promote innovation. Strategic alliances create a competitive advantage through partnerships. Concern for the environment also helps build strong relationships with customers.

Assessment Check Answers

4.1 **What was the Industrial Revolution?** The Industrial Revolution began around 1750 in England and moved business operations from an emphasis on independent, skilled workers to a factory system that mass-produced items.

4.2 **During which era was the idea of branding developed?** The idea of branding began in the marketing era.

4.3 **What is the difference between transaction management and management in the relationship era?** Transaction management is an approach that focuses on building, promoting, and selling enough products to cover costs and earn profits. In the relationship era, businesses seek ways to actively nurture customer loyalty by carefully managing every interaction.

LEARNING OBJECTIVE 5 Explain current workforce trends in business.

The workforce is changing in several significant ways: it is aging and the labor pool is shrinking, and it is becoming increasingly diverse. The nature of work has shifted toward services and a focus on information. More businesses now rely on outsourcing, offshoring, and nearshoring to produce goods or fulfill services and functions that were previously handled in-house or in-country. In addition, today's workplaces are becoming increasingly flexible, allowing employees to work from different locations. And with artificial intelligence (AI) to become more efficient, companies are fostering innovation through teamwork and collaboration.

Assessment Check Answers

5.1 **Define *outsourcing*, *offshoring*, and *nearshoring*.** Outsourcing involves using outside vendors to produce goods or fulfill services and functions that were once handled in house. Offshoring is the relocation of business processes to lower-cost locations overseas. Nearshoring is the outsourcing of production or services to locations near a company's home base.

5.2 **Describe the importance of collaboration and employee partnership.** Businesses are increasingly focusing on collaboration rather than on individuals working alone. No longer do employees just put in their time at a job they hold their entire career. The new employer–employee partnership encourages teamwork, creative thinking, and problem solving.

LEARNING OBJECTIVE 6 Identify the skills and attributes needed for today's manager.

For today's managers, the ability to communicate and strategically apply critical thinking skills and creativity to both challenges and opportunities will be a top priority. Critical-thinking skills and creativity allow managers to pinpoint problems and opportunities and plan novel solutions. Finally, managers are dealing with rapid change, and they need skills to help lead their organizations through shifts in external and internal conditions.

Assessment Check Answers

6.1 **Why is vision an important managerial quality?** To thrive in the 21st century, managers need vision, the ability to perceive marketplace needs and to determine what an organization must do to satisfy those needs.

6.2 **What is the difference between creativity and critical thinking?** Critical thinking is the ability to analyze and assess information to pinpoint problems or opportunities. Creativity is the capacity to develop novel solutions to perceived organizational problems.

LEARNING OBJECTIVE 7 Outline the characteristics that make a company admired.

A company is usually admired for its solid profits, stable growth, a safe and challenging work environment, high-quality goods and services, and business ethics and social responsibility.

Assessment Check Answers

7.1 **Define *business ethics* and *social responsibility*.** Business ethics refers to the standards of conduct and moral values involving decisions made in the work environment. Social responsibility is a management philosophy that includes contributing resources to the community, preserving the natural environment, and developing or participating in nonprofit programs designed to promote the well-being of the general public.

7.2 **Identify three criteria used to judge whether a company might be considered admirable.** Criteria in judging whether companies are admirable include three of the following: solid profits, consistent growth, a safe and challenging work environment, high-quality goods and services, and business ethics and social responsibility.

Business Terms You Need to Know

business 2
profits 3
not-for-profit organizations 3
factors of production 4
land 5
labor 5
capital 5
entrepreneurship 5
private enterprise system 6
capitalism 6
competition 6
competitive differentiation 6
private property 6
entrepreneur 7
consumer orientation 11
branding 12
brand 12
transaction management 12
relationship era 12
social era 12
relationship management 12
strategic alliance 13
diversity 16
outsourcing 16
offshoring 17
nearshoring 17
crowdsourcing 17
vision 18
critical thinking 18
creativity 18

Review Questions

1. Why is business so important to a country's economy?

2. In what ways are not-for-profit organizations a substantial part of the U.S. economy? What unique challenges do not-for-profits face?

3. Identify and describe the four basic inputs that make up factors of production. Give an example of each factor of production that an auto manufacturer might use.

4. What is a private enterprise system? What four rights are critical to the operation of capitalism? Why would capitalism function poorly in a society that does not ensure these rights for its citizens?

5. In what ways is entrepreneurship vital to the private enterprise system?

6. Identify the seven eras of business in the United States. How did business change during each era?

7. Describe the focus of the most recent era of U.S. business. How is this different from previous eras?

8. Define partnership and strategic alliance. How might a motorcycle dealer and a local radio station benefit from an alliance?

9. Identify the major changes in the workforce that will affect the way managers build a world-class workforce. Why is the knowledge economy so important?

10. Identify four qualities that managers of the 21st century must have. Why are these qualities important in a competitive business environment?

Projects and Teamwork Applications

1. The entrepreneurial spirit fuels growth in the U.S. economy. Choose a company that interests you—one you have worked for or dealt with as a customer—and read about the company by visiting its website. Learn what you can about the company's early history: Who founded it and why? Is the founder still with the organization? Do you think the founder's original vision is still embraced by the company? If not, how has the vision changed?

2. Branding distinguishes one company's goods or services from those of its competitors. Each company you purchase from hopes that you will become loyal to its brand. Some well-known brands are Amazon, Google, Toyota, and Apple. Choose a type of good or service you use regularly and identify the major brands associated with it. Are you loyal to a particular brand? Why or why not?

3. More and more businesses are forming strategic alliances to become more competitive. Sometimes, businesses pair up with not-for-profit organizations in a relationship that is beneficial to both. Choose a company whose goods or services interest you, such as REI, FedEx, Kashi, or Sam's Club. On your own or with a classmate, research the company to learn about its alliances with not-for-profit organizations. Then describe one of the alliances, including goals and benefits to both parties. Create a presentation for your class.

4. This chapter describes how the nature of the workforce is changing: the population is aging, the labor pool is shrinking, the workforce is becoming more diverse, the nature of work is changing, the workplace is becoming more flexible and mobile, and with artificial intelligence (AI), to innovate and become more efficient, employers are fostering collaboration among their employees. Form teams of two to three students. Select a company and research how that company is responding to changes in the workforce as discussed in the chapter. When you have completed your research, be prepared to present it to your class. Choose one of the following companies or select your own: Allstate, Cargill, Staples, or Microsoft.

5. Today's business leaders must guide their employees and organizations through the changes brought about by technology, marketplace demands, and global competition. Choose a for-profit or not-for-profit organization and provide one example for each of the specific changes brought about by: (a) technology, (b) marketplace demands, and (c) global competition.

Web Assignments

1. **Nearshoring despite uncertainty around trade, trends.** General Electric, who manufactures water heaters, among many other products, has recently moved production back to the United States from China. As global economic conditions have changed, companies like Apple, Walmart, and Caterpillar have also followed suit—seeing opportunities closer to home as good business sense. Research nearshoring (also called insourcing, reshoring, and nearsourcing) trends and identify examples of three companies, the advantages, and why they have made the decision to do so.

2. **Companies and not-for-profits.** In addition to companies, virtually all not-for-profit organizations have websites. Four websites are listed below, two for companies (Lululemon and Best Buy) and two for not-for-profits (Mayo Clinic and Wounded Warrior Project). What is the purpose of each website? What type of information is available? How are the sites similar? How are they different?

www.amazon.com
www.bestbuy.com
www.mayoclinic.org
www.woundedwarriorproject.org

3. **Characteristics of U.S. workforce.** Visit the website for the U.S. Bureau of Labor Statistics—a good source of basic demographic and economic data. On the home page, scroll down to the Career Information box and click on "Occupational Outlook Handbook." Within the Occupational Groups, explore the "Business and Financial" occupations. Which ones look interesting? Are you surprised by the median pay levels listed for these careers? Why or why not?

www.bls.gov

Note: Internet web addresses change frequently. If you don't find the exact sites listed, you may need to access the organization's home page and search from there or use a search engine such as Google or Bing.

Cases

Case 1.1 Mars Expands Its Sweet Line of Business

Stricken with childhood polio, Frank C. Mars learned the art of hand dipping chocolate in his mother's kitchen and went on to start Mars back in the early 1900s. A privately held business in its fourth generation of family ownership, Mars has more than 85,000 employees around the globe. Some of the company's sweet brands include Snickers, Starburst, M&Ms, LifeSavers, Skittles, Juicy Fruit, and Orbit chewing gun. The company also owns Uncle Ben's Rice and Whiskas pet food. Recently, for the first time in 35 years, Mars opened a new $270 million, 500,000-square-foot chocolate factory in Topeka, Kansas, creating 200 new jobs. On a daily basis, the plant's output will amount to 8 million miniature Snickers candy bars and 39 million peanut M&Ms.

As America's seventh-largest private company with over $35 billion in sales, Mars, based in McLean, Virginia, rarely grants interviews to the media, even preferring to keep information like how the little "m" gets stamped on the outer shell of an M&M private. Internally, however, there remain few, if any, secrets—flat screens throughout its facilities display up-to-date financial information about the company. This reflects the company's philosophy of closely tying employee compensation to financial results. Employees can earn bonuses of 10% to 100% of their salaries for team performance.

For the sixth time, Mars recently made it onto *Fortune's* roster of 100 Best Companies to Work For. Known for its extensive training, community engagement, and health and wellness programs, Mars offers other benefits and perks in its highly collaborative environment, including free candy and being able to bring one's pet to work. Turnover is less than 6% among its U.S. employees, known as "Martians." Perhaps the most significant feature of this "Best Company" is its internal advancement and reward opportunities. The company develops and encourages cross-division talent and expects its employees to follow its five guiding principles of quality, responsibility, mutuality, efficiency, and freedom. "The consumer is our boss, quality is our work and value for money is our goal," reads the Mars quality principle.

Questions for Critical Thinking

1. Discuss how guiding principles, internal advancement, and reward opportunities such as those practiced at Mars can help with employee retention.
2. Discuss the pros and cons of company secrecy. Are there certain situations in which a company benefits by keeping information confidential? Are there other situations in which secrecy can be harmful? Using examples, please explain.

Sources: Oliver Stately, "To Fill 70,000 Jobs, Chocolate Giant Mars Will Have to Overcome Its Deeply Secretive Past," *Quartz*, http://quartz.com, accessed February 9, 2018; company website, "History of Mars" and "The Five Principles," http://www.mars.com, accessed February 9, 2018; Annie Gasparro, "At Mars Inc., 'Fun Size' Chocolate and Right-Size Conglomerate," *Wall Street Journal*, http://www.wsj.com, accessed February 9, 2018; Andrea Murphy, "America's Largest Private Companies 2015," *Forbes*, https://www.forbes.com, accessed February 9, 2018; "100 Best Companies to Work For: 2015," *Fortune*, http://money.cnn.com, accessed February 9, 2018; David A. Kaplan, "Mars: A Pretty Sweet Place to Work," *Fortune*, http://management.fortune.cnn.com, accessed February 9, 2018; Vandana Sinha, "Read Our First-Ever Conversation with Mars," *Biz Beat*, http://www.bizjournals.com, accessed February 9, 2018; company website, "Reviews: Mars, Inc.," http://reviews.greatplacetowork.com/mars-incorporated, accessed February 9, 2018.

Case 1.2 Jack Ma of Alibaba Helps China Breathe Easier

A little over two decades ago, Jack Ma founded Alibaba Group in his Hangzhou apartment. Alibaba includes an online payment system, Alipay, and two e-commerce sites, Tmall and Taobao. Valued at close to $500 billion, Alibaba had the largest ever U.S.-listed initial public offering (IPO) to date—the first sale of stock by a company to the general public. As a result of its IPO, Alibaba has become far better known in the United States. Similarly, the company has been described as a Chinese combination of eBay, Amazon, and PayPal.

Jack Ma, who is in his 50s, has been referred to as the "godfather of China's scrappy entrepreneurial spirit." As the face of China's new age of entrepreneurs, he commands a cult-like following among the younger Chinese generation. At a speech given upon his retirement as Alibaba's CEO five years ago, Ma reminded the audience that business cannot prosper when it continues to be ruined by overdevelopment, which includes China's hazardous levels of pollution. Recently, he set up a way to give a certain percentage of his wealth to causes related to health care, education, and the environment in China.

Alluding to China's increased economic prosperity and rising middle class, Ma points out that the dreams of the Chinese people may fade away if the sun cannot be seen. When Ma's family and friends were diagnosed with lung and liver cancer, he became increasingly concerned about cleaning up China's air and water. He has committed 2% of the value of Alibaba's stock to help preserve the environment. As he is a self-made Internet billionaire, many see Ma's move, the largest of its kind in China, as the beginning of a new era of giving among China's billionaires.

Questions for Critical Thinking

1. A philanthropist is someone who donates time and money to charitable causes. Why do you think there might be more challenges for philanthropists in China as compared to those in the United States?
2. What are some of the issues that can arise in a country experiencing unpredictable economic prosperity among segments of its population?

Sources: Scott Cendrowski, "Alibaba's Jack Ma Is China's Biggest Philanthropist," *Fortune*, http://fortune.com, accessed February 8, 2018; Liyan Chen, Ryan Mac, and Brian Solomon, "Alibaba Claims Title for Largest Global IPO Ever with Extra Share Sales," *Forbes*, https://www.forbes.com, accessed February 8, 2018; Steven Millward, "Godfather of China's Scrappy Entrepreneurial Spirit: Alibaba's Jack Ma Is FT's Person of the Year," *Techinasia*, http://www.techinasia.com, accessed February 8, 2018; Andrew Browne and Paul Mozur, "Alibaba's Jack Ma Sets Up Philanthropic Trust," *Wall Street Journal*, http://www.wsj.com, accessed February 8, 2018; Susan Chan Shifflett, "China's Hottest Tech Giants Join the 'War on Pollution'," *The Diplomat*, http://thediplomat.com, accessed February 8, 2018; Paul R. La Monica, "Look Out, Amazon: China's Alibaba May Soon Be Bigger," *CNN Money*, http://money.cnn.com, accessed February 8, 2018; Claire Brownell, "Jack Ma on Kindred Spirit Trudeau, Retirement and Why Alibaba Is Not the 'Amazon of China'," *Financial Post*, http://business.financialpost.com, accessed February 8, 2018.

Case 1.3 TripAdvisor: "Speed Wins"

At TripAdvisor, a global travel website with user-generated reviews and opinions, competition within the global travel industry remains cutthroat and intense. Steve Kaufer is the co-founder and CEO of Trip Advisor, and taped on his office door is a sign that reads "Speed Wins." The sign, handwritten by Kaufer when he first started TripAdvisor in 2000, is the company's informal and internal motto. As the company has grown to over 3,000 employees, the sign has been moved multiple times.

One of the basic rights under the private enterprise system happens to be fair competition. Because it is so inexpensive for competitors to start up, there are many unknowns, and in a business environment in which things move so quickly, one of the core aspects of a company's response must be speed and fast response. "If you don't respond quickly, you will kind of go through this decay," says the company's President of Vacation Rentals. TripAdvisor boasts over 570 million reviews and opinions, 60 million photos from travelers worldwide, and more than 7 million hotels, bed and breakfasts, specialty lodging, vacation rentals, restaurants, and attractions in 136,000 destinations. With those kinds of numbers, TripAdvisor remains focused on creating value for its users and, using its global footprint, to continuously acquire new knowledge of what users respond to most favorably.

This chapter explores the ways companies are admired—and TripAdvisor certainly falls into that category. The company has earned the reputation as one of the most highly recognized, used, and trusted travel websites in the global travel industry. TripAdvisor's customers are thrilled with the company's quick and constant improvements and new features on its site that services hundreds of millions of visitors each month in more than two dozen languages. The company remains focused on the quality of what is produced and what goes on its site, and with volumes of information, its meticulously built infrastructure must support it well and accurately.

TripAdvisor fosters managerial success through a culture that promotes finding successful outcomes while sponsoring novelty, new ideas, and even failure. Tolerance for failure in the organization—not out of sloppiness but from outcomes that just didn't work out—is the way TripAdvisor's management team subscribes to learning, which results in better long-term decision making.

One of the basic inputs of an economic system happens to be entrepreneurship. TripAdvisor began by accidental discovery in 2000 when Steve Kaufer, a classic entrepreneur, was planning a vacation to Mexico for his family. During the planning process Kaufer's wife realized her husband's frustration with unbiased hotel reviews—and the lack of user-generated information and feedback from travelers. Sure, plenty of breathtaking pictures and beautifully printed and designed brochures from travel agents were available. Rather than reading what hotel operators were saying about themselves, what Kaufer really wanted to know was what customers were saying about the hotels. This lack of information is what ultimately led Kaufer to create a firsthand, user-generated feedback system and platform.

Another basic input of an economic system happens to be human resources, and TripAdvisor is acutely focused on its hiring practices to ensure a cultural fit. As part of its "Speed Wins" culture, TripAdvisor hires people who wish to get out of a larger bureaucratic company environment as well as those with a predisposition to moving quickly. The company develops its employees to take knowledge and convert it into interesting user experiences not only for its travelers, but for business advertisers, too.

Leveraging technology, the TripAdvisor site attracts over 455 million users a month in search of firsthand travel research and experience. Kaufer admits that the biggest change impacting his business is the way in which people use technology. TripAdvisor has adapted to the changing nature of today's business and technology environment. As internet usage has moved to a mobile device, TripAdvisor has invested in in-destination functionality for their products, so that people can use the application not just to plan their trip, but also in short bursts while they are moving around and using their mobile phones. Kaufer's goal is for his customers to bring the TripAdvisor experience with them on their trip. In addition, virtual reality and virtual tours—where travelers can experience places before they even go—are becoming part of what Kaufer refers to as his company's universal value proposition—that which allows travelers the ability to share their opinion thereby allowing other travelers the ability to make their decisions based on those opinions.

Questions for Critical Thinking

1. How does TripAdvisor use the four basic inputs of an economic system?
2. Steve Kaufer, an entrepreneur, has said, "I watch with amazement at how some of the companies these days start up without much of a notion of how they're going to make money. But just if they get a lot of eyeballs, if they got a lot of usage, they'll figure it out. I'm the first to say that several companies have figured that out in spades, and they're wonderfully successful. Amen. I want to remind people, that is the exception to the rule." From what you can tell, how has Kaufer made TripAdvisor a success?
3. How has the company earned the reputation as the most recognized, used, and trusted travel website? What are the admirable traits of TripAdvisor? (You may want to go to the TripAdvisor.com website to learn more about the company.)
4. This chapter discusses that at the heart of every business endeavor is an exchange between buyer and seller. How does this relate to TripAdvisor's business?

Sources: Adele Blair, "Airbnb, TripAdvisor, Product Review: We Still Trust Strangers' Recommendations," *Sydney Morning Herald*, http://www.smh.com.au, accessed February 9, 2018; Dennis Schaal, "Buying TripAdvisor: Would Antitrust Issues Kill a Priceline or Google Acquisition?" *Skift.com*, https://skift.com, accessed February 9, 2018; Yue Wu, "The Story of TripAdvisor," http://www.onlineeconomy.org, *The Online Economy: Strategy and Entrepreneurship*, accessed February 9, 2018; company website, "Fact Sheet," https://www.tripadvisor.com/PressCenter-c4-Fact_Sheet.html, accessed February 9, 2018; Victoria Abbott Riccardi, "A Day in the Life of TripAdvisor CEO Steve Kaufer," *Boston Globe*, http://bostonglobe.com, accessed February 9, 2018; company website, "About TripAdvisor," https://tripadvisor.mediaroom.com, accessed February 9, 2018.

Business Ethics and Social Responsibility

LEARNING OBJECTIVES

1. Explain the concern for ethical and societal issues.
2. Describe the contemporary ethical environment.
3. Discuss how organizations shape ethical conduct.
4. Describe how businesses can act responsibly to satisfy society.
5. Explain the ethical responsibilities of businesses to investors and the financial community.

Changemaker

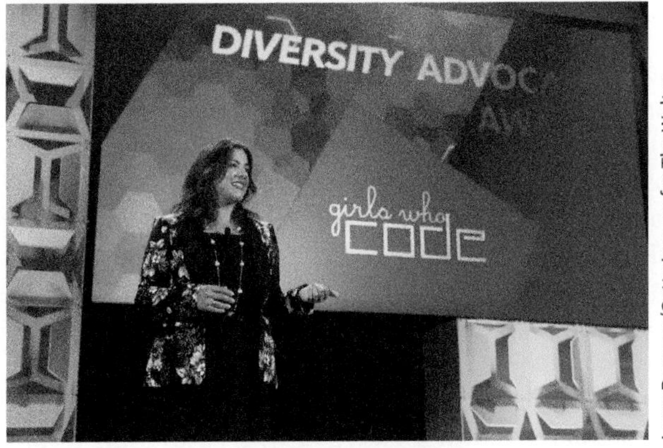

Larry Busacca/Getty Images for The Walter Kaitz Foundation

Reshma Saujani, Founder and CEO

Organization/Nonprofit: Girls Who Code

Industry: Nonprofit/Education/Technology

Website: http://www.girlswhocode.com

Recent statistics reveal that only 18% of computer science graduates are women, with the percentage gradually declining since the 1980s. In 2012, with 20 girls in New York City, Reshma Saujani, a lawyer and politician, founded Girls Who Code with the single mission of closing the gender gap in technology. Girls Who Code, a nonprofit organization, is now a national movement that includes programs during the academic school year teaching middle school and high school girls computing skills like programming, robotics, and web design. Currently, there are 1,500 Girls Who Code clubs across America, and corporate partners play a key role in funding.

The goal is to teach one million girls to code in the next two years. With a new model for computer science education, Girls Who Code has taught 50,000 girls in all 50 states. Girls Who Code includes a summer program for junior and senior high school girls, a 2-week specialized Campus Program, and after-school Clubs for middle school girls. Before entering the program, 77% of the girls have no intention of majoring or minoring in computer science. After completing the program, however, 90% of participants intend on doing so.

As a self-proclaimed "failed politician," Saujani, an Indian American, learned firsthand about failure. "Success is the product of bravery, not perfection. Fail first, fail hard, and fail fast," she proclaims. Saujani advocates for a new model of female leadership that is focused on risk-taking, competition, and mentorship. As part of the Girls Who Code summer immersion program, girls participate in project-based-learning and workshops, hear from guest speakers, connect with female engineers and entrepreneurs, and go on field trips to technology companies like Airbnb, Vimeo, Daily Beast, Google, General Motors, Lyft, and Dell. It won't be easy to close the gender gap in computer science, but Saujani is confident that it can be done. "I think this is one of the problems we can solve. And we can do it in the next 10 years," she says.[1]

Overview

Although most organizations practice ethical business conduct while making a profit, in recent years some have continued to face challenges in overcoming major ethical lapses. Ethical failures in several large or well-known companies have led to lawsuits, CEO firings, huge fines associated with legal settlements, and sometimes even failure. The reputation of corporations has suffered in the recent past as news and social media reports of scandals spread like wild fire.

In the wake of ongoing news reports of corporate wrongdoing, companies have become increasingly aware of the importance of conducting themselves in an ethical manner—and one that reflects a responsibility to customers, to society, to consumers, and to the environment. The U.S. Sentencing Commission expanded and strengthened its guidelines for ethics compliance programs, and more companies began to pay attention to formulating more explicit standards and procedures for ethical behavior. Companies also began to recognize the enormous impact of setting a good example. Today you are likely to hear about the efforts of companies such as Starbucks, Lego, and Microsoft—all of whom give back to their respective communities by creating jobs for veterans, enhancing education, and reducing their environmental impact through sustainable production.[2]

As we discussed in Chapter 1, the underlying goal of business is to serve customers at a profit. But most companies today try to do more than that, looking for ways to give back to customers, employees, society, and the environment. Sometimes they face difficult decisions in the process. When does a company's self-interest conflict with the well-being of society and customers? And must the goal of the pursuit of profits conflict with conducting business ethically and above board? A growing number of entities of all sizes are proving that profitability does not have to come at the expense of ethics.

1 Concern for Ethical and Societal Issues

business ethics standards of conduct and moral values regarding right and wrong actions in the work environment.

An organization that wants to succeed over the long term has as its core, strong **business ethics**, the standards of conduct and moral values governing actions and decisions in the work environment. Businesses also must take into account a wide range of social issues, including how a decision will affect the environment, employees, and customers. These issues are at the heart of *social responsibility*, whose primary objective is the enhancement of society's welfare through philosophies, policies, values, and actions. Panera, a chain of fast casual restaurants, has been using antibiotic-free chicken for over a decade and recently announced it would do the same for all of its turkey products, a move that has received positive feedback from customers. Many consumers believe that ethically raised animals are not just better for their diets but also better for society as a whole.[3]

In business, as in life, deciding what is right or wrong in a given situation does not always involve a clear-cut choice. Companies have many responsibilities—to customers, to employees, to investors, and to society as a whole. Sometimes conflicts arise in trying to serve the different needs of these separate constituencies. The ethical values of executives and individual employees at all levels can influence the decisions and actions a business takes. Throughout your own career, you will encounter many situations in which you will need to weigh right and wrong before making a decision or taking action. So we begin our discussion of business ethics by focusing on individual ethics.

Business ethics are also shaped by the ethical climate within an organization. Codes of conduct and ethical standards play increasingly significant roles in businesses in which doing the right thing is both supported and applauded. This chapter demonstrates how a company can create a framework to encourage—and even demand—high standards of ethical behavior and social responsibility throughout its organization. The chapter also considers the complex question of what obligation business has to society and how societal forces influence the actions of businesses. Finally, it examines the influence of business ethics and social responsibility on global business.

Assessment Check

1. To whom do businesses have responsibilities?
2. If a company is meeting all its responsibilities to others, why do ethical conflicts arise?

2 The Contemporary Ethical Environment

Ethical lapses by businesses are in the news like never before. Companies are well aware that gaining the trust of both their consumer base and the general public requires constant attention to detail and high ethical conduct. To maintain and gain trust, a company's *social responsibility* efforts should be designed to benefit consumers, investors, employees, the environment, and the companies themselves.

Most business owners and managers have built and maintained companies without compromising ethics. One example of a corporate leader with a long-standing commitment to employee welfare, ethical practice, and corporate social responsibility is Howard Schultz of Starbucks. The company distributes to all employees (called partners) a resource entitled *The Standards of Business Conduct*—an expectation of how to conduct business. Operating in 70 countries with more than 27,000 stores, Starbucks was recently recognized as the World's Most Ethical Company by the Ethisphere Institute. Figure 2.1 outlines the company's standards of business conduct, one of the first retailers to offer comprehensive health coverage to part-time employees (and their families) working 20 hours or more per week. The Starbucks College Achievement Plan provides full tuition reimbursement to eligible part- and full-time employees who wish to earn a college degree. In addition, the Starbucks C.A.F.E. practices (Coffee and Farmer Equity) include four key areas: quality, economic accountability and transparency, social responsibility, and environmental leadership.[4]

Many companies are conscious of how ethical standards can translate into concern for the environment. Recently, The Coca-Cola Company released its global sustainability report, highlighting goals related to women, water, packaging and recycling, and giving back:

1. Since 2010, the company has empowered 1.7 million women producers, suppliers, distributors, retailers, recyclers, and artisans.
2. 221 billion liters of water have been replenished through community and watershed projects across the globe.
3. Sixty percent of bottles and cans equivalent to what was introduced in the marketplace were refilled or recovered and recycled.
4. $106 million was donated across more than 200 countries and territories.

In addition, the CO_2 embedded in the Coca-Cola, "the drink in your hand," was reduced by 14%, and the company estimates that energy efficiency initiatives since 2004 have saved the global system over $1 billion.[5]

To inspire and nurture the human spirit—one person, one cup, and one neighborhood at a time. Here are the principles of how we live that every day:

Our Coffee

It has always been, and will always be, about quality. We're passionate about ethically sourcing the finest coffee beans, roasting them with great care, and improving the lives of people who grow them. We care deeply about all of this; our work is never done.

Our Partners

We're called partners, because it's not just a job, it's our passion. Together, we embrace diversity to create a place where each of us can be ourselves. We always treat each other with respect and dignity. And we hold each other to that standard.

Our Customers

When we are fully engaged, we connect with, laugh with, and uplift the lives of our customers—even if just for a few moments. Sure, it starts with the promise of a perfectly made beverage, but our work goes far beyond that. It's really about human connection.

Our Stores

When our customers feel this sense of belonging, our stores become a haven, a break from the worries outside, a place where you can meet with friends. It's about enjoyment at the speed of life—sometimes slow and savored, sometimes faster. Always full of humanity.

Our Neighborhood

Every store is part of a community, and we take our responsibility to be good neighbors seriously. We want to be invited in wherever we do business. We can be a force for positive action—bringing together our partners, customers, and the community to contribute every day. Now we see that our responsibility—and our potential for good—is even larger. The world is looking to Starbucks to set the new standard, yet again. We will lead.

Our Shareholders

We know that as we deliver in each of these areas, we enjoy the kind of success that rewards our shareholders. We are fully accountable to get each of these elements right so that Starbucks—and everyone it touches—can endure and thrive.

Onward.

Source: Company website, "Our Starbucks Mission," http://globalassets.starbucks.com, accessed January 23, 2018.

FIGURE 2.1 **Starbucks Standards of Business Conduct**

The Global Business Ethics Survey™ provides insight into worker conduct and workplace integrity on a global scale in both the public and the private sector, a first-of-its-kind study. A key finding of the survey is that 4 out of 5 retaliation victims across all sectors, a median of 79%, said that retaliation occurred three weeks after reporting an incident.[6]

Sarbanes-Oxley Act of 2002 federal legislation designed to deter and punish corporate and accounting fraud and corruption and to protect the interests of workers and shareholders through enhanced financial disclosures, criminal penalties on CEOs and CFOs who defraud investors, safeguards for whistle- blowers, and establishment of a new regulatory body for public accounting firms.

In response to a number of corporate and accounting scandals, the **Sarbanes-Oxley Act of 2002** established new rules and regulations for securities trading and accounting practices in addition to enhancing the reliability and transparency of public company financial statements. Companies are now required to publish their code of ethics, if they have one, and inform the public of any changes made to it. The law may actually encourage even more companies to develop written codes and guidelines for ethical business behavior. The federal government also created the U.S. Sentencing Commission to institutionalize ethics compliance programs that would establish high ethical standards and end corporate misconduct. The requirements for such programs are shown in **Table 2.1**.

The current ethical environment of business also includes the appointment of new corporate officers specifically charged with deterring wrongdoing and ensuring that ethical standards are met. Ethics compliance officers, whose numbers are rapidly rising, are responsible for conducting employee training programs that help spot potential fraud and abuse within an organization, investigating sexual harassment and discrimination charges, and monitoring any potential conflicts of interest. But practicing corporate social responsibility is more than just monitoring behavior. Many companies now adopt a three-pronged approach to ethics and social responsibility:

1. engaging in traditional corporate philanthropy, which involves giving to worthy causes
2. anticipating and managing risks
3. identifying opportunities to create value by doing the right thing.[7]

TABLE 2.1 Minimum Requirements for Ethics Compliance Programs

Compliance standards and procedures. Establish standards and procedures, such as codes of ethics and identification of areas of risk, capable of reducing misconduct or criminal activities.
High-level personnel responsibility. Assign high-level personnel, such as boards of directors and top executives, the overall responsibility to actively lead and oversee ethics compliance programs.
Due care in assignments. Avoid delegating authority to individuals with a propensity for misconduct or illegal activities.
Communication of standards and procedures. Communicate ethical requirements to high-level officials and other employees through ethics training programs or publications that explain in practical terms what is required.
Establishment of monitoring and auditing systems and reporting system. Monitor and review ethical compliance systems, and establish a reporting system employees can use to notify the organization of misconduct without fear of retribution.
Enforcement of standards through appropriate mechanisms. Consistently enforce ethical codes, including employee discipline.
Appropriate responses to the offense. Take reasonable steps to respond to the offense and to prevent and detect further violations.
Self-reporting. Report misconduct to the appropriate government agency.
Applicable industry practice or standards. Follow government regulations and industry standards.

Sources: Government website, "An Overview of the United States Sentencing Commission and the Federal Sentencing Guidelines," http://www.ussc.gov, accessed February 15, 2018; "The Relationship Between Law and Ethics, and the Significance of the Federal Sentencing Guidelines for Organizations," Ethics & Policy Integration Centre, http://www.ethicaledge.com, accessed February 15, 2018; government website, "Sentencing Commission Toughens Requirements for Corporate Compliance and Ethics Programs," United States Sentencing Commission news release, http://www.ussc.gov, accessed February 15, 2018.

Individuals Make a Difference

In today's business environment, individuals certainly make the difference in ethical expectations and behavior. As executives, managers, and employees demonstrate their personal ethical principles—or lack of ethical principles—the expectations and actions of those who work for and with them can change.

What is the current status of individual business ethics in the United States? Although ethical behavior can be difficult to track or define in all circumstances, evidence suggests that some individuals do act unethically or illegally on the job. The National Business Ethics Survey identifies such behaviors as putting one's own interests ahead of the organization, abuse of company resources, misreporting hours worked, Internet abuse, and safety violations, among others.[8]

Technology seems to have expanded the range and impact of unethical behavior. For example, anyone with computer access to data has the potential to steal or manipulate the data or to shut down the system, even from a remote location. Banks, insurance companies, and other financial institutions are often targeted for such attacks. Equifax, a 118-year-old credit reporting agency, revealed one of the largest cyberattacks and data breaches of all time, impacting over 145 million customers. Personal information like names, date of birth, Social Security numbers, and home addresses of customers was compromised. Additionally, the company learned about a major breach of its computer systems five months before the date the attack was publicly disclosed, leading to further investigations of stock sales by top level executives.[9]

Nearly every employee, at every level, faces ethical dilemmas or questions. Some rationalize questionable behavior by saying, "Everybody's doing it." Others act unethically to avoid punishment or job loss because they feel pressured in their jobs to meet performance quotas. Further, some act unethically solely for the purpose of personal gain. To help you understand the differences in the ways individuals arrive at ethical choices, the next section focuses on how personal ethics and morals develop.

Development of Individual Ethics

According to psychologist Lawrence Kohlberg, moral reasoning, the basis for ethical behavior, has three developmental stages—and each has greater adequacy at responding to moral dilemmas. The three stages are shown in **Figure 2.2**: the preconventional, conventional, and postconventional stages. In stage 1, the preconventional stage, individuals primarily consider their own needs and desires in making decisions. They obey external rules only because they are afraid of punishment or hope to receive rewards if they comply.

In stage 2, the conventional stage, individuals are aware of and act in response to their duty to others, including their obligations to their family members, co-workers, and organizations. The expectations of these groups influence how they choose between what is acceptable and unacceptable in certain situations. Self-interest, however, continues to play a role in decisions.

Stage 3, the postconventional stage, represents the highest level of ethical and moral behavior. The individual is able to move beyond mere self-interest and duty and take the larger needs of society into account as well. He or she has developed personal ethical principles for determining what is right and can apply those principles in a wide variety of situations. Being passionate about a specific cause is a unique qualification for a career in fundraising (known as development), as the "Job Description" feature describes.

An individual's stage in moral and ethical development is determined by a number of factors. Experiences help shape responses to different situations. A person's family, educational, cultural, and religious backgrounds can also play a role, as can the environment within the firm. Individuals can also have different styles of deciding ethical dilemmas, no matter what their stage of moral development.

To help you understand and prepare for the ethical dilemmas you may confront in your career, let's take a closer look at some of the factors involved in solving ethical questions on the job.

Stage 1: Preconventional

Individual is mainly looking out for his or her own interests. Rules are followed only out of fear of punishment or hope of reward.

↓

Stage 2: Conventional

Individual considers the interests and expectations of others in making decisions. Rules are followed because it is a part of belonging to the group.

↓

Stage 3: Postconventional

Individual follows personal principles for resolving ethical dilemmas. He or she considers personal, group, and societal interests.

FIGURE 2.2 Stages of Moral and Ethical Development

Job Description

Fundraiser/Director of Development

Overview Fundraisers work primarily for nonprofit organizations, including educational institutions, charitable organizations, healthcare foundations, and political campaigns. Most nonprofits have a development department, which conducts fundraising campaigns and focuses on ways to supplement funding with donations, grants, sponsorships, and gifts-in-kind (gifts other than cash donations). To make up shortfalls in funding, organizations need fundraiser to solicit money from individuals as well as other groups or organizations.

Responsibilities The role of a fundraiser includes: researching, identifying, and contacting potential donors; devising fundraising strategies and creating a message that appeals to targeted donors; organizing a campaign to solicit contributions; maintaining records of donor information; training volunteers in fundraising procedures and practices: planning and organizing events, galas, sponsorships, and other fundraiser; and ensuring that all legal reporting requirements are satisfied.

Requirements Strong writing skills are necessary to craft letters of solicitation and thanks to donors, as well as to highlight the various types of projects undertaken as a result of donations and/or grants. Fundraisers usually have a bachelor's degree in a variety of subjects, including but not limited to business, marketing, finance, public relations, English, journalism, or communications. Some candidates enter the nonprofit sector from higher education programs that offer a focus in nonprofit management, philanthropic studies, or fundraising and development. Students who have participated in volunteering at local charities or have served in leadership positions of student-led organizations sometimes find themselves in the fundraising or development department of a nonprofit organization.

Effective communication skills are also crucial to cultivate relationships with prospective donors so that people will make donations on an ongoing basis. Fundraisers evaluate large amounts of data to determine past (and future) giving trends, so being detail-oriented matters. Leadership skills are also crucial because fundraisers often manage teams of unpaid volunteers. As nonprofits continue to use social media channels to raise funds, knowledge of digital and social media tools is important.

Outlook Driven by the need to raise funds on a continuing basis, job prospects for fundraisers are expected to increase 9% annually, faster than many other occupations. For those with excellent communication and organizations skills, along with a passion for a specific cause, fundraising is an excellent career opportunity.

Sources: Government website, "Fundraisers," *Occupational Outlook Handbook*, 2017–2018 Edition, http://www.bls.gov, accessed February 16, 2018; organization website, "Summary Report for: 13-1131.00—Fundraisers," http://www.onetonline.org, accessed February 16, 2018; government website, "What Fundraisers Do," http://www.bls.gov, accessed February 16, 2018.

On-the-Job Ethical Dilemmas

In today's hyperchanging business world, you will sometimes be called on to weigh the ethics of decisions that can affect not just your own future but possibly the future of your co-workers, your company, and its customers. As already noted, it's not always easy to distinguish the difference between what is right and wrong in many business situations, especially when the needs and concerns of various parties conflict. In the past, some CEOs (or their companies) who were accused of wrongdoing simply claimed that they had no idea crimes were being committed, but today's environment is such that top management must make a greater effort to be aware of activities taking place in their companies.

In an effort to increase business, Wells Fargo encouraged employees to cross-sell its products and services. For example, a checking account customer was encouraged to open a savings or credit card account. To encourage employees to cross-sell, the company provided financial incentives. Using fictitious or unauthorized information, employees responded to these incentives by manufacturing approximately 3.5 million fake bank accounts. On a grand scale, this "pay for performance" strategy brought about employee behavior that eventually led to a tarnished reputation, the resignation of the company's CEO, and the firing of 5,300 employees. The bank is providing $3.7 million in refunds to impacted customers. Additionally, the bank has been criticized for not acknowledging the crisis soon enough.[10]

Banks are still trying to regain consumer trust after the financial downturn that began over a decade ago. Within the banking industry, constant reminders about ethical conduct and the consequences of falling short should be practiced so that employees instinctively understand and adhere strictly to the highest levels of ethical conduct.[11]

Solving ethical dilemmas is not easy. In many cases, each possible decision can have both unpleasant consequences and positive benefits that must be evaluated. Figure 2.3

identifies four of the most common ethical challenges that businesspeople face: conflict of interest, honesty and integrity, loyalty versus truth, and whistle-blowing.

FIGURE 2.3 **Common Business Ethical Challenges**

Conflict of Interest

A **conflict of interest** occurs when a businessperson is faced with a situation in which an action benefiting one person or group has the potential to harm another. Conflicts of interest may pose ethical challenges when they involve the businessperson's own interests and those of someone to whom he or she has a duty or when they involve two parties to whom the businessperson has a duty. The majority of mutual fund purchases are made by investors through intermediaries, such as brokers and advisors, whose high fees (commissions) associated with such funds have created a conflict of interest. Firms with a legal obligation to put clients' interests ahead of their own have made it mandatory to disclose when a client is put into a higher fee fund when less expensive shares are available. A conflict may also exist between someone's personal interests and those of an organization or its customers. An offer of gifts or bribes for special treatment creates a situation in which the buyer, but not necessarily the company, may benefit personally.

Ethical ways to handle conflicts of interest include (1) avoiding them and (2) disclosing them. Some companies have policies against taking on clients who are competitors of existing clients. Most businesses and government agencies have written policies prohibiting employees from accepting gifts or specifying a maximum gift value. Or a member of a board of directors or committee might abstain from voting on a decision in which he or she has a personal interest. In other situations, people disclose their potential conflict of interest so that the people affected can decide whether to get information or help they need from another source instead.

conflict of interest situation in which an employee must choose between a business's welfare and personal gain.

Honesty and Integrity

Employers highly value honesty and integrity. An employee who is honest can be counted on to tell the truth. An employee with **integrity** goes beyond truthfulness. Having integrity means adhering to deeply felt ethical principles in business situations. It includes doing what you say you will do and accepting responsibility for mistakes. Behaving with honesty and integrity inspires trust, and as a result it can help build long-term relationships with customers, employers, suppliers, and the public. Employees, in turn, want their managers and the company as a whole to treat them honestly and with integrity.

integrity adhering to deeply felt ethical principles in business situations.

Unfortunately, violations of honesty and integrity are all too common. Some people misrepresent their academic credentials and previous work experience on their resumes, LinkedIn profiles, or job applications. Although it may seem tempting to embellish a résumé in a competitive job market, the act shows a lack of honesty and integrity. A technology CEO resigned after it was discovered that a degree he allegedly "earned" was not offered by the university cited on his résumé.[12]

Others steal from their employers by taking home supplies or products without permission or by carrying out personal business on company time. For example, Internet misuse during the workday is increasing. As shown in the photo, employees use the Internet for personal shopping, e-mail, gaming, and social networking. This misuse costs U.S. companies billions of dollars annually in lost productivity.[13] While the occurrence of such activity varies widely—and employers may feel more strongly about cracking down on some activities than others—most agree that Internet misuse is a problem. Some organizations have resorted to electronic monitoring and surveillance.

Loyalty versus Truth

Employees are expected to be loyal and to act in the best interests of the company. However, an ethical conflict can arise when an employee sees something going on within the organization that is untruthful or something that just doesn't seem legitimate, honest, and open. Individuals may have to decide between loyalty to the company and truthfulness, especially when it comes to business relationships. Some place the highest value on loyalty, even at the expense of truth. Others avoid volunteering negative information but

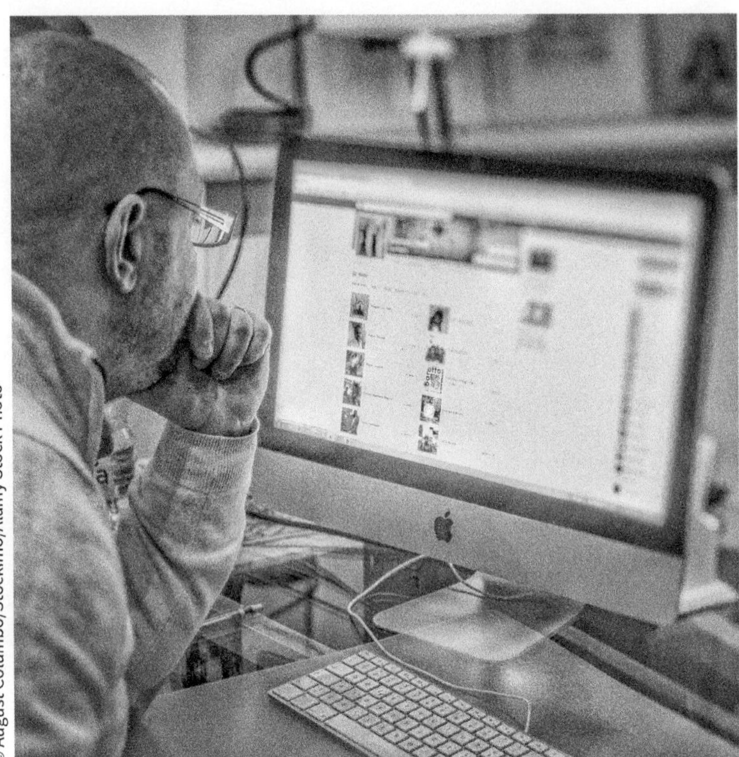
© August Columbo/Stockimo/Alamy Stock Photo

Employers and employees value honesty and integrity, but what should happen when employees misuse Internet privileges for personal purposes?

answer truthfully if someone asks them a specific question. People may emphasize truthfulness and actively disclose negative information, especially if the cost of silence is high, as in the case of operating a malfunctioning aircraft or selling tainted food items.

Whistle-blowing When an individual encounters unethical or illegal actions at work, that person must decide what action to take. Sometimes it is possible to resolve the problem by working through channels within the organization. If that fails, the person should weigh the potential damages to the greater public good. If the damage is significant, a person may conclude that the only solution is to blow the whistle. **Whistle-blowing** is an employee's disclosure to company officials, government authorities, or the media of illegal, immoral, or unethical practices.

whistle-blowing employee's disclosure to company officials, government authorities, or the media of illegal, immoral, or unethical practices committed by an organization.

A whistleblower must weigh a number of issues when deciding whether to come forward. Resolving an ethical issue within the organization can be more effective, assuming higher-level managers cooperate. A company that values ethics will try to correct an issue; staying at a company that does not value ethics may not be worthwhile. In some cases, however, people resort to whistle-blowing because they believe the unethical behavior is causing significant damage that outweighs the risk that the company will retaliate against the whistleblower. In some cases, those risks have been real.

State and federal laws protect whistleblowers in certain situations, such as reports of discrimination, and the Sarbanes-Oxley Act of 2002 now requires that companies in the private sector provide procedures for anonymous reporting of accusations of fraud. Under the act, anyone who retaliates against an employee for taking concerns of unlawful conduct to a public official can be prosecuted. In addition, whistleblowers can seek protection under the False Claims Act, under which they can file a lawsuit on behalf of the government if they believe that a company has somehow defrauded the government. Charges against health care companies for fraudulent Medicare or Medicaid billing are examples of this type of lawsuit.

Despite protections, whistle-blowing has its risks, including resentment from co-workers, and ultimately, job loss. However, it is one way to expose illegal business behavior. In the defense, healthcare, financial, and pharmaceutical industries, whistleblower cases have become a common way to uncover fraud. Banking giant JP Morgan Chase & Company failed to properly inform wealth management clients about conflicts of interest when they were steered into investments that created greater profitability for the bank, resulting in a $30 million whistleblower award. According to JP Morgan Chase, its communication omissions were unintentional, and the bank has since enhanced its disclosures.[14]

Obviously, whistle-blowing and other ethical issues arise relatively infrequently in companies with strong organizational climates of ethical behavior. The next section examines how an organization can develop an environment that discourages unethical behavior among individuals.

Assessment Check

1. What role can an ethics compliance officer play in a company?
2. What are the three components of a typical company's approach to ethics and social responsibility?

3 How Organizations Shape Ethical Conduct

No individual makes decisions in a vacuum. Choices are strongly influenced by the standards of conduct established within the organizations where people work. Most ethical lapses in business reflect the corporate culture and values of an organization.

As shown in **Figure 2.4**, development of a corporate culture to support business ethics happens on four levels:

1. ethical awareness
2. ethical education
3. ethical action
4. ethical leadership

If any of these four factors is missing, the ethical climate in an organization will weaken.

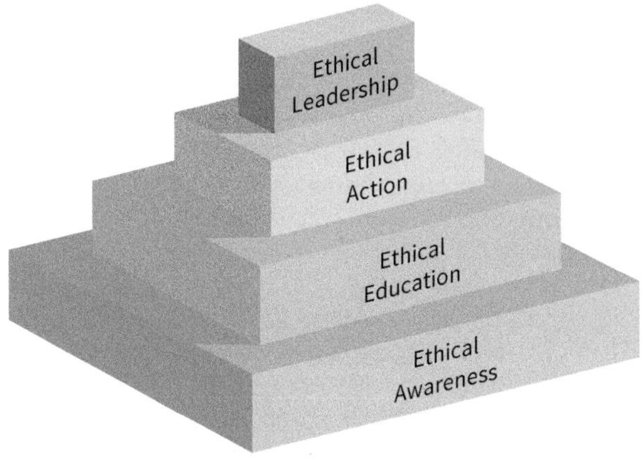

FIGURE 2.4 **Structure of an Ethical Environment**

Ethical Awareness

The foundation of an ethical climate is ethical awareness. As we have already seen, ethical dilemmas occur frequently in the workplace. So employees need assistance in identifying ethical problems when they occur. Workers also need guidance about how the company expects them to respond.

One way for a company to create awareness and support is to develop a **code of conduct**, a formal statement that defines how the organization expects employees to resolve ethical questions. At Google, "Don't be evil" is part of the company's code of conduct—and how the company serves its users with unbiased access to information, focusing on their needs and giving them the best possible products. Google believes in doing the right thing by following the law, acting honorably, and treating everyone with respect.[15] At the most basic level, a code of conduct may simply specify ground rules for acceptable behavior, such as identifying the laws and regulations to which employees must adhere. Other companies use their codes of conduct to identify key corporate values and provide frameworks that guide employees as they resolve moral and ethical dilemmas.

code of conduct formal statement that defines how an organization expects its employees to resolve ethical issues.

The aerospace giant Lockheed Martin, headquartered in Bethesda, Maryland, and with branch offices around the world, has issued a code of conduct to define its values and help employees put them into practice. The code of conduct emphasizes "maintaining a culture of integrity" and defines three basic core values: "Do what's right; respect others; perform with excellence." All employees at every level are expected to treat fellow employees, suppliers, and customers with dignity and respect and to comply with environmental, health, and safety regulations. The code reminds leaders that their language and behavior must not put pressure on subordinates that might induce them to perform in a way that is contrary to the standards set forth in the code. The code also outlines procedures for reporting violations to a local company ethics officer, promising confidentiality and nonretaliation for problems reported in good faith. Lockheed Martin issues a copy of this code of conduct to each employee and also posts it (in 16 languages) on its website.[16] Other companies incorporate similar codes in their policy manuals or mission statements; some issue a code of conduct or statement of values in the form of a small card that employees and managers can carry with them.

Ethical Education

Although a code of conduct can provide an overall framework, it cannot provide a detailed solution for every ethical situation. Some ethical questions have straightforward answers, but others do not. Businesses must provide the tools employees need to evaluate the options and arrive at suitable decisions.

Judgment Call

Goldman Sachs Analysts Fired for Cheating

There is about a 3% chance of landing a spot as a new analyst at Goldman Sachs, the New York–based investment banking and securities firm. For the 2,000 college graduates who accomplish this feat, the starting salary is $85,000 a year—not including a bonus. Known as one of the most selective firms in the financial services industry, Goldman Sachs is considered an employer of choice on Wall Street.

New analysts in the company's securities division participate in what is called the "Goldman Sachs Experience," designed to provide the skills, connections, and continuous learning to a fast-track career. Typically the company's analysts spend two to three years in their current position before advancing at the company or leaving to seek success at other financial firms.

Despite the tremendous odds of landing a job at Goldman Sachs, a group of 20 securities analysts were recently fired after it was discovered they cheated on a training test. Most investment firms like Goldman Sachs test employees on their knowledge of key policies, industry concepts, and compliance and regulatory matters. Traditionally, new analysts have not taken the tests very seriously while completing the five-week training program in New York. Reports suggest the tests have typically been taken in a collaborative manner—with test takers consulting each other about answers or using company computers to research information on the Internet. One source says that Goldman Sachs was explicit in telling new recruits what was (and was not) permissible.

Many on Wall Street are shocked at the firings and wonder whether cheating on required tests is an everyday occurrence or whether Goldman Sachs has decided to crack down.

Questions for Critical Thinking

1. Why do you think test takers assumed that a collaborative approach to taking the exam was acceptable behavior?
2. Discuss the importance of taking securities training seriously and why you believe Goldman Sachs fired the analysts.

Sources: Company website, "What We Do," http://www.goldmansachs.com, accessed February 18, 2018; Sofia Horta e Costa, "Goldman, JPMorgan Said to Fire 30 Analysts for Cheating on Tests," *Bloomberg Business*, http://www.bloomberg.com, accessed February 18, 2018; Justin Baer, "Goldman Firing About 20 Junior Staffers for Cheating on Tests," *Wall Street Journal*, http://www.wsj.com, accessed February 18, 2018; Liz Moyer, "Goldman Fires 20 Junior Employees Accused of Test Cheating," *New York Times*, http://www.nytimes.com, accessed February 18, 2018.

Many companies have either instituted their own ethics training programs or hired organizations such as SAI Global, which provides outsourced ethics and compliance programs to businesses. Among other services, SAI Global hosts employee reporting services with an anonymous hotline and an ethics case management system. It also helps companies develop appropriate ethics codes with training customized to each company's needs, including specialized online, interactive training systems.[17]

The debate continues over whether ethics can be taught. However, training can provide practice in the application of ethical values to hypothetical situations to employees before they are faced with "real-life" workplace situations. A free behavioral ethics series, "Ethics Unwrapped," from the University of Texas at Austin, provides business students with cases, concepts, and definitions through a series of videos. Convicted white-collar criminal Walter Pavlo, a former employee at telecommunications firm MCI, speaks at colleges and universities about his experiences in the firm and prison. Pavlo, who along with other MCI associates stashed money in offshore accounts, speaks about his actions in an effort to warn students of the consequences of cheating. After cheating was discovered among 20 members of an analyst class at Goldman Sachs, all were fired. See the "Judgment Call" feature for more details.

Ethical Action

Codes of conduct and ethics training help employees recognize and reason through ethical problems. In addition, companies must provide structures and approaches that allow decisions to be turned into ethical actions. At Starbucks, after identifying an ethical problem, the "Ethical Decision Making Framework" outlines the following to help partners (employees) determine the best approach:[18]

- Is it consistent with Our Starbucks Mission, the *Standards of Business Conduct,* and any applicable law or regulation?
- Would your approach embarrass you or Starbucks?
- How would your approach look published in the newspaper?

- Would you be comfortable with the example it sets for future decisions?
- If the path isn't clear, ask for guidance.
- Follow through on your decision.

Goals set for the business as a whole and for individual departments and employees can affect ethical behavior. A company whose managers set unrealistic goals for employee performance may find an increase in cheating, lying, and other misdeeds as employees attempt to protect themselves. In today's technology-enabled business environment, the high value placed on speed can create a climate in which ethical behavior is sometimes challenged. Ethical decisions often require careful and quiet thought, a challenging task in today's fast-paced business world.

Some companies encourage ethical action by providing support for employees faced with dilemmas. One common tool is an employee hotline, a telephone number that employees can call, often anonymously, for advice or to report unethical behavior they have witnessed. Ethics compliance officers can guide employees through ethical dilemmas while mobilizing them behind a culture of ethics.

Ethical Leadership

Executives must not only talk about ethical behavior but also demonstrate it through their actions. The devastating effects of the 2007–2009 U.S. financial crisis, a result of excessive leverage, lax financial regulation, and disgraceful banking practices, brought to light the increased commitment by organizations and business leaders to a company's core values, ethical leadership, and social responsibility.

The owner of several juice bars paid her employees to take part in a "22 days of kindness" program," where their only job was to perform random acts of kindness—acts that would brighten someone else's day. Featured in the media, the positive publicity yielded a flood of job applicants. This is an example of "tone at the top," a term used to describe an organization's ethical climate as established and acted out by its senior management, which has a "trickle-down" effect on employees.[19]

Unfortunately, not all organizations are able to build a solid framework of business ethics. Because the damage from ethical misconduct can profoundly affect a company's **stakeholders**—customers, investors, employees, and the public—pressure is exerted on businesses to act in acceptable ways. But when businesses fail, laws must be applied to enforce good business practices. Many of the laws that affect specific industries or individuals are described in subsequent chapters in this book. For example, legislation affecting international business operations is discussed in Chapter 4. Laws designed to assist small businesses are examined in Chapter 5. Laws related to labor unions are described in Chapter 8. Legislation related to banking and the securities markets is discussed in Chapters 16 and 17. Finally, for an examination of the legal and governmental forces designed to safeguard society's interests when businesses fail at self-regulation, see Appendix A, "Business Law."

stakeholders customers, investors, employees, and public affected by or with an interest in a company.

Assessment Check

1. Identify the four levels of a company's ethical environment.
2. How does ethical leadership contribute to ethical standards throughout a company?

4 Acting Responsibly to Satisfy Society

A second major issue affecting business is the issue of social responsibility. **Social responsibility** is management's acceptance of the obligation to consider profit, consumer satisfaction, and societal well-being of equal value in evaluating performance. It is the recognition

social responsibility business's consideration of society's well-being and consumer satisfaction, in addition to profits.

Clean & Green Business

No GMOs in Cheerios

General Mills, the maker of Cheerios, has stopped using genetically modified ingredients (GMOs) to make its famous cereal. Because Cheerios is one of the first foods given to toddlers, consumers placed pressure on General Mills to make Cheerios without GMOs. Among the fastest-growing U.S. food segments, retail sales of GMO-free cereal, salad dressing, eggs, and other food products increased 15% in a recent year.

The issue of GMOs has come to light as consumers pay closer attention to how their food is grown and processed while demanding more natural food products. They have become vocal to food makers like General Mills that have used modified food organisms. This modification gives the original plants or seeds new characteristics such as resistance to disease, longer shelf life, and greater yield. However, both consumers and environmentalists fear that plants not damaged when sprayed with weed killer will lead to the development of "superweeds" and ultimately to the use of more and more chemical herbicides. This has led to an anti-GMO movement and consumer concerns over environmental damage and the health and safety of using GMOs.

While the U.S. Food and Drug Administration says food made with GMOs is safe, consumers are increasingly seeking out non-GMO foods and becoming more curious about what is in their food. This has resulted in a debate around whether or not food with GMOs should (or should not) be labeled.

The response to General Mills eliminating GMOs from Cheerios has been positive from both consumers and environmental groups. Cheerios is one of the first major packaged food brands to eliminate GMOs from its manufacturing process, and certainly General Mills leads the trend for more transparency when it comes to food labeling.

Questions for Critical Thinking

1. An organization called the Non-GMO Project charges a fee to certify that a company's product contains no genetically modified ingredients. It has recently been inundated with requests for its non-GMO certification. Discuss or research the types of organizations that would be requesting such services.
2. Some farmers recently started planting GMO-free crops that command a premium price from food companies, even though the yield for such crops is smaller than other crops. Do you think this trend in the farming industry will continue? Why or why not?

Sources: Ilan Brat, "Food Goes 'GMO Free' with Same Ingredients," *Wall Street Journal*, http://www.wsj.com, accessed February 17, 2018; Bruce Horovitz, "Cheerios Drops Genetically Modified Ingredients," *USA Today*, http://www.usatoday.com, accessed February 17, 2018; Katie Couric, "GMO Controversy Explained," *Yahoo News*, http://news.yahoo.com, accessed February 17, 2018; Jacob Bunge, "Fields of Gold: GMO-Free Crops Prove Lucrative for Farmers," *Wall Street Journal*, http://www.wsj.com, accessed February 17, 2018; Stephanie Strom, "Chipotle to Stop Using Genetically Altered Ingredients," *New York Times*, http://www.nytimes.com, accessed February 17, 2018.

that business must be concerned with the qualitative dimensions of consumer, employee, and societal benefits, as well as the quantitative measures of sales and profits, by which business performance is traditionally measured. Businesses may exercise social responsibility because such behavior is required by law, because it enhances the company's image, or because management believes it is the ethical course of action. The "Clean & Green Business" feature describes how General Mills, maker of Cheerios, has eliminated genetically modified organisms (GMOs) from its iconic cereal.

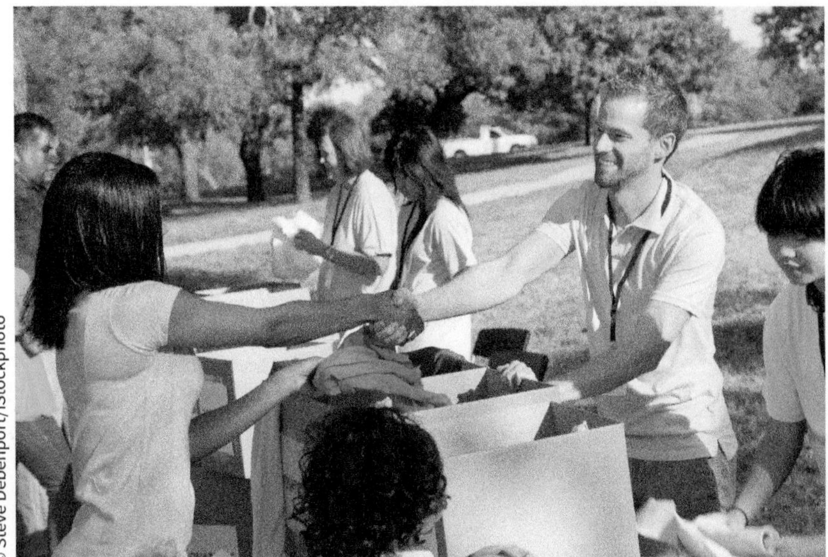

Businesses are judged by their interactions with the surrounding community, including employees volunteering at charitable events.

Historically, a company's social performance has been measured by its contribution to the overall economy and the employment opportunities it provides. Many factors contribute to the assessment of a company's social performance—and the private sector is an important partner in helping to address the pressing global challenges of health care and nutrition, poverty, increasing access to education, unemployment, gender inequality and cultural diversity, improving food, water and energy security, and reducing climate change. Additionally, organizations must provide a safe, healthy workplace and produce high-quality products that are safe to use.

A business is also evaluated on the basis of its interactions with the community. To demonstrate their social responsibility, many corporations highlight charitable contributions and community service in their annual reports and on their websites, which can be seen in the photo. Cisco Systems' most recent corporate social responsibility report focuses on improving lives, building communities, and preserving the environment. The company is also committed to improving access to health care in rural parts of the world, reducing poverty and unemployment, developing technologies that can help reduce greenhouse gas emissions, and fostering diversity and ethical standards throughout its business and supply chain.[20]

A company that takes into account the full cost of doing business is said to use a **triple bottom line** approach to measure its overall performance. This strategy places equal value on the three Ps: people, planet, and profit. In addition to a company's financial performance (profit), its social and environmental (people and planet) performance is also measured. Southwest Airlines and Patagonia are among the top companies that use this business approach.[21]

triple bottom line strategic business approach used by companies to evaluate performance by placing equal value on financial, social, and environmental factors.

Two contrasting views define the range of an organization's attitude toward social responsibility. Under the **socioeconomic model**, the belief is that business, as part of its role, owes its existence to improving the society in which it operates. This view recognizes that businesses aren't separate from society and that with their abundant resources, they should play a role in promoting a healthy and prosperous society. On the other hand, the **economic model**, favored by U.S. economist Milton Friedman, is one where businesses believe strongly that their sole role is to maximize profits and increase value to shareholders—and that society will further benefit when business is left alone to produce and market profitable products needed by society.[22]

socioeconomic model the belief that business, as part of its role, owes its existence to improving the society in which it operates.

economic model one in which businesses believe strongly that their sole role is to maximize profits and increase value to shareholders.

Some companies measure social performance by conducting **social audits**, formal procedures that identify and evaluate all company activities that relate to social issues such as conservation, employment practices, environmental protection, and philanthropy. Based on this information, management may improve or revise current programs or develop new ones.

social audits formal procedures that identify and evaluate all company activities that relate to social issues such as conservation, employment practices, environmental protection, and philanthropy.

As **Figure 2.5** shows, the social responsibilities of business can be classified according to its relationships to the general public, customers, employees, and investors and other members of the financial community. Many of these relationships extend beyond national borders.

Responsibilities to the General Public

The responsibilities of business to the general public include dealing with public health issues, protecting the environment, and developing the quality of the workforce. Many would argue that businesses also have responsibilities to support charitable and social causes and organizations that work toward the greater public good. In other words, they should support the communities in which they earn profits. Such efforts are called *corporate philanthropy*.

Public-Health Issues One of the most complex issues facing business as it addresses its ethical and social responsibilities to the general public is public health. Central to the public-health debate is the question of what businesses should do about products such as tobacco and alcohol. Tobacco products represent a major health risk, contributing to heart disease, stroke, and cancer among smokers. Families and co-workers of smokers share this danger as well, as their exposure to secondhand smoke increases their risks for cancer, asthma, and respiratory infections. Many cities have not only banned smoking in public places and enclosed places (like offices), but also in commercial businesses such as restaurants. Several states, including Arkansas, California, Louisiana, and Maine, have bans on smoking in cars when children under the age of 18 are present.[23]

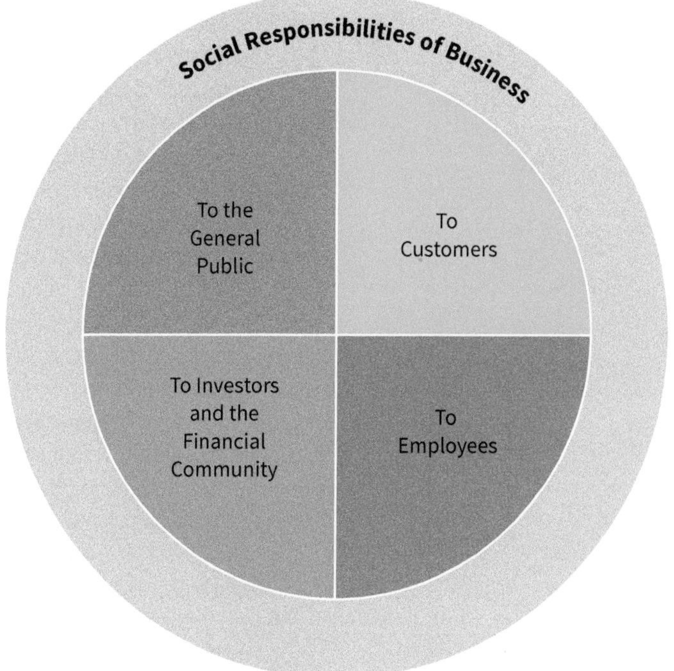

FIGURE 2.5 **Social Responsibilities of Business**

Heart disease, diabetes, and obesity have become major public health issues as the rates of these three conditions have

© Jani Bryson/iStockphoto

To do their part to aid the general public, some businesses collaborate with urban neighborhoods to set up community gardens as a way of showing kids how to eat healthy.

been rising. According to the Centers for Disease Control and Prevention, the obesity rate for children between the ages of 6 and 11 in the United States has increased—and for those ages 12 to 19, it has quadrupled over the last four decades. Three-quarters of obese teenagers will become obese adults at risk for diabetes and heart disease. In 2014, drugstore giant CVS Health made the bold decision to stop selling cigarettes and related products, a move that was estimated to cost the company more than $2 billion in annual sales. Recent research published in the *American Journal of Public Health* proves that the CVS decision had a powerful public health impact by disrupting access to cigarettes and helping guide more customers to better health. Data from the drugstore giant reveals that the decision contributed to a drop in tobacco purchases for all retailers.[24]

With more than 42,000 people killed in a recent year, opioid addiction is another critical public health crisis. The CDC recently issued guidelines for opioid prescriptions (narcotics used for pain medication) to reduce the risk of drug addiction and overdose. Forty percent of all opioid deaths involve a prescription opioid.

Leafy greens were recently identified as the likely source for recent foodborne *E. coli* outbreaks. The Food and Drug Administration (FDA) will continue to work to determine the specific products that made people ill, as well as where they were grown, distributed, and sold. Monitored by the FDA, the Food Safety Modernization Act (FSMA) will draw increased attention on farms with enforced safety standards for fresh fruits and vegetables.

Other serious public health threats include infectious and chronic disease. Chronic diseases include heart disease, cancer, diabetes, and Alzheimer's. In many developing countries, infectious diseases still loom large, including malaria, diarrhea, pneumonia, tuberculosis, and HIV.[25]

Protecting the Environment Businesses impact the environment through the energy they consume, the waste they produce, the natural resources they use, and more. Today, many businesses have set goals as part of their corporate social responsibility efforts to protect the environment. Some have even launched sustainability initiatives—operating in such a way that the company not only minimizes its impact on the environment but actually regenerates or replaces used resources. Ford and Kaiser Permanente maintain sustainability assessments of their suppliers, rating them on energy and water use, recycling, waste production, greenhouse gases produced, and other factors. Both organizations expect suppliers to meet green standards—or risk losing them as customers.[26]

For many managers, finding ways to minimize pollution and other environmental damage caused by their products or operating processes has become an important economic and legal issue as well as a social one. Nike continues to focus on decreasing waste. Nike Grind incorporates recycled materials like rubber, foam, fiber, leather, and textile blends into 71% of Nike's footwear and apparel products, including yarns and trims—even in its iconic basketball shoes. Flyknit technology (shoes made entirely of polyester in a knit construction process) produces 60% less waste than traditional cut-and-sew methods.[27]

Despite the efforts of companies like Ford, Kaiser Permanente, Nike, and many others, production and manufacturing methods still leave behind large quantities of waste materials that can further pollute the air, water, and soil. Some products themselves, such as electronics that contain lead and mercury, are difficult to recycle or reuse. Another solution to the problems of pollutants is **recycling**—reprocessing used materials for reuse. Recycling can sometimes provide much of the raw material that manufacturers need, thereby conserving the world's natural resources and reducing the need for landfills. The "Business Model" feature describes how toymaker Hasbro has been named one of the best corporate citizens in an annual survey.

recycling reprocessing of used materials for reuse.

In recent years, electronic items containing toxic substances such as lead, mercury, cadmium, arsenic, and flame retardants are being discarded at increasingly faster speeds. Due to changes in technology, built-in obsolescence, and consumer demand for the latest technology, smartphones, tablets, laptops, and TVs are being discarded into landfill. Increased consumption not only creates massive quantities of electronic waste, but also increases mining and procurement for the materials needed to produce the gadgets.[28]

Business Model

Hasbro Wins "Best Corporate Citizen" Award

The relationship between the environment and corporate citizenship might not be immediately apparent when you play Monopoly, Scrabble, or Twister. However, toymaker Hasbro has worked diligently to improve its social and environmental performance and was recently awarded the top spot as the best corporate citizen in the United States, ranking first in climate change, third in philanthropy, and fourth in human rights. The company, based in Pawtucket, Rhode Island, received high marks in several categories, including environment, human rights, and philanthropy and community support.

Hasbro has improved its packaging and printing processes while reducing greenhouse emissions and landfill waste. To save 34,000 miles of wire in a single year, Hasbro eliminated the wire ties that typically come with games and toys. To eliminate 800,000 pounds of waste worldwide, the company no longer wraps toy and game instructions in plastic bags. The company's factory in Massachusetts where many of its board games, puzzles, boxes, and components are manufactured uses vegetable-based printing inks and water-based coatings in its printing process.

On the topic of human rights, Hasbro employees carefully monitor factory facilities on an ongoing basis both here and in China where its products are made. In addition, employees are given four hours a month of paid time off to volunteer. The company's recent philanthropic efforts include more than $14 million in grants and toys to various organizations and 67,000 employee volunteer hours.

Hasbro's corporate social responsibility group is charged with advancing the company's social and environmental performance while remaining committed to achievements in several key areas, including product safety, environmental sustainability, and diversity. More than just creating words with its iconic Scrabble board game, Hasbro has taken action to build a safe and sustainable world for millions of children and their families.

Questions for Critical Thinking

1. What is your experience with packaging when purchasing toys, electronics, or other products? What additional solutions might you offer a toymaker like Hasbro?
2. How can Hasbro continue to advance its social and environmental performance agenda while maintaining profitability? What ideas would you present to company management?

Sources: Company website, "Playing With Purpose: 2017 Corporate Social Responsibility Report," http://csr.hasbro.com, accessed February 19, 2018; Karsten Strauss, "America's 100 Best Corporate Citizens in 2017," *Forbes*, http://www.forbes.com, accessed February 19, 2018; Julie Duffy, "Hasbro Earns Top Spot on Prestigious CSR Ranking," *Business Wire*, https://www.businesswire.com, accessed February 19, 2018.

Subaru recently transformed its 3.5-million-square-foot Lafayette, Indiana manufacturing facility into the first zero-waste automobile plant in the United States. To achieve this feat, the company worked carefully with an outside waste management solutions company to adopt the three Rs of environmental sustainability: reduce, reuse, and recycle.

After evaluating the manufacturing process and all materials used in production, everything that Subaru threw away was inventoried. The result is 94 million pounds of material, including 80 million pounds of metal recycled.

The facility, which employs 5,500 workers and produces 375,000 cars annually, involved all associates in the process by offering financial incentives for recommendations to improve the quality and safety of its vehicles, along with its environmental footprint. Each vehicle generates 240 pounds of waste, and the company is proud that every bit has been kept out of landfill.[29]

Many consumers favor and develop loyalty to environmentally conscious businesses. To target these customers, companies often use **green marketing**, a marketing strategy that promotes environmentally safe products and production methods. A business cannot simply claim that its goods or services are environmentally friendly, however. The Federal Trade Commission (FTC) has issued guidelines for businesses to follow in making environmental claims. A company must be able to prove that any environmental claim made about a product has been substantiated with reliable scientific evidence. In addition, as shown in **Figure 2.6**, the FTC has given specific directions about how various environmental terms may be used in advertising and marketing. The agency recently issued enforcement actions against companies with false and unsupported claims that their manufactured plastic products were biodegradable.[30]

green marketing a marketing strategy that promotes environmentally safe products and production methods.

Other environmental issues—such as finding renewable sources of clean energy and developing **sustainable** agriculture—are the focus of the efforts of many businesses, both large and small. Solar energy, geothermal energy, biodiesel, and wind power are just a few of the renewable sources of energy being developed by entrepreneurs, large energy firms, and small engineering companies. In North Carolina, more than 350 clean tech companies are working on developing a new generation of energy that includes smart grid technology, efficient water management, and smart transportation.[31]

sustainable the capacity to endure in ecology.

If a business says a product is . . .	The product or package must . . .
Biodegradable	break down and return to nature in a reasonably short period of time.
Compostable	break down into, or otherwise become part of, usable compost (e.g., soil-conditioning material, mulch) in a safe and timely manner
Recyclable	be entirely reusable as new materials in the manufacture or assembly of a new product or package.
Refillable	be included in a system for the collection and return of the package for refill. If consumers have to find a way to refill it themselves, it is not **refillable.**
Ozone Safe/Ozone Friendly	must not contain any ozone-depleting ingredient.

Source: Educational website, "16 CFR Part 260—for the Use of Environmental Marketing Claims," *Legal Information Institute*, https://www.law.cornell.edu, accessed February 19, 2018; government website, "Guides for the Use of Environmental Marketing Claims," http://www.ftc.gov, accessed February 19, 2018.

FIGURE 2.6 **FTC Guidelines for Environmental Claims in Green Marketing**

Developing the Quality of the Workforce In the past, a nation's wealth has often been based on its money, production equipment, and natural resources. A country's true wealth, however, lies in its people. An educated, skilled workforce provides the intellectual capital and know-how required to innovate, develop new technology, improve productivity, and compete in the global marketplace. It is becoming increasingly clear that to remain competitive, U.S. business must assume more responsibility for enhancing the quality of its workforce, including encouraging diversity initiatives.

In developed economies like that of the United States, many new jobs require college-educated workers. With an increased demand for workers with advanced skills, the difference between the highest-paid and lowest-paid workers has been increasing. Education plays a significant role in earnings, despite success stories of those who dropped out of college or high school to start businesses. Workers with a college degree earn an average of $1,170 a week, whereas those with a high school diploma earn $714.[32] Amazon sponsors a "Career Choice" program for full-time hourly employees working at its many fulfillment centers around the country. The company will pay up to 95% of tuition, textbooks, and associated fees up to $3,000 a year for four years. The company says it will pay for study in areas that are well paying and in high demand, such as aircraft mechanics, nursing, and medical laboratory science—funding education in those areas regardless of whether those skills are relevant to a career at Amazon.[33]

Organizations also face enormous responsibilities for assisting women, members of various cultural groups, returning military veterans, and those with physical disabilities to contribute fully to the economy. Failure to do so is not only a waste of more than half the nation's workforce but also devastating to a company's public image. Some socially responsible companies also encourage diversity in their business suppliers. A recent list of DiversityInc's top companies for supplier diversity include Ernst & Young (EY), Kaiser Permanente, AT&T, PwC, Johnson & Johnson, Sodexo, MasterCard, Marriott International, Wells Fargo, and Abbot.[34]

Corporate Philanthropy As discussed in Chapter 1, not-for-profit organizations play an important role in society by serving the public good. They provide the human resources that enhance the quality of life in communities around the world. To fulfill this mission, many not-for-profit organizations rely on financial contributions from the business community. Companies respond by donating billions of dollars each year to not-for-profit organizations. This **corporate philanthropy** includes cash contributions, donations of equipment and products,

corporate philanthropy effort of an organization to make a contribution to the communities in which it earns profits.

and supporting the volunteer efforts of company employees. Recipients include cultural organizations, adopt-a-school programs, neighborhood sports programs, and housing and job training programs.

Corporate philanthropy can have many positive benefits beyond the purely "feel-good" rewards of giving, such as higher employee morale, enhanced company image, and improved customer relationships. United Parcel Service recently announced sustainability goals to be met by 2025. These include the following: a reduction of greenhouse gas (GHG) emissions from global operations by 12%; one in four of its vehicle purchases annually will be an alternative fuel or advanced technology vehicle; and 25% of its electricity consumption will come from renewable energy sources. Approximately 40% of all ground fuel will be from sources other than conventional gasoline and diesel. In addition, 20 million volunteer hours will have been achieved, and $127 million in charitable contributions been made by 2020.[35]

German Garcia/AP Images for UPS

The UPS Foundation believes that tree planting, part of the Global Forestry Initiative, is a very effective way to remove carbon from our environment—in addition to creating better farming conditions to increase available foods, jobs, and shelter.

Companies often seek to align their marketing efforts with their charitable giving. Many contribute to the Olympics and create advertising that promotes the company's sponsorship. This is known as *cause-related marketing*. In a recent survey, nearly nine out of ten young people said they believed companies had a duty to support social causes, and nearly seven in eight said they would switch brands in order to reward a company that did so. In 2010, American Express launched Small Business Saturday (#ShopSmall), a cause-related marketing effort to increase revenue at small businesses the Saturday after Thanksgiving. In the early 1980s, the company partnered with a nonprofit to raise $1.7 million for restoration of the Statue of Liberty by giving a portion of every purchase made with its credit cards.[36]

Another form of corporate philanthropy is volunteerism. In their roles as corporate citizens, thousands of businesses encourage their employees to contribute their efforts to projects as diverse as Habitat for Humanity, the Red Cross, and the Humane Society. John Deere, known for its iconic green tractors, recently purchased a crop-spraying startup that uses machine learning. See the "Business & Technology" feature for the details. In addition to making tangible contributions to the well-being of fellow citizens, such programs generate considerable public support and goodwill for the companies and their employees. In some cases, the volunteer efforts occur mostly during off-hours for employees. In other instances, companies permit their employees to volunteer during regular working hours. Sometimes volunteers with special skills are indispensable. Employees at Deloitte undertake thousands of pro bono (voluntary professional services) projects to assist underserved individuals and groups in the community. Deloitte uses the talents and resources of its staff to help strengthen organizations that need additional guidance.[37]

consumerism public demand that a business consider the wants and needs of its customers in making decisions.

Responsibilities to Customers

Businesspeople share a social and ethical responsibility to treat their customers fairly and act in a manner that is not harmful to them. **Consumerism**—the public demand that a business consider the wants and needs of its customers in making decisions—has gained widespread acceptance. Consumerism is based on the belief that consumers have certain rights. The Consumer Bill of Rights was part of a speech made to U.S. Congress by President John F. Kennedy in 1962. **Figure 2.7** summarizes those consumer rights. Numerous state and federal laws have been implemented since then to protect the rights of consumers.

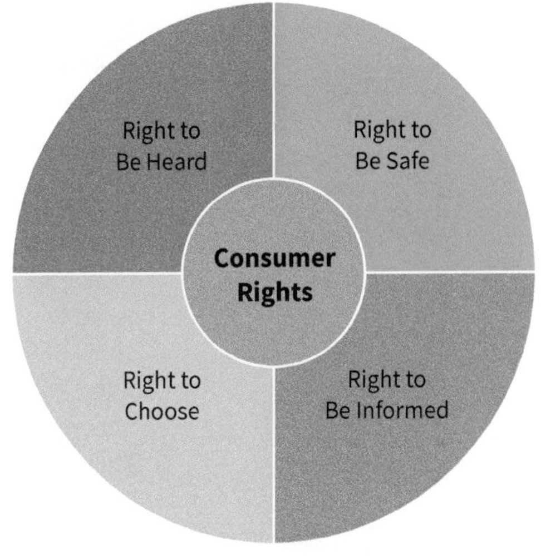

FIGURE 2.7 Consumer Bill of Rights as Proposed by President Kennedy

The Right to Be Safe Businesses must recognize obligations, both moral and legal, to ensure the safe operation of their products. Consumers should be

Business & Technology

John Deere Uses Artificial Intelligence to Increase Yield and Kill Weeds

Based in Illinois, John Deere is a 180-year-old company best known for its iconic green tractors often spotted on large picturesque farms located far from urban sprawl. After spending $305 million to purchase Blue River Technology—a 60-person, Sunnyvale, CA–based company that uses machine learning and computer vision to spot weeds—the company set up John Deere Labs in Silicon Valley (California). Once Blue River's crop-spraying technology and intellectual property is further developed and commercialized in John Deere Labs, the company plans to offer it through its global dealer network—and to bring agriculture into the modern age.

Crop-spraying equipment with machine learning "decides" which plants to keep and which to kill through imaging. In turn, farm management decisions are moved from field level to plant level through computer vision, robotics, and machine learning to help smart machines detect, identify, and make management decisions about individual plants in a farmer's field. Blue River's "See & Spray" technology identifies weeds that allow farmers to reduce reliance on chemicals such as herbicides by 95%.

In addition to significant cost savings on herbicides, crop yields are also increased by up to 10%. By 2050, with an anticipated population growth of 2.4 billion people, more food can be grown, and yields will be higher—and all with the same amount of land. Since there is not much more land to bring into production, the timing of the technology, coupled with the anticipated population growth, is a welcome sign to the age-old agriculture industry.

Questions for Critical Thinking

1. **Agriculture is being brought into the modern age, with more technology being developed to bring what some refer to as "the world's least digitized industry" into the modern age. Research and discuss additional technology being developed for the agriculture industry. What are the benefits and to whom?**
2. **Blue River Technology disrupts a $28 billion herbicide industry with big agrochemical players such as Syngenta, Bayer, BASF, DowDuPont, and Monsanto. But it will also restore water so that it is clean and healthy. Can you think of any other residual effects of this technology?**

Sources: Company website, "Our Smart Machines," http://www.bluerivertechnology.com, accessed February 18, 2018; Adele Peters, "How John Deere's New AI Lab is Designing Farm Equipment for a More Sustainable Future," *Fast Company*, http://www.fastcompany.com, accessed February 18, 2018; Michael Lev-Ram, "John Deere is Paying $305 Million for This Silicon Valley Company," *Fortune*, http://www.fortune.com, accessed February 18, 2018; Chris Duckett, "LettuceBOT Wants to Kill the Plants Farmers Hate," *ZDNet*, http://www.zdnet.com, accessed February 18, 2018; company website, "Deere to Advance Machine Learning Capabilities in Acquisition of Blue River Technology," https://www.deere.com, accessed February 18, 2018; Amanda Little, "This Family of AI Robots Will Feed the World," *Bloomberg*, http://www.bloomberg.com, accessed February 18, 2018.

product liability the responsibility of manufacturers for injuries and damages caused by their products.

confident that the products they purchase will not cause injuries during normal use. **Product liability** refers to the responsibility of manufacturers for injuries and damages caused by their products. Items that lead to injuries, either directly or indirectly, can have disastrous consequences for their makers. Table 2.2 outlines a number of companies faced with well-known product liability cases.

Many companies put their products through rigorous testing to avoid safety problems. Still, testing alone cannot foresee every eventuality. Companies must try to consider all possibilities and provide adequate warning of potential dangers. When a product does pose a threat to customer safety, a responsible manufacturer responds quickly to either correct the problem or recall the dangerous product. Although we take for granted that our food is safe, sometimes contamination leaks in, which can cause illness or even death. Texas-based ice cream maker Blue Bell Creameries nearly went out of business when a bacteria outbreak resulted in a massive recall and several deaths. The product is back in grocery store freezers, but an attempt to regain customer confidence continues to be an uphill battle.[38]

The Right to Be Informed Consumers should have access to enough education and product information to make responsible buying decisions. In their efforts to promote and sell their goods and services, companies can easily neglect consumers' right to be fully informed. False or misleading advertising is a violation of the Wheeler-Lea Act, a federal law enacted in 1938. The Federal Trade Commission and other federal and state agencies have established rules and regulations that govern truth in advertising. These rules prohibit businesses from making unsubstantiated claims about the performance or superiority of their merchandise. They also require businesses to avoid misleading consumers. Businesses that fail to comply face scrutiny from the FTC and consumer protection organizations. The maker of 5-Hour Energy drink misled consumers with questionable marketing claims that led consumers to believe that its product ingredients were superior to coffee and caffeine and that there would be a "no crash" boost. The company was recently ordered to pay a total of $4.3 million.[39]

TABLE 2.2 Well-Known Product Liability Cases

Company	Product	Claim	Settlement
General Motors	Automobiles	Faulty ignition switches linked to 124 deaths and a recall of 30 million cars worldwide.	To date, GM has paid out more than $2.5 billion in fines and settlements.
Philip Morris (Altria Group, Inc.)	Tobacco	A woman with lung cancer, a result of smoking cigarettes, claimed that the company failed to warn her about the risks of smoking.	Plaintiff awarded $28 million in damages.
Dow Corning (Dow Chemical Company)	Silicone breast implants	Consumers claimed the implants ruptured, causing injury and sometimes death.	$3.2 billion was awarded to more than170,000 women.
Takata Corporation	Airbags	Takata's malfunctioning airbag inflators sent shards of metal at drivers and passengers—resulting in 20 deaths to date.	Takata pleaded guilty and agreed to pay $1 billion for the investigation, $25 million in fines, $125 million for victim compensation, and $850 million to compensate automobile manufacturers.
McDonald's	Coffee	Third-degree burns were claimed after a woman spilled a scalding hot cup of coffee on herself.	In addition to compensatory damages, McDonald's paid the plaintiff punitive damages of $2.7 million.

Sources: Nathan Bomey and Kevin McCoy, "GM Agrees to $900M Criminal Settlement over Ignition Switch Defect," *USA Today*, http://www.usatoday.com, accessed February 19, 2018; "The 5 Largest U.S. Product Liability Cases," *Investopedia*, http://www.investopedia.com, accessed February 19, 2018; organization website, "Mesothelioma Cancer," http://www.mesothelioma.com, accessed February 19, 2018; David R. Olmos, "Dow Corning OKs $3.2-Billion Payout on Breast Implants," *Los Angeles Times*, http://articles.latimes.com, accessed February 19, 2018; Andrea Gerlin, "A Matter of Degree: How a Jury Decided That a Coffee Spill Is Worth $2.9 Million," *Wall Street Journal*, http://www.wsj.com, accessed February 19, 2018; Jie Ma, Emi Nobuhiro, Dawn McCarty, and Tiffany Kary, "Roiled by Airbag-Recall Crisis, Takata Files for Bankruptcy," *Bloomberg*, http://www.bloomberg.com, accessed February 19, 2018; Associated Press, "Honda Reports 20th Death from Exploding Takata Air Bag," *Los Angeles Times*, http://www.latimes.com, accessed February 19, 2018; Paul Lienert and David Shepardson, "Takata to Plead Guilty, Pay $1 Billion U.S. Penalty Over Air Bag Defect," *Reuters*, https://www.reuters.com, accessed February 19, 2018.

The Food and Drug Administration (FDA), which sets standards for advertising conducted by drug manufacturers, eased restrictions for prescription drug advertising on television. In print ads, drug makers are required to spell out potential side effects and the proper uses of prescription drugs. Because of the requirement to disclose this information, prescription drug television advertising was limited. Now, however, the FDA says drug ads on radio and television can directly promote a prescription drug's benefits if they provide a quick way for consumers to learn about side effects, such as displaying a toll-free number or website. In an effort to promote affordable alternatives, the American Medical Association for an end to the practice despite the drug industry's attempt to seek official approval to expand its efforts to so-called off-label drug uses—uses for which a drug wasn't originally intended and for which it may not be fully tested.[40]

The responsibility of business to preserve consumers' right to be informed extends beyond avoiding misleading advertising. All communications with customers—from salespeople's comments to warranties and product effectiveness—must be controlled to clearly and accurately inform customers. Most packaged-goods companies, personal-computer makers, and other makers of products bought for personal use by consumers include toll-free customer service numbers on their product labels so that consumers can get answers to questions.

The Right to Choose Consumers should have the right to choose which goods and services they need and want to purchase. Socially responsible firms attempt to respect this right, even if they reduce their own sales and profits in the process. Consumers certainly have an immense amount of choice and a variety of options when it comes to products and services. The federal government continues to take steps to ensure the availability of choice through anti-trust legislation designed to limit monopolistic business practices that potentially create price control and price gouging.

The Right to Be Heard The Consumer Financial Protection Bureau (CFPB) works directly with consumers to ensure their voice is heard when it comes to issues with mortgages,

Laurentiu Iordache/iStockphoto

Workplace safety is an important business responsibility. In potentially dangerous areas, workers are required to wear safety equipment, including hard hats and protective eyewear.

student loans, payday loans, debt collection, credit reports, and other financial products and services. The CFPB is a government agency established in 2011 that makes sure that banks, lenders, and other financial companies treat consumers fairly. CFPB also allows, through a separate process, current and former employees or industry insiders of companies to submit tips if there is reason to believe that federal consumer financial laws have been violated.[41]

Responsibilities to Employees

Companies that can attract skilled and knowledgeable employees are better able to meet the challenges of global competition. In return, businesses have wide-ranging responsibilities to their employees, including workplace safety, quality-of-life issues, fair wages, ensuring equal opportunity on the job, avoiding age discrimination, and preventing sexual harassment and sexism.

Workplace Safety A century ago, few businesses paid much attention to the safety of their workers. In fact, most business owners viewed employees as mere cogs in the production process. Workers—many of whom were young children—toiled in frequently dangerous conditions. In 1911, a fire at the Triangle Shirtwaist Factory in New York City killed 146 people, mostly young girls. Contributing to the massive loss of life were the sweatshop working conditions at the factory, including overcrowding, blocked exits, and a lack of fire escapes. This horrifying tragedy forced businesses to begin to recognize their responsibility for their workers' safety.

The safety and health of workers on the job is now a crucial business responsibility. The Occupational Safety and Health Administration (OSHA) is the main federal regulatory agency in setting workplace safety and health standards. These mandates range from broad guidelines on storing hazardous materials to specific standards for worker safety in industries such as construction, manufacturing, and mining. OSHA tracks and investigates workplace accidents and has the authority to fine employers who are found liable for injuries and deaths that occur on the job.

In a recent year, 24 U.S. teens under the age of 18 died as a result of a work injury. Most of these fatalities occur because of unsafe equipment, inadequate safety training, and dangerous work that is illegal or inappropriate for youth. OSHA is taking steps to educate employers and teen workers about safety, health, and a positive work environment. The OSHA website has a special section for teens with the answers to most frequently asked questions about such issues as wages, labor standards, harassment issues, and safety at work. In addition, the U.S. Department of Labor's YouthRules! initiative is designed to further educate and empower young workers. The YouthRules! web page offers information and activities for teens, parents, educators, and employers.[42]

Quality-of-Life Issues Balancing work and family remains a challenge for many employees. They find themselves squeezed between working long hours and handling child-care issues, caring for elderly parents, and solving other family crises. A *sandwich generation*, those caring for two generations—their children and their aging parents—has arisen. As the population ages, the share of American households providing some type of care to a relative or friend age 50 or older has grown dramatically over the last few decades.

As women pursue their professional careers, and technology blurs work and home life, there are fewer hours to spend on family. However, working mothers aren't the only employees juggling work with life's other demands. Childless couples, single people, and men all express frustration at the pressures of balancing work with family and personal needs. To help with work–life balance, some employers are offering flexible work schedules so that parents can meet the needs of their children (or aging parents) as well as their jobs. *Forbes Magazine* offers a list of the "Best Companies for Work–Life Balance." Topping the list are tax preparation service H&R Block, Network Capital Funding Corporation (mortgages), In-N-Out Burger, H-E-B (food retailer), Kaiser Permanente, Intuit, Southwest Airlines, and Nike. H&R Block's benefits include tax preparation services, legal services, and tuition assistance.[43]

Some companies have come up with truly innovative ways to deal with work schedules, including paid time off for vacation or illness. Companies such as DropBox, Virgin Group, and Netflix have implemented unlimited vacation policies. The number of days employees take off is not tracked; instead vacation time is considered open ended. Employees at these companies put in just as many hours, if not more, with an unlimited vacation policy.[44]

Another solution has been to offer **family leave** to employees who need to deal with family matters. Under the Family and Medical Leave Act of 1993, employers with 50 or more employees must provide unpaid leave annually for any employee who wants time off for the birth or adoption of a child; to become a foster parent; or to care for a seriously ill relative, spouse, or self if he or she has a serious health condition or injury. The law requires employers to grant up to 12 weeks of leave each year, and leave may be taken intermittently as medical conditions make necessary. Workers must meet certain eligibility requirements. Employers must continue to provide health benefits during the leave and guarantee that employees will return to equivalent jobs. The issue of who is entitled to health benefits can also create a dilemma as companies struggle to balance the needs of their employees against the staggering costs of health care.

family leave the Family and Medical Leave Act of 1993 states that employers with 50 or more employees must provide unpaid leave up to 12 weeks annually for any employee who wants time off for the birth or adoption of a child, to become a foster parent, or to care for a seriously ill relative, spouse, or self.

Ensuring Equal Opportunity on the Job

Businesspeople face many challenges managing today's increasingly diverse workforce. Technology is expanding the ways people with physical disabilities can contribute in the workplace. Businesses also need to find ways to responsibly recruit and manage older workers and workers with varying lifestyles.

There are legal directives that help ensure a diverse workforce. The Civil Rights Act (1964) outlawed many kinds of discriminatory practices, and Title VII of the act specifically prohibits **discrimination**—biased treatment of a job candidate or employee—in the workplace. As shown in **Table 2.3**, other nondiscrimination laws include the Equal Pay Act (1963), the Age Discrimination in Employment Act (1967), the Equal Employment Opportunity Act (1972), the Pregnancy Discrimination Act (1978), the Civil Rights Act of 1991, and numerous executive orders. The Americans with Disabilities Act (1990) protects the rights of physically challenged people. The Vietnam Era Veterans Readjustment Act (1974) protects the employment of veterans of the Vietnam War. The Genetic Information Nondiscrimination Act (2008) prohibits discrimination on the basis of genetic tests or the medical history of an individual or that individual's family.

discrimination biased treatment of a job candidate or employee.

The **Equal Employment Opportunity Commission (EEOC)** was created to increase job opportunities for women and minorities and to help end discrimination based on race, color, religion, disability, gender, or national origin in any employment practice such as hiring, firing, promotions, transfers, or wage practices. To enforce fair-employment laws, it investigates charges of discrimination and harassment and files suit against violators. The EEOC can also help employers set up programs to increase job opportunities for women, minorities, people with disabilities, and people in other protected categories.

Equal Employment Opportunity Commission (EEOC) this commission was created to increase job opportunities for women and minorities and to help end discrimination based on race, color, religion, disability, gender, or national origin in any personnel action.

Fair treatment of employees is more than a matter of complying with EEOC regulations, however. All employees want to be treated with respect. A minority employee who misses out on a desirable assignment may miss out on the big raise that goes with it. As the employee's salary grows more slowly, managers may eventually begin to use the size of the salary as an indicator that the employee contributes less to the organization. While in the past the EEOC has focused on this type of individual situation, currently it is addressing what it terms *systemic discrimination*, which it defines as "a pattern or practice, policy and/or class cases where the alleged discrimination has a broad impact on an industry, profession, company, or geographic location." In a recent year, class action gender discrimination lawsuits were brought against tech giants Google, Twitter, Microsoft, Oracle, and Uber. Systemic compensation disparities (men being paid more than women for performing the same job) were found across the entire workforce.[45] Chapter 8 takes a closer look at diversity and employment discrimination issues as part of a discussion of human resource management.

TABLE 2.3 Laws Designed to Ensure Equal Opportunity

Law	Key Provisions
Title VII of the Civil Rights Act of 1964 (as amended by the Equal Employment Opportunity Act of 1972)	Prohibits discrimination in hiring, promotion, compensation, training, or dismissal on the basis of race, color, religion, sex, or national origin.
Age Discrimination in Employment Act of 1967 (as amended)	Prohibits discrimination in employment against anyone age 40 or older in hiring, promotion, compensation, training, or dismissal.
Equal Pay Act of 1963	Requires equal pay for men and women working for the same company in jobs that require equal skill, effort, and responsibility.
Vocational Rehabilitation Act of 1973	Requires government contractors and subcontractors to take affirmative action to employ and promote qualified disabled workers. Coverage now extends to all federal employees. Coverage has been broadened by the passage of similar laws in more than 20 states and, through court rulings, to include people with communicable diseases, including AIDS.
Vietnam Era Veterans Readjustment Act of 1974	Requires government contractors and subcontractors to take affirmative action to employ and retain disabled veterans. Coverage now extends to all federal employees and has been broadened by the passage of similar laws in more than 20 states.
Pregnancy Discrimination Act of 1978	Requires employers to treat pregnant women and new mothers the same as other employees for all employment-related purposes, including receipt of benefits under company benefit programs.
Americans with Disabilities Act of 1990	Makes discrimination against the disabled illegal in public accommodations, transportation, and telecommunications; stiffens employer penalties for intentional discrimination on the basis of an employee's disability.
Civil Rights Act of 1991	Makes it easier for workers to sue their employers for alleged discrimination. Enables victims of sexual discrimination to collect punitive damages; includes employment decisions and on-the-job issues such as sexual harassment, unfair promotions, and unfair dismissal. The employer must prove that it did not engage in discrimination.
Family and Medical Leave Act of 1993	Requires all businesses with 50 or more employees to provide up to 12 weeks of unpaid leave annually to employees who have had a child or are adopting a child, are becoming foster parents, are caring for a seriously ill relative or spouse, or are themselves seriously ill. Workers must meet certain eligibility requirements.
Uniformed Services Employment and Reemployment Rights Act of 1994	Prohibits employers from denying employment benefits on the basis of employees' membership in or obligation to serve in the uniformed services and protects the rights of veterans, reservists, and National Guard members to reclaim their jobs after being absent due to military service or training.
Genetic Information Nondiscrimination Act of 2008	Prohibits employers from discriminating against employees or applicants on the basis of genetic information, including genetic tests of an individual or family member or an individual's personal or family medical history.

Age Discrimination

With the average age of U.S. workers steadily rising, more than half the workforce is projected to be age 40 or older in a few years. Yet some employers find it less expensive to hire and retain younger workers, who generally have lower medical bills as well as lower salary requirements. At the same time, many older workers have training and skills that younger workers have yet to acquire. The Age Discrimination in Employment Act (ADEA) of 1967 protects individuals who are age 40 or older, prohibiting discrimination on the basis of age and denial of benefits to older employees.

Ruling in a lawsuit brought under the ADEA, the Supreme Court determined that employers can be held liable for age discrimination against older workers even if they intended no harm. At the same time, the court allowed employers to use "reasonable" factors, such as cost cutting, to defend business practices that might have more severe impacts on older than on younger workers. As workers stay in the labor force longer, protecting them against age discrimination has become an important issue. After suffering a minor stroke, a 65-year-old *Los Angeles Times* sports columnist was pushed out of his job. As a result, he was awarded $7.1 million by a jury.[46]

Legal issues aside, employers might do well to consider not only the experience that older workers bring to the workplace but also their enthusiasm. Many surveys report that older workers who remain on the job by choice—not because they are forced to do so for economic reasons—are often happy with their employment. Still, employees with decades of work experience can be a valuable asset to any company (see photo).[47]

In all cases, employers need to plan ahead for the aging of the workforce, finding ways to retain accumulated business wisdom, prepare for the demand for health services, and be ready for growth in the industries that serve seniors. The 55-and-older age group is projected to comprise over 25% of the workforce by 2024. These numbers signify a coming shift in the workforce, as well as in the goods and services needed.[48]

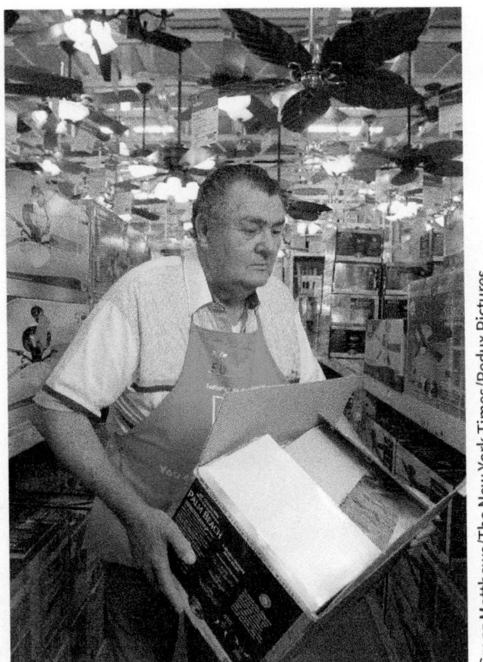

Gregg Matthews/The New York Times/Redux Pictures

Employers are responsible for avoiding age discrimination in the workplace. As the average age of workers rises, employers will benefit from the older generation's knowledge.

Sexual Harassment and Sexism Every employer has a responsibility to ensure that all workers are treated fairly and are safe from sexual harassment. **Sexual harassment** refers to unwelcome sexual advances, requests for sexual favors, and other verbal or physical harassment of a sexual nature. It is a form of sex discrimination that violates the Civil Rights Act of 1964, which gives both men and women the right to file lawsuits for intentional sexual harassment. About 6,700 sexual harassment complaints are filed with the EEOC each year, of which about 16.5% are filed by men.[49] Thousands of other cases are either handled internally by companies or never reported.

sexual harassment unwelcome and inappropriate actions of a sexual nature in the workplace.

Two types of sexual harassment exist. The first type occurs when an employee is pressured to comply with unwelcome advances and requests for sexual favors in return for job security, promotions, and raises. The second type results from a hostile work environment in which an employee feels hassled or degraded because of unwelcome flirting, lewd comments, or obscene jokes. The courts have ruled that allowing sexually oriented materials in the workplace can create a hostile atmosphere that interferes with an employee's ability to do the job. Employers are also legally responsible to protect employees from sexual harassment by customers and clients. The EEOC's website informs employers and employees of criteria for identifying sexual harassment and how it should be handled in the workplace.

A number of high-profile cases against men accused of sexual misconduct ranging from inappropriate comments to rape have created a significant shift in what behavior is tolerated in the workplace. What began as a string of women coming forward with claims of sexual assault and rape against Hollywood producer Harvey Weinstein has resulted in the creation of the Me Too Movement—to support survivors and end sexual violence.[50]

Many companies have revisited their already established policies and employee education programs aimed at increasing awareness and preventing any behavior or sexual misconduct in the workplace. An effective harassment prevention program should include the following measures:[51]

- A clear explanation of prohibited conduct
- Assurance that employees who make claims of harassment or provide information related to such claims will be protected against retaliation
- A clearly described complaint process
- To the extent possible, assurance of confidentiality of the individuals bringing harassment claims

- A prompt, thorough, and impartial investigation
- When determined that harassment has occurred, assurance that the employer will take immediate and appropriate corrective action

sexism discrimination against members of either sex, but primarily affecting women.

Sexual harassment is often part of the broader problem of **sexism**—discrimination against members of either sex but primarily affecting women. One important sexism issue is equal pay for equal work.

Lilly Ledbetter was near retirement when she found out that for a considerable length of time men at her management level had been getting paid more than she had been. But the Supreme Court threw out her case because she did not sue within the statute of limitations—that is, within 180 days of the first instance of a lower paycheck. Recently the statute of limitations was extended in these types of cases.[52]

U.S. Census statistics show that overall, women still earn 79 cents for every $1 earned by men. The number drops to 63 cents for African American women and 54 cents for Hispanic women. Education, occupation, work hours, and other factors don't seem to affect the gap, which remains unexplained other than the penalty of gender.[53] In some extreme cases, differences in pay and advancement can become the basis for sex discrimination suits, which, like sexual harassment suits, can be costly and time consuming to settle.

Assessment Check

1. What is meant by social responsibility, and why do companies exercise it?
2. What is green marketing?
3. What are the four main consumer rights?

5 Responsibilities to Investors and the Financial Community

Although a fundamental goal of any business is to make a profit for its shareholders, investors and the financial community demand and deserve that businesses behave ethically and legally. When companies fail in this responsibility, the fallout can impact all stakeholders.

State and federal government agencies are responsible for protecting investors from financial misdeeds. At the federal level, the Securities and Exchange Commission (SEC) investigates suspicions of unethical or illegal behavior of publicly traded companies. It investigates accusations that a business is using faulty accounting practices to inaccurately portray its financial resources and profits to investors. Regulation FD (Fair Disclosure) is an SEC rule that requires publicly traded companies to announce major information to the general public, rather than first disclosing the information to selected major investors. The agency also operates an Office of Internet Enforcement to target fraud in online trading and online sales of stock by unlicensed sellers. Recall that the Sarbanes-Oxley Act of 2002 also protects investors from unethical accounting practices. Chapter 17 discusses securities trading practices further.

Assessment Check

1. Why do companies need to do more than just earn a profit?
2. What is the role of the Securities and Exchange Commission?

What's Ahead

The decisions and actions of businesspeople are often influenced by external forces such as the economic and legal environment and society's expectations about the responsibility and role of business. The next chapter discusses broad economic issues that influence businesses around the world. Our discussion will focus on how factors such as supply and demand, unemployment, inflation, and government monetary policies pose both challenges and opportunities for companies seeking to compete in the global marketplace.

Chapter in Review

Summary of Learning Objectives

LEARNING OBJECTIVE 1 Explain the concern for ethical and societal issues.

Business ethics refers to the standards of conduct and moral values that businesspeople rely on to guide their actions and decisions in the workplace. Businesspeople must take a wide range of social issues into account when making decisions. Social responsibility refers to management's acceptance of the obligation to place a significant value on profit, consumer satisfaction, and societal well-being in evaluating the company's performance.

Assessment Check Answers

1.1 **To whom do businesses have responsibilities?** Businesses are responsible to customers, employees, investors, and society.

1.2 **If a company is meeting all its responsibilities to others, why do ethical conflicts arise?** Ethical conflicts arise when business is trying to serve the different needs of its constituents.

LEARNING OBJECTIVE 2 Describe the contemporary ethical environment.

Among the many factors shaping individual ethics are personal experience, peer pressure, and organizational culture. Individual ethics are also influenced by family, cultural, and religious standards. Additionally, the culture of the organization where a person works can be a factor.

Assessment Check Answers

2.1 **What role can an ethics compliance officer play in a company?** Ethics compliance officers are charged with deterring wrongdoing and ensuring that ethical standards are met.

2.2 **What are the three components of a typical company's approach to ethics and social responsibility?** The three components are (1) engaging in typical corporate philanthropy; (2) anticipating and managing risks; and (3) identifying opportunities to create value by doing the right thing.

LEARNING OBJECTIVE 3 Discuss how organizations shape ethical conduct.

Choices are strongly influenced by the standards of conduct established within any organization. Most ethical lapses in business reflect the values of the companies' corporate cultures. Development of a corporate culture to support business ethics happens on four levels: ethical awareness; ethical education; ethical action; and ethical leadership. Ethical awareness involves providing help to employees in identifying ethical problems when they occur and giving them guidance about how the company expects them to respond. One way to provide this support is to develop a code of conduct for the organization. Ethical education involves implementing an ethics training program for employees or hiring an outside firm to develop ethics and compliance programs for the organization. Ethical action involves companies providing structures and approaches for employees that allow decisions to be turned into appropriate business actions. Ethical leadership involves commitment to the company's core values at all levels of the organization.

Assessment Check Answers

3.1 **Identify the four levels of a company's ethical environment.** Development of a corporate culture to support business ethics happens on four levels: ethical awareness; ethical education; ethical action; and ethical leadership.

3.2 **How does ethical leadership contribute to ethical standards throughout a company?** Employees more readily commit to the company's core values when they see that executives and managers behave ethically.

LEARNING OBJECTIVE 4 Describe how businesses can act responsibly to satisfy society.

Today's businesses are expected to weigh their qualitative impact on consumers and society, in addition to their quantitative economic contributions such as sales, employment levels, and profits. One measure is their compliance with labor and consumer protection laws and their charitable contributions. Another measure some businesses take is to conduct social audits. Public-interest groups also create standards and measure companies' performance relative to those standards. The responsibilities of business to the general public include protecting the public health and the environment and developing the quality of the workforce. Additionally, many would argue that businesses have a social responsibility to support charitable and social causes in the communities in which they earn profits. Business also must treat customers fairly and protect consumers, upholding their rights to be safe, to be informed, to choose, and to be heard. Businesses have wide-ranging responsibilities to their workers. They should make sure that the workplace is safe, address quality-of-life issues, ensure equal opportunity, and prevent sexual harassment and other forms of discrimination.

Assessment Check Answers

4.1 **What is meant by social responsibility, and why do companies exercise it?** Social responsibility is management's acceptance of its obligation to consider profit, consumer satisfaction, and societal well-being to be of significant value when evaluating the company's performance. Businesses demonstrate social responsibility because such behavior is required by law, because it enhances the company's image, or because management believes it is the right thing to do.

4.2 **What is green marketing?** Green marketing is a marketing strategy that promotes environmentally safe products and production methods.

4.3 **What are the four main consumer rights?** The four main consumer rights are the right to be safe, to be informed, to choose, and to be heard.

LEARNING OBJECTIVE 5 Explain the ethical responsibilities of businesses to investors and the financial community.

Investors and the financial community demand that businesses behave ethically as well as legally in handling their financial transactions. Businesses must be honest in reporting their profits and financial performance to avoid misleading investors. The Securities and Exchange Commission is the federal agency responsible for investigating suspicions that publicly traded firms have engaged in unethical or illegal financial behavior.

Assessment Check Answers

5.1 **Why do companies need to do more than just earn a profit?** Although a fundamental goal of any business is to make a profit for its shareholders, investors and the financial community demand that businesses behave ethically and legally.

5.2 **What is the role of the Securities and Exchange Commission?** Among other functions, the Securities and Exchange Commission investigates suspicions of unethical or illegal behavior by publicly traded firms.

Business Terms You Need to Know

Review Questions

1. What do the terms *business ethics* and *social responsibility* mean? Why are they important components of a company's overall philosophy in conducting business?

2. In what ways do individuals make a difference in a company's commitment to ethics? Describe the three stages in which an individual develops ethical standards.

3. What type of ethical dilemma does each of the following illustrate? (A situation might involve more than one dilemma.)

   a. Due to a corporate merger, an advertising agency suddenly finds itself representing rival companies.

   b. A newly hired employee learns that the office manager plays computer games on company time.

   c. An employee is asked to destroy documents that implicate his or her company in widespread pollution.

   d. A company spokesperson agrees to give a press conference that puts a positive spin on his or her company's lack of overseas factory monitoring and questionable treatment of labor.

4. Describe how ethical leadership contributes to the development of each of the other levels of ethical standards in a corporation.

5. In what ways do companies demonstrate their social responsibility?

6. What are the four major areas in which businesses have responsibilities to the general public? In what ways can meeting these responsibilities give a company a competitive edge?

7. Identify and describe the four basic rights that consumerism tries to protect. How has consumerism improved the contemporary business environment? What challenges has it created for businesses?

8. What are the five major areas in which companies have responsibilities to their employees? What types of changes in society are now affecting these responsibilities?

9. Identify which equal opportunity law (or laws) protects workers in the following categories:

   a. an employee who must care for an elderly parent

   b. a National Guard member who is returning from deployment overseas

   c. a job applicant who is HIV positive

   d. a person who is over 40 years old

   e. a woman who has been sexually harassed on the job

   f. a woman with a family history of breast cancer

10. How does a company demonstrate its responsibility to investors and the financial community?

Projects and Teamwork Applications

1. Write your own personal code of ethics. Create standards for your behavior at school, in personal relationships, and on the job. Then assess how well you meet your own standards and revise them if necessary.

2. On your own or with a classmate, visit the website of one of the following companies, or choose another that interests you. On the basis of what you can learn about the company from the site, construct a chart or figure that illustrates examples of the firm's ethical awareness, ethical education, ethical actions, and ethical leadership. Present your findings to the class.

   a. Instagram

   b. NFL, NHL, NBA, MLB, MLS (or any other major professional sports league)

   c. Gilead Sciences

   d. L'Oreal

   e. Activision

   f. Costco

   g. IKEA

3. Take the company you chose for question 2 (or choose another), and search for information about the company's social and environmental responsibility practices. Some companies publish annual corporate social responsibility and sustainability reports. Present to the class the company's successes and challenges for the most recent year.

4. Warren Buffett is a world-famous investor and CEO of conglomerate Berkshire Hathaway, which includes companies as diverse as Kraft Heinz, Geico Auto Insurance, and Benjamin Moore Paints. Buffett plans to give away 99% of his wealth and has already donated over $3 billion to the Bill and Melinda Gates Foundation. List and discuss three other well-known corporate philanthropists, their goals, and their causes.

5. As technology becomes more pervasive, new and complex ethical issues have arisen in the workplace, which have contributed to ethical and, at times, legal challenges for employers and employees. Consider the action of transmitting confidential or proprietary company data, for example. With a classmate or alone, come up with a list of ways technology has affected or compromised ethics at work, school, or home.

Web Assignments

1. **Ethical standards.** Go to the Boeing website and review its supplier page listed below. With more than 23,000 different suppliers listed, review and list the criteria and expectations Boeing uses when choosing suppliers.
www.boeingsuppliers.com

2. **Volunteers.** People volunteer for a variety of reasons. Visit the following website and choose a few of the organizations that interest you. List some of the reasons you might volunteer with each of the selected organizations.
www.volunteermatch.org

3. **Whistle-blowers.** Go to the National Whistleblowers Center website to outline and discuss the rights of whistleblowers (FAQ page under "Resources" tab). Either in small groups or individually, prepare a report profiling some of the individuals featured in "Meet the Whistleblowers." Is there a common theme with some of the claims, and in your opinion, are they justified? Why or why not?
www.whistleblowers.org

Note: Internet web addresses change frequently. If you don't find the exact sites listed, you may need to access the organization's home page and search from there or use a search engine such as Google or Bing.

Cases

Case 2.1 Whole Foods Shares Salary Data with Employees

If you've ever wondered how much your boss or co-workers make, you would know if you worked at Whole Foods. While most companies keep salary information confidential, the Austin, Texas–based grocery chain has an open-salary policy whereby employees are actually encouraged to look up salaries and bonuses of co-workers as well as the CEO's compensation. For this grocer well known for its high-end organic selections, the benefits of an open-salary policy far outweigh keeping salaries a secret.

Whole Foods Co-CEO John Mackey is a firm believer in an open-salary policy as part of the company's "we're all in this together" culture of full transparency and no secrets. Mackey wants any and all information about Whole Foods accessible and available to company employees. In addition to sharing salary data, managers are required to post detailed financial, sales, and profitability reports by individual store locations as part of the shared culture.

One effect of the open-salary policy at Whole Foods is a highly motivated workforce that places value on productivity and community, which outweighs any benefit of keeping salaries and profit margins confidential. Whole Foods believes that sharing salary data can motivate employees to excel and work harder to get to the next earnings level.

Mackey admits that he is constantly challenged with questions about salary levels and fairness and believes that sharing information about salaries provides each employee a road map to success. Mackey uses salary information to bring to light the type of performance and achievement necessary to reach each level within the organization. With this information, employees can be inspired, knowing that they too can reach the next level. Mackey believes that there should be no secrets when creating a high-trust organization where people are all-for-one and one-for-all—which includes openness about salaries to reduce gender pay inequities.

Questions for Critical Thinking

1. Mackey believes that, if employees have a clear understanding of the path required to be as successful as the "next person," they will be inspired in part to become that "next person." Do you agree? Why or why not?
2. What are some disadvantages of a company sharing salary and profitability data with all of its employees?

Sources: Christina Majaski, "3 Benefits of Whole Foods' Open Salaries," *Payscale*, http://www.payscale.com, accessed February 17, 2018; Alison Griswold, "Here's Why Whole Foods Lets Employees Look Up Each Other's Salaries," *Business Insider*, http://www.businessinsider.com, accessed February 17, 2018; Tamara Lytle, "Making Pay Public," Society for Human Resource Management, *HR Magazine*, http://www.shrm.org, accessed February 17, 2018; Tanza Loudenback, "More Tech Companies Have Stopped Keeping Employee Salaries Secret—and They're Seeing Results," *BusinessInsider*, http://www.businessinsider.com, accessed February 17, 2018.

Case 2.2 Tech Philanthropists Lead the Way

In an effort to solve some of the world's most pressing problems, Mark Zuckerberg and his wife Dr. Priscilla Chan created a philanthropic organization to pledge 99% of their shares in Facebook. The announcement came in the form of a letter to their then- newborn daughter, Maxima Chan Zuckerberg. One of the largest in philanthropic history, the pledge, to be distributed over Zuckerberg's lifetime, could increase in value if Facebook shares continue to climb.

Unlike other philanthropists who pledge funds more closely aligned with a cause or issue, to date the initiative is not earmarked for any one particular organization, cause, or philanthropic organization. Because it is set up as a limited liability company or LLC, the structure gives Zuckerberg and Chan leeway to make investments of many kinds—from funding nonprofits or private investments to taking a public stand on policy issues. This also includes the ability to invest in for-profit ventures as joint ventures. Any profits from the investments will be used to fund additional work and initiatives, and under this structure the couple can disburse any profits from the LLC as they wish. (See Chapter 5 for more about this type of business structure.)

A professor who advises philanthropists agrees that the LLC structure of the initiative is gaining momentum in the world of philanthropy—and effectively creates a synergy between the nonprofit and the for-profit world to solve complex problems. The LLC structure also has fewer rules than the traditional approach of setting up a nonprofit foundation.

Tech donors like Zuckerberg and his wife represent 49% of the more than $10 billion in donations made in a recent year. The Chan Zuckerberg initiative is one example of a growing number of Silicon Valley tech entrepreneurs who find giving back, spreading wealth, and solving problems an imperative.

Questions for Critical Thinking

1. Others like Bill Gates (Microsoft) and Warren Buffett (Berkshire Hathaway) have pledged to give away their fortunes. Some call this the spirit of the times. Do you agree? Why or why not?
2. Is it reasonable to assume that the ability to solve societal problems corresponds with one's wealth? As billionaires tackle some of society's toughest problems, what are some of the downsides?

Sources: Jessica Guynn, "Mark Zuckerberg Takes Unconventional Approach to Philanthropy," *USA Today*, http://www.usatoday.com, February 17, 2018; John Naughton and Justin Forsyth, "Is Billionaire Philanthropy Always a Good Thing?" *The Guardian*, http://www.theguardian.com, February 17, 2018; Natasha Singer and Mike Isaac, "Mark Zuckerberg's Philanthropy Uses L.L.C. for More Control," *New York Times*, http://www.nytimes.com, accessed February 17, 2018; Alex Daniels and Maria Di Mento, "Young Tech Donors Take Leading Role in Philanthropy 50," *The Chronicle of Philanthropy*, http://philanthropy.com, February 17, 2018.

Case 2.3 Being Socially Responsible Helps Timberland Thrive

Timberland got its name from the iconic yellow work boot introduced more than four decades ago. Nathan Swartz founded the company in South Boston as the Abington Shoe Company, and he set out to create the most premium, durable, waterproof leather boots on the market to help workers withstand the harsh New England winters. Today, the New Hampshire-based footwear manufacturer, retailer, and global lifestyle company has found a place in the fashion world with celebrities and non-celebrities alike. As important, Timberland has also found its place as a model for best practices in corporate social responsibility (CSR). The company's passion for the outdoors, along with its responsibility to stakeholders, plays a major part in Timberland's overall business culture.

At its core, the company is committed to a culture of protecting the very essence of what keeps it in business—the outdoors and the environment. Each of Timberland's strategies demonstrates a synergy between commerce and social responsibility. The company's CSR activities are not limited to a separate department but integrated into all of its business strategies. Timberland focuses its CSR efforts on the three areas of responsible products, community engagement, and resource efficiency.

Maintaining transparency in product manufacturing is integral to Timberland's culture of taking steps to preserve the environment. Apparel and footwear manufacturing can have a variety of environmental consequences, which include the amount of water used to grow cotton, toxic chemicals used in tanning leather, and large amounts of crude oil and volatile compounds released during the production of synthetic fibers and fabrics. Timberland chooses to use leather tanneries that have wastewater purifying systems as part of their manufacturing process. Timberland collaborates with manufacturers of leather goods in various industries ranging from automobile to apparel to footwear. Together, the companies influence leather tanners to create a standard to monitor their processes in how leather goods are made and sourced.

Protecting the environment is one of Timberland's responsibilities to the general public. The company labels its products with respect to their environmental impact in much the same way that food products contain nutritional information. Through the Sustainable Apparel Coalition and the Outdoor Industry Association, Timberland, along with other footwear and apparel makers, has worked diligently to create awareness through an industry-wide standard of measurement and transparency of the environmental impact of products found in retail outlets. To reduce a product's environmental impact, better raw material choices at the beginning of product design are essential. At the front end, Timberland collaborates with designers and developers by making sure that they choose less environmentally harmful product materials.

Timberland is engaged in a variety of activities to protect the environment. The company is most proud of the advancements made in the use of recycled, renewable, and organic materials such as plastic water bottles and coffee grounds to make its apparel and shoes. A few years ago, the company invested in the planting of 5 million trees in Haiti to create a sustainable business model that provides jobs for their partners there. The result, the Smallholder Farmers Alliance, is a network of community nurseries where planted trees are maintained by 2,000 volunteer farmers in exchange for non-genetically modified seeds and agricultural training to plant and grow crops of their own. Timberland's investment in Haiti has provided a better life for the country's people and a sustainable model that can be replicated and scaled in other farming applications around the world.

To create greater transparency about where products are made, Timberland was one of the first companies to go public with its list of suppliers. Historically, the names of suppliers and their whereabouts have been closely guarded in the ready-made garment industry. With hundreds of thousands of workers involved in the production of its products, Timberland is committed to improving the quality of life for those workers through "responsible product," which translates to making sure that supplier engagement goes beyond compliance with rules and regulations. In the communities in which it operates, Timberland has provided transportation and housing, along with access to clean drinking water. In addition, the company has opened up daycare centers and provided educational and financial literacy programs for workers. Timberland has found that investing in workers and giving back to the communities in which they live and work translates to better business and higher morale.

Timberland takes community engagement seriously. For 25 years, through its Path of Service program, the company's employees have logged over a million hours to communities where its global employees live and work. Each employee is granted, on an annual basis, the opportunity to engage in up to 40 paid hours of community service. Working side-by-side outside the organizational structure with others throughout the company has proven to be not only an exercise in team building and leadership but also a way to increase morale within the organization.

Resource efficiency targets include reducing greenhouse gas emissions, increasing the use of renewable energy, and reducing waste. The company was recognized with a corporate sustainability award to acknowledge its efforts to partner with a tire manufacturer to use recycled rubber in the soles of Timberland shoes.

Timberland believes that corporate responsibility should not be treated as an add-on to the agenda of a company; rather it should provide the company a powerful competitive advantage. Consumer satisfaction and social well-being are of significant value and part of Timberland's performance assessment.

The next time you consider making a fashion statement with the purchase of a new pair of the iconic yellow boots, you might also consider the trendsetting example Timberland has demonstrated in the realm of corporate social responsibility.

Questions for Critical Thinking

1. Compare and contrast the CSR efforts of three of Timberland's competitors. How do they compare to and/or differ from Timberland's efforts?
2. Discuss Timberland's philosophy that CSR does not have to be an add-on but instead can work as a competitive advantage. Provide three examples of how Timberland's commitment to corporate social responsibility has created a competitive advantage for the company.
3. The Timberland Responsibility website (http://responsibility.timberland.com) is a wealth of information about the company's approach to corporate social responsibility. Evaluate Timberland's most recent CSR report, and expand on some of the company's most recent initiatives. Discuss the company's progress against its targets set around its core areas of corporate social responsibility.

Sources: Company website, www.vfc.com, accessed February 17, 2018; company website, "About Us," http://www.timberland.com, accessed February 17, 2018; company website, "Timberland Responsibility," http://responsibility.timberland.com, accessed February 17, 2018; company website, http://www.timberland.com/en/yellow-boot, accessed February 17, 2018; Ashley Rodriguez, "Timberland Looks Beyond Millennials in New Ad Campaign," *Advertising Age,* http://adage.com, accessed February 17, 2018; Sarah Halzack, "How Timberland Used Customer Data to Reboot Its Brand," *Washington Post,* http://www.washingtonpost.com, accessed February 17, 2018; Tara Gallagher, "The February 17, 2018 Corporate Sustainability Awards: 5 Companies That Bravely and Brilliantly Led the Pack," http://www.sustainablebrands.com, accessed February 17, 2018; Fawnia Soo Hoo, "Will the Return of Timberland's Classic Boot Help Sell Its Other Styles?" *Fashionista*, http://fashionista.com, accessed February 17, 2018; Natalie Burg, "Timberland and Its Corporate Transparency," *Business Insider*, http://www.businessinsider.com, accessed February 17, 2018; Christina Binkley, "How Green Is My Sneaker?" *Wall Street Journal*, http://www.wsj.com, accessed February 17, 2018.

CHAPTER **3**

Economic Challenges Facing Business Today

LEARNING OBJECTIVES

1. Discuss microeconomics and explain the forces of demand and supply.
2. Describe macroeconomics and the issues for the entire economy.
3. Identify how to evaluate economic performance.
4. Discuss managing the economy's performance.
5. Describe the global economic challenges encountered by businesses today.

Changemaker

Waldo Swiegers/Bloomberg via Getty Images

Brian Chesky, CEO

Company: Airbnb

Industry: Hotel/Hospitality/Lodging

Website: http://www.airbnb.com

Little did Brian Chesky and Joe Gebbia know that the purchase of three air mattresses would result in Airbnb, a global online community that matches hosts of overnight accommodations with potential guests. As roommates and recent college graduates, the two learned of an international design conference in town, making hotel rooms scarce. Enterprising and unemployed, they purchased three air mattresses and built a website they named "Air Bed and Breakfast." All three mattresses were quickly "rented," and in addition, breakfast was provided for the guests. A little more than a decade later, Airbnb has over 4 million listings in more than 65,000 cities and 191 countries. An affordable alternative to a more costly hotel room, Airbnb allows people to list, find, or rent entire homes, spare bedrooms, sofas, and even air mattresses via the Internet—and to "live" as locals.

Airbnb is a dominant player in today's "sharing economy," the idea of using the Internet to create person-to-person marketplaces. Hosts list their available space and rental price with photographs and descriptions on the Airbnb website. Travelers search the site by entering travel dates and location. To help guests learn more about a host, a user profile contains reviews and responsiveness ratings posted by previous guests. When a space is rented, Airbnb takes a 3% fee, and travelers pay a guest service fee of 6% to 12%, in addition to the rental fee.

At play are basic economic principles of supply and demand. In travel destinations like Las Vegas and New York, demand by guests is driven by seasonality and tourism. Specific events like music festivals can cause a spike in demand. Airbnb uses a dynamic pricing model that fluctuates with changes in supply and demand for the listed rentals.

The global success of Airbnb has not been without challenges. Ongoing issues include the debate over uncollected hotel taxes and rising rents in cities where otherwise open apartments are occupied long term by Airbnb travelers. The lower supply of available units for rent has led to higher rent prices in some cities. Despite obstacles, the Airbnb co-founders clearly saw an untapped supply and an unaddressed demand in the lodging industry.[1]

Overview

When we examine the exchanges that companies like Airbnb and societies make as a whole, we are focusing on the *economic systems* operating in different nations. These systems reflect the combination of policies and choices a nation makes to allocate resources among its citizens. Countries vary in the ways they allocate scarce resources.

Economics, which analyzes the production, distribution, and consumption of goods and services, or the choices people and governments make in allocating scarce resources, affects each of us. The economic problem of scarcity refers to the gap between limited (or scarce) resources and limitless wants. This forces people to make decisions around efficient resource allocation so that basic needs and additional wants are satisfied.

Everyone is involved in producing, distributing, or simply the consumption of goods and services—and economics impacts life daily. Whether you buy tickets to a concert or decide to stay home and watch a movie on Netflix instead, you are making an economic choice.

Businesses and not-for-profit organizations also make economic decisions when they choose how to use human and natural resources; invest in equipment, machinery, and buildings; and form strategic alliances. Economists refer to the study of the behavior of small economic units, such as individuals, families, and businesses, in making decisions regarding the allocation of limited resources as *microeconomics*.

The study of a country's overall economic issues is called *macroeconomics* (*macro* means "large"). Macroeconomics addresses such issues as how an economy as a whole uses its resources and how government policies affect people's standards of living. The substitution of alternative fuels for gasoline or biodiesel for diesel fuel has macroeconomic consequences—affecting many parts of the U.S. economy and worldwide suppliers. Macroeconomics examines not just the economic policies of individual nations, but the ways in which those individual policies affect the overall world economy. Aggregated indicators such as GDP, unemployment rates, national income, inflation, and the price indices are examples of macroeconomic issues. Macroeconomic issues help shape the decisions made by individuals, businesses, and families.

This chapter introduces economic theory and the economic challenges facing individuals, businesses, and governments in the global marketplace. We begin with a discussion of the two branches of economics—microeconomics and macroeconomics. Next we explain the various types of economic systems, along with tools for comparing and evaluating their performance. Then we examine the ways in which governments seek to manage economies to create stable business environments in their countries. The final section in the chapter looks at some of the driving economic forces currently affecting people's lives.

1 Microeconomics: The Forces of Demand and Supply

Think about your own economic activities. You shop for groceries, pay for transportation, choose a cell phone service provider, and pay college tuition. Now think about your family's economic activities. When you were growing up, your parents might have owned a home or rented an apartment. You might have taken a family vacation. Your parents may have shopped at discount clubs or at local stores. Each of these choices relates to the study of **microeconomics**. Microeconomics studies human choices and resource allocation. Individuals weigh the benefits and costs related to routine purchases before making a decision—all with the desire to maximize benefits and minimize costs. Weighing choices such as which college to attend, which car to buy, and where to live are all examples of economic decisions. A microeconomic decision to get from point A to point B might be between an on-demand rideshare service like Lyft, public transportation, or riding your bicycle. These choices also help determine both the prices of goods and services and the quantities sold. Information about these activities is vital to companies because their survival and ability to grow depends on selling enough products priced high

microeconomics study of small economic units, such as individual consumers, families, and businesses.

enough to cover costs and earn profits. The same information is important to consumers who must make purchase decisions based on prices and the availability of the goods and services they need.

At the heart of every business endeavor is an exchange between a buyer and a seller. The buyer recognizes that he or she needs or wants a particular good or service—whether it's a hamburger or a haircut—and is willing to pay a seller for it. The seller requires the exchange in order to earn a profit and stay in business. So the exchange process involves both demand and supply. **Demand** refers to the willingness and ability of buyers to purchase goods and services at different prices. The other side of the exchange process is **supply**, the amount of goods and services for sale at different prices. Understanding the factors that determine demand and supply, as well as how the two interact, can help you understand the actions and decisions of individuals, businesses, and government. This section takes a closer look at these concepts.

demand willingness and ability of buyers to purchase goods and services.

supply willingness and ability of sellers to provide goods and services.

Factors Driving Demand

economics social science that analyzes the choices people and governments make in allocating scarce resources.

For most of us, **economics** amounts to a balance between what we want and what we can afford. Because of this dilemma, each person must choose how much money to save and how much to spend. We must also decide among all the goods and services competing for our attention. To cause further confusion, you may be exposed to a bewildering number of brands, store promotions, gift bonuses, and online incentives—all competing for your attention.

Demand is driven by a number of factors that influence how people decide to spend their money, including price and consumer preferences. It may also be driven by outside circumstances or larger economic events. Chinese consumers, part of a rising middle class with a fondness for Western brands, are drinking up Starbucks's growth plans in China. To meet demand, the company's China expansion of 500 stores a year and 10,000 jobs annually is far greater than its U.S. growth plans.[2]

Businesses, including restaurants and food delivery services, are recognizing a growing demand by including both vegetarian and vegan options on their menus. Vegans, in addition to being vegetarian (no meat), do not eat animal-derived food products and by-products such as eggs and dairy products. As consumers have become more health-conscious, plant-based diets center around unprocessed or minimally processed vegetables, fruits, whole grains, beans, legumes, nuts, and seeds.[3]

demand curve graph of the amount of a product that buyers will purchase at different prices.

In general, as the price of a good or service goes up, people buy smaller amounts. In other words, as price rises, the quantity demanded declines. At lower prices, consumers are generally willing to buy more of a good. A **demand curve** is a graph of the amount of a product that buyers will purchase at different prices. Demand curves typically slope downward, meaning that buyers will purchase greater quantities of a good or service as its price falls.

Courtesy of Carlos Maldonado

You shop for groceries, pay for transportation, choose a cell phone service provider, and pay college tuition. Each of these choices relates to the study of microeconomics. They also help determine the prices of goods and the amounts sold.

As an example, let's use pizza to understand how demand curves work. The left side of **Figure 3.1** shows a possible demand curve for the total number of pizzas per week people will purchase at different prices, say in a college town. For discussion purposes, the prices shown reflect the typical cost of a large pizza, although price may vary depending upon a number of factors, such as toppings, location, and whether the pizza is purchased from a fast food chain like Domino's or from a small family-owned business that offers authentic family recipes, culinary expertise, and high-quality, specialty ingredients. When a pizza is priced at $15.00, students and families may consume a few per month. At $16.00 each, a decision might be made to consume fewer pizzas, eat at home, or have something else altogether. When the price drops to $14.00, more pizzas are sold per week as people opt to grab a pizza together instead of eating at home or purchasing another more expensive meal. Other factors like geographic location or use of healthy ingredients may cause consumers to accept higher prices.

Economists clearly distinguish between changes in the quantity demanded at various prices and changes in overall market demand. A change in quantity demanded, such as the change that occurs at different prices for a pizza, is simply movement along the demand curve. A change in overall market demand, on the other hand, results in

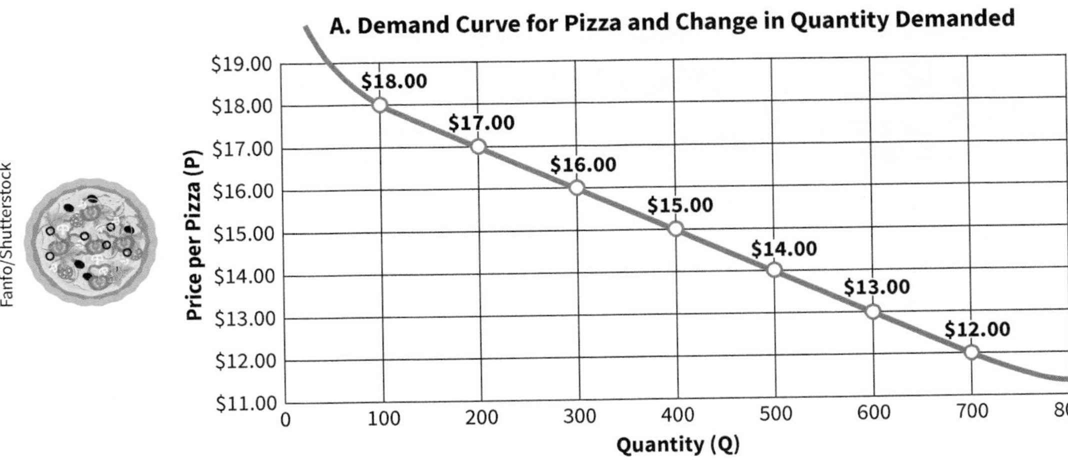

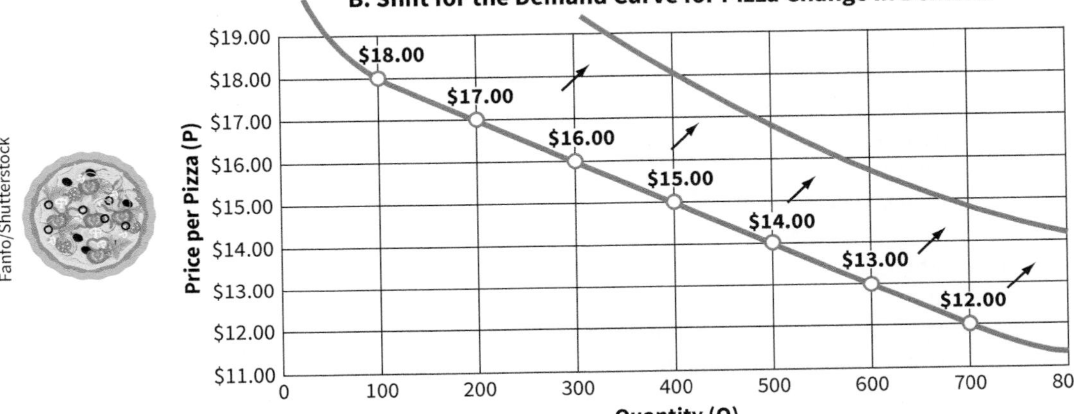

FIGURE 3.1 **Demand Curves for Pizza**

an entirely new demand curve. An increase or decrease in market demand can cause the entire demand curve to shift to the right or to the left. Many factors come into play when restaurants try to make predictions and forecasts about both types of demand.

The overall increase in pizza consumption, or a shift in tastes where more pizza as a food choice is being consumed, can create a new demand curve, as shown in Figure 3.1. The new demand curve shifts to the right of the original demand curve, indicating that overall demand has increased at every price. A demand curve can also shift to the left when the demand for pizza drops. However, the demand curve still has the same shape.

Although price is the underlying cause of movement along a demand curve, many factors can combine to determine the overall demand for a product—that is, the shape and position of the demand curve. These influences include customer preferences and incomes, the prices of substitute and complementary items, the number of buyers in a market, and the strength of their optimism regarding the future. Changes in any of these factors produce a new demand curve.

Changes in household income also change demand. As consumers have more money to spend, companies can sell more products at every price. This means the demand curve has shifted to the right. However, when income falls, fewer product purchases are made (in the case of pizza consumption, this may include choosing not to eat out at all), and the demand curve shifts to the left.

Table 3.1 shows five demand determinants that shift the demand curve either right or left. A shift in consumer tastes and preferences toward a particular food or diet, say healthy frozen foods or non-dairy milk alternatives like soy milk, will increase demand for such products and the curve will shift to the right. Anything that causes a shift in tastes away from a good will decrease demand for that good, and conversely, the demand curve will shift to the left.

TABLE 3.1 Demand Determinants and Expected Shifts in Demand Curves

Factor	Demand Curve Shifts	
	To the Right *if*:	**To the Left *if*:**
Customer preferences	Increase	Decrease
Number of buyers	Increase	Decrease
Buyers' incomes	Increase	Decrease
Prices of substitute goods	Increase	Decrease
Prices of complementary goods	Decrease	Increase
Future expectations become more	Optimistic	Pessimistic

If there is an increase in the number of buyers in the market, then demand for the good increases (a right shift). However, if there is a decrease in the number of buyers, this is seen as a leftward shift of the demand curve.

If people expect their incomes to rise, their demand for travel, for example, may increase. However, if the economy falters and people worry about their job security, demand for new automobiles or designer shoes, for example, may fall.

Buyers must decide between one good over another. If prices of goods rise, buyers will purchase other goods or substitute goods. Two goods are substitutes (let's say pizza and burgers) if an increase in the price of one causes an increase in the demand for the other. If the price of hamburgers increases, students may demand pizza instead (demand curve shifts right). The demand curve for pizza will shift to the left if the price of hamburgers decreases.

Two goods are complements (complementary goods) if an increase in the price of one causes a fall in demand for the other. Examples are peanut butter and jelly, french fries and ketchup, computer and software, bagels and cream cheese, and eggs and bacon. If the price of peanut butter increases, the demand for jelly may decrease.

Buyers make purchasing decisions based upon a comparison of current and future prices—and they're motivated to purchase a good at the lowest price possible. Buyers will decide when to purchase a new smart phone or an airline ticket, for example, at a given current price based upon their expectations of future prices.[4]

Factors Driving Supply

Important economic factors also affect supply, the willingness and ability of companies to provide goods and services at different prices. Just as consumers must decide about how to spend their money, businesses must decide what products to sell, and how.

supply curve graph that shows the relationship between different prices and the quantities that sellers will offer for sale, regardless of demand.

A **supply curve** shows the relationship between different prices and the quantities that sellers will supply or offer for sale, regardless of demand. As price increases, other things constant, a producer becomes more willing and able to supply the good. Movement along the supply curve is the opposite of movement along the demand curve. So as price rises, the quantity that sellers are willing to supply also rises. At progressively lower prices, the quantity supplied decreases. In **Figure 3.2**, a possible supply curve for pizza shows that increasing prices should bring increased supplies to market. In this example, each $1 increase in price results in an increase of the quantity supplied by 100 pizzas. Note that at a price of $11.00 per pizza, zero will be supplied. A restaurant will certainly supply more pizzas if the price is higher, mainly because more money can be made with higher prices. Therefore, a higher price encourages a company to increase its output—in this case, purchasing more cheese, tomato sauce, oil, salt, yeast, and flour—and hiring more employees. At a price of $12.00 per pizza, a seller will supply only 100 per week, as compared to a price of $18.00 each, where a seller will supply 700 per week.

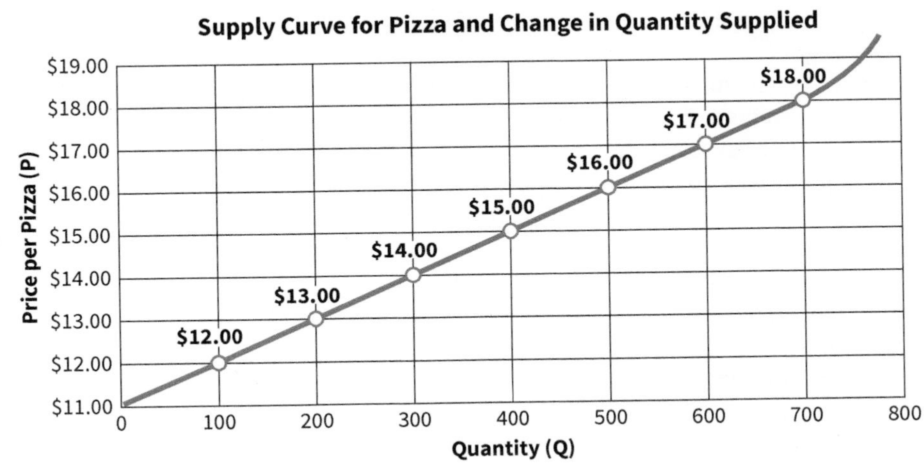

Fanfo/Shutterstock

FIGURE 3.2 **Supply Curve for Pizza**

Businesses need certain inputs to operate effectively in producing their output. As discussed in Chapter 1, these *factors of production* include natural resources, capital, human resources, and entrepreneurship. Factors of production play a central role in determining the overall supply of goods and services.

A change in the cost or availability of any of these inputs (for example, mozzarella cheese, tomato sauce, or flour) can shift the entire supply curve, either increasing or decreasing the amount available at every price. If the cost of land increases, a company might not be able to purchase a site for a more efficient manufacturing plant, which would lower production levels, shifting the supply curve to the left. But if the company finds a way to speed up the production process, allowing it to turn out more products with less labor, the change reduces the overall cost of the finished products, which shifts the supply curve to the right. For example, there is a pizza restaurant in Mountain View, California, which uses robots to make pizza.

Table 3.2 summarizes how changes in various factors can affect the supply curve. Sometimes forces of nature can affect the supply curve. If the cost of inputs, say mozzarella cheese and yeast, increases, the supply curve may shift to the left. The cost of producing pizzas increases, and at each price, producers need to sell their good for more money. They profit less per pizza, so they are motivated to make fewer pizzas at a given price, decreasing quantity supplied. Therefore, an increase in the price of inputs leads to a decrease in supply. Conversely, if the cost of the same inputs declines, so does the cost of producing the pizzas, and the supply curve may shift to the right (more pizzas will be supplied).

If a more efficient technology is developed, say robots in the pizza kitchen (this has become a reality at Zume Pizza in California), or a high-tech oven, then suppliers will be willing and able to supply more of the good, causing a rightward shift of the supply curve and more supplied at each possible price.[5] The opposite will happen if cost of technologies increases.

Taxes, regulations, and government policies can affect the cost of production. Taxes and regulatory compliance are costs by businesses, and higher costs potentially decrease supply

TABLE 3.2 **Supply Determinants and Expected Shifts in Supply Curves**

	Supply Curve Shifts	
Factor	**To the Right *if*:**	**To the Left *if*:**
Costs of inputs	Decrease	Increase
Costs of technologies	Decrease	Increase
Taxes	Decrease	Increase
Number of suppliers	Increase	Decrease

(leftward shift). Sometimes a government subsidy can increase supply, shifting the curve to the right.

Generally speaking, as more or fewer suppliers enter the market, this has a direct impact on the amount of a product that producers are willing and able to sell. Greater competition (more producers) usually translates to a reduced supply (a left shift), while less competition gives the producer an opportunity to have a larger market share and a larger supply (a right shift).

How Demand and Supply Interact

Separate shifts in demand and supply have obvious effects on prices and the availability of products. In the real world, changes do not alternatively affect demand and supply. Several factors often change at the same time—and they keep changing. Sometimes such changes in multiple factors cause contradictory pressures on prices and quantities. In other cases, the final direction of prices and quantities reflects the factor that has changed the most. Demand and supply can affect employment as well.

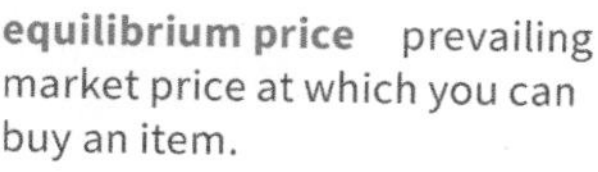

equilibrium price prevailing market price at which you can buy an item.

Figure 3.3 shows the interaction of both supply and demand curves for pizza on a single graph. Notice that the two curves intersect at *P*. The law of supply and demand states that prices (*P*) are set by the intersection of the supply and demand curves. The point where the two curves meet identifies the **equilibrium price**, the prevailing market price at which you can buy an item or the price toward which a good or service will trend. At the equilibrium price of $15.00 per pizza, the price acceptable to both buyer and seller, the supply curve indicates that 400 pizzas will be supplied, which is exactly the quantity that consumers are willing to buy at that price. The seller may want $30 for a large pizza, but the quantity demanded at that price may be few. Therefore, if the seller lowers the price, the quantity of pizzas demanded may increase.

If the actual market price differs from the equilibrium price, buyers and sellers tend to make economic choices that restore the equilibrium level. Disequilibrium results in either a surplus or shortage. If the price of a pizza is $17, the quantity demanded is 200, and the quantity that businesses are willing to supply is 400—a difference of 200 pizzas (400 − 200). In this case, there is a **surplus** of 200 pizzas (more available than consumers are willing to purchase), and the price will change or decrease close to the equilibrium price per pizza of $15. The quantity that pizza makers are willing to sell exceeds the quantity that potential buyers are willing to buy at $17 each. This will prompt sellers to lower prices until demand at that price matches the available supply.

If the price is $13 for a pizza, the quantity demanded is 600 pizzas (consumers are willing to purchase more than what is available), and the quantity that businesses are willing to supply is 400. The result will be a shortage of 200 pizzas (600 − 400). If there is a **shortage**, the price will change—or increase closer to the equilibrium price of $15. In other words, an excess of demand will prompt sellers of pizza to increase the price until demand at that price matches the available supply. As the "Business Model" feature points out, companies are scrambling to take advantage of the "athleisure" market that is trending.

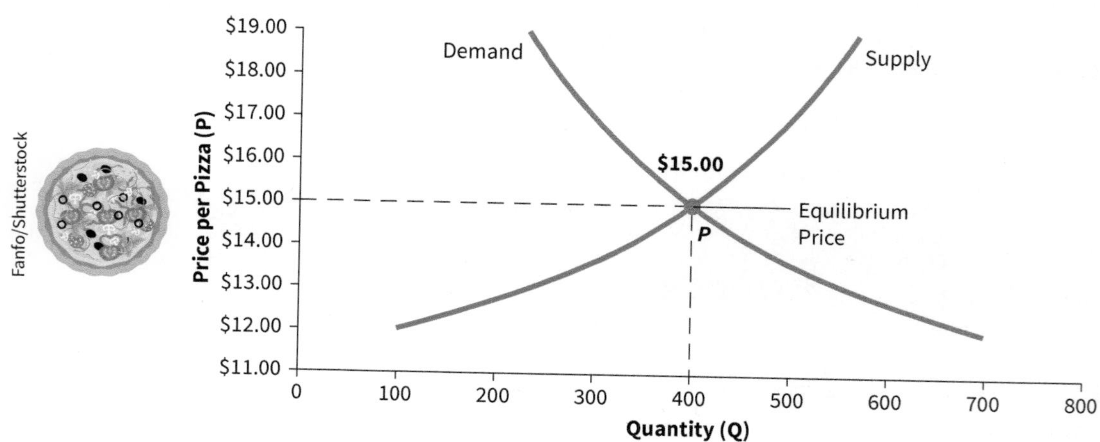

FIGURE 3.3 **Law of Supply and Demand**

Business Model

Companies Compete for Share of "Athleisure" Market

If you've noticed more people around you dressed as if they're going to yoga or to the gym, you're witnessing a fashion trend called "athleisure," a cross between activewear and fashion. Popularized by Lululemon, a yoga-inspired athletic apparel company, athleisure has given rise to wearing comfortable athletic apparel beyond the gym and as part of one's daily wardrobe. As fitness-conscious consumers embraced the fashion and styles in a wide variety of social situations, athleisure soon became part of a growing trend.

As the athleisure market has grown, so has the competition. Companies from Nike and Gap-owned Athleta to high-end designers like Tory Burch, Beyoncé, and Alexander Wang have chased the strong demand for apparel that represents a fashion spectrum ranging from high style to comfort. Number-two sneakers behemoth Adidas, another leader keenly aware of the athleisure trend, has seen sneaker sales increase 50% in a recent year. Its website describes a pair of sneakers as "contemporary street fashion," and its Superstar line is billed as "an authentic reissue of the classic sneaker fit for anyone from basketball MVP to streetwear queen." Kanye West, Pharrell Williams (discussed in Chapter 13), and Stella McCartney are well-known celebrity brand ambassadors and designers whose endorsements have helped pump up sales.

Traditional blue jean makers have jumped on the athleisure bandwagon, too. Noticing a drop in sales, Levi's, Lee, and Wrangler have created new denim lines with greater stretch and movement and a "flatter, hold and lift" feature for greater mobility, comfort, and durability. As function and fashion fuse, competition in the athleisure market intensifies to reach those who go to yoga or go to the gym—along with those who just prefer to dress that way.

Questions for Critical Thinking

1. Discuss the growth in the athleisure market in light of the fact that American participation in sports has declined. Do you see the athleisure market as a trend? Why or why not?
2. In addition to celebrities and fashion designers, giants like Nike, and innovators like Lululemon, are there other brands or companies that have made their way into the growing athleisure market? If so, who are they and what is their differentiator in a crowded market?

Sources: Lauren Schwartzberg, "How Levi's Is Fighting Athleisure by Reinventing Denim," *Fast Company,* http://www.fastcompany.com, accessed February 26, 2018; Marina Nazario, "How Levi's Plans to Survive the Denim Apocalypse," *Business Insider*, http://www.businessinsider.com, accessed February 26, 2018; Alec Leach, "Beyoncé Is Launching an Athleisure Brand with Topshop Billionaire Philip Green," *High Snobiety*, http://www.highsnobiety.com, accessed February 26, 2018; Booth Moore, "Designer Tory Burch's New 'Athleisure' Line Is Riding One of Fashion's Hottest Trends," *Los Angeles Times,* http://www.latimes.com, accessed February 26, 2018; Elizabeth Holmes, "Are You Going to the Gym, or Do You Just Dress That Way?" *Wall Street Journal,* http://www.wsj.com, accessed February 26, 2018; company website, "Innovated for Adaptive Breathability," http://www.nike.com, accessed February 26, 2018; Rob Walker, "Rise of 'Athleisure' Threatens to Put Jeans Out of Fashion," *Guardian,* http://www.theguardian.com, accessed February 26, 2018; Greg Petro, "Lululemon, Nike and the Rise of 'Athleisure'," *Forbes,* http://www.forbes.com, accessed February 26, 2018; Elizabeth Paton, "Nike and Rivals Such as Lululemon Battle for 'Athleisure' Crown," *Financial Times*, http://ft.com, accessed February 26, 2018; Kristin Tice Studeman, "From Alexander Wang to Beyoncé, Everyone's Doing It: A Look at How Gym-to-Street Became the New Uniform," *Vogue,* http://www.vogue.com, accessed February 26, 2018; Andria Cheng, "The Athleisure Trend Isn't Taking a Resting Break," *Forbes*, accessed February 26, 2018, www.forbes.com.

The forces of demand and supply can be affected by a variety of factors. One important variable is the larger economic environment. The next section explains how macroeconomics and economic systems influence market forces and, ultimately, demand, supply, and prices.

Assessment Check

1. Define microeconomics and macroeconomics.
2. Explain demand and supply curves.
3. How do factors of production influence the overall supply of goods and services?

2 Macroeconomics: Issues for the Entire Economy

macroeconomics study of a nation's overall economic issues, such as how an economy maintains and allocates resources and how a government's policies affect the standards of living of its citizens.

Macroeconomics is the study of a country's overall economic issues. Macroeconomic topics usually relate topics to be discussed—output, unemployment, and inflation. Macroeconomics refers to the performance, structure, behavior, and decision making of an economy as a whole. Each

TABLE 3.3 Types of Competition

Characteristics	Types of Competition: Pure Competition	Monopolistic Competition	Oligopoly	Monopoly
Number of competitors	Many	Few to many	Few	No direct competition
Ease of entry into industry by new firms	Easy	Somewhat difficult	Difficult	Regulated by government
Similarity of goods or services offered by competing firms	Similar	Different	Similar or different	No directly competing products
Control over price by individual firms	None	Some	Some	Considerable in a pure monopoly; little in a regulated monopoly
Examples	Small-scale farmer in Indiana	Local fitness center	Boeing aircraft	Rawlings Sporting Goods, exclusive supplier of major-league baseballs

nation's policies and choices help determine its economic system. However, the political, social, and legal environments differ in every country. In general, however, these systems can be classified into three categories: private enterprise systems; planned economies; or combinations of the two, referred to as mixed economies. As business becomes increasingly global in nature, it is important to understand the primary features of the various economic systems operating worldwide.

Capitalism: The Private Enterprise System and Competition

pure competition market structure in which large numbers of buyers and sellers exchange homogeneous products and no single participant has a significant influence on price.

Most industrialized nations operate economies based on the *private enterprise system*, also known as *capitalism* or a *market economy*. A private enterprise system rewards businesses for meeting the needs and demands of consumers. Government tends to favor a hands-off attitude toward controlling business ownership, profits, and resource allocations. Instead, competition regulates economic life, creating opportunities and challenges that businesspeople must manage in order to succeed.

The relative competitiveness of a particular industry is an important consideration for every company because it determines the ease and cost of entering or doing business within that industry. Four basic types of competition take shape in a private enterprise system: pure competition, monopolistic competition, oligopoly, and monopoly. **Table 3.3** highlights the main differences among these types of competition.

Orientaly/Shutterstock

Wheat is an example of pure competition in which large numbers of buyers and sellers exchange homogenous products. Consumers view each bushel of wheat as being the same as the next.

Pure competition is a market structure, like that of small-scale agriculture or fishing, in which large numbers of buyers and sellers exchange homogeneous products like sugar, rice, and wheat, and no single participant has a significant influence on price. Instead, prices are set by the market as the forces of supply and demand interact. Firms can easily enter or leave a purely competitive market because no single company dominates. Also, in pure competition, buyers see little difference between the goods and services offered by competitors.

Agricultural products like wheat and corn (see photo) are good examples of pure competition where market prices are determined primarily by consumer demand. With thousands of wheat and corn farmers, most account for no more than a tiny fraction of total output—and no single farmer has influence over market price. Since wheat and corn are standardized products, each farmer's product is regarded as identical by consumers. Extreme weather like heat waves and droughts can take a toll on crop yields, and with less supply, prices can increase.

Steve Proehl/Getty Images

The airline industry is a good example of an oligopoly market structure, which occurs when a select few companies have the majority of market share.

Monopolistic competition is a market structure, like that for retailing, in which large numbers of buyers and sellers exchange differentiated (heterogeneous) products, so each participant has some control over price. Sellers can differentiate their products from competing offerings on the basis of price, quality, or other features. In an industry that features monopolistic competition, it is relatively easy for a firm to begin or stop selling a good or service. The success of one seller often attracts new competitors to such a market. Individual firms also have some control over how their goods and services are priced.

One example of monopolistic competition is the market for pet food. Consumers can choose from private-label (store brands such as Walmart's Ol' Roy) and brand-name products such as Purina in bags, boxes, and cans. Producers of pet food and the stores that sell it have wide latitude in setting prices. Consumers can choose the store or brand with the lowest prices, or sellers can convince them that a more expensive offering—for example the Fromm brand, because it offers better nutrition, more convenience, or other benefits.

monopolistic competition market structure in which large numbers of buyers and sellers exchange heterogeneous products so each participant has some control over price.

An **oligopoly** is a market structure in which relatively few sellers compete and high start-up costs form barriers to keep out new competitors. In some oligopolistic industries, such as paper and steel, competitors offer similar products. In others, such as aircraft and automobiles, they sell different models and features (see photo). The huge investment required to enter an oligopoly market tends to discourage new competitors. The limited number of sellers also enhances the control these firms exercise over price. Competing products in an oligopoly usually sell for very similar prices because substantial price competition would reduce profits for all firms in the industry. So a price cut by one firm in an oligopoly will typically be met by its competitors. However, prices can vary from one market to another, as from one country to another.

oligopoly market situation in which relatively few sellers compete and high start-up costs form barriers to keep out new competitors.

The final type of market structure is a **monopoly**, in which a single seller dominates trade in a good or service for which buyers can find no close substitutes. A pure monopoly, a single supplier in a market, occurs when a firm possesses unique characteristics so important to competition in its industry that they form barriers to prevent entry by would-be competitors. There are a number of companies once thought to dominate their respective markets, but disruptive technology, a new technology that unexpectedly replaces an existing one, has changed that. PayPal's e-commerce payment system, Google's search engine, Hulu's video on-demand, Facebook's social networking platform, and Apple's iTunes no longer dominate their respective markets as they once did.[6]

monopoly market situation in which a single seller dominates trade in a good or service for which buyers can find no close substitutes.

Many companies create short-term monopolies when research breakthroughs permit them to receive exclusive patents on new products. In the pharmaceuticals industry, drug giants such as Merck and Pfizer invest billions in research and development programs. When the research leads to successful new drugs, the companies can enjoy the benefits of their patents: the ability to set prices without fear of competitors undercutting them. Once the patent expires, generic substitutes enter the market, driving down prices.

Because a monopoly market lacks the benefits of competition, many governments regulate monopolies. Besides issuing patents and limiting their life, the U.S. government prohibits most pure monopolies through antitrust legislation such as the Sherman Act and the Clayton Act. The U.S. government has applied these laws by disallowing proposed mergers of large companies in some industries. In other cases, the government permits certain monopolies in exchange for regulating their activities.

With **regulated monopolies**, a local, state, or federal government grants exclusive rights in a certain market to a single firm. Pricing decisions—particularly rate-increase requests—are

regulated monopolies market situation in which a local, state, or federal government grants exclusive rights in a certain market to a single firm.

subject to control by regulatory authorities such as state public service commissions. An example is the delivery of first-class mail, a monopoly held by the U.S. Postal Service. The USPS is a self-supporting corporation wholly owned by the federal government. Its postal rates are set by a postal commission and approved by a board of governors.

During the 1980s and 1990s, the U.S. government trended away from regulated monopolies and toward deregulation. Regulated monopolies that have been deregulated include transportation, energy, and communications. The idea is to improve customer service and reduce prices for customers through increased competition. Recently, the Federal Communications Commission (FCC) repealed net neutrality rules, which will allow blocking and controlling the rate at which application processing takes place by Internet providers.[7]

Planned Economies: Socialism and Communism

planned economy economic system in which government controls determine business ownership, profits, and resource allocation to accomplish government goals rather than those set by individual firms.

socialism economic system characterized by government ownership and operation of major industries such as communications.

communism economic system in which all property would be shared equally by the people of a community under the direction of a strong central government.

In a **planned economy**, government controls determine business ownership, profits, and resource allocation to accomplish government goals rather than those set by individual firms. Two forms of planned economies are communism and socialism.

Socialism is characterized by government ownership and operation of major industries such as communications. Socialists argue that major industries are too important to a society to be left in private hands and that government-owned businesses can serve the public's interest better than private firms. However, socialism allows private ownership in industries considered less crucial to social welfare, such as retail shops, restaurants, and certain types of manufacturing facilities. Scandinavian countries such as Denmark, Sweden, and Finland have many socialist features in their societies, as do some African nations and India.

The writings of Karl Marx in the mid-1800s formed the basis of communist theory. Marx believed that private enterprise economies created unfair conditions and led to worker exploitation because business owners controlled most of society's resources and reaped most of the economy's rewards. Instead, he suggested an economic system called **communism**, in which all property would be shared equally by the people of a community under the direction of a strong central government. Marx believed that elimination of private ownership of property and businesses would ensure the emergence of a classless society that would benefit all. Each individual would contribute to the nation's overall economic success, and resources would be distributed according to each person's needs. Under communism, the central government owns the means of production, and the people work for state-owned enterprises. The government determines what people can buy because it dictates what is produced in the nation's factories and farms.

Several nations adopted communist-like economic systems during the early 20th century in an effort to correct abuses they believed occurred in their existing systems. In practice, however, the new governments typically gave less freedom of choice in regard to jobs and purchases and might be best described as totalitarian socialism. These nations often made mistakes in allocating resources to compete in the growing global marketplace. Government-owned monopolies often suffer from inefficiency.

Consider the former Soviet Union, where large government bureaucracies controlled nearly every aspect of daily life. Shortages became chronic because producers had little or no incentive to satisfy customers, and because prices were not arrived at by the economy itself, government had little knowledge to make effective allocation decisions. The quality of goods and services also suffered for the same reason. When Mikhail Gorbachev became the last president of the dying Soviet Union, he tried to improve the quality of Soviet-made products. Effectively shut out of trading in the global marketplace and caught up in a treasury-depleting arms race with the United States, the Soviet Union faced severe financial problems. Eventually, these events led to the collapse of Soviet communism and the breakup of the Soviet Union itself.

Today, communist-like systems exist in just a few countries, such as North Korea. By contrast, the People's Republic of China has shifted toward a more market-oriented economy. The national government has given local government and individual plant managers more say in business decisions and has permitted some private businesses. Households now have more control over agriculture, in contrast to the collectivized farms introduced during an earlier era.

In addition, Western products such as Ralph Lauren apparel and Coca-Cola soft drinks are now part of Chinese consumers' lives.

Mixed Market Economies

Private enterprise systems and planned economies adopt basically opposite approaches to operating economies. In reality, though, many countries operate **mixed market economies**, economic systems that draw from both types of economies, to different degrees. In nations generally considered to have a private enterprise economy, government-owned firms frequently operate alongside private enterprises. In the United States, programs such as Medicare are government run.

mixed market economies economic system that draws from both types of economies, to different degrees.

France has blended socialist and free enterprise policies for hundreds of years. The nation's energy production, public transportation, and defense industries are run as nationalized industries, controlled by the government. Meanwhile, a market economy operates in other industries. Over the past two decades, the French government has loosened its reins on state-owned companies, inviting both competition and private investment into industries previously operated as government monopolies.

The proportions of private and public enterprise can vary widely in mixed economies, and the mix frequently changes. Dozens of countries have converted government-owned and operated companies into privately held businesses in a trend known as **privatization**. Even the United States has seen proposals to privatize everything from the postal service to air traffic control.[8]

privatization conversion of government-owned and operated companies into privately held businesses.

Governments may privatize state-owned enterprises in an effort to raise funds and improve their economies. The objective is to cut costs and run the operation more efficiently. In an effort to create a more modern U.S. infrastructure, there is discussion to allow private investment.[9] **Table 3.4** compares the alternative economic systems on the basis of ownership and management of enterprises, rights to profits, employee rights, and worker incentives.

TABLE 3.4 Comparison of Alternative Economic Systems

System Features	Capitalism (Private Enterprise)	Planned Economies		Mixed Economy
		Communism	Socialism	
Ownership of enterprises	Businesses are owned privately, often by large numbers of people. Minimal government ownership leaves production in private hands.	Government owns the means of production with few exceptions, such as small plots of land.	Government owns basic industries, but private owners operate some small enterprises.	A strong private sector blends with public enterprises.
Management of enterprises	Enterprises are managed by owners or their representatives, with minimal government interference.	Centralized management controls all state enterprises in line with three- to five-year plans. Planning now is being decentralized.	Significant government planning pervades socialist nations. State enterprises are managed directly by government bureaucrats.	Management of the private sector resembles that under capitalism. Professionals may also manage state enterprises.
Rights to profits	Entrepreneurs and investors are entitled to all profits (minus taxes) that their firms earn.	Profits are not allowed under communism.	Only the private sector of a socialist economy generates profits.	Entrepreneurs and investors are entitled to private-sector profits, although they often must pay high taxes. State enterprises are also expected to produce returns.
Rights of employees	The rights to choose one's occupation and to join a labor union have long been recognized.	Employee rights are limited in exchange for promised protection against unemployment.	Workers may choose their occupations and join labor unions, but the government influences career decisions for many people.	Workers may choose jobs and labor union membership. Unions often become quite strong.
Worker incentives	Considerable incentives motivate people to perform at their highest levels.	Incentives are emerging in communist countries.	Incentives usually are limited in state enterprises but do motivate workers in the private sector.	Capitalist-style incentives operate in the private sector. More limited incentives influence public-sector activities.

Assessment Check

1. What is the difference between pure competition and monopolistic competition?
2. On which economic system is the U.S. economy based?
3. What is privatization?

3 Evaluating Economic Performance

Ideally, an economic system should provide two important benefits for its citizens: a stable business environment and sustained growth. In a stable business environment, the overall supply of needed goods and services is aligned with the overall demand for these items. Consumers and businesses not only have access to ample supplies of desired products at affordable prices but also have money to buy the items they demand.

Growth is another important economic goal. An ideal economy incorporates steady change directed toward continually expanding the amount of goods and services produced from the nation's resources. Growth leads to expanded job opportunities, improved wages, and a rising standard of living.

Flattening the Business Cycle

Over time, a nation's economy tends to flow through various stages of a business cycle: prosperity, recession, depression, and recovery. A business cycle is a cycle of fluctuation in the long-term natural growth rate of Gross Domestic Product (GDP). No "true" economic depressions have occurred in the United States since the 1930s, and some economists believe that society is capable of preventing future depressions through effective economic policies. Consequently, they expect recessions to give way to periods of economic recovery. The "Clean & Green Business"

Clean & Green Business

Gates Creates Coalition to Invest in Climate Change

Prior to the UN Climate Change Conference held a few years ago in Paris, Bill Gates announced that he would invest $1 billion to help fight global warming. By persuading other wealthy entrepreneurs to join him in the creation of the Breakthrough Energy Coalition, Gates is committed to investing in technologies developed by companies that have a near-term impact on carbon reduction and help create jobs. Virgin Group's Richard Branson, Amazon's Jeff Bezos, LinkedIn's Reid Hoffman, Facebook's Mark Zuckerberg, and Alibaba's Jack Ma, among others, have joined the coalition. In total, there are 28 private investors.

Gates came up with the coalition idea out of frustration with the lack of energy research and government programs that have disappeared due to budget cuts. The coalition will focus on developing novel innovations that enable current clean technologies to be more efficient, scalable, and cheaper.

Because there are so many different solutions to climate change, Gates wants to invest in as many as possible. "We want to give a little bit of money to the guy who thinks that high wind will work; we want to give a little bit of money to the guy who thinks that taking sunlight and making oil directly out of sunlight will work," Gates says. His goals are lofty, but so are his investors. And it is hoped that such commitment to energy innovation will not only reduce emissions but also spur the creation of many new jobs in the process.

Questions for Critical Thinking

1. **Discuss the Breakthrough Energy Coalition's sense of urgency and need to scale rapidly to drive innovation and create jobs. Is this realistic? Why or why not?**
2. **Why do you think Gates was able to persuade so many other wealthy entrepreneurs to invest?**

Sources: Stephan Dolezalek, Stefan Heck, and Andrew Shapiro, "Can Bill Gates' Climate Pledge Make a Real Difference?" *Fortune*, http://fortune.com, accessed February 27, 2018; James Bennet, "'We Need an Energy Miracle,'" *Atlantic*, http://www.theatlantic.com, accessed February 27, 2018; Joby Warrick, "Bill Gates on Climate Change: 'We Need to Move Faster Than the Energy Sector Ever Has,'" *Washington Post*, http://www.washingtonpost.com, accessed February 27, 2018.

feature describes how Bill Gates recently led the charge to recruit other wealthy entrepreneurs to join his coalition to create new jobs and alternative sources of energy.

Both business decisions and consumer buying patterns differ at each stage of the business cycle. In periods of economic prosperity, unemployment remains low, consumer confidence about the future leads to more purchases, and businesses expand—by hiring more employees, investing in new technology, and making similar purchases—to take advantage of new opportunities.

Kristoffer Tripplaar/Alamy Stock Photo

During a recession, consumers will increasingly shop at lower-priced retailers like The Dollar Tree to purchase essentials like cereal, school supplies, and kitchenware, and even some grocery items.

During a **recession**—a cyclical economic contraction that lasts for six months or longer—consumers frequently postpone major purchases and shift buying patterns toward basic, functional products carrying low prices. Businesses mirror these changes in the marketplace by slowing production, postponing expansion plans, reducing inventories, and often cutting the size of their workforces. During recessions, people facing layoffs and depletions of household savings become much more conservative in their spending, postponing luxury purchases and vacations, and often turning to generic brands and lower-priced retailers such as Dollar Tree and Dollar General for the goods they need (see photo). Dollar Tree's sales increased in a recent year, and the company continues to compete in an Amazon-centric environment among lower-income earners who may get a boost from recent tax cuts and wage hikes.[10]

recession cyclical economic contraction that lasts for six months or longer.

If an economic slowdown continues in a downward spiral over an extended period of time, the economy falls into depression. Occurring after the stock market crash known as Black Tuesday in October of 1929, the Great Depression of the 1930s was severe and worldwide. Until 1932, GDP fell by approximately 15%.

In the recovery stage of the business cycle, the economy emerges from recession and consumer spending picks up steam. The economy experiences high levels of growth in gross domestic product, employment, output levels, and corporate profits.

Productivity and the Nation's Gross Domestic Product

An important concern for every economy is **productivity**, the relationship between the goods and services produced in a nation each year and the inputs needed to produce them. In general, as productivity rises, so does an economy's growth and the wealth of its citizens. In a recession, productivity stalls or even declines.

productivity relationship between the number of units produced and the number of human and other production inputs necessary to produce them.

Productivity describes the relationship between the number of units produced and the number of human and other production inputs necessary to produce them. Productivity is a ratio of output to input. When a constant amount of inputs generates increased outputs, an increase in productivity occurs.

Total productivity considers all inputs necessary to produce a specific amount of outputs. Stated in equation form, it can be written as follows:

$$\text{Total Productivity} = \frac{\text{Output (goods or services produced)}}{\text{Input (human/natural resources, capital)}}$$

Many productivity ratios focus on only one of the inputs in the equation: labor productivity or output per labor-hour. An increase in labor productivity means that the same amount of work produces more goods and services than previously. Many of the gains in U.S. productivity can be attributed to technology.

Productivity is a widely recognized measure of a company's efficiency. In turn, the total productivity of a nation's businesses has become a measure of its economic strength and standard of living. Economists refer to this measure as a country's **gross domestic product (GDP)**—

gross domestic product (GDP) sum of all goods and services produced within a country's boundaries during a specific time period, such as a year.

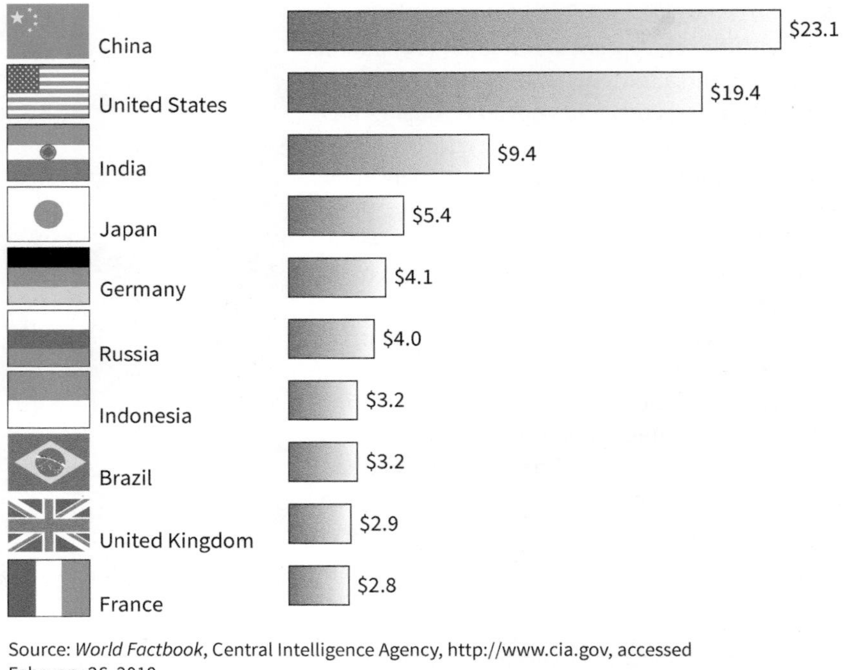

Source: *World Factbook*, Central Intelligence Agency, http://www.cia.gov, accessed February 26, 2018.

FIGURE 3.4 Nations with Highest Gross Domestic Products (in trillions)

the sum of all goods and services produced within its boundaries. The GDP is based on the per-capita output of a country—in other words, total national output divided by the number of citizens. As **Figure 3.4** shows, the United States has an estimated GDP of $19.4 trillion. Only the European Union, with its 28 member nations and estimated GDP of $20.9 trillion, and China, with an estimated GDP of $23.1 trillion, have GDPs higher than the United States. In the United States, GDP is tracked by the Bureau of Economic Analysis (BEA), a division of the U.S. Department of Commerce. Current updates and historical data on the GDP are available at the BEA's website (http://www.bea.gov).[11] A new economic aggregate, gross output (GO), has been introduced recently by the BEA. It will measure total sales volume at all production stages rather than just final output.

Price-Level Changes

inflation economic situation characterized by rising prices caused by a combination of excess consumer demand and increases in the costs of raw materials, component parts, human resources, and other factors of production.

core inflation rate inflation rate of an economy after energy and food prices are removed.

hyperinflation economic situation characterized by soaring prices.

Another important indicator of an economy's stability is the general level of prices. For the past hundred years, economic decision makers concerned themselves with **inflation**, rising prices caused by a combination of excess consumer demand and increases in the costs of raw materials, component parts, human resources, and other factors of production. The **core inflation rate** is the inflation rate of an economy after energy and food prices are removed. This measure is often an accurate prediction of the inflation rate that consumers, businesses, and other organizations can expect to experience during the near future.

Excess consumer demand generates what is known as demand-pull inflation whereas increases in the costs of factors of production generate cost-push inflation. America's most severe inflationary period during the last half of the 20th century peaked in 1980 at over 14%. In extreme cases, an economy may experience **hyperinflation**—an economic situation characterized by soaring prices. A severe case of hyperinflation occurred in Zimbabwe, with prices doubling almost every 24 hours.[12]

Inflation devalues money as persistent price increases reduce the amount of goods and services people can purchase with a given amount of money. This can be especially difficult for people whose earnings do not keep up with inflation, who live on fixed incomes, or who have most of their wealth in investments paying a fixed rate of interest. Inflation can be good news for people whose income is rising or those with debts at a fixed rate of interest. A homeowner with a fixed-rate mortgage during inflationary times is paying off that debt with money that is worth less and less each year. As hedges against inflation, investments in real estate, gold, oil, and stocks historically have been viewed very favorably.[13]

Lya Cattel/iStockphoto

When increased productivity keeps prices steady, it can have a major positive impact on an economy. Low interest rates encourage firms to invest in capital improvements—such as building a new company headquarters or expanding existing space—which are likely to produce productivity gains.

When increased productivity results in stabilized prices, it can have a major positive impact on an economy. In a low-inflation environment, businesses can make long-range plans without the constant worry of sudden inflationary shocks. Low interest rates encourage companies to invest in research and development and capital improvements (pictured in photo), both of which are likely to result in productivity gains. Consumers can purchase goods and services with the same amount of money, and low interest rates encourage major purchases such as new homes and autos. The fluctuating cost of oil—which is used to produce many goods—remains an issue. Businesses need to raise prices to cover their costs. Also, smaller firms have gone out of business or have merged with larger companies, reducing overall competition and increasing the purchasing power of the larger corporations. Business owners continue to keep a watchful eye on signs of inflation.

The opposite situation—**deflation**—occurs when prices continue to fall. Deflation occurs when the inflation rate falls below 0%, also called a negative inflation rate. Falling prices might sound ideal for consumers, but falling prices begin to impact companies who reduce pay and employment in response to falling revenues—which results in a decline in income, spending, and consumer confidence.[14]

deflation opposite of inflation, occurs when prices continue to fall.

Measuring Price Level Changes In the United States, the government tracks changes in price levels with the **Consumer Price Index (CPI)**, which measures the monthly average change in prices of goods and services. The U.S. Bureau of Labor Statistics (BLS) calculates the CPI monthly based on prices of a "market basket," a compilation of the goods and services most commonly purchased by urban consumers. While the CPI measures price change from a consumer perspective, the **Producer Price Index (PPI)** is the average change over time of prices of goods and services received by domestic producers. **Figure 3.5** shows the categories included in the CPI market basket. Each month, BLS representatives collect prices in 75 urban areas across the United States from about 5,000 housing units and approximately 22,000 retail establishments—department stores, supermarkets, hospitals, filling stations, and other types of stores and service establishments.[15] They compile the data to create the CPI. Thus, the CPI provides a running measurement of changes in consumer prices.

Consumer Price Index (CPI) measurement of the monthly average change in prices of goods and services.

Producer Price Index (PPI) measurement of the average change in prices of goods and services received by domestic producers.

Employment Levels To purchase goods and services produced in an economy, money is required. Because most consumers earn that money by working, the number of people in a nation who currently have jobs is an important indicator of how well the economy is doing. Employment has slowly rebounded since the recession, which began nearly a decade ago. Industries where jobs have been added include professional and business services, construction, leisure and hospitality, education and health services, manufacturing, and retail trade.[16] The "Business & Technology" feature discusses one of the top five largest U.S. employers, United Parcel Service, and recent productivity gains resulting from new technology used to optimize driving routes.

Economists refer to a nation's **unemployment rate** as an indicator of its economic health. The unemployment rate is usually expressed as a percentage of the total workforce actively seeking work but currently unemployed. The total labor force includes all people who are willing

unemployment rate percentage of the total workforce actively seeking work but currently unemployed.

FIGURE 3.5 Contents of the CPI Market Basket

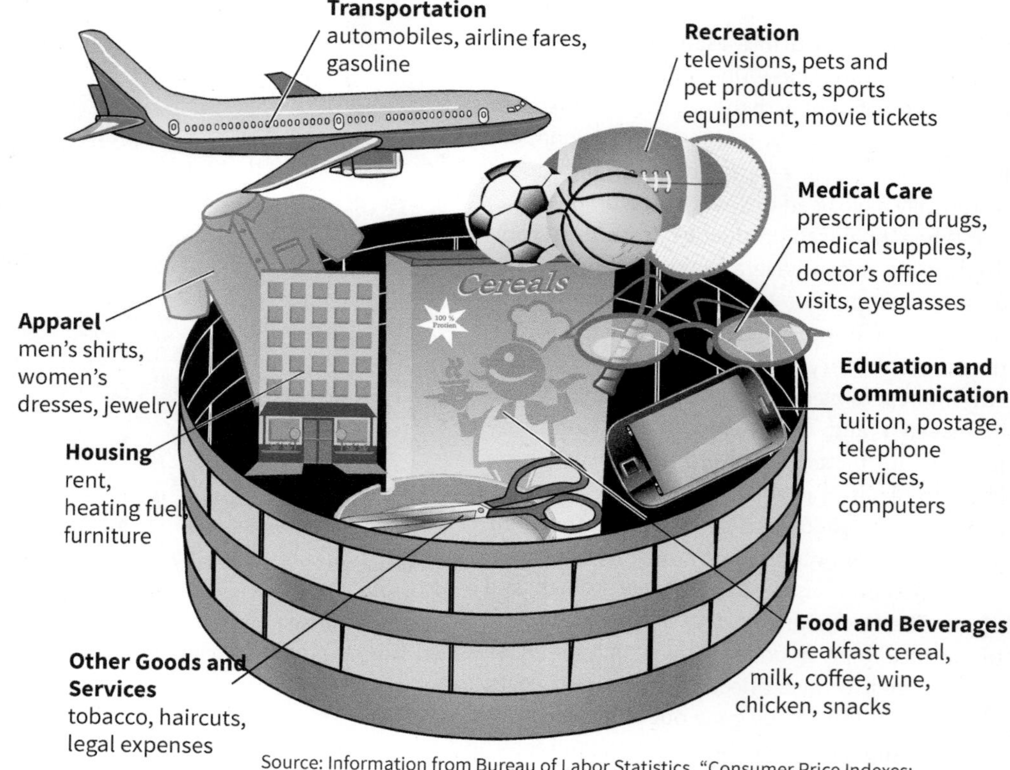

Source: Information from Bureau of Labor Statistics, "Consumer Price Indexes: Frequently Asked Questions," http://www.bls.gov/cpi, accessed February 25, 2018.

Business & Technology

ORION Helps UPS Deliver Productivity Gains

Given the fact that a UPS driver makes anywhere between 120 and 175 stops per day, the challenge of optimizing routes for greater efficiency and productivity might seem like a daunting task. The number of alternatives a driver can choose to take on any given day is, according to company officials, more than "the number of nanoseconds the earth has existed." Factor in variables such as special delivery times, road regulations, and private roads that don't appear on a map, and optimizing routes becomes even more complicated. The convergence of mobile devices, cloud computing, and big data are playing a significant role in productivity gains at UPS, resulting in enhanced customer service, reduced emissions, and greater routing efficiencies.

Consider this: A reduction of one mile a day for each driver would save the company as much as $50 million per year. For UPS, figuring out the most efficient route for its 55,000 North American delivery routes requires analytics and big data technologies. For a company like UPS, increased productivity occurs when a constant amount of inputs (drivers and routes) generates increased outputs (more packages delivered in a shorter or same period of time).

Its latest computer system, ten years in the making with an estimated cost of hundreds of millions of dollars, was developed by a team of 50 UPS engineers. Called ORION (On-Road Integrated Optimization and Navigation), this proprietary routing platform has been implemented across 70% of UPS's routes in North America to squeeze every penny from its delivery routes. For each 120-stop route, ORION analyzes more than 200,000 options (travel costs, distance, and other factors) and selects the most efficient route while meeting customer requirements for time-sensitive pickups or deliveries. Eliminating one mile per driver per day saves UPS up to $50 million a year. With ORION, up to 10 million gallons of fuel is saved annually, which translates to a reduction of 100,000 metric tons in CO_2 emissions. This is of particular importance to UPS in an industry with increased competition from FedEx, small profit margins, and a union workforce compensated at the high end of the industry's wage scale. Optimizing 55,000 routes is no easy feat, but UPS and its customers have certainly reaped the benefits of an important package arriving just in time.

Questions for Critical Thinking

1. If you were involved with the development of ORION, what type of input would you solicit from UPS drivers who have intimate knowledge of alternate routes, as compared to computer-generated routes?
2. Discuss the environmental benefits and additional cost reductions expected with a program like ORION. Does this system have implications for other industries? Explain.

Sources: Jeff Berman, "UPS Is Focused on the Future for Its ORION Technology," *Logistics Management*, http://www.logisticsmgmt.com, accessed February 25, 2018; Jenn Gidman, "Algorithm Will Tell All UPS Trucks Where to Go," *Supply Chain 247*, http://www.supplychain247.com, accessed February 25, 2018; Katherine Noyes, "The Shortest Distance Between Two Points? At UPS, It's Complicated," *Fortune*, http://www.fortune.com, accessed February 25, 2018; "To Increase Productivity, UPS Monitors Drivers' Every Move," *National Public Radio*, http://www.npr.org, accessed February 25, 2018; Steven Rosenbush and Laura Stevens, "At UPS, the Algorithm Is the Driver," *Wall Street Journal*, http://www.wsj.com, accessed February 25, 2018.

and available to work at the going market wage, whether they currently have jobs or are seeking work. The survey excludes people living in a correctional institution or a residential nursing or mental health care facility, along with those on active duty in the military.[17] The U.S. Department of Labor, which tracks unemployment rates, also measures so-called discouraged workers and underemployed workers. Discouraged workers are individuals who want to work but have given up looking for jobs. Underemployed workers are individuals who have taken lower-paying positions than their qualifications would suggest. Unemployment can be grouped into the four categories shown in **Figure 3.6**: frictional, seasonal, cyclical, and structural.

Frictional Unemployment
- Temporarily not working
- Looking for a job

Example: New graduates entering the workforce

Seasonal Unemployment
- Not working during some months
- Not looking for a job

Example: Farm workers needed only when a crop is in season

Structural Unemployment
- Not working due to no demand for skills
- May be retraining for a new job

Example: Assembly line employees whose jobs are now done by robots

Cyclical Unemployment
- Not working due to economic slowdown
- Looking for a job

Example: Executives laid off during corporate downsizing or recessionary periods

FIGURE 3.6 Four Types of Unemployment

Frictional unemployment is experienced by members of the workforce who are temporarily not working but are looking for jobs. This pool of potential workers includes new graduates, people who have left jobs for any reason and are looking for other employment, and former workers who have decided to return to the labor force. **Seasonal unemployment** is the joblessness of people in a seasonal industry. Construction workers, farm laborers, fishing boat operators, and landscape employees may contend with bouts of seasonal unemployment when conditions make work unavailable.

Cyclical unemployment includes people who are out of work because of a cyclical contraction in the economy. During periods of economic expansion, overall employment is likely to rise, but as growth slows and a recession begins, unemployment levels commonly rise. At such times, even workers with good job skills may face temporary unemployment. Workers in high-tech industries, air travel, and manufacturing have all faced unemployment during economic contraction.

Structural unemployment applies to people who remain unemployed for long periods of time, often with little hope of finding new jobs like their old ones. This situation may arise because these workers lack the necessary skills for available jobs or because the skills they have are no longer in demand. For example, technological advances have increased the demand for people with computer-related skills but have created structural unemployment among many types of manual laborers or workers who may have been injured and unable to return to work.

frictional unemployment applies to members of the workforce who are temporarily not working but are looking for jobs.

seasonal unemployment joblessness of workers in a seasonal industry.

cyclical unemployment people who are out of work because of a cyclical contraction in the economy.

structural unemployment people who remain unemployed for long periods of time, often with little hope of finding new jobs like their old ones.

Assessment Check

1. Describe the four stages of the business cycle.
2. What are some measures that economists use to determine the health of an economy?

4 Managing the Economy's Performance

Government can use both monetary policy and fiscal policy in its efforts to fight unemployment, increase business and consumer spending, and reduce the length and severity of economic recessions. For instance, the Federal Reserve System can increase or reduce interest rates, and the federal government can enact tax cuts and rebates, or propose other reforms.

Monetary Policy

A common method of influencing economic activity is **monetary policy**, government actions to increase or decrease the money supply and change banking requirements and interest rates

monetary policy government actions to increase or decrease the money supply and change banking requirements and interest rates to influence bankers' willingness to make loans.

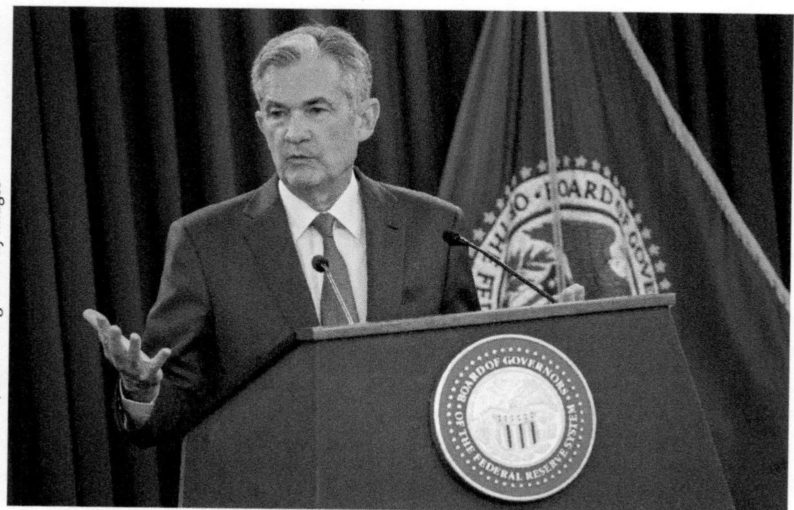
Andrew Harrer/Bloomberg via Getty Images

Jerome Powell is the most recent chair of the Federal Reserve Bank, replacing Janet Yellen.

to influence spending by altering bankers' willingness to make loans. An **expansionary monetary policy** increases the money supply in an effort to cut the cost of borrowing, which encourages business decision makers to make new investments, in turn stimulating employment and economic growth. By contrast, a **restrictive monetary policy** reduces the money supply to curb rising prices, overexpansion, and concerns about overly rapid economic growth. This is accomplished by increasing interest rates.

In the United States, the Federal Reserve System ("the Fed") is responsible for formulating and implementing the nation's monetary policy. It is headed by a chair and board of governors, all of whom are nominated by the president. The current chair is Jerome Powell (shown in the photo), a former private equity partner and bank regulator. All national banks must be members of this system and keep some percentage of their checking and savings funds on deposit at the Fed. The Federal Open Market Committee (FOMC) oversees the nation's open market operations, which consist of buying and selling treasury securities.

expansionary monetary policy government actions to increase the money supply in an effort to cut the cost of borrowing, which encourages business decision makers to make new investments, in turn stimulating employment and economic growth.

restrictive monetary policy government actions to reduce the money supply to curb rising prices, overexpansion, and concerns about overly rapid economic growth.

The Fed's board of governors uses a number of tools to regulate the economy. By changing the required percentage of checking and savings accounts that banks must deposit with the Fed, the governors can expand or shrink funds available to lend. The Fed also lends money to member banks, which in turn make loans at higher interest rates to business and individual borrowers. By changing the interest rates charged to commercial banks, the Fed affects the interest rates charged to borrowers and, consequently, their willingness to borrow. Quantitative easing (QE) is an expansionary monetary policy whereby a central bank buys back predetermined amounts of government bonds or other financial assets to increase liquidity and stimulate the economy.

Fiscal Policy

fiscal policy government spending and taxation decisions designed to control inflation, reduce unemployment, improve the general welfare of citizens, and encourage economic growth.

Governments also influence economic activities by making decisions about taxes and spending. Through revenues and expenses, the government implements **fiscal policy**. Used to encourage economic growth, control inflation, reduce unemployment, and improve the general standard of living, fiscal policy includes government revenue collection through tax collection, and expenditure through spending. Increased taxes may restrict economic activities, while lower taxes and increased government spending usually boost spending and profits, cut unemployment rates, and fuel economic expansion. To create jobs and increase GDP, an ongoing discussion of reducing corporate taxes—a way to stimulate investment and spending—remains. Although different from improving the standard of living, pharmaceutical companies argue that they are improving the quality of life for many consumers. The "Judgment Call" feature describes some of the strategies they use to develop new drugs while charging more for their products.

International Fiscal Policy Nations in the industrial world, including the United States, are currently struggling to find ways to help developing nations modernize their economies. One proposal is to forgive the debts of some of these countries, particularly those in Africa, to stimulate their economies to grow. But not all fiscal experts agree with this idea. They suggest that any debt forgiveness should come with certain conditions so that these countries can build their own fiscal policies. Countries should encourage and allow citizens to own property, lower their tax rates, avoid devaluing their currencies, lay a

Judgment Call

Drug Prices Soar Despite Falling Demand

The basic principle of supply and demand is not always applicable in the pharmaceutical industry as prices for some drugs have jumped dramatically despite lower demand. Over the past decade, even though demand has decreased for the multiple sclerosis drug Avenox, Cambridge, Massachusetts-based drug maker Biogen has steadily raised its price 21 times, an average of 16% per year. It is common for pharmaceutical companies like Biogen to defend high pricing on older medications as a way to help finance the development of new life-saving drugs. In addition, the high prices typically support a company's costly and risky research and development (R&D) investment. Over the past decade, Biogen has invested over $1 billion annually in R&D, or about 24% of its annual revenues.

There are several reasons why the drug industry has so much control over pricing. First, drug makers have a two-decade-long patent protection on new products before other companies can offer competing drugs in the marketplace. In addition, for some drugs, there is very little competition. Another industry strategy routinely used to raise prices is the purchase of another company's "undervalued" drugs. When Lomastine, used to treat brain tumors, lung cancer, and Hodgkin's lymphoma, was sold from one pharma giant to a small startup called NextSource Biotechnology, the price went up 15-fold in four short years. Still, some argue that focusing on increased drug prices is shortsighted because it overlooks the role of drugs in helping contain overall healthcare costs by preventing disease and further complications. For now, it remains true that the market power for branded drugs is a result of a few basic economic principles: a single manufacturer, no substitutes, and guaranteed patent protection to rule out competitors.

Questions for Critical Thinking

1. **Drug maker Biogen argues that increasing prices on existing drugs funds its research for new medicines. Is it fair for American consumers to subsidize industry R&D costs?**
2. **Do you think customer loyalty plays a role in pharmaceutical sales? Do TV commercials have anything to do with a customer's loyalty to a drug? Would loyalty trump a lower cost drug option?**

Sources: Joseph Walker, "For Prescription Drug Makers, Price Increases Drive Revenue," *Wall Street Journal*, http://www.wsj.com, accessed February 26, 2018; Peter Loftus and Ron Winslow, "FDA Approves Bristol-Myers's Yervoy, Opdivo for Treatment of Melanoma," *Wall Street Journal*, http://www.wsj.com, accessed February 26, 2018; Jonathan D. Rockoff and Ed Silverman, "Pharmaceutical Companies Buy Rivals' Drugs, Then Jack Up the Prices," *Wall Street Journal*, http://www.wsj.com, accessed February 26, 2018; Rafi Mohammed, "It's Time to Rein in Exorbitant Pharmaceutical Prices," *Harvard Business Review*, http://hbr.org, accessed February 26, 2018; Brady Huggett, "America's drug problem," *Nature Biotechnology*, accessed February 26, 2018; www.nature.com, Benjamin Kentish, "Cancer Drug Price Rises 15-fold as Owner Raises Cost for Ninth Time in Four Years," *Independent*, accessed February 26, 2018, www.independent.co.uk.

path for new businesses to start, and reduce trade barriers. In addition, they must improve agriculture, education, and health care so their citizens can begin to set and reach financial goals. The World Bank is an organization that offers such programs as low-interest loans and interest-free credit and grants to developing countries. The World Bank recently approved a $10 million grant to support Sierra Leone in its efforts to recover from severe landslides and floods.[18]

The Federal Budget Each year, the president proposes a **budget** for the federal government, a plan for how it will raise and spend money during the coming year, and presents it to Congress for approval. A typical federal budget proposal undergoes months of deliberation and many modifications before receiving approval. The federal budget includes a number of different spending categories, ranging from defense and Social Security to interest payments on the national debt. The decisions about what to include in the budget have a direct effect on various sectors of the economy. During a recession, the federal government may approve increased spending on interstate highway repairs to improve transportation and increase employment in the construction industry. During prosperity, the government may allocate more money for scientific research toward medical breakthroughs.

budget organization's plan for how it will raise and spend money during a given period of time.

The primary sources of government funds to cover the costs of the annual budget are taxes, fees, and borrowing. Both the overall amount of these funds and their specific combination have major effects on the economic well-being of the nation. One way governments raise money is to impose taxes on sales, income, and other sources. But increasing taxes leaves people and businesses with less money to spend. This might reduce inflation, but overly high taxes can also slow economic growth. Governments then try to balance taxes to give people necessary services without slowing economic growth.

Taxes don't always generate enough funds to cover every spending project the government hopes to undertake. When the government spends more than the amount of money it raises through taxes, it creates a **budget deficit**. To cover the deficit, the U.S. government borrows money by selling Treasury bills, Treasury notes, and Treasury bonds to investors. All of this borrowing makes up the **national debt**. If the government takes in more money than it spends, it is said to have a **budget surplus**. A **balanced budget** means total revenues raised by taxes equal the total proposed spending for the year.

budget deficit situation in which the government spends more than the amount of money it raises through taxes.

national debt money owed by government to individuals, businesses, and government agencies who purchase Treasury bills, Treasury notes, and Treasury bonds sold to cover expenditures.

budget surplus excess funding that occurs when government spends less than the amount of funds raised through taxes and fees.

balanced budget situation in which total revenues raised by taxes equal the total proposed spending for the year.

Achieving a balanced budget—or even a budget surplus—does not erase the national debt. Congress continually debates how to use revenues to reduce its debt. Most families want to wipe out debt—from credit cards, automobile purchases, and college, to name a few sources. To put the national debt into personal perspective, with roughly 327 million U.S. citizens, each one currently owes about $63,437 as his or her share.[19]

But for the federal government, the decision is more complex. When the government raises money by selling Treasury bills, it makes safe investments available to investors worldwide. If foreign investors cannot buy Treasury notes, they might turn to other countries, reducing the amount of money flowing into the United States. U.S. government debt has also been used as a basis for pricing riskier investments. If the government issues less debt, the interest rates it commands are higher, raising the overall cost of debt to private borrowers. In addition, the government uses the funds from borrowing, at least in part, to invest in such public services as education and scientific research.

Assessment Check

1. What is the difference between an expansionary monetary policy and a restrictive monetary policy?
2. What are the three primary sources of government funds?
3. Does a balanced budget erase the national debt?

5 Global Economic Challenges

Businesses face a number of important economic challenges today. As the economies of countries around the globe become increasingly interconnected, governments and businesses must compete worldwide. To maintain global competitiveness, government and business will need to address several challenges. The annual World Economic Forum meeting identifies global risks in the following five categories: economic, environmental, geopolitical, societal, and technological.[20] **Table 3.5** outlines the World Economic Forum's Global Risks Report, developed from an annual survey of more than 1,000 experts from industry, government, academia, and the general public. It lists the top global economic risks (and their likelihood and impact) as follows: (1) asset bubbles in a major economy, (2) deflation in a major economy, (3) failure of a major financial mechanism or institution, (4) failure/shortfall of critical infrastructure, (5) fiscal crises in key economies, (6) high structural unemployment or underemployment, (7) Illicit trade, (8) Trade tensions, (9) Energy price shock, (10) Unmanageable Inflation.[21]

No country is an economic island in today's global economy. A growing number of businesses have become true multinational firms, operating manufacturing plants and other facilities around the world. These global companies will require employees who can evaluate political, social, and economic trends that affect their operations. See the "Job Description" feature to learn more about a career as an economic analyst.

TABLE 3.5 Global Economic Challenges

Economics		
	Businesses face ten key global risks in today's economy:	
	(1) **Asset bubble** in a major economy	Unsustainably overpriced assets such as commodities, housing, shares, etc. in a major economy or region
	(2) **Deflation** in a major economy	Prolonged near-zero inflation or deflation in a major economy or region
	(3) **Failure of** a major **financial mechanism or institution**	Collapse of a financial institution and/or malfunctioning of a financial system that impacts the global economy
	(4) **Failure**/shortfall **of critical infrastructure**	Failure to adequately invest in, upgrade and/or secure infrastructure networks (e.g. energy, transportation and communications), leading to pressure or a breakdown with system-wide implications
	(5) **Fiscal crises** in key economies	Excessive debt burdens that generate sovereign debt crises and/or liquidity crises
	(6) **High structural unemployment or underemployment**	A sustained high level of unemployment or underutilization of the productive capacity of the employed population
	(7) **Illicit trade**	Large-scale activities outside the lagal framework such as illicit financial flows, tax evasion, human trafficking, counterfeiting and/or organized crime that undermine social interactions, regional or international collaboration, and global growth
	(8) **Trade tensions**	Trade tensions can dampen confidence and take a toll on economic expansion.
	(9) **Energy price shock**	Significant energy price increases or decreases that place further economic pressures on highly energy-dependent industries and consumers
	(10) **Unmanageable inflation**	Unmanageable increases in the general price levels of goods and services in key economies

Source: Organization website, "World Economic Forum: The Global Risks Report 2018," http://reports.weforum.org, accessed February 26, 2018.

As global trade and investments grow, events in one nation can reverberate around the globe. But despite the risks of world trade, global expansion can offer huge opportunities to U.S. companies. With U.S. residents accounting for just over 1 in every 23 of the world's more than 7.6 billion people, growth-oriented American companies cannot afford to ignore the world market.[22] U.S. businesses also benefit from the lower labor costs in other parts of the world, and some are finding successful niches importing goods and services provided by foreign firms. Still, it is extremely important for U.S. firms to keep close track of the foreign firms that supply their products. A number of U.S. companies have tried having their goods manufactured in China because production costs are lower than they would be in the United States. But there have been many product recalls of Chinese-made goods over the past few years. In a recent product safety summit between the United States and China manufacturers, product developers, and designers, safety standards for the import of lithium-ion batteries into the United States and use in consumer products was discussed. The Consumer Product Safety Commission's office in Beijing works directly with Chinese stakeholders to continue to improve the safety of consumer products exported to the United States.[23]

U.S. companies must also develop strategies for competing with each other and with foreign companies to meet the needs and wants of consumers overseas. In the huge and fragmented beverage industry, experts predict that the global markets for healthy soft drinks, including juice-based and ready-to-drink tea-based drinks, will grow significantly over the next few years.[24]

Job Description

Economic Analyst

Overview If you've ever wondered about the type of job an economics degree will help land, the answer is not cut-and-dried, but becoming an economic analyst is one option. Due to the varied classes taken in this field of study, the jobs and industries open to an economic analyst are wide ranging, including nonprofit, private sector, government, education, healthcare, environment, banking, and consumer products. Most job titles for economics majors do not contain the word *economist*, mainly because jobs for economists usually require a master's degree (or higher).

Responsibilities Typically, an economic analyst studies the production and distribution of resources, goods, and services by collecting, manipulating, and analyzing data (surveys); researching trends; and evaluating economic issues and historical (past) trends to find relationships and make future forecasts and recommendations. An economic analyst takes into account data about GDP, inflation, employment, housing, taxes, exchange rates, and stock prices. Within the private sector, an economic analyst might help a company make decisions on the basis of economic predictions and expectations, market trends, and how they will impact their business.

Requirements An undergraduate degree in economics is typically required for an economic analyst. Economics majors are likely to possess good analytical and research skills, the ability to understand relationships and trends, and proficiency at collecting and analyzing data. An economic analyst understands relationships and the ability to think conceptually rather than in absolute specifics. For example, what factors might lead to higher sales or higher costs? Understanding major changes within various industries is important to learning about new products, trends, and business models. An economic analyst may analyze issues such as consumer demand and sales to help a company maximize its profits.

Required skills include collecting, researching, and interpreting data; reporting it in the form of oral and written reports, tables, and charts; and making accurate predictions and recommendations. Attention to detail, trustworthiness, integrity, logic, and analytic and problem-solving skills are also essential.

Outlook As businesses increasingly rely on economic analysis and quantitative methods to analyze and forecast business, sales, and other economic trends, employment in this sector is projected to grow 6% annually. However, employment in the federal government is projected to decline due to spending cutbacks, so job growth will be mainly in the private sector.

Sources: Bill Conerly, "Career Advice for Economics Majors," *Forbes*, http://www.forbes.com, accessed February 25, 2018; government website, "Economists," *Occupational Outlook Handbook, 2017–18 Edition*, http://www.bls.gov, accessed February 25, 2018; Kelci Lynn Lucier, "Jobs for an Economics Major," About.com, http://collegelife.about.com, accessed February 25, 2018.

Assessment Check

1. Why is virtually no country an economic island these days?
2. Describe two ways in which global expansion can benefit a U.S. firm.

What's Ahead

Global competition is a given in today's economy. In Chapter 4, we focus on the global dimensions of business. We cover basic concepts of doing business internationally and examine how nations can position themselves to benefit from the global economy. Then we describe the specific methods used by individual businesses to expand beyond their national borders and compete successfully in the global marketplace.

Chapter in Review

Summary of Learning Objectives

LEARNING OBJECTIVE 1 Discuss microeconomics and explain the forces of demand and supply.

Microeconomics is the study of economic behavior among individual consumers, families, and businesses whose collective behavior in the marketplace determines the quantity of goods and services demanded and supplied at different prices. Macroeconomics is the study of the broader economic picture and how an economic system maintains and allocates its resources; it focuses on how a government's monetary and fiscal policies affect the overall operation of an economic system.

Demand is the willingness and ability of buyers to purchase goods and services at different prices. Factors that drive demand for a good or service include customer preferences, the number of buyers and their incomes, the prices of substitute goods, the prices of complementary goods, and consumer expectations about the future. Supply is the willingness and ability of businesses to offer products for sale at different prices. Supply is determined by the cost of inputs and technology resources, taxes, and the number of suppliers operating in the market.

Assessment Check Answers

1.1 **Define microeconomics and macroeconomics.** *Microeconomics* is the study of economic behavior among individual consumers, families, and businesses. *Macroeconomics* is the study of a nation's overall economic issues and how an economic system maintains and allocates its resources.

1.2 **Explain demand and supply curves.** A demand curve is a graph of the amount of a product that buyers will purchase at different prices. A supply curve shows the relationship between different prices and the quantities that sellers will offer for sale, regardless of demand.

1.3 **How do factors of production influence the overall supply of goods and services?** A change in the cost or availability of any of the inputs considered to be factors of production can shift the entire supply curve, either increasing or decreasing the amount available at every price.

LEARNING OBJECTIVE 2 Describe macroeconomics and the issues for the entire economy.

Four basic models characterize competition in a private enterprise system: pure competition, monopolistic competition, oligopoly, and monopoly. Pure competition is a market structure, like that in small-scale agriculture, in which large numbers of buyers and sellers exchange homogeneous products and no single participant has a significant influence on price. Monopolistic competition is a market structure, like that of retailing, in which large numbers of buyers and sellers exchange differentiated products, so each participant has some control over price. Oligopolies are market situations, like those in the steel and airline industries, in which relatively few sellers compete and high start-up costs form barriers to keep out new competitors. In a monopoly, one seller dominates trade in a good or service, for which buyers can find no close substitutes.

The major economic systems are private enterprise economy, planned economy (such as communism or socialism), and mixed market economy. In a private enterprise system, individuals and private businesses pursue their own interests—including investment decisions and profits—without undue governmental restriction. In a planned economy, the government exerts stronger control over business ownership, profits, and resources to accomplish governmental and societal—rather than individual—goals. Socialism, one type of planned economic system, is characterized by government ownership and operation of all major industries. Communism is an economic system with limited private property; goods are owned in common, and factors of production and production decisions are controlled by the state. A mixed market economy blends government ownership and private enterprise, combining characteristics of both planned and private enterprise economies.

Assessment Check Answers

2.1 **What is the difference between pure competition and monopolistic competition?** Pure competition is a market structure in which large numbers of buyers and sellers exchange homogeneous products, and no single participant has a significant impact on price. Monopolistic competition is a market structure in which large numbers of buyers and sellers exchange differentiated (heterogenous) products, so each participant has some control over price.

2.2 **On which economic system is the U.S. economy based?** The U.S. economy is based on the private enterprise system.

2.3 **What is privatization?** Privatization is the conversion of government-owned and operated companies into privately held businesses.

LEARNING OBJECTIVE 3 Identify how to evaluate economic performance.

The four stages of the business cycle are prosperity, recession, depression, and recovery. Prosperity is characterized by low unemployment and strong consumer confidence. In a recession, consumers often postpone major purchases, layoffs occur, and household savings may be depleted. A depression occurs when an economic slowdown continues in a downward spiral over a long period of time. During recovery, consumer spending begins to increase and business activity accelerates, leading to an increased number of jobs.

As productivity rises, so do an economy's growth and the wealth of its citizens. In a recession, productivity stalls or possibly declines. Changes in general price levels—inflation or deflation—are important indicators of an economy's general stability. The U.S. government measures price-level changes by the Consumer Price Index. A nation's unemployment rate is an indicator of both overall stability and growth. The unemployment rate shows, as a percentage of the total labor force, the number of people actively seeking employment who are unable to find jobs.

Assessment Check Answers

3.1 **Describe the four stages of the business cycle.** The four stages are prosperity, recession, depression, and recovery. Prosperity is characterized by low unemployment and strong consumer confidence. Recession may include consumers postponing major purchases, layoffs, and decreased household savings. A depression occurs when an economic slowdown continues in a downward spiral over a long period of time. In recovery, consumer spending increases and business activity accelerates.

3.2 **What are some measures that economists use to determine the health of an economy?** Gross domestic product (GDP), general level of prices, core inflation rate, the Consumer Price Index, and the unemployment rate are all measures used to determine the health of an economy.

LEARNING OBJECTIVE 4 Discuss managing the economy's performance.

Monetary policy encompasses a government's efforts to control the size of the nation's money supply. Various methods of increasing or decreasing the overall money supply affect interest rates and therefore affect borrowing and investment decisions. By changing the size of the money supply, government can encourage growth or control inflation. Fiscal policy involves decisions regarding government revenues and expenditures. Changes in government spending affect economic growth and employment levels in the private sector. However, a government must also raise money, through taxes or borrowing, to finance its expenditures. Because tax payments are funds that might otherwise have been spent by individuals and businesses, any taxation changes also affect the overall economy.

Assessment Check Answers

4.1 **What is the difference between an expansionary monetary policy and a restrictive monetary policy?** An expansionary monetary policy increases the money supply in an effort to cut the cost of borrowing. A restrictive monetary policy reduces the money supply to curb rising prices, overexpansion, and concerns about overly rapid economic growth by increasing the cost of borrowing.

4.2 **What are the three primary sources of government funds?** The U.S. government acquires funds through taxes, fees, and borrowing.

4.3 **Does a balanced budget erase the national debt?** No, a balanced budget does not erase the national debt; it just doesn't increase it.

LEARNING OBJECTIVE 5 Describe the global economic challenges encountered by businesses today.

Businesses face ten key global risks in today's economy: (1) asset bubble in a major economy, (2) deflation in a major economy, (3) failure of a major financial mechanism or institution, (4) failure/shortfall of critical infrastructure, (5) fiscal crises in key economies, (6) high structural unemployment or underemployment, (7) illicit trade, (8) trade tensions, (9) energy price shock , and (10) unmanageable Inflation.

Assessment Check Answers

5.1 **Why is virtually no country an economic island these days?** No business or country is an economic island because many goods and services travel across national borders. Companies now are becoming multinational firms.

5.2 **Describe two ways in which global expansion can benefit a U.S. firm.** A firm can benefit from global expansion by attracting more customers and using less expensive labor and production in other parts of the world to produce goods and services.

Business Terms You Need to Know

Review Questions

1. How does microeconomics affect business? How does macroeconomics affect business? Why is it important for businesspeople to understand the fundamentals of each?

2. Draw supply and demand graphs that estimate what will happen to demand, supply, and the equilibrium price of coffee if these events occur:

    a. Widely reported medical studies suggest that coffee drinkers are less likely to develop certain diseases.

    b. The cost of manufacturing paper cups increases.

    c. The state imposes a new tax on takeout beverages.

    d. The biggest coffee chain leaves the area.

3. Describe the four different types of competition in the private enterprise system. In which type of competition would each of the following businesses be likely to engage?

    a. United Airlines

    b. small CrossFit gym

    c. steel mill

    d. large farm whose major crop is wheat

    e. Apple

4. Distinguish between the two types of planned economies. What factors do you think keep them from flourishing in today's economic environment?

5. What are the four stages of the business cycle? In which stage do you believe the U.S. economy is now? Why?

6. What is the gross domestic product? What is its relationship to productivity?

7. What are the effects of inflation on an economy? What are the effects of deflation? How does the Consumer Price Index work?

8. What does a nation's unemployment rate indicate? Describe what type of unemployment you think each of the following illustrates:

    a. discharged armed forces veteran

    b. bus driver who has been laid off due to cuts in his or her city's transit budget

    c. worker who was injured on the job and must start a new career

    d. lifeguard

    e. a new college graduate seeking employment

9. Explain the difference between monetary policy and fiscal policy. How does the government raise funds to cover the costs of its annual budget?

10. What is the difference between the budget deficit and the national debt? What are the benefits of paying down the national debt? What might be the negative effects?

Projects and Teamwork Applications

1. Describe a situation in which you have had to make an economic choice in an attempt to balance your wants with limited means. What factors influenced your decision?

2. Choose one of the following products and describe the different factors that you think might affect its supply and demand.
   a. Nike running shoes
   b. the latest smart phone release
   c. web conference tools
   d. newly created name-brand drug
   e. Houston Astros baseball tickets

3. Go online to research one of the following government agencies—its responsibilities, its budget, and mission. Then make the case for privatizing it:
   a. Veterans Administration
   b. Bureau of the Census
   c. Department of Labor
   d. Transportation Security Administration
   e. Social Security

4. Some businesses automatically experience seasonal unemployment. More and more, however, owners of these businesses are making efforts to increase demand—and employment—during the off season. Choose a classmate to be your business partner, and together select one of the following businesses. Create a plan for developing business and keeping employees for a season during which your business does not customarily operate:
   a. children's summer camp
   b. jet ski rental company
   c. inn located near a beach resort
   d. home roofing service and repair
   e. income tax service

5. On your own or with a classmate, go online to research the economy of one of the following countries. You may use the World Factbook website (http://www.cia.gov) to learn about the type of economy the country has, its major industries, and its competitive issues. (Note which industries or services are privatized and which are government owned.) Take notes on unemployment rates, monetary policies, and fiscal policies. Present your findings to the class.
   a. China
   b. New Zealand
   c. India
   d. Denmark
   e. Mexico
   f. Canada
   g. Chile
   h. Brazil
   i. Venezuela

Web Assignments

1. **What did things cost the year you were born?** Go to the Federal Reserve Bank of Minneapolis website listed below to see the calculator called "What is a dollar worth?" You can also download the feature as a free app. The calculator allows you to see what an item purchased in the past costs today. Insert the year you were born, a dollar amount, and the current year. What are your results? Discuss the implications in economic terms. Are there product or service segments that have increased in price more than others?
http://www.minneapolisfed.org

2. **Unemployment.** In the United States, the Bureau of Labor Statistics (BLS) compiles and publishes data on unemployment. Go to the BLS website and click on "Unemployment" (under "Subjects"). Read through the most recent report and answer the following questions:
   a. What is the current unemployment rate in the United States? How does it compare with those of other developed countries?
   b. Which state has the highest unemployment rate? Which state has the lowest unemployment rate?
   c. What is the underemployment rate?

www.bls.gov

3. **Financial debt.** Go to the U.S. Debt Clock website to see the dizzying array of real-time estimates of debt. This website was created by an individual who wanted to alert people to the amount of debt in the United States. On the upper right-hand side you will see an icon that reads "Debt Clock Time Machine." Click on the icon and go back in time to the year 2000. Compare the figures from 2000 to those of today's date for the following:
   - U.S. GDP
   - Credit card debt
   - Personal debt per citizen
   - U.S. population
   - U.S. national debt
   - Debt per citizen
   - Unemployment figures

Discuss the differences. Which number revealed the greatest difference? Why?
www.usdebtclock.org

4. **Global food supply and demand.** With an anticipated population increase of 2 billion by 2050, global demand for food is increasing. Go online to conduct current research on supply and demand with regard to the agricultural market, crop yield, and global food production. How does technology impact agriculture? How do water scarcity, rising global temperatures, and extreme weather impact crop yields and overall supply and demand?

Note: Internet web addresses change frequently. If you don't find the exact sites listed, you may need to access the organization's home page and search from there or use a search engine such as Google or Bing.

Cases

Case 3.1 Big Mergers Get Blocked

Sysco, the country's largest food distributor to hotels, restaurants, and other food-service operations, tried to acquire rival US Foods for $8.2 billion. As part of its overall strategic plan, Sysco believed that merging with its largest rival would help reduce costs and allow savings to be passed on to customers. The deal would have created a single company valued at more than $65 billion in annual sales with 25% of the U.S. market.

The Federal Trade Commission (FTC) filed a lawsuit challenging the transaction on antitrust grounds, stating the merger would lead to higher prices and diminished service for restaurants, hotels, and schools that contract with the two food distributors. Recently a federal judge agreed with the FTC and blocked the merger, saying it would reduce competition and potentially harm businesses and consumers.

Less than a decade ago, AT&T was blocked from acquiring T-Mobile. To date, Sprint and T-Mobile have engaged in "on-again, off-again" back-and-forth discussions. However, AT&T, which has not lost its urge to merge, recently made an $85 billion bid for Time Warner. The Justice Department adamantly disagrees with the merger, saying that it has the potential for AT&T to unilaterally price out competitors who might offer content owned by Time Warner. As mergers become more commonplace, there will be those who stand to gain and some who stand to lose. However, the Department of Justice will continue to determine the winner without a heavy expense to consumers.

Questions for Critical Thinking

1. Discuss the various types of contingency planning that might have been done by restaurants or schools in anticipation of the merger between US Foods and Sysco.
2. Discuss the recent mergers that have taken place in financial services, media, automobile, and retail. Are there other industries that are ripe for mergers? Why? Why not?

Sources: Annie Gasparro, "Sysco Ends Plans to Merge with US Foods," *Wall Street Journal*, http://www.wsj.com, accessed February 26, 2018; Antoine Gara, "Sysco Cancels $8.2 Billion US Foods Takeover in Big Antitrust Win for FTC," *Forbes*, http://www.forbes.com, accessed February 26, 2018; Jonathan Maze, "Experts: Despite Injunction, Sysco–US Foods Has Changed Distribution," *Nation's Restaurant News*, http://nrn.com, accessed February 26, 2018; government website, "Guide to Antitrust Laws," http://www.ftc.gov, accessed February 26, 2018; Benjamin Gomes-Casseres, "What the Big Mergers of 2017 Tell Us About 2018," *Harvard Business Review*, http://www.hbr.org, accessed February 26, 2018.

Case 3.2 Pawnshops: Fast Access to Capital

If you have a cash flow issue and a rare piece of art you can do without, consider checking out what was once thought of as a lender of last resort. People facing layoffs with depleted savings, or those who are cash-strapped with inconsistent incomes, often use valuable items as collateral in exchange for a cash loan. For some, the pawnshop remains an important lending source, and like retailers, the pawn shop is now online.

Pawnshops represent a short-term loan alternative for small businesses and individuals. Without a rigorous credit check or bank approval, and very little paperwork, people bring an item of value to the pawnshop (or this can be done online), where it is held as collateral against a loan. If the loan is repaid, and about 85% are, the item is retrieved. If not, the pawnshop sells the item to the public.

Over the last few years, a new breed of high-end pawnshops like Borro can be found in places such as New York City and Beverly Hills. In exchange for luxury items like art and watches and using an online platform, Borro loaned nearly $404 million to cash-poor, asset-rich individuals in a recent year. Many high-end collateral lenders have added additional online services where borrowers can get items appraised before shipping. Online players like iPawn and Pawngo have made it easy for consumers and small businesses to access short-term loans with discretion and privacy to avoid the negative stigma of pawn shops. Collectively, iPawn and Pawngo have loaned tens of millions of dollars to customers.

The industry has been glamorized by highly rated reality TV shows like *Pawn Stars*, which profiles three generations of the Harrison family engaged in the colorful pawn business world in Las Vegas. Americans in all economic groups, and even small business owners, are utilizing pawnshops in place of traditional credit lenders. In both good and bad economic times, companies like Borro will continue to occupy a unique niche in a growing number of alternative-lending technology startups.

Questions for Critical Thinking

1. What is your perception of pawnshops, and do you have personal experience or know anyone who has bought something there? Are pawnshops a substitute for banks?
2. The dark side of the pawn industry is its lack of regulation and exorbitant loan rates. Do some additional research to discuss the benefits and drawbacks of this trend.

Sources: Organization website, "Pawnbrokers Report Trends & Steady Industry Growth," http://www.nationalpawnbrokers.org, accessed February 26, 2018; Lizette Chapman, "Borro Banks $19 Million for Online Luxury Pawn Shop," *Wall Street Journal*, http://www.wsj.com, accessed February 26, 2018; Adam Palin, "Wealthy Pawn Classic Cars and More to Pay Tax Bills," *Financial Times*, http://www.ft.com, accessed February 26, 2018; company website, "How It Works," http://ipawn.com, accessed February 26, 2018; company website, "How Pawngo Works," http://pawngo.com, accessed February 26, 2018; Geoff Williams, "Pawn Shops Go Mainstream," *U.S. News and World Report*, http://money.usnews.com, accessed February 26, 2018; Allison Ross, "High-End Pawn Shops Cater to the Asset-Rich," BankRate.com, http://www.bankrate.com, accessed February 26, 2018.

Case 3.3 Secret Acres: Selling Comics Is Serious Business

Just about everyone remembers a favorite comic book from childhood—whether it was *Spiderman, Tintin*, or even *Garfield*. Leon Avelino and Barry Matthews readily acknowledge that they are kids in grown-up bodies with real day jobs (Avelino works for *Sports Illustrated,* and Matthews is an accountant for an e-commerce firm) who happen to love comic books and their latest incarnation, graphic novels. Their love for comics in all forms—along with the desire to start their own business—led them to found Secret Acres, a comic book and graphic novel publisher based in Brooklyn, New York. In addition to publishing several works from up-and-coming authors (they have 30 books on their list so far), the Secret Acres duo sells books from independent distributors.

Acknowledging that Secret Acres faces many economic challenges if it's going to continue to grow and succeed, Matthews observes, "Every decision we make, we know what the outcome is going to be because it's all small and it's very close to us." Right now, Secret Acres can use its small size to build relationships with its customers. "We are able, because we're small, to produce a very specific kind of comic book, a specific kind of graphic novel, that appeals to a specific audience," explains Matthews. "I love that. We have a lot of control over what we do and we're not doing anything specifically to turn a buck." That said, the accountant in Matthews knows that in order to stay in business, Secret Acres must sell enough books to push unit costs down, keeping production expenses and prices as low as possible.

Matthews also refers to relationships with bookstores, which are personal because he and Avelino do all the communicating themselves. "When you have a small group of stores you are selling from, you have to collect from them on a one-to-one basis," says Matthews. Sometimes the relationship becomes awkward when Matthews or Avelino has to remind a book store owner personally of an unpaid balance.

Another challenge facing the duo is the uncertain future of the print publishing market. A new delivery system for printed work has been created by e-commerce and the Internet—and online delivery of printed matter is alive and well.

Another phenomenon that has taken hold over the last decade or so is the graphic novel, the fiction genre that combines comic book techniques with the longer, more complex structure of a novel. Graphic novels are particularly popular among teens and college students, but they have received serious attention from the literary world. Some college courses are now taught around the graphic novel, and each year the American Library Association publishes a list of recommended graphic novels for teens. A company like Secret Acres could capitalize on a literary trend that continues to gain ground.

Matthews and Avelino haven't quit their day jobs yet. They know it will be awhile before they can call themselves full-time publishers. But they love the comic book business and are willing to wait for the good times they believe are ahead. "We have faith in the fact that if these books find the right audience, they'll do fine," says Avelino. "I'm okay with being patient. We need to keep going long enough to build a back list that is self-supporting." And Secret Acres already has a following among comic fans—their secret is out.

Questions for Critical Thinking

1. What steps might Matthews and Avelino take to create demand for their books? How must a small business like Secret Acres balance supply with demand?
2. What advantages and disadvantages might Secret Acres have over a large publishing company?
3. How would you categorize the competition that Secret Acres faces?
4. Do you think Secret Acres should pursue alternative content delivery systems? Why or why not?

Sources: Company website, http://secretacres.com, accessed February 26, 2018; "Great Graphic Novels for Teens," *Young Adult Library Services Association,* http://www.ala.org/yalsa, accessed February 26, 2018; "What Tablet Device Should You Buy for Your Digital Comic Books?" *Comic Book Herald*, http://comicbookherald.com, accessed February 26, 2018; Harry McCracken, "E-Readers May Be Dead, But They're Not Going Away Yet," *Tech Hive,* http://www.techhive.com, accessed February 26, 2018; Calvin Reid and Heidi MacDonald, "From the Fringes to the Mainstream: Ten Years of Growth In Graphic Novel Publishing," *Publishers Weekly*, http://www.publishersweekly.com, accessed February 26, 2018.

CHAPTER **4**

Competing in World Markets

LEARNING OBJECTIVES

1. Explain why nations trade.
2. Describe how trade is measured between nations.
3. Identify the barriers to international trade.
4. Discuss reducing barriers to international trade.
5. Explain the decisions to go global.
6. Discuss developing a strategy for international business.

Changemaker

Peter Foley/Bloomberg via Getty Images

Angela Ahrendts, Senior Vice President, Retail and Online Stores

Company: Apple Inc.

Industry: Technology/Consumer Products/Computer Manufacturing/Electronic Equipment

Website: http://www.apple.com

Angela Ahrendts is a member of Apple's executive team, where she serves as Senior Vice President of Retail and Online Stores. Her background includes stints in the fashion industry with luxury brands such as Donna Karan and Henri Bendel. Prior to joining Apple, Ahrendts was CEO of British luxury brand Burberry.

Ahrendts is regarded as a consummate brand ambassador. Some suggest Apple hired Ahrendts because she not only understands retail but is also extremely perceptive when it comes to using digital technology to sell a brand. Like Burberry, Apple is a company with high price points, and Ahrendts understands the importance of avoiding any form of price cutting. She also grasps the importance of the consumer experience, which is vital to the success and growth of a global brand like Apple.

Apple reported its largest quarterly revenue in history, and with 65% of sales outside the United States, the company is truly a global player. A little less than half of Apple's 500 retail stores worldwide are outside the United States. Further global retail growth is planned in countries such as Taiwan, Singapore, Germany, Dubai, and Mexico.

Apple's retail stores, referred to as "Town Squares," which constitute less than 15% of the company's total sales, have recently been overhauled so that the sleek, statuesque, open-air glass domes are perceived as inviting gathering places. The numbers certainly prove it—in a recent year, over 500 million people paid a visit to an Apple store.

Angela Ahrendts is leading the company's new store initiative called "Today at Apple," which seeks to build relationships with customers even when they're not in the store looking for a new iPhone or repairing a device. "We think of Apple Retail as Apple's largest products, and like all of our products, we've designed new features to take the customer experience even further," says Ahrendts.

Part of Apple's success as a company recently valued at $1 trillion can be attributed to the crucial role its retail stores play as the face of its iconic brand. Today, that legacy continues with Ahrendts at the helm and her ability to identify consumer preferences on a global scale.[1]

Overview

Consider for a moment how many products you have used today that came from outside the United States. Maybe you drank Brazilian coffee with your breakfast, wore clothes manufactured in Honduras or Malaysia, drove to class in a German or Japanese car fueled by gasoline refined from Canadian crude oil, and watched a movie on a new laptop assembled in China for a U.S. company such as Apple. A fellow student in China may be wearing Zara jeans, drinking Pepsi, or using an iPhone purchased in one of the stores opened by Apple in China, under the leadership of Angela Ahrendts.

U.S. and foreign companies alike recognize the importance of international trade to their future success. Economic interdependence is increasing throughout the world as companies pursue additional markets for their goods and services and the most cost-effective locations for production facilities. No longer can businesses rely solely on domestic sales. Today, foreign sales are essential to U.S. manufacturing, agricultural, and service companies for growth and profit opportunities in new markets. Foreign businesses also frequently look to the United States when they pursue new markets.

Thousands of products cross national borders every day. Together, U.S. exports and imports make up about a quarter of the U.S. gross domestic product (GDP). The United States ranks third in the world among exporting nations, with exports exceeding $1.6 trillion, and first in the world with annual imports of more than $2.4 trillion. That total amount is more than double the nation's imports and exports of just a decade ago.[2]

Transactions that cross national boundaries may expose a company to an additional set of factors such as new social and cultural practices, economic and political environments, and legal restrictions.

This chapter travels through the world of international business to see how both large and small companies approach globalization. First, we consider the reasons nations trade, the importance and characteristics of the global marketplace, and the ways nations measure international trade. Then we examine barriers to international trade that arise from cultural and environmental differences. To reduce these barriers, countries turn to organizations that promote global business. Finally, we look at the strategies companies implement for entering foreign markets and the way they develop international business strategies.

1 Why Nations Trade

As domestic markets mature and sales growth slows, companies in every industry recognize the increasing importance of efforts to develop business in other countries. **Exports** are domestically produced goods and services sold in other countries. **Imports** are foreign-made products purchased by domestic consumers. Boeing recently signed a deal valued at $37 billion to sell 300 planes to China.[3] These are only a few examples of the many U.S. companies taking advantage of large populations, substantial resources, and rising standards of living abroad that boost global interest in their goods and services. Likewise, the U.S. market, with the world's greatest purchasing power, attracts thousands of foreign companies.

exports domestically produced goods and services sold in other countries.

imports foreign-made products purchased by domestic consumers.

International trade is vital to a nation and its businesses because it boosts economic growth by providing a market for its products and access to needed resources. Companies can expand their markets, seek growth opportunities in other nations, and make their production and distribution systems more efficient. They also reduce their dependence on the economies of their home nations.

International Sources of Factors of Production

Business decisions to operate globally depend on the availability, price, and quality of labor, natural resources, capital, and entrepreneurship—the basic factors of production—

in the foreign country. Colleges and universities in India and China produce thousands of highly qualified computer scientists and engineers each year. To take advantage of this talent, many U.S. computer software and hardware companies have set up operations overseas, and many others are outsourcing information technology and customer service jobs there.

Trading with other countries also allows a company to spread risk, because different nations may be at different stages of the business cycle or in different phases of development. If demand falls off in one country, the company may realize demand in other nations. For example, Apple has eyed expansion in India as growth in China has fallen by 50% in recent years.[4]

Size of the International Marketplace

In addition to human and natural resources, entrepreneurship, and capital, companies are attracted to international business by the sheer size of the global marketplace. Only one in six of the world's more than 7.6 billion people lives in a relatively well-developed country. The world population is expected to continue growing and estimates point to a total population of 8.6 billion by mid-2030, 9.8 billion by mid-2050, and 11.2 billion by 2100.[5]

As developing nations expand their involvement in global business, the potential for reaching new customers dramatically increases. Companies looking for new revenue are inevitably attracted to sizable markets such as China and India, with respective populations of about 1.4 billion and 1.3 billion. However, people alone are not enough to create a market. Consumer demand also requires purchasing power. As **Table 4.1** shows, population size is no guarantee of economic prosperity. Of the 10 most populous countries, only the United States appears on the list of those with the highest per-capita GDPs.

Although people in developing nations have lower per-capita incomes than those in the highly developed economies of North America and Western Europe, their huge populations do represent lucrative markets. Even when the higher-income segments are only a small percentage of the entire country's population, their sheer numbers may still represent significant and growing markets.

TABLE 4.1 The World's Top 10 Nations Based on Population and Wealth

Country	Population (In Millions)	Country	Per Capita GDP (In U.S. Dollars)
China	1,379	Qatar	124,927
India	1,281	Luxembourg	109,192
European Union	511	Singapore	90,531
United States	326	Brunei	76,743
Indonesia	260	Ireland	72,632
Brazil	207	Norway	70,590
Pakistan	204	Kuwait	69,669
Nigeria	190	United Arab Emirates	68,245
Bangladesh	157	Switzerland	61,360
Russia	142	Hong Kong	61,016

Source: *World Factbook*, https://www.cia.gov, accessed March 1, 2018.

Also, many developing countries have typically posted high growth rates of annual GDP. Over the past five years, the U.S. GDP has averaged 2.2%. By contrast, GDP growth in less-developed countries is much greater—China's GDP growth rate, recently slowing, had exceeded double digits for most of the last decade, and India's averaged 7.2% over the last decade.[6] These markets represent opportunities for global businesses, even though their per-capita incomes lag behind those in more-developed countries. Many companies are establishing operations in these and other developing countries to position themselves to benefit from local sales driven by expanding economies and rising standards of living. Medifast, an American nutrition and weight loss company, recently announced its expansion into Hong Kong and Singapore with its lifestyle brand, OPTAVIA, sold through independent coaches who offer knowledge, support, and guidance to clients trying to create change with healthier eating habits.[7]

The United States trades with many other nations. As **Figure 4.1** shows, the top five are China, Canada, Mexico, Japan, and Germany, which represent over 80% of U.S. imports and exports annually. Over half of the world's wheat, corn, soybean, and cotton exports comes from the United States. Individual states like Texas export more than $264 billion of goods annually, and California exports more than $171 billion. Machinery and electronic equipment are major exports of the United States, while examples of major exports of states as a whole are lobsters from Maine, gold from Nevada, trucks from Michigan, and corn from Iowa.[8]

Absolute and Comparative Advantage

Few countries can produce all the goods and services their people need. For centuries, trading has been the way that countries can meet the demand. If a country focuses on producing what it does best, it can export surplus domestic output and buy foreign products that it lacks or cannot efficiently produce. The potential for foreign sales of a particular item depends largely on whether the country has an absolute advantage or a comparative advantage.

A country has an *absolute advantage* in making a product for which it can maintain a monopoly or that it can produce at a lower cost than any competitor. For centuries, China

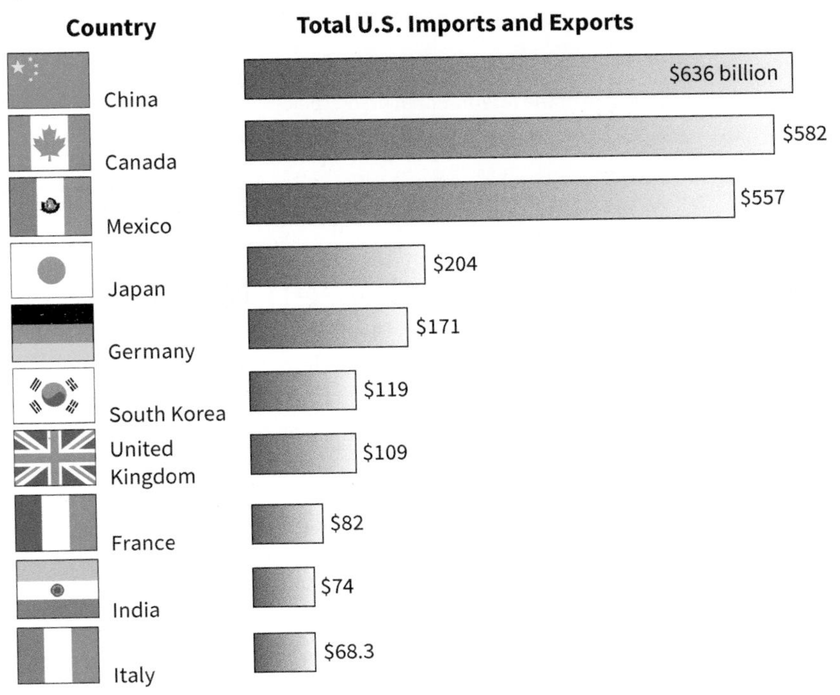

Source: Data from U.S. Census Bureau, "Top Trading Partners—December 2017," http://www.census.gov, accessed March 1, 2018.

FIGURE 4.1 Top 10 Trading Partners with the United States

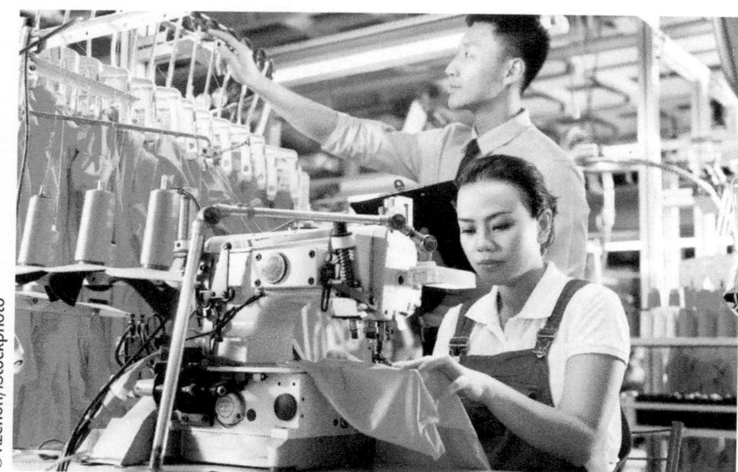
© Kzenon/iStockphoto

A country can develop a comparative advantage if it supplies its products more efficiently and at a lower price than it supplies other goods. China enjoys a comparative advantage in producing textiles.

enjoyed an absolute advantage in silk production. The fabric was woven from fibers recovered from silkworm cocoons, making it a prized raw material in high-quality clothing. Demand among Europeans for silk led to establishment of the famous Silk Road, a 5,000-mile link between Rome and the ancient Chinese capital city of Xi'an.

Absolute advantages are rare these days because it is common for two or more countries to efficiently supply a product. For example, wine is produced in France, Italy, and the United States, among other countries, and three of the world's largest oil-producing countries are the United States, Russia, and Saudi Arabia. But some countries manage to approximate absolute advantages in some products. Climate, geography, and the skills and size of a labor force all give a nation an advantage in the manufacturing and production of products or growth of food and plants. For example, over 80% of the world's saffron production comes from Iran.[9]

A nation can develop a *comparative advantage* if it can supply its products more efficiently and at a lower price than it can supply other goods, compared with the outputs of other countries. As a top global exporter, China is profiting from its comparative advantage in producing textiles (see photo). On the other hand, ensuring that its people are well educated is another way a nation can develop a comparative advantage in skilled human resources. India offers the services of its educated, English-speaking tech workers at a lower wage. But sometimes these strategies backfire. Recently, some U.S. companies have decided to bring their customer service call centers back from overseas or to keep them in the United States. Reasons include customer demand for better service, rising labor costs in traditional call center locations like the Philippines and India, and new technologies that lower costs.[10]

Assessment Check

1. Why do nations trade?
2. Cite some measures of the size of the international marketplace.
3. How does a nation acquire a comparative advantage?

2 Measuring Trade between Nations

Clearly, engaging in international trade provides tremendous competitive advantages to both the countries and individual companies involved. But how do we measure global business activity? To understand what the trade inflows and outflows mean for a country, we need to examine the concepts of balance of trade and balance of payments. Another important factor is currency exchange rates for each country.

balance of trade difference between a nation's exports and imports.

A nation's **balance of trade** is the difference between its exports and imports. If a country exports more than it imports, it achieves a positive balance of trade, called a *trade surplus*. If it imports more than it exports, it produces a negative balance of trade, called a *trade deficit*. The United States has run a trade deficit every year since 1976. Despite being one of the world's top exporters, the United States has an even greater appetite for foreign-made goods, which creates a trade deficit.

balance of payments overall flow of money into or out of a country.

A nation's balance of trade plays a central role in determining its **balance of payments**—the overall flow of money into or out of a country. Other factors also affect the balance of payments, including overseas loans and borrowing, international investments, profits from such investments, and foreign aid payments. To calculate a nation's balance of payments, subtract the monetary outflows from the monetary inflows. A positive balance of payments, or a *balance-of-payments* surplus, means more money has moved into a country than out of it. A negative balance of payments, or *balance-of-payments deficit*, means more money has gone out of the country than entered it.

Major U.S. Exports and Imports

The United States, with combined exports and imports of about $5.2 trillion, leads the world in the international trade of goods and services. As listed in **Table 4.2**, the leading categories of goods exchanged by U.S. exporters and importers range from machinery and vehicles to crude oil and chemicals. Strong U.S. demand for imported goods is partly a reflection of the nation's prosperity and diversity.

Although the United States imports more goods than it exports, the opposite is true for services. U.S. exporters sell more than $778 billion in services annually. Much of that money comes from travel and tourism—money spent by foreign nationals visiting the United States.[11] U.S. service exports also include business and technical services such as engineering, financial services, computing, healthcare, education, legal services, and entertainment, as well as royalties and licensing fees. Major service exporters include Berkshire Hathaway, The Walt Disney Company, State Farm, American Express, and retailers like Walmart.

Businesses in many foreign countries want the expertise of U.S. financial and business professionals. Accountants are in high demand in Russia, China, the Netherlands, and Australia—Sydney has become one of Asia's biggest financial centers. Entertainment is another major growth area for U.S. service exports. Disney's overseas theme parks began when the company realized how many Japanese tourists visited its two U.S. parks. The Walt Disney Company now has six theme parks worldwide, including two in the United States and four overseas in Japan, Hong Kong, Paris and Shanghai, China.[12]

TABLE 4.2 Top 10 U.S. Merchandise Exports and Imports

Exports	Amount (In Billions)	Imports	Amount (In Billions)
Machinery including computers	$201.7	Electrical machinery, equipment	$356.8
Electrical machinery, equipment	174.2	Machinery including computers	349.1
Mineral fuels including oil	138	Vehicles	294.6
Aircraft, spacecraft	131.2	Mineral fuels including oil	204.2
Vehicles	130.1	Pharmaceuticals	96.4
Optical, technical, medical apparatus	83.6	Optical, technical, medical apparatus	86.2
Plastics, plastic articles	61.5	Furniture, bedding, lighting, signs, prefab buildings	67.2
Gems, precious metals	60.4	Gems, precious metals	60
Pharmaceuticals	45.1	Plastics, plastic articles	54.9
Organic chemicals	36.2	Organic chemicals	46.1

Source: United States International Trade Commission, "U.S. Trade by Industry, Sector, and Selected Trading Partners (data)," https://www.usitc.gov, accessed March 1, 2018.

With annual imports of more than $2.89 trillion, the United States is by far the world's leading importer. American tastes for foreign-made goods for everything from clothing to consumer electronics show up as huge trade deficits with the consumer-goods-exporting nations of China and Japan.

Exchange Rates

exchange rate the rate at which a nation's currency can be exchanged for the currencies of other nations.

A nation's exchange rate is the value of one nation's currency relative to the currencies of other countries. **Exchange rate** is the rate at which its currency can be exchanged for the currencies of other nations. As part of a global economy where many currencies are trading hands in trillions of dollars each day for trade, finance, and speculation, it is important to understand how exchange rates work. Each currency's exchange rate is usually quoted in terms of another currency, such as the number of Mexican pesos needed to purchase one U.S. dollar. Roughly 18 pesos are needed to exchange for a U.S. dollar. A Canadian dollar can be exchanged for close to 78 cents in the United States. The euro, the currency used in most of the European Union (EU) member countries, has fluctuated in exchange value. European consumers and businesses use the euro to pay bills online, by credit card, or bank transfer. Euro coins and notes are also used in many EU-member countries.

Foreign exchange rates are influenced by a number of factors, including domestic economic and political conditions, central bank intervention, balance-of-payments position, and speculation over future currency values. Currency values fluctuate, depending on the supply and demand for each currency in the international market. In this system of *floating exchange rates*, currency traders create a market for the world's currencies based on each country's relative trade and investment prospects. In theory, this market permits exchange rates to vary freely according to supply and demand. In practice, exchange rates do not float in total freedom. National governments often intervene in currency markets to adjust their exchange rates.

devaluation drop in a currency's value relative to other currencies or to a fixed standard.

Nations influence exchange rates in other ways as well. They may form currency blocs by linking their exchange rates to each other. Many governments practice protectionist policies that seek to guard their economies against trade imbalances. For instance, nations sometimes take deliberate action to devalue their currencies as a way to increase exports and stimulate foreign investment. **Devaluation** describes a drop in a currency's value relative to other currencies or to a fixed standard. In an effort to deal with slowing growth and to boost exports, the Chinese government has repeatedly devalued the country's currency (see photo).

For an individual business, the impact of currency devaluation depends on where that business buys its materials and where it sells its products. Business transactions are usually conducted in the currency of the particular region in which they take place. The world's largest retailer, Walmart, purchases goods globally, and deals extensively with different currencies. As the company builds and expands new stores worldwide, pays salaries to employees in each country where it operates, and takes profits out of a country to reinvest in another country, changes in foreign currency can impact the company's costs, and in turn, its profitability. As the U.S. dollar appreciates and remains strong against other currencies, Walmart, with a large base of business overseas, convert sales from other currencies into dollars when they report financial results. If the dollar strengthens relative to other currencies, the international revenue is in turn converted into fewer dollars—which lowers sales.[13]

Thomas Ruecker/Getty Images

The Chinese government has repeatedly devalued the country's currency, the yuan, in an effort to boost exports and counter slowing growth.

Exchange rate changes can quickly create opportunity—or eliminate—a competitive advantage, so they are crucial factors in foreign investment decisions. In Europe, a declining dollar means that a price of 10 euros is worth more, so companies may lower prices. At the same time, if the dollar falls, it makes European vacations less affordable for U.S. tourists because their dollars are worth less relative to the euro. There are numerous online currency converters to calculate conversions and help you understand the spending power of a U.S. dollar in other countries. A *strong* dollar means that our currency buys more of a foreign country's goods—which benefits consumers and international travelers. A *weak* dollar means that our currency buys less of a foreign country's goods and services. When this happens, imports increase and foreign travelers may decide to stay home.

Currencies that owners can easily convert into other currencies are called *hard currencies*. Examples include the euro, the U.S. dollar, and the Japanese yen. The Russian ruble and many central European currencies are considered soft currencies because they cannot be readily converted. Exporters trading with these countries sometimes prefer to barter, accepting payment in oil, timber, or other commodities that they can resell for hard-currency payments. The foreign exchange market, also called FOREX, FX, or currency market, is a global market where investors can buy, sell, exchange, and speculate on currencies. The most traded currencies are the U.S. dollar (USD), European Euro (EUR), Japanese Yen (JPY), Pound Sterling, and Australian Dollar.[13]

Assessment Check

1. Compare balance of trade and balance of payments.
2. Explain the function of an exchange rate.
3. What happens when a currency is devalued?

3 Barriers to International Trade

All businesses encounter barriers in their operations, whether they sell only to local customers or trade in international markets. Italy's shopkeepers, whose hours of operation were once regulated, are now able to keep their stores open longer. In addition to complying with a variety of laws and currencies, international companies may also have to reformulate or adapt their products to accommodate different buying preferences by location.

In addition to social and cultural differences, companies engaged in international business face economic barriers as well as legal and political ones. Some of the hurdles shown in **Figure 4.2** are easily breached, but others require major changes in a company's business strategy. Yum! Brands, which operates Taco Bell, KFC, and Pizza Hut worldwide, and once a huge success in China, made a decision to split off its China business into a separate publicly traded franchise, a model that includes the collection of royalties from the franchisee and provides greater stability and less risk to the parent company. A number of issues related to operating overseas, including food safety, increased competition, and operational missteps, have caused the brand to implement the new business model.[14] To successfully compete in global markets, companies must understand not only how these barriers affect international trade but also how to manage them. As a global business, United Airlines knows that a swift response to customers' needs is

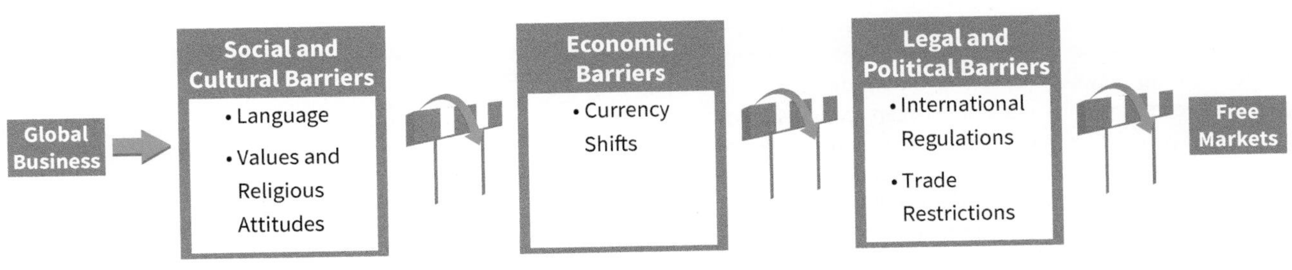

FIGURE 4.2 Barriers to International Trade

a critical strategy. The "Business & Technology" feature describes how mobilizing customer service agents with iPhones has made a big difference.

Social and Cultural Differences

The social and cultural differences among nations range from language and customs to educational background and religious holidays. Understanding and respecting these differences is critical to paving the way for international business success. Businesspeople with knowledge of host countries' cultures, languages, social values, religious beliefs, lifestyles, and practices are well equipped for the marketplace and the negotiating table. Sensitivity and openness to such elements as local attitudes, organizational hierarchy, workplace etiquette, forms of address, and expectations regarding dress, body language, and punctuality also helps them win customers and achieve their business objectives.

Language Mandarin Chinese is the most widely spoken language in the world, followed by English, Spanish, Hindi, Arabic, and Bengali. Understanding a business colleague's primary language may prove to be the difference between closing an international business transaction and losing the deal to someone else. Company representatives operating in foreign markets must not only choose correct and appropriate words but also must translate words correctly to convey the intended meanings. Products may need to be renamed and slogans rewritten for foreign markets.

Potential communication barriers include more than translation errors. While some cultures value directness and brevity, others may be more indirect and nuanced when communicating.

Business & Technology

United Airlines Uses iPhones to Mobilize Agents

In a recent year, 148 million customers chose to travel with United Airlines. The global company operates an average of 4,500 flights daily to 338 airports across six continents. With the most comprehensive route network in the world, United has issued 50,000 gate agents and flight attendants with Apple iPhones. The goal: to meet customers' needs in real time.

The iPhones with enterprise mobile apps will enable agents and other customer service representatives to help customers who have checked into their flights with several pre-departure actions that include printing boarding passes and baggage tags anywhere throughout the airport. In addition, using United's own custom-built software for iOS, customer service representatives carrying the iPhones will be able to assist other United employees at locations throughout the airport with problem solving, troubleshooting, and, when needed, developing alternate flight options.

The iPhones include tools that allow full check-in capabilities in airport lobbies and the ability to offer customers the same service levels and functionality as traditional kiosk locations. The change is a result of feedback from United staff who reported the need for operational information access and tools to better assist customers—particularly during peak travel times and severe weather conditions.

The relationship between Apple and United dates back to more than five years ago when the airline began giving its pilots iPads. Later that year, United picked the iPhone as the device of choice for its 23,000 flight attendants. United chose the iPhone because of its expansion possibilities and the ability to use it with other applications. According to the company's head of airport operations, the iPhone is also a great way to empower employees.

Although traditionally a consumer-focused company, under CEO Tim Cook's leadership Apple has come to realize the power its devices hold in the business environment. There will be continued investment and focus on business and enterprise users like United Airlines. Cook agrees that Apple has changed the lives of consumers, the way students learn and teachers teach, and next is the business environment. Enterprise users can do more on larger phones like the iPhone Plus, the first phablet (tablet and phone) introduced by Apple six years ago.

To partner with United Airlines, Apple teamed up with IBM to create business apps with productivity features and deeper integration with United's enterprise software system, new app distribution methods, and enhanced management tools. The goal of the IBM–Apple partnership is to bring the same experience to work lives as that experienced in our personal lives. The creation of enterprise software, which looks and feels like consumer apps but links to back-end corporate systems, has helped many United Airlines customers catch that next plane home--in order to arrive right on time.

Sources: Company website, "United Airlines to 'Mobilize' Airport Customer Service Representatives with Apple's iPhone 6 Plus," http://newsroom.united.com, accessed March 1, 2018; Jon Russell, "United Airlines Is Giving Its 6,000 Customer Service Reps the iPhone 6 Plus," *Tech Crunch*, http://techcrunch.com, accessed March 1, 2018; company website, "Even More Ways to Transform Your Business," http://www.apple.com, accessed March 1, 2018; Ron Miller, "One Year Later Apple and IBM Remain Oddest Couple in Tech," *Tech Crunch*, http://techcrunch.com, accessed March 1, 2018; Jeff Ulrich, "Here's How United Airlines Is Empowering Employees with Enterprise Mobile Apps," *Mobile Shopping*, https://mobileshopping.wbresearch.com, accessed March 5, 2018; company website, "Fact Sheet," http://newsroom.united.com/corporate-fact-sheet, accessed March 5, 2018.

Companies may present messages through inappropriate media, overlook local customs and regulations, or ignore differences in taste. One U.S. executive recently lost a deal in China by giving the prospective client a set of four antique clocks wrapped in white paper. Unfortunately, the number four and the Chinese word for clock are similar to the word "death," and white is the traditional color for funerals.[15] Cultural sensitivity is especially critical in cyberspace and even when considering user interface design. Website developers must be aware that visitors to a site may come from anywhere in the world. Some icons that seem friendly to U.S. Internet users may be offensive to people from other countries. A person making a high-five hand gesture would be insulting people in Greece; the same is true of making a circle with the thumb and index finger in Brazil, a thumbs-up sign in Egypt, and a two-fingered peace sign with the back of the hand facing out in Great Britain.

Gift-giving traditions employ the language of symbolism. For example, in Latin America, knives and scissors should not be given as gifts because they represent the severing of friendship. Flowers are generally acceptable but are used in Day of the Dead festivities in Mexico, and yellow flowers can be associated with death.

Values and Religious Attitudes Even though today's world is shrinking in many ways, people in different countries do not necessarily share the same values or religious attitudes. Marked differences remain in workers' attitudes from country to country, for example. In the United States, efficiency, output, and low unemployment may be emphasized, whereas in Europe, employee benefits and work–live balance may be more valued. The average worker in France can expect 30 days of paid vacation, as compared to 10 days for U.S. workers.

The U.S. government does not legally mandate vacation time or paid leave, and employees typically receive no paid vacation during their first year of employment, then two weeks of vacation, and eventually up to three or four weeks if they stay with the same employer for many years. In contrast, the EU mandates a minimum paid vacation of four weeks per year, and most Europeans get five or six weeks. In these countries, a U.S. company that opens a manufacturing plant may comply with local customs by offering vacations in line with a nation's business practices.

U.S. culture values national unity, with sensitivity to regional differences. The United States is viewed as a national market with a single economy. European countries that are part of the EU are trying to create a similar marketplace. French consumers differ from Italians in important ways, and U.S. companies that fail to recognize consumer differences will be challenged with brand acceptance.

Religion plays an important role in every society, so businesspeople must be aware of the dominant religions in countries where they operate. Understanding religious traditions and the timing of major holidays can help prevent embarrassing moments when scheduling meetings, trade shows, conferences, or events such as the opening of a new manufacturing plant. People doing business in Saudi Arabia must take into account Islam's month-long observance of Ramadan, when work ends at noon. Friday is the Muslim formal day of worship, so the Saudi workweek runs from Saturday through Thursday. Also, many Muslims abstain from alcohol and pork products, so gifts of this kind would be considered inappropriate.

Economic Differences

A country's size, inflation rate, income and employment levels, per capita income, and stage of economic growth and development are among the economic factors to consider when evaluating an international business venture. Ford Motor Company, along with other automobile companies, has invested heavily in Mexico, which is no longer seen as an assembly-only destination. See the "Business Model" feature for more details.

Infrastructure Along with other economic conditions, businesses should understand a country's infrastructure. **Infrastructure** refers to basic systems of communications, transportation, and energy facilities. The Internet and technology use can also be considered part of a country's infrastructure.

infrastructure basic systems of communication, transportation, and energy facilities in a country.

Business Model

Battery-Powered Rush to Build Cars in Mexico

Ford recently announced plans to assemble battery-powered cars in Mexico. Over the last several years, many automobile companies have rushed to build plants in Mexico to take advantage of the low cost of labor in addition to a growing demand for cars in parts of Latin and South America. Wages in Mexico are in the range of \$8–\$10 per hour, as compared to \$29 per hour in the United States.

Because profit margins on electric vehicles are still slim, a result of costly batteries and sales volume that hasn't reached its potential, the move to Cuautitlán, north of Mexico City, will allow Ford to begin assembling a small, battery-powered sport-utility vehicle in 2020. The electric vehicle boasts a 300-mile driving range before the need for charging.

The investment is part of the company's ongoing "One Ford" global engineering structure and strategy, which emphasizes global competitiveness. "One Ford" is the company's effort to get its global operations in sync for greater efficiencies and economies of scale. In less than a decade, Ford has reduced its product platforms (examples include subcompact, compact, midsize, SUV, truck) from 27 down to just 9.

Ford manufactures the Fiesta, Fusion, and Lincoln MKZ in Mexico. As Mexico continues to transform into a world-class manufacturing destination, foreign carmakers like Nissan, Mazda, Toyota, and Volkswagen have also taken notice by investing billions of dollars into the country. As auto manufacturing continues to gain momentum in Mexico, look for more investments by global carmakers, led by "One Ford."

Questions for Critical Thinking

1. Discuss your perception of Ford Motor Company, its cars, and its brand. Does the fact that many of its cars are made in Mexico and throughout the world impact your perception of Ford as an American brand? Why or why not?
2. Mexico is the fourth-largest vehicle producer, the fourth-largest engine producer, and the second-largest nation supplying Ford's global manufacturing facilities. Despite Ford's success, what challenges do you see for automobile manufacturing in Mexico?

Sources: Jim Henry, "One Ford, Part Two; Tweaking the Master Plan," *Forbes*, http://www.forbes.com, accessed March 7, 2018; Luis Rojas, "Ford to Spend \$2.5 Billion on Plants in Mexico, Angering UAW," *Reuters*, http://www.reuters.com, accessed March 7, 2018; company website, "Operations Worldwide," http://corporate.ford.com, accessed March 7, 2018; company website, "Ford Announces \$2.5 Billion USD Investment for New Engine, Transmission Plants in Mexico," http://media.ford.com, accessed March 7, 2018; Nacha Cattan and Ben Bain, "Auto Industry's \$23 Billion Investment in Mexico May Face Snarls at Ports," *Automotive News*, http://www.autonews.com, accessed March 7, 2018; Brendan Case, "Mexico's Surprising Engineering Strength," *Bloomberg Business*, http://www.bloomberg.com, accessed March 7, 2018; Richard Johnson, "Why Ford Stands by its 'One Ford' Philosophy," *Automotive News*, http://www.automotivenews.com, accessed March 6, 2018; Neal E. Boudette, "Ford Will Build Electric Cars in Mexico, Shifting Its Plan," *New York Times*, http://www.newyorktimes.com, accessed March 6, 2018; Glenn Brooks, "Ford's Future Models and Platforms," *Just Auto*, https://www.just-auto.com, accessed March 6, 2018.

Financial systems provide a type of infrastructure for businesses. In the United States, buyers have widespread access to many forms of payment processing, including online, electronic, and credit and debit cards. Global investment in financial technology companies that develop and use software to provide payment and lending services continues to expand in Asia and throughout Europe.[16] This is discussed further in Chapter 16.

Currency Conversion and Shifts Despite growing similarities in infrastructure, businesses crossing national borders may still encounter basic economic differences, including national currencies. Foreign currency fluctuations may present challenges to global businesses. As explained earlier in the chapter, the values of the world's major currencies fluctuate—sometimes drastically—in relation to each other. Rapid and unexpected currency shifts can make pricing in local currencies difficult. Shifts in exchange rates can also influence the attractiveness of various business decisions. A devalued currency may make a nation less desirable as an export destination because of reduced demand in that market. However, devaluation can make the nation desirable as an investment opportunity because investments there will be a bargain in terms of the investor's currency.

Political and Legal Differences

Like social, cultural, and economic differences, legal and political differences in host countries can pose barriers to international trade. To compete in today's world marketplace, international business managers must be well versed in laws that affect their industries. Some countries impose general trade restrictions. Others have established detailed rules that regulate how foreign companies can operate.

Political Climate An important factor in any international business investment is the stability of the political climate. The political structures of many nations promote stability similar to that in the United States. Other nations, such as Indonesia, Thailand, and Congo, feature quite different—and frequently changing—structures.[17] Host nations often pass laws designed to protect their own interests, sometimes at the expense of foreign businesses.

Legal Environment When conducting business internationally, managers must be familiar with three dimensions of the legal environment: U.S. law, international regulations, and the laws and legal systems of the countries in which they plan to conduct business. Some laws protect the rights of foreign companies to compete in the United States. Others dictate actions allowed for U.S. companies doing business in foreign countries. Legal rules derived from multiple sources and bodies with fragmented and overlapping jurisdictions enforce such rules.

The *Foreign Corrupt Practices Act* forbids U.S. companies from bribing foreign officials, political candidates, or government representatives. Although the law has been in effect since 1977, in the past few years the U.S. government has increased its enforcement, including major proceedings in the pharmaceutical, medical device, and financial industries. The United States, United Kingdom, France, Germany, and 30 other countries have signed the Organization for Economic Cooperation and Development Anti-Bribery Convention.

Still, corruption continues to be an international problem. Its pervasiveness, combined with U.S. prohibitions, creates a difficult obstacle for U.S. businesspeople who want to do business in many foreign countries. Chinese pay *huilu*; Russians rely on *vzyatka*. In the Middle East, palms are greased with *baksheesh*. **Figure 4.3** compares 168 countries based on surveys of perceived corruption. The Corruption Perceptions Index is computed by Transparency International, a Berlin-based organization that rates the degree of corruption observed around the world.

The growth of e-commerce has introduced new challenges to the legal climate of international business. Protections for brand names, trademarks, copyrights, privacy, and other intellectual property are difficult to enforce, given the availability of information on the Internet. Privacy laws for websites, which govern how information on private individuals can be used, have now been

Source: Data from Transparency International, "Corruption Perceptions Index 2017, Results," http://www.transparency.org, accessed March 1, 2018.

FIGURE 4.3 **Corruption in Business and Government**

Clean & Green Business

Campbell Warms Up to Reducing Food Waste

Global food giant Campbell Soup Company is well aware that reducing food waste has positive social, environmental, and financial implications.

The company has implemented strategic initiatives to reduce food waste by creating a food recovery hierarchy that includes source reduction, donation to food banks, animal feed, composting, or energy production. Product that doesn't meet the company's food specifications or standards fall into this category.

In fact, a number of companies in the food sector are taking food waste very seriously by publicly reporting their food loss and waste inventories. In partnership with the Environmental Protection Agency, Campbell is taking the lead by implementing the Food Loss and Waste Standard as a way to establish a baseline and report progress toward reduction. By 2030, the goal is to cut food waste in half.

A recent report estimates that 40% of all food produced globally is never consumed. According to the United Nation's Food and Agriculture Organization, food discarded by retailers and consumers in the world's most developed countries is enough to feed 84% of the population with a 2,000 calorie-a-day diet.

Why is so much food being wasted, and where does it go? Grocery stores and supermarket chains throw away blemished produce, stale packaged goods, and products past their "sell-by" dates. Discarded food in the restaurant sector is a result of overproduction, improper preparation, or restaurant diners who simply over order. Households contribute to food waste by tossing leftovers or perishables into the garbage.

In addition to its social and financial cost, food waste also has an environmental impact that contributes to climate change issues—most food waste goes to landfills, where it decomposes and emits an estimated 3.3 billion metric tons annually of the potent greenhouse gas methane. Composting or using waste as a source of renewable energy has reduced the amount of food waste Campbell sends to local landfills. As a champion of reducing food waste, Campbell's is providing so much more than just a warm bowl of soup.

Questions for Critical Thinking

1. A typical family in the United States loses $1,600 to $2,000 each year to food that is purchased but not eaten. What ideas do you have on an individual level to help reduce food waste?
2. Food industry groups have increased their efforts to combat food waste by promoting consumer education on labeling and to standardize and clarify date labeling and expiration dates worldwide by year-end 2020. Are there additional ideas you might suggest to food industry groups to reduce food waste?

Sources: Company website, "Resource Stewardship: Waste," http://www.campbellcsr.com, accessed March 7, 2018; Ron Nixon, "Food Waste Is Becoming Serious Economic and Environmental Issue, Report Says," *New York Times*, http://www.nytimes.com, accessed March 7, 2018; Jan Lee, "Why Food Waste Is an Urgent Global Problem," *Triple Pundit*, http://www.triplepundit.com, accessed March 7, 2018; Jessica Lyons Hardcastle, "How Campbell's, ConAgra Foods, Yum! Brands Cut Food Waste," *Environmental Leader*, http://www.environmentalleader.com, accessed March 7, 2018; government website, "Food Recovery Hierarchy," http://www.epa.gov, accessed March 7, 2018; organization website, "Food Bank of South Jersey Names Campbell Soup Company 2017 Champion Against Hunger Awardee," http://foodbanksj.org, accessed March 5, 2018; company website, "Farm to Fork: Progress on Food Waste," https://www.campbellsoupcompany.com, accessed March 5, 2018; government website, "United States 2030 Food Loss and Waste Reduction Goal," *Environmental Protection Agency*, http://www.epa.gov, accessed March 8, 2018; John Perritano, "Wasted Food in the U.S. Could Feed Much of Population," https://recipes.howstuffworks.com, accessed March 6, 2018.

enacted in over 80 countries around the world. Under the European Union Data Protection Directive of 1998, anyone processing personal data needs to do so in a fair and lawful manner. To be considered lawful, data collection must be for specified, explicit and legitimate purposes, and users are required to give explicit consent after being informed that data collection is taking place.[18]

International Regulations To regulate international commerce, the United States and many other countries have ratified treaties and signed agreements that dictate the conduct of international business and protect some of its activities. The United States has entered into many *friendship, commerce, and navigation* (FCN) *treaties* with other nations. Such treaties address many aspects of international business relations, including the right to conduct business in the treaty partner's domestic market. Other international business agreements involve product standards, patents, trademarks, reciprocal tax policies, export controls, international air travel, and international communications. Some international efforts to protect the environment are voluntary, such as Campbell Soup Company's food waste reduction program. See the "Clean & Green Business" feature for the story.

Many types of regulations affect the actions of managers doing business in international markets. Not only must worldwide producers and marketers maintain required minimum quality levels for all the countries in which they operate, but they must comply with numerous specific local regulations. Britain prevents advertisers from encouraging children to engage in such unhealthy behavior as overeating or replacing regular meals with candy and snack foods. Malaysia's Censorship Board prohibits nudity and profanity on TV. Germany and France allow publishers to set prices that retailers charge for their books.

Italian clothing manufacturers have long enjoyed high status for their fabrics and workmanship. However, they believed they were being victimized by a lax labeling system when international clothing designers bought less-expensive fabric in China or Bulgaria, had the garments cut in countries with lower labor costs, then sent them to Italy for final sewing. There, they tacked on the prestigious "Made in Italy" label and charged a high price for the goods. In 2009, an Italian law stated that only products totally made in Italy (planning, manufacturing, and packaging) are allowed to use the label "Made in Italy".[19]

Types of Trade Restrictions

Trade restrictions such as taxes on imports and complicated administrative procedures create additional barriers to international business. They may limit consumer choices while increasing the costs of foreign-made products. Trade restrictions are also imposed to not only promote trade, but to protect citizens' security, health, and jobs. Still others protect countries from unfair competition. Regardless of the political reasons for trade restrictions, most take the form of tariffs. In addition to tariffs, governments impose a number of non-tariff—or administrative—barriers. These include quotas, embargoes, and exchange controls.

Tariffs Taxes, surcharges, or duties on foreign products are referred to as **tariffs**. Governments may assess two types of tariffs—revenue and protective tariffs—both of which make imports more expensive for domestic buyers. Revenue tariffs generate income for the government. Cars and trucks imported into the United States carry a tax that goes directly to the U.S. Treasury. The sole purpose of a protective tariff is to raise the retail price of imported products to match or exceed the prices of similar products manufactured in the home country. In other words, protective tariffs seek to limit imports and level the playing field for local competitors.

tariffs taxes, surcharges, or duties on foreign products.

Of course, tariffs create a disadvantage to companies that want to export to the countries imposing the tariffs. In addition, governments do not always agree on the reasons behind protective tariffs, so they do not always have the desired effect. The United States imposes a tariff on foreign competitors accused of selling products at lower prices in the United States than U.S. manufacturers charge. Congress passed a bill giving the money from these tariffs directly to U.S. plaintiff companies, instead of to the Treasury as in the past. Recently, U.S. trade restrictions in the form of tariffs were placed on any foreign shipment of aluminum and steel coming into the United States—to combat what some refer to as "cheap metals" coming in from China.[20]

quota limit set on the amounts of particular products that countries can import during specified time periods.

dumping selling products abroad at prices below production costs or below typical prices in the home market to capture market share from domestic competitors.

Non-Tariff Barriers Non-tariff, or administrative, trade barriers also restrict imports. These measures may take such forms as quotas on imports, restrictive standards for imports, and export subsidies. Because many countries have recently substantially reduced tariffs or eliminated them entirely, they increasingly use non-tariff barriers to control flows of imported products. Recently, there are many news reports about trade sanctions, also non tarriff barriers. Trade sanctions are trade penalties imposed by one nation onto one or more other nations. Sanctions can be unilateral, imposed by only one country on one other country, or multilateral, imposed by one or more countries on a number of different countries. Sometimes, allies will impose multilateral sanctions on their foes.

Quotas limit the amounts of particular products that countries can import during specified time periods. Limits may be set as quantities, such as the number of cars or bushels of wheat, or as values, such as dollars' worth of cigarettes. Governments regularly set quotas to regulate the volume of trade between countries for agricultural products and sometimes for imported automobiles. The United States, for example, sets a quota on imports of sugar. Imports under the quota amount are subject to a lower tariff than shipments above the quota.[21]

The U.S. steel industry faces challenges from lower priced imports from China, where production has surged. Tariffs on foreign shipments of steel were recently imposed in what some see as a way to protect the U.S. steel industry from less expensive imports.

Quotas help prevent **dumping**. In one form of dumping, a company sells products abroad at prices below its cost of production. In another, a company exports a large quantity of a product at a lower price than the same product in the home market and drives down the price of the domestic product. Dumping benefits domestic consumers in the importing market, but it hurts domestic producers. It also allows companies to gain quick entry to foreign markets. China's Ministry of Commerce is concerned about the harm caused to its styrene industry as a result of dumping from the U.S., Taiwan, and South Korea. Styrene, a petroleum byproduct found in plastics, resins, and Styrofoam, is being sold at unfairly low prices, and an ongoing investigation into trade of the chemical continues.[22]

embargo total ban on importing specific products or a total halt to trading with a particular country.

More severe than a quota, an **embargo** imposes a total ban on importing a specified product or even a total halt to trading with a particular country. Embargo durations can vary to accommodate changes in foreign policy. The United States has had a long-standing embargo with Cuba and recently took initial steps to normalize diplomatic relations with the island nation. For the first time in over 50 years, the United States and Cuba will restore postal service between the two countries.[23]

exchange control restriction on importation of certain products or against certain companies to reduce trade and expenditures of foreign currency.

Another form of administrative trade restriction is **exchange control**. Imposed through a central bank or government agency, exchange controls affect both exporters and importers. Companies that gain foreign currencies through exporting are required to sell them to the central bank or another agency. Importers must buy foreign currencies to pay for their purchases from the same agency. The exchange control authorities can then allocate, expand, or restrict foreign exchange in accordance with national policy.

Assessment Check

1. How might values and attitudes form a barrier to trade, and how can they be overcome?
2. What is a tariff? What is its purpose?
3. Why is dumping a problem for companies marketing goods internationally?

4 Reducing Barriers to International Trade

Although tariffs and administrative barriers, recently widespread in the media, still restrict trade, overall the world has moved toward free trade. Several types of organizations ease barriers to international trade, including groups that monitor trade policies and practices and institutions that offer monetary assistance. Another type of federation designed to ease trade barriers is the multinational economic community, such as the European Union. This section looks at the roles these organizations play.

Organizations Promoting International Trade

General Agreement on Tariffs and Trade (GATT) international trade accord that substantially reduced worldwide tariffs and other trade barriers.

The **General Agreement on Tariffs and Trade (GATT)**, an international trade accord, has sponsored a series of negotiations, called rounds, which substantially reduced worldwide tariffs and other barriers. Major industrialized nations founded the multinational organization in 1947 to work toward reducing tariffs and relaxing import quotas. The last set of completed negotiations—the Uruguay Round—cut average tariffs by one-third, in excess of $700 billion; reduced farm subsidies; and improved protection for copyright and patent holders. In addition, international trading rules now apply to various service industries. Finally, the new agreement established the **World Trade Organization (WTO)** to succeed GATT. This organization includes representatives from 164 countries.

World Trade Organization (WTO) 164-member international institution that monitors GATT agreements and mediates international trade disputes.

World Trade Organization Since 1995, the WTO has monitored GATT agreements among the member nations, mediated disputes, and continued the effort to reduce trade barriers throughout the world. Unlike provisions in GATT, the WTO's decisions are binding on parties involved in disputes.

The WTO has become increasingly controversial in recent years as it issues decisions that have implications for working conditions and the environment in member nations. Concerns have been expressed that the WTO's focus on lowering trade barriers encourages businesses to keep costs down through practices that may increase pollution and human rights abuses. Particularly worrisome is the fact that the organization's member countries must agree on policies, and developing countries tend not to be eager to lose their low-cost advantage by enacting stricter labor and environmental laws. Other critics claim that if well-funded U.S. firms such as fast-food chains, entertainment companies, and online retailers can freely enter foreign markets, they will eliminate smaller foreign businesses serving the distinct tastes and practices of other countries.

Trade unions in developed nations complain that the WTO's support of free trade makes it easier to export manufacturing jobs to low-wage countries. But many small and midsize companies have benefited from the WTO's reduction of trade barriers and lowering of the cost of trade. They currently make up 98% of all firms that export goods and services, according to the U.S. Department of Commerce.

The most recent round of WTO talks is called the *Doha Round* after the city in Qatar where it began. After more than a decade, discussion still continues on ways to improve global trade among developing countries, with the goal of reducing domestic price supports, eliminating export subsidies, and improving market access for goods. Such changes could help farmers in developing countries compete in the global marketplace.[24]

World Bank Shortly after the end of World War II, industrialized nations formed an organization to lend money to less-developed and developing countries. The **World Bank** primarily funds projects that build or expand nations' infrastructure, such as transportation, education, and medical systems and facilities. The World Bank and other development banks provide the largest source of advice and assistance to developing nations. Often, in exchange for granting loans, the World Bank imposes requirements intended to build the economies of borrower nations.

World Bank organization established by industrialized nations to lend money to less-developed countries.

The World Bank has been criticized for making loans with conditions that ultimately hurt the borrower nations. When developing nations are required to balance government budgets, they are sometimes forced to cut vital social programs. Critics also say that the World Bank should consider the impact of its loans on the environment and working conditions.

International Monetary Fund Established a year after the World Bank, the **International Monetary Fund (IMF)** was created to promote trade through financial cooperation and, in the process, eliminate barriers. The IMF makes short-term loans to member nations that are unable to meet their expenses. It operates as a lender of last resort for troubled nations. In exchange for these emergency loans, IMF lenders frequently require significant commitments from the borrowing nations to address the problems that led to the crises. These steps may include curtailing imports or even devaluing currencies. Throughout its existence, the IMF has worked to prevent financial crises by warning the international business community when countries encounter problems meeting their financial obligations. Often, the IMF lends to countries to keep them from defaulting on prior debts. In an effort to make the currency more tradeable, the IMF recently designated the Chinese renminbi, commonly known as the yuan, as a global reserve currency. Along with the U.S. dollar, euro, British pound, and Japanese yen, the yuan will now be part of the IMF's official basket of world currencies.[25]

International Monetary Fund (IMF) organization created to promote trade, eliminate barriers, and make short-term loans to member nations that are unable to meet their budgets.

However, some countries owe far more money than they can ever hope to repay, and the debt payments make it impossible for their governments to deliver needed services to their citizens. Recently, the IMF has come under scrutiny over how much influence and voting power emerging market economies (EMEs) have within the IMF. With the rapid development and expansion of developing economies, some believe that their voice and power in the IMF has not grown proportionately. As emerging markets continue to remain vulnerable to tightened global financial conditions and a turbulent world economy, the issue of governance reform of the IMF remains at the forefront.

International Economic Communities

International economic communities reduce trade barriers and promote regional economic integration. In the simplest approach, countries may establish a *free-trade area* in which they trade freely among themselves without tariffs or trade restrictions. Each maintains its own tariffs for trade outside this area. A *customs union* sets up a free-trade area and specifies a uniform tariff structure for members' trade with nonmember nations. In a *common market*, or economic union, members go beyond a customs union and try to bring all of their trade rules into agreement.

North American Free Trade Agreement (NAFTA) agreement among the United States, Canada, and Mexico to break down tariffs and trade restrictions.

One example of a free-trade area is the **North American Free Trade Agreement (NAFTA)** enacted by the United States, Canada, and Mexico. Other examples of regional trading blocs include the MERCOSUR customs union (joining Brazil, Argentina, Paraguay, Uruguay, Chile, and Bolivia) and the 10-country Association of South East Asian Nations (ASEAN).

NAFTA

NAFTA went into effect in 1994, creating the world's largest free-trade zone with the United States, Canada, and Mexico. With a combined population of more than 478 million and a total GDP of more than $23 trillion, North America represents the world's largest and most attractive free-trade areas. The United States—the single largest market—dominates North America's business environment. Although fewer than 1 person in 20 lives in the United States, the nation's more than $19 trillion GDP represents about 25% of total world output.[26]

Central America–Dominican Republic Free Trade Agreement (CAFTA-DR) agreement among the United States, Costa Rica, El Salvador, Guatemala, Honduras, Nicaragua, and the Dominican Republic to reduce tariffs and trade restrictions.

Canada is far less densely populated but has achieved a similar level of economic development. Over the last decade, Canada's economy has grown at about the same rate as the U.S. economy. Almost 70% of Canada's GDP is generated in the services sector, and three of every four Canadian workers are engaged in service occupations. The country's per-capita GDP places Canada among the top 20 nations in terms of its people's spending power. Canada's economy is fueled by trade with the United States, and its home markets are strong as well. About 75% of Canada's exports and about 50% of its imports are to or from the United States.[27] Ford, General Motors, Toyota, Honda, and Chrysler all have large production facilities in Canada. While Mexico has taken important steps, its low GDP per capita ($19,500) is evidence that it still has not reached the classification of a fully developed country. Mexico's trade with the United States and Canada has tripled since the signing of NAFTA, although more than half of the country's 125 million people live below the poverty line, and per capita income is about one-third that of the United States. But Mexico's border with the United States is busy with a nearly endless stream of traffic transporting goods from Mexican manufacturing facilities into the United States. The United States is Mexico's largest trading partner by far, accounting for about 80% of total exports and 50% of all Mexico's imports.[28]

D100/Shutterstock

The North American Free Trade Agreement, or NAFTA, created the world's largest free trade zone between Canada, the United States, and Mexico.

By eliminating all trade barriers and investment restrictions, NAFTA opened the economic borders between the United States, Canada, and Mexico—and Canada and Mexico became two of the most important trading partners to the United States. The agreement also eased regulations governing services, such as banking, and established uniform legal requirements for protection of intellectual property. The three neighboring nations were allowed to trade with one another without tariffs or other trade barriers. However, NAFTA has not been without its fair share of criticism with regard to job loss and the United States' trade deficit. To date, U.S., Canadian, and Mexican officials have met for numerous rounds of talks to update NAFTA—or possibly, pull out altogether.

CAFTA-DR

The **Central America–Dominican Republic Free Trade Agreement (CAFTA-DR)** created a free-trade area among the United States, Costa Rica, El Salvador, Guatemala, Honduras, Nicaragua, and the Dominican Republic (the DR of the title). The agreement—the first of its kind between the United States and these smaller, developing economies—ends tariffs on the

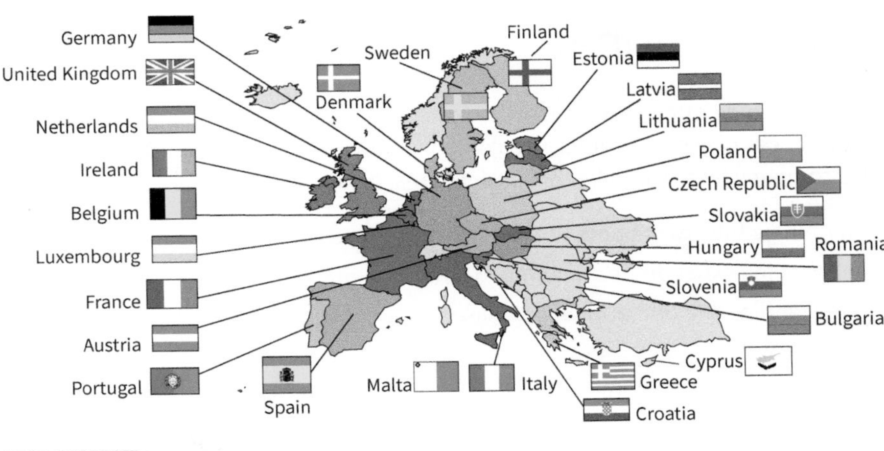

FIGURE 4.4 **Nations of the European Union**

nearly $54 billion in products traded between the United States and its Latin American neighbors. Agricultural producers such as corn, soybean, and dairy farmers stand to gain under the relaxed trade rules. Overall, CAFTA-DR's effects have increased both exports and imports substantially.[29]

European Union

European Union (EU) 28-nation European economic alliance.

Perhaps the best-known example of a common market is the **European Union (EU)**. A few years ago, the United Kingdom held a referendum to vote to leave the European Union—leaving the EU won 52% to 48%. Prior to *Brexit*, a word that is short for *Britain* and *exit*, the EU combined 28 countries. The scheduled departure date is yet to come. If all goes as planned, this deal could then be given the go ahead by both sides by early 2019. However, the UK and EU have agreed on how much the UK owes the EU, what happens to the Northern Ireland border and what happens to UK citizens living elsewhere in the EU and EU citizens living in the UK. Talks about post-Brexit relations are continuing. Figure 4.4 shows the member countries. Current candidates for membership are Albania, Montenegro, Serbia, the former Yugoslav Republic of Macedonia, and Turkey.[30]

The EU's goals include promoting economic and social progress, introducing European citizenship as a complement to national citizenship, and giving the EU a significant role in international affairs. To achieve its goal of a borderless Europe, the EU is removing barriers to free trade among its members. This highly complex process involves standardizing business regulations and requirements, standardizing import duties and taxes, and eliminating customs checks so that companies can transport goods from France to Italy or Poland as easily as from New York to Boston.

Unifying standards and laws can contribute to economic growth. But just as NAFTA sparked fears in the United States about free trade with Mexico, some people in Western Europe worried that opening trade with such countries as Poland, Hungary, and the Czech Republic would cause jobs to flow eastward to lower-wage economies.

The EU also introduced the euro to replace currencies such as the French franc and Italian lira. For the 19 member-states that have adopted the euro, potential benefits include eliminating the economic costs of currency exchange and simplifying price comparisons. Businesses and their customers now make electronic and credit card transactions in euros and use euro notes and coins in making cash purchases.

Assessment Check

1. What international trade organization succeeded GATT, and what is its goal?
2. Compare and contrast the goals of the World Bank and the International Monetary Fund.
3. What are the goals of the European Union, and how do they promote international trade?

5 Going Global

Although expanding into overseas markets can increase profits and marketing opportunities, it also introduces new complexities to a company's business operations. Before deciding to go global, a company faces a number of key decisions, beginning with the following:

- determining the growth potential of each of the foreign markets being considered
- analyzing the expenditures required to enter new markets
- understanding the operational complexities and deciding the best way to organize overseas operations
- understanding foreign regulations and standards

These issues vary in importance, depending on the level of involvement a company chooses. Education and employee training in the host country would be much more important for an electronics manufacturer building an Asian factory than for a company that is simply planning to export American-made products.

The choice of which markets to enter usually involves extensive research focusing on local demand for the company's products, availability of needed resources (such as raw materials and labor), and ability of the local workforce to produce quality merchandise. Other factors include existing and potential competition, tariff rates, currency stability, and investment barriers. A variety of government and other sources are available to facilitate this research process. A good starting place is the CIA's *World Factbook*, which contains country-by-country information on geography, population, government, economy, and infrastructure.

U.S. Department of Commerce counselors working at district offices offer a full range of international business advice, including computerized market data and names of business and government contacts in dozens of countries.

Levels of Involvement

After a company has completed its research and decided to do business overseas, it can choose one or more strategies:

- exporting or importing
- entering into contractual agreements such as franchising, licensing, and subcontracting deals
- direct investment in the foreign market through acquisitions, joint ventures, or establishment of an overseas division

Under Armour, now a global sports clothing and accessory company, began in then college football player Kevin Plank's grandmother's basement.

Although the company's risk increases with the level of its involvement, so does its overall control of all aspects of producing and selling its goods or services.

Los Angeles, California–based Sky Zone is a chain of indoor trampoline parks with locations in 11 countries, including the United States, Canada, Mexico, Australia, and Saudi Arabia. Sky Zone, which began over a decade ago, offers birthday parties, corporate events, physical activities, exercise classes, and dodgeball on the company's patented all-trampoline, walled playing courts. In an attempt to go global, Sky Zone entered a master franchise license with Strike Bowling Bar to build 10 parks in Australia along with future parks in New Zealand, Guatemala, Norway, Pakistan, Poland, Qatar, and the United Arab Emirates.[31]

With global headquarters in Baltimore (see photo), Under Armour began in college football player Kevin Plank's grandmother's basement over two decades ago.

The worldwide sports clothing and accessories company operates its European headquarters from Amsterdam, where it is building its brand across Europe. In Latin America, Under Armour has expanded through partnerships such as one with Chilean football club Colo-Colo and Brazilian fashion model Gisele Bündchen. In Asia, the company is focused on product development, sourcing, production, and delivery of footwear and accessories.[32]

Importers and Exporters When a company brings in goods produced abroad to sell domestically, it is an importer. Conversely, companies are exporters when they produce—or purchase—goods at home and sell them in overseas markets. An importing or exporting strategy provides the most basic level of international involvement, with the least risk and control.

Exports are frequently handled by special intermediaries called export trading companies. These firms search out competitively priced local merchandise and then resell it abroad at prices high enough to cover expenses and earn profits. When a retail chain such as Dallas-based Pier 1 Imports wants to purchase West African products for its store shelves, it may contact an export trading company operating in a country such as Ghana. The local firm is responsible for monitoring quality, packaging the order for transatlantic shipment, arranging transportation, and arranging for completion of customs paperwork and other steps required to move the product from Ghana to the United States.

Firms engage in exporting of two types: indirect and direct. A company engages in *indirect exporting* when it manufactures a product, such as an electronic component, that becomes part of another product sold in foreign markets. The second method, *direct exporting*, occurs when a company seeks to sell its products in markets outside its own country. Often the first step for companies entering foreign markets, direct exporting is the most common form of international business. Firms that succeed at this may then move to other strategies.

In addition to reaching foreign markets by dealing with export trading companies, exporters may choose two other alternatives: export management companies and offset agreements. Rather than simply relying on an export trading company to assist in foreign markets, an exporting

Job Description

Import/Export Coordinator

Overview An import/export coordinator plans and coordinates business transactions involving receiving or delivering goods to foreign countries. Companies with import/export coordinators include freight forwarders, third-party logistics businesses, retailers, and manufacturers. An import/export coordinator may work for the government, an international company, or as a representative of a client. An import/export coordinator maintains good working relationships with clients, vendors, and government agency representatives in a fast-paced, changing global environment.

Responsibilities Typical job responsibilities include preparing commercial documentation for shipments to international customers; working with customs brokers, forwarders, and international partners in a variety of industries; arranging financial transactions with worldwide banks, including letters of credit and wire transfers; ensuring smooth trade operations with a variety of entities, including retailers, manufacturers, freight forwarders, third-party logistics companies, distributors, and sales professionals; arranging shipments; preparing and confirming order approvals; handling and verifying pricing information; and issuing invoices.

Requirements Typically a degree in business, international business, or business management is preferred. Coursework includes international business, geography, foreign languages, import and export management, and global business management. Understanding domestic and global business practices, U.S. and foreign regulations for the movement of goods between countries, and national and international procedures for receipt and delivery of goods is required. Import/export coordinators must understand U.S. Customs and Border Protection requirements for goods entering and leaving the United States and follow export administration regulations, or EAR, to avoid shipment delays and costly penalties. Fluency in a foreign language is a real plus, and problem resolution skills will come in handy to troubleshoot discrepancies. Attention to detail, organizational skills, and the ability to prioritize are important, along with excellent communication skills, especially when corresponding with international companies abroad.

Outlook As a result of increased emphasis on globalization, the outlook for import/export coordinators is strong and advancement and employment prospects are good. Career advancement includes management, import/export business owner, marketing manager, and import/export specialist.

Sources: Company website, "Import/Export Coordinator: Job Description and Information," http://study.com, accessed March 5, 2018; Sharon O'Neil, "Responsibilities of an Import/Export Manager," *Chron*, http://work.chron.com, accessed March 5, 2018; company website, "Import/Export Coordinator Job Description for True Religion Brand Jeans," http://prsm.files.cms-plus.com, accessed March 5, 2018; company website, "Import/Export Specialists," http://www.vault.com, accessed March 5, 2018.

firm may turn to an *export management company* for advice and expertise. These international specialists help the exporter complete paperwork, make contacts with local buyers, and comply with local laws governing labeling, product safety, and performance testing. At the same time, the exporting firm retains much more control than would be possible with an export trading company. See the "Job Description" feature to see what it takes to work as an import/export coordinator.

An *offset agreement* matches a small business with a major international firm. It basically makes the small firm a subcontractor to the larger one. Such an entry strategy helps a new exporter by allowing it to share in the larger company's international expertise. The small firm also benefits in such important areas as international transaction documents and financing, while the larger company benefits from the local expertise and capabilities of its smaller partner.

countertrade barter agreement whereby trade between two or more nations involves payment made in the form of local products instead of currency.

Countertrade

A sizable share of international trade involves payments made in the form of local products, not currency. This system of international bartering agreements is called **countertrade**.

A common reason for resorting to international barter is inadequate access to needed foreign currency. To complete an international sales agreement, the seller may agree to accept part or all of the purchase cost in merchandise rather than currency. Because the seller may decide to locate a buyer for the bartered goods before completing the transaction, a number of international buyers and sellers frequently join together in a single agreement.

Countertrade may often be a company's only opportunity to enter a particular market. Many developing countries simply cannot obtain enough credit or financial assistance to afford the imports that their people want. Countries with heavy debt burdens also resort to countertrade. Russian buyers, whose currency is often less acceptable to foreign traders than the stronger currencies of countries such as the United States, Great Britain, Japan, and EU countries, may resort to trading local products ranging from crude oil to diamonds to vodka as payments for purchases from foreign companies unwilling to accept Russian rubles. Still, other countries such as China may restrict imports. Under such circumstances, countertrade may be the only practical way to win government approval to import needed products.

Contractual Agreements

Once a company, large or small, gains some experience in international sales, it may decide to enter into contractual agreements with local parties. These arrangements can include franchising, foreign licensing, and subcontracting.

franchise contractual agreement in which a franchisee gains the right to produce and/or sell the franchisor's products under that company's brand name if they agree to certain operating requirements.

Franchising

Common among U.S. companies, franchising can work well for companies seeking to expand into international markets, too. A **franchise**, as described in detail in Chapter 5, is a contractual agreement in which a wholesaler or retailer (the franchisee) gains the right to sell the franchisor's products under that company's brand name if it agrees to the related operating requirements. The franchisee can also receive training, marketing, management, and business services from the franchisor. While these arrangements are common among leading fast-food brands such as Dunkin' Donuts, McDonald's, and KFC, other kinds of service providers like Cisco also often look to franchising as an international marketplace option.

Domino's Pizza, the largest pizza seller worldwide, has expanded to more than 14,000 stores in over 85 international markets. Its largest international market is Mexico, but wherever it operates, the company adapts its menus to meet local tastes with pizza toppings such as barbequed chicken in the Bahamas; potatoes, onions, bacon, mushrooms, corn, pepperoni, and mayonnaise in Korea; squid in Japan; and chorizo in Portugal.[33] **Table 4.3** lists the top 10 largest global franchisors and initial investment requirements.

foreign licensing agreement international agreement in which one company allows another to produce or sell its product, or use its trademark, patent, or manufacturing processes, in a specific geographical area in return for royalties or other compensation.

Foreign Licensing

In a **foreign licensing agreement**, one company allows another to produce or sell its product, or use its trademark, patent, or manufacturing processes, in a specific geographical area. In return, the company gets a royalty or other compensation.

Licensing can be advantageous for a small manufacturer eager to launch a well-known product overseas. Not only does it get a proven product from another market, but little or no investment is required to begin operating. The arrangement can also allow entry into a market otherwise closed to imports due to government restrictions. Global e-commerce giant Alibaba

TABLE 4.3 **Top 10 Global Franchise Companies**

Name	Type	Initial Investment
McDonald's	Hamburger Fast Food Restaurant	Up to $2.5 MM
KFC	Fried Chicken	Up to $2.6 MM
Burger King	Hamburger Fast Food Restaurant	Up to $2.9 MM
Pizza Hut	Pizza Restaurant Chain	Up to $1.2 MM
7-Eleven	Convenience Store	Up to $1.2 MM
Marriott International	Hotel Franchises	Up to $96.5 MM
RE/MAX	International Real Estate Company	Up to $219K
Dunkin' Donuts	Doughnut and Coffee House Company	Up to $1.7 MM
InterContinental Hotels and Resorts	Hotels	Up to $98 MM
Subway®	Submarine Sandwiches	Up to $320K

Source: "Top 100 Global Franchises," *Global Direct*, https://www.franchisedirect.com, accessed March 3, 2018.

recently struck a licensing agreement with The Walt Disney Company to provide the Chinese group's Youku video streaming platform with the largest Disney animation collection of more than 1,000 episodes in China.[34]

Subcontracting The third type of contractual agreement, **subcontracting**, involves hiring local companies to produce, distribute, or sell goods or services. This move allows a foreign firm to take advantage of the subcontractor's expertise in local culture, contacts, and regulations. Subcontracting works equally well for mail-order companies, which can farm out order fulfillment and customer service functions to local businesses. Manufacturers practice subcontracting to save money on import duties and labor costs, and businesses go this route to market products best sold by locals in a given country. Some firms, such as Maryland-based Pacific Bridge Medical, help medical manufacturers find reliable subcontractors and parts suppliers in Asia.

subcontracting international agreement that involves hiring local companies to produce, distribute, or sell goods or services in a specific country or geographical region.

A key disadvantage of subcontracting is that companies cannot always control their subcontractors' business practices. Several major U.S. companies have had to launch investigations and take compliance measures when findings surfaced that their subcontractors did not uphold agreed-upon workplace standards (including factory monitoring and workplace conditions) to manufacture clothing.

Offshoring While it is not generally considered a way of initiating business internationally, *offshoring*, or the relocation of business processes to a lower-cost location overseas, has become a widespread practice. Despite increasing labor costs, China is still one of the top destinations for production offshoring and India and the Philippines for services offshoring. Many business leaders argue, in favor of offshoring, that global firms must keep their costs as low as possible to remain competitive. But the apparent link between jobs sent overseas and jobs lost at home has made the practice controversial. The top 10 global outsourcing destinations are Bangalore, followed by Mumbai (2nd), Delhi (3rd), Manila (4th), Hyderabad (5th), Sao Paulo (6th), Dublin (7th), Krakow (8th), Chennai (9th), and Buenos Aires (10th).

Offshoring shows no signs of slowing down, but it is changing, particularly for manufacturers. Not surprisingly, maintaining flexibility by offshoring to a few different low-cost locations may be a low-risk strategy for U.S. companies for the future. The rising cost of Chinese labor has created a wave of change. Wages in Mexico, a manufacturing alternative to China, are predicted to be as much as 40% lower than China's, and many countries, like Vietnam, have seen gains due to the country's lower wages. India and the Philippines remain the top two outsourcing destinations.[35]

International Direct Investment Investing directly in production and marketing operations in a foreign country is the ultimate level of global involvement. Over time, a company may become successful at conducting business in other countries through exporting and contractual agreements. Its managers may then decide to establish manufacturing facilities in those countries, open branch offices, or buy ownership interests in local companies.

In an *acquisition*, a company purchases another existing firm in the host country. An acquisition permits a largely domestic business operation to gain an international presence very quickly. In a recent year, despite an overall decrease in global foreign direct investment by 16%, the United States ranked highest with $311 billion, followed by China, who recorded a record inflow of $144 billion.[36]

joint venture partnership between companies formed for a specific undertaking.

Joint ventures allow companies to share risks, costs, profits, and management responsibilities with one or more host country nationals. By setting up an *overseas division*, a company can conduct a significant amount of its business overseas. This strategy differs from that of a multinational company in that a firm with overseas divisions remains primarily a domestic organization with international operations. Toyota and Mazda recently signed a joint venture agreement to build an automobile plant in Huntsville, Alabama. The estimated cost is $1.6 billion and 4,000 jobs will be created. The United States is an example of an overseas division for Japanese automakers Toyota and Mazda.[37]

From Multinational Corporation to Global Business

multinational corporation (MNC) firm with significant operations and marketing activities outside its home country.

A **multinational corporation (MNC)** is an organization with significant foreign operations. As **Table 4.4** shows, companies headquartered in the United States and China make up 5 of the top 10 world's largest multinationals, with the two top industries of banking and oil and gas.

TABLE 4.4 The World's Top 10 Leading Companies By Sales

Rank	Company	Industry	Country of Origin
1	ICBC China	Banking	China
2	China Construction Bank	Banking	China
3	Berkshire Hathaway	Conglomerate	United States
4	JPMorgan Chase	Banking	United States
5	Wells Fargo	Banking	United States
6	Agricultural Bank of China	Banking	China
7	Bank of America	Banking	United States
8	Bank of China	Banking	China
9	Apple	Technology	United States
10	Toyota Motor	Automobile	Japan

Source: "The World's Biggest Public Companies," *Forbes*, http://www.forbes.com, accessed March 5, 2018.

Many U.S. multinationals, including Nike and Walmart, have expanded their overseas operations because they believe that domestic markets are mature and foreign markets allow the potential to generate more sales and profits. Other MNCs are making substantial investments in developing countries in part because these countries provide low-cost labor compared with the United States and Western Europe. In addition, many MNCs are locating high-tech facilities in countries with large numbers of technical school graduates.

Assessment Check

1. Name three possible strategies for beginning overseas operations.
2. What is countertrade?
3. Compare and contrast licensing and subcontracting.
4. Describe joint ventures.

6 Developing a Strategy for International Business

In developing a framework in which to conduct international business, managers must first evaluate their corporate objectives, organizational strengths and weaknesses, and strategies for product development and marketing. They can choose to combine these elements in either a global strategy or a multidomestic strategy.

Global Business Strategies

In a **global business** (or *standardization*) **strategy**, a firm sells the same product in essentially the same manner throughout the world. Many companies simply modify their domestic business strategies by translating promotional brochures and product-use instructions into the languages of the host nations.

global business strategy offering a standardized, worldwide product and selling it in essentially the same manner throughout a firm's domestic and foreign markets.

A global marketing perspective can be appropriate for some goods and services and certain market segments that are common to many nations. The approach works for products with nearly universal appeal, for luxury items such as jewelry, for commodities like chemicals and metals, and for consumer staples like soft drinks and other beverages. The Coca-Cola Company, one of the world's most recognizable brands, provides an example of global standardization. Using relatively standard formulations, packaging, positioning, and distribution in its global markets, the product is marketed in a similar fashion to consumers worldwide. Additional "standard" attributes of Coca-Cola include its high-quality requirements for retailers, its iconic script logo, and the glass design of its bottle.[38] However, even products like Coca-Cola that look similar across the globe tend to have subtle country-by-country variations that can make or break their success in a local region. Regardless of global business strategies, companies need to be aware of local cultural and business customs in the countries in which they do business and whether certain behaviors are acceptable, as discussed in "Judgment Call."

Multidomestic Business Strategies

multidomestic business strategy developing and marketing products to serve different needs and tastes of separate national markets.

Under a **multidomestic business** (or *adaptation*) **strategy**, the company treats each national market in a different way. It develops products and marketing strategies that appeal to the

Judgment Call

Understanding *Guanxi*: Connections or Bribes?

It is customary as part of the work culture in China to spend time, mainly after work, developing relationships, getting to know co-workers, and building trust. According to one American executive with frequent travel to China, business is never discussed during dinner, which is a time to get better acquainted, and to see how well everyone can know, like, and trust each other. Competing in world markets includes understanding local customs and business practices of the countries in which a company plans to operate.

Guanxi is the Chinese word for "connections" or "relations" and involves making business and personal connections with local companies and officials. It is important to understand the mixed implications of *guanxi* when doing business in China. While some say it is a local custom and a generally accepted business practice in China, others say it is a form of bribery to extort money from foreign companies anxious to do business there. Companies must base their business strategy on solid business and ethical foundations. Building mutually beneficial relationships with connected networks of local businesses and government officials provides foreign companies with strategic advantages. The concept of *guanxi* is a local custom, and companies and officials may expect foreign companies to seek their advice and expertise to navigate the complicated business environment in China.

On the other hand, the concept of *guanxi* is another word for doing whatever it takes—no matter the cost—to succeed in the Chinese business marketplace. When doing business in a foreign land, U.S. companies must abide by the Foreign Corrupt Practices Act, federal legislation that prohibits the exchange of money for obtaining or retaining business. Some say that foreigners who do business in China and tout their "connections" are overrated—and that *guanxi* can take generations and years to develop. The best advice is to respect the time it takes to build connections and relationships and, when doing business in China, to fully comply with the laws.

Questions for Critical Thinking

1. Discuss how foreigners can create a *guanxi* network and its importance when doing business in China.
2. How can foreign business professionals better understand *guanxi's* implications and importance?

Sources: Dan Harris, "China Guanxi: Overrated," *Forbes*, http://www.forbes.com, accessed March 5, 2018; Gary Stroller, "Expert Etiquette Tips for Doing Business in China," *USA Today*, http://www.usatoday.com, accessed March 5, 2018; "The Mystery of China's Guanxi (video clip)," *BBC News*, http://www.bbc.com, accessed March 5, 2018; Josie Stoker, "Guanxi 101: Navigating Relationships in Chinese Business," *LinkedIn*, https://www.linkedin.com, accessed March 5, 2018.

customs, tastes, and buying habits of particular national markets. McDonald's Corporation provides an example of adaptation in each of the countries where it operates. The company serves kosher burgers in Jerusalem and halal menus in Arab countries in accordance with Islamic food preparation guidelines. In the Philippines, McDonald's offers McSpaghetti, crispy, golden brown chicken, served over spaghetti with ground beef.[39]

Assessment Check

1. What is a global business strategy? What are its advantages?
2. What is a multidomestic business strategy? What are its advantages?

What's Ahead

This chapter travels through the world of international business and shows how companies both large and small approach a global business environment. Chapter 5 examines the special advantages and challenges that small-business owners encounter. In addition, a critical decision facing any new business is the choice of the most appropriate form of business ownership. Chapter 5 also examines the major ownership structures—sole proprietorship, partnership, and corporation—and assesses the pros and cons of each. The chapter closes with a discussion of recent trends affecting business ownership, such as the growing impact of franchising and business consolidations through mergers and acquisitions.

Chapter in Review

Summary of Learning Objectives

LEARNING OBJECTIVE 1 Explain why nations trade.

The United States is both the world's largest importer and the largest exporter, although less than 5% of the world's population lives within its borders. With the increasing globalization of the world's economies, the international marketplace offers tremendous opportunities for U.S. and foreign businesses to expand into new markets for their goods and services. Doing business globally provides new sources of materials and labor. Trading with other countries also reduces a company's dependence on economic conditions in its home market. Countries that encourage international trade enjoy higher levels of economic activity, employment, and wages than those that restrict it.

Nations usually benefit if they specialize in producing certain goods or services. A country has an absolute advantage if it can maintain a monopoly or produces a good or service at a lower cost than other nations. It has a comparative advantage if it can supply a particular product more efficiently or at a lower cost than it can produce other items.

Assessment Check Answers

1.1 **Why do nations trade?** Nations trade because trading boosts economic growth by providing a market for products and access to needed resources. This makes production and distribution systems more efficient and reduces dependence on the economy of the home nation.

1.2 **Cite some measures of the size of the international marketplace.** Although developing countries have lower per capita incomes than developed nations in North America and Western Europe, their populations are large and growing. China's population is about 1.4 billion, and India's is roughly 1.3 billion.

1.3 **How does a nation acquire a comparative advantage?** Comparative advantage exists when a nation can supply a product more efficiently and at a lower price than it can supply other goods, compared with the outputs of other countries.

LEARNING OBJECTIVE 2 Describe how trade is measured between nations.

Countries measure the level of international trade by comparing exports and imports and then calculating whether a trade surplus or a deficit exists. This is the balance of trade, which represents the difference between exports and imports. The term *balance of payments* refers to the overall flow of money into or out of a country, including overseas loans and borrowing, international investments, and profits from such investments. An exchange rate is the value of a nation's currency relative to the currency of another nation. Currency values typically fluctuate relative to the supply and demand for specific currencies in the world market. When the value of the dollar falls compared with other currencies, the cost paid by foreign businesses and households for U.S. products declines, and demand for exports may rise. An increase in the value of the dollar raises the prices of U.S. products sold abroad, but it reduces the prices of foreign products sold in the United States.

Assessment Check Answers

2.1 **Compare balance of trade and balance of payments.** Balance of trade is the difference between a nation's exports and imports. Balance of payments is the overall flow of money into or out of a country.

2.2 **Explain the function of an exchange rate.** A nation's exchange rate is the rate at which its currency can be exchanged for the currencies of other nations to make it easier for them to trade with one another.

2.3 **What happens when a currency is devalued?** Devaluation describes a drop in a currency's value relative to other currencies or to a fixed standard.

LEARNING OBJECTIVE 3 Identify the barriers to international trade.

Businesses face several obstacles in the global marketplace. Companies must be sensitive to social and cultural differences, such as languages, values, and religions, when operating in other countries. Economic differences include standard-of-living variations and levels of infrastructure development. Legal and political barriers are among the most difficult to judge. Each country sets its own laws regulating business practices. Trade restrictions such as tariffs and administrative barriers also present obstacles to international business.

Assessment Check Answers

3.1 **How might values and attitudes form a barrier to trade, and how can they be overcome?** Marked differences in values and attitudes, such as religious attitudes, can form barriers between traditionally capitalist countries and those adapting new capitalist systems. Many of these can be overcome by learning about and respecting such differences.

3.2 **What is a tariff? What is its purpose?** A tariff is a tax, surcharge, or duty charged on foreign products. Its purpose is to protect domestic producers of those items.

3.3 **Why is dumping a problem for companies marketing goods internationally?** Dumping is selling products abroad at prices below the cost of production or exporting products at a lower price than charged in the home market. It drives the cost of products sharply down in the market where they are dumped, thus hurting the domestic producers of those products.

LEARNING OBJECTIVE 4 Discuss reducing barriers to international trade.

Many international organizations seek to promote international trade by reducing barriers among nations. Examples include the World Trade Organization, the World Bank, and the International

Monetary Fund. Multinational economic communities create partnerships to remove barriers to the flow of goods, capital, and people across the borders of members. Three such economic agreements are the North American Free Trade Agreement (NAFTA), CAFTA-DR, and the European Union.

Assessment Check Answers

4.1 **What international trade organization succeeded GATT, and what is its goal?** The World Trade Organization (WTO) succeeded GATT with the goal of monitoring GATT agreements, mediating disputes, and continuing the effort to reduce trade barriers throughout the world.

4.2 **Compare and contrast the goals of the World Bank and the International Monetary Fund.** The World Bank funds projects that build or expand nations' infrastructure such as transportation, education, and medical systems and facilities. The International Monetary Fund makes short-term loans to member nations that are unable to meet their expenses. The fund operates as a lender of last resort for troubled nations.

4.3 **What are the goals of the European Union, and how do they promote international trade?** The European Union's goals include promoting economic and social progress, introducing European citizenship as a complement to national citizenship, and giving the EU a significant role in international affairs. Unifying standards and laws can contribute to economic growth.

LEARNING OBJECTIVE 5 Explain the decisions to go global.

Exporting and importing, the first level of involvement in international business, involves the lowest degree of both risk and control. Companies may rely on export trading or management companies to help distribute their products. Contractual agreements, such as franchising, foreign licensing, and subcontracting, offer additional options. Franchising and licensing are especially appropriate for services. Companies may also choose local subcontractors to produce goods for local sales. International direct investment in production and marketing facilities provides the highest degree of control but also the greatest risk. Firms make direct investments by acquiring foreign companies or facilities, forming joint ventures with local firms, and setting up their own overseas divisions.

Assessment Check Answers

5.1 **Name three possible strategies for beginning overseas business operations.** Strategies are exporting or importing; contractual agreements such as franchising, licensing, or subcontracting; and making direct investments in foreign markets through acquisition, joint venture, or establishment of an overseas division.

5.2 **What is countertrade?** Countertrade consists of payments made in the form of local products, rather than currency.

5.3 **Compare and contrast licensing and subcontracting.** In a foreign licensing agreement, one company allows another to produce or sell its product or use its trademark, patent, or manufacturing process in a specific geographical area in return for royalty payments or other compensation. In subcontracting, a firm hires local companies abroad to produce, distribute, or sell its goods and services in a specific region.

5.4 **Describe joint ventures.** Joint ventures allow companies to share risks, costs, profits, and management responsibilities with one or more host-country nationals.

LEARNING OBJECTIVE 6 Discuss developing a strategy for international business.

A company that adopts a global strategy develops a single, standardized product and marketing strategy for implementation throughout the world. The company sells the same product in essentially the same manner in all countries in which it operates. Under a multidomestic (or adaptation) strategy, the firm develops a different treatment for each foreign market. It develops products and marketing strategies that appeal to the customs, tastes, and buying habits of particular nations.

Assessment Check Answers

6.1 **What is a global business strategy? What are its advantages?** A global business strategy specifies a standardized competitive strategy in which the firm sells the same product in essentially the same manner throughout the world. It works well for goods and services that are common to many nations.

6.2 **What is a multidomestic business strategy? What are its advantages?** A multidomestic business strategy allows the firm to treat each foreign market in a different way to appeal to the customs, tastes, and buying habits of particular national markets. It allows the firm to customize its marketing appeals for individual cultures or areas.

Business Terms You Need to Know

Review Questions

1. How does a business decide whether to trade with a foreign country? What are the key factors for participating in the information economy on a global basis?

2. Why have developing countries such as China and India become important international markets?

3. What is the difference between absolute advantage and comparative advantage? Give an example of each.

4. Can a nation have a favorable balance of trade and an unfavorable balance of payments? Why or why not?

5. Identify several potential barriers to communication when a company attempts to conduct business in another country. How might these be overcome?

6. Identify and describe briefly the three dimensions of the legal environment for global business.

7. What are the major nontariff restrictions affecting international business? Describe the difference between tariff and nontariff restrictions.

8. What is NAFTA? How does it work?

9. How has the EU helped trade among European businesses?

10. What are the key choices a company must make before reaching the final decision to go global?

Projects and Teamwork Applications

1. What are some examples of business or personal mishaps that have resulted from cultural misunderstandings? How did they occur, and how were they resolved? Give specific examples and discuss among classmates.

2. The tremendous growth of online business has introduced new elements to the legal climate of international business. Patents, brand names, copyrights, and trademarks are difficult to monitor because of the boundaryless nature of the Internet. What steps could businesses take to protect their trademarks and brands in this environment? Come up with at least five suggestions, and compare your list with those of your classmates.

3. Microlending is the disbursement of small loans to people, typically entrepreneurs and small business owners, living in extreme poverty. Due to their lack of collateral and creditworthiness, many have been locked out of the banking system. A small dairy farmer in Nepal can benefit from a microloan, for example. With typical repayment rates of over 90%, commercial banks and investors from international markets have moved into microfinance, which has led to questions about the ethics of whether they should be capitalizing on the poorest people on the planet. After reading and researching more about microfinance, what are your thoughts? Do the benefits outweigh the possible issues that may result?

4. Describe briefly the EU and its goals. What are the pros and cons of the EU?

5. Use the most recent edition of "The *Fortune* Global 500," which usually is published in *Fortune* magazine in July, or go to *Fortune's* online version at http://fortune.com.

   a. On what data is the Global 500 ranking based?

   b. Among the world's 10 largest corporations, list the countries in which they are based.

   c. Identify the top-ranked company, along with its Global 500 ranking and country, for the following industry classifications: Food and Drug Stores; Industrial and Farm Equipment; Petroleum Refining; Utilities: Gas and Electric; Telecommunications; Pharmaceuticals.

Web Assignments

1. **WTO.** Visit the website of the World Trade Organization. Research two current trade disputes. Which countries and products are involved? What, if anything, do the two disputes have in common? What procedures does the WTO follow in resolving trade disputes between member countries?
http://wto.org

2. **Made in the USA.** What does "Made in the USA" really mean, and how does one know whether the many parts that go into assembling a product are actually all made in the United States? The Federal Trade Commission has issued a "Made in the USA" standard to enforce origin claims by companies in advertising and labeling. Search for the FTC document entitled "Complying with Made in the USA Standard" and discuss the factors determined by the FTC as to whether a product is "all or virtually all" made in the United States.
www.ftc.gov

3. **Nike.** Nike is one of the world's largest and best-known global corporations. Visit the company's website. Where is the company headquartered? What are its products? Where are they manufactured? As a global corporation, what issues does Nike face? Review Nike's most recent annual report to discuss some of its global issues and challenges.
www.nike.com

Note: Internet web addresses change frequently. If you do not find the exact sites listed, you may need to access the organization's or company's home page and search from there or use a search engine such as Google or Bing.

Cases

Case 4.1 American Hipster Bikes Go Global

If you've looked around your neighborhood or college campus, you may have noticed more bicycles—and the increased popularity of custom-designed bicycles. A recent report indicates that 34% of Americans ages 3 or older rode a bike at least once in a recent year. Communities throughout the United States have promoted programs to ride bicycles on a daily basis, for commuting, recreation, and exercise. In some urban cities, bicycle ridership has recently doubled from the previous year.

Alex Chou, who grew up and attended design school in Los Angeles, is a bicycle designer and owner of start-up GoChic Bicycle, a shop he set up in an abandoned factory in Taiwan. Chou chose Taiwan, home of Giant Manufacturing Company, which is the world's largest bicycle manufacturer, because he believes it has the most sophisticated worldwide supply chain for bicycles.

It was during a visit to Taiwan, his parents' homeland, that Chou discovered excellent manufacturing technology for bikes and the small but growing biking culture triggered by a Taiwanese government push to get people out of their cars. It takes half the time to produce a bicycle in Taiwan as it does in the United States, and the initial cost to develop and bring to market new products is far lower, too. Chou soon became aware of the potential of his bicycle in the high-end, hand-built, niche market that has taken off in the United States—and he thought it was ideal to bring his idea to Taiwan.

Priced between $1,200 and $1,800, Chou's bicycles are sleek with Gates carbon belt drives in place of traditional, clunky chains for a smoother, grease-free ride. As a start-up owner, Chou believes that choosing to locate in a global bicycle manufacturing hub like Taiwan has great advantages. And because Chou's bikes are beautifully and meticulously designed, customers are often confused about whether they're rideable—or works of art.

Questions for Critical Thinking

1. What are some other types of small businesses and industries that could benefit from the decision to be close to a worldwide supply chain for their products?
2. What advantage does Alex Chou have to make his business a success in Taiwan?

Sources: Company website, http://gochicbicycle, accessed March 5, 2018; Elizabeth Weise, "L.A. Designer Brings Hipster Bikes to Taiwan," *USA Today*, www.usatoday.com, accessed March 5, 2018; "Study: 103.7 Million Americans Ride Bikes," *Velo News*, http://velonews.competitor.com, accessed March 5, 2018; organization website, "City Bicycle Count Report Shows a Dramatic 96% Increase in Ridership," https://www.sfbike.org, accessed March 5, 2018; Rachel Bachman, "Rise of the Five-Figure Bicycle," *Wall Street Journal*, http://www.wsj.com, accessed March 5, 2018.

Case 4.2 Chinese Consumers and Medical Tourism

According to the Cancer Institute and Hospital in Beijing, the five-year survival rate for cancer patients in China is 30%, as compared to 70% in the United States. To tap into the healthcare market in China, several top hospitals in the United States, including Cedars-Sinai Medical Center in Los Angeles and the Mayo Clinic in Rochester, Minnesota, have recently begun partnerships with Chinese businesses in an effort to attract affluent Chinese consumers seeking lifesaving treatments unavailable at home in the United States. The number of patients from China seeking high-end medical treatment overseas is estimated to be about 3,000 a year.

Although medical procedures in China are fairly inexpensive, Chinese hospitals have become overburdened, increasingly crowded, and incur long waiting periods for specialized treatment. Some Chinese consumers travel overseas in search of advanced pharmaceuticals because bureaucratic red tape has delayed their availability in China. Government-run hospitals in China are also known to run short of physicians and suitable facilities.

Many Chinese are demanding access to top-notch treatment in the areas of cancer, heart conditions, orthopedics, and plastic surgery as China's population and affluence have grown. Chinese travel agencies are taking advantage of the trend, and medical tourism packages to the United States, Canada, and Japan are in high demand. The packages include airfare, five-star hotels, fine cuisine, and post-surgery sightseeing tours.

As a result, U.S. companies and international entrepreneurs are tapping into healthcare markets in China. One company plans to launch an online platform that will connect Chinese tourists with a wide variety of medical institutions in the United States. Within two weeks, after downloading records, Chinese consumers can receive a diagnostic report concerning their conditions from any of the participating U.S. hospitals. Medical records translation, visa application assistance, airport pickups, and accommodations—all of which are sure to ease post-surgery healing—will generate revenue for the healthcare facilities involved.

Questions for Critical Thinking

1. What are the potential risks that could arise from medical tourism? What recourse should the medical tourism company offer should something go wrong with the surgery?
2. Other types of medical tourism include U.S. health insurance companies encouraging patients to have surgeries performed overseas at half the cost. Discuss the benefits and drawbacks of this strategy.

Sources: Alice Yan, "Top 5 Destinations for China's Medical Tourists," *South China Morning Post*, http://www.scmp.com, accessed March 5, 2018; Amy Nordrum, "Medical Tourism on the Rise as Chinese Patients Seek Care at U.S. Hospitals, American Companies Court China's Healthcare Market," *International Business Times*, http://www.ibtimes.com, accessed March 5, 2018; Elizabeth Baier, "Mayo Readies Service to Draw Patients from China," *MPR News*, http://www.mprnews.org, accessed March 5, 2018; Shan Juan, "Top U.S. Hospital Taps Chinese Medical Tourism Market," *China Daily*, http://europe.chinadaily.com, accessed March 5, 2018; Farfan Wang, "Desperate Chinese Seek Medical Care Abroad," *Wall Street Journal*, http://www.wsj.com, accessed March 5, 2018; Sui-Lee Wee, "China's Ill, and Wealthy, Look Abroad for Medical Treatment," *New York Times*, http://www.nytimes.com accessed March 5, 2018.

Case 4.3 Unbiased Travel Reviews: TripAdvisor Speaks Your Language

Can you guess which global travel website has over 600 million reviews and opinions; contains 60 million photos from travelers worldwide; and includes more than 7.5 million hotels, bed and breakfasts, specialty lodging, vacation rentals, restaurants, and attractions in 136,000 destinations? It's TripAdvisor—and this travel review and booking site is one of the most recognized names in the global travel industry.

The Needham, Massachusetts–based company began in 2000 when its co-founder and CEO, Steve Kaufer, underwent the process of planning a trip to Mexico. During the planning process Kaufer's wife realized her husband's frustration with unbiased hotel reviews and the lack of user-generated information and feedback from travelers. Sure, plenty of beautiful pictures, well-heeled brochures, and online information with carefully selected testimonials were available. This ultimately led Kaufer to create an authentic, firsthand, user-generated feedback system and platform. Leveraging technology, today the TripAdvisor site attracts over 300 million users a month in search of firsthand travel research and experience.

During TripAdvisor's startup stage, in addition to offering edited content, the company added a button that allowed users to provide their own reviews. To the surprise of Kaufer and his team, user-generated content—primarily about hotels and restaurants—expanded exponentially and soon replaced the edited content upon which the company had sought to establish itself. Today, TripAdvisor operates 25 travel brands, including TripAdvisor, Airfarewatchdog, BookingBuddy, Cruise Critic, Family Vacation Critic, and FlipKey, to name just a few. The company operates websites internationally in 48 markets and 28 languages, in places such as Australia, China, Germany, Indonesia, Japan, Norway, Poland, Singapore, Thailand, Turkey, and the United States.

International expansion for TripAdvisor didn't happen overnight—and it was not without its challenges. However, because travel is inherently a global business, TripAdvisor's global reach and international scope have been a natural extension of its business. Since its users are moving all around the world, the company wanted to achieve a very global perspective by delivering the best, most accurate travel research to people regardless of where they live. Today the majority of the company's traffic comes from outside the United States, so the vast majority of features developed for the site are translated into over 30 languages.

TripAdvisor employs a multidomestic business strategy that allows the company to treat each foreign market in a unique way to appeal to the customs, tastes, and buying habits of each particular national market. Its 3,100 employees include those in the local community and time zone who understand local culture and traditions. This also allows customized marketing appeals for individual cultures or parts of the world. The company admits that it is a challenge to stay relevant to each local audience and to deal with local competition that exists in each market. With its user base in excess of 300 million and weekly software releases in a variety of languages, making sure the site feels relevant and local to each market is critical.

The external environment—which includes technology, politics, and the economy—has impacted TripAdvisor's business. In fact, concerns about the global economy, political differences, and acts of terrorism have impacted the near-term prospects for online travel. In addition, technology, including online travel agents (OTAs) and travel supplier websites, has forever changed the global travel industry. When aviation became more common in the mid-1920s, travel agencies and private retailers providing travel- and tourism-related services to the public on behalf of suppliers such as airlines, car rentals, cruise lines, hotels, railways, and package tours began to flourish. Today, TripAdvisor utilizes a technology platform to bring about easy access worldwide to leading online travel agencies, including Expedia, Orbitz, Travelocity, Hotels.com, Priceline, Booking.com, and more.

Kaufer agrees that the biggest change impacting his business is the way in which people use technology. Because a lot of Internet usage has moved to a mobile device, TripAdvisor has invested in in-destination functionality for its products so that people can use the application not just to plan their trip but also in short bursts while they are moving around and using their mobile phones. Kaufer's goal is for his global customer-base to bring the TripAdvisor experience with them on their trip.

TripAdvisor's comparative advantage lies in what Kaufer refers to as its universal value proposition—which allows travelers the ability to share their opinion, thereby helping other travelers to make their decisions based on those opinions. By learning the truth about where to go, where to stay, what to do, and even what to eat, Kaufer hopes that people worldwide will plan and book a trip that results in lifetime memories.

Questions for Critical Thinking

1. Kaufer agrees that the biggest change impacting his business is the way in which people use technology. Consider virtual reality and virtual tours, where travelers can experience places before they even go there. Discuss ways that technology such as this will continue to impact TripAdvisor's business. In what ways can TripAdvisor continue to utilize technology to benefit both the company and its user base of travelers?
2. TripAdvisor recently introduced an airline reviews platform to include all major airlines across the globe, to include pricing and service and overall quality experienced by travelers. What other platforms such as these could Trip Advisor capitalize upon?
3. As hotels try to get customers to book stays directly and Google enhances its own travel products, who are additional TripAdvisor competitors? How does TripAdivsor differentiate itself?
4. Have you ever used a travel site to help plan a trip? If so, discuss your experience. If not, discuss your thoughts about websites that provide user-generated content. Is the content accurate? Credible? What are the pros and cons?

Sources: Adele Blair, "Airbnb, TripAdvisor, Product Review: We still trust strangers' recommendations," *Sydney Morning Herald*, accessed March 5, 2018, http://www.smh.com.au; Dennis Schaal, "Buying TripAdvisor: Would Antitrust Issues Kill a Priceline or Google Acquisition?" Skift.com, https://skift.com, accessed March 5, 2018; Yue Wu, "The Story of TripAdvisor," http://www.onlineeconomy.org/t, accessed March 5, 2018; Company website, "Fact Sheet," https://www.tripadvisor.com/PressCenter-c4-Fact_Sheet.html, accessed March 5, 2018; Victoria Abbott Riccardi "A Day in the Life of TripAdvisor CEO Steve Kaufer," *Boston Globe*, http://bostonglobe.com, accessed March 5, 2018.

CHAPTER 5

Forms of Business Ownership and Organization

LEARNING OBJECTIVES

1. Discuss why most businesses are small businesses.
2. Determine the contributions of small businesses to the economy.
3. Discuss why small businesses fail.
4. Describe the features of a successful business plan.
5. Identify the available assistance for small businesses.
6. Explain franchising.
7. Outline the forms of private business ownership.
8. Describe public and collective ownership of business.
9. Discuss organizing a corporation.
10. Explain what happens when businesses join forces.

Overview

Do you prefer to work for a big company or a small one? Do you plan to start your own business? If you're thinking about striking out on your own, you're not alone. On any given day in the United States, many people are in the process of starting a new business. But before you enter the business world—as an employee or an owner—you need to understand the industry in which a company operates, as well as the size and framework of the firm's organization. For example, V&J Holdings is a business in the fast-growing service franchise segment. It's important to remember that most large businesses—like Patagonia and Tesla—began as small businesses.

Several variables affect the way a business is organized, including how easily it can be set up, access to financing, tolerance of financial risk, and strengths and weaknesses of competitors, as well as the strengths and weaknesses of your company.

This chapter begins by focusing on small-business ownership, including the advantages and disadvantages of small-business ventures, the contributions of small business to the economy, and the reasons small businesses fail. The chapter examines the services provided by the U.S. government's Small Business Administration, the role of women and minorities in small business, and alternatives for small businesses such as franchising.

Changemaker

© Journal Sentinel/USA Today

Valerie Daniels-Carter, President and CEO

Company: V & J Holdings

Industry: Multi-Unit Franchising

Website: http://www.vjfoods.com

To call Valerie Daniels-Carter a multi-faceted woman would be an understatement. As a CEO, philanthropist, motivational speaker, and author, she owns over 120 multi-unit, multi-concept, multi-state franchises employing 4,000 people. In 1984, along with her brother John, an attorney, Daniels-Carter purchased a single Burger King franchise. That was the beginning of Milwaukee, WI–based V&J Holdings, one of the largest women-owned and African-American-owned food service franchise operators in the United States.

V&J has grown from a single Milwaukee, WI Burger King restaurant into 12 stores. Add to that, 68 Pizza Huts throughout four states, six Captain D's (seafood), five Haagen-Dazs locations, and five Coffee Beanery stores. Teaming up with NBA basketball legend Shaquille O'Neal, Daniels-Carter jointly owns numerous Auntie Anne's soft pretzel stores. If that weren't enough, V&J has recently become a franchisor of MyYoMy Frozen Yogurt, and has an investment in Nino's Southern Sides (fried chicken).

In the early 1980s, Daniels-Carter remembers that "there was a clear definition of what franchisee owners looked like," and as an African-American woman with a background in finance and banking, she laments that "there was not a welcoming mat for females and minorities." With a push for minority recruitment by Burger King in the early 1980s, Daniels-Carter made a trip to Minneapolis to meet with the regional manager and after some resistance, her perseverance paid off. Of all African American franchisees, 78% own a single unit while only 22% own more than one unit.

Daniels-Carter, a woman of faith with a hands-on approach, believes in and insists on integrity, recognition, accountability, responsibility, respect, communication, and commitment to excellence and passion. With a corporate philosophy of "YATSE," she lives and breathes the mantra "You Are The Standard of Excellence."

Named in honor of her late mother, Daniels-Carter helped fund a community center in Milwaukee that houses numerous schools, a Boys and Girls Club, a credit union, and an affordable health clinic. Daniels-Carter has gained much respect in the competitive world of franchising, and the challenge has been "daunting," she says. "If you'd have asked me 30 years ago, would I have the opportunity to have 4,000 employees and over 120 restaurants. . . . I would not have seen that."

Sources: Company website, "About Us," http://www.vjfoods.com, accessed March 11, 2018; company website, "Our President," http://www.vjfoods.com, accessed March 11, 2018; Chris Kenning, "Black Female Franchise Owner Battled 'Cement Ceiling' in Quest for Success," *USA Today,* http://www.usatoday.com, accessed March 11, 2018; Tracy Jan, "Only 2 of the 300 Case Studies Read by First-Year Harvard Business School Students Include Black Executives," *Washington Post,* http://www.washingtonpost.com, accessed March 11, 2018; Carolyn Brown, "Mega Franchise Owner Valerie R. Daniels Carter Named a Women of Power Legacy Award Winner," *Black Enterprise,* http://www.blackenterprise.com, accessed March 11, 2018; Nancy Weingartner, "Valerie Daniels-Carter, the Ultimate Do-Good Franchisee," *Franchise Times,* http://www.franchisetimes.com, accessed March 11, 2018.

The chapter then moves on to an overview of the forms of private business-ownership—sole proprietorships, partnerships, and corporations. In addition, the features of businesses owned by employees and families, as well as not-for-profit organizations, are discussed. Public and collective ownership are examined. The chapter concludes with an explanation of structures and operations typical of larger companies and a review of the major types of business alliances.[1]

1 Most Businesses Are Small Businesses

Although many people associate the term *business* with corporate giants such as Walmart, Amazon, and General Motors, 99.7% of all U.S. companies are considered small businesses. Small businesses have generated 62% of new jobs over the past two decades and employ close to half of all private-sector workers.[2] Small businesses are also the launching pad for new ideas and products. They hire 43% of high-tech workers, such as scientists, engineers, and computer programmers, who devote their time to developing new goods and services.[3]

What Is a Small Business?

How can you tell a small business from a large one? The Small Business Administration (SBA), the federal agency most directly involved with this sector of the economy, defines a

Michael Buckner/Getty Images for Paper Crown + Rifle Paper Co.

Anna Bond is founder and CEO of Rifle Paper Company, a stationery and lifestyle brand.

small business independent business with fewer than 500 employees, not dominant in its market.

small business as an "independent business having fewer than 500 employees." However, those bidding for government contracts or applying for government assistance may vary in size depending on the industry. For example, small manufacturers fall in the 500-worker range, whereas wholesalers must employ fewer than 100. Construction firms may generate up to $36.5 million in annual sales and still be considered small businesses, while farms or other agricultural businesses are designated small if they generate less than $750,000 annually.[4]

Because government agencies offer benefits designed to help small businesses compete with larger firms, small-business owners want to determine whether their companies meet the standards for small-business designation—certainly not a "one size fits all" approach. If it qualifies, a company may be eligible for government loans or for government purchasing programs that encourage proposals from smaller suppliers. With this type of assistance, small companies might eventually expand and become larger businesses.

Typical Small-Business Ventures

A childhood pastime of stamp collecting and letter writing to pen pals piqued Anna Bond's interest in print, graphic design, and illustration. Along with her husband, Bond, founder and CEO of Rifle Paper Company, started the stationery company from her garage apartment in Winter Park, Florida with just $10,000. After working odd jobs as a freelance graphic designer, Bond and her husband, then a musician in a bluegrass band, are proud of a company with no debt or outside investors. Their multi-million dollar company, best known for its greeting cards, art prints, and planners, has kept overhead low—and growth has been slow and careful. A dream project of a lifetime became a reality when Bond designed a recent "LOVE" stamp for the U.S. Postal Service.[5]

There has been a steady erosion of small businesses in some industries as larger firms have bought out small, independent businesses and replaced them with larger operations. The number of independent home improvement stores has fallen dramatically as Lowe's and other national discounters have increased the size and number of their stores. However, the businesses less likely to be gobbled up are those that sell personalized services, rely on certain locations, and keep their expenses (excluding labor and direct materials) low.

Nonfarming-related small firms create more than half the nation's gross domestic product (GDP). Nonfarming, as its name indicates, does not include farm workers, private household employees, or nonprofits, and refers to goods, construction, and manufacturing companies in the United States. In the past, many of these businesses focused on retailing or a service industry, such as insurance. More recently, however, small companies have carved out an important niche for themselves: providing busy consumers with customized services that range from pet sitting to personal shopping. These businesses cater to the needs of individual customers more effectively than larger firms.

As **Figure 5.1** shows, small businesses provide most jobs in construction, agricultural services, wholesale trade, other services, and within the real estate, lending, and leasing industries. Retailing to the consumer is another important industry for small firms. Online and retailing giants such as Amazon and Target may be the best-known companies, but smaller stores and websites outnumber them. And these small companies can be very successful, as Anna Bond of Rifle Paper Company illustrates, often because they can keep their overhead expenses low.

Small business also plays a significant role in agriculture. Although most farm acreage is in the hands of large, corporate farms, almost 90% of U.S. farms are owned by individual farmers or families, not partners or shareholders.[6] The family farm is a classic example of a

TABLE 5.1 Small Business Facts and Figures

Mostly Small	Small businesses comprise 99.9% of all firms and 99.7% of firms with paid employees. Out of almost 30 million businesses, all but 19,000 are small.
Exporters: Small and Powerful	Almost all U.S. exporters are small businesses representing 97.6% of all exporting companies with $440 million in exports representing 33% of total export value.
Job Creation	Small businesses generate over 60% of new jobs, which drives employment growth. About 48% (or 58 million) private-sector employees work for a small business.
Family Businesses	One in five small businesses is family-owned. Most family businesses are in management of companies and enterprises, real estate, leasing, accommodations, and food services.
Home-Based Businesses	Half of small businesses are home-based. Four out of five businesses without paid employees are home-based. Most home-based businesses fall into the information, construction, professional, scientific, and technical services industries.
Hi-Tech	Almost 99% of high-technology industries are small businesses. They consist primarily of computer systems design, architecture, or engineering.
Franchise	Less than 3% of small businesses are franchises. More specifically, 2.3% of nonemployer firms are franchises, as are 5.3% of small employers and 9.6% of large employers.
Average Employee Count	Average small business employment in a recent year reached an average of 6.1 employees.
Demographics of Owners	Approximately 29% of all small businesses are minority-owned. American Indian and Alaska Natives comprise 1%; Asians comprise 7.1%; Black or African Americans comprise 9.5%; Hispanics comprise 12.2%; Native and Pacific Islander comprise 0.2%; females comprise 36%; and veterans comprise 9.3%.

Sources: "The Big Impact of Small Business: 9 Amazing Facts," *Forbes,* www.forbes.com, accessed March 8, 2018; government website, "Frequently Asked Questions About Small Business," https://www.sba.gov, accessed March 8, 2018.

small-business operation. It is independently owned and operated, with a limited number of employees, including family members. Cider Hill Farm in Massachusetts is one such farm. Together, three generations of the Cook family operate the farm producing fruits and vegetables, apples from its orchards, and honey from its on-site beehives. In addition, Cider Hill makes its own fresh cider and cider doughnuts every day and operates a well-stocked country store on the property. During growing season, the farm hosts field trips for schools, offers hay rides, and creates a corn maze in its fields. All of these activities contribute to the income of the farm. The Cooks are also dedicated to environmentally friendly farming technologies. Cider Hill operates three wind turbines and uses solar cells to help power its buildings.[7]

home-based businesses firm operated from the residence of the business owner.

Fifty percent of established small businesses in the United States are **home-based businesses**—firms operated from the residence of the business owner.[8] People who operate home-based firms often do so because this type of work allows them more control over their business as well as their personal time. Whether you're a morning person or a night owl, in many cases you can structure your business hours accordingly. Access to the Internet and availability of mobile computing devices and technology make it convenient to run a home-based business. Reduced overhead costs such as leasing office or warehouse space is another major attraction of home-based businesses. Drawbacks include difficulty separating business and personal life, isolation, and less customer visibility—except, of course, if your customers visit you online. In that case, they don't care where your office is located.

Technology not only allows small businesses to compete in a global marketplace, but it also provides the necessary tools to run a business and to engage with customers

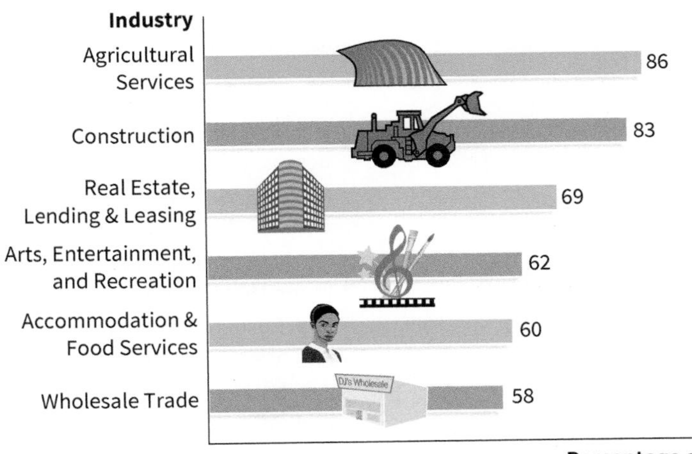

Source: Office of Advocacy, U.S. Small Business Administration, "Small Business Profile: United States," http://www.sba.gov/advocacy, accessed March 8, 2018.

FIGURE 5.1 Industries Dominated by Small Businesses

worldwide. Consider how social media and online marketplaces, for example, allow small businesses to market, sell, and export products worldwide. As e-commerce and mobile commerce continue to explode, small businesses have the tools to build new relationships outside local areas, and to increase market share. Nebraska–based Fat Brain toys is a manufacturer and e-retailer of educational toys. How does a small business like Fat Brain compete with the likes of online giants such as Amazon and Walmart? The company specializes in brain teasers and multiplayer games meant to inspire creativity in children. Started by husband and wife Mark and Karen Carson from the basement of their home over 15 years ago, the company has close to 50 full-time employees and a distribution center in Omaha, Nebraska. In a recent Fat Brain "Kidventor" contest, eleven-year-old Alexander Xiong of Brooklyn Park, Minnesota was chosen as the grand prize winner of the Door Pong game, a ping pong game that can be easily mounted to any doorway.[9]

American business history is filled with inspirational stories of innovators who launched companies in barns, garages, warehouses, and attics. For visionaries such as the late Apple Computer founder Steve Jobs and co-founder Steve Wozniak, the logical option for transforming their technical idea into a commercial reality was to begin work in a family garage. The impact of today's entrepreneurs, including home-based businesses, is discussed in more depth in Chapter 6.

Assessment Check

1. How does the Small Business Administration (SBA) define *small business*?
2. In what industries do small businesses play a significant role?

2 Contributions of Small Business to the Economy

Small businesses form the core of the U.S. economy. Businesses with fewer than 500 employees generate more than half the nation's GDP. In a recent year, these companies accounted for 32.9% of known export value ($440 billion out of $1.3 trillion).[10] Small firms are credited with U.S. competitiveness in a number of global markets.[11]

Creating New Jobs

Small businesses make tremendous contributions to the U.S. economy and to society as a whole. One impressive contribution is the number of new jobs created each year by small businesses. While it varies from year to year and remains dependent on the state of the economy, on average two of every three new jobs are created by companies with fewer than 500 employees.[12] A significant share of these jobs is created by the smallest companies, those with four or fewer employees. In a study conducted by the Kauffman Foundation, a research nonprofit, researchers found that a more accurate method of job creation prediction is a company's age rather than its size. Research has found that younger companies or newer businesses create more jobs, regardless of size.[13] **Table 5.2** illustrates some of the best growth industries for starting a new business.

Small businesses also contribute to the economy by hiring workers who traditionally have had difficulty finding jobs at larger firms, such as military veterans returning to the workforce, former welfare recipients, and workers with various challenges. The SBA provides incentives for companies to hire these types of workers. Small firms often hire younger, teenage workers.

Creating New Industries

Small firms give businesspeople the opportunity and outlet for developing new ideas. Sometimes these new ideas become entirely new industries. Many of today's largest and most

TABLE 5.2 Best Industries for Starting a New Business

Industry	Small Business Idea	Projected Trend
Senior Care Services	Health and mobility products, errands and assistance, adult daycare	The entire baby boomer generation will have reached age 65 by 2030. Seniors will make up 1/4 of the entire U.S. population with a longer life expectancy than previous generations.
Virtual Reality	3D movies, real estate marketing, gaming, team building exercises, social media VR interaction, training, and meditation	The VR marketing is growing at an astounding rate, and immersing the user in a realistic sensory experience is the work of software and hardware vendors.
Technology Consulting	Social media consulting, training, and coaching	Social media is second nature to Millennials: 88% of people between the ages of 18 and 29 used Facebook every day in a recent year, compared with 62% of those over the age of 65, according to a Pew Research Center study.
Pet Care	Dog walking, grooming, and boarding	Tech innovations are taking over this industry, which is valued at $60 billion in the United States.
Online Education	Offer coursework through online platform including supplemental instruction in grade-level reading, math, science, history, or standardized test preparation	As more and more American schools struggle to prepare students for both standardized testing and life outside the classroom, there's ample opportunity for teachers and subject matter experts to earn income through online courses.
Enrichment Activities Children's Services	Private businesses offering enrichment activities outside of school such as gymnastics, music, tennis, soccer, golf, swimming, yoga, art, and athletics are filling a niche.	The number of children in the United States continues to grow, and at the same time, school budgets for traditional academics and enrichment activities continue to shrink.
Mobile Businesses	Businesses that travel to their customers—wherever they happen to be. They include auto repair, car wash, electronics services, IT support, personal training, dog walking and grooming, and massage.	As consumers become more accustomed to instant gratification, accessibility, and convenience, mobile businesses are at the forefront of an emerging trend. Keeping your business mobile avoids the cost of overhead for a physical location.
Food & Beverage	Mobile Food Trucks	Consumer demand for unique and gourmet food trucks has contributed to a boom in affordable meals from specialty food trucks and street vendors. (See the video case at the end of this chapter for more about food trucks.)
Supermarkets & Grocery Stores	Ethnic Supermarkets	As the U.S. Asian and Hispanic populations continue to grow, so does the demand for culturally diverse specialty foods for home consumption.
Healthcare & Wellness	Corporate Wellness Services	As healthcare costs continue to rise, corporate wellness services provide companies and workplaces with low-cost and convenient alternatives to healthcare through on-site care, consulting, wellness fairs, or fitness offerings.
Construction	Home Builders and Residential Construction	Building material dealers, home center and hardware stores, and residential real estate developers are expected to continue their growth trajectory as the housing market continues its rebound.
Financial Services	Financial Planning	As more Baby Boomers plan for retirement, growth in this sector is expected to continue.

Sources: "50 Best Small Business Ideas & Opportunities in USA for 2018," https://www.profitableventure.com, accessed March 8, 2018; Susan Ward, "Best Small Business Opportunities for 2018," *The Balance*, https://www.thebalance.com, accessed March 8, 2018; Meredith Wood, "The 5 Most Profitable Industries for Small Business Owners in 2018," *Fundera*, https://www.fundera.com, accessed March 8, 2018; Jackie Zimmerman, "The 5 Best Industries for Starting a Business 2018," *Nerd Wallet*, https://www.nerdwallet.com, accessed March 8, 2018.

successful firms, such as Whole Foods, Google, and Amazon, began as small businesses. When 16-year-old John W. Nordstrom left Sweden for America with $5 in his pocket, he dreamed of something bigger. With enough savings, he opened his first shoe store in Seattle in 1901. Today, Nordstrom is a multibillion-dollar retailer that is well known for its customer service.[14]

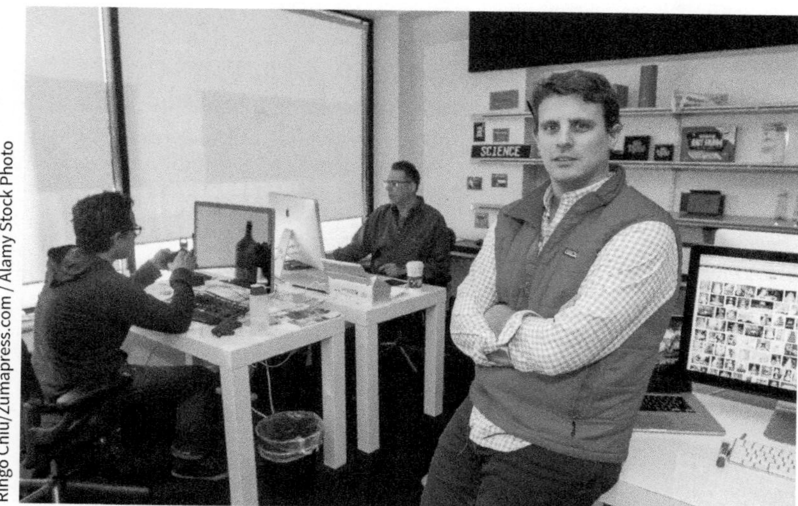
Ringo Chiu/Zumapress.com / Alamy Stock Photo

Michael Dubin is CEO and co-founder of Dollar Shave Club—purchased by consumer product giant, Unilever. Dollar Shave Club has adapted to the needs of consumers by offering an online monthly subscription service of body grooming products.

New industries are created when small businesses adapt to the needs of consumers. The digital disruption of banking systems, known for being slow and archaic, has created an ecosystem of financial technology specialists, as described in the "Business & Technology" feature.

New industries can be created when small businesses adapt to shifts in consumer interests and preferences. For example, the idea of offering shaving accessories and services for a man's face, scalp, and body—dubbed "manscaping" by marketers—has taken root in the U.S. economy, with small businesses like Dollar Shave Club, an online monthly subscription service (see photo), providing body grooming products and services. Services include facial hair "styling"—beard, mustache, and goatee shaping and scalp and body hair waxing and shaving.[15]

Finally, new industries may be created when both the business world and consumers recognize a need for change. The recent emphasis on environmental responsibility—ranging from recycling and reuse of goods to reducing the amount of energy consumed—has fostered a whole new industry of green products and services, many produced by small companies.

Business & Technology

Financial Technology Firms Fund Small Businesses

Technology has changed the landscape for small business owners, who less than a decade ago had few financing options beyond traditional lending institutions such as banks. Fueled by software technology, a new industry called FinTech (Financial technology) has emerged over the past several years. Alternative sources of small business lenders include Kiva, OnDeck, Funding Circle, and LendingClub. In addition, companies such as Intuit, PayPal, Stripe, and Square are now entering the small business lending space.

Small businesses, dependent on credit for growth, might typically spend as much as 25 hours filling out loan applications at traditional banks. Technology allows for a quicker, easier application process—sometimes less than an hour—with quicker access to cash. Typically, money transfers among FinTech start-up companies occur within a few days as compared to several weeks or even months at a traditional bank. Compared to a traditional lending officer, the technology of alternative lenders allows for newer methods of predictive modeling and, quite possibly, a more accurate assessment of businesses' credit risk.

San Francisco–based Kiva, which provides small business loans of up to $10,000 at 0% interest, relies more on "social capital" than a traditional credit evaluation. Prospective borrowers are required to crowdfund $25 each from 10 to 20 friends before Kiva will allow fund-raising efforts using its platform of 1.3 million online lenders. If the current trend of using mobile apps and websites for business lending continues, the technology created by these alternative lenders may also contribute to continued U.S. job growth and further innovation for the FinTech industry and the small business sector.

Questions for Critical Thinking

1. **Rather than using a conventional approach to credit evaluation, Kiva evaluates a company's "character" (social capital) and its "trust network" to measure creditworthiness. What are the benefits and shortfalls of this approach?**
2. **What impact, if any, will FinTech companies have on the way traditional banks do business? What must traditional banks do to remain competitive in the small-business lending sector?**

Sources: Organization website, "69,079 People Have Supported a Small Business Owner on Kiva Zip," https://zip.kiva.org, accessed March 8, 2018; Amy Feldman, "Kiva to Offer Its Zero-Interest Crowdfunded Loans to Small Businesses Nationwide," *Forbes*, http://www.forbes.com, accessed March 8, 2018; Matilda James, "Lending to Small Businesses: Technology Companies' New Venture," *Yahoo Finance*, http://finance.yahoo.com, accessed March 8, 2018; Mike Milan, "Traditional Banks v. Alternative Lenders: How Goliath Can Beat David," *Banking*, http://www.banking.com, accessed March 8, 2018; Karen Mills, "Can Lending Technology Revive America's Small Businesses?" *Harvard Business Review*, https://hbr.org, accessed March 8, 2018; Marcus Wohlsen, "Square's Found a Way to Beat Banks at the Loan Business," *Wired*, http://www.wired.com, accessed March 8, 2018.

Innovation

Small businesses are adept at developing new and improved goods and services. Innovation is often the sole reason for the founding of a new business. In a typical year, small firms develop twice as many product innovations per employee as larger firms. They also produce more than 16 times more patents per employee than larger firms.[16]

Key innovations developed by small businesses in the 20th century include the airplane, the personal computer, soft contact lenses, and the zipper. Innovations, many technology-related, that already drive small businesses in the 21st century include artificial intelligence, machine learning, virtual reality, autonomous vehicles, digital assistants, and cloud computing, to name a few.

Assessment Check

1. What are the three key ways in which small businesses contribute to the economy?
2. How are new industries created?

3 Why Small Businesses Fail

Small businesses play an integral role in the U.S. economy. But one of the reasons they are so successful is also the reason they might fail: Their founders are willing to take a risk. Some of the most common shortcomings that plague a small firm include management inexperience, inadequate financing, and the challenge of meeting government regulations.

As **Figure 5.2** shows, nearly 7 out of every 10 new businesses survive at least two years. About 50% make it to the five-year mark. But by the tenth year, 70% will have closed. However, keep in mind that these statistics can be misleading—they include companies that have changed their names, changed their legal structure, merged into another firm, or been sold. Let's look a little more closely at why this happens.[17]

Management Shortcomings

One of the most common causes of small-business failure is mismanagement. These may include overconfidence, lack of people skills, inadequate knowledge of finance, inability to track inventory or sales, poor assessment of the competition or customer, or simply poor time management or the lack of time to do everything required. While large firms often have the resources to recruit specialists in areas such as marketing and finance, the owner of a small business often winds up doing too many things at once.

This could result in poor decision making, which could lead to a company's failure. Krispy Kreme was once a small business that expanded too quickly by taking on too much debt. The company's near failure had nothing to do with the quality of its doughnuts. In addition, consumers turned their taste buds toward more healthful snacks and breakfast foods produced by competitors. More recently, Krispy Kreme became a privately held company when it was acquired by JAB Beech, an investment group based in Germany specializing in consumer goods. Over time, JAB Beech may take Krispy Kreme public again.[18]

Owners of small businesses can increase their chances of success if they become educated in the principles of business and entrepreneurship; know the industry in which they intend to operate; develop good customer service and interpersonal skills; understand their customers; hire and train motivated employees; and seek professional advice on issues such as finance, regulations, and other legal matters.[19]

Out of Business Within 2 to 10 Years

Gone Out of Business

100
80
60
40
20
0

33%
2 yrs.

50%
5 yrs.

70%
10 yrs.

*Data includes companies that have changed their names, changed their legal structure, merged into another firm, or have been sold.

Source: Office of Advocacy, U.S. Small Business Administration, "Frequently Asked Questions: Advocacy Small Business Statistics and Research," http://www.sba.gov/advocacy, accessed March 8, 2018.

FIGURE 5.2 Rate of Business Failures*

Inadequate Financing

Money provides the growth engine of any business. Every business—large or small—needs a certain amount of financing in order to operate, thrive, and grow. Another leading problem of small businesses is inadequate financing. First-time business owners often overestimate the funds their firms will generate from initial sales to allow for operations to continue. But building a business takes time and perseverance. Products must be developed, employees have to be hired, technology must be implemented, distribution strategy has to be determined, office or retail space might have to be secured, and suppliers established. Most small businesses—even those with minimal start-up costs—sometimes don't turn a profit for months or even years.[20]

Although there are stories about business founders starting firms with just a few hundred dollars loaned by family or with a cash advance from a credit card, commercial banks and other financial institutions are the largest lenders to small businesses, accounting for over half of total traditional credit to small firms. This type of financing includes credit lines and loans for nonresidential mortgages, vehicles, specialized equipment, and leases.[21]

With less money to spend on employees, marketing, inventory, and other business costs, successful small companies need to be creative. Ann Dickerson and her husband, Bill Zack, of Signal Mountain, Tennessee, are both former sports journalists. They decided to pursue their love of cooking to embark on a new career. When the state of Tennessee changed the law to allow legal moonshine, a once illegal 100-proof liquor, Ann and Bill saw the opportunity to create the first ever moonshine bakery. After diligent experimentation and testing, the two came up with the perfect cake batter. Combining their own concoction of moonshine with homemade cake batter, Tennessee Moonshine Cakes (shown in photo) was created. The "witch's brew" glaze on the cakes is where the moonshine comes in, although the alcohol evaporates during the baking process. The cakes are sold through retailers, online, and at Tennessee airports and festivals.[22]

Courtesy of Tennessee Moonshine Cakes

Ann Dickerson and her husband, Bill Zack, took a unique cake idea and turned it into a successful business.

Government Regulation

Small-business owners cite their struggle to comply with government regulations as one of the biggest challenges they face. A small firm has limited staff and fewer resources to deal with regulatory requirements. For example, compliance consumes immense amounts of financial capital. This can drain hours of an owner's time, and it also diverts a small firm from its core business. It may also result in missed opportunities and delayed growth. A large company can better cope with reporting requirements. Larger firms often find that it makes economic sense to hire or contract with specialists in specific types of regulation, such as employment law and workplace safety regulations. Small firms, on average, spend almost five times more per employee than larger firms do to comply with federal regulations.[23]

Recognizing the burden of regulation on small businesses, Congress sometimes exempts the smallest companies from certain regulations. For example, small businesses with 49 or fewer employees are exempt from both the Personal Protection and Affordable Care Act and the Family and Medical Leave Act, which gives employees up to 12 weeks of unpaid leave each year to take care of a newborn child, adopt a child, or care for a family member who has serious health problems.[24] Most small-business owners comply with employment and other laws, believing that such compliance is ethically correct and fosters better employee relations than trying to determine which regulations don't apply to a small business.

Taxes are another burdensome expense for a small business. In addition to local, state, and federal income taxes, employers must pay taxes covering workers' compensation insurance, Social Security payments, and unemployment benefits. Although large companies have similar expenses, they generally have more resources to cover them. But there are also tax incentives designed to help small businesses. These incentives cover a broad range, including HUBZones (Historically Underutilized Business Zones), tax credits for use of biodiesel and renewable fuels, increased research activities, pension plan start-up, and access for individuals with disabilities.[25]

Assessment Check

1. What percentage of small businesses remain in operation five years after starting? Ten years?
2. What are the three main causes of small-business failure?

4 The Business Plan: A Foundation for Success

Large or small, every business needs a plan in order to succeed. While there are tales of firms launched from an idea scribbled on a napkin at a restaurant or sketched out on a white board in a dorm room, the idea has a greater chance of becoming a reality if it is backed by a solid plan. A **business plan** is a written document that provides an orderly statement of a company's goals, the methods by which it intends to achieve these goals, and the standards by which it will measure its achievements. The business plan is often the document that secures financing for a firm and creates a framework for the organization (see photo).

business plan written document that provides an orderly statement of a company's goals, methods, and standards.

Business plans give the organization a sense of purpose. They identify the firm's mission and goals. They create measurable standards and outline a strategy for reaching company objectives. A typical business plan includes the following sections:

- an *executive summary* that briefly answers the who, what, where, when, why, and how questions for the business
- an *introduction* that includes a general statement of the concept, purpose, and objectives of the proposed business
- separate *financial* and *marketing sections* that describe the firm's target market and marketing plan as well as detailed financial forecasts of the need for funds and when the firm is expected to break even—the level of sales at which revenues equal costs
- *résumés of principals*—especially in plans written to obtain financing

Within this structure, an effective business plan contains the written soul of a firm. A good plan addresses the following issues:

- *The company's mission and the vision of its founders.* Look at the home page of any firm's website and you will find its mission. At the website for New York–based Warby Parker, an

Dimitrije Paunovic/iStockphoto

The business plan is often the document that secures financing for a company and creates a framework for the organization. Business plans identify the firm's missions and goals. They create measurable standards and outline a strategy for reaching company objectives.

online subscription eyewear company, visitors learn that "For every pair purchased, a pair is distributed to someone in need. Buy a Pair, Give a Pair." To date, Warby Parker has sold and distributed more than three million pairs of eyeglasses.[26] This milestone demonstrates why the company was founded and what it intends to accomplish.

- *An outline of what makes the company unique*. Why start a business that's just like hundreds of others? An effective business plan describes what distinguishes the firm and its products from competitors. Warby Parker illustrates a unique business model with its Buy a Pair, Give a Pair program.
- *The customers*. A business plan identifies who the firm's customers will be and how it will serve their needs.
- *The competition*. A business plan addresses existing and potential competitors with a strategy for creating superior or unique offerings. Studying the competition can provide valuable information about what works and what doesn't in the marketplace.
- *Financial evaluation of the industry and market conditions*. This knowledge helps develop a credible financial forecast and budget.
- *Assessment of the risks*. Every business undertaking involves risks. A solid business plan acknowledges these and outlines a strategy for dealing with them.[27]

Whether a company's intention is to revolutionize an entire industry on a global scale or improve the lives of individuals by providing them with eyeglasses, the business plan is a major factor in its success. For more detailed information on how to write a business plan, see Appendix D, "Developing a Business Plan."

Assessment Check

1. What are the five main sections of a business plan?
2. Why is an effective business plan important to the success of a firm?

5 Assistance for Small Businesses

An important part of organizing a small business is financing its activities. Once a business plan has been created, various sources can be tapped for loans and other types of financing. These include government agencies as well as private investors.

Small Business Administration

Small Business Administration (SBA) principal government agency concerned with helping small U.S. firms.

Small businesses can benefit from using the resources provided by the **Small Business Administration (SBA)**. The SBA is the principal government agency concerned with helping small U.S. firms, and it is the advocate for small businesses within the federal government. Several thousand employees staff the SBA's Washington, D.C., headquarters and its 1,800 regional and field offices. The SBA's mission is to aid, counsel, assist, and protect the interests of small business concerns, to preserve free competitive enterprise, and to maintain and strengthen the overall economy of the nation.[28]

Financial Assistance from the SBA Contrary to popular belief, the SBA seldom provides direct business loans. Nor does it provide outright grants to start or expand small businesses. Instead, the SBA *guarantees* small-business loans made by private lenders, including banks and other institutions. To qualify for an SBA-backed loan, borrowers must be "unable to secure conventional commercial financing on reasonable terms and be a 'small business' as defined by SBA size standards."[29] Direct SBA loans are available in only a few special situations, such as natural disaster recovery and energy conservation or development programs.

The SBA also guarantees **microloans** of up to $50,000 to start-ups and other very small firms. The average loan is $13,000, with a maximum repayment term of six years.[30] Microloans may be used to buy equipment or operate a business but not to buy real estate or pay off other loans. These loans are available from nonprofit organizations located in most states. Other sources of microloans include the federal Economic Development Administration, some state governments, and certain private lenders, such as credit unions. State and local programs offer business grants for creation of energy-efficient technology, child care centers, or marketing campaigns for tourism, for example.

microloans small-business loans often used to buy equipment or operate a business.

Small-business loans are also available through SBA-licensed organizations called *Small Business Investment Companies (SBICs)*, which are run by experienced venture capitalists. SBICs use their own capital, supplemented with government loans, to invest in small businesses. Like banks, SBICs are profit-making enterprises, but they are likely to be more flexible than banks in their lending decisions. Large companies that used SBIC financing when they were small start-ups include Apple, FedEx, and Staples (see photo).

Other Specialized Assistance Although government purchases represent a huge market, small companies have difficulty competing for this business with giant firms, which employ specialists to handle the volumes of paperwork involved in preparing proposals and completing bid applications. Today, many government procurement programs set aside portions of government spending for small companies; an additional SBA role is to help small firms secure these contracts. With set-aside programs for small businesses, up to 23% of certain government contracts should be awarded to small businesses.[31]

Every federal agency with buying authority must maintain an Office of Small and Disadvantaged Business Utilization to ensure that small businesses receive a reasonable portion of government procurement contracts. To help connect small businesses with government agencies, the SBA's website offers Central Contractor Registration, which includes a search engine for finding business opportunities as well as a chance for small businesses to provide information about themselves. Set-aside programs are also common in the private sector, particularly among major corporations.

In addition to help with financing and government procurement, the SBA delivers a variety of other services to small businesses. It provides information and advice through toll-free telephone numbers and its website,

Small Business Investment Companies (SBICs) are for-profit businesses licensed by the Small Business Administration. Using their own capital, SBICs provide loans to small businesses. FedEx used SBIC financing when it was a small start-up company.

http://www.sba.gov. Through its SBA Learning Center, the SBA offers free online courses; sponsors inexpensive training courses on topics such as taxes, networking, and start-ups in cities and towns throughout the nation; and provides a free online library of more than 200 SBA publications and additional business resources. Business owners can find local resources by logging on to the SBA website and searching for SBA partners in their region. Local resource partners include small-business development centers, women's business centers, U.S. export assistance centers, and veterans business outreach centers.[32]

Local Assistance for Small Businesses

In conjunction with the federal government or on their own, state and local governments often have programs in place to help small businesses get established and grow. One such region is Washington State's Thurston County. The Thurston County Economic Development Council (EDC) was founded more than 30 years ago with the mission of "creating a vital and sustainable economy throughout our County that supports the livelihood and values of our residents." The Thurston County EDC provides information and assistance in business planning, licenses and registrations, taxes, and employment considerations. In addition, the council works to connect local businesses with each other and with industry experts, create marketing messages that attract new businesses and customers, and ensure that Thurston County plays an important role in the region's economy.[33] Organizations like the Thurston County EDC offer important resources and links for small businesses around the country.

business incubator local programs designed to provide low-cost shared business facilities, along with training, support, and networking, to small start-up ventures.

Business Incubators Some community agencies interested in encouraging business development have implemented a concept called a **business incubator** to provide low-cost shared business facilities, along with training, support, and networking, to small start-up ventures. See the "Business Model" feature to read about the incubator experience of Turning Technologies. Tenants often share clerical staff, computers, and other business services. The objective is that, with the incubator as a launch pad, after a few months or years, the fledgling business will be ready to move out and operate on its own.

More than 1,250 business incubator programs operate in the United States, and many are housed at colleges and universities. Well-known college business incubators can be found at Boston University, Syracuse University's Sandbox, the Innovation Depot at The University of Alabama, and The Garage at Northwestern University. Ninety-three percent are run by not-for-profit organizations focused on economic development. Nearly half of all incubators focus on new technology businesses, and more than half operate in urban areas. The Rice Alliance for Technology and Entrepreneurship at Houston's Rice University is a top incubator focused on clean technology.[34]

Private Investors

venture capital money invested in a business by another business firm or group of individuals in exchange for an ownership share or equity stake.

A small business may start with cash from a personal savings account or a loan from a family member. But small-business owners soon begin to look for greater sums of money in order to continue operating and eventually grow. They may want to continue with assistance from private investors. **Venture capital**—money invested in the small business by another business firm or group of individuals in exchange for an ownership or equity stake—can give the small business needed capital to expand. Venture capital technology trend investments by industry include artificial intelligence, augmented reality and virtual reality, bitcoin and blockchain, cybersecurity, digital health, fintech, and Internet of things (which will be discussed further in Chapter 14). Venture capital firms want to know explicit detail—and the makeup of leadership team and a startup's earning potential will be studied closely. San Francisco topped the list for the city with the largest venture capital-backed startups, followed by New York, San Jose (CA), Boston-Cambridge (MA), and Los Angeles (CA). Other cities include Seattle (WA), Miami (FL), Chicago (IL), Austin (TX), and Washington, DC.[35]

Business Model

Audience Response Technologies Create Interactive Learning

Turning Technologies, founded in Youngstown, Ohio, has enjoyed substantial growth and brought dozens of new jobs to a city whose decline in manufacturing and steel can still be felt. First supported by a business incubator, the firm has delivered more than six million ResponseCard clickers to K–12 schools, universities, and businesses worldwide.

Audience-response systems ("clickers") are the wireless keypads that spectators use on TV game shows to register their opinions or answers to questions. Teachers from kindergarten through college also use Turning's audience-response technology. Instructors can ask questions in class using other programs; have students key in answers—anonymously or not—using their remotes; and instantly collate the responses to credit attendance, measure understanding, and increase participation in the classroom. Government agencies and nonprofit organizations also use the systems for their training programs.

Most of Turning's more than 250 employees are young Ohioans who enjoy some of the same benefits as their Silicon Valley counterparts. The firm takes pride in being the kind of success story people have long thought "doesn't happen here."

The bottom line? Good products that are affordable, easy to use, and well marketed can help small companies become engines of growth and job creators.

Questions for Critical Thinking

1. List some possible advantages and disadvantages to the strategy of locating a company such as Turning Technologies outside high-tech hotspots where most companies can be found.
2. Turning Technologies is passionate about integrating technology to enhance and create better learning experiences. Compare and contrast the benefits of this technology for both students and teachers. How does it differ for each?

Sources: Company website, "Turning Technologies Story" and "Who We Are," http://www.turningtechnologies.com, accessed March 9, 2018; educational website, "Clickers: Turning Technologies," http://oregonstate.edu, accessed March 9, 2018; educational website, "Classroom Response Systems: Clickers," https://cft.vanderbilt.edu, accessed March 9, 2018; Anthony Ponce and Shawna Prince, "Classrooms Evolve Beyond Chalkboards, No. 2 Pencils," *NBC Chicago*, http://www.nbcchicago.com, accessed March 9, 2018; "Turning Technologies Releases New Polling Tools," *Successful Meetings*, http://www.successfulmeetings.com, accessed March 9, 2018.

Small-Business Opportunities for Women and Minorities

Over the past two decades, the number of women-owned businesses has grown 114% compared to the overall national growth rate of 44% for all businesses. In a recent year, there were an estimated 11.6 million women-owned businesses in the United States that employed nearly 9 million people and generated more than $1.7 trillion in revenues. Half of women-owned businesses can be found in the services industry, which include nail salons and pet care businesses; health care and social assistance (day care and home health services); and professional/scientific/technical services such as lawyers, accountants, architects, public relations firms, and management consultants.[36]

Women, like men, have a variety of reasons for starting their own companies. Some have a unique business idea that they want to bring to life. Others decide to strike out on their own when they lose their jobs or become frustrated with the bureaucracies in large companies. To this day, Michele Hoskins is grateful for the secret syrup recipe of honey, cream, and butter made by her great-great-great-grandmother, then a slave, for her plantation owner's family. Newly divorced, Hoskins was determined to create financial stability for her children. "There were no mentors for an African American entrepreneur in the food industry in those days," she remembers. With the passed-on recipe, Hoskins made the syrup in 55-gallon drums in her basement—hand filling and delivering each bottle to local grocery stores. Today, Michele's crème syrups, used for pancakes, waffles, and as condiments in sweet and savory dishes, can be found in 8,000 retail locations.[37]

Michele Hoskins created financial stability for herself by commercializing a family syrup recipe passed on to her by her great-great-great-grandmother. Her product is now in over 8,000 stores.

A recent study reveals that 86% of female millennials are leaving their corporate jobs to start their own companies and to follow their passion. Many cite not progressing fast enough, restrictions of corporate life, and the inability to meaningfully influence as their reasons. Female millennials leave when morals feel compromised—including wage inequality, being passed over for promotions, and a general lack of female mentors.

One of the many nationwide programs to assist women-owned firms offered by the Small Business Administration is the Contract Assistance for Women Business Owners program, which teaches women how to market their businesses to the federal government. Federal contracting opportunities for WOSBs (women-owned small businesses) have been expanded. Organizations such as the Center for Women's Business Research provide information, contacts, and other resources as well.

Business ownership is also an important opportunity for racial and ethnic minorities in the United States. In recent years, the growth in the number of businesses owned by African Americans, Hispanics, and Asian Americans has far outpaced the growth in the number of U.S. businesses overall. The relatively strong presence of minorities in the services and retail industries is especially significant because these industries contain the greatest number of businesses.

The Small Business Administration has programs targeted to minority-owned small businesses. SBA's 8(a) Business Development program helps minority-owned firms develop and grow through one-to-one counseling, training, and management and technical guidance, with access to government contracting opportunities.[38]

Assessment Check

1. What are the various ways the SBA helps small businesses?
2. What are business incubators?
3. Why are small businesses good opportunities for women and minorities?

6 Franchising

franchising contractual business arrangement between a manufacturer or other supplier, and a dealer such as a restaurant operator or retailer.

Using another company's established business model, **franchising** is a contractual business arrangement between a manufacturer or another supplier and a dealer such as a restaurant operator or a retailer. The contract specifies the methods by which the dealer markets the product of the supplier. Franchises can involve both goods and services, and many well-known brands like 7-Eleven and Wendy's have grown with this model. See Chapter 4 for further discussion about global franchising.

Starting a small, independent company can be a risky, time-consuming endeavor, but franchising can reduce the amount of time and effort needed to expand. The parent company has already developed and tested the concept, and the brand is often familiar to prospective customers.

Jim Gensheimer/San Jose Mercury News/KRT/NewsCom

International franchises have become more common. Baskin-Robbins has stores in over 50 countries, including Australia, China, Japan, Russia, and Vietnam.

The Franchising Sector

Franchised businesses are a huge part of the U.S. economy, accounting for over 18 million jobs in the U.S. workforce. The International Franchise Association reported that franchising is responsible for close to 759,000 businesses at a forecasted output of close to $1 trillion annually. The business sectors currently experiencing the most growth are quick service restaurants, retail products, personal services, and lodging.[39]

An increased appetite for lodging, haircuts, Big Macs, and Baskin-Robbins ice cream in the developing world coincides with rising levels of household income. Due to saturated U.S. markets, over the last decade companies like Yum! Brands, the parent company of Taco Bell, KFC, and Pizza Hut, expanded overseas in markets such as China, India, Africa, Russia, Indonesia, and Vietnam. However, recently Yum! Brands is beginning to retrench the efforts of its outlets in China due to increased competition and slow sales. Also becoming more common are other international franchises like Baskin-Robbins (see photo). Now owned by Dunkin' Brands, Baskin-Robbins ice cream has more than 7,800 stores worldwide in over 50 countries.[40]

Franchising Agreements

The two parties in a franchising agreement are the franchisee and the franchisor. The individual or business firm purchasing the franchise is called the **franchisee**. This business owner agrees to sell the goods or services of the franchisor under certain terms. The **franchisor** is the firm whose products are sold by the franchisee. For example, McDonald's Corp. is a franchisor. Your local McDonald's restaurant owner is a franchisee.

franchisee individual or business firm purchasing a franchise.

franchisor firm whose products are sold to customers by the franchisee.

Franchise agreements can be complex. They involve an initial purchase fee plus agreed-on start-up costs. Because the franchisee is representing the franchisor's brand, the franchisor usually stipulates the purchase of certain ingredients or equipment, pricing, and marketing efforts. The total start-up cost for a Great Clips hair salon franchise may be as low as $109,000.[41] In contrast, McDonald's is one of the more expensive franchises—total start-up costs can run more than $1 million. For this reason, businesspeople interested in purchasing a more costly franchise often do so in groups.

Benefits and Challenges of Franchising

Like any other type of business arrangement, franchising has its benefits and drawbacks. Benefits for the franchisor include opportunities for expansion (using other people's money) that might not otherwise be available. A franchised business can move into new geographic locations, including those overseas, at less expense and with the advantages of employing local workers and businesspeople who have intimate knowledge of local preferences. A good franchisee can manage a larger and more complex business—with fewer direct employees—than could be handled without the franchise option. In most cases, franchisees will be highly attentive to the management of their franchises because of their stake as business owners. If the business is run efficiently, the franchisor will probably experience a greater return on investment than if the firm were run entirely as a company-owned chain of retail shops, restaurants, or service establishments.

Finally, a successful franchisor can usually negotiate better pricing with suppliers for ingredients, supplies, even real estate, because of its financial strength and large volume purchases. This benefits the franchisees if the savings are passed along to them.[42]

Franchising can be the quickest way to become a business owner. Some people contend that it's also the least risky. Franchisees have the benefit of name recognition—Papa John's, LA Fitness, H&R Block, and Days Inn—that usually includes a loyal following of customers. The management system of the franchisor has already been established, and a performance record is readily available. In addition, franchisors provide a wide range of support to franchisees, including financing, assistance in obtaining a location, business training, supplies, and marketing programs.[43]

Franchisees themselves say they are drawn to the idea of franchising because it combines the freedom of business ownership with the support of a large company. Like other small-business owners, franchisees want to make their own business decisions and determine their own work hours. And they want to have more control over the amount of wealth they can possibly accumulate, as opposed to what they might earn in a salaried job. In an economic slowdown, franchisees might very well be executives who have been laid off during a downsizing or reorganization effort by previous employers. These are highly trained and motivated businesspeople looking for a way to advance their careers.[44] To learn more about being a franchise owner, see the "Job Description" feature.

Franchising can have its downside—for both franchisors and franchisees. For the franchisor, if its franchisees fail in any way, that failure reflects poorly on the overall brand as well as the bottom line. The same holds true for the franchisee: A firm that is mismanaged at the top level can spell doom for the smaller business owners who are actually running the individual

Job Description

Franchise Owner

Overview If you're hard working, possess excellent interpersonal skills, and can follow an already proven system for a business operation, owning a franchise may be a good fit. As a franchise owner, experience in operations or marketing helps ensure success. With the right temperament and expectation level, some franchisees have managed to make it big with ownership of multiple locations. However, it is important to be aware of a false sense of security created by franchise marketing when people think all they have to do is write a check for the franchise fee in exchange for the guaranteed success of a "business-in-a-box" or turnkey business. As a franchise owner, long hours are common, but the payoff from being a small-business owner can be very gratifying.

Responsibilities The work environment of a franchise owner will vary according to the type of franchise—for example, retail store, traveling to customers in a mobile business van, or working from home. Responsibilities may include inventory control (ordering new products according to existing stock and customer demand); compliance with instructions about branding, signs, logos, and color schemes; maintaining accurate records; hiring, training, and supervising employees; and operating at set standards to sell products or services.

Requirements A degree is not required, although franchisors may give some weight to a college degree and transferable skills during the selection process. Education is important, but it is not always a determinant of a franchisee's success. There are factors with greater importance than education in determining whether a franchisee will be successful. They include franchise choice, location, employees, managers, and marketing. The education and training provided by the franchisor are specific to the type of business you'll be running, so no previous or direct experience is required. This type of training is typically more important than a college degree. Some local colleges offer classes on small-business ownership, which may be beneficial for someone exploring a career as a franchise owner. A franchise owner with management skills, basic accounting and recordkeeping skills, product or service knowledge, and sales and marketing skills will have a leg up on the competition.

Outlook The International Franchise Association projects continued growth for franchising in the United States. Employment growth for the sector, projected to increase 3.7% on an annual basis, will outpace the growth of employment in the general economy. The growth of the franchise sector is projected to increase by more than 6.1% to over $450 billion in an upcoming year.

Sources: Peter Tourian, "Top Five Traits of Successful Franchise Owners," *LinkedIn*, https://www.linkedin.com, accessed March 9, 2018; Sara Wilson, "Do You Need a College Degree to Succeed as a Franchisee?" *All Business*, http://www.allbusiness.com, accessed March 9, 2018; Jason Daly, "The Top Traits of Successful Franchise Owners," *Entrepreneur*, http://www.entrepreneur.com, accessed March 9, 2018; Jeff Elgin, "Top 5 Characteristics of Successful Franchisees," *Entrepreneur*, http://www.entrepreneur.com, accessed March 9, 2018; organizational website, "Franchise Business Economic Outlook for 2015," http://emarket.franchise.org, accessed March 9, 2018.

units. Krispy Kreme, mentioned earlier, is an example of a franchised company that stumbled due to overexpansion. When a firm initially decides to offer franchise opportunities, the company overall may lose money for several years. Of course, in offering franchise opportunities, the franchisor—often the founder of what was once a small business—loses absolute control over every aspect of the business. This uncertainty can make the process of selecting the right franchisees to carry out the company's mission an important task.[45]

The franchisee faces an outlay of cash in the form of an initial investment, franchise fees, supplies, maintenance, leases, and the like. The most expensive franchises generally are those that involve well-known fast food chains and hotels and resorts, which can run in the millions.[46] For this reason, it is not unusual for groups of businesspeople to purchase a franchise (or several franchise locations). Payments to the franchisor can add to the burden of keeping the business afloat until owners begin to earn a profit. Choosing a low-cost start-up such as Heaven's Best might be a good alternative. Heaven's Best is a cleaning company that specializes in business and residential carpet and upholstery. The firm offers top-quality methods, equipment, and products along with training, brand awareness, and marketing tools. Businesspeople can purchase a franchise for an investment of as little as $30,000.[47] As in any business, it is important for franchisees to evaluate carefully how much profit they can make once their cost obligations are met.

Because franchises are so closely linked to their brand, franchisors and franchisees must work well together to maintain standards of quality in their goods and services. If customers are unhappy with their experience at one franchise location, they might avoid stopping at another one several miles away, even if the second one is owned and operated by someone else. This is especially true where food is involved. The discovery of tainted meat or produce at one franchise restaurant can cause panic to spread throughout the entire chain. A potential franchisee would be wise to thoroughly research the financial performance and reputation of the franchisor, using resources such as other franchisees and the Federal Trade Commission. A prospective franchisee typically receives the franchisor's franchise disclosure document, a presale document presented to any prospective franchisee, prior to signing a contract or submitting payment.

Some franchisees have found the franchising agreement to be too confining. Regardless of the number of stores owned, a McDonald's franchisee, for example, cannot decide to add a tuna salad sandwich to the menu. The agreements are usually fairly strict, and that generally helps to maintain the integrity of and uniformity of the brand. Toward this end, some franchise companies control promotional activities, select the site location, or even become involved in hiring decisions. But these activities may seem overly restrictive to some franchisees, especially those seeking independence and autonomy.

Restrictions can also cost franchisees more than they feel is fair. Recently, McDonald's franchisees have expressed frustration over the recent rollout of a new value menu along with required demands for costly store remodels. McDonald's has implemented an initiative to modernize its stores, which means adding kiosks and more gourmet options, such as espresso-based McCafe drinks, on the menu. For franchisees, this is complex and costly. As profits on food shrink and labor costs grow, a few franchisees have put their stores up for sale.[48]

Assessment Check

1. What is the difference between a franchisor and a franchisee?
2. What are the benefits to both parties of franchising?
3. What are the potential drawbacks of franchising for both parties?

7 Forms of Private Business Ownership

sole proprietorship business ownership in which there is no legal distinction between the sole proprietor's status as an individual and his or her status as a business owner.

Regardless of its size, every business is organized according to one of three categories of legal structure: sole proprietorship, partnership, or corporation. As **Figure 5.3** shows, sole proprietorships are the most common form of business ownership, accounting for more than 86.4% of all firms in the United States. Although far fewer firms are organized as corporations, the revenues earned by these companies represent over 80% of revenues earned by U.S. businesses each year.

Each legal structure offers unique advantages and disadvantages. But because there is no universal formula for every situation, some business owners prefer to organize their companies further as S corporations, limited-liability partnerships, and limited-liability companies. In some cases, corporations are owned by their employees.

In addition to the three main legal structures, several other options for ownership exist. These include employee-owned businesses, family-owned businesses, and not-for-profit organizations.

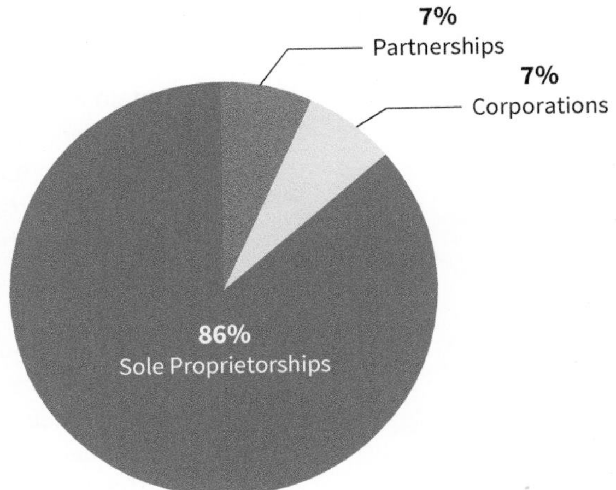

Source: Data from SBA Office of Advocacy, "Frequently Asked Questions," http://sba.gov/advocacy, accessed March 9, 2018; government website, U.S. Census Bureau, SBO, SUSB, http://census.gov, accessed March 9, 2018.

FIGURE 5.3 Forms of Business Ownership

Sole Proprietorships

The most common form of business ownership, the **sole proprietorship** is also the oldest and the simplest. In a sole proprietorship, no legal distinction separates the sole proprietor's status as an individual from his or her status as a business owner. Although sole proprietorships are common in a variety of industries, they are concentrated primarily among small businesses such as repair shops, small retail stores, and service providers such as plumbers, hair stylists, and photographers. The term solopreneur refers to an entrepreneur who works alone, "solo," and runs his or her business single-handedly without any employees.

Sole proprietorships offer some unique advantages. Because such businesses involve a single owner, they are easy to form *and* dissolve. A sole proprietorship gives the owner maximum management flexibility, along with the right to all profits after payment of business-related bills and taxes. A highly motivated owner of a sole proprietorship directly reaps the benefits of his or her hard work.

Minimal legal requirements simplify entering and exiting a sole proprietorship. The owner registers the business or trade name—to guarantee that two firms do not use the same name—and takes out any necessary licenses. Local governments require certain licenses for businesses such as restaurants, motels or hotels, and retail stores. In addition, some occupational licenses require business owners to obtain specific insurance such as liability coverage.

Sole proprietorships are also easy to dissolve. This advantage is particularly important to temporary or seasonal businesses that set up for a limited period of time. It's also helpful if the owner needs or wants to close the business for any reason—say, to relocate or to accept a full-time position with a larger firm.

Management flexibility is another advantage of a sole proprietorship. The owner can make decisions without reporting to a manager, take quick action, and keep trade secrets. A sole proprietorship always bears the individual stamp or branding of its owner, whether it's a certain way of styling hair or the way a store window is decorated.

The greatest disadvantage of the sole proprietorship is the owner's personal financial liability for all debts of the business. Also, the business must operate with financial resources limited to the owner's personal funds and money that he or she can borrow. Such financing limitations can keep the business from expanding.

Another disadvantage is that the owner must wear many hats, handling a wide range of management and operational responsibilities. He or she may not have expertise in every area, which may inhibit the firm's growth or even cause the firm damage. In addition, a sole proprietorship usually lacks long-term continuity, because a change in personal circumstances or finances can terminate the business on short notice.

Partnerships

partnership association of two or more persons who operate a business as co-owners by voluntary legal agreement.

Another option for organizing a business is to form a partnership. The Uniform Partnership Act, which regulates this ownership form in most states, defines a **partnership** as an association of two or more persons who operate a business as co-owners by voluntary legal agreement. Many small businesses begin as partnerships between co-founders.

Partnerships are easy to form. All the partners need to do is register the business name and obtain any necessary licenses. Having a partner generally means greater financial capability and someone to share in the operations and decision making of a business. It is even better if one partner has a particular skill, such as design, while the other has a knack for finance.

Most partnerships have the disadvantage of being exposed to unlimited financial liability. Each partner bears full responsibility for the debts of the firm, and each is legally liable for the actions of the other partners. If the firm fails and is left with debt—no matter who is at fault—every partner is responsible for those debts. If one partner defaults, the others are responsible for the firm's debts, even if it means dipping into personal funds. To avoid these problems, many firms establish a limited-liability partnership, which limits the liability of partners to the value of their interests in the company.

Breaking up a partnership is more complicated than dissolving a sole proprietorship. Rather than simply withdrawing funds from the bank, the partner who wants out may need to find someone to buy his or her interest in the firm. The death of a partner also threatens the survival of a partnership. A new partnership must be formed, and the estate of the deceased is entitled to a share of the firm's value. To ease the financial strains of such events, business planners often recommend life insurance coverage for each partner, combined with a buy–sell agreement. The insurance proceeds can be used to repay the deceased partner's heirs and allow the surviving partner to retain control of the business. Because partnerships are vulnerable to personal conflicts that can escalate quickly, it is important for partners to choose each other carefully—not just because they are friends—and try to plan for the future.

Corporations

A **corporation** is a legal organization with assets and liabilities separate from those of its owner(s). A corporation can be a large or small business. It can be Ford Motor Company or a local auto repair shop.

corporation legal organization with assets and liabilities separate from those of its owner(s).

Corporate ownership offers considerable advantages. Because a corporation is a separate legal entity, its stockholders have limited financial risk. If the firm fails, they lose only the money they have invested. This applies to the firm's managers and executives as well. Because they are not the sole proprietors or partners in the business, their personal savings are not at risk if the company folds or goes bankrupt. This protection also extends to legal risk. Class-action suits involving automakers, drug manufacturers, and food producers are filed against the companies, not the owners of those companies. Ulta Beauty, a cosmetic company with more than 1,000 retail stores, was recently hit with a class-action lawsuit that claims that damaged or returned products were cleaned, repackaged, and resold as new.[49]

Corporations offer other advantages. They gain access to expanded financial capabilities based on the opportunity to offer direct outside investments such as stock sales. A large corporation can legally generate internal financing for many projects by transferring money from one part of the corporation to another.

One major disadvantage for a corporation is the double taxation of corporate earnings. After a corporation pays federal, state, and local income taxes on its profits, its owners (stockholders) also pay personal taxes on any distributions of those profits they receive from the corporation in the form of dividends.

S Corporations and Limited Liability Companies

To avoid double taxation of business income while minimizing financial liability for their owners, many smaller firms (those with fewer than 100 stockholders) organize as **S corporations**. These companies can elect to pay federal income taxes as partnerships while retaining the liability limitations typical of corporations. S corporations are taxed only once. Unlike regular corporations, S corporations do not pay corporate taxes on their profits. Instead, the untaxed profits of S corporations are paid directly as dividends to shareholders, who then pay the individual tax rate. This tax advantage has resulted in a tremendous increase in the number of S corporations. Consequently, the IRS closely monitors S corporations because some businesses don't meet the legal requirements to form S corporations.[50]

S corporations corporations that do not pay corporate taxes on profits; instead, profits are distributed to shareholders, who pay individual income taxes.

Business owners may also form a **limited-liability company (LLC)** to secure the corporate advantage of limited liability while avoiding the double taxation characteristic of corporations. An LLC combines the pass-through taxation of a partnership or sole proprietorship with the limited liability of a corporation.

limited-liability company (LLC) secures the corporate advantage of limited liability while avoiding the double taxation characteristic of a traditional corporation.

An LLC is governed by an operating agreement that resembles a partnership agreement, except that it reduces each partner's liability for the actions of the other owners. Corporations of professionals, such as lawyers, accountants, and physicians, use a similar approach, with the letters *PC* (professional corporation) attached to the business name. LLCs appear to be the wave of the future. Immediately after the first LLC law was passed, most major CPA (certified public accountant) firms in the United States converted to LLC status. Today you'll see the LLC or PC designation attached to businesses ranging from bowling alleys to veterinary hospitals.

Certified Benefit Corporations

Some for-profit organizations are choosing a corporate form called a **benefit corporation**, or B corporation for short. A nonprofit, B Lab, certifies B Corps, for-profit companies, that meet rigorous standards of social and environmental performance, accountability, and transparency. Companies with a culture, structure, and decision making centered around creating a meaningful impact on the environment have chosen this form of business ownership. The purpose of a B corporation is to create a qualitative benefit

benefit corporation type of for-profit corporate entity that includes a positive impact on society and the environment as part of its defined goals.

Clean & Green Business

Certified B Corporations as a Force for Good

What do for-profit companies like Ben & Jerry's Ice Cream, Numi Organic Tea, Method Soap, Patagonia, Etsy, and Warby Parker have in common? All are certified Benefit Corporations—or B Corporations for short—and all must meet high standards in how they treat employees, their impact on the environment, and how they benefit the communities in which they operate. To date, there are more than 1,700 certified B Corporations in 50 countries—and the number is growing. Certification involves meeting rigorous standards of social and environmental performance, accountability, and transparency.

A form of incorporation that took hold a number of years ago, certified B Corporations differ from traditional corporations in that a third-party auditor must verify that the corporation stands behind its goals—those that go beyond earning a profit. B Corporations must state their social and environmental goals in their bylaws—the rules a corporation uses to regulate itself. An annual benefit report, which differs from a company's traditional annual report, must be published in order to accurately measure its actual versus stated goals.

Certified B Corporations are taxed in the same way as their traditional C corporation counterparts. Companies become certified B Corporations as part of a larger mission. Method, an eco-friendly home and personal care products company, became a certified B Corporation rather than just being a business that talks about "people, planet, and profit," according to its co-founder.

Patagonia's CEO doesn't believe traditional corporate structures encourage a company's board of directors to possibly lessen shareholder value for the public good. To date, 30 states have passed benefit corporation legislation with hopes of more businesses focused on a triple bottom line of profit, people, and planet.

Questions for Critical Thinking

1. Although investors may be attracted to companies committed to making a social impact, discuss why some investors might not be attracted to certified B Corporations. Similarly, will all shareholders, particularly those with a primary goal of earning a profit, agree with a company's decision to become a certified B Corp? Why or why not?
2. Discuss whether or not certified B Corporations possess a certain type of "branding" that allows further differentiation from competitors. If given the choice, would you purchase products and services from a certified B Corporation?

Sources: Organization website, http://www.bcorporation.net, accessed March 9, 2018; "20 Moments from the Past 20 Years That Moved the Whole World Forward," *Fast Company*, http://www.fastcompany.com, accessed March 9, 2018; Mark Kohler, "Benefit Corporations: Doing Good (and Potentially) Boosting Profits," *Entrepreneur*, http://www.entrepreneur.com, accessed March 9, 2018; Michelle Goodman, "Everything You Need to Know About B Corporation Certification," *Entrepreneur*, http://www.entrepreneur.com, accessed March 9, 2018.

to the public beyond financial gains for its shareholders.[51] See the "Clean & Green Business" feature for more about how companies are using capitalism as a force for good.

Employee-Owned Corporations

employee ownership business ownership in which workers own shares of stock in the company that employs them.

Another alternative for creating a corporation is **employee ownership**, in which shares of stock are owned by some or all of a company's employees. With the exception of employee ownership, the corporation remains the same.

Today about 36% of all employees of for-profit companies report owning stock in their companies; approximately 32 million Americans own employer stock through *employee stock ownership plans (ESOPs)*, options, stock purchase plans, 401(k) plans, and other plans.[52]

Several trends underlie the rise in employee ownership. One is that employees want to share in whatever profit their company earns. Another is that management wants employees to care deeply about the firm's success and contribute their best effort. These firms remain committed to this kind of involvement and compensation for their workers. Because human resources are so essential to the success of a modern business, employers want to build their employees' commitment to the organization. Studies show that ESOP companies experience faster growth than they would have without their ownership plans, and that ESOP companies grow fastest when combined with worker participation programs.[53] Some of the country's most successful public corporations, including Publix Super Markets, Full Sail Brewing Company, and Herman Miller, an office furniture company, have embraced employee ownership.

Family-Owned Businesses

Family-owned firms are considered by many to be the backbone of American business. The Waltons and the Fords are viewed as pioneers because each of their firms—Walmart and Ford

Motor Company—was once a small, family-owned company. (The small, family-owned beginning of Walmart is shown in the photo.) Family-owned firms come in a variety of sizes and legal structures. Because of the complex nature of family relationships, family-owned firms experience some unique challenges.

Whether a family-owned business is structured as a partnership, limited liability company, or traditional corporation, its members must make decisions regarding succession, marriages and divorces, compensation, hierarchy and authority, shareholder control, and more. Whereas some family members may prefer a loose structure—perhaps not even putting certain agreements in writing—experienced businesspeople caution that failing to choose the right legal structure for a family-owned firm can create problems later.[54]

Jb Reed/Bloomberg via Getty Images

Family-owned companies are considered by many to be the backbone of American business. Sam Walton started the family business with Walton's 5&10 store, which later became Walmart.

Succession is a major benefit—and drawback—to family-owned firms. On the one hand, a clearly documented plan for succession from one generation to the next is a huge source of security for the firm's continuity. But lack of legal planning, or situations in which succession is challenged, can cause chaos. In fact, only a small percentage of family-owned businesses survive into the second or third generation.

A small family firm that has managed to thrive for five generations is Squamscot Beverages. Originally called Connermade, the company was founded in 1883 when William H. Conner began producing his own "tonic" beverage—a spruce beer that came in glass bottles with porcelain-and-wire stoppers. Conner ran the company until his son Alfred took over in 1911. Alfred remained in charge until 1948, when he handed the reins to his own son, Alfred Jr. Today, Tom Conner and his son Dan manage most aspects of running the firm, which is still headquartered on the family's rural property in New Hampshire. Squamscot Beverages produces soda drinks in a variety of flavors, including birch beer, cola, cream, orange, grape, and ginger ale. Bottles are distributed to small grocery outlets, or customers can visit the bottling plant to select whichever flavors they want.[55]

Not-for-Profit Corporations

The same business concepts that apply to commercial companies also apply to **not-for-profit corporations**—organizations whose goals do not include pursuing a profit. About 1.5 million not-for-profits operate in the United States, including charitable groups, social-welfare organizations, government agencies, and religious congregations. This sector also includes museums, libraries, hospitals, conservation groups, private schools, and the like.[56]

not-for-profit corporations organization whose goals do not include pursuing a profit.

Most states set out separate legal provisions for organizational structures and operations of not-for-profit corporations. These organizations do not issue stock certificates, because they pay no dividends to owners, and ownership rarely changes. They are also exempt from paying corporate taxes. However, they must meet strict regulations in order to maintain their not-for-profit status.

Assessment Check

1. What are the key differences between sole proprietorships and partnerships?
2. What is a corporation?
3. What are the main characteristics of a not-for-profit corporation?

TABLE 5.3 Largest Nonprofits in the United States

Name	Type	Donations
United Way	Help individuals and groups with specific community interests	$3.54 Billion
The Task Force for Global Health	Routes donated medicines abroad	$2.67 Billion
Feeding America	Umbrella organization for several food banks	$2.38 Billion
The Salvation Army	Social service agency and church	$1.88 Billion
St. Jude Children's Research Hospital	Standalone hospital	$1.37 Billion
Habitat for Humanity	Builds homes for the poor	$1.17 Billion
Direct Relief	Routes medicine and supplies to 140 countries	$1.1 Billion
The Y (YMCA)	Youth and health club facilities	$1.0 Billion
Food for the Poor, Inc.	Food for the poor	$1.2 Billion
Americares Foundation	Disaster and humanitarian relief abroad	$970 Million

Source: "America's Top Charities 2017," *Forbes,* http://www.forbes.com, accessed March 10, 2018.

8 Public and Collective Ownership of Business

Though most businesses in the United States are in the private sector, some firms are actually owned by the local, state, or federal government. Alaskan Railroad Corp., East Alabama Medical Center, and Washington State Ferries are all government-owned businesses.[57]

In another type of ownership structure, groups of customers may collectively own a company. Recreational Equipment Inc. (REI) is a collectively owned retailer that sells outdoor gear and apparel. Finally, groups of smaller firms may collectively own a larger organization. Both of these collective ownership structures are also referred to as cooperatives.

Public (Government) Ownership

One alternative to private ownership is some form of *public ownership*, in which a unit or agency of government owns and operates an organization. In the United States, local governments often own parking structures and water systems. The Pennsylvania Turnpike Authority operates a vital highway link across the Keystone State. The federal government operates Hoover Dam in Nevada to provide electricity over a large region.

Sometimes public ownership results when private investors are unwilling to invest in a high-risk project—or find that operating an important service is simply unprofitable. The National Railroad Passenger Corporation—better known as Amtrak—is a for-profit corporation that operates on more than 21,300 route miles of intercity passenger rail service in 46 states and the District of Columbia. Congress created Amtrak in the Rail Passenger Service Act of 1970, thereby removing from private railroads the obligation of transporting passengers, because passenger rail travel was generally unprofitable. In exchange, the private railroads granted Amtrak access to their existing tracks at a low cost. The Amtrak board of directors is made up of seven voting members appointed for five-year terms by the president of the United States.[58]

Collective (Cooperative) Ownership

Collective ownership establishes an organization referred to as a *cooperative* (or *co-op*), whose owners join forces to operate all or part of the activities in their firm or industry. Currently, there are about 250 million people worldwide employed part-time or full-time by cooperatives.[59] Cooperatives allow small businesses to pool their resources on purchases, marketing, equipment, distribution, and the like. Cooperatives can share equipment and expertise, and discount savings can be split among members.

Cooperatives are frequently found among agricultural businesses. Cabot Creamery is a cooperative of 1,200 small dairy farms spread throughout New England and upstate New York. Cabot is owned and operated by its members—farmers and their families. In addition, Cabot works with other cooperatives around the country to produce and distribute high-quality cheese, butter, and other dairy products.[60]

Assessment Check

1. What is public ownership?
2. What is collective ownership? Where are cooperatives typically found, and what benefits do they provide small businesses?

9 Organizing a Corporation

A corporation is a legal structure, but it also requires a certain organizational structure that is more complex than the structure of a sole proprietorship or a partnership. This is why people often think of a corporation as a large entity, even though it does not have to be a specific size. In rare instances, there are one-person corporations.

Types of Corporations

Corporations fall into three categories: domestic, foreign, and alien. A firm is considered a *domestic corporation* in the state where it is incorporated. When a company does business in states other than the one where it has filed incorporation papers, it is registered as a *foreign corporation* in each of those states. A firm incorporated in one nation that operates in another is known as an *alien corporation* where it operates. Many firms—particularly large corporations with operations scattered around the world—may operate under all three of these designations.

Where and How Businesses Incorporate

Businesses owners who want to incorporate must decide where to locate their headquarters and follow the correct procedure for submitting the legal document that establishes the corporation.

Although most small and medium-size businesses are incorporated in the states in which they operate, a U.S. firm can actually incorporate in any state it chooses. The founders of large corporations, or those that will do business nationwide, often compare the benefits—such as tax incentives—provided by each state. Some states are considered to be more "business friendly" than others. Delaware is one of the easiest states in which to incorporate.

The Corporate Charter Each state has a specific procedure for incorporating a business. Most states require at least one *incorporator* to create the corporation. In addition, the

stockholders owners of a corporation due to their purchase of stock in the corporation.

preferred stock shares that give owners limited voting rights, and the right to receive dividends or assets before owners of common stock.

common stock shares that give owners voting rights but only residual claims to the firm's assets and income distributions.

board of directors governing body of a corporation.

- Name and Address of the Corporation
- Corporate Objectives
- Type and Amount of Stock to Issue
- Expected Life of the Corporation
- Financial Capital at the Time of Incorporation
- Provisions for Transferring Shares of Stock among Owners
- Provisions for Regulating Internal Corporate Affairs
- Address of the Business Office Registered with the State of Incorporation
- Names and Addresses of the Initial Board of Directors
- Names and Addresses of the Incorporators

FIGURE 5.4 Traditional Articles of Incorporation

new corporation must select a name that is different from names used by other businesses. **Figure 5.4** lists the ten elements that most states require for chartering a corporation.[61]

The information provided in the articles of incorporation forms the basis on which a state grants a *corporate charter*, which is the legal document that formally establishes a corporation. After securing the charter, the owners prepare the company's bylaws, which describe the rules and procedures for its operation.

Corporate Management

Regardless of its size, every corporation has levels of management and ownership. **Figure 5.5** illustrates those that are typical—although a smaller firm might not contain all five of these. Levels range from stockholders down to supervisory management.

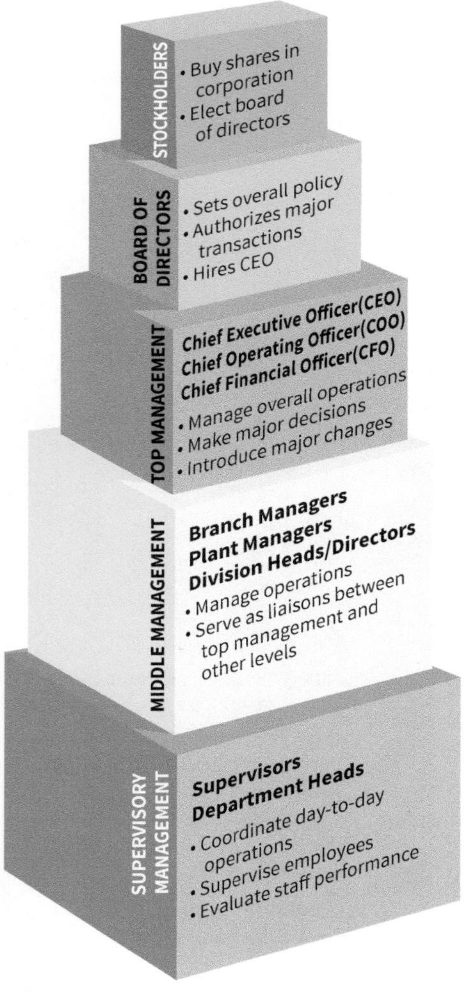

FIGURE 5.5 Levels of Management in a Corporation

Stock Ownership and Stockholder Rights

At the top of Figure 5.6 are **stockholders**. They buy shares of stock in the corporation, becoming part owners of it. Some companies, such as family businesses, are owned by relatively few stockholders, and the stock is generally unavailable to outsiders. In such a firm, known as a *closed* or *closely held corporation,* the stockholders also control and manage all of the company's activities. Trader Joe's grocery chain and Mars, maker of M&M's, are examples of privately held companies.

In contrast, an open corporation, also called a *publicly held corporation,* sells stock to the general public, establishing diversified ownership and often leading to a broader scope of operations than those of a closed corporation. Publicly held corporations usually hold annual stockholders' meetings. During these meetings, managers report on corporate activities, and stockholders vote on any decisions that require their approval, including elections of officers. Walmart holds the nation's largest stockholder meeting at the University of Arkansas Bud Walton Arena. Approximately 14,000 people attend. In addition to standard shareholder business, the Walmart meeting has featured celebrities and entertainers such as Reese Witherspoon, Mariah Carey, Rod Stewart, Brian McKnight, and Ricky Martin.

Stockholders' role in the corporation depends on the class of stock they own. Shares are usually classified as common or preferred stock. Although owners of **preferred stock** have limited voting rights, they are entitled to receive dividends before holders of common stock. If the corporation is dissolved, they have first claims on assets, once debtors are repaid. Owners of **common stock** have voting rights but only residual claims on the firm's assets, which means they are last to receive any distributions. Because one share is typically worth only one vote, small stockholders generally have little influence on corporate management actions. More about stock ownership is covered in Chapter 16.

Board of Directors

Stockholders elect a **board of directors**—the governing body of a corporation. The board sets overall policy, authorizes major transactions involving the corporation, and hires the chief executive officer (CEO). Most boards include both inside directors (corporate executives) and outside directors—people who are not otherwise employed by the organization. Sometimes the corporation's top executive also chairs the board. Generally, outside directors are also stockholders, so they have a financial stake in the company's performance.

Corporate Officers and Managers

The CEO and other members of top management, such as the chief operating officer (COO), chief financial officer (CFO), and the chief information officer (CIO), make most major corporate decisions. Managers at the next level down the hierarchy, middle management, handle the ongoing

Judgment Call

Are Activist Investors Good for Business?

Not long ago, corporate America bid farewell to one of the few women CEOs running a major corporation. Ellen Kullman of chemical company DuPont stepped down after a long-fought battle against a challenge from activist investor Nelson Peltz and his $11 billion investment firm, Trian Fund Management.

An activist investor is an individual or group that has raised large sums of money and typically purchases large numbers of a company's shares of stock to obtain greater control over the company's business. Greater control comes with getting a seat or multiple seats on a company's board of directors. This strategy gives activists the greatest opportunity to influence business decisions and possibly increase the company's stock price.

The long-term impact of activist investors on corporate America continues to be questioned. One side of the debate views the role of activists as one that seemingly holds corporate leaders accountable for their decision making and spending. The other side views their tactics and power as aggressive and impatient—with too much focus on short-term results, stock prices, and financial gains.

A recent study by the *Wall Street Journal* reveals that stock shares of large public companies confronted by activist investors are likely to just slightly outperform industry peers by a margin of less than 5%. The survey also suggests that rather than shunning activist investors, targeted companies should evaluate each proposal and the track record of the investors in question.

Peltz's recent bid to win seats on the DuPont board fell short by a narrow margin. However, he continues to launch boardroom battles, most recently at Procter & Gamble, where he believes the consumer products company needs more research innovation. While their strategies are legal, have activist investors gone too far?

Questions for Critical Thinking

1. Either in small groups or with a partner, debate the pros and cons of an activist investor challenge.
2. One report shows that almost half of company boards remain unprepared for an activist investor challenge. What should a company do to prepare for such a challenge?

Sources: Monica Langley, "Activists Put Mondelez CEO Irene Rosenfeld on the Spot," *Wall Street Journal,* http://www.wsj.com, accessed March 10, 2018; David Benoit and Ted Mann, "Nelson Peltz's Trian Makes a Big Bet on GE," *Wall Street Journal,* http://www.wsj.com, accessed March 10, 2018; "Almost Half of Public Company Boards Are Unprepared for an Activist Investor Challenge," *Nasdaq Global Newswire,* http://globenewswire.com, accessed March 10, 2018; Stephen Gandel, "How DuPont Went to War with Activist Investor Nelson Peltz," *Fortune,* http://fortune.com, accessed March 10, 2018; company website, "About Us," https://www.trianpartners.com, accessed March 10, 2018; David Benoit and Vipal Monga, "Are Activist Investors Helping or Undermining American Companies?" *Wall Street Journal,* http://www.wsj.com, accessed March 10, 2018; Ronald Orol, "Nelson Peltz Begins Showdown Over P&G CEO, R&D," *The Street,* https://www.thestreet.com, accessed March 11, 2018.

operational functions of the company. At the first tier of management, supervisory personnel coordinate day-to-day operations, assign specific tasks to employees, and evaluate job performance. This will be discussed further in Chapter 7.

Today's CEOs and CFOs are bound by stricter regulations than in the past. They must verify in writing the accuracy of their firm's financial statements, and the process for nominating candidates for the board has become more complex. In short, more checks and balances are in place for the governance of corporations. A continuing controversy surrounds the impact of activist investors on business and corporate structure. See the "Judgment Call" feature for more detail.

Assessment Check

1. What are the two key elements of the incorporation process?
2. Identify the five main levels of corporate ownership and management.

10 When Businesses Join Forces

Today's business environment contains many complex relationships among businesses as well as not-for-profit organizations. Two firms may team up to develop a product or co-market products. One company may buy out another. Large corporations may split into smaller units. The list of alliances is as varied as the organizations themselves, but the major trends in corporate ownership include mergers and acquisitions and joint ventures.

Mergers and Acquisitions (M&A)

In a recent year, mergers and acquisitions among U.S. corporations hit an all-time high. Airlines, financial institutions, telecommunications companies, and media corporations are just a few of the types of businesses that have merged into giants. The merger between two food and beverage giants, Heinz and Kraft Foods, creates the world's fifth largest food and beverage company in the world.[62]

merger agreement in which two or more firms combine to form one company.

acquisition agreement in which one firm purchases another.

The terms *merger* and *acquisition* are often used interchangeably, but their meanings are different. In a **merger**, two or more firms combine to form one company. In an **acquisition**, one firm purchases the other. This means that not only does the buyer acquire the firm's property and assets, it also takes on any debt obligations. Acquisitions also occur when one firm buys a division or subsidiary from another firm. Not all such attempts are successful. E-commerce giant Amazon recently shelled out $1.37 billion to acquire close to 500 grocery stores of Austin, TX–based Whole Foods Company. Amazon can use the consumer data from well-off Whole Foods shoppers to upsell products with its Prime Now delivery option. Customers can have groceries delivered in a few short hours. The digital and e-commerce "Amazon effect" has changed and shaped the way consumers shop—and the impact on traditional retailers is profound.[63]

vertical merger merger that combines firms operating at different levels in the production and marketing process.

Mergers can be classified as vertical, horizontal, or conglomerate. A **vertical merger** combines firms operating at different levels in the production and marketing process—the combination of a manufacturer and a large retailer, for instance. A vertical merger pursues one of two primary goals: (1) to ensure adequate flows of raw materials and supplies needed for a firm's products or (2) to increase distribution.

horizontal merger merger that joins firms in the same industry for the purpose of diversification, increasing customer bases, cutting costs, or expanding product lines.

A **horizontal merger** joins firms in the same industry. This is done for the purpose of diversification, increasing customer bases, cutting costs, or expanding product lines. This type of merger is particularly popular in the auto and health care industries. To increase their video streaming services direct to consumers, The Walt Disney Company recently acquired the assets of 21st Century Fox for $52.4 billion in stock.[64]

conglomerate merger merger that combines unrelated firms, usually with the goal of diversification, spurring sales growth, or spending a cash surplus in order to avoid a takeover attempt.

A **conglomerate merger** combines unrelated firms. The most common reasons for a conglomerate merger are to diversify, spur sales growth, or spend a cash surplus that might otherwise make the firm a tempting target for a takeover effort. Conglomerate mergers may join firms in totally unrelated industries. General Electric is well known for its conglomerate mergers—including ownership of health care services and household appliances. Experts debate whether conglomerate mergers are beneficial. The usual argument in favor of such mergers is that a company can use its management expertise to succeed in a variety of industries. But the obvious drawback is that a huge conglomerate can spread its resources too thin to be dominant in any one market.

Figure 5.6 lists some well-known mergers and acquisitions in industries including e-commerce, retail, media, publishing, entertainment, fast food, aerospace, pharmaceuticals, software, and consumer goods.

Joint Ventures: Specialized Partnerships

joint venture partnership between companies formed for a specific undertaking.

A **joint venture** is a partnership between companies formed for a specific undertaking. Sometimes a company enters into a joint venture with a local firm, sharing the operation's costs, risks, management, and profits with its local partner. This is particularly common when a firm wants to enter into business in a foreign market. Fiat Chrysler Automobiles invested $280 million in a manufacturing joint venture in India with Tata Motors Limited to jointly manufacture a Jeep vehicle (as shown in the photo). To date, the two companies are discussing the sharing of engines and transmissions.[65]

Joint ventures between for-profit firms and not-for-profit organizations are becoming more and more common. These partnerships provide great benefits for both parties. Not-for-profit

Purchaser	Company Acquired	Cost
Amazon	Whole Foods	$13.7 Billion
Intel	Mobileye	$15.3 Billion
United Technologies	Rockwell Collins	$23 Billion
Disney	21st Century Fox	$52 Billion
JAB Holdings	Panera Bread	$7.5 Billion
Michael Kors	Jimmy Choo	$1.2 Billion
Coach	Kate Spade	$2.4 Billion
CVS	Aetna	$69 Billion
Gilead	Kite Pharma	$11.9 Billion
Cisco	BroadSoft	$2 Billion
Apple	Shazam	$400 Million
Arby's	Buffalo Wild Wings	$2.4 Billion
Meredith Corp	Time	$2.8 Billion
Discovery	Scripps Network	$14.6 Billion
Google	HTC Smartphone Team (part of)	$1.1 Billion

Sources: Madeline Johnson, "15 of the Best Mergers & Acquisitions of 2017," *NASDAQ,* https://www.nasdaq.com, accessed March 11, 2018; Benjamin Gomes-Casseres, "What the Big Mergers of 2017 Tell Us About 2018," *Harvard Business Review,* https://hbr.org, accessed March 11, 2018.

FIGURE 5.6 Well-Known Mergers and Acquisitions

IndianAutosBlog.com

Fiat Chrysler Automobiles has invested in a manufacturing joint venture in India with Tata Motors Limited to produce Jeep vehicles such as this.

organizations receive the funding, marketing exposure, and sometimes human resources they might not otherwise generate. When employees donate to nonprofits of their choosing, Google offers generous matching grants. The company also provides nonprofits with $10,000 of advertising using Google's search results. This allows nonprofits to expand their audience and reach out to potential supporters.[66]

Assessment Check

1. Distinguish between a merger and an acquisition.
2. What are the different kinds of mergers?
3. What is a joint venture?

What's Ahead

The next chapter focuses on entrepreneurs, the driving force behind the formation of new businesses. It examines the differences between a small-business owner and an entrepreneur and identifies certain personality traits typical of entrepreneurs. The chapter also details the process of launching a new venture, including identifying opportunities, locating needed financing, and turning good ideas into successful businesses. Finally, the chapter explores a method for infusing the entrepreneurial spirit into established businesses—intrapreneurship.

Chapter in Review

Summary of Learning Objectives

LEARNING OBJECTIVE 1 Discuss why most businesses are small businesses.

A small business is an independently owned business having fewer than 500 employees. Generally, it is not dominant in its field and meets industry-specific size standards for income or number of employees. A business is classified as large when it exceeds these specifications.

Assessment Check Answers

1.1 **How does the Small Business Administration (SBA) define *small business*?** A small business is defined as an independent business having fewer than 500 employees. However, those bidding for government contracts or applying for government assistance may vary in size according to industry.

1.2 **In what industries do small businesses play a significant role?** Small businesses provide most jobs in construction, agriculture, wholesale trade, accommodation and food services, arts, entertainment and recreation, real estate, lending, and leasing. In addition, home-based businesses make up 50% of American small businesses.

LEARNING OBJECTIVE 2 Determine the contributions of small businesses to the economy.

Small businesses create new jobs and new industries. They often hire workers who traditionally have had difficulty finding employment at larger firms. Small firms give people the opportunity and outlet for developing new ideas, which can turn into entirely new industries. Small businesses also develop new and improved goods and services.

Assessment Check Answers

2.1 **What are the three key ways in which small businesses contribute to the economy?** Small businesses create new jobs and new industries and provide innovation.

2.2 **How are new industries created?** New industries are created when small businesses adapt to shifts in consumer interests and preferences. Innovation and new technology can play a significant role. In addition, new industries may be created when both the business world and consumers recognize a need for change.

LEARNING OBJECTIVE 3 Discuss why small businesses fail.

About 7 of every 10 new (small) businesses survive at least two years. But by the tenth year, 70% have closed. Failure is often attributed to management shortcomings, inadequate financing, and difficulty meeting government regulations.

Assessment Check Answers

3.1 **What percentage of small businesses remain in operation five years after starting? Ten years?** About 50% are in business after 5 years; about 70% have folded by the 10-year mark.

3.2 **What are the three main causes of small-business failure?** The three main causes of small-business failure are management shortcomings, inadequate financing, and difficulty complying with government regulations.

LEARNING OBJECTIVE 4 Describe the features of a successful business plan.

A complete business plan contains an executive summary, an introduction, financial and marketing sections, and résumés of the business principals. Within this structure, an effective business plan includes the company's mission, an outline of what makes the company unique, identification of customers and competitors, financial evaluation of the industry and market, and an assessment of the risks.

Assessment Check Answers

4.1 **What are the five main sections of a business plan?** The five sections are the executive summary, introduction, financial section, marketing section, and résumés of principals.

4.2 **Why is an effective business plan important to the success of a firm?** The business plan is a written document that provides an orderly statement of a company's goals, methods, and standards. It is the document that secures financing and creates a framework for the organization.

LEARNING OBJECTIVE 5 Identify the available assistance for small businesses.

The SBA guarantees loans made by private lenders, including microloans and those funded by Small Business Investment Companies

(SBICs). It offers training and information resources, so business owners can improve their odds of success. The SBA also provides specific support for businesses owned by women and minorities. State and local governments also have programs designed to help small businesses get established and grow. Venture capitalists are firms that invest in small businesses in return for an ownership or equity stake.

Assessment Check Answers

5.1 **What are the various ways the SBA helps small businesses?** The SBA guarantees business loans; helps small businesses compete for government set-aside programs; and provides business information, advice, and training to owners of small businesses. It also advocates for small-business interests within the federal government.

5.2 **What are business incubators?** Business incubators are local programs organized by community agencies that provide low-cost shared business facilities, along with training, support, and networking, in an effort to help small businesses get started.

5.3 **Why are small businesses good opportunities for women and minorities?** Many women feel they can achieve more as small-business owners and can balance family and work more easily if they own their own firms. Minority business owners can receive special assistance from programs such as the SBA's 8(a) Business Development program.

LEARNING OBJECTIVE 6 Explain franchising.

A franchisor is a large firm that permits another business (the franchisee) to sell its products under its brand name in return for a fee. Benefits to the franchisor include opportunities for expansion and greater profits. Benefits to the franchisee include name recognition, quick start-up, support from the franchisor, and the freedom of small-business ownership.

Assessment Check Answers

6.1 **What is the difference between a franchisor and a franchisee?** A franchisor permits a franchisee to market and sell its products under its brand name, in return for a fee.

6.2 **What are the benefits to both parties of franchising?** Benefits to the franchisor include opportunities for expansion and greater profits. Benefits to the franchisee include name recognition, quick start-up, support and training from the franchisor, and the freedom of small-business ownership.

6.3 **What are the potential drawbacks of franchising for both parties?** The drawbacks for the franchisor include mismanagement and failure on the part of any of its franchisees, overexpansion, and loss of absolute control over the business. Drawbacks for the franchisee include an initial outlay of expenses, problems due to failure on the part of the franchisor or other franchisees, and restrictive franchise agreements.

LEARNING OBJECTIVE 7 Outline the forms of private business ownership.

A sole proprietorship is owned and operated by one person. While sole proprietorships are easy to set up and offer great operating flexibility, the owner remains personally liable for all of the firm's debts and legal settlements. In a partnership, two or more individuals share responsibility for owning and running the business. Partnerships are relatively easy to set up, but they do not offer protection from liability. When a business is set up as a corporation, its assets and liabilities are separate from those of its owners and it is a separate legal entity. Investors receive shares of stock in the firm. Owners have no legal and financial liability beyond their individual investments. In an employee-owned business, most stockholders are also employees. Family-owned businesses may be structured legally in any of these three ways but face unique challenges, including succession and complex relationships. The legal structure of a not-for-profit corporation stipulates that its goals do not include earning a profit.

Assessment Check Answers

7.1 **What are the key differences between sole proprietorships and partnerships?** Sole proprietorships and partnerships expose their owners to unlimited financial liability from their businesses. Sole proprietorships are more flexible and easier to dissolve than partnerships. Partnerships involve shared work load and decision making, whereas sole proprietorships are entirely the responsibility of one business owner.

7.2 **What is a corporation?** A corporation is a legal organization with assets and liabilities separate from those of its owners. A corporation can be a large or small business.

7.3 **What is the main characteristic of a not-for-profit corporation?** A not-for-profit organization is set up legally so that its goals do not include pursuing a profit. Most states set out specific legal provisions for organizational structures and operations of not-for-profit corporations. They are exempt from paying corporate taxes.

LEARNING OBJECTIVE 8 Describe public and collective ownership of business.

Public ownership occurs when a unit or agency of government owns and operates an organization. Collective ownership establishes an organization referred to as a cooperative, whose owners join forces to operate all or part of the functions in their firm or industry.

Assessment Check Answers

8.1 **What is public ownership?** Public ownership occurs when a unit or agency of government owns and operates an organization.

8.2 **What is collective ownership? Where are cooperatives typically found, and what benefits do they provide small businesses?** Collective ownership establishes an organization referred to as a cooperative (co-op), whose owners join forces to operate all or part of the functions in their firm or industry. Cooperatives are frequently found among agricultural businesses. Cooperatives allow small firms to pool their resources, share equipment and expertise, and split discount savings among members.

LEARNING OBJECTIVE 9 Discuss organizing a corporation.

There are three types of corporations: domestic, foreign, and alien. Stockholders, or shareholders, own a corporation. In return for their financial investments, they receive shares of stock in the company. Stockholders elect a board of directors, who set overall policy. The board hires the chief executive officer (CEO), who then hires managers.

Assessment Check Answers

9.1 **What are the two key elements of the incorporation process?** The two key elements are where to incorporate and the corporate charter.

9.2 Identify the five main levels of corporate ownership and management. The five levels are stockholders, board of directors, top management, middle management, and supervisory management.

LEARNING OBJECTIVE 10 Explain what happens when businesses join forces.

In a merger, two or more firms combine to form one company. A vertical merger combines firms operating at different levels in the production and marketing process. A horizontal merger joins firms in the same industry. A conglomerate merger combines unrelated firms. An acquisition occurs when one firm purchases another. A joint venture is a partnership between companies formed for a specific undertaking.

Assessment Check Answers

10.1 Distinguish between a merger and an acquisition. In a merger, two or more firms combine to form one company. In an acquisition, one firm purchases the property and assumes the obligations of another. Acquisitions also occur when one firm buys a division or subsidiary from another firm.

10.2 What are the different kinds of mergers? Mergers can be classified as vertical, horizontal, or conglomerate.

10.3 What is a joint venture? A joint venture is a partnership between organizations formed for a specific undertaking.

Business Terms You Need to Know

small business 116
home-based businesses 117
business plan 123
Small Business Administration (SBA) 124
microloans 125
business incubator 126
venture capital 126
franchising 128
franchisee 129
franchisor 129
sole proprietorship 131
partnership 132
corporation 133
S corporations 133
limited-liability company (LLC) 133
benefit corporation 133
employee ownership 134
not-for-profit corporations 135
stockholders 137
preferred stock 137
common stock 137
board of directors 137
merger 140
acquisition 140
vertical merger 140
horizontal merger 140
conglomerate merger 140
joint venture 140

Review Questions

1. Describe how a small business might use innovation to create new jobs.

2. Why do so many small businesses fail before they reach their tenth year?

3. What are the benefits of developing and writing an effective business plan?

4. What is the Small Business Administration? How does it assist small companies, financially and in other specialized ways?

5. Describe how local governments and business incubators help small firms get established and grow.

6. Why are so many small-business owners attracted to franchising? Under what circumstances might it be better to start an entirely new business instead of purchasing a franchise?

7. What are the benefits and drawbacks to traditional corporate structure? How do S corporations and limited liability companies enhance the corporate legal structure?

8. Cooperatives appear frequently in agriculture. Describe another industry in which you think collective ownership would be beneficial, and explain why.

9. In a proprietorship and in partnerships the owners and the managers of the business are the same people. How are ownership and management separated in corporations?

10. How might a joint venture between a commercial firm and a not-for-profit organization help both achieve their goals?

Projects and Teamwork Applications

1. Research a large company to find out more about its beginnings as a start-up or small business. Who founded the company? What were the company's original offerings, and how do they differ today?

2. Go to the website for *Entrepreneur* and research information on "Franchise 500," the magazine's top franchises. Choose one that interests you and evaluate the information about its start-up requirements. Discuss whether you would consider a partnership in your franchise with someone you know. Why or why not? Present your findings in class.

3. Think of your favorite small business—you know, the one where they know you by name. Maybe it's your hair or nail salon, coffee shop, or corner market. Interview the owner of the business and ask how and why the current form of ownership was chosen. Present your findings in class.

4. Identify an organization—such as the Corporation for Public Broadcasting or the United States Postal Service—that is owned by a unit or agency of government. Discuss the pros and cons of whether the organization should remain publicly owned. Research its successes and failures, and create an outline explaining your conclusion.

5. Discuss your experience and thoughts about crowdfunding sites as an alternative to funding by big banks. Have you ever contributed to a crowdfunding campaign, and if so, what were the details of the venture? If you were to set up a crowdfunding campaign, what steps would you take to encourage donations?

Web Assignments

1. **Cooperatives.** Go to the Cranberry Growers cooperative website and click on "Who We Are" to learn more about the 700 families who have been Ocean Spray cranberry growers, some for generations. Compare and contrast the benefits of this form of ownership with that of a sole proprietorship or partnership by focusing on the following elements: ownership, risk, profits, and decision making.

http://www.oceanspray.com

2. **Venture capital firms.** Kleiner Perkins Caufield & Byers is regarded by Wall Street as one of the largest and most established venture capital firms in the country. Go to the company's website and click on "companies" to review "focus areas." Choose one focus area and describe its initiatives and categories.

http://www.kpcb.com

3. **Successful partnerships.** Neil Blumenthal and Dave Gilboa are the entrepreneurs who started Warby Parker, the online eyewear company. Perform research to determine the unique talents of each partner and how their combined talents made them innovators.

http://www.warbyparker.com

Note: Internet web addresses change frequently. If you do not find the exact sites listed, you may need to access the organization's or company's home page and search from there or use a search engine like Google or Bing.

Cases

Case 5.1 Drones Do More than Just Deliver

Imagine for a moment a relaxing day at the beach, when suddenly you hear the sound of someone in the ocean who appears to be in distress. Next, picture the arrival of a drone, an unmanned aerial vehicle, carrying a flotation device to rescue the individual—eventually replacing or supplementing the role of the traditional beach lifeguard. For now, the buzz about drones seems to be centered on delivery strategies, but what if, in addition to delivering packages, drones could be used to protect people from harm? That's where the company Airware comes in.

Recently awarded Small Business Innovator of the Year by *USA Today,* Jonathan Downey is the founder of Airware, the fast-growing commercially operated drone company based in San Francisco. Airware's Aerial Information Platform (AIP) combines hardware, software, and cloud services to enable companies to quickly customize, efficiently manage, and safely and reliably operate commercial drones for a variety of uses, including industrial and infrastructure inspections, land and agriculture management, public safety, surveying and mapping, search and rescue, and even wildlife conservation.

A number of companies are using Airware's AIP to help inspect factories and pipelines, to monitor large tracts of farmland, and to collect overhead video and measurement data. For farmers, drones can be used for crop surveillance to increase crop yields and to minimize the cost of labor used to walk the fields or more costly traditional airplane flyover inspections. As ivory poachers threaten African elephants and rhinos, drones can be used to catch them in their tracks from thousands of miles away. Within the utility, oil and gas, and telecommunications industries, Airware drones can be used to perform jobs traditionally deemed unsafe for workers—like climbing 250-foot communication towers or surveying, detecting, and locating leaks in oil and gas fields.

While some companies like e-commerce giant Amazon continue to fine-tune their drone delivery systems, companies such as Airware are using drones to turn aerial data into actionable business intelligence as well as making business operations safer and more efficient for companies.

Questions for Critical Thinking

1. Can you think of other types of commercial uses of drones?
2. Discuss the different ways Airware's drones are being used in the following industries: insurance, natural gas, utilities, and telecommunications. What are the potential risks of using drones as part of a company's overall business practices?

Sources: Company website, https://www.airware.com, accessed March 11, 2018; Bart Jansen, "Airware CEO Is Small Business Innovator of the Year," *USA Today*, http://www.usatoday.com, accessed March 11, 2018; Kyle Russell, "Airware Launches Its Commercial Drone Operating System," *Tech Crunch,* http://techcrunch.com, accessed March 11, 2018; Philip Elmer-DeWitt, "Amazon Stands By Its Dubious Drone," *Fortune,* http://fortune.com, accessed March 11, 2018; Sandy Smith, "Telecommunication Towers Claim More Lives: Two Workers Dead in Kansas," *EHS Today,* http://ehstoday.com, accessed March 11, 2018; Charlotte Jee, "Drone Deliveries Take Off in the UK Any Time Soon. Here's Why . . ." *Tech World,* http://www.techworld.com, accessed March 11, 2018; Alex Hern, "DHL Launches First Commercial Drone 'Parcelcopter' Delivery Service," *Guardian*, http://www.theguardian.com, accessed March 8, 2018.

Case 5.2 Why Family Businesses Leave the Family

S.C. Johnson & Son, makers of Windex and Pledge, is a family-owned business currently in its fifth generation of leadership. An often overlooked form of business ownership, family-owned businesses surround us—from your neighborhood mom-and-pop stores to corporate giants like S.C. Johnson, Walmart, and Ford. According to a Harvard

Business School study, 70% of family businesses either fail or are sold before the second generation of ownership even gets a chance to succeed its founders. The biggest reason for lack of succession is commonly referred to as "business divorce," or the separation of its business owners. The reason? Poor management and, even worse, long-term succession and strategic planning. Other conflicts can include money, nepotism (favoring relatives), and infighting over succession of power from one generation to the next.

Are senior family members cannibalizing the very businesses they took years to build? Many successful business owners have the means to provide for college—which creates a highly educated, next generation of family members. With levels of education superior to their small business-owning parents, children choose careers commensurate with education levels. In addition, family business parents may avoid encouraging or pressuring children to take over due primarily to more education and career choices available than in previous generations.

Many newly minted college graduates may prefer the opportunity to make a difference or change the world—and that might not include working as a middle-level manager of what can sometimes amount to a traditional, not-so-glamorous, small-town family business in an "old economy" industry.

In the past, next-generation family members worked years before gradually taking over the business from a previous generation. Today's family members are impatient to advance their own careers and to make an impact on society. For the 30% of family businesses that do make it beyond the second generation of ownership—there's something to be said about the longevity of "keeping it in the family."

Questions for Critical Thinking

1. What do you believe are additional reasons to support the statistic that 70% of family businesses fail or are sold before the second generation of ownership gets a chance to succeed? Discuss why next-generation family members may not be qualified or suited to take over the business.
2. Do the odds of the long-term survival of a family business have more to do with the many career and educational opportunities available today and less to do with the quality of succession and long-term strategic planning? What are other contributing factors?

Sources: Company website, "5 Generations of Johnsons," http://www.scjohnson.com, accessed March 8, 2018; Wayne Rivers, "10 Reasons Family Businesses Are Not Staying in the Family," *Wall Street Journal,* http://www.wsj.com, accessed March 8, 2018; Chase Peterson-Withorn, "New Report Reveals the 500 Largest Family-Owned Companies in the World," *Forbes,* http://www.forbes.com, accessed March 8, 2018; Christian Caspar, Ana Karina Dias, and Heinz-Peter Elstrodt, "The Five Attributes of Enduring Family Businesses," *McKinsey & Company,* http://www.mckinsey.com, accessed March 8, 2018.

Case 5.3 The Mei Mei Group: A Family Affair in Boston

Many consider family-owned businesses the backbone of American business. "Mei Mei" translates from Chinese to "little sister" in English, and its name aptly represents a family business of three siblings: Andy, Margaret (Mei), and Irene Li. When Andy, the oldest sibling, formed the Mei Mei Group, it was only appropriate to name it after his two little sisters. Together as the Mei Mei Group, the Lis operate Mei Mei Street Kitchen, a food truck on the streets of Boston, and Mei Mei restaurant near the Boston University campus. When the siblings decided to go into business together, they realized that despite their distinctly different backgrounds, what they have all shared since childhood was a love of food.

With a passion for food instilled in them by their parents, the Li siblings began brainstorming about how to utilize their complimentary skills to create a family business. With restaurant management experience, Andy oversees the restaurant. Mei studied social entrepreneurship in London. While in London, she created a number of pop-up restaurants in unique locations, including one underneath the railway arches of the Thames River. Mei also attended business school, so she focuses on finances, marketing, business development, and the company's social media platform. Irene, the youngest sibling, attended Cornell University and has worked and lived on organic farms. Her experience helps the company ethically source food ingredients from local vendors. While in college Irene also began her own pop-up restaurant. The siblings were unanimous in their goal to bring authentic Chinese dishes with an American twist to Boston consumers, using seasonal, locally sourced ingredients. The restaurant was named Eater Boston's Restaurant of the Year and made *Boston Magazine*'s list of 50 Best Restaurants.

One impressive contribution of small businesses like the Mei Mei Group is its creation of jobs in the local Boston area. Between its food truck and restaurant, the Mei Mei Group now employs more than 35 workers. In addition, the Lis firmly believe that supporting the local food system and area farms provides fresher products to its customers. As a result, they are able to create jobs and provide revenue to the local Boston area economy.

The Mei Mei Group is an example of a small business that has provided an outlet for creative new ideas as businesses and consumers recognize a need for change. In this case, making a difference in the local food system is part of Mei Mei's core values. Since opening less than eight years ago, the Mei Mei Group has brought hundreds of thousands of pounds of local and regional food from nearby farms in the Northeast to the consumers of Boston.

Menu items begin with traditional Chinese cuisine, and based on the supply of produce from local growers, menus are constantly changed and updated. Dumplings, for example, might be filled with sweet potato and sage, based on what's local and in season. With hundreds sold daily, Mei Mei's signature Double Awesome, recently named by *Food & Wine Magazine* as one of Boston's Best Snacks!, is an egg sandwich with pesto made from local growers and Vermont cheese on a scallion pancake. All eggs are purchased from a local free-range farm in nearby Providence, Rhode Island, and after a few years in business, the Lis are beginning to realize the impact of local sourcing on the local economy and the Boston food scene.

Although it may feel like David versus Goliath, the Mei Mei Group wants to do its part to innovate by working with local and regional growers to change the startling statistic that only 1% of food consumed is grown locally. Most food is produced on a massive or industrialized scale, which includes growing food on farms as inexpensively as possible, many times resulting in the inhumane treatment of animals solely for profit. The Lis' business model has proved that providing healthy, locally grown food and meats to customers is both responsible and financially sustainable.

The growth of the Mei Mei Group has had a direct impact on the prosperity of the 40 local farmers with whom they work. Irene has built strong and enduring partnerships with their suppliers, who range from pig, poultry, and beef farmers to local and regional growers. One farmer is building two new chicken coops for the Mei Mei Group, which purchased every one of his chickens last year. Since the demand for greens like kale and swiss chard remains strong, Mei Mei Group's suppliers are working on ways to continue greenhouse operations during winter months.

The Lis wrote a business plan, which was a helpful way for them to learn more about the industry and to think about the different aspects of their business, from marketing, to finance, to operations. Knowing very well that industries and markets continually change, the Lis used the business plan as a dynamic and changing road map. In addition, the Lis decided to create their form of ownership as an S corporation. This decision was made to avoid double taxation of business income while minimizing financial liability for the siblings.

The challenge of financing remains an obstacle for many small businesses, and without adequate funds generated from initial sales, failure can occur. Through personal loans and some help from family members, the Lis launched their first venture, the food truck, a little more than three years ago. Partial financing for their restaurant came in the form of donations of $35,000 from Kickstarter, a crowdsourcing website.

Some of the biggest challenges faced by the Mei Mei Group are regulatory in nature. The city of Boston has many food truck regulations that Mei Mei and other businesses must follow. Issues range from the threat of fewer public parking spaces, truck hours and locations, and the types of food and meals the trucks are allowed to serve. In addition, the Mei Mei Group has been persistent about trying to obtain a liquor license for its restaurant operation.

Without thinking too much about future plans, the siblings are enjoying their firm's success and the fruits of their labor. While there's always the possibility of opening more restaurants, the company's core value of making a difference in the local food system may take them in a different direction that could involve farming. Recently the siblings launched three bottled sauces for marinades, dips, and glazes. The sauces are for sale online, at store locations, and through wholesale and retail outlets. For now, the Li siblings are sure of one business goal: continuing to bring good food to the people of Boston.

Questions for Critical Thinking

1. Discuss and outline the unique ways the Mei Mei Group contributes to the local Boston area economy. Provide additional ideas and examples of how the Mei Mei Group can continue making a contribution to the local food scene in Boston.
2. How might the company's social media outreach differ for its food truck compared to its restaurant? Do you think each attracts a different group of diners? Explain.
3. Small businesses contribute to the economy by creating new jobs and industries and providing innovation. Provide examples of how the Mei Mei Group has achieved each of the contributions typically made by small businesses.
4. Discuss some of the biggest challenges for the Mei Mei Group as a small business. How do these challenges differ from other types of small businesses?

Sources: Company website, "Container" and "Pantry," http://meimeiboston.com, accessed March 11, 2018; Kara Baskin, "Awesome Bowls in a Repurposed Seaport Shipping Container," *Boston Globe,* http://www.bostonglobe.com, accessed March 11, 2018; company website, "2015 Best Dumplings," http://www.bestofboston.com, accessed March 11, 2018; Kate Krader, "The New Originals," *Food and Wine*, http://www.foodandwine.com, accessed March 11, 2018; Mei Mei Street Kitchen Facebook page, https://www.facebook.com/meimeiboston, accessed March 11, 2018; "Meet Young Guns Semi-Finalists Irene Li and Max Hull of Boston's Mei Mei," *Eater.com*, http://www.eater.com, accessed March 11, 2018; Sascha Garey, "Lunch Anyone? Mei Mei," *BU Today*, http://www.bu.edu, accessed March 11, 2018; Rachel Leah Blumenthal, "Changing the Way the World Eats: Mei Mei Street Kitchen at TED," *YouTube*, http://www.youtube.com, accessed March 11, 2018; Christopher Hughes, "Five Reasons You Should Be Eating at Mei Mei Street Kitchen," *Boston Magazine*, http://www.bostonmagazine.com, accessed March 11, 2018; Devya First, "Mei Mei Crew Inventively Spins Off Its Truck Menu," *Boston Globe*, http://www.bostonglobe.com, accessed March 11, 2018; Jon Giardiello, "Mei Mei Street Kitchen Opens New Location," http://www.boston.com, accessed March 11, 2018; Morgan Rousseau, "Cray Cray for Mei Mei: Boston Food Truck to Open Green Eatery," *Metro US Magazine*, http://www.metro.us, accessed March 11, 2018; Rachel Travers, "Rolling with the Mei Mei Street Kitchen," *Boston.com*, http://www.boston.com, accessed March 11, 2018; Brian Samuels, "Serving Local on the Road: Mei Mei Street Kitchen," *Edible Boston*, http://edibleboston.com, accessed March 11, 2018.

CHAPTER **6**

Starting Your Own Business: The Entrepreneurship Alternative

LEARNING OBJECTIVES

1. Define entrepreneur.
2. Identify the different categories of entrepreneurs.
3. Explain why people choose entrepreneurship as a career path.
4. Discuss the environment for entrepreneurs.
5. Identify the characteristics of entrepreneurs.
6. Summarize the process of starting a new venture.
7. Explain intrapreneurship.

Changemaker

Daniel Zuchnik/WireImage/Getty Images

Jennifer Hyman, Co-founder and Chief Executive Officer

Company: Rent the Runway

Industry: e-commerce/retail/fashion

Website: www.renttherunway.com

Jennifer Hyman is a classic entrepreneur. Known for "fashion in the cloud," Rent the Runway is an e-commerce company that makes high fashion accessible to the everyday woman interested in renting luxury items like dresses and accessories—at a fraction of their retail price. Rent the Runway is part of the "access economy," which favors access over ownership.

The inspiration for Rent the Runway, which started less than a decade ago, came to Hyman (pictured in photo) after witnessing her sister spend thousands of dollars on designer dresses for a multitude of weddings—and being pictured on social media wearing the same dress. Hyman's business venture also solves a problem common to many retailers with liberal return policies—that of women purchasing, wearing, and promptly returning special-occasion dresses.

Rent the Runway partners with fashion designers using a subscription-based model to rent clothing, jewelry, and handbags to its 6 million members. Members choose items filtered by designer, color, length, and body type from among thousands of dresses from more than 400 designers. In addition, the designers gain exposure to a new market of customers, many of whom might not otherwise ever wear or purchase a special-occasion dress.

Rental costs are typically 10% of the retail price of the dress, and rental periods are between four and eight days. The dress is delivered via UPS, and returns are free. All dry cleaning is handled by Rent the Runway, and a $5 insurance fee is added to handle small mishaps like stains.

Rent the Runway is backed by over $125 million in venture capital funding, and Jack Ma of Alibaba recently invested $20 million in the company. When asked about being an entrepreneur, Hyman says implementing a business idea is relatively easy; however, entrepreneurs need to listen, be humble, and continuously learn.[1]

Overview

You think you want to start and run your own company. Like the founder of Rent the Runway, you have a great idea for a new business. Maybe you dream of being highly successful and making a difference. If you have been bitten by the entrepreneurial bug, you are not alone. More than ever, people like you, your classmates, and your friends are choosing the path of entrepreneurship.

How do you become an entrepreneur? Experts advise aspiring entrepreneurs to learn as much as possible about business by completing academic programs such as the one in which you are currently enrolled and by gaining practical experience by working part- or full-time for businesses. In addition, you can obtain valuable insights about the pleasures and pitfalls of entrepreneurship by reading newspaper and magazine articles and biographies of successful entrepreneurs. These sources will help you learn how entrepreneurs handle the challenges of starting their businesses. For advice on how to launch and grow a new venture, turn to magazines such as *Entrepreneur, Forbes, Fast Company, Success, Wired,* and *Inc*. Entrepreneurship associations such as the United States Association for Small Business and Entrepreneurship and Entrepreneurs' Organization also provide valuable assistance. Finally, any aspiring entrepreneur should visit these websites:

- TED Talks (https://www.ted.com/topics/entrepreneur)
- Entrepreneur.com (http://www.entrepreneur.com)
- Kauffman Foundation (http://www.kauffman.org)
- The Small Business Administration (http://www.sba.gov)
- The Wall Street Journal Accelerator (https://blogs.wsj.com/accelerators)
- Mashable (http://www.mashable.com)
- Venture Beat (https://venturebeat.com/)
- Inc. Magazine (http://inc.com)

In this chapter, we focus on pathways for entering the world of entrepreneurship, describing the activities, the different kinds of entrepreneurs, and the reason a growing number of people choose to be entrepreneurs. We discuss the business environment in which entrepreneurs work, the characteristics that help them succeed, and the ways they start new ventures. The chapter ends with a discussion of methods by which large companies try to incorporate the entrepreneurial spirit.

1 What Is an Entrepreneur?

An **entrepreneur** is a risk taker in the private enterprise system, a person who seeks a profitable opportunity and takes the necessary risks to set up and operate a business. Consider Sam Walton, Walmart's founder, who started by franchising a few small Ben Franklin variety stores and then opened his own Walton Five and Dime stores. Today, Walmart has grown into a multibillion-dollar global business that is also one of the world's largest companies.

entrepreneur risk taker in the private enterprise system; a person who seeks a profitable opportunity and takes the necessary risks to set up and operate a business.

Entrepreneurs differ from many small-business owners. Although many small-business owners possess the same drive, creative energy, and desire to succeed, what makes entrepreneurs different is that one of their major goals is expansion and growth. Sam Walton was not satisfied with just one successful Ben Franklin franchise, so he purchased others. And when that was not enough, he started and grew his own stores. Entrepreneurs combine their ideas and drive with money, employees, and other resources to create a business that fills a market need. That entrepreneurial role can make something significant out of a small beginning. Walmart, the company that Sam Walton started, has revenues of close to $500 billion.[2]

Entrepreneurs also differ from managers. Managers are employees who direct the efforts of others to achieve organizational goals. Owners of some small start-up firms serve as owner-managers to implement their plans for their businesses and to offset human resource limitations at their fledgling companies. Entrepreneurs may also perform a managerial role, but their overriding responsibility is to use the resources of their organizations—employees, money, equipment, and facilities—to accomplish their goals. With the goal of satisfying health-conscious macaroni and cheese lovers, Annie Withey co-founded Annie's Homegrown. Annie chose her pet rabbit, Bernie, to be the company mascot, and he appeared on each box of the company's products, which came in shell and bunny rabbit shapes, as the brand's "Rabbit of Approval." Twenty-five years later, Annie's Homegrown uses only natural and organic ingredients to make a wide range of products, including pastas, pizzas, salad dressings, snacks and soups—and gluten-free and vegan selections. General Mills paid $820 million for the company in hopes that consumers will continue to demand natural and organic foods like the ones created by Annie Withey. Recently, General Mills announced Annie's elbow pasta and cheddar and bunny-shaped baked graham snacks made with organic ingredients from regenerative farms in Montana.[3]

Studies have identified certain personality traits and behaviors common to entrepreneurs. One of these traits is the willingness to assume the risks involved in starting a new venture. Some, like Annie Withey, take that risk out of necessity—they have left or lost previous jobs or simply need a way to generate cash. Others want a challenge or a different quality of life. Entrepreneurial characteristics are examined in detail in a later section of this chapter.

Assessment Check

1. How do entrepreneurs create new businesses?
2. How do entrepreneurs differ from managers?

2 Categories of Entrepreneurs

Entrepreneurs apply their talents in different situations. These differences can be classified into distinct categories: classic entrepreneurs, serial entrepreneurs, and social entrepreneurs.

classic entrepreneur person who identifies a business opportunity and allocates available resources to tap that market.

Classic entrepreneurs identify business opportunities and allocate available resources to tap those markets. Greg Wittstock, a classic entrepreneur, became intrigued with ponds at the age of 12 when his father built one for his pet turtles. However, the pond leaked and turned green, and the turtles ended up migrating away. Wittstock turned his backyard into a classroom experiment by ripping out and rebuilding the pond—and that was the beginning of what is now Aquascape, based in St. Charles, Illinois. Wittstock sells his water garden ponds—an 11-by-16 foot kit for about $10,000—to specialty contractors. He also throws an annual event called "Pondemonium" for both contractors and pond enthusiasts.[4]

serial entrepreneur person who starts one business, runs it, and then starts and runs additional businesses in succession.

A classic entrepreneur starts a new company by identifying a business opportunity and allocating resources to tap a new market; **serial entrepreneurs** start one business, run it, and then start and run additional businesses in succession. Elon Musk, the founder of such businesses as PayPal, Tesla Motors, Solar City, and SpaceX, is a serial entrepreneur. Mark Cuban is another well-known serial entrepreneur who also happens to be a "shark" investor on the hit reality TV series, *Shark Tank*. As owner of the Dallas Mavericks, he has invested in numerous startups and built and sold multiple businesses (including a company, which he sold to CompuServe in 1990). Cuban speaks honestly about many failures before becoming a billionaire—and confesses that he was "fired from more jobs than most people have had." He is the author of *How to Win at the Sport of Business: If I Can Do It, You Can Do It*, excerpts from his popular Blog Maverick—a profile of business, life, and what it takes to become a thriving entrepreneur.[5]

social entrepreneur person who recognizes societal problems and uses business principles to develop innovative solutions.

Some entrepreneurs focus on solving society's challenges through their businesses. **Social entrepreneurs** recognize a societal problem and use business principles to develop innovative solutions. Social entrepreneurs are pioneers of innovations that benefit humanity. With personal savings and $500,000 from angel investors, Kristin Richmond and Kirsten Tobey, as shown in photo, launched Revolution Foods. Each day, the Oakland, California–based company provides what it calls "real food" meals, including brown rice and fresh vegetables, to schoolchildren in 25 U.S. cities. More than just serving healthy meals, Revolution Foods partners with schools to deliver nutrition education programs through classroom instruction and off-campus, hands-on activities to empower students to make smarter and healthier eating choices. Recently, the company has expanded into grocery retail outlets.[6]

Jim Wilson/The New York Times/Redux Pictures

Revolution Foods, started by Kristen Richmond and Kirsten Toby, creates nutritious, fresh, and delicious food for schools using high-quality ingredients and no artificial colors, flavors, or sweeteners.

Assessment Check

1. What is the difference between a classic entrepreneur and a serial entrepreneur?
2. Describe a social entrepreneur.

3 Reasons to Choose Entrepreneurship as a Career Path

You're in good company if you want to be an entrepreneur. A recent report finds that 14%, or 27 million working-age Americans, are starting or running new businesses, and that entrepreneurship is considered an attractive career option by 51% of the working population.[7]

The past few decades have witnessed a heightened interest in entrepreneurial careers, spurred in part by publicity celebrating the successes of technology entrepreneurs such as Elon Musk, who launched the first electric sports car; Larry Page and Sergey Brin of Google; and Tory Burch, iconic fashion designer and Chairman and CEO of Tory Burch, LLC.

People choose to become entrepreneurs for many different reasons. Some are motivated by dissatisfaction with the traditional work setting—they want a more flexible schedule or freedom to make all the decisions. Others launch businesses to fill a gap in goods or services that they could use themselves. Still others start their own firms out of financial necessity, like Annie Withey did with her healthy mac and cheese business. During her junior year in college, Jessica Matthews who is Nigerian-American, participated in a class project that became the inspiration for her idea to create clean energy from the well-loved sport of soccer. Her company is Uncharted Play, and its main product is a soccer ball called SOCCKET (displayed in photo), which harnesses the kinetic energy created during normal game play and stores it for later to power electrical appliances like LED lamps, water sterilization devices, and mini refrigerators. Embedded in the soccer ball is technology called M.O.R.E: Motion-based, Off-grid-Renewable Energy. With each purchase of an Uncharted Play product, a toy and an innovative STEM (science, technology, engineering, math) and social invention curriculum called "Think Out of Bounds" is donated to a child in a less-developed country.[8]

Angela Weiss/Getty Images

While in college at Harvard University, Jessica Matthews started Uncharted Play, whose main product is a soccer ball called SOCCKET, which stores energy that can be used later to power electrical appliances and lamps.

As pointed out in **Figure 6.1**, people become entrepreneurs for one or more of four major reasons: a desire to be their own boss, to succeed financially, to attain job security, and to improve their quality of life. Each of these reasons is described in more detail in the following sections.

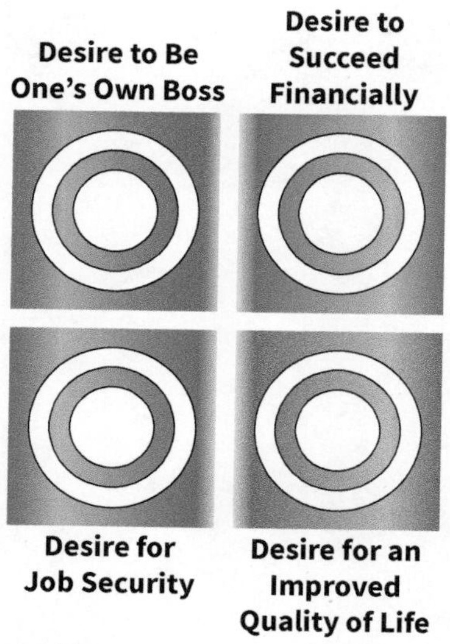

Desire to Be One's Own Boss

Desire to Succeed Financially

Desire for Job Security

Desire for an Improved Quality of Life

FIGURE 6.1 Why People Become Entrepreneurs

Being Your Own Boss

The freedom to make all the decisions—being your own boss—is one of the biggest lures of entrepreneurship. When Michael Grondahl purchased a struggling gym, little did he know that more than two decades later, he'd be disrupting the fitness industry's model of locked-in annual membership contracts and high monthly fees. Based in New Hampshire, Planet Fitness offers its members a no "gymtimidation," judgment-free zone, and a unique environment where anyone can be comfortable. With the same equipment and amenities as its competitors, Planet Fitness does not require a contract for sometimes-fickle gym members. For a $10 monthly starting fee, members join without the pressure of an annual commitment. As a national sponsor of NBC's reality TV hit *The Biggest Loser*, Planet Fitness has over 1,400 franchise locations and recently went public.[9]

Being your own boss generally means getting to make all the important decisions. It also means engaging in much—if not all—of the communication related to your business, including customers, suppliers, distributors, retailers, and the like. Think you have what it takes to be an entrepreneur? See the "Job Description " feature to find out more.

Job Description

Entrepreneur

Overview Entrepreneurs rarely fit into one specific job title, career path, or industry. Emotionally demanding, entrepreneurial careers can be found in just about every facet of business. Entrepreneurship results in new products and services, and sometimes even new industries. Some entrepreneurs work alone, while others work in family businesses, or in teams as part of larger organizations. Entrepreneurs typically create new ventures by launching a company, buying a business, or developing (and commercializing) a technology. Some entrepreneurs typically begin work in a startup environment and later leave to launch their own enterprise.

Responsibilities Entrepreneurs plan, direct, and coordinate the operations of their organizations while keeping the big picture in mind and maintaining a focus on customers, financial matters, employees, and innovation. Duties and responsibilities might include formulating policies, managing daily operations, planning, and managing finances, human resources, and materials. Tasks are diverse and may include problem solving, management, administration, and purchasing.

Requirements Educational requirements for entrepreneurs vary. Some may have high school diplomas, while others may have dropped out of college. Some entrepreneurs have degrees in business or entrepreneurship; others in a specific field related to the business they're starting. For example, an aspiring restaurateur may be a culinary or hospitality college graduate. Since most entrepreneurs need to raise capital, writing a business plan, communicating, networking, and tolerating risk are all required skills.

Entrepreneurs typically need a cross-functional skill base. Since many start with limited resources, a solid business background with an understanding of functional areas (management, human resources, marketing, finance, and operations) certainly helps. Other required skills include flexibility and adaptability, a high energy level, need for achievement, a strong work ethic, honesty and integrity, initiative, optimism, self-confidence, tolerance for ambiguity, and total commitment.

Outlook Earnings among entrepreneurs vary, and income is often unpredictable, particularly during the start-up phase of a business. New business creation dropped during the last recession, and recovery has been slow. According to the Bureau of Labor Statistics, entrepreneurial survival rates vary according to industry, with construction enterprises ranking at the lower end of the spectrum and health care and social assistance services enjoying a higher success rate. While the risk can be high, so are the rewards. With drive, determination, and the desire to innovate and be your own boss, entrepreneurship may be the career for you.

Sources: Educational website, "Entrepreneurship—Explore Entrepreneurial Careers," www.babson.edu, accessed March 12, 2018; "Careers in Entrepreneurship," http://careers-in-business.com, accessed March 12, 2018; company website, "Entrepreneurs: Information About a Career As an Entrepreneur," http://study.com, accessed March 12, 2018 ; government website, "Entrepreneurship and the U.S. Economy," https://www.bls.gov, accessed March 12, 2018; J. D. Harrison, "The Decline of American Entrepreneurship in Five Charts," *Washington Post*, accessed March 12, 2018, https://www.washingtonpost.com; company website, "5 Important Roles for an Entrepreneur," http://virgin.com, accessed March 12, 2018.

Financial Success

Entrepreneurs are wealth creators. Some start their ventures with the specific goal of becoming rich—or at least financially successful. Often they believe they have an idea for a superior product and they want to be the first to bring it to market, reaping the financial rewards as a result. Entrepreneurs believe they will not achieve their greatest success by working for someone else, and they are generally right. Of course, the downside is that when they fail, entrepreneurs do not have the cushion of employment.

Online shoe and clothing retailer Zappos was started by Nick Swinmurn, whose inspiration struck when he was unable to find a pair of brown Airwalk shoes at his local mall. Swinmurn approached Tony Hsieh and Alfred Lin to invest, which they did—and shoesite.com, later renamed Zappos, was born. Ten years later, Amazon purchased the company for more than $1 billion.[10]

Job Security

As you probably know, working for a company, even a well-known *Fortune* 500 firm, is no guarantee of job security. In fact, over the last few decades, large companies have downsized in response to declining revenues and technological innovation. As a result, a growing number of American workers—first-time job seekers, college grads, and experienced, unemployed workers—have created their own job security by starting their own business or taking a chance on a start-up. Although running your own business doesn't guarantee job security, the U.S. Small Business Administration has found that most newly created jobs come from small businesses, with a significant share of those jobs coming from new companies.[11]

As economies around the world continue to evolve, workers are discovering the benefits of entrepreneurship compared with employment by large corporations. In some countries, where entire industries, such as banking, steel, and telecommunications, are government owned, young businesspeople are starting their own small firms. An entrepreneur solves problems while creating efficiency. This is achieved by providing a better service or building a new product that potentially helps people in their everyday lives.[12]

Quality of Life

Entrepreneurship is an attractive career option for people seeking to improve their quality of life. Starting a business gives the founder independence and some freedom to decide when, where, and how to work. A **lifestyle entrepreneur** is a person who starts a business to gain flexibility in work hours and control over his or her life. But this does *not* mean working fewer hours or with less intensity. Generally, it is the opposite—people who start their own businesses often work longer and harder than ever before, at least in the beginning. But they enjoy the satisfaction of success, both materially and in the way they live their lives.

lifestyle entrepreneur person who starts a business to gain flexibility in work hours and control over his or her life.

Tim Ferriss, best-selling author of the *4-Hour* self-help series (*Tribe of Mentors, The 4-Hour Workweek, The 4-Hour Body,* and *The 4-Hour Chef*), is considered by many to be an example of a lifestyle entrepreneur. He ran a dietary supplement company, which made him wealthy but also had him working 24/7. Ferriss took a month off to travel and ended up traveling the world for almost a year and a half. While he was traveling, his company thrived without him. When he returned home, he went back to work but made time to write his first book, which advised people to maximize their business results while minimizing the time to do it. After being rejected by 27 publishers, Ferriss hit the jackpot: one publisher finally took a risk and published his book. The book became a huge hit. He sold his company and became a successful author, consultant, and investor in numerous tech start-ups.[13]

Assessment Check

1. What are the four main reasons people choose to become entrepreneurs?
2. What is a lifestyle entrepreneur?

4 The Environment for Entrepreneurs

Are you ready to start your own company? Do some research about the environment in which you will be conducting business. There are several important overall factors to consider. There's the economy—whether it is lagging or booming, you may find opportunities. A recent study

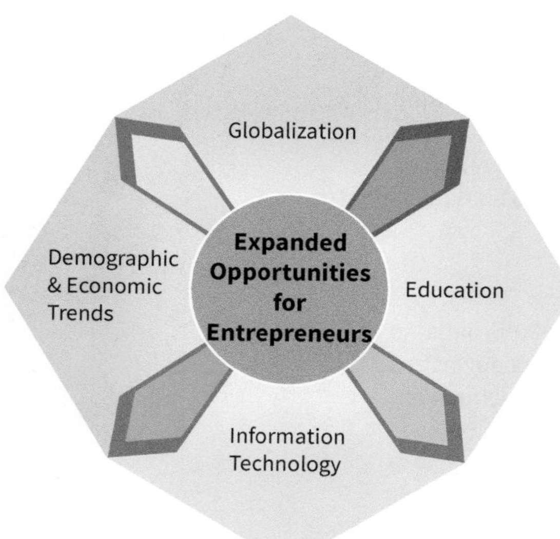

FIGURE 6.2 Factors Supporting and Expanding Opportunities for Entrepreneurs

analyzed data from key innovation indicators, including the density of tech companies, the share of professionals in STEM fields (science, technology, engineering, and math), and research and development spending per capita. Top ranking cities include Washington DC, Maryland, Massachusetts, California, Colorado, and Washington (state).[14]

In addition to favorable public attitudes toward entrepreneurs and the growing number of financing options, several other factors—identified in **Figure 6.2**—also support and expand opportunities for entrepreneurs: globalization, education, information technology, and demographic and economic trends. Each of these factors is discussed in the following sections.

Globalization

The rapid globalization of business has created many opportunities for entrepreneurs. Entrepreneurs market their products abroad and hire international workers. Among the fastest-growing small U.S. companies, almost two of every five have international sales. LinkedIn, the world's largest professional social network (purchased by Microsoft), was started by Reid Hoffman less than two decades ago. Of the 500 million registered LinkedIn users, 70% are outside of the United States. India, one of LinkedIn's fastest-growing user bases, has over 35 million users. There are 40 million students and recent college graduates on LinkedIn.[15]

Growth in entrepreneurship is a worldwide phenomenon. The role of entrepreneurs is growing in most industrialized and newly industrialized nations, as well as in the emerging free-market countries in Eastern Europe. The business ownership rate is highest in economies that compete based on unskilled labor and natural resources—like those in Sub-Saharan Africa, Latin America, and the Caribbean. Established business ownership rates are lower in places like Italy, Japan, Germany, and France—countries whose economies are driven by innovation.[16]

Organizations worldwide recognize the importance of developing the next generation of entrepreneurs. Global Entrepreneurship Week (GEW), the world's largest campaign to promote entrepreneurship, is one way of reaching out to innovators and job creators as well as recent graduates to encourage entrepreneurship and drive economic growth. Founded by the Kauffman Organization and Enterprise UK, GEW holds thousands of events, activities, and competitions in more than 149 countries for nearly 10 million participants since its inception. More than companies and organizations plan youth-oriented business events in countries ranging from the United States to South Africa.[17]

Education

The past two decades have brought tremendous growth in the number of educational opportunities for would-be entrepreneurs. Today, many U.S. universities offer full-fledged majors in entrepreneurship, dozens of others offer an emphasis in entrepreneurship, and hundreds more offer one or two courses in how to start a new business venture.

In addition to traditional classroom experience, a number of schools offer opportunities to intern with a start-up or actually work toward launching a company. The Entrepreneurship and Innovation Group at Northeastern University in Boston, which is staffed by professors who are entrepreneurs themselves, provides students with the chance to work in entrepreneurial settings in a variety of social enterprises and industries, including retail, commercial real estate development, financial services, health care, and high-growth technology. Students also have the opportunity to do enterprise development and microfinancing in South Africa and Latin America.[18]

Besides schools, many organizations have sprouted up in recent years to teach entrepreneurship to young people. The Kauffman Center for Entrepreneurial Leadership in Kansas City, Missouri, offers training programs for learners from kindergarten through community college. Enactus is a worldwide, not-for-profit organization in which over 72,000 college students across 1,700 universities, working with faculty advisors, teach grade school and high school students and other community members the value of private enterprise and entrepreneurship.[19] The Collegiate Entrepreneurs' Organization has chapters on many college campuses in the United States and Canada.

Highly motivated self-starters are often found in an entrepreneurship major. In fact, you don't have to wait for graduation to launch your first start-up, and your business idea doesn't have to change the world. In fact, there are many examples of entrepreneurs who started their businesses as college students—such as Facebook, Reddit, Federal Express, and Dell Computer.[20] Is it possible to stay in college and successfully run a startup? Some of the wealthiest and most influential entrepreneurs are college dropouts—and it worked for them. Keep in mind, however, that the rise in entrepreneurship and technology billionaires has been glamorized in the media. Becoming an entrepreneur is not only intense, but an incredible amount of work, sacrifice, and responsibility. **Table 6.1** shows a common dilemma that entrepreneurs in college face—the impulse to leave college once the entrepreneur bug has bitten them.[20]

Information Technology

The explosion in information technology (IT) has provided one of the biggest boosts for entrepreneurs, such as Jack Dorsey of Twitter. As business and technology have merged, entrepreneurs have gained tools that help them compete with large companies. Information technology helps entrepreneurs work quickly and efficiently, provide immediate and attentive customer service, and increase sales. In fact, technology has leveled the playing field to the point that, with the use of smart phones and other wireless devices, along with instant web distribution, a dorm-room innovator can compete with a much larger firm.

Social networking continues to transform the business environment for entrepreneurs. According to a recent study, more than 90% of successful companies now use at least one social media tool. Two childhood friends embracing the power of social media are Ian Hecox and Anthony Padilla, part of Smosh, a sketch comedy duo that became famous doing Pokémon skits on YouTube. YouTube, owned by Google, has minted a good number of do-it-yourself (DIY) millionaire-filmmakers or "vloggers" (video blog or log) about topics including comedy, video games, shopping, health and beauty, dance, and more. Smosh has ten YouTube channels, 23 million subscribers, and more than 7 billion views. The brand continues to thrive despite the

TABLE 6.1 Entrepreneurship or Education?

Entrepreneurship	Education
The cost of college is outrageously expensive and there is no guarantee of a return on the investment.	Student loans vs. business loans? That is the question.
There is no guarantee for success or a job with a college degree.	A college education provides social experiences and lifetime friendships. School provides networking opportunities and important resources like business plan competitions, incubator-accelerator programs, and, of course, connections.
Hands-on learning can be more valuable than textbook learning. Lessons learned as an entrepreneur can't be taught reading case studies, and some argue that being in the classroom pushes one further away from taking on the challenge of a startup.	A formal education provides increased knowledge of a field, along with a skill set. A degree is a statement that you were willing to learn in a formal setting to better yourself. An accounting course may help an entrepreneur later. Education is about inspiring potential, knowledge, and skills to generate creative ideas and the initiative to turn those ideas into action.
Starting a business is like earning a college degree or an MBA (Master of Business Administration).	A college degree, even as an entrepreneur, provides social capital when raising funds and developing a network. To work at a company (before launching your own), a college degree may be a minimum requirement.
Studying and test taking can feel unsatisfying and unproductive, while a startup that fuels a passion can be satisfying and motivating.	To increase earnings—studies show college graduates make 98% more than those who do not graduate college. Many small business owners report that college makes a difference in business success.
Procrastination leads to failure, so some entrepreneurs act on an idea right away. In other words, "strike while the iron is hot."	To have a better lifestyle, improved confidence, and improved discipline to show that you didn't quit—you started something and finished it (college). This may help promote your startup endeavor.
Some possess the attitude that entrepreneurship and formal education are longtime "frenemies."	College helps hone better critical thinking skills, allows a process of finding your direction, and creates greater options through exploration.

Sources: John Rampton, "What's the Smarter Move, Start My Business or Stay in School?," Entrepreneur, http://www.entrepreneur.com, accessed March 13, 2018; Adam Toren, "Want to Drop out of School and Start a Business? Don't Make These Stupid Mistakes," *Entrepreneur*, http://www.entrepreneur.com, accessed March 13, 2018; contributor, "Considering Starting a Business or Staying in School—What's the Smarter Move?" *Young Upstarts*, http://www.youngupstarts.com, accessed March 13, 2018; H. O. Maycotte, "Education vs. Entrepreneurship: What Path Wins?" *Forbes*, http://www.forbes.com, accessed March 13, 2018.

recent departure of Daniel Padilla, who is in search of greater creativity. Owned by Defy Media, Padilla is in search of greater creative freedom.[21]

Demographic and Economic Trends

Who might be starting a business alongside you? Immigrants to the United States are the most likely to start their own businesses, as well as those between the ages of 55 and 64.[22] As Baby Boomers continue to age and control a large share of wealth in this country, the trend can only be expected to continue. Older entrepreneurs will also have access to their retirement funds and home equity for financing. Many Boomers also plan to work after retirement from traditional jobs or careers, either because they want to continue to work or in order to boost income and savings.

Insomnia Cookies was founded in a college dorm room at the University of Pennsylvania by Seth Berkowitz to meet the need of college students for late night or early morning break-time munchies—with delivery until 3:00 a.m. In addition to deliveries, the company has expanded to 100 retail locations and an e-commerce gift site serving more than just college students.[23]

Demographic trends—including the aging of the U.S. population, increasingly diverse ethnic groups, millennials starting new homes, and the predominance of two-income families—create opportunities for entrepreneurs. Convenience products for busy parents, ethnic foods that cater to individuals, and services designed specifically for older consumers all enjoy opportunities for success. Feather is a mid-priced to high-end apartment furniture rental company focused on a target audience—namely apartment-renting, college-educated millennials. As a group that isn't tied down to a single location, moving from city to city or from place to place entails moving heavy furniture or having to buy and sell pieces that don't travel well or fit into the next space. Jay Reno, founder and CEO, has taken the stress out of buying, selling, assembling, and moving furniture. An entire living room set can be rented for less than $100 a month.[24]

For more about how one company has successfully made shopping convenient for one demographic, see the "Business Model" feature.

Business Model

Bed-in-a-Box a Big Hit with Millennials

If you think back to the last time you purchased a mattress, the words *technology* and *innovation* might not immediately come to mind. The mattress industry is ripe for disruption, and e-commerce company Casper Mattress has played a key role in changing the way people shop for a mattress. Mattresses have traditionally been part of a low-tech industry that has relied on an old-school, person-to-person showroom sales approach. A few years ago, as a way to shake up a somewhat sleepy, yet large $29 billion industry, CEO Philip Krim and four friends started Casper Mattress. Sold online and direct to consumers, the New York–based firm has ignited a fire with one demographic in particular: social-media-savvy Millennials, born between the early 1980s and early 2000s who frequently move from place to place, and prefer to shop online. In addition to Casper's product superiority—its on-site user experience, packaging, delivery, and customer service—consumer response to its high-quality, competitively priced memory foam mattress has been tremendous.

What makes the Casper mattress unique is the convenient way it is packaged and delivered. Casper mattresses are compressed to fit into a condensed box the size of a mini-fridge for greater portability. After unboxing, the mattress decompresses, expanding to full thickness in 60 seconds. Casper recently teamed up with Uber to deliver mattresses in the New York City area. CEO Krim's goal was to bring the mattress into the tech age, and he has done just that by meeting the needs of his targeted demographic, which has proclaimed the product's virtues through Instagram and Facebook posts and "unboxing" videos that have gone viral. Sales have been anything but sleepy—In a recent year, revenues exceeded $200 million, and Target stores invested $75 million in Casper, opening a partnership that placed Casper's sheets and pillows in their stores. Casper's growth, albeit rife with competitors, has brought a good night's rest to many.

Questions for Critical Thinking

1. **Casper Mattress has turned the mundane activity of buying a mattress into a conversation on social media. Company co-founders are basking in the unexpected free publicity. Discuss how traditional mattress companies might respond.**
2. **Casper wants to expand past the bed-in-a-box idea and become a sleep lifestyle brand. Discuss steps the company might take to continue catering to the needs of its targeted demographic.**

Sources: Charlie Wells, "The New Mattress Professionals," *Wall Street Journal*, http://www.wsj.com, accessed March 13, 2018; Donna Fenn, "Remember These Names: The 2015 30 Under 30 List Is Here—How Casper Is Bringing Sexy Back to Bed," *Inc.*, http://www.inc.com, accessed March 13, 2018; Josh Ong, "2 Weeks with the Casper Mattress: Bedtime Never Felt So Good," *The Next Web*, http://thenextweb.com, accessed March 13, 2018; Lora Kolodny, "Casper Sleep Raises $13.1M from Celebs and VCs to Make a Better Bed," *Wall Street Journal*, http://blogs.wsj.com, accessed March 13, 2018; USA Today, *"Casper's Bed in a Box Huge Millennial Hit," YouTube*, https://www.youtube.com, accessed March 13, 2018; Jefferson Graham, "Bed-in-a-Box Start-Up Resonates with Millennials," *USA Today*, http://www.usatoday.com, accessed March 13, 2018; Cameron Albert-Deitch, "Casper Disrupted a $29 Billion Industry. Now, Its Business Model Is Getting a Complete Makeover," *Inc.*, http://www.inc.com, accessed March 14, 2018.

Assessment Check

1. What opportunities does globalization create for today's entrepreneurs?
2. Identify the educational factors that help expand current opportunities for entrepreneurs.
3. Describe current demographic trends that present opportunities for entrepreneurial businesses.

5 Characteristics of Entrepreneurs

People who strike out on their own are pioneers in their own right. They aren't satisfied with the status quo and want to achieve certain goals on their own terms. Successful entrepreneurs are often likely to have had parents who were entrepreneurs—or dreams of starting their own business. They also tend to possess specific personality traits. Researchers who study successful entrepreneurs report that they are more likely to be curious, passionate, self-motivated, honest, courageous, and flexible. The eight traits summarized in **Figure 6.3** are especially important for people who want to succeed as entrepreneurs.

Vision

Entrepreneurs generally begin with a *vision*—an overall idea for how to make their business idea a success. Then they pursue that vision with relentless passion. Billionaire Cher Wang, a Taiwanese entrepreneur and philanthropist, co-founded and currently serves as chairperson of HTC Corporation, an Android and Windows-based smartphone manufacturer. Prior to that, she co-founded integrated chipset maker, VIA. Wang is considered one of the most powerful female entrepreneurs in technology. Recently, HTC and Google announced a licensing agreement valued at $1.1 billion.[25]

Arguably, every invention from the light bulb to the smart phone originated from a person with vision—someone who viewed the world in a slightly different way. Sometimes inventions have occurred out of necessity or even a mistake. True entrepreneurs know how to turn these situations into opportunities. It's well known that penicillin was created by accident; so was champagne. The heating potential for microwaves was discovered by its inventor while working on another project. Play-Doh was intended to be a cleaning product, and Velcro was created by a hunter who noticed that burrs stuck to his socks as he walked through the wilderness.[26]

Imaginechina via AP Images

Entrepreneurs need to have a vision of how to make their business idea a success. After graduating from the University of California, Berkeley, Cher Wang, a Taiwanese-born entrepreneur and philanthropist, co-founded smart phone maker, HTC.

High Energy Level

Entrepreneurs work long and hard to realize their visions. Many entrepreneurs work full-time at their regular day jobs and spend weeknights and weekends launching their start-ups. Many entrepreneurs work alone or with a very small staff, which means that they often wear most—if not all—of the hats required to get the business going. Most entrepreneurs spend at least 70 hours a week on their new business, which can affect their other job (if they have one), personal life, and work-life balance. To maintain momentum and enthusiasm, high energy levels are needed.

Entrepreneurial Personality

Vision
High Energy Level
Need to Achieve
Self-Confidence and Optimism
Tolerance for Failure
Creativity
Tolerance for Ambiguity
Internal Locus of Control

FIGURE 6.3 Characteristics of Entrepreneurs

Need to Achieve

Entrepreneurs work hard because they want to excel. Their strong competitive drive helps them enjoy the challenge of reaching difficult goals and promotes dedication to personal success. In a recent interview, Virgin Group founder Richard Branson said Steve Jobs is the entrepreneur he most admires. Branson explains that what allowed Jobs to create the most respected brand in the world was his ability to, as Apple's advertising once claimed, "think different." "Steve Jobs wasn't known for his sense of fun, but he was always at the center of everything Apple did. Jobs was a great comeback artist who fought his way back up to create the greatest global brand ever."[28]

Self-Confidence and Optimism

Entrepreneurs believe in their ability to succeed, and they instill their optimism in others. Often their optimism resembles fearlessness in the face of difficult odds. They see opportunities where others might not. In 2008, Tesla and SpaceX, two companies founded by serial entrepreneur, Elon Musk, were on the brink of bankruptcy. Fast forward to over a decade later, and SpaceX is exploring space like never before while orders for Tesla cars remain brisk. The "secret sauce" is Elon Musk's unrelenting confidence and optimism. Some critics have labeled Musk as overconfident. However, even during the darkest times, with faith and the vision to transform ideas into reality, he pursued his goals with tenacity, perseverance, and utmost confidence. Despite ongoing detractors, setbacks, and failures, Musk continues to believe in himself.[29]

Tolerance for Failure

Entrepreneurs often succeed by sheer will and the ability to try and try again when others would give up. They also view setbacks and failures as learning experiences and are not easily discouraged or disappointed when things don't go as planned. Bobbi Brown built a big name in the cosmetics industry. Estée Lauder bought her company, and Brown stayed on, maintaining complete creative control. The brand faced some setbacks after its acquisition and sales went flat, but Brown never gave up. She met with the CEO, who said the problem was that the company was not setting itself apart from the competition. Brown took the criticism in stride, learned from the setback, and decided to change the culture of the company. She made advertising photographs more editorial and approached the cosmetics business as if it were a magazine. Today the brand is available in more than 60 countries and distributed at exclusive retailers including Nordstrom, Bergdorf Goodman, Neiman Marcus, Saks Fifth Avenue, and Bloomingdale's. Brown's latest venture, http://justBOBBI.com, an editorial site, is a lifestyle platform for wellness, beauty, and travel.[30]

When things go well, it's easy to take personal credit. But when poor business decisions result in failure, it's a bit more difficult. Truly successful entrepreneurs are willing to take responsibility for their mistakes. That is why an important part of launching any new business is remaining aware that entrepreneurs are continuously faced with ethical challenges as discussed in the "Judgment Call" feature.

Judgment Call

Whose Idea? Ethical Challenges Facing Entrepreneurs

On an ongoing basis, entrepreneurs are faced with ethical challenges and temptations to take shortcuts. A business professor who studies entrepreneurs says that managing temptations, particularly in the technology industry, can be particularly difficult because of the tremendous pressure to "stretch the truth." This can result in a host of unethical actions ranging from falsifying financials to lack of truthfulness with customers and investors.

Entrepreneurs were asked in a survey about the greatest pressures they faced. Many pointed to the ongoing dilemma centered around the ownership of intellectual property. As entrepreneurs (and serial entrepreneurs in particular) move from start-up to start-up, and ideas are tossed around like footballs, the question must be asked if an idea is fair use or whether it is a violation of someone else's intellectual property or trade secret. Knowing where the idea came from is important.

While Mark Zuckerberg readily admits that he wasn't the first to come up with the idea for an online face book, the problem with what is called a "collective invention" process is that credit for ideas can be difficult to assign. Zuckerberg claims that while there weren't many new ideas floating around, at the time the idea of a social networking site was "in the air" at his school, Harvard University, and that it was taken from a number of other ideas. However, Zuckerberg designed and built the Facebook site while at Harvard.

For entrepreneurs who strike it rich, another question around how they spend their wealth arises. Should it be spent for social change? Lavish lifestyles? Both? If so, should the investment in social change take place right away or when the company is more mature? For some like Marc Benioff, CEO and co-founder of Salesforce.com, his integrated approach to philanthropy consists of a 1-1-1 model to leverage 1% of Salesforce's technology, people, and resources to improve communities around the world. Yes, how to spend wealth is yet another challenging decision facing entrepreneurs.

Questions for Critical Thinking

1. List and discuss additional ethical issues facing entrepreneurs.
2. Are ethical dilemmas faced by entrepreneurs more difficult to manage than those faced by others? Why or why not?

Sources: Kirk O. Hansen, "The Ethical Challenges Facing Entrepreneurs," *Wall Street Journal*, http://www.wsj.com, accessed March 14, 2018; company website, "1% Model," http://www.salesforce.com, accessed March 14, 2018; Farhad Manjoo, "Mark Zuckerberg Invented Facebook," *Slate*, http://slate.com, accessed March 14, 2018; Elinore Longobardi, "Who Invented Facebook?" *Columbia Journalism Review*, http://www.cjr.com, accessed March 14, 2018.

Creativity

Entrepreneurs typically conceive new ideas for goods and services, and they devise innovative ways to overcome challenges. If we look at the top entrepreneurs in the world, we can see that creativity is the common denominator. *Inc.* magazine presents an annual list of the 500 top small businesses, most of which were started by entrepreneurs. The word *solution* is one of the most common to appear in the names of these companies.

Some entrepreneurs find creative solutions to problems; others find creative ways to accomplish a task or provide a service. Still others create entirely new products. More than 20 years ago, Jimmy Ray sketched his idea for an affordable telephone system for private airplanes on a paper napkin. Today, Chicago-based Gogo provides in-flight connectivity services to aircraft across the globe. As airlines race to improve Wi-Fi connectivity on their flights to support high-bandwidth activities like video streaming, Gogo continues to grow. Hong Kong's Cathay Pacific Airlines recently announced the installation of Gogo's satellite-based 2Ku inflight connectivity for its Airbus A330 and Boeing 777 aircraft.[31]

One out of five Americans suffer from mental health issues. Talkspace, a mobile text and video therapy app and website started in 2012 by New York–based husband-and-wife team Oren and Roni Frank, has provided a creative solution to replace the traditional face-to-face therapy session. For as little as $49 a month, once a match is made with one of Talkspace's licensed therapists, "your room is always open" for text or video therapy.[32]

Tolerance for Ambiguity

Entrepreneurs take in stride the uncertainties associated with launching a venture. Dealing with unexpected events is the norm for most entrepreneurs. Tolerance for ambiguity is different from the love of risk taking that many people associate with entrepreneurship. Successful entrepreneurs look for strategies that they believe have a good chance of success, and they quickly make adjustments when a strategy isn't working. An important way entrepreneurs manage ambiguity is by staying close to customers so that they can adjust their offerings to customer desires. When Netflix's founder Reed Hastings tried to phase out the DVD-by-mail offering in favor of a more up-and-coming streaming service, he was met with intense customer resistance. Netflix heard its customers loud and clear, and today the company, in addition to its streaming services, continues to offer DVDs by mail to nearly 3.7 million U.S. subscribers, most of whom are in rural areas with nonoptimal broadband.[33]

Internal Locus of Control

Entrepreneurs have an internal locus of control, which means they believe that they control their own destinies. You will not find entrepreneurs blaming others or outside events for their successes or failures—they own it all.

Diagnosed with a degenerative illness at age 6, Ralph Braun was confined to a wheelchair by the time he was 14. College became too difficult for Braun to navigate in his traditional wheelchair, so he decided to design his own transportation. Within about four months, he had built his first scooter. Braun later redesigned the interior of his van and created a wheelchair lift. Braun's increased mobility attracted the attention of the community of people with disabilities, and he began to receive requests for scooters, wheelchair-enabled vans, wheelchair lifts, and other products that aid the wheelchair-bound. Indiana-based BraunAbility manufactures a full line of mobility products including wheelchair accessible vans and wheelchair lifts.[34]

After reading this summary of typical personality traits, maybe you're wondering if you have what it takes to become an entrepreneur. Take the test (from the Small Business Administration

Readiness Assessment Guide

This guide is designed to help you better understand your readiness for starting a small business. It is not a scientific assessment tool. Rather, it is a tool that will prompt you with questions and assist you in evaluating your skills, characteristics and experience—as they relate to your readiness for starting a business.

The Assessment Guide has twenty five questions. When taken online, your responses will be evaluated at completion of the questions.

Readiness Questions	Yes	No
General		
1. Do you think you are ready to start a business?		
2. Do you have support for your business from family and friends?		
3. Have you ever worked in a business similar to what you are starting?		
4. Would people that know you say you are entrepreneurial?		
5. Have you ever taken a small business course or seminar?		
Personal Characteristics		
6. Are you a leader?		
7. Do you like to make your own decisions?		
8. Do others turn to you for help in making decisions?		
9. Do you enjoy competition?		
10. Do you have will power and self discipline?		
11. Do you plan ahead?		
12. Do you like people?		
13. Do you get along with others?		
14. Would people that know you say you are outgoing?		
Personal Conditions		
15. Are you aware that running your own business may require working more than 12 hours a day, six days a week and maybe Sundays and holidays?		
16. Do you have the physical stamina to handle a "self-employed" workload and schedule?		
17. Do you have the emotional strength to deal effectively with pressure?		
18. Are you prepared, if needed, to temporarily lower your standard of living until your business is firmly established?		
19. Are you prepared to lose a portion of your savings?		
Skills and Experience		
20. Do you know what basic skills you will need in order to have a successful business?		
21. Do you possess those skills?		
22. Do you feel comfortable using a computer?		
23. Have you ever worked in a managerial or supervisory capacity?		
24. Do you think you can be comfortable hiring, disciplining and delegating tasks to employees?		
25. If you discover you do not have the basic skills needed for your business, will you be willing to delay your plans until you have acquired the necessary skills?		

Result Reset

FIGURE 6.4 Quiz for Small-Business Success

Source: "Small Business Readiness Assessment," https://eweb1.sba.gov/cams/training/business_primer/assessment.htm, accessed March 14, 2018.

website) in **Figure 6.4** to find out. Your results may help you determine whether you would succeed in starting your own company.

Assessment Check

1. What is meant by an entrepreneur's vision?
2. Why is it important for an entrepreneur to have a high energy level and a strong need for achievement?
3. How do entrepreneurs generally feel about the possibility of failure?

6 Starting a New Venture

The examples of entrepreneurs presented so far have introduced many ways to start a business. This section discusses the process of choosing an idea for a new venture and transforming the idea into a working business.

Selecting a Business Idea

In choosing an idea for your business, the two most important considerations are (1) finding something you love to do and are good at doing, and (2) determining whether your idea can satisfy a need in the marketplace. People willingly work hard doing something they love, and the experience will bring personal fulfillment. The old adages "Do what makes you happy" and "Be true to yourself" are the best guidelines for deciding on a business idea.

Success also depends on customers, so would-be entrepreneurs must also be sure that the idea they choose fills a need in the marketplace. The most successful entrepreneurs tend to operate in industries in which change is ongoing and in which customers have difficulty pinpointing their precise needs. These industries allow entrepreneurs to capitalize on their strengths, such as creativity, hard work, and tolerance of ambiguity, to build customer relationships. Nevertheless, examples of outstanding entrepreneurial success occur in every industry. Whether you want to build a business based on your grandmother's cookie recipes or know that you have a better idea for tax-preparation software, you are more likely to succeed if you ask yourself the right questions from the beginning.

Consider the following guidelines as you think about your business ideas:

- List your interests and abilities. Include your values and beliefs, your goals and dreams, things you like and dislike doing, and your job experiences.
- Make another list of the types of businesses that match your interests and abilities.
- Read business and consumer magazines and websites to learn about demographic and economic trends that identify future needs for products that no one yet offers.
- Carefully evaluate existing goods and services, looking for ways you can improve them.
- Decide on a business that matches what you want and offers profit potential.
- Conduct marketing research to determine whether your business idea will attract enough customers to earn a profit.
- Learn as much as you can about the industry in which your new venture will operate, your product(s) or service, and your competitors. Read surveys that project growth in various industries.

Many entrepreneurs who start new businesses invent new products or processes. When that happens, the inventor–entrepreneur needs to protect the rights to his or her invention by securing a patent. The U.S. Patent and Trademark Office's website (http://www.uspto.gov) provides information about this process, along with forms to apply for a patent. Inventors can also apply for a patent online. The same suggestions apply to entrepreneurs who are interested in copyright protection for their product names or processes. The U.S. Copyright Office's website (http://www.copyright.gov) provides information about this process, along with forms to apply for copyright protection. Some entrepreneurs have come up with innovative ways to create clean energy from plastic, like Utah–based PK Clean. See the "Clean & Green Business" feature for more details.

Buying an Existing Business Some entrepreneurs prefer to buy established businesses rather than assume the risks of starting new ones. Buying an existing business brings many advantages: employees are already in place to serve established customers and deal with familiar suppliers, the good or service is known in the marketplace, and the necessary permits and licenses have already been secured. Getting financing for an existing business can be easier than it is for most start-ups. Some sellers may even help the buyers by providing financing and offering to serve as consultants. Most people want to buy a healthy business so that they can build on its success, but an experienced entrepreneur might purchase a struggling business with the intent of

Clean & Green Business

PK Clean Turns Plastic Waste into Fuel

Waste remains one of the biggest environmental problems of this century. Currently 2 trillion pounds of plastic waste remain in U.S. landfills, and only 8% of plastic waste actually gets recycled each year, partly because not all plastic is recyclable. While plastic from water bottles, soda cans, and milk cartons is recyclable, other types are not easily recyclable, including disposable utensils, plastic pipes, food storage containers, and shampoo bottles.

With the goal of zero landfill and greater energy independence, Priyanka Bakaya, a clean energy enthusiast, began PK Clean, a business startup in Salt Lake, Utah, less than 10 years ago. In the company's full-scale commercial facility, plastic waste is converted into oil through a process called catalytic depolymerization, in which heat and a catalyst break down plastics into crude oil, which is then sold to refineries. The creator of the process is Percy Kean, a family friend and the "PK" in the company's name, whom Bakaya met while growing up in Australia. Bakaya's imagination was sparked when Kean would show her the oil samples in his kitchen, which he used as a lab.

Cleaner than regular fuel, PK Clean's sustainable process results in zero toxic emissions. When operating at full capacity, the plant turns 10 tons of non-recycled plastic waste into 60 barrels of fuel per day. Bakaya hopes to deploy her process to other recyclers and to eventually expand on a global basis where a huge overseas market exists to recycle massive amounts of plastic waste.

Questions for Critical Thinking

1. Discuss ways Bakaya can partner with other recyclers across the country. How might the recycling opportunities differ based upon location?
2. If you had a clean tech idea, how would you go about gaining visibility and establishing relationships within the industry?

Sources: Company website, "Why," http://www.pkclean.com, accessed March 14, 2018; Jill Krasny, "Turning Landfill Into Black Gold," *Inc.*, http://www.inc.com, accessed March 14, 2018; Molly Triffin, "These 5 Women Are Saving the World," *Daily Worth*, https://www.dailyworth.com, accessed March 14, 2018; Joe McGauley, "12 Companies You've Never Heard of That Are Changing the World," *Thrillist*, https://www.thrillist.com, accessed March 14, 2018.

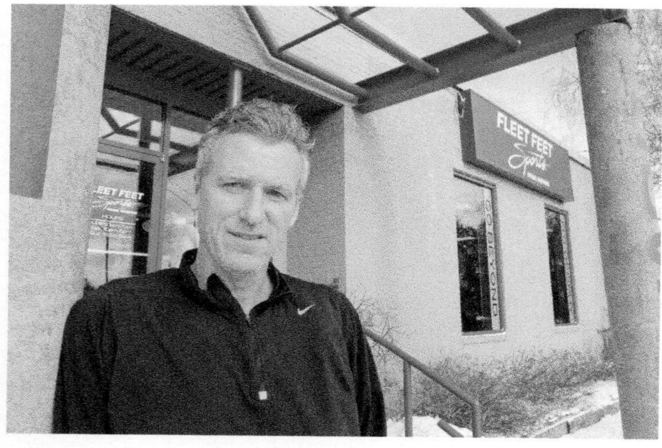

John Patriquin/Portland Press Herald via Getty Images

Buying a franchise, such as a Fleet Feet Sports store, offers entrepreneurs a less risky way to begin a business than starting an entirely new firm.

turning it around. There are many resources for entrepreneurs who are considering the purchase of a business, ranging from information provided by government agencies such as the Small Business Administration to websites listing actual companies for sale.

Buying a Franchise Similar to buying an established business, buying a franchise offers a less risky way to begin a business than starting an entirely new firm. But franchising, which was discussed in detail in Chapter 5, still involves risks, and it is wise to do thorough research before taking the plunge. Although there are a multitude of franchises from which to choose, one area that is experiencing tremendous growth is health and fitness. These businesses offer everything from athletic apparel to fitness facilities to home care to nutritional products. One example, as shown in the photo, is retailer Fleet Feet Sports.

Creating a Business Plan

In the past, many entrepreneurs launched their ventures without creating formal business plans. Although planning is an integral part of managing in business, today entrepreneurs typically seize opportunities as they arise and change course as necessary. Flexibility seems to be the key to business start-ups, especially in rapidly changing markets. But because of the risks inherent in starting a business, it has become apparent that at least some planning is not only advisable but necessary, particularly if an entrepreneur is seeking funds from outside sources.

More than 20 years ago, Jeff Bezos, CEO of Amazon.com, quit his well-paying job as a New York City hedge fund manager to move to Seattle to start an online bookseller. The first thing he did was write a business plan. On a cross-country car trip, Bezos called investors and wrote the first draft of Amazon.com's 30-page business plan on a laptop while his friend drove. In retrospect, he acknowledges that a business plan will always be different than the company's first encounters with reality and customers. However, writing the plan forced him to think through some of his company's potential issues.[35]

Chapter 5 and Appendix D discuss business plans in more detail. The Internet also offers a variety of resources for creating business plans. **Table 6.2** lists some of these online resources.

TABLE 6.2 Online Resources for Preparing a Business Plan

Bplans http://bplans.com	Click "Sample Business Plans" under "Business Planning."
Score https://www.score.org/business-plan-resources	Click on "Business Plan Template for a Startup Business."
MoreBusiness.com http://www.morebusiness.com	Under "Business Plan," click on "Templates."
Small Business Administration http://sba.gov	Go to "Write Your Business Plan" under "Business Guide."

Finding Financing

A key issue in any business plan is financing. Requirements for **seed capital**, funds used to launch a company, depend on the nature of the business. For start-ups in search of seed capital, Kickstarter is one of the best-known crowdfunding platforms. A major source of alternative funding for start-ups, over $3.5 billion was raised on Kickstarter in a recent year. Micro-VCs (venture capital firms that invest other people's money) invest in projects at the earliest stage of financing that are too small for traditional venture capital firms.[36] **Table 6.3** lists the common sources of start-up capital.

seed capital initial funding used to launch a company.

Debt Financing When entrepreneurs use **debt financing**, they borrow money that they must repay. Loans from banks, finance companies, credit card companies, and family or friends are all sources of debt financing. Although some entrepreneurs charge business expenses to personal credit cards because they are relatively easy to obtain, high interest rates make this source of funding expensive, and the Small Business Administration (SBA) recommends finding less expensive credit.

debt financing borrowed funds that entrepreneurs must repay.

Many banks turn down requests for loans to fund start-ups, fearful of the high risk such ventures entail. To a certain extent, this still remains true. Only a small percentage of start-ups raise seed capital through bank loans, although some new firms can get SBA-backed loans, as discussed in Chapter 5. Applying for a bank loan requires careful preparation. Bank loan officers want to see a business plan and will evaluate the entrepreneur's credit history. Because a start-up has not yet

TABLE 6.3 Funding Used by Entrepreneurs for Start-Ups

Source	Percentage of Entrepreneurs
Personal savings	67%
Bank loans	52%
Loans from family, friends, or business associates	40%
Credit cards	34%
Have not used financing	14%
Angel investors	8%
Venture capitalists	7%
Government grants	4%

*Percentages do not total 100 because entrepreneurs often use multiple sources to finance start-ups.

Source: Organization website, "How Entrepreneurs Access Capital and Get Funded," Entrepreneurship Policy Digest, http://www.kauffman.org, accessed March 14, 2018.

established a business credit history, banks often base lending decisions on evaluations of entrepreneurs' personal credit histories. Banks are more willing to make loans to entrepreneurs who have been in business for a while, show a profit on rising revenues, and need funds to finance expansion. Some entrepreneurs have found that local community banks are more interested in their loan applications than major national banks are.

Even entrepreneurs who have previously received funding from banks—and have maintained a good relationship with their lenders—have experienced a credit crunch in recent years. Today, banks are making far fewer loans to small businesses than they did a decade ago, and as a result small businesses have turned to alternative lenders. Jorge Rodriguez, owner of a Peruvian restaurant in Los Angeles, was turned down by his bank when he applied for financing to remodel and expand his restaurant. He ended up securing an SBA loan from a local community bank and an additional loan from a nonprofit lender.[37]

equity financing funds invested in new ventures in exchange for part ownership.

Equity Financing

To secure **equity financing**, entrepreneurs exchange a share of ownership in their company for money supplied by one or more investors. Entrepreneurs invest their own money along with funds provided by other people and firms that become co-owners of the start-ups. An entrepreneur does not have to repay equity funds. Rather, the investors share in the success of the business. Sources of equity financing include family and friends, business partners, venture capital firms, and private investors.

Teaming up with a partner who has funds to invest may benefit an entrepreneur with a good idea and skills but little or no money. Investors may also have business experience, which they will be eager to share because the company's prosperity will benefit them. Like borrowing, however, equity financing has its drawbacks. One is that investment partners may not agree on the future direction of the business, and in the case of partnerships, if they cannot resolve disputes, one partner may have to buy out the other to keep operating.

Some entrepreneurs find creative ways to obtain equity financing. With an initial seed investment of $2,500, classmates Dave Gilboa and Neil Blumenthal started Warby Parker, an eyewear company, in the Venture Initiation Program of the Wharton School of the University of Pennsylvania. Recently, the company raised $75 million in a Series E (fifth) funding round, bringing its total equity funding to nearly $300 million. The company, founded in 2010, plans to open 100 retail outlets in addition to its growing e-commerce business. The company plans to turn a profit in the coming year.[38]

venture capitalists business organizations or groups of individuals that invest in early-stage, high-potential growth companies.

Venture capitalists are business organizations or groups of private individuals that invest in early-stage, high-potential growth companies. Venture capitalists typically back companies in high-technology industries such as biotechnology. In exchange for taking a risk with their own funds, these investors expect high rates of return, along with a stake in the company. Typical terms for accepting venture capital include agreement on how much the company is worth, how much stock both the investors and the founders will retain, control of the company's board, payment of dividends, and the period of time during which the founders are prohibited from "shopping" for additional investors.[39] Venture capitalists require a combination of qualities, such as innovative technology, potential for rapid growth, a well-developed business model, and an experienced management team.

angel investors wealthy individuals who invest money directly in new ventures in exchange for equity.

Angel investors, wealthy individuals who invest money directly in new ventures in exchange for equity, are a larger source of investment capital for start-up firms. In contrast to venture capitalists, angels focus primarily on new ventures. Many angel investors are successful entrepreneurs who help aspiring business owners through the familiar difficulties of launching their businesses. Angel investors back a wide variety of new ventures. Because most entrepreneurs have trouble finding wealthy private investors, angel networks are formed to match business angels with start-ups in need of capital. New York Angels is an organization that invests in early-stage technology companies in the Northeast.

The Small Business Administration's Active Capital provides online listings to connect would-be angels with small businesses seeking financing. Venture capitalists that focus on women include Women's Venture Capital Fund (http://www.womensvcfund.com) and Springboard Enterprises (https://sb.co). Those interested in minority-owned business include, for example, the U.S. Hispanic Chamber of Commerce (http://www.ushcc.com).

Michael Buckner/Getty Images for Warby Parker

David Gilboa and Neil Blumenthal have found creative ways to obtain equity financing. With an initial seed investment of $2,500, Warby Parker has grown into an American brand of prescription eyewear.

Government Support for New Ventures

Federal, state, and local governments support new ventures in a number of ways, as discussed in Chapter 5. The Small Business Administration (SBA), state and local agencies, and business incubators all offer information, resources, and sometimes access to financing for entrepreneurs.

Another way to encourage entrepreneurship is through *enterprise zones*, specific geographic areas designated for economic revitalization. Enterprise zones encourage investment, often in distressed areas, by offering tax advantages and incentives to businesses locating within the boundaries of the zone. The state of Florida, with multiple enterprise zones, allows a business located within urban zones to take and use tax credits, tax refunds for business machinery and equipment, sales tax refunds for building materials, and a sales tax exemption for electrical energy.[40]

Assessment Check

1. What are the two most important considerations in choosing an idea for a new business?
2. What is seed capital?
3. What is the difference between debt financing and equity financing?

7 Intrapreneurship

Established companies try to retain the entrepreneurial spirit by encouraging **intrapreneurship**, the process of promoting innovation within organizational structures. Today's fast-changing business climate compels established firms to innovate continually to maintain their competitive advantages. Another form of intrapreneurship is a **skunkworks**, a project initiated by an employee who conceives an idea, convinces top management of its potential, and then recruits human and other resources from within the company to turn that idea into a commercial project.

intrapreneurship process of promoting innovation within the structure of an existing organization.

skunkworks project initiated by an employee who conceives an idea, convinces top management of its potential, and then recruits human and other resources from within the company to turn the idea into a commercial project.

Many companies encourage intrapreneurship, and many large corporations now allocate investment dollars to fund internal start-up ideas.[41] 3M is a firm that has long been known for its innovative products. Ranging from Post-it Notes and Scotch Tape to Nexcare bandages and

Thinsulate insulation, more than 55,000 3M products are either on store shelves or embedded in other firms' goods.[42] Today, industrial giants like GE are borrowing a few important lessons from younger start-ups. See the "Business & Technology" feature for more.

Coming up with the ideas for these products, developing them, and testing them before bringing them to market takes time and resources. Former 3M CEO George Buckley believes that the only way to do this is to allocate both time and money in support of intrapraneurship. 3M, along with the Coca-Cola Company, GE, Google, and IBM encourage their employees to take risks and pursue their own ideas. Facebook's infamous thumbs-up "Like" button, originally called the "awesome button," was developed at a hackathon, an event where computer programmers and software developers collaborate intensively on new developments.[43]

Business & Technology Intersection

Intrapreneurship: GE and the "Industrial Internet"

Does intrapreneurship within a large corporation have a better chance of success with far less risk? Can age-old corporate giants like GE borrow some of the lessons of culture and innovation from younger, more nimble startups? Top executives at the company believe that GE needs to become more than just a company selling jet engines and LED lights; it must become a software and analytics company.

Recently GE invested more than $1 billion to build a software start-up within its large conglomerate. Named the "Center of Excellence," the start-up will manage big data and analytics and create a more connected world described as "the Internet of Things," where customers will expect their smart, connected products to be enhanced digitally and with data services. With data-driven solutions, GE is developing hardware to reduce costs and improve performance. The company has hired 1,000 software engineers and data scientists in addition to 500 coaches to train executives to embrace concepts like risk taking, constant learning, asking questions, and yes, even failure.

One GE project, with its own board of directors, funding, and decision-making power, is a 31-person start-up seeking to commercialize a cheaper, cleaner form of solid oxide fuel cells, which convert natural gas into electricity. Its leader agrees that the project has the same agility as a start-up, and its impact on the long-term bottom line could be huge.

While 90% of Millennials prefer to work for a start-up, GE is one of a few big companies working diligently to discover and lure entrepreneurs to join its ranks. Recruiters within GE appeal to potential in-demand candidates by emphasizing the opportunity to work on challenging assignments within the healthcare and energy sectors, a focus on leadership development, and a vision of the "Industrial Internet" as the next big wave.

Questions for Critical Thinking

1. A central theme in the business start-up environment is striking it rich. How might large companies deal with this issue when they create start-up organizations within their organizational structure?
2. With its goal of becoming more like a software company, how might GE, a century-old company with over 300,000 employees, embrace a cultural shift within its organization?

Sources: Company website, "All Products," http://www.ge.com, accessed March 15, 2018; Jennifer Alsever, "Startups . . . Inside Giant Companies," *Fortune*, http://fortune.com, accessed March 15, 2018; Brad Power, "Building a Software Start-Up Inside GE," *Harvard Business Review*, https://hbr.org, accessed March 15, 2018; Geoff Colvin, "For GE, Breaking Up Is Hard to Do," *Fortune*, accessed http://fortune.com, March 15, 2018.

Assessment Check

1. Why do large, established companies support intrapreneurship?
2. What is a skunkworks?

What's Ahead

In upcoming chapters, we look at other trends that are reshaping today's business world. For example, in the next part of *Contemporary Business* we explore the critical issues of how companies organize, lead, and manage their work processes; manage and motivate their employees; empower their employees through teamwork and enhanced communication; handle labor and workplace disputes; and create and produce world-class goods and services.

Chapter in Review

Summary of Learning Objectives

LEARNING OBJECTIVE 1 Define entrepreneur.

Unlike some small-business owners, entrepreneurs are risk takers who run their business with a major goal of expansion and growth. They are visionaries who seek profitable opportunities and take the initiative to gather the resources they need to start their businesses quickly.

Assessment Check Answers

1.1 **How do entrepreneurs create new businesses?** Entrepreneurs combine their ideas and drive with money, employees, and other resources to create a business that fills a market need.

1.2 **How do entrepreneurs differ from managers?** Managers are employees who direct the efforts of others to achieve an organization's goals. The drive and impatience that entrepreneurs have to make their companies successful may hurt their ability to manage.

LEARNING OBJECTIVE 2 Identify the different categories of entrepreneurs.

A classic entrepreneur identifies a business opportunity and allocates available resources to tap that market. A serial entrepreneur starts one business, runs it, and then starts and runs additional businesses in succession. A social entrepreneur uses business principles to solve social problems.

Assessment Check Answers

2.1 **What is the difference between a classic entrepreneur and a serial entrepreneur?** A classic entrepreneur identifies a business opportunity and allocates available resources to tap that market. A serial entrepreneur starts one business, runs it, and then starts and runs additional businesses in succession.

2.2 **Describe a social entrepreneur.** A social entrepreneur recognizes a societal problem and uses business principles to develop innovative solutions.

LEARNING OBJECTIVE 3 Explain why people choose entrepreneurship as a career path.

There are many reasons people choose to become entrepreneurs. Some reasons are desire to be one's own boss, desire to achieve financial success, desire for job security, and desire to improve one's quality of life.

Assessment Check Answers

3.1 **What are the four main reasons people choose to become entrepreneurs?** People generally choose to become entrepreneurs because they want to be their own boss, they believe they will achieve greater financial success, they believe they have more control over job security, and they want to enhance their quality of life.

3.2 **What is a lifestyle entrepreneur?** A lifestyle entrepreneur is a person who starts a business to gain flexibility in work hours and control over his or her own life.

LEARNING OBJECTIVE 4 Discuss the environment for entrepreneurs.

A favorable public perception, availability of financing, the falling cost and widespread availability of information technology, globalization, entrepreneurship education, and changing demographic and economic trends all contribute to a fertile environment for people to start new ventures.

Assessment Check Answers

4.1 **What opportunities does globalization create for today's entrepreneurs?** The rapid globalization of business has created many opportunities for entrepreneurs. They market their products abroad and hire international workers. Among the fastest-growing small U.S. companies, almost two of every five have international sales.

4.2 **Identify the educational factors that help expand current opportunities for entrepreneurs.** Many U.S. universities offer majors in entrepreneurship, dozens of others offer an entrepreneurship emphasis, and hundreds more offer courses in how to start a business. Also, organizations such as the Kauffman Center for Entrepreneurial Leadership and Enactus encourage and teach entrepreneurship.

4.3 **Describe current demographic trends that present opportunities for entrepreneurial businesses.** The aging of the U.S. population, increasingly diverse ethnic groups, and the predominance of two-income families are creating opportunities for entrepreneurs to market new goods and services.

LEARNING OBJECTIVE 5 Identify the characteristics of entrepreneurs.

Successful entrepreneurs share several typical traits, including vision, high energy levels, the need to achieve, self-confidence and optimism, tolerance for failure, creativity, tolerance for ambiguity, and an internal locus of control.

Assessment Check Answers

5.1 **What is meant by an entrepreneur's vision?** Entrepreneurs begin with a vision, which is an overall idea for how to make their business idea a success, and then passionately pursue it.

5.2 **Why is it important for an entrepreneur to have a high energy level and a strong need for achievement?** Because start-up companies typically have a small staff and struggle to raise enough capital, the entrepreneur has to compensate by working long hours. A strong need for achievement helps entrepreneurs enjoy the challenge of reaching difficult goals and promotes dedication to personal success.

5.3 **How do entrepreneurs generally feel about the possibility of failure?** They view failure as a learning experience and are not easily discouraged or disappointed when things don't go as planned.

LEARNING OBJECTIVE 6 Summarize the process of starting a new venture.

Entrepreneurs must select an idea for their business, develop a business plan, and obtain financing.

Assessment Check Answers

6.1 **What are the two most important considerations in choosing an idea for a new business?** Two important considerations are finding something you love to do and are good at doing and determining whether your idea can satisfy a need in the marketplace.

6.2 **What is seed capital?** Seed capital is the money that is used to start a company.

6.3 **What is the difference between debt financing and equity financing?** Debt financing is money borrowed that must be repaid. Equity financing is an exchange of ownership shares in a company for money supplied by one or more investors.

LEARNING OBJECTIVE 7 Explain intrapreneurship.

Intrapreneurship is the process of promoting innovation within the structure of an established company.

Assessment Check Answers

7.1 **Why do large, established companies support intrapreneurship?** Large firms support intrapreneurship to retain an entrepreneurial spirit and to promote innovation.

7.2 **What is a skunkworks?** A skunkworks project is initiated by an employee who conceives an idea and then recruits resources from within the company to turn that idea into a commercial product.

Business Terms You Need to Know

entrepreneur 149
classic entrepreneur 150
serial entrepreneur 150
social entrepreneur 151
lifestyle entrepreneur 153
seed capital 163
debt financing 163
equity financing 164
venture capitalists 164
angel investors 164
intrapreneurship 165
skunkworks 165

Review Questions

1. Identify the three categories of entrepreneurs. How are they different from each other? How might an entrepreneur fall into more than one category?

2. People often become entrepreneurs because they want to be their own boss and be in control of most or all of the major decisions related to their business. How might this relate to potential financial success? If there are downsides, what might they be?

3. How have globalization and information technology created new opportunities for entrepreneurs? How does an aging population create opportunities for entrepreneurs? Describe current demographic trends that suggest new goods and services for entrepreneurial businesses.

4. Identify the eight characteristics that are attributed to successful entrepreneurs. Which trait or traits do you believe are the most important for success? Why? Are there any traits that you think might actually contribute to potential failure? If so, which ones—and why?

5. When selecting a business idea, why is the advice to "do what makes you happy" and "be true to yourself" so important?

6. Suppose an entrepreneur is considering buying an existing business or franchise. Which of the eight entrepreneurial traits do you think would most apply to this person, and why?

7. Imagine that you and a partner are planning to launch a business that sells healthy lunch choices from an on-campus food truck. You'll need seed capital for your venture. Outline how you would utilize the seed capital.

8. Describe the two main types of financing that entrepreneurs may seek for their businesses. What are the risks and benefits involved with each? Discuss alternative forms of financing.

9. What is an enterprise zone? Describe what types of businesses might benefit from opening in such a zone—and how their success might be interconnected.

10. What is intrapreneurship? How does it differ from entrepreneurship?

Projects and Teamwork Applications

1. You got bit by the entrepreneurial bug after taking an entrepreneurship class. You are at the point of deciding whether to leave college to launch a business. After all, some famous entrepreneurs—for example, Mark Zuckerberg of Facebook and Steve Jobs of Apple—were college dropouts. What are the arguments for and against leaving school to launch your new business venture? Form two teams to debate this issue.

2. Certain demographic trends can represent opportunities for entrepreneurs—the aging of the U.S. population, the increasing diversity of the U.S. population, the growth in population of some states, and the predominance of two-income families, to name a few. On your own or with a classmate, choose a demographic trend and brainstorm business ideas that could capitalize on the trend. Present your idea—and its relationship to the trend—to your class.

3. Either individually or in groups, come up with ideas from large companies that are seemingly intrapreneurial. Discuss how each company is innovating beyond its core business.

4. Many entrepreneurs turn a hobby or area of interest into a business idea. Others get their ideas from situations or daily problems for which they believe they have a solution—or a better solution than those already offered. Think about an area of personal interest—or a problem

you think you could solve with a new good or service—and create the first part of a potential business plan, the introduction to your new company and its offerings. Then outline briefly the kind of financing you think would work best for your business and the steps you would take to secure the funds.

5. You've recently graduated, and you're trying to decide whether to take a job at a large company or start your own company. Form two teams to evaluate, compare, and contrast the risk of entrepreneurship and business ownership versus working for a large company. Outline and debate the risks and rewards of each.

Web Assignments

1. **Interviewing entrepreneurs.** Salman Khan, creator of Khan Academy, has a series of interviews with entrepreneurs as part of his online teaching academy. Go to the website and search for "Interviews with Entrepreneurs." Choose one entrepreneur interview to watch and evaluate the interview for the class. Are there things you learned about this entrepreneur that surprised you? Discuss.
http://khanacademy.org

2. **Funding for Startups.** Y Combinator provides seed funding for start-ups. Twice a year, the start-ups move to Silicon Valley for three months. During that time, Y Combinator works extensively with them to help develop their ideas and, ultimately, fine-tune their pitch to investors. Demo Day, the completion of the program, is when the start-ups present their companies to groups of investors who are part of the Y Combinator program, whose alums include Dropbox, Stripe, and Airbnb. Go to the Y Combinator website and watch the video to learn more about the company's benefits and application process. Explain the long-term benefits of why a start-up might hope to be selected for the program.
http://www.ycombinator.com

3. **Getting started.** Each year, *Fast Company* magazine publishes its "50 Most Innovative Companies" issue. Visit the company's website and search for "50 Most Innovative Companies." In which industries are the companies? Does one particular industry dominate the list? Are the companies more product or service related or both? How much social entrepreneurship can you find? Cite examples.
http://www.fastcompany.com

Note: Internet web addresses change frequently. If you don't find the exact sites listed, you may need to access the organization's home page and search from there or use a search engine such as Google or Bing.

Cases

Case 6.1 Shinola Watches: Built in Detroit

Shinola is catering to consumers who have become increasingly interested in American-made products with a story behind them. The Detroit-based company not only manufactures luxury watches, bicycles, and leather goods but also has revitalized Detroit, a city once an integral part of America's automobile industry. Headquartered in a building that was home to General Motors' design facility, the company has put Detroit residents back to work after a recession caused the decline of U.S. manufacturing. The Shinola website states: "of all the things we make, American jobs might just be the thing we're most proud of."

Shinola was founded by Dallas-based entrepreneur Tom Kartsotis, also a co-founder of the Fossil watch and accessories brand. Kartsotis secured the rights to Shinola, an old shoe polish name. The company began as a watch factory in Detroit and hired nearly all of its employees from the Detroit area, half from the automobile industry. Employees had an overlap of skills, sewing leather headrests, managing quality assurance, and managing workflow engineering.

In a few short years, Shinola has established itself as a high-end maker of consumer goods across a range of product categories including dog accessories, handbags, and even a soda brand. To date, there are over 500 employees, with close to 400 in Detroit. With more than 30 retail stores, Shinola's revenues recently topped \$100 million—and if watches weren't enough, upcoming plans call for a 130-room boutique hotel in downtown Detroit.

While some might perceive Shinola as a sustainable luxury brand (its watches sell for up to \$1,125 and its bicycles are priced up to \$2,950), it may be attributed to the company's powerful narrative, which includes the renaissance of U.S. manufacturing in the Motor City of Detroit, Michigan.

Questions for Critical Thinking

1. Shinola has built credibility and market share by focusing on craftsmanship and creating social change. Do you agree that people want real, authentic luxury brands that tell a story? Why or why not?
2. Shinola employees joke that someday the company will even make a toaster. What are additional product categories that might make sense for Shinola?

Sources: Company website, "American-Made Journals" and "Our Story," http://shinola.com, accessed March 15, 2018; J. C. Reindl, "Shinola to Keep 'Built in Detroit' Slogan Despite Flak," *Detroit Free Press*, http://www.freep.com, accessed March 15, 2018; Dale Buss, "'Built in Detroit': Shinola Brand Shines Bright in Post-Recession America," *Brand Channel*, http://www.brandchannel.com, accessed March 15, 2018; Jessica Twentyman, "Live Chat Helps e-Commerce Customers Understand 'Stuff' from Shinola," *Diginomica*, http://diginomica.com, accessed March 15, 2018; Liz Stinson, "A Bold Attempt to Bring Leather-Making Back to Detroit," *Wired*, www.wired.com, accessed March 15, 2018; Theodore Koumelis, "Shinola and Bedrock Partner to Create the First Shinola Hotel," *Travel Daily News*, http://www.traveldailynews.com, accessed March 16, 2018.

Case 6.2 Glassybaby's Light Shines

When cancer patient Lee Rhodes was unexpectedly soothed by the reflective light of a simple candle inside a glass-blown votive holder, a business was born. Today, Glassybaby produces hand-blown votive candles that require over 70 glassblowers, three layers of glass, and a 24-hour process to make. Coming in 400 colors, with names like Begin Again, BFF, and Fearless, they sell for \$44 each. Recent sales are expected to top \$9 million at eight retail storefronts and online.

As integral to Glassybaby as its Seattle glass-blowing studios, which are open to customers, is its commitment to donate 10% of revenues to help cancer patients cover noninsured expenses. To date,

Rhodes has given more than $7 million to her Glassybaby White Light Fund, a nonprofit organization based in Seattle, to assist Glassybaby in its goal to promote hope and healing. Despite suggestions to expand her product line, Rhodes, a three-time cancer survivor who is now healthy, keeps the business simple. "There's something to be said for sticking to what you're good at," she says. "We make one thing really, really well." While many told Rhodes that she would never succeed selling a single American-made product, she refused to believe she could not. Seems she was right.

Questions for Critical Thinking

1. Which classification of entrepreneur does Rhodes fall into? What qualities of an entrepreneur does she probably possess?
2. Discuss how struggling with adversity might have helped Rhodes begin her business. What kind of success do you think Glassybaby might realize if it didn't have a philanthropic focus as part of its business?

Sources: Company website, "About" and "Stores," http://www.glassybaby.com, accessed March 16, 2018; Kim Holcomb, "Glassybaby Donates More than Two Million Dollars," *King 5 News*, www.king5.com, accessed March 16, 2018; "Glassybaby Opens Third Bay Area Store in San Francisco's Historic Ferry Building," *PR Newswire*, https://prnewswire.com, accessed March 16, 2018; Julie Weed, "A Seattle Retailer Builds on the Lessons of a Failed Store in New York," *New York Times*, http://boss.blogs.nytimes.com, accessed March 16, 2018.

Case 6.3 Seed + Mill: Open Sesame for Entrepreneurial Success

When most people think of sesame seeds, what might come to mind are those commonly found sprinkled atop a burger bun or bagel. However, the founders of Seed + Mill had something a little different in mind. A business partnership of three women—a serial entrepreneur, a former corporate lawyer, and a Stanford MBA—Seed + Mill is an artisanal sesame stall in one of New York City's "foodie-havens," Chelsea Market, which draws over six million people annually.

If you've never heard of tahini or halvah, popular Middle East food staples, Seed + Mill has capitalized on both. Milled on site, tahini is a sesame butter spread made from the natural oil of sesame seeds. The result is a delicious and beautifully rich and creamy product, considered a nut butter in much the same way as peanut or almond butter. The tahini, along with sugar and fruits and nuts for flavor, is used to make 30 different flavors of halvah cakes that are similar to soft, sesame candy. The texture and taste of halvah can be likened to the flakiness and sweetness found inside a Butterfinger candy bar. Seed + Mill's halvah is imported from Israel and made by small producers to the specifications of the owners (often, it includes butter to make it light and melting).

The story of Seed + Mill exemplifies the entrepreneurial spirit of individuals who began with a vision—an overall idea for how to make their business a success—and then pursued it passionately. While on vacation in Israel, the inspiration for Seed + Mill struck when Lisa Mendelson saw a group of Americans sampling halvah at an outdoor marketplace. This immediately brought back memories from her childhood—growing up and eating halvah and tahini. Mendelson's vision was to take an ancient Middle East food product and *modernize* it in the United States.

Fast forward a few years and add business partners, Rachel Simmons and Monica Molenaar, and Seed + Mill has become a reality. Mendelson identified a business opportunity and then allocated available resources (sesame seeds, business partners, suppliers, machinery, information, equipment, and a location) to tap the U.S. market. In addition, with e-commerce and the ability to connect with customers outside the realm of their stall at Chelsea Market, customers from remote parts of the country are accessible via social media, the company website, Instagram, and Facebook.

The characteristics of entrepreneurs described in this chapter are seen in Lisa, Rachel, and Monica. With a vision of building Seed + Mill into a top tahini and halvah brand, the partners, each with her own unique background and experience, bring to the endeavor optimism, creativity, and self-confidence—along with a passion for artisanal food products and their health benefits.

Inspired to create unique, healthy, and delicious artisanal food products, Seed + Mill's partners are determined to see tahini land a spot as a staple in kitchens all over the country—and worldwide. However, this endeavor will require educating customers about the versatility and health and nutrition benefits of tahini—what some have even refer to as a superfood. "It's such a great, multipurpose ingredient that no one is using the way that they can," Rachel exclaimed. "I want to see tahini on every table at home," she says with passion.

Questions for Critical Thinking

1. Tahini and halvah were long considered peasant food—good enough for those who could not afford sweets containing expensive ingredients like butter, white flour, and sugar. Today, chefs are embracing ancient flavors and devising new treats, such as multilayered halvah, sesame ice creams, and pâte brisée made with tahini instead of butter. Based upon this trend, what role will Seed + Mill play? What are its growth prospects, and where do you see the company in the next five years?
2. If you were to start a food product business, how would you determine whether there would be a need in the market? How did the partners of Seed + Mill determine whether their products would fill a need in the market?
3. What were some of the considerations of the partners when choosing an idea for their new business? What would be some of your own considerations when choosing an idea for a new businesss?
4. Based on the following, describe current demographic trends (and additional ones you can think of) that present opportunities for Seed + Mill:
   a. Aging of the U.S. population
   b. Health benefits of tahini (and halvah)
   c. America is more racially and ethnically diverse than in the past
   d. Two-income families
   e. Food and artisan trends
   f. New goods and services
   g. Additional demographic trends

Sources: Company website, "About," http://www.seedandmill.com/about, accessed March 15, 2018 ; Emma Christensen, "Open Sesame: What to Do with a Jar of Tahini," *Kitchn*, http://www.thekitchn.com, accessed March 15, 2018; Julia Moskin, "Sesame Extends Its Sweet Reach Beyond the Middle East," *New York Times*, http://nytimes.com, accessed March 15, 2018 ; Tejal Rao, "SPEND: A Spectacular Take on a Beloved Middle-Eastern Sweet," *Bloomberg*, http://www.Bloomberg.com, accessed March 15, 2018; "From Chelsea Market: A Seed, Without a Doubt," *Kitchen Kvell*, http://www.kitchenkvell.com, accessed March 15, 2018; Coral Garnick, "Glassybaby Expands into Southern California—East Coast is Next," *Puget Sound Business Journal*, https://www.bizjournals.com, accessed March 18, 2018.

Management, Leadership, and the Internal Organization

LEARNING OBJECTIVES

1. Define *management*.
2. Explain the role of setting a vision and ethical standards for a company.
3. Summarize the importance of planning.
4. Describe the strategic planning process.
5. Discuss managers as decision makers.
6. Evaluate managers as leaders.
7. Discuss corporate culture.
8. Identify organizational structures.

Changemaker

Mike Point/WireImage / Getty Images

Mark Parker, Chief Executive Officer

Company: Nike, Inc.

Industry: Athletic shoes, equipment and apparel manufacturer

Website(s): http://www.nike.com

Mark Parker, CEO of Nike, began his career with the company over 40 years ago as a shoe designer. Like his CEO predecessor, co-founder Phil Knight, he was a competitive college track and cross-country runner. Under Parker's leadership, the company's annual revenues have doubled from $15 billion to $34 billion over the last decade—and the stock price has increased six-fold. Nike began as Blue Ribbon Sports, a distributor of Japanese athletic shoes sold at track meets.

Using a participative and creative leadership style to preserve Nike's unique culture of innovation, Parker has advanced up the chain of command in a broad range of leadership roles in design, product development, manufacturing, and distribution. Known as a visual thinker and inspiring leader, Parker, an introvert, asks lots of questions. He is known to use different leadership styles depending on the circumstances. When he needs to go hard and fast, top-down leadership is utilized. However, he doesn't believe in micromanaging—and he goes out of his way to solicit raw ideas from junior members of his staff. He celebrates the fact that ideas can come from all levels of an organization. "Little side projects can grow into multi-billion dollar franchises," he says.

Parker continues to grow Nike while focusing on a central operating principle, "Serve the Athlete," set forth by its original founders, a University of Oregon runner, Phil Knight, and his then-coach, Bill Bowerman. Parker stays true to the guiding principle like gospel, regardless of how excited he gets about a new sneaker design or the technology utilized to produce the shoe. As a company deeply rooted in innovation, Parker carefully navigates the growth of his 70,000-employee firm while maintaining its coveted culture of "Serve the Athlete"—by "Just Doing It."[1]

Overview

When asked about their career goals, some students say, "I want to be a manager." You may think that the role of a manager is basically being the boss. But in today's business environment, companies are looking for much more than bosses. They want managers who understand technology, can adapt and respond quickly to change, can skillfully motivate employees, and realize the importance of satisfying customers. Managers who can master those skills will continue to be in great demand because their commitment strongly affects their companies' performance. Mark Parker's management style of asking questions and encouraging his team to find the answers has proven effective against intense competition from Adidas and Reebok.

This chapter begins by examining how successful organizations use management to turn visions into reality. It describes the levels of management, the skills that managers need, and the functions that managers perform. The chapter explains how the first of these functions, planning, helps managers meet the challenges of a rapidly changing business environment and the importance of developing strategies that guide a company's future. Other sections of the chapter explore the types of decisions that managers make, the role of managers as leaders, and the importance of corporate culture. The chapter concludes by examining the second function of management—organizing.

1 What Is Management?

management process of achieving organizational objectives through people and other resources.

Management is the process of achieving organizational objectives through people and other resources. The manager's job is to combine human and technical resources in the best way possible to achieve the company's goals.

Management principles and concepts apply to not-for-profit organizations as well as profit-seeking companies. A city mayor, the executive director of Goodwill Industries International, and a superintendent of schools all perform the managerial functions described later in this chapter. Management happens at many levels, from that of the manager of a family-owned restaurant to a national sales manager for a major manufacturer.

The Management Hierarchy

A single, independently owned hamburger joint may have a fairly simple organization that consists of a store owner or manager, several assistant managers, and other team members such as a cook, order taker, and table busser. If that burger joint happens to be a McDonald's franchise, it will be part of a global organizational structure that is divided into four performance-based geographic divisions—United States, International Lead Markets (Australia, Canada, France), High Growth Markets (China and Russia), Foundational Markets (Asia, Europe, Latin America, Africa, and the Middle East), and Corporate. Each of the four divisions has its own senior level executive in charge of functional areas like franchises, legal, information technology, marketing, and finance, for example. Typical of most global business organizations, Steve Easterbrook, CEO of McDonald's, passes down mandates to middle managers, and then to restaurant managers, who may also happen to be franchise owners.[2]

FIGURE 7.1 The Management Hierarchy

All of these people are managers because they combine human and other resources to achieve company objectives. Their jobs differ, however, because they work at different levels of the organization.

A company's management usually has three levels: top, middle, and supervisory. These levels of management form a management hierarchy, as shown in **Figure 7.1**. The hierarchy is the traditional structure found in most organizations. Managers at each level perform different activities.

The highest level of management is *top management*. Top managers include such positions as chief executive officer (CEO), chief financial officer (CFO), and executive vice president. Top managers devote most of their time to developing long-range plans for their organizations. They make decisions such as whether to introduce new products, purchase other companies, or enter new geographical markets. Top managers set a direction for their organization and inspire the company's executives and employees to achieve their vision for the company's future.

The job is intense and demanding. Many top managers must lead their companies through a variety of challenges, which might include a slowing economy, a quality crisis, and formidable competitors. Sometimes this involves selling a positive outlook to investors, stockholders, and managers during challenging times. Not long ago, Chipotle Mexican Grill, whose core mission is "Food with Integrity," was a rising star in the fast casual restaurant segment. Founder Steve Ells created a healthy, ethical, and better-for-the-environment food concept that had investors and consumers clamoring. In 2015, multiple reports of *E. coli* outbreaks and food-borne illnesses sent Chipotle's sales on a downward spiral. Recently, a new CEO was appointed. A veteran of Taco Bell, Brian Niccol has a significant undertaking to lead Chipotle back to healthy sales.[3]

Middle management, the second tier in the management hierarchy, includes positions such as general managers, plant managers, division managers, and unit managers. Middle managers' attention focuses on specific operations, products, or customer groups within an organization. They are responsible for developing detailed plans and procedures to implement the company's strategic plans. If top management decided to broaden the distribution of a product, a sales manager would be responsible for determining the number of sales personnel required. Middle managers are responsible for targeting the products and customers who are the source of the sales and profit growth expected by their CEOs. To achieve these goals, middle managers might budget money for product development, identify new uses for existing products, and improve the ways they train and motivate salespeople. Because they are more familiar with day-to-day operations than CEOs, middle managers often come up with new ways to increase sales or solve company problems.

Supervisory management, or first-line management, includes positions such as supervisor, section chief, and team leader. These managers are directly responsible for assigning nonmanagerial employees to specific jobs and evaluating their performance. Managers at this first level of the hierarchy work directly with the employees who produce and sell the company's goods and services. They are responsible for implementing middle managers' plans by motivating workers to accomplish daily, weekly, and monthly goals. David Novak, former CEO of Yum Brands (KFC, Pizza Hut, and Taco Bell), believes that today's first-line supervisors do not yet receive proper training. The majority of people who begin supervising others wish they had been better prepared—with some sort of leadership training. After retiring from Yum Brands, Novak is doing his life's work. Using his many years of experience, he has put together a curriculum for a digital leadership training program called oGoLead.[4]

Skills Needed for Managerial Success

Managers at every level in the management hierarchy must exercise three basic types of skills: technical, human, and conceptual. All managers must acquire these skills in varying proportions, although the importance of each skill changes at different management levels.

Technical skills are the manager's ability to understand and use the techniques, knowledge, tools, and equipment of a specific discipline or department. Technical skills are especially important for first-line managers and become less important at higher levels of the management hierarchy. Nonetheless, most top executives started out as technical experts. The résumé of a vice president for information systems probably lists experience as a computer

Gregory Rec/Portland Press Herald via Getty Images

Trader Joe's ranks in the top tier of the Temkin Group's annual list of companies providing top-notch customer service. Store leaders, known as mates, make sure that customer service is a priority for all employees.

analyst and that of a vice president for marketing usually shows a background in sales. Many companies have made investing in employee training a strategic priority—and an important way to increase employee ROI (return on investment). Real estate franchise Keller Williams was recently inducted into the Training Top 10 Hall of Fame by *Training Magazine* as one of the top training organizations worldwide for growth, productivity, and profit gains resulting from educational training for its associates. Keller Williams constantly updates its training programs by compiling information from proven models and systems of its top agents and other leaders in the field.[5]

Human skills include the ability to communicate, build rapport, collaborate, motivate, and lead employees to meet organizational goals through individual and team assignments. It would be challenging for a manager to succeed with others both inside and outside of the organization without the ability to get a point across, create a compelling presentation to support goals, and get buy-in for ideas that inspire others to achieve results. Effectively communicating using e-mail, text messaging, voicemail, videoconferencing—and even face-to-face—is crucial in today's business environment. Human skills might also include *emotional intelligence,* the ability to understand and manage one's own emotions, along with the emotions of others.

Conceptual skills determine a manager's ability to see the organization as a unified whole and to understand how each part of the overall organization interacts with other parts. These skills involve an ability to understand abstract relationships, interpret information, develop ideas, and creatively solve problems. Conceptual skills are especially important for top-level managers, who must develop long-range plans for the future direction of their organization. Emma Walmsley made history when she became the first female CEO of a major pharmaceutical company. Following a string of patent expirations for its top-selling drugs, she is tasked with reversing GlaxoSmithKline's lackluster growth. The company's pipeline for new drugs has been hit hard with two failures—a heart drug and a cancer treatment drug. Walmsley will develop a long-range plan for the future direction of her organization to improve its research pipeline.[6]

Managerial Functions

In the course of a typical day, managers spend time meeting and talking with people, reading, evaluating, analyzing, and communicating. As they perform these activities, managers are carrying out four basic functions: planning, organizing, directing, and controlling. Planning activities lay the groundwork, and the other functions are aimed at carrying out the plans.

planning process of anticipating future events and conditions and determining courses of action for achieving organizational objectives.

Planning

Planning is the process of anticipating future events and conditions and determining courses of actions for achieving organizational objectives. Effective planning helps a business focus its vision, avoid costly mistakes, and seize opportunities. Planning should be flexible and responsive to changes in the business environment, and should involve managers from all levels of the organization. As global competition intensifies, technology expands and the speed at which companies bring new innovations to market increases. Thus, planning for the future becomes even more critical. For example, a CEO and other top-level managers need to plan for succession—those who will follow in their footsteps. Some CEOs resist this kind of planning, fearing that doing so might shorten their time at the helm of a company. But management experts encourage planning ahead for the next generation of management, in order to keep the company's position in the marketplace strong.[7]

Business mogul Warren Buffet is now in his late 80s and showing few signs of slowing down. But it's clear that someone (or several people) must be in place to take the reins of his huge diversified company, Berkshire Hathaway, which has significant holdings in businesses ranging from Geico Insurance to Dairy Queen to Duracell batteries. Recently, Buffet widely broadened the management scope of two insiders, viewed as front runners to become his replacement. Gregory Abel was named vice chairman of non-insurance business operations and Ajit Jain was named vice chairman of insurance operations. Buffet has made it clear that his replacement must be vigilant and determined at warding off the "ABCs of business decay": arrogance, bureaucracy, and complacency.[8]

Organizing Once plans have been developed, the next step in the management process typically is **organizing**—the process of blending human and material resources through a formal structure of tasks and authority; arranging work, dividing tasks among employees, and coordinating them to ensure implementation of plans and accomplishment of objectives. Organizing involves classifying and dividing work into manageable units with a logical structure. Managers staff the organization with the best possible employees for each job. Sometimes the organizing function requires analyzing a company's existing structure and determining whether to change it in order to operate more efficiently, cost effectively, or sustainably.

organizing process of blending human and material resources through a formal structure of tasks and authority; arranging work, dividing tasks among employees, and coordinating them to ensure implementation of plans and accomplishment of objectives.

Directing Once an organization has been established, managers focus on **directing**, or guiding and motivating employees to accomplish organizational objectives. Directing might include training (or retraining), setting up schedules, delegating certain tasks, and monitoring progress. To guide and motivate employees—and to get them to be part of something new and exciting, the late Steve Jobs (Apple Computer) was known for tapping into their FOMO (fear of missing out) through storytelling. To encourage a group of developers to build applications for a new Macintosh platform, Jobs told the story of the successful outcome of one developer whom he had called to fly across the country to work on a "secret project."[9]

Often when managers take time to listen to their employees, the manager gains insight and the employee gets a motivational boost. Fashion designer Eileen Fisher says, "Share information and your own ideas. Be present. Be accessible. Listen."[10]

directing guiding and motivating employees to accomplish organizational objectives.

Controlling The **controlling** function evaluates an organization's performance against its objectives. Controlling assesses the success of the planning function and provides feedback for future rounds of planning.

The four basic steps in controlling are to establish performance standards, monitor actual performance, compare actual performance with established standards, and make corrections if necessary. Under the provisions of the Sarbanes-Oxley Act, for example, CEOs and CFOs must monitor the performance of an organization's accounting staff more closely than typically had been done in the past. They must personally attest to the truth of financial reports filed with the Securities and Exchange Commission.

controlling function of evaluating an organization's performance against its objectives.

Assessment Check

1. What is management?
2. How do the jobs of top managers, middle managers, and supervisory managers differ?
3. What is the relationship between the manager's planning and controlling functions?

2 Setting a Vision and Ethical Standards for the Company

A business begins with a **vision**, its founder's perception of marketplace needs and the ways a company can satisfy them. Vision serves as the target for a company's actions, helping direct the company toward opportunities and differentiating it from its competitors. Distributing software on CDs is a thing of the past, and Adobe Systems CEO Shantanu Narayen (see photo) had the vision to overhaul the widely used distribution model. The Adobe Creative Suite, no

vision ability to perceive marketplace needs and what an organization must do to satisfy them.

David Paul Morris/Bloomberg via Getty Images

Adobe CEO Shantanu Narayen overhauled boxed software sets by making his company's Creative Suite available through a cloud-based subscription.

longer packaged in boxed sets, is available instantly to subscribers via the cloud. Narayen's vision has resulted in record sales of its Creative Cloud applications that gives subscribers access to a collection of software used for graphic design, video editing, web development, photography, and mobile applications.[11]

A company's vision must be focused and yet flexible enough to adapt to changes in the business environment. Also critical to a company's long-term relationship with its customers, suppliers, and the general public are the ethical standards that top management sets. Sometimes ethical standards are set in compliance with industry or federal regulations, such as safety or quality standards. Sometimes new standards are set in response to a crisis. United changed its overbooking policy (airlines typically sell more tickets than there are seats) after a passenger was dragged off a plane when he refused to give up his seat to a crew member. A video of the bloody scene went viral. United now allows up to $10,000 in flight vouchers to passengers willing to give up their seats, and airline crews must check in one hour prior to takeoff.[12]

The ethical tone that a top management team establishes can reap monetary as well as nonmonetary rewards. Setting a high ethical standard does not merely discourage employees from wrongdoing, but it also motivates and inspires them to achieve goals they never thought possible. Such satisfaction creates a more productive, stable workforce—one that can create a long-term competitive advantage for the organization. In practice, ethical decisions are not always clear-cut, and managers must make difficult decisions. Sometimes a company operates in a country where standards differ from those in the United States. In other situations, a manager might have to make an ethical decision that undermines

Judgment Call

Duke Energy Guilty of Toxic Dumping

Duke Energy, the largest electrical utility in the United States with more than $22 billion in revenues, recently pleaded guilty to polluting rivers with coal ash, a hazardous waste that comes from the remains of coal burning in power plants. In addition to polluting the air and killing fish and wildlife, coal ash slurry contains toxic arsenic, lead, mercury, and heavy metals known to cause cancer and reproductive and development disorders.

Duke Energy was charged nine times with criminally negligent discharge of pollutants related to Clean Water Act violations and failure to maintain coal ash treatment equipment at its North Carolina operations. Duke has been required to run two full-page newspaper advertisements in numerous North Carolina papers with apologies to those affected. A fine of $102 million was slapped on the utility, and a five-year probation period means that a court-appointed monitor will oversee compliance and reports to federal parole officers related to coal ash. The fine will be paid for by shareholders rather than customers and includes $68.2 million in fines and restitution and $34 million for community service and mitigation projects.

For years, the company refused to listen to its own employees and ignored warnings about a problem pipe. When it was suggested that $20,000 be spent to inspect four pipes, including the one that eventually ruptured, requests were ignored. Duke's attorney acknowledged "a series of independent errors" on behalf of Duke's management over a long time, but moving forward Duke Energy plans to implement proper and sustainable coal ash solutions. The company will be required to close down all of its ash ponds by 2029, according to a recent state law. The utility has laid out plans to build lined landfills to contain the coal ash.

Questions for Critical Thinking

1. **Environmental groups contend that both Duke and the state have known for years that the ash ponds at various Duke power plants have been leaking toxins into groundwater and nearby rivers and streams. Should the people who made the decisions to knowingly pollute a public resource and endanger lives go to jail?**
2. **The fine of $102 million is 0.2% of Duke's annual revenues. Are fines of this nature punitive to the company? Why or why not?**

Sources: Josh Bergeron, "Coal Ash Neighbors Issue Demands for State, Duke Energy," *Salisbury Post,* http://www.salisburypost.com, accessed March 18, 2018; Matthew Burns and Derek Medlin, "Duke Energy, NC Agree to $7M Fine over Coal Ash Leaks," *WRAL,* http://www.ral.com, accessed March 18, 2018; John Downey, "How Much Has Duke Energy Paid of $102M in Federal Fines, Restitution in Coal-Ash Case?" *Charlotte Business Journal*, http://www.bizjournals.com, accessed March 18, 2018; David Zucchino, "Duke Energy Fined $102 Million for Polluting Rivers with Coal Ash," *Los Angeles Times*, http://www.latimes.com, accessed March 18, 2018.

profits or even causes people to lose their jobs. And while it's tempting to think that a large company—by virtue of its size—will have a harder time adopting ethical practices than a small company, consider the ethical dilemma faced by Bill Hoberg of Glass-Rite Windows and Doors in Albuquerque, New Mexico. When the Environmental Protection Agency made lead-based paint testing mandatory for window replacement projects, the small business could have skirted the requirement, but instead, Holberg spent $20,000 to accommodate for lead testing.

Alex Brigham, executive chairman and founder of the New York–based Ethisphere Institute, observes the connection between ethics and good business. He states a company's ethical environment "shows a clear understanding that operating under the highest standards for business behavior goes beyond goodwill and 'lip-service' and is linked to performance and profitability."[13]

When it became clear that health technology company Theranos was making false claims about its revolutionary blood tests and financial results, an early, low-level employee in his early 20s reported the misconduct. Theranos saw its business dissolve, and its billionaire owner, Elizabeth Holmes, has been banned from working at a public company for 10 years.[14] Sometimes, however, companies' actions raise more ethical questions than they answer, as the example in the "Judgment Call" feature shows.

Assessment Check

1. What is meant by a vision for the company?
2. Why is it important for a top executive to set high ethical standards?

3 The Importance of Planning

Although some companies manage to launch without a clear strategic plan, they run a higher risk of failure without a strategy. By reshaping its growth strategy, Coca-Cola plans to become a "total beverage company" to operate more in line with consumer tastes and buying habits by focusing on more low- and no-sugar options and drinks. James Quincey, the company's new CEO, plans to win over customers with better-for-you beverages such as Zico, the company's coconut water brand.[15]

Types of Planning

Planning can be categorized by scope and breadth. Some plans are very broad and long range, whereas others are short range and very narrow, affecting selected parts of the organization rather than the company as a whole. Planning can be divided into the following categories: strategic, tactical, operational, and contingency, with each step including more specific information than the last. From the mission statement (described in the next section) to objectives to specific plans, each phase must fit into a comprehensive planning framework. The framework also must include narrow, functional plans aimed at individual employees and work areas relevant to individual tasks. These plans must fit within the company's overall planning framework and help it reach objectives and achieve its mission.

Strategic Planning The most far-reaching level of planning is *strategic planning*—the process of determining the primary objectives of an organization and then acting and allocating resources to achieve those objectives. Generally, strategic planning is undertaken by top executives in a company. As customers use multiple channels for retail shopping, Home Depot,

Daniel Acker/Bloomberg via Getty Images

As part of its strategic planning, Home Depot has introduced mobile apps with location-based technology that provides shoppers with real-time inventory, pricing, and information about where to find products in a specific store.

on a digital transformation journey, has implemented a strategy called "interconnected retailing" (see photo). The company wants to create a seamless experience for customers—whether they browse online, open promotional e-mails on their smart phones, or visit brick-and-mortar locations in person.[16]

Tactical Planning *Tactical planning* involves implementing the activities specified by strategic plans. Tactical plans guide the current and near-term activities required to implement interconnected retail strategies. As part of Home Depot's strategy to create a multichannel customer shopping experience, the company has introduced an optimized mobile redesign, which integrates location-based technology in smart phones. The technology allows promotions to be sent to in-store shoppers while giving them access to real-time inventory, location, and pricing by store. How-to videos are offered for mobile shoppers doing research on products. The tactical plan keeps customers in contact with the retailer across multiple points of the shopping process in addition to helping them navigate the retail store with product location by aisle.[17]

Operational Planning *Operational planning* creates the detailed standards that guide implementation of tactical plans. This activity involves choosing specific work targets and assigning employees and teams to carry out plans. Unlike strategic planning, which focuses on the organization as a whole, operational planning deals with developing and implementing tactics in specific functional areas. If customers make purchases online and pick up or return merchandise to the retailer, Home Depot will need staff at its stores to take care of these transactions. This will require additional planning on the part of management that might include additional staffing in shipping, separate customer service teams, and different delivery strategies. The company has opened three fulfillment facilities to support its growing online business.

Contingency Planning Planning cannot foresee every possibility. Major accidents, natural disasters, and rapid economic downturns can throw even the best-laid plans into chaos. To handle the possibility of business disruption from events of this nature, many companies use *contingency planning*, which allows them to resume operations as quickly and as smoothly as possible after a crisis while openly communicating with the public about what happened. This planning activity involves two components: business continuation and public communication. Many companies have developed management strategies to speed recovery from accidents such as loss of data, breaches of security, product failures, and natural disasters such as floods or fire. If a major disaster or business disruption occurs, a company's contingency plan usually designates a chain of command for crisis management, assigning specific functions to particular managers and employees in an emergency. But crisis more often occurs on a less global scale. For example, a product delivery might go astray, a key person might be sick and unable to attend an important customer meeting, or the power might go out for a day. These instances require contingency planning as well.

Tesla recently announced further Model 3 Sedan production delays. Four hundred thousand Tesla enthusiasts have made a $1,000 deposit to purchase the car—and in a recent quarter, only 222 were delivered. The delays are a result of a Gigafactory in Nevada where Tesla builds its car batteries. An outside supplier responsible for assembling the batteries "dropped the ball," according to Elon Musk. "We had to rewrite all of the software from scratch and redo many of the mechanical and electrical elements," he says.[18]

TABLE 7.1 Planning at Different Management Levels

Primary Type of Planning	Managerial Level	Examples
Strategic	Top management	Organizational objectives, fundamental strategies, long-term plans
Tactical	Middle management	Quarterly and semiannual plans, departmental policies and procedures
Operational	Supervisory management	Daily and weekly plans, rules, and procedures for each department
Contingency	Primarily top management, but all levels contribute	Ongoing plans for actions and communications in an emergency

Planning at Different Organizational Levels

Although managers spend some time on planning virtually every day, the total time spent and the type of planning done differ according to the level of management. As **Table 7.1** points out, top managers, including a company's board of directors and CEO, spend a great deal of time on long-range planning, while middle-level managers and supervisors focus on short-term, tactical, and operational planning. Employees at all levels can benefit themselves and their company by making plans to meet their own specific goals.

Assessment Check

1. Outline the planning process.
2. Describe the purpose of tactical planning.
3. Compare the kinds of plans made by top managers and middle managers. How does their focus differ?

4 The Strategic Planning Process

Strategic planning often makes the difference between an organization's success and failure. Strategic planning has formed the basis of many fundamental management decisions. Successful strategic planners typically follow the six steps shown in **Figure 7.2**: defining a mission, assessing the organization's competitive position, setting organizational objectives, creating strategies for competitive differentiation, implementing the strategy, and evaluating the results and refining the plan.

Defining the Organization's Mission

The first step in strategic planning is to translate the company's vision into a **mission statement**. A mission statement is a written explanation of an organization's business intentions and aims. It is an enduring statement of a company's purpose, possibly highlighting the scope of operations, the market it seeks to serve, and the ways it will attempt to set itself apart from competitors. A mission statement guides the actions of employees and publicizes the company's reasons for existence.

mission statement written explanation of an organization's business intentions and aims.

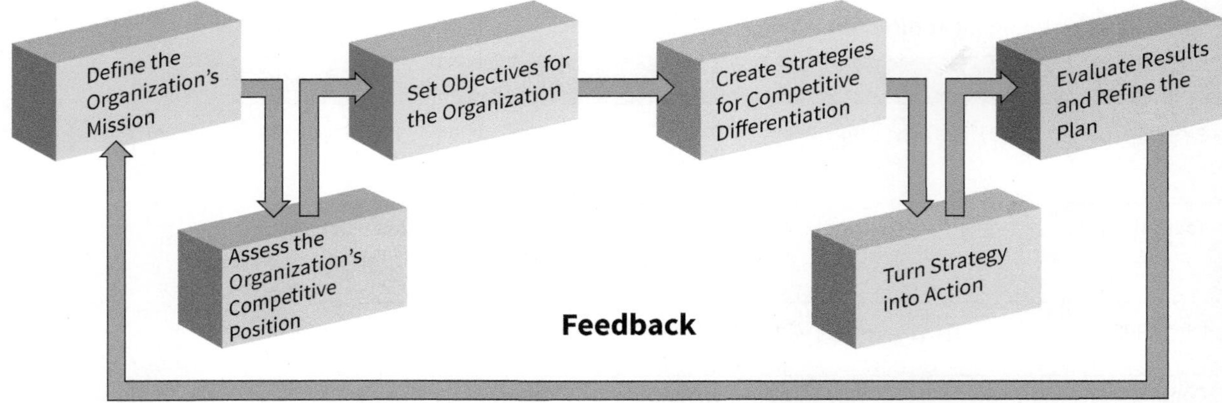

FIGURE 7.2 **Steps in the Strategic Planning Process**

Mission statements can be short or long:

- Starbucks: "To inspire and nurture the human spirit—one person, one cup, and one neighborhood at a time."
- Disney: "To be one of the world's leading producers and providers of entertainment and information, using its portfolio of brands to differentiate its content, services, and consumer products."
- Nike: "To bring inspiration and innovation to every athlete in the world."
- Apple: "Apple designs Macs, the best personal computers in the world, along with OS X, iLife, iWork and professional software. Apple leads the digital music revolution with its iPods and iTunes online store. Apple has reinvented the mobile phone with its revolutionary iPhone and App store and is defining the future of mobile media and computing devices with iPad."

A good mission statement states the company's purpose for being in business and its overall goal. The "Clean & Green" feature describes the denim jean maker Levi Strauss and its focus on sustainability.

Clean & Green Business

Levi's Wants Your Old Jeans

Denim jean maker Levi Strauss & Co. has studied its product closely enough to know that the average life span of a pair of its iconic blue jeans is about three years—after which, jeans get tossed. Referred to as "birth to death," Levi's is trying to change consumer attitudes about unwanted clothing by creating a closed product cycle and a wider circular economic strategy, whereby donated clothes are used to make new items.

The company recently created an incentive for customers to bring their used jeans into stores—regardless of the brand—in exchange for 20% off a single regular-priced Levi's item. The company's vice president of sustainability wants to make recycling the norm throughout all stages of Levi's product life cycle, including stages beyond the product's end point. Instead of having old jeans end up in landfills, cotton production will be reduced when denim is instead "harvested" from throwaway jeans. Levi's recycling partner, I:Collect (I:CO), operates globally to divert clothing from landfills so that it can be reworn or recycled to make other products.

After conducting a number of lifecycle assessments to determine where their products had the biggest environmental impact, Levi's also introduced its Water < Less jeans and initiatives to educate customers on the value of saving water and energy. Half the water usage happens during the production of a pair of jeans, while the other half happens in the wash at home. Levi's continues to urge customers to wash their jeans less often as part of its focus on sustainability. The company estimates that washing one pair of jeans every two weeks instead of every week saves more than 5 gallons of water.

Questions for Critical Thinking

1. Think about the last time you decided your favorite pair of jeans was no longer wearable. What steps did you take to discard the jeans and what was the basis for your decision? Would you have considered an incentive such as the one being offered by Levi's?
2. Discuss the concepts of *rewear*, which means a product is still wearable, and *upcycling*, which means a discarded textile can be used to create a new product of equal or better quality. What implications do these ideas have for retailers?

Sources: Company website, "The Life Cycle of a Jean," "Water < Less: Doing Your Part," "'Stop Washing Your Jeans': LS & Co. CEO Chip Bergh at Brainstorm Green," http://levistrauss.com, accessed March 19, 2018; Michael Kobori, "Levi Strauss & Co: Bring Us Your Old Jeans," *EcoWatch*, http://ecowatch.com, accessed March 19, 2018; James Phillips, "Levi Strauss Extends Clothing Recycling Programme across US," *BusinessGreen*, http://www.businessgreen.com, accessed March 19, 2018; "Levi's Stitches Plastic Bottles into Latest Denim Collection," *Business-Green*, http://www.businessgreen.com, accessed March 19, 2018; company website, "The I:CO Mission," http:// www.ico-spirit.com, accessed March 19, 2018.

Assessing Your Competitive Position

Once a mission statement has been created, the next step in the planning process is to determine the company's current—or potential—position in the marketplace. The company's founder or top managers evaluate the factors that may help it grow or could cause it to fail. A frequently used tool in this phase of strategic planning is the **SWOT analysis**. SWOT is an acronym for *strengths*, *weaknesses*, *opportunities*, and *threats*. By systematically evaluating all four of these factors, a company can then develop the best strategies for gaining a competitive advantage. The framework for a SWOT analysis appears in **Figure 7.3**.

SWOT analysis SWOT is an acronym for *strengths*, *weaknesses*, *opportunities*, and *threats*. By systematically evaluating all four of these factors, a company can then develop the best strategies for gaining a competitive advantage.

To evaluate a company's strengths and weaknesses, its managers may examine each functional area such as finance, marketing, information technology, and human resources. Or they might evaluate strengths and weaknesses of each office, plant, or store. Entrepreneurs may focus on the individual skills and experience they bring to a new business.

For Starbucks, key strengths include the company's positive image, reputation for global responsibility and ethical sourcing, recognized global brand, premium-priced quality coffee, market dominance, strong financial performance, and employer of choice among its labor force. Starbucks is one of *Fortune's* "Best 100 Companies to Work for" in the United States and is well known for the socially responsible corporate policies of its founder, Howard Schultz. The company's strategic plans include various ways to build on Starbucks's strong brand loyalty by expanding its food offerings, which include breakfast and lunch items. Starbucks remains focused on overseas retail expansion in China; its online, mobile, and digital loyalty reward program; and its gift card business. An updated mobile app allows customers to place an order, pay, and pick up. Weaknesses include uneven international growth impacted by foreign currency fluctuations; a premium-priced product (which makes the brand less accessible to cost-conscious consumers); an easily imitated ambiance; and an oversaturation in some markets with too many stores. Starbucks eventually addressed some of these weaknesses by lowering the price of bagged coffee and closing some stores.[19]

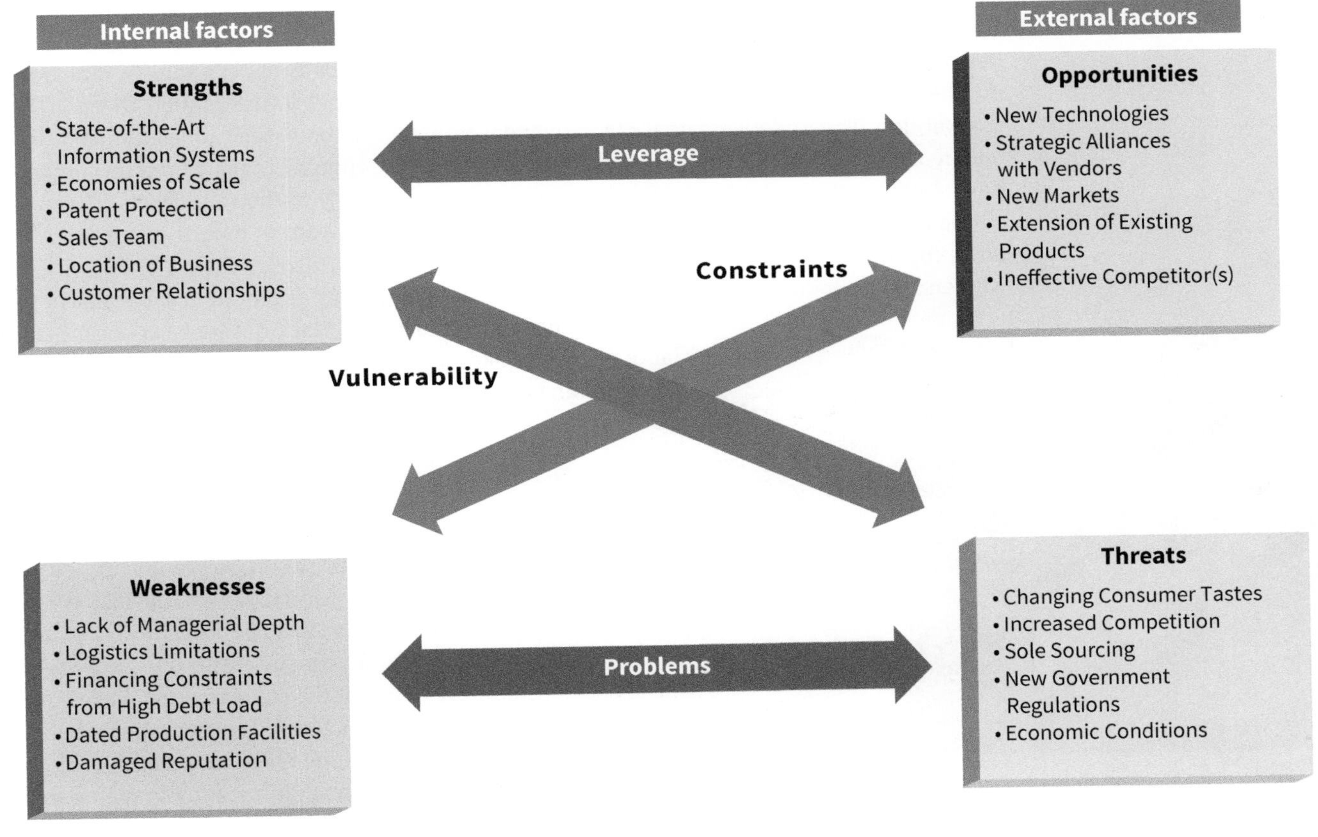

FIGURE 7.3 Elements of SWOT Analysis

A SWOT analysis also defines a company's major opportunities and threats. Threats to Starbucks might include a potential increase in the price of coffee beans; the slowdown of China's economy; trademark infringements; increased competition from independent coffee houses and lower-priced fast-food chains; single coffee brewers like Keurig; and increased online shopping, which reduces retail-store foot traffic. Starbucks addressed the threat of lower-priced competitors by offering less-expensive, instant coffee in its stores and through retailers like Costco and Target. Opportunities include expansion of retail store operations and various store concepts (tea and wine bars, drive-through, coffee roasteries in major cities, and even coffee museum stores); increased product offerings, including the K-cup and cold brew; expansion to emerging economies (China, India, Japan, and Brazil); and greater connections to customers by continuing to build loyalty through online communities.[20]

A SWOT analysis isn't carved in stone. Strengths and weaknesses, like opportunities and threats, may change over time. A strength may eventually become a weakness and a threat may turn into an opportunity, but the analysis gives managers a place to start.

Setting Objectives for the Organization

objectives guideposts by which managers define the organization's desired performance in such areas as new-product development, sales, customer service, growth, environmental and social responsibility, and employee satisfaction.

The next step in planning is to develop objectives for the company. **Objectives** set guideposts by which managers define the organization's desired performance in such areas as new-product development, sales, customer service, growth, environmental and social responsibility, and employee satisfaction. While the mission statement identifies a company's overall goals, objectives are more concrete.

With a sparkly mixed era and styles aesthetic that is more in tune with popular culture, "The Gucci effect" has taken hold since Alessandro Michele took over as creative director a few years ago. His aesthetic is described as "maximalism," which makes sense since he is good friends with Elton John.[21]

Creating Strategies for Competitive Differentiation

Developing a mission statement and setting objectives point a business in a specific direction. But the company needs to identify the strategies it will use to reach its destination ahead of the competition. The underlying goal of strategy development is *competitive differentiation*—the unique combination of a company's abilities and resources that set it apart from its competitors. A company named Slack earned *Inc. magazine's* Company of the Year. Since its launch a little over five years ago, its astronomical growth, mainly by word of mouth, is a result of a powerful and efficient instant messaging communication platform, used mainly by knowledge workers. The experience of being able to search back over a team's communications is a huge differentiator in doing business. Slack has replaced legacy collaboration tools like email and instant messaging. However, the competition from Microsoft and Google remains a challenge.[22]

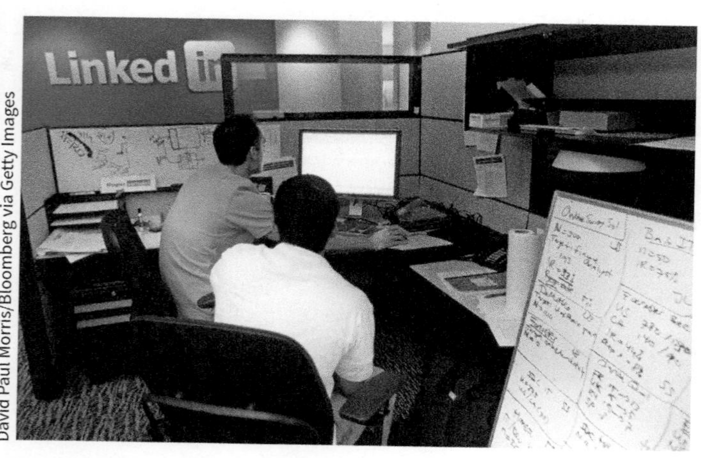

David Paul Morris/Bloomberg via Getty Images

In an effort to empower employees to act like owners, LinkedIn, along with numerous other technology companies, has an unlimited vacation policy.

Implementing the Strategy

Once the first four phases of the strategic planning process are complete, managers are ready to put those plans into action. Often, it's the middle managers or supervisors who actually implement a strategy. But studies show that top company officials are still reluctant to empower these managers with the authority to make decisions that could benefit the company. Companies that are willing to empower employees generally reap the benefits.[23]

In an effort to empower employees to act like owners, social networking career site LinkedIn recently implemented a new unlimited vacation policy. While LinkedIn (shown in photo), recently purchased by Microsoft, is not the first to do so, it is unusual for a company of its size (more than 9,000 full-time employees) to make such a move. To date, only 2% of companies, many in tech, offer this unlimited time-off policy. According to LinkedIn's chief human *resources* officer, employees are adults who don't need to be micromanaged.[24]

Monitoring and Adapting Strategic Plans

The final step in the strategic planning process is to monitor and adapt plans when the actual performance fails to meet goals. Monitoring involves securing feedback about performance. Managers might compare actual sales against forecasts; compile information from surveys; listen to customer feedback; interview employees who are involved; and review reports prepared by production, finance, marketing, or other company units. If a social media ad campaign doesn't result in enough response or sales, managers might evaluate whether to continue the campaign, change it, or discontinue it. For example, if a large consumer products company plans to shed some of its less-profitable brands, this may allow a research and development team to focus resources on new product ideas that resonate more with customers. Ongoing use of such tools as SWOT analysis and forecasting can help managers adapt their objectives and functional plans as changes occur.

Assessment Check

1. What is the purpose of a mission statement?
2. Which of a company's characteristics does a SWOT analysis compare?
3. How do managers use objectives?

5 Managers as Decision Makers

Managers make decisions every day, whether it involves shutting down a manufacturing plant or adding grilled cheese sandwiches to a lunch menu. **Decision making** is the process of recognizing a problem or opportunity, evaluating alternative solutions, selecting and implementing an alternative, and assessing the results. Managers make two basic kinds of decisions: programmed decisions and nonprogrammed decisions.

decision making process of recognizing a problem or opportunity, evaluating alternative solutions, selecting and implementing an alternative, and assessing the results.

Programmed and Nonprogrammed Decisions

A *programmed decision* involves simple, common, and frequently occurring problems for which solutions have already been determined. Examples of programmed decisions include reordering office supplies, renewing a lease, and referring to an established discount for bulk orders. Programmed decisions are made in advance—the company sets rules, policies, and procedures for managers and employees to follow on a routine basis. Programmed decisions actually save managers time and companies money because new decisions don't have to be made each time the situation arises.

A *nonprogrammed decision* involves a complex and unique problem or opportunity with important consequences for the organization. Examples of nonprogrammed decisions include entering a new market, deleting a product from the line, or developing a new product. In a surprising announcement, Amazon, Berkshire Hathaway, and JP Morgan announced that they would be forming a healthcare not-for-profit. They would be developing technological solutions to provide "simplified, high-quality healthcare for their hundreds of thousands of U.S. workers," clearly a nonprogrammed decision.[25]

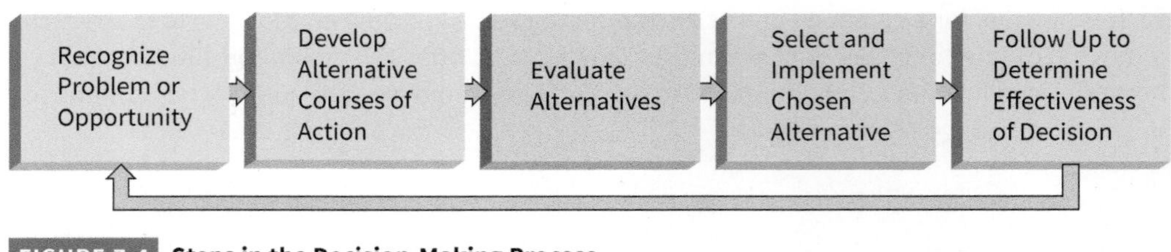

FIGURE 7.4 **Steps in the Decision-Making Process**

How Managers Make Decisions

In a narrow sense, decision making involves choosing among two or more alternatives, with the chosen alternative becoming the decision. In a broader sense, decision making involves a systematic, step-by-step process that helps managers make effective choices. This process begins when someone recognizes a problem or opportunity, develops possible courses of action, evaluates the alternatives, selects and implements one of them, and assesses the outcome. It's important to keep in mind that managers are *human* decision makers, and while they can follow the decision-making process step-by-step as shown in Figure 7.4, the outcome of their decisions depends on many factors, including the accuracy and timeliness of their information and the experience, creativity, and wisdom of the person. Warren Buffett, billionaire investor and CEO of Berkshire Hathaway, empowers his managers to make decisions without his input. See the "Business Model" feature for more on Buffett's management style.

Making good decisions is never easy. A decision might hurt or help the sales of a product; it might offend or disappoint a customer or co-worker; it might affect the manager's own career or reputation. Managers' decisions can have complex legal and ethical dimensions. *CR Magazine* publishes an annual list of the "100 Best Corporate Citizens." These companies make

Business Model

Buffett Gives Managers Autonomy

Warren Buffett, billionaire investor and CEO of Berkshire Hathaway for more than 50 years, is known for his hands-off management style. Buffett prefers to give what he refers to as his "chief lieutenants" the autonomy to make decisions on their own about the companies they run. He also believes in providing allowances for mistakes, which never gets a manager in trouble. Berkshire Hathaway is a conglomerate that owns a diverse range of companies ranging from Geico Auto Insurance to NetJets.

Buffett believes that giving people autonomy motivates them to do the best possible job. In a previous annual letter to shareholders, he wrote, "there are managers to whom I have not talked in the last year, while there is one with whom I talk almost daily. Our trust is in people rather than process. A 'hire well, manage little' code suits both them and me."

Another one of Buffett's management hallmarks is the lack of bureaucracy in the organization. Surprisingly, there is no standard process among the company's more than 60 operating units or businesses, which include 377,000 employees. The lieutenants are experienced and competent—and they understand Buffett's familiar rituals that promote short-term, rather than long-term, thinking. Trust, according to Buffett, has allowed his managers to produce more "than would be achieved by streams of directives, endless reviews, and layers of bureaucracy."

Buffett does not hassle his managers for updates. The only thing he insists on is that bad news be reported promptly. Buffett creates a hassle-free environment for his managers, which is part of the reason why he has so many great self-starters who love what they do. "Talented people can accomplish a whole lot," he says.

Questions for Critical Thinking

1. **What are the advantages and disadvantages of Buffett's management style?**
2. **Buffett is known to set aside time each morning for personal learning and self-improvement. If this practice were customary throughout corporate America, what benefits might result?**

Sources: Company website, "Berkshire Hathaway, Inc.," http://www.berkshirehathaway.com, accessed March 18, 2018; Jena McGregor, "The Leadership Wisdom of Warren Buffett," *Washington Post*, https://www.washingtonpost.com, accessed March 18, 2018; Roger Lowenstein, "Forget Buffett the Investor. Follow Buffett the Manager," *Forbes*, http://www.forbes.com, accessed March 18, 2018; Timothy McAleenan, Jr., "Lessons from Warren Buffett's Management Style," *The Conservative Income Investor*, http://theconservativeincomeinvestor.com, accessed March 18, 2018; Andrew Ross Sorkin, "Warren Buffett Delegator in Chief," *New York Times*, http://www.nytimes.com, accessed March 18, 2018; Timothy R. Clark, "Why We Trust Warren Buffett," *Deseret News*, http://www.deseretnews.com, accessed March 18, 2018.

decisions that are ethical, environmentally responsible, fair toward employees, and accountable to local communities in addition to providing responsible goods and services to customers and a healthy return to investors. These organizations prove that good corporate citizenship is good behavior. The top 10 corporate citizens named one recent year were Hasbro, Intel, Microsoft, Altria, Campbell's Soup, Cisco Systems, Accenture plc, Hormel Foods, Lockheed Martin, and EcoLab.[26]

Assessment Check

1. Distinguish between programmed and nonprogrammed decisions.
2. What are the steps in the decision-making process?

6 Managers as Leaders

A manager must demonstrate **leadership**, directing or inspiring people to attain certain goals. Great leaders do not all share the same qualities, but three traits are often mentioned: empathy (the ability to imagine yourself in someone else's position), self-awareness, and objectivity. While it might seem as though empathy and objectivity are opposite traits, they do balance each other. Many leaders share other traits—courage, passion, commitment, innovation, and flexibility, to name a few.

leadership ability to direct or inspire people to attain certain goals.

Leadership involves the use of influence or power. This influence may come from one or more sources. One source of power is the leader's position in the company. A national sales manager has the authority to direct the activities of the sales force. Another source of power is a leader's expertise and experience. A first-line supervisor with expert machinist skills will most likely be respected by employees in the machining department. Some leaders derive power from their personalities. Employees may admire a leader because they recognize an exceptionally kind and fair, humorous, energetic, or enthusiastic person. To allow customers to put a face to a respected company leader, executives are being encouraged to develop an online presence using the benefits of social media. However, when it comes to social media, the lines can become blurred in terms of what is appropriate. See the "Business & Technology" feature on this topic.

When Tim Cook took over as CEO for Steve Jobs a little less than a decade ago, he stood in direct contrast to his predecessor. He has adopted some of the legendary characteristics and leadership practices of the late Steve Jobs, a true visionary. While Cook may not have the bold visionary style of Jobs, his strengths as a participative leader are many. He is charismatic and thoughtful—and, as a democratic leader, he has placed greater focus on existing products and fostering strong bonds with employees and suppliers.[27]

David Paul Morris/Bloomberg via Getty Images

In August 2011, Tim Cook took on the near-impossible task of filling the shoes of (the late) legendary Apple CEO, Steve Jobs. His leadership style is humble and understated.

Leadership Styles

The way a person uses power to lead others determines his or her leadership style. Leadership styles range along a continuum with autocratic leadership at one extreme end and free-rein leadership at the other. *Autocratic leadership* is centered on the boss. Autocratic leaders make decisions on their own without consulting employees. They reach decisions, communicate them to subordinates, and expect automatic implementation.

Democratic leadership includes subordinates in the decision-making process. This leadership style centers on employees' contributions. Democratic leaders delegate assignments, ask employees for suggestions, and encourage participation. An important outgrowth of democratic leadership in business is the concept of

Business & Technology

Good Tweet, Bad Tweet

With more than twelve million followers on Twitter, Virgin Group CEO Richard Branson tweets about everything from baseball to his newest business ventures. If you're an investor in Virgin Group, Branson's Twitter feed is a must-read with a direct line to the company's insights. The value of inexpensive positive publicity from social media outlets is a recognized part of a company's marketing strategy.

A recent study showed that the country's most successful CEOs are participating in social media, with LinkedIn as an entry-level stage. Approximately 80% of the country's top 50 CEOs now use a social network profile or appear in videos through their company's website or YouTube channel. However, social media is not for everyone.

In a recent year, ride-hailing giant Uber saw its founder and CEO, Travis Kalanick, depart under allegations of widespread sexual harassment within a toxic corporate culture of misogyny. Additionally, during a travel ban incident, several New York taxi companies, to show support, banned pickups at airports. Using social media, Uber issued a tweet to promote its service. This prompted a flurry of downloads of competitor Lyft's app—and a hashtag movement, #DeleteUber, began online.

As the use of social media continues to expand in business, companies are suggesting their executives develop an online presence. While the benefits for a company are many—letting customers put a face to a respected, well-known thought leader or senior executive, showing a commitment to customers who use social media, and touting new product announcements—things can also go bad. To reduce the risk of social media missteps, some companies have set up training for senior executives and other members of management.

Questions for Critical Thinking

1. Should a company be responsible for what an executive says through social media channels? Why or why not?
2. What are the risks when an executive misrepresents a company on social media? Should companies require executives to undergo social media training?

Sources: Educational website, "Business Ethics in the News," *Santa Clara University*, http://www.scu.edu, accessed March 18, 2018; Zack Guzman, "J Crew Fires VP after Social Media Backlash," *CNBC*, http://www.cnbc.com, accessed March 18, 2018; Seth Archer, "11 Best CEOs to Follow on Twitter," *The Street*, http://www.thestreet.com, accessed March 18, 2018; educational website, "The Executive Social Media Gap," https://www.gsb.stanford.edu, accessed March 18, 2018; Jurica Dujmovic, "Here's What the World's Top 50 CEOs Do on Social Media," *Market Watch*, http://www.marketwatch.com, accessed March 18, 2018; Jillian D'Onfro, "After Going on a Twitter Tirade, Former PayPal Exec Rakesh Agrawal Tells Us He's Sorry for an Experiment Gone Awry," *Business Insider*, http://www.businessinsider.com, accessed March 18, 2018; Zoe Henry, "These Are the Biggest Social Media Fails of 2017," *Inc.*, http://www.inc.com, accessed March 21, 2018.

empowerment giving employees authority and responsibility to make decisions about their work.

empowerment, in which employees share authority, responsibility, and decision making with their managers.

At the other end of the continuum from autocratic leadership is *free-rein leadership*. Free-rein leaders believe in minimal supervision. They allow subordinates to make most of their own decisions. Free-rein leaders communicate with employees frequently, as the situation warrants. For the first decade of its existence, Google was proud of its free-rein leadership style. Engineers were encouraged to pursue any and all ideas; teams formed or disbanded on their own; employees were encouraged to spend 20% of their work time on any given project. But as the company entered its second decade, it became apparent that not every innovation was worth pursuing—and some valuable ideas were getting lost in the chaos. Concerned that some of the biggest ideas were getting squashed, the company established a process for reviewing new project ideas in order to identify those most likely to succeed.[28]

Which Leadership Style Is Best?

No single leadership style is best for every company in every situation. Sometimes leadership styles require change in order for a company to grow, as has been the case for Google. Martha Stewart became a household name through her media empire, Martha Stewart Living Omnimedia, which includes a variety of business ventures ranging from publishing to broadcast to merchandising and e-commerce. Over a decade ago, convicted of charges related to insider trading, Stewart served five months in prison. Known as an autocratic and demanding leader and on the brink of bankruptcy, Stewart turned around her company. As a hands-on leader, Stewart is known to pay personalized attention to every small detail and has the final say in anything in which she is involved. Many agree that Stewart's autocratic leadership style has allowed her to succeed in an extremely competitive media environment, while others argue that a participative leadership style might have yielded even greater success. Stewart recently sold her media empire to Sequential Brands, a retail-licensing company, but will remain on board as chief creative officer.[29] A company that recognizes which leadership style works best for its employees, customers, and business conditions is most likely to choose the best leaders for its particular needs.

Assessment Check

1. How is *leadership* defined?
2. Identify the styles of leadership as they appear along a continuum of greater or lesser employee participation.

7 Corporate Culture

corporate culture organization's system of principles, beliefs, and values.

An organization's **corporate culture** is its system of principles, beliefs, and values. The leadership style of its managers, the way it communicates, and the overall work environment influence a company's corporate culture. A corporate culture is typically shaped by the leaders who founded and developed the company and by those who have succeeded them. Although Google has grown by leaps and bounds since its launch, the company still tries to maintain the culture of innovation, creativity, and flexibility that its co-founders, Larry Page and Sergey Brin, promoted from the beginning (see photo). Google now has offices around the world, staffed by over 88,000 full-time employees. "We hire people who are smart and determined, and we favor ability over experience. Although Googlers share common goals and visions for the company, we hail from all walks of life and speak dozens of languages, reflecting the global audience that we serve," the website states. "When not at work, Googlers pursue interests ranging from cycling to beekeeping, from frisbee to foxtrot."[30]

Managers use symbols, rituals, ceremonies, and stories to reinforce corporate culture. The corporate culture at the Walt Disney Company is almost as famous as the original Disney characters themselves. In fact, Disney employees are known as cast members. All new employees attend training seminars in which they learn the language, customs, traditions, stories, product lines—everything there is to know about the Disney culture, the importance of face-to-face contact, and its original founder, Walt Disney. According to a former operations executive at the company, Disney's attention to detail throughout the organization is one of the major reasons for its global success.[31]

Corporate cultures can be very strong and enduring, but sometimes they are forced to change to meet new demands in the business environment. A company that is steeped in tradition and bureaucracy might have to shift to a leaner, more flexible culture in order to respond to shifts in technology or customer preferences. A company that grows quickly—like Google—generally has to make some adjustments in its culture to accommodate more customers and employees.

Michael Short/Bloomberg via Getty Images

Google's campus-wide bike-sharing program is an integral part of the search giant's corporate culture.

Assessment Check

1. What is the relationship between leadership style and corporate culture?
2. How do managers reinforce corporate culture?

8 Organizational Structures

organization structured group of people working together to achieve common goals.

An **organization** is a structured group of people working together to achieve common goals. An organization features three key elements: human interaction, goal-directed activities, and structure. The organizing process, much of which is led by managers, should result in an overall structure that permits interactions among individuals and departments needed to achieve company goals.

The steps involved in the organizing process are shown in **Figure 7.5**. Managers first determine the specific activities needed to implement plans and achieve goals. Next, they group these work activities into a logical structure. Then they assign work to specific employees and give the people the resources they need to complete it. Managers coordinate the work of different groups and employees within the company. Finally, they evaluate the results of the organizing process to ensure effective and efficient progress toward planned goals. Evaluation sometimes results in changes to the way work is organized.

Many factors influence the results of organizing. The list includes a company's goals and competitive strategy, the type of product it offers, the way it uses technology to accomplish work, and its size. Small companies typically create very simple structures. The owner of a dry-cleaning business generally is the top manager, who hires several employees to process orders, clean the clothing, and make deliveries. The owner handles the functions of purchasing supplies such as detergents and hangers, hiring and training employees and coordinating their work, creating marketing and promotional campaigns, and keeping accounting records.

As a company grows, its structure increases in complexity. With increased size comes specialization and growing numbers of employees. A larger company may employ many salespeople, along with a sales manager to direct and coordinate their work, or organize an accounting department.

An effective structure is one that is clear and easy to understand: Employees know what is expected of them and to whom they report. They also know how their jobs contribute to the company's mission and overall strategic plan. An *organization chart* is a visual representation of a company's structure that illustrates job positions and functions. **Figure 7.6** illustrates a sample organization chart.

Not-for-profit organizations also organize through formal structures so they can function efficiently and carry out their goals. These organizations, such as World Wildlife Federation and the Wounded Warrior Project, have a combination of paid staff and volunteers in their organizational structure.

Departmentalization

departmentalization process of dividing work activities into units within the organization.

Departmentalization is the process of dividing work activities into units within the organization. In this arrangement, employees specialize in certain jobs—such as marketing, finance, or design. Depending on the size of the company, usually a senior-level executive runs the department,

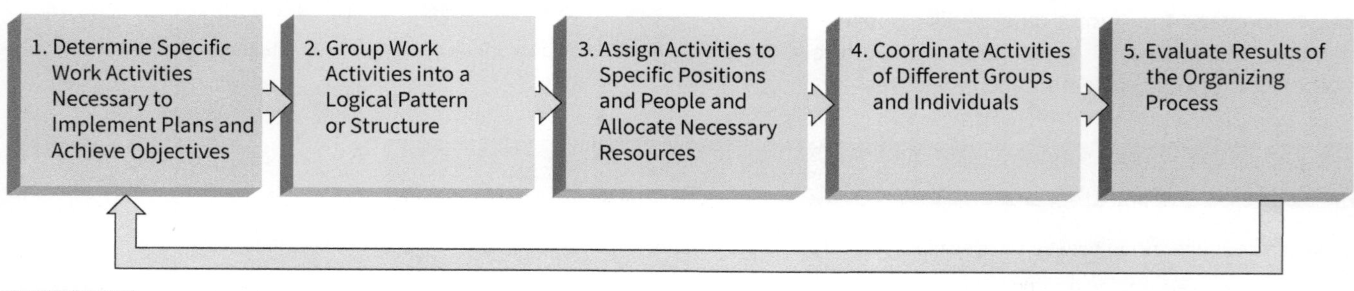

FIGURE 7.5 **Steps in the Organizing Process**

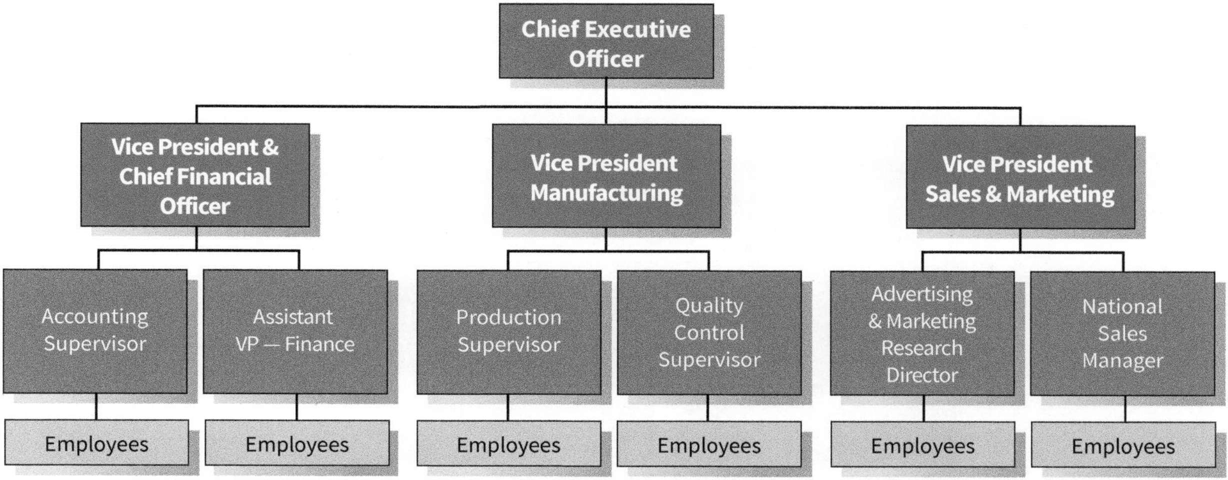

FIGURE 7.6 **Sample Organization Chart**

followed by middle-level managers and supervisors. The five major forms of departmentalization subdivide work by product, geographical area, customer, function, and process.

- *Product departmentalization*. This approach organizes work units based on the goods and services a company offers. California's Activision Blizzard Inc. is organized by product. The video-game publisher is divided into the following divisions: Call of Duty, Candy Crush, Destiny, Skylanders, Guitar Hero, World of WarCraft, StarCraft, Diablo, and HearthStone: Heroes of WarCraft.[32]
- *Geographical departmentalization*. This form organizes units by geographical regions within a country or, for a multinational company, by region throughout the world. Denim jean maker Levi Strauss & Co. is divided into the following divisions: Levi Strauss Americas (LSA), headquartered in San Francisco; Levi Strauss Europe (LSE), based in Brussels; and Levi Strauss Asia Pacific, Middle East, and Africa (LSAMA), based in Singapore.[33]
- *Customer departmentalization*. A company that offers a variety of goods and services targeted at different types of customers might structure itself based on customer departmentalization. Management of Procter & Gamble's wide array of products (see photo) is divided among four business units: Baby, Feminine, and Family Care (Always, Bounty, Charmin, and Pampers); Beauty (Head & Shoulders, Olay, and Pantene); Fabric and Home Care (Dawn, Downy, Febreze, Gain, and Tide); and Health and Grooming (Gillette, Crest, and Oral-B).[34]
- *Functional departmentalization*. Some companies organize work units according to business functions such as finance, marketing, human resources, and production. Nike, Inc. is organized by function, including Finance, Global Human Resources, Product & Merchandising, Administration & Legal, Global Sports Marketing, and Operations.
- *Process departmentalization*. Some goods and services require multiple work processes to complete their production. For instance, a textile manufacturer may set up separate departments for cotton ginning (separating cotton fibers from their seeds), spinning, weaving, dyeing, and finishing.

Neal Hamberg/Bloomberg via Getty Images

Consumer products giant, Procter & Gamble, targets its products to different types of customers. Products range from laundry detergent to diapers to toothpaste.

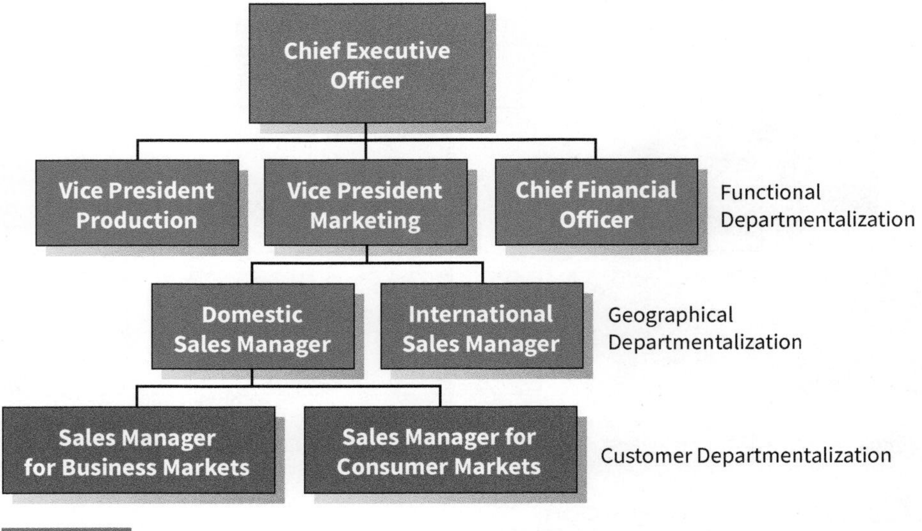

FIGURE 7.7 **Different Forms of Departmentalization within One Company**

As **Figure 7.7** illustrates, a single company may implement several different departmentalization schemes. In deciding on a form of departmentalization, managers take into account the type of product they produce, the size of their company, their customer base, and the locations of their customers.

Delegating Work Assignments

delegation managerial process of assigning work to employees.

Managers assign work to employees, a process called **delegation**. Employees might be responsible for answering customer calls, scooping ice cream, processing returns, making deliveries, opening or closing a store, cooking or serving food, contributing to new-product design, calculating a return on investment, or any of a multitude of other tasks. Just as important, employees are given a certain amount of authority to make decisions.

Companies like Zappos, the online shoe retailer, that empower their workers to make decisions that could better serve their customers generally have happier employees and more satisfied customers.[35] As employees receive greater authority, they also must be accountable for their actions and decisions—they receive credit when things go well, and must accept responsibility when they don't.

Span of Management The *span of management*, or span of control, is the number of employees a manager supervises. These employees are often referred to as direct reports. First-line managers have wider spans of management, monitoring the work of many employees. The span of management varies depending on many factors, including the type of work performed and employees' training. In recent years, a growing trend has brought wider spans of control, as companies have reduced their layers of management to flatten their organizational structures, in the process increasing the decision-making responsibility they give employees.

Centralization and Decentralization How widely should managers disperse decision-making authority throughout an organization? A company that emphasizes *centralization* retains decision making at the top of the management hierarchy. A company that emphasizes *decentralization* locates decision making at lower levels. A trend toward decentralization has pushed decision making down to operating employees in many cases. Companies that have decentralized believe that the change can improve their ability to serve customers. For example, the front-desk clerk at a hotel is much better equipped to answer a guest's questions about Internet connectivity or in-room dining than the hotel's general manager.

Types of Organization Structures

The four basic types of organization structures are line, line-and-staff, committee, and matrix. While some companies do follow one type of structure, most use a combination.

Line Organizations A *line organization,* the oldest and simplest organization structure, establishes a direct flow of authority from the chief executive to employees. The line organization defines a simple, clear *chain of command*—a hierarchy of managers and workers. With a clear chain of command, everyone knows who is in charge and decisions can be made quickly. This structure is particularly effective in a crisis situation. But a line organization has its drawbacks. Each manager has complete responsibility for a range of activities; in a medium-size or large organization, however, this person can't possibly be expert in all of them. In a small organization such as a local hair salon or a dentist's office, a line organization is probably the most efficient way to run the business.

Line-and-Staff Organizations A *line-and-staff organization* combines the direct flow of authority of a line organization with staff departments that support the line departments. Line departments participate directly in decisions that affect the core operations of the organization. Staff departments lend specialized technical support. **Figure 7.8** illustrates a line-and-staff organization. Accounting, engineering, and human resources are staff departments that support the line authority extending from the plant manager to the production manager and supervisors. Oftentimes, when an organization is in the process of either growth or retrenchment, as part of corporate restructure or reorganization, a management consultant will perform the role of evaluating the flow of authority and specific support of line and staff departments. See the "Job Description" feature to learn more.

A line manager and a staff manager differ significantly in their authority relationships. A line manager forms part of the primary line of authority that flows throughout the organization. Line managers interact directly with the functions of production, financing, or marketing—the functions needed to produce and sell goods and services. A staff manager provides information, advice, or technical assistance to aid line managers. Staff managers do not have authority to give orders outside their own departments or to compel line managers to take action.

The line-and-staff organization is common in midsize and large organizations. It is an effective structure because it combines the line organization's capabilities for rapid decision making and direct communication with the expert knowledge of staff specialists.

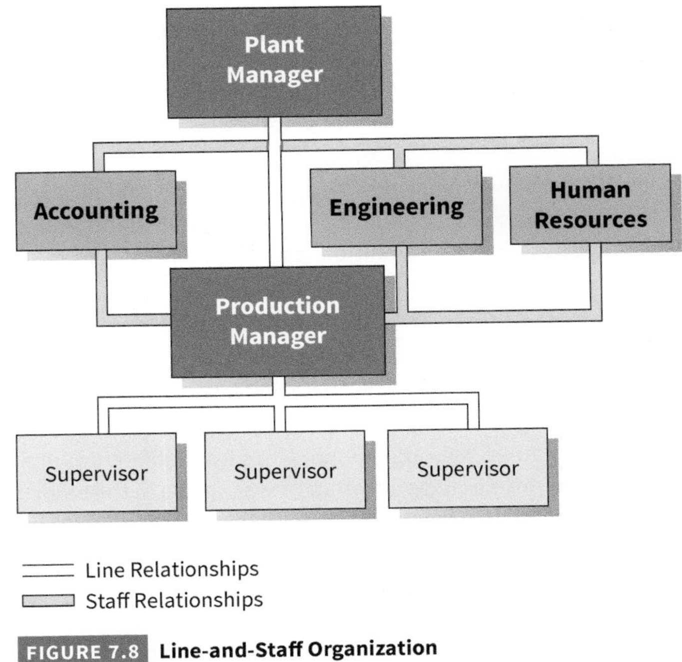

FIGURE 7.8 **Line-and-Staff Organization**

Job Description

Management Analyst or Management Consultant

Overview Management analysts, often called management consultants, work to improve an organization's efficiency and performance by evaluating and analyzing existing problems and developing improvement plans. Organizations typically hire management analysts to help develop strategies, implement technology, and improve operations. Recommendations are typically made to help an organization remain competitive, increase profitability and revenue, and control costs. Management analysts frequently work at a client's office, which can involve extended periods of travel. Some projects require teams of consultants (each with an area of expertise), whereas others may require an individual consultant working directly with a company's management team.

Responsibilities Tasks typically include information gathering about the problem(s) or issue(s) to be resolved. Many times employees are interviewed and on-site observations conducted to determine needed methods, equipment, and labor. Financial data are gathered and analyzed to determine trends and to make recommendations for improved systems and organizational changes. Follow-up is conducted to evaluate actual results.

Requirements For a typical entry-level job, most management analysts have a minimum of a bachelor's degree. The designation of Certified Management Consultant (CMC) may improve job prospects and opportunities. Fields of study that might lead to a career as a management analyst include business, management, finance, economics, political science, government, accounting, marketing, psychology, and computer and information science.

Some consultants have specific expertise in industries such as transportation, healthcare, and financial services. Others have specific skills such as cost reduction, inventory management, or reorganizing corporate structures to increase productivity within existing jobs.

Desired skills include analytical skills (interpreting information, data, and making proposals); communication skills (written, presentation, talking with and listening to clients); interpersonal skills (working well with others); problem-solving skills (creative thinking helps); and time management (tight deadlines are common). Working as part of a team to solve issues and meet goals is important.

Outlook As organizations continue to seek greater efficiencies and focus on controlling costs, they will employ the assistance of professionals such as management analysts. According to the Bureau of Labor Statistics, employment of management analysts is expected to grow 14% over the next five years, which is faster than the average for all other occupations. There will be continued growth in healthcare, information technology, and human resource consulting services. Well-known management consulting firms include McKinsey & Company; Boston Consulting Group; Bain, Booz & Company; and Deloitte Consulting.

Sources: Government website, "Management Analyst," *Occupational Outlook Handbook, 2017–2018 Edition,* http://www.bls.gov, accessed March 18, 2018; organization website, http://www.imcusa.org, accessed March 18, 2018; Susan Adams, "The Most Prestigious Consulting Firms of 2015," *Forbes*, http://www.forbes.com, accessed March 18, 2018; organization website, "What Is a Typical Day in the Life of a Management Consultant Like?" http://www.consultingfact.com, accessed March 18, 2018.

Committee Organizations A *committee organization* is a structure that places authority and responsibility jointly in the hands of a group of individuals rather than a single manager. This model typically appears as part of a regular line-and-staff structure.

Committees also work in areas such as new-product development. A new-product committee may include managers from such areas as accounting, engineering, finance, manufacturing, marketing, and technical research. By including representatives from all areas involved in creating and marketing products, such a committee generally improves planning and employee morale because decisions reflect diverse perspectives.

Committees tend to act slowly and conservatively, however, and may make decisions by compromising conflicting interests rather than by choosing the best alternative. The definition of a camel as "a racehorse designed by committee" provides an apt description of some limitations of committee decisions.

Matrix Organizations Some organizations use a matrix or product management design to customize their structures. The *matrix structure* links employees from different parts of the organization to work together on specific projects. Figure 7.9 diagrams a matrix structure. A project manager assembles a group of employees from different functional areas. The employees keep their ties to the line-and-staff structure, as shown in the vertical white lines. As the horizontal gold lines show, employees are also members of project teams. When the project is completed, employees return to their regular jobs.

In the matrix structure, each employee reports to two managers: one line manager and one project manager. Employees who are chosen to work on a special project receive instructions from the project manager (horizontal authority), but they continue as employees in their

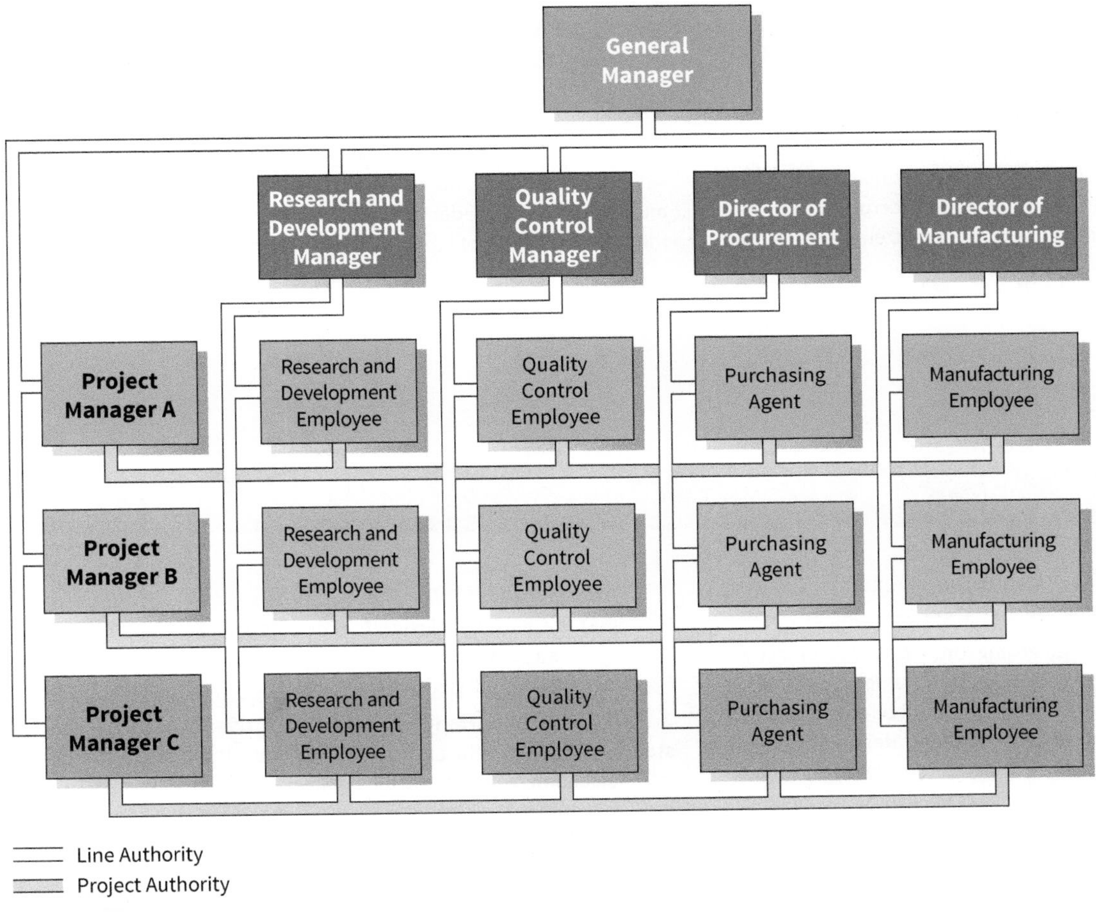

FIGURE 7.9 **Matrix Organization**

permanent functional departments (vertical authority). The term *matrix* comes from the intersecting grid of horizontal and vertical lines of authority.

The matrix structure is popular at high-technology and multinational corporations, as well as hospitals and consulting firms. Optics manufacturer Olympus uses a matrix organizational structure that maximizes the use of corporate resources by interconnecting businesses and functions efficiently.[36] The major benefits of the matrix structure come from its flexibility in adapting quickly to rapid changes in the environment and its capability of focusing resources on major problems or products. It also provides an outlet for employees' creativity and initiative. However, it challenges project managers to integrate the skills of specialists from many departments into a coordinated team. It also means that team members' permanent functional managers must adjust their employees' regular workloads.

The matrix structure is most effective when company leaders empower project managers to use whatever resources are available to achieve the project's objectives. Good project managers know how to make the project goals clear and keep team members focused. A company that truly embraces the matrix structure also nurtures a project culture by making sure staffing is adequate, the workload is reasonable, and other company resources are available to project managers.

Assessment Check

1. What is the purpose of an organization chart?
2. What are the five major forms of departmentalization?
3. What does *span of management* mean?

What's Ahead

In the next chapter, we sharpen our focus on the importance of people—the human resource—in shaping the growth and profitability of the organization. We examine how companies recruit, select, train, evaluate, and compensate employees in their attempts to attract, retain, and motivate a high-quality workforce. The concept of motivation is examined, and we discuss how managers apply theories of motivation in the modern workplace. The next chapter also looks at the important topic of labor–management relations.

Chapter in Review

Summary of Learning Objectives

LEARNING OBJECTIVE 1 Define management.

Management is the process of achieving organizational objectives through people and other resources. The management hierarchy is generally as follows: top managers provide overall direction for company activities, middle managers implement the strategies of top managers and direct the activities of supervisors, and supervisors interact directly with workers. The three basic managerial skills are technical, human or interpersonal, and conceptual.

Assessment Check Answers

1.1 **What is management?** Management is the process of achieving organizational objectives through people and other resources. The manager's job is to combine human and technical resources in the best way possible to achieve the company's goals.

1.2 **How do the jobs of top managers, middle managers, and supervisory managers differ?** Top managers develop long-range plans, set a direction for their organization, and inspire all employees to achieve the company's vision. Middle managers focus on specific operations, products, or customers. They develop procedures to implement the company's strategic plans. Supervisory managers interact directly with nonmanagerial employees who produce and sell the company's goods and services. They are responsible for implementing the plans developed by middle managers and motivating workers to accomplish daily, weekly, and monthly goals.

1.3 **What is the relationship between the manager's planning and controlling functions?** The basic purpose of controlling is to assess the success of the planning function. Controlling also provides feedback for future rounds of planning.

LEARNING OBJECTIVE 2 Explain the role of setting a vision and ethical standards for the company.

Vision is the founder's perception of the marketplace needs and the company's methods for meeting them. Vision helps clarify a company's purpose and the actions it can take to make the most of opportunities. High ethical standards can help build success for a company through job satisfaction and customer loyalty.

Assessment Check Answers

2.1 **What is meant by a vision for the company?** A vision serves as the target for a company's actions, helping direct the company toward opportunities and differentiating it from its competitors.

2.2 **Why is it important for a top executive to set high ethical standards?** High ethical standards often result in a stable workforce, job satisfaction, and customer loyalty.

LEARNING OBJECTIVE 3 Summarize the importance of planning.

The planning process identifies organizational goals and develops the actions necessary to reach them. Planning helps a company turn vision into action, take advantage of opportunities, and avoid costly mistakes. Strategic planning is a far-reaching process. It views the world through a wide-angle lens to determine the long-range focus and activities of the organization. Tactical planning focuses on the current and short-range activities required to implement the organization's strategies. Operational planning sets standards and work targets for functional areas such as production, human resources, and marketing.

Assessment Check Answers

3.1 **Outline the planning process.** Some plans are very broad and long range, focusing on key organizational objectives; others are more detailed and specify how particular objectives will be achieved. From the mission statement to objectives to specific plans, each phase must fit into a comprehensive planning framework.

3.2 **Describe the purpose of tactical planning.** The purpose of tactical planning is to determine which short-term activities should be implemented to accomplish the company's overall strategy.

3.3 **Compare the kinds of plans made by top managers and middle managers. How does their focus differ?** Top managers focus on long-range, strategic plans. In contrast, middle-level managers focus on short-term, tactical planning.

LEARNING OBJECTIVE 4 Describe the strategic planning process.

The first step of strategic planning is to translate the company's vision into a mission statement that explains its overall intentions and aims. Next, planners must assess the company's current competitive position using tools such as SWOT analysis. Managers then set specific objectives. The next step is to develop strategies for reaching objectives that will differentiate the company from its competitors. Managers then develop an action plan that outlines the specific methods for implementing the strategy. Finally, the results achieved by the plan are evaluated, and the plan is adjusted as needed.

Assessment Check Answers

4.1 **What is the purpose of a mission statement?** A mission statement is a written explanation of a company's purpose, the reason it exists, the customers it will serve, and how it is different from competitors. A mission statement guides the actions of company managers and employees.

4.2 **Which of a company's characteristics does a SWOT analysis compare?** A SWOT analysis determines a company's strengths, weaknesses, opportunities, and threats relative to its competitors.

4.3 **How do managers use objectives?** Objectives set guideposts by which managers define the organization's desired performance in such areas as new-product development, sales, customer service, and employee satisfaction.

LEARNING OBJECTIVE 5 Discuss managers as decision makers.

A programmed decision applies a company rule or policy to solve a frequently occurring problem. A nonprogrammed decision forms a response to a complex and unique problem with important consequences for the organization. The five-step approach to decision making includes recognizing a problem or opportunity, developing alternative courses of action, evaluating the alternatives, selecting and implementing an alternative, and following up the decision to determine its effectiveness.

Assessment Check Answers

5.1 **Distinguish between programmed and nonprogrammed decisions.** Programmed decisions, such as reordering office supplies, are simple and happen frequently, so procedures for them can streamline the process. Nonprogrammed decisions, such as entering a new market or developing a new product, require more individual evaluation.

5.2 **What are the steps in the decision-making process?** The decision-making steps are recognition of a problem or opportunity, development of alternatives, evaluation of alternatives, selection and implementation of the chosen alternative, and follow-up to determine effectiveness of the decision.

LEARNING OBJECTIVE 6 Evaluate managers as leaders.

Leadership is the act of motivating others to achieve certain goals. The basic leadership styles are autocratic, democratic, and free-rein leadership. The best leadership style depends on three elements: the leader, the followers, and the situation.

Assessment Check Answers

6.1 **How is leadership defined?** Leadership means directing or inspiring people to attain certain organizational goals. Effective leaders share several traits, such as empathy, self-awareness, and objectivity in dealing with others. Leaders also use the power of their jobs, expertise, and experience to influence others.

6.2 **Identify the styles of leadership as they appear along a continuum of greater or lesser employee participation.** At one end of the continuum, autocratic leaders make decisions without consulting employees. In the middle of the continuum, democratic leaders ask employees for suggestions and encourage participation. At the other end of the continuum, free-rein leaders leave most decisions to their employees.

LEARNING OBJECTIVE 7 Discuss corporate culture.

Corporate culture refers to an organization's principles, beliefs, and values. It is typically shaped by a company's founder and perpetuated through formal programs such as training, rituals, and ceremonies, as well as through informal discussions among employees. Corporate culture can influence a company's success by giving it a competitive advantage.

Assessment Check Answers

7.1 **What is the relationship between leadership style and corporate culture?** The best leadership style to adopt often depends on the organization's corporate culture and its system of principles, beliefs, and values. Managerial philosophies, communications networks, and workplace environments and practices all influence corporate culture.

7.2 **How do managers reinforce corporate culture?** Managers use symbols, rituals, ceremonies, and stories to reinforce corporate culture.

LEARNING OBJECTIVE 8 Identify organizational structures.

The subdivision of work activities into units within the organization is called *departmentalization*. It may be based on products, geographical locations, customers, functions, or processes. Most companies implement one or more of four structures: line, line-and-staff, committee, and matrix structures.

Assessment Check Answers

8.1 **What is the purpose of an organization chart?** An organization chart is a visual representation of a company's structure that illustrates job positions and functions.

8.2 **What are the five major forms of departmentalization?** Product departmentalization organizes units by the different goods and services a company offers. Geographical departmentalization organizes units by geographical regions. Customer departmentalization organizes units by different types of customers. Functional departmentalization organizes units by business activities such as finance, marketing, human resources, and production. Process departmentalization organizes units by the steps or work processes it takes to complete production or provide a service.

8.3 **What does *span of management* mean?** The span of management, or span of control, is the number of employees a manager supervises.

Business Terms You Need to Know

management 172
planning 174
organizing 175
directing 175
controlling 175
vision 175
mission statement 179
SWOT analysis 181
objectives 182
decision making 183
leadership 185
empowerment 186
corporate culture 187
organization 188
departmentalization 188
delegation 190

Review Questions

1. What are the three levels of management hierarchy? For each level, which management skills might be considered most important, and why?

2. Identify the four basic managerial functions. Suppose you were hired to be the manager of a local fitness center. Which managerial functions would likely be the biggest part of your job? In what ways?

3. Describe the relationship between a company's vision and its ethical standards. Why is it important for top management to put forth a clear vision and ethical standards for a company?

4. Suppose you planned a ski trip with the ski club at school, but when you woke up on the morning of the trip, the weather called for a storm—and to reach the ski resort requires a three-hour drive. What type of planning would you employ prior to the report of bad weather? What type of planning would allow you to cope with the potential storm? Specifically, what might you do?

5. What is the link between a company's vision and its mission statement? Think about your own career as a start-up venture. What is your vision? What might be your mission statement?

6. Define *objectives*. Outline objectives you might have for your own college education and career. How might this outline help you implement your own career strategy?

7. Identify each of the following as a programmed or nonprogrammed decision:

   a. purchasing school supplies

   b. buying a new smart phone

   c. buying your favorite toothpaste or shampoo at the supermarket

   d. selecting a college to attend

   e. choosing where to have lunch

8. From what sources might a leader derive power? Which leadership style might work best for a manager whose company is forced to make cost-cutting decisions? Why?

9. Why is a strong corporate culture important to a company's success? How might corporate culture be linked to leadership style?

10. Which type of organization structure provides a company with the most flexibility to respond to changes in the marketplace and engage in innovation? What might be the drawbacks of this structure?

Projects and Teamwork Applications

1. A micromanager is someone who, for many different reasons, closely observes or tries to control the work of subordinates or employees. Discuss why someone might micromanage, and why it might be difficult for someone who does so to accept that there are numerous ways to accomplish tasks and goals. What kind of impact does a micromanager have on employees, and how does this relate to the task of delegating?

2. Search your personal or professional network to find a supervisor or manager to interview. Find out more about how he or she performs each of the four management functions discussed in this chapter. Which of the technical, conceptual, and human skills are important for on-the-job performance?

3. Contingency planning requires a combination of foresight and adaptability. Research the news headlines for situations that could (or did) require contingency planning. Report to the class what the challenge was and how the managers involved handled it. Remark on whether the planning was effective or successful.

4. Identify someone who you think is a good leader—it can be someone you know personally or even a public figure. Describe the traits that you think are most important in making this person an effective leader. Would this person's leadership style work in situations other than his or her current position? Why or why not?

5. Research two companies you admire in each of the following industries: a technology start-up and a traditional bank. Learn what you can about each organization's culture. How does each differ? Explain which culture, if any, best suits you. Share your findings with the class.

Web Assignments

1. **SWOT analysis.** Create your own personal SWOT analysis as part of your career plan by going to the website listed below. Evaluate your personal strengths, weaknesses, opportunities, and threats. Either with a partner or in a small group, discuss your personal assessment and its impact on your career.
http://www.quintcareers.com/SWOT_Analysis.html

2. **Mission statements.** Go to the websites of two organizations, a for-profit firm and a not-for-profit organization. Evaluate the mission statement of each organization on the basis of four of the following: function, personality, target market, values, employees, strategic positioning, or financial objectives. How does the for-profit mission statement differ from the nonprofit mission statement? Either with a partner, or in small groups, discuss and analyze the differences.

3. **Management structure.** Visit the website listed below and answer the following questions.
http://www.pfizer.com/about/leadership_and_structure/leadership_structure
   a. How would you characterize Pfizer's organizational structure?
   b. What is the composition of Pfizer's board of directors?

Note: Internet web addresses change frequently. If you don't find the exact sites listed, you may need to access the organization's home page and search from there or use a search engine such as Google or Bing.

Cases

Case 7.1 Zappos Tries On Holacracy for Size

A number of years ago, in a courageous and somewhat risky move, Tony Hsieh, CEO and founder of Zappos, eliminated all managerial positions at the Las Vegas–based e-commerce shoe company. The strategy is called holacracy—better known as management by committee. Holacracy eliminates traditional manager roles and job titles with the intention of creating a faster, more efficient, and more innovative company. Hsieh is trying to fully integrate a self-managed organization that has estimated sales of $3 billion and 1,500 employees. The "work hard, play hard" attitude that embodies the Zappos culture will remain intact. What's different is that all employees will have equal say, and employees will be evaluated and rewarded by peers rather than a traditional boss.

To date, Zappos, a wholly owned subsidiary of Amazon, is one of the largest companies known to be implementing holacracy. Teams choose their own goals in a decentralized structure. Hsieh is confident that the more control he relinquishes and redistributes, the better off and more productive the company will be.

Previously a manager at Zappos had a variety of responsibilities, including managing people, overseeing and approving decisions, budgeting, developing employees, and working directly with team members to meet goals and improve project results. Hsieh is interested to see what contributions will materialize from those who are no longer responsible for managing others. Former managers will be given insight and training through a process called "Reinventing Yourself," whereby they explore new roles that match their passions, skills, and interests.

Hsieh acknowledges that for some the transition to self-management has been difficult. About 18% of the Zappos workforce has left since holacracy was implemented. Experts agree that it can take up to a decade to see its full, positive impact. Whether or not holacracy succeeds at Zappos remains to be seen. Yet, Hsieh's decision to eliminate the negativity and lack of productivity sometimes associated with the power of a traditional organizational hierarchy may be a risk worth taking.

Questions for Critical Thinking

1. Suppose you had been a manager at Zappos before holacracy had been implemented. Would you stay on with the company in a different nonmanagerial role? Why or why not?
2. Research the current status of Hsieh's decision to eliminate all managers and to implement holacracy. What have been the benefits? Drawbacks?

Sources: Forbes Leadership Forum, "Three Lessons for Zappos CEO Tony Hsieh From a 250-Year-Old Team," *Forbes*, http://www.forbes.com, accessed March 19, 2018; Jennifer Reingold, "A Move to 'Self-Management' Has Shaken the Online Shoe Retailer. Can It Regain Its Mojo?" *Fortune*, http://www.fortune.com, accessed March 20, 2018; Bourree Lam, "Why Are So Many Zappos Employees Leaving," *Atlantic*, http://www.theatlantic.com, accessed March 18, 2018; David Gelles, "The Zappos Exodus Continues after a Radical Management Experiment," *New York Times*, http://bits.blogs.nytimes.com, accessed March 18, 2018; Ilan Mochari, "3 Reasons the Zappos Exodus Doesn't Spell Doom for Holacracy," *Inc.*, http://www.inc.com, accessed March 18, 2018; Jeff Bercovici, "Why Tony Hsieh Is Turning Zappos into a City," *Inc.*, http://www.inc.com, accessed March 18, 2018; Tyler Durden, "Hundreds Leave 'Boss-less' Zappos As 'Get-Paid-to-Quit' Scheme Backfires," *Zero Hedge*, http://www.zerohedge.com, accessed March 18, 2018; Aaron Taub, "Even CEO Tony Hsieh's Inner Circle Can't Describe Zappos' Insanely Complicated Management Philosophy," *Business Insider*, http://www.businessinsider.com, accessed March 18, 2018; Gregory Ferenstein, "Zappos Just Abolished Bosses. Inside Tech's Latest Management Craze," *Vox*, http://www.vox.com, accessed March 18, 2018; Steve Denning, "Is Holacracy Succeeding at Zappos?" *Forbes*, http://www.forbes.com, accessed March 18, 2018; organization website, "How It Works," http://www.holacracy.com, accessed March 18, 2018.

Case 7.2 BambooHR Says No to More Than a 40-Hour Workweek

To say that Utah-based start-up BambooHR has a work culture that includes consequences for working too many hours might sound peculiar. But while some start-up businesses demand long work hours, BambooHR, maker of online human resources software, has a strict policy against it. As work–life balance remains an issue for many companies and employees, BambooHR has created a unique culture for its 150 workers with definitive work-time policies.

Voted by *Utah Business* as a "Best Company to Work For," BambooHR is well known for its workplace culture. Co-founders Ryan Sanders and Ben Peterson have created a unique approach to enforcing a strict policy that work–life balance is not just lip service and reminding employees that a 40-hour workweek does not limit creativity. The company's "anti-workaholics" policy means that all employees must leave the office at 5:00 p.m. Breaks are mandatory, and employees are admonished for not taking them.

Why the fuss? The guidelines, part of the co-founders' core beliefs, have developed from witnessing and hearing firsthand about other business cultures where their friends worked. Sleep deprivation, rewards for working long hours, failed marriages, and stress-related illnesses were just some of the things they observed.

Sanders says working a lot of hours might seem great on the surface, but ultimately it affects the business—in a negative way. One employee, who used to work 70 to 80 hours a week, nearly lost her job because she was sleep deprived, increasingly difficult to work with, and not very productive. Confronted by the company's two owners, she was told she needed to scale back to a 40-hour workweek or risk losing her job.

The company's "no workaholics" strategy has not hurt the bottom line. In its most recent year, the young company posted sales in the millions. BambooHR employees—and their bosses—are united in the belief that one's home life does not need to be sacrificed to build a great company.

Questions for Critical Thinking

1. Discuss the impact on employees of working long hours. What is the impact on productivity? Morale?
2. Discuss how a 40-hour workweek might be difficult to adapt to for someone coming from a work environment where working long hours is part of the culture and the norm.

Sources: Company website, http://bamboohr.com, accessed March 18, 2018; Erik Sherman, "These 5 Employers Are Rescuing the 40-Hour Workweek," *Fortune*, http://fortune.com, accessed March 18, 2018; Rachel Feintzeig, "Radical Idea at the Office: A 40-Hour Workweek," *Wall Street Journal*, http://www.wsj.com, accessed March 18, 2018; Jennifer Alsever, "Why This Startup Has a No-Workaholics Policy," *Inc.*, http://www.inc.com, accessed March 18, 2018.

Case 7.3 Management, Leadership, and the Internal Organization: TripAdvisor

TripAdvisor's mission is to empower travelers around the globe with the insights that they need to confidently explore and experience our world. Co-founder and CEO Steve Kaufer has achieved this mission on a grand scale—with more than 455 million monthly users and 570 million unbiased reviews by travelers across the globe. As the world's largest travel site, TripAdvisor offers travelers advice, travel choices, planning features, and seamless links to booking tools that check hundreds of websites to find the best hotel prices.

Growth of this nature hasn't happened without careful management—planning, organizing, directing, and controlling. As a technology company in a cutthroat and hyperchanging travel industry, TripAdvisor settles for hiring nothing less than the best talent in each department throughout the organization—and much care and consideration are taken to manage its coveted base of employees.

The company's informal and internal motto, "Speed Wins," is also part of its rich culture, which promotes finding successful outcomes while sponsoring novelty, new ideas, and even failure. Tolerance for failure, not out of sloppiness but from outcomes that just didn't work out, is the way TripAdvisor's management team subscribes to learning—which results in better long-term decision making. TripAdvisor's top leaders subscribe to responsiveness and speed, with the belief that if a response isn't quick and immediate, decay can set in. As part of its "Speed Wins" culture, TripAdvisor hires employees in search of a less bureaucratic company environment who can move and execute quickly. With 3,000 employees worldwide, getting everyone on the same page to understand the company's mission, business objectives, and how each job connects to its mission can be a challenge. TripAdvisor's top management team invests a huge amount of time thinking about creating alignment by communicating consistently, constantly, and with candor and transparency.

TripAdvisor's management team is organized on a functional basis—according to the traditional functions of sales & marketing, product, engineering, and finance. In fact, TripAdvisor's managers, fearless of change, are well versed in a wide variety of disciplines when it comes to managing their individual departments while viewing the changing travel space on a holistic basis. A common characteristic of all managers is the willingness and openness to change and to question the way things have been done in the past—while focusing on what can be done differently in the future.

TripAdvisor's business is built upon travelers sharing candid, transparent, and unbiased reviews with other travelers. Throughout its community of users, the company expects trustworthy, unbiased, clear, and accurate information that represents the experiences of the travel community. Given the company's 570 million unbiased reviews, this philosophy of trust extends to the company's management and leadership philosophies. The company's leaders are focused on being inclusive, constructive, and positive.

Strategic planning is an ongoing process—particularly in the cutthroat, hi-tech travel space. Kaufer admits that the biggest change impacting his business is the way in which travelers use technology—namely, the shift to mobile devices. TripAdvisor has had to adapt to the changing nature of today's business and technology environment. This includes investing in in-destination functionality for their products so that people can use the TripAdvisor app not just to plan their trip but also in short bursts while they are traveling around with their mobile devices. Longer-term strategic planning efforts include virtual reality and virtual tours—where travelers can "experience" a place virtually before ever booking that trip using their beloved TripAdvisor.

Questions for Critical Thinking

1. Using the SWOT analysis framework, discuss a few of TripAdvisor's strengths, weaknesses, opportunities, and threats.
2. How might TripAdvisor's mission change as Internet travel sites and competitors create intensified competition?
3. How would you describe TripAdvisor's corporate culture? Based upon what you know and with some further research, do you think the company's growth has impacted its culture?

Sources: Adele Blair, "Airbnb, TripAdvisor, Product Review: We Still Trust Strangers' Recommendations," *Sydney Morning Herald*, http://www.smh.com.au, accessed March 18, 2018; Dennis Schaal, "Buying TripAdvisor: Would Antitrust Issues Kill a Priceline or Google Acquisition?" Skift.com, https://skift.com, accessed March 18, 2018; Yue Wu, "The Story of TripAdvisor," http://www.onlineeconomy.org, accessed March 18, 2018; company website, "Fact Sheet," https://www.tripadvisor.com/PressCenter-c4-Fact_Sheet.html, accessed March 18, 2018; Victoria Abbott Riccardi, "A Day in the Life of TripAdvisor CEO Steve Kaufer," *Boston Globe*, http://bostonglobe.com, accessed March 18, 2018.

CHAPTER **8**

Human Resource Management: From Recruitment to Labor Relations

LEARNING OBJECTIVES

1. Explain the role of human resources: the people behind the people.
2. Describe recruitment and selection.
3. Discuss orientation, training, and evaluation.
4. Describe compensation.
5. Discuss employee separation.
6. Explain the different methods for motivating employees.
7. Discuss labor–management relations.

Changemaker

© 2018 The Ford Motor Company

Kiersten Robinson, Chief Human Resources Officer (CHRO), Ford Motor Company

Industry: Automotive

Website: http://www.ford.com

Ford Motor Company ("Ford" for short), designs, manufactures, markets, and services a full range of cars, trucks, SUVs, electrified vehicles, and luxury vehicles (under the Lincoln brand). Based in Dearborn, Michigan, Ford employs 203,000 people worldwide.

Ford Motor Company has moved beyond its core automobile business into autonomous vehicles and mobile apps for car sharing and parking (FordPass). FordPass lets users find and reserve parking ahead of time. The company also provides big data solutions to help people find faster routes. Last, "experience centers" have been developed to help customers experience all the digital solutions available through Ford vehicles and connected electronics.

With such tremendous change, a multi-year initiative is being implemented to streamline people processes under the leadership of a newly appointed Chief Human Resources Officer (CHRO), Kiersten Robinson. A 23-year Ford employee, Robinson has served in leadership roles in Asia Pacific, Europe, and North America. As part of an open global employee feedback process, Robinson learned about what employees really want, the problems and challenges they face at work, and how HR can better enable and empower them.

To encourage more sharing and collaboration, Robinson will focus on four key areas, known as "people shifts"—employee empowerment, high-performing teams, more employee input, and a more agile and uncomplicated people process. Eliminating lengthy policies and complex rules, Ford hopes to empower employees far more.

To encourage joint responsibility and accountability, more focus will be placed on high-performing teams and partnerships. To better understand the priorities and concerns of employees, and to create employee-focused solutions, employees' opinions will be considered on an ongoing basis. Robinson will lead an important global cultural transformation that involves creating a high-performing, diverse, and inclusive workforce that make employees' lives better.[1]

Overview

In this chapter, we explore the important issues of human resource management and motivation. We begin with a discussion of the ways organizations attract, develop, and retain employees. Topics covered include finding qualified candidates; selecting and hiring employees; creating effective training programs; conducting performance evaluations; and implementing compensation and benefits strategies. Then we describe the concepts behind motivation and the way human resource managers apply them to increase employee satisfaction and organizational effectiveness.

We also discuss the reasons why labor unions exist and focus on legislation that affects labor–management relations. The process of collective bargaining is then discussed, along with tools used by unions and management in seeking their objectives.

1 Human Resources: The People Behind the People

In the past decade, HR has undergone profound changes in how talent is identified, onboarded (orientation and socialization), and supported. Many in the industry believe that while the people skills at the core of HR will remain key, executives will need to be adept at quantitative reasoning, fiscal responsibility, and the impact of automation. The best companies value their employees just as much as their customers—without employees, there would be no goods or services to offer customers. Companies like Nike, The Walt Disney Company, and Google understand this. Management at these companies knows that hiring good talent is vital to overall success. Achieving the highest level of job satisfaction and dedication among employees is the goal of **human resource management**, which attracts, develops, and retains the employees who can perform the activities necessary to accomplish organizational objectives.

human resource management function of attracting, developing, and retaining employees who can perform the activities necessary to accomplish organizational objectives.

Not every company is large enough to have a separate human resources department. But whoever performs this function generally does the following: plans for staffing needs, recruits and hires employees, provides for training and evaluates performance, determines compensation and benefits, and oversees employee separation. In accomplishing these five tasks, shown in **Figure 8.1**, human resource managers achieve their objectives of:

1. providing qualified, well-trained employees for the organization;
2. maximizing employee effectiveness in the organization; and
3. satisfying individual employee needs through monetary compensation, benefits, opportunities to advance, and job satisfaction.

FIGURE 8.1 Human Resource Management Responsibilities

Human resource plans must be based on an organization's overall competitive strategies. In conjunction with other managers, human resource managers predict how many employees a company or department will need and what skills those workers should bring to the job—along with what skills they might learn on the job. Human resource managers are often involved in a company's strategic planning efforts involving both workforce reduction and additional hiring. Today, many companies use web-based human resources software, which includes recruiting tools and applicant tracking, benefits administration, performance evaluation tools, learning management, and payroll management.

Assessment Check

1. What are the five main tasks of a human resource manager?
2. What are the three overall objectives of a human resource manager?

human resource inventory also called a skills inventory, contains employee data such as age, gender, education, experience, training, and specialized skills.

job analysis is a process to identify and determine in detail the particular job duties and requirements and the relative importance of these duties for a given job.

2 Recruitment and Selection

The recruitment and selection process usually begins with planning current and future human resource needs. The first step is to prepare a **human resource inventory** (also called a skills inventory) of all the company's employees containing data such as age, gender, education, experience, training, and specialized skills. Next, a **job analysis** is a process to identify and determine in detail the particular job duties and requirements and the relative importance of these duties for a given job. The job analysis includes a job description and job specifications. A **job description** includes information such as job title, location, reporting to and of employees, job summary, nature and objectives of the job, and tasks and duties to be performed. **Job specification** is a written statement of educational qualifications, specific qualities, level of experience, and physical, emotional, technical, and communication skills required to perform a job. The recruitment process varies by company, and different methods are used to recruit and select individuals. As shown in **Figure 8.2**, most employers, large and small, have a formal process or steps in the recruitment and selection process.

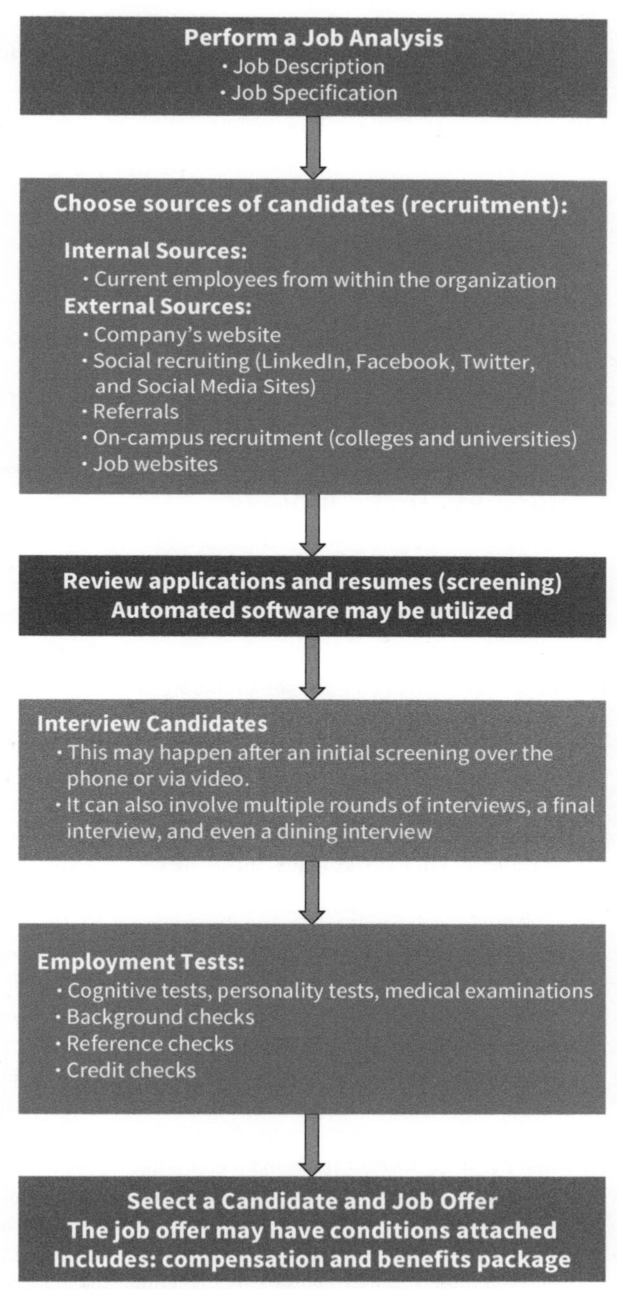

Perform a Job Analysis
• Job Description
• Job Specification
Choose sources of candidates (recruitment):
Internal Sources:
• Current employees from within the organization
External Sources:
• Company's website
• Social recruiting (LinkedIn, Facebook, Twitter, and Social Media Sites)
• Referrals
• On-campus recruitment (colleges and universities)
• Job websites
Review applications and resumes (screening)
Automated software may be utilized
Interview Candidates
• This may happen after an initial screening over the phone or via video.
• It can also involve multiple rounds of interviews, a final interview, and even a dining interview
Employment Tests:
• Cognitive tests, personality tests, medical examinations
• Background checks
• Reference checks
• Credit checks
Select a Candidate and Job Offer
The job offer may have conditions attached
Includes: compensation and benefits package

FIGURE 8.2 **Steps in the Recruitment and Selection Process**

Finding Qualified Candidates

One of the biggest challenges faced by HR professionals today is the growing skills gap. As part of an upskilling effort, Google has teamed up with educational technology company, Coursera. To create job readiness in 8–12 months, Google has designed an industry-relevant curriculum with a certificate upon completion. In an effort to revive its talent pipeline, employers will continue to seek both internal and external candidates.[2]

In addition to traditional methods of recruiting, such as college job fairs and referrals, most companies rely on their websites. A company's website might contain a career section with general employment information and a listing of open positions. Applicants are often able to submit a résumé and apply for an open position online.

Long gone are the days of applying to jobs found in newspaper want ads. No longer do employers spend time sifting through mounds of resumes. Thanks to social media recruitment, which uses social media profiles, blogs, and other sites to find information on candidates, attracting and engaging a broad range of candidates with desired skills is a more efficient and accurate process. Recruitment has become a digital experience, as candidates come to expect convenience, speed, and mobile contact. Savvy recruiters will use fast-response new talent acquisition technologies, some of which include cognitive and robotic technologies—such as machine learning, artificial intelligence (AI), and robotic process automation (RPA). These technologies allow

job description includes information such as job title, location, reporting to and of employees, job summary, nature and objectives of a job, and tasks and duties to be performed.

job specification is a written statement of educational qualifications, specific qualities, level of experience, physical, emotional, technical, and communication skills required to perform a job.

psychological and emotional connections with candidates for new talent acquisition. Many companies use recruiting and applicant tracking system software, which also includes cognitive technology. In some cases, applicants will submit a resume and cover letter via email.

Today, having a profile on LinkedIn is an imperative, and joining discussion groups on social networking sites related to your industry or field of interest can also be helpful. In many cases, the traditional resume is being replaced by online social media profiles, virtual portfolios that highlight real-world skills, work samples, and published online recommendations and referrals.[3]

In response to claims of bias and gender and pay inequality in the workplace, some companies are using a blind hiring process. Factors such as age, race, gender, and even affiliations and alma mater can create (unconscious) bias. By eliminating such information, screening can be done strictly on the basis of achievements, experience, and skills. To increase diversity, recruiting software can even automate screening and anonymize candidates to eliminate the bias that typically occurs during the recruitment and selection process.[4] Cognitive and robotic technology is being utilized as part of the recruitment process, as described in the "Business & Technology" feature.

Selecting and Hiring Employees

The selection stage is the process by which an employer, usually in conjunction with department managers or supervisors, assesses each of the applicants within the pool to decide which will be offered a position. Sometimes this is done with the help of human resource software. As part of the selection process, every company must follow state and federal employment laws. Title VII of the Civil Rights Act of 1964 prohibits employers from discriminating against applicants

Business & Technology

Recruitment Using Cognitive and Robotic Technology

With a skills gap, many companies are scrambling to keep up with talent acquisition, and most will eventually adopt a wide range of tools to compete. One of the most promising trends for recruiters today is the use of talent acquisition technology tools. These tools include automation software (like chatbots) for high-volume recruitment, open sourcing tools for skilled job recruitment, automated applicant tracking systems (recruitment management systems), and better assessments (including widely accessible video assessment and culture assessment tools).

Here's how it works: by reviewing resumes, a team of recruiters in need of filling open job requisitions for a broad number of positions may look at equally qualified candidates. The interview process may provide additional insight. Using the cognitive approach, and to streamline their efforts, the recruiters are provided a prioritized list of job requisitions based upon an analysis of drivers such as job complexity, skills, location, and seniority. The pipeline list of best-fit talent (a "fit score" is provided) is based upon the skills, career experiences, and other attributes found on the candidate's resume that match the job description. In addition, social networks are scanned. This not only speeds up the selection process, but it removes any bias.

A company called Paradox has recently launched Olivia, a chatbot who guides candidates through an application process with a series of sequenced questions. Olivia begins a dialogue with a candidate when interest is first expressed in a company, and in doing so, she builds up data points leading the conversation through her unique machine learning ability. The conversation leads Olivia to ask the prospective candidate to create a profile within the recruiter's database, which allows recruiters to build a tailored list of interested prospects. Another useful tool for recruiting is video, complemented by AI. Olivia is helping companies like Delta Airlines, Sprint, CVS, and Staples acquire talent.

Questions for Critical Thinking

1. **Video interviews provide additional insight into promising candidates, and they also save money and speed up hiring time frames. What are your thoughts about video interviews as compared to face-to-face interviews?**
2. **What are the pros and cons of talent acquisition technology tools like those described? Do you agree that they're the wave of the future?**

Sources: Michael Stephan, David Brown, and Robin Erickson, "Talent Acquisition: Enter the Cognitive Recruiter 2017 Global Human Capital Trends," https://www2.deloitte.com, accessed March 22, 2018; company website, "The AI Poised to Disrupt Recruiting," http://www.vsource.io, accessed March 22, 2018; Michael Stefan, "Say Hello to the Cognitive Recruiter," *The Wall Street Journal*, http://www.wsj.com, accessed March 21, 2018; company website, "Olivia Is Working for World Class Organizations," https://www.paradox.ai, accessed March 22, 2018; Bob Schultz, "How Cognitive Computing Transforms the Employee Experience," *Marginalia*, http://www.marginalia.online, accessed March 22, 2018.

based on their race, religion, color, sex, or national origin. The Americans with Disabilities Act of 1990 prohibits employers from discriminating against disabled applicants. The Civil Rights Act created the *Equal Employment Opportunity Commission (EEOC)* to investigate discrimination complaints. The Uniform Employee Selection Guidelines were adopted by the EEOC in 1978 to further clarify ways in which employers must ensure that their employees will be hired and managed without discrimination.[5] The EEOC also helps employers set up *affirmative action programs* to increase job opportunities for women, minorities, people with disabilities, and other protected groups.

The Civil Rights Act of 1991 expanded the alternatives available to victims of employment discrimination by including the right to a jury trial, punitive damages, and damages for emotional distress, though limiting the amount that a jury could award. At the same time, opponents to such laws have launched initiatives to restrict affirmative action standards and protect employers against unnecessary litigation.

These laws have been the basis for many legal cases over the years. Regardless of any contrary state or local laws, the EEOC interprets and enforces Title VII's prohibition of sex discrimination as forbidding any employment discrimination based on gender identity or sexual orientation. Examples of sex discrimination include failing to hire an applicant because she is a transgender woman, or firing an employee because he or she is planning or has made a gender transition.[6] Failure to comply with equal employment opportunity legislation can result in costly legal fees, expensive fines, bad publicity, and poor employee morale.

Even the process of interviewing a job candidate is covered by law. An interviewer may not ask any questions about marital status, children, race or nationality, religion, age, criminal records, mental illness, medical history, or alcohol and substance abuse problems. For more information about employment law, visit the websites of the Society for Human Resource Management (http://www.shrm.org), the EEOC (http://www.eeoc.gov), and the Department of Labor (http://dol.gov).

Navigating the maze of hiring restrictions is a challenge. To protect society's interests and to provide a safe workplace, some companies require drug testing, sometimes random, for job applicants. Mandatory drug testing is required in certain industries such as air travel or trucking, where public safety is crucial. But drug testing is controversial because of an employee's right to privacy.

Many companies have revised their selection criteria process. Some employers have adopted the mindset of "hiring for attitude and training for technical skills." Today, many employers, focused on soft skills, are less insistent on each box on the job qualifications scorecard being checked. A recent survey revealed that 66% of organizations plan to train new employees who may not have all of the required skills but possess the ability and desire to learn and excel. Hard skills (tangible and technical skills), are relevant to jobs such as engineering or health sciences. Soft skills, which include communication, ability to work under pressure, leadership, self-motivation, responsibility, teamwork, and problem solving, are skills that many employers see as vital to job performance and culture fit. Exceptional soft skills tell an employer that there may be greater potential for effective training and learning.[7]

Recruitment and selection are costly. There are costs for advertising, interviewing, administering employment tests, and even medical exams. Once an applicant is hired, there are costs for training, onboarding, and orientation. But a poor hiring decision is even more costly because the company has to go through the whole process again to find the right person. The cost of hiring the wrong top-level manager not only results in a financial cost, but a company's productivity, employee morale, and reputation can suffer as well.[8] Some companies are questioning whether the tremendous time investment of traditional (and multiple rounds of) interviews is worth it. Some companies are finding out that interviews do not always result in the ability to effectively evaluate a candidate. Instead, online assessment tools to measure soft skills and traits like curiosity, communication, problem solving, and teamwork are being utilized. Job auditions where candidates are paid to do work while being observed is another tool being used. Last, many companies are hiring based upon potential rather than experience.

To avoid these mistakes—and to get the right person for the job—many employers require applicants to complete employment tests. These tests may verify certain job-related skills, including mechanical, technical, language, and computer skills.

Assessment Check

1. Describe several recruiting techniques used by human resource managers.
2. What is the function of the Equal Employment Opportunity Commission (EEOC)?

3 Orientation, Training, and Evaluation

Once hired, employees need to know what is expected of them and how well they are performing. Companies provide this information through onboarding, orientation, training, and evaluation. Onboarding is the process of socializing a new employee to the company. A new hire may complete an orientation program administered jointly by the human resource department and the department in which the employee will work. During orientation, employees learn about company policies regarding their rights and benefits. They could also learn specific knowledge, skills, company norms, and behaviors to become effective members of the organization. They might receive an employee manual that includes the company's code of ethics and code of conduct. Many companies have a vast number of online resources and support for new hires. A personalized agent or automated advisor provides new employees with the information and support they need.

Training Programs

Training is a good investment for both employers and employees. Training provides workers with an opportunity to build their skills and knowledge, preparing them for new job opportunities within the company. It also provides employers with a better chance at retaining long-term, loyal, high-performing talent. For continuous learning, many companies are utilizing machine learning and artificial intelligence (AI) to deliver learning that is "always on and always available" over a range of mobile platforms. Machine learning and gamification is also being used for employee training. Technology "learns" the user habits and preferences to streamline the user learning experience—and skill level, progress, point scoring, competition with others, and mastery is tracked. With cognitive computing, employees are alerted via email about training programs and customized coursework suitable for team members. Further discussion on artificial intelligence and machine learning can be found in Chapter 14.[9]

On-the-Job Training One popular teaching method is *on-the-job training,* which prepares employees for job duties by allowing them to perform tasks under the guidance of experienced employees. A variation of on-the-job training is apprenticeship training, in which an employee learns a job by serving for a time as an assistant to a trained worker. To bridge the gap between what students learn in the classroom and what companies require, BMW's Spartanburg, South Carolina, plant works with students from a nearby community college who train and study part-time at the manufacturing plant while earning two-year degrees.[10]

Classroom and Computer-Based Training Many companies offer some form of classroom instruction such as lectures, conferences, and workshops or seminars. Ernst & Young (EY), a global professional services firm, offers a training program called EY and You (EYU), focusing on classroom learning, experiential learning, and coaching.[11]

Many firms are replacing classroom training with online training programs, which can significantly reduce the cost of training. Online training offers consistent presentations, along with videos that can simulate the work environment. Employees can learn at their own pace without having to sign up for a class. Through online training programs, employees can engage in interactive and adaptive learning—they might videoconference or Skype with a mentor or instructor who is located elsewhere, or they might participate in a simulation requiring them to make decisions related to their work. Accenture, a global consulting firm, has created a flexible digital learning environment to enable its people to deliver highly specialized strategy and consulting services to clients as described in the "Business Model" feature.

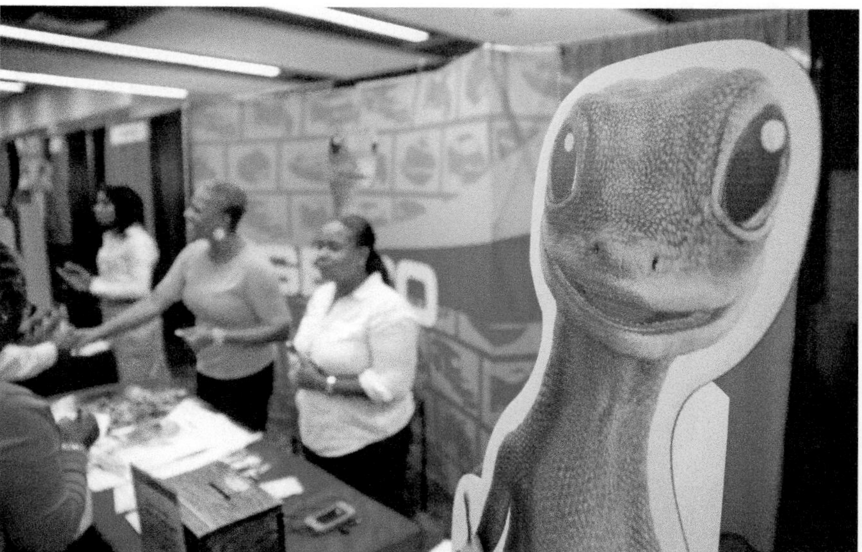
Andrew Harrer/Bloomberg via Getty Images

Geico's management development program grooms future business leaders to become managers in various segments of its insurance business, including sales, customer service, claims, or auto damage.

Management Development A *management development program* provides training designed to improve the skills and broaden the knowledge of current or future managers and executives. Training may be aimed at increasing specific technical knowledge or more general knowledge in areas such as leadership and interpersonal skills. Geico Insurance, owned by Berkshire Hathaway, has a management development program focused on grooming future business leaders to ultimately manage a team of associates in each of its key areas: sales, customer service, claims, or auto damage (see photo). Those with a bachelor's degree in business, or a related field, will participate in industry seminars and training, professional insurance licensing, on-the-job training, mentoring and coaching, and hands-on business projects.[12]

While more women are being encouraged to seek and retain leadership roles within companies, solutions such as building women leadership programs or network groups do not always work. When companies identify high-potential female employees, develop them, and create mentors, the downside can be the unchanged nature of the existing environment. If women leaders do not feel valued or accepted, they might not stay—and data shows that they

Business Model

Digital Learning Provides Great Returns

Accenture is a global strategy and consulting firm that is also a world-class learning organization. A learning organization refers to a company that encourages and facilitates the learning of its employees on a continuous basis.

In a recent year, Accenture made an $841 million investment on the training and development of its 425,000 employees, delivering on average more than 40 hours per employee, or 15 million hours in total. Known as Accenture Connected Learning, the program is a flexible learning environment that combines both classroom and digital learning and provides links to training and world-class experts. Included are 50 connected classrooms, 24,000 online courses, and 900 learning boards with online forums by subject matter experts. The company's five regional learning centers offer a more traditional face-to-face classroom learning experience, and its 100 professional communities brings together Accenture colleagues worldwide with similar work, goals, and industry specializations.

Training is particularly important for Accenture's specialists, who work across more than 40 industries and business functions to create value and solutions for clients worldwide. Accenture's CEO believes strongly that in order to remain competitive the organization must continue to invent new ways for its people to learn and grow quickly as needed. Accenture's return on its training investment results in highly skilled, idea-driven people who deliver creative and sustainable solutions and strategies to clients and communities worldwide.

Questions for Critical Thinking

1. **Discuss the benefits of Accenture's Connected Learning environment and how, in the long run, the investment in learning sets Accenture apart from its competitors.**
2. **In what ways would you assume Accenture's focus on learning benefits the company in terms of employee loyalty and turnover?**

Sources: Company website, "Accenture Invests More than $840 Million in Employee Learning and Professional Development," https://newsroom.accenture.com, accessed March 22, 2018; "2015 Workforce 100: Ranking the World's Top Companies for HR," *Workforce*, http://www.workforce.com, accessed March 22, 2018; Tom Starner, "Accenture Goes All in on Learning and Development," *HRDive*, http://www.hrdive.com, accessed March 22, 2018.

usually do not. In certain industries in particular, human resource organizations must continue to examine their structures and culture to determine why women and people of color may consistently feel left out of leadership positions.[13]

Performance Appraisals

performance appraisal evaluation of and feedback on an employee's job performance.

Many companies use annual **performance appraisal** to evaluate and provide feedback about an employee's job performance. A performance appraisal can include assessments of everything from attendance to goals met. Based on this evaluation, a manager will make decisions about compensation, promotion, additional training needs, transfers, or even termination.

Studies indicate that as much as 62% of a rater's evaluation of an employee is a reflection of the rater rather than of the person being reviewed. If reviews are to be effective, bias must be removed. Links should be made to organizational goals, based on objective criteria, and take place in the form of a two-way conversation.[14]

Some companies conduct peer reviews, in which employees assess the performance of their co-workers, while other companies ask employees to review their supervisors and managers. One such performance appraisal is the *360-degree performance review,* a process that gathers feedback from a review panel of 8 to 12 people, including co-workers, supervisors, team members, subordinates, and sometimes even customers. The idea is to get as much honest feedback from as many perspectives as possible. By its very nature, this kind of review involves a lot of work, but employees benefit from it because they are more involved with the process and ultimately better understand their own strengths, weaknesses, and roles in the company. Managers benefit because they get much more in-depth feedback from all parts of the organization. Companies such as Halogen Software offer cloud-based performance appraisal software to help firms evaluate employee performance. General Electric recently eliminated annual performance reviews. Instead, managers will hold regular, informal "touchpoints" with employees during which priorities will be set and updated based upon customer needs. With this new approach, GE managers will coach employees rather than critique their performance.[15]

Assessment Check

1. What are the benefits of computer-based or online training?
2. What is a management development program?
3. What are the three criteria of an effective performance appraisal?

4 Compensation

compensation amount employees are paid in money and benefits.

Compensation—how much employees are paid in money and benefits—is one of the most highly charged issues faced by human resource managers. The amount employees are paid, along with whatever benefits they receive, has a tremendous influence on where they live, what they eat, and how they spend their leisure time. It also can have an effect on job satisfaction. Balancing compensation for employees at all job levels can be a challenge for human resource managers. To learn more about the role of a compensation and benefits analyst, see the "Job Description" feature.

wage pay based on an hourly rate or the amount of work accomplished.

The terms *wage* and *salary* are often used interchangeably, but actually are different. **Wages** are based on an hourly pay rate or the amount of work accomplished. Typical wage earners are factory workers, construction workers, auto mechanics, retail salespeople, and

Job Description

Compensation and Benefits Analyst

Overview Compensation and benefits analysts are responsible for helping to coordinate a company's compensation and benefits programs. There are opportunities in every industry, including government and healthcare.

Responsibilities Compensation analysts evaluate a company's pay structure by researching trends and reviewing surveys to compare pay levels with other companies in a particular industry, market, or geographic region. The analysis typically consists of evaluating data and costs of compensation policies along with various options of pay-for-performance strategies such as bonuses, paid leave (sabbaticals), and other incentives.

Benefits analysts help administer a company's benefits program, which typically includes retirement programs, wellness programs, and insurance policies such as health, life, and disability. Research is conducted on various benefit plans, policies, and programs, and recommendations are made to senior management. There is ongoing oversight to make sure a company is in compliance with government regulations, legislation, and benefit trends and to ensure that company programs are current, legal, and competitive.

Compensation and benefit analysts often collaborate with partners and vendors such as payroll administrators, insurance brokers, and investment managers; prepare and present reports that include evaluation of compensation and benefits research, and make recommendations. Critical thinking, writing, decision making, presentation, and problem-solving skills are essential.

Requirements Most employers require compensation and benefit analysts to have at least a bachelor's degree for an entry-level job. Many specialists have coursework in human resource management, general business, finance, accounting, or communications. Previous work experience is helpful, and employers typically require some sort of compensation analysis and research, benefits administration, or human resources generalist work. Experience can also be gained through internships. Understanding compliance with federal and state laws, minimum wages, overtime, and equal pay is required. Certification is not necessary; however, it can provide an edge to job seekers. An advancement or promotion from a compensation and benefits analyst is usually to a position as manager or human resources manager.

Outlook Employment prospects are projected to grow approximately 4% annually for the next decade, particularly as compensation and benefit plans become more complex and costly. Specialists to analyze, select, and update a company's benefits and employment policies will continue to be in demand. Wellness plans will be of particular interest as companies continue to look for ways to reduce overall health care costs.

Sources: Government website, "Compensation, Benefits, and Job Analysis Specialists," *Occupational Outlook Handbook, 2016-17 Edition*, http://www.bls.gov, accessed March 21, 2018; Gail Sessoms, "Detailed Job Description for a Compensation Specialist," *Houston Chronicle*, http://work.chron.com, accessed March 21, 2018; company website, "Compensation, Benefits, or Job Analysis Specialists," http://hrpeople.monster.com, accessed March 21, 2018.

restaurant wait staff. **Salaries** are calculated periodically, such as weekly or monthly. Salaried employees receive a set amount of pay that does not fluctuate with the number of hours worked. Wage earners receive overtime pay, and salaried workers do not. Office managers, executives, and professional employees usually receive salaries.

salary pay calculated on a periodic basis, such as weekly or monthly.

An effective compensation system should attract well-qualified workers, keep them satisfied in their jobs, and inspire them to succeed. It's also important to note that certain laws, including minimum wage, must be taken into account. The Lilly Ledbetter Fair Pay Act of 2009 is one such law, which gives workers more time to file a complaint for pay discrimination.[16]

The movement toward pay transparency was highlighted when Google announced that it would begin displaying salary information next to job postings. Proponents of pay transparency argue that it can help motivate employees and attract new talent while closing the gender gap. Opponents worry about the demoralizing effect it could have by potentially driving valuable employees away. Companies such as Facebook and Salesforce are performing company overhauls to correct existing pay gaps between genders. Salesforce considers equality a business value, and the company recently spent $6 million to review and correct the pay of 26,000 employees.[17]

Most companies base their compensation policies on the following factors: (1) what competing companies are paying, (2) government regulation, (3) cost of living, (4) company profits, (5) an employee's productivity or performance, and (6) supply and demand of talent. Many companies try to balance rewarding workers with maintaining profits by linking more of their pay to superior performance. Companies try to motivate employees to excel by offering some type of incentive compensation in addition to salaries or wages.

Various Forms of Incentive Compensation

- **Annual incentive plan.** A pay plan that rewards the accomplishment of specific results. Rewards usually are tied to expected results identified at the beginning of the performance cycle.
- **Discretionary bonus plan.** A plan in which management determines the size of the bonus pool and the amounts to be allocated to individuals after a performance period.
- **Spot awards.** Recognize special contributions as they occur for a project or task, generally accomplished in a short period.
- **Profit-sharing plan.** A plan through which employees share in the organization's profits. The plan normally includes a predetermined, defined formula for allocating profit shares among participants and for distributing funds accumulated under the plan.
- **Gain-sharing plans.** Any one of a number of incentive programs that share the results of productivity gains with employees as a group.
- **Team/small-group incentives.** Any incentive program that focuses on the performance of a small group, usually a work team.
- **Retention bonus.** A payment or reward outside of regular salary that is offered as an incentive to keep a key person on the job during a particularly crucial business cycle.
- **Project bonus.** A form of additional compensation paid to an employee or a department for successfully completing a project within a certain time frame.

FIGURE 8.3 Various Forms of Incentive Compensation

Employee Benefits

employee benefits additional compensation such as vacation, retirement plans, profit-sharing, health insurance, gym memberships, child and elder care, and tuition reimbursement, paid entirely or in part by the company.

In addition to wages and salaries, companies provide benefits to employees and their families as part of their compensation. **Employee benefits**—such as vacation, retirement plans, profit-sharing, health insurance, gym memberships, child and elder care, and tuition reimbursement—are sometimes offered by the company. Benefits represent a large component of an employee's total compensation. Although wages and salaries account for around 68% of the typical employee's earnings, the other 32% takes the form of employee benefits.[18]

Some benefits are required by law. U.S. companies are required to make Social Security and Medicare contributions, as well as payments to state unemployment insurance and workers' compensation programs, which protect workers in case of job-related injuries or illnesses. The Family and Medical Leave Act of 1993 requires covered employers to offer up to 12 weeks of unpaid, job-protected leave to eligible employees. Companies voluntarily provide other employee benefits, such as child care and health insurance, to help them attract and retain employees.[19] **Table 8.1** shows a number of examples of unique and creative employee perks that match current demographic trends of today's workforce.

PhotoBeaM/iStockphoto

Benefits such as on-site fitness facilities improve both a company's health and that of its employees.

In the past, companies have paid the greater share of the cost of health care benefits, with employees paying a much smaller share. However, as health care costs rise, employers are passing along premium increases to employees. Many companies now offer incentives for workers to live healthier lives. Gym memberships, wellness programs, wellness visits to the doctor, and smoking-cessation programs are all examples of these incentives (see photo). Well-being apps have created workplace camaraderie through the formation of fitness groups and various competitions. Fitbit, a wireless-enabled wearable technology company, is known for its activity trackers that measure data such as number of steps walked, heart rate, sleep quality, to name a few. Fitbit wellness programs continue to successfully infiltrate the ranks of Fortune 500 companies.[20]

Retirement plans make up a chunk of employee benefits. Some companies have reduced the contributions they make to workers' *401(k) plans*—

TABLE 8.1 Unique and Creative Employee Perks

Company	Perk
Zappos	Pet insurance, pre-paid legal, monthly team outings, nap rooms.
Google	Free food for breakfast, lunch, and dinner, on-site haircuts, laundry and dry cleaning services, on-site medical staff, death benefits of half the salary of the deceased for ten years, financial advisors, and egg freezing services.
SAS	Three weeks of paid company vacation and unlimited sick days, subsidized on-site child care centers, college scholarship program for children of employees, and no dress code.
Starbucks	All U.S. employees who work more than 20 hours per week earn free tuition to earn a bachelor's degree through Arizona State University Online.
Evernote	Free twice-monthly housecleaning.
BodyLogicMD	Free spa services including massages and manicures.
Netflix	Unlimited vacation and no official work hours.
Facebook	$4,000 "baby cash" for a newborn, egg freezing services, in vitro fertilization (IVF) benefits for women, and four months of paid parental leaves for both moms and dads.
Zynga	Every day is "Bring your dog to work day."
Ben & Jerry's	Three pints of ice cream daily.
PricewaterhouseCoopers	Student loan reimbursement of $1,200 per year.
Etsy	New moms and dads receive six months of paid parental leave.
Patagonia	Free mid-day surfing during lunch (daily surf and wave reports are posted) and on-site childcare.
Quicken Loans	Free tickets to any Cleveland Cavaliers game or any concert or event held at Quicken Loans Arena in Cleveland, Ohio (owned by company founder, Dan Gilbert).
Accenture	Gender reassignment surgery as part of their commitment to LGBTQ rights and diversity.
Zillow	Paid shipping of overnight breast milk to babies of employees who are traveling on business.

Sources: Kristi Hines, "4 Companies Attracting Quality Talent with Unique Perks," *RecruiterBox*, https://recruiterbox.com, accessed March 25, 2018; David Rook, 20 "Unique Employee Benefits That Boost Employee Morale," *GriffinBenefits*, www.griffinbenefits.com, accessed March 25, 2018; Sammi Caramela, "15 Cool Job Perks That Keep Employees Happy," *Business News Daily*, http://www.businessnewsdaily.com, accessed March 25, 2018; company website, "How We Care for Googlers," https://careers.google.com, accessed March 26, 2018; Clare O'Connor, "Etsy's 6 Month Paid Parental Leave: The New Normal in Tech as U.S. Law Lags," *Forbes*, http://www.forbes.com, accessed March 25, 2018; Brie Weiler Reynolds, "26 Crazy Employee Benefits Offered by Companies," *FlexJobs*, https://www.flexjobs.com, accessed March 25, 2018; Craig Weller, "What You Need to Know About Egg-Freezing, the Hot New Perk at Google, Apple, and Facebook," *Business Insider*, http://www.businessinsider.com, accessed March 25, 2018; Vanessa Fuhrmans, "The Latest Way to Woo Workers: Fertility Benefits," *The Wall Street Journal*, http://www.wsj.com, accessed March 25, 2018; Lydia Dishman, "These Are the Best Employee Benefits and Perks," *Fast Company*, http://www.fastcompany.com, accessed March 25, 2018.

retirement savings plans to which employees can make pretax contributions. Some companies have cut back on cash contributions to the plans and contribute company stock instead. However, others provide a high level of funding. Boeing, a global aircraft manufacturer, provides a generous 75% match on the first 8% of base pay that employees save in their 401(k) accounts.[21]

Flexible Benefits

In response to increased workplace diversity, companies are developing creative ways to tailor their benefit plans to the needs of employees. One approach sets up *flexible benefit plans,* also called cafeteria plans. This system offers employees a choice of benefits, including different types of medical insurance, dental and vision plans, and life and disability insurance. This flexibility allows one working spouse to choose medical coverage for the entire family, while the other spouse uses benefit dollars to buy other types of coverage. Typically, each employee receives a set allowance (called flex dollars or credits) to pay for benefits depending on his or her needs. Contributions to cafeteria accounts can be made by both the employee and employer. Cafeteria plans also offer tax benefits to both employees and employers.

Another way of increasing the flexibility of employee benefits involves time off from work. Instead of establishing set numbers of holidays, vacation days, personal days, and sick days, some employers give each employee a bank of *paid time off (PTO)*. Employees use days from their PTO account without having to explain why they need the time. The greatest advantage of PTO is the freedom it gives workers to make their own choices; the greatest disadvantage is that it is an expensive benefit for employers.

Flexible Work

Many companies have moved toward the option of *flexible work plans,* which are benefits that allow employees to adjust their working hours or places of work according to their needs. Flexible work plan options include flextime, compressed workweeks, job sharing, and home-based work (telecommuting). These benefit programs have reduced employee turnover and absenteeism, and boosted productivity and job satisfaction. Flexible work has become critical in attracting and keeping talented human resources.

Flextime allows employees to set their own work hours within certain parameters. Rather than mandating that all employees work, say, from 8:00 A.M. to 5:00 P.M., a manager might stipulate that everyone works between the core hours of 10:00 A.M. and 3:00 P.M. Outside the core hours, employees could choose to start and end early, or start and end late. Flextime works well in jobs that are independent, but not so well when teams or direct customer service are involved. Flextime has gained popularity in the accounting industry. Accounting firm EY builds flexibility into its workplace through its Flexible Work Arrangement plan, believing it fosters greater productivity in the long run.[22]

For workplaces that require continuous staffing, cloud-based scheduling software can simplify scheduling and staffing tasks. One such software program, called Shiftboard, lets managers post schedules online and lets employees log in and request certain shifts or schedule changes.[23]

Some companies offer a *compressed workweek*, which allows employees to work longer hours on fewer days. Employees might work four 10-hour days and then have three days off each week. Such arrangements not only reduce the number of hours employees spend commuting each week but can stretch out the company's overall workday, providing more availability to customers in other time zones. Hospitals, police and fire departments, and airlines often offer work schedules that allow several long days matched by several days off. Unique for a company its size, KPMG, a global audit, tax, and advisory firm (see photo), offers its U.S. employees the option of a four-day compressed workweek. According to the company's director of workplace solutions, employees have greater control over their time, and satisfaction, productivity, and morale are increased.[24]

Far less common is a *job sharing program*, which allows two or more employees to divide the tasks of one job. This plan appeals to a growing number of people who prefer to work part-time rather than full-time—such as students, working parents, and people of all ages who want to devote time to personal interests or leisure. Job sharing requires a lot of cooperation and communication between the partners, but an employer can benefit from the talents of both people.

Ifeelstock/Depositphotos

As part of its flexible work arrangements, KPMG offers its U.S. employees a four-day compressed workweek.

Home-based work programs allow employees to perform their jobs from home instead of at the workplace. These *telecommuters* are connected to their employers via the Internet, voice and video conferencing, and mobile devices. Working from home generally appeals to employees who want freedom but also to persons with disabilities, older workers, and parents. Companies are beginning to adopt telecommuting as a business strategy rather than as an employee perk. There's been a more than double increase in telecommuting over the last 10 years, and 43% of the U.S. workforce currently works remotely to some degree. Companies benefit because it can reduce operating costs, attract or retain talent, allow expansion into new markets, be better for the environment, and improve employee satisfaction, health, and work-life balance. Employees juggling multiple responsibilities benefit with increased work-life balance and an estimated realized annual savings of $4,000 on reduced gasoline, parking, dry cleaning, and public transit.[25]

In what is referred to as the gig economy, HR professionals will embrace the new norm of temporary, flexible jobs, freelance work, and short-term contracts. In the next few years, in place of full-time, permanent work, mobile workers are expected to account for more than three-quarters of the workforce. Combined with machines and software, this new generation of workers points to a redesign of workforce planning and the very nature of work itself.[26]

Assessment Check

1. Explain the difference between *wage* and *salary*.
2. What are flexible benefit plans? How do they work?

5 Employee Separation

Employee separation is a broad term covering the loss of an employee for any reason, voluntary or involuntary. Voluntary separation includes workers who resign to take a job at another company or start a business. Involuntary separation includes downsizing and outsourcing.

employee separation broad term covering the loss of an employee for any reason, voluntary or involuntary.

Voluntary and Involuntary Turnover

Turnover occurs when an employee leaves a job. Voluntary turnover occurs when the employee resigns—perhaps to take another job, start a new business, or retire. The human resource manager might conduct an exit interview with the employee to learn why he or she is leaving; this conversation can provide valuable information to a company. An employee might decide to resign because of lack of career advancement. Learning this, the human resource manager might offer ongoing training. Sometimes employees choose to resign and accept jobs at other companies because they fear upcoming layoffs. In this case, the human resource manager might be able to allay fears about job security.

Occasionally an employee resigns because of low pay. In some cases, to keep a high-performing employee, the human resource manager might offer a raise.

Involuntary turnover occurs when employees are terminated because of poor job performance or unethical behavior. No matter how necessary a termination may be, it is never easy for the manager or the employee. Managers must be educated in employment laws. Protests against wrongful termination are often involved in complaints filed by the EEOC or by lawsuits brought by fired employees. Involuntary turnover also occurs when companies are forced to eliminate jobs as a cost-cutting measure, as in the case of downsizing or outsourcing.

Downsizing

When there is an economic downturn, companies are often faced with the hard choice of terminating employees in order to cut costs or streamline the organization. **Downsizing** is the process of reducing the number of employees within a company by eliminating jobs. Downsizing can be accomplished through early retirement plans or voluntary severance programs.

downsizing process of reducing the number of employees within a company by eliminating jobs.

Although some companies report improvements in profits, market share, employee productivity, quality, and customer service after downsizing, research shows that downsizing doesn't guarantee those improvements. And while in some cases downsizing is necessary and justified, it can have the following negative effects:

- Anxiety, health problems, low morale, and reduced productivity among remaining employees.
- Diminished trust in management.
- Expensive severance packages paid to laid-off employees.
- Loss of institutional memory and knowledge.
- A domino effect on the local economy—unemployed workers have less money to spend, creating less demand for consumer goods and services, increasing the likelihood of more layoffs and other failing businesses.[27]

When downsizing is the only alternative for company survival, there are steps managers can take to make sure it is done in the best way possible. A company committed to its workforce as part of its mission will do everything it can to support the workers who must leave and those who will stay.

Sometimes companies downsize to create a competitive advantage over the long term, as the Coca-Cola Company recently did. The company laid off more than 350 managers at facilities across Atlanta to create a "leaner organization."[28]

Outsourcing

outsourcing using outside vendors—contracting work out to another party—for the production of goods or fulfillment of services and functions previously performed in house.

Another way that companies become leaner is by **outsourcing**. Outsourcing involves transferring jobs from inside to outside a company. Jobs that are typically outsourced include office maintenance, deliveries, food service, and security. However, other job functions can be outsourced as well, including manufacturing, design, information technology (IT), and accounting. In general, in order to reduce expenses and remain flexible, companies will try to outsource functions that are not part of their core business.

Although outsourcing might work on paper, often the reality is quite different. Industry observers claim aggressive outsourcing was the reason that Boeing's highly touted 787 Dreamliner arrived three years behind schedule and billions of dollars over budget. Boeing outsourced the manufacture of 30% of the plane's parts; by contrast, it had outsourced only 5% of its iconic 747 aircraft. A recent reversal of the outsourcing trend, called *reshoring*, can be attributed to a number of factors including economic uncertainty and increased labor costs in China. In addition, security concerns among outsourced service providers, managing long-distance supply chains, and lower labor and environmental standards have made reshoring an attractive alternative.[29]

Assessment Check

1. What is the difference between voluntary and involuntary turnover?
2. What is downsizing? How is it different from outsourcing?

6 Motivating Employees

Everyone wants to enjoy going to work. Smart employers know that and look for ways to motivate workers to commit to their company's goals and perform their best. Motivation starts with high employee morale—a positive attitude towards the job. Positive job attitude is usually enhanced with meaningful work, growth opportunity, and trust in leadership.

High morale generally results from good management, including an understanding of human needs and an effort to satisfy those needs in ways that move the company forward. Low employee morale, on the other hand, usually signals a poor relationship between managers and employees and often results in absenteeism, voluntary turnover, and a lack of motivation.

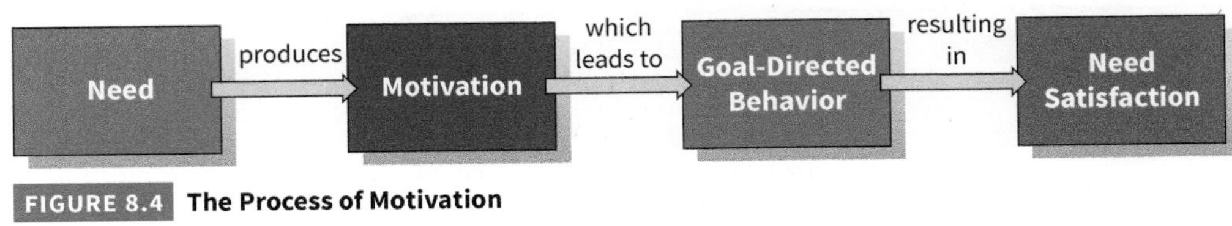

FIGURE 8.4 **The Process of Motivation**

To reduce absenteeism and turnover among employees, managers are particularly careful when recruiting new hires. As social media continues to blur the lines between social networking and job searching, see the "Judgment Call" feature about the ways recruiters are using social media as a screening tool.

Generally speaking, managers use rewards and punishments to motivate employees. Extrinsic rewards are external to the work itself, such as pay, fringe benefits, and praise. Intrinsic rewards are feelings related to performing the job, such as feeling proud about meeting a deadline or achieving a sales goal. Punishment involves a negative consequence for such behavior as being late, skipping staff meetings, or treating a customer poorly.

There are several theories of motivation, all of which relate back to the basic process of motivation itself, which involves the recognition of a need, the move toward meeting that need, and the satisfaction of that need. For instance, if you are hungry you might be motivated to make yourself a peanut butter sandwich. Once you have eaten the sandwich, the need is satisfied and you are no longer hungry. **Figure 8.4** illustrates the process of motivation. Motivators also include empowerment, open communication, respect, involving employees in decisions, minimizing rules and policies, providing recognition, feedback, coaching, good benefits, perks, and compensation.

Maslow's Hierarchy of Needs Theory

The studies of psychologist Abraham H. Maslow suggest how managers can motivate employees. **Maslow's hierarchy of needs** has become a widely accepted list of human needs based on these important assumptions:

- People's needs depend on what they already possess.
- A satisfied need is not a motivator; only needs that remain unsatisfied can influence behavior.
- People's needs are arranged in a hierarchy of importance; once they satisfy one need, at least partially, another emerges and demands satisfaction.

Maslow's hierarchy of needs theory of motivation proposed by Abraham Maslow. According to the theory, people have five levels of needs that they seek to satisfy: physiological, safety, social, esteem, and self-actualization.

In his theory, Maslow proposed that all people have basic needs such as hunger and protection that they must satisfy before they can consider higher-order needs such as social relationships or self-worth. He identified five types of needs:

1. *Physiological needs*. These basic human needs include food, shelter, and clothing. On the job, employers satisfy these needs by paying salaries and wages and providing a temperature-controlled workspace.
2. *Safety needs*. These needs refer to desires for physical and economic protection. Companies satisfy these needs with benefits such as health insurance and meeting safety standards in the workplace.
3. *Social (belongingness) needs*. People want to be accepted by family, friends, and co-workers. Managers might satisfy these needs through teamwork and group lunches.
4. *Esteem needs*. People like to feel valued and recognized by others. Managers can meet these needs through special awards or privileges.
5. *Self-actualization needs*. These needs drive people to seek fulfillment of their dreams and capabilities. Employers can satisfy these needs by offering challenging or creative projects, along with opportunities for education and advancement.[30]

Judgment Call

Social Screening During the Selection Process

A recent study reveals that 57% of companies found new hires through LinkedIn, 30% through professional association networking sites, 19% through Facebook, and 8% through Twitter. In an attempt to make the best possible hiring decisions, recruiters use as many tools as possible. A recent study revealed that 70% of employers now use social media to screen job candidates before hiring them.

But what happens when companies research a candidate's presence on social media and use this information as part of a hiring decision? Just 5% of companies surveyed admitted to using information on social media sites to make hiring decisions. While it isn't illegal to use Facebook as a screening tool, a company can find itself in legal hot water if a staff member creates a fictitious social media account to "friend" or connect with a prospective employee.

Some states have laws that prevent companies from asking candidates for access to their social media accounts. Although it is not unlawful to look at a candidate's social media profile (especially in the absence of privacy settings), discriminating against a candidate for characteristics protected under Title VII of the Civil Rights Act of 1964—such as religion, race, health condition, or age—certainly is.

Is everything a person posts online fair game for prospective employers? Care should be taken when posting information via social media. A public profile is just that—public. A well-crafted online profile and well-written blogs, tweets, and posts can actually work in a job candidate's favor, which could result in that coveted job offer.

Questions for Critical Thinking

1. What recommendations would you make to a friend looking for a job when it comes to social media activities?
2. Do you think it's realistic that only 5% of companies surveyed used information on social media sites to make hiring decisions? Explain.

Sources: Aliah D. Wright, "SHRM Survey: Social Media Remains a Popular Recruitment Tool," *Society for Human Resource Managers*, http://shrm.org, accessed March 26, 2018; Greg Wright, "Despite Legal Risks, Companies Still Use Social Media to Screen Employees," *Society for Human Resource Management*, http://shrm.org, accessed March 26, 2018; William Welkowitz, "Job Applicant Screening: Is Social Media Fair Game?" *Bloomberg BNA*, http://bna.com, accessed Roni Jacobson, "Facebook Snooping on Job Candidates May Backfire for Employers," *Scientific American*, http://scientificamerican.com, accessed March 26, 2018; Jonathan A. Segal and Joyce LeMay, "Should Employers Use Social Media to Screen Job Applicants?" *Society for Human Resource Management*, http://www.shrm.org, accessed March 26, 2018; Chad Brooks, "Keep it Clean: Social Media Gains in Popularity," *Business News Daily*, http://www.businessnewsdaily.com, accessed March 26, 2018; Rachel Nauen, "Number of Employers Using Social Media to Screen Candidates at All-Time High, Finds Latest Career-Builder Study," *CareerBuilder*, http://press.careerbuilder.com, accessed March 26, 2018.

According to Maslow, people must satisfy the lower-order needs in the hierarchy (physiological and safety needs) before they are motivated to satisfy higher-order needs (social, esteem, and self-actualization needs).

Herzberg's Two-Factor Model of Motivation

More than 50 years ago, Frederick Herzberg—a social psychologist and consultant—came up with a theory of motivation and work that is still popular today. Herzberg surveyed workers to find out when they felt good or bad about their jobs. He learned that certain factors were important to job satisfaction though they might not contribute directly to motivation. These *hygiene factors* (or maintenance factors) refer to aspects of work that are not directly related to a task itself but instead are related to the job environment, including pay, job security, working conditions, status, interpersonal relations, technical supervision, and company policies.

Motivator factors, on the other hand, can produce high levels of motivation when they are present. These relate directly to the specific aspects of a job, including job responsibilities, achievement and recognition, and opportunities for growth. Hygiene factors are extrinsic, while motivators are intrinsic. Managers should remember that hygiene factors, though not motivational, can result in satisfaction. But if managers want to motivate employees, they should emphasize recognition, achievement, and growth. Regardless of their size, companies that make the various lists published annually of "best places to work" have managers who understand what it takes to motivate employees.

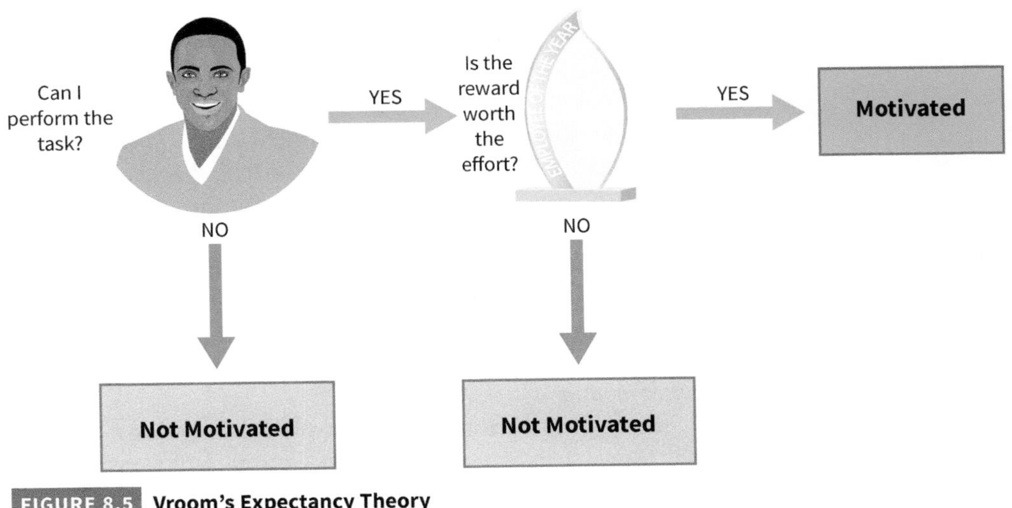

FIGURE 8.5 **Vroom's Expectancy Theory**

Expectancy Theory and Equity Theory

Victor Vroom's **expectancy theory** of motivation describes the process people use to evaluate the likelihood that their efforts will yield the results they want, along with the degree to which they want those results. Expectancy theory suggests that people use three factors to determine how much effort to put forth. First is a person's subjective prediction that a certain effort will lead to the desired result. This is the "can do" component of an employee's approach to work. Second is the value of the outcome (reward) to the person. Third is the person's assessment of how likely a successful performance will lead to a desirable reward. Vroom's expectancy theory is summarized in **Figure 8.5**. In short, an employee is motivated if he or she thinks he or she can complete a task. Next, the employee assesses the reward for accomplishing the task and is motivated if the reward is worth the effort.

expectancy theory the process people use to evaluate the likelihood that their efforts will yield the results they want, along with the degree to which they want those results.

Equity theory is concerned with an individual's perception of fair and equitable treatment. In their work, employees first consider their effort and then their rewards. Next, employees compare their results against those of their co-workers. As shown in **Figure 8.6**, if employees feel they are under-rewarded for their effort in comparison with others doing similar work, equity theory suggests they will decrease their effort to restore the balance. Conversely, if employees feel they are over-rewarded, they will feel guilty and put more effort into their job to restore equity and reduce guilt.

equity theory an individual's perception of fair and equitable treatment.

Many workers are willing to work hard as long as the burden is shared. Income inequality is higher in the United States than in any other developed society in the world. The Securities and Exchange Commission recently adopted rules mandating that public companies disclose the ratio of chief executive pay to the average worker salary within the firm. Driven in large part by differences in worker pay, in the energy sector, most CEOs make less than 100 times what their median workers do, partly because of high-paying jobs in engineering and on oil rigs. However, in health care and financial services, with many low-paid workers, CEO pay is typically 150 times that of a company's median employee.[31]

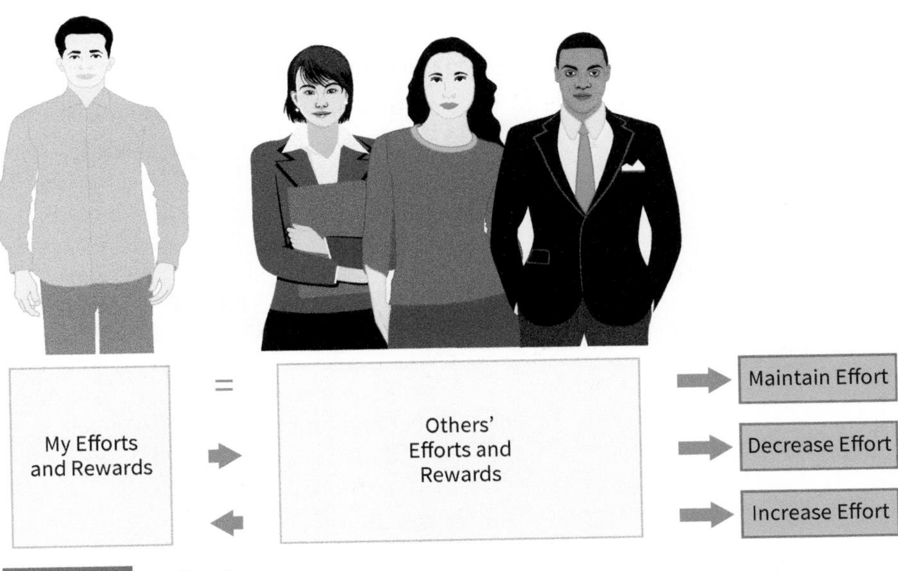

FIGURE 8.6 **Equity Theory**

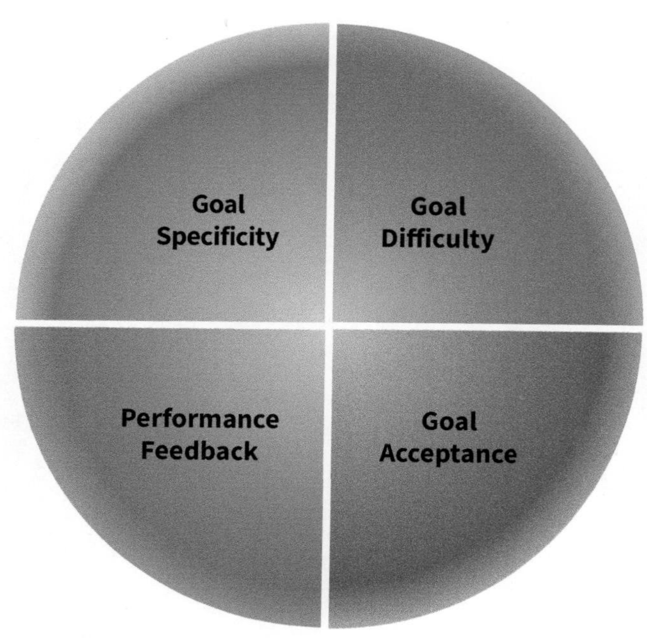

FIGURE 8.7 **Components of Goal-Setting Theory**

Goal-Setting Theory and Management by Objectives

Needs motivate people to direct their behavior toward something that will satisfy those needs. That something is a goal. A goal is a target, objective, or result that someone tries to accomplish. **Goal-setting theory** says that people will be motivated to the extent to which they accept specific, challenging goals and receive feedback that indicates their progress toward goal achievement. As shown in **Figure 8.7**, the basic components of goal-setting theory are goal specificity, goal difficulty, goal acceptance, and performance feedback.

Goal specificity is the extent to which goals are clear and concrete. A goal such as "we want to reduce carbon emissions" is vague and hard to pin down. But "we want to reduce carbon emissions by 2%" gives employees a clear target. Goal difficulty outlines how hard the goal is to reach. A more difficult goal, such as "we want to reduce carbon emissions by 5% in three years" can actually be more motivating than the easier goal.

Goal acceptance is the extent to which people understand and agree to the goal. If a goal is too challenging—such as reducing the company's carbon emissions by 20% in two years—people are likely to reject it. Finally, performance feedback is information about performance and how well the goal has been met. Goal setting typically won't work unless performance feedback is provided.

goal-setting theory says that people will be motivated to the extent to which they accept specific, challenging goals and receive feedback that indicates their progress toward goal achievement.

management by objectives (MBO) systematic approach that allows managers to focus on attainable goals and to achieve the best results based on the organization's resources.

Goals help focus workers' attention on the important parts of their jobs. Goals also energize and motivate people. They create a positive tension between the current state of affairs and the desired state. This tension is satisfied by meeting the goal or abandoning it.

More than 60 years ago, Peter Drucker introduced a goal-setting technique called **management by objectives (MBO)** in his book, *The Practice of Management*. MBO is a systematic approach that allows managers to focus on attainable goals and to achieve the best results based on the organization's resources. MBO helps motivate individuals by aligning their objectives with the goals of the organization, increasing overall organizational performance. MBO clearly outlines people's tasks, goals, and contributions to the company. MBO is a collaborative process between managers and employees. MBO principles include the following:

- a series of related organizational goals and objectives;
- specific objectives for each person;
- participative decision making;
- a set time period to accomplish goals; and
- performance evaluation and feedback.

Job Design and Motivation

Today's human resource managers constantly search for ways to motivate employees through their jobs. Three ways that jobs can be restructured to be more motivating are through job enlargement, job enrichment, and job rotation.

Job enlargement is a job design that expands an employee's responsibilities by increasing the number and variety of tasks. Redesigning the production process is one way to accomplish this. Instead of having an assembly line on which each worker repeatedly completes the same task, modular work areas allow employees to complete a variety of tasks, which may result in the construction of an entire product.

Job enrichment involves an expansion of job duties that empowers an employee to make decisions and learn new skills leading toward career growth. The Pampered Chef is a direct seller of kitchen tools and housewares that gives its managers and sales consultants the power to make decisions about many aspects of their work. Pampered Chef consultants, who organize home sales parties, can decide how much or how little they want to work and receive various incentive rewards for performance. The company's mission is to provide "opportunities for individuals to develop their talents and skills to their fullest potential for the benefit of themselves, their families, our customers, and the company."[32]

Job rotation involves systematically moving employees from one job to another. Job rotation increases the range of activities by introducing workers to more jobs and therefore more tasks. The goal is to increase employees' interest in their jobs and allow them to learn more about the company. Nurses might rotate from oncology to the ICU in a hospital. Job rotation is often part of a training program, as is the case at EMC, a global provider of business solutions for data backup and storage, information security, infrastructure management, and many other products. EMC offers motivated employees the chance to participate in rotational training programs in business, leadership, finance, marketing, and other areas.[33]

Managers' Attitudes and Motivation

A manager's attitude toward his or her employees greatly influences their motivation. Maslow's theory, described earlier, has helped managers understand that employees have a range of needs beyond their paychecks. Psychologist Douglas McGregor, a student of Maslow, studied motivation from the perspective of how managers view employees. After observing managers' interactions with employees, McGregor created two basic labels for the assumptions that different managers make about their workers' behavior, and how these assumptions affect management styles.

- *Theory X* assumes that employees dislike work and try to avoid it whenever possible, so management must coerce them to do their jobs. Theory X managers believe that the average worker prefers to receive instructions, avoid responsibility, take little initiative, and views money and job security as the only valid motivators—Maslow's lower order of needs.
- *Theory Y* assumes that the typical person actually likes work and will seek and accept greater responsibility. Theory Y managers assume that most people can think of creative ways to solve work-related problems, and should be given the opportunity to participate in decision making. Unlike the traditional management philosophy that relies on external control and constant supervision, Theory Y emphasizes self-control and self-direction—Maslow's higher order of needs.

Another perspective on management, proposed by management professor William Ouchi, has been labeled *Theory Z*. Organizations structured on Theory Z concepts attempt to blend the best of American and Japanese management practices. This approach views worker involvement as the key to increased productivity for the company and improved quality of work life for employees. Many U.S. companies have adopted the participative management style used in Japanese companies by asking workers for suggestions to improve their jobs and then giving them the authority to implement proposed changes.

Assessment Check

1. What are the four steps in the process of motivation?
2. Explain goal-setting theory.
3. Describe three ways that managers restructure jobs to increase employee motivation.

7 Labor–Management Relations

The U.S. workplace is far different from what it was a century ago, when child labor, unsafe working conditions, and a 72-hour workweek were common. The development of labor unions, labor legislation, and the collective bargaining process have contributed to the changed environment. Today's human resource managers must be educated in labor–management relations, the settling of disputes, and the competitive tactics of unions and management.

Development of Labor Unions

labor union group of workers who have banded together to achieve common goals in the areas of wages, hours, and working conditions.

A **labor union** is a group of workers who have banded together to achieve common goals in the areas of wages, hours, and working conditions. The organized efforts of Philadelphia printers in 1786 resulted in the first wage agreed upon in the United States—$1 a day. One hundred years later, New York City streetcar conductors were able to negotiate a reduction in their workday from 17 to 12 hours.

Labor unions can be found at the local, national, and international levels. A *local union* represents union members in a specific area, such as a single community, while a *national union* is a labor organization consisting of numerous local chapters. An *international union* is a national union with membership outside the United States, usually in Canada. About 14.8 million U.S. workers—just over 11% of the nation's full-time workforce—belong to labor unions.[34] Although only about 6.5% of workers in the private sector are unionized, more than 40% of government workers belong to unions. The largest union in the United States is the 3-million-member National Education Association (NEA), representing public school teachers and other support personnel. Other large unions include the 2 million members of the Service Employees International Union (SEIU), the 1.9 million members of the American Federation of State, County & Municipal Employees, the 1.3 million members of the International Brotherhood of Teamsters, the 1.3 million members of the United Food and Commercial Workers, and the 390,000 members of the United Automobile, Aerospace and Agricultural Implement Workers of America.[35]

Labor Legislation

Over the past century, some major pieces of labor legislation have been enacted, including the following:

- *National Labor Relations Act of 1935 (Wagner Act).* Legalized collective bargaining and required employers to negotiate with elected representatives of their employees. Established the National Labor Relations Board (NLRB) to supervise union elections and prohibit unfair labor practices such as firing workers for joining unions, refusing to hire union sympathizers, threatening to close if workers unionize, interfering with or dominating the administration of a union, and refusing to bargain with a union.
- *Fair Labor Standards Act of 1938.* Set the first federal minimum wage (25 cents an hour), and a maximum basic workweek for certain industries. Also outlawed child labor.
- *Taft-Hartley Act of 1947 (Labor–Management Relations Act).* Limited unions' power by banning such practices as coercing employees to join unions, coercing employers to discriminate against employees who are not union members, discrimination against nonunion employees, picketing or conducting secondary boycotts or strikes for illegal purposes, and excessive initiation fees.
- *Landrum-Griffin Act of 1959 (Labor–Management Reporting and Disclosure Act).* Amended the Taft-Hartley Act to promote honesty and democracy in running unions' internal affairs. Required unions to set up a constitution and bylaws and to hold regularly scheduled elections of union officers by secret ballot. Set forth a bill of rights for members. Required unions to submit certain financial reports to the U.S. Secretary of Labor.

The Collective Bargaining Process

Labor unions work to increase job security for their members and to improve wages, hours, and working conditions. These goals are achieved primarily through **collective bargaining**, the process of negotiation between management and union representatives.

collective bargaining process of negotiation between management and union representatives.

Union contracts, which typically cover a two- or three-year period, are often the result of weeks or months of discussion, disagreement, compromise, and eventual agreement. Once agreement is reached, union members must vote to accept or reject the contract. If the contract is rejected, union representatives may resume the bargaining process with management representatives, or union members may strike to obtain their demands.

Settling Labor–Management Disputes

Strikes make the headlines, but most labor–management negotiations result in a signed contract. If a dispute arises, it is usually settled through a mechanism such as a grievance procedure, mediation, or arbitration. Any of these alternatives is quicker and less expensive than a strike.

The union contract serves as a guide to relations between the company's management and its employees. The rights of each party are stated in the agreement. But no contract, regardless of how detailed, will eliminate the possibility of disagreement. Such differences can be the beginning of a *grievance,* a complaint—by a single employee or by the entire union—that management is violating some portion of the contract. Almost all union contracts require these complaints to be submitted through a formal grievance procedure similar to the one shown in **Figure 8.8**. A grievance might involve a dispute about pay, working hours, or the workplace itself. The grievance procedure usually begins with an employee's supervisor and then moves up the company's hierarchy. If the highest level of management can't settle the grievance, it is submitted to an outside party for mediation or arbitration.

Mediation is the process of settling labor–management disputes through an impartial third party. Although the mediator does not make the final decision, he or she can hear the whole story and make objective recommendations. If the dispute remains unresolved, the two parties can turn to *arbitration*—bringing in an outside arbitrator, who renders a legally binding decision. The arbitrator must be acceptable both to the union and to management, and his or her decision is final. Most union negotiations go to arbitration if union and management representatives fail to reach a contract agreement.

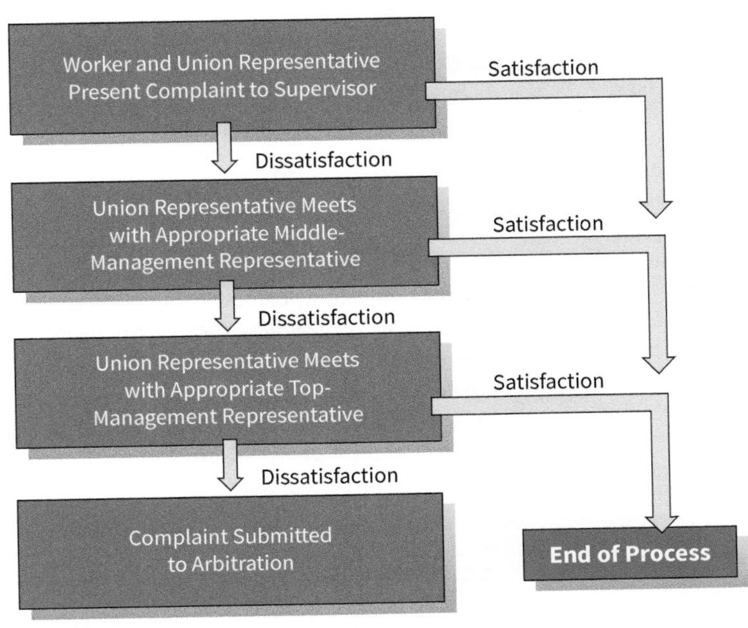

FIGURE 8.8 **Steps in the Grievance Procedure**

Erik McGregor/AP Images

Verizon union workers shown picketing for a new contract.

Competitive Tactics of Unions and Management

Both unions and management use tactics to make their views known and to win support.

Union Tactics The chief tactics of unions are strikes, picketing, and boycotts. The *strike,* or walkout, is one of the most effective tools of the labor union. It involves a temporary work stoppage by workers until a dispute has been settled or a contract signed. A strike generally seeks to disrupt business as usual, calling attention to workers' needs and union demands. Strikes can last for days or weeks and can be costly to both sides. Although a strike is powerful, it can also be damaging to the very people it is trying to help. Surrounding businesses may suffer too. If striking workers aren't eating at their usual lunch favorites, those businesses will lose profits. Strikes seem to be on the decline, however. In a recent year, the largest major work stoppage by days idle occurred between Charter Communications and the International Brotherhood of Electrical Workers union, with 345,600 total days idle and involving 1,800 workers.[36]

Picketing, which involves workers marching in a public protest against their employer, is another effective form of union pressure. As long as picketing does not involve violence or intimidation, it is protected under the U.S. Constitution as freedom of speech. Picketing may accompany a strike, or it may be a protest against alleged unfair labor practices. Recently, Verizon workers picketed for a new contract to include fair health insurance costs, job security, an unchanged retirement plan, and protections to workers injured on the job (see photo).[37]

A *boycott* is an organized attempt to keep the public from purchasing the goods or services of a company. Some unions have been quite successful in organizing boycotts, and some unions even fine members who defy a boycott.

Clean & Green Business

Solid Waste Workers Get Organized

A few privately held companies control the solid waste industry, but the Teamsters have made some headway in organizing some of the industry's workers. The Solid Waste, Recycling and Related Industries Division of the Teamsters currently represents more than 32,000 workers. To date, an additional 180,000 nonunion workers are employed in solid waste and related industries.

Recently more than 200 workers in five locations in California, Oregon, Washington, and Ohio took action to become Teamsters. With 1.4 million members, the Teamsters Union is North America's strongest and most diverse labor union, consisting mainly of freight drivers and warehouse workers. Including waste management, workers in every imaginable occupation, both private and public sector, professional and nonprofessional are members.

Employees at Republic Services, one of the top two largest waste management companies, recently won card-check recognition, which means that the majority of workers in a bargaining unit signed authorization forms stating their desire for union representation. At Republic Services, with 30,000 employees nationwide, workers at the Huntington Beach, California, facility organized workers following the overhaul of waste collection efforts in Los Angeles. The local union worked with community groups and environmental supporters to get the Los Angeles City Council to support a bill to approve a plan to use cleaner trucks and to divert more waste from landfills. The workers are seeking fair pay, improved benefits, and a safer workplace. In Salem, Ohio, 15 residential and commercial drivers in the bargaining unit at another Republic facility joined Local 92 in Canton, Ohio. The Salem workers want affordable health care, safer equipment, and fair wages—and believe Teamster representation will help them in their cause.

Questions for Critical Thinking

1. Will union organizing of these waste workers have a positive impact on recycling efforts within the industry? Why or why not?
2. Discuss the fact that the solid waste industry has 32,000 union members and an additional 180,000 unorganized workers. Do these statistics surprise you? Why or why not?

Sources: Organization website, "Waste Workers at Five Locations Join Teamsters Across the Country," "Who Are the Teamsters?", and "Definitions for Common Labor Terms," http://www.teamster.org, accessed March 26, 2018; company website, "About Us," http://www.republicservices.com, accessed March 26, 2018; organization website, "2015 Waste 100," http://waste360.com, accessed March 26, 2018.

Management Tactics Management also has tactics for competing with organized labor when negotiations break down. In the past, it has used the lockout—a management "strike" to put pressure on union members by closing the company. However, companies more commonly try to recruit strikebreakers in highly visible fields such as professional sports, or they transfer supervisors and other nonunion employees to continue operations during strikes.

The Future of Labor Unions

Union membership and influence grew through most of the 20th century by giving industrial workers a voice in decisions about their wages, benefits, and working conditions. However, as the United States, western Europe, and Japan have shifted from manufacturing economies to information and service economies, union membership and influence have declined. Today, about 40% of all union members are government employees.[38]

How can labor unions change to maintain their relevance? They can be more flexible and adapt to a global economy and diverse workforce. They can respond to the growing need for environmentally responsible business and manufacturing processes, as the workers in the solid waste industry are doing, described in the "Clean & Green Business" feature. Unions can establish collaborative relationships with human resource managers and other managers. And they can recognize the potential for prosperity for all—management and union workers included.

Assessment Check

1. What is a labor union? What is collective bargaining?
2. What are the three main tactics used by unions to win support for their demands?

What's Ahead

Creating a productive, engaging, enjoyable work experience along with an integrated focus on the entire employee experience will have an impact on employee retention. In addition, managers can tap the full potential of their employees by empowering them to make decisions, leading them to work effectively as teams, and fostering clear, positive communication. The next chapter covers these three ways of improving performance. By involving employees more fully through empowerment, teamwork, and communication, companies can benefit from their knowledge while employees enjoy a more meaningful role in the company.

Chapter in Review

Summary of Learning Objectives

LEARNING OBJECTIVE 1 Explain the role of human resources: the people behind the people.

Human resource managers are responsible for attracting, developing, and retaining the employees who can perform the activities necessary to accomplish organizational objectives. They plan for staffing needs, recruit and hire workers, provide for training, evaluate performance, determine compensation and benefits, and oversee employee separation.

Assessment Check Answers

1.1 **What are the five main tasks of a human resource manager?** The five main tasks are planning for staffing needs, recruiting and hiring workers, providing for training and evaluating performance, determining compensation and benefits, and overseeing employee separation.

1.2 What are the three overall objectives of a human resource manager? They are providing qualified, well-trained employees for the organization; maximizing employee effectiveness; and satisfying individual employee needs through monetary compensation, benefits, opportunities to advance, and job satisfaction.

LEARNING OBJECTIVE 2 Describe recruitment and selection.

Human resource managers use internal and external methods to recruit qualified employees. They may use college job fairs, personal referrals, social media, and other resources. Internet recruiting is now the fastest, most efficient, and inexpensive way to reach a large pool of job seekers. Companies must abide by employment laws during selection. Before hiring candidates, human resource managers may require employment tests that evaluate certain skills or aptitudes. When all of this is complete, there is a better chance that the right person will be hired for the job.

Assessment Check Answers

2.1 Describe several recruiting techniques used by human resource managers.

2.2 What is the function of the Equal Employment Opportunity Commission (EEOC)? The EEOC investigates discrimination complaints and helps employers set up affirmative action programs.

LEARNING OBJECTIVE 3 Discuss orientation, training, and evaluation.

New employees often participate in an orientation, also called onboarding, where they learn about company policies and practices. Training programs provide opportunities for employees to build their skills and knowledge and prepare them for new job opportunities within the company. They also give employers a better chance of retaining employees. Performance appraisals give employees feedback about their strengths and weaknesses and how they can improve.

Assessment Check Answers

3.1 What are the benefits of computer-based or online training? Computer-based or online training offers consistent presentations, interactive learning, and learning at one's own pace. It is also less expensive than other types of training.

3.2 What is a management development program? A management development program provides training designed to improve the skills and broaden the knowledge of current or future managers and executives.

3.3 What are the three criteria of an effective performance appraisal? A performance appraisal must be linked to organizational goals, be based on objective criteria, and be a two-way conversation.

LEARNING OBJECTIVE 4 Describe compensation.

Companies compensate employees with wages, salaries, incentive pay systems, and benefits. Benefit programs vary among firms, but most companies offer health care programs, insurance, retirement plans, paid time off, and sick leave. A growing number of companies are offering flexible benefit plans and flexible work plans, such as flextime, compressed workweeks, job sharing, and home-based work.

Assessment Check Answers

4.1 Explain the difference between *wage* and *salary*. Wages are based on an hourly pay rate or the amount of work accomplished. Salaries are paid periodically, such as weekly or monthly. Salaries do not fluctuate with hours worked.

4.2 What are flexible benefit plans? How do they work? Flexible benefit plans offer employees a choice of benefits, including different types of medical insurance, dental and vision plans, and life and disability insurance. Typically, each employee receives a set allowance to pay for these benefits, depending on his or her needs.

LEARNING OBJECTIVE 5 Discuss employee separation.

Employee separation occurs when a worker leaves his or her job, voluntarily or involuntarily. Sometimes an employee is terminated because of poor job performance or unethical behavior. Downsizing is the process of reducing the number of employees within a company in order to cut costs and achieve a leaner organization. However, some negative effects include anxiety and lost productivity among remaining workers; expensive severance packages; and a domino effect in the local economy. Outsourcing involves transferring jobs from inside a firm to outside the company. While some expenses may be cut, a company may experience a backlash in performance and public image.

Assessment Check Answers

5.1 What is the difference between voluntary and involuntary turnover? Voluntary turnover occurs when employees resign and leave companies to start their own businesses, take jobs with other companies, move to another community, or retire. Involuntary turnover occurs when employees are terminated because of poor job performance or unethical behavior. It can also occur when a company is forced to eliminate jobs.

5.2 What is downsizing? How is it different from outsourcing? Downsizing is the process of reducing the number of employees within a company by eliminating jobs. Downsizing is done to cut overhead costs and streamline the organizational structure. With outsourcing, companies contract with other companies to perform noncore jobs or business functions, such as maintenance or accounting. This allows companies to focus on what they do best and can result in a downsized workforce.

LEARNING OBJECTIVE 6 Explain the different methods for motivating employees.

Employee motivation starts with high employee morale. According to Maslow's hierarchy of needs, people satisfy lower-order needs (such as food and safety) before moving to higher-order needs (such as esteem and fulfillment). Herzberg's two-factor model of motivation is based on the fulfillment of hygiene factors and motivation factors. Expectancy theory suggests that people use those factors to determine whether to put forth the effort to complete a task. Equity theory refers to a person's perception of fair and equitable treatment. Goal-setting theory says that people will be motivated to the extent to which they accept specific, challenging goals. Job design is also used by managers for motivation.

Assessment Check Answers

6.1 What are the four steps in the process of motivation? The four steps are need, motivation, goal-directed behavior, and need satisfaction.

6.2 Explain goal-setting theory. People will be motivated to the extent to which they accept specific, challenging goals and receive feedback that indicates their progress toward goal achievement.

6.3 **Describe three ways that managers restructure jobs to increase employee motivation.** Three ways that employers apply motivational theories to restructure jobs are job enlargement, job enrichment, and job rotation. Job enlargement is a job design that expands an employee's responsibilities by increasing the number and variety of tasks the person works on. Job enrichment is an expansion of job duties that empowers employees to make decisions and learn new skills leading toward career growth. Job rotation involves systematically moving employees from one job to another.

LEARNING OBJECTIVE 7 Discuss labor–management relations.

Labor unions have resulted in the improvement of wages and working conditions for many workers over the past century, along with the passage of significant labor laws. Unions achieve these improvements through the collective bargaining process, resulting in an agreement. Most labor–management disputes are settled through the grievance process, in which mediation or arbitration sometimes is necessary.

Assessment Check Answers

7.1 **What is a labor union? What is collective bargaining?** A labor union is a group of workers who have banded together to achieve common goals in the areas of wages, hours, and working conditions. Collective bargaining is the process of negotiation between management and union representatives.

7.2 **What are the three main tactics used by unions to win support for their demands?** Unions use strikes (walkouts), picketing, and boycotts.

Business Terms You Need to Know

human resource management 200
human resource inventory 201
job analysis 201
job description 202
job specification 202
performance appraisal 206
compensation 206
wage 206
salary 207
employee benefits 208
employee separation 211
downsizing 211
outsourcing 212
Maslow's hierarchy of needs 213
expectancy theory 214
equity theory 215
goal-setting theory 216
management by objectives (MBO) 216
labor union 218
collective bargaining 219

Review Questions

1. Why has Internet recruiting become such an important tool for human resource managers?

2. Recruitment and selection are costly. So, what precautions do human resource managers take to make sure they are hiring the right person for each job?

3. Give an example of a type of job that would be appropriate for on-the-job training. Then describe specifically how you think that type of training would work for your selected job, including types of tasks a new hire might learn this way.

4. On what five factors are compensation policies usually based? Name at least three employee benefits that are required by law and three more that are provided voluntarily by some companies.

5. Describe four types of flexible work plans. Identify an industry that would be well suited to each type of plan, and explain why.

6. Why do companies downsize? What are some of the drawbacks to downsizing? Why do companies outsource? What are some of the drawbacks to outsourcing? What is reshoring?

7. Select three different theories of motivation, and explain how each can be used by managers to motivate employees.

8. Suppose a manager of a popular café and bakery maintains a Theory X assumption about employees. At the beginning of each workweek, what types of things might the manager tell his or her employees? Now suppose the manager has a Theory Y assumption; then Theory Z. Describe what he or she might say to employees.

9. In what major ways has labor legislation changed the workplace over the past century? How might the workplace be different today without this legislation?

10. What are mediation and arbitration? Describe a situation that you think might result in arbitration.

Projects and Teamwork Applications

1. When hiring new employees, it is common for companies to use internal recruitment (from within the organization) and external recruitment (from outside the organization). With a partner, choose internal or external recruitment and compare and contrast the benefits and drawbacks of each from the standpoint of current employees and the employer. Present your findings in class.

2. Choose one of the following companies, or one that you might like to work for sometime in the future. Using the company's website in

addition to a popular jobsite like Indeed.com or Glassdoor.com, research the company's benefits and perks. Outline the company's benefits and then determine if you still want to work for that company, and why. Suggested companies:

Nordstrom
Facebook
Intuit
L.L. Bean
Build-A-Bear Workshop

3. With a classmate or individually, evaluate and prioritize beyond just salary what would be important for you as part of a total job offer. You may want to consider vacation, work–life balance, performance review, schedule, flexible work arrangements, and required perks, among other things.

4. Choose what you think would be your dream job five years from now. Then create a chart according to Maslow's hierarchy of needs, and identify the ways in which you envision this job fulfilling each level of need.

5. Some employees might question the need for company policies related to workers' appearances. As tattoos and piercings have become mainstream, discuss the pros and cons of putting appearance-related policies in place in the work setting.

Web Assignments

1. **Human resources (HR) as a profession.** Go to the website listed below and review the data about HR managers.

   Answer the following questions:

   a. What do HR managers do?

   b. What is the job outlook for HR managers?

   c. Review and discuss the "How to Become a Human Resource Manager" link on the website.

http://www.bls.gov/ooh/management/human-resources-managers.htm

2. **Society for Human Resource Professionals.** If you are interested in working in human resources, you might want to learn about the Society for Human Resource Management (SHRM). An industrywide organization, SHRM supports its members with advocacy, education, seminars, career search, and more. Go to the websites listed below to find out more about the organization. How would becoming a student member help you decide if HR management is a field for you?

www.shrm.org

https://www.shrm.org/communities/student-resources/pages/crc.aspx

3. **Go to the Equal Employment Opportunity website and explore its enforcement process.** Under the "About EEOC" tab, click on "Statistics," and then under that tab click on "EEOC Enforcement and Litigation Statistics." Choose the "Charges Alleging Sexual Harassment" link and evaluate the statistics. What are the factors that have contributed to a rise in the percentage of charges filed by males? Discuss.

www.eeoc.gov

Note: Internet web addresses change frequently. If you don't find the exact sites listed, you may need to access the organization's home page and search from there or use a search engine such as Google or Bing.

Cases

Case 8.1 "Upskilling" Helps Walmart Workers Advance

At most retailers, when it comes to allocating training and development dollars, entry-level front-line workers—cashiers, cart pushers, and sales associates—typically have been ignored. While many large retailers have implemented development programs for new college graduates aspiring to be managers, front-line workers, typically with little or no education, are often an afterthought. Walmart is changing that with the announcement of a test program called Pathways in its Joplin, Missouri, supercenter, which boasts 345 full- and part-time employees.

Walmart is hoping the investment in training front-line workers—a trend called upskilling—will yield results in the form of reduced turnover, increased sales, and better customer service. Estimates of employee turnover costs within the retail industry for front-line workers can be as much as $5,000 per employee, or 20% to 30% of worker salaries. According to one of its human resource executives, Walmart estimates savings into the "tens of millions of dollars" if it can slow down the number of front-line workers leaving the company.

The Pathways program includes six months of on-the-job training, using technology to deliver "game-like" simulations, drills, and instruction via computer modules, which the company hopes to convert to mobile apps for access on tablets and smart phones. After six months of on-the-job training, associates undergo an assessment. Passing the evaluation opens more doors to higher-paying sales opportunities and even into management. Walmart recently awarded a $600,000 grant to UpSkill America, a nonprofit organization that provides education, training, and development to frontline workers so that they can progress in their careers.

Questions for Critical Thinking

1. Discuss Walmart's training program in light of research that shows that when companies invest in people they experience lower turnover and greater employee engagement. Discuss the benefits to shareholders, investors, employees, and customers.

2. For front-line workers who do not have the interest or resources to earn a four-year degree, discuss how training, particularly in advanced or specialized skills, can provide a potential career path. What impact will the shift in management's attitude toward front-line workers have on employee performance? On company revenues?

Sources: Tamar Jacoby, "Wal-Mart Tests Upskilling," *Wall Street Journal*, http://www.wsj.com, accessed March 26, 2018; Dan Alaimo, "Walmart Taps Technology to Train Front-Line Workers," *Fierce Retail*, http://www.fiercere-tail.com, accessed March 26, 2018; government website, "FACT SHEET: Administration Announces New Commitments in Support of President Obama's Upskill Initiative to Empower Workers with Education and Training," http://www.whitehouse.gov, accessed March 26, 2018; organization website, "UpSkill America Receives $600,000 Grant from Walmart to Expand Upskilling Programs for Businesses and Opportunities for Frontline Workers," *Aspen Institute*, https://www.aspeninstitute.org, accessed March 26, 2018.

Case 8.2 PwC Helps Employees with Student Loans

You've landed a few job offers—and you're considering one with free gourmet meals, shuttles to and from work, on-site fitness and laundry facilities, and yes, on-site massages. With heated competition for talent, companies are dangling innovative perks to lure and keep Millennials, workers in their 20s and 30s, estimated at close to 50% of the labor force in the next few years.

While many of these perks contribute to employee savings, there's a new one that has particular appeal to recent college graduates, 71% of whom are saddled with student loan debt of about $35,000 on average. PricewaterhouseCoopers (PwC), the largest of the big four accounting firms, recently launched a new employee perk that will pay $100 a month or $1,200 a year to reduce student-loan principal for its associates and senior associates for up to six years. Since paying off the loan also reduces interest payments, the company estimates the perk's value is closer to $10,000, in addition to shortening the loan payoff period by up to three years.

As the first in the industry to offer this innovative perk, PwC has made it available to all of its employees in the United States. According to the company's global talent director, PwC's help with student loan repayment is a way to provide leadership on a major societal issue as well as an effective business strategy to retain top employees.

Questions for Critical Thinking

1. Some argue that PwC's employee perk is really not much of an incentive for employees who already earn generous salaries. Do you agree? Why or why not?
2. In an effort to reduce student debt more quickly, many recent grads end up jumping from company to company to make more money. Do you think this new perk will help with employee recruitment and retention? Explain how you would evaluate a perk like this as part of a job offer.

Sources: Company website, "PwC LLP Launches New Benefit to Help Employees Pay Down College Debt," http://www.pwc.com, accessed March 26, 2018; Rebecca Greenfield, "The Hot, New Company Benefit: Student Debt Repayment," *Bloomberg Business*, http://www.bloomberg.com, accessed March 26, 2018; Bob Collins, "Growing Company Perk: Paying Student Loans," *Minnesota Public Radio*, http://blogs.mprnews.org, accessed March 26, 2018; Patrick May, "Tech Companies Dangle Perks to Lure Millennials," *Detroit News*, http://www.detroitnews.com, accessed March 26, 2018; Jena McGregor, "PwC to Help Employees Pay Back Their Student Loans, *Washington Post*, https://www.washingtonpost.com, accessed March 26, 2018.

Case 8.3 Timberland's Culture Rooted in Community Building

Timberland's employees agree that what makes the company unique is the way its culture is brought to life every day, supported by company values of humanity, humility, integrity, and excellence. The role of the human resource department, closely aligned with the company's social responsibility team, is to ensure all events and programs reinforce and support the company's culture of giving, which is at the very foundation of this New Hampshire–based global lifestyle company.

The roots of Timberland's tree logo have often been compared to the foundation of its rich culture of community building. Founded in Boston as a private-label shoe company by Nathan Swartz, it wasn't until the 1970s that his son, Sydney, put the company on the map with its iconic yellow boot. Waterproof and able to withstand the harsh New England winters, the boot's brand name, Timberland, soon became the name of the company.

The connection between corporate social responsibility and human resources is at the core of Timberland's values. Community involvement not only enhances a community outside of Timberland but also creates one within. As a result of the company's community involvement, workplace collaboration is enhanced, and associates have a unique opportunity to build relationships with leaders and managers throughout the organization, regardless of rank. It's also an opportunity for all employees to demonstrate leadership and team-building skills.

Timberland's team-building events happen away from its workplace, and they're not in the form of a company picnic or an awards dinner. Timberland's Path of Service program, in which all employees are offered up to 40 hours of paid time to use in community service, also provides a team-building vehicle. Its two global annual events include Earth Day in the spring, and Serv-a-palooza, a day of annual service in the fall. On both days, in an effort to give back and make a difference in the communities where its employees live and work, the company closes its main offices.

In addition to analyzing ways to keep employees productive and motivated, the human resources function at Timberland includes training and development. When associates assume a leadership and development role to put together a community service project, "they get to exercise that leadership muscle." Many employees are motivated by their experiences outside the organization and are helped by helping others.

Timberland's culture of service touches many different aspects of its human resource functions, including training, development, and orientation. At Timberland, community service provides a way to foster learning, create leaders, motivate employees, and increase employee morale. New recruits, as part of their orientation process, participate in a new-hire service event, where they engage and get to know one another. While Timberland does its best to hire motivated self-starters, keeping them motivated is largely a function of the opportunities available inside and outside of its workplace environment. The culture is described as empowering and motivating, and employees agree that growth is a direct result of the company's investment and commitment to its people.

Human resource departments typically deal with issues of employee loyalty, retention, absenteeism, and morale. Timberland's culture of giving has a residual effect of increasing loyalty among its associates. The company also makes commitments in developing countries to help workers, employed by third-party manufacturers, who are engaged in the manufacture of its products with factories scattered across 30 countries. After recognizing the needs of factory workers with children in India, Timberland helped establish a community-based day care center. Investing in factory workers and their well-being has paid incredible dividends in the form of higher morale, increased loyalty, greater retention, and less absenteeism.

Whether it's doing some gardening in the company's "Victory Garden," which sells its organically grown produce and donates proceeds to the local food bank, or helping with a reading program at a local elementary school, Timberland employees work together to forge lasting bonds in and out of the workplace. In addition, employees can use service hours any way they see fit.

An integral part of human resource management is talent acquisition, learning and development, and management of compensation and benefits. Talent acquisition at Timberland is about finding the best people in the industry and helping them grow in their careers. Equally important to an associate's skills set is cultural fit. Talent is scouted primarily using social media sites such as LinkedIn, and the employee referral program has become widely used. The company's policy is to fill openings first with internal candidates. Timberland's human resource group manages its unique and exciting wellness programs, along with its competitive compensation and benefits programs. On-site wellness programs include the use of a fitness center, soccer games, yoga, and boot camp style exercise. Learning and development are critical to the success of the Timberland brand, and the company is committed to making sure that associates are growing in the same direction, and as quickly as the company.

As an outdoor lifestyle company, Timberland embraces the crucial nature of work–life balance, and the perks the company offers are again connected to its values. Intent on making sure employees connect with the outdoor lifestyle promoted by its brand, Timberland provides kayaks to employees during the summer and snowshoes during the winter. The cafeteria prides itself on healthy food choices at reasonable prices. In addition, there are incentives for biking to work and other wellness activities.

For those who place a high value on community, Timberland is an incredibly unique and special place to work. Its human resource department has spent decades reinforcing the company's unique culture through events and programs that connect associates in a meaningful way. When associates are connected to loving the work they do, they're also connected to the community in which they're doing the work. At Timberland, the company's corporate culture has proved to be as durable as its iconic yellow work boot.

Questions for Critical Thinking

1. Volunteerism and service are key components of Timberland's corporate values. For each of the human resource functions outlined in the chapter, provide examples of the skills employees gain through the company's culture of volunteerism and community service.
2. Provide specific examples of how Timberland's values of humanity, humility, integrity, and excellence come to life within the organization.
3. Discuss Timberland's flexible schedule options and the benefits to employees. Does the company support telecommuting and flexible schedule options? What impact, if any, does this have on company results?
4. Discuss the various ways Timberland keeps its employees motivated. Discuss the ways employees are encouraged to seek out opportunities on their own and to pursue their own path for career development.

Sources: Taryn Luna, "Five Things You Should Know About Stewart Whitney," *Boston Globe*, https://www.bostonglobe.com, accessed March 24, 2018; company website, "Timberland," http://www.vfc.com, accessed March 24, 2018; company website, "About Us," http://www.timberland.com, accessed March 24, 2018; company website, "Timberland Responsibility," http://responsibility.timberland.com, accessed March 24, 2018; company website, "Our Original Yellow Boot," http://www.timberland.com/en/yellow-boot, accessed March 24, 2018; Fawnia Soo Hoo, "Will the Return of Timberland's Classic Boot Help Sell Its Other Styles?" *Fashionista*, http://fashionista.com, accessed March 24, 2018; Natalie Burg, "Timberland and Its Corporate Transparency," *Business Insider*, http://www.businessinsider.com, accessed March 24, 2018.

CHAPTER 9

Top Performance through Empowerment, Teamwork, and Communication

LEARNING OBJECTIVES

1. Discuss empowering employees.
2. Distinguish the five types of teams.
3. Identify team characteristics.
4. Evaluate team cohesiveness and norms.
5. Describe team conflict.
6. Explain the importance of effective communication.
7. Compare the basic forms of communication.
8. Explain external communication and crisis management.

Overview

Top managers like Richard Branson at organizations such as Virgin Group recognize that teamwork and communication are essential for empowering employees to perform their best. This chapter focuses on how organizations involve employees by sharing information and empowering them to make critical decisions, encouraging them to work in teams, and fostering communication.

We begin by discussing the ways managers can empower their employees' decision-making authority and responsibility. Then we explain why and how a growing number of companies rely on teams of workers rather than individuals to make decisions and carry out assignments. We discuss the five basic types of teams found in the business environment and provide real-world examples of each type. We also highlight the characteristics shared by effective teams and discuss the five stages of team development.

Finally, we discuss how effective communication allows workers to share information that improves the quality of decision making.

1 Empowering Employees

An important component of effective management is the **empowerment** of employees. Managers promote this goal by giving employees the authority and responsibility to make decisions about their work. Empowerment seeks to tap the brainpower of all workers to find improved

empowerment giving employees authority and responsibility to make decisions about their work.

Changemaker

Peter MacDiarmid/REX/Shutterstock

Richard Branson, Chief Executive Officer

Company: Virgin Group

Industry: Telecoms & Media, Music & Entertainment, Financial Services and Health & Wellness

Website: www.virgin.com

Richard Branson, CEO of multinational conglomerate Virgin Group lives and breathes a leadership philosophy that centers on his employees as his company's greatest asset. Branson believes that the secret to getting customers to come back to any company lies in the quality of their interactions with employees—and his continuous interactions and communication proves it. Branson came up with the brand name "Virgin" because when he first started his record company, he considered himself a virgin in the record industry. Today, the Virgin name represents companies in a variety of industries including fitness, media, health care, aerospace, wireless communications, financial services, retail, and travel.

The foundation of Branson's philosophy throughout his 60 businesses is strong employee empowerment and a passionate commitment to serving customers. Across his businesses, Branson believes strongly that employees should be empowered to make decisions and that managers should never rule over them. Branson believes that after training employees, allowing them to use their own imagination and creativity for problem solving is crucial. The company's mantra that it's better to ask for forgiveness rather than permission is a way of encouraging employees to take risks while using their abilities and unique styles to handle different situations. Empowerment comes with its rewards. During a fog delay in San Francisco, one employee took it upon herself to roll out the first class drink cart to provide complimentary cocktail service. Shortly thereafter, she received a call from Branson himself congratulating her for coming up with a solution to keep customers happy.

Branson believes that a good leader "doesn't get stuck behind a desk." To build and maintain rock solid relationships, he makes it a point to communicate and interface with employees on an ongoing basis. An avid listener, Branson is well known for taking notes and constantly soliciting feedback when meeting with employees, cabin crew members and customers.

Branson believes that the employee pride found throughout Virgin Group, along with its unparalleled customer focus is a result of his company's employee engagement and empowerment philosophy. When once asked about Virgin America, he said: "We're really a customer service company that's operating an airline."[1]

ways of doing their jobs, better serving customers, and achieving organizational goals. It also motivates workers by adding challenges to their jobs and giving them a feeling of ownership. Managers empower employees by sharing company information and decision-making authority and by rewarding them for their performance—as well as the company's.

Sharing Information and Decision-Making Authority

One of the most effective methods of empowering employees is to keep them informed about the company's performance. Companies such as KIND Healthy Snacks, a New York–based maker of whole fruit and nut bars, believes that a transparent and authentic work environment is one in which employees are kept informed and taught to think like owners. The company's founder and CEO, Daniel Lubetzky, has embedded core principles of transparency and open communication into the company and its products—from its transparent, see-through product wrapper to the way executives are open with employees, who are promoted from within the organization. Team leaders serve as mentors to encourage real-time decision making among employees (called team members). If team members wish to move on, they tell a supervisor who helps them find a job inside or outside the company, asking only for help to train a replacement. While some decisions will continue to be made at the top, transparency about why and how decisions are made and listening to employee feedback allows all team members to feel a part of, and more invested in, company results. Lubetzky practices keeping quiet during meetings so that others feel free to speak. KIND Healthy Snacks has systems in place for sharing information and provides training to allow employees to understand such information. The team dynamic and decisions reflect the company's brand and its mission to spread kindness—all the while building employee loyalty and trust.[2]

The second way in which companies empower employees is to give them broad authority to make workplace decisions that implement a company's vision and its competitive strategy. Even among non-management staff, empowerment extends to decisions and activities traditionally handled by managers. In a work environment that includes decision-making tools and managerial support, Toyota's front-line assembly workers are challenged to stop production and identify and solve problems as they arise on the assembly line.[3]

This can be an especially powerful tool in many health care environments. At Lebanon Valley Brethren Home, a continuing care community in Pennsylvania, workers at all levels are empowered to do whatever it takes to improve the quality of their elderly residents' lives. Each care worker attends to the same residents every day, so caregivers and residents form a strong personal bond (see photo). Caregivers are responsible for the overall management of their households, including meals and housekeeping. They make decisions for individual residents ranging from sleep schedules to room lighting. As a result, each household within the larger community feels like a home.[4]

Jacob Wackerhausen/iStockphoto

At Lebanon Valley Brethren Home, a continuing care community in Pennsylvania, workers at all levels are empowered to do whatever it takes to improve the quality of their elderly residents' lives.

Cloud-based technology has increased employee engagement and collaboration. See the "Business & Technology" feature to learn more.

Linking Rewards to Company Performance

Perhaps the ultimate step in convincing employees of their stake in the results of their company is employee ownership. Two ways that companies provide such ownership are employee stock ownership plans and stock options. **Table 9.1** compares these two methods of employee ownership.

Employee Stock Ownership Plans Over the last two decades, there has been a decline in the total number of ESOP plans but an increase in the number of participants. More than 14 million workers participate in approximately 7,000 employee stock ownership plans (ESOPs).[5] These plans benefit employees by giving them ownership stakes in their companies, leading to potential profits as the value of their company increases. Under ESOPs, the employer buys shares of the company stock on behalf of the employee as a retirement benefit. The accounts continue to grow in value tax-free, and when employees leave the company they can cash in their stock shares. Employees are motivated to work harder and smarter than they would without ESOPs because as part owners, they share in their company's financial success. More than 76% of companies surveyed that offer ESOPs report an increase in employee productivity.[6]

As retirement plans, ESOPs must comply with government regulations designed to protect pension benefits. Because ESOPs can be expensive to set up, they are more common in larger companies than in smaller ones. Privately held companies represent over 90% of ESOP ownership, while publicly held companies represent less than 10%.[7] One danger with ESOPs is that

TABLE 9.1 Employee Stock Ownership Plans and Stock Options

Employee Stock Option Plans	Stock Options
Company-sponsored trust fund holds shares of stock for employees	Company gives employees the option to buy shares of its stock
Usually covers all full-time employees	Can be granted to one, a few, or all employees
Employer pays for the shares of stock	Employees pay a set price to exercise the option
Employees receive stock shares (or value of stock) upon retiring or leaving the company	Employees receive shares of stock when (and if) they exercise the option, usually during a set period

Sources: "Employee Stock Options and Ownership (ESOP)," Reference for Business, http://www.referenceforbusiness.com, accessed March 28, 2018; "Employee Stock Options Fact Sheet," National Center for Employee Ownership, http://www.nceo.org, accessed March 28, 2018.

Business & Technology

Employee Collaboration Via the Cloud

Some companies are using technology to increase collaboration and to help rebuild corporate cultures. For some companies, collaboration may simply entail more day-to-day conversations and interactions and increased training and learning. For others, depending on their size, it may mean regaining a competitive edge within a specific department, such as sales or human resources. Sharing information, decision making, and empowerment are all elements of cloud-based social collaboration tools.

As companies evaluate their somewhat disconnected digital communication strategies, many have decided to utilize cloud technology. One such tool is Jam, a suite of "human capital management" software developed by Success Factors, a company owned by global software giant SAP.

Using employee profiles resembling Facebook, Jam allows the formation of ad hoc groups to work on projects and to encourage new ideas. On a mobile device, tablet, or desktop, Jam can be used to connect customers, partners, and colleagues with information, applications, document sharing, ideas, and processes to help solve issues and drive more sales.

Within a company's sales or human resource department, for example, Jam allows connecting, information sharing, decision making, and collaboration. Using Jam, blended learning (online and offline) can take place, and training costs can be reduced. Connecting new employees with mentors to get needed help allows them to do their job more effectively. The software allows for greater sharing, metrics, and tracking, which translates to meeting goals faster in a more cohesive atmosphere.

For sales professionals, Jam allows stakeholders in the selling process to be updated in real time to shorten the sales cycle, and ultimately increase sales. Enhanced customer engagement helps build stronger relationships, and new salespeople can be brought up to speed faster by connecting them with the right people, process, and products. Social collaboration tools such as Jam enhance employee engagement, help companies reach goals more quickly, and reestablish a connected company culture.

Questions for Critical Thinking

1. **What might be lost when it comes to employee engagement when using social collaboration tools? What might be gained?**
2. **Social collaboration tools allow multiple streams of information and multiple users to be updated at the same time on an ongoing basis. Discuss the impact of real-time updates to multiple users, including the information's accuracy and timeliness.**

Sources: "The Digital Imperative: Firing Up Employee Engagement," *Fortune*, http://fortune.com, accessed March 28, 2018; company website, "SAP Jam" and "Drive Results with Social Collaboration," http://www.successfactors.com, accessed March 28, 2018; company website, "Independent Study for SAP Finds Social Collaboration Key to Driving Business and Lowering Costs," http://news.sap.com, accessed March 28, 2018.

if the majority of an employee's retirement funds are in company stock and if the value falls dramatically, the employee—like other investors—will be financially harmed.[8]

Stock Options Although used less frequently than in the past, another way for companies to share ownership with their employees is through the use of *stock options,* or the right to buy a specified amount of company stock at a given price within a given time period. In contrast to an ESOP, in which the company holds stock for the benefit of employees, stock options give employees a chance to own the stock themselves if they exercise their options by completing the stock purchase. If an employee receives an option on 100 shares at $10 per share and the stock price goes up to $25, the employee can exercise the option to buy those 100 shares at $10 each, sell them at the market price of $25, and pocket the difference. In this case, the calculation would be ($25 – $10) or $15 per share multiplied by 100 shares—for a total gain of $1,500. If the stock price never goes above the option price, the employee isn't required to exercise the option.[9]

Although options were once limited to senior executives and members of the board of directors, some companies now grant stock options to employees at all levels. Federal labor laws allow stock options to be granted to both hourly and salaried employees. It is estimated that 7.2 million employees in thousands of companies hold stock options. Over the last few years, some of the largest executive compensation packages have been fueled by stock options.[10] About one-third of all stock options issued by U.S. corporations go to the top five executives at each company. Much of the remainder goes to other executives and managers, who make up only about 2% of the U.S. workforce. Yet there is solid evidence that stock options motivate regular employees to perform better. Some argue that to be most effective as motivators, stock options need to be granted to a much broader base of employees.

Over the past few decades, there have been many stories of stock-options millionaires. After five years at Google, Bonnie Brown—the company's 40th employee and in-house masseuse—cashed out millions of dollars in stock options and retired.[11] But today, such success stories are no guarantee, especially with stock price volatility. As with ESOPs, employees face risks when they rely on a single company's stock to provide them. In addition to stock options and ESOPs, many companies offer their executives other perks or special privileges.

Restricted stock awards are a popular alternative to stock options. Restricted stock gives employees the full value of a company's stock at a future date when, for example, a performance target or continued employment time is met. These awards are growing in popularity because of favorable accounting rules and income tax treatment. In order to retain talent, a few years ago, Apple announced a new restricted stock plan that would be extended to all employees, and not just to top-level executives. The restricted stock would be granted outright to employees at zero cost, and employees would need to stay with the company for three years before cashing out the stock. More recently, as a result of U.S. tax law changes, Apple granted all employees $2,500 bonuses in restricted stock units.[12]

Assessment Check

1. What is empowerment?
2. How can managers empower employees?
3. How do employee stock ownership plans and stock options reward employees and encourage empowerment?

team group of people with certain skills who are committed to a common purpose, approach, and set of performance goals.

work team relatively permanent group of employees with complementary skills who perform the day-to-day work of organizations.

problem-solving team temporary or permanent combination of workers who gather to solve a specific problem.

2 Teams

A **team** is a group of people with certain skills who are committed to a common purpose, approach, and set of performance goals. All team members hold themselves mutually responsible and accountable for accomplishing their objectives. Teams are widely used in business and in many not-for-profit organizations, such as hospitals and government agencies. Teams are one of the most frequently discussed topics in employee training programs, because teams require that people learn how to work together effectively. Many companies emphasize the importance of teams during their hiring processes, asking job applicants about their previous experiences as members of a team. Why? Because companies want to hire people who can work well with others and pool their talents and ideas to achieve more together than they could achieve working alone. **Figure 9.1** outlines five basic types of teams: work teams, problem-solving teams, self-managed teams, cross-functional teams, and virtual teams.

About two-thirds of U.S. firms currently use **work teams**, which are relatively permanent groups of employees. In this approach, people with complementary skills perform the day-to-day work of the organization. A work team might include all the workers involved in assembling and packaging a product—it could be anything from cupcakes to cars. Most of Walmart's major vendors maintain offices near its headquarters in Bentonville, Arkansas. Typically, the vendor offices operate as work teams, and the heads of these vendor offices often have the title of "team leader."

In contrast to work teams, a **problem-solving team** is a temporary combination of workers who gather to solve a specific problem and then disband. They differ from work teams in important ways, though. Work teams are permanent units designed to handle any business problem that arises, but problem-solving teams pursue specific missions. To reduce customer confusion about what to purchase for an activity, Lululemon, famous for its yoga-inspired athletic apparel, formed a problem-solving

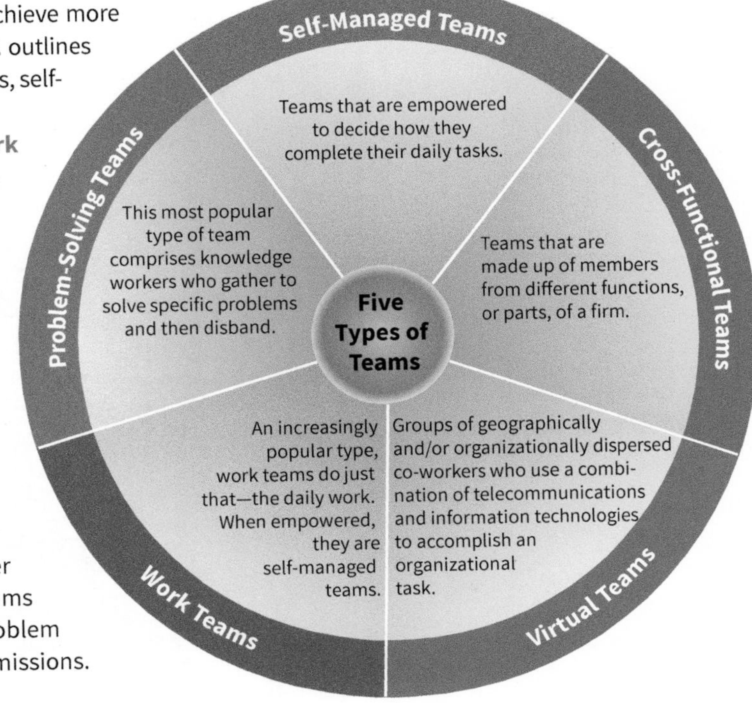

FIGURE 9.1 Five Types of Teams

team. In the past, pants were organized from tightest to loosest. With increased competition in the athleisure arena (which Lululemon invented), its pants, which come with a sticker price of $98 or more, are now organized according to sensation. Based upon the activity, the selling points of each garment are explained by each sensation, which describes the performance quality of the pant. These sensations include hugged sensation, naked, relaxed sensation, tight sensation, and held-in sensation. For example, naked pants are designed to fit very tightly, and they're ideal for yoga, whereas hugged sensation is form-fitting but not skintight, and good for exercise like barre.[13] Typically, when a problem is solved, the team disbands—but in some cases, the team may develop or take on a more permanent role within the company.

self-managed team work team that has the authority to decide how its members complete their daily tasks.

A work team empowered with the authority to decide how its members complete their daily tasks is called a **self-managed team**. A self-managed team works most effectively when it combines employees with a range of skills and functions. Members are cross-trained to perform each other's jobs as needed. Distributing decision-making authority in this way can free members to concentrate on satisfying customers. Whole Foods Market has a structure based on self-managed work teams. Company managers decided that Whole Foods could be most innovative if employees made decisions themselves. Every employee is part of a team, and each store has about ten teams handling separate functions, such as groceries, bakery, and customer service. Each team handles responsibilities related to setting goals, hiring and training employees, scheduling team members, and purchasing goods to stock. Teams meet at least monthly to review goals and performance, solve problems, and explore new ideas. Whole Foods awards bonuses based on the teams' performance relative to their goals.[14]

cross-functional team a team made up of members from different functions, such as production, marketing, and finance.

A team made up of members from different functions, such as production, marketing, and finance, is called a **cross-functional team**. Most often, cross-functional teams, which consist of people with different strengths from various company departments, work on specific problems or projects, but they can also serve as permanent work team arrangements. The value of cross-functional teams comes from their ability to bring different perspectives—as well as different types of expertise—to a work effort. Communication is key to the success of cross-functional teams. At 3M, famous for its Post-it Notes, the CEO discovered that a refocus of the company's new product research and development efforts meant getting 3M scientists to communicate early in the new-product sequence with marketing and manufacturing employees.[15]

virtual team group of geographically or organizationally dispersed co-workers who use a combination of telecommunications and information technologies to accomplish an organizational task.

Virtual teams are groups of geographically or organizationally dispersed co-workers who use a combination of telecommunication and information technologies to accomplish an organizational task. Because of the availability of e-mail, videoconferencing, and group—communication software, members of virtual teams rarely meet face to face (see photo). The

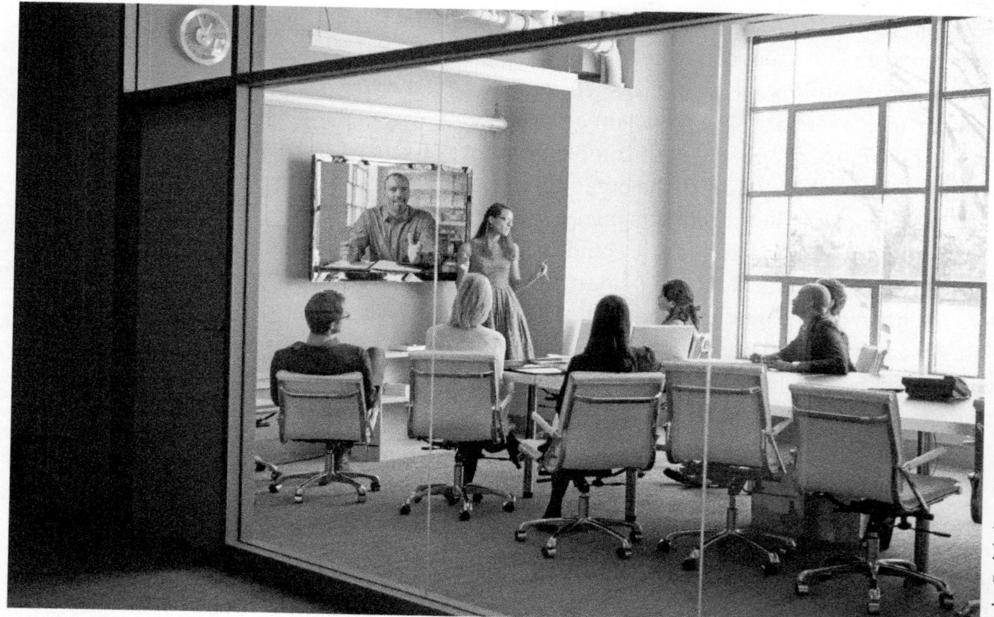

John Fedele/Age Fotostock America, Inc.

Although members of a virtual team rarely meet in person, they stay in touch through technologies such as videoconferencing. In today's global marketplace, the flexibility of virtual teams is a distinct advantage.

Judgment Call

Virtual Teams: Cost Savings or Challenges?

A virtual team, also known as a geographically dispersed team, a distributed team, or a remote team, consists of professionals who work across time, space, and organizational boundaries to reach a common objective or goal. Individuals on virtual teams can work from home or in various off-site locations. They work and keep in touch using web-based technology, project management software, and video conferencing tools such as Skype. By reducing the need for office space and overhead, virtual teams can generate significant cost savings for an organization. But some companies fear that geographically dispersed workers, oftentimes across several time zones, pose greater challenges for management.

Are virtual teams good for business and for individual workers? With the right composition of members and clarification of roles, virtual teams can often achieve as much if not more than other types of teams. In addition to making sure the right technology is utilized, managers should promote and instill trust; hire those suited to working independently; delete responsibilities comfortably; choose an experienced team leader; and set clear goals, team rules, policies, and processes. Occasional in-person team meetings help too.

Using virtual teams allows managers to tap the most highly skilled and diverse workers regardless of time zone and geographic location. Team members can enjoy better work–life balance with fewer interruptions and flexible schedules without commute and travel. In addition, members of virtual teams are usually more productive because of their ability to focus on work tasks without the distractions of a large company atmosphere, which can slow down communications and decision making.

On the downside, managing communications among virtual team members can be difficult due to cultural differences, multiple time zones, and the use of technology as a primary communication vehicle. In addition, not everyone has the temperament and discipline to work virtually. This can lead to misunderstandings, miscommunication, and costly errors. If the process is managed well, the advantages of virtual teams can be many, but risks do remain.

Questions for Critical Thinking

1. **Imagine what it would be like to work with co-workers on a virtual basis without ever having met face-to-face. In what ways could trust be built and conflicts be managed?**
2. **It is a well-known fact that people who are members of virtual teams can suffer from isolation and a lack of personal interactions. Do you agree? Why or why not? Would you like to be a member of a virtual team some day?**

Sources: George Bradt, "The Three Keys to Leading Virtual Teams," *Forbes*, http://www.forbes.com, accessed March 29, 2018; Mark Mortensen, "A First-Time Manager's Guide to Leading Virtual Teams," *Harvard Business Review*, http://hbr.org, accessed March 29, 2018; company website, "Virtual Teams: Benefits and Advantages," https://www.marsdd.com, accessed March 29, 2018.

principal advantage of virtual teams is that they are very flexible. Employees can work with each other regardless of physical location, time zone, or organizational affiliation. Because of their very nature, virtual teams that are scattered across the globe can be challenging to manage. But companies that are committed to them believe that the benefits outweigh the challenges. See the "Judgment Call" feature for a discussion of the benefits and challenges of virtual teams.

Assessment Check

1. What is a team?
2. What are the five types of teams, and how are they different?

3 Team Characteristics

Effective teams share a number of characteristics. They must be an appropriate size to accomplish their work. In addition to size, teams also can be categorized according to the similarities and differences among team members, called *level* and *diversity*. We discuss these three characteristics next.

Team Size

Teams can range in number from as few as 2 people to as many as 150 people. In practice, however, most teams have fewer than 12 members. Although no ideal size limit applies to every team, research on team effectiveness indicates that they achieve their best results with about six or seven members. A group of this size is big enough to benefit from a variety of diverse skills, yet small enough to allow members to communicate easily and feel part of a close-knit group.

Certainly, groups smaller or larger than this can be effective, but they also create added challenges for team leaders. Participants in small teams of two to four members often show a desire to get along with each other. They tend to favor informal interactions marked by discussions of personal topics, and they make only limited demands on team leaders. A large team with more than 12 members poses a different challenge for team leaders because decision making may work slowly and participants may feel less committed to team goals. Larger teams also tend to foster disagreements, absenteeism, and membership turnover. Subgroups may form, leading to possible conflicts among various functions. As a general rule, a team of more than 20 people should be divided into subteams, each with its own members and goals. Jeff Bezos, CEO of Amazon, has a two-pizza team rule that states teams shouldn't be any larger than what two pizzas can feed. Small teams make communication easier; however, as group size grows, conversations and interactions are less meaningful.[16]

Team Level and Team Diversity

team level average level of ability, experience, personality, or any other factor on a team.

team diversity variances or differences in ability, experience, personality, or any other factor on a team.

Team level is the average level of ability, experience, personality, or any other factor on a team. Businesses consider team level when they need teams with a particular set of skills or capabilities to do their jobs well. For example, an environmental engineering firm might put together a team with a high level of experience to write a proposal for a large contract.

While team level represents the average level or capability on a team, **team diversity** represents the differences in ability, experience, personality, or any other factor on a team. Strong teams not only have talented members—as demonstrated by their team level—but also members who are different in terms of ability, experience, personality, and even socio-economic level. Team diversity is an important consideration for teams that must complete a wide range of different tasks or particularly complex tasks. As Director of Diversity and Inclusion for Google, Yolanda Mangolini (see photo) is focused on expanding the tech giant's concept of diversity. Goals include hiring initiatives to expand the pool of tech candidates, fostering a fair and inclusive culture, and bridging the digital divide. To recruit more computer science students of color from historically black colleges and universities (HBCUs), Google has opened "Howard West" on its campus in Silicon Valley in California. Twenty-five college juniors majoring in computer science from all HBCUs are chosen to spend 12 weeks immersing themselves in tech culture while receiving instruction and training from Google engineers.[17]

Team diversity is an important component of many successful companies. Read how Sheryl Sandberg and Facebook have taken a stand on diversity as described in the "Business Model" feature.

Dan Clark/Weinberg Clark Photography

Yolanda Mangolini is Director of Global Diversity & Inclusion and Talent & Outreach Programs for Google, which has made a significant financial commitment to internal and external diversity initiatives. Google's goal is to foster a fair and inclusive culture while expanding the pool of computer science job applicants.

Stages of Team Development

According to Bruce Tuckman, an educational psychologist from Ohio State University, team development and behavior typically progresses through five stages: forming, storming, norming, performing, and adjourning. Although not every team passes through each of these stages, those teams that do are usually better performers. These stages are summarized in **Figure 9.2**.

Stage 1: Forming Forming is an orientation period during which team members get to know each other and find out the behaviors that are acceptable to the group. Team members begin with curiosity about

Business Model

Facebook's Sheryl Sandberg Promotes Inclusion

Sheryl Sandberg, Facebook's Chief Operating Officer, believes that businesses succeed when management reflects the diversity of the population at large. A leadership team with different experiences and backgrounds typically is better at identifying and solving problems. In addition to her COO duties at Facebook, Sandberg is author of *Lean In,* the top-selling book that challenges women to take risks in their careers and not let gender bias get in the way of workplace advancement, and *Option B*, a book about building resilience in the face of adversity, written after the unexpected and sudden death of her husband.

Sandberg believes that a culture of inclusion and a diverse workplace improve employees' engagement levels, performance, productivity, and retention. It also helps with performance among teams in organizations as well as with innovation, creativity, revenue, and profits. However, according to Sandberg, using the talents of the total workforce—not just half—will be critical to economic growth, corporate productivity, and individual happiness.

In the wake of the Me Too movement, a social media hashtag used to signify widespread sexual assault and harassment in the workplace, Sandberg has launched the hashtag #MentorHer. With senior-level men uncomfortable about perceptions of interactions with top-level female executives, Sandberg is concerned that women will be held back. "Women are missing out on high-impact, flexible, well-paid, and exciting careers, and the industry is missing out on their ideas," she says.

Questions for Critical Thinking

1. **Discuss situations in which you have witnessed gender or cultural bias at work or at school. What could have been done to prevent the situation?**
2. **Provide specific examples of what Sandberg refers to when she says that we need the talents of the entire labor force and not just half. What other solutions can you propose for companies to deal with gender bias?**

Sources: Julia Boorstin, First on CNBC: Facebook's Sheryl Sandberg and Lori Goler Speak on "'Closing Bell' Today," *CNBC,* http://www.cnbc.com, accessed March 29, 2018; Lauren Hockenson, "Sheryl Sandberg Articulates the Diversity Silicon Valley Is Chasing After," *TNW News*, http://nextweb.com, accessed March 29, 2018; "Sheryl Sandberg: When Women Get Stuck, Corporate America Gets Stuck," *Wall Street Journal*, http://www.wsj.com, accessed March 29, 2018; Sara Murray, "Who's Still Leaning In? It's Complicated," *Wall Street Journal*, http://blogs.wsj.com, accessed March 29, 2018; Sheryl Sandberg, "Why I Want Women to Lean In," *Time*, http://ideas.time.com, accessed March 29, 2018; organization website, "About Option B," https://optionb.org/, accessed March 29, 2018; Natalie Robehmed, "Amid #MeToo Backlash, Lean In's Sheryl Sandberg Launches #MentorHer Campaign," http://www.forbes.com, *Forbes*, accessed March 29, 2018.

expectations of them and whether they will fit in with the group. An effective team leader provides time for members to become acquainted.

Stage 2: Storming The personalities of team members begin to emerge during the storming stage, as members clarify their roles and expectations. Conflicts may arise, as people disagree over the team's mission and jockey for position and control of the group. Subgroups may form based on common interests or concerns. At this stage, the team leader must encourage everyone to participate, allowing members to work through their uncertainties and conflicts. Teams must move beyond this stage to achieve real productivity.

Stage 3: Norming During the norming stage, members resolve differences, accept each other, and reach broad agreement about the roles of the team leader and other participants. This stage is usually brief, and the team leader should use it to emphasize the team's unity and the importance of its objectives.

Stage 4: Performing While performing, members focus on solving problems and accomplishing tasks. They interact frequently and handle conflicts in constructive ways. The team leader encourages contributions from all members. He or she should attempt to get any nonparticipating team members involved.

Stage 5: Adjourning The team adjourns after members have completed the assigned task or solved the problem. During this phase, the focus is on wrapping up and

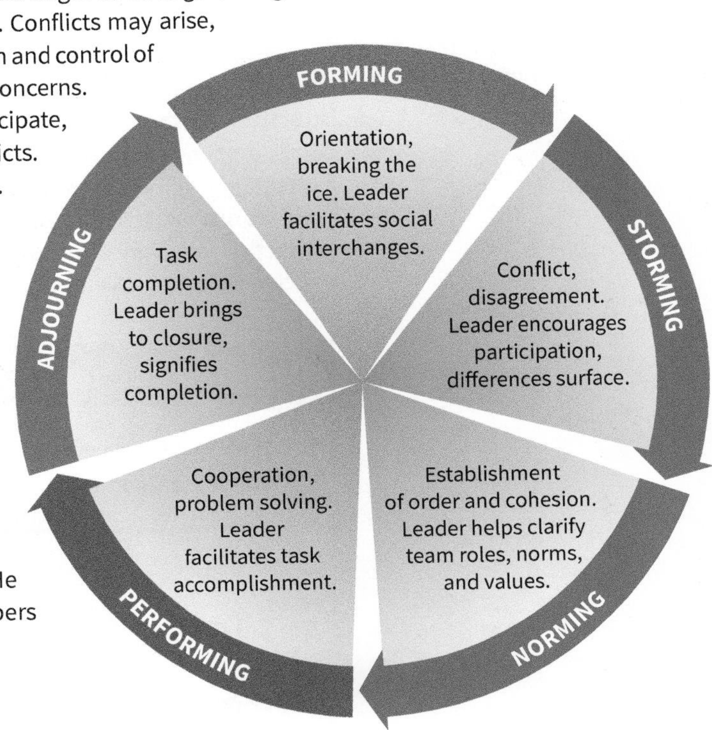
FORMING
Orientation, breaking the ice. Leader facilitates social interchanges.
STORMING
Conflict, disagreement. Leader encourages participation, differences surface.
NORMING
Establishment of order and cohesion. Leader helps clarify team roles, norms, and values.
PERFORMING
Cooperation, problem solving. Leader facilitates task accomplishment.
ADJOURNING
Task completion. Leader brings to closure, signifies completion.

FIGURE 9.2 **Stages of Team Development**

summarizing the team's experiences and accomplishments. The team leader may recognize the team's accomplishments with a celebration, perhaps handing out plaques or awards.

Assessment Check

1. Explain team level and team diversity.
2. Explain how teams progress through the stages of team development.

4 Team Cohesiveness and Norms

team cohesiveness extent to which team members feel attracted to the team and motivated to remain part of it.

Teams tend to maximize productivity when they form into highly cohesive units. **Team cohesiveness** is the extent to which members feel attracted to the team and motivated to remain part of it. This cohesiveness typically increases when members interact frequently, share common attitudes and goals, and enjoy being together. Cohesive groups have a better chance of retaining their members than those that do not achieve cohesiveness. As a result, cohesive groups typically experience lower turnover. In addition, team cohesiveness promotes cooperative behavior, generosity, and a willingness on the part of team members to help each other. When team cohesiveness is high, team members are more motivated to contribute to the team, because they want the approval of other team members. Not surprisingly, studies have clearly established that cohesive teams quickly achieve high levels of performance and consistently perform better.

Team-building retreats are one way to encourage cohesiveness and improve satisfaction and retention. Companies that specialize in conducting these retreats offer a wide range of options. Massachusetts–based TeamBonding is a company specializing in creating customized corporate retreats and team-building experiences. Clients like American Express, Disney, and Apple can choose among a variety of events, including a high-tech scavenger hunt using tablets and smart phones, a corporate *Project Runway*, building a remote-powered robot, and photo and video challenges.[18]

team norm standard of conduct shared by team members that guides their behavior.

A **team norm** is a standard of conduct shared by team members that guides their behavior. Norms are not formal written guidelines; they are informal standards that identify key values and clarify team members' expectations. In highly productive teams, norms contribute to constructive work and the accomplishment of team goals. At Texas–based retailer The Container Store, employees come first. CEO Kip Tindell believes strongly that if his employees are paid better and given excellent training, they will take care of their customers. Each new employee receives one week of intensive training and more than 263 hours of formal training during his or her first year with the company. Team norms include supportive and spontaneous ways in which employees take time to recognize and support the efforts of co-workers.[19]

Assessment Check

1. How does cohesiveness affect teams?
2. What is a team norm?

5 Team Conflict

conflict situation in which one person's or group's needs do not match those of another, and attempts may be made to block the opposing side's intentions or goals.

Conflict occurs when one person's or group's needs do not match those of another, and attempts may be made to block the opposing side's intentions or goals. Conflict and disagreement are inevitable in most teams. But this shouldn't surprise anyone. People who work together are naturally going to disagree about what and how things are done. What causes conflict in teams? Although almost anything can lead to conflict—casual remarks that unintentionally offend a team member or fighting over scarce resources—the primary cause of team conflict is disagreement over goals and priorities. Other common causes of team conflict include disagreements over task-related issues, interpersonal incompatibilities, simple fatigue, and team diversity.

Earlier in this chapter we noted how teams can experience diversity among members. While diversity brings stimulation, challenge, and energy, it can also lead to conflict. The job of the manager is to create an environment in which differences are appreciated and in which a team of diverse individuals work together productively. Diversity training programs can reduce conflict and increase inclusion and tolerance among a diverse group of team members. By creating awareness of differences in culture, knowledge, and skills, greater cohesiveness is usually a result.

Although most people think conflict should be avoided, management experts note that conflict can actually enhance team performance. The key to dealing with conflict is making sure that the team experiences the right kind of conflict. **Cognitive conflict** focuses on problem-related differences of opinion, and reconciling those differences strongly improves team performance. With cognitive conflict, team members disagree because their different experiences and expertise lead them to different views of the problem and its solutions. Cognitive conflict is also characterized by a willingness to examine, compare, and reconcile differences to produce the best possible solution. By contrast, **affective conflict** refers to the emotional reactions that can occur when disagreements become personal rather than professional, and these differences strongly decrease team performance. Because affective conflict often results in hostility, anger, resentment, distrust, cynicism, and apathy, it can make people uncomfortable, cause them to withdraw, decrease their commitment to a team, lower the satisfaction of team members, and decrease team cohesiveness. So, unlike cognitive conflict, affective conflict undermines team performance by preventing teams from engaging in activities that are critical to team effectiveness.

cognitive conflict disagreement that focuses on problem- and issue-related differences of opinion.

affective conflict disagreement that focuses on individuals or personal issues.

What can managers do to manage team conflict—and even make it work for them? Perhaps the team leader's most important contribution to conflict resolution can be facilitating good communication so that teammates respect each other and are free to disagree with each other. Ongoing, effective communication ensures that team members perceive each other accurately, understand what is expected of them, and obtain the information they need. Taking this a step further, organizations should evaluate situations or conditions in the workplace that might be causing conflict. Solving a single conflict isn't helpful if there are problems systemic to the team or to the company. Team-building exercises, listening exercises, and role-playing can help employees learn to become better team members.[20]

Assessment Check

1. What is cognitive conflict, and how does it affect teams?
2. Explain affective conflict and its impact on teams.

6 The Importance of Effective Communication

Countries such as China, India, and Mexico are home to businesses that provide goods and services to companies or consumers in the United States. But the more parties involved in the production process, the harder it is to coordinate communication. Brooks Brothers, well-known for its traditional menswear, is contributing to the apparel industry's trend to reshore, or bring production back to the United States from overseas. Doing so has become more financially feasible as wages in China have increased and factories there are demanding higher production volumes.[21]

communication meaningful exchange of information through messages.

Communication can be defined as a meaningful exchange of information through messages. Few businesses can succeed without effective communication. In fact, miscommunication can result in damage to the company and can be costly. Over a decade ago, McDonald's invested in fast-casual Mexican chain Chipotle, but it didn't take long for Chipotle founder and co-CEO Steve Ells to part ways when he realized that there were major miscommunication and cultural differences between the two companies. Chipotle's organic and sustainable food sourcing, far fewer menu items, and corporate ownership of stores (no franchisees) were just a few of the things that made the relationship too challenging to be successful.[22]

Managers spend about 80% of their time—nearly six and a half hours of every eight-hour day—in direct communication with others, whether on the telephone, in meetings, via e-mail, or in individual conversations. Company recruiters consistently rate effective communication, such as listening, conversing, and giving feedback, as the most important skill they look for when hiring new employees. In the last part of this chapter, you'll learn about the communication process, the basic forms of communication, and ways to improve communication within organizations.

The Process of Communication

Every communication follows a step-by-step process that involves interactions among six elements: sender, message, channel, audience, feedback, and context. This process is illustrated in **Figure 9.3**.

In the first step, the *sender* composes the message and sends it through a communication carrier, or channel. Encoding a message means that the sender translates its meaning into understandable terms and a form that allows transmission through a chosen channel. The sender can communicate a particular message through many different channels, including face-to-face conversations, phone calls, and e-mail or texting. A promotional message to the company's customers may be communicated through such forms as radio and television ads, dynamic outdoor billboards, magazines and newspapers, sales presentations, and social media sites. The audience consists of the people who receive the message. In decoding, the receiver of the message interprets its meaning. Feedback from the audience—in response to the sender's communication—helps the sender determine whether the audience has correctly interpreted the intended meaning of the message.

Every communication takes place in some sort of situational or cultural context. The *context* can exert a powerful influence on how well the process works. A conversation between two people in a quiet office, for example, may be a very different experience from the same conversation held at a noisy party. An American who orders chips in an English tavern will receive French fries.

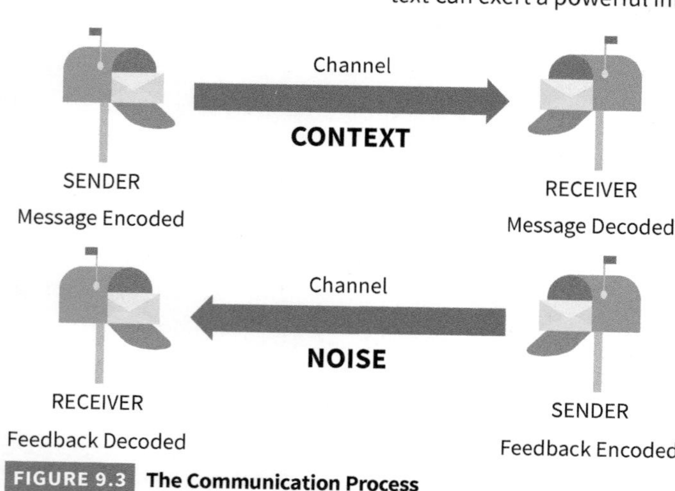

FIGURE 9.3 **The Communication Process**

Anthropologists classify cultures as low context and high context. Communication in *low-context cultures* tends to rely on explicit written and verbal messages. Examples include Switzerland, Austria, Germany, and the United States. In contrast, communication in *high-context cultures*—such as those of Japan, Latin America, and India—depends not only on the message itself but also on the conditions that surround it, including nonverbal cues, past and present experiences, and personal relationships among the parties. Westerners must carefully temper their low-context style to the expectations of colleagues and clients from high-context countries (see photo). Although Americans tend to favor direct interactions and want to "get down to business" soon after shaking hands or sitting down to a business dinner, businesspeople in Mexico and Asian countries prefer to become acquainted before discussing details. When conducting business in these cultures, well-versed visitors allow time for relaxed meals during which business-related topics are avoided.

Stephen Lock/Newscom

During a recent visit to New Zealand, an elder performs Hongi with the Duchess of Cambridge, Catherine Middleton. Hongi is a traditional Māori greeting in which people press their nose and forehead together at the same time.

Senders must pay attention to audience feedback, even requesting it if none is forthcoming, because this response clarifies whether the communication has conveyed the intended message. Feedback can indicate whether the receiver heard the message and was able to decode it accurately. Even when the receiver tries to understand, the communication may fail if the message contained jargon or ambiguous words.

Noise during the communication process is some type of interference that influences the transmission of messages and feedback. Noise can result from simple physical factors such as poor reception of a cell phone message or static that drowns out a radio commercial. It can also be caused by more complex differences in people's attitudes and perceptions. Consequently, even when people are exposed to the same communications, they can end up with very different perceptions and understandings because of communication noise.

Noise can be present at any point in the communication process. This is why managers must learn how to cut through noise when communicating with employees, particularly in today's digital age. Every day throughout its worldwide luxury hotels, Ritz-Carlton holds 15-minute departmental meetings at which managers share "wow stories," examples of outstanding service by department employees. The meetings are also a way to reinforce important skills and to demonstrate through storytelling the value of exceptional customer service.[23]

Assessment Check

1. What is the difference between communication in low-context and high-context cultures?
2. In the context of the communication process, what is noise?

7 Basic Forms of Communication

Managers and co-workers communicate in many different ways—by making a phone call, sending an e-mail or text message, holding a staff meeting, or chatting in the hallway. They also communicate with facial expressions, gestures, and other body language. Subtle variations can significantly influence the reception of a message. As **Table 9.2** points out, communication takes various forms: oral and written, formal and informal, and nonverbal.

Oral Communication

Managers spend a lot of time engaged in oral communication, both in person and on the phone. Some people prefer to communicate this way, believing that oral channels convey messages

TABLE 9.2 Forms of Communication

Form	Description	Examples
Oral communication	Communication transmitted through speech	Personal conversations, speeches, meetings, voice mail, telephone conversations, video or web conferences
Written communication	Communication transmitted through writing	e-mails, letters, memos, formal reports, news releases, online discussion groups, text messages
Formal communication	Communication transmitted to members within an organization through the chain of command, or to people outside the organization	Internal—memos, reports, meetings, written proposals, oral presentations, meeting minutes; external—letters, written proposals, oral presentations, speeches, news releases, press conferences
Informal communication	Communication transmitted outside formal channels without regard for the organization's hierarchy of authority	Rumors spread informally among employees via the grapevine
Nonverbal communication	Communication transmitted through actions and behaviors rather than through words	Gestures, facial expressions, posture, body language, dress, makeup

more accurately. Face-to-face oral communication allows people to combine words with such cues as facial expressions, body language, and tone of voice. Oral communication over the phone lacks visual cues, but it does allow people to hear the tone of voice and provide immediate feedback by asking questions or restating the message. Because of its immediacy, oral communication has drawbacks. If one person is agitated or nervous during a conversation, noise enters the communication process. A hurried manager might brush off an employee who has an important message to deliver. A frustrated employee might feel compelled to fire a harsh retort at an unsupportive supervisor instead of thinking before responding.

listening receiving a message and interpreting its intended meaning by grasping the facts and feelings it conveys.

In any medium, a vital component of oral communication is **listening**—receiving a message and interpreting its genuine meaning by accurately grasping the facts and feeling conveyed. Although listening may be the most important communication skill, most of us don't use it enough—or as well as we should.

Listening may seem easy, because the listener appears to make no effort. But the average person talks at a rate of roughly 150 words per minute, while the brain can handle up to 400 words per minute. This gap can lead to boredom, inattention, and misinterpretation. In fact, immediately after listening to a message, the average person can recall only half of it. After several days, the proportion of a message that a listener can recall falls to 25% or less.

Certain types of listening behaviors are common in both business and personal interactions:

- *Cynical or defensive listening*. This type of listening occurs when the receiver of a message feels that the sender is trying to gain some advantage from the communication.
- *Offensive listening*. In this type of listening, the receiver tries to catch the speaker in a mistake or contradiction.
- *Polite listening*. In this mechanical type of listening, the receiver listens to be polite rather than to contribute to communication. Polite listeners are usually inattentive and spend their time rehearsing what they want to say when the speaker finishes.
- *Active listening*. This form of listening requires involvement with the information and empathy with the speaker's situation. In both business and personal life, active listening is the basis for effective communication.

Learning how to be an active listener is an especially important goal for business leaders because effective communication is essential to the effectiveness of their role. Active listening (see photo) shows a desire to help others and pays off with better interpersonal relationships and greater influence.[24] Starbucks has come up with innovative ways to listen to both customers and employees in order to save energy, as described in the "Clean & Green Business" feature.

Joshua Hodge Photography/iStockphoto

Listening may seem easy, because the listener appears to make no effort. But the average person talks much slower than the amount of information the brain can handle at any given time. This gap may lead to boredom, inattention, and misinterpretation on the part of the listener.

Written Communication

Channels for written communication include reports, letters, memos, online discussion boards and social media, e-mails, and text messages. Many of these channels permit only delayed feedback and create a record of the message. So it is important for the sender of a written communication to prepare the message carefully and review it to avoid misunderstandings—particularly before hitting that "send" button.

Effective written communication reflects its audience, the channel carrying the message, and the appropriate degree of formality. When writing a formal business document such as a complex marketing research report or business plan, a manager must plan in advance and carefully construct the document. The process of writing a formal document involves planning, research, organization, composition and design, and revision. Written communication via e-mail may call for a less-formal writing style, including short sentences, phrases, and bulleted lists.

Clean & Green Business

Starbucks Listens to Energy-Saving Ideas

Less than a decade ago, Starbucks created My Starbucks Idea, a social engagement and crowdsourcing platform on social media. My Starbucks Idea allows anyone, including customers and employees, to contribute ideas about sustainability, social responsibility, and community building, among others. Since the inception of My Starbucks Idea, more than 200,000 ideas have been submitted, and close to 300 have been implemented.

Using the two-way social platform, participants engage even further by voting or commenting on sustainability ideas. After receiving ideas about creating more energy-efficient stores, Starbucks recently implemented an LED lighting replacement program in all of its U.S. and Canada store locations. By listening to others, the sustainability team at Starbucks was able to gather and implement ideas from many more individuals than just their own team members.

Energy efficiency is a large component of the company's sustainability efforts, and lighting also presents a big opportunity. The switch to LED lighting started almost a decade ago when Starbucks began replacing traditional incandescent lamps with energy-efficient LED ones. Since the switch, Starbucks has been on a mission to evaluate even newer technology to meet its goal of even greater energy efficiency. In the coming year, Starbucks will make yet another switch to even more energy-efficient lighting. To create a cozy and warm ambiance, the company recently introduced vintage-looking LED lamps, which use far less energy. The next time you go to Starbucks, look up at the lighting and know that the company listened to what turned out to be an illuminating and sustainable idea.

Questions for Critical Thinking

1. **Discuss the ways companies can provide incentives to employees and customers for innovative and cost-saving ideas. Should Starbucks have a similar incentive as part of its My Starbucks Idea program?**
2. **Can you think of other ways Starbucks can listen to customer feedback and suggestions while also engaging them?**

Sources: Tina Geisel, "My Starbucks Idea: The Starbucks Crowdsourcing Success Story," *Social Media for Business Performance,* http://smbp.uwaterloo.ca, accessed March 29, 2018; company website, http://mystarbucksidea.force.com, accessed March 29, 2018; company website, Jessica Hyman, "Five Ways to Make Employee Engagement Programs Effective," http://www.bsr.org, accessed March 29, 2018; company website, "Saving Energy with LED Lighting," http://blogs.starbucks.com, accessed March 29, 2018; Joseph Giorgi, "Building a Community: Why Starbucks Gets Customer Service Right," *Branding Beat,* https://www.qualitylogoproducts.com, accessed March 29, 2018.

E-mail is a very effective communication channel, especially for delivering straightforward messages and information. But e-mail's effectiveness also leads to its biggest problem: too much e-mail! Many workers find their valuable time being consumed with e-mail. To relieve this burden and leave more time for performing the most important aspects of the job, some companies are looking into ways to reduce the time employees spend sending and reading e-mail. To fulfill this need, there are now companies that provide e-mail management services. One such company is Boston-based SaneBox, which provides customized e-mail solutions for firms that have been struggling to keep up with the volume of e-mail they receive and the time it takes to operate an in-house server.[25]

Other e-mail issues are security and permanence. Because e-mail messages are often informal, senders occasionally forget that they are creating a written record. Even if the recipient deletes an e-mail message, other copies exist on company e-mail servers. E-mails on company servers can be used as evidence in a legal case or disciplinary action.

Formal Communication

A *formal communication channel* carries messages that flow within the chain of command structure defined by an organization. The most familiar channel, downward communication, carries messages from someone who holds a senior position in the organization to subordinates. Managers may communicate downward by sending employees e-mail messages, presiding at department meetings, giving employees policy manuals, posting notices online or on bulletin boards, and reporting news in company newsletters. The most important factor in formal communication is transparency—to be open and honest. "Spinning" bad news to make it look better almost always backfires. In a work environment characterized by open communication, employees feel free to express opinions, offer suggestions, and even voice complaints. Research has shown that open communication has the following seven characteristics:

1. *Employees are valued.* Employees are happier and more motivated when they feel they are valued and their opinions are heard.
2. *A high level of trust exists.* Telling the truth maintains a high level of trust; this forms the foundation for open communication and employee motivation and retention.
3. *Conflict is invited and resolved positively.* Without conflict, innovation and creativity are stifled.
4. *Creative dissent is welcomed.* By expressing unique ideas, employees feel they have contributed to the company and improved performance.
5. *Employee input is solicited.* The key to any company's success is input from employees, which establishes a sense of involvement and improves working relations.
6. *Employees are well informed.* Employees are kept informed about what is happening within the organization.
7. *Feedback is ongoing.* Both positive and negative feedback must be ongoing and provided in a manner that builds relationships rather than assigns blame.[26]

Many companies also define formal channels for upward communications. These channels encourage communication from employees to supervisors and upward to top management levels. Some examples of upward communication channels are employee surveys, online surveys, and other methods that allow employees to propose ideas for new products or express concerns. Upward communication is also necessary for managers to evaluate the effectiveness of downward communication. **Figure 9.4** illustrates the forms of organizational communication, both formal and informal.

Informal Communication

grapevine internal information channel that transmits information from unofficial sources.

Informal communication channels carry messages outside formally authorized channels within an organization's hierarchy. A familiar example of an informal channel is the **grapevine**, an

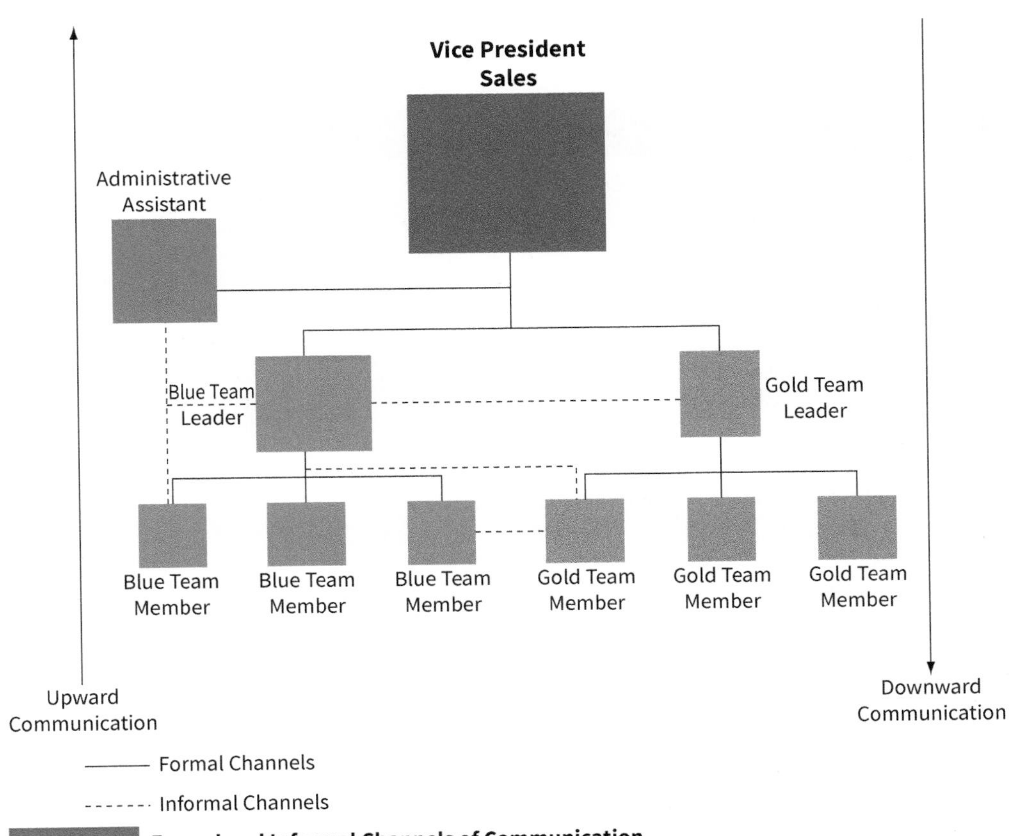

FIGURE 9.4 Formal and Informal Channels of Communication

internal channel that passes information from unofficial sources. All organizations, large or small, have grapevines. Grapevines disseminate information with speed and economy and are surprisingly reliable. But company communications must be managed effectively so that the grapevine is not the main source of information. When properly nurtured, the grapevine can help managers get a feel for the morale of companies, understand the anxieties of the workforce, and evaluate the effectiveness of formal communications. Managers can improve the quality of information circulating through the company grapevine by sharing knowledge, even if it is preliminary or partial information. By feeding information to selected people, smart leaders can harness the power of the grapevine.

Gossip—which usually travels along the grapevine—is the main drawback of this communication channel. Because gossip can spread misinformation quickly—particularly if it is discovered online—a manager should address the issue quickly so the grapevine can become a legitimate source of information once again. Conversely, employees can nurture informal communication by taking the time to learn more about the communication needs of their managers.[27]

As organizations become more decentralized and more globally dispersed, informal communication—more than ever before—provides an important source of information, through e-mail, texting, and social media.

Nonverbal Communication

So far, this section has considered different forms of verbal communication, or communication that conveys meaning through words. Equally important is *nonverbal communication,* which transmits messages through actions and behaviors. Gestures, posture, eye contact, tone and volume of voice, and even clothing choices are all nonverbal actions that become communication cues. Nonverbal cues can have a far greater impact on communications than many people realize. In fact, it is estimated that 70% of interpersonal communication is conveyed through nonverbal cues. Top salespeople are particularly adept at reading such cues.

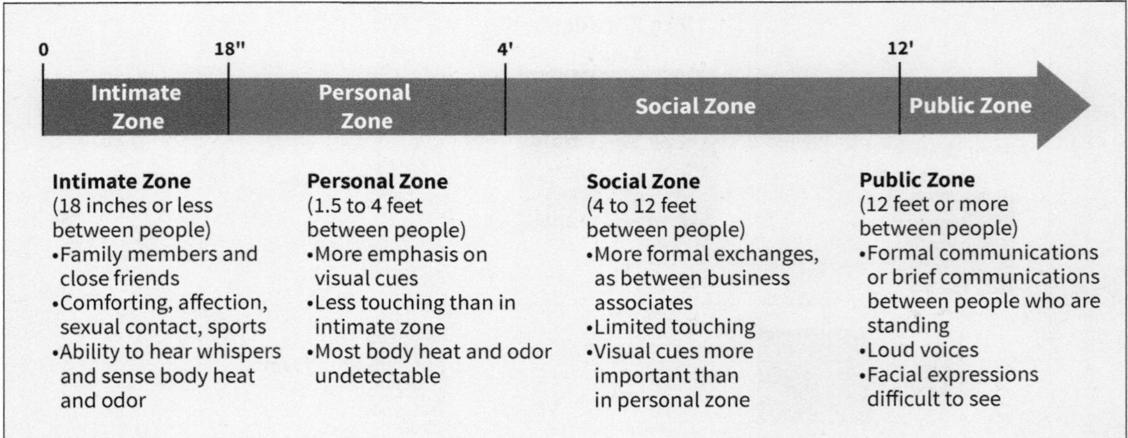

FIGURE 9.5 **Influence of Personal Space in Nonverbal Communication**

For example, they practice "mirroring" a customer's gestures and body language in order to indicate agreement.[28]

Even personal space—the physical distance between people who are engaging in communication—can convey powerful messages. **Figure 9.5** shows a continuum of personal space and social interaction with four zones of physical space within which we feel safe: intimate, personal, social, and public. In the United States, most business conversations occur within the social zone, roughly between 4 and 12 feet apart. If one person tries to approach closer than that, the other individual will likely feel uncomfortable or even threatened.

Interpreting nonverbal cues can be especially challenging for people with different cultural backgrounds. Concepts of appropriate personal space differ dramatically throughout most of the world. For example, Latin Americans may conduct business discussions in close positions that some Americans and northern Europeans might find uncomfortable. Americans often back away to preserve their personal space, a gesture that Latin Americans might perceive as unfriendly.

People send nonverbal messages even when they consciously try to avoid doing so. Sometimes nonverbal cues convey a person's true attitudes and thoughts, which may differ from spoken meanings. Generally, when verbal and nonverbal cues conflict, receivers of the communication tend to believe the nonverbal content. This is why companies seeking to hire people with positive attitudes and a team orientation closely watch nonverbal behavior during job interviews in which job applicants participate in group sessions with other job candidates applying for the same job.

Assessment Check

1. Define the four common listening behaviors.
2. What are the differences between formal and informal communication?

8 External Communication and Crisis Management

external communication meaningful exchange of information through messages transmitted between an organization and its major audiences.

External communication is a meaningful exchange of information through messages transmitted between an organization and its major audiences, such as customers, suppliers, other firms, the general public, and government officials. Businesses use external communication to keep their operations functioning, to maintain their positions in the marketplace, and to build customer relationships by supplying information about topics such as product modifications and price changes. Every communication with customers—including sales presentations and advertisements—should create goodwill and contribute to customer satisfaction (see photo). Companies hire corporate communication specialists who create content and communicate internally with people inside the company and externally with the public—all in an effort to convey a positive image. See the "Job Description" feature for more about this type of career. Letting the public know about new initiatives for environmentally friendly processes as well as community projects and other socially responsible activities in which the company is involved is an important function of external communication.

© Steve Debenport/iStockphoto

Businesses use external communication to keep their operations functioning, to maintain their positions in the marketplace, and to build customer relationships.

However, all of this is threatened when companies experience a public relations crisis that threatens their reputation or goodwill. Equifax, a credit rating agency, makes its profit from selling personal and sensitive data to financial institutions. In a recent year, the company revealed one of the worst data breaches in history—putting at risk the personal information of some 145 million people. As a result, the company's CEO, Richard Smith, and its Chief Information Officer (CIO) stepped down. Well before the data breach was reported, the news revealed that Equifax was aware of a software issue six months prior to the breach. The ongoing discoveries point to negligence, and to Equifax's failure not only to communicate to the public but to protect itself against a known flaw.[29]

How companies handle such events can determine whether or not their reputation can be remedied. Putting together a plan of action and dealing with facts and rumors immediately could be the difference between regaining trust and disaster. The following communication steps can help during a public relations crisis:

1. When a crisis occurs, a company should respond quickly. Executives should prepare a written statement—and stick to it. The statement should mention the time, place, initial description of what occurred (not the cause), and the number and status of the people involved.
2. As soon as possible, top company management should appear in public—if possible, to the press. Because the public will hold top management accountable, it's best to have top managers responding to reporters' questions.
3. When answering questions at an initial press conference or in an interview, the management representative must stick to the facts. It's likely that details about the event, the cause, and people's roles will not yet be known; the spokesperson shouldn't speculate. As information becomes available, the company can provide accurate updates.
4. If a question is currently unanswerable, the executive can offer to find out the answer, which should be delivered in a timely manner. It's not advisable to answer a question by saying "No comment." It's much better to say "I don't know."
5. The company should acknowledge problems, explain solutions, and welcome feedback. If a question or factual statement puts the organization in a negative light, the manager should acknowledge the problem and then explain how the company is correcting it.
6. The press conference or interview will be most effective if the executive speaks briefly and clearly, and provides positive visual images.[30]

Crises faced by companies such as Equifax are sometimes magnified by critics and crisis management experts through news stories that quickly go viral. To avoid further damage to their reputation, companies must accept responsibility and respond quickly and decisively. Instead of directing potential victims to its own website, found to be full of bugs, Equifax built a separate website—which some say resembled a phishing operation. Before victims could find out whether their personal information was compromised, they were asked to submit their last name and the last six digits of their Social Security number. Next, the victim was asked to enroll in the company's TrustedID Premier Service and, as part of the enrollment, to agree to relinquish the right to participate in a class action lawsuit against the company.[31]

Job Description

Corporate Communications Specialist

Overview A corporate communications specialist is responsible for coordinating and developing new and innovative content for a company's internal and external communications. The role of a corporate communications specialist is to project a positive image about the organization. Sometimes the role is referred to as a public relations specialist.

Responsibilities Corporate communications specialists usually work with management to determine strategies for marketing and publicity purposes that reflect company goals. Communication can be in the form of videos, social media posts, press releases, case studies, white papers, newsletters, corporate events, and company speaking engagements. Responsibilities can also include creating company literature, brochures, and electronic materials for educational and promotional purposes. E-mail marketing campaigns are launched, and website design and updates are ongoing. Maintaining relationships with media specialists is also an important part of the job. Ongoing analysis is often required to determine the effectiveness of various communication methods used by the company.

Requirements A minimum of a bachelor's degree is usually required, and prospective corporate communications specialists often have completed coursework in public relations, marketing, journalism, crisis communications, advertising strategies, public relations, or other communications fields.

Developing fresh story ideas to set the organization apart in a positive light is essential. Corporate communications specialists usually possess skills in corporate communications, media and public relations, project management, editing, and copywriting. Knowledge and use of social media are also essential in today's environment. Strong writing skills are critical; part of the job requires creation of concise, easy-to-understand content for internal and external communication. In addition, awareness of costs and budgets and the ability to manage expenses are essential to the role of a corporate communications specialist.

Outlook According to the Bureau of Labor Statistics, employment in this field is projected to grow 9% over the next 10 years due to the need for organizations to maintain and project a positive image. Organizations with large media exposure, typically *Fortune 500* firms, will continue to work closely with corporate communications specialists to develop and coordinate innovative and interesting communication strategies.

Sources: Government website, "Public Relations Specialists," *Occupational Outlook Handbook,* revised January 28, 2018, http://www.bls.gov, accessed March 29, 2018; company website, "Corporation Communications Specialist," http://www.americasjobexchange.com, accessed March 29, 2018; "Corporate Communications Specialist Job Salary," *Payscale.com,* http://www.payscale.com, accessed March 29, 2018; organization website, "Corporate Communications Specialist Job Facts," http://learn.org, accessed March 29, 2018.

Assessment Check

1. What is external communication?
2. What is the first thing a company should do when a public crisis occurs?

What's Ahead

Today's consumers expect the products they buy to be of the highest value for the price. Companies ensure this value by developing efficient systems for producing goods and services as well as maintaining high quality. The next chapter examines the ways in which businesses produce world-class goods and services, efficiently organize their production facilities, purchase what they need to produce their goods and services, and manage large inventories to maximize efficiency and reduce costs.

Chapter in Review

Summary of Learning Objectives

LEARNING OBJECTIVE 1 Discuss empowering employees.

Managers empower employees by giving them the authority and responsibility to make decisions about their work. Empowerment seeks to tap the brainpower of all workers to find improved ways of doing their jobs, better serving customers, and achieving organizational goals. Empowerment often includes linking rewards to company performance through employee stock ownership plans (ESOPs) and stock options.

Assessment Check Answers

1.1 What is empowerment? Empowerment comes from giving employees authority and responsibility to make decisions about their work.

1.2 How can managers empower employees? Managers empower employees by sharing company information and decision-making authority and by rewarding them for their performance as well as the company's.

1.3 How do employee stock ownership plans and stock options reward employees and encourage empowerment? Employee stock ownership plans (ESOPs) benefit employees by giving them ownership stakes in their companies. Employees are motivated to work harder and smarter than they would without ESOPs because they share in their company's financial success. In contrast to an ESOP, in which the company holds stock for the benefit of employees (when employees leave the company, they cash in their stock), stock options give employees a chance to own the stock themselves if they exercise their options by completing the stock purchase.

LEARNING OBJECTIVE 2 Distinguish the five types of teams.

The five basic types of teams are work teams, problem-solving teams, self-managed teams, cross-functional teams, and virtual teams. Work teams are permanent groups of co-workers who perform the day-to-day tasks necessary to operate the organization. Problem-solving teams are temporary groups of employees who gather to solve specific problems and then disband. Self-managed teams have the authority to make decisions about how their members complete their daily tasks. Cross-functional teams are made up of members from different units, such as production, marketing, and finance. Virtual teams are groups of geographically or organizationally dispersed co-workers who use a combination of telecommunications and information technologies to accomplish an organizational task.

Assessment Check Answers

2.1 What is a team? A team is a group of people with certain skills who are committed to a common purpose, approach, and set of performance goals.

2.2 What are the five types of teams, and how are they different? Work teams are permanent, while problem-solving teams are temporary. Unlike work teams, self-managed teams have the authority to change how they get their work done. Cross-functional teams are composed of people from different backgrounds, while virtual teams are composed of people from different locations.

LEARNING OBJECTIVE 3 Identify team characteristics.

Three important characteristics of a team are its size, team level, and team diversity. The ideal team size is about six or seven members. Team level is the average level of ability, experience, personality, or any other factor on a team. Team diversity is the variances or differences in ability, experience, personality, or any other factor on a team. Team diversity is an important consideration for teams that must complete a wide range of different tasks or particularly complex tasks. Teams pass through five stages of development: (1) Forming is an orientation period during which members get to know each other and find out the behaviors that are acceptable to the group. (2) Storming is the stage during which individual personalities emerge as members clarify their roles and expectations. (3) Norming is the stage at which differences are resolved, members accept each other, and consensus emerges about the roles of the team leader and other participants. (4) Performing is characterized by problem solving and a focus on task accomplishment. (5) Adjourning is the final stage, with a focus on wrapping up and summarizing the team's experiences and accomplishments.

Assessment Check Answers

3.1 Explain team level and team diversity. Team level is the average level of ability, experience, personality, or other factors on a team. Team diversity represents differences in ability, experience, personality, or any other factor on a team.

3.2 Explain how teams progress through the stages of team development. Teams pass through five stages of development: forming, storming, norming, performing, and adjourning.

LEARNING OBJECTIVE 4 Evaluate team cohesiveness and norms.

Team cohesiveness is the extent to which team members feel attracted to the team and motivated to remain on it. Team norms are standards of conduct shared by team members that guide their behavior. Highly cohesive teams whose members share certain standards of conduct tend to be more productive and effective.

Assessment Check Answers

4.1 How does cohesiveness affect teams? Members of cohesive teams interact more often, share common attitudes and goals, have higher morale, and are more likely to help each other. Cohesive teams also perform better.

4.2 What is a team norm? A team norm is a standard of conduct shared by team members that guides their behavior. Norms are informal standards that identify key values and clarify team members' expectations.

LEARNING OBJECTIVE 5 Describe team conflict.

Conflict and disagreement are inevitable in most teams. Conflict can stem from many sources: disagreements about goals and priorities, task-related issues, interpersonal incompatibilities, scarce resources, and simple fatigue. The key to dealing with team conflict is not avoiding it but making sure that the team experiences the right kind of conflict. Cognitive conflict focuses on problem-related differences of opinion and, when reconciled, strongly improves team performance. By contrast, affective conflict refers to the emotional reactions that can occur when disagreements become personal rather than professional, and these differences strongly decrease team performance. A team leader can manage team conflict by fostering good communication so team members perceive each other accurately, understand what is expected of them, and obtain the information they need.

Assessment Check Answers

5.1 What is cognitive conflict, and how does it affect teams? In cognitive conflict, team members disagree because their different experiences and expertise lead them to different views of the problem and its solutions. Cognitive conflict is characterized by a willingness to examine, compare, and reconcile differences to produce the best possible solution.

5.2 Explain affective conflict and its impact on teams. Affective conflict refers to the emotional reactions that can occur when disagreements become personal rather than professional. These differences strongly decrease team performance.

LEARNING OBJECTIVE 6 Explain the importance of effective communication.

Managers spend about 80% of their time in direct communication with others. Company recruiters consistently rate effective communication—such as listening, conversing, and giving feedback—as the most important skill they look for when hiring new employees. The communication process follows a step-by-step process that involves interactions among six elements: sender, message, channel, audience, feedback, and context. The sender composes the message and sends it through the channel. The audience receives the message and interprets its meaning. The receiver gives feedback to the sender. The communication takes place in a situational or cultural context.

Assessment Check Answers

6.1 What is the difference between communication in low-context and high-context cultures? Communication in low-context cultures tends to rely on explicit written and verbal messages. By contrast, communication in high-context cultures depends not only on the message itself but also on the conditions that surround it, including nonverbal cues, past and present experiences, and personal relationships among the parties.

6.2 In the context of the communication process, what is noise? Noise is some type of interference that influences the transmission of messages and feedback. It can result from physical factors such as poor reception of a cell phone message or from differences in people's attitudes and perceptions.

LEARNING OBJECTIVE 7 Compare the basic forms of communication.

People exchange messages in many ways: oral and written, formal and informal, verbal and nonverbal communication. Effective written communication reflects its audience, its channel, and the appropriate degree of formality. Formal communication channels carry messages within the chain of command. Informal communication channels, such as the grapevine, carry messages outside the formal chain of command. Nonverbal communication plays a larger role than most people realize. Generally, when verbal and nonverbal cues conflict, the receiver of a message tends to believe the meaning conveyed by nonverbal cues.

Assessment Check Answers

7.1 Define the four common listening behaviors. Cynical listening occurs when the receiver of a message feels that the sender is trying to gain some advantage from the communication. Offensive listening occurs when the receiver tries to catch the speaker in a mistake or contradiction. Polite listening occurs when the receiver is rehearsing what he or she wants to say when the speaker finishes. Active listening requires involvement with the information and empathy with the speaker's situation.

7.2 What are the differences between formal and informal communication? Formal communication occurs within the formal chain of command defined by an organization. Informal communication occurs outside formally authorized channels within an organization's hierarchy.

LEARNING OBJECTIVE 8 Explain external communication and crisis management.

External communication is a meaningful exchange of information through messages transmitted between an organization and its major audiences, such as customers, suppliers, other companies, the general public, and government officials. Every communication with customers should create goodwill and contribute to customer satisfaction. However, all of this is threatened when companies experience a public crisis that threatens their reputations or goodwill. To manage a public crisis, businesses should respond quickly and honestly, with a member of top management present.

Assessment Check Answers

8.1 What is external communication? External communication is a meaningful exchange of information through messages transmitted between an organization and its major audiences.

8.2 What is the first thing a company should do when a public crisis occurs? The company should respond quickly by preparing a written statement that includes the time, place, description of the event, and the number and status of people involved.

Business Terms You Need to Know

empowerment 228
team 231
work team 231
problem-solving team 231
self-managed team 232
cross-functional team 232
virtual team 232
team level 234
team diversity 234
team cohesiveness 236
team norm 236
conflict 236
cognitive conflict 237
affective conflict 237
communication 238
listening 240
grapevine 242
external communication 244

Review Questions

1. How do companies benefit from empowering their employees? How do employees benefit from empowerment?

2. How might a company that manufactures shoes use teams to determine ways to improve its environmental standards in terms of

products and processes? What type (or types) of teams would be best for this initiative? Why?

3. How do team level and team diversity affect team performance?

4. What are the characteristics of an effective team? Why are these features so significant?

5. At what stages of development might a team *not* be able to move forward? How might a team leader or manager resolve the situation?

6. Describe the norms associated with your business class. How do these norms influence the way students behave in class?

7. What steps can managers take to resolve team conflict?

8. In what ways is context a powerful influence on the effectiveness of communication? Describe an instance in which situational or cultural context has influenced one of your communication processes.

9. What are the benefits and drawbacks of oral and written communication?

10. What is the role of external communication? Why is it so important to companies?

Projects and Teamwork Applications

1. Find a classmate or friend who is on a team—sports, speech and debate, math, or any other type of team. Go through the five stages of team development that teams typically progress through—forming, storming, norming, performing, and adjourning—and provide specific examples and occurrences at each stage.

2. Is teamwork more important than skill? In pairs or in groups, discuss the importance of an organizational culture that includes teamwork and collaboration over an organization that lacks such traits. Using sports as an analogy, why is it that a team with weaker players but stronger cohesiveness and collaboration can, at times beat a team with stronger, more-skilled players? If you had to choose, would you select the team with stronger collaboration or the one with more skilled players? Discuss your reasoning.

3. Try this listening exercise with a partner. First, spend a few minutes writing a paragraph or two about the most important thing that happened to you this week. Second, read your paragraph out loud to your partner. Next, have your partner read his or her paragraph. Finally, take turns summarizing the most important points in one another's stories. How well did you listen to one another? How much did you each remember?

4. On your own or with a classmate, visit the college library, a mall, or anywhere else on or off campus where people gather. For about 10 or 15 minutes, observe the nonverbal cues that people give each other: Does the librarian smile at students? What is the body language of students gathered in groups? When you leave the venue, jot down and make a list of as many of your observations as you can. Notice things such as changes in nonverbal communication when someone joins a group or leaves it.

5. Every day we hear news about companies in crisis. Either online or through media reports, find and research a recent event and how the company used external communication to address the crisis. Review the communication steps outlined in the chapter and discuss the effectiveness of how the company did or did not follow these steps.

Web Assignments

1. **Team-building exercises.** The website Team-Building-Bonanza.com calls itself "the motherlode of corporate team building ideas." You are asked select a team-building exercise to help resolve conflicts. What are some of the suggested activities?
http://www.team-building-bonanza.com

2. **Apologizing can be difficult, but it certainly can help when resolving conflicts.** In a business setting, there can be strategic reasons for extending an apology. If you've made a mistake that you regret, and an apology is in order, consider the website listed on the next page. Think back to the last time you offended someone or realized you needed to take responsibility for your actions. After reviewing the site below, how might you make that apology? Discuss.
http://www.perfectapology.com

3. **Teamwork at Whole Foods.** Go to the Whole Foods website and learn more about the importance of teams and teamwork on the "Company Mission and Values" page. Along with additional research, if necessary, discuss the importance the company places on collaboration and teamwork.
http://www.wholefoodsmarket.com

Note: Internet web addresses change frequently. If you don't find the exact sites listed, you may need to access the organization's home page and search from there or use a search engine such as Google or Bing.

Cases

Case 9.1 Teamwork Key to Ritz-Carlton's Success

The Ritz-Carlton Hotel Company is known for its 91 luxury resorts in 30 countries—and 40,000 employees whose top mission is the genuine care and comfort of its guests. The Ritz-Carlton philosophy embodies teamwork, which it strongly believes has a profound impact on productivity and employee engagement.

The Ritz-Carlton Leadership Center is an organization that offers courses to business professionals outside the company who wish to learn more about and benchmark how Ritz-Carlton provides its award-winning service levels to guests globally. The center also teaches seminars about the company's effective strategies for employee empowerment and teamwork.

When it comes to holding meetings, Ritz-Carlton expects each meeting to include agenda items, promote efficiency, and detail clear accountability and responsibility for specific issues. Respecting time is of paramount importance, and meetings should start and end on time. "Do not place additional stress on your colleagues' day by making them late for their next engagement" is the norm at Ritz-Carlton. Active listening is also encouraged, and the company asks that all employees respect the ideas of colleagues by listening carefully. Rather than simply waiting for colleagues to stop talking, digest what is being said to ensure the greatest amount of success.

Daily briefings are conducted at the beginning of each work shift to communicate company values and announcements pertinent to operations. Most important, the company encourages a philosophy of giving one another the benefit of the doubt. "Praise in public, coach in private" refers to a company principle of discussing mistakes in private rather than in a group forum or an e-mail. At the Ritz-Carlton, kindness—rather than criticism—is an important part of the company's philosophy when it comes to teamwork and providing exceptional service to its guests. And who knows—kindness can increase that feeling of luxury during a stay at the world-famous Ritz-Carlton Hotel.

Questions for Critical Thinking

1. Does the Ritz-Carlton work environment sound like the type of place you would like to work? Why or why not?
2. In an environment that acknowledges mistakes and encourages open communication, discuss the types of risks a team member might take to accommodate a guest.

Sources: Micah Solomon, "Customer Service Best Practices: The Ritz-Carlton's Powerful System for Making Sure They Spread," *Forbes*, http://www.forbes.com, accessed March 29, 2018; company website, "DO's and DON'Ts for Excellent Teamwork," http://ritzcarltonleadershipcenter.com, accessed March 29, 2018; company website, "Gold Standard" and "Fact Sheet," http://www.ritzcarlton.com, accessed March 29, 2018.

Case 9.2 Yelp's Open Office Encourages Collaboration

You might not immediately associate transparency and communication with the look or layout of a company's workspace. At Yelp, a company that publishes crowdsourced reviews about local businesses, an open workspace is as much a part of its floor design as its culture. Designed to improve communication and encourage a culture of openness, Yelp's futuristic-looking open space office is intended to facilitate new ways for employees to collaborate, innovate, and share knowledge.

Growing in popularity over the last decade, an open office space was the look for a typical start-up—and a cost-effective way of cramming more people into an open space equipped with benches and desks. Now a relic of the past, a corner office, even for Yelp's co-founder and CEO, doesn't exist. There are no private offices at Yelp.

Although some see the open floor plan as the new look, not everyone has embraced it warmly. In fact, there has been some backlash as some companies migrate to an open office plan. Even with the best noise-canceling headphones, some find the environment and culture "polluting"—noisy, distracting, and a negative for employee morale. An open workspace makes it difficult to concentrate, and at times, instead of communicating, co-workers might have a tendency to ignore one another in order to get their work done.

To deal with the backlash and for some, a need for privacy, Yelp has compromised between open and closed offices by adding additional private spaces. Yelp realizes different groups have different communication needs and expectations, and many may need additional quiet space. The private spaces consist of conference rooms, phone booth rooms, and "chill-out" rooms. To maintain its culture of communication, openness, and transparency, Yelp has adjusted its open office space with the right amount of small spaces, which just might earn the company its own five-star review.

Questions for Critical Thinking

1. Discuss how the same openness that can increase innovation, collaboration, and knowledge sharing in an open office environment can also undermine it.
2. Approximately 70% of U.S. companies have open space offices. However, they're not for everyone. Discuss how a company might confront the challenge of hiring someone who previously had a private office in another firm.

Sources: Ariel Schwartz, "Is the Open-Office Trend Reversing Itself?" *FastCo Exist*, http://www.fastcoexist.com, accessed March 29, 2018; Lindsey Kaufman, "Google Got It Wrong. The Open-Office Trend Is Destroying the Workplace," *Washington Post*, https://www.washingtonpost.com, accessed March 29, 2018; Ethan Bernstein, "The Smart Way to Create a Transparent Workplace," *Wall Street Journal*, http://www.wsj.com, accessed March 29, 2018.

Case 9.3 Necco Empowers and Engages Employees

If you've ever received a box of candy hearts imprinted with cute sayings for Valentine's Day, you know about the New England Confectionery Company, or Necco for short. Behind the scenes of the 150-year tradition of "Conversation Hearts" is a collaborative and empowered group of 500 employees who work in teams at Necco's headquarters in Revere, Massachusetts.

Facilitating change at the oldest candy-making company in the United States is no easy feat. A company executive with the title of lean champion works tirelessly to engage and empower the workforce, build awareness, and capture energy and passion among employees. In addition, the lean champion tries to find the root cause of wasteful activities and to eliminate anything that does not add value to the company's products. Eliminating waste, whether it be materials, supplies, or production processes, is Necco's overall goal. For example, once the circles used to make Necco wafers are printed, the remaining dough is automatically reused and sent through the machine to produce more product.

In addition to reducing waste, part of the company's initiative is to add value. This includes determining employee training needs, identifying tools to do jobs more efficiently, and working collaboratively to determine strategies for improvement. Necco has reduced scrap and reworks, which has resulted in improved quality and production lead times. However, none of this can be accomplished without Necco employees, who are all members of the company's various teams.

Necco's lean initiative, pervasive throughout its culture of expansion, rebuilding, and improvement, is practiced from the top down. One recent change was the decision to discontinue its all-natural wafers. In a move to meet consumer demand, Necco decided to produce its centuries-old wafer as all natural, substituting corn syrup for sugar and using beet juice and purple cabbage in place of colorings and sweeteners. Customers were not happy with the change, and management made the decision to revert back to the original ingredients, which resulted in a sales rebound of 20%. In addition, to appeal to the next generation of candy lovers, the Sweetheart candies were introduced in new, trendier flavors. These steps are part of Necco's long-term vision for innovation, new products, and new markets.

Integral to the growth and transformation of Necco's products is employee engagement. The company solicits input from employees, all of whom are considered "experts" in their respective work areas. When employees know there is someone within the organization to champion their efforts, they want to come to work, and the more support they have, the more they do for the company. For improvement to occur, Necco's leadership team not only talks the talk but walks the walk. Goals and values, referred to as key performance indicators or KPIs, are developed by top management and supported at every level of the company.

Rewards are linked to both company and department performance. When goals are met, manufacturing workers on a single production line are given monetary incentives. Within the wafers team—the company's largest—various departments work together, including sales, marketing, production, and engineering. In addition to each product team, Necco assembles cross-functional teams to problem solve and improve processes. Staying involved in all phases of the business keeps employees engaged, knowledgeable, and interested.

Necco's focus on product quality requires teamwork and collaboration, and it doesn't end after the candy is produced. Teams in sales, packaging, distribution, and shipping play an integral role in managing everything from the purchase of raw materials to product delivery. The company's improvement plan is fueled by the trust and cohesiveness among team members in each of Necco's units.

Necco's recipe for empowerment includes the key ingredients of knowledge and education for employees to perform their jobs effectively. If things don't go as planned, employees have the authority to stop the process to make the proper adjustments. Necco's open-door policy encourages employees at all levels to meet and speak with others throughout the organization, regardless of rank or hierarchy.

At Necco, continuing to woo the next generation of customers requires knowledge, support, engagement, and collaboration among its employees and work teams. With its focus on innovation, product development, and employee empowerment, Necco hopes for many more conversations with its "Conversation Hearts."

Questions for Critical Thinking

1. Give three specific reasons why empowerment is key to Necco's success. Provide examples of how Necco empowers its employees.
2. Select the concept of a problem-solving team or a self-managed team. How might this team function at Necco? Who might be on the team, and what role might the team have in the running of the company?
3. Give an example of a situation in which informal communication would work well among Necco employees—either on the production floor or among its top leadership team.
4. Describe the five stages of team development, and provide an example of what each stage might look like at Necco.

Sources: Company website, http://necco.com, accessed March 29, 2018; Seth Daniel, "Attraction to Necco Much Sweeter This Year," *Revere Journal*, http://www.reverejournal.com, accessed March 29, 2018; "Candy Company Necco Offers Custom #Tweethearts for Valentine's Day," *ClickZ*, http://www.clickz.com, accessed March 29, 2018; Jonathan Berr, "Necco's Iconic Sweethearts Show Their Sassy Side," *CBS News*, http://www.cbsnews.com, accessed March 29, 2018; Claire Suddath, "How Do They Get Those Tiny Words on Sweethearts Candy?" *Time*, http://content.time.com, accessed March 29, 2018; Associated Press, "Necco Wafers Scrapping Artificial Additives," *Daily Beast*, http://www.thedailybeast.com, accessed March 29, 2018.

CHAPTER 10

Production and Operations Management

LEARNING OBJECTIVES

1. Explain the strategic importance of production.
2. Identify and describe the production processes.
3. Explain the role of technology in the production process.
4. Identify the factors involved in a location decision.
5. Explain the job of production managers.
6. Discuss controlling the production process.
7. Determine the importance of quality.

Changemaker

Kiyoshi Ota/Bloomberg via Getty Images

Elon Musk, Founder, CEO & CTO, SpaceX

Cofounder and CEO, Tesla Motors

Companies: Tesla Motors/SpaceX

Industry: Automotive Manufacturing/Airlines and Aerospace

Websites: http://www.teslamotors.com and http://www.spacex.com

South African–born serial entrepreneur Elon Musk is on a very short list of CEOs who run multiple corporations. Musk is cofounder, CEO, and product architect of Tesla Motors, the first company to build an electric sports car. In addition, he is founder, CEO, and chief technology officer of SpaceX, which develops and manufactures launch vehicles. It doesn't end there. He is a co-founder of Solar City, a solar power systems company, and co-founder of electronic payments company, PayPal. Musk arrived in the United States over 25 years ago as an immigrant, and he is one of the greatest examples of an innovator who revolutionized three different manufacturing-intensive industries: automobile, aerospace, and solar.

Tesla Motors is a technology, design, and automobile manufacturing company. Many of the topics covered in this chapter are the very ones Musk and his skilled production teams confront on a daily basis. Tesla Motors creates form utility by converting raw materials (aluminum) and combining thousands of inputs (parts) into a finished product—an electric car. As the company grows, the following decisions must be made on an ongoing basis: plant location, production layout, use of technology, ensuring high quality, and choosing suppliers for the 2,000 parts in each car. The company is also in the process of building an electric big rig truck and a high-speed underground rail system.

Tesla Motors utilizes customer-driven production systems. Because each vehicle is made to order, delivering customized cars to consumers on time is crucial. There is often a two- to three-month wait time for delivery and recently, there have been delays due to production issues. Although a car takes less than a week to make, to save on costs and to lessen potential damage Musk insists on delivery by train rather than by truck, which extends delivery times. Musk's entrepreneurial drive and his attention to production and operations detail have propelled him into a mainstream automobile industry player from a niche luxury-car company. [1]

Overview

By producing and marketing the goods and services that consumers want, businesses satisfy their commitment to society as a whole. They create what economists call *utility*—the want-satisfying power of a good or service. Businesses can create or enhance four basic kinds of utility: time, place, ownership, and form. A company's marketing operation generates time, place, and ownership utility by offering products to customers at a time and place that is convenient for purchase.

Production creates form utility by converting raw materials and other inputs into finished products, such as Tesla's electric cars. Production uses resources, including workers and machinery, to convert materials into finished goods and services. This conversion process may result in major changes in raw materials or simply combine already finished parts into new products. The task of production and operations management in a company is to oversee the production process by managing people and machinery (and even robots with artificial intelligence) in converting materials and resources into finished goods and services, which is illustrated by **Figure 10.1**.

People sometimes use the terms *production* and *manufacturing* interchangeably, but the two are actuallyt different. Production spans both manufacturing and nonmanufacturing industries. For instance, companies that engage in fishing or mining engage in production, as do firms that provide package deliveries or lodging. **Figure 10.2** lists five examples of production systems for a variety of goods and services.

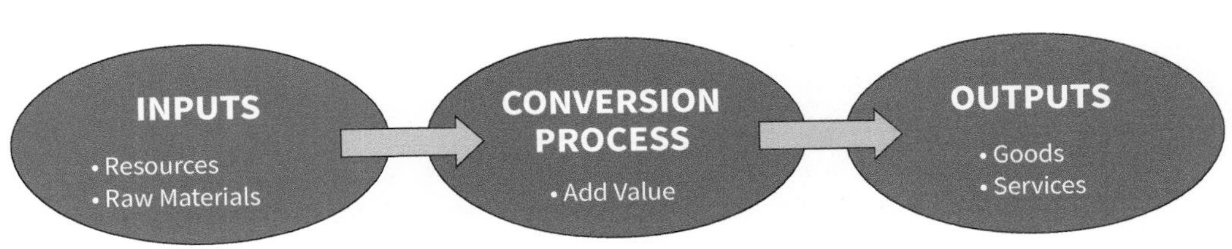

FIGURE 10.1 The Production Process: Converting Inputs to Outputs

FIGURE 10.2 Typical Production Systems

Example	Primary Inputs	Transformation	Outputs
Computer Factory	Hard drives, computer memory, computer chips, keyboards, cases, power supply, central circuit board, boards for network and Internet access and graphics, monitors, andsoftware	Assembles components to meet customer orders, including specialized orders for hardware and software	Desktop or laptop computers
Trucking Firm	Trucks, personnel, buildings, fuel, goods to be shipped, packaging supplies, truck parts, utilities	Packages and transports goods from sources to destinations	Delivered goods
Retail Store	Buildings, displays, scanners, merchandise, employees, suppliers, supplies, utilities	Attracts customers, stores goods, sells products	Merchandise sold
Automobile Body Shop	Damaged autos, paints, supplies, machines, tools, buildings, employees, utilities	Transforms damaged auto bodies into facsimiles of the originals	Repaired automobile bodies
County Sheriff's Department	Staff, police equipment, automobiles, office furniture, buildings, utilities	Detects crimes and brings criminals to justice	Reduces crime and creates safer communities

Whether the production process results in a tangible good such as a car or an intangible service such as a Netflix or Hulu subscription, it always converts inputs into outputs. A cabinetmaker combines wood, tools, and skill to create finished kitchen cabinets for a new home. A transit system combines buses, trains, and employees to create its output: passenger transportation. Both of these production processes create utility.

This chapter describes the process of producing goods and services. It looks at the importance of production and operations management and discusses the new technologies that are transforming the production function. It then discusses the tasks of the production and operations manager, the importance of quality, and the methods businesses use to ensure high quality.

1 The Strategic Importance of Production

production use of resources, such as workers and machinery, to convert materials into finished goods and services.

production and operations management oversee the production process by managing people and machinery in converting materials and resources into finished goods and services.

Along with marketing and finance, **production** is a vital business activity. Without products to sell, companies cannot generate money to pay their employees, lenders, and stockholders. And without the profits from products, companies quickly fail. The production process is just as crucial in nonprofit organizations such as Habitat for Humanity or Goodwill Industries because the goods or services they offer justify their existence. Effective **production and operations management** can lower a company's costs of production, boost the quality of its goods and services, allow it to respond dependably to customer demands, and enable it to grow while creating new value for customers by providing new products. Let's look at the differences among mass, flexible, and customer-driven production.

Mass Production

mass production a system for manufacturing products in large quantities through effective combinations of employees, with specialized skills, mechanization, and standardization.

From its beginnings as a colonial supplier of raw materials to Europe, the United States has evolved into an industrial giant. Much of this change has resulted from **mass production**, a system for manufacturing products in large quantities through effective combinations of employees with specialized skills, mechanization, and standardization. Mass production makes outputs (goods and services) available in large quantities at lower prices than individually crafted items would cost. Mass production brought cars, computers, televisions, books, and even homes to the majority of the population. After returning from World War II, William Levitt saw the need for affordable housing for veterans. In his first planned development named Levittown, near Long Island, New York, Levitt used an assembly-line construction method organized into 27 operations with teams of specialized workers to complete each operation at each construction site.[2]

Mass production begins with the specialization of labor, dividing work into its simplest components so that each worker can concentrate on performing a single task. By separating jobs into small tasks, managers create conditions for high productivity through mechanization, in which machines perform much of the work previously done by people. Standardization, the third element of mass production, involves producing uniform, interchangeable goods and parts. Standardized parts simplify the replacement of defective or worn-out components. For instance, if your room's light bulb burns out, you can easily buy a replacement at a local hardware store or supermarket.

A logical extension of these principles of specialization, mechanization, and standardization led to development of the *assembly line*. This manufacturing method moves the product along a conveyor belt past a number of workstations, where workers perform specialized tasks such as welding, painting, installing individual parts, and tightening bolts. Henry Ford's application of this concept revolutionized auto assembly. Before the assembly line, it took Ford's workers 12 hours to assemble a Model T car, but with an assembly line, it took just 1.5 hours to make the same car. Not surprisingly, many other industries soon adopted the assembly-line process.

Although mass production has important advantages, it has limitations, too. While mass production is highly efficient for producing large numbers of similar products, it is highly inefficient when producing small batches of different items. This trade-off might cause some companies to focus on efficient production methods rather than on making what customers really want. In addition, the labor specialization associated with mass production can lead to boring jobs, because workers keep repeating the same task. To improve their competitive capabilities, many companies adopt flexible production and customer-driven production systems. These methods won't replace mass production in every case, but in many instances might lead to improved product quality and greater job satisfaction. It might also enhance the use of mass production.

Courtesy of Honda

Honda's East Liberty, Ohio plant uses flexible manufacturing to build both the Acura RDX and MDX (owned by Honda). The plant's 200,000-square-foot welding shop was recently expanded and 200 new robots were added.

Flexible Production

While mass production is effective for creating large quantities of a single item, *flexible production*, which allows manufacturing equipment to be used for more than one purpose, is usually more cost-effective for producing smaller runs. Flexible production can take many forms, but it generally involves using information technology to share the details of customer orders, technology (sometimes robots) to fulfill the orders, and skilled people to carry out whatever tasks are needed to fill a particular order. This system is even more beneficial when combined with lean production methods that use automation and information technology to reduce requirements for workers and inventory. Flexible production requires a lot of communication among everyone in the organization.

Flexible production is now widely used in the auto industry. While Henry Ford revolutionized auto production in the early 20th century, automakers such as Toyota and Honda are innovating with new methods of production. Changing from mass production to flexible production has enabled these companies to produce different kinds of cars at the same plant. Honda's flexible manufacturing plant in East Liberty, Ohio (seen in photo), builds cars and light trucks on the same assembly line. The facility accomplishes this through team-based operations, relying on the expertise and knowledge of individual workers to innovate and improve manufacturing processes.[3]

Customer-Driven Production

A *customer-driven* production system evaluates customer demands in order to make the connection between products manufactured and products bought. Many companies use this approach with great success. One method is to establish information systems between production facilities and retailers using sales data as the basis for creating short-term forecasts and production schedule designs to meet those forecasts. Another approach to customer-driven production systems is simply to make the product only when a customer orders it—whether it's a taco or a tablet. Samsung, an example of a customer-driven company, studies and understands its customers and markets, and then designs and markets its products to fit. As an alternative to a more costly Apple iPhone, the company developed a less expensive product for customers in search of a more affordable alternative to the Apple iPhone.[4]

Assessment Check

1. What is mass production?
2. What is the difference between flexible production and customer-driven production?

2 Production Processes

Not surprisingly, the production processes and time required to make an Apple iPad and a gallon of gasoline are different. Production processes use either an analytic or synthetic system; time requirements call for either a continuous or an intermittent process.

An analytic production system reduces a raw material to its component parts in order to extract one or more marketable products. Petroleum refining breaks down crude oil into several marketable products, including gasoline, heating oil, and aviation fuel. When corn is processed, the resulting marketable food products include animal feed and corn sweetener.

A synthetic production system is the reverse of an analytic system. It combines a number of raw materials or parts or transforms raw materials to produce finished products. Canon's assembly line produces a camera by assembling various parts such as a shutter or a lens cap. Other synthetic production systems make prescription drugs, chemicals, computer chips, and canned soup.

A continuous production process generates finished products over a lengthy period of time. The steel industry provides a classic example. Its blast furnaces never completely shut down except for malfunctions. Petroleum refineries, chemical plants, and nuclear power facilities also practice continuous production. A shutdown can damage sensitive equipment, with extremely costly results.

An intermittent production process generates products in short production runs, shutting down machines frequently or changing their configurations to produce different products. Most services result from intermittent production systems. For example, accountants, plumbers, and dentists traditionally have not attempted to standardize their services because each service provider confronts different problems that require individual approaches. However, some companies, such as Jiffy Lube and H&R Block, offer standardized services as part of a strategy to operate more efficiently and compete with lower prices. McDonald's, well-known for its nearly continuous production of food, has moved toward a more intermittent production model. The fast-food chain invested millions in new cooking equipment to set up kitchens for preparing sandwiches quickly to order, rather than producing large batches ahead of time and keeping them warm under heat lamps. McDonald's recently announced that Quarter Pounders and Signature Crafted Recipe burgers would be made with 100% fresh beef patties at all U.S. locations. This is the most significant change in the McDonald's operation since all-day breakfast was announced in 2015.[5]

Assessment Check

1. What are the two main production systems?
2. What are the two time-related production processes?

3 Technology and the Production Process

Technological advances continue to change the production process. Some manufacturing plants are now "lights out" facilities that are completely automated—meaning no workers are required to build or make the products. While this signals a change in the types of jobs available in manufacturing, it also means that companies can design, produce, and adapt products more quickly to meet customers' changing needs. Until recently, only tasks that human eyes, hands, and minds could handle are now being performed with robots enabled with artificial intelligence. By some measures, this is part of what some are calling The Fourth Industrial Revolution.

Green Manufacturing Processes

More and more companies are investing in the development of manufacturing processes that result in a reduction of waste, energy use, and pollution. Companies ranging in size from

Walmart to the local café are finding ways to operate in a more sustainable manner. Whether it is using a fleet of electric delivery trucks or eliminating unnecessary packaging, companies have begun to view the steps they take with pride. Retailer Gap recently announced improved efficiency in its manufacturing practices. In addition, the company has set a goal of saving up to 2.6 billion gallons of water to address the issue of global water scarcity. Along with the opportunity to reduce water usage to create its products, the company recognizes its responsibility to reduce water consumption in its manufacturing process.[6] IKEA, a company that sources massive amounts of wood to make its furniture, is doing its part to make sure forests are managed responsibly. See the "Clean & Green" feature for details.

Companies that are involved in construction—or are thinking of building new offices or manufacturing plants—are turning their attention to **LEED (Leadership in Energy and Environmental Design)** certification for their facilities. LEED is a voluntary certification program administered by the U.S. Green Building Council, aimed at promoting the most sustainable construction processes available. The LEED certification process is rigorous and involves meeting standards in energy savings, water efficiency, CO_2 emissions reduction, improved indoor environmental quality (including air and natural light), and other categories.[7]

LEED (Leadership in Energy and Environmental Design) voluntary certification program administered by the U.S. Green Building Council, aimed at promoting the most sustainable construction processes available.

Robots

A growing number of manufacturers have freed workers from boring, sometimes dangerous jobs by replacing them with robots. A *robot* is a reprogrammable machine capable of performing a variety of tasks that require the repeated manipulation of materials and tools. Robots are capable of frequent and repetitive tasks with precision. Many manufacturing and production environments use robots for welding, painting, assembly, product inspection, testing, stacking products on pallets, and shrink-wrapping for shipping. In industries including steel, automobiles, food processing, consumer goods, aerospace, and mining, approximately 1.7 million industrial robots are expected to appear on factory floors in an upcoming year. Beyond human ability, companies are realizing the precision, productivity, and flexibility that robots deliver. Collaborative robots

Clean & Green Business

IKEA Is "Forest Positive"

IKEA, the multinational Swedish company that makes ready-to-assemble furniture, uses about 1% of all commercially harvested wood in the world to create its products, packaging, and printed materials. Although you might not think about how the wood was sourced as you're assembling a new IKEA table, the company is committed to sustainable forestry techniques, which translates to not taking anything from the world's precious rainforests. IKEA's "forest positive" commitment promotes the adoption of more sustainable forestry methods across an entire industry—and not just in the forests used to make its products. IKEA is also working to end deforestation and illegal logging practices around the world.

In a partnership with the World Wildlife Federation, IKEA has set a goal of 100% recycled wood in its supply chain or wood that has been certified by the Forest Stewardship Council (FSC) within five years. So far about 50% of the wood it uses meets either criterion. FSC is a nonprofit group that promotes responsible forestry. IKEA currently works with 21 foresters to increase the amount of certified wood in its supply chain and to ensure that all wood purchased is in compliance with its own forestry standards. In total, through its partnership projects, IKEA will contribute to the FSC certification of 4.5 *billion* acres of forest. The next time you sit down at your IKEA table, you can feel good about the company's "forest positive" approach.

Questions for Critical Thinking

1. IKEA continually looks for ways to get the most out of the wood it uses by designing products that minimize the amount of wood needed while increasing manufacturing efficiencies. What do you think this means, and what are some examples of this?
2. IKEA's suppliers must comply with the company's forestry standard to ensure that wood has not been grown or harvested in a way that harms the environment. How can this practice be applied to other industries that source heavy volumes of natural resources?

Sources: Company website, "Energy and Resources" and "IKEA Group Sustainability Report 2017," http://www.ikea.com, accessed April 1, 2018; organization website, "IKEA Sustainability Report," http://www.wwf.se, accessed April 1, 2018; Susie Olson, "10 Companies with Eco-Conscious Production Processes," *Financial Spots,* http://financialspots.com, accessed April 1, 2018; organization website, "WWF & IKEA Partnership," http://wwf.panda.org, accessed April 1, 2018; Saabira Chaudhuri, "IKEA Gets Deeper Into the Woods," *Wall Street Journal,* http://www.wsj.com, accessed April 1, 2018; organization website, Martha Stevenson and Kerry Cesareo, "Creating a Forest Positive Culture," https://www.worldwildlife.org, accessed April 1, 2018.

Baranozdemir/iStockphoto

Robots are used in manufacturing as well as in many other fields. In auto manufacturing, robots can be perform a variety of tasks that have freed workers from monotonous and sometimes dangerous jobs.

are those working alongside humans, and they too will boost productivity and efficiency even further. While robots have replaced jobs of low-skilled workers in the past, there is a looming threat that with the growing "intelligence" of robots, half of the white collar jobs in the next 20 years could be wiped out by work performed with the help of artificial intelligence, algorithms, and automation—and all at a lower cost. With the help of sensors and data that can be shared with AI and analytics software, increased output, defect detection, and corrective action is far faster and the entire production cycle is far more efficient.[8] Companies operate many different types of robots, depending on their application and use. Different robot types include industrial, domestic or household, medical, service, military, space exploration, and transportation. (The photo offers an example of a manufacturing robot.) The simplest kind, a pick-and-place robot, moves in only two or three directions as it picks up something from one spot and places it in another. So-called field robots assist people in nonmanufacturing, often hazardous, environments such as nuclear power plants, the international space station, and even military battlefields. Police use robots to remotely dispose of suspected bombs. However, the same technology can be used in factories. Using vision systems, infrared sensors, and bumpers on mobile platforms, robots can automatically move parts or finished goods from one place to another, while either following or avoiding people, whichever is necessary to do the job. For instance, machine vision systems are being used more frequently for complex applications such as quality assurance in the manufacturing of medical devices. The advancements in machine vision components such as cameras, illumination systems, and processors have greatly improved their capabilities. Companies such as Texas-based National Instruments help customers around the world boost productivity, simplify development, and reduce time to market.[9]

Computer-Aided Design and Manufacturing

computer-aided design (CAD) process that allows engineers to design components as well as entire products on computer screens faster and with fewer mistakes than they could achieve working with traditional drafting systems.

A process called **computer-aided design (CAD)** allows engineers to design components as well as entire products on computer screens faster and with fewer mistakes than they could achieve working with traditional drafting systems. Using an electronic pen, an engineer can sketch three-dimensional (3-D) designs on an electronic drafting board or directly on the screen. The computer then provides tools to make major and minor design changes and to analyze the results for particular characteristics or problems. Engineers can put a new car design through a simulated road test to project its real-world performance. If they find a problem with weight distribution, for example, they can make the necessary changes virtually—without actually test-driving the car. With advanced CAD software, prototyping is as much "virtual" as it is "hands-on." Actual prototypes or parts aren't built until the engineers are satisfied that the required structural characteristics in their virtual designs have been met. Dentistry has benefited from CAD, which can design and create on-site such products as caps and crowns that precisely fit a patient's mouth or jaw.[10]

computer-aided manufacturing (CAM) computer tools to analyze CAD output and enable a manufacturer to analyze the steps that a machine must take to produce a needed product or part.

The process of **computer-aided manufacturing (CAM)** picks up where the CAD system leaves off. Computer tools enable a manufacturer to analyze the steps that a machine must take to produce a needed product or part. Electronic signals transmitted to processing equipment provide instructions for performing the appropriate production steps in the correct order. Both CAD and CAM technologies are now used together at most modern production facilities.

These so-called CAD/CAM systems are linked electronically to automatically transfer computerized designs into the production facilities, saving both time and effort. They also allow more precise manufacturing of parts.

Flexible Manufacturing Systems

A **flexible manufacturing system (FMS)** is a production facility that workers can quickly modify to manufacture different products. The typical system consists of computer-controlled machining centers to produce metal parts, robots to handle the parts, and remote-controlled carts to deliver materials. All components are linked by electronic controls that dictate activities at each stage of the manufacturing sequence, even automatically replacing broken or worn-out drill bits and other implements.

flexible manufacturing system (FMS) production facility that can be quickly modified to manufacture different products.

Flexible manufacturing systems have been enhanced by powerful new software that allows machine tools to be reprogrammed while they are running. This capability allows the same machine to make hundreds of different parts without the operator having to shut the machine down each time to load new programs. With updates and software, engineers can make decisions or diagnose problems from anywhere they can access a company's network. Pharmaceutical companies are using flexible manufacturing for multiproduct manufacturing because of the need for rapid deployment of products worldwide (for example, threats of serious disease outbreaks). In addition, an increasing number of products and formulations dictate the need for manufacturing flexibility. Overall, the need to reduce costs, increase capacity, and reduce the time needed to develop pharmaceuticals has increased the industry's attention toward a flexible manufacturing process.[11]

Computer-Integrated Manufacturing

Companies integrate robots, CAD/CAM, FMS, computers, and other technologies to implement **computer-integrated manufacturing (CIM)**, a production system in which computers help workers design products, control machines, handle materials, and control the production process in an integrated fashion. This type of manufacturing does not necessarily imply more automation and fewer people than other alternatives. It does, however, involve a new type of automation organized around the computer. The key to CIM is a centralized computer system running software that integrates and controls separate processes and functions. The advantages of CIM include increased productivity, decreased design costs, increased equipment utilization, and improved quality.

computer-integrated manufacturing (CIM) production system in which computers help workers design products, control machines, handle materials, and control the production function in an integrated fashion.

Vistaprint, with its online design studio, allows customers to print small quantities of business cards and promotional materials at affordable prices. The company uses computer-integrated manufacturing, common in the printing industry, to automate printing from design to delivery.[12]

Assessment Check

1. List some of the reasons businesses invest in robots.
2. What is a flexible manufacturing system (FMS)?
3. What are the major benefits of computer-integrated manufacturing (CIM)?

4 The Location Decision

The decision of where to locate a production facility hinges on the concept of time-to-market, which includes transportation, human, and physical or infrastructure factors, as shown in **Table 10.1**. Transportation factors include proximity to markets and raw materials, along with availability of alternative modes for transporting both inputs and outputs. Automobile assembly

TABLE 10.1 Factors in the Location Decision

Location Factor	Examples of Affected Businesses
Transportation	
Proximity to markets	Baking companies and manufacturers of other perishable products, dry cleaners, hotels, other services
Proximity to raw materials	Paper mills
Availability of transportation alternatives	Brick manufacturers, retail stores
Physical or Infrastructure Factors	
Water supply	Computer chip fabrication plants
Energy	Aluminum, chemical, and fertilizer manufacturers
Hazardous wastes	All businesses
Human Factors	
Labor supply	Auto manufacturers, software developers, and engineers
Local zoning regulations	Manufacturing and distribution companies
Community living conditions	All businesses
Taxes	All businesses

plants are located near major rail lines. Inputs—such as engines, plastics, and metal parts—arrive by rail, and the finished vehicles are shipped out by rail. Shopping malls are often located next to major streets and freeways in suburban areas, because most customers arrive by car. Influencedby a variety of factors, including its high-tech labor force, proximity to international ports, favorable investment environment, and solid infrastructure, a few years ago, Volvo (see photo) broke ground on a $500 million plant in Charleston, South Carolina—its first in the United States.[13]

Courtesy of Volvo North America Corporation

Volvo recently chose Charleston, South Carolina, for its first U.S. factory, where it plans to produce the S60 model. This picture shows a ground breaking ceremony, which typically occurs prior to construction.

Physical or infrastructure variables involve such issues as weather, water supplies, available energy, and options for disposing of hazardous waste. A company that wants to locate near a community must prepare an *environmental impact study* that analyzes how a proposed plant would affect the quality of life in the surrounding area. Regulatory agencies typically require these studies to cover topics such as the impact on transportation facilities, energy requirements, water and sewage treatment needs, natural plant life and wildlife, and water, air, and noise pollution. Volvo prepared an environmental impact study that estimates an initial number of 2,000 direct jobs and, long term, more than 8,000 new jobs. In addition, the plant is projected to contribute approximately $4.8 billion in total economic output on an annual basis.[14]

Human factors in the location decision include an area's labor supply, local regulations, taxes, and living conditions. Management considers local labor costs as well as the availability of workers with needed skills. Technology companies concentrate in areas with the technical talent they need, including California's Silicon Valley, Seattle, New York City, Boston, and Austin, Texas. By contrast, some labor-intensive industries have located plants in rural areas with readily available labor pools and limited high-wage alternatives. And some companies with headquarters in the United States and other industrialized countries have moved production offshore in search of low wages, although that trend may be changing, with some U.S. firms bringing jobs back home. But no matter what type of industry a company is in, a production and operations manager's facility location decision must consider the following factors:

- proximity to suppliers, warehouses, and service operations
- insurance and taxes
- availability of employee needs such as housing, hospitals and health centers, schools, mass transportation, daycare, shopping, and recreational facilities
- size, skills, and costs of the labor force
- ample space for current and future growth needs
- distance to market for goods
- receptiveness of the community

Business Model

The Motor City Bounces Back

U.S. automobile manufacturing has recently returned to its roots in Detroit, after suffering through a very slow recovery from a debilitating economic downturn and industry-wide crisis (The Great Recession) that began over a decade ago. During that time, the "Big Three" automakers—General Motors, Ford, and Chrysler—were plagued by the credit crisis, rising fuel prices, and increased competition from smaller, less expensive, fuel-efficient Japanese and European automobile makers.

Filing for bankruptcy in 2013, Detroit has recovered 40% of the jobs it lost during the Great Recession, and today the Big Three, along with a host of foreign competitors, have built factories in or near Detroit. While the auto industry dominates the Motor City as a whole, Detroit now employs more people than it did since 2008, and a variety of other manufacturing companies—like FANUC America, an industrial robot maker, online mortgage lender Quicken Loans, and Shinola, a high-end watch company—have contributed to the city's resurgence.

A few other factors have also contributed to Detroit's revitalization, including rising wages in China, an ample supply of energy, and the need to respond to customer demand by producing goods locally. In addition, Detroit boasts the second-largest number of engineers in the country, second only to Silicon Valley in California. In a little over a decade, Detroit has seen a rebound of more than 30% in industrial jobs and, in a recent year, close to a 10% expansion. Hopes of continued growth, improved job prospects, and lower unemployment levels have provided additional torque to the ever-important Motor City.

Questions for Critical Thinking

1. **Can you think of other U.S. cities that recently have experienced a recovery of sorts? If so, what have been some of the contributing factors?**
2. **Discuss how clusters of industries or types of companies can sometimes take root in certain U.S. cities. Why do you think this trend occurs? Are there examples you can cite?**

Sources: Bob Woods, "Tech and Innovation Power Detroit's Manufacturing Revival," *CNBC*, http://www.cnbc.com, accessed April 1, 2018; Joel Kotkin and Michael Shires, "The Cities Leading a U.S. Manufacturing Revival," *Forbes*, http://www.forbes.com, accessed April 1, 2018; Jonathan Berr, "Car Sales Are on a Streak We Haven't Seen in 50 Years," *Business Insider*, http://www.businessinsider.com, accessed April 1, 2018; Jeff Bennett and Chelsey Dulaney, "U.S. Auto Sales Pace Accelerates," *Wall Street Journal*, http://www.wsj.com, accessed April 1, 2018. Michael Hicks, "U.S. Manufacturing Growing, Transforming," *Advanced Manufacturing*, https://advancedmanufacturing.org, accessed April 1, 2018; Zack Guzman, "Billionaire Dan Gilbert's Mission to Rebuild Detroit as a Hub of 'Muscles and Brains'" *CNBC*, www.cnbc.com, accessed April 1, 2018.

- economical transportation for materials and supplies as well as for finished goods
- climate and environment that match the industry's needs and employees' lifestyle
- amount and cost of energy services
- government incentives.

A continuing trend in location strategy is bringing production facilities closer to the final markets where the goods will be sold. One reason for this is reduced time and cost for shipping. Another reason is a closer cultural affinity between the parent company and supplier (in cases where production remains overseas). A few years ago, companies like global snack food giant Mondelez International invested close to $200 million as part of its ongoing supply-chain growth strategy in emerging markets such as Brazil, Russia, China, and India. Recently, with the rising value of the dollar against other currencies, those markets have cooled, and so have international investments in them.[15] Not so with investments in Detroit. Improved automobile sales in the United States have contributed to the revitalization of the Motor City, where U.S. automobile manufacturing began. See the "Business Model" feature for more details.

Assessment Check

1. How does an environmental impact study influence the location decision?
2. What human factors are relevant to the location decision?

5 The Job of Production Managers

Production and operations managers oversee the work of people and technology to convert inputs (materials and resources) into finished goods and services. As **Figure 10.3** shows, these managers perform four major tasks

1. Plan the overall production process
2. Determine the best layout for the firm's facilities
3. Implement the production plan
4. Control the manufacturing process to maintain the highest possible quality

Part of the control process involves continuous evaluation of results. If problems occur, managers return to the first step and make adjustments.

Planning the Production Process

Production planning begins by choosing what goods or services to offer to customers. This decision is the essence of every company's reason for operating. Other decisions—such as

PRODUCTION MANAGEMENT TASKS

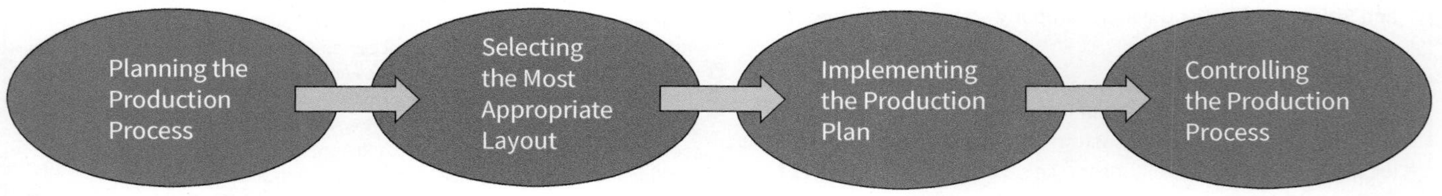

FIGURE 10.3 Tasks of Production Managers

equipment purchases, pricing decisions, and selection of retail outlets—all grow out of product planning. But with product planning, it's not enough to plan products that satisfy customers. Products must satisfy customers *and* be produced as efficiently and cost effectively as possible. So while marketing research studies determine consumer reactions to proposed products and services, and estimate potential sales and profitability levels, production departments focus on planning the production process when they (1) convert original product ideas into final specifications and (2) design the most efficient facilities to produce those products.

It is important for production managers to understand how a project fits into the company's existing framework because this will affect the success of the project. In a traditional manufacturing organization, each production manager is given a specific area of authority and responsibility such as purchasing or inventory control. One drawback to this structure is that it may actually create a divide between the purchasing manager and the inventory control manager. As more organizations have moved toward team-oriented structures, many assign team members to specific projects reporting to the production manager. Each team is responsible for the quality of its products and has the authority to make changes to improve performance and quality. The major difference between the two approaches is that all workers on teams are responsible for their output, and the competitiveness between managers often found in traditional structures is minimized with greater teamwork.

Determining the Facility Layout

The next production management task is determining the best layout for the facility. An efficient facility layout can reduce material handling, decrease costs, and improve product flow through the facility. This decision requires managers to consider all phases of production and the necessary inputs at each step. **Figure 10.4** shows three common layout designs: process, product, and fixed-position layouts. It also shows a customer-oriented layout typical of service providers' production systems.

A *process layout* groups machinery and equipment according to their functions. The work in process moves around the plant to reach different workstations. A process layout often facilitates production of a variety of nonstandard items in relatively small batches. Its purpose is to process goods and services that have a variety of functions. For instance, a typical machine shop generally has separate departments where machines are grouped by functions such as grinding, drilling, pressing, and lathing. Process layouts accommodate a variety of production functions and use general-purpose equipment that can be less costly to purchase and maintain than specialized equipment.

A *product layout*, also referred to as an assembly line, sets up production equipment along a product-flow line, and the work in process moves along this line past workstations. This type of layout efficiently produces large numbers of similar items, but it may prove inflexible and able to accommodate only a few product variations. Although product layouts date back at least to the Model T assembly line, companies are refining this approach with modern touches. Many auto manufacturers continue to use a product layout, but robots perform many of the tasks and activities once performed by humans. Automation overcomes one of the major drawbacks of this system—unlike humans, robots don't get bored doing a dull, repetitive job. However, in what some label "a rare win" for humans over robots in the battle for productivity and efficiency, Wall Street analysts have identified "over-automation" as the root of Tesla's problems and production delays of its Model 3. In recent years, the company has quadrupled the number of robots used on its production lines.[16]

A *fixed-position layout* places the product in one spot, and workers, materials, and equipment come to it. This approach suits production of very large, bulky, heavy, or fragile products. For example, a bridge cannot be built on an assembly line. Fixed-position layouts dominate several industries, including construction, shipbuilding, aircraft and aerospace, and oil drilling, to name a few. In all of these industries, the nature of the product generally dictates a fixed-position layout.

Service organizations also must decide on appropriate layouts for their production processes. A service firm should arrange its facilities to enhance the interactions between customers

FIGURE 10.4 Basic Facility Layouts

(A) Process Layout

Laundry Receiving
Labeling and Sorting
Washing and Drying
Pressing
Delivery and Invoicing
Loading
Order Assembly

(B) Product Layout

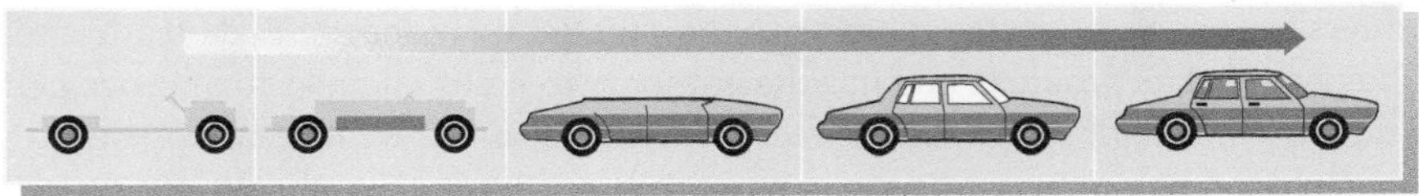

(C) Fixed-Position Layout

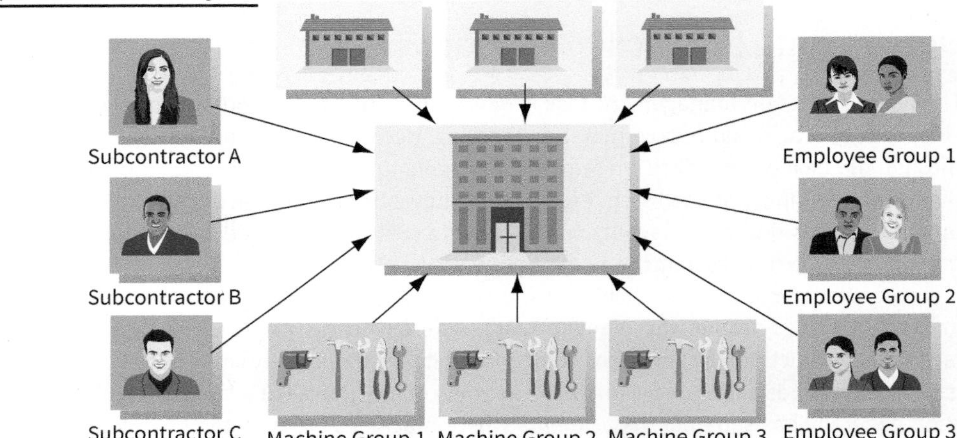

(D) Customer-Oriented Layout

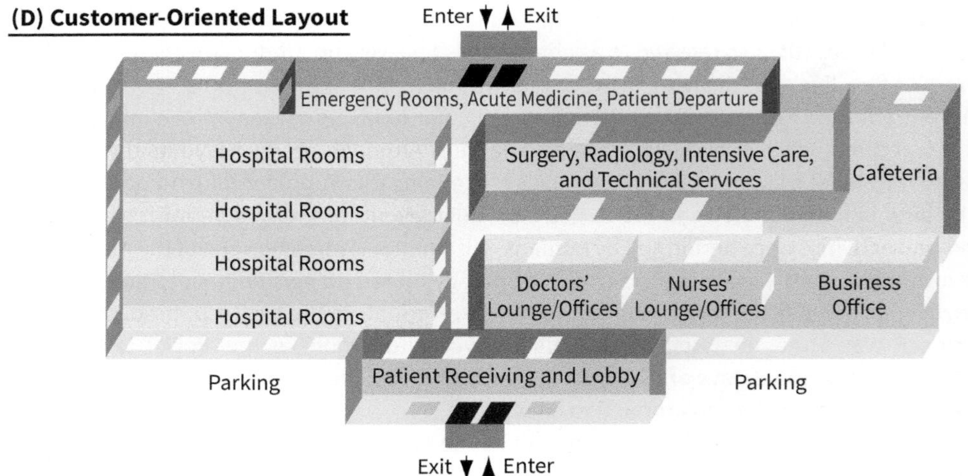

and its services—also called *customer-oriented layout*. If you think of patients as inputs, a hospital implements a form of the process layout. Banks, libraries, dental offices, and hair salons also use process layouts. Sometimes the circumstances surrounding a service require a fixed-position layout. For instance, doctors, nurses, and medical devices are brought to patients in a hospital emergency room.

Implementing the Production Plan

After planning the production process and determining the best layout, a company's production managers begin to implement the production plan. This activity involves (1) deciding whether to make, buy, or lease components; (2) selecting the best suppliers for materials; and (3) controlling inventory to keep enough, but not too much, on hand.

Make, Buy, or Lease Decision One of the fundamental issues facing every producer is the **make, buy, or lease decision**—choosing whether to manufacture a product or component in-house, purchase it from an outside supplier, or lease it. This decision is critical in many contemporary business situations.

make, buy, or lease decision choosing whether to manufacture a product or component in-house, purchase it from an outside supplier, or lease it.

Several factors affect the make, buy, or lease decision, including the costs of leasing or purchasing parts from vendors compared with the costs of producing them in-house. The decision sometimes hinges on the availability of outside suppliers that can dependably meet a company's standards for schedule, quality, and quantity. The need for confidentiality sometimes affects the decision, as does the short- or long-term duration of the company's need for supplies. A company might not yet have the technology to produce certain components or materials, or the technology might be too costly. The "Business & Technology" feature describes how **3D printing** has shortened the production and delivery time for airplanes.

3D printing etching of plastic layers into different shapes by laying down successive layers of material to form a 3D solid object

Even when a company decides to purchase from outside vendors, production managers should maintain access to and relationships with multiple supply sources. An alternative supplier ensures that the firm can obtain needed materials despite strikes, quality-assurance problems, supply chain disruptions, or other situations that may affect inputs. Outsourcing has its disadvantages. The main reasons companies say they use outsourcing is to reduce costs and focus on their core business activities, but outsourcing also may trigger layoffs and compromise quality.

American Giant, known as the company behind "the greatest hoodie ever made," is looking at an American-made resurgence with its hoodies, polos, and T-shirts. Sold only online—

Business & Technology

3D-Printed Airplane Parts Reduce the Wait

Choosing whether to manufacture a product or component in house, purchase it from an outside supplier, or lease it is a common decision made in the aerospace industry. Chuck Hull, an engineer by trade, may not be a household name. However, in the 1980s he had the idea to use ultraviolet lights to etch plastic layers into different shapes by laying down successive layers of material to form a three-dimensional solid object—and 3D printing or additive manufacturing—was born.

Aerospace giant Boeing is using 3D-printed, nonmetallic parts in the production of its airplanes. With 300 different parts on 10 different aircraft production programs, over 50,000 3D parts are currently installed on commercial, space, and defense vehicles. Expected to shave up to $3 million in manufacturing costs for each plane, the company will begin using 3D printed titanium parts in the production of its 787 Dreamliner. In addition to efficiencies realized with producing parts in house, Boeing retains greater control with quicker turnaround times, less stockpiling, and less time waiting for parts from outside suppliers.

Competitor Airbus has used over a thousand aircraft parts—also 3D-printed from plastic—which allows for reduced production time and improved on-schedule delivery of its planes. Rather than milling from metal, the parts are forged from resin certified to an Airbus specification. Both companies have turned to Stratasys, a company in Minneapolis, which manufactures orthodontic appliances, human prosthetics, automobile parts, and film props out of resin. In addition to better on-time parts delivery and streamlined supply chains, the 3D-printing technology helps reduce weight, which is a big issue when it comes to fuel efficiency and reduced CO_2 emissions.

Questions for Critical Thinking

1. **Could a reduction in the weight of an airplane from 3D-printed parts also translate to a reduction in the cost of fuel and, ultimately, airline fares? Discuss the future impact of 3D-printing innovation on airfares.**
2. **What are some of the ways a 3D printer could serve the consumer market? When do you foresee the use of a 3D printer in the home?**

Sources: Frank Catalano, "Boeing Files Patent for 3D-printed Aircraft Parts—and Yes, It's Already Using Them," *GeekWire*, http://www.geekwire.com, accessed March 29, 2018; Matthew Ponsford and Nick Glass, "'The Night I Invented 3D Printing," *CNN*, http://www.cnn.com, accessed March 29, 2018; Caroline Ku, "3-D Printed Parts on Airplanes Are Just the Beginning of a Movement," *Apex*, http://apex.aero, accessed March 29, 2018; Benedict, "Boeing Says Its 3D Printed Microlattice Is 'World's Lightest Metal,'" http://www.3ders.org, accessed March 29, 2018. James Vincent, "3D-Printed Titanium Parts Could Save Boeing up to $3 Million per Plane," *The Verge*, www.theverge.com, accessed April 2, 2018; Michael Molitch-Hou, "Airbus Takes on Stratasys 3D Printing for Serial Part Production," *engineering.com*, www.engineering.com, accessed April 2, 2018.

and almost entirely sourced and produced in North and South Carolina, American Giant wants to prove that American-made goods can be high quality and profitable.[17]

Selection of Suppliers Once a company decides what inputs to purchase, it must choose the best vendors for its needs. To make this choice, production managers compare the service levels, quality, prices, dependability of delivery, and other services offered by competing companies. Different suppliers may offer virtually identical quality levels and prices, so the final decision often rests on factors such as the company's experience with each supplier, speed of delivery, warranties on purchases, and other services.

For a major purchase, negotiations between the purchaser and potential vendors may stretch over several weeks or even months, and the buying decision may rest with a number of colleagues who must say yes before the final decision is made. The choice of a supplier for an industrial drill press, for example, may require a joint decision by the production, engineering, purchasing, and quality-control departments. These departments often must reconcile their different views to settle on a purchasing decision.

The Internet has given buyers powerful tools for finding and comparing suppliers. Buyers can log on to business exchanges to compare specifications, prices, and availability. Ariba, acquired by German software maker SAP, provides cloud-based applications to the world's largest business-to-business community of more than 2 million businesses. This allows companies to collaborate with a global network of suppliers and partners.[18]

Companies often purchase raw materials and component parts on long-term contracts. If a manufacturer requires a continuous supply of materials, a one-year or two-year contract with a vendor helps ensure availability. Today, many companies are building long-term relationships with suppliers and reducing the number with whom they do business. At the same time, they are asking their vendors to expand their roles in the production process.

Networking provides a way for production managers to learn about suppliers and get to know them personally. Trade shows, conferences, seminars, and other meetings enable managers to meet vendors, competitors, and colleagues.

inventory control function requiring production and operations managers to balance the need to keep stock on hand to meet demand against the costs of carrying inventory.

Inventory Control Production and operations managers' responsibility for **inventory control** requires them to balance the need to keep stock on hand to meet demand against the costs of carrying inventory. Among the expenses involved in storing inventory are warehousing costs, taxes, insurance, and maintenance. Companies waste money if they hold more inventory than they need. On the other hand, having too little inventory on hand may result in a shortage of raw materials, parts, or goods for sale that could lead to delays, lost sales, and unhappy customers.

Companies stand to lose business when they miss promised delivery dates or turn away orders. Having an efficient inventory control system can save customers and money. Many companies maintain *perpetual inventory* systems to continuously monitor the amounts and locations of their stock. Such inventory control systems typically rely on computers, and many automatically generate orders at the appropriate times. Many companies link their scanning devices to perpetual inventory systems that reorder needed merchandise. As the system records a shopper's purchase, it reduces the inventory count online. Once inventory on hand drops to a predetermined level, the system automatically reorders the merchandise. Because more than 50% of its future sales are anticipated to come from online channels, Seattle-based retailer Nordstrom has recently invested in a perpetual inventory control system. As the company continues to create a more integrated shopping experience for its customers, its inventory system will be more closely integrated with any way a customer chooses to shop.[19]

Some companies go further and hand over their inventory control functions to suppliers. This concept is known as *vendor-managed inventory*. Dow Chemical uses a vendor-managed inventory (VMI) service for its customers with predictable and consistent product supply needs. Dow uses the latest technology to manage its customers' inventory levels and consumption rates to automatically place product reorders for just-in-time supply.[20]

just-in-time (JIT) system broad management philosophy that reaches beyond the narrow activity of inventory control to influence the entire system of production and operations management.

Just-in-Time Systems A **just-in-time (JIT) system** implements a broad management philosophy that reaches beyond the narrow activity of inventory control to influence the entire system of production and operations management. A JIT system seeks to eliminate anything

Courtesy of Seattle Children's Hospital

JIT inventory systems are used in a wide range of industries, including the healthcare field. Seattle Children's Hospital uses a JIT system to manage distribution of its supplies and other materials.

that does not add value in operations activities by providing the right part at the right place at just the right time—right before it is needed in production.

JIT systems are being used in a wide range of industries, including medical supplies. Seattle Children's Hospital (pictured in photo) uses a two-bin system called Demand Flow to manage the distribution of its supplies, equipment, and clinical materials. The Demand Flow system distributes supplies in a two-bin, low unit of measure (LUM) system, where supplies are delivered in the right quantity and at the right time, removing the clinician from the ordering process. Unlike other distribution systems, Demand Flow monitors inventory turns of the supply bins at the point of use, whereas a more traditional distribution system monitors usage at the warehouse. Demand Flow enables Seattle Children's to monitor performance of the supplies within the bins so the bins can be right sized at the point of use, eliminating supply stock-outs and stale inventory. The hospital partners with its key distributors to deploy the system. While the hospital does keep an inventory of certain emergency supplies on hand, the rest are distributed on a JIT basis.[21]

Production using JIT shifts much of the responsibility for carrying inventory to vendors, which operate on forecasts and keep stock on hand to respond to manufacturers' needs. Suppliers that cannot keep enough high-quality parts on hand may be assessed steep penalties by purchasers. Another risk of using JIT systems is what happens if manufacturers underestimate demand for a product. Strong demand will begin to overtax JIT systems, as suppliers and their customers struggle to keep up with orders with no inventory cushion to tide them over. Natural disasters can also have a negative impact on JIT systems, preventing materials from reaching manufacturing facilities in a timely manner.

Materials Requirement Planning Besides efficiency, effective inventory control requires careful planning to ensure the company has all the inputs it needs to make its products. How do production and operations managers coordinate all of this information? They rely on **materials requirement planning (MRP)**, a software-based production planning system that lets a company ensure that it has all the parts and materials it needs to produce its output at the right time and place and in the right amounts. The software can be cloud-based, used on the premises, or accessed with a mobile device.

materials requirement planning (MRP) computer-based production planning system that lets a company ensure that it has all the parts and materials it needs to produce its output at the right time and place and in the right amounts.

Production managers use MRP programs to create schedules that identify the specific parts and materials required to produce an item. These schedules specify the exact quantities needed and the dates on which to order those quantities from suppliers so that they are delivered at the optimal time in the production cycle. A small company might get by without an

MRP system. If a firm makes a simple product with few components, an e-mail or phone call may ensure overnight delivery of crucial parts. For a complex product, however, such as a high-definition TV or an aircraft, longer lead times may be necessary.

Creative Energy Foods is an energy-bar maker, and the company's recent growth has prompted the need for a new software solution to maintain inventory accuracy and replenish stock. The MRP software provides immediate production summaries, inventory levels, and sales and stock forecasts.[22]

Assessment Check

1. List the four major tasks of production and operations managers.
2. What is the difference between a traditional manufacturing structure and a team-based structure?
3. What factors affect the make, buy, or lease decision?

6 Controlling the Production Process

production control creates a well-defined set of procedures for coordinating people, materials, and machinery to provide maximum production efficiency.

The final task of production and operations managers is controlling the production process to maintain the highest possible quality. **Production control** creates a well-defined set of procedures for coordinating people, materials, and machinery to provide maximum production efficiency. Suppose that a watch factory must produce 80,000 watches during October. Production control managers break down this total into a daily production assignment of 4,000 watches for each of the month's 20 working days. Next, they determine the number of workers, raw materials, parts, and machines the plant needs to meet the production schedule. Similarly, a manager in a service business such as a restaurant must estimate how many dinners will be served each day and then determine how many people are needed to prepare and serve the food, as well as what food to purchase.

Figure 10.5 illustrates production control as a five-step process composed of planning, routing, scheduling, dispatching, and follow-up. These steps are part of a company's overall emphasis on total quality management.

Production Planning

The phase of production control called *production planning* determines the amount of resources (including raw materials and other components) an organization needs to produce a certain output. The production planning process develops a bill of materials that lists all needed parts and materials. By comparing information about needed parts and materials with perpetual inventory data, purchasing staff can identify necessary purchases. Employees or automated systems establish delivery schedules to provide needed parts and materials when required during the production process. Production planning also ensures the availability of needed machines and personnel. Workers at a Wilson Sporting Goods Company factory in Ohio have made every football ever used in a Super Bowl game. Each January, production begins; the footballs are about 70% complete before the final playoff games are decided. Once the

FIGURE 10.5 Steps in Production Control

Super Bowl teams emerge and workers know which two team names will be printed on the balls, production goes into overdrive. The plant makes official game balls for each team and around 10,000 replicas for sale to fans.[23]

Although material inputs contribute to service-production systems, production planning for services tends to emphasize human resources more than materials.

Routing

Another phase of production control, called *routing*, determines the sequence of work throughout the facility and specifies who will perform each aspect of the work at what location. Routing choices depend on two factors: the nature of the good or service and the facility layouts discussed earlier in the chapter—product, process, fixed position, or customer oriented. JETCAM is a company headquartered in Monaco that provides routing software to the aerospace composite industry, in which quality and accuracy are absolutely critical. One feature of the software is that it allows instructions for processes to be provided automatically instead of keyed in by workers—thus avoiding errors.[24]

Scheduling

In the *scheduling* phase of production control, managers develop timetables that specify how long each operation in the production process takes and when workers should perform it. Efficient scheduling ensures that production will meet delivery schedules and make efficient use of resources.

Scheduling is important whether the product is complex or simple to produce and whether it is a tangible good or a service. A pencil is simpler to produce than a computer, but each production process has scheduling requirements. A stylist may take 25 minutes to complete each haircut with just one or two tools, whereas every day a hospital has to schedule procedures and treatments ranging from X-rays to surgery to follow-up appointments. Turner Suspension Bicycles, Inc., manufactures high-quality, world-class, full-suspension mountain bikes. Previously performing scheduling manually, the company turned to MRP software, which has made a dramatic difference in the company's productivity, labor cost savings, and on-time delivery. Entering information about types of machines, laborers, materials, vendors, and customers gave Turner advanced information to better control scheduling. By knowing the sequence of what needed to be done and how long each step in the process would take, the company now has a handle on its product flow—from projections to orders to shipments.[25]

Production managers use a number of analytical methods for scheduling. One of the oldest methods, the *Gantt chart*, tracks projected and actual work progress over time. Gantt charts like the one in **Figure 10.6** remain popular because they show at a glance the status

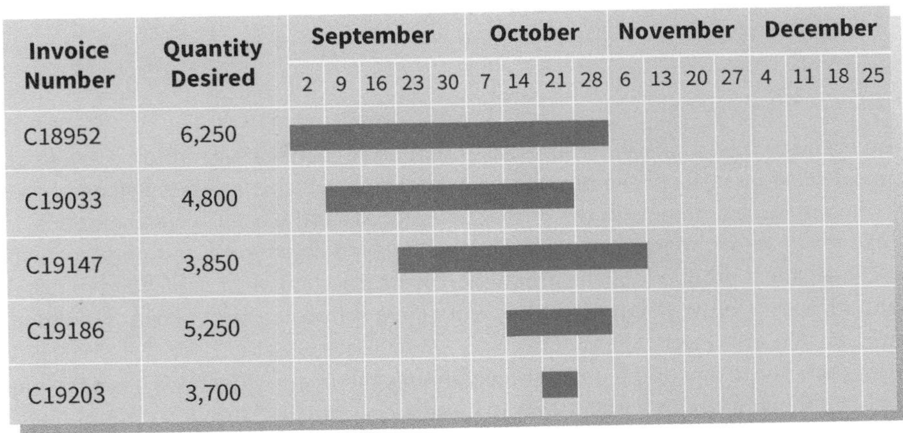

FIGURE 10.6 **Sample Gantt Chart**

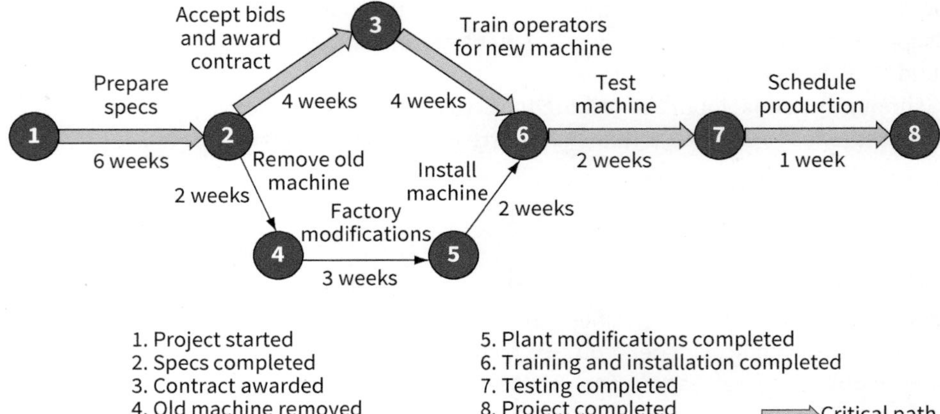

FIGURE 10.7 PERT Diagram for the Purchase and Installation of a New Robot

of a particular project. However, they are most effective for scheduling relatively simple projects.

A complex project might require a *PERT (program evaluation and review technique)* chart, which seeks to minimize delays by coordinating all aspects of the production process. First developed for the military, PERT has been modified for industry. The simplified PERT diagram in **Figure 10.7** summarizes the schedule for purchasing and installing a new robot in a factory. The heavy gold line indicates the *critical path*—the sequence of operations that requires the longest time for completion. In this case, the project cannot be completed in fewer than 17 weeks.

In practice, a PERT network may consist of thousands of events and cover months of time. Complex computer programs help production managers develop such a network and find the critical path among the maze of events and activities. The construction of a huge office building requires complex production planning of this nature.

Dispatching

Dispatching is the phase of production control in which management instructs each department on what work to do and the time allowed for its completion. The dispatcher authorizes performance, provides instructions, and lists job priorities. Dispatching may be the responsibility of a manager or a self-managed work team.

Follow-Up

Because even the best plans sometimes fail, production managers need to be aware of any problems. *Follow-up* is the phase of production control in which managers and employees or team members spot problems in the production process and come up with solutions. Problems take many forms: machinery malfunctions, delayed shipments, and employee absenteeism can all affect production. The production control system must detect and report these delays to managers or work teams so they can adjust schedules and correct the underlying problems.

If your interest in any of the production planning and control functions has been piqued, you might be thinking about possible jobs in these areas. See the "Job Description" feature to learn more about the role of a production manager.

Job Description

Production Manager

Overview Production managers, also called plant managers, work in an industrial setting and oversee daily manufacturing operations. They coordinate, plan, and direct the range of activities that result in the production of goods such as computers, automobiles, paper products, and electronics. Industrial settings vary and may include transportation, chemical manufacturing, food manufacturing, or metal fabrication.

Responsibilities Industrial production managers typically hire, train, and evaluate workers and also decide the best utilization of workers to meet production goals and schedules. Production managers focus on staying on schedule and being within budget. They often write reports and analyze data from previous production activities. They streamline the production process, fix existing bottlenecks, and learn from past production slowdowns and challenges. With growth in mind, they are also charged with evaluating and analyzing the need for additional capital and equipment.

Performance and safety are top priorities in many manufacturing settings, and production managers are responsible for making sure that employees adhere to safety requirements. In addition, to meet expected quality levels and metrics, production managers monitor quality control closely, while working with and training workers in quality control strategies. Quality control training programs help ensure that product defects can be identified and fixed quickly. Production managers also interface with managers from other departments, including sales, warehousing, research and development, purchasing, and scheduling.

Requirements Most employers require a bachelor's degree in any field. Typically production managers have degrees in business or industrial engineering. At larger facilities where more oversight is required, some companies prefer managers with advanced degrees in business or industrial management. Essential skills required include leadership skills to motivate workers, problem-solving skills to identify production issues, and time management skills to meet critical deadlines. Some production managers begin as first-line supervisors before being promoted to management. Training progams are often available for recent college graduates.

Outlook Employment outlook is projected to decline slightly over the next decade as many manufacturing industries experience a decline in production and overall employment—mainly due to increased technology and productivity. Some manufacturing jobs will continue to be outsourced to countries with lower labor costs. However, this situation may be mitigated with recent trends in reshoring, in which previously outsourced production work is being brought back to the United States.

Sources: Government website, "Industrial Production Managers," *Occupational Outlook Handbook,* 2017–2018 Edition, http://www.bls.gov, accessed April 1, 2018; Aurelio Locsin, "What Is a Facilities Operations Manager?" *Houston Chronicle,* http://work.chrom.com, accessed April 1, 2018; organization website, "Operations Manager," http://www.shrm.org, accessed April 1, 2018.

Assessment Check

1. What five steps are involved in controlling the production process?
2. What is the difference between a Gantt chart and a PERT chart?

7 Importance of Quality

Quality—as it relates to the production of goods and services—is defined as being free of deficiencies. Quality matters because fixing, replacing, or redesigning defective products is costly. If Seagate makes a defective computer hard drive, it has to either fix the drive or replace it to keep a customer happy. If Delta Airlines books too many passengers for a flight, it has to offer vouchers worth hundreds of dollars to encourage passengers to give up their seats and take a later flight.

quality good or service that is free of deficiencies.

For most companies, the costs of poor quality can amount to lost revenues and a tarnished reputation. Poor quality results in additional material-related costs, downtime, labor, rework, repair, opportunity costs, and recalls. Takata, a Japanese airbag supplier, is responsible for a faulty airbag inflator. When deployed, an inside metal cartridge, loaded with propellant wafers, sprayed metal shards throughout the car. Vehicles in the United States manufactured by BMW, Chrysler, Daimler Trucks, Ford, General Motors, Honda, Mazda, Mitsubishi, Nissan, Subaru, and Toyota were part of the largest automotive recall in history. The recall impacts over 30 million vehicles, and 20 lives have been claimed.[26]

One process that companies use to ensure that they produce high-quality products from the start is **benchmarking**—determining how well other companies perform business

benchmarking process of determining how well other companies perform business functions or tasks.

functions or tasks. In other words, benchmarking is the process of comparing other firms' standards, performance metrics, and best practices, usually in terms of quality, costs, and time. Taking apart or dismantling a competitor's automobile, otherwise known as a teardown, provides information about quality, production costs, design, materials, and even suppliers. A recent teardown, or reverse engineering analysis, of a BMW i3 revealed unique assembly techniques and innovative systems.[27] Companies may use many different benchmarks, depending on their objectives. For instance, organizations that want to increase profits may compare their operating profits or expenses to those of other firms. Retailers concerned with productivity may benchmark sales per square foot. Manufacturers interested in productivity may benchmark using output per workers.

It's important when benchmarking for a company to establish what it wants to accomplish, what it wants to measure, and which company can provide the most useful benchmarking information. A company might choose a direct competitor for benchmarking, or it might select a company in an entirely different industry—but one that has processes the firm wants to study and emulate.

Quality Control

quality control measuring output against established quality standards.

Quality control involves measuring output against established quality standards. Companies need such checks to spot defective products and to avoid delivering inferior shipments to customers. Standards should be set high enough to meet customer expectations. A 90% or 95% success rate might seem to be a good number, but consider what your phone service or ATM network would be like if it worked only 90% of the time. You would feel frustrated and inconvenienced and would probably switch to another service provider or bank.

Manufacturing companies can monitor quality levels through visual inspections, electronic sensors, robots, and X-rays. Surveys can provide quality-control information to services. Negative feedback from customers or a high rejection rate on a product or component sends a signal that production is not achieving quality standards. Companies that outsource operations may face a greater challenge in monitoring quality and assuring customers of the quality of their goods or services, especially if they are highly visible companies. The "Judgment Call" feature discusses concerns over ingredients and labeling of popular dietary supplements.

Judgment Call

Profits and Production Deadlines Impact Quality at Kobe Steel

Osaka, Japan–based Kobe Steel, maker of high-end steel products for trains, cars, and rockets, recently admitted to manipulating quality-certification documents and inspections for hundreds of thousands of its aluminum and copper parts sold to over 500 different clients. Among those clients are Boeing, Ford, and General Motors—all of whom are investigating any potential impact.

One of the world's top steelmakers, Kobe admits to decades of the practice of employees faking reports to make it appear as if some of its copper, aluminum, and steel products met the specifications requested by customers—when in reality they did not. Overworked line workers are at the root of the issue, along with out-of-touch senior-level executives. An internal report reveals that while trying to maintain profit levels, top-level executives were out of touch with overstressed workers and, during peak production periods, unrealistic goals.

Under pressure to ship products with tight turnaround cycles, employees approved products that did not meet required quality standards, and quick shipments were prioritized over quality. Metals from Kobe Steel are included in a wide array of products including air conditioners, Blu-ray discs, car doors, computer chips, copper pipes, heat exchangers, gear boxes, nuclear power plant parts, ship engines, and space ships. Customers have their fingers crossed that no safety issues will surface.

Questions for Critical Thinking

1. At one time, Japan had a reputation for flawless manufacturing quality and astute attention to detail and efficiency. Advice books asserting the power of Japanese manufacturing and production filled bookstore shelves and college classrooms. Discuss and research a few other recent scandals of Japanese companies and their root causes. Is there a trend or pattern?
2. Kobe Steel is admitting that data fraud had been going on for more than five decades. What kind of turmoil does this produce in global supply chains?

Sources: Alastair Gale and Sean McLain, "Companies Everywhere Copied Japanese Manufacturing. Now the Model Is Cracking," *The Wall Street Journal*, http://www.wsj.com, accessed April 4, 2018; Dan Shane, "Kobe Steel Chief Is Resigning Over Fake Data Scandal," *CNNMoney*, http://www.cnnmoney.com, accessed April 4, 2018; Yuka Obayashi, "Kobe Steel Admits Data Fraud Went on Nearly Five Decades, CEO to Quit," *Reuters*, http://www.reuters.com, accessed April 4, 2018; "Factbox: Kobe Steel's Affected Customers—From Computer Chips to Space Ships," *Reuters*, http://www.reuters.com, accessed April 4, 2018.

Because the typical factory can spend up to half its operating budget identifying and fixing mistakes, a company cannot rely solely on inspections to achieve its quality goals. Instead, quality-driven production managers identify all processes involved in producing goods and services and work to maximize their efficiency. The causes of problems in the processes must be found and eliminated. If a company concentrates its efforts on better designs of products and processes with clear quality targets, it can ensure virtually defect-free production.

General Electric, Heinz, 3M, Sears, and the U.S. military are among the organizations that use the Six Sigma concept to achieve quality goals. *Six Sigma* means a company tries to make error-free products 99.9997% of the time—a tiny 3.4 errors per million opportunities. The goal of Six Sigma programs is for companies to eliminate virtually all defects in output, processes, and transactions. (Six Sigma projects follow a methodology shown in photo.) Information technology (IT) service organizations are employing Six Sigma tools to create better flow, to prioritize activities, and to remove waste (tickets sitting in queues, for example).[28]

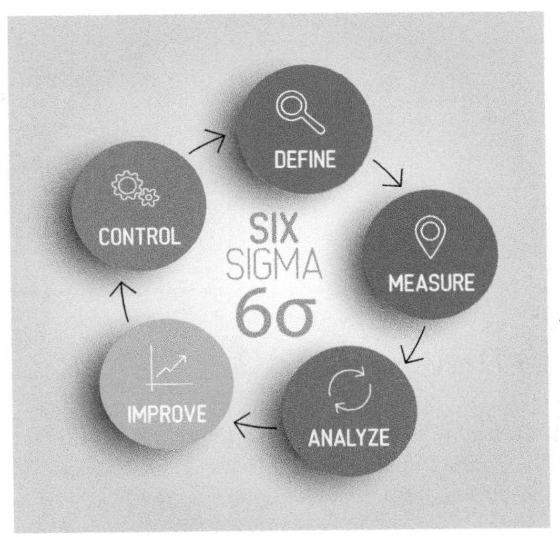

Petr Vaclavek/Shutterstock

Six Sigma projects follow a methodology aimed at improving an existing business process composed of five phases: define, measure, analyze, improve, and control.

ISO Standards

For many goods and services, an important measure of quality is to meet the standards of the **International Organization for Standardization**, known as ISO for short—not an acronym but a shorter name derived from the Greek word *isos*, meaning "equal." Operating since 1947, ISO is a network of national standards bodies from 162 countries. Its mission is to develop and promote international standards for business, government, and society to facilitate global trade and cooperation. ISO has developed voluntary standards for everything from the format of banking and telephone cards to freight containers to paper sizes to metric screw threads. The U.S. member body of ISO is the American National Standards Institute (ANSI).

International Organization for Standardization (ISO) organization whose mission is to develop and promote international standards for business, government, and society to facilitate global trade and cooperation.

The ISO 9000 family of standards gives requirements and guidance for quality management to help organizations ensure that their goods and services achieve customer satisfaction and also provide a framework for continual improvement. The ISO 14000 family of standards for environmental management helps organizations to ensure that their operations cause minimal harm to the environment and to achieve continual improvement of their environmental performance.

ISO 9001:2008 and ISO 14001:2004 respectively give the requirements for a quality management system and an environmental management system. Both can be used for certification, which means that the organization's management system (the way it manages its processes) is independently audited by a certification body (also known in North America as a registration body, or registrar) and confirmed as conforming to the requirements of the standard. The organization is then issued with an ISO 9001:2008 or an ISO 14001:2004 certificate.

It should be noted that certification is not a requirement of either standard, which can be implemented solely for the benefits it provides the organization and its customers. However, many organizations opt to seek certification because of the perception that an independent audit adds confidence in its abilities. Business partners, customers, suppliers, and consumers may prefer to deal with or buy products from a certified organization. Certifications have to be periodically renewed through accompanying audits.

A second point is that ISO itself develops standards but does not itself carry out auditing and certification. This is done independently of ISO by hundreds of certification bodies worldwide. The certificates they issue carry their own logo, but not ISO's because the latter does not approve or control their activities.

Whether or not an organization decides to seek certification of its management system, many have reported significant benefits from implementing ISO's management system standards, such as increased efficiency, better teamwork, improved customer satisfaction, and reduced consumption of resources.[29]

Assessment Check

1. What are some ways in which a company can monitor the quality level of its output?
2. List some of the benefits of acquiring ISO 9000 certification.

What's Ahead

Maintaining high quality is an important part of satisfying customers. Product quality and customer satisfaction are also objectives of the business function of marketing. The next part consists of three chapters that explore the many activities involved in customer-driven marketing. These activities include product development, distribution, promotion, and pricing.

Chapter in Review

Summary of Learning Objectives

LEARNING OBJECTIVE 1 Explain the strategic importance of production.

Production and operations management is a vital business function. Without a quality product or service, a company is less likely to be profitable, and this can result in closure. The production process is also crucial in a not-for-profit organization because the good produced or service provided justifies the organization's existence. Production and operations management plays an important strategic role by lowering the costs of production, boosting output quality, and allowing the company to respond flexibly and dependably to customers' demands.

Assessment Check Answers

1.1 **What is mass production?** Mass production is a system for manufacturing products in large quantities through effective combinations of employees with specialized skills, mechanization, and standardization.

1.2 **What is the difference between flexible production and customer-driven production?** Flexible production generally involves using technology to receive and fulfill orders and skilled people to carry out tasks needed to fill a particular order. Customer-driven production evaluates buyer demands in order to make the connection between products manufactured and products purchased.

LEARNING OBJECTIVE 2 Identify and describe the production processes.

The four main categories of production processes are the analytic production system, which reduces a raw material to its component parts in order to extract one or more marketable products; the synthetic production system, which combines a number of raw materials or parts to produce finished products; the continuous production process, which generates finished items over a lengthy period of time; and the intermittent production process, which generates products in short production runs.

Assessment Check Answers

2.1 **What are the two main production systems?** The two systems are analytic production and synthetic production.

2.2 **What are the two time-related production processes?** The two time-related production processes are the continuous production process and the intermittent production process.

LEARNING OBJECTIVE 3 Explain the role of technology in the production process.

Computer-driven automation allows companies to design, create, and modify products rapidly and produce them in ways that effectively meet customers' changing needs. Important design and production technologies include robots, computer-aided design (CAD), computer-aided manufacturing (CAM), and computer-integrated manufacturing (CIM). Many companies are pouring resources into the development of manufacturing processes that result in a reduction of waste, energy use, and pollution.

Assessment Check Answers

3.1 **List some of the reasons businesses invest in robots.** Businesses use robots to free people from boring, sometimes dangerous assignments and to perform tasks that require repeated manipulation of materials and tools.

3.2 **What is a flexible manufacturing system (FMS)?** An FMS is a production facility that can be quickly modified to manufacture different products.

3.3 **What are the major benefits of computer-integrated manufacturing (CIM)?** The main benefits are increased productivity, decreased design costs, increased equipment utilization, and improved quality.

LEARNING OBJECTIVE 4 Identify the factors involved in a location decision.

Criteria for choosing the best site for a production facility fall into three categories: transportation, physical, and human factors. Transportation factors include proximity to markets and raw materials, along with availability of transportation alternatives. Physical or infrastructure variables involve such issues as water supply, available energy, and options for disposing of hazardous wastes. Human factors include the area's labor supply, local regulations, taxes, and living conditions.

Assessment Check Answers

4.1 **How does an environmental impact study influence the location decision?** An environmental impact study influences the location decision because it outlines how transportation, energy use, water and sewer treatment needs, and other factors will affect plants, wildlife, water, air, and other elements of the natural environment.

4.2 **What human factors are relevant to the location decision?** Human factors include an area's labor supply, labor costs, local regulations, taxes, and living conditions.

LEARNING OBJECTIVE 5 Explain the job of production managers.

Production and operations managers use people, technology, and machinery to convert inputs (materials and resources) into finished goods and services. Four major tasks are involved. First, the managers must plan the overall production process. Next, they must pick the best layout for their facilities. Then they implement their production plans. Finally, they control the production process and evaluate results to maintain the highest possible quality.

Implementation involves deciding whether to make, buy, or lease components; selecting the best suppliers for materials; and controlling inventory to keep enough, but not too much, on hand.

Assessment Check Answers

5.1 **List the four major tasks of production and operations managers.** The four tasks are planning the overall production process, determining the best layout for the firm's facilities, implementing the production plan, and controlling manufacturing to maintain the highest quality.

5.2 **What is the difference between a traditional manufacturing structure and a team-based structure?** In the traditional structure, each manager is given a specific area of authority. In a team-based structure, all workers are responsible for their output.

5.3 **What factors affect the make, buy, or lease decision?** The costs of leasing or purchasing parts from vendors, versus producing them in-house, the availability of dependable outside suppliers, and the need for confidentiality affect this decision.

LEARNING OBJECTIVE 6 Discuss controlling the production process.

The production control process consists of five steps: planning, routing, scheduling, dispatching, and follow-up. Quality control is an important consideration throughout this process. Coordination of each of these phases should result in high production efficiency and low production costs.

Assessment Check Answers

6.1 **What five steps are involved in controlling the production process?** The five steps are planning, routing, scheduling, dispatching, and follow-up.

6.2 **What is the difference between a Gantt chart and a PERT chart?** Gantt charts, which track projected and actual work progress over time, are used for scheduling relatively simple projects. PERT charts, which seek to minimize delays by coordinating all aspects of the production process, are used for more complex projects.

LEARNING OBJECTIVE 7 Determine the importance of quality.

Quality control involves evaluating goods and services against established quality standards. Such checks are necessary to spot defective products and to see that they are not shipped to customers. Devices for monitoring quality levels of the firm's output include visual inspection, electronic sensors, robots, and X-rays. Companies are increasing the quality of their goods and services by using Six Sigma techniques and by becoming ISO 9000 and ISO 14000 certified.

Assessment Check Answers

7.1 **What are some ways in which a company can monitor the quality level of its output?** Benchmarking, quality control, Six Sigma, and ISO standards are ways of monitoring quality.

7.2 **List some of the benefits of acquiring ISO 9000-certification.** These standards define how a company should ensure that its products meet customers' requirements. Business partners, customers, suppliers, and consumers may prefer to deal with or buy products from a certified organization.

Business Terms You Need to Know

production 254
production and operations management 254
mass production 254
LEED (Leadership in Energy and Environmental Design) 257
computer-aided design (CAD) 258
computer-aided manufacturing (CAM) 258
flexible manufacturing system (FMS) 259
computer-integrated manufacturing (CIM) 259
make, buy, or lease decision 265
3D printing 265
inventory control 266
just-in-time (JIT) system 266
materials requirement planning (MRP) 267
production control 268
quality 271
benchmarking 271
quality control 272
International Organization for Standardization (ISO) 273

Review Questions

1. What is utility? How does production create utility?

2. Why is production such an important business activity? In what ways does it create value for the company and its customers?

3. Why are companies now moving more toward flexible production and customer-driven production instead of mass production? Describe a product that you think would be better suited to flexible production or customer-driven production than mass production. Explain your choice.

4. Identify which production system—analytic or synthetic—applies to each of the following products:

   a. logging
   b. healthcare
   c. soybean farming
   d. fishing
   e. a smart phone

5. Industries such as home construction and dentistry benefit from the use of CAD. In both of these, CAM could be used as well—in the manufacture of home components as well as dental implants, crowns, and the like. Choose another industry that seems like a candidate for the use of both CAD and CAM systems. Explain how the industry could use both.

6. SeaWorld amusement parks are located in Florida, Texas, and California. What specific factors might have contributed to those choices?

7. What would be the best facility layout for each of the following?

   a. a tax preparation business
   b. nail salon
   c. car wash
   d. sandwich shop

8. What might be the factors involved in the selection of suppliers for a steakhouse restaurant?

9. What is inventory control? Why is the management of inventory crucial to a company's success?

10. What is benchmarking? How can it help a company improve the quality of its goods and services?

Projects and Teamwork Applications

1. In groups or in pairs, compare your backpacks, handbags, and any articles of clothing or shoes. Can you determine from the item's label where it was manufactured? What type of production process do you think was used to make the item? Is anyone wearing an item made in the United States? If so, how does it differ from the items made elsewhere?

2. With a partner or in small teams, discuss the impact , if any, on quality when a company decides to outsource the production of its goods or services. Is domestic production always a sure sign that higher quality standards will be followed and met? Compare and contrast both options with regard to quality.

3. On your own or with a classmate, select one of the following businesses and sketch or describe the layout that you think would be best for attracting and serving customers:

   a. Mexican restaurant
   b. clothing boutique
   c. pet store
   d. motorcycle dealership
   e. skateboard shop

4. With same-day and one-hour delivery services from Amazon and Google commonplace, discuss whether this fulfillment model is long lasting or just a passing trend. Discuss the types of products that lend themselves to same-day or one-hour delivery, as compared to traditional 1- to 3-day (or more) delivery options.

5. Choose two companies for comparison (one company should provide a good benchmarking opportunity for its production processes). Keep in mind that the benchmarking company doesn't necessarily have to be in the same industry as the other selected company. Present your decisions to the class and explain why you made both choices. What criteria would you use in your comparison?

Web Assignments

1. Mass customization is here to stay. Starbucks has declared that when multiplying its core beverages by its modifiers and customization options, there are over 80,000 drink combinations. While this might be an extreme case, go online to research and come up with three other companies that create mass customization products or services for customers. Describe each company's core product(s) and general customization options.

2. Plant location decision. Search for Toyota and Mazda's recent decision to build a plant in Huntsville, Alabama (which will produce over 300,000 cars and SUV's a year and employ 4,000 people). Research the decision and prepare a brief report outlining the factors that went into the company's location decision.

3. Reshoring. Discuss and give examples of the benefits realized by companies involved in reshoring—bringing manufacturing and production work back to the United States. Study the website below and discuss some of the reasons this movement has started to take shape. Outline, individually or in groups, the initiatives listed on this website.

   www.reshorenow.org

Note: Internet web addresses change frequently. If you don't find the exact sites listed, you may need to access the organization's home page and search from there or use a search engine such as Google or Bing.

Cases

Case 10.1 Home Depot Gives Customers Retail Options

Picture yourself in the middle of a home improvement project and in need of additional nails or lumber. Home improvement retail giant Home Depot is well aware of customers and do-it-yourselfers who find themselves in this situation. The Internet has changed the way customers shop, and with the tap of a smart phone, those nails and lumber are ready for immediate store pickup.

As the retail industry has become more interconnected, Home Depot has benefited from its multichannel approach to the customer experience. The company continues to leverage its digital platform and technology to support customers shopping in its stores as well as online. Sales associates have been trained on the company's web-enabled handheld device that allows for quick checks on inventory levels, how-to videos, product research, and the ability to complete a sales transaction in the middle of a store aisle.

While still a traditional bricks-and-mortar retailer, Home Depot has fine-tuned its retail network to accommodate four interconnected options for shoppers: buy online, ship to store (BOSS); buy online, pick up in store (BOPIS); buy online, return in store (BORIS); and its newest—buy online, deliver from store (BODFS). Approximately 40% of Home Depot's online orders are filled through its 2,200 retail stores, which double as fulfillment centers.

Although initially reluctant to embrace the web and its technology, in a recent year Home Depot's online sales grew 21% and represent almost 7% of annual sales of $100 billion. Home Depot has invested over $300 million to upgrade its e-commerce offerings, with a focus on distribution capability, supply-chain management, and full integration of web and store inventory. In addition to two fulfillment centers in Georgia and California, the company has added a third in Ohio, and warehouse technology systems have been updated. Home Depot is counting on a continued housing market recovery as well as the inevitability that customers and contractors will continue to run short of lumber and nails in the midst of that all-important home improvement project.

Questions for Critical Thinking

1. As more retailers embrace an interconnected retail strategy, discuss your experience as a consumer with how retailers are bridging the gap between physical stores and the online world.
2. How can Home Depot ensure that its online fulfillment strategy keeps the retail chain competitive?

Sources: Company website, "2017 Annual Report," http://media.corporate-ir.net, accessed April 1, 2018; Phalguni Soni, "Home Depot Shares Multichannel Strategy at dotCommerce Day 2015," *Yahoo Finance*, http://finance.yahoo.com, accessed April 1, 2018; Tracy Wallace, "Home Depot's Innovative, Successful Multichannel Strategy Your Brand Should Copy—Now," *Business 2 Community*, http://www.business2community.com, accessed April 1, 2018; company website, "Seamless Shopping: Inside Home Depot's Interconnected Retail Revolution," http://builtfromscratch.homedepot.com, accessed April 1, 2018; company website, "The Home Depot Opens its Third and Largest Fulfillment Center," http://ir.homedepot.com, accessed March 31, 2018; Bill Briggs, "Home Depot's Sales Grow Almost 21.5% in 2017," *Digital Commerce 360*, https://www.digitalcommerce360.com, accessed March 31, 2018.

Case 10.2 Customization Gives Companies an Edge

Henry Ford, founder of Ford Motor Company, is quoted as saying that customers could choose a car in any color as long as it was black. Things have come a long way since that time—when customization and choice were seen as expensive and inaccessible. Today, brands are offering just about any way to customize, personalize, build loyalty, and create a deeper bond and greater engagement with customers. From music playlists to sneakers to burgers, mass customization continues to create a unique edge for businesses.

Mass customization combines elements of mass production with custom tailoring. Using information technology, Levi's originally created customized jeans for women by taking their measurements and sending the information electronically to a factory where the jeans were electronically cut, produced, and shipped to the customer. Built Custom Burgers, a popular Los Angeles–based franchise, serves "Build Your Own" burgers, fries, shakes, and more.

Close to 20 years ago, footwear giant Nike was one of the first to create a mass customization service that allowed customers to engage directly in the design of their sneakers by choosing colors and materials. Nike's e-commerce customization service is known as NikeID, and customers can order to their specifications. Nike blends the benefits of a traditional handcrafted product with modern-day manufacturing efficiencies. Nike recently unveiled the Nike Makers' Experience in New York City that merges "digital design with traditional footwear making." In 90 minutes, a collaborative design experience is created, along with a fully customized pair of Nike Presto X shoes.

Automobile makers have embraced customization, too. Through Tesla's online design studio configurator, automobile options include equipment levels, paint, wheels, interior, autopilot feature, LED lighting, suspension, hi-fidelity sound, and a $5,000 premium interior, and a long-range battery, which Tesla refers to as the ~75 kWh pack, is available at a premium of $9,000. Customization may have a cost, but it seems no one is complaining about a personalized purchase.

Questions for Critical Thinking

1. One advantage of mass customization is that customers typically pay for products before they're produced, which eliminates excess inventory and potential markdowns. Are there other industries where mass customization has caught on? Provide some examples.
2. What are the advantages and disadvantages of mass customization for a manufacturer? Is mass production taking a backseat to mass customization? Explain.

Sources: Laura Manes and Amye Parker, "Emerging Trends in Customer Experience for 2016," *Chain Store Age*, http://chainstoreage.com, accessed April 1, 2018; Kate Abnet, "Will Mass Customization Work for Fashion?" *Business of Fashion*, http://www.businessoffashion.com, accessed April 1, 2018; "McDonald's Revamps Build-Your-Own Burger Program"; Fred Lambert, "Tesla Updates Model 3 Configurator in Preparation for More Options," *Elektrek*, https://electrek.co, accessed April 1, 2018, Joe Berkowitz, "Nike Unveils Live Design That Creates A Custom Pair Of Sneakers In 90 Minutes," *Fast Company*, www.fastcompany.com, accessed April 12, 2018. *Advertising Age*, http://advertisingage.com, accessed April 1, 2018; Steve Hanley, "Tesla Opens Model X Design Studio for Pre-orders, 70D to Start at $80k," http://www.teslarati.com, accessed April 1, 2018.

Case 10.3 Necco Produces Classic Valentine's Day Treats

Not long ago, New England Confectionery Company, or Necco for short, marked the production of its one *trillionth* candy wafer. The humble roots of Necco, the country's oldest continuously operating candy company, began in Cambridge, Massachusetts in 1847. In fact, during the Civil War, Union soldiers carried Necco "hub wafers." Over the years, the candy maker has expanded production and become famous for more than just its wafers. Its product line includes the world-famous Sweethearts, a favorite for Valentine's Day, Clark Bar, Candy Buttons, Mighty Malts, and Haviland Thin Mints.

In addition to inventing a machine to print sayings onto candy, Necco founder Oliver Chase invented and patented the first American candy machine, a lozenge cutter. The result is Necco's iconic pastel-colored wafers, made mainly from sugar, corn syrup, gelatin, colorings, and flavoring. In its most recent year, the company produced over 4 billion wafers. Integral to the timely production and delivery of Necco's sweet treats is an ongoing strategic planning and production process. Production for Valentine's Day, an annual event lasting 24 hours, consists of 11 months of work. During this time, the company produces roughly 15 million pounds of Sweetheart hearts and over 8 billion of them are sold in a six-week window. After Valentine's Day, the demand for Sweethearts falls off dramatically.

For more than 150 years, the production process for Necco's hearts has remained unchanged. The ingredients to make the dough are mixed and then thrown on a machine for stretching and rolling. Sweethearts are embossed, rather than laser printed, in red ink with an old-fashioned print plate, including letters that can be rearranged and moved. It is during embossing that the dough gets cut into the shape of a heart. Two to three days later, after the drying (not baking) process, the hearts are placed into what Necco calls its rocket launcher, which mixes them together so that no one box has too many hearts of the same color. There are 72 different affectionate sayings like "Kiss Me," "Be True," and, "XOXO," and each year 12 new sayings are added. Newer sayings include "Te Amo," "Pugs & Kittens," "BFF," "Girl Power," "Luv 2 Dance," and "Je T'aime," and a few emoticon images, like a smiley face and a mustache. In fact, on the company's website, consumers can order personalized hearts and Necco wafers.

As a production company, Necco focuses its strategies on identifying opportunities for process improvement. The task of the company's executive called the lean champion is to identify, through observation and dialogue with employees, areas throughout the company in need of improvement. A cross-functional team is assembled to address many different kinds of process improvements, which can range from safety issues to eliminating waste and reworks of any kind. Oftentimes, this process improvement may include managing people and machinery.

In addition to process improvement, Necco focuses intently on quality. At the heart of its operation is balancing the production process, which includes projecting the time required to produce its various products while meeting delivery schedules. A Necco production supervisor firmly states there are no shortcuts to making a product that should have gone out the door yesterday. Each step in the production process requires a certain amount of time, and there are procedures followed to ensure that a quality food product is delivered to the customer. Necco also remains well aware that the company would not be in business without its customers. The company strives for freshness and consistency by weighing, measuring, and timing each of the 10 steps in the production of its wafers, for example.

About a decade ago, in order to expand, Necco was faced with a location decision after many years at its original 500,000-square-foot location and longtime home in Cambridge, Massachusetts. The company made the decision to move to a suburb about eight miles away—a location that boasts an 800,000+–square-foot facility for its 500 employees. One of the location factors in Necco's decision was to remain close to its roots in Cambridge. In addition, the company has plans to expand and house production of multiple products under one roof while retaining and growing its longtime base of coveted employees and nearby suppliers. Despite moves by most candy companies to Mexico where sugar is less expensive, Necco refused to even consider the consequence of such a move on its loyal employees.

Part of Necco's production process involves monitoring and controlling inventory. Necco must pay constant attention to products such as sugar, corn syrup, gelatin, colorings, and flavoring to avoid wasting dollars in carrying inventory on its warehouse floor. Its methods include carrying enough "safety stock" and controlling the inventory it does keep on hand without having to tie up a lot of money with product "sitting on the warehouse that's not going to move." Ideally, Necco would prefer not to keep any inventory on hand, although that's next to impossible until the company is able to improve its processes that would allow raw materials to be delivered just in time for production. However, for a company producing 8 billion individually embossed Sweetheart candies annually, Valentine's Day, for years gone by and those to come, would not be the same without Necco's miniature proclamations of romantic intentions.

Questions for Critical Thinking

1. What is the key role of a production supervisor at Necco, how might it change during peak production times, and with which departments and employees might the supervisor interface? How might the role of a production supervisor at Necco differ from that of a company with a steadier production process?
2. A daily staff meeting at Necco can be considered part of production control, contributing to the smooth running of the candy production process. Who might attend such a meeting? What kinds of topics might they discuss, and how might the discussion change during peak production times?
3. What steps does a supervisor at Necco take to balance quality and doing a job well? As a player in the food business, discuss and provide examples of the ways and the processes Necco uses to monitor quality throughout its supply chain. Evaluate and discuss Necco's quality control process, and list any changes you might make.
4. Discuss Necco's efforts to remain relevant in today's environment. How do its efforts to remain relevant impact its production processes and decisions? Discuss the role of mass customization in the production of Necco's Sweetheart candies.

Sources: Company website, http://necco.com, accessed April 1, 2018; Seth Daniel, "Attraction to Necco Much Sweeter This Year," *Revere Journal*, http://www.reverejournal.com, accessed April 1, 2018; "Candy Company Necco Offers Custom #Tweethearts for Valentine's Day," *ClickZ*, http://www.clickz.com, accessed April 1, 2018; Jonathan Berr, "Necco's Iconic Sweethearts Show Their Sassy Side," *CBS News*, http://www.cbsnews.com, accessed April 1, 2018; Claire Suddath, "How Do They Get Those Tiny Words on Sweethearts Candy?" *Time*, http://content.time.com, accessed April 1, 2018; Associated Press "Necco Wafers Scrapping Artificial Additives," *Daily Beast*, http://www.thedailybeast.com, accessed April 1, 2018.

CHAPTER 11

Customer-Driven Marketing

LEARNING OBJECTIVES

1. Define *marketing*.
2. Discuss the evolution of the marketing concept.
3. Describe not-for-profit marketing and nontraditional marketing.
4. Outline the basic steps in developing a marketing strategy.
5. Describe marketing research.
6. Discuss market segmentation.
7. Summarize consumer behavior.
8. Discuss relationship marketing.

Changemakers

Ethan Pines/The Forbes Collection / Contour by Getty Images

Do Won "Don" Chang, CEO and Founder, and
Jin Sook Chang, Chief Merchandising Officer
Organization: Forever 21
Industry: Retail/Fashion
Website: http://www.forever21.com

Forever 21, a "fast fashion" retailer, started over 30 years ago as a single 900-square-foot store in Los Angeles, California called Fashion 21. Fast fashion refers to quickly and frequently moving fashion trends from the runway to a retailer's store shelves. Today, Forever 21 is the world's fifth-largest specialty retailer with more than 700 stores and over $4 billion in annual sales.

The South Korean–born couple behind the brand well loved for its "cheap chic" and trendiness is Do Won Chang, Chief Executive Officer, and his wife, Jin Sook Chang, Chief Merchandising Officer. The company is privately held and remains family owned, with marketing run by their daughter, Linda.

Beyond its original teen target, Forever 21 has faced the reality of having to "age-up" its market segment. This has meant hiring celebrities like Charlize Theron and Megan Fox, with whom its initial teen customer of the 1980s can identify. As the Forever 21 customer has grown up, so have the pricing and product elements of the company's marketing mix. The company has expanded into plus sizes, accessories, and intimate apparel. However, as the fashion-obsessed Millennials have matured, Forever 21 has come to realize that its name doesn't necessarily hold true.

As its initial target market has grown up, the company has had to adapt its product offering to include more forgiving fits and styles that are more sophisticated and classic. "We've been working hard to break down that barrier of age with our brand," says marketing chief Linda Chang. "Part of it has to do with overcoming the stigma of our name—Forever 21." Nevertheless, as Forever 21 continues to target a wider range of consumers, this strategy has helped the company maintain a strong and healthy business.[1]

Overview

Today, business success is directly tied to a company's ability to identify and serve its target markets. In fact, all organizations—profit-oriented and not-for-profit, manufacturing and retailing—*must* serve customer needs to succeed, just as Forever 21 has done, since it began almost 35 years ago. Marketing is the link between the organization and the people who buy and use its goods and services. It is the way organizations determine buyer needs and inform potential customers that they can meet those needs by providing a quality product (or service) at a reasonable price. And it is the path to developing loyal, long-term customers.

Consumers who purchase goods for their own use and business purchasers seeking products to use in their company's operation may seem to fall in the same category, but marketers see distinct wants and needs for each group. To understand buyers—from manufacturers to web surfers to shoppers in the grocery aisles—companies gather a tremendous amount of data on every aspect of consumer lifestyles and buying behaviors. Marketers use the data to understand the wants and needs of both consumers and business buyers. Satisfying customers goes a long way toward building relationships with them. However, in today's hyper-competitive environment, it can be challenging.

This chapter begins with an examination of the marketing concept and the way businesspeople develop a marketing strategy. We then turn to marketing research strategies and how businesses apply data to market segmentation and understanding customer behavior. The chapter closes with a detailed look at the importance of customer relationships in today's highly competitive business environment.

1 What Is Marketing?

Every organization—from profit-seeking companies such as Nintendo and Adidas to such not-for-profits as the Make-A-Wish Foundation and the American Cancer Society—must serve customer needs to succeed. Perhaps the retail pioneer J. C. Penney best expressed this priority when he told his store managers, "Either you or your replacement will greet the customer within the first 60 seconds."

marketing activity, set of institutions, and processes for creating, communicating, delivering, and exchanging offerings that have value for customers, clients, partners, and society at large.

According to the American Marketing Association, **marketing** is the activity, set of institutions, and processes for creating, communicating, delivering, and exchanging offerings that have value for customers, clients, partners, and society at large.[2] In addition to selling goods and services, marketing strategies help people advocate ideas or viewpoints and educate and inform others. The American Heart Association has an online heart attack risk calculator along with prevention guideline tools to educate the general public.[3]

Retailer Nordstrom is best known for its obsession with customer service (see photo on the next page), and its mission statement makes this clear by stating that "Nordstrom works relentlessly to give customers the most compelling shopping experience possible."[4] The best marketers not only give consumers what they want but even anticipate consumers' needs before those needs arise. Ideally, they can create a link in the mind of consumers between the new need and the fulfillment of that need by their products and services. CVS Caremark, with headquarters in Rhode Island, is a retail pharmacy, and with its "MinuteClinic" service, customers can get quick, in-store medical consultations without going to the doctor. Owned by Berkshire Hathaway, NetJets offers fractional jet ownership to executives who want the luxury and flexibility of private ownership without the cost of owning their own plane. Airbnb is an online vacation rental site where people can list or lease spare rooms, apartments, homes, and other accommodations.[5]

As these examples suggest, marketing is more than just selling. It is a process that begins with discovering unmet customer needs and continues with researching the potential market; producing a good or service capable of satisfying the targeted customers; and promoting, pricing, and distributing that good or service. The 4 P's of marketing refer to the management process through which goods and services move from concept to the customer. They include identification, selection and development of a product, determination of its price, selection of a distribution channel to reach the customer's place, and development and implementation of a promotional strategy. Throughout the entire marketing process, a successful organization focuses on building customer relationships.

When two or more parties benefit from trading things of value, they have entered into an **exchange process**. When you purchase a cup of coffee, the other party may be a convenience store clerk, a vending machine, or a Peet's Coffee barista. The exchange seems simple—some money changes hands, and you receive your cup of coffee. But the exchange process is more complex than that. It could not occur if you didn't feel the need for a cup of coffee or if the convenience store or vending machine were not available. You might not choose Peet's Coffee unless you were aware of the brand. Because of marketing, your desire for a flavored blend, plain black coffee, or decaf is identified, and the coffee manufacturer's business is more likely to be successful.

Ben Nelms/Bloomberg via Getty Images

Seattle-based retailer Nordstrom is renowned for its customer service. Employees are empowered to use their "best judgment" in an environment with high company standards.

exchange process activity in which two or more parties give something of value to each other to satisfy perceived needs.

utility power of a good or service to satisfy a want or need.

How Marketing Creates Utility

Marketing affects many aspects of an organization and its dealings with customers. The ability of a good or service to satisfy the wants and needs of customers is called **utility**. A company's production function creates *form utility* by converting raw materials, component parts, and other inputs into finished goods and services. Customers see value in a finished product, or the form

Business Model

Harley-Davidson Looks to a Younger Generation of Riders

For more than a century, Milwaukee, Wisconsin–based Harley-Davidson, the iconic motorcycle brand, has embodied everything American. In its heyday, the company had such a following that consumers would wait patiently for 18 months to get their hands on a new bike. Harley-Davidson motorcycles are oftentimes associated with Baby Boomer men, many of whom associate status with the ability to purchase the big, expensive, shiny chrome touring bike with a price tag of more than $30,000.

Over the last three years, slumping sales have become a reality. With increased global competition from Italian rival Ducati and U.S.-based Indian bikes, the company is searching for ways to let go of its macho image by diversifying its segments toward millennials and women. Younger, urban motorcycle enthusiasts who are more interested in scooters and smaller, less-expensive bikes have also contributed to Harley's soft sales.

To target a younger generation of riders, Harley-Davidson recently rolled out its biggest ever product revamp, which includes eight faster and lighter revamped cruisers. With plans to produce an electric motorcycle, the company recently made an investment in a small electric vehicle and components part maker. To generate interest from younger riders or rider wannabes, an upcoming Ubisoft video game called *The Crew 2* was created. An open-road racing adventure, the game is "gender agnostic," and like its hit predecessor, *The Crew*—with 12 million players—is expected to appeal to young male and female gamers and potentially anyone with a passion for motor sports. Harley-Davidson hopes that the next generation of riders can revitalize its iconic American brand.

Questions for Critical Thinking

1. **Without alienating its traditional base of aging Baby Boomer men, how might Harley-Davidson continue to market its bikes to a younger and more diverse market segment? With a psychographic segmentation of "renegade" or "outsider," how might the company also apply this?**
2. **With its goal of 2 million U.S. riders in the next decade, Harley is also focused on understanding "consumer life stages, cultural shifts and where people are in their riding journey, despite age or gender." How might understanding these elements help Harley-Davidson?**

Sources: Norman Mayersohn, "Harley-Davidson's Newest Rival Is an Old Brand Wheels," *The Wall Street Journal*, http://www.wsj.com, accessed April 7, 2018; Rich Duprey,"Harley-Davidson going all-in on electric motorcycles," *USA Today*, http://www.usatoday.com, accessed April 7, 2018; Kenra Investors, "Harley-Davidson: No Reason To Get Onboard," *Seeking Alpha*, http://www.seekingalpha.com, accessed April 7, 2018; company website, "Harley-Davidson Announces 2017 Model-Year Prices," http://motorcyclistonline.com, accessed April 7, 2018; Joseph Hincks, "Harley-Davidson Rolls Out a New Range to Target Younger Riders," *Fortune*, http://www.fortune.com, accessed April 7, 2018; T. L. Stanley, "Harley-Davidson Is Trying to Cultivate Millennials While Catering to Loyalists, Iconic Brand Seeks New Generation of Riders Via Digital and Mobile," *AdWeek*, http://www.adweek.com, accessed April 7, 2018; company website, "The Crew 2 News and Updates," https://thecrew-game.ubisoft.com, accessed April 7, 2018.

created by each product part—rather than finding and putting parts together. The marketing function creates time, place, and ownership utility. *Time utility* is created by making a good or service available when customers want and need to purchase it. Examples include winter coats in time for months of snow and cold weather and Halloween costumes in time for the holiday. *Place utility* is created by making a product available in a location convenient for customers to purchase. For example, groceries at a grocery store and bank ATMs placed at convenient locations. The Internet has made products easily available, too. *Ownership utility* (also called possession utility) refers to an orderly transfer of goods and services from the seller to the buyer. This includes allowing the use of a credit card or electronic payment processing system for a purchase, or offering low- or no-interest rate loans for an automobile purchase. Companies may be able to create all three forms of utility—and understanding why consumers value products and services helps marketers create more effective campaigns. As discussed in the "Business Model" feature, to expand beyond its macho Baby Boomer segment, Harley-Davidson recently announced a 10-year plan that calls for the introduction of 100 new models to attract new riders.[6]

Assessment Check

1. What is utility?
2. Identify three ways in which marketing creates utility.

2 Evolution of the Marketing Concept

Marketing has always been an integral part of business, from the earliest village traders to large technology giants of today, known as FAANG companies—Facebook, Apple, Amazon, Netflix, and Google. Over time, however, marketing activities evolved through the five eras shown in **Figure 11.1**: the production, sales, marketing, and relationship eras, and now the social era. Note that these eras parallel some of the time periods discussed in Chapter 1.

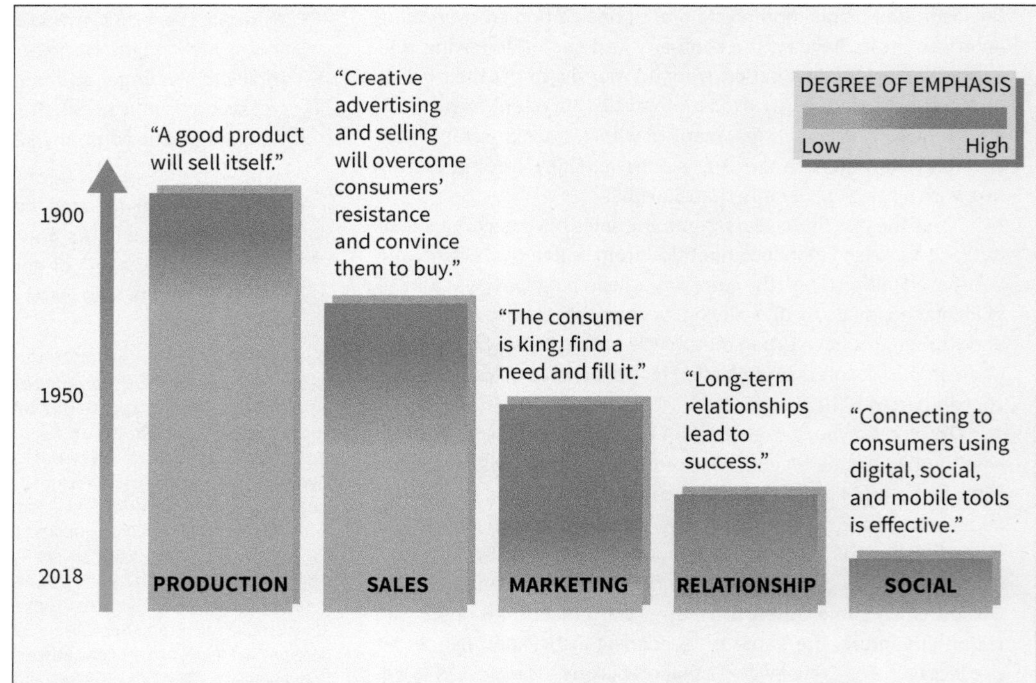

FIGURE 11.1 Five Eras in the History of Marketing

For centuries, organizations of the *production era* stressed efficiency in producing quality products. Their philosophy could be summed up by the remark "A good product will sell itself." Although this production orientation continued into the 20th century, it gradually gave way to the *sales era*, in which businesses assumed that consumers would buy as a result of energetic sales efforts. Organizations didn't fully recognize the importance of their customers until the *marketing era* of the 1950s, when they began to adopt a consumer orientation. This focus intensified, leading to the emergence of the *relationship era* in the 1990s. In the relationship era, companies emphasized customer satisfaction and building long-term business relationships. Today, the *social era* continues to grow exponentially, thanks to the Internet and social media sites like Facebook, Twitter, and LinkedIn. Companies now routinely use mobile, social media, virtual reality, artificial intelligence, chatbots, interactive content, marketing software, and the web as a way of marketing their goods and services to consumers.

Emergence of the Marketing Concept

The term **marketing concept** refers to a companywide customer orientation with the objective of achieving long-run success. The basic idea of the marketing concept is that marketplace success begins with the customer. A company should analyze each customer's needs and then work backward to offer products that fulfill them. The emergence of the marketing concept can be explained best by the shift from a *seller's market,* one with a shortage of goods and services, to a *buyer's market,* one with an abundance of goods and services. During the 1950s, the United States became a strong buyer's market, forcing companies to satisfy customers rather than just producing and selling goods and services.

marketing concept company-wide consumer orientation to promote long-run success.

Today, there is intense competition among companies to identify customers' stated and unstated wants and needs. E-commerce giant Amazon listens to their customers' needs by continuously testing new solutions. The company interacts with buyers through multiple channels including web, social, mobile app, and even Alexa, its virtual assistant. As customers demand more interactive experiences, omni-channel interactions also become more crucial. Building loyalty means listening to customers and adapting. Amazon has done so with its Amazon Prime offering, Amazon Fresh (grocery delivery), continued growth of Amazon Web Services (AWS), Amazon Video, Amazon Echo, drone patents, and the introduction of Amazon Go (a store with no checkout required). "We're not competitor obsessed, we're customer obsessed. We start with what the customer needs and we work backwards," says founder and CEO, Jeff Bezos.[7]

Assessment Check

1. What is the marketing concept?
2. How is the marketing concept tied to the relationship and social eras of marketing?

3 Not-for-Profit and Nontraditional Marketing

The marketing concept has traditionally been associated with products of profit-seeking organizations. Today, however, it is also being applied to not-for-profit sectors and other nontraditional areas ranging from religious organizations to political campaigns.

Not-for-Profit Marketing

Nonprofit marketing tactics differ from for-profit marketing strategies. Nonprofits, focused primarily on promoting a cause and getting people to volunteer and donate money, develop

Dave Hogan/TAS18 / Getty Images

Singer-songwriter Taylor Swift has contributed to numerous nonprofits that help sexual assault victims defend themselves.

marketing strategies differently than a business selling a product or service. Nonprofit organizations are tasked with finding ways to market and create awareness of their cause both to volunteers who wish to help and to individuals willing to donate to their cause.[8] The largest not-for-profit organization in the world is the Red Cross/Red Crescent. Other not-for-profits range from Habitat for Humanity to the Boys & Girls Clubs of America to the Juvenile Diabetes Research Foundation. These organizations all benefit by applying many of the strategies and business concepts used by profit-seeking companies. They apply marketing strategies to connect with audiences, secure funding, and accomplish their overall missions. Marketing strategies are important for not-for-profit organizations because they are all competing for dollars—from individual donors, foundations (through grants), and corporate donations.[9]

Not-for-profit organizations operate in both public and private sectors. Public groups include federal, state, and local government units as well as agencies that receive tax funding. A state's department of natural resources, for instance, regulates land conservation and environmental programs; the local animal control officer enforces ordinances protecting people and animals; a city's public health board ensures safe drinking water for its citizens. The private not-for-profit sector comprises many different types of organizations, including the Philadelphia Zoo, the United States Olympic Committee, and the American Academy of Orthopaedic Surgeons. Although some private not-for-profits generate surplus revenue, their primary goals are not earning profits. If they earn funds beyond their expenses, they invest the excess in their organizational missions.

In some cases, not-for-profit organizations form a partnership with a profit-seeking company to promote the company's message or distribute its goods and services. This partnership usually benefits both organizations. Merck, a global pharmaceutical company, has invested $33 million over 15 years in a program with the United Negro College Fund (UNCF), the largest minority educational assistance program in the United States. Merck supports more than 400 students pursuing undergraduate, graduate, and postdoctoral degrees in the biosciences. This initiative benefits both organizations by increasing the number of STEM (science, technology, engineering, and mathematics) students with mentors and research and learning internship opportunities at Merck.[10]

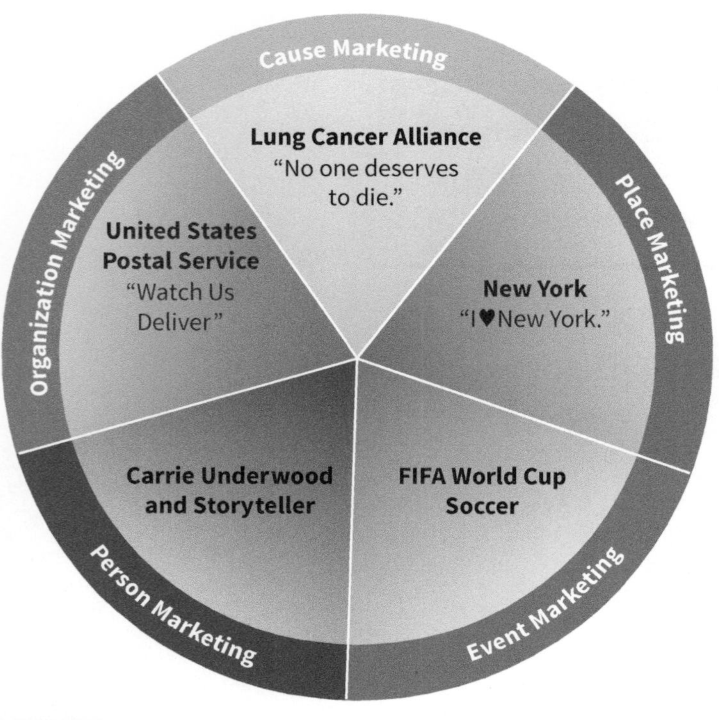

FIGURE 11.2 Categories of Nontraditional Marketing

Celebrities are particularly visible campaigning for not-for-profit organizations—their own as well as others. Matt Damon, Jennifer Hudson, and Ben Affleck have their own nonprofits dedicated to specific environmental, societal, and health issues. Recently, singer-songwriter Taylor Swift won a counter lawsuit against a former Denver radio personality who allegedly groped her during a post-concert photo opportunity. Since then, she has committed to making significant donations to multiple organizations that help sexual assault victims defend themselves. Joyful Heart Foundation, created by *Law and Order: Special Victims Unit* actress, Mariska Hargitay is one such organization. "Swift's donation is an extremely generous financial investment in the movement to end sexual violence," says Hargitay.[11]

Nontraditional Marketing

Not-for-profit organizations often engage in one or more of five major categories of nontraditional marketing: person marketing, place marketing, event marketing, cause marketing, and organization marketing. **Figure 11.2** provides examples of these types of marketing.

Person Marketing Efforts designed to attract the attention, interest, and preference of a target market toward a person are called **person marketing**. Campaign managers for a political candidate conduct marketing research, identify groups of voters and financial supporters, and then design advertising campaigns, fund-raising events, and political rallies to reach them. Although basketball icon and legend Michael Jordan left the NBA in 2003, he still rules the basketball shoe market with his Nike collaboration. Retro Jordan shoe sales remain strong, and Jordan's shoe earnings from the brand that bears his name were estimated at about $110 million in a recent year.[12]

person marketing use of efforts designed to attract the attention, interest, and preference of a target market toward a person.

Many successful job seekers apply the tools of person marketing. They research the wants and needs of prospective employers, and they identify ways they can meet them. They find employers through a variety of channels, sending messages that emphasize how they can benefit the employer.

Place Marketing As the term suggests, **place marketing** attempts to attract people to a particular area, such as a city, state, or nation. It may involve appealing to consumers as a tourist destination or to businesses as a desirable business location. A strategy for place marketing often includes advertising.

place marketing attempt to attract people to a particular area, such as a city, state, or nation.

Place marketing may be combined with event marketing, such as the Super Bowl. Each year on its official Super Bowl website, the NFL lists local host-city events, lodging, restaurants, travel packages, and even what to wear. Well before the actual game, the website captures the energy and spirit of the upcoming competition.[13]

Event Marketing Marketing or sponsoring short-term events such as athletic competitions and cultural and charitable performances is known as **event marketing**. The American Diabetes Association sponsors the "Tour de Cure," a series of fund-raising cycling events held across the United States to raise funds to support its mission to prevent and cure diabetes.[14] To forge deeper customer connections, American Express sponsors the U.S. Open tennis tournament and Coachella, a music festival.

event marketing marketing or sponsoring short-term events such as athletic competitions and cultural and charitable performances.

Clean & Green Business

Dell and Lonely Whale Foundation Direct Plastic Away from Waterways

Plastic litter in the earth's oceans continues to be a critical environmental issue, but thanks to Dell Computer, plastic from the ocean is finding new life. Dell is among a number of companies using plastic waste from the ocean in the production of its product packaging, and by doing so, the company has rescued 16,000 pounds of plastic out of the world's oceans.

Dell has partnered with the Lonely Whale Foundation, an ocean advocacy foundation created by actor Adrian Grenier. The foundation has reduced plastic in oceans by 8 million tons annually. Other products with plastic waste as part of their production include plastic milk jugs, laundry detergent bottles, and shopping bags. Even fashion retailer H&M, as part of its newest Conscious Exclusive Collection modeled by Natalia Vodianova, has made an elegant gown from BIONIC®—a polyester made from recycled shoreline waste.

To date, there is no established market for plastics recovered from oceans. But if Dell has anything to do with this issue, there soon may be one. They continue to invest in developing the infrastructure necessary to channel this plastic from the ocean and into various forms of production. With Dell as a leader, the hope is that other companies will follow suit. A few years ago, in conjunction with the Lonely Whale Foundation and to encourage further expansion, Dell ran a feasibility study in Haiti to determine the best way to collect, wash, and treat the plastic.

By using cutting-edge technology to bring the public into the depths of the sea to witness underwater life and the impact of ocean noise, plastics, and pollution, Dell hopes to educate and advocate about this critical environmental cause and its impact on the plight of the whale.

Questions for Critical Thinking

1. **According to a recent poll, 87% of consumers say they would switch from one brand to another on the basis of a worthy cause. Do you agree with this statistic? Why or why not?**
2. **Determine what Dell stands for as a brand, and then discuss the ways PC maker Dell's participation in the Lonely Whale Foundation integrates its cause marketing campaign into its culture and values.**

Sources: Aimee Lutkin, "Dell and Lonely Whale Launch Collaboration to Keep Plastic out of the Ocean," *Green Matters*, http://www.greenmatters.com, accessed April 8, 2018; Jamie Feldman, "This Stunning H&M Gown Is Made From Plastic Waste," *Huffington Post*, http://www.huffingtonpost.com, accessed April 8, 2018; company website, "H&M's Conscious Exclusive 2017 Collection Shows the Beauty of Sustainability," https://about.hm, accessed April 8, 2018; "Companies Use Ocean Plastics to Make Products for Eco-Minded Consumers," http://www.plasticsmakeitpossible.com, accessed April 8, 2018; Sierra Club, "5 Companies Leading the Charge in Using Ocean Plastic in Their Products," *Eco Watch*, http://www.ecowatch.com, accessed April 8, 2018.

Event marketing often forges partnerships between not-for-profit and profit-seeking organizations. Many businesses sponsor events such as 10K runs to raise funds for health-related charities. These events require a marketing effort to plan and attract participants and sponsors. Events may be intended to raise money or awareness, or both.

cause marketing marketing that promotes a cause or social issue, such as preventing child abuse, anti-littering efforts, and stop-smoking campaigns.

Cause Marketing

Marketing that promotes awareness of, or raises money for, a cause or social issue, such as drug abuse prevention or childhood hunger is **cause marketing**. Cause marketing seeks to educate the public and may or may not attempt to directly raise funds. An advertisement often contains a website address, through which people can obtain more information about the organization or issue. Then they can either donate money or take other actions of support. State Farm Insurance has partnered with nonprofit advocacy organization Mothers Against Drunk Driving (MADD) to sponsor its Power of You(th) program to combat underage teen drinking.[15]

Profit-seeking companies look for ways to contribute to their communities by joining forces with charities and causes, providing financial, marketing, and human resources. For-profit companies can also combine their goods and services with a cause. For customers who reuse bags to save paper or bring their own cloth bags, Whole Foods Markets gives customers a 5-cent credit, which can be donated to a local nonprofit organization. All nonprofits can apply to be considered for the Whole Foods "Nickels for Nonprofits" program.[16] PC maker Dell recently partnered with the Lonely Whale Foundation to find a new life for plastic ocean waste, by recycling it into its product packaging, as described in the "Clean and Green Business" feature.

organization marketing marketing strategy that influences consumers to accept the goals of, receive the services of, or contribute in some way to an organization.

Organization Marketing

The final category of nontraditional marketing, **organization marketing**, influences consumers to accept the goals of, receive the services of, or contribute in some way to an organization. The U.S. Postal Service, Teach for America, and the NBA are all examples of organizations that engage in marketing. The National Basketball Association (NBA) has social media coordinators who serve as virtual ambassadors. For the Brooklyn Nets, the coordinators create Internet buzz by monitoring content and capturing game moments and fan reactions across social media platforms such as Facebook, SnapChat, Instagram, and Twitter. Social media is used to push season ticket sales, merchandise, apps, promotional giveaways, corporate partners, and social engagement.[17]

Assessment Check

1. Why do not-for-profit organizations engage in marketing?
2. What are the five types of nontraditional marketing used by not-for-profit organizations?

4 Developing a Marketing Strategy

Decision makers in any successful organization, for-profit or not-for-profit, follow a two-step process to develop a *marketing strategy*. First, they study and analyze potential target markets and choose among them. Second, they create a marketing mix to satisfy the chosen market. **Figure 11.3** shows the relationships among the target market, the marketing mix variables, and the marketing environment. Later discussions refer back to this figure as they cover each topic. This section describes the development of a marketing strategy designed to attract and build relationships with customers. Sometimes, in an effort to do this, marketers use questionable methods, as described in the "Judgment Call" feature.

environmental scanning analysis of external environmental factors by marketers to understand how they impact business and marketing decisions.

Earlier chapters of this book introduced many of the environmental factors that affect the success or failure of a company's business strategy, including today's rapidly changing and highly competitive world of business, a vast array of social and cultural factors, economic challenges, political and legal factors, and technological innovations. To better understand the external factors that operate outside a marketing manager's control, **environmental scanning** is conducted. This process allows a marketer to assess competitive, social, economic, technological,

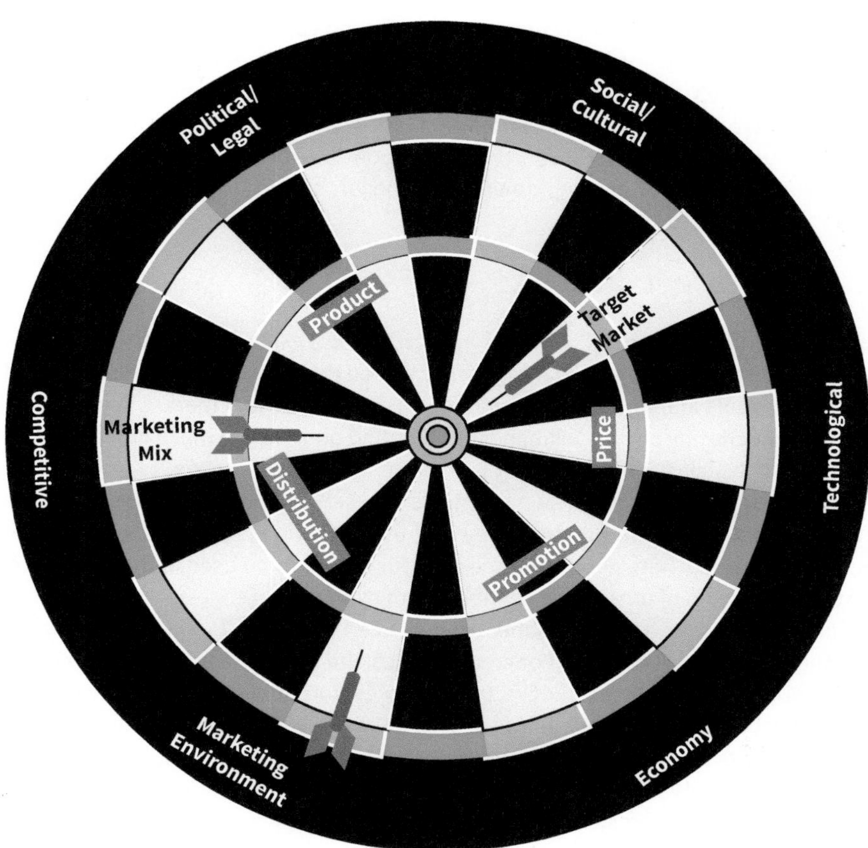

FIGURE 11.3 Target Market and Marketing Mix within the Marketing Environment

Judgment Call

Big Pharma: Persuading the Prescribers?

On a daily basis, people from all walks of life depend upon prescription drugs to sustain life, and in most cases, to treat chronic lifestyle diseases such as high cholesterol, diabetes, or hypertension. Big Pharma, the name for pharmaceutical companies collectively as a sector or industry, has always been scrutinized for many of its practices, including the way it conducts its marketing—which seems to be working. Over the past 20 years, research reveals that the percentage of Americans taking more than five prescription medications has nearly tripled.

The relationship between doctors and Big Pharma continues to be scrutinized. According to the recent data, nine out of 10 pharmaceutical companies spend more money on marketing than on research and development. As a consumer, a fair share of media from Big Pharma (think: TV) includes a familiar pattern: Do you feel [insert symptom]? Has [insert ailment] been holding you back? (Footage of sad people is shown.) Next, the invitation to "talk to your doctor" about the prescription drug that will change all that is shown. Last, a laundry list (sometimes spoken quickly) of some of the potential (and somewhat alarming), side effects. In the ads, a reversal of sorts results when, rather than the doctor recommending the drug to the patient, patients are being "asked" to recommend drugs to their doctors.

Big Pharma spends $3 billion annually marketing premium-branded drugs to consumers and 8 times that amount—$24 billion, marketing directly to health care professionals like physicians. For years, drug makers have engaged in financial incentivizing not only doctors and health care providers to promote their profitable drugs (generics are far less expensive), but in addition, pharmaceutical sales reps are compensated based upon the number of prescriptions written by the doctors they call on (or visit). Pharmaceutical companies assert that their visits to doctors serve an educational purpose. However, with the widespread availability of high-quality sources for ongoing medical education, it's hard to imagine that the lure of an expensive dinner and theater production from a drug representative would serve that purpose.

Questions for Critical Thinking

1. How does the marketing practice described relate to the result of over-prescription of medications that may not even be the most appropriate for patients?
2. What might be more ethical alternatives to the way drug companies market their products to prescribers? Discuss.

Sources: Jessica Migala, "Pharma Reps Are Basically Bribing Your Doctor, Study Confirms," *Tonic*, http://www.tonic.com, accessed April 13, 2018; Nicole Van Groningen, "Big Pharma Gives Your Doctor Gifts. Then Your Doctor Gives You Big Pharma's Drugs," *Washington Post*, http://www.washingtonpost.com, accessed April 13, 2018; organization website, Mladen Golubic, MD, PhD, "Lifestyle Choices: Root Causes of Chronic Diseases," https://my.clevelandclinic.org, accessed April 13, 2018; John Marshall, "Why You See Such Weird Drug Commercials on TV All the Time," *Thrillist*, http://www.thrillist.com, accessed April 13, 2018; Dale Archer, "The Dark Side of Big Pharma," *Forbes*, http://www.forbes.com, accessed April 13, 2018; Bernard Munos, "Managing Revenue Growth (and Contraction) in Big Pharma: What Have We Learned in the Last 10 Years?" *Forbes*, http://www.forbes.com, accessed April 13, 2018; Jonha Revesencio, "4 Examples of Dubious Marketing Ethics," *Huffington Post*, http://www.huffingtonpost.com, accessed April 13, 2018.

and political environments that may impact business, and consequently, marketing decisions. A marketing plan is a key component of a company's overall business plan. The marketing plan outlines the company's marketing strategy and includes information about the specific activities to be undertaken, the audience to whom each activity is targeted, sales and revenue goals, the marketing budget, the timing of who will be responsible for specific tasks, metrics used to measure goals, and the timing to implement elements of the marketing mix.

Selecting a Target Market

The expression "find a need and fill it" is perhaps the simplest explanation of the two elements of a marketing strategy. A company's marketers find a need through marketing research and analysis of the individuals and business decision makers in its potential market. A market consists of people with purchasing power, willingness to buy, and authority to make purchase decisions.

consumer (B2C) product good or service that is purchased by end users.

business (B2B) product good or service purchased to be used, either directly or indirectly, in the production of other goods for resale.

target market group of people toward whom an organization markets its goods, services, or ideas with a strategy designed to satisfy their specific needs and preferences.

marketing mix blending of the four elements of marketing strategy—product, distribution, promotion, and pricing—to fit the needs and preferences of a specific target market.

Markets can be classified by type of product. **Consumer products**—often known as business-to-consumer (B2C) products—are goods and services, such as GPS systems, tomato sauce, and a haircut, that are purchased by end users. **Business products**—or business-to-business (B2B) products—are goods and services purchased to be used, either directly or indirectly, in the production of other goods for resale, for example, an espresso machine at a coffee café or a printing press at a printer. Some products can fit either classification depending on who buys them and why. A computer or credit card can be used by a business or a consumer.

An organization's **target market** is the group of potential customers toward whom it directs its marketing efforts. Customer needs and wants vary considerably, but marketers concentrate their efforts on one or a few key segments consisting of the customers whose needs and desires most closely match their product or service offerings. *Popular Science* is geared toward readers who are interested in science and technology, whereas *Bon Appétit* is aimed at readers who are interested in fine food, cooking, and entertaining.

Decisions about marketing involve strategies for four areas of marketing activity: product, distribution, promotion, and pricing. A company's **marketing mix** blends the four strategies to fit the needs and preferences of a specific target market. Marketing success depends not on the four individual strategies but on their unique combination.

Product strategy involves more than just designing a good or service with needed attributes. It also includes decisions about package design, brand names, trademarks, warranties, product image, new-product development, and customer service. Think about your favorite pair of jeans. Do you like them because they fit the best, or do other attributes—such as styling and overall image—also contribute to your brand preference? *Distribution strategy*, the second marketing mix variable, ensures that customers receive their purchases in the proper quantities at the right times and locations. *Promotional strategy*, another marketing mix element, effectively blends advertising, personal selling, sales promotion, and public relations to achieve its goals of informing, persuading, and influencing purchase decisions.

Pricing strategy, the final mix element, is also one of the most difficult areas of marketing decision making in setting profitable and justifiable prices for the company's product offerings. Such actions are sometimes subject to government regulation and considerable public scrutiny. They also represent a powerful competitive weapon and frequently produce responses by the other companies in the industry, who match price changes to avoid losing customers. Think about your jeans again. Would you continue to purchase them if they were priced either much higher or much lower?

The traditional drugstore chain continues to double as a healthcare clinic, and with its expected growth the following marketing strategies would be employed.

Product/Service Retail health clinics are low-cost, walk-in medical facilities usually found in retailers like drug-chain giant CVS. There are no board-certified doctors on site, so patients typically see a nurse practitioner or a physician assistant who can prescribe medicines while diagnosing and treating minor medical conditions like colds and flus. Conveniently open after work hours, they offer appropriate vaccinations and inexpensive sports and summer camp physicals for children.

Price They have proven to be a popular and more convenient alternative to primary care and emergency room services. Because of their low cost—usually about 40% less than a physician office visit, or $60 per visit, they have become popular as a trusted source.

Place The company operates more than 1,100 retail clinics throughout the United States, many of which are conveniently located in supermarkets or retail drugstores.

Promotion Drugstore-chain CVS has been promoting its Minute Clinics to shoppers and among nationwide healthcare organizations. The seasonality of its services combined with reaching patients who don't typically shop at a retail store can be a challenge, however. Retail clinics are evolving with the changing economic and healthcare landscape, and the operators of the clinics will continue to develop marketing strategies to match their growing demand.[18]

Courtesy of CVS Health

With a changing healthcare landscape, drugstore-chain CVS continues to promote its MinuteClinic—where most insurance is accepted and no appointment is necessary.

Developing a Marketing Mix for International Markets

Marketing a good or service in foreign markets means deciding whether to offer the same marketing mix in every market *(standardization)* or to develop a unique mix to fit each market *(adaptation)*. The advantages of standardizing the marketing mix include reliable marketing performance and low costs. This approach works best with B2B goods, such as steel, chemicals, and aircraft, which require little sensitivity to a nation's culture.

Adaptation, on the other hand, lets marketers vary their marketing mix to suit local competitive conditions, consumer preferences, and government regulations. Consumer tastes are often shaped by local cultures. Because consumer products generally tend to be more culture dependent than business products, they more often require adaptation. Dunkin' Donuts is known for its delicious Boston Kreme doughnuts in the United States. However, in China, the company serves up fresh batches of dry pork and bacon-topped doughnuts. In India, doughnuts are not a favorite, so Dunkin' Donuts has retooled its menu to serve beef-free burgers. For example, the Naughty Lucy Veg burger's "center-filled veg patty gushes out warm, loving cheese. Its raw green mango tickle adds a touch of mischief. Its fresh veggies, chipotle sauce, and sourdough buns do whatever they can to make you feel loved. Because in an extra harsh world, you need extra comforting," according to Dunkin' Donuts.[19]

Marketers also try to build adaptability into the designs of standardized goods and services for international and domestic markets. *Mass customization* allows a company to mass produce goods and services while adding unique features to individual or small groups of orders. Despite joint pain from their hips, knees, and shoulders, fitness-minded Baby Boomers, born between 1946 and 1964, are determined to maintain a high quality of life by staying active. Conformis a company making joint implants, is using 3D printing and imaging software to more precisely tailor replacement joints for this exploding market.[20]

Assessment Check

1. Distinguish between consumer products and business products.
2. What are the steps in developing a marketing strategy?

5 Marketing Research

Marketing research involves more than just collecting data. Researchers must decide how to collect data, interpret the results, convert the data into decision-oriented information, and communicate those results to managers for use in decision making. **Marketing research** is the process of collecting and evaluating information to help marketers gain insight in order

marketing research collecting and evaluating information to help marketers make effective decisions.

to make effective decisions. It links business decision makers to the marketplace by providing data about potential target markets that help them design effective marketing mixes.

big data information collected in massive amounts and at unprecedented speed from both traditional and digital sources that is used in business decision making.

The technological advances of the past decades—the Internet, social media, mobile devices, and the like—have given rise to what's been called **big data**, information collected in massive amounts and at unprecedented speed from both traditional and digital sources. These advances make it possible for businesses to gather and analyze information from customers, visitors to company websites, social media sites, downloaded apps, and more. Big data has the potential to increase revenue, create new business and marketing strategies, and build market share. A number of different analytics, usually quantitative in nature, are revealed by analyzing big data. Descriptive analytics reveal what happened, diagnostic analytics reveal why something happened, predictive analytics reveal what will happen, and prescriptive analytics allow marketers to make something happen. However, the greatest challenge for marketers is the ability to manage and analyze all of this data.[21]

Obtaining Marketing Research Data

Marketing researchers need both internal and external data. Companies generate *internal data* within their organizations. Financial records provide a tremendous amount of useful information, such as inventory levels; sales generated by different categories of customers or product lines; profitability of particular divisions; or comparisons of sales by territories, salespeople, customers, or product lines; or unpaid bills. At Amazon, a company that believes that all data must be collected and analyzed, every transaction is recorded, every buyer is profiled, every inventory movement is known, and even more importantly, every possible next order can be suggested based on each visitor's purchasing and browsing history. The company has the ability to improve its customer's experience by providing recommendations through personalized interactions while engaging across multiple channels, due mainly to the sheer magnitude and power of its data.

Researchers gather *external data* from outside sources, including previously published data. Trade associations publish reports on activities in particular industries. Advertising agencies collect information on the audiences reached by various media. National marketing research companies offer information through paid subscription services. Some of these professional research companies specialize in specific markets, such as teens or ethnic groups. This information helps companies make decisions about developing or modifying products.

A recent report by comScore, a marketing research company, indicates that consumers view website, video, and app content across a variety of platforms, including mobile. In today's multiplatform digital media environment, understanding digital consumer behavior across desktop computers, tablets, and mobile devices (smart phones) is critical information to marketers.

Mobile commerce (m-commerce), purchasing goods and services using mobile wireless technology, has now surpassed desktop or other media. In the next few years, mobile commerce is expected to reach 54% of e-commerce sales. Mobile commerce is driven by retailers that create more opportunities for consumers to purchase products by developing mobile responsive sites. In addition, more Millennials are using their phones as a primary device—and their increased earning power has meant increased spending. Big data of this nature can provide very clear indications of mobile purchasing habits and what consumers seek in a product.[22]

Using insight software programs and social media research techniques, market research has evolved beyond traditional methods of surveys and focus groups. Companies with social media campaigns can sift through vast amounts of opinions, ideas, and even critiques across multiple channels including web, social, mobile, SMS (text messaging), and email. With new and original ways to gather research about consumers, and with solicited feedback data from surveys, social media campaigns can be segmented and tracked to spot real-time trends and patterns. Backpack maker Herschel Supply Company uses social media to attract different audience segments. Their Instagram account attracts aspiring photographers; their Pinterest following caters more toward females; and their Twitter posts attract those interested in product releases and news stories.[23]

Secondary data, or previously published data, are low cost and easy to obtain. Federal, state, and local government publications are excellent data sources, and most are available online.

The most frequently used government statistics include census data, published every 10 years, which contain the population's age, gender, education level, household size and composition, occupation, employment status, and income. Private research firms such as Pricewaterhouse-Coopers (PwC) provide a range of research on topics from business megatrends to industry analysis, some of which are available online. This information helps companies evaluate consumers' buying behavior, anticipate possible changes in the marketplace, and identify new markets.

Even though secondary data are a quick and inexpensive resource, marketing researchers sometimes discover that this information isn't specific or current enough for their needs. If so, researchers may conclude that they must collect *primary data*—data collected firsthand through original sources, using such methods as observation and surveys. Online survey sites, such as Survey Monkey, are quick and effective ways to collect primary data.

Observational studies view the actions of consumers either directly or through other devices. Several examples of observational techniques include actual observation through video cameras, through cookies on computers to track site views and visits, and through bar-coded transactions for purchasing behavior.[24]

As interest in fresh and organic products continues to grow, canned soup consumption is down. Campbell Soup Company, in an effort to change its culture, undertook a marketing research study that involved eating, cooking, and shopping with Millennials to understand their habits. The company recently purchased Snyder's-Lance, which includes Cape Cod potato chips, Diamond Foods, and Pop Secret popcorn. "Snacking is a big deal," says Campbell's CEO, and market research points to the increasing number of people who indulge in snacks from their corner store and on their way to the office.[25]

Simply observing customers cannot provide some types of information. A researcher might observe a customer buying a red sweater but have no idea why the purchase was made—or for whom. When researchers need information about consumers' attitudes, opinions, and motives, they need to ask the consumers themselves. They may conduct surveys in person, online, or in focus groups.

A *focus group* gathers 8 to 12 people in a room or over the Internet to discuss a particular topic. A focus group can generate new ideas, address consumers' needs, and even point out flaws in existing products. In an effort to rebrand, Seattle, Washington–based Alaska Airlines, as told to the airline by customer focus groups, unveiled a new logo and update to its iconic Eskimo face.[26] Social media has emerged as the new focus group for some brands able to collect information from wide and varied audiences—and to gather insights about their customers, such as their demographics and geography, lifestyle, and purchase behavior.

Applying Marketing Research Data

As the accuracy of information collected by researchers increases, so does the effectiveness of resulting marketing strategies. One field of research is known as **business intelligence**, which uses various activities and technologies to gather, store, and analyze data to make better competitive decisions. Unilever, maker of consumer products including Dove soap, Axe deodorant, and Ben and Jerry's ice cream, has a highly regarded global research staff and values input from outside sources. The company has adopted a crowdsourced, open-innovation platform, where external contributions are sought for diverse projects. Unilever's "challenges and wants" web page solicits ideas for new designs and technologies to help improve the way its products are made. Recently Unilever developed an additional crowdsourcing website called Unilever Sustainable Living Plan (USLP), focused on ideas for embedding innovative and creative sustainability processes for further growth.[27]

business intelligence activities and technologies for gathering, storing, and analyzing data to make better competitive decisions.

Data Mining

Once a company has built a database, marketers must be able to analyze the data and use the information it provides. **Data mining**, part of the broader field of business intelligence, is the task of using computer-based technology to evaluate large sets of data, or big data, and

data mining the task of using computer-based technology to evaluate data in a database and identify useful trends.

identify useful trends. These trends or patterns may suggest predictive models of real-world business activities. Accurate data mining can help researchers forecast economic trends and pinpoint sales prospects.

data warehouse customer database that allows managers to combine data from several different organizational functions.

Data mining uses **data warehouses** or relational databases, which are sophisticated customer databases that allow managers to combine data from several different organizational functions such as sales, finance, and customer service. In an effort to recruit consumers with specific conditions for clinical drug trials, pharmaceutical companies hire companies like Blue Chip Marketing Worldwide. Based in suburban Chicago, Blue Chip Marketing uses data from social networks, data brokers, and pharmacies to identify potential participants. Among the issues arising from data mining are ownership of web user data, the targeting capabilities of web research, government intervention, how collected data is used, and privacy.[28]

Supermarkets increasingly engage in data mining and business intelligence. Loyalty programs, most of which are online or downloadable with an app, are driven by the desire to get purchasing data about customers to use in data mining. Retail giant Target recently used data mining, by way of purchases, to predict whether customers were pregnant. Typical purchases at the beginning of their second trimester included unscented lotions. What followed was soap and cotton balls, and then hand sanitizers and wash cloths. Each purchase is a signal that the customer is getting closer to their delivery date, at which time the company begins targeting this segment with diaper promotions.[29]

Unity Analytics's segmentation technology and predictive analysis mine and analyze the individual behavior and traits of online and app game players by tracking the number of hours they spend on games and creating behavioral profiles. App and game developers pay a monthly fee for the resulting data. The company's CEO says providing information about user activity gives brands a way to build their stories with developers to find and engage the right player for greater retention and increased revenues.[30]

Assessment Check

1. What is the difference between primary data and secondary data?
2. What is data mining?

6 Market Segmentation

market segmentation process of dividing a total market into several relatively homogeneous groups.

Market segmentation is the process of defining and subdividing a large homogeneous market into specific and identifiable segments or groups whose characteristics, needs, and wants are similar. Market segmentation, used by nonprofits and for-profit organizations to reach specific markets, is often based on the results of research, which attempts to identify trends among certain groups of people. Facebook and YouTube remain the primary social media platform for most U.S. adult users. In the 18- to 24-year-old user category, about 78% use Snapchat, 71% use Instagram, and 45% are Twitter users. Approximately 41% of users on Pinterest are women, as compared to 16% of whom are men. Some 50% of higher income college graduates use LinkedIn, compared with only 9% of those with a high school diploma or less.[31] This kind of information can help marketers decide what types of products to develop and to whom they should be marketed.

Market segmentation attempts to isolate the traits that distinguish a certain group of customers from the overall market. However, segmentation doesn't automatically translate to marketing success. **Table 11.1** lists several criteria for segmentation that marketers should consider. The effectiveness of a segmentation strategy depends on how well the market meets these criteria. Once marketers identify a market segment to target, they can create an appropriate marketing strategy.

Whole Foods, purchased by Amazon, targets customers whose income is well above the national average, and those who are conscious about the environment and lead a healthy lifestyle. Most of Whole Foods customers are college graduates. Whole Foods' affluent

TABLE 11.1 Criteria for Market Segmentation

Criterion	Description	Example
Measurable	Some form of data should be available to measure the size of the market segment.	To evaluate the growth potential of each segment, measuring is important—for example, the readiness of residents in a particular area willing to participate in prenatal care.
Accessible	In terms of distribution and communication, the market segment should be reachable.	Each segment needs to be reached and communicated with on an efficient basis—for example, reaching senior citizens or those who do not speak English.
Sizeable or Substantial	To warrant a company's resources and focus, the market segment should be large enough to offer sales and profit potential.	A company has minimum financial return requirements from its investment in a market—for example, the number of banks that realize the value of online banking services.
Unique or Differentiable Needs	Differences between market segments should be clearly defined, so that the campaigns, products, and marketing tools applied to each can be implemented without overlap.	Develop a unique marketing mix for a specified target market—for example, a waterless bathing gel adopted by the military, airlines, and less-developed countries with limited access to water.

Sources: Fraser Sherman, "How to Identify the Segmentation Criteria That Will Affect Your Target Market Selection," *Houston Chronicle,* http://smallbusiness.chron.com, accessed April 8, 2018; Alessandro Iannuzzi, "Market Segmentation Criteria—Five Essential Criteria," *LinkedIn,* https://www.linkedin.com, accessed April 8, 2018.

customers should certainly help Amazon, which can now reach millions of Whole Foods customers, who live primarily in dense urban areas. In fact, 72% of the U.S. population lives within a one-hour drive from a Whole Foods store, and one-third of American households with annual incomes over $100,000 live within 3 miles of a Whole Foods.[32]

How Market Segmentation Works

An immediate segmentation distinction involves whether the company is offering goods and services to customers for their own use or to purchasers who will use them directly or indirectly in providing other products and services for resale (the so-called B2B market). Depending on whether their company offers consumer or business products, marketers segment their target markets differently. Four common bases for segmenting consumer markets are geographical segmentation, demographic segmentation, psychographic segmentation, and product-related segmentation. By contrast, business markets can segment on three criteria: customer-based segmentation, end-use segmentation, and geographical segmentation. **Table 11.2** lists the segmentation methods for consumer (B2C) markets.

Segmenting Consumer Markets

Market segmentation has been around since people first began selling products. Tailors made some clothing items for men and others for women. Tea was imported from India for tea drinkers in England and other European countries. In addition to demographic and geographical segmentation, today's marketers also define customer groups based on psychographic—lifestyle and values—criteria as well as product-related distinctions.

Geographical Segmentation The oldest segmentation method is **geographical segmentation**—dividing a market into homogeneous groups on the basis of their locations. Geographical location does not guarantee that consumers in a certain region will all buy the same kinds of products, but it does provide some indication of needs. For instance, suburbanites buy more lawn-care products than central-city dwellers. However, many suburbanites choose instead to purchase the services of a lawn maintenance company. Consumers who live in northern states, where winter is more severe, are more likely to buy ice scrapers, snow shovels, and snow blowers than those who live in warmer climates. They are also more likely to contract

geographical segmentation dividing a market into homogeneous groups on the basis of their locations.

TABLE 11.2 Segmentation Methods for Consumer (B2C) Markets

Segmentation Method	Variables	Example
Geographical	Region, Population Density, Zip Code	Producers of seasonal products like snow blowers, water and snow skis, jet skis, umbrellas, and heavy winter coats often market based upon geographical segmentation. Tractor dealers like John Deere are far more prevalent in rural than urban areas.
Demographic	Age, Gender, Income, Education, Family Size and Life Cycle, Occupation	Income level influences consumer purchasing. Companies selling automobiles, housing, jewelry, clothing, and food segment based upon income. Pharmaceutical companies segment based upon a number of demographics, including but not limited to gender, age, and life cycle.
Psychographic	Lifestyles, Attitudes, Traits, Habits, Opinions, Behavior Patterns, Values, Personality, Self-Image	Companies producing vitality beverages, herbal supplements, and healthy snacks may target health-conscious consumers, while carmakers like Subaru may segment consumers who value practicality or the outdoors. Companies who sell high-end trendy clothing may segment on the basis of personality, attitudes, and self-image.
Product-Related	Comfort, Safety, Luxury, Economy, Convenience, Durability, Brand Loyalty, Eco-friendly, Usage Rates	Automobile companies may segment according to benefits including comfort (Chevrolet), safety (Volvo), economy (Honda Civic), luxury (Mercedes-Benz), durability (GMC Yukon), and eco-friendly (Chevrolet Volt). Usage rates might include non, light, medium, and heavy users.

with companies who remove the snow from driveways. Marketers also look at the size of the population of an area, as well as who lives there: What age are the residents? What is their level of income? What is their ethnic makeup?

Job growth and migration patterns are important considerations as well. Some businesses combine areas or even entire countries that share similar population and product-use patterns instead of treating each as an independent segment.

demographic segmentation distinguishes markets on the basis of various demographic or socioeconomic characteristics.

Demographic Segmentation

By far the most common method of market segmentation, **demographic segmentation** distinguishes markets on the basis of various demographic or socioeconomic characteristics. Common demographic measures include gender, income, age, occupation, household size, stage in the family life cycle, education, and racial or ethnic group. The U.S. Census Bureau is one of the best sources of demographic information for the domestic market. **Table 11.3** lists some of the measures used in demographic segmentation.

TABLE 11.3 Common Demographic Measures

Demographic Measure	Segments
Gender	Male, Female, Non-Binary, Transgender, Other
Income	Less than $20,000; $20,000–$34,999; $35,000–$49,999; $50,000–$74,999; $75,000–$99,999; $100,000–$149,999; $150,000–$199,999; $200,000 or more
Age	17 or younger; 18–20; 21–29; 30–39; 40–49; 50–59; 60–64; 65+
Occupation	Professional, services, technical, management, education, administrative, unemployed, retired
Household Size	1; 2; up to 4; 5 or more
Stage in Family Life Cycle	Infancy (0–3); early childhood (3–6); middle childhood (6–8); late childhood (9–11); adolescence (12–20); early adulthood (20–35); midlife (35–50); mature adulthood (50–80); late adulthood (80+)
Education	Less than high school degree; high school degree or equivalent (e.g., GED); some college but no degree; associate degree; bachelor degree; graduate degree; doctoral degree; professional degree (e.g., MD or JD)
Race and Ethnicity	Caucasian, Asian, African American, Hispanic, Native American

More children today are being raised in a gender-neutral manner, and some retailers have become more wary of marketing some products only to boys or only to girls. For example, H & M, Zara, and Target released a gender-neutral clothing collection, and U.K. retailer John Lewis is removing gender labels from its children's clothing. Maybelline, L'Oreal, and Cover Girl all have hired male models. As consumers move away from traditional gender stereotypes, some retailers are becoming less gendered. Facebook now has over 70 gender options to allow people to better express their identities on its platform.[33]

Courtesy of Diaper Dude

Designed with today's dad in mind, Chris Pegula of DiaperDude.com created a hip and functional messenger-style diaper bag.

As men continue to participate more fully in child-rearing responsibilities, Chris Pegula created Diaper Dude bags when he noticed that most diaper bags and accessories had a sense of style and design geared more toward women. Rather than carry his items in a backpack, Pegula designed the Diaper Dude for dads (and moms, too) (see photo). The messenger-style bag provides easy access to essentials and is also hip and functional. The product line has been extended to include accessories like travel and laptop bags. Other items designed with men in mind include Just for Men products that include a quick five-minute leave-in coloring process for hair, moustaches, and beards.[34]

Another shift involves purchasing power. Women now control an estimated 80% of U.S. consumer purchases, up to $15 trillion a year.[35] A number of companies like jewelers who sell charms—Pandora and Alex and Ani—target their products to this dominant consumer segment, which includes moms.[36]

With our rapidly aging population, age is perhaps the most volatile factor in demographic segmentation in the United States. Of the 335-plus million people estimated to be living in the United States over the next few years, almost 30 percent will be age 55 or older.[37] Working from these statistics, marketers for travel and leisure products, as well as retirement and business investments, are working hard to attract the attention of this age group, the aging Baby Boomers—those born between 1946 and 1964. Active-adult housing communities are one result of these efforts. Some developers have built communities with a resort-style atmosphere in desirable locations such as Colorado ski country or the outskirts of large cities such as Chicago and San Francisco. One poll indicates that 74% of adults now plan to work past retirement age—63% part-time and 11% full-time. Twenty years earlier, only 14% planned to work after age 65. One segment marketers are paying close attention to is Baby Boomer women. With successful careers, investments, and inheritances from parents, they are more financially empowered than their moms from a previous generation.[38]

Millennials, a diverse group between the ages of 23 and 38, hold approximately $1.3 trillion in consumer purchasing power. (There is no official age range for Millennials, but the group is defined generally as born between the early 1980s and early 2000s.) With potential earning power expected to increase, they're also the most educated generation in U.S. history. Millennials are more likely than the generation that came before them to pay a premium to purchase green products and to place more emphasis on purchasing from companies who support a cause they care about.[39]

Statistics can be helpful, but they don't tell the entire story. Marketers must learn where people live, how old they are, what language or languages they speak, and how much income they have in order to serve them well. They must learn cultural tastes and preferences, too. Music artists and bands have embraced technology using social media platforms, becoming more customer-centric, and catering directly to fans. See the "Business & Technology" feature to learn more.

Above all, companies must avoid stereotyping if they are going to market successfully to a diverse group of consumers. One way to do this is to break a large group into smaller segments or subgroups. For instance, the Hispanic market is made up of many smaller segments, based on country of origin, language, lifestyle, and cultural values. In an attempt to target a younger Hispanic audience, three television networks have begun to offer bilingual, Spanish, and English-language programming with Hispanic themes. Approximately 65% of the 58 million Hispanics living in the United States are between the ages of 18 and 34, and unlike previous generations many are English-first or bilingual. In an attempt

Business & Technology

Music Artists Embrace Direct-to-Fan Marketing

A few years ago, with no advance notice and using only social media, music icon Beyoncé bypassed traditional marketing channels and announced her self-titled album. She boasts millions of followers on Instagram, Facebook, and Tumblr, and her YouTube videos have been viewed by millions. Some marketing experts have compared Beyoncé's album release to a form of relationship marketing—Beyoncé has a loyal fan base with whom she has built a rock-solid relationship.

Long gone are the days when musicians worked tirelessly knocking on the doors of record executives for a golden record deal. In fact, it wasn't long ago that the only way a musical artist could reach an audience was through a record label. No more.

Today, the music industry continues to evolve at hyper speed, primarily a result of disruption caused by technology. The previous multilayered model put the power in the hands of record label executives and marketers. Today, however, with technology platforms and social media, the marketing power has landed in the hands of the creative genius behind the music. With a direct-to-fan concept, consumers have benefited from a more authentic customer-centric approach. Music lovers across the globe can now connect directly with their favorite artists and bands to learn about new releases and tour schedules.

The music industry's traditional model of marketing began with vinyl albums and then shifted to CDs. Today, an alternative to free illegal music downloads on the Internet is the mass marketing of digital downloads for a small fee—mostly by tune rather than by album. Artists who once felt the grip of industry executives making tremendous profits at their expense can now embrace the power of social media with greater control and lower costs associated with direct-to-fan marketing.

Questions for Critical Thinking

1. With a tweet and an e-mail, social media tools allow an artist or touring band to market their music at a cost that is close to zero. Discuss and provide examples of three different music artists or bands and how they are using social media effectively for marketing purposes.
2. How have consumers benefited from the power shift of marketing to artists and bands themselves? Are there downsides to this approach?

Sources: Alison Coleman, "How the Music Retail Industry Is Being Disrupted Beyond All Recognition," *Forbes*, http://www.forbes.com, accessed April 10, 2018; company website, http://www.donnapeeples.com, accessed April 10, 2018; Natasha Nanner, "5 Music Artists Who Have Mastered Social Media," *Branded3.com*, http://www.branded3.com, accessed April 10, 2018; Hugh McIntyre, "Marketing After Beyoncé: The State of the Surprise Album," *Forbes*, http://www.forbes.com, accessed April 10, 2018; Carolyn Englar, "Flawless Branding: Lessons for Marketers from Beyoncé," *Percolate.com*, https://blog.percolate.com, accessed April 10, 2018; Heather McDonald, "Direct to Fan Marketing Bypasses the Music Industry," The Balance, www.thebalance.com, accessed April 10, 2018.

to target a younger Hispanic audience, two television networks have begun to offer bilingual, Spanish, and English-language programming with Hispanic themes. To capture teen and young adult bilingual listeners and their Spanish-speaking-only parents and grandparents, the Spanish language network Telemundo has launched a newly designed digital platform that includes an updated and streamlined look (see photo) for its 18 Telemundo-owned stations' online properties, including desktop, mobile, and station apps so that viewers can access content across platforms they prefer to use.[40]

Brad Barket/Telemundo/NBCU Photo Bank via Getty Images

TELEMUNDO

Aimed at Hispanic and Latino American audiences worldwide, Telemundo broadcasts programs and original content consisting of telenovelas, sports, reality television, news programming, and films.

Marketers typically segment and adopt different strategies in order to sell products and services to various groups based upon stages in family life cycle. As families pass through each life cycle stage, needs change. The stages include unmarried, newly marrieds, and full nest (two stages: those whose youngest child is six or younger, and those whose youngest child is six or older). Once children leave home, the empty nest 1 stage of the life cycle begins and adults are likely to be in a strong financial position to purchase vacations and luxury items. The empty nest 2 stage usually indicates retirement and, consequently, a decline in income. These individuals appeal to marketers of medical appliances, medication, and medical care products.[41]

Psychographic Segmentation Lifestyle is the sum of a person's needs, preferences, motives, attitudes, social habits, and cultural background. In recent years, marketing researchers have tried to understand consumer lifestyles. This effort has led to another strategy for segmenting target markets, **psychographic segmentation**, which divides consumer markets into groups with similar psychological characteristics, values, and lifestyles.

psychographic segmentation dividing consumer markets into groups with similar psychological characteristics, values, and lifestyles.

Psychographic studies have evaluated motivations for purchases of hundreds of goods and services, ranging from soft drinks to health care services. Using the resulting data, companies tailor their marketing strategies to carefully chosen market segments. A frequently used method of developing psychographic profiles involves the use of *AIO statements*—people's verbal descriptions of various activities, interests, and opinions. Researchers survey a sample of consumers, asking them whether they agree or disagree with each statement. The answers are then tabulated and analyzed for use in identifying various lifestyle categories.

When psychographic customer profiles are understood, more effectively focused marketing communications and promotions can be implemented. A psychographic profile provides more of a holistic perspective and overview than just demographic information alone. Understanding what customers like and don't like gives companies a huge competitive advantage. Hired by Donald Trump's 2016 campaign, a political data firm called Cambridge Analytica gained access to private information on more than 80 million Facebook users and offered tools to identify personalities of American voters to potentially influence their behavior. The data, used to map personality traits based upon what people had "liked" on Facebook, included users' identities, friends, and networks to target with digital advertisements. To do this, Cambridge Analytica designed personality quizzes for Facebook users to assess them on the basis of a score called an "OCEAN," which includes Openness, Conscientiousness, Extroversion, Agreeableness, and Neuroticism.[42]

Although demographic classifications such as age, gender, and income are relatively easy to identify and measure, researchers may also want to consider psychographic categories. Often marketing research firms conduct extensive studies of consumers and then share their psychographic data with clients. In addition, businesses look to studies done by sociologists and psychologists to help them understand their customers. Recent marketing research reveals that today's parents are willing and able to spend more on goods and services for their children than parents were a generation or two ago. Shoppers spent over $4.5 billion on toys from Amazon.com in a recent year.[43] These are just a few trends identified by the researchers, but they provide valuable information to companies that may be considering developing toys, designing the interiors of family vehicles, or implementing new wireless plans.

Product-Related Segmentation

Using **product-related segmentation**, sellers can divide a consumer market into groups based on buyers' relationships to the good or service. The three most popular approaches to product-related segmentation are based on benefits sought, usage rates, and brand-loyalty levels.

product-related segmentation dividing consumer markets into groups based on buyers' relationships to the good or service.

Segmenting by *benefits sought* focuses on the attributes that people seek in a good or service and the benefits they expect to receive from it. As more companies shift toward consumer demand for products that are eco-friendly, marketers find ways to emphasize their benefits. Marketers of electric vehicles (EVs) emphasize benefits to consumers who are attracted to EVs because they help reduce global warming, pollution, and dependence on oil. Benefits also include great acceleration, savings from fuel and maintenance, and convenient charging stations at home. For health-conscious consumers, vitality drink makers promise the benefit of high-quality organic seeds mixed with organic fruit juices lightly sweetened with agave nectar and "heart and brain healthy" omega-3s, antioxidants, dietary fibers, protein, calcium, and magnesium.[44]

Consumer markets can also be segmented according to the amounts of a product that people buy and use. Segmentation by *product usage rate* usually defines such categories as heavy users, medium users, and light users. The 80/20 principle states that roughly 80% of a product's revenues come from only 20% of its buyers. Companies can now pinpoint which of their customers are the heaviest users—and even the most profitable customers—and direct their heaviest marketing efforts to this critical market segment.

The third technique for product-related segmentation divides customers by *brand loyalty*—the degree to which consumers recognize, prefer, and insist on a particular brand.

TABLE 11.4 Segmentation Method for B2B Markets

Segmentation Method	Variables	Example
Geographical	Geographically concentrated industries	Geographic segmentation is used to identify business target markets based on where the businesses are located—for example, high technology (Silicon Valley), aircraft manufacturing (Washington state), and oil and gas/utilities (Texas).
End-Use	Product design specifications for performance, design, and price	How customers use a product is influenced by the amount purchased—for example, a construction company uses wood differently than a paper mill does.
Demographic	Geographic location, sales revenue, number of employees, number of buyers	Commercial banks have B2B lending teams segmented by size—for small, medium- and large-size multinational corporations.

Marketers define groups of consumers with similar degrees of brand loyalty. They then attempt to tie loyal customers to a good or service by giving away premiums, which can be anything from a discount, coupon, or reward to loyalty points.

Segmenting Business Markets

In many ways, the segmentation process for business markets resembles that for consumer markets. However, some specific methods differ. Business markets can be divided through geographical segmentation; demographic, or customer-based, segmentation; and end-use segmentation (see **Table 11.4**).

Geographical segmentation methods for business markets resemble those for consumer markets. Many B2B marketers target geographically concentrated industries, such as aircraft manufacturing, automobiles, and oil field equipment. Especially on an international scale, customer needs, languages, and other variables may require differences in the marketing mix from one location to another.

Demographic, or *customer-based, segmentation* begins with a good or service design intended to suit a specific organizational market. Sodexo is the largest provider of food services in North America. Its customers include health care institutions, business and government offices, schools, and colleges and universities. Within these broad business segments, Sodexo identifies more specific segments, which might include colleges in the South or universities with culturally diverse populations—and differing food preferences or dining styles. Sodexo uses data obtained from surveys that cover students' lifestyles, attitudes, preferences for consumer products in general, services, and media categories. In addition, it uses targeted surveys that identify preferences for restaurant brands or certain foods, meal habits, amount of spending, and the like. With the increased popularity of food trucks, Sodexo was the first to launch a food truck program as part of a meal plan within a university setting. The truck includes current food trends like vegan "chicken" wings, ice cream sandwiches, mac-and-cheese bowls, and Hawaiian food. Sodexo is piloting a food truck concept called "Street Eatz" at a number of high schools as well.[45]

To simplify the process of focusing on a particular type of business customer, the federal government has developed a system for subdividing the business marketplace into detailed segments. The six-digit *North American Industry Classification System (NAICS)* provides a common classification system used by the United States, in collaboration with Canada and Mexico. It divides industries into broad categories such as agriculture, forestry, and fishing; manufacturing; transportation; and retail and wholesale trade. Each major category is further subdivided into smaller segments—such as gas stations with convenience food and warehouse clubs—for more detailed information and to facilitate comparison among the member nations.

Another way to group companies by their demographics is to segment them by size based on their sales revenue or number of employees. Some companies collect data from visitors to its website and use the data to segment customers by size. Modern information processing also enables companies to segment business markets based on how much they buy, not just how big they are. **End-use segmentation** focuses on the precise way a B2B purchaser will use a product. For example, companies purchasing coiled springs made from hardened steel may be using them to produce bicycles, watches, and cars. The same holds true for steel and aluminum, used to make many different products. Resembling benefits-sought segmentation for consumer markets, this method helps small and midsize companies target specific end-user markets rather than competing directly with large companies for wider customer groups. A company might also design a marketing mix based on certain criteria for making a purchase.

end-use segmentation marketing strategy that focuses on the precise way a B2B purchaser will use a product.

Assessment Check

1. What is the most common form of segmentation for consumer markets?
2. What are the three approaches to product-related segmentation?
3. What is end-use segmentation in the B2B market?

7 Consumer Behavior

A fundamental marketing task is to find out why people buy one product over another. This requires an understanding of consumer behavior; the actions of ultimate consumers directly involved in obtaining, consuming, and disposing of products; and the decision processes that precede and follow these actions.

Determinants of Consumer Behavior

By studying consumers' purchasing behavior, businesses can identify the processes consumers undergo to obtain, use, and dispose of purchased goods and services. This information also helps marketers reach their targeted customers. Both personal and interpersonal factors influence the way buyers behave. Personal influences on **consumer behavior** include individual needs and motives, perceptions, attitudes, learned experiences, and self-concept. For example, one-hour delivery services like Google Express and Amazon Prime Now will continue to grow with consumers who have a demand for convenience and instant gratification. For orders placed, Amazon Prime members receive free two-hour delivery with Prime Now. One-hour delivery is available for an additional fee. Amazon Prime members can choose from thousands of items on its site—from groceries to electronics to apparel. Google Express offers same day or overnight delivery of items from well-known stores like Walmart, Costco, Kohl's, PetSmart, Walgreens, and Target. With a Google Express membership, shipping is free on orders meeting minimum sales requirements.[46]

consumer behavior actions of ultimate consumers directly involved in obtaining, consuming, and disposing of products and the decision processes that precede and follow these actions.

The interpersonal determinants of consumer behavior include cultural, social, and family influences. Culture includes values, language, rituals, and laws that guide behavior and daily habits. How people dress, the food they consume, the music they listen to, and the language they speak are all a function of cultural influences. When marketers understand such influences on purchases of clothing, food, and music, they can emphasize the same values in their marketing promotions.

Sometimes external events influence consumer behavior. One study suggests that as a result of the recession that began over a decade ago, consumers may have permanently

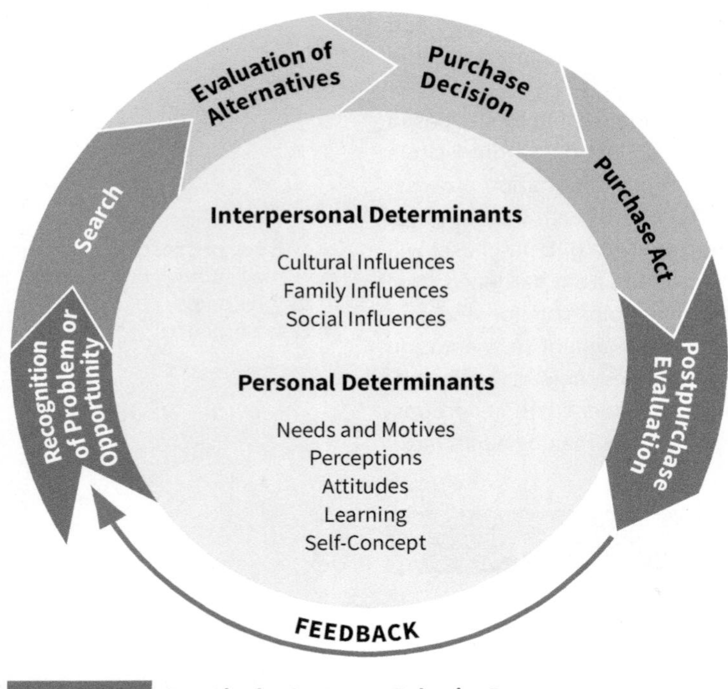

FIGURE 11.4 **Steps in the Consumer Behavior Process**

altered their buying and spending behavior. Industry analysts believe the increasing importance and growth of private label brands (like Costco's Kirkland) and consumers' focus on product value will continue. Manufacturers and retailers—and especially small businesses—will need to create new marketing strategies in response to these challenges.[47]

Determinants of Business Buying Behavior

Because a number of people can influence purchases of B2B products, business buyers face a variety of organizational influences in addition to their own preferences. A design engineer may help set the specifications that potential vendors must satisfy. A procurement manager may invite selected companies to bid on a purchase. A production supervisor may evaluate the operational aspects of the proposals that the company receives, and the vice president of manufacturing may head a committee making the final decision.

Steps in the Consumer Behavior Process

Consumer decision making follows the sequential process outlined in **Figure 11.4**, with interpersonal and personal influences affecting every step. The process begins when the consumer recognizes a problem or opportunity. If someone needs a new pair of shoes, that need becomes a problem to solve. If you receive a promotion at work and a 20% salary increase, that change may also become a purchase opportunity.

To solve the problem or take advantage of the opportunity, the consumer seeks information about his or her intended purchase and evaluates alternatives, such as available brands. The goal is to find the best response to the problem or opportunity.

Eventually, the consumer reaches a decision and completes the transaction. Later, he or she evaluates the experience by making a postpurchase evaluation. Feelings about the experience serve as feedback that will influence future purchase decisions. The various steps in the sequence are affected by both interpersonal and personal factors.

Assessment Check

1. Define *consumer behavior.*
2. What are some determinants of consumer behavior?

8 Relationship Marketing

The past decade has brought rapid change to most industries, as customers, armed with instant information through technology, have become better-informed and more-demanding purchasers through closely evaluating and comparing competing goods and services. They expect, even demand, new benefits from the companies that supply them, making it harder for companies to gain a competitive advantage based on product features alone.

In today's hypercompetitive business environment, companies are constantly searching to find new ways of relating to customers in an effort to build long-term relationships. Businesses are developing strategies that create closer connections and longer-lasting relationships with their customers, suppliers, and even employees. As a result, many companies are turning their attention to relationship marketing. **Relationship marketing** goes beyond an effort toward making the sale. Instead, it develops and maintains long-term, cost-effective exchange relationships with partners. These partners include individual customers, suppliers, and employees. As its ultimate goal, relationship marketing seeks to achieve customer satisfaction.

relationship marketing developing and maintaining long-term, cost-effective exchange relationships with partners.

Managing relationships instead of simply completing transactions often leads to creative and longer-lasting partnerships. However, customers enter into relationships with companies only if it is mutually beneficial. As the level of commitment increases, so does the likelihood of a business continuing a long-term relationship with its customers. Businesses are building relationships by partnering with customers, suppliers, and other businesses. Timberland, maker of footwear and clothing, creates many partnerships that foster long-term relationships. The company partners with not-for-profit organizations such as City Year and the Planet Water Foundation to complete service projects for communities and the environment. Through its Serv-a-Palooza, hundreds of Timberland employees engage in volunteer tasks in their communities. Those opportunities even extend to customers who have expressed an interest in participating in programs in their own regions. If you want to volunteer for a food drive or to help restore a marsh, just log on to the Timberland website to see what's available. All of these activities help build relationships with customers, communities, and other organizations.[48]

Benefits of Relationship Marketing

Relationship marketing helps all parties involved. In addition to providing mutual protection against competitors, businesses that forge solid links with vendors and customers are often rewarded with lower costs and higher profits than they would generate on their own. Long-term agreements with a few high-quality suppliers frequently reduce a company's production costs. Unlike one-time sales, ongoing relationships encourage suppliers to offer customers preferential treatment, quickly adjusting shipments to accommodate changes in orders and correcting any quality problems that might arise.

Good relationships with customers can be vital strategies for a company. By identifying current purchasers and maintaining positive relationships with them, organizations can efficiently target their best customers. Analyzing current customers' buying habits and preferences can help marketers identify potential new customers and establish ongoing contact with them. Attracting a new customer can cost five times as much as keeping an existing one. Not only do marketing costs go down, but long-term customers usually buy more, require less service, refer other customers, and provide valuable feedback. Together, these elements contribute to a higher **lifetime value of a customer**—the revenues and intangible benefits (referrals and customer feedback) from the customer over the life of the relationship, minus the amount the company must spend to acquire and serve that customer. Keeping that customer may occasionally require some extra effort, especially if the customer has become upset or dissatisfied with a good or service. Keeping customers requires researching their wants and needs. Marketing research analysts study markets to better understand the factors that drive consumers and their purchases as described in the "Job Description" feature.

lifetime value of a customer revenues and intangible benefits (referrals and customer feedback) from a customer over the life of the relationship, minus the amount the company must spend to acquire and serve that customer.

Businesses also benefit from strong relationships with other companies. Purchasers who repeatedly buy from one business may find that they save time and gain service quality as the business learns their specific needs. Some relationship-oriented companies also customize items based on customer preferences. Because many businesses reward loyal customers with discounts or bonuses, some buyers may even find that they save money by developing long-term relationships. Alliances with other companies to serve the same customers also can be rewarding. The partners combine their capabilities and resources to accomplish goals that they could not reach on their own. In addition, alliances with other companies may help businesses develop the skills and experience they need to successfully enter new markets or improve service to current customers.

Job Description

Marketing Research Analyst

Overview Marketing research analysts gather data and perform research to help companies market their goods and services and to reveal what products or services consumers want and how much they're willing to pay. They study market conditions in order to evaluate the potential for a product or service and gather data on consumer demographics, needs, preferences, and buying habits. Some marketing research analysts work directly for companies, and others serve as consultants or work for consulting firms who perform research for numerous clients.

Responsibilities Marketing research analysts typically perform a variety of tasks related to monitoring, measuring, and forecasting sales and marketing trends along with evaluating the effectiveness of marketing strategies and programs. They also develop strategies and methods to collect data by way of surveys, focus groups, and questionnaires. The goal is to gather data from consumers while evaluating competitors and the competitive environment. To better understand a company's competitive position in the marketplace, marketing research analysts research and evaluate the products, services, and pricing of competitors. This type of research allows a company to determine potential markets, products, product demand, and ways to promote and advertise.

Requirements A college degree is required to become a marketing research analyst. Common majors include marketing, psychology, math, statistics, computer science, business administration, communications, and more. The job requires good writing skills and the ability to translate complex data into an understandable and readable written report, including tables, charts, and graphs. Analytic skills are certainly important, and being curious about people and their behavior certainly helps. There is a professional research certification for those who wish to pursue it, but employers do not require it.

Outlook Employment for marketing research analysts is expected to grow by 23% over the next decade. Growth will be driven by marketing research conducted across all industries to better understand the wants and needs of consumers. As companies look to differentiate themselves, increase sales, and reduce expenses in an increasingly competitive environment, research and market intelligence will be essential. Research is also helpful when monitoring and measuring customer satisfaction and pinpointing ways a company can more effectively target customers.

Sources: Government website, "Market Research Analysts," *Occupational Outlook Handbook*, 2017–2018 Edition, http://www.bls.gov, accessed April 10, 2018; "Best Business Jobs—Market Research Analyst," *U.S. News and World Report*, http://money.usnews.com, accessed April 10, 2018; organization website, "Market Research Analyst," http://marketresearchcareers.com, accessed April 10, 2018.

Tools for Nurturing Customer Relationships

Although relationship marketing has important benefits for both customers and businesses, most relationship-oriented businesses quickly discover that some customers generate more profitable business than others. If 20% of a company's customers account for 80% of its sales and profits—the 80/20 principle mentioned earlier in the chapter—a customer in that category undoubtedly has a higher lifetime value than a customer who buys only once or twice or who makes small purchases.

While businesses shouldn't ignore any customer, they need to allocate their marketing resources wisely. A company may choose to customize goods or services for high-value customers while working to increase repeat sales of stock products to less-valuable customers. Differentiating between these two groups also helps marketers focus on each in an effort to increase their commitment.

frequency marketing marketing initiative that rewards frequent purchases with cash, rebates, merchandise, or other premiums.

affinity programs marketing effort sponsored by an organization that solicits involvement by individuals who share common interests and activities.

Frequency Marketing and Affinity Marketing Programs

Popular strategies through which companies try to build and protect customer relationships include frequent-buyer or-user programs. These so-called **frequency marketing** programs reward purchasers with cash, rebates, merchandise, or other premiums. Airlines, hotel groups, restaurants, and many retailers including supermarkets offer frequency programs, which have become more sophisticated and personalized over the years. For example, Marriott Rewards, one of the top loyalty programs in the hospitality industry, allows members to earn rewards points with affiliated brands, including The Ritz-Carlton, Courtyard Marriott, and Renaissance, and share points with friends or mix cash and points in rewards.[49]

Affinity programs are another tool for building emotional links with customers. An affinity program is a marketing effort sponsored by an organization that solicits involvement by individuals who share common interests and activities. Affinity programs are common in the credit-card industry. For instance, a person can sign up for a credit card emblazoned with the logo of a favorite charity, a sports or entertainment celebrity, or an image of his or her college (see photo). Bank of America offers credit cards featuring the logos of all 30 Major League Baseball clubs.

Many businesses also use comarketing and cobranding. In a **comarketing** deal, two businesses jointly market each other's products. When two or more businesses link their names to a single product, **cobranding** occurs. Sometimes two seemingly unlikely businesses team up and two different groups of consumers may come together to buy the same product; for example, Dell computers with Intel processors. Hershey has teamed up with Betty Crocker to introduce a new line of co-branded desserts, including cookies, cupcakes, and frostings, based on Reese's Peanut Butter Cups, Almond Joy, and Hershey's Milk Chocolate Bars.[50]

Courtesy Bank of America Corporation (Major League Baseball trademarks and copyrights are used with permission of Major League Baseball Properties, Inc. VisitMLB.com.)

Affinity programs are another tool for building emotional links with customers and are common in the credit-card industry. For instance, Bank of America offers credit cards featuring Major League Baseball logos, like the one pictured here, as well as the logos of all 30 MLB clubs.

One-on-One Marketing The ability to customize products and rapidly deliver goods and services has become increasingly dependent on technology such as computer-aided design and manufacturing (CAD/CAM). The Internet offers a way for businesses to connect with customers in a direct and intimate manner. Companies can take orders for customized products, gather data about buyers, and predict what items a customer might want in the future. Computer databases provide strong support for effective relationship marketing. Marketers can maintain databases on customer tastes, price-range preferences, and lifestyles, and they can quickly obtain names and other information about promising prospects. Amazon.com greets each online customer with a list of suggested products he or she might like to purchase. Many online retailers send their customers e-mails about upcoming sales, new products, and special events.

comarketing cooperative arrangement in which two businesses jointly market each other's products.

cobranding cooperative arrangement in which two or more businesses team up to closely link their names on a single product.

Small and large companies often rely on *customer relationship management (CRM)* software technology that helps them gather, sort, and interpret data about customers. Software companies develop this software in order to help businesses build and manage their relationships with customers. Salesforce.com, a leader in customer relationship management (CRM) software, creates highly scalable and customizable solutions for large and small businesses to offer customer insights using analytics. Business opportunities can be viewed with predictive analytics, and operations can be streamlined. With CRM software, companies can create a more personalized service level using information about a customer's known history and prior interactions. Salesforce Essentials is one such product—data is automatically captured and synced from inbound and outbound emails, calendars, and smartphone calls. All communication is analyzed to deliver powerful relationship intelligence to sell and service customers smarter.[51]

Assessment Check

1. What is the lifetime value of a customer?
2. Discuss the increasing importance of one-on-one marketing efforts.

What's Ahead

The next two chapters examine each of the four elements of the marketing mix that marketers use to satisfy their selected target markets. Chapter 12 focuses on products and their distribution through various channels to different outlets. Chapter 13 covers promotion and the various methods marketers use to communicate with their target customers, along with strategies for setting prices for different products.

Chapter in Review

Summary of Learning Objectives

LEARNING OBJECTIVE 1 Define *marketing*.

Marketing is the activity, set of institutions, and processes for creating, communicating, delivering, and exchanging offerings that have value for customers, clients, partners, and society at large. Marketing creates time, place, and ownership utility by making the product available when and where consumers want to buy and by arranging for orderly transfers of ownership.

Assessment Check Answers

1.1 **What is utility?** Utility is the ability of a good or service to satisfy the wants and needs of customers.

1.2 **Identify three ways in which marketing creates utility.** Marketing creates time utility by making a good or service available when customers want to purchase it, place utility by making the product available in a convenient location, and ownership utility by transferring the product from the seller to the buyer.

LEARNING OBJECTIVE 2 Discuss the evolution of the marketing concept.

The marketing concept refers to a companywide customer orientation with the objective of achieving long-run success. This concept is essential in today's marketplace, which is primarily a buyer's market, meaning buyers can choose from an abundance of goods and services. Marketing now centers on the satisfaction of customers and building long-term relationships with those customers.

Assessment Check Answers

2.1 **What is the marketing concept?** The marketing concept is a companywide customer orientation with the objective of achieving long-run success. According to the marketing concept, marketplace success begins with the customer.

2.2 **How is the marketing concept tied to the relationship and social eras of marketing?** Most marketing now centers on the satisfaction of customers and building long-term relationships with them through several channels including the Internet and social media, rather than simply producing and selling goods and services.

LEARNING OBJECTIVE 3 Describe not-for-profit marketing and nontraditional marketing.

Not-for-profit organizations must engage in marketing just as for-profit firms do. Not-for-profit organizations operate in both the public and private sectors and use marketing to obtain volunteers and donations, make people aware of their existence, achieve certain goals for society, and so on. Not-for-profit organizations may engage in several types of nontraditional marketing—person, place, event, cause, or organization marketing. They may rely on one type or a combination.

Assessment Check Answers

3.1 **Why do not-for-profit organizations engage in marketing?** Not-for-profit organizations use marketing to reach audiences, secure funding, and accomplish their overall missions.

3.2 **What are the five types of nontraditional marketing used by not-for-profit organizations?** The five types of nontraditional marketing are person, place, event, cause, and organization marketing.

LEARNING OBJECTIVE 4 Outline the basic steps in developing a marketing strategy.

All organizations develop marketing strategies to reach customers. This process involves analyzing the overall market, selecting a target market, and developing a marketing mix that blends elements related to product, distribution, promotion, and pricing decisions.

Assessment Check Answers

4.1 **Distinguish between consumer products and business products.** Consumer products are goods and services purchased by end users. Business products are goods and services purchased to be used, either directly or indirectly, in the production of other goods for resale.

4.2 **What are the steps in developing a marketing strategy?** The two steps are (1) studying and analyzing potential target markets and choosing among them and (2) creating a marketing mix to satisfy the chosen market.

LEARNING OBJECTIVE 5 Describe marketing research.

Marketing research is the information-gathering function that links marketers to the marketplace. It provides valuable information about potential target markets. Companies may generate internal data or gather external data. They may use secondary data or conduct research to obtain primary data. Data mining, which involves evaluating and analyzing customer data to detect patterns or relationships, is one helpful tool in forecasting various trends such as sales revenues and consumer behavior.

Assessment Check Answers

5.1 **What is the difference between primary data and secondary data?** Primary data are collected firsthand through observation or surveys. Secondary data are previously published facts that are inexpensive to retrieve and easy to obtain.

5.2 **What is data mining?** Data mining is the task of using computer technology to evaluate data in a database and identify useful trends.

LEARNING OBJECTIVE 6 Discuss market segmentation.

Consumer markets can be divided according to four criteria: geographical factors; demographic characteristics, such as age and family size;

psychographic variables, which involve behavioral and lifestyle profiles; and product-related variables, such as the benefits consumers seek when buying a product or the degree of brand loyalty they feel toward it. Business markets are segmented according to three criteria: geographical characteristics, customer-based specifications for products, and end-user applications.

Assessment Check Answers

6.1 **What is the most common form of segmentation for consumer markets?** Demographics is the most commonly used consumer market segmentation method.

6.2 **What are the three approaches to product-related segmentation?** The three approaches to product-related segmentation are by benefits sought, product usage rate, and brand loyalty levels.

6.3 **What is end-use segmentation in the B2B market?** End-use segmentation focuses on the precise way a B2B purchaser will use a product.

LEARNING OBJECTIVE 7 Summarize consumer behavior.

Consumer behavior refers to the actions of ultimate consumers with direct effects on obtaining, consuming, and disposing of products as well as the decision processes that precede and follow these actions. Personal influences on consumer behavior include an individual's needs and motives, perceptions, attitudes, learned experiences, and self-concept. The interpersonal determinants include cultural influences, social influences, and family influences. A number of people within a company may participate in business purchase decisions, so business buyers must consider a variety of organizational influences in addition to their own preferences.

Assessment Answers Check

7.1 **Define *consumer behavior*.** Consumer behavior refers to the actions of ultimate consumers directly involved in obtaining, consuming, and disposing of products, along with the decision processes that precede and follow these actions.

7.2 **What are some determinants of consumer behavior?** Both personal and interpersonal factors influence the way buyers behave. Personal influences include an individual's needs and motives; perceptions, attitudes, and learned experiences; and self-concept. Interpersonal influences include cultural, social, and family influences.

LEARNING OBJECTIVE 8 Discuss relationship marketing.

Relationship marketing is an organization's attempt to develop long-term, cost-effective links with individual customers for mutual benefit. Good relationships with customers can be an effective strategy for a company. By identifying current purchasers and maintaining a positive relationship with them, an organization can efficiently target its best customers, fulfill their needs, and create loyalty. Information technologies, frequency and affinity programs, and one-on-one efforts all help build relationships with customers.

Assessment Check Answers

8.1 **What is the lifetime value of a customer?** The lifetime value of a customer incorporates the revenues and intangible benefits from the customer over the life of the relationship with a company minus the amount the company must spend to acquire and serve the customer.

8.2 **Discuss the increasing importance of one-on-one marketing efforts.** One-on-one marketing is increasing in importance as consumers demand more customization in goods and services. It is also increasingly dependent on technology such as computer-aided design and manufacturing (CAD/CAM). The Internet also offers a way for businesses to connect with customers in a direct and personal manner.

Business Terms You Need to Know

Review Questions

1. Define the four different types of utility and explain how marketing contributes to the creation of utility. Then choose one of the following companies and describe how it creates each type of utility with its goods or services:
   a. Taco Bell
   b. Polo Ralph Lauren
   c. New England Patriots football team
   d. Supercuts hair salons
   e. Adobe Creative Cloud

2. Describe the shift from a seller's market to a buyer's market. Why was this move important to marketers and what impact did it have?

3. Describe how an organization might combine person marketing and event marketing. Give an example.

4. Describe how an organization might combine cause marketing and organization marketing. Give an example.

5. Identify each of the following as a consumer product or a business product, or classify it as both:

   a. frozen yogurt
   b. iPad
   c. gasoline
   d. boat trailer
   e. hand sanitizer
   f. Post-its

6. Identify and describe the four strategies that blend to create a marketing mix.

7. What is a target market? Why is target-market selection usually the first step in the development of a marketing strategy?

8. Identify the two strategies that a firm could use to develop a marketing mix for international markets. What are the advantages and disadvantages of each?

9. Describe the types of data that someone who is thinking of starting an accounting practice might choose to gather. How might this data be used to decide to start an accounting practice?

10. Explain each of the methods used to segment consumer and business markets. Which methods do you think would be most effective for each of the following? Why? (Note that a combination of methods might be applicable.)

   a. supermarket featuring organic foods
   b. hair-care products
   c. tour bus company
   d. line of baby food
   e. pet insurance
   f. dry cleaner

11. What are the three major determinants of consumer behavior? Give an example of how each one might influence a person's purchasing decision.

12. What are the benefits of relationship marketing? Describe how frequency and affinity programs work toward building relationships.

Projects and Teamwork Applications

1. On your own or with a classmate, choose one of the following products and create an advertisement that illustrates how your company creates time, place, and form utility in its delivery of the product to the customer.

   a. auto-repair service
   b. outdoor adventure tours
   c. craft supply store
   d. dog-walking service

2. Think back to one of the largest purchases you've ever made. Discuss which steps in the consumer behavior process were applied and whether cultural, family, or social influences came into play. How would you evaluate the purchase decision today?

3. As a marketer, if you can find ways to classify your company's goods and services as both business and consumer products, most likely your company's sales will increase as you build relationships with a new category of customers. On your own or with a classmate, choose one of the following products and outline a marketing strategy for attracting the classification of customer that is *opposite* the one listed in parentheses.

   a. electric car (consumer)
   b. trash bag liners (consumer)
   c. limousine service (business)
   d. office furniture (business)

4. Think of two situations in which you have been a customer: one in which you were satisfied with the merchandise you received and one in which you were not. Make a list of the reasons you were satisfied in the first case and a list of the reasons you were not satisfied in the second case. Would you say that the failure was the result of the seller's not understanding your needs?

5. Comarketing and cobranding are techniques that companies often use to market their own and each other's products, such as Sherwin Williams paints featured in Pottery Barn home furnishings catalogs. On your own or with a classmate, choose two companies with products that would work well together for comarketing separate products or cobranding a single product.

Web Assignments

1. **Marketing research.** You have probably taken a marketing survey at one time or another. Go to SurveyMonkey.com, an online survey tool, to learn more about how it works. What are some of the different ways surveys are used? How would you reach the right consumers and collect relevant results? What types of questions would you ask if you were opening an Internet near your campus?

2. **Market segmentation.** VALS™ (Values, Attitudes, and Life-styles) is a proprietary psychographic research software used to segment U.S. adults into eight distinct types using a specific set of psychological traits and key demographics that drive consumer behavior.[52] Go to the website below to take the survey. In pairs or groups, summarize and compare the results of your primary and secondary VALS type. Do you agree or disagree with the results?

http://www.strategicbusinessinsights.com/vals/presurvey.shtml

3. **Customer loyalty programs.** Retailers, airlines, and hotel chains have well-developed customer loyalty programs. Pick one of the following companies and evaluate its customer loyalty program

against one of its competitors in the same industry. Be prepared to discuss your findings in class.

https://www.southwest.com/rapidrewards

https://www.cvs.com/extracare/landing.jsp

http://www.marriott.com/rewards/rewards-program.mi

4. **Customer lifetime value.** Building customer loyalty over the long term involves becoming more aware of customer lifetime value (CLV). Go to the following website to learn more about CLV and the relationship between average order value, repeat purchases, and customer acquisition costs.

http://customerlifetimevalue.co

Note: Internet web addresses change frequently. If you don't find the exact sites listed, you may need to access the organization's home page and search from there or use a search engine such as Google or Bing.

Cases

Case 11.1 Orthotics Ease Pain in Consumer Segments

Want to "improve your posture, align your balance and live your life?" That's the ad campaign for SOLS, a $3 million company that makes custom 3D-printed orthotics, a custom-made insert or footbed placed in a shoe. As a child, founder Kegan Schouwenburg said she was flat footed, and her goal is to bring orthotics out of the closet and to a mainstream audience.

Based in New York City, SOLS is well aware that the market for orthotics users is diverse. Its segmentation strategy includes a variety of users across age and lifestyle demographics. Users of orthotics usually face health and medical issues related to diabetes, obesity, and arthritis. In addition, another market segment includes athletes and runners.

In the past, orthotics were sold primarily through foot doctors (podiatrists), who made a plastic cast of the patient's foot before crafting a pair of inserts. With SOLS, customers, many of whom happen to be runners, can realize quick foot comfort through an iPad app. Using 3D printing technology, each pair of orthotics is custom made with thinner, more flexible, and better-fitting materials than traditional orthotics.

By completing a simple profile, including weight, height, and lifestyle information, and uploading three "feet selfies" of each foot in weight-bearing and nonweight-bearing stances, SOLS runs a series of processing algorithms. Over a thousand data points are extrapolated to generate a 3D model of the custom insole. The insoles, which match the customer's foot almost exactly, are produced and shipped within a week from a factory in Austin, Texas. Because of its unique product, SOLS has made believers out of many runners and nonrunners alike, who are eager to take "feet selfies" to get the proper fit and ease their foot pain.

Questions for Critical Thinking

1. Dr. Scholl's, a famous packaged foot care brand, has installed "foot mapping kiosks" at major retailers. Compare the Dr. Scholl's user to the SOLs user. How might they differ?
2. What other market segments should SOLS target?

Sources: Justin Rocket Silverman, "Not Just for Grandma Anymore, Sols Aims to Make Orthotics Cool," *New York Daily News*, http://nydailynews.com, accessed April 10, 2018; Sarah Perez, "SOLS Lets You Buy 3D-Printed Insoles, Customized to Your Feet, Right from an iPhone App," *Tech Crunch*, http://techcrunch.com, accessed April 10, 2018; Joseph Flaherty, "How an iPad and a 3D Printer Can Fix Your Sweaty, Messed Up Feet," *Wired*, http://www.wired.com, accessed April 10, 2018; company website, "About," http://drscholls.com, accessed April 10, 2018.

Case 11.2 Mobile Game Maker Adapts to U.S. Market

When marketing a good or service in a foreign market, the decision must be made about whether to standardize or adapt a product's marketing mix. Tencent Holdings Ltd., the world's largest mobile games company, and maker of WeChat, a WhatsApp messaging copycat, dominates the Chinese market.

The company is setting its sights beyond its home base by exporting games to new markets overseas. However, what works for Chinese gamers may not necessarily work in the United States. Adaptation allows marketers to vary their marketing mix to suit local consumer preferences because consumer products typically are more "culturally dependent" than business products.

Through collaboration with a California-based online game company in which Tencent acquired a stake, the company seeks to market its most popular mobile game, WeFire, to the U.S. market. The global mobile game market is estimated to surpass $30 billion in annual sales this year, which is nearly double from two years ago.

The company plans to redesign its game with characters that seem more appealing to Western audiences. As companies expand into Asia, Tencent sees it suitable to capitalize on the trend by expanding and standing up to big competitors like Finland-based Supercell. Tencent believes that the success of its growth prospects lie in structuring how its games are played in ways that are similar to U.S. games.

Questions for Critical Thinking

1. To ensure success in the U.S. market, discuss the research methods you would recommend to Tencent to better understand U.S. gamers and their habits.
2 Discuss what some skeptics view as the challenges of taking a mobile game from one market to another. If you're not familiar with mobile games, discuss and provide examples of companies that have successfully employed adaptation strategies.

Sources: Kenneth Rapoza, "Three China Tech Stocks That Will Outperform the Market," *Forbes*, http://www.forbes.com, accessed April 10, 2018; Juro Osawa, "Tencent Acquires Full Control of U.S.-Based Riot Games," *Wall Street Journal*, http://www.wsj.com, accessed April 10, 2018; Juro Osawa, "Tencent Aims for Overseas Mobile-Game Domination," *Wall Street Journal*, http://www.wsj.com, accessed April 10, 2018.

Case 11.3 Mei Mei Group Communicates and Delivers Value

The owners of Boston-based food truck Mei Mei Street Kitchen and Mei Mei restaurant, collectively known as the Mei Mei Group, imaginatively provide context to the definition of marketing by creating, communicating, and delivering value to their guests while managing customer relationships. The very nature of its mobile food truck creates visibility for the unique Mei Mei brand, which is making a difference on the local food scene by serving creative Chinese American cuisine.

The sibling threesome, older brother Andy, and his younger sisters Irene and Margaret (Mei), came up with the idea of a food truck to share their passion for new and exciting cuisine based on what they ate as children. Almost as important as the food itself, the siblings have incorporated practices integral to their marketing strategy and target market, which fit their vision of how to conduct business with a sustainable future. Mei Mei is Mandarin for "little sister," and Mei Mei Group's owners use their combined experience in fine dining, farming, and entrepreneurship to develop marketing strategies, including relationship marketing, marketing research, place marketing, and target marketing.

To differentiate their food from competitors, the siblings strive to be the "best out there," by sourcing local ingredients and working closely with farmers in the Northeast. Also important for a food truck is place marketing, which attempts to attract people to a particular area or location. Mei Mei utilizes its website, social media, Twitter, and a StreetFood app to engage customers and make them aware of the truck's location.

Mei Mei Group's 40 employees, many of whom are professed foodies, represent its brand with passion, knowledge, and pride. Similar to creating new menu items, the company develops fun and engaging promotions to keep customers coming back to its food truck and restaurant.

The success of Mei Mei Group's food truck and restaurant evolved by effectively utilizing a series of marketing research tools. To gain a deeper understanding of how guests perceive and enjoy Mei Mei's food, the owners believe that in-the-moment real-time feedback is crucial. Improvements and changes have been made based upon online and offline feedback from customers. Before the Street Kitchen began, the Li siblings asked themselves about the types of meals they would be interested in eating. Their research also included a competitive analysis of the types of cuisine available in the Boston-area food truck scene. And they researched food trucks throughout the country to see what was going on and to learn more about the constantly evolving mobile food truck industry.

Mei Mei's food truck and restaurant serve different market segments. On weekdays, the food truck caters to those who want a quick, healthy, and affordable meal at lunchtime. Depending on the truck's location, customers range from students to professionals. The restaurant, which is located next to Boston University, serves college students who may want to grab a quick bite between classes. In the evening, the restaurant attracts more than just college students because of its creative and contemporary dinner menu. Mei Mei's business practices of using locally sourced produce and sustainably raised meats from small family farms resonate with its animal-loving, health-conscious, eco-friendly customers.

Maintaining ongoing relationships with customers through social media and in person allows the Li siblings to develop even deeper connections. Listening to and responding to guests creates a better dining experience and consequently improves business for Mei Mei. It's no surprise that Mei Mei Street Kitchen has been awarded Boston's Best Meal on Wheels and Boston's Best Food Truck. Recently, the restaurant was also named Eater Boston's Restaurant of the Year and made *Boston Magazine*'s list of 50 Best Restaurants.

Questions for Critical Thinking

1. Discuss Mei Mei's target market based on the fact that it sources, cooks, and serves food that respects animals in the environment. What other unique features of Mei Mei's food truck or restaurant can be used to further segment the company's target market? Discuss.
2. Discuss and list ways Mei Mei Street Kitchen creates time, place, and ownership utility. How does this differ between its food truck and its bricks-and-mortar restaurant?
3. Apply the basic steps to develop a marketing strategy to Mei Mei Street Kitchen and Mei Mei Restaurant.
4. What additional marketing research or information gathering might you conduct to increase business for Mei Mei Street Kitchen? How would this differ from data gathered for its restaurant? Discuss how you would utilize both primary and secondary research for each.

Sources: Company website, "Container" and "Pantry," http://meimeiboston.com, accessed April 10, 2018; Kara Baskin, "Awesome Bowls in a Repurposed Seaport Shipping Container," *Boston Globe*, http://www.bostonglobe.com, accessed April 10, 2018; Kate Krader, "The New Originals," *Food and Wine*, http://www.foodandwine.com, accessed April 10, 2018; Mei Mei Street Kitchen Facebook page, https://www.facebook.com/meimeiboston, accessed April 10, 2018; "Meet Young Guns Semi-Finalists Irene Li and Max Hull of Boston's Mei Mei," *Eater.com*, http://www.eater.com, accessed April 10, 2018; Sascha Garey, "Lunch Anyone? Mei Mei," *BU Today*, http://www.bu.edu, accessed April 10, 2018; Rachel Leah Blumenthal, "Changing the Way the World Eats: Mei Mei Street Kitchen at TED," *YouTube*, www.youtube.com, accessed April 10, 2018; Christopher Hughes, "Five Reasons You Should Be Eating at Mei Mei Street Kitchen," *Boston Magazine*, http://www.bostonmagazine.com, accessed April 10, 2018; Devya First, "Mei Mei Crew Inventively Spins Off Its Truck Menu," *Boston Globe*, http://www.bostonglobe.com, accessed April 10, 2018; Jon Giardiello, "Mei Mei Street Kitchen Opens New Location," Boston.com, http://www.boston.com, accessed April 10, 2018; Morgan Rousseau, "Cray Cray for Mei Mei: Boston Food Truck to Open Green Eatery," *Metro US Magazine*, http://www.metro.us, accessed April 10, 2018; Rachel Travers, "Rolling with the Mei Mei Street Kitchen," *Boston.com*, http://www.boston.com, accessed April 10, 2018; Brian Samuels, "Serving Local on the Road: Mei Mei Street Kitchen," *Edible Boston*, http://edibleboston.com, accessed April 10, 2018; Jenna Pelletier, "Best Restaurants in Boston," *Boston Magazine*, www.bostonmagazine.com, accessed April 10, 2019.

Product and Distribution Strategies

LEARNING OBJECTIVES

1. Explain product strategy and how to classify goods and services.
2. Briefly describe the four stages of the product life cycle.
3. Discuss product identification.
4. Outline the major components of an effective distribution strategy.
5. Explain the concept of wholesaling.
6. Describe how to develop a competitive retail strategy.
7. Identify distribution channel decisions and logistics.

Changemaker

© Zach Gross

Jodi Goodman, President, Northern California

Company: Live Nation Entertainment, Inc.

Industry: Entertainment/Live Events Promoter/Venue Operator

Website: http://www.livenation.com

If you've ever thought about a career as a concert promoter, consider the "accidental trajectory" of Northern California Live Nation Entertainment President, Jodi Goodman. In her mid-teens, Goodman confesses to sneaking out from her suburban home in New Jersey to ride the subway to see live music concerts in New York. Today, Goodman is at the forefront of promotion with one of the world's largest producers of live music, Live Nation Entertainment. In addition to developing new venues in one of the top music markets in the country, she brings fans together with music artists as varied as Pink, Bruno Mars, Fleetwood Mac, Drake, John Mayer, Florence and the Machine, and Beyoncé. In addition to ticketing, sponsorship, and advertising, Live Nation Entertainment's core business includes the global promotion of live events.

Chances are the last concert you attended may have been produced by the Beverly Hills, CA–based powerhouse, which, in a recent year, produced close to 30,000 live music events connecting close to 580 million fans to more than 4,000 artists in 40 countries. Along with the world's largest ticketing distribution network (in 2009, the company purchased Ticketmaster), Live Nation Entertainment's global distribution includes a network of promoters, venues, and festivals.

After urging a failing jazz club owner in Boston to allow her to book a few rock music events, Goodman, then a college student, not only turned the club around, but word soon went viral about her flair for managing, promoting, and booking artists. "I still didn't see this as a career, though, until other venues started calling, wanting me to do the same thing," Goodman recalls. Much of the success in the San Francisco Bay Area music scene can be attributed to the Boston college kid who, at the time, had an intuition about the local music market and took the initiative to bring some "good old rock 'n' roll" to a jazz club on the brink of closure. Goodman lives by the business philosophy of "paying it forward," which is a fitting testament to how she has landed as one of the top women in the music business today.[1]

Overview

In this chapter we examine ways in which organizations design and implement marketing strategies that address customers' needs and wants. Two of the most powerful such tools are strategies that relate to products, which include both goods and services, and those that relate to the distribution of those products.

As the case of Live Nation Entertainment illustrates, the company's global distribution network of promoters, venues, and festivals creates dominance in the live concert industry, highly dependent on the availability of popular artists and sensitive to quickly changing music tastes.

This chapter focuses on the first two elements of the marketing mix: product and distribution. Our discussion of product strategy begins by describing the classifications of goods and services, customer service, product lines and the product mix, and the product life cycle. Companies often shape their marketing strategies differently when they are introducing a new product, when the product has established itself in the marketplace, and when it is declining in popularity. We also discuss product identification through brand name and distinctive packaging, and the ways in which companies foster loyalty to their brands to keep customers coming back for more.

Distribution, the second marketing mix variable discussed, focuses on moving goods and services from producer to wholesaler to retailer to buyers. Managing the distribution process includes making decisions such as what kind of wholesaler to use and where to offer products for sale. Retailers can range from specialty stores to factory outlets and everything in between, and they must choose effective customer service, pricing, and location strategies. The chapter concludes with a look at logistics, the process of coordinating the flow of information, goods, and services among suppliers and on to consumers.

1 Product Strategy

product bundle of physical, service, and symbolic characteristics designed to satisfy consumer wants.

Most people respond to the question "What is a product?" by listing its physical features. By contrast, marketers take a broader view. To them, a **product** is a bundle of physical, service, and symbolic characteristics designed to satisfy consumer wants. The chief executive officer of a major tool manufacturer once surprised his stockholders with this statement: "Last year our customers bought over one million quarter-inch drill bits, and none of them wanted to buy the product. They all wanted quarter-inch holes." Product strategy involves considerably more than just producing a good or service; instead, it focuses on benefits. The marketing conception of a product includes decisions about package design, brand name, trademarks, warranties, product image, new-product development, and customer service. Think, for instance, about your favorite beverage. Do you like it for its taste alone? Or do other attributes, such as innovative ads, attractive packaging, ease of purchase from vending machines and other convenient locations, and overall image, also attract you? These other attributes may influence your choice more than you realize.

Classifying Goods and Services

Marketers have found it useful to classify goods and services as either B2C or B2B, depending on whether the purchasers of the particular item are consumers or businesses. These classifications, based on the way consumers purchase, can be subdivided further, and each type requires a different competitive strategy.

Classifying Consumer Goods and Services The classification typically used for ultimate consumers who purchase products for their own use and enjoyment and not for resale is based on consumer buying habits. *Convenience products* are items the consumer seeks to purchase frequently, immediately, and with little effort. Items stocked in gas-station convenience stores, vending machines, and local newsstands are usually convenience products—for example, newspapers, snacks, candy, coffee, bread, milk, and eggs.

Shopping products are those typically purchased only after the buyer has compared competing products in competing stores. A person intent on buying a new sofa or dining room table may visit many stores, examine perhaps dozens of pieces of furniture, and spend days making the final decision. *Specialty products*, the third category of consumer products, are those that a purchaser is willing to make a special effort to obtain. The purchaser is already familiar with the item and considers it to have no reasonable substitute. Specialty products are usually compared against each other less frequently. For example, the buyer of a Lamborghini (see photo) is convinced of their choice and would not compare the exotic supercar, with a starting price tag of $200,000, against other brands.[2]

Valentin Flauraud/Bloomberg via Getty Images

The buyer of a new Lamborghini makes an extra special effort, sometimes traveling great distances, to buy one.

Unsought products are goods and services that consumers either do not know about or know about but don't think of buying until a need arises. Examples include car towing, home security systems, and burial services.

The interrelationship of the marketing mix factors is shown in **Figure 12.1**. By knowing the appropriate classification for a specific product, the marketing decision maker knows quite a bit about how the other mix variables will adapt to create a profitable, customer-driven marketing strategy. Each item's classification is based on the buying patterns of the majority of people who purchase it.

Classifying Business Goods *Business products* are goods and services such as payroll services and huge multi-function copying machines used in operating an organization; they

Marketing Strategy Factor	Convenience Product	Shopping Product	Specialty Product	Unsought Product
Examples	Newspapers, snacks, candy, coffee, bread, milk, toothpaste, laundry detergent, and eggs	Sofa, furniture, clothing, electronics, and appliances	Luxury goods, antique furniture, wedding dress, certain types of automobiles, and handbags.	Car towing, burial services, and life insurance.
Purchase Frequency	Frequent with little effort	Relatively infrequent with much effort and planning and comparison of brands on price, quality, and style	Infrequent and special purchase effort, usually strong brand preference and loyalty, little comparison of brands, low price sensitivity	Infrequent with little product awareness and knowledge or little interest
Store Image	Unimportant	Very important	Important	Unimportant
Price	Low price	Higher price	High price	Price varies
Promotion	By manufacturer and mass promotion	By manufacturer and retailers with advertising and personal selling	By manufacturer and retailers with more carefully targeted promotion	By manufacturer, brokers, and retailers with aggressive advertising and personal selling
Distribution Channel	Widespread distribution with many wholesalers, retailers, and convenient locations	Selective distribution with relatively few wholesalers and retailers and fewer outlets	Exclusive distribution with very few wholesalers and retailers and one or a few outlets	Varies with many wholesalers and retailers
Number of Retail Outlets	Many	Few	Very small number—often one per market area	Many

FIGURE 12.1 **Marketing Impacts of Consumer Product Classification**

also include machinery, tools, raw materials, components, and buildings used to produce other items for resale. While consumer products are classified by buying habits, business products are classified based on how they are used and by their basic characteristics. Products that are long-lived and relatively expensive are called *capital items*. Less costly products that are consumed within a year are referred to as *expense items*.

Five basic categories of B2B products include: installations, accessory equipment, component parts and materials, raw materials, and supplies. *Installations* are major capital items, such as new factories, heavy equipment and machinery, and custom-made equipment. Installations are expensive and often involve buyer and seller negotiations that may last for more than a year before a purchase actually is made. Purchase approval frequently involves a number of different people—production specialists, representatives from the purchasing department, and members of top management—who must agree on the final choice.

Although *accessory equipment* also includes capital items, they are usually less expensive and shorter lived than installations and involve fewer decision makers. Examples include hand tools and printers. *Component parts and materials* are finished business goods that become part of a final product, such as disk drives that are sold to computer manufacturers or batteries purchased by automakers. *Raw materials* are farm and natural products used in producing other final products. Examples include milk, wood, leather, and soybeans. *Supplies* are expense items used in a company's daily operation that do not become part of the final product. Often referred to as MRO (maintenance, repair, and operating supplies), they include paper clips, light bulbs, and copy paper.

Classifying Services Services can be classified as either B2C or B2B. Child and elder care centers and auto detail shops provide services for consumers, while the Pinkerton security patrol at a local factory and ADP payroll services are examples of business services. In some cases, a service can accommodate both consumer and business markets. For example, when ServiceMaster cleans the upholstery in a home, it is a B2C service, but when it provides disaster restoration services at a manufacturing plant, it is a B2B service.

Like tangible goods, services can also be convenience, shopping, or specialty products depending on the buying patterns of customers. However, they are distinguished from goods in several ways. First, services, unlike goods, are intangible and quality is difficult to evaluate prior to consumption or purchase. In addition, they are perishable because companies cannot stockpile or store them in inventory. They are also difficult to standardize, because they must meet individual customers' needs. Finally, from a buyer's perspective, the service provider is the service; the two are inseparable in the buyer's mind. For example, Alaska Airlines is the service provider of a domestic flight from New York to Chicago.

Marketing Strategy Implications

The consumer product classification system is a useful tool in marketing strategy. As described in Figure 12.1, because a new refrigerator is classified as a shopping good, its marketers have a better idea of its promotion, pricing, and distribution needs.

Each group of business products, however, requires a different marketing strategy. Because most installations and many component parts are frequently marketed directly from manufacturer to business buyer, the promotional emphasis is on personal selling rather than on advertising. By contrast, marketers of supplies and accessory equipment rely more on advertising, because their products are often sold through an intermediary, such as a wholesaler. Producers of installations and component parts may involve their customers in new-product development, especially when the business product is custom made. Finally, companies selling supplies and accessory equipment place greater emphasis on competitive pricing strategies than do other B2B marketers, who tend to concentrate more on product quality and customer service.

Product Lines and Product Mix

Few companies operate with a single product. If their initial entry is successful, they tend to increase their profit and growth chances by adding new offerings. Family-owned Gorilla Glue is well known for its famous adhesive, which offers a strong bond for almost any surface and quick drying time. The company has expanded by adding two products—tape, silicone sealants, and epoxy—to its offerings.[3]

A company's **product line** is a group of related products marked by physical similarities or intended for a similar market. A **product mix** is the assortment of product lines and individual goods and services that a company offers to consumers and business users. The Coca-Cola Company's product mix has expanded to include a variety of healthier beverage options beyond its iconic carbonated drinks. Its product mix (see photo) includes soft drinks such as Coca-Cola and Diet Coke; juice drinks such as Minute Maid Orange Juice; bottled water such as Dasani; enlightened water such as Vitamin Water; energy drinks such as Monster; and teas such as Honest Tea. The company's Diet Coke product line includes Diet Cherry Coke, Diet Coke Black Cherry Vanilla, Diet Coke with Lime, Caffeine-free Diet Coke, and Diet Coke with Splenda.[4]

Marketers must assess their product mix continually to evaluate and monitor company growth, to satisfy changing consumer needs and wants, and to adjust to competitors' offerings. To remain competitive, marketers look for gaps in their product lines and fill them with new offerings or modified versions of existing ones. A helpful tool that is frequently used in making product decisions is the product life cycle.

© Eric Carr/Alamy Stock Photo

The Coca Cola Company's product mix goes beyond its iconic soft drinks to include energy drinks, teas, juices, and healthy beverage options.

product line group of related products marked by physical similarities or intended for a similar market.

product mix the assortment of product lines and individual goods and services that a firm offers to consumers and business users.

Assessment Check

1. How do consumer products differ from business products?
2. Differentiate among convenience, shopping, and specialty products.

2 Product Life Cycle

Once a product is on the market, it usually goes through four stages known as the **product life cycle**: introduction, growth, maturity, and decline. As **Figure 12.2** shows, industry sales and profits vary depending on the life cycle stage of an item.

product life cycle four basic stages—introduction, growth, maturity, and decline—through which a successful product progresses.

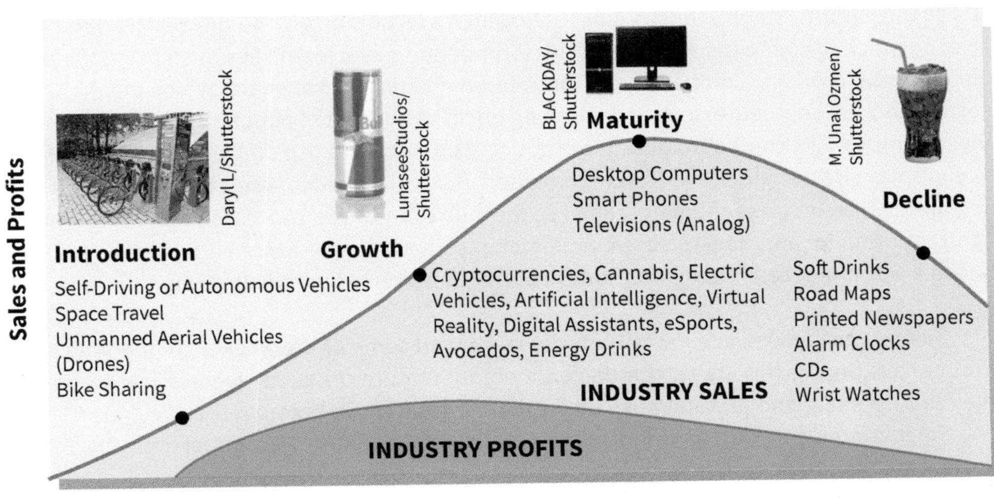

FIGURE 12.2 **Stages in the Product Life Cycle**

Product life cycles are not set in stone; not all products follow this pattern precisely, and different products may spend different periods of time in each stage. In today's business environment, with the rapid adaptation and implementation of technology, product life cycles are being shortened. It becomes increasingly important for marketers to understand the stage of a product in its life cycle. Profits assume a predictable pattern through the stages, and promotional emphasis shifts from dispensing product information in the early stages to increased brand promotion in the later ones.

Stages of the Product Life Cycle

In the *introduction stage*, the company tries to promote demand for its new offering; inform the market about it; give free samples to entice consumers to make a trial purchase; and explain its features, uses, and benefits. Sometimes companies partner at this stage to promote new products and technology. A recent fatality in Tempe, Arizona as a result of the testing of an Uber self-driving car has, of course, led to preventing this from happening to someone else. A company called Flir sees a new market opportunity to equip self-driving cars with heat-seeking cameras that can see things to avoid hitting. Flir's sensor can detect slight differences in temperature so that something like the cold metal of a bicycle stands out. Next, Flir is teaching the car's computer to learn (through machine learning) to identify people, pedestrians, and cyclists.[5]

New-product development costs and extensive introductory promotional campaigns to acquaint prospective buyers with the merits of the innovation, though essential to later success, are expensive and commonly lead to losses in the introductory stage. Some companies are seeking to lower these costs through ultra-low-cost product development, which involves meeting customer needs with the lowest-cost innovations possible, designing from scratch with a stripped-down budget, and the simplest engineering possible. But all these expenditures are necessary if the company is to profit later.

During the *growth stage*, sales climb quickly as new customers join early users who, depending on the cost and type of item, are now repurchasing. Word-of-mouth referrals and continued advertising and other special promotions by a company induce others to make trial and even long-term purchases. At this point, the company may begin to earn a profit on the new product. This success encourages competitors to enter the field with similar offerings, and price competition may result. A sign from investments made by automobile manufacturers for the research, development, and deployment indicates a continued surge in the growth of electric vehicles (EVs). As battery prices continue to fall, it is estimated that EVs will outsell fossil fuel–powered vehicles within two decades. Additionally, governments worldwide are providing tax benefits and subsidies to encourage the production of EVs and to reduce vehicle emission levels.[6]

In the *maturity stage*, industry sales at first increase, but they eventually reach a saturation level at which further expansion is difficult. Competition also intensifies, increasing the availability of the product. Companies concentrate on greater market share, which means taking customers from competitors or even dropping prices to further the appeal. Smart phones are in the maturity stage: competitors compete not only on price but also on features such as phone size, display size, weight, build (glass/aluminum), flex, colors, video resolution, fingerprint sensor, battery life, wireless charging, camera's megapixels, storage, processor, operating system, contract options, and new releases. Smart phones have grown exponentially over the past decade, but in a recent year global sales fell by 5.6 percent, the industry's first decline since 2004.[7]

Sales volume fades late in the maturity stage, and some of the weaker competitors leave the market. During this stage, companies promote mature products aggressively to protect their market share and to distinguish their products from those of competitors.

Sales continue to fall in the *decline stage*, the fourth phase of the product life cycle. Profits decline and may become losses as further price cutting occurs in the reduced overall market for the item. Competitors gradually exit, making some profits possible for the remaining companies in the shrinking market. The decline stage usually is caused by a product innovation or a shift in consumer preferences. Sometimes technology change can accelerate the decline stage for a product. Consumption of soda in the United States has fallen to an all-time 30-year low. The decline can be attributed to evolving tastes, sugar taxes, and the desire for healthier food choices. To offset sluggish sales of their core carbonated soft drink product, both the Coca-Cola Company and PepsiCo have diversified their product mix with snacks, chips, juice, water, sports drinks, and iced coffee. After merging with Frito-Lay, PepsiCo owns Quaker Oats, SodaStream, and Tostitos, to name a few.[8]

Marketing Strategy Implications of the Product Life Cycle

Like the product classification system, the product life cycle is a useful concept for designing a marketing strategy that will be flexible enough to accommodate changing marketplace characteristics. These competitive moves may involve developing new products, lowering prices, increasing distribution coverage, creating new promotional campaigns, or any combination of these approaches. In general, the marketer's objective is to extend the product life cycle as long as the item is profitable. Some products can be highly profitable during the later stages of their life cycle, because all the initial development costs have already been recovered. As landfills become increasingly crowded and solid waste a greater concern, the "trashion" trend, in the growth stage of its product life cycle, is becoming increasingly more common. See the "Clean & Green Business" feature for more details.

A common strategy for extending the life cycle is to increase customers' frequency of use. Walmart and Target offer grocery sections in many of their stores to increase the frequency of shopper visits. Another strategy is to add new users. To gain new customers, Kellogg's promoted its Special K brand using a two-week weight loss plan, known as the Special K diet. A version of a meal-replacement diet, the plan calls for replacing two regular meals with a bowl of Special K cereal. The company has also introduced a line of foods, including cereals and bars that are promoted as part of a healthy well-balanced diet and smart snack choices.[9]

A third product life cycle extension strategy is to find new uses for products. 3M's Post-it Notes can be used in a variety of innovative ways, which include using the sticky edge to clean between the keys of a computer keyboard. Finally, a company may decide to change package sizes, labels, and product designs. To coincide with International Women's Day, Barbie doll maker, Mattel recently released "Inspiring Women" and "Modern Day Role Models" dolls to highlight women who have broken barriers, like snowboarding champion Chloe Kim and painter Frida Kahlo.[10]

Clean & Green Business

Transforming Trash into Fashion

A marketing strategy flexible enough to accommodate marketplace characteristics and changing trends includes the development of new products. This is exactly what environmentalist and Filipino artist Francis Sollano has done with his "trashion" fashion collection. Trashion is a fusion of "trash" and "fashion," and Sollano has come up with a fashionable way to recycle found, used, and repurposed elements. Sollano's constant new product development utilizes "making something from nothing." As a result, new ways to think about supply chains, fashion, and retail have evolved.

Salvaged materials have been used for many years to create new objects. In Africa, rice and juice packets have been converted to bags, sculptural jewelry from oil cans come from Haiti, and quilts and rugs from thrown-away clothing and fabric scraps have been a mainstay of U.S. culture. However, as landfills become increasingly crowded and the solid waste problem mounts, Sollano is one of the innovators of the growing trashion movement.

Working with restaurants and shops in his hometown of Cebu in the Philippines to turn their garbage into wearable fashion and art, Sollano employs local labor to contribute to a cleaner environment while creating livelihood opportunities. In addition to creating installations and fashion made from trash, Sollano is a founding member of Youth for a Livable Cebu, which works on the development and livability of local communities. Trashion continues to serve the dual purpose of job creation and unique and interesting fashion.

Questions for Critical Thinking

1. Discuss ways the "trashion" movement might change how retailers consider sourcing innovative, new, and unique products to sell.
2. What are additional products that might be developed and marketed using found, used, or repurposed elements? Are there other applications for trashion beyond retail?

Sources: Company website, http://francissollano.com, accessed April 15, 2018; Jonathan Shieber, "At the WEF the Future of Fashion Could Be 'Trashion,'" *TechCrunch*, http://techcrunch.com, accessed April 15, 2018; Maria Niza Marinas, Orly J. Cajegas, and Rob Gonzales, "Francis Sollano Turning Trash into Treasure," *Cebu Daily News*, http://cebudailynews.inquirer.net, accessed April 15, 2018.

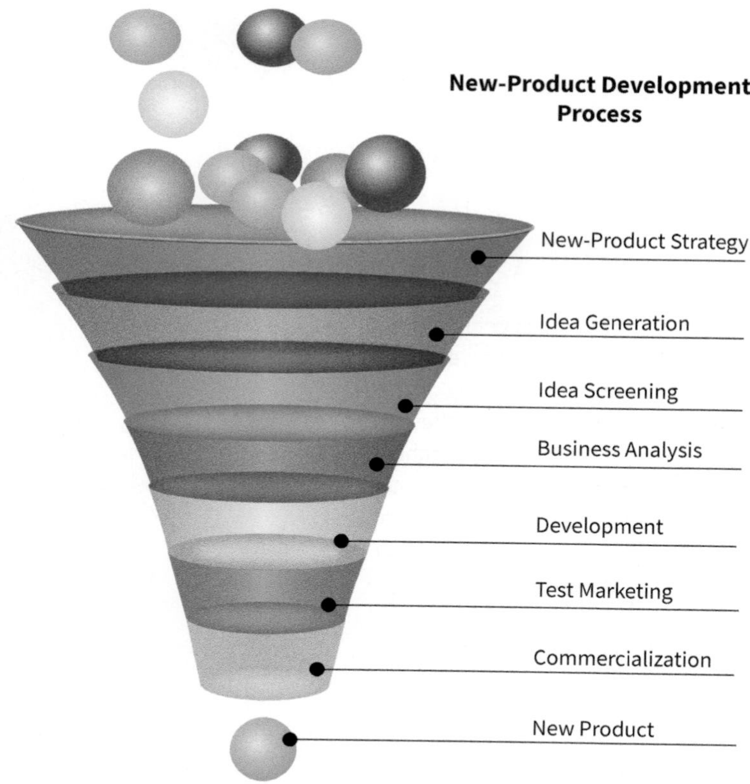

FIGURE 12.3 Process for Developing New Goods and Services

Stages in New-Product Development

New-product development is costly, time consuming, and risky because of the high rate of failure. Products can fail for many reasons. Some are not properly developed and tested, some are poorly packaged, and others lack adequate promotional support or distribution or do not satisfy a consumer need or want. Even successful products may eventually reach the decline stage and must be replaced with new-product offerings.

Most of today's newly developed items are aimed at satisfying specific consumer demands. New-product development is becoming increasingly efficient and cost-effective because marketers use a systematic approach in developing new products. As **Figure 12.3** shows, the new-product development process has six stages. Each stage requires a "go/no-go" decision by management before moving on to subsequent stages. Because items that go through each development stage only to be rejected at one of the final stages involve significant investments in both time and money, the sooner decision makers can identify a marginal product and drop it from further consideration, the less time and money will be wasted.

The starting point in the new-product development process is generating ideas for new offerings. Ideas come from many sources, including customer suggestions, suppliers, employees, research scientists, marketing research, inventors outside the firm, and competitive products. The most successful ideas are directly related to satisfying unmet customer needs. Competing against razor giant Gillette, Dollar Shave Club sends razors, shaving cream, and wipes directly to consumers, mostly men, on a subscription basis for as little as $5 to $9 per month—depending on the type of blade. The rising cost of a good shave and changing consumer shopping habits have contributed to the company's strong growth.[11]

In the second stage, screening eliminates ideas that do not match overall company objectives or that cannot be developed given the company's resources. Some companies hold open discussions of new-product ideas with specialists who work in different functional areas in the organization.

During the concept development and business analysis phase, further screening occurs. The analysis involves assessing the new product's potential sales, profits, growth rate, and competitive strengths and determining whether it fits with the company's product, distribution, and promotional resources. *Concept testing*—marketing research designed to solicit initial consumer reaction to new-product ideas—may be used at this stage. For example, potential consumers might be asked about proposed brand names and other methods of product identification. *Focus groups* are sessions in which consumers meet with marketers to discuss what they like or dislike about current products and perhaps test or sample a new offering to provide some immediate feedback.

Next, an actual product is developed, subjected to a series of tests, and revised. Functioning prototypes or detailed descriptions of the product may be created. These designs are the joint responsibility of the company's development staff and its marketers, who provide feedback on consumer reactions to the proposed product design, color, and other physical features. Sometimes prototypes do not meet the stated requirements. In search of a quick-drying camouflage uniform for tropical environments, the U.S. Marines have issued a federal contract opportunity to suppliers to conduct market research and user evaluation to help identify tropical uniform fabrics, uniform designs, and boots that provide durability and protection and improved moisture management.[12]

test marketing introduction of a new product supported by a complete marketing campaign to a selected city or geographic area.

Test marketing introduces a new product supported by a complete marketing campaign to a selected city or geographic area. Marketers look for a location with a manageable size, where residents match their target market's demographic profile, to test their product. During the test marketing stage, the item is sold in a limited area while the company analyzes both consumer responses to the new offering and the marketing effort used to support it. Test market results can help managers determine the product's likely performance in a full-scale introduction. Some companies skip test marketing, however, because of concerns that the test could reveal their strategies to the competition. Also, the expense of doing limited production runs of complex products, such as a new auto or refrigerator, is sometimes so high that the test marketing stage is skipped and the development process moves directly to the next stage.

In the final stage, commercialization, the product is made available in the marketplace. Sometimes this stage is referred to as a product launch. Considerable planning goes into this stage, because the company's distribution, promotion, and pricing strategies must all be geared to support the new product offering. Activision Blizzard has put forth considerable planning into the streamed network launch of its eSports Overwatch League (OWL), with over 35 million existing players. In the fast-growing world of video games, eSports mimic traditional sports by following teams, watching games, and even attending finals to cheer on favorite sports idols in a virtual setting. Much like Major League Baseball or Major League Football, OWL is a gaming league for professional players, pitting six-person teams against one another in a single-shooter game, and major sponsors include T-Mobile and Hewlett-Packard.[13]

The need for new products to continually be offered to a company's customers, the chances of product failure, and the significant financial investment needed to complete a successful new-product launch make new-product development critical to any business. **Table 12.1** lists a few product failures of the last decade, many of which are brand extensions that illustrate that a new-product offering must first gain customer acceptance. For

TABLE 12.1 Examples of Products That Failed

Product	Why It Flopped
Google Glass	The product, which didn't work properly, was touted as a pair of high-tech glasses able to scan surroundings and send information to the eye's retina. However, its functionality was flawed due mainly to the need for a larger battery to fully perform its intended functions. Some call the design distracting, and the eyeglass, with a $1,500 price tag, was prone to break.
Amazon Fire Phone	CEO Jeff Bezos is blamed for micromanaging the design of the fatally flawed Amazon Fire phone while overspending on development, manufacturing, and marketing. Users criticized the device for its "gimmicky" product features like 3D screen and facial recognition as bland and distracting. It also lacked the variety of apps and service cohesion available with Apple's competing products. Lastly, the Fire phone was simply overpriced.
McDonald's Mighty Wings	Mighty Wings were "too spicy and too pricey," according to an industry executive. Sold in packs of 3, 5, or 10 wings starting at $2.99, it was clear that discounting was being used to sell the product. The discounted price cut into profits for franchise owners. The wings never met sales goals for McDonald's, and they were discontinued.
Blackberry	Despite a functional keyboard and secure messaging and e-mail capabilities, Blackberry's focus was on battery performance but had limited use of carrier network resources. When the iPhone was introduced as an exclusive to AT&T, it became an almost instant success. Blackberry tried to deliver the Storm, a touch-screen smart phone for Verizon, which was initially the best-selling Verizon product ever, but it was flawed. It just didn't match the hardware or software features of the iPhone.

Sources: "When Corporate Innovation Goes Bad—The 110 Biggest Product Failures of All Time," *CB Insights*, http://www.cbinsights.com, accessed April 16, 2018; Pavithra Mohan, "Amazon Dismisses 'Dozens' of Engineers Who Worked on Failed Fire Phone," *Fast Company*, http://www.fastcompany.com, accessed April 17, 2018; Adam Hartung, "The Reason Why Google Glass, Amazon Fire Phone and Segway All Failed," *Forbes*, http://www.forbes.com, accessed April 17, 2018; Eric Zeman, "BlackBerry Doomed by First iPhone, Storm Failure," *Information Week*, http://www.informationweek.com, accessed April 17, 2018; Kia Kokalitcheva, "Ex-BlackBerry CEO Admits Why Its Most Important Device Failed," *Fortune*, http://fortune.com, accessed April 17, 2018.

example, in 2010, Cisco created the Umi, a personal telepresence product that cost $600 and allowed for video calls via TV. However, with a monthly subscription fee of $25, its lack of success was overshadowed by both Skype and Facetime.[14]

Assessment Check

1. What are the stages of the product life cycle?
2. What are the marketing implications of each stage?

3 Product Identification

brand name, term, sign, symbol, design, or some combination that identifies the products of one company and differentiates them from competitors' offerings.

brand name part of the brand consisting of words or letters included in a name used to identify and distinguish the company's offerings from those of competitors.

trademark brand that has been given legal protection.

A major aspect of developing a successful new product involves methods used for identifying a product and distinguishing it from competing offerings. Both tangible goods and intangible services are identified by brands, brand names, and trademarks. A **brand** is a name, term, sign, symbol, design, or some combination that identifies the products of one company and differentiates them from competitors' offerings. Tropicana, Pepsi, and Gatorade are all made by PepsiCo, but a unique combination of name, symbol, and package design distinguishes each brand from the others.

A **brand name** is that part of the brand consisting of words or letters included in a name used to identify and distinguish a company's offerings from those of competitors. The brand name is the part of the brand that can be vocalized. Many brand names, such as Coca-Cola, McDonald's, American Express, Google, and Nike, are famous around the world. Likewise, the golden arches brand mark of McDonald's is widely recognized.

A **trademark** is a brand that has been given legal protection. The protection is granted solely to the brand's owner. Trademark protection includes not only the brand name but also design logos, slogans, packaging elements, and product features such as color and shape. A well-designed trademark, such as the Nike swoosh, can make a difference in how positively consumers perceive a brand.

Helen Sessions/Alamy Stock Photo

To be effective, *brand names* must be easy for consumers to pronounce, recognize, and remember.

Selecting an Effective Brand Name

Good brands are easy to pronounce, recognize, and remember: Crest, Visa, and Pepsi are examples. Named after the world's largest river, Jeff Bezos chose the name Amazon because it started with the letter "A." Southwest Airlines , headquartered in Dallas in the American Southwest, also chose a name descriptive of what the company does. The late Steve Jobs, founder of Apple, chose the name because he thought it sounded "fun, spirited and not intimidating." In addition, Jobs had just visited an apple farm and he was on a fruitarian diet.[15]

Brand names should also convey the right image to the buyer. One effective technique is to create a name that links the product with its positioning strategy. The name Purell (see photo) reinforces the concept of sanitizing hands to protect against germs, Dove soap and beauty products give an impression of mildness, Nike was the Greek goddess of victory, and sports drink Gatorade was developed for the Florida Gators who were struggling to play in the heat.

Brand names also must be legally protectable. Trademark law specifies that brand names cannot contain words in general use, such as *television* or *automobile*. Generic words—words that describe a type of product—cannot be used exclusively by any organization. On the other hand, if a brand name becomes so popular that it passes into common language and turns into a generic word, the company can no longer use it as a brand name. Once upon a time, aspirin, linoleum, and zipper were exclusive brand names, but today they have become generic terms and are no longer legally protectable.

Brand Categories

A brand offered and promoted by a manufacturer is known as a *manufacturer's* (or *national*) *brand*. Examples are Tide, Cheerios, Windex, North Face, and Nike. But not all brand names belong to manufacturers; some are the property of retailers or distributors. A *private* (or *store*) *brand* identifies a product that is not linked to the manufacturer but instead carries a wholesaler's or retailer's label. Kirkland sold by Costco and 365 Everyday Value sold by Whole Foods are examples.

Another branding decision marketers must make is whether to use a family branding strategy or an individual branding strategy. A *family brand* is a single brand name used for several related products. KitchenAid, Johnson & Johnson, Hewlett-Packard, and Arm & Hammer use a family name for their entire line of products. When a company using family branding introduces a new product, both customers and retailers recognize the familiar brand name. The promotion of individual products within a line benefits all the items because the family brand is well known.

Other companies use an *individual branding* strategy by giving each product within a line a different name. For example, Procter & Gamble has individual brand names for its different laundry detergents, including Tide, Cheer, and Gain. Each brand targets a unique market segment. Consumers who want a cold-water detergent can choose Cheer over Tide or Gain, instead of purchasing a competitor's brand. Individual branding also builds competition within a company and enables the company to increase overall sales.

Brand Loyalty and Brand Equity

Brands achieve varying consumer familiarity and acceptance. While a homeowner may insist on Andersen windows when renovating, the consumer buying a loaf of bread may not have a brand preference. Consumer loyalty increases a brand's value, so marketers focus on strengthening brand loyalty. When a brand image suffers, marketers try to re-create a positive image. After various crises, companies attempting to remedy their brand image include Uber, Equifax, Volkswagen, Chipotle, and United Airlines.

Brand Loyalty Marketers measure brand loyalty in three stages: brand recognition, brand preference, and brand insistence. *Brand recognition* is brand acceptance strong enough that the consumer is aware of the brand but not strong enough to cause a preference over other brands. A consumer might have heard of L'Oréal hair care products, for instance, without necessarily preferring them to Redken or Garnier. Advertising, free samples, and discount coupons are among the most common ways to increase brand recognition.

Brand preference occurs when a consumer chooses one company's brand over a competitor's. At this stage, the consumer usually relies on previous experience in selecting the product. Furniture and other home furnishings fall into this category. A shopper who purchased an IKEA dining room table and chairs and was satisfied with them is likely to return to purchase a bedroom set. While there, this shopper might pick up a set of mixing bowls for the kitchen or a lamp for the family room—because he or she knows and likes the IKEA brand (see photo).

Brand insistence is the ultimate degree of brand loyalty, in which the consumer will look for it at another outlet, special-order it from a dealer, order by mail, or search the Internet. Shoppers who insist on IKEA products for their homes may drive an hour or two—making a day excursion of the venture—to visit an IKEA store. The combination of value for the money and the concept of IKEA as a shopping destination have given the brand a unique allure for shoppers.[16]

Kumar Sriskandan/Alamy Stock Photo

The retailer of affordable, well-designed contemporary furniture enjoys *brand insistence*—the ultimate expression of brand loyalty. For devoted IKEA fans, no other brand will do.

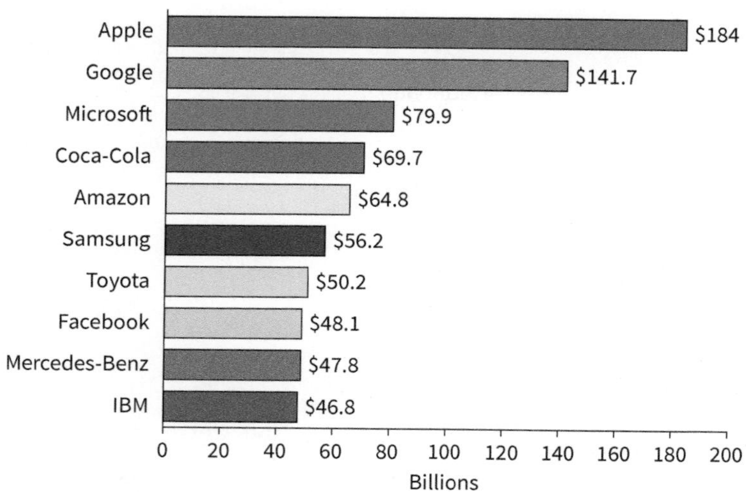

FIGURE 12.4 The World's 10 Most Valuable Brands (sales in billions)

Source: "Best Global Brands 2017," *Interbrand*, http://www.interbrand.com, accessed April 15, 2018.

Brand-building strategies were once limited to the consumer realm, but now they are becoming more important for B2B brands as well. Intel, Xerox, IBM, and service providers such as Xfinity and Salesforce are among the suppliers who have built brand names among business customers.

Brand Equity Brand loyalty is at the heart of **brand equity**, the added value that a respected and successful name gives to a product. This value results from a combination of factors, including awareness, loyalty, and perceived quality, as well as any feelings or images the customer associates with the brand. High brand equity offers financial advantages to a company, because the product commands a relatively large market share and sometimes reduces price sensitivity, generating higher profits. Figure 12.4 shows the world's 10 most valuable brands.

Brand awareness means the product is the first one that comes to mind when a product category is mentioned. If someone says "coffee," do you think of Starbucks, Dunkin' Donuts, or Folgers? Brand association is the link between a brand and other favorable images. A recent survey of recognizable logos with strong brand identities includes Disney, Google, IBM, and Federal Express.[17]

brand equity added value that a respected and successful name gives to a product.

Large companies have typically assigned the task of managing a brand's marketing strategies to a *brand manager*, who may also be called a *product manager* at some companies. This marketer plans and implements the balance of promotional, pricing, distribution, and product arrangements *that* leads to strong brand equity. A *category manager*, a type of marketer, oversees an entire group of products. Unlike traditional brand or product managers, category managers have profit responsibility for their product group. These managers are assisted by associates, usually called *analysts*. Part of the shift to category management was initiated by large retailers, when they realized there could be a benefit from the marketing muscle of large

Job Description

Brand Manager

Overview Does influencing a consumer's emotional perception, experience, or connection with a brand interest you? Would it be exciting to enhance a consumer's relationship to a brand by developing a product's look, price, and packaging? If so, becoming a brand manager might be for you.

Responsibilities A brand manager monitors the competitive landscape of a brand's category or segment; develops strategies to take advantage of opportunities in the marketplace; executes those strategies with the help of a cross-functional marketing team; and delivers the sales volume, market share, and profit projections forecasted by company management. As part of a company's marketing function, a brand manager sets the strategic direction of a brand and works with various departments within the organization to execute the strategy. This includes product and strategy development, manufacturing, product extension, package design, marketing research, business and financial forecasts and analysis, and promotion.

Requirements The career path of a brand manager typically requires a college degree and an entry-level position as a marketing analyst or sales representative. To become an assistant brand manager, with the responsibility for developing a brand's strategy, several years of experience or a degree may be required. The most sought-after skills for brand managers include analytical skills, problem-solving abilities, creativity, strategic vision, and the intuition and ability to take action. Most brand managers also have some background and coursework in marketing or sales.

Outlook Employment for brand and marketing managers is expected to grow 10% over the next decade. Declining revenues and increased competition have led companies to examine their product categories more closely than ever before and to hire the right individuals to manage their brands. Because of the increased number of channels now available to send out marketing messages, and increased branding within organizations, the need for brand managers should continue to increase.

Sources: Government website, "Advertising, Promotions, and Marketing Managers," *Occupational Outlook Handbook,* 2017 Edition, http://bls.gov, accessed April 15, 2018; government website, "Marketing Managers," http://onetonline.org, accessed April 15, 2018: "A Day in the Life: Assistant Brand Manager," *Vault,* http://www.vault.com, accessed April 15, 2018; "Career Overview: Brand Management," *Wet Feet,* http://www.wetfeet.com, accessed April 15, 2018; "What Does a Brand Manager Do?," *wiseGEEK,* http://www.wisegeek.org, accessed April 15, 2018; Victoria Black, "A Day in the Life: Assistant Brand Manager," *Bloomberg Business,* http://www.bloomberg.com, accessed April 15, 2018.

grocery and household goods producers such as General Mills and Procter & Gamble. As a result, producers began to focus their attention on in-store merchandising instead of mass-market advertising. See the "Job Description" feature for more details about a career as a brand manager.

A **category advisor** functions in the B2B context. This vendor is the major supplier designated by a business customer to assume responsibility for dealing with all the other vendors for a project and presenting the entire package to the business buyer.

category advisor vendor that is designated by the business customer as the major supplier to assume responsibility for dealing with all the other vendors for a project and presenting the entire package to the business buyer.

Packages and Labels

Packaging and labels are important in product identification. They also play an important role in a company's overall product strategy. Packaging affects the durability, image, and convenience of an item and is responsible for one of the biggest costs in many consumer products. Due to a growing demand to produce smaller, more environmentally friendly packages, box manufacturers and chemical companies are now working harder to create more compact packaging that is made from renewable sources and is recyclable. One-third of America's waste consists of containers and packaging, much of it from fast-food chains. McDonald's recently announced that its packaging is now 100% sustainably sourced, which means that its cartons, cups, bags, napkins, and tray liners are and will be made with wood fiber from recycled sources or forests certified by the Forest Stewardship Council. The Coca-Cola Company will deliver its "World without Waste" packaging vision, which includes collecting and recycling a bottle or can for every one it sells globally by 2030. The company aims to collect an amount of bottles equivalent to the 110 billion bottles it produces.[18] Choosing the right package is especially crucial in international marketing because marketers must be aware of such factors as language variations and cultural preferences. Package size can vary according to the purchasing patterns and market conditions of a country, and people with small refrigerators may purchase single beverages rather than a six-pack. Package weight is another important issue, because shipping costs are often based on weight. Made from multi-layers of film, stand-up pouches have become very popular in products from dog food to candy to dish soap. Although pouches are not recyclable in the United States, the packaging weight of a pouch is less than a standard bottle, and the resources used to produce, transport, and use the pouch are about 14% of the impact of an equivalent volume bottle. With features like tear notches, zippers, spouts, closures, and carrying holes on top, pouches (as shown in photo) facilitate easy on-the-go consumption, including drinking and eating—and dispensing and re-closing.

Labeling is an integral part of the packaging process as well. In the United States, labeling must meet federal laws requiring companies to provide enough information to allow consumers to make value comparisons among competitive products and, in the case of food packaging, provide nutrition information on the label. Marketers who ship products globally have to comply with labeling in those nations. This means knowing the answers to such questions as whether the labels should be in more than one language, specification of ingredients, and whether the labels provide enough information about the product to meet government standards.

The U.S. Food and Drug Administration (FDA) regulates the labeling of food and drug products, investigates violations, and enforces compliance with the Food, Drug, and Cosmetic Act. Typical violations include unauthorized health claims, unauthorized nutrient content claims, and unauthorized use of such terms as *healthy* or *natural*, and others that have strict regulatory definitions. The FDA has recently revised its labeling requirements to update and help consumers better understand its nutrition facts label with the percent daily value for added sugars and to reflect new scientific information, including the link between diet and chronic diseases such as obesity and heart disease.[19]

Another important aspect of packaging and labeling is the *universal product code (UPC)*, the bar code read by optical scanners that print the name of the item and the price on a receipt. For many stores, these identifiers are useful not just for packaging and labeling but also for simplifying and speeding retail transactions and for evaluating customer purchases and controlling inventory. *Radio-frequency identification (RFID) technology*—embedded chips or sensors—also coordinate inventory tracking, and when linked with a companywide system can provide information about delivery, product ordering and reordering, fulfillment, sales, and billing.

Keith Homan/Shutterstock

Stand-up pouches have become very popular in products ranging from dog food to candy to dish soap.

Assessment Check

1. Differentiate among a brand, a brand name, and a trademark.
2. Define *brand equity*.

4 Distribution Strategy

distribution strategy deals with the marketing activities and institutions involved in getting the right good or service to the company's customers.

distribution channels path that products—and legal ownership of them—follow from producer to consumers or business user.

physical distribution actual movement of products from producer to consumers or business users.

The next element of the marketing mix, **distribution strategy**, deals with the marketing activities and institutions involved in getting the right good or service to the company's customers. Distribution decisions involve modes of transportation, warehousing, inventory control, order processing, and selection of marketing channels. Marketing channels typically are made up of intermediaries such as retailers and wholesalers that move a product from producer to final purchaser.

The two major components of an organization's distribution strategy are distribution channels and physical distribution. **Distribution channels** are the paths that products—and legal ownership of them—follow from producer to consumer or business user. They are the means by which all organizations distribute their goods and services. **Physical distribution** is the actual movement of products from producer to consumers or business users. Physical distribution covers a broad range of activities, including customer service, transportation, inventory control, materials handling, order processing, and warehousing. Local Foods, a wholesale distribution company in Chicago, provides innovative distribution options to connect Midwest farmers and local restaurants, as described in the "Business Model" feature.

Distribution Channels

In their first decision for distribution channel selection, marketers choose which type of channel will best meet both their company's marketing objectives and the needs of their customers.

Business Model

Local Foods Connects Farmers and Eateries

With a background in farming, finance, and the growing farm-to-table movement, it still took time for Andrew Lutsey to realize success. The Wisconsin native has built a business serving as a fresh-produce intermediary between more than a hundred Midwestern farmers and local chefs and restaurateurs in the Chicago area.

The company is called Local Foods, and in its third year of operations and with sales nearing $5 million, Lutsey has learned that as an intermediary, relationships not only matter but also take time. With intense competition, price and service matter as well, particularly against other local and regional wholesalers, some of whom have been around for over a century. But as an intermediary between farmers and wholesale buyers, Lutsey has figured out how to differentiate Local Foods, and part of it has to do with tomatoes.

In nearby Rochelle, Illinois, a hydroponic tomato farm named MightyVine has emerged. The demand for fresh, locally grown tomatoes is brisk during the winter months, and Local Foods delivers the "hot" tomatoes to local restaurants. For a farmer in nearby Sandwich, Illinois, Local Foods has provided a lifeline to someone who acknowledges that he struggled to figure out the logistics of the wholesale process. During the summertime, Local Foods delivers more than a thousand pounds of the Sandwich farmer's produce on a weekly basis to Chicago restaurants. Without Local Foods, some farmers might not otherwise have an effective way to ultimately connect with foodies in Chicago-area restaurants.

Questions for Critical Thinking

1. Given the fact that restaurants face the ongoing issues of food waste and running out of produce, discuss the additional opportunities that exist for Local Foods and how the company can leverage its services with local eateries.
2. With a new 27,000-square-foot facility, Local Foods has evolved into a "food hub," with a small market, a café that serves seasonal fare, and a whole animal butcher shop, which the company acquired over a year ago. In what other ways might Local Foods continue to expand and grow?

Sources: Company website, http://localfoods.com, accessed April 17, 2018; Greg Trotter, "How Tasty Winter Tomatoes Are Helping Local Foods Grow," *Chicago Tribune*, http://www.chicagotribune.com, accessed April 17, 2018; Brett Hickman, "Take a Stroll Through Local Foods, Bringing Farm Fresh to Bucktown," *Chicago Eater*, http://chicagoeater.com, accessed April 17, 2018; Peter Frost, "Summertime Tomatoes in the Dead of Winter?" *Crain's Chicago Business*, http://www.chicagobusiness.com, accessed April 17, 2018.

As shown in **Figure 12.5**, marketers can choose either a *direct distribution channel*, which carries goods directly from producer to consumer or business user, or distribution channels that involve several different marketing intermediaries. A *marketing intermediary* (also called a *middleman*) is a company that moves goods between producers and consumers or business users. Marketing intermediaries perform various functions that help the distribution channel operate smoothly, such as buying, selling, storing, and transporting products; sorting and grading bulky items; and providing information to other channel members. The two main categories of marketing intermediaries are wholesalers and retailers.

No one channel suits every product. The best choice depends on the circumstances of the market and on customer needs. The most appropriate channel choice may also change over time as new opportunities arise and marketers strive to maintain their competitiveness. Currently, most smart phones sold in the United States are tied to four major carriers, AT&T, Sprint, Verizon, and T-Mobile, who each control the distribution of its particular phone network. However, recently, a more affordable trend in smartphones is the option of an unlocked phone. Rather than going through one of the "Big 4" carriers to purchase a device, an unlocked phone allows a user the freedom to choose a distribution channel not tied directly to a specific wireless carrier. Buyers select a phone first and then sign up with a carrier in the same way they can now buy any brand of computer regardless of their Internet service provider.[20]

Direct Distribution The shortest and simplest means of connecting producers and customers is direct contact between the two parties. This approach is most common in the B2B market. Growers of fresh fruits and vegetables who sell the products on a rural roadside stand use direct distribution, as do services ranging from banking and 10-minute oil changes to ear piercing and producers who frequently connect directly to consumers through company websites or auction sites such as eBay or e-commerce site Etsy.

Direct distribution is commonly found in the marketing of relatively expensive, complex products that may require demonstrations. Most major B2B products such as installations, accessory equipment, component parts, business services, and even raw materials are typically marketed through direct contacts between producers and business buyers. The Internet

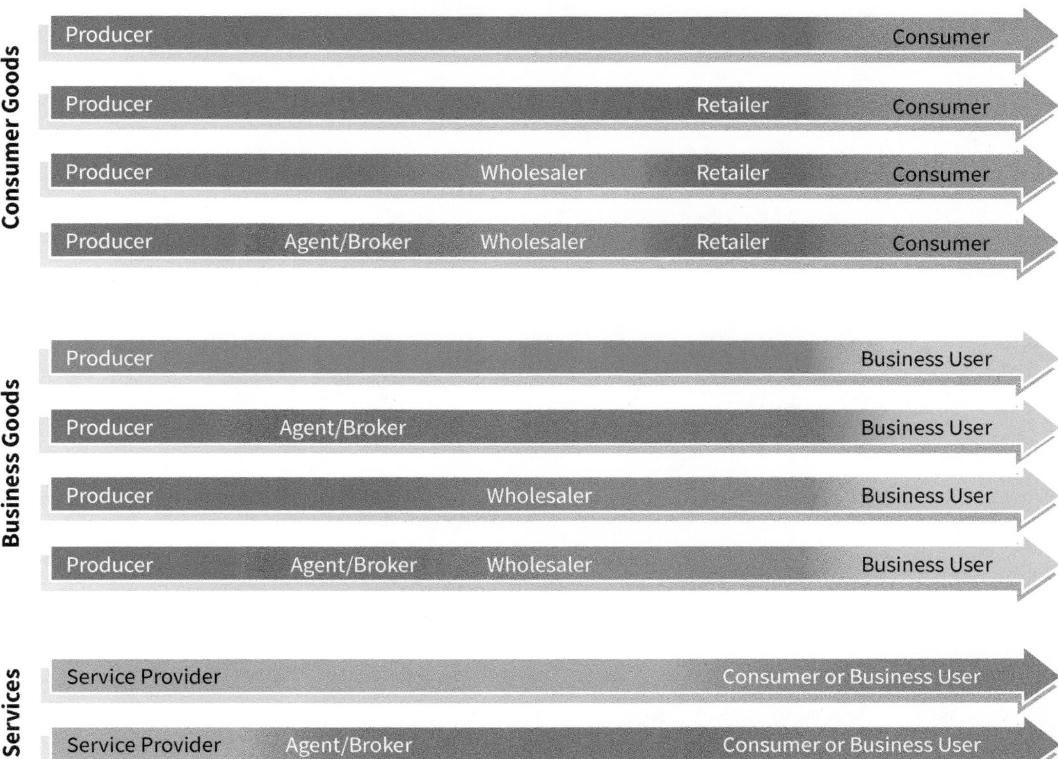

FIGURE 12.5 **Alternative Distribution Channels**

has also made direct distribution an attractive option for many retail companies and service providers. In an effort to bypass the traditional wholesale route of selling through multibrand boutiques and department stores, online companies like San Francisco–based Everlane have found alternative ways to sell directly to consumers. Rethinking the way retail works, the company, bypassing markups by intermediaries, designs and produces high-quality, affordable basic clothing items sold through two retail stores and its website.[21]

Distribution Channels Using Marketing Intermediaries Although direct channels allow simple and straightforward connections between producers and their customers, the list of channel alternatives in Figure 12.5 indicates that direct distribution is not the best choice in every instance. Some products sell in small quantities for relatively low prices to thousands of widely scattered consumers. Producers of such products cannot cost-effectively contact each of their customers, so they distribute products through marketing intermediaries called *wholesalers* and *retailers*.

Although you might think that adding intermediaries to the distribution process would increase the final cost of products, more often than not this choice actually lowers consumer prices. Intermediaries such as wholesalers and retailers often add significant value to a product as it moves through the distribution channel. They do so by creating utility, providing additional services, and reducing costs.

Marketing utility is created when intermediaries help ensure that products are available for sale when and where customers want to purchase them. If you need salad dressing for your dinner salad, you would not call Newman's Own and ask them to send you a bottle of the company's Balsamic Vinaigrette. Instead, you go to the nearest grocery store, where you find utility in the form of product availability. In addition, intermediaries perform such important services as transporting merchandise to convenient locations. Finally, by representing numerous producers, a marketing intermediary can cut the costs of buying and selling. As **Figure 12.6** shows,

FIGURE 12.6 Reducing Transactions through Marketing Intermediaries

if four manufacturers each sold directly to four consumers, this would require 16 separate transactions. Adding a marketing intermediary, such as a retailer, to the exchange cuts the number of necessary transactions to eight.

Assessment Check

1. Define *distribution channels*.
2. What is a marketing intermediary?

5 Wholesaling

A **wholesaler** is a distribution channel member that sells primarily to retailers, other wholesalers, or business users. An example of a wholesale distributor to the convenience retail industry is Core-Mark Holding Company. Core-Mark provides sales, marketing, distribution, and logistics services to 43,000 locations across the United States and Canada through 30 distribution centers with products including cigarettes, food, candy, snacks, groceries, beverages, tobacco products, health, beauty, beverages, dairy, juices, salads, and more.

wholesaler distribution channel member that sells primarily to retailers, other wholesalers, or business users.

Wholesaling is a crucial part of the distribution channel for many products, particularly consumer goods and business supplies. Wholesaling intermediaries can be classified on the basis of ownership; some are owned by manufacturers, some are owned by retailers, and others are independently owned. Wholesalers purchase finished goods from manufacturers and sell those goods to retailers, typically in large quantities.[22]

Manufacturer-Owned Wholesaling Intermediaries

A manufacturer's marketing manager may decide to distribute goods directly through company-owned facilities to control distribution or customer service. Companies operate two main types of manufacturer-owned wholesaling intermediaries: sales branches and sales offices.

Sales branches stock the products they distribute and fill orders from their inventories. They also provide offices for sales representatives. Sales branches are common in the chemical, petroleum products, motor vehicle, and machine and equipment industries.

A *sales office* is exactly what its name implies: an office for a producer's salespeople. Manufacturers set up sales offices in various regions to support local selling efforts and improve customer service. Some kitchen and bath fixture manufacturers maintain showrooms to display their products. Builders and decorators can visit these showrooms to see how the items would look in place. Unlike sales branches, however, sales offices do not store any inventory. When a customer orders from a showroom or other sales office, the merchandise is delivered from a separate warehouse.

Independent Wholesaling Intermediaries

An independent wholesaling intermediary is a business that represents a number of different manufacturers and makes sales calls on retailers, manufacturers, and other business accounts. Independent wholesalers are classified as either merchant wholesalers or agents and brokers, depending on whether they take title to the products they handle.

Merchant wholesalers, like apparel wholesaler WholesaleSarong.com, are independently owned wholesaling intermediaries that take title to the goods they handle. Within this category, a *full-function merchant wholesaler* provides a complete assortment of services for retailers or industrial buyers, such as warehousing, shipping, and even financing. A subtype of full-function merchant is a *rack jobber*, such as Virginia-based Choice Books, which is a direct-store-delivery distributor of inspirational books to retail stores. This type of company stocks, displays, and services particular retail products, such as calendars, books, and note cards, in drugstores and gift shops. Usually, the retailer receives a commission based on actual sales as payment for providing merchandise space to a rack jobber.

A *limited-function merchant wholesaler* also takes legal title to the products it handles, but it provides fewer services to the retailers to which it sells. Some limited-function merchant wholesalers only warehouse products but do not offer delivery service. Others warehouse and deliver products but provide no financing. One type of limited-function merchant wholesaler is a *drop shipper* such as Kate Aspen, an Atlanta-based wholesaler of wedding favors. Drop shippers also operate in such industries as coal and lumber, characterized by bulky products for which no single producer can provide a complete assortment. They give access to many related goods by contacting numerous producers and negotiating the best possible prices. Cost considerations call for producers to ship such products directly to the drop shipper's customers.

Another category of independent wholesaling intermediaries consists of *agents* and *brokers*. They may or may not take possession of the goods they handle, but they never take title, working mainly to bring buyers and sellers together. Stockbrokers such as Charles Schwab and real estate agents such as RE/MAX perform functions similar to those of agents and brokers, but at the retail level. They do not take title to the seller's property; instead, they create time and ownership utility for both buyer and seller by helping carry out transactions.

Manufacturers' reps act as independent sales forces by representing the manufacturers of related but noncompeting products. These agent intermediaries, sometimes referred to as *manufacturers' agents*, receive commissions based on a percentage of the sales they make.

Retailer-Owned Cooperatives and Buying Offices

Retailers sometimes band together to form their own wholesaling organizations. Such organizations can take the form of either a buying group or a cooperative. The participating retailers set up the new operation to reduce costs or to provide some special service that is not readily available in the marketplace. To achieve cost savings through quantity purchases, independent retailers may form a buying group that negotiates bulk sales with manufacturers. Ace Hardware is a retailer-owned cooperative. The independent owners of its more than 5,000 stores have access to bulk merchandise purchases that save them—and their customers—money.[23] In a cooperative, an independent group of retailers may decide to band together to share functions such as shipping or warehousing.

Assessment Check

1. Define *wholesaling*.
2. Differentiate between a merchant wholesaler and an agent or broker in terms of title to the goods.

6 Retailing

retailer distribution channel member that sells goods and services to individuals for their own use rather than for resale.

Retailers, in contrast to wholesalers, are distribution channel members that sell goods and services, typically in small quantities, to individuals for their personal use rather than for resale. Consumers usually buy their food, clothing, shampoo, furniture, and appliances from some type of retailer. The supermarket where you buy your groceries may have bought some of its items from a retail-owned wholesale grocery cooperative such as Unified Grocers and then resold them to you.

Retailers are the final link of the distribution channel. Because they are often the only channel members that deal directly with consumers, it is essential that retailers remain aware of changing shopping trends. As more shoppers head to the screen instead of the mall, bricks-and-mortar retailers (those with physical store locations) need to offer better customer experiences to compete. Known as "The Amazon Effect," since the company began in 1994, the e-commerce marketplace, with near-immediate results and, oftentimes, lower prices, has had a profound impact on traditional forms of retail.

Nonstore Retailers

Two categories of retailers exist: store and nonstore. As **Figure 12.7** shows, nonstore retailing includes four forms: direct-response retailing, Internet retailing, automatic merchandising, and direct selling. *Direct-response retailing* reaches prospective customers through catalogs; telemarketing; and even magazine, newspaper, and television ads. Shoppers order merchandise by mail, telephone, online, or mobile device and then receive home delivery or pick up the merchandise at a local store. Lands' End has long stood out as a highly successful direct-response retailer; its well-known clothing catalog and stellar customer service have set the standard for this type of distribution channel.

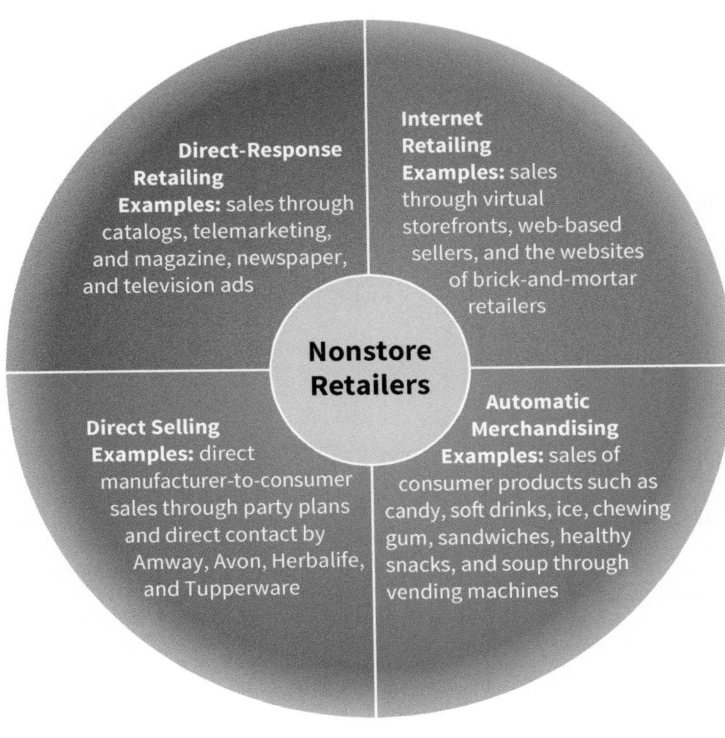

FIGURE 12.7 **Types of Nonstore Retailing**

Internet retailing, the second form of nonstore retailing, continues to experience strong sales growth. To offset the decline in bricks-and-mortar sales, most retailers have created online websites, which continue to grow faster than traditional physical (bricks-and-mortar) retail store sales. With more people owning smart phones, there has been a shift to shopping with mobile devices, and this has helped fuel the growth of online sales. E-commerce will increase 16% in an upcoming year, representing 10% of U.S. retail sales. Surging growth will continue for mobile commerce, which, in a recent year, was up 32%, representing almost 40% of e-commerce sales. By 2020, mobile commerce will represent nearly half of total e-commerce sales.[24]

The last two forms of nonstore retailing are automatic merchandising and direct selling. *Automatic merchandising* provides convenience through the use of vending machines. WeGoBabies vending machines are for parents on the go. Within each vending machine, essentials for babies, including pacifiers, diapers, wipes, formula, and snacks, are available. The machines are strategically placed in airports, malls, amusement parks, zoos, museums, and anywhere else babies and toddlers can be found. The machines come with a touch screen for customized advertising, branding, and logos.[25] *Direct selling* includes direct-to-consumer sales by Pampered Chef kitchen consultants (as seen in photo) and high-end Stella & Dot jewelry salespeople through party-plan selling methods. The party plan, a form of direct selling, is a method of marketing products by hosting what is presented as a social event at which products will be offered for sale.

Companies that previously relied on telemarketing to generate new customers have encountered consumer resistance to intrusive phone calls. Among the growing barriers are caller ID, call-blocking devices such as the TeleZapper, and the National Do Not Call list for cell phones and land lines, which made it illegal for most companies to call people who are registered. Today, telemarketing can be used for appointment setting, following up on direct mail or an e-mail, marketing research, customer reactivation, generating leads, and selling to existing customers.

Rick Wilking/Reuters/Alamy Stock Photo

Pampered Chef's direct sales force of independent consultants offers high-quality, multipurpose kitchen tools and in-home cooking demonstrations.

TABLE 12.2 Types of Retail Stores

Store Type	Description	Example
Specialty store	Sells a wide selection and deep assortment of goods in a single merchandise category	Bass Pro Shops, Dick's Sporting Goods, Williams-Sonoma
Convenience store	Offers staple convenience goods, easily accessible locations, extended store hours, and rapid checkouts	7-Eleven, Mobil Mart, QuikTrip
Discount store	Offers wide selection of merchandise at low prices; off-price discounters offer designer or brand-name merchandise	Target, Walmart, Dollar General, Marshalls
Warehouse club	Large, warehouse-style store selling food and general merchandise at discount prices to membership cardholders	Costco, Sam's Club, BJ's
Factory outlet	Manufacturer-owned store selling seconds, production overruns, or discontinued lines	Adidas, Coach, Gap, Ralph Lauren
Supermarket	Large, self-service retailer offering a wide selection of food and nonfood merchandise	Publix, Whole Foods Market, Kroger
Supercenter	Giant store offering food and general merchandise at discount prices	Walmart Supercenter, Super Target, Meijer
Department store	Offers a wide variety of merchandise selections (furniture, cosmetics, housewares, clothing) and many customer services	Macy's, Nordstrom, Neiman Marcus

Store Retailers

For not much longer, in-store sales still outpace nonstore retailing methods such as direct-response retailing and Internet selling. Store retailers range in size from tiny newsstands to temporary pop-up stores to department stores and multiacre warehouse-like retailers such as Sam's Club. Table 12.2 lists the different types of store retailers, with examples of each type. Clearly, there are many approaches to retailing and a variety of services, prices, and product lines offered by each retail outlet.

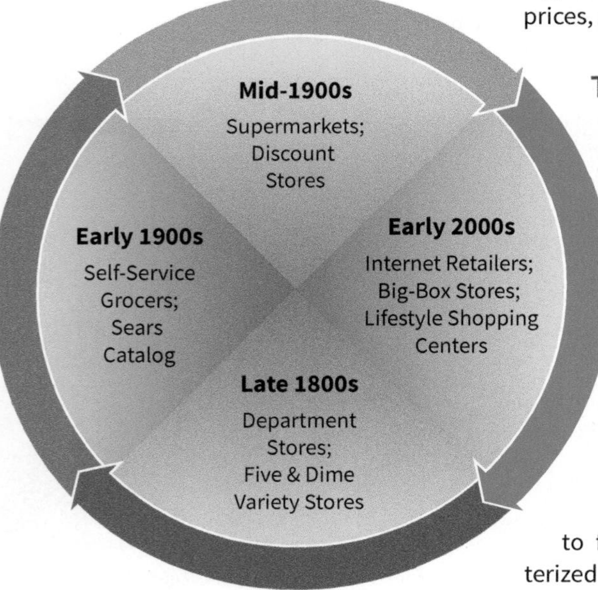

FIGURE 12.8 The Wheel of Retailing

The Wheel of Retailing Retailers are subject to constant change as new stores replace older establishments. In a concept called the *wheel of retailing*, introduced by Malcolm McNair of Harvard University, retailers use low-price strategies to build market share, to the point where the goal shifts from attracting new customers to building margins and profits through higher prices. This creates room for retailers with new low-price business models to create—thus spinning the wheel of retailing again. Seen as a cycle and an evolutionary theory, it represents one of the theories of structural change in the evolution of retailing. Whether or not it applies to Amazon is a controversial topic of debate. Some question whether Amazon stopped the wheel, is a victim of the wheel, or is riding the wheel.

As Figure 12.8 shows, most major developments in retailing appear to fit the wheel-pattern. The low-price, limited-service strategy characterized supermarkets, catalog retailers, discount stores, and, most recently, Internet retailers and giant big-box stores. Corner grocery stores gave way to supermarkets and then to warehouse clubs such as Costco. Department stores lost market share to discount clothing retailers such as Target. Independent bookstores have lost business to giant chains such as Barnes & Noble and e-commerce sellers such as Amazon.com.

How Retailers Compete

Retailers are operating in an increasingly competitive environment and face a period of rapid change. Nonstore retailers focus on making the shopping experience as convenient as possible. Shoppers at stores such as Saks Fifth Avenue enjoy a luxurious atmosphere and personal service. In fact, those who visit the new shoe department at the flagship store in New York have the run of the entire eighth floor, devoted entirely to shoes—with its own zip code. The elite shopping experience includes a private VIP room, a repair service, and a chocolate café.[26]

Like manufacturers, retailers must develop customer-focused marketing strategies based on goals. Successful retailers convey images that alert consumers to the stores' identities and the shopping experiences they provide. To create that image, all components of a retailer's strategy must complement each other. After identifying their target markets, retailers must choose merchandising, customer service, pricing, and location strategies that will attract customers in those market segments.

Identifying a Target Market The first step in developing a competitive retailing strategy is to select a target market. This choice requires careful evaluation of the size and profit potential of the chosen market segment and the current level of competition for the segment's business. Bargain stores such as Dollar General target the price-conscious consumer, for example, while convenience stores like 7-Eleven target consumers who want a quick and easy way to purchase items they buy frequently. Actor Bruce Willis and basketball icon Michael Jordan have embraced a shaved head. The size and potential of the market for head shavers continues to grow. By the age of 35, two-thirds of American men will experience some degree of hair loss, and by age 50, most will have thinning hair. SkullShaver, maker of the Pitbull, a head shaver, targets this demographic of men who want a smooth, bald, and confident look. Its flexible heads adjust to the contours of any man's head perfectly.[27]

Selecting a Product Strategy After identifying a target market, the retailer must next develop a product strategy to determine the best mix of merchandise to carry to satisfy that market. Retail strategists must decide on the general product categories, product lines, and variety to offer. Sometimes that involves expanding the product mix and sometimes it involves contracting it. As consumers gravitate toward larger and roomier vehicles, Toyota is challenged to produce the right mix of cars and trucks. In a recent year, Toyota posted its best ever SUV sales results.[28]

Shaping a Customer Service Strategy A retailer's customer service strategy focuses on attracting and retaining target customers to maximize sales and profits. Some stores offer a wide variety of services, such as gift wrapping, alterations, returns, interior design services, and delivery. Other stores offer bare-bones customer service, stressing low price instead. Some grocery shoppers, for instance, find convenience online through a service such as Instacart, which handles product selection, packing, and delivery. Other shoppers choose to visit a supermarket and make their own selections. Or they can go to a discount supermarket like Iowa-based ALDI, where they not only assemble their orders but also bag their purchases.

Selecting a Pricing Strategy Retailers base their pricing decisions on the costs of purchasing products from other channel members and offering services to customers. Pricing can play a major role in consumers' perceptions of a retailer, and not just because they appreciate low prices. The grocery retailer Trader Joe's offers organic and gourmet foods under its own private labels at rock-bottom prices. Customers enjoy shopping for private label brands Trader Jose's Mexican specialties and Trader Darwin's nutritional supplements at prices lower

James Kirkikis/Shutterstock

For an ultimate experience, Mall of America in Minnesota has an indoor theme park to provide entertainment and to attract shoppers.

than other gourmet or organic markets.[29] Pricing strategy is covered in more detail in Chapter 13.

Choosing a Location A good location often marks the difference between success and failure in retailing. The location decision depends on the retailer's size, financial resources, product offerings, competition, and, of course, its target market. Traffic patterns, the visibility of the store's signage, parking, and the location of complementary and competing stores also influence the choice of a retail location.

A *planned shopping center* is a group of retail stores planned, coordinated, and marketed as a unit to shoppers in a geographic trade area. By providing convenient locations with free parking, shopping centers have replaced downtown shopping in many urban areas. But time-pressed consumers are increasingly looking for more efficient ways to shop, including catalogs, online retailers, and one-stop shopping at large freestanding stores such as Walmart Supercenters. To lure more customers, shopping centers are recasting themselves as entertainment destinations, with movie theaters, art displays, carousel rides, and musical entertainment. The giant Mall of America in Bloomington, Minnesota, features a seven-acre amusement park and an aquarium (see picture).

As part of a customer service strategy and to remain competitive, online and bricks-and-mortar retailers like Best Buy have created liberal return policies. However, as described in the "Judgment Call" feature, some "returnaholics" have taken advantage of such policies.

Large regional malls have witnessed a shift in shopping center traffic to smaller strip centers, name-brand outlet centers, and *lifestyle centers*, open-air complexes containing retailers that often focus on specific shopper segments and product interests. In recent years, lifestyle centers have grown because consumers are drawn to a shopping experience different from that offered by a traditional mall.[30]

Judgment Call

Liberal Return Policies May Cost Retailers

As part of a retailer's customer service strategy, and in an effort to stay competitive in an increasingly competitive environment, retailers like Best Buy have created liberal return policies. Most retailers will allow returns from customers suffering from buyers' remorse. However, what you might not know is that retailers like Best Buy are tracking serial returners, or those who return items frequently.

Using customized software, Best Buy is tracking and cracking down on serial returners. Too many returns can be costly for a company. The electronics giant is one of several chains (along with Sephora and Home Depot) that have hired a service called Retail Equation to score customers' shopping behavior and impose limits on the amount of merchandise they can return. Serial returns can be associated with fraud, when customers either steal items from a store and return with a counterfeit receipt or without a receipt or take back used or worn merchandise on a regular basis. Best Buy will refuse to accept a return if its database records a high number of returns or large dollar amounts on specific returns from the same customer.

Most retailers are well aware of so-called friendly fraud that applies to consumers not shy about "wardrobing"—using a product for a while before returning it. Still, others worry that consumers who do not return products on a frequent basis will suffer at the expense of those who overreturn. For Best Buy, giving customers the benefit of the doubt and applying a "customer is always right" philosophy isn't always easy when it comes to serial returners.

Questions for Critical Thinking

1. **What are additional strategies retailers can use to continue to balance the delicate issue of giving customers the benefit of the doubt while protecting themselves against serial fraud?**
2. **It seems that some consumers are willing to purchase a product with the intent to "gently" use it and then return it. Does this practice seem socially acceptable? Why or why not?**

Sources: Kristin Colella, "Returnaholics, Beware: You Could Get Blacklisted by Your Favorite Stores," *Main Street,* https://www.mainstreet.com, accessed April 19, 2018; Tom Ryan, "Should Chronic Returners Be Banned?" *Retail Wire,* http://www.retailwire.com, accessed April 19, 2018; "The Unethical But (Mostly) Legal Retail Shopping Tactics of Devil Consumers," *SixWise,* http://www.sixwise.com, accessed April 19, 2018; Chavie Lieber, "You Can Be Banned From Making Returns at Sephora," *Racked,* www.racked.com, accessed April 19, 2018; Khadeeja Safdar, "How Returns Are Used Against You at Best Buy, Other Retailers," *The Wall Street Journal,* www.wsj.com, accessed April 19, 2018.

Building a Promotional Strategy A retailer develops a variety of promotions to stimulate demand for its product or service. Retailer North Face, a social media trailblazer, is recognized for its marketing excellence. As an outdoor product company, North Face is convinced that more "adventurous, brave, boundary-breaking" women need to be featured in advertising and social media campaigns to create strong role models for young women and girls. Using social media, the company launched a global effort, "Move Mountains," which includes a series of posts highlighting athletes and trailblazing women as explorers. The company's Global VP of Marketing is quoted as saying, "We had a simple theory that if women and girls see more role models in exploration, it will create more female role models for future generations." This builds trust and intimacy within the North Face community.[31]

As a way to gain an advantage over competitors, online retailers compete on the basis of customer service. Incentive programs also drive customers back as a way to reward them and to create a value exchange. Promotional strategy is discussed further in Chapter 13.

Creating a Store Atmosphere A successful retailer closely aligns its merchandising, pricing, and promotion strategies with *store atmospherics*, the physical characteristics of a store and its amenities, to influence consumers' perceptions of the shopping experience. Atmospherics begin with the store's exterior, which may use eye-catching architectural elements and signage to attract customer attention and interest. Interior atmospheric elements include store layout, merchandise presentation, lighting, color, sound, decor, and cleanliness. A high-end store such as Nordstrom, for instance, features high ceilings in selling areas that spotlight tasteful and meticulously cared for displays of carefully chosen items of obvious quality. Hollister has dim lights and loud music for a clublike atmosphere to attract teenagers. Bookstore Barnes & Noble has an inviting atmosphere that is warm and cozy, which makes reading easy and fun.

Assessment Check

1. Define *retailer*.
2. What are the elements of a retailer's marketing strategy?

7 Distribution Channel Decisions and Logistics

Every company faces two major decisions when choosing how to distribute its goods or services: selecting a specific distribution channel and deciding on the level of distribution intensity. In deciding which distribution channel is most efficient, business managers need to consider four factors: the market, the product, the producer, and the competition. These factors are often interrelated and may change over time. In today's global business environment, strong relationships with customers and suppliers are important for survival. Amazon.com has proven that traditional distribution for consumer packaged goods has evolved. See the "Business and Technology" feature for more details.

Selecting Distribution Channels

Market factors may be the most important consideration in choosing a distribution channel. To reach a target market with a small number of buyers or buyers concentrated in a geographical area, the most feasible alternative may be a direct channel. In contrast, if the company must reach customers who are dispersed or who make frequent small purchases, then the channel may need to incorporate marketing intermediaries to make goods available when and where customers want them.

In general, standardized products or items with low unit values usually pass through relatively long distribution channels. On the other hand, products that are complex, expensive, custom made, or perishable move through shorter distribution channels involving few—or no—intermediaries. As products continue to be sold across multiple channels, traditional distribution practices have undergone a profound change. Today, physical store operators are selling online, and online merchants such as Amazon are expanding with stores and showrooms. The challenge is meeting the expectations of consumers who are buying and receiving products through multiple channels—online, bricks and mortar, and mobile. As retailers integrate these channels, consumers can choose how they will receive a product. This has created a massive shift in the distribution efforts of many big companies that must know in real time whether an item is in a store, warehouse, or distribution center.[32]

Producers that offer a broad product line, with the financial and marketing resources to distribute and promote it, are more likely to choose a shorter channel. Instead of depending on marketing intermediaries, financially strong manufacturers with broad product lines typically use their own sales representatives, warehouses, and credit departments to serve both retailers and consumers.

In many cases, start-up manufacturers turn to direct channels because they can't persuade intermediaries to carry their products or because they want to extend their sales reach. Some companies employ direct channels to carry intangible goods as well. Anne Wojcicki, co-founder and CEO of genetic testing company 23andMe, utilizes a direct-to-consumer selling model. Recently, the company was approved as the first and only direct-to-consumer genetic test for cancer risk. Without a prescription, customers are provided with infomation on three genetic variants known to be associated with higher risk for cancer. With a simple saliva sample, 23andMe provides consumers the opportunity to learn more about their own chromosomes, family history, and ancestry.[33]

Competitive performance and excellent service are key considerations to choosing a distribution channel. A producer can lose customers when an intermediary fails to achieve promotion or product delivery. Channels used by established competitors as well as new market entries also can influence decisions. Sometimes a joint venture between competitors can work

Business & Technology

Amazon "Dashes" to Connected Consumers

As online purchases of consumer packaged goods (CPGs) continue to grow, traditional distribution practices have undergone a change. In a recent year, the purchase of online CPGs grew at a rate of 42%, as compared to 30% for e-commerce.

E-commerce giant Amazon.com has made it as easy as the click of a button, called Dash, to order paper towels, laundry detergent, and toilet paper. This one-click option, made possible through a small Internet-enabled hardware device, bypasses having to log into Amazon, and creates a direct connection between Amazon and its buyers.

The Dash button, offered for free, can conveniently be placed near products that typically need replenishing—for example, on a washing machine or alongside a paper towel holder. The device uses Wi-Fi to send a message to a consumer's Amazon account, automatically ordering the needed item.

As consumers hop from one channel to another to make purchases—from desktop to tablet to mobile device—delivery, fulfillment, inventory control, and supply chains have undergone a transformation. To stay competitive, retailers must sell across multiple channels, while engaging and providing a personalized shopping experience to consumers. Amazon has subsequently introduced a programmer-friendly "Internet-of-Things Dash Button" that allows programming modifications to the device, which can be configured to respond to commands such as ordering pizza and controlling household lights.

Questions for Critical Thinking

1. Are there other applications for the Dash button beyond consumer packaged goods? Would you use the Dash button? Why or why not?
2. What are the benefits of the Dash button to Amazon? Discuss ways that retailers can compete with Amazon's goal to create a more "connected customer."

Sources: Leena Rao, "Amazon Expands One Click Buying Program, Makes Dash Button Free," *Fortune*, http://fortune.com, accessed April 21, 2018; Lisa Arthur, "What Amazon's New Dash Button Means to CPG Manufacturers and Marketers," *Forbes*, http://www.forbes.com, accessed April 21, 2018; Aaron Mendes, "CPG Killed It in E-Commerce in 2015," *1010 Data*, https://www.1010data.com, accessed April 21, 2018; Paul Myerson, "Amazon Dashes to Make Consumers (and Their Supply Chains) Leaner," *Industry Week*, http://www.industryweek.com, accessed April 21, 2018.

well. Topshop, a trendy UK-based multinational retailer, has partnered with Nordstrom to sell clothing, shoes, and cosmetics through the department store as a store-within-a-store concept. Currently, there are 90 Nordstrom locations with TopShop stores. Topshop management cites Nordstrom's multichannel retail presence as the reason for the partnership.[34]

Simon Greig/Shutterstock

Expensive specialty products like Rolex watches are typically part of a limited market coverage strategy of exclusive distribution.

Selecting Distribution Intensity

A second key distribution decision involves *distribution intensity*—the number of intermediaries or outlets through which a manufacturer distributes its goods. Only one BMW dealership may be operating in your immediate area, but you can find Coca-Cola everywhere—in supermarkets, convenience stores, gas stations, vending machines, and restaurants. BMW has chosen a different level of distribution intensity than that used for Coca-Cola. In general, market coverage varies along a continuum with three different intensity levels:

1. *Intensive distribution* involves placing a company's products in nearly every available outlet. Generally, intensive distribution suits low-priced convenience goods such as milk, newspapers, and soft drinks. This kind of market saturation requires cooperation by many intermediaries, including wholesalers and retailers, to achieve maximum coverage.
2. *Selective distribution* is a market-coverage strategy in which a manufacturer selects only a limited number of retailers to distribute its product lines. Selective distribution can reduce total marketing costs and establish strong working relationships within the channel. A good example of selective distribution would be cars and certain types of clothing brands.
3. *Exclusive distribution*, at the other end of the continuum from intensive distribution, limits market coverage in a specific geographical region. The approach suits relatively expensive specialty products such as Rolex watches (see photo). Retailers are carefully selected to enhance the product's image to the market and to ensure that well-trained personnel will contribute to customer satisfaction. Although producers may sacrifice some market coverage by granting an exclusive territory to a single intermediary, the decision usually pays off in developing and maintaining an image of quality and prestige.

When companies are offloading excess inventory, even high-priced retailers may look to discounters to help them clear the merchandise from their warehouses. To satisfy consumers' taste for luxury goods, designer outlet malls offer shoppers a chance to buy status items at lower prices. Chicago Premium Outlets features 170 stores carrying such upscale brands as Michael Kors, Armani Exchange, and Diesel. Similar centers include Desert Hills Premium Outlets in California, Las Vegas Premium Outlets, and Seattle Premium Outlets.[35]

Logistics and Physical Distribution

A company's choice of distribution channels creates the final link in the **supply chain**, the complete sequence of suppliers that contribute to creating a good or service and delivering it to business users and final consumers. The supply chain begins when the raw materials used in production are delivered to the producer and continues with the actual production activities that create finished goods. Finally, the finished goods move through the producer's distribution channels to end customers.

supply chain complete sequence of suppliers that contribute to creating a good or service and delivering it to business users and final consumers.

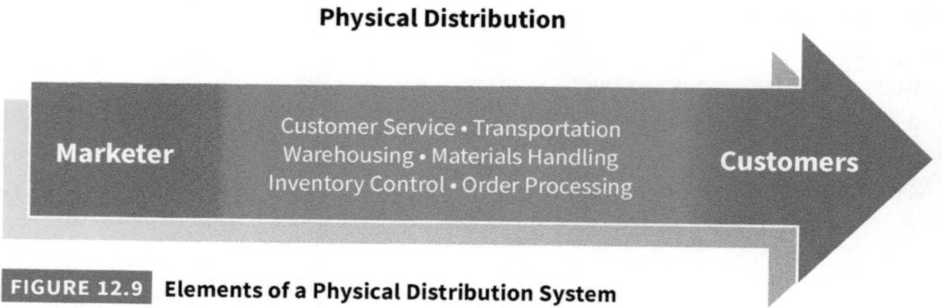

FIGURE 12.9 **Elements of a Physical Distribution System**

logistics process of coordinating the flow of goods, services, and information among members of the supply chain.

The process of coordinating the flow of goods, services, and information among members of the supply chain is called **logistics**. The term originally referred to strategic movements of military troops and supplies. Today, however, it describes all of the business activities involved in the supply chain with the ultimate goal of getting finished goods to customers.

Physical Distribution A major focus of logistics management—identified earlier in the chapter as one of the two basic dimensions of distribution strategy—is *physical distribution*, the activities aimed at efficiently moving finished goods from the production line to the consumer or business buyer. As **Figure 12.9** shows, physical distribution is a broad concept that includes transportation and numerous other elements that help link buyers and sellers. An effectively managed physical distribution system can increase customer satisfaction by ensuring reliable movements of products through the supply chain. For instance, Walmart studies the speed with which goods can be shelved once they arrive at the store because strategies that look efficient at the warehouse, such as completely filling pallets with goods, can actually be time-consuming or costly in the aisles.

As discussed earlier, RFID technology relies on a computer chip implanted somewhere on a product or its packaging that emits a low-frequency radio signal identifying the item. The radio signal doesn't require a line of sight to register on the store's computers the way a bar code does, so a hand-held RFID reader can scan crates and cartons before they are unloaded. Because the chip can store information about the product's progress through the distribution channel, retailers can efficiently manage inventories, maintain stock levels, reduce loss, track stolen goods, and cut costs. The technology is similar to that already used to identify lost pets and vehicles speeding through toll booths. Walmart, Target, the U.S. Department of Defense, and the German retailer Metro Group already require their suppliers to use RFID technology. The U.S. Army is now using solar power to activate battery-powered RFIDs, which are particularly useful in remote areas. Automakers are also using RFID technology to improve their production processes by tracking parts and other supplies. A new version of the RFID chip can be printed on paper or plastic. RFID technology brings with it privacy and counterfeiting concerns. However, one company has developed a process that uses unique silicon "fingerprints" to generate unclonable RFID chips.[36]

Warehousing is the physical distribution activity that involves the storage of products. *Materials handling* is moving items within factories, warehouses, transportation terminals, and stores. Inventory control involves managing inventory costs, such as storage facilities, insurance, taxes, and handling. The physical distribution activity of *order processing* includes preparing orders for shipment and receiving orders when shipments arrive.

vendor-managed inventory process in which the producer and the retailer agree that the producer (or the wholesaler) will determine how much of a product a buyer needs and automatically ship new supplies when needed.

The wide use of electronic data interchange (EDI) and the constant pressure on suppliers to improve their response time have led to **vendor-managed inventory**, in which the producer and the retailer agree that the producer (or the wholesaler) will determine how much of a product a buyer needs and will automatically ship new supplies when needed.

The form of transportation used to ship products depends primarily on the kind of product, the distance involved, and the cost. The logistics manager can choose from a number of companies and modes of transportation. As **Table 12.3** shows, the five

TABLE 12.3 Comparison of Transportation Modes

Mode	Speed	Dependability in Meeting Schedules	Frequency of Shipments	Availability in Different Locations	Flexibility in Handling	Cost
Truck	Fast	High	High	Very extensive	Average	High
Rail	Average	Average	Low	Low	High	Average
Water	Very slow	Average	Very low	Limited	Very high	Very low
Air	Very fast	High	Average	Average	Low	Very high
Pipeline	Slow	High	High	Very limited	Very Low	Low

major transport modes are—in order of total expenditures—trucks (with about 75% of total expenditures), railroads (approximately 12%), water carriers (6%), air freight (4%), and pipelines (3%). The faster methods typically cost more than the slower ones. Speed, reliable delivery, shipment frequency, location availability, handling flexibility, and cost are all important considerations when choosing the most appropriate mode of transportation.

More than 33.8 million trucks operate in the United States, carrying mostly finished goods all or part of the way to the consumer and earning more than $739 billion in gross freight revenues. Over 3 million of these are tractor trailers.[37] Railroads, which compete with many truck routes despite their recent loss of market share, are a major mode of transportation. The 575 freight railroads in the United States operate across more than 140,000 miles of track through 49 states. A freight train needs only 1 gallon of diesel fuel to transport 1 ton of cargo almost 484 miles.[38]

Customer Service Customer service is a vital component of both product and distribution strategies. *Customer service standards* measure the quality of service a company provides to its customers. Managers frequently set quantitative guidelines—for example, that all orders be processed in less than 24 hours after they are received or that salespeople approach shoppers within two minutes after they enter the store. Sometimes customers set their own service standards and choose suppliers that meet or exceed them.

The customer service components of product strategy include warranty and repair service programs. *Warranties* represent a company's promise to repair a defective product, refund money paid, or replace a product if it proves unsatisfactory. Repair services are also important. Consumers want to know that help is available if something goes wrong. Those who shop for computers or tablets, for example, often choose retailers that not only feature low prices but also offer repair services and tech support.

Consumers' complaints of the impersonal service they received at websites led e-commerce retailers to take a number of steps to "humanize" their customer interactions and deal with complaints. Using artificial intelligence, many companies have enhanced their customer service with chatbots and virtual assistants. Chatbots can answer questions and provide support inexpensively, quickly, and accurately.

Assessment Check

1. What is distribution intensity?
2. Define *supply chain.*
3. What do customer service standards measure?

What's Ahead

This chapter covered two of the elements of the marketing mix: product and distribution. It introduced the key marketing tasks of developing, marketing, and packaging want-satisfying goods and services. It also focused on the three major components of an organization's distribution strategy: the design of efficient distribution channels; wholesalers and retailers that make up many distribution channels; and logistics and physical distribution. We now turn to the remaining two—promotion and pricing—in Chapter 13.

Chapter in Review

Summary of Learning Objectives

LEARNING OBJECTIVE 1 Explain product strategy and how to classify goods and services.

A product is a bundle of physical, service, and symbolic attributes designed to satisfy consumer wants. The marketing of a product includes its brand, product image, warranty, service attributes, packaging, and labeling, in addition to the physical or functional characteristics of the good or service.

Goods and services can be classified as consumer (B2C) or business (B2B) products. Consumer products are those purchased by ultimate consumers for their own use. They can be convenience products, shopping products, specialty products, or unsought products, depending on consumer habits in buying them. Business products are those purchased for use either directly or indirectly in the production of other goods and services for resale. They can be classified as installations, accessory equipment, component parts and materials, raw materials, and supplies. This classification is based on how the items are used and product characteristics. Services can be classified as either consumer or business services.

A product mix is the assortment of goods and services a company offers to individual consumers and B2B users. A product line is a series of related products.

Assessment Check Answers

1.1 **How do consumer products differ from business products?** Consumer products, such as personal-care items, are sold to end users. Business products, such as copying machines, are sold to companies or organizations.

1.2 **Differentiate among convenience, shopping, specialty and unsought products.** Convenience products are items the consumer seeks to purchase frequently, immediately, and with little effort. Shopping products are typically purchased after the buyer has compared competing products in competing stores. Specialty products are those a purchaser is willing to make a special effort to obtain. Unsought products are goods and services that consumers either do not know about or know about but don't think of buying until a need arises.

LEARNING OBJECTIVE 2 Briefly describe the four stages of the product life cycle.

Every successful new product passes through four stages in its product life cycle: introduction, growth, maturity, and decline. In the introduction stage, the company attempts to elicit demand for the new product. In the product's growth stage, sales climb, and the company earns its initial profits. In the maturity stage, sales reach a saturation level. In the decline stage, both sales and profits decline. Marketers sometimes employ strategies to extend the product life cycle, including increasing the frequency of use, adding new users, finding new uses for the product, and changing package size, labeling, or product quality.

The new-product development process for most products has six stages: idea generation, screening, concept development and business analysis, product development, test marketing, and commercialization. At each stage, marketers must decide whether to continue to the next stage, modify the new product, or discontinue the development process. Some new products skip the test marketing stage due to the desire to quickly introduce a new product with excellent potential, a desire not to reveal new-product strategies to competitors, and the high costs involved in limited production runs.

Assessment Check Answers

2.1 **What are the stages of the product life cycle?** In the introduction stage, the company attempts to promote demand for the new product. In the product's growth stage, sales climb, and the company earns its initial profits. In the maturity stage, sales reach a saturation level. In the decline stage, both sales and profits decline.

2.2 **What are the marketing implications of each stage?** Marketers sometimes employ strategies to extend the product life cycle, including increasing frequency of use, adding new users, finding new uses for the product, and changing package size, labeling, or product design.

LEARNING OBJECTIVE 3 Discuss product identification.

Products are identified by brands, brand names, and trademarks, which are important elements of product images. Effective brand names are easy to pronounce, recognize, and remember, and they project the right images to buyers. Brand names cannot contain generic words. Under certain circumstances, companies lose exclusive rights to their brand names if common use makes them generic terms for product categories. Some brand names belong to retailers or distributors rather than to manufacturers. Brand loyalty is measured in three degrees: brand recognition, brand preference, and brand insistence. Some marketers use family brands to identify several related items in a product line. Others employ individual branding strategies by giving each product within a line a different brand name.

Assessment Check Answers

3.1 **Differentiate among a brand, a brand name, and a trademark.** A brand is a name, term, sign, symbol, design, or some combination thereof used to identify the products of one company and differentiate them from competitive offerings. A brand name is that part of the brand consisting of words or letters used to identify and distinguish the company's offerings from those of competitors. A trademark is a brand that has been given legal protection.

3.2 **Define *brand equity*.** Brand equity is the added value that a respected and successful name gives to a product.

LEARNING OBJECTIVE 4 Outline the major components of an effective distribution strategy.

A company must consider whether to move products through direct or indirect distribution. Once the decision is made, the company needs to identify the types of marketing intermediaries, if any, through which it will distribute its goods and services. The Internet has made direct distribution an attractive option for many retail companies. Another component is distribution intensity. The business must decide on the amount of market coverage—intensive, selective, or exclusive—needed to achieve its marketing strategies. Finally, attention must be paid to managing the distribution channel. It is vital to minimize conflict between channel members.

Assessment Check Answers

4.1 **Define *distribution channels*.** Distribution channels are the paths that products, and legal ownership of them, follow from producer to consumer or business user.

4.2 **What is a marketing intermediary?** A marketing intermediary (also called a middleman) is a business that moves goods between producers and consumers or business users.

LEARNING OBJECTIVE 5 Explain the concept of wholesaling.

Wholesaling is the process of selling goods primarily to retailers, other wholesalers, or business users and is a crucial part of the distribution channel for many products. Wholesaling intermediaries can be classified on the basis of ownership; some are owned by manufacturers, some are owned by retailers, and others are independently owned. Companies operate two main types of manufacturer-owned wholesaling intermediaries: sales branches and sales offices. An independent wholesaling intermediary is a business that represents a number of different manufacturers and makes sales calls to retailers, manufacturers, and other business accounts. Independent wholesalers are classified as either merchant wholesalers or agents and brokers, depending on whether they take title to the products they handle. Retailers sometimes band together to form their own wholesaling organizations. Such organizations can take the form of either a buying group or a cooperative.

Assessment Check Answers

5.1 **Define *wholesaling*.** Wholesaling is the process of selling goods primarily to retailers, other wholesalers, or business users.

5.2 **Differentiate between a merchant wholesaler and an agent or broker in terms of title to the goods.** Merchant wholesalers are independently owned wholesaling intermediaries that take title to the goods they handle. Agents and brokers may or may not take possession of the goods they handle, but they never take title, working mainly to bring buyers and sellers together.

LEARNING OBJECTIVE 6 Describe how to develop a competitive retail strategy.

Retailers, in contrast to wholesalers, are distribution channel members that sell goods and services, usually in small quantities, to individuals for their personal use rather than for resale. Nonstore retailing includes four forms: direct-response retailing, Internet retailing, automatic merchandising, and direct selling. Store retailers range in size from tiny newsstands to department stores and warehouse-like retailers such as Sam's Club.

The first step in developing a competitive retailing strategy is to select a target market. Next, the retailer must develop a product strategy to determine the best mix of merchandise to carry to satisfy that market. A retailer's customer service strategy focuses on attracting and retaining target customers to maximize sales and profits. Retailers base their pricing decisions on the costs of purchasing products from other channel members and offering services to customers. A good location often marks the difference between success and failure in retailing. A retailer develops promotions to stimulate demand and to provide information such as the store's location, merchandise offerings, prices, and hours. A successful retailer closely aligns its merchandising, pricing, and promotion strategies with store atmospherics, and the physical characteristics of a store and its amenities to influence consumers' perceptions of the shopping experience.

Assessment Check Answers

6.1 **Define *retailer*.** Retailers are distribution channel members that sell goods and services to individuals for their own use rather than for resale.

6.2 **What are the elements of a retailer's marketing strategy?** After identifying their target markets, retailers must choose merchandising, customer service, pricing, and location strategies that will attract customers in those market segments.

LEARNING OBJECTIVE 7 Identify distribution channel decisions and logistics.

Marketers can choose either a direct distribution channel, which moves goods directly from the producer to the consumer, or indirect distribution channels, which involve marketing intermediaries in the paths through which products—and legal ownership of them—flow from producer to the final customer. Ideally, the choice of a distribution channel should support a company's overall marketing strategy. Before selecting distribution channels, companies must consider their target markets, the types of goods being distributed, their own internal systems and concerns, and competitive factors.

Assessment Check Answers

7.1 **What is distribution intensity?** Distribution intensity is the number of intermediaries or outlets through which a manufacturer distributes its goods.

7.2 **Define *supply chain*.** A supply chain is the complete sequence of suppliers that contribute to creating a good or service and delivering it to business users and final consumers.

7.3 **What do customer service standards measure?** Customer service standards measure the quality of service a company provides to its customers.

Business Terms You Need to Know

product 310
product line 313
product mix 313
product life cycle 313
test marketing 316
brand 318
brand name 318
trademark 318
brand equity 320
category advisor 321
distribution strategy 322
distribution channels 322
physical distribution 322
wholesaler 325
retailer 326
supply chain 333
logistics 333
vendor-managed inventory 334

Review Questions

1. Classify each of the following business-to-consumer (B2C) and business-to-business (B2B) goods and services. Then choose one and describe how it could be classified as both.
   a. *Runner's World* or *Esquire* magazine
   b. six-pack of apple juice
   c. limousine service
   d. tech support for a corporate cloud computing system
   e. golf course
   f. Thai restaurant
2. What is the relationship between a product line and a product mix? Give an example of each.
3. Identify and briefly describe the six stages of new-product development.
4. What is the difference between a manufacturer's brand and a private brand? What is the difference between a family brand and an individual brand?
5. What are the three stages of brand loyalty? Why is the progression to the last stage so important to marketers?
6. What are the advantages of direct distribution? When is a producer most likely to use direct distribution?
7. What is the wheel of retailing? How has the Internet affected the wheel of retailing?
8. Identify and briefly describe the four different types of nonstore retailers. Give an example of at least one type of good or service that would be suited to each type of nonstore retailer.
9. What are the three intensity levels of distribution? Give an example of two products for each level.
10. Define *logistics*. How does it relate to physical distribution?

Projects and Teamwork Applications

1. On your own or with a classmate, choose one of the following goods or services. Decide whether you want to market it as a consumer product or a business product. Now create a brand name to convey the right image to the buyer, and one that links the product with its positioning strategy.
   a. lawnmower repair service
   b. natural foods store
   c. soft drink
   d. foreign-language class
   e. accounting firm
2. Choose one of the following products that is either in the maturity or decline stage of its life cycle (or select one of your own), and develop a marketing strategy for extending its life cycle.
   a. popcorn
   b. fast-food restaurant chain
   c. newspaper
   d. soda beverages
   e. paper stationery or note cards
3. Does online success as an e-commerce company automatically translate into successful bricks-and-mortar commerce? Discuss and research the strategy behind Amazon's recent decision to open retail bookstores. To date, what do results look like?
4. Choose one of the following products and select a distribution intensity for the product. Describe specifically where and how your product would be sold. Then describe the reasons for your strategy.
   a. line of clothing manufactured from recycled or reclaimed materials
   b. custom-designed jewelry
   c. house-painting service
   d. plumbing supplies
   e. radio talk show

Web Assignments

1. Go to the website and social media accounts of your favorite retailer. How has a competitive retailing strategy been developed, and how has a target market been selected? How does this retailer differentiate itself from others who sell similar products? What is the level of competition for the chosen market segment? Do you happen to be part of this retailer's target market? Explain.

2. **Fair Packaging and Labeling Act.** You may not think about what is in your favorite candy bar or bag of chips, but the Fair Packaging and Labeling Act enacted more than 35 years ago regulates how "consumer commodities" are labeled, including ingredients and name and place of the product's manufacturer, packer, or distributor. Compare a product's label to the requirements listed on the government website and discuss some of the regulations used to prevent consumer deception. What are some newer labeling requirements under review by the Federal Trade Commission?
www.ftc.gov/enforcement/rules/rulemaking-regulatory-reform-proceedings/fair-packaging-labeling-act

3. **Interbrand and the World's Best Global Brands.** Go to the Interbrand website and research the "Best Global Brands" for the most recent year. Go to the "Best 100 Brands" and sort by sector and ranking to evaluate the various concentrations within. Which sectors are dominant among the top global brands? Do the dominant sectors surprise you? Why or why not?
www.interbrand.com/en/

Note: Internet web addresses change frequently. If you don't find the exact sites listed, you may need to access the organization's home page and search from there or use a search engine such as Google or Bing.

Cases

Case 12.1 "Chucks" Remodeled after Nearly a Century

A few years ago, Boston-based Converse, one of the most iconic brands in existence today, underwent the first-ever remodel of its Chuck Taylor shoe, simply known as Chucks, in nearly a century. The Converse Chuck All Star II is the company's effort to bring the sneaker into the next century with a more high-tech version. With a focus on comfort, the changes include a new outer made from Tencel canvas, a more sustainable natural fiber, and higher-tech shock absorption for the foot bed. There is foam padding at the ankle, tongues are padded, and micro-suede liners can be found along the sides of the interior. The shoe has Lunarlon sock-liner technology for cushioning and arch support, which is used in some Nike shoes.

On the brink of bankruptcy, Converse was purchased by Nike in 2003 and remains the only brand in Nike's lineup without the legendary swoosh. However, what makes the shoe particularly unique is its simple retro look and feel. The company's chief marketing officer says the brand's universal appeal and retro look explains why the company reportedly sells more than 100 million pairs of its shoes annually, making it the best-selling basketball shoe of all time. Converse has also maintained a countercultural appeal by dropping its all-American image of an on-court shoe in favor of attracting a newer, Millennial audience.

There is good news for those unable to adapt to the shoe's changes. Converse will continue to sell the old version right alongside its updated counterpart, both of which will maintain a retro coolness.

Questions for Critical Thinking

1. Where are Converse shoes in their product life cycle? Explain.
2. The premium models will more closely resemble and take a page from the playbook of its parent company, Nike. How will this impact customer perception of a shoe that has traditionally been a retro favorite across several generations?

Sources: Company website, "Converse Turns 100," http://www.chucksconnection.com, accessed April 19, 2018; company website, http://www.converse.com, accessed April 19, 2018; Dana Hunsinger Benbow, "Run! Converse Launched New Chuck Taylor All Stars Tuesday," *Indianapolis Star*, http://www.indystar.com, accessed April 19, 2018; Susanna Kim, "Converse Chuck Taylors Getting First Update in Nearly 100 Years," *ABC News*, http://abcnews.go.com, accessed April 19, 2018; company blog, "Tencel: Sustainable, But Not Necessarily Healthy," http://organicclothing.blogs.com, accessed April 19, 2018; Laura Lorenzetti, "How Converse Went from Bankruptcy to a $1.4 Billion Business," *Quartz*, http://qz.com, accessed April 19, 2018; Leslie Wayne, "For $305 Million, Nike Buys Converse," *The New York Times*, http://www.nytimes.com, accessed April 19, 2018.

Case 12.2 Warby Parker Adds Retail Stores

Three years after its launch, eyewear e-commerce pioneer, Warby Parker, opened its first Manhattan showroom. According to Dave Gilboa, the company's co-founder and co-CEO, the physical stores are driving the company's e-commerce sales growth. As a data-driven company, Warby Parker found that 30% to 50% of those who shop in its stores are less likely to purchase eyewear online, while 90% of those who enter the retail outlets have at least visited the website. (The company sends its sometimes-reluctant online customers "dummy" frames to try on.)

In the retail environment, store associates can pull up customer data, which includes a history of online purchases and frames "tried on." The shopping experience can start online and finish in a retail store—and conversely, it can start in a retail store and finish online. Many retail customers will make a second or third purchase online after spending time in the retail stores. For Warby Parker, it appears that the synergy between both channels is working well.

While e-commerce sales still make up the majority of Warby Parker's business, the company, with close to 63 retail stores to date, plans to "accelerate" store openings over the next several years. If the new offline trend of a web-native company like Warby Parker seems counterintuitive and puzzling, consider what might just be new rules about an online-first success prior to opening bricks-and-mortar retail stores.

Questions for Critical Thinking

1. For now, it appears that Warby Parker's retail locations are helping the company grow. Discuss and come up with additional ways Warby Parker can use its retail locations to grow its business. Are there downsides to this strategy?
2. Would you be curious to go to a retail location to see and touch the offerings of an e-commerce site where you've shopped? Would you be more likely to go online to shop after seeing items at a retail store? Why or why not?

Sources: Company website, "Retail," https://www.warbyparker.com, accessed April 19, 2018; Stacy Zeiger, "The Pros & Cons of a Retail Store vs. an Online Store," *Houston Chronicle*, http://smallbusiness.chron.com, accessed April 19, 2018; Hillary Milnes, "3 e-Commerce Companies Explain Their Move to Brick-and-Mortar," *Digiday*, http://digiday.com, accessed April 19, 2018; Dhani Mau, "Warby Parker's Retail Expansion Isn't Slowing Down Anytime Soon," *Fashionista*, http://fashionista.com, accessed April 19, 2018; Jacob Brogan, "Does Warby Parker Need Actual Stores?" *Slate*, http://www.slate.com, accessed April 19, 2018.

Case 12.3 Secret Acres: Getting the Word Out

No matter how powerful they are, comic book heroes can't get themselves into bookstores—and readers' hands—without a little help. Leon Avelino and Barry Matthews, co-founders of Secret Acres, know that one of the greatest challenges of publishing is getting books onto the shelves and into readers' shopping carts. The task is even more difficult for small publishers—in this case, small publishers of comic books and graphic novels—because they don't have the wide distribution network of major publishers. But Avelino and Matthews, whose authors consider them the superheroes of comicbook publishing, are undaunted. They know what they are trying to achieve and work doggedly to make it happen.

"Distribution is a difficult thing right now," admits Matthews. "The publishing industry is changing and comic books themselves have a different distribution methodology and wholesale methodology than traditional books do." Unlike conventional book shops, comic book shops do not operate on a return basis. Conventional bookstores receive a small discount when they purchase books from a publisher, but then have the option to return any unsold books to the publisher. Comic book shops take a deeper discount but make no returns. Matthews also notes that currently there is only one major distributor of comic books—Diamond Distributors—which has the leverage to dictate much of what happens in the business of comic book distribution.

In addition, Matthews observes that Secret Acres' graphic novels could easily be sold to the general book market, but many general book distributors prefer not to deal with smaller publishers because they simply don't produce enough books to be profitable.

All of that said, Matthews explains that they are learning alternative ways to distribute their books. "Amazon is great," he says. "They make it very easy for smaller publishers. They treat your books as if they are Amazon books, giving them the sheen of being part of a larger retail channel." Amazon does take a significant cut of sales, but Matthews says it's worth it to broaden the distribution of Secret Acres products. Of course, Secret Acres also sells its entire line directly through its website, along with some books from other independent authors and publishers. This sales method is the most profitable for Secret Acres. More importantly, it allows Matthews and Avelino to keep closer tabs on their readers.

Matthews explains that because orders are filled on an individual basis, he can slip promotional materials, notices of upcoming events or new books, and tie-ins right into the package of a customer whose preferences he knows. This one-on-one interaction helps in the management of customer relationships.

Matthews and Avelino also enjoy one other form of distribution—attending comic book conventions around the country, such as the Stumptown Comics Fest in Portland, Oregon. There, they have the opportunity to interact with readers, other publishers, comic book authors and artists, and even some smaller distributors who have begun to attend these events. They note that readers in particular love to meet the authors and artists. "It feeds the interest in what we're doing," says Matthews. While at an event, Matthews and Avelino try to carve out some time to meet with other small publishers. "A lot of small publishers are in the same position" with regard to distribution, Matthews explains. "So we have been talking with them to see if we can band together to share resources."

Matthew and Avelino are fully aware of the impact of digital technologies on the comic book industry. So far, the Internet age has not wreaked the same type of havoc on comics as it has on traditional print media.

Despite its small size, Secret Acres' authors consider the company a mighty one. Theo Ellsworth, author of such titles as *Capacity* and *Sleeper Car*, praises Secret Acres for its personal attention and efforts to market and distribute his books. "It feels good to have the distribution part in someone else's hands," says Ellsworth. He explains that having someone else take care of that aspect of publishing frees him up to concentrate on his art, producing more posters and books—which is, after all, the author's job.

Questions for Critical Thinking

1. Visit Secret Acres' website at www.secretacres.com to learn more about the company's product line. Write a marketing blurb describing the line to a potential distributor.
2. What steps can Secret Acres take to develop brand loyalty and ultimately brand equity for its products?
3. How might Secret Acres expand its Internet retailing presence?
4. Secret Acres is a tiny firm with limited distribution. How can the company use customer service to create a competitive advantage, increase distribution, and help it grow?

Sources: Company website, http://secretacres.com, accessed April 27, 2018; "Great Graphic Novels for Teens," *Young Adult Library Services Association*, accessed April 27, 2018, www.ala.org/yalsa; "What Tablet Device Should You Buy for Your Digital Comic Books?" *Comic Book Herald*, accessed April 27, 2018; Harry McCracken, "E-Readers May Be Dead, But They're Not Going Away Yet," *Tech Hive*, accessed April 27, 2018, www.techhive.com; Calvin Reid and Heidi MacDonald, "From the Fringes to the Mainstream: Ten Years of Growth In Graphic Novel Publishing," *Publishers Weekly*, http://www.publishersweekly.com/, accessed April 27, 2018.

CHAPTER 13

Promotion and Pricing Strategies

LEARNING OBJECTIVES

1. Discuss integrated marketing communications (IMC).
2. Summarize the different types of advertising.
3. Outline sales promotion.
4. Describe pushing and pulling strategies.
5. Discuss the pricing objectives in the marketing mix.
6. Outline pricing strategies.
7. Discuss consumer perceptions of prices.

Changemaker

Rick Wilking/Reuters/Newscom

Pharrell Williams, Pop/R&B Singer, Musician, Producer, Philanthropist, Entrepreneur

Industries: Music/Recording/Apparel/Nonprofit

Websites: http://www.pharrellwilliams.com; http://fohta.org; http://www.24hoursofhappy.com

After resounding success as a Grammy award–winning singer-songwriter, Pharrell Williams (see photo), known simply as Pharrell, began to dabble in a number of various business and philanthropic ventures. Pharrell has been called a digital marketing genius, exemplified by a simple song, "Happy," which he singlehandedly wrote, produced, and performed. The song, part of the *Despicable Me 2* soundtrack album and an Internet phenomenon, is one of the most downloaded tunes of all time. Pharrell admits that the success of "Happy" is not something he engineered, and he acknowledges the crucial role of marketing using social media to increase customer interaction and reach top-notch fans and brand advocates.

Pharrell is a brand ambassador for Adidas and Chanel—and has collaborated with Uniqlo on a clothing line that bears the name of his company, i am OTHER. His most recent collaboration with creative director Karl Lagerfeld for Chanel and Adidas Originals includes a very exclusive pair of sneakers, NMD Hu, of which Justin Timberlake was the first to purchase a pair. It is also the first time that the Chanel name appeared on a product made by another brand—in this case, Adidas. Pharrell's company includes a dedicated YouTube channel, his apparel and textile lines Billionaire Boys Club, and shoe company Ice Cream.

A native of Virginia Beach, Virginia, Pharrell spent $35 million to build an after-school program in his hometown. His nonprofit foundation, From One Hand To AnOTHER (FOHTA), develops educational S.T.E.A.M.M. (Science, Technology, Engineering, Arts, Mathematics, and Motivation) for underserved 7- to 20-year-olds. Called Swan and Bar Bevy, Pharrell's latest business venture is a cocktail lounge and restaurant in Miami. Pharrell has joined the ranks of Madonna, Gwen Stefani, Jennifer Lopez, Jay Z, and Russell Simmons—celebrities who combine music, TV and film, social good and philanthropy, art and design, and fashion. Pharrell says what makes him "happy" is that "we are lucky to live in an era of connectivity and interaction."[1]

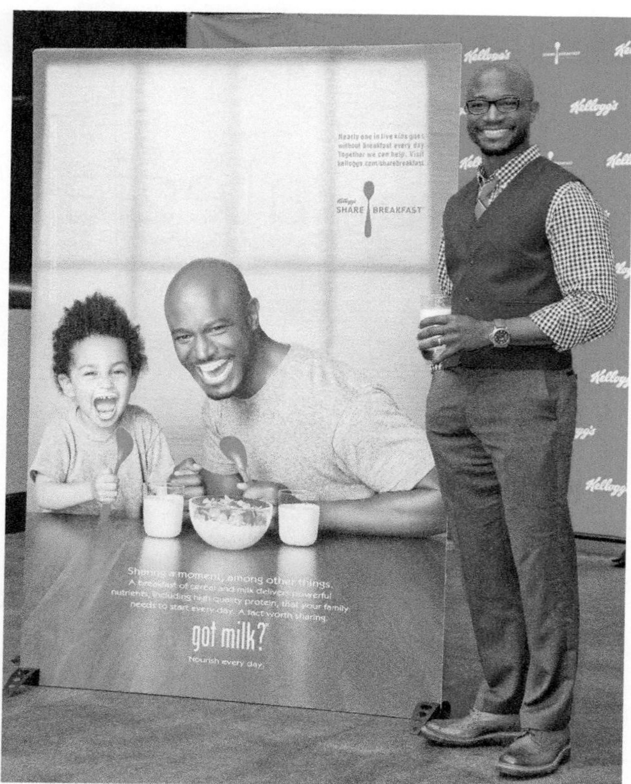

Imeh Akpanudosen/Getty Images

Created by advertising agency Goodby Silverstein & Partners to encourage the consumption of cow's milk, "Got Milk" has become one of the most prolific primary demand marketing campaigns of all time.

Overview

This chapter focuses on the various types of promotional activities and the way prices are established for goods and services. Promotion is the function of informing, persuading, and influencing a purchase decision. This activity is as important to not-for-profit organizations as it is to profit-seeking companies. Even Pharrell Williams embraces numerous forms of innovative marketing to promote his many brands.

The goal of some promotional strategies is to develop *primary demand*, or consumer desire for a general product category. The objective of such a campaign is to stimulate sales for an entire industry so that individual companies benefit from this market growth. For more than two decades, "Got Milk?" (see photo) was one of the greatest marketing taglines ever and one of the most respected primary demand marketing campaigns of all time. Other examples include the California Avocado Commission, whose goal is to increase demand for California-grown avocados through social media advertising, industry activities, promotion, and public relations. Similarly, the Wisconsin Milk Marketing Board promotes more than 600 varieties, types, and styles of Wisconsin cheese.[2]

Most promotional strategies, in contrast, seek to stimulate *selective demand*—desire for a specific brand. Cereal giant Cheerios created the "Good Goes Round" campaign, resulting in the donation of over one million meals to food bank–focused nonprofit, Feeding America. As part of its social campaign, for every photo and video of someone drawing an "o" and the hashtag #goodgoesround the company donated 10 meals.[3]

Marketers choose from among many promotional options to communicate with potential customers. Each marketing message a buyer receives—through social media, a video advertisement, a television or radio commercial, newspaper or magazine ad, website, direct-mail flyer, or sales call—reflects the product, place, person, cause, or organization promoted in the content. Through integrated marketing communications (IMC), marketers coordinate all promotional activities—media advertising, direct mail, personal selling, sales promotion, and public relations—to produce a unified, customer-focused promotional strategy. This coordination is designed to utilize various promotional methods that reinforce one another.

This chapter begins by explaining the role of IMC and then discusses the objectives of promotion and the importance of promotional planning. Next, it examines the components of the promotional mix: advertising, sales promotion, personal selling, and public relations. Finally, the chapter addresses pricing strategies for goods and services.

1 Integrated Marketing Communications

An **integrated marketing communications (IMC)** strategy focuses on customer needs to create a unified and seamless promotional message in a company's ads, in-store displays, product samples, and presentations by company sales representatives. To gain a competitive advantage, marketers that implement IMC need a broad view of **promotion**. Media options continue to multiply, and marketers cannot simply rely on traditional broadcast, print media, and direct mail. Plans usually include multiple forms of customer contact. Packaging, store displays, sales promotions, sales presentations, and online and interactive media also communicate information about a brand or organization. With IMC, marketers create a unified personality and message for the good, brand, or service they promote by incorporating various types of communications. Coordinated activities also enhance the effectiveness of reaching and serving target markets.

integrated marketing communications (IMC) coordination of all promotional activities—media advertising, direct mail, personal selling, sales promotion, and public relations—to produce a unified, customer-focused promotional strategy.

promotion function of informing, persuading, and influencing a purchase decision.

Clean & Green Business

Thirsty for Sustainability: Water in a Box

Consumer concern over the environment continues to influence spending habits. According to recent research, 63% of U.S. consumers believe ethical issues are becoming increasingly more important, and 56% have stopped purchasing products from companies deemed unethical. As consumers continue to question everything from ingredients to packaging to pricing fairness, companies have long realized that are well aware that purchasing decisions are based on sustainability.

Each year, 50 billion plastic bottles of water are consumed, and about 80% of those plastic bottles end up in landfills. To participate in the conversation in a genuine way, a number of consumer product companies are stepping up their efforts to create a more sustainable and ecological product, which includes packaging. Typically consumed in a plastic bottle, and oftentimes referred to as "bottled water," Grand Rapids, Michigan–based Boxed Water has changed that. Its milk carton–like paper packaging represents sustainability, and its simplistically designed bold, black capital letters against a white backdrop read, "Boxed Water Is Better."

The box is made of 76% paper, which is a renewable resource. More efficient than shipping empty glass bottles to be filled, Boxed Water cartons are shipped flat to the filler. Additionally, 1% of the company's sales support reforestation and water relief efforts. Over the next five years, in collaboration with the National Forest Foundation, the company has committed to planting one million trees.

The company recently kicked off its Better for Our Planet campaign, at the South By Southwest (SXSW) conference and festival. Consumers can give back to the planet simply by posting a picture of Boxed Water on social media using #betterplanet. For each picture posted, the company will plant two trees.

Questions for Critical Thinking

1. Why do you think consumers would purchase water in a box as compared to a plastic or glass bottle? If you knew nothing about Boxed Water, would the packaging alone encourage you to make a purchase? Why or why not?
2. Would you consider the company's sustainability efforts part of its promotional appeal? Explain.

Sources: Company website, "Our Water," http://www.boxedwaterisbetter.com, accessed May 9, 2018; Kyle Jenkins, "The Environmental Benefits of Boxed Water," *Millennial Magazine*, http://millennialmagazine.com, accessed May 9, 2018; "Boxed Water Kicks off 'Better for Our Planet' Campaign at SXSW," *BevNet*, http://www.bevnet.com, accessed May 9, 2018.

Marketing managers set the goals and objectives for the company's promotional strategy with overall organizational objectives and marketing goals in mind. Using these objectives, marketers combine the various elements of the strategy—personal selling, advertising, sales promotion, publicity, and public relations—into an integrated communications plan. This document becomes a central part of the company's total marketing strategy to reach its selected target market. Feedback, including marketing research and sales reports, completes the system by identifying any deviations from the plan and suggesting improvements.

Global Burger giant McDonald's spends $2 billion in advertising annually, and plans include a focus on mobile pay and ordering, social media, digital marketing, and technology. Its IMC includes targeted TV ads (promoting breakfast), outdoor advertising, traditional print and media advertising, sales promotions, events, and experiences.[4] The "Clean & Green Business" feature profiles the efforts of a company attempting to offset the billions of plastic water bottles that end up in landfills.

The Promotional Mix

Just as every organization creates a marketing mix combining product, distribution, promotion, and pricing strategies, each also requires a similar mix to blend the many facets of promotion into a cohesive plan. The **promotional mix** consists of two components—personal and nonpersonal selling—that marketers combine to meet the needs of their company's target customers and effectively and efficiently communicate its message to them. **Personal selling** is the most basic form of promotion: a direct person-to-person promotional presentation to a potential buyer. The buyer–seller communication can occur during a face-to-face meeting or via telephone, videoconference, or Skype. Salespeople represent their company with the goal of promoting and selling its products and services.

Nonpersonal selling is not directed to a specific individual and is conducted without being face-to-face with a buyer. It consists of advertising, sales promotion, direct marketing, and public relations. Advertising is the best-known form of nonpersonal selling, but sales promotion accounts for a significant portion of these marketing expenditures. Spending for

promotional mix combination of personal and nonpersonal selling components designed to meet the needs of a company's target customers and effectively and efficiently communicate its message to them.

personal selling the most basic form of promotion: a direct person-to-person promotional presentation to a potential buyer.

nonpersonal selling consists of advertising, sales promotion, direct marketing, and public relations.

sponsorships, which involves marketing messages delivered in association with another activity such as a golf tournament or a music festival. BMW was a recent sponsor at Coachella Valley Music & Art Festival, and its hashtag #RoadToCoachella social media campaign is part of an effort to promote its all-electric models to the festival's millennial audience, who crave unique experiences. BMW iFleets were wrapped in colorful custom designs, and details of road trips in the cars to the festival were shared with followers.[5]

Each component in the promotional mix offers its own advantages and disadvantages, as **Table 13.1** demonstrates. By selecting the most effective combination of promotional mix elements, a company may reach its promotional objectives. Spending within the promotional mix varies by industry. Manufacturers of many business-to-business (B2B) products typically spend more on personal selling than on advertising because those products—such as a

TABLE 13.1 Comparing the Components of the Promotional Mix

Component	Advantages	Disadvantages
Personal Selling	- For complex goods and services of high value, more information can be conveyed - Message can be tailored for each customer - Produces immediate buyer response - Effectiveness is easily measured	- High cost per contact - Limited reach (can only cover one geographic region or place at a time) - Costly and difficulty attracting and retaining effective salespeople
Nonpersonal Selling		
Advertising	- Reaches the masses at a low cost per contact - Allows control of the message - Messaging can be tailored to match each audience	- Difficult to measure effectiveness - Limited value for closing sales - Costs can be high - Can be confusing or untruthful - Can add to a product's cost
Sales Promotion	- Attracts attention and creates awareness - Effectiveness is easily measured - Produces short-term sales increases - Attracts customers away from competitors - Creates upselling and cross-selling opportunities	- May only create temporary loyalty based upon price - Difficult to differentiate from similar programs of competitors - Nonpersonal appeal - Can work against long-term company goals
Public Relations	- Enhances product or company credibility through third-party media - Creates a positive attitude about the product or company - More detailed information to targeted market - Low cost compared to other promotions	- Difficult to measure effectiveness - Media may deliver an inaccurate message - Overreliance on the media to deliver a message - Often devoted to nonmarketing activities
Direct Marketing	- Response rates can be quantified and tracked - Can use to first test with a smaller campaign - Can appeal to a specific and appropriate market segment - Enhances brand awareness	- Increased demand from consumers to end unsolicited contacts from companies - Privacy issues - Negative perception of direct marketers - Consumers throw away direct mail pieces or delete marketing emails
Sponsorships	- Viewed positively by consumers - Enhances brand awareness - Target specific market segments	- Difficult to control message

cybersecurity protection system—may require a significant investment. Consumer-goods marketers may focus more on advertising and sponsorships. Later sections of this chapter discuss how the parts of the mix contribute to effective promotion.

Objectives of Promotional Strategy

Promotional strategy objectives vary among organizations. Some use promotion to expand their markets, and others use it to maintain their current positions. As **Figure 13.1** illustrates, common objectives include providing information, differentiating a product, increasing sales, stabilizing sales, and providing information about a product's value. Additional objectives include brand reinforcement, increasing customer visits, creating interest, and building brand awareness.

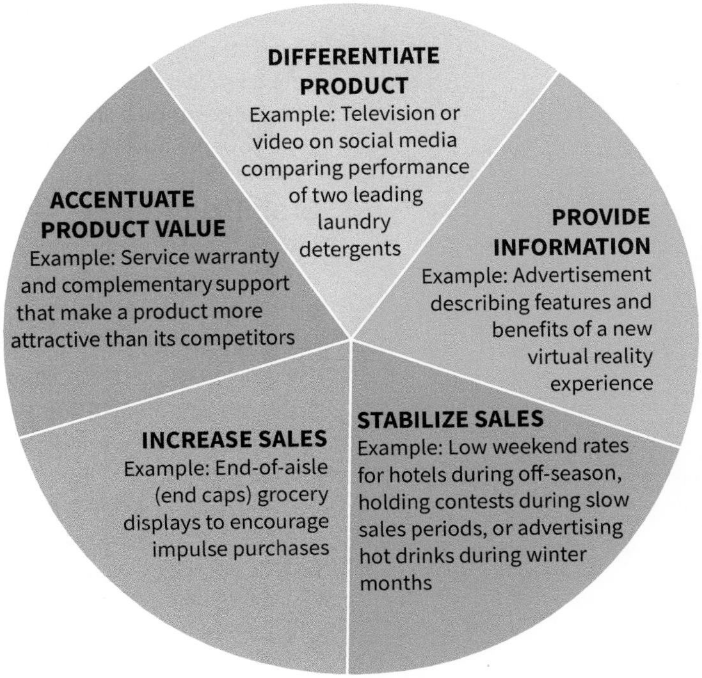

Marketers often pursue multiple promotional objectives at the same time because they may need to convey different messages to different audiences. John Deere, which began as a manufacturer of farm tractors, produces equipment for several different audiences in industries as varied as agriculture, residential, golf and sport, commercial construction, forestry, government and military, and landscaping. Promotional messages vary by audience served. Through an independently owned and operated global dealer network, John Deere sells its tractors, harvesters, sprayers, cotton pickers, planters, and seeders to agricultural farmers. Its construction and forestry products, excavators and pavers, serve construction firms and logging operators. Lawn mowers and snow blowers are sold to both consumers and businesses. To differentiate itself from its largest competitor, Caterpillar, the company encourages product trials and free demonstrations so that customers can experience firsthand the ongoing innovation and value for which John Deere is known. John Deere partakes in several trade and industrial shows and, along with ads through print media and special interest and trade magazines, is well known for its annual John Deere Classic, a professional golf tournament of the Professional Golfers Association tour.[6]

FIGURE 13.1 **Five Major Promotional Strategy Objectives**

Providing Information A major portion of U.S. advertising is information oriented. Credit-card ads provide information about benefits, cash back, awards, and rates. Ads for hair-care products include information about benefits such as shine and volume. Ads for breakfast cereals often contain nutritional information. Television ads for prescription drugs, an industry expected to grow 4 to 7 percent over the next few years, are sometimes criticized for relying on emotional appeals rather than providing information about the causes, risk factors, and especially the prevention of disease.[7] But print advertisements for drugs often contain an entire page of warnings, side effects, and usage guidelines.

Differentiating a Product Promotion can also be used to differentiate a company's offerings from the competition. Applying a concept called **positioning**, marketers attempt to establish the identity and value of their products in the minds of customers. The idea is to communicate to buyers meaningful distinctions about the attributes, price, quality, or use of a good or service.

positioning form of promotion in which marketers attempt to establish the identity and value of their products in the minds of customers by communicating to buyers meaningful distinctions about the attributes, price, quality, or use of a good or service.

Marketers of luxury goods position their products as upscale, expensive, high quality, and exclusive. But how do they position goods that are intended for the vast number of "ordinary" consumers? In one of the most talked about collaborations of "masstige," a hybrid of "mass market" and "prestige," fast fashion retailer H&M collaborated with high-end designer Moschino to create a clothing line, also referred to as a "high-low mash-up" to be sold in its stores.[8]

Increasing Sales Increasing sales volume is the most common objective of a promotional strategy. In an effort to increase sales, Mercedes Benz has expanded its lineup of compact cars from five to eight. With the revamped A-class hatchback, the addition of smaller, more affordable models like the GLA compact crossover and the CLA coupe has helped attract first-time younger buyers to the brand.[9]

Stabilizing Sales Sales stabilization is another goal of promotional strategy. Companies often use sales contests during slow periods, motivating salespeople by offering prizes such as vacations, smart phones, and cash bonuses to those who meet certain goals. Companies distribute sales promotion materials—such as calendars, pens, and t-shirts—to customers to stimulate sales during the off-season. Jiffy Lube puts that little sticker on your windshield to remind you when to schedule your car's next oil change—the regular visits help stabilize sales. A stable sales pattern brings several advantages. It evens out the production cycle, reduces some management and production costs, and simplifies financial, purchasing, and marketing planning.

During off-season months when hotels are less crowded—and, as a result, less expensive compared to peak season—retreats and special events are organized and promoted. Financial district hotels are usually crowded on weekdays with business traveler; but on the weekends, to attract loyalty members, tourists, and visitors, many will use online promo codes and double or triple bonus points to increase sales.

Accentuating the Product's Value Some promotional strategies enhance product values by explaining hidden benefits of ownership. To accentuate product value, BMW offers free maintenance for the entire duration of its four years or 50,000 miles factory warranty. Roadside assistance lasts four years with no mileage limits, and the corrosion warranty is 12 years with unlimited mileage.

Promotional Planning

product placement form of promotion in which marketers pay placement fees to have their products showcased in various media, ranging from newspapers and magazines to original online television and movies.

guerrilla marketing innovative, low-cost marketing efforts designed to get consumers' attention in unusual ways.

digital marketing marketing of products or services using digital channels to reach consumers through promotion of brands through various forms of digital media.

Marketers can promote their products in various ways. Because television viewing has changed, brands once dominant in TV advertising have changed the way they connect with consumers. Consider the practice of **product placement**. A growing number of marketers pay placement fees to have their products showcased in various media, ranging from newspapers and magazines to original online television shows and movies. All of the characters on Fox's TV drama "9-1-1" have Apple iPhones. An example of product placement, Apple supplies production staffs and actors with its products, which surface throughout various scenes. In another example, *Spiderman: Homecoming* featured 52 brands including Ford, Sony, Jansport, Dell, and Audi.[10]

Another type of promotional planning is often used by companies or start-ups that have small promotional budgets. **Guerrilla marketing** involves leaving the screen behind, and in public places, using innovative, low-cost marketing efforts designed to get consumers' attention in unusual ways. When Google gave away free cupcakes in Austin, Texas, to people who tried its new photo app, Zappos soon set up an adjacent kiosk and advertised #paywithacupcake. People exchanged the cupcake they received from Google for a free Zappos product, including backpacks and watches.[11]

Digital marketing is the marketing of products or services using digital channels to reach consumers through promotion of brands using various forms of digital media. It includes mobile phones, social media marketing, display advertising, and search engine marketing that do not require use of the Internet. Digital marketing requires analytics and digital tools to quantify and analyze customer behavior such as site visits from other social media platforms, app downloads on mobile devices, tweets on Twitter, and interactions. With Pizza Hut's digital marketing campaign, customers downloaded its app to create and order a pizza by dragging and dropping toppings.[12]

From this overview of the promotional mix, we now turn to discussions of each of its elements. The following sections detail the major components of advertising, sales promotion, personal selling, and public relations.

Assessment Check

1. What is the objective of an integrated marketing communications program?
2. Why do companies pursue multiple promotional objectives at the same time?
3. What are product placement and guerrilla marketing?

2 Advertising

Consumers see hundreds of marketing messages daily, many of them in the form of advertising.[13] **Advertising** is the most visible form of nonpersonal promotion—and the most effective for many companies. Advertising, a global activity, is paid nonpersonal communication usually targeted at large numbers of potential buyers. In a recent year, global advertising spending grew by 3.8%, reaching $563 billion. The surge is primarily a result of the growth of mobile technologies and the use of social media. Overtaking television for the first time, as digital technology changes the way media is accessed and consumed, global digital advertising expenditures grew 16% in a recent year, representing almost 37.6% of the total advertising market.[14] The largest U.S. advertisers in a recent year include Procter & Gamble, Berkshire Hathaway (Geico), General Motors, Comcast, and L'Oreal.[15]

advertising paid nonpersonal communication, usually targeted at large numbers of potential buyers.

The advertising industry is facing one of its biggest transformations to date due mainly to advancements in mobile web, artificial intelligence, virtual reality, and growing online video content. The result is an increase in digital advertising spending. Mobile advertising will allow more effective ad targeting and message distribution to the right audience at the right time as a result of access to information on user location, usage, app history, and browsing data.

However, as privacy scandals continue, policymakers are under pressure to create new regulations that will impact the profitability of online advertising where user data is required.[16]

product advertising consists of messages designed to sell a particular good or service.

institutional advertising involves messages that promote concepts, ideas, philosophies, or goodwill for industries, companies, organizations, or government entities.

cause advertising form of institutional advertising that promotes a specific viewpoint on a public issue as a way to influence public opinion and the legislative process.

Types of Advertising

The two basic types of ads are product and institutional advertisements. **Product advertising** consists of messages designed to sell a particular good or service. Advertisements for ketchup (see photo), Band-Aids, and Capital One credit cards are examples of product advertising. **Institutional advertising** involves messages that promote concepts, ideas, philosophies, or goodwill for industries, companies, organizations, or government entities. Each year, the Juvenile Diabetes Research Foundation promotes its Walk for the Cure fund-raising event, and your college may use different types of advertising to promote its activities.

A form of institutional advertising that is growing in importance, **cause advertising**, promotes a specific viewpoint on a public issue as a way to influence public opinion and the legislative process about issues such as literacy, hunger and poverty, and alternative energy sources. Both not-for-profit organizations and businesses use cause advertising, sometimes called *advocacy advertising*. Singer-songwriter Alicia Keys is a global ambassador for Keep a Child Alive, a program that brings treatment, care, and support to families and children affected by HIV in sub-Saharan Africa.[17]

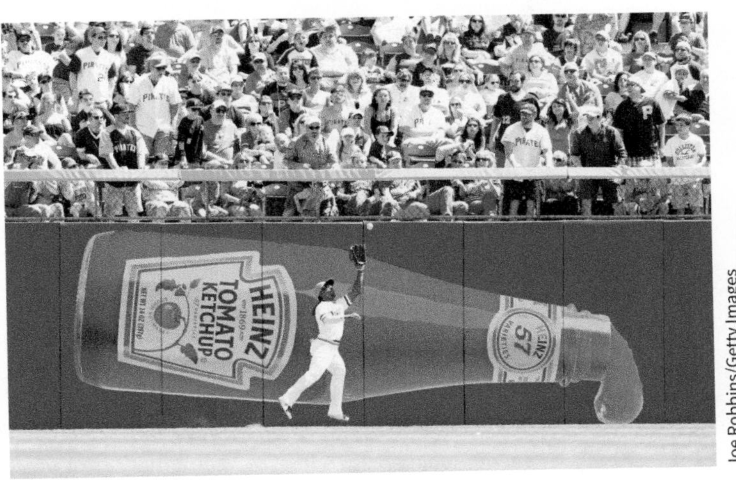

Joe Robbins/Getty Images

Product advertising is used to sell a particular good or service. In this case, the product is Heinz ketchup.

Most companies hire advertising agencies whose role is to conceive and develop advertisements. Full-range agencies offer a complete array of creative and media services across all advertising media, including print, radio, television, outdoor, and digital. Direct relationships with customers and in-house teams of data scientists, content creators, researchers, and digital-media buying experts are a recent trend by some marketers. Interestingly, some marketers, born with the Internet, have never run massive TV and magazine campaigns, which, in the past, were typically performed by traditional ad agencies. With more data than a media agency, this allows adjusting digital ad campaigns with lightning speed.[18]

Advertising and the Product Life Cycle

Both product and institutional advertising fall into one of three categories based on whether the ads are intended to inform, persuade, or remind. A company uses *informative advertising* to build initial demand for a product in the introductory phase of the product life cycle. Highly publicized new-product entries attract the interest of potential buyers who seek information about the benefits and advantages of the new products over existing ones, warranties provided, prices, and places that offer the new products. Ads for new smart phones boast of new features, colors, designs, and pricing options to attract new customers.

Persuasive advertising attempts to improve the competitive status of a product, institution, or concept, usually in the growth and maturity stages of the product life cycle. One of the most popular types of persuasive product advertising, *comparative advertising*, compares products directly with their competitors—either by name or by inference. Comparative advertising has traditionally been used in a number of industries where there are rivalries between companies. Fast-food companies have used comparative advertising when promoting their burgers and fries. Cell phone providers compete against one another by promoting more flexible pricing, plans, and no contracts. Consumer products, namely laundry detergents, have used comparative advertising against rival brands to promote stain removal and whiteness.

Reminder-oriented advertising often appears in the late maturity or decline stages of the product life cycle to maintain awareness of the importance and usefulness of a product, concept, or institution. Reminder advertising is used in the pharmaceutical industry whereby the drug's name is given but not the drug's use. The assumption is that the target audience is aware of what the drug is used for.

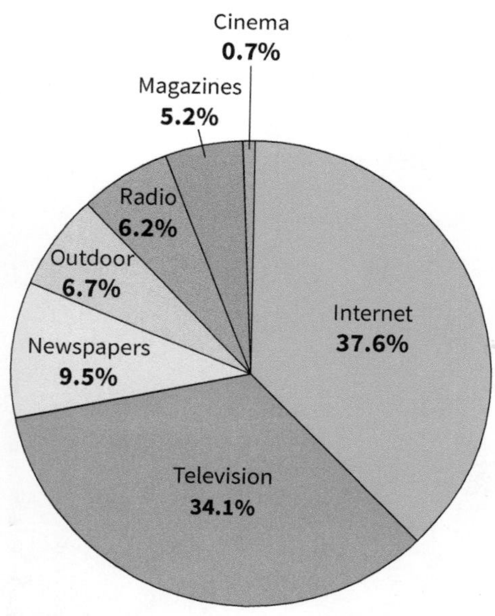

Source: Company website, "Advertising Expenditure Forecasts March 2018," http://www.zenithmediacorp.com, accessed May 5, 2018.

FIGURE 13.2 Share of Global Ad Spending by Media Type

Advertising Media

Marketers must choose how to allocate their advertising budgets among various media. All media offer advantages and disadvantages. Cost is an important consideration in media selection, but marketers must also choose the media best suited for communicating their message to an intended audience. As **Figure 13.2** indicates, the three largest media outlets for advertising are Internet (including both digital and desktop), television, and newspapers. Reflecting the continued disruption by digital technology of print and TV media, digital advertising, 37.6% of total advertising, took over TV as the largest advertising medium. The key growth driver will be mobile advertising—driven by the rapid spread of smart phone devices and improvements in user experiences. Social media platforms, search engines, programmatic ad platforms (software to purchase digital advertising), and other Internet properties will gain from this trend. Digital print advertising will soon reach 46% of global ad spending.[19]

Television Offering the capacity to build, reach, and establish brand awareness and associations, television is still one of America's leading national advertising media. The TV industry faces competition from technology giants investing billions of dollars in original content. Our viewing experiences in the future will be a combination of voice activation, customization, and virtual and augmented reality watched on the Internet or mobile devices. There are numerous types of TV systems, which are combinations of equipment, protocols, and transmission lines that are used to obtain media from content providers and distribute the media, programs, and advertising to content viewers. Each type of TV system can distribute TV shows to viewers, but what varies is the type of advertising they can accept and the way (and speed) at which it can be delivered. Some types include cable TV (a few hundred channels delivered via high-speed data), satellite TV (received by communications satellite to a dish), broadcast TV (networks like ABC, CBS, and NBC), mobile TV (broadcasts in resolution formats that are less than standard definition), IPTV (sends programs to users over a single data connection), and Internet TV (sends TV programs through the Internet). In a recent year, the average amount of ad time for an hour on broadcast was a little over 13 minutes, and on cable, it was 16 minutes. As more viewing takes place on ad-free platforms and spending on digital video increases, marketers are being forced to rethink the traditional, interruptive TV commercial experience. Average time spent watching TV has fallen—however, TV has evolved from what was once a limited number of options to infinite choice. Today, about three-quarters of American adults have broadband Internet service at home.[20]

Broadcast and cable TV viewership continues to decline while Netflix, Amazon Prime Video, ESPN+, and YouTube Red continue to experience strong subscriber growth. Cord-cutters, people who have opted out of standard cable TV subscriptions, and Cord Nevers, people who never had any standard TV subscriptions to begin with, are using streaming video services instead. Apple, on track to outspend Facebook and YouTube, will be investing as much as $1 billion in an upcoming year on original TV programming, which includes Octavia Spencer starring in a 10-episode series and a drama based on the early life and career of NBA star Kevin Durant. Premium cable streaming services have shown substantial growth, with companies like HBO Go, Starz, and Showtime.[21]

Although—or perhaps because—television reaches the greatest number of consumers at once, it is the most expensive advertising medium. The Super Bowl is widely known for its hefty advertising price tag—and its ability to reach more than 103 million people in a three-hour period. In a recent year, companies such as T-Mobile, Netflix, TD Ameritrade, Avocados from Mexico, and Budweiser paid a minimum of $5 million for a 30-second spot.[22]

Digital Advertising The increased number of digital advertisements delivered to smart phones and tablets is a direct result of the growth of social media usage. Digital advertising, which increased 14% in a recent year, remains the largest and fastest-growing advertising medium. Online video and social media are currently the drivers of advertising spending, expected to grow 17% a year for the next three years. High-quality content is contributing to the growth of online video, along with better displays and faster connections, which create an improved viewing experience. Habitual social media usage creates a seamless blend of advertisements into newsfeeds.

In a recent year, global mobile advertising revenues, representing over half of Internet ad expenditures, reached $107 billion. However, as users spend more time on connected devices, spending on ads delivered to desktops and laptops has slowed. Companies that dominate digital advertising include Google, Facebook, Microsoft, Instagram, and Twitter. Some of the most followed brands on social media include Victoria's Secret, Nike, National Geographic, Airbnb, Tesla, Adobe, and Chef David Chang of Momofuku.[23]

A subcategory of digital advertising is display, which includes banners, online video, and social media. All three types of display have benefitted from the growth of programmatic buying, which uses software to aggregate, book, analyze, and optimize advertising on sites such as Facebook and Google. With programmatic buying, audiences are targeted more effectively with personalized creative advertising across various platforms and devices. Lagging behind display is paid search and classified ads.[24]

Viral advertising creates a message that is novel or entertaining enough for consumers to forward it to others, often through social networking sites, spreading it like a virus. Michael Dubin of Dollar Shave Club wrote one of the best known promotional product videos ever produced. At a cost of $4,500, to date, the video has garnered over 25 million views, and the company has cracked into a demographic of young professional men who found humor in an absurd video about the high cost of store-bought razors. In another example, in addition to a celebrity-filled New York launch party, luxury jeweler and retailer Tiffany & Co. released a video featuring Elle Fanning and rapper A$AP Ferg to promote a new jewelry collection. And last, with more than 108 million followers, the youngest Kardashian's posts (Kylie Jenner), according to a social media analytics firms, are worth more than $1 million each in "ad equivalent value."[25] **Table 13.2** lists important digital marketing trends, along with some new and innovative ways brands will reach consumers.

TABLE 13.2 Digital Marketing Trends

Trend	Description
Mobilfication	On the rise and quickly becoming a top priority for marketers with personalized text messages, apps, and even mobile-friendly websites.
Media Properties	The best way to control the conversation with prospects and customers is to provide helpful, authentic, quality content.
Chatbots	A website or Facebook chatbots (with artificial intelligence) can be considered a tool on the other side of the computer that can be used as a marketing strategy for engagement, customer service issues, basic questions, or support.
Reviews	Many consumers regularly check online reviews before purchasing a new item. Organic traffic from search engine optimization continues to be one of the best sources of web traffic for many businesses. While there are many elements involved in ranking, the number of reviews is a key factor.
Video on Demand	To increase sales, nothing on social media is as eye-catching as a good video to tell a compelling story—and more mobile ads will be in the form of videos. Most videos (90% of Twitter and 60% of YouTube) are viewed on mobile devices. Facebook Live, YouTube, or a video on a website landing page are all options.
Branding Versus Direct Response	Telling your story versus telling people what to do is critical. Rather than focusing attention on the call to action, deliver value first by telling your brand's story and portraying your business in the best possible light.
Social Media Influencers	There are advantages to social influencer marketing. Developing long-term organic and authentic relationships with social media influencers that mesh with a brand can help establish or revitalize a brand. Social media influencer Bryanboy works with Gucci, Prada, and Calvin Klein.
Storytelling	Social media "stories," pioneered by Snapchat, have now become popular on Instagram, Facebook, and YouTube. Stories capture a brand's best moments from a day—and vanish within 24 hours.
Voice Search	Voice Search will profoundly change search engine optimization. Marketers must decide how to market and build applications to voice-activated and searchable devices like Amazon's Alexa—who will retrieve and serve information to the user.
Consuming in Virtual and Augmented Worlds	Social media platforms have already started to adopt virtual reality and augmented reality into their algorithms. IKEA has a virtual shopping application to preview furniture in your own home before purchasing. Facebook offers 360-video publishing and Snapchat users can project their virtual self into the real world as an animated, 3-D bitmoji.
Native Advertising	A native ad, paid for by an advertiser to promote a product or service, includes written or other material in an online publication that blends in by resembling the publication's editorial content. Examples include advertorial, instant content, search advertising, recommended content, or sponsored listings.
Personalization	With privacy and consumer confidence threatened, targeted advertising depends on gaining insights into customers' demographics and viewing behaviors—and then augmenting this customer information with social media data. To reach the right person at the right time at the right place with the right message, personalization requires data and information to be highly accurate and relevant.

Sources: Nick Brucker, "Four Emerging Digital Marketing Trends to Keep on Your Radar," *Forbes*, http://www.forbes.com, accessed May 6, 2018; Michael Tasner, "Six Digital Marketing Trends to Watch in 2018," *Forbes*, http://www.forbes.com, accessed May 6, 2018; company website, "Deloitte Insights," https://www2.deloitte.com, accessed May 6, 2018; "12 Marketing Trends to Take Advantage of This Year," *Forbes*, http://www.forbes.com, accessed May 6, 2018; Jay Kernis, "The Rise of Social Media Influencers," *CBS News*, https://www.cbsnews.com, accessed May 6, 2018.

Newspapers The way newspapers are read ranges from print to digital to mobile—and as advertising dollars continue to shift to digital platforms, print newspaper advertising revenues continue to fall. Over 70% of U.S. adults with an annual income over $100k read newspaper content, and over 75% of U.S. adults with a college degree access newspaper content each week. Newspaper readers are a highly sought-after demographic for advertisers. Newspaper advertising offer a variety of ways to target an audience through both its print and digital properties.[26]

Radio Radio advertising has long been a form of promotion for products and services within the broadcast range of a station. For advertisers, morning and afternoon drive-time listeners are a captive audience as they drive to and from work. Many stations, depending on their format, serve various demographic groups with targeted programming. For example, the classical music radio station may contract with luxury car advertisers who choose to target the station's listening demographic, with higher incomes that skew older.

In the last few years, radio programming delivered via satellite has become an option for more widespread advertising. As radio stations allow their signals to be broadcast over the Internet, the advertising options become greater. Radio has experienced the same trajectory as television, namely a mass medium that isn't highly targeted or easily tracked. In addition, Internet radio services like Pandora and Spotify continue to chisel away at traditional broadcast radio. Personalized Internet music streaming services like Pandora and Spotify have the unique ability to create personalized content and advertising for listeners. Voice-activated devices like Amazon's Alexa also give radio an opportunity to win back in-home radio listenership.

Through geo-targeting, interactive mobile apps, and advanced analytics, radio can optimize its large and diverse audience to compete with digital advertising. Integrating more sophisticated location technology with mobile apps, radio stations can provide return-on-investment data to advertisers in the same way offered by digital platforms.[27]

Magazines Magazines include consumer publications and business trade journals. *Time*, *Reader's Digest*, and *Sports Illustrated* are consumer magazines, whereas *Advertising Age* and *Oil & Gas Journal* fall into the trade category, whose target audience is people who work in a particular trade or industry.

Magazines are a natural choice for targeted advertising. Media buyers study the demographics of subscribers and select magazines that attract the desired readers. American Express advertises in *Fortune* and *Bloomberg Businessweek* to reach businesspeople, while PacSun clothing and Proactiv skin medications are advertised in *Teen Vogue*. Magazine print ads have been driven by a recent shift from print editions to online or mobile editions.

Because the printed sector lacks an accountable data mechanism, print magazines are difficult vehicles for advertising sales tracking. However, print magazines are effective branding and marketing tools to support a magazine's digital presence.

As mobile growth continues and consumers read content across multiple devices, publishers are focused on geotargeted mobile content and programmatic ads based on readers' locations optimized for all device types and screens.[28]

Direct Mail Direct mail, expected to see increased spending in the next few years, includes promotions such as printed catalogs, ads, and letters sent by marketers to a large volume of consumers. When combined with email and social media, direct mail can be complementary to digital marketing channels. With multichannel shopping on the rise, catalogs have become popular once again, and companies such as JC Penney, J. Crew, American Girl, and West Marine Boating collectively send hundreds of millions of catalogs annually. Retailers send direct mail to advertise new products or distribute coupons. Nonprofits may find direct mail appealing as a way to encourage volunteers or donations. While consumers may ignore an online ad or an e-mail, a printed direct mail piece may grab their attention. Although printing and postage are costly, a carefully targeted direct mail campaign can be very effective. Companies like Amazon use e-mail, a low-cost form of direct marketing, to target customers with new product offerings based upon previous purchases. Direct mail is used as a vehicle to drive consumers online to make purchases.[29]

Address lists are at the heart of direct-mail advertising. Using data-mining techniques to segment markets, direct-mail marketers create profiles with demographics and characteristics of consumers who are likely to buy their products or donate to their organizations. Catalog retailers sometimes experiment by sending direct-mail pieces randomly to people who subscribe to particular magazines. Next, they analyze the response rates (orders) from the mailings and develop profiles of purchasers. Finally, they rent lists of additional names that match the profiles they have developed.

The Direct Marketing Association (DMA; www.thedma.org) helps marketers combat negative perceptions by offering its members guidelines on ethical business practices. The DMA also provides consumer information on its website, as well as services that enable consumers to opt out of receiving unsolicited offers. In addition, Federal Trade Commission regulations have taken effect for direct mail in certain industries. With the passage of the Credit Accountability Responsibility and Disclosure (CARD) Act of 2009, credit-card issuers must follow stricter regulations in their direct mail practices. Unsolicited, preapproved applications sent to consumers must be accompanied by a prominent notice explaining how to be removed from the issuer's mailing list. Top credit card acquisition mailers include American Express, Capital One, Chase, Citibank, and Discover.[30]

Outdoor Advertising In one recent year, outdoor (also called out-of-home) advertising accounted for $7.7 billion in advertising revenues.[31] The majority of spending on outdoor advertising is for billboards, but spending for other types of outdoor advertising, such as signs in transit stations, stores, airports, and sports stadiums, is growing fast. To learn more about how the National Basketball Association is selling advertising space on its professional jerseys, see the "Business Model" feature. Advertisers are exploring new forms of outdoor media, many of which involve technology: computerized paintings; digital billboards; "trivision," which displays three revolving images on a single billboard; and moving billboards mounted on trucks.

Billboards provide an effective medium for advertisers to reach their segments with dynamic, timely, and relevant messages. Technology advances in digital or electronic billboards

Business Model

NBA Players as Human Billboards?

Marking the first media buy of this nature for the business of professional sports, NBA teams can now wear jerseys with 2.5-by-2.5-inch ads (patches) above the left chest. This represents a new revenue opportunity by giving sponsors highly visible real estate—location, location, location—right on the basketball jersey of a favorite star player.

The NBA is the first of the four U.S. male professional sports leagues to display a nonapparel logo on jerseys during game play. Usually the logos of apparel companies Nike, Under Armour, and Adidas appear on players' jerseys. The jerseys that include the sponsor patches will be available for sale to the general public. So far, topping the sales chart is the Warriors jersey of Stephen Curry, which includes a patch for a Tokyo, Japan–based Internet company called Rakuten. The small jersey patch is yielding the Warriors $20 million a year for three years.

In a $7 million annual deal, Boston-based General Electric will have its logo emblazoned on Celtics jerseys, and Goodyear, based in Akron, Ohio will pay more than $10 million to appear on Cleveland Cavalier jerseys. The entire NBA experience is already heavily branded. Teams sell rights to stadium names, halftime entertainment, special seating sections, and almost every inch of free space within an arena.

Agreeing upon a sponsor that does not conflict with current TV advertisers can be a challenge. In addition, although players in the union share in the revenue, star players promoting competing brands may see the new patch as a threat to endorsement opportunities. Nonetheless, the jerseys, which will be seen doing unique court contortions, represent the final remnant of noncommercialized space.

Questions for Critical Thinking

1. **Opposition to this practice comes from athletic apparel companies that pay hundreds of millions of dollars for exclusive rights to outfit a league. What type of conflicts might Nike, the new official jersey outfitter for the NBA, face with this new marketing strategy?**
2. **Are NBA players becoming human billboards? Do you agree with this practice? Why or why not?**

Sources: Steven Kutz, "19 NBA Teams Have Now Sold Ad Space on Their Jerseys," *MarketWatch*, www.marketwatch.com, accessed May 6, 2018; Will Jarvis, "Follow the Money: Ads on NBA Jerseys Open the Doors for Other Top Sports," *AdAge*, www.adage.com, accessed May 6, 2018; Andy Lewis, "NBA Looking to Raise $150M Annually With Ads on Uniforms," *Hollywood Reporter*, www.hollywoodreporter.com, accessed May 6, 2018; Scooby Axson, "Nike, NBA Reveal New Game Uniforms for Next Season," *Sports Illustrated*, www.si.com, accessed May 6, 2018.

provide brighter, sleeker, sharper, and higher-resolution images. As part of their outdoor advertising strategy, companies are using location data to target people who have passed by an outdoor ad. Via Bluetooth, when device IDs are logged, a retailer can see if a user has visited its store where their device ID would be tracked. One company's campaign for a Samsung product used geofencing to target ads on digital radio and Soundcloud at people within the billboard site. For example, based upon outside temperature, advertisements can feature hot drinks on a cold day and cold drinks on a hot day. A sporting goods retailer can promote a home team's gear after a win. Outdoor advertisers must comply with regulations such as brightness, flashing lights, and video, which could potentially distract drivers. Law enforcement and community groups have benefited from this medium, where announcements about public safety, community events, and even Amber Alerts (a child abduction alert system) can be made in real time.[32] Other forms of outdoor advertising, commonly seen in urban locations, include street furniture, bus shelters, news racks, and mall kiosk advertising. Transit advertising is placed on moving buses, subways, food trucks, and taxis—and this also includes airport advertising.[33,34]

Rudi Von Briel/Getty Images

Digital billboards allow advertisers the flexibility to change a message throughout the day with real time updates and conditional content based upon weather and events.

Sponsorship One trend in promotion offers marketers the ability to integrate several elements of the promotional mix. **Sponsorship** involves providing funds to support an issue, cause, or event in exchange for direct association. Sponsorships play an important role in relationship marketing, bringing together the event, its participants, and the sponsoring companies. Sponsorships dominate spending in the sporting event category at 70%, followed by entertainment at 10%, causes at 9%, the arts at 4%, festivals and fairs at 4%, and associations and membership organizations at 3%. Spending on sponsorships is expected to increase to $24.2 billion.[35]

sponsorship involves providing funds for a sporting or cultural event in exchange for a direct association with the event.

NASCAR, the biggest spectator sport in the United States, thrives on sponsorships, and its most recent—Monster Energy. Sponsorships can run in the tens of millions of dollars. Hendricks Motorsports, based in North Carolina, is the wealthiest and most successful NASCAR team to date, with more than $120 million in sponsorships from companies such as PepsiCo, 3M, Nationwide Insurance, Lowe's, and Kelley Blue Book.[36] Companies may also sponsor charitable or other not-for-profit awards or events. In conjunction with sports network ESPN, Gatorade sponsors its Player of the Year award, presented to the top male and female high school athletes who "strive for their best on and off the field."

Sponsors benefit in two major ways: exposure to the event's audience and association with the image of the activity. If a celebrity is involved, sponsors usually earn the right to use his or her name along with the name of the event in advertisements. They can set up signs at the event, offer sales promotions, and the like.

Other Media Options **Infomercials** are a form of broadcast direct marketing, also called *direct-response television (DRTV)*. These 30-minute programs resemble regular television programs but are devoted to selling goods or services such as exercise equipment, skin-care products, or kitchenware. The lengthy format allows an advertiser to thoroughly present product benefits, increase awareness, and make an impact on consumers. Advertisers also receive immediate responses in the form of sales or inquiries because most infomercials feature toll-free phone numbers and websites. Infomercial stars may become celebrities in their own right, attracting more customers wherever they go. The most effective infomercials tend to be for auto-care products, beauty and personal-care items, investing and business opportunities, collectibles, fitness and self-improvement products, and housewares and electronics.[37]

infomercials form of broadcast direct marketing; 30-minute programs that resemble regular TV programs, but are devoted to selling goods or services.

Advertisers use just about any medium they can find. They place messages on New York City MetroCard transit cards and toll receipts on the Massachusetts Turnpike. Another development is the use of ATMs for advertising. Some ATMs can play 15-second commercials on their screens, and many can print advertising messages on receipts. An ATM screen has a captive audience because the user must watch the screen to complete a transaction. Commonly found in supermarkets, floor graphics include brand and product advertisements on printed sheets of thin plastic adhered to the floor. Grocery ad sticks, which separate customers' groceries at the checkout, also contain advertisements, as do most supermarket shopping carts.[38]

Assessment Check

1. What are the two basic types of advertising? Into what three categories do they fall?
2. What is the leading advertising medium in the United States?
3. In what two major ways do firms benefit from sponsorship?

3 Sales Promotion

sales promotion consists of types of promotion such as coupons, product samples, and rebates that support advertising and personal selling.

Traditionally viewed as a supplement to a company's sales or advertising efforts, sales promotion is now an integral part of the promotional mix. Promotion now accounts for more than half as many marketing dollars as are spent on advertising, and promotion spending is rising faster than ad spending. **Sales promotion** consists of promotions such as coupons, product samples, and rebates that support advertising and personal selling. **Figure 13.3** highlights the most common types of sales promotions.

Both retailers and manufacturers use sales promotions to offer consumers extra incentives to buy. Beyond the short-term advantage of increased sales, sales promotions can also help marketers build brand equity and enhance customer relationships. Examples include samples, coupons, contests, displays, trade shows, and dealer incentives. Billy Fuccillo, who owns the bestselling Kia car dealership in the world, offers a free six-day cruise for every customer who buys or leases a Kia from one of his Florida Kia stores during an annual late-winter sales event. Some customers come back every two or three years just to buy a new Kia.[39]

Consumer-Oriented Promotions

The goal of a consumer-oriented sales promotion is to get new and existing customers to try or buy products. In addition, marketers want to encourage repeat purchases by rewarding current users, increase sales of complimentary products, and boost impulse purchases. Netflix recently increased its advertising budget by over 50 percent to $2 billion. Even though the company's software tailors content recommendations to households based upon viewing data, CEO Reid Hastings agrees that the company sees value in paid advertising.[40]

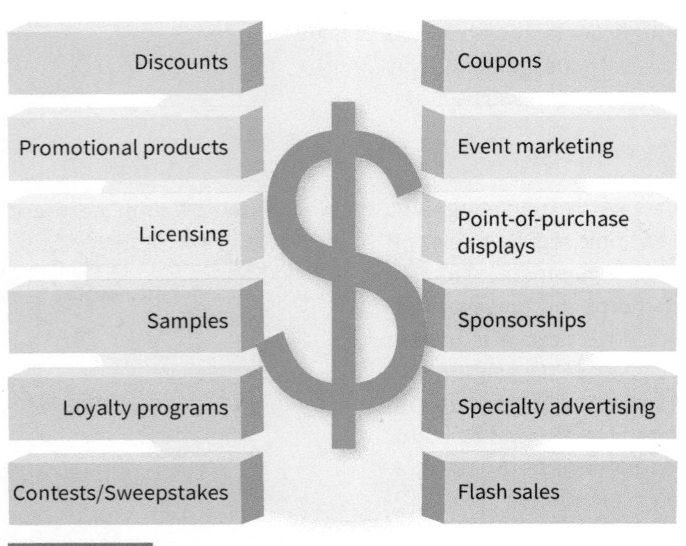

FIGURE 13.3 **The Most Common Types of Sales Promotions**

Premiums, Coupons, Rebates, and Samples

Over half of all sales promotion dollars are spent on *premiums*—items given free or at a reduced price with the purchase of another product. Cosmetics companies such as Clinique offer sample kits with purchases of their products. Bobbleheads have become a popular give away item to boost baseball game attendance. In general, marketers choose premiums that are likely to get consumers thinking about and caring about the brand and the product.

The coupon, which first began in 1887 with Coca-Cola, is traditionally issued to promote products by consumer packaged goods companies to provide consumers with a discount or rebate. Coupons, used by 94% of consumers, are available digitally either online, through a mobile device, or through a company's app. They may persuade a customer to try a new or different product. However, some people still enjoy clipping paper coupons from newspaper inserts and magazines.

In a recent year, 31 billion eCoupons were redeemed, and there will be over 1 billion mobile coupon users worldwide. Paperless coupon use (discounts via smart phones, mobile devices, and loyalty cards) rose to 75% in a recent year, and paper coupon use via mail, store, printed from computer, or newspaper/coupon book increased to 93% of consumers. Grocery/drug/mass store mobile savings apps are on the rise in addition to a cash back and points app, coupon app, in-store shopping rewards app, shopping list app, and deal comparison app.[41]

Rebates offer cash back to consumers who previously would mail in required proofs of purchase. Today, companies have simplified the rebate mail-in requirement by offering consumers the opportunity to submit rebates online. Rebates help packaged-goods manufacturers increase purchase rates, promote multiple purchases, and reward product users. Other types of companies also offer rebates, especially for electronics, computers and their accessories, and automobiles. Processing rebates gives marketers a way to collect data about their customers, but many shoppers find it inconvenient to collect the required receipts, forms, and UPC codes and then wait several weeks for their refund. In the past, many manufacturers counted on the fact that consumers would not follow through on rebates.[42]

A *sample* is a gift of a product distributed by mail, door to door, during a demonstration, or inside packages of another product. On any given day you might receive a sample moisturizer, a bar of soap, or a packet of laundry detergent. Three of every four consumers who receive samples will try them.

Games, Contests, and Sweepstakes Games, contests, and sweepstakes offer cash, merchandise, or travel as prizes to participating winners. Companies often sponsor these activities to engage customers, introduce new goods and services, and attract additional customers. Games and contests require entrants to solve problems or write essays and sometimes provide proof of purchase. Sweepstakes choose winners by chance and require no product purchase. Consumers typically prefer them because games and contests require more effort. Companies like sweepstakes, too, because they are inexpensive to run, and the number of winners is determined from the beginning. To increase customer engagement and to crowd source the selection of its new flavors, Oreo cookies launched its #MyOreoCreation contest. Three new finalists (Pina Colada, Cherry Cola, and Kettle Corn) were awarded $25,000, and the winning flavor will be awarded a cash prize of $500,000 and the chance to see where Oreos cookies are made.[43] Sweepstakes, games, and contests can reinforce a company's image and advertising message, but consumer attention may focus on the promotion rather than the product.

In recent years, court rulings and legal restrictions have limited the use of games and contests. Companies must proceed carefully in advertising their contests and games and the prizes they award. Marketers must indicate the chances of winning and avoid false promises such as implying that a person has already won.

Specialty Advertising Do you have any pens, T-shirts, or refrigerator magnets imprinted with a business name that you received for free? These offers are examples of **specialty advertising** or *advertising specialties*. This type of sales promotion involves the gift of useful merchandise carrying the name, logo, or slogan of a profit-seeking business or a not-for-profit organization. Because those products are useful and sometimes personalized with recipients' names, people tend to keep and use them, giving advertisers repeated exposure. Originally designed to identify and create goodwill for advertisers, advertising specialties now generate sales leads and develop traffic for stores and trade show exhibitors. Like premiums, these promotions should reinforce the brand's image and its relationship with the recipient.

specialty advertising promotional items that prominently display a company's name, logo, or business slogan.

Trade-Oriented Promotions

trade promotion sales promotion geared to marketing intermediaries rather than to final consumers.

Sales promotion techniques can also contribute to campaigns directed to retailers and wholesalers. **Trade promotion** is sales promotion geared to marketing intermediaries rather than to consumers. Marketers use trade promotion to encourage retailers to stock new products, continue carrying existing ones, and promote both new and existing products effectively to consumers. Successful trade promotions offer financial incentives. They require careful timing, attention to costs, and easy implementation for intermediaries. These promotions should bring quick results and improve retail sales. Major trade promotions include point-of-purchase advertising and trade shows.

point-of-purchase (POP) advertising displays or demonstrations that promote products when and where consumers buy them, such as in retail stores.

Point-of-purchase (POP) advertising is tied to impulse purchasing using displays or demonstrations that are strategically placed. Candy, chewing gum, batteries, comics, soft drinks, and magazines are typically displayed this way. The display—usually cardboard and created by the manufacturer—is intended to catch a consumer's eye and promote products at a checkout counter or where payment is made. Types of POP displays include floor stands, display bins, counter displays, shelf-mounted signs, posters, banners, and open and closed display cases. POP displays can significantly impact sales, as an estimated 70% of purchase decisions are made within the retail store itself. Recently, electronic POP displays, updated in real time, have been used to present targeted product information and instant coupons. Marketing research has shown that consumers are more likely to purchase certain products when such displays are present. Because retailers are forced to compete with online sellers for impulse purchases, more attention is being paid to innovative POP media, materials, and techniques within the in-store sales environment.[44]

Manufacturers and other sellers often exhibit at *trade shows* to promote goods or services to members of their distribution channels. These shows are often organized by industry trade associations. Each year, thousands of trade shows attract millions of exhibitors and hundreds of millions of attendees. Such shows are particularly important in fast-changing industries like those for computers, toys, furniture, and fashions. The International Consumer Electronics Show, which is held annually in Las Vegas and attracts more than 4,000 exhibitors and 184,000 attendees, is the largest. Other trade shows are in the construction, consumer goods, energy, entertainment, manufacturing, and sports and outdoors industries. Trade shows are especially effective for introducing new products and generating sales leads.[45]

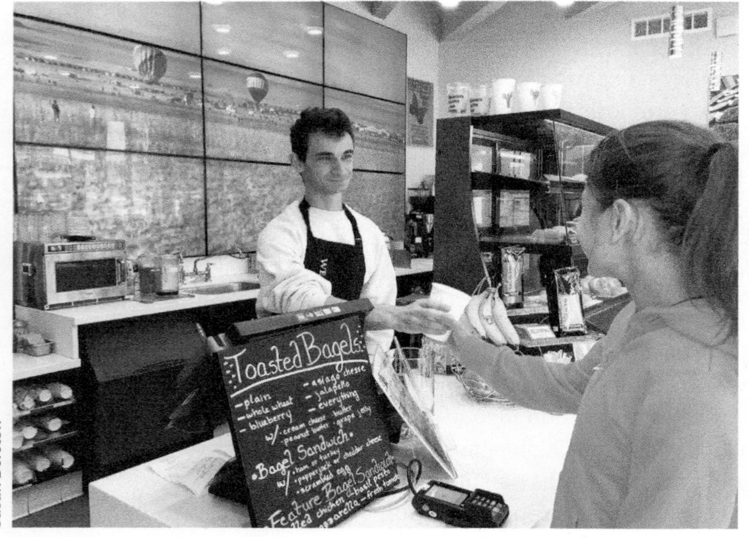

Susan Berston

All sales activities involve assisting customers. At Weaver's Coffee & Tea in San Francisco, a helpful barista is conscientious about quality and friendly service to accommodate a customer's specific needs — and to increase and maintain repeat sales.

Personal Selling

Many companies consider personal selling—a person-to-person promotional presentation to a potential buyer—an integral part of their promotion efforts. To produce benefits, it is crucial that a seller matches a company's goods or services to the needs of a particular customer or buyer. Today, sales and sales-related jobs employ about 15 million U.S. workers, and that number is expected to increase to 16 million over the next several years.[46] Businesses often spend 5 to 10 times as much on personal selling as they do on advertising. Given the significant cost of hiring, training, benefits, and salaries, companies are focused on the effectiveness of their sales force and their ability to build long-term customer relationships.

How do marketers decide whether to make personal selling the primary component of their company's marketing mix? In general, companies are likely to emphasize personal selling rather than advertising or sales promotion under four conditions:

1. Customers are relatively few in number and geographically concentrated.
2. The product is technically complex, involves trade-ins, or requires special handling.
3. The product carries a relatively high price.
4. The product moves through direct-distribution channels.

Selling luxury items such as a Porsche 918 Spyder at over $1 million, or a limited-edition Kuhn Bösendorfer grand piano would require a personal touch. If there's a need for construction of a heated driveway to avoid heavy snow during winter months, personal selling to convey costs and construction options might also be required.[47]

The sales functions of most companies are experiencing rapid change. Today's salespeople are more concerned with establishing long-term buyer–seller relationships and acting as consultants to their customers. Today's sales professionals emphasize *relationship selling* or *consultative selling*, a sales process that uses a personalized, customercentric approach built upon long-term, lasting relationships and trust. Anyone with a smart phone or price comparison app can search for competing prices of merchandise while standing in a retail store. Called *showrooming*, these apps have saved consumers the trouble of shopping for deals online or the time of driving and calling around to local stores. Product reviews are helpful with price comparisons as well. Many consumers have become savvy online shoppers, searching for bargains on websites like Overstock, eBay, Expedia, Orbitz, and Priceline. Recently, dynamic pricing has been implemented by online retailers in search of gaining margin advantage. The practice of changing prices, particularly during peak shopping seasons and based on market conditions, consumer behavior, and competitive intelligence, has become more commonplace.[48]

Personal selling can occur in several environments, each of which can involve business-to-business or business-to-consumer selling. Sales representatives who make sales calls on prospective customers at their businesses are involved in *field selling*. Companies that sell major industrial equipment typically rely heavily on field selling. *Over-the-counter selling* describes sales activities in retailing and some wholesale locations, where customers visit the seller's facility to purchase items. *Telemarketing* sales representatives make their presentations over the phone. A later section reviews telemarketing in more detail.

Sales Tasks

All sales activities involve assisting customers in some manner (such as in the photo). Although a salesperson's work can vary significantly from one company or situation to another, it usually includes a mix of three basic tasks: order processing, creative selling, and missionary selling.

Order Processing

Although both field selling and telemarketing involve this activity, **order processing** is most often related to retail and wholesale companies. The salesperson identifies customer needs, points out merchandise to meet them, and processes the order. Retail sales associates process orders for such consumer goods as bread, milk, soft drinks, and snack foods. Most of these jobs include at least minor order-processing functions.

order processing form of selling, mostly at the wholesale and retail levels, that involves identifying customer needs, pointing them out to customers, and completing orders.

Creative Selling

Sales representatives for most business products and some consumer items perform **creative selling**, a persuasive type of promotional presentation. Creative selling promotes a good or service whose benefits are not readily apparent or whose purchase decision requires a close analysis of alternatives. Sales of intangible products such as insurance rely heavily on creative selling, but sales of tangible goods benefit as well.

creative selling persuasive type of promotional presentation.

Many retail salespeople just process orders, but many consumers are looking for more in the form of customer service, which is where creative selling comes in. Personal shoppers at Topshop—located in London and various cities in the United States, and now in Nordstrom stores—help customers create entire looks from three floors of clothing. In the comfort of your own private dressing suite, the service provides one-on-one style advice and access to the latest arrivals.

Missionary Selling

Sales work also includes an indirect form of selling in which the representative promotes goodwill for a company or provides technical or operational assistance

missionary selling indirect form of selling in which the representative promotes goodwill for a company or provides technical or operational assistance to the customer.

to the customer; this practice is called **missionary selling**. Many businesses that sell technical equipment, such as Oracle and Fujitsu, provide systems specialists who act as consultants to customers. These salespeople work to solve problems and sometimes help their clients with questions not directly related to their employers' products. Other industries also use missionary selling techniques. Pharmaceutical company representatives—called *detailers*—visit physicians to introduce the company's latest offerings. Drug companies are turning to digital technologies and providing salespeople with digital devices to enhance face-to-face office visits with doctors for greater relevancy. This includes tracking customer accounts, triggering alerts, and managing relationships in new ways. A sales representative can emphasize certain products and services for increased goal achievement when there is knowledge of a doctor's performance metrics, clinical outcomes, and adherence to treatment protocol. For pharmaceutical sales representatives, relying solely on providing samples is a thing of the past. More recently, to assist the selling effort, machine learning and artificial intelligence (AI) technologies have emerged. As a virtual sales assistant, relevant recommendations can be made to help close a sale—including the prioritization of the most relevant information in a meeting, ways of reducing administrative tasks, and sharing best practices and specific sales presentations among reps. Robin is a virtual assistant, and part of Saleshero, an AI startup. She automates data entry tasks and ensures that accounts, contacts, and opportunities are up to date.[49]

telemarketing personal selling conducted entirely by telephone, which provides a company's marketers with a high return on their expenditures, an immediate response, and an opportunity for personalized two-way conversation.

Telemarketing

Telemarketing, personal selling conducted by telephone, provides a company's marketers with a high return on their expenditures, an immediate response, and an opportunity for personalized two-way conversation. Many companies use telemarketing because expense or other obstacles prevent salespeople from meeting many potential customers in person. Telemarketers can use databases to target prospects based on demographic data. Telemarketing takes two forms. A sales representative who calls you is practicing *outbound telemarketing*. On the other hand, *inbound telemarketing* occurs when you call a toll-free phone number to get product information or place an order.

The new reality is that telemarketing is being replaced by teleprospecting, which occurs after a potential buyer has engaged with online web content. Traditional outbound telemarketers must abide by the Federal Trade Commission's 1996 Telemarketing Sales Rules, which require telemarketers to make specific disclosures of material information; prohibits misrepresentations; sets limits on the times telemarketers may call consumers; prohibits calls to a consumer who has asked not to be called again; and sets payment restrictions for the sale of certain goods and services. Over time, the job of telemarketer will be handed off from humans to robots—computers with speech recognition software, programmed to make calls, handle surveys, and collect payments.

In recent years, automated calls, or robocalls, have skyrocketed—and regulators are working with the telecommunications industry to curb abuse by authenticating calls. Calls travel through various carriers, and with similar area codes, make it hard to pinpoint their origins.[50]

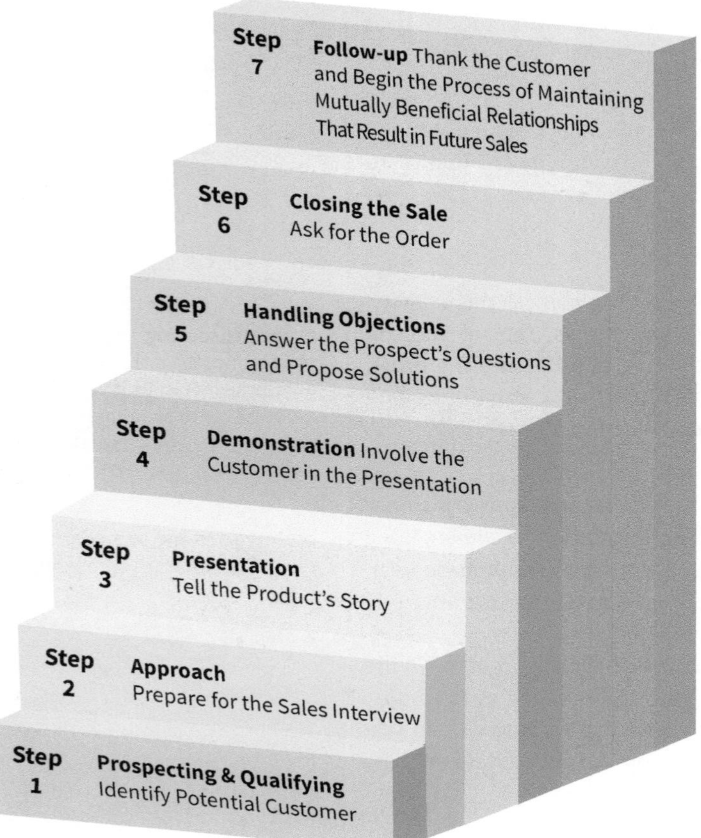
Step 7
Follow-up Thank the Customer and Begin the Process of Maintaining Mutually Beneficial Relationships That Result in Future Sales
Step 6
Closing the Sale
Ask for the Order
Step 5
Handling Objections
Answer the Prospect's Questions and Propose Solutions
Step 4
Demonstration Involve the Customer in the Presentation
Step 3
Presentation
Tell the Product's Story
Step 2
Approach
Prepare for the Sales Interview
Step 1
Prospecting & Qualifying
Identify Potential Customer

FIGURE 13.4 Seven Steps in the Sales Process

The Sales Process

The sales process typically follows the seven-step sequence shown in **Figure 13.4**: prospecting and qualifying, the approach, presentation, the demonstration, handling objections, closing, and the follow-up. Keeping in mind that selling to a new customer is different from serving an existing or longtime customer, a salesperson should customize the sales process to the needs of the customer.

Prospecting, Qualifying, and Approaching At the prospecting or lead generation stage, salespeople identify potential customers who possess the financial ability and authority to purchase its products and services. Sales leads can come from existing customer referrals, online contacts, friends and family, or business associates.

Companies use different strategies to identify and qualify prospects. Some companies rely on business development teams, passing responses from direct mail along to their sales reps. Others use technology databases, lead generation software, and social media websites such as LinkedIn. Some software tools even create prospect lists catered to a target market. Cloud technologies and quick access to data can increase productivity. Sales platforms utilizing machine learning can deliver key insights to reps and reduce the burden of data entry, and mobile platforms can update accounts with intuitive user experiences. CRM (customer relationship management) systems have been a sales game changer—and companies can work openly to leverage and share information in a transparent manner.[51]

Successful salespeople make careful preparations, analyzing available data about a prospective customer's product lines and other pertinent information before making the initial contact.

Presentation and Demonstration At the presentation stage, salespeople communicate promotional messages. They may describe the major features of their products, highlight the advantages, and cite examples of satisfied consumers. A demonstration helps reinforce the message that the salesperson has been communicating—a critical step in the sales process. Department-store shoppers can get a free makeover at the cosmetics counter. Anyone looking to buy a car will take it for a test drive before deciding whether to purchase it.

Some products are too large to transport to prospective buyers or require special installation to demonstrate. Using online videos or even live streaming, product demonstrations can be made. Selling services may include customer testimonials or a trial experience.

Handling Objections A good salesperson can use objections as an opportunity to answer questions and explain how the product will benefit the customer. As a general rule, the key is to sell benefits, not features: How and why will this product help the customer?

Closing The critical point in the sales process—the time at which the salesperson actually asks the prospect to buy—is the closing. If the presentation effectively matches product benefits to customer needs, the closing should be a natural conclusion. If there are more bumps in the process, the salesperson can try some different techniques, such as offering alternative products, offering a special incentive for purchase, or restating the product benefits. Closing the sale—and beginning a relationship in which the customer builds loyalty to the brand or product—is the ideal outcome of this interaction. But even if the sale is not made at this time, the salesperson should regard the interaction as the beginning of a potential relationship anyway. The prospect might very well become a customer in the future. See the "Job Description" feature to learn more about a career as an advertising sales representative.

Follow-up A salesperson's actions after the sale may determine whether the customer will make another purchase. Follow-up is an important part of building a long-lasting relationship. After closing, the salesperson should process the order efficiently. By making contact soon after a purchase, the salesperson provides reassurance about the customer's decision to buy and creates an opportunity to correct any problems. Automating responses and using software to personalize and track each and every message helps with communicating with customers over time.

Public Relations

A final element of the promotional mix, public relations (PR)—including publicity—supports advertising, personal selling, and sales promotion, usually by pursuing broader objectives.

Job Description

Advertising Sales Representative

Overview Advertising sales representatives, also called advertising sales agents, sell advertising space to businesses and individuals in newspapers, magazines, direct-mail circulars, and on TV, radio, websites, and billboards. They work in a range of industries including advertising agencies, publishing, radio, television, and Internet publishing. Sales quotas, usually expressed in dollars or by number of units of goods or services sold, are commonly used to measure a representative's effectiveness.

Responsibilities Advertising sales representatives typically go through the steps in the sales process to contact clients, make presentations, and maintain and service customer accounts where their company's advertising services can be offered. Using creativity and a needs-based selling approach, they consult with clients and review the value of how different types of advertising will help in the promotion of products and services. Pricing is often discussed and reviewed and proposals are presented, with estimates of the costs and options (sizes, time, and formats) of advertising products or services.

Determining client needs helps build strong relationships. Because clients may use various types of media (print, Internet, radio, TV, outdoor), an advertising sales representative may sell advertisements or integrated packages. Staying up to date on industry trends, fine-tuning negotiation skills, and learning about competitors will usually provide advertising sales representatives with a competitive advantage.

Requirements The education level for entry-level advertising sales positions may vary depending on the company. Publishing companies, for example, and broadcast and cable TV and radio stations may prefer candidates with a minimum of a college degree. For those with a previous sales track record, experience may be more important than education. As an advertising sales representative, must-have skills include effective communication, initiative, organizational skills, and self-confidence. Listening, making recommendations, persuading, actively seeking new clients, staying in touch with existing clients, and expanding a client base set a representative apart from others.

Outlook Employment for advertising sales representatives is projected to remain about the same over the next decade. As newspapers and print advertising declines, the need for advertising sales representatives will be offset by the growth in digital media advertising, which includes online video ads, search engine ads, and other mobile-ad formats. As companies target consumers directly using digital advertising (without a sales representative) through websites, the growth outlook remains in question.

Sources: Government website, "Advertising Sales Agents," *Occupational Outlook Handbook*, 2017–2018 Edition, http://www.bls.gov, accessed May 5, 2018; company website, "Career: Advertising Sales Agents," *Big Future*, https://bigfuture.collegeboard.org, accessed May 5, 2018; company website, "Advertising Sales Representative," http://www.shmoop.com, accessed May 5, 2018.

Through PR, companies attempt to improve their prestige and image with the public by distributing specific messages or ideas to target audiences. Cause-related promotional activities are often supported by public relations and publicity campaigns. In addition, PR helps a company establish awareness of goods and services and then builds a positive image of them.

public relations organization's communications and relationships with its various public audiences.

Public relations refers to an organization's communications and relationships with its various public audiences, such as customers, vendors, news media, employees, stockholders, the government, and the general public. Public relations is a strategic marketing communications process designed to build mutually beneficial relationships between organizations and their audiences with news topics of interest (free coverage) rather than paid-for advertising.

With direct media relationships, an organization's public relations department provides the media with news releases and videos and holds news conferences to announce new products, the formation of strategic alliances, management changes, financial results, and similar developments. Publications issued by a company's PR department include social media and news updates, reports, and newsletters.

publicity nonpersonal stimulation of demand for a good, service, place, idea, event, person, or organization by unpaid placement of information in print or broadcast media.

Publicity The type of public relations that is tied most closely to promoting a company's products is **publicity**—nonpersonal stimulation of demand for a good, service, place, idea, event, person, or organization by unpaid placement of information in print or broadcast media. Press releases generate publicity, as does news coverage. The National Football League has dealt with its share of negative publicity in major media coverage. Recent stories include the impact of concussions and head injuries on players, "deflategate" (underinflated footballs), domestic abuse and assault charges, and its longstanding policy of leaving teams alone with regard to its employment of team cheerleaders.

Despite these negative reports, the NFL still organizes the most popular sport among U.S. adults.[54]

Assessment Check

1. Why do retailers and manufacturers use sales promotions?
2. When does a company use personal selling instead of nonpersonal selling?
3. How does public relations serve a marketing purpose?

4 Pushing and Pulling Strategies

Marketers can choose between two general promotional strategies: a pushing strategy or a pulling strategy. A **pushing strategy** relies on personal selling to market an item to wholesalers and retailers in a company's distribution channels. So companies promote the product to members of the marketing channel, rather than end users. Salespeople explain to marketing intermediaries why they should carry particular merchandise, usually supported by offers of special discounts and promotional materials. Drug manufacturers use a pushing strategy to market to physicians and hospitals. Marketers also provide **cooperative advertising** allowances, in which they share the cost of local advertising of their company's product or line with channel partners. All of these strategies are designed to motivate wholesalers and retailers to push the good or service to their own customers.

pushing strategy personal selling to market an item to wholesalers and retailers in a company's distribution channels.

cooperative advertising allowances provided by marketers in which they share the cost of local advertising of their company's product or product line with channel partners.

A **pulling strategy** attempts to promote a product by generating consumer demand for it, primarily through advertising and sales promotion appeals. Potential buyers will seek out the item and perhaps become loyal to the brand—thereby pulling it through the distribution channel. Tickle Me Elmo, a plush toy resembling a Muppet character from Sesame Street (a TV show for children), was first introduced in 1996 by Tyco Toys. The company made sure of Elmo's visibility in magazines, TV shows, and toy stores. The demand for the toy surged, far exceeding supply.[55] Retailers and consumer goods manufacturers typically use a pulling strategy to promote their products.

pulling strategy promoting a product by generating consumer demand for it, primarily through advertising and sales promotion appeals.

Assessment Check

1. Give an example of a pushing strategy.
2. Give an example of a pulling strategy.

price exchange value of a good or service.

5 Pricing Objectives in the Marketing Mix

Products offer utility, or want-satisfying power. However, we as consumers determine how much value we associate with each one. In the aftermath of a major storm, we may value electricity and food and water above everything else. If we commute a long distance or are planning a driving vacation, fuel may be of greater concern. But all consumers have limited amounts of money and a variety of possible uses for it. So the **price**—the exchange value of a good or service—becomes a major factor in consumer buying decisions.

Businesspeople attempt to accomplish certain objectives through their pricing decisions. Pricing objectives vary from company to company, and many companies pursue multiple pricing objectives. Some try to increase profits by setting high prices; others set low prices to attract new business. As **Figure 13.5** shows, the four basic categories of pricing objectives are (1) profitability, (2) volume, (3) meeting competition, and (4) prestige.

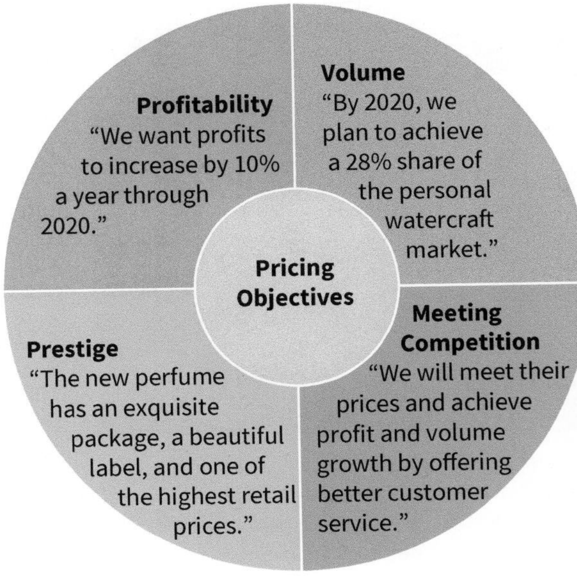

Profitability
"We want profits to increase by 10% a year through 2020."
Volume
"By 2020, we plan to achieve a 28% share of the personal watercraft market."
Pricing Objectives
Prestige
"The new perfume has an exquisite package, a beautiful label, and one of the highest retail prices."
Meeting Competition
"We will meet their prices and achieve profit and volume growth by offering better customer service."

FIGURE 13.5 **Pricing Objectives**

Profitability Objectives

profitability objectives common objectives included in the strategic plans of most companies.

Profitability objectives are the most common objectives included in the strategic plans of most companies. Marketers know that profits are the revenue the company brings in, minus its expenses. Usually a big difference exists between revenue and profit. Automakers try to produce at least one luxury vehicle for which they can charge $50,000 or more instead of relying entirely on the sale of $15,000 to $25,000 models.

Some companies maximize profits by reducing costs rather than through higher prices. Companies can maintain prices and increase profitability by operating more efficiently or by modifying the product to make it less costly to produce. One strategy is to maintain a steady price while reducing the size or amount of the product in the package, which is what ice-cream maker Haagen-Dazs did when it reduced its containers from 16 ounces to 14 ounces.[56]

Volume Objectives

volume objectives objects based on pricing decisions on market share, the percentage of a market controlled by a certain company or product.

A second approach to pricing strategy—**volume objectives**—bases pricing decisions on maximizing sales or market share, the percentage of a market controlled by a certain company or product. One company may seek to achieve a 25% market share in a certain product category, and another may want to maintain or expand its market share for particular products. Nestlé recently paid Starbucks $7.15 billion plus royalties for the global distribution rights to its brands of packaged coffees and Teavana packaged teas. The products join Nestlé's Nescafe and Nespresso coffee brands, which command 15% and 4.5% of global market share compared to Starbucks' global market share of 2.4%. For Starbucks, brand familiarity in international markets where it is not currently sold will increase.[57]

prestige pricing strategies that establish relatively high prices to develop and maintain an image of quality and exclusiveness.

Thomas Kienzle/AFP/Getty Images, Inc.

Prestige pricing sets a relatively high price to develop and maintain an image of quality and exclusiveness. People expect to pay more for cars adorned with the Mercedes hood emblem known as "the star."

Pricing to Meet Competition

A third set of pricing objectives seeks simply to meet competitors' prices so that price essentially becomes a nonissue. In many lines of business, companies set their own prices to match those of established industry leaders. However, companies may not legally work together to agree on prices.

Because price is such a highly visible component of a company's marketing mix, businesses may be tempted to use it to obtain an advantage over competitors. But sometimes the race to match competitors' prices results in a *price war*, which has happened periodically in the airline and fast-food industries. The ability of competitors to match a price cut leads many marketers to try to avoid price wars by favoring other strategies, such as adding value, improving quality, educating consumers, and establishing long-term relationships. Although price is a major component of the marketing mix, it is not the only one. Ride-sharing service Uber employs "surge pricing," a market-demand pricing structure whereby a premium price is placed on rides during periods of high demand, as the "Judgment Call" feature explains.

Prestige Objectives

The final category of objectives encompasses the effect of prices on prestige. **Prestige pricing** establishes a relatively high price to develop and maintain an image of quality and exclusiveness. Marketers set such objectives because they recognize the role of price in communicating an overall image of quality, status, and exclusiveness for the company and its products. People expect to pay more for a Mercedes (see photo), Christian Louboutin shoes, or a week at a villa on the British Virgin Islands' Necker Island, owned by Virgin CEO Richard Branson.

Judgment Call

Is Surge Pricing Unfair or Smart Business?

On a recent New Year's Eve, ride-sharing service Uber came under attack when it was reported on social media that customers paid over $100 for a ride that took them only a few miles. Generally, on weekends and during peak times, Uber's pricing structure becomes more dynamic. It's called "surge pricing," and it is sure to skyrocket in busy areas when rides are in demand.

Some, including Uber executives, believe that surge pricing suggests no wrongdoing—that it is merely an example of marketplace factors in action. After all, there is nothing illegal about charging higher prices during the wee hours of a New Year's morning to get revelers home safe and sound. The company defends its position by saying the Uber app allows a customer to accept or reject a ride based upon the stated percentage price increase at the time, which can be up to 10 times the usual rate. From a business perspective, it can be argued that surge pricing makes sense for Uber and other businesses. In fact, airlines, hotels, and other companies employ surge pricing during holidays and other times of the year.

In another incident after the New York Port Authority bombing, which prompted a shutdown of the Times Square subway station, Uber had to cough up refunds to passengers who were hit with surge pricing of 2.5 times the normal rate as they frantically hailed the ride sharing app to flee.

Uber's pricing strategy is seen as price gouging by some. However, Uber argues that along with surge pricing, the supply of drivers increases, and more people are better off because they are able to get rides. In the end, although a greater number of drivers benefit, customers end up paying a higher price. In Uber's case, the market is allocating goods by those who are willing and able to pay the price. For others, they may question the fairness and ask "Is it really okay to use surge pricing, even with advance warning?"

Questions for Critical Thinking

1. Although Uber's app allows a customer to either accept or reject a ride based upon the stated percentage price increase, does this transparency make it ethical? Why or why not?
2. Surge pricing has caused Uber unexpected damage to its reputation, particularly among its user base on social media. If Uber were to rethink its surge pricing, would it be a matter of ethics or a strategy to save itself from lost business? Explain.

Sources: Zach Epstein, "New Year's Eve Surge Pricing Enrages Uber Users; One Man Hit with $1,100 Fare, *BGR*, http://bgr.com, accessed May 9, 2018; Dan Eaton, "Was Uber's New Year's Eve Pricing Unethical?" *CNBC*, http://www.cnbc.com, accessed May 9, 2018; John Hooker, "Surge Pricing by Uber and Lyft," *Ethical Decisions*, http://ethicaldecisions.net, accessed May 9, 2018; Jeff Cherry, "The Missing Link at Uber: Ethics, Innovation, and Conscious Capitalism," *Conscious Company*, http://www.consciouscompanymagazine, accessed May 9, 2018; Nicholas Vega, "Uber, Lyft give refunds for surge pricing after Port Authority bombing," *New York Post*, www.nypost.com, accessed May 10, 2018.

Scarcity can create prestige. Products that are limited in distribution or so popular that they become scarce generate their own prestige—allowing businesses to charge more for them. For A-list celebrities, a haircut can run $750—an example of prestige pricing. Beverly Hills stylist Chris McMillan, whose client roster includes Hilary Swank, Michelle Williams, Anne Hathaway, Olivia Wilde, and Jennifer Lopez, is known as the master of creating the natural layered look for Hollywood's leading ladies.[58]

Assessment Check

1. Define *price*.
2. In addition to profitability, what is another approach to pricing strategy?

6 Pricing Strategies

Pricing strategies are developed with expertise from individuals across various functions of an organization. Accountants, financial managers, and marketers provide relevant sales and cost data, along with customer feedback. Designers, engineers, and systems analysts all contribute important data as well.

Prices are determined in two basic ways: by applying the concepts of supply and demand discussed in Chapter 3 and by performing cost analyses. Economic theory assumes that a market price will be set at the point at which the amount of a product desired at a given price equals the amount that suppliers will offer for sale at that price. In other words, this price occurs at the point at which the amount demanded and the amount supplied are equal. Online auctions, such as those on eBay, are a popular application of the demand-and-supply approach.

Price Determination in Practice

cost-based pricing formulas that calculate total costs per unit and then add markups to cover overhead costs and generate profits.

Economic theory might lead to the best pricing decisions, but most businesses do not have all the information they need to make those decisions, so they adopt **cost-based pricing** formulas. These formulas calculate total costs per unit and then add markups to cover overhead costs and generate profits.

Cost-based pricing totals all costs associated with offering a product in the market, including research and development, production, transportation, and marketing expenses. An added amount, the markup, then covers any unexpected or overlooked expenses and provides a profit. The total becomes the price. Although the actual markup used varies by such factors as brand image and type of store, the typical markup for clothing is determined by doubling the wholesale price (the cost to the merchant) to arrive at the retail price for the item.

Breakeven Analysis

breakeven analysis pricing-related technique used to determine the minimum sales volume a product must generate at a certain price level to cover all costs.

Businesses often conduct a **breakeven analysis** to determine the minimum sales volume a product must generate at a certain price level to cover all costs. This method involves a consideration of various costs and total revenues. *Total cost* is the sum of total variable costs and total fixed costs. *Variable costs* change with the level of production, as labor and raw materials do, while *fixed costs* such as rents, insurance premiums, and utility rates charged by water, natural gas, and electric power suppliers are constants regardless of the production level. *Total revenue* is determined by multiplying price by the number of units sold.

Finding the Breakeven Point

The level of sales that will generate enough revenue to cover all of the company's fixed and variable costs is called the *breakeven point*. It is the point at which total revenue just equals total costs. Sales beyond the breakeven point will generate profits; sales volume below the breakeven point will result in losses. The following formulas give the breakeven point in units and dollars:

$$\text{Breakeven Point (in units)} = \frac{\text{Total fixed costs}}{\text{Contribution to fixed costs per unit}}$$

$$\text{Breakeven Point (in dollars)} = \frac{\text{Total fixed costs}}{1 - \text{Variable cost per unit/Price}}$$

A product selling for \$20 with a variable cost of \$14 per unit produces a \$6 per-unit contribution to fixed costs. If the company has total fixed costs of \$42,000, then it must sell 7,000 units to break even on the product, as shown in **Figure 13.6**. The calculation of the breakeven point in units and dollars is as follows:

$$\text{Breakeven Point (in units)} = \frac{\$42{,}000}{\$20 - \$14} = \frac{\$42{,}000}{\$6} = 7{,}000 \textit{ units}$$

$$\text{Breakeven Point (in dollars)} = \frac{\$42{,}000}{1 - \$14/\$20} = \frac{\$42{,}000}{1 - 0.7} = \frac{\$42{,}000}{0.3} = \$140{,}000$$

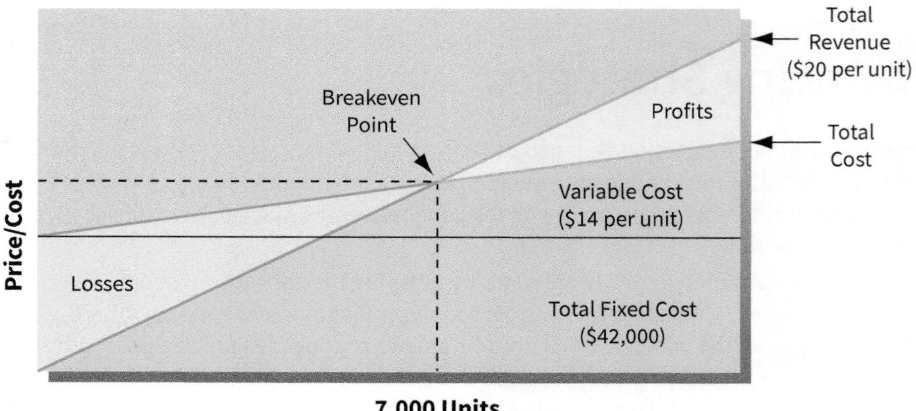

FIGURE 13.6 **Breakeven Analysis**

Marketers use breakeven analysis to determine the profits or losses that would result from several different proposed prices. Because different prices produce different breakeven points, marketers could compare their calculations of required sales to break even with sales estimates from marketing research studies. This comparison can identify the best price—one that would attract enough customers to exceed the breakeven point and earn profits for the company.

Most companies add consumer demand—determining whether enough customers will buy the number of units the company must sell at a particular price to break even—by developing estimates through surveys of likely customers, interviews with retailers that would be handling the product, and assessments of prices charged by competitors. Then the breakeven points for several possible prices are calculated and compared with sales estimates for each price. This practice is referred to as *modified breakeven analysis*.

Alternative Pricing Strategies

The strategy a company uses to set its prices should grow out of the company's overall marketing strategy. In general, companies can choose from four alternative pricing strategies: skimming pricing, penetration pricing, discount or everyday low pricing, and competitive pricing.

Skimming Pricing A **skimming pricing** strategy sets an intentionally high price relative to the prices of competing products. The term comes from the expression "skimming the cream." This pricing strategy often works for the introduction of a distinctive good or service with little or no competition, although it can be used at other stages of the product life cycle as well. A skimming strategy can help marketers set a price that distinguishes a company's high-end product from those of competitors. It can also help a company recover its product development costs before competitors enter the field. This is often the case with prescription drugs.

skimming pricing strategy that sets an intentionally high price relative to the prices of competing products.

Penetration Pricing By contrast, a **penetration pricing** strategy sets a low price as a major marketing weapon. Businesses may price new products noticeably lower than competing offerings when they enter new industries characterized by dozens of competing brands. Once the new product achieves some market recognition through consumer trial purchases stimulated by its low price, marketers may increase the price to the level of competing products. However, stiff competition might prevent the price increase. Another type of pricing strategy, loss leader pricing, is an aggressive pricing strategy in which a store sells selected goods below cost with hopes of attracting customers who will make up for the losses on those products with additional purchases of more profitable goods.

penetration pricing strategy that sets a low price as a major marketing weapon.

Everyday Low Pricing and Discount Pricing **Everyday low pricing (EDLP)** is a strategy devoted to maintaining continuous low prices rather than relying on short-term price-cutting tactics such as cents-off coupons, rebates, and special sales. This strategy has been used successfully by retailers such as Walmart and Lowe's to consistently offer low prices to consumers; manufacturers also use EDLP to set stable prices for retailers.

With *discount pricing*, businesses hope to attract customers by dropping prices for a set period of time. Automakers usually offer consumers special discounts on most or all of their vehicles during the holiday shopping season. After the holidays, prices usually rebound. But experts warn that discounting must be done carefully, or profits can disappear. Businesses should offer discounts only for a specified period of time and with a clear understanding of what they are trying to accomplish with the strategy. They should advertise the discount, so customers know it is a special deal. When the time period has elapsed, so should the discount. Retailers have struggled with pricing as they continue to battle showrooming and price wars waged by online competitors. See the "Business & Technology" feature for more details.

everyday low pricing (EDLP) is a strategy devoted to maintaining continuous low prices rather than relying on short-term price-cutting tactics such as cents-off coupons, rebates, and special sales.

Business & Technology

Instagram Stories Drive Sales for Brands

When social media site Instagram, owned by Facebook, introduced *Instagram Stories* in 2016, about one-third of the top-viewed short video and photo montages, which disappear after 24 hours, were brands. As Instagram edges into the e-commerce space, the company is offering brands a new way to promote their products. The photo- and video-sharing app has recently started testing ads that blend videos and product catalogs—and consumers can complete a purchase inside the app, without leaving.

Called "collection" campaigns, e-commerce is becoming a tremendous growth opportunity for brands on Instagram. Beauty brands are among the first to try "collection" ads on Instagram, where approximately 200 million fashion-followers watch their favorite brands—and two-third of the visits to Instagram business profiles are from non-followers. This is also a way for businesses to find new customers.

Airbnb, an online marketplace and hospitality service for travelers to lease or rent short-term lodging, used *Instagram Stories* to promote its Airbnb Experiences product, which connects travelers with local activities. Its 15-second spots show travelers exploring the natural wonders of San Francisco and attending a cooking class in Japan. Set to music, short bursts of video build into an episodic story that involves the making of miso soup—and hashtags can be added, too. Further discovery is created when users search through a hashtag, or stories with that specific hashtag appear at the top of the feed. For Instagram Stories with more than 10,000 followers, a "swipe up" option inside the story includes an outbound link—namely, to a brand's website, shop item, or content. With close to 300 million daily active users, Instagram Stories may very well continue its "storytelling" of products that align themselves with Instagram's aspirational and curated content platform—and with good reason.

Questions for Critical Thinking

1. "Instagram is a business's visual shop on mobile, and we're seeing more people seek out businesses there," said Sheryl Sandberg, Facebook's chief operating officer. What types of brands lend themselves to this type of advertising platform?
2. Who are some social media competitors to *Instagram Stories?* How do they differ?

Sources: Garrett Sloane, "Instagram Gives Brands New Way to Sell in 'Collection' Ads," *AdAge*, accessed May 10, 2018, http://www.adage.com; Pius Boachie, "How Brands Can Take Advantage of Instagram Stories," *AdWeek*, http://www.adweek.com, accessed May 10, 2018; Grace Caffyn, "How 5 Brands Are Using Ads on Instagram Stories," *DigiDay*, http://www.digiday.com, accessed May 10, 2018; *Social Report Blog*, "Instagram Stories Vs. Snapchat Stories—2017 Statistics," Social Report, http://www.socialreport.com, accessed May 10, 2018; Christina Moravec, "6 Brands Crushing It With Instagram Stories," *Convince & Convert*, http://www.convinceandconvert.com, accessed May 10, 2018.

competitive pricing strategy that tries to reduce the emphasis on price competition by matching other companies' prices and concentrating their own marketing efforts on the product, distribution, and promotional elements of the marketing mix.

Competitive Pricing Although many organizations rely heavily on price as a competitive weapon, even more implement **competitive pricing** strategies. They try to reduce the emphasis on price competition by matching the prices of other companies and concentrating their own marketing efforts on the product, distribution, and promotional elements of the marketing mix. In fact, in industries with relatively homogeneous products, competitors must match one another's price reductions to maintain market share and remain competitive. By pricing their products at the levels of competing offerings, marketers largely negate the price variable in their marketing strategies.

Assessment Check

1. What is a cost-based pricing formula?
2. Why do companies implement competitive pricing strategies?

7 Consumer Perceptions of Prices

How do you perceive prices for certain products? Marketers must consider this. If large numbers of potential buyers consider a price too high or too low, businesses must make modifications. Price–quality relationships and the use of odd pricing are important considerations in setting prices.

Price–Quality Relationships

Research shows that a consumer's perception of product quality is closely related to an item's price. Most marketers believe that this perceived price–quality relationship holds true over a relatively wide range of prices, although extremely high or low prices may have less credibility. The price–quality relationship can critically affect a company's pricing strategy.

Many consumers associate prestige, quality, and high price together—believing that paying a high price for an item such as a BMW or a Chanel bag not only conveys prestige but also ensures quality. Others believe that eating at an expensive restaurant automatically means the food will be better than food served at a modestly priced eating establishment. Conversely, consumers may view an extremely low price as an indication that corners have been cut and quality has been compromised. But what about the perception associated with a sale? If a line of designer boots goes on sale for 50% off the original price, a bargain hunter will snap them up with a sense of victory—high quality at a rock bottom price.

Odd Pricing

Have you ever wondered why retailers set prices at $1.99 instead of $2 or $9.95 instead of $10? Before the age of cash registers and sales taxes, retailers reportedly followed this practice of **odd pricing**—pricing method using uneven amounts, which appear less than they really are to consumers—to force clerks to make correct change as part of their cash control efforts. But now odd pricing is commonly used because many retailers believe that consumers favor uneven amounts or amounts that sound less than they really are. However, some retailers also use this method to identify items that have been marked down. The odd price suggests the item is on sale.

odd pricing pricing method using uneven amounts, which sometimes appear smaller than they really are to consumers.

Assessment Check

1. How does the price–quality relationship affect a company's pricing strategy?
2. Why is odd pricing used?

What's Ahead

The chapters in Part 4 have explained the main principles underlying marketing management and described how each fits a company's overall business strategy. The next few chapters will help you understand how companies manage the technology and information that are available to businesses to create value for their customers and enhance their competitiveness in the marketplace. You'll also learn how companies manage their financial resources.

Chapter in Review

Summary of Learning Objectives

LEARNING OBJECTIVE 1 Discuss integrated marketing communications (IMC).

In practicing IMC, a company coordinates promotional activities to produce a unified, customer-focused message. IMC identifies consumer needs and shows how a company's products meet them. Marketers select the promotional media that best target and reach customers. Teamwork and careful promotional planning to coordinate IMC strategy components are important elements of these programs.

A company's promotional mix integrates two components: personal selling and nonpersonal selling, which includes advertising, sales promotion, and public relations. By selecting the appropriate combination of promotional mix elements, marketers attempt to achieve the company's five major promotional objectives: provide information, differentiate a product, increase demand, stabilize sales, and accentuate the product's value.

Assessment Check Answers

1.1 **What is the objective of an integrated marketing communications program?** An IMC strategy focuses on customer needs to create a unified promotional message about a company's goods or services.

1.3 **Why do companies pursue multiple promotional objectives at the same time?** Companies pursue multiple promotional objectives because they may need to convey different messages to different audiences.

1.4 **What are product placement and guerrilla marketing?** Product placement involves paying a fee to have a product showcased in various types of media. Guerrilla marketing consists of innovative, low-cost marketing efforts designed to get consumers' attention in unusual ways.

LEARNING OBJECTIVE 2 Summarize the different types of advertising.

Advertising, the most visible form of nonpersonal promotion, is designed to inform, persuade, or remind. Product advertising promotes a good or service, while institutional advertising promotes a concept, idea, organization, or philosophy. Television, Internet, and newspapers are the largest advertising media categories. Others include magazines, radio, and outdoor advertising.

Assessment Check Answers

2.1 **What are the two basic types of advertising? Into what three categories do they fall?** The two basic types of advertising are product and institutional. They fall into the categories of informative, persuasive, and reminder-oriented advertising.

2.2 **What is the leading advertising medium in the United States?** According to the most recent statistics listed in Figure 13.2, television is the leading advertising medium in the United States.

2.3 **In what two major ways do companies benefit from sponsorship?** Companies benefit from sponsorship in two ways: they gain exposure to the event's audience, and they become associated with the activity's image.

LEARNING OBJECTIVE 3 Outline sales promotion.

Sales promotion accounts for greater expenditures than advertising. Consumer-oriented sales promotions such as coupons, games, samples, contests, sweepstakes, loyalty programs, and promotional products offer an extra incentive to buy a product. Point-of-purchase advertising displays and trade shows are sales promotions directed to the trade markets. Personal selling involves face-to-face interactions between seller and buyer. The primary sales tasks are order processing, creative selling, and missionary selling. Public relations is nonpaid promotion that seeks to enhance a company's public image.

Assessment Check Answers

3.1 **Why do retailers and manufacturers use sales promotions?** Retailers and manufacturers use sales promotions to offer consumers extra incentives to buy their products.

3.2 **When does a company use personal selling instead of nonpersonal selling?** Companies generally use personal selling when customers are few and geographically concentrated; the product is technically complex, involves trade-ins, or requires special handling; the price is high; or the product moves through direct-distribution channels.

3.2 **How does public relations serve a marketing purpose?** Public relations can be an efficient, indirect communications channel for promoting products. It can publicize products and help create and maintain a positive image of the company.

LEARNING OBJECTIVE 4 Describe pushing and pulling strategies.

A pushing strategy relies on personal selling to market a product to wholesalers and retailers in a company's distribution channels. A pulling strategy promotes the product by generating consumer demand for it, through advertising and sales promotion.

Assessment Check Answers

4.1 **Give an example of a pushing strategy.** An example of a pushing strategy is one used by drug manufacturers, which is used to market solely to physicians and hospitals.

4.2 **Give an example of a pulling strategy.** Pulling strategies are used by retailers and by manufacturers of consumer goods such as cosmetics, automobiles, and clothing.

LEARNING OBJECTIVE 5 Discuss the pricing objectives in the marketing mix.

Pricing objectives can be classified as profitability, volume, meeting competition, and prestige. Profitability objectives are the most common. Volume objectives base pricing decisions on market share. Meeting competitors' prices makes price a nonissue in competition. Prestige pricing establishes a high price to develop and maintain an image of quality or exclusiveness.

Assessment Check Answers

5.1 **Define price.** Price is the exchange value of a good or service.

5.2 **In addition to profitability, what is another approach to pricing strategy?** A second approach to pricing strategy is *volume objectives*, which bases pricing decisions on market share.

LEARNING OBJECTIVE 6 Outline pricing strategies.

Although economic theory determines prices by the law of supply and demand, most companies use cost-based pricing, which adds a markup after costs. They usually conduct a breakeven analysis to determine the minimum sales volume a product must generate at a certain price to cover costs. The four alternative pricing strategies are skimming, penetration, everyday low pricing and discounting, and competitive pricing. A skimming strategy sets a high price initially to recover costs and then lowers it; a penetration strategy sets a lower price and then raises it later. Everyday low pricing and discounting offers a lower price for a period of time. Competitive pricing matches other companies' prices and emphasizes nonprice benefits of an item.

Assessment Check Answers

6.1 **What is a cost-based pricing formula?** A cost-based pricing formula calculates the total costs per unit and then adds markups to cover overhead costs and generate profits.

6.2 Why do companies implement competitive pricing strategies? Companies use competitive pricing strategies to reduce the emphasis on price competition by matching other companies' prices and concentrating their own marketing efforts on the product, distribution, and promotional elements of the marketing mix.

LEARNING OBJECTIVE 7 Discuss consumer perceptions of prices.

Marketers must consider how consumers perceive the price–quality relationship of their products. Consumers may be willing to pay a higher price if they perceive a product to be of superior quality. Marketers often use odd pricing to convey a message to consumers.

Assessment Check Answers

7.1 How does the price–quality relationship affect a company's pricing strategy? Consumers must believe that the price of an item reflects its quality, except in extreme cases. So a company must try to set its prices accordingly.

7.2 Why is odd pricing used? Retailers believe that consumers favor uneven amounts or amounts that sound like less than they really are. Odd pricing may also be used to suggest an item is on sale.

Business Terms You Need to Know

integrated marketing communications (IMC) 342
promotion 342
promotional mix 343
personal selling 343
nonpersonal selling 343
positioning 345
product placement 346
guerrilla marketing 346
digital marketing 345
advertising 347
product advertising 347
institutional advertising 347
cause advertising 347
sponsorship 353
infomercials 353
sales promotion 354
specialty advertising 355
trade promotion 356
point-of-purchase (POP) advertising 356
order processing 357
creative selling 357
missionary selling 358
telemarketing 358
public relations 360
publicity 360
pushing strategy 361
cooperative advertising 361
pulling strategy 361
price 361
profitability objectives 362
volume objectives 362
prestige pricing 362
cost-based pricing 364
breakeven analysis 364
skimming pricing 365
penetration pricing 365
everyday low pricing (EDLP) 365
competitive pricing 366
odd pricing 367

Review Questions

1. What is the purpose of integrated marketing communications?
2. What are the five major objectives of a promotional strategy?
3. Identify and define each of the three categories of advertising based on their purpose. Which type of advertising might marketers use for the following products?
   a. cars
   b. virtual reality headset
   c. organic produce
   d. renter's insurance
4. What are the benefits of online and interactive advertising? What might be some drawbacks?
5. For each of the following, describe potential benefits and drawbacks of a sponsorship relationship:
   a. BMW and the Snowboard World Cup
   b. Bank of America and the Chicago Marathon
   c. Mattel Corporation and the Special Olympics
6. If you were a marketer for Rolex, what kind of sales promotion might you use for your watches?
7. Under what circumstances are companies likely to emphasize personal selling?
8. Describe the seven-step sales process.
9. Define the four basic categories of pricing objectives.
10. What are the four alternative pricing strategies that marketers use? Give an example of the circumstances under which each might be selected.

Projects and Teamwork Applications

1. Choose a product that you purchased recently. Identify the various media that were used to promote the product and analyze the promotional mix. Do you agree with the company's marketing strategy? Or would you recommend changes to the mix? Why?
2. Evaluate the price of the product you selected in the preceding exercise. What appears to be the pricing strategy that its manufacturer used? Do you think the price is fair? Why or why not? Choose a different strategy and develop a new price for the product based on your strategy. Poll your classmates to learn whether they would purchase the product at the new price—and why.
3. Evaluate outdoor advertisements by neighborhood and type—either where you live or in your college town. Include billboards, bus shelters, wall advertisements, advertisements and billboards in transit terminals, sporting arenas, and outdoor benches. Are they digital?

Do you see any trends or patterns by neighborhood and type of outdoor media utilized? For example, are there certain products or services advertised based on neighborhood and demographics?

4. A "freemium" pricing model like Pandora, Dropbox, or LinkedIn offers a basic service free of charge with the option to upgrade at a cost. It's a common pricing strategy among web technology start-up companies to get users onto the site and then later to convince them to subscribe to a premium or enhanced version of the service. What are some of the benefits of a freemium pricing model to a company? To consumers? Can you think of a situation when freemium pricing wouldn't work?

5. Product placement is also called embedded marketing, and you've probably seen it in TV programming, movies, and even video games. Skipping ads has never been easier due to advances in technology, so marketers have come up with alternative ways of placing their products in various media. One way is to use technology that allows them to digitally place products in TV shows or films after they have been released. What are your thoughts on this practice? What are the benefits to the brand? To the TV show or video game with the virtual product placement?

Web Assignments

1. **Evaluating a social media campaign.** Choose an airline, an automobile company, or a fast-food company (or product). On Facebook, Twitter, YouTube, and Instagram, compare and contrast social media campaigns. How does the company engage its customers? What is its most recent campaign, and what is unique about it? How does the company use each unique social media outlet to promote its product?

2. **Online coupon fraud.** Do some research to learn about online coupon fraud and its estimated annual costs to businesses. Prepare a brief report that includes answers to the following: How big of a problem is online coupon fraud? What are some of the risks, and how can marketers minimize that risk?

3. **Super Bowl Ads.** Go to YouTube.com and conduct research to view the most recent Super Bowl advertisements. Discuss the types of companies that paid over $5 million for a 30-second spot. How do you think these companies decided to advertise in the Super Bowl instead of using other media, and in your opinion, what were their goals in doing so?

Note: Internet web addresses change frequently. If you don't find the exact sites listed, you may need to access the organization's home page and search from there or use a search engine such as Google or Bing.

Cases

Case 13.1 Target Promotes a Dozen New Private-Label Brands

Shoppers who buy brand-name products usually cite quality as a reason, while shoppers who buy store-brand products usually cite price. Retailer Target believes it is possible to have the best of both, and the company, seen as a more upscale retailer in recent years, is focused on promoting its new private-label brands.

Competing in a crowded retail space with disruption from e-commerce companies, store brands or private label brands, once "uncool," are now a differentiating strategy for retailers like Target. Taking sales share away from national brands, private label brands continue to set new revenue records across the board. In the 1990s, Target teamed up with architect Michael Graves for an exclusive design partnership. Additionally, in-house brands like Merona and Mossimo, no longer produced, earned Target a devoted following of shoppers interested in affordable priced fashion available only at Target.

The company hopes to win back customers with about a dozen new brands of clothes and furnishings, which include A New Day (womenswear), its first-ever menswear line, Goodfellow, Project 62 (home décor), Joylab (athleisure), and Hearth and Hand with Magnolia, a home and lifestyle label created in conjunction with HGTV stars Chip and Joanna Gaines.

With $2 billion in sales its first year, the company's children's clothing line Cat & Jack is a reminder of what might come of its new private label launches—and it is not at all private that these very products will continue to be Target's focus for growth.

Questions for Critical Thinking

1. Why do you think retailers carry brand-name items alongside their own in-house brands? From your own experience, are the national brands worth the additional cost? Why or why not?
2. Many retailers are tapping into what is called "Millennial pragmatism," which addresses how consumers in this demographic group demand to know more about what a brand stands for beyond its bottom line. How are retailers appealing to Millennials with products, imagery, and appeals of a private-label brand without the higher price tag?

Sources: David Kirkpatrick and Peter Adams, "Target Puts Heavy Marketing Push Behind 12 New Private-Label Brands," *Marketing Dive*, http://www.marketingdive.com, accessed May 9, 2018; organization website, "Consumers Continue to Reach for Store Brands, Producing Record Sales Across Major U.S. Retail Channels," http://plma.com, accessed May 8, 2018; Kristen Cloud, "Store Brands Widen Growth Gap vs. National Brands as Sales Hit New Highs in All Outlets," *The Shelby Report*, http://www.theshelbyreport.com, accessed May 8, 2018; Pan Demetrakakes, "Top CPG Brands Languish in Sales," Retail Leader, http://www.retailleader.com, accessed May 8, 2018; Jeff Fromm, "No Longer Uncool: Millennials Love Store Brands," *Forbes*, http://www.forbes.com, accessed May 8, 2018; Phil Wahba, "Target Has a New CEO: Will He Reenergize the Retailer?" *Fortune*, http://fortune.com, accessed May 8, 2018; Paul Ziobro, "Target Extends Return Window for Private-Label Brands," *Wall Street Journal*, http://www.wsj.com, accessed May 8, 2018.

Case 13.2 Marriott Partners with TripAdvisor

As technology has changed the way consumers search for and book hotels, hotel loyalty programs also have evolved. Road warriors, those who travel extensively for business, have traditionally favored one or two hotel chains to rack up points for rewards that today go beyond a free night's stay. With the primary goal of building a customer's affinity to a brand, hotel loyalty programs are designed to provide unique experiences and build deeper levels of customer engagement.

When travelers stay at any of Marriott's 19 affiliated brands, including Ritz-Carlton, Courtyard, Renaissance, and Residence Inn, rewards are earned in the form of points. These points can be redeemed for flights through more than 30 airline rewards programs, along with spa and dining gift cards. Statistics show that loyalty members are three times more likely to book a hotel directly with Marriott than through a third-party travel website. This also saves hotels the commissions paid to a third-party website for bookings.

When bookings are made through third-party websites, hotels do not give loyalty awards or points to its members. They're only awarded when booked directly with a hotel. However, many travelers are willing to jump around from place to place and forgo points for a better price. For business travel, some companies are even requiring that employee travel be booked through a favored third-party site.

As third-party websites become increasingly difficult to ignore, Marriott recently announced an agreement with TripAdvisor, which allows travelers to book rooms directly at any of Marriott's 4,200 properties without leaving the TripAdvisor site. The instant booking platform (with a "Book on TripAdvisor" button) provides a streamlined booking experience for travelers. However, to earn rewards points, Marriott requires that reservations still be made directly through its site. This new collaboration is a result of changing trends, greater price competition, and far more choices—which can result in less customer loyalty. The benefit to Marriott is greater exposure for its many brands and the ease with which consumers can book a room at any of its hotels without leaving the TripAdvisor website. The benefit to TripAdvisor is the additional revenue in the form of fees for more bookings at any of Marriott's worldwide hotels.

Questions for Critical Thinking

1. What led Marriott to enter into a relationship with TripAdvisor? Discuss how the relationship between Marriott and TripAdvisor benefits each company.
2. Discuss how more choices for travelers have caused hotels to rethink their loyalty programs.

Sources: Company website, "Marriott International and TripAdvisor Announce Instant Booking Partnership," http://ir.tripadvisor.com, accessed May 5, 2018; Tony Mecia, "Third-Party Booking Sites Trip up Hotel Rwards," *Creditcards.com*, http://www.creditcards.com, accessed May 5, 2018; Amy Zipkin, "Online Booking Makes Hotel Loyalty Harder to Keep," *New York Times*, http://www.nytimes.com, accessed May 5, 2018; "Best Hotel Rewards Programs," *U.S. News and World Report*, http:///travel.usnews.com, accessed May 5, 2018; Ed Watkins, "The History and Evolution of Hotel Loyalty," *Hotel News Now*, http://www.hotelnewsnow.com, accessed May 5, 2018.

Case 13.3 Zipcar Informs, Persuades, and Reminds

A Zipster is one of over a million members of the world's largest car-sharing service, Cambridge, Massachusetts–based Zipcar. The company was founded in 2000 by two moms, Antje Danielson and Robin Chase, who met when their children were in school together. Today, Zipcar is owned by Avis Budget and offers self-serve, on-demand automobile reservations by the hour or day to three distinct customer segments: city dwellers, business people, and college students. Using various marketing channels and promotional activities, Zipcar targets each segment using a slightly different approach.

Zipcar employs several forms of advertising to inform, persuade, and remind, but the most effective approach is direct and personalized. Based on demographic information, the company uses technology to find the right target audiences to deliver the most timely and relevant messages. For example, Zipcar uses social media to market to college and university students with a message about the benefits of picking up and driving a Zipcar on or nearby campus and reserving a car using a mobile device or the web. The message to college students centers on the convenience and ultimate benefit of being a Zipster, when considering the expense of owning and maintaining a car while still in school. For city dwellers, Zipcar's marketing focus is on running errands or getting out of the city for a daylong excursion.

Not everyone understands how Zipcar's service works. From an advertising perspective, the company has discovered the effectiveness of direct-response TV, which is TV advertising purchased on a national basis that appears in local markets. This approach has proved valuable to Zipcar's marketing mix. TV commercials are used to build awareness and inform users about how the service works. Unlike a traditional car rental service, Zipcar is based on the use of technology. Zipcar members have automated access to rentals using a "Zipcard," which works with the car's technology to unlock the door so customers can locate the keys inside the car. While there are annual membership fees and hourly rental rates, gas, parking, insurance, and maintenance are included.

Outdoor and Internet advertising strategies are effective for marketing Zipcar's services. For those looking online for car rentals, Zipcar's search engine optimization is leveraged on Twitter, YouTube, Facebook, and other social media sites. In the early days of the company, promotional events included brand ambassadors from its field marketing organization (on college or university campuses, for example) to educate and inform students about Zipcar's benefits. In mature markets like New York and Boston, the marketing message focuses more on reminding users about Zipcar's value and less about educating and informing. In markets where car sharing is a new concept for most consumers, the promotional strategy centers on informing and differentiating Zipcar from competitors, mainly rental car companies and other modes of transportation.

Zipcar pursues multiple promotional objectives simultaneously. Recently the company collaborated with JetBlue to provide services for the airline's customers traveling to specific destinations. To empower and collaborate among its own community members, Zipcar will be distributing up to $100,000 in free driving to 40 nonprofit organizations.

Zipcar's Chief Marketing Officer oversees membership, which is an integral part of the company's marketing efforts. Zipcar's field marketing representatives show up at farmer's markets, public transportation stations, and companies located in the city to educate and promote its value proposition and the benefits of its brand. Marketing strategies are developed around the seasonality of Zipcar's business, which varies between summer and winter months in each of its market segments.

To remain competitive, Zipcar carefully analyzes how it prices its services. Determining the pricing strategy for Zipcars located in a local city is actually a fairly complex process. With more than 12,000 vehicles across the globe, at 50 airports, and over 30 cities around North America, pricing varies by market. For example, in Boston where the company is headquartered, pricing begins at $8.25 per hour. There is a onetime application fee to become a member, and various pricing plans are available depending on customers' needs and the type of vehicles available in each of its markets.

Zipcar remains a lifestyle brand, and the customer experience remains the company's most valuable marketing tool. So whether it's a car to run errands or to enjoy a night on the town, pricing will vary, but the customer experience remains the same. Using Zipcar allows you to avoid paying for gas or visiting the auto repair shop. That's clearly something worth advertising.

Questions for Critical Thinking

1. Discuss and provide examples of the different types of marketing channels and promotional activities Zipcar uses to target each of its three user segments. As marketing manager at Zipcar, discuss additional promotional strategies you would employ for each of the market segments.
2. Discuss how Zipcar is more a lifestyle brand than a travel brand, and what this means. How does this impact the company's promotional efforts? What solutions does Zipcar provide, and how does this make it a lifestyle brand?
3. Who are Zipcar's competitors, and how do their promotional and advertising efforts compare? Do competitors vary for each of Zipcar's distinct market segments? What transportation options are there for each of the three segments?
4. Go online and perform additional research to learn more about Zipcar's pricing structure in your local market. Using pricing objectives discussed in the chapter (profitability, volume, meeting competition, and prestige), how would you evaluate Zipcar's pricing objectives? Provide examples.

Sources: Company website, "Rates and Plans," http://www.zipcar.com, accessed May 5, 2018; company website, "Is Zipcar for Me?" http://www.zipcar.com, accessed May 5, 2018; company website, "Zipcar Overview," http://zipcar.com, accessed May 5, 2018; company website, "The Zipcar Grant Program," http://zipcar.com, accessed May 5, 2018; company website, "Just Landed from a JetBlue Flight?" http://zipcar.com, accessed May 5, 2018; Chris Ready, "Zipcar Rolls Out One-Way Service with Guaranteed Parking," *Boston Globe,* http://www.bostonglobe.com, accessed May 5, 2018; Mark Rogowsky, "Zipcar, Uber, and the Beginning of Trouble for the Auto Industry," *Forbes*, http://www.forbes.com, accessed May 5, 2018; Carol Hymowitz, "Zipcar Founder Robin Chase on Starting Buzzcar and a Portugal Venture," *Bloomberg Businessweek*, http://www.bloomberg.com, accessed May 5, 2018; Natalie Zmuda, "Marketers Hitting Campus Harder than Ever," *AdAge*, http://adage.com, accessed May 5, 2018.

CHAPTER **14**

Using Technology to Manage Information

LEARNING OBJECTIVES

1. Outline the ways technology has forever changed business.
2. Distinguish between data and information, and discuss information systems and the role of big data.
3. List components and types of information systems.
4. Discuss computer hardware and software.
5. Describe computer networks, cloud computing, and the future of the Internet.
6. Outline the security, ethical, and privacy issues affecting information systems.
7. Explain disaster recovery and backup systems.
8. Discuss information technology trends.

Overview

This chapter explores how businesses manage information as a resource, particularly how they use technology to do so. Today, virtually all business functions—from human resources to production to supply chain management—rely on information systems. The chapter begins by describing the way technology has forever changed business. Next, we differentiate between data and information, define an information system, and explain the role of big data. The components and two major types of information systems are described along with a look at the evolution of the Internet and the computer hardware and software that drive information systems. The chapter examines different types of networks, including virtual networking and cloud computing. An overview of security and ethical issues related to information systems is provided (as described by the efforts of Ricardo Villadiego of Easy Solutions), along with a review of the importance of disaster recovery and backup. A discussion of information technology trends concludes the chapter.

1 Technology Has Forever Changed Business

Today, every business is a technology business, and the development of technology over the last few decades has been the impetus for powerful and less-costly growth options for companies. In varying degrees, all businesses are being transformed by technology. Sophisticated

Changemaker

Courtesy of Easy Solutions, Inc.

Ricardo Villadiego, Founder and CEO

Company: Easy Solutions

Industry: Online Fraud Detection/Cybersecurity/Enterprise Security

Website: http://www.easysol.net

After more than a decade in the information technology (IT) industry, Ricardo Villadiego (see photo), a classic entrepreneur and former IBM veteran, took a risk to start cybersecurity company Easy Solutions, where he currently serves as chief executive officer. A former software sales executive, Villadiego's experience in the IT industry includes product innovation, regional management, and even installing and fixing ATM machines. Villadiego is from Bogotá, Colombia, where he earned an electronic engineering degree with honors.

Villadiego has built a company that offers solutions to more than 320 leading financial institutions, which continue to face cyberthreats in an increasingly complex and changing Internet ecosystem. The Doral, Florida–based company was ranked as one of the 500 hottest and most innovative cybersecurity companies to watch by *Cybersecurity Ventures* magazine. The company protects the online activities of more than 85 million users in 30 different countries.

A new report from Websense Security Labs reveals that the average number of attacks against financial services institutions is four times that of companies in other industries. As big banks have fallen victim to sophisticated external cyberattacks, attacks of this nature have become the cause for increased scrutiny of a financial institution's security efforts by financial regulators. The issue of data security has resulted in an increasingly sharp focus on the cybersecurity industry.

By understanding complex fraud attacks, Easy Solutions provides Total Fraud Protection, a real-time, anti-fraud product that delivers proactive, integrated, cross-channel protection across multiple devices, channels, and clouds. Cross-channel refers to transactions performed through various channels such as online and mobile platforms, ATMs, point-of-sale computer terminals, and interactive voice response systems. As hackers continue to leverage multiple platforms to conduct highly sophisticated fraud, Easy Solutions has devised tools to detect activity at each stage of the fraud attack lifecycle.

With Villadiego at the helm, Easy Solutions continues to innovate to keep pace with the growing trend of cyberthreats directed toward financial institutions. According to the CEO, it's all about winning battles for Easy Solutions' customers: When the bad guys are thwarted at one bank, they will try another one to gain access to clients' secure information.[1]

technology now allows artists to record music, build websites, crowdfund upload music videos, create and sell merchandise, and release their own music online. No longer is a record label deal a prerequisite to success as a musical artist. Technology has forever changed the face of many businesses and industries including music, entertainment, automobiles, healthcare, hospitality, and retail.

Industry 4.0, or the fourth industrial revolution, powered by digitization in manufacturing, is driven by the recent rise in data volumes, computational power and connectivity, analytics and business intelligence capabilities, new forms of human–machine interaction and augmented reality systems, and robotics and 3-D printing. Following the lean revolution of the 1970s, the outsourcing boom that took place in the 1990s, and the automation occurring in the 2000s, this is the fourth upheaval in modern manufacturing. Consider the smart phone, a game-changing technological innovation. On a global basis and at lightning speed, the smart phone has contributed to an increased flow of ideas and improved knowledge exchange resulting in growth and productivity for both businesses and the global economy. **Table 14.1** lists everyday items replaced by the smart phone.[2]

The *disruptive innovation* model from Clayton Christensen, a Harvard business professor and author, refers to a theory that describes the impact an innovation has when a new market and value are created, which "disrupts" an existing market and its value.[3] Companies continue to innovate and figure out ways to manage the growth of information technology, in an effort to turn its disruptive potential into profits.

TABLE 14.1 Everyday Items Replaced by the Smart Phone

Answering machine	Fax machine	ATM machine
Calculator	Radio	Wrist watch & wall clock
Digital and Video cameras	MP3 player	GPS & fold-out maps
Credit card	Alarm clock	Flashlight
Pedometer	Landline phone	Photo album
Personal computer	Scanner	Tape recorder
Daily calendar	Phone book	Pay phone
Portable gaming device	USB flash drive	Books, magazines, and newspapers

Sources: Gavyn Davies, "The Greatest Unknown—The Impact of Technology on the Economy," *Financial Times*, http://blogs.ft.com, accessed May 16, 2018; Linda Bilyeu, "40 Things the iPhone Has Replaced," *HubPages*, http://hubpages.com, accessed May 16, 2018.

Disruptive innovations refer to less-expensive and simpler versions of existing products and services that target entirely new customers, many times replacing industry leaders. Examples include smart phones replacing personal computers; downloadable digital media replacing CDs and DVDs; Wikipedia and other online sources replacing traditional print encyclopedias; and retail medical clinics replacing traditional doctors' offices. SpaceX and Airbnb are examples of companies referred to as "unicorns," which use innovative business models to bring about disruption in a particular industry.[4]

disruptive innovations less-expensive and simpler versions of existing products and services that target an entirely new group of customers.

As valuations for business start-ups continue to grow, the term *unicorn* also refers to start-up companies with values of $1 billion or more. The ten largest technology firms by revenue will reach sales of over $1 trillion in an upcoming year. These companies are Apple, Amazon, Alphabet (aggregate Google's corporate parent), Microsoft, IBM, Intel, Hewlett Packard, Facebook, Cisco, and Oracle. Primary business activities include hardware and software, semiconductors, Internet, telecom, e-commerce, and computer services.[5]

Assessment Check

1. How has the smart phone impacted business?
2. What is disruptive innovation?

2 Data, Information Systems, and Big Data

Every day, businesspeople ask themselves questions such as:

- How well is our product selling in Boston compared to Phoenix? Have sales among consumers aged 25 to 45 increased or decreased within the past year?
- How will fluctuating energy prices affect production and distribution costs?
- How can we communicate more efficiently and effectively with our increasingly diverse and global workforce?

An effective information system can help answer these and many other questions. **Data** consist of raw facts and figures that may or may not be relevant to a business decision. **Information** is knowledge gained from processing those facts and figures. So although businesspeople need to gather data about the demographics of a target market or the specifications of a certain product, the data are useless unless they are transformed into relevant information

data raw facts and figures that may or may not be relevant to a business decision.

information knowledge gained from processing data.

that can be used to make a competitive decision. For example, data might be the sizes of various demographic groups. Information drawn from those data could be how many of those individuals are potential customers for a company's products. Technology has advanced so quickly that all businesses, regardless of size or location, now have access to data and information that allows for global competitiveness.

information system organized method for collecting, storing, and communicating past, present, and projected information on internal operations and external intelligence.

chief information officer (CIO) executive responsible for managing a company's information system and related computer technologies.

An **information system** is an organized method for collecting, storing, and communicating past, present, and projected information on internal operations and external intelligence. Most information systems today use computer and telecommunications technology. A large organization typically assigns responsibility for directing its information systems and related operations to an executive called the **chief information officer (CIO)**. Often, the CIO reports directly to the company's chief executive officer (CEO). A strategic CIO will understand and harness technology so that the company can seamlessly communicate internally and externally.

Today's CIO cannot ignore the countless business opportunities resulting from technology-based advances which include lower costs, increased product innovation, more efficient supply chains, more secure networks and data storage, more personalized customer service, and, ultimately, greater customer loyalty.

Today's CIO is more closely connected to the company's overall business strategies and marketing efforts due to the fact that technology, which comes up in every conversation, intersects with everything, including new customer models and regulatory issues. Additionally, making use of available emerging Industry 4.0 technologies is a priority.[6]

Information systems can be tailored to assist many business functions and departments—from marketing and manufacturing to finance and accounting. They can manage the overwhelming information overload by organizing data in a logical and accessible manner. Through an information system, a company can more effectively plan and better manage all aspects of its operations and business strategy. Information systems contain data gathered from inside and outside the organization; the data is processed to produce information that is relevant to all aspects of the organization. Processing steps could involve storing data for later use, classifying and analyzing it, and retrieving it easily when needed. Many companies combine various solutions to manage and share the flow of information. E-mail, online meetings, and wireless communications have not totally replaced face-to-face meetings, written correspondence, and phone conversations, but they have become increasingly common.

big data large or complex structured or unstructured sets of information that traditional processing applications are unable to analyze.

The massive amounts of data available to companies today continue to grow. Referred to as **big data**, it changes on an ongoing basis and can be structured or unstructured—due mainly to the many sources from which it originates. Because big data consist of large or complex data sets, traditional processing applications are usually inadequate to analyze it.

Sources of big data may include social media, mobile devices, online sales, and customer service feedback. Because there is so much data, it can be difficult to process with existing database and software processing capacity. However, the promise of data-driven decision making is great. When captured, formatted, manipulated, stored, analyzed, and evaluated, the data can lead a company to see trends, providing greater insight to make better, more timely and informed decisions. There's an ever-expanding pool of data sources and types, including the public web (external), social media (high velocity, high volume), sensor data (geolocation, temperature, noise), archived data, media, and business applications (structured).

Business analytics refers to standard tools and procedures designed to search and analyze the amount of complex data a business gathers. For example, in an effort to deal with rising healthcare costs and to encourage employees to become healthier, companies are working with outside data analytic firms to mine data about employees' use of prescription drugs and how they shop to predict their health needs and to recommend treatments. Using mobile technology, Ginger.io is one of a number of healthcare companies harnessing the power of smartphone data to deliver customized mental health services from healthcare professionals. Data is gathered from users to deliver a full-service online and app-based mental healthcare service, either direct-to-consumer or via insurers and self-insured employers.[7] *Data mining,* discussed in Chapter 11, refers to using computer-based technology to evaluate information in a database to identify useful trends, which often suggests predictive models of real-world business activities.

Assessment Check

1. Distinguish between data and information.
2. What is an information system?
3. What is big data?

3 Components and Types of Information Systems

The definition of *information system* in the previous section does not specifically mention the use of computers or technology. In fact, information systems have been around since the beginning of civilization but were, by today's standards, very low tech. At one time, your college or university's library probably had card catalog files to help users find information. Those files were information systems because they stored data about books and periodicals on 3-by-5-inch index cards.

Today, however, when businesspeople think about information systems, they are most likely thinking about **computer-based information systems**. These systems rely on computer and related technologies to store information electronically in an organized, accessible manner. So, instead of card catalogs, your college library probably uses a computerized information system that allows users to search through periodicals, journals, books, and even digital collections of historic photographs, manuscripts, and maps.

computer-based information systems information systems that rely on computer and related technologies to store information electronically in an organized, accessible manner.

Some information systems support parts of an organization, others support entire organizations, and some support groups of organizations. Information support systems are capable of performing high-speed, high-volume numerical and quantitative computations and provide fast, accurate communication and collaboration within an organization. They store massive amounts of information in an easy-to-access, yet small space and allow quick and inexpensive access to information worldwide. Information systems interpret vast amounts of data quickly and efficiently while automating business processes and manual tasks. **Table 14.2** provides examples of how information technology systems are used in functional areas of a business organization.

Computer-based information systems consist of computer hardware, computer software, a network, and a database.

Computer hardware consists of machines that range from supercomputers to smart phones. It also includes the input, output, and storage devices needed to support computing machines.

Software includes operating systems, such as Microsoft's Windows 10, and application programs, such as Adobe Acrobat and Microsoft Office. Consumer software includes Dropbox and Evernote, while enterprise software includes Salesforce.com and Workday. In addition, mobile software consists primarily of iOS and Android operating systems.

Networks encompass the hardware and software needed to provide wired or wireless voice and data communications. This includes support for external networks such as the Internet and private internal networks. Data resource management involves developing and maintaining an organization's databases so that decision makers are able to access the information they need in a timely manner.

A network is the connecting system (wireline or wireless) that allows shared resources among different computers, and usually among a wide range of users. Networks include hardware and software needed to provide voice and data communications. They are becoming increasingly faster, which means that their *bandwidth*, the transmission capacity of a network, is increasing. Types of computer networks are discussed later in this chapter.

TABLE 14.2 IT Systems in Functional Areas of an Organization

Business Function	How Information Technology Is Used
Human Resources	• Manage recruiting process (analyze/screen applicants) • Performance evaluation • Training • Manage careers of current employees • Administer employee testing • Monitor employee productivity • Administer compensation and benefits packages
Marketing	• Manage customer relationships • Maintain customer profiles and preferences • Automate business tasks of the selling process • Develop new goods and services • Identify the best advertising channels • Determine product pricing
Production/Operations and Logistics	• Determine the best locations for production and distribution facilities • Design and manufacture products using computer-assisted design (CAD) and computer-assisted manufacturing (CAM) • Inventory management (includes just-in-time inventory) • Quality control • Materials requirement planning
Finance and Accounting	• Financial planning, budgeting, and revenue forecasts • Investment management • Determine the best sources and uses of funds • Perform audits • Administer payroll • Financial reporting

Sources: "The Six Important Business Objectives of Information Technology," *Houston Chronicle*, http://smallbusiness.chron.com, accessed May 18, 2018; R. Kelly Rainer and Brad Prince, *Introduction to Information Systems*, 7th Edition (Hoboken, NJ: Wiley, 2018).

Databases

database centralized integrated collection of data resources.

The heart of any information system is its **database**, a centralized integrated collection of data resources. A company designs its databases to meet particular information processing and retrieval needs of its workforce. Businesses obtain databases in many ways. They can hire a staff person to build them on site, hire an outside source to do so, or buy cloud-based services from specialized vendors, such as Oracle, SAP, or Salesforce.com. A database serves as an electronic filing cabinet, capable of storing massive amounts of data and retrieving it within seconds. A database should be continually updated; otherwise, a company may find itself with information that is obsolete, outdated, and possibly useless. One problem with databases is that they can contribute to information overload—too much data for people to absorb or data that are not relevant to decision making. Because both computer processing speed and storage capacity have increased so dramatically, and because data have become more abundant, businesspeople need to be careful that their databases contain only the facts they need. If they don't, they can waste time wading through unnecessary data.

One of the largest online databases is that of the U.S. Census Bureau. The census of population, conducted every 10 years, collects data on more than 126 million households across the United States. The general public may access the data via the American FactFinder on the Census Bureau's website (http://factfinder2.census.gov) as well as at state data centers and public libraries.[8]

Types of Information Systems

Many different types of information systems exist. In general, however, information systems fall into two broad categories: operational support systems or management support systems.

© Flightlevel80/iStockphoto

The complex process of airline maintenance is critical to passenger safety. To track parts, schedule inspections, and manage inventory levels, many airlines, including American, use an operational support system.

Operational Support Systems

Operational support systems are designed to produce a variety of information on an organization's activities for both internal and external users. Examples of operational support systems include transaction processing systems, process control systems, and enterprise collaboration systems, which facilitate efficient sharing of documents and knowledge between teams and individuals within an organization. **Transaction processing systems** record and process data from business transactions. For example, major retailers use point-of-sale systems, which link electronic cash registers to the retailer's computer centers. Sales data are transmitted from cash registers to the computer center either immediately or at regular intervals. **Process control systems** monitor and control physical processes. A steel mill, for instance, may have electronic sensors linked to a computer system monitoring the entire production process. The system makes necessary changes and alerts operators to potential problems. On the topic of information systems and information technology, BMW's 7-series automobile has the latest information technology, as discussed in the "Business Model" feature.

operational support systems information systems designed to produce a variety of information on an organization's activities for both internal and external users.

transaction processing systems operational support system to record and process data from business transactions.

process control systems operational support system to monitor and control physical processes.

Business Model

Digital Technologies Replace Power Windows and Leather Seats

As consumers continue to be lured by connectivity and technology, BMW's 7-series automobile is a prime example of information technology and digital excellence. According to the *Financial Times*, in the future, 50% to 60% of the value of a car will consist of digital devices and tools.

Tom Brenner, head of BMW's digital services, believes that cars will need to "play well" with the digital lifestyle owners choose. This is where BMW's high-tech feature called Connected Plus comes in. The new system will help a driver plot out the best route to a destination with real-time traffic reports to give a heads-up of when it's time to leave. Running late? Alerts are sent to let the folks on the other end know when to expect you. Appointments in an owner's calendar are tracked, along with ride time, walking-to-vehicle time, and parking options. Additionally, an intelligent personal assistant, Alexa, can turn on the car, along with the air conditioner or heater, if needed.

Add driverless technology to the mix, and new technology entrants into the auto industry have traditional carmakers eyeing electronic wizardry and information technology add-ons in order to attract buyers. Add-ons include radar sensors, cameras, software, and advanced driver-assistance technology. For in-car technologies, German automakers are partnering with companies like Google, Apple, Nvidia, and Amazon—as well as restaurant chains and smaller technology start-ups.

BMW's 7-series cars come with gesture control, remote-control self-parking, and an app store. To avoid having to take their eyes off the road, drivers can use hand movements or gestures to adjust radio volume or accept or reject incoming phone calls. Truly unique is the car's remote parking feature, which allows for self-parking into a tight space or garage. A valet parking system has been developed that will eventually allow an autonomous drive around a parking garage to find a space—and, ultimately, to pick up the driver. As the modern automobile continues to evolve, BMW's next model will be a digital car.

Questions for Critical Thinking

1. BMW's CEO is quoted as saying, "We are responding to the digitization of modern mobility." What do you think he means by this, and how would you define "modern mobility"?
2. Would you be interested in any of the features mentioned? Do such features improve the driving experience of the automobile?

Sources: Bob O'Donnell, "The Future of the Modern Car Is Actually Digital," *Recode*, http://www.recode.net, accessed May 23, 2018; Mark Matousek "Most Hi-Tech Sedans You Can Buy Today," *Business Insider*, http://www.businessinsider.com, accessed May 20, 2018; Paul A. Eisenstein, "Who's Winning the Fight for Best-In-Car Technology?" *NBC News*, http://www.nbcnews.com, accessed May 21, 2018; Norbert Schwieters and Bob Moritz, "10 Principles for Leading the Next Industrial Revolution," *Strategy + Business*, http://www.strategy-business.com, accessed May 21, 2018; William Boston, "BMW Pours Technology into New Sedan," *The Wall Street Journal*, http://www.wsj.com, accessed May 21, 2018; company website, "Innovative Functionality in the BMW 7 Series," http://www.bmw.com, accessed March 8, 2018; William Boston, "German Car-Parts Makers See Bigger Role in Technology," *The Wall Street Journal*, http://www.wsj.com, accessed May 21, 2018.

management support systems information systems that are designed to provide support for effective decision making.

management information system (MIS) information system that is designed to produce reports for managers and others within the organization.

decision support system (DSS) gives direct support to businesspeople during the decision-making process.

executive support system (ESS) lets senior executives access the company's primary databases, often by touching the computer screen, pointing and clicking a mouse, or using voice recognition.

expert system computer program that imitates human thinking through complicated sets of if-then rules.

Management Support Systems Information systems that are designed to provide support for effective decision making are classified as **management support systems**. Several different types of management support systems are available. A **management information system (MIS)** is designed to produce reports for managers and other personnel.

A **decision support system (DSS)** gives direct support to businesspeople during the decision-making process. Decision support systems may range from simple software systems to complex knowledge-based and artificial intelligence systems. An Intelligent Decision Support System (IDSS) makes extensive use of artificial intelligence (AI) techniques. For example, in interpretive analysis of large-scale patient data with intelligent and knowledge-based methods, IDSS allows doctors to quickly gather and process information to make diagnosis and treatment decisions.

An **executive support system (ESS)** lets senior executives access the company's primary databases, often by touching the computer screen, pointing and clicking a mouse, or using voice recognition. The typical ESS allows users to choose from many types of data, such as the company's financial statements and sales figures, as well as stock market trends for the company and for the industry as a whole. Managers can start by looking at summaries and then access more detailed information as needed.

Finally, an **expert system** is a computer program that imitates human thinking through complicated sets of if-then rules. The system applies human knowledge in a specific subject area to solve a problem. In artificial intelligence, expert systems are used for a variety of business purposes: determining credit limits for credit card applicants, monitoring machinery in a plant to predict potential problems or breakdowns, making mortgage loans, and determining optimal plant layouts. They are typically developed by capturing the knowledge of recognized experts in a field whether within a business itself or outside it.

Assessment Check

1. List the four components of a computer-based information system.
2. What is a database?
3. What are the two general types of information systems? Give examples of each.

4 Computer Hardware and Software

The first commercial computer, UNIVAC I, was sold to the U.S. Census Bureau in the early 1950s. It cost $1 million, took up most of a room, and could perform about 2,000 calculations per second.[9] The invention of transistors and then integrated circuits (microchips) quickly led to smaller and more powerful devices. By the 1980s, computers could routinely perform several million calculations per second. Now, computers perform trillions of calculations per second, and many fit in the palm of your hand.

When the first personal computers were introduced in the late 1970s and early 1980s, the idea of a computer on every desk, or in every home, seemed far-fetched. Today they have become indispensable to both businesses and households. Not only have computers become much more powerful and faster over the past 25 years, but they are less expensive as well. IBM's first personal computer (PC), introduced in 1981, cost well over $5,000 fully configured. Today, due to decreased demand and lower production costs, a typical desktop PC sells for between $300 and $600; products in Apple's MacBook lineup range from $1,299 to $2,799.[10]

Types of Computer Hardware

hardware all tangible elements of a computer system.

Hardware consists of all tangible elements of a computer system—the input devices, the components that store and process data and perform required calculations, and the output devices that present the results to information users. Input devices allow users to enter data and commands for processing, storage, and output. The most common input devices are the keyboard and mouse. Backing up important documents with external hardware is less prevalent today, as the Internet has provided storage solutions like Box, a service that allows you to save local files to the cloud. Flash memory devices, also called thumb drives, are small and can hold large amounts of data and are easily accessed by plugging the drive into a USB (universal serial bus) port. Output devices, such as monitors and printers, are the hardware elements that transmit or display documents and other results of a computer system's work.

Different types of computers incorporate widely varying memory capacities and processing speeds. These differences define four broad classifications: mainframe computers, midrange systems, personal computers, and hand-held devices. A mainframe computer is the largest type of computer system with the most extensive storage capacity and the fastest processing speeds.

Midrange systems consist of high-end network servers and other types of computers that can handle large-scale processing needs. They are less powerful than mainframe computers but more powerful than most personal computers. A **server** is the heart of a midrange computer network, supporting applications and allowing the sharing of output devices, software, and databases among networked users. Many Internet-related functions of organizations are handled by midrange systems. On the topic of hardware and software, the "Job Description" feature outlines the role of a computer systems analyst.

server the heart of a midrange computer network.

Once the center of the digital universe, a full-scale Windows or Mac OS personal desktop computer was the way most people accessed social media and the Internet, wrote papers, played games, organized music and photos, and more. While some believe the PC is on its way to extinction and ownership rates have declined, PCs are still widely used in homes, businesses, schools, and government agencies.

Desktop computers used to be the standard PC seen in offices and homes. While millions of desktop computers remain on the job, laptops—including notebooks and netbooks—surpassed desktop units in sales. The increasing popularity of these computers can be explained by smaller, lighter, more powerful computing, and by their improved displays, faster processing speeds, ability to handle more intense graphics, larger storage capacities, and more durable designs. Business owners, managers, salespeople, and students all benefit from their portability and instantaneous access to information. While the tablet market is shrinking, shipments of tablets with detachable keyboards have become popular, with many consumers treating tablets as PC replacements. Even as tablet sales decline, Apple continues to dominate with its iPad, which has a processor that enables augmented reality and ten hours of battery life.[11]

Microsoft and Qualcomm have introduced a laptop powered by a smartphone processor running a desktop operating system. Specifically, the Windows 10 laptops that will be built initially by HP, Lenovo, and Asus are powered by the Qualcomm Snapdragon 835 processor. This is the same chip that powers high-end smartphones such as the Galaxy S8 and Note 8.[12]

Hand-held devices such as smart phones are even smaller. The most popular smart phones today are powered by Google's Android and Apple's iOS mobile operating systems. With advanced and cloud computing capabilities, smart phones like the Apple iPhone and Samsung Galaxy have become ubiquitous. With small tweaks in each subsequent smartphone introduction and consumers holding on to phones longer, smartphone sales have reached their peak. However, as artificial intelligence matures, thanks to a machine learning chip, a new wave of demand is anticipated for AI smart phones.[13]

In addition to smart phones, specialized hand-held devices are used in a variety of businesses for different applications. Some restaurants, for example, have small wireless devices that allow servers to swipe a credit card and print out a receipt right at the customer's table. Drivers for UPS and FedEx use special hand-held scanning devices to track package deliveries and accept delivery signatures. The driver scans each package as it is delivered, and the

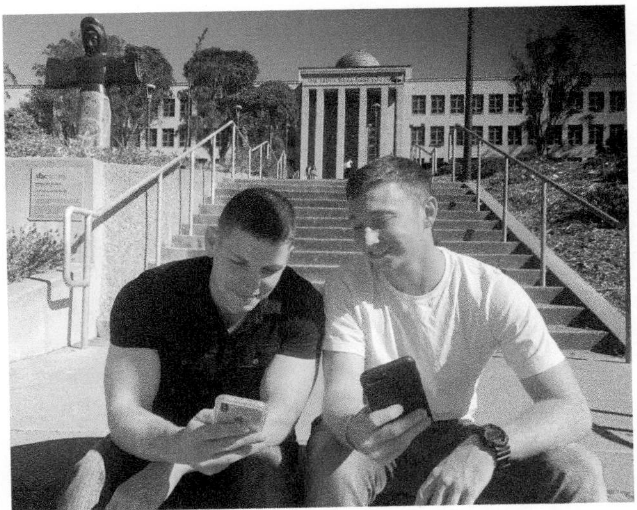

Susan Berston

It is anticipated that mobile phones will account for over half of all web traffic.

Job Description

Computer Systems Analyst

Overview Computer systems analysts must understand a company's current computer systems, including hardware, software, and networks and how they work together, so they can make recommendations for operations systems to use, and improve existing technologies and business practices. A computer systems analyst is tasked with choosing, customizing, and configuring the most efficient and effective hardware and software system for an organization.

Responsibilities Computer systems analysts consult with managers to determine information technology (IT) needs, research existing and emerging technologies, analyze and prepare cost-benefit analyses, and determine ways to add additional functionality to existing systems. Testing is often conducted, and end users are trained on the system.

In an effort to design an efficient and effective computer system (taking into consideration both memory and speed), an analyst is concerned with data modeling, which studies the processes and data flows within an organization. Depending upon the type of organization or the industry, a systems analyst will create a financial or production system, for example. A systems analyst works closely with business leaders and managers to explain how the system can best serve the organization's internal and external customers.

Requirements The education level for computer systems analysts usually includes a bachelor's degree in a computer or information science field. However, some companies hire liberal arts majors with good critical-thinking and problem-solving skills, who have actual experience in information technology or computer programming. Analysts may also have coursework in business, which is helpful since many are involved in the business aspects of a company or organization—and this job integrates business and technology.

An analyst with industry-specific experience is a plus. For example, a hospital may find an analyst with knowledge of health care plans including Medicare and Medicaid. This experience would be beneficial when it comes to communicating with managers to determine the role of IT within an organization. Analytical, communication, and creativity skills are essential to interpreting and gathering complex information from multiple sources and communicating between company managers and the IT department. Strong problem-solving and critical-thinking skills assist in finding innovative solutions and troubleshooting computer issues.

Outlook As organizations increasingly rely on information technology, employment of computer systems analysts is projected to grow 9% over the next decade. Analysts will be relied upon to design and install new computer systems for companies both large and small. Demand for systems analysts can be attributed to continued growth in cloud computing, the increased need for cybersecurity, and the use of mobile networks.

Sources: Government website, "Computer Systems Analysts," *Occupational Outlook Handbook, 2017–2018 Edition*, http://www.bls.gov, accessed May 18, 2018; company website, "Computer Systems Analysts," *About Careers*, http://careerplanning.about.com, accessed May 18, 2018; company website, "Career: Computer Systems Analyst," *Big Future*, https://bigfuture.collegeboard.org, accessed May 18, 2018.

information is transmitted to the delivery firm's network. Within a few seconds, the sender, using an Internet connection, can obtain the delivery information and even see a facsimile of the recipient's signature.

Types of Computer Software

software all the programs, routines, and computer languages that control a computer and tell it how to operate.

Software includes all of the programs, routines, and computer languages that control a computer and tell it how to operate. The software that controls the basic workings of a computer system is its *operating system*. Many personal computers use a version of Microsoft's popular Windows operating system. Personal computers made by Apple use the Mac operating system. The Android and iPhone models have their own operating systems. Other operating systems include Unix, which runs on many midrange computer systems, and Linux, which runs on both PCs and midrange systems. Open Source Software (OSS), usually free, is a type of computer software developed in an open and collaborative public manner.

A program that performs the specific tasks that the user wants to carry out—such as writing a letter or looking up data—is called *application software*. Examples of application software include Adobe Acrobat, Microsoft Word (word processing), Excel (spreadsheets), and PowerPoint (presentations), and Quicken. Most application software has become web based, with the programs themselves stored on Internet-connected, cloud-based servers.

An app is a software program, and most are designed to run on a smart phone or a tablet. Originally intended for e-mail, calendar, and contact databases, apps continue to be in high demand for other areas like games, GPS, factory automation, banking, order tracking, ticket purchases, and travel. Free to download, many of the most popular smartphone apps are owned by Google, Facebook, Apple, or Amazon. They include Instagram, Apple Music, YouTube, Google Maps, and Amazon.

Assessment Check

1. List two input and output devices.
2. What accounts for the popularity of laptop and notebook computers?
3. What is software? List the two categories of software.

5 Networks, the Internet, and Cloud Computing

Virtually all computers today are linked to networks. In fact, if your PC has Internet access, you're linked to a network. Local area networks and wide area networks allow businesses to communicate, transmit and print documents, and share data. These networks, however, require businesses to install special equipment and connections between office sites. But Internet technology has also been applied to internal company communications and business tasks, tapping a ready-made network. Among these Internet-based applications are intranets and virtual networks. As technology infrastructures continue to evolve, cloud computing has become an important component of business IT strategies. Each has contributed to the effectiveness and speed of business processes, so we discuss them next.

local area networks (LANs) computer networks that connect machines within limited areas, such as a building or several nearby buildings.

wide area networks (WANs) tie larger geographical regions together by using telephone lines and microwave and satellite transmission.

Wi-Fi wireless network that connects various devices and allows them to communicate with one another through radio waves.

Local Area Networks and Wide Area Networks

Most organizations connect their offices and buildings by creating **local area networks (LANs)**, computer networks that connect machines within limited areas, such as a building or several nearby buildings. LANs are useful because they link computers and allow them to share printers, documents, and information as well as provide access to the Internet.

Wide area networks (WANs) tie larger geographical regions together by using telephone lines and microwave and satellite transmission. One familiar WAN is long-distance telephone service. Companies such as AT&T and Verizon provide WAN services to businesses and consumers. Companies also use WANs to conduct their own operations. Typically, companies link their own network systems to outside communications equipment and services for transmission across long distances.

Wireless Local Networks

A wireless network allows computers, printers, and other devices to be connected without the hassle of stringing cables in traditional office settings. The current standard for wireless networks is called Wi-Fi. **Wi-Fi**—is a wireless network that connects various devices and allows them to communicate with one another through radio waves. Any device with a Wi-Fi receptor can connect with the Internet at so-called hot spots—locations with a wireless router and a high-speed Internet modem. There are hundreds of thousands of hot spots worldwide today. Wi-Fi can be found in a variety of places, including restaurants, hotels, airports, libraries, and cafés (see photo). With

OJO Images RF/Getty Images

Wi-Fi connections are often called hot spots—locations with a wireless router and a high-speed Internet modem. There are hundreds of thousands of hot spots worldwide today found in a variety of places, including airports, libraries, and coffee shops.

the desire for fast Internet access, major U.S. cities are quickly scaling up to build out high-speed, next-generation wireless infrastructures. In the next three years, the 5G network promises to be anywhere between 10 and 100 times faster than what's available today.[14]

The Internet

The Internet is a powerful source of information. However, using the Internet requires a company to process overwhelming amounts of information in order to make good business decisions. Integral to a company's success is the ability to manage its knowledge. Recent data suggest that companies lose approximately $31.5 billion annually by failing to share knowledge. Making sure that knowledge gets to the right people at the right time is crucial to remaining competitive. *Knowledge management* is a discipline that promotes an integrated approach to identifying, capturing, evaluating, retrieving, and sharing all of an enterprise's information assets. These assets may include databases, documents, policies, procedures, and previously uncaptured expertise and experience of individual workers.[15]

Let's first look at a brief history of the Internet, and how it has evolved. The Internet dates back to research and development performed in the 1960s, originally commissioned by the governments of the United States, France, and the United Kingdom, to build communication networks. In the United States, this work led to an early network called ARPANET. In the 1980s with the interconnectedness of academic computer networks, the Internet was "turned on." Today, most types of communication and media have adapted to the Internet and web technology, including entertainment, television, newspapers, books, and print publishing. Almost 88% of the U.S. population uses the Internet to connect and exchange information.[16]

Using the Internet protocol suite as a way to link billions of devices worldwide, the Internet consists of a global system of interconnected mainframe, personal, and wireless computer networks including government, commercial, and education. The Internet enables information to be shared and exchanged through the collection of billions of interconnected web pages collectively known as the World Wide Web.

In the late 1980s, rapid adoption of the Internet took place as computers became more affordable. This spawned a range of communication and information services that have reached every aspect of modern life today. Although there is no centralized governing board for the Internet, there does exist the Internet Corporation for Assigned Names and Numbers or ICANN, a nonprofit organization whose principal role is to preserve the operational stability of the Internet and to develop policies using a consensus-based approach. For safe operation, ICANN coordinates and maintains the database of unique identifiers or namespaces of the Internet.[17] The Internet has profoundly changed the way we work, socialize, create, and share information. As with any hub of information, protection is an ongoing issue. A company may want to consider implementing an intranet or virtual private network to protect sensitive information.

Virtual Networks

virtual network common type of technology infrastructure, which consists of links that are not wired connections.

A **virtual network** is a common type of computer network that consists of links that are not physical connections. Virtual network links are implemented using network virtualization, using mainly wired or wireless connections between two computer devices. On a single hardware platform, virtual networking allows for the consolidation of a set of diverse services and devices. This reduces the cost of maintaining costly hardware and software commonly associated with maintaining separate devices widely scattered across geographic locations. All troubleshooting can be performed on remote machines from a single location.

virtual private networks (VPNs) secure connections between two points on the Internet.

To gain increased security for Internet communications, companies often turn to **virtual private networks (VPNs)**, secure connections between two points on the Internet. These VPNs use firewalls and programs that encapsulate data to make them more secure during transit. Loosely defined, a VPN can include a range of networking technologies, from secure Internet connections to private networks from service providers such as IBM. A VPN is less expensive for a company to use than leasing several of its own lines. It can also take months to install a leased line in some parts of the world, but a new user can be added to a VPN in a day. Because a VPN uses the Internet, it can be wired, wireless, or a combination of the two.

The most-used form of Internet access is **broadband**. With high access speeds, it is offered in four different forms: DSL (or Digital Subscriber Line), fiber-optic, cable, and satellite. Broadband allows for voice and video files to be sent with optimal download and upload speeds.

broadband The most used form of Internet access. With its high access speeds, it is offered in four different forms: DSL (or Digital Subscriber Line), fiber-optic, cable, and satellite.

A broad approach to sharing information in an organization is to establish a company network patterned after the Internet. Such a network is called an **intranet**. Intranets are similar to the Internet, but they limit access to employees or other authorized users. An intranet blocks outsiders without valid passwords from entering its network by incorporating both software and hardware known as a **firewall**. Firewalls limit data transfers to certain locations and log system use so that managers can identify attempts to log on with invalid passwords and other threats to a system's security. Highly sophisticated real-time threat defense alert systems let administrators know about suspicious activities and permit authorized personnel to use smart cards to connect from remote terminals.

intranet computer network that is similar to the Internet but limits access to authorized users.

firewall limits data transfers to certain locations and log system use so that managers can identify attempts to log on with invalid passwords and other threats to a system's security.

Intranets solve the problem of linking different types of computers. Like the Internet, intranets can integrate computers running all kinds of operating systems and some companies are employing a cloud-based intranet solution. In addition, intranets are relatively easy and inexpensive to set up because most businesses already have some of the required hardware and software. All the business's computers will be linked with each other and with the Internet. Microsoft's SharePoint is the dominant software used for creating intranets.[18]

Intranets enable collaboration among employees who are traveling or telecommuting. They can nurture innovation and the development of creative ideas. They can be used to share marketing and brand information worldwide. Mobile intranets—with access from smart phones—are becoming increasingly popular for companies with employees who are often on the go.

Enterprise Computing

Information technology infrastructures have evolved. In the early 1990s, after mainframes, personal computers, and local area networks, **enterprise computing** became the norm when networking standards to integrate different types of networks throughout a company began to take place. As the Internet became widespread after 1995, organizations began using the Internet networking protocol to integrate different types of networks. This called for many different types of hardware to be networked, as discussed in an earlier section, from mainframes to personal computers to smart phones. The result: a seamless data flow between organizations.

enterprise computing many different types of hardware networked together to create a seamless data flow between organizations.

Cloud Computing

Today companies are realizing the revolutionary power of **cloud computing**. **Table 14.3** describes some of its benefits. With cloud computing, powerful servers store applications software and databases for users to access via the web using anything from a PC to a smart phone. Cloud computing provides access to a shared pool of resources, including computers, storage, applications, and services over a network, typically the Internet. As the digital and mobile transformation of data continues, with more information becoming available almost instantaneously from more sources than ever before, cloud computing has helped the traditional company IT department evolve. As cloud services become a way of doing business, exponential growth continues, and data storage will continue to grow accordingly.[19]

cloud computing powerful servers store applications software and databases for users to access via the web using anything from a PC to a smart phone.

The three types of cloud computing include the public cloud, private cloud, and hybrid cloud. *Public clouds* are shared, easily accessible, multicustomer IT infrastructures available to any entity in the general public. The service may be a free service or pay-as-you-go. Companies known for running hyperscale public clouds include well-known technology mainstays MIcrosoft, Amazon, IBM, Salesforce, and SAP.[20] *Private clouds*, referred to as corporate clouds or internal clouds, are IT infrastructures that can be accessed only by a single entity or a group of related entities that share the same purpose and requirements. *Hybrid clouds* are public and private clouds bound together, offering users the benefits of both models—for example, business units of an organization.

Public cloud architecture can be categorized by service model: SaaS (Software as a Service), in which a third-party provider hosts applications and makes them available to customers over the Internet; PaaS (Platform as a Service), in which a third-party provider delivers hardware and software

TABLE 14.3 Benefits of Cloud Computing

Characteristic	Application	Company Benefit
On-demand self-service	A customer can access needed computing resources on demand.	Easy access for all employees, facilitated collaboration, and increased productivity.
Encompasses characteristics of grid computing	Hardware and software components are pooled to create a single IT environment with shared resources for greater efficiency.	Reduced or no software costs (upgrades and patches are avoided).
Encompasses characteristics of utility computing	A service provider makes computing resources and infrastructure management available to a customer as needed. Rather than owning the hardware infrastructure, companies can meet fluctuating demands for computing power.	Lower or no equipment costs; expanded power and capacity.
Utilizes broad network access	The cloud provider's computing services are available over a network, accessed with a web browser, or configured for any computing device.	Ease of accessibility and hardware and software algorithms to help businesses perform complex data analysis.
Pools computing resources	The cloud provider's resources are available to multiple customers and dynamically assigned and reassigned based upon customer demand.	Greater efficiencies with flexible capacity based upon fluctuating demand. Business operations and growth can be expanded when needed.
Occurs on virtual servers	Hundreds of thousands of networked servers have been placed in massive data centers called server farms.	Improved security at an off-site center, along with scheduled backup of data.

Sources: R. Kelly Rainer and Brad Prince, *Introduction to Information Systems*, 7th Edition (Hoboken, NJ: Wiley, 2018); company website, "Why Move to the Cloud? 10 Benefits of Cloud Computing," https://www.salesforce.com/uk/blog, accessed May 18, 2018.

tools—usually those needed for application development—as a service to its users; and IaaS (Infrastructure as a Service), in which a third-party provider offers virtualized computing resources, such as VMs and storage, over the Internet. Of all cloud-based workloads, 60% are Software as a Service, where data resides in the cloud rather than on a user's hard drive or data center.[21]

Application Service Providers

application service provider (ASP) outside supplier that provides both the computers and the application support for managing an information system.

As with other business functions, many companies find that outsourcing at least some of their information technology functions makes sense. Because of the increasing cost and complexity of obtaining and maintaining information systems, many companies hire an **application service provider (ASP)**, an outside supplier that provides both the computers and the application support for managing an information system.

The Future of the Internet

The Internet has changed how we live, how we access information, how we utilize various services such as transportation, and how we are entertained. Consider, too, the infinite learning possibilities, and even the ability to earn an online or advanced degree.

The Internet has democratized information and enabled global communication. As companies like Facebook enter their late adolescence, their overwhelming success and growth in an unregulated space have created challenges. On platforms such as Facebook and Twitter, allegations of Russian impropriety during the 2016 presidential election, for example, have made room for a global dialogue about the power and influence exercised by major social media and Internet giants.[22]

Assessment Check

1. What is a LAN?
2. What is a virtual network?
3. What is cloud computing?

6 Security and Ethical Issues Affecting Information Systems

Numerous security, ethical, and privacy issues affect information systems. As information systems become increasingly important business assets, they also become progressively harder and more expensive to replace. Damage to information systems or theft of data can have disastrous consequences. When computers are connected to a network, a problem at any individual computer can affect the entire network. Three of the major security threats are cybercrime, cyberterrorism, and so-called malware.

Cybercrime

Computers provide efficient ways for employees to share information. But they may also allow people with more malicious intentions to access information. Or they may allow pranksters—who have no motive other than to see whether they can hack into a system—to gain access to private information.

Common cybercrimes involve stealing or altering data in several ways. Employees or outsiders may change or invent data to produce inaccurate or misleading information, modify computer programs to create false information or illegal transactions, or insert viruses. Unauthorized people can access computer systems for their own benefit or knowledge or just to see if they can get in. Other common crimes include illegal Internet downloads, online threats, identity theft, social engineering (conning someone into providing sensitive data, for example), and sophisticated fraud scams.

Individuals, businesses, and government agencies are all vulnerable to computer crime. Computer hackers—unauthorized users—sometimes work alone and sometimes work in groups. Hackers can break into computer systems just to show that they can do it; other times they have more sinister motives. A recent survey reported that although computer crime decreased slightly recently, the majority of such attacks may go undetected because many companies have concentrated on foiling hackers while leaving themselves open to cybercriminals who are developing increasingly sophisticated weapons. Even Apple computers, usually immune to cybercrime, are becoming vulnerable as more and more Mac users store data in the cloud—that is, on the Internet itself—rather than on hard drives. Until now there has been no single uniform system for reporting cybercrime.

Information system administrators implement basic protections against computer crime: They try to prevent access and viewing of data by authorized users. The simplest method of preventing access requires authorized users to enter passwords. The company may also install firewalls, described earlier. To prevent system users from reading sensitive information, the company may use encryption software, which encodes, or scrambles, messages. To read encrypted messages, users must use an electronic key to convert them to regular text. But as fast as software developers invent new and more elaborate protective measures, hackers seem to break through their defenses. Thus, security is an ongoing battle.

Data breaches continue to make the news, and not only are records compromised, but risk and damage can be enormous. Equifax, one of the largest credit bureaus in the United States, fell victim to a data breach that exposed personal information of 147.9 million consumers, which included Social Security numbers, birth dates, and addresses.[23]

As the size of computer hardware becomes smaller, handheld devices in particular become increasingly vulnerable to theft. Find My iPhone was introduced for iOS users to help them locate their device and remotely delete data in the event the device is lost or stolen. Apple updated its operating system to include software with an activation lock to prevent access to confidential information in the event of theft, similar to a kill switch feature.[24]

After the introduction of the kill switch, thefts of smart phones, particularly iPhones, plummeted. The kill switch makes the phones less valuable for resale, and therefore, less desirable to steal. When a phone is lost or stolen, the kill switch is a software lock that can be remotely activated. This erases all of a phone's data, which makes it unable to be reused or reprogrammed. Thefts still remain—and some fraudsters quickly send a spoofed Apple email notifying the victim that their device has been recovered. Desperate to get their device back, the victim unknowingly clicks on a link that requires their iCloud account information.[25]

Phishing Attacks

A *phishing attack* uses deception to acquire sensitive personal information by impersonating an official-looking e-mail or instant message. Typically, attackers may pose as a university, bank, or Internet service provider. Recently, phishing attacks and campaigns have been on the rise. The attacker is typically seeking employee data, including user names and passwords, credit card numbers, and Social Security information.[26]

In one attack on California-based Magnolia Health Corporation, an operator of senior living and rehabilitation facilities, the attacker impersonated its CEO by sending a spoofed e-mail that appeared to look legitimate with the proper name and address scheme. The request was for personal information for employees of four of the company's facilities, and the attacker got away with employee salary and address data and Social Security numbers. E-mails or phone calls that ask users to update account information should be ignored. No personal information should ever be divulged over the phone unless a user initiates the call. E-mails asking users to call a phone number to update information are also suspicious.[27]

Around tax season, the Internal Revenue Service (IRS) reports a four-fold increase in phishing attacks. Official-looking messages "from the IRS" request that taxpayers provide a wide range of sensitive information related to refunds, filing status, personal information, and PIN verifications.[28]

Cyberterrorism

Cyberterrorism can involve deliberate threats to information systems and can be associated with terrorist activities. It is usually accompanied by a large-scale disruption to a computer network. Some refer to cyberterrorism as an attack of an information system by a known terrorist group, with the primary goal of wreaking havoc and creating panic and alarm. Others identify cyberterrorism primarily as a means to achieve personal objectives often related to furthering a political or ideological agenda. This is accomplished through the use of computers, telecommunication infrastructures, networks, and the public Internet.[29]

Examples include using electronic communications or media to make terrorist threats or hacking into computer systems to disrupt banks, utility companies, emergency services, stock exchanges, or air traffic control networks. Another example, referred to as a denial-of-service (DOS) attack, is a network and its intended services that will become unavailable to its users or visitors. A DOS attack occurs when an attacker sends so many requests to a target computer system that the target is unable to handle them and simply crashes. The most powerful distributed denial of service attack recorded to date hit the developer platform GitHub all at once.[30] In a recent survey, 81% of Americans ranked cyberterrorism as a critical threat to the nation. There is no consensus about what cyberterrorism is or how it should be defined, so a set of universal safeguards against cyberterrorism does not yet exist. However, there are preventive measures that can be taken to safeguard data and information.[31]

Computer Viruses

malware any malicious software program designed to infect computer systems.

Viruses, worms, Trojan horses, and spyware, collectively referred to as **malware**, are malicious software programs designed to infect computer systems. These programs can destroy data, steal sensitive information, and even render information systems inoperable. Recently, behind a surge of sketchy online ads to the Internet that tried to trick viewers into installing malicious software was a consortium of 28 fake ad agencies. Malware and data breach attacks cost consumers and businesses billions of dollars annually.[32]

Computer **viruses** are programs that secretly attach themselves to other programs (called *hosts*) and change them or destroy data. Viruses can be programmed to become active immediately or to remain dormant for a period of time, after which the infections suddenly activate themselves and cause problems. A virus can reproduce by copying itself onto other programs stored on the same device. It spreads as users install infected software on their systems or exchange files with others, usually by exchanging e-mail, accessing electronic bulletin boards, trading disks, or downloading programs or data from unknown sources on the Internet.

viruses programs that secretly attach themselves to other programs (called hosts) and change them or destroy data.

A **botnet** is a network of PCs that have been infected with one or more data-stealing viruses. Computer criminals tie the infected computers into a network, often without the owners being aware of it, and sell the botnet on the black market. They or others use the botnet to commit identity theft, sell fake pharmaceuticals, buy blocks of concert tickets for scalping, and attack the Internet itself. Each year, financial institutions across more than a hundred countries are targeted by cybercriminals using banking botnets. As the banking industry continues to push customers to mobile banking and payment services, attacks on mobile banking platforms remain a prime target as cybercriminals take advantage of a lack of protection on mobile devices.[33]

botnet a network of PCs that have been infected with one or more data-stealing viruses.

A **Trojan horse** is a program that claims to do one thing but in reality does something else, usually something malicious. For example, a Trojan horse might claim, and even appear, to be a game. When an unsuspecting user clicks on the Trojan horse to launch it, the program might erase the hard drive or steal any personal data stored on the computer.

Trojan horse program that claims to do one thing but in reality does something else, usually something malicious.

Spyware is software that secretly gathers user information through the user's Internet connection without his or her knowledge, usually for advertising purposes. Spyware applications are typically bundled with other programs downloaded from the Internet. Once installed, the spyware monitors user activity on the Internet and transmits that information in the background to someone else.

spyware software that secretly gathers user information through the user's Internet connection without his or her knowledge, usually for advertising purposes.

As viruses, botnets, and Trojan horses become more complex, the technology to fight them must become more sophisticated as well. The simplest way to protect against computer viruses is to install one of the many available antivirus software programs, such as Norton AntiVirus and McAfee VirusScan.

But management must begin to emphasize security at a deeper level: during software design, in corporate servers, at web gateways, and through Internet service providers. Because the vast majority of the world's computers run on Microsoft operating systems, a single virus, worm, or Trojan horse can spread among them quickly. Individual computer users should carefully choose the files they load onto their systems, scan their systems regularly, make sure their antivirus software is up to date, and install software only from known sources. They should also be very careful when opening attachments to e-mails because many viruses are spread that way.

Information Systems and Ethics

The scope and power of today's information systems not surprisingly raise a number of ethical issues and concerns. These affect both employees and organizations. For instance, it is not uncommon for organizations to have specific ethical standards and policies regarding the use of information systems by employees and vendors. These standards include obligations to protect system security and the privacy and confidentiality of data. Policies also may cover the personal use of computers and related technologies, both hardware and software, by employees.

Ethical issues also involve organizational use of information systems. Organizations have an obligation to protect the privacy and confidentiality of data about employees and customers. Employment records contain sensitive personal information, such as bank account numbers, which, if not protected, could lead to identity theft.

Another ethical issue involves tracking people without their consent, usually through electronic surveillance. There are no laws regulating electronic surveillance in the private sector

Judgment Call

The Ethics of Employee Monitoring

In a Florida hospital, 300 nurses and patient care technicians are monitored by way of an electronic sensor embedded in a required wearable badge. During a shift, in much the same way that a GPS system tracks a car, employees and their whereabouts are monitored. With real-time location data, information can reveal, for example, how many times per shift an employee visits (or doesn't visit) patient rooms. As companies increasingly use technology to assess and analyze employee performance, equally at stake is the potential to compromise trust between employees and employer.

While not entirely used for tracking frequency of patient visits, the sequence of data reveals other important information used by the hospital. For example, workers appeared to take multiple trips during a shift to get medication refills, which revealed the supply of medication was running low more frequently. This information triggered a redesign of supply and medication stocking procedures.

Security badges and fingerprint scanners track hours worked, while video, GPS, and cameras record employee activities. In today's big data environment, employees are being tracked in other ways, too—by the keystrokes they use on computers, websites visited during work, frequency and types of e-mails sent, and instant messaging. Under federal law, employers have the legal right to monitor employees by placing a camera in public work areas. However, in areas like restrooms or public eating areas, cameras and recorders are not allowed when people might be engaged in private conversations.

It is recommended that companies communicate about all monitoring activities—and get written confirmation and consent from employees. As companies continue to increase their use of technology for assessing and analyzing employee performance, will monitoring produce the very behaviors it was designed to prevent?

Questions for Critical Thinking

1. By tracking employees to potentially improve productivity or spot lapses, engagement and employee trust can be compromised, which can result in poor morale. If you had to decide for a company whether to use employee surveillance, what factors would you take into consideration?
2. Employee monitoring often collects work-related activities, but it can also collect an employee's personal information not linked to their work. How would you manage employees who want to maintain their privacy against an employer who wants to ensure that company resources aren't being misused?

Sources: Lee Michael Katz, "Monitoring Employee Productivity: Proceed with Caution," *Society for Human Resource Management*, http://www.shrm.org, accessed May 21, 2018; Clayton Jones, "Hasty Employee Surveillance Can Doom Your Case," *Society for Human Resource Management*, http://www.shrm.org, accessed May 21, 2018; Ben DiPietro, "Employers Turn to Surveillance to Curb Employee Risk," *Wall Street Journal*, http://www.wsj.com, accessed May 21, 2018; Kirstie S. Ball, "The Harms of Electronic Surveillance in the Workplace," *PEN America Center*, http://www.pen.org, accessed May 21, 2018.

workplace. This issue is discussed in greater detail in the "Judgment Call" feature. In the workplace, electronic surveillance remains an issue because the law generally gives employers the right to read and own anything work-related and all employee Internet use in the workplace. Most employers routinely monitor employees' Internet usage and patterns.[34] Enforcing privacy regulations can be difficult due to rapid advances in information technology, which have made it easier to collect and store information about individuals. Surveillance cameras on toll roads, credit card transactions, phone calls on a mobile device, banking transactions, and even search engine queries create a digital profile of individual consumers.[35]

A larger debate over how much users can trust Facebook with their data surfaced when the company recently exposed data on up to 87 million of its users to a researcher who worked at Cambridge Analytica, a political consulting firm hired by the Trump campaign. Facebook allowed a third-party developer to engineer an application for the sole purpose of gathering data—and the developer was able to exploit a loophole to gather information on not only people who used the app but all their friends—without them knowing. Another issue, *net neutrality*, revolves around the principle that Internet service providers treat all data and Internet traffic equally—with access to apps and content regardless of the source. A well-known example of violation of net neutrality occurred when Verizon Wireless was accused of "throttling" (slowing of upload speeds) after users noticed that Netflix and YouTube videos were slower than usual.[36]

Assessment Check

1. Explain cybercrime, computer hacking, and cyberterrorism.
2. What is malware, and how does a computer virus work?
3. What are the ethical issues with the use of information technology?

7 Disaster Recovery and Backup

Natural disasters, power failures, equipment malfunctions, software glitches, human error, and terrorist attacks can disrupt even the most sophisticated computer information systems. These problems can cost businesses and other organizations billions of dollars. Even more serious consequences can occur.

FalconStor, a global company headquartered in Melville, New York, provides data backup applications and sophisticated disaster recovery solutions for businesses. The company's services go way beyond simply replicating data because organizations that have suffered a major loss have needs well beyond replicating their data. FalconStor's software solutions permit them to access their applications, restart operations, and return to serving customers.[37]

Disaster recovery planning—deciding how to prevent system failures and continue operations if computer systems fail—is a critical function of all organizations. Disaster prevention programs can avoid some of these costly problems. The most basic precaution is routinely backing up software and data—at the organizational and individual levels. However, the organization's data center cannot be the sole repository of critical data because a single location is vulnerable to threats from both natural and human-caused disasters. Consequently, off-site or cloud data backup is a necessity, whether in a separate physical location or online. Companies that perform online backups store the encrypted data in secure facilities that in turn have their own backups. Cloud computing services can actually be more environmentally friendly, as discussed in the "Clean & Green Business" feature.

According to security experts, there are five important considerations for off-site data storage. First is planning. The organization needs to decide what data need to be protected. Priority should be given to data having severe legal or business consequences should they be lost. Second, a backup schedule must be established and adhered to closely. Third, when data are

Clean & Green Business

IBM Helps Customers Build a Green Infrastructure

You may not immediately associate cloud computing and data center strategies with energy efficiency. As the demand for cloud services continues to increase, so does energy consumption, which can translate to increased carbon emissions. While many cloud providers might not put environmental responsibility at the top of their list, IBM does.

With close to 380,000 employees, IBM markets computer hardware and software and also offers infrastructure, hosting, cloud computing, and consulting services. IBM has green IT policies and takes energy-saving servers, cooling racks, and eco-friendly systems and data center needs seriously. The company helps clients focus on energy efficiency by evaluating energy needs and gaining insight into energy usage across a company's IT environment.

As companies move their systems to the cloud for cost savings and flexibility, it is also a much more environmentally friendly choice when compared to running servers in a business location. Research suggests that moving to the cloud can actually save a large enterprise the equivalent of 6,000 cars on the road each year, or 30,000 metric tons of CO_2 within five years.

IBM offers its clients a green approach to building infrastructure and network-connected properties and assets. Offering data center strategies, design, building, and relocation services, IBM helps clients realize the reality of a green data center. This not only helps a company reduce costs, but it also allows for legal and regulatory requirements to be met.

By implementing green strategies, a data center can meet growing data volume and increased processing demands while managing rising resource costs. To avoid higher operating costs, IBM helps companies manage physical space and power and cooling capacity while making sure business decisions take the environment into consideration.

Questions for Critical Thinking

1. **What other benefits might a company realize by implementing green strategies and IT policies?**
2. **Discuss the types of customers who might be an ideal fit for IBM's green IT policies.**

Sources: Company website, "A Smart Systems Approach to Green IT," https://www.ibm.com, accessed May 21, 2018; company website, "Go Green or Go Home: Green Cloud Computing Guide for Service Providers," http://searchtelecom.techtarget.com, accessed May 21, 2018; Phil Bickerton, "Is Cloud Computing a More Environmentally Friendly Choice?" *Saxons Blog*, http://www.saxonsgroup.com.au, accessed May 21, 2018; Martin Ceron, "A Green IT Approach to Data Center Efficiency," http://www.redbooks.ibm.com, accessed May 21, 2018; Alex Barinka, "IBM Employee Count Falls for Second Year in Shift to Cloud," *Bloomberg Business*, http://www.bloomberg.com, accessed May 21, 2018.

transmitted off site, they must be protected by the highest level of security possible. Fourth, care should be taken in selecting the right security vendor. There are dozens of vendors offering different services and having different areas of expertise. Finally, the backup system should be continually tested and evaluated.

Assessment Check

1. What are the types of disasters to which information systems are vulnerable?
2. List the five considerations for off-site data storage.

8 Information Technology Trends

Today, digital reality, robotics, cognitive, and blockchain are redefining information technology, business, and society at large—and revolutionary growth is being created across businesses and industries. The leaders in the next industrial revolution are the very companies making advances in these fields. A recent report by Accenture about the trends driving the future of technology highlights the following topics: artificial intelligence and machine learning, Internet of Things (IoT) and the blockchain revolution, and augmented and virtual reality. As people use products and services, information and access is being fed back to companies allowing them to create deeper connections by providing further insights and deeper connections into people's lives. Businesses are becoming more personal in the way they engage with customers.[38] **Table 14.4** lists a number of additional disruptive technologies and trends.

Artificial Intelligence (AI) and Machine Learning (ML) have seen considerable advancement. AI involves machines that can perform tasks characteristic of human intelligence—things like planning, understanding language, recognizing objects and sounds, learning, and problem solving. At its core, machine learning is simply a way of achieving AI. "Training" involves feeding huge amounts of data to the algorithm and allowing the algorithm to adjust itself and improve. For example, machine learning has been used to make drastic improvements to computer vision (the ability of a machine to recognize an object in an image or video). You gather hundreds of thousands or even millions of pictures and then have humans tag them. For example, the humans might tag pictures that have a car in them versus those that do not. Then, the algorithm tries to build a model that can accurately tag a picture as containing a car or not as well as a human. Once the accuracy level is high enough, the machine has now "learned" what a car looks like. AI is making strides in industries ranging from real estate to law, and more recently, hospitality. Hotels are activating chatbots to create concierges that can assist guests with restaurant recommendations or tomorrow's weather. Hotel guests can access chatbot concierge services from their mobile phones. AI will show its presence in new startups ranging from automotive to finance to healthcare. In the near future, as artificial intelligence and cognitive technologies gain traction, human workers and machines will work together, and organizations will develop strategies to recruit, manage, and train this new hybrid human–machine workforce where technology augments human performance.[39]

Internet of Things a webconnected ecosystem of everyday objects with network connectivity, including TVs, cars, household appliances, and wearable tech devices.

The Internet of Everything or the **Internet of Things (IoT)** refers to a move beyond standalone devices and toward an entire Internet-connected ecosystem of everyday items such as TVs, cars, household appliances, and wearable tech devices. With big data and analytics, algorithms in the software used by smart devices monitor and record how they are used to build a profile that allows them to intelligently set themselves. With IoT, factories are seeing reductions in equipment downtime, process waste, and energy consumption. Imagine a diabetic with a blood glucose monitor that connects to a phone that sends the information to their primary physician, who records that ping to an online portal to better manage levels and the impact on that individual's healthcare experience. For more on this subject, see the "Business & Technology" feature, which describes the value of IoT data.

TABLE 14.4 Disruptive Technologies and Trends

Disruptive Technology or Trend	Explanation/Example
Artificial Intelligence (AI) for Services	As more guests demand an always-on and personalized concierge service, hotels are activating concierge chatbots that can help with any request in a timely manner.
Chatbots	Using AI, chatbots will understand tone, content, and conversational paths to perform customer care activities, often improving the customer experience.
Virtual Reality	Creates a fully rendered digital environment (with body and motion tracking capabilities) that replaces a user's real-world environment.
Augmented Reality	A direct or indirect live view of a physical, real-world environment whose elements are "augmented" by computer-generated graphics, sounds, and touch feedback—for an enhanced user experience.
Blockchain	Blockchain creates a digital record across hundreds or thousands of computers, reducing the risk of hacking. Blockchain solutions from different companies or industries will be able to communicate and share digital assets within a blockchain ecosystem.
Video	Researchers at MIT found that at the top of the list of what makes a great employee experience is video, which leads to innovation, improved collaboration, and productivity.
Internet of Things (IoT)	IoT refers to a move beyond stand-alone devices and an entire Internet-connected ecosystem of everyday items such as TVs, cars, household appliances, and wearable tech devices.
Voice Control Virtual Assistants	Assistants help increase productivity and improve work–life balance. Longer term, they may replace computer screens and keyboards.
Immersive Experiences	Immersive experiences are changing how people connect with one another, information, and experiences. Companies will design user experiences for immersive environments to promote their brands and products.
Smart Manufacturing (3D Printing)	Industrial 3D printing for prototypes and parts created on demand is on the rise.
Robots and Automation	Human employees are embracing their future robot colleagues, but fear the loss of human connection in the workplace.
Enterprise Data Sovereignty	With more data than ever before from a wider variety of sources including transactional systems, industrial machinery, social media, IoT sensors and images, video, audio, and the deep web, decisions are being informed and future paths charted.

Sources: Anthony Abbatiello, Tim Boehm, Jeff Schwartz, and Sharon Chand, "No-Collar Workforce: Humans and Machines in One Loop—Collaborating in Roles and New Talent Models," *Tech Trends 2018*, https://www2.deloitte.com, accessed May 22, 2018; Alison DeNisco Rayome, "Less Than Half of Employees Optimistic About AI, Robots in the Workplace," *TechRepublic*, http://www.techrepublic.com, accessed May 23, 2018; Paul Helzel, "12 Technologies That Will Disrupt Business in 2018," *CIO*, http://www.cio.com, accessed May 22, 2018; Eric Piscini, Darshini Dalal, David Mapgaonkar, and Prakash Santhana, "Blockchain to Blockchains: Broad Adoption and Integration Enter the Realm of the Possible Tech Trends 2018," https://www2.deloitte.com, accessed May 22, 2018; Jay Samit, "4 Technology Trends That Will Transform Our World in 2018," *Fortune*, http://www.fortune.com, accessed May 23, 2018; Paul Daugherty, Marc Carrel-Billiard, and Michael Biltz, "Intelligent Enterprise Unleashed: Five Technology Trends Shaping the Future of Business," *Accenture*, https://www.accenture.com, accessed May 22, 2018; Kasey Panetta, "Gartner Top 10 Strategic Technology Trends for 2018," http://www.cio.com, accessed May 22, 2018.

The Internet of Things (IoT) and the blockchain revolution see an increase in the use of mobile devices like smartphones to manage smart gadgets and interconnected devices like smart doors, smart locks, and smart cars. The data explosion that automatically comes with IoT will make 5G imperative for mobile service providers. Blockchains will see their value grow beyond their use in cryptocurrency and digital currency. As data is stored across a decentralized network of millions of computers, the influence of blockchain will expand and transform the Internet of Things—and hopefully, reduce the risk of data hacking.[40]

Augmented Reality (AR), Virtual Reality (VR), and mixed reality, which combines the two, will be used by 20% of all businesses to create immersive experiences with the help of head-mounted displays. Virtual and augmented reality technologies are removing the distance to people, information, and experiences, transforming the ways people live and work. For example, General Electric is equipping field technicians with cutting-edge augmented reality glasses, changing the way workers engage with the physical world by giving them hands-free access to information, or allowing remote experts to see exactly what the technicians see as they repair wind turbines.[41]

Business & Technology

Internet of Things Provides Insight

As the Internet of Things (IoT) ecosystem continues to grow with communicating sensors and digital smarts, so will devices, connectivity, and IT services. Connected devices are projected to triple from 8 billion today to almost 20 billion in 2020. Processing and analyzing the data in real time will hold the answers for many companies. Here are a few examples of the value extracted from the massive amounts of data made available from connected devices such as refrigerators, cars, thermostats—and even farm tractors.

In agriculture, when sensors are placed on plants and farm equipment, the benefit is higher productivity and more efficient use of water, land, and fertilizer. Add satellite images and weather tracking, and no longer is a farmer kicking the dirt and making decisions based upon intuition rather than data.

In the heating and air conditioning industry, Nest, a thermostat company owned by Google, learns a user's habits about heating and cooling usage to help optimize scheduling and power usage. In addition, thermostat companies use data from the IoT, which tracks weather information and statistics. Ultimately, this results in saving both consumers and businesses time and money.

In the next few years, 90% of automakers will be using IoT solutions that help to securely deliver data generated from cars directly to the cloud for real-time analysis. The benefit of IoT data could give automakers insights about product usage, which could lead to improved information for drivers about vehicle maintenance, engine trouble diagnostics, the most efficient travel routes, and even the nearest parking spaces.

The explosion of IoT data has spurred a number of start-ups focusing on software and online services to reap value from the massive amounts of information made available from connected devices. To help companies make sense of all the data in real time, Salesforce, a cloud computing company, recently introduced a service called the "IoT Cloud," which will allow customers to monitor "billions of events relayed daily by smart devices."

To orchestrate the interactions between devices with sensors, customers are able to set rules that trigger actions for a variety of purposes, including early detection and information. So, the next time you run out of milk, your "smart" refrigerator identifies you have no milk, contacts the closest supermarket, and orders the quantity you need. Then a message is sent to your phone. Is that smart, or what? Call it the Internet of Things.

Questions for Critical Thinking

1. **Having more information helps make better decisions, but where does a company draw the line between good decision making and managing too much information?**
2. **Our lives are increasingly controlled by technology, as demonstrated by the Internet of Things. How much of our daily lives should we be willing to hand over to technology?**

Sources: Don Clark, "Companies See Market in Managing 'Internet of Things,'" *Wall Street Journal*, http://www.wsj.com, accessed May 18, 2018; Steven Norton, "Internet of Things Market to Reach $1.7 Trillion by 2020: IDC," *Wall Street Journal*, http://www.wsj.com, accessed May 18, 2018; Michael Kirby Smith and Ben Laffin, "Bushels and Bytes: The Data Driven Farm," *New York Times*, http://bits.blogs.nytimes.com, accessed May 18, 2018; Steve Lohr, "The Internet of Things and the Future of Farming," *New York Times*, http://bits.blogs.nytimes.com, accessed May 18, 2018; company website, "IBM Helps Automakers Build Internet of Things Connected Vehicles," http://www-03.ibm.com, accessed May 18, 2018; Liam Tung, "IoT Devices will outnumber the world's population this year for the first time," *ZDNet*, accessed May 23, 2018, https://www.zdnet.com/.

Assessment Check

1. What are a few information technology trends?
2. Explain the rising trend of mobility.
3. What is the Internet of Things?

What's Ahead

This is the first of two chapters devoted to managing technology and information. The next chapter, "Understanding Accounting and Financial Statements," focuses on accounting, financial information, and financing reporting. Accounting is the process of measuring, interpreting, and communicating financial information to enable people inside and outside the firm to make informed decisions. The chapter describes the functions of accounting and role of accountants; the steps in the accounting cycle; the types, functions, and components of financial statements; and the role of budgets in an organization.

Chapter in Review

Summary of Learning Objectives

LEARNING OBJECTIVE 1 Outline the ways technology has forever changed business.

Today, every business is a technology business, and the development of technology over the last few decades has been the impetus for powerful and less-expensive growth options for companies. As technology and business have become increasingly interwoven, technology has forever changed the face of many businesses and industries, including music, entertainment, transportation, automobiles, healthcare, hospitality, and retail.

Assessment Check Answers

1.1 **How has the smart phone impacted business?** The smart phone is a game-changing technological innovation. On a global basis and at lightning speed, the smart phone has contributed to an increased flow of ideas and improved knowledge exchange, resulting in growth and productivity for both businesses and the global economy.

1.2 **What is disruptive innovation?** Disruptive innovation refers to a theory that describes the impact an innovation has when a new market and value are created that "disrupt" an existing market and its value. Disruptive innovations are less expensive and simpler versions of existing products and services that target entirely new customers, many times replacing industry leaders. Examples include smart phones replacing personal computers, downloadable digital media replacing CDs and DVDs, Wikipedia and other online sources replacing traditional print encyclopedias, and retail medical clinics replacing traditional doctors' offices.

LEARNING OBJECTIVE 2 Distinguish between data and information and discuss information systems and the role of big data.

It is important for businesspeople to know the difference between data and information. Data are raw facts and figures that may or may not be relevant to a business decision. Information is knowledge gained from processing those facts and figures. An information system is an organized method for collecting, storing, and communicating past, present, and projected information on internal operations and external intelligence. Most information systems today use computer and telecommunications technology. The massive amounts of data available to companies today, referred to as big data, continue to grow. When captured, formatted, manipulated, stored, analyzed, and evaluated, big data can lead a company to see trends, providing greater insight to make better, more informed decisions.

Assessment Check Answers

2.1 **Distinguish between data and information.** Data consist of raw facts and figures that may or may not be relevant to a decision. Information is the knowledge gained from those facts and figures.

2.2 **What is an information system?** An information system is an organized method for collecting, storing, and communicating past, present, and projected information on internal operations and external intelligence.

2.3 **What is big data?** Big data can be defined as the massive amounts of data available to companies today, which is available in a structured or unstructured format. Big data changes on an ongoing basis, due mainly to the many sources from which it originates, including social media, mobile devices, online sales, and customer service feedback. Big data can lead a company to see trends, providing greater insight to make better, more informed decisions.

LEARNING OBJECTIVE 3 List the components and types of information systems.

Computer-based information systems rely on four components: computer hardware, computer software, a network, and a database. The heart of an information system is its database, a centralized, integrated collection of data resources. Information systems fall into two broad categories: operational support systems and management support systems. Operational support systems are designed to produce a variety of information for users. Examples include transaction processing systems and process control systems. Management support systems are those designed to support effective decision making. They include management information systems, decision support systems, executive support systems, and expert systems.

Assessment Check Answers

3.1 **List the four components of a computer-based information system.** The four components of a computer-based information system are computer hardware, computer software, a network, and a database.

3.2 **What is a database?** A database is a centralized, integrated collection of data resources.

3.3 **What are the two general types of information systems? Give examples of each.** The two categories of information systems are operational support systems (such as transactions processing and process control systems) and management support systems (such as management information, decision support, executive support, and expert systems). Some information systems support parts of an organization, others support entire organizations, and some support groups of organizations.

LEARNING OBJECTIVE 4 Discuss computer hardware and software.

Hardware consists of all tangible elements of a computer system, including input and output devices. Major categories of computers include mainframes, supercomputers, midrange systems, personal computers (PCs), and handheld devices. Computer software provides the instructions that tell the hardware what to do. The software that controls the basic workings of the computer is its operating system. Other programs, called application software, perform specific tasks that users want to complete.

Assessment Check Answers

4.1 List two input and output devices. Input devices include the keyboard and mouse. Output devices include the monitor and printer.

4.2 What accounts for the popularity of laptop and notebook computers? The popularity of these devices can be explained by smaller, lighter, more powerful computing, and by the improved displays, faster processing speeds, and ability to handle more intense graphics, larger storage capacities, and more durable designs.

4.3 What is software? List the two categories of software. Computer software provides the instructions that tell the hardware what to do. The software that controls the basic workings of the computer is its operating system. Other programs, called application software, perform specific tasks that users want to complete.

LEARNING OBJECTIVE 5 Describe computer networks, cloud computing, and the future of the Internet.

Local area networks connect computers within a limited area. Wide area networks tie together larger geographical regions by using telephone lines, microwave, or satellite transmission. A wireless network allows computers to communicate through radio waves. A virtual network is a common type of computer network that consists of links that are not physical connections. Virtual private networks (VPNs) provide a secure Internet connection between two or more points. Intranets allow employees to share information on a ready-made company network. Access to an intranet is restricted to authorized users and is protected by a firewall. Cloud computing involves powerful servers that store applications software and databases for users to access via the web using anything from a PC to a smart phone. The Internet has changed how we live, how we access information, how we utilize various services, and how we are entertained. It is predicted that soon everyone around the world will have Internet access, with usage currently at 88% of the global population.

Assessment Check Answers

5.1 What is a LAN? A local area network (LAN) is a computer network that connects machines within a limited area, such as a building or several nearby buildings.

5.2 What is a virtual network? A virtual network is a common type of computer network that partly or in whole consists of virtual network links that are not physical connections.

5.3 What is cloud computing? Cloud computing involves powerful servers that store applications software and databases for users to access via the web using anything from a PC to a smart phone.

LEARNING OBJECTIVE 6 Outline the security and ethical issues affecting information systems.

Numerous security and ethical issues affect information systems. Main security threats are cybercrime, cyberterrorism, and malware. Cybercrimes range from hacking—unauthorized penetration of an information system—to the theft of hardware. Cyberterrorism can involve deliberate threats to information systems and can be associated with terrorist activities. Malware is any malicious software program designed to infect computer systems. Examples include viruses, botnets, Trojan horses, and spyware. Ethical issues affecting information systems include the proper use of the systems by authorized users. Organizations also have an obligation to employees, vendors, and customers to protect the security and confidentiality of the data stored in information systems.

Assessment Check Answers

6.1 Explain cybercrime, computer hacking, and cyberterrorism. Cybercrime is stealing or altering data in several ways. Computer hacking is a breach of a computer system by unauthorized users. Sometimes the hackers' motive is just to see if they can get in. Other times, hackers have more sinister motives, including stealing or altering data. Cyberterrorism, a new generation of terrorism, can involve deliberate threats to information systems and can be associated with terrorist activities.

6.2 What is malware, and how does a computer virus work? Malware is any malicious software program designed to infect computer systems. A virus is a computer program that secretly attaches itself to another program (called a host). The virus then changes the host, destroys data, or even makes the computer system inoperable.

6.3 What are the ethical issues with the use of information technology? It is not uncommon for organizations to have specific ethical standards and policies regarding the use of information systems by employees and vendors. Ethical issues also involve organizational use of information systems to protect the privacy and confidentiality of employee and customer data and records. Another ethical issue is the use of computer technology to monitor employees while they are working.

LEARNING OBJECTIVE 7 Explain disaster recovery and backup systems.

Information system disasters, whether caused by humans or natural disasters, can cost businesses billions of dollars. The consequences of a disaster can be minimized by routinely backing up software and data, both at an organizational level and at an individual level. Organizations should back up critical data at an off-site location. Some firms may also want to invest in extra hardware and software sites, which can be accessed during emergencies.

Assessment Check Answers

7.1 What are the types of disasters to which information systems are vulnerable? Natural disasters, power failures, equipment malfunctions, software glitches, human error, and even terrorist attacks can disrupt even the most powerful, sophisticated computer information systems.

7.2 List the five considerations for off-site data storage. The five considerations are planning and deciding which data to back up, establishing and following a backup schedule, protecting data when they are transmitted off site, selecting the right security vendor, and continually testing and evaluating the backup system.

LEARNING OBJECTIVE 8 Discuss information technology trends.

Today, digital reality, robotics, cognitive, and blockchain are redefining information technology, business, and society at large—and revolutionary growth is being created across businesses and industries.

The leaders in the next industrial revolution are the very companies making advances in these fields. A recent report by Accenture about the trends driving the future of technology highlights the following topics: artificial intelligence and machine learning, Internet of Things (IoT) and the blockchain revolution, and augmented and virtual reality.

Assessment Check Answers

8.1 **What Is Artificial Intelligence and Machine Learning?** Artificial Intelligence (AI) and Machine Learning (ML) have seen considerable advancement. AI involves machines that can perform tasks characteristic of human intelligence—things like planning, understanding language, recognizing objects and sounds, learning, and problem solving. Machine learning is simply a way of achieving AI by "training" an algorithm so that the algorithm can "learn how." "Training" involves feeding huge amounts of data to the algorithm and allowing the algorithm to adjust itself and improve.

8.2 **Explain the Internet of Things (IoT) and Blockchain.** The Internet of Everything or the Internet of Things (IoT) refers to a move beyond stand-alone devices and toward an entire Internet-connected ecosystem of everyday items such as TVs, cars, household appliances, and wearable tech devices. Blockchains will see their value grow beyond their use in cryptocurrency and digital currency. As data is stored across a decentralized network of millions of computers, the influence of blockchain will expand and transform the Internet of Things—and hopefully, reduce the risk of data hacking.

8.3 **What is Augmented and Virtual Reality?** *Augmented Reality (AR), Virtual Reality (VR)*, and mixed reality, which combines the two, will be used by 20% of all businesses to create immersive experiences with the help of head-mounted displays. Virtual and augmented reality technologies are removing the distance to people, information, and experiences, transforming the ways people live and work.

Business Terms You Need to Know

Review Questions

1. Distinguish between data and information. Why is the distinction important to businesspeople in their management of information?
2. What are the four components of an information system?
3. Describe the two different types of information systems, and give an example of how each might help a particular business.
4. Explain decision support systems, executive support systems, and expert systems.
5. What are the major categories of computers? What is a smart phone?
6. What is an intranet? Give specific examples of benefits for companies that set up their own intranets.
7. What steps can organizations and individuals take to prevent cybercrime?
8. How does a computer virus work? What can individuals and organizational computer users do to reduce the likelihood of acquiring a computer virus?
9. Why is disaster recovery important for businesses? Relate your answer to a natural disaster such as a hurricane, tornado, or fire.
10. Describe three information technology trends.

Projects and Teamwork Applications

1. Suppose you've been hired to design an information system for a midsize retailer. Describe what that information system might look like, including the necessary components. Would the system be an operational support system, a management support system, or both?
2. Think about your relationship with technology. Has technology been a time-saver, or have its benefits made your work and personal life even more stressful? Do you have extra time as a result of using technology? Discuss the ways technology is supposed to save time and create efficiencies.

3. Some individuals choose piracy—a form of unauthorized duplication and/or distribution of music, software, art, or other copyrighted material, which includes downloading and file sharing. Some argue that piracy does not affect a product maker's revenues because pirates might actually help promote the product they steal by the buzz they generate. Furthermore copying or downloading a product does not present a financial loss to the product maker because the pirate would probably not buy the product in the first place. Working with a partner, discuss both sides of the piracy issue.

4. A number of different storage options are available for students, including Google, Dropbox, and the steadfast USB flash drive. Take a poll among students to determine which storage options they prefer. What are the benefits of each, and why have students chosen each option? Do some utilize more than one?

5. Has your computer ever been hacked or attacked by a virus? What steps did you take to recover lost files and data? What steps have you taken to prevent something similar from happening again?

Web Assignments

1. **Enterprise resource planning (ERP).** SAP is one of the world's largest enterprise resource planning software companies. Go to the company's website (http://www.sap.com) and click on "About," then "Find a Testimonial." Choose one of the customers listed and read its testimonial. Prepare a brief summary and explain how this exercise improved your understanding of the business applications of ERP software.

2. Go online to research the world's largest technology companies. List the top 10 by recent revenues and discuss the primary business for each. How many are associated with hardware, software, telecom, e-commerce, or the Internet? Do the results surprise you? Why or why not?

3. **Cloud computing.** IBM is one of the largest providers of so-called cloud computing. Visit the IBM website (http://www.ibm.com) and click on "products" and then "cloud." Print out the material and bring it to class to participate in a class discussion on the subject.

Note: Internet web addresses change frequently. If you don't find the exact sites listed, you may need to access the organization's home page and search from there or use a search engine such as Google or Bing.

Cases

Case 14.1 Khan Academy: Distributing Knowledge

A little over a decade ago, while attempting to help his cousin Nadia with math, Salman "Sal" Khan stumbled upon the idea to upload a few tutorials onto YouTube for a more interactive learning experience. This was the beginning of Khan's free online education delivery system. Known globally as Khan Academy, this nonprofit organization's mission is to provide a world-class education for anyone, anywhere. Khan Academy has more than 10 million users per month, including students, teachers, and parents.

With over 9,000 10-minute "micro-lectures" to date, subjects include math, finance, physics, history, biology, astronomy, economics, and computer science. Khan controls the online instruction and creates the videos and their content. More than $20 million in funding has been provided by technology philanthropists and their foundations, including Bill and Melinda Gates, Netflix's Reed Hastings, and Google. Khan's goal of access to secondary education for everyone has been accomplished globally and locally. In remote rural areas, learning opportunities have been made available through the distribution of tablet devices. Offline versions of Khan's lectures have been distributed to rural areas in Asia, Latin America, and Africa.

In an effort to help low-income families, Khan Academy has leveled the field for college admissions. In a partnership with the College Board and Law School Admission Council, Khan Academy will bring free SAT, ACT, and LSAT (Law School Admissions Test) test prep software to the masses. More recently, Khan Academy created a collaboration with Disney & Pixar Animation Studios to launch Pixar in a Box, whose goal is to teach the public about techniques used to create Pixar animated films and to apply academic theory learned in the classroom to the making of these films. For example, one topic covers how Pixar's images are painted using simultaneous math equations.

Khan's initial intention to help his cousin with math has sparked a worldwide learning revolution. As Sal Khan continues to produce more homemade videos, he is, according to Bill Gates, "my favorite teacher and 'educator to the world.'"

Questions for Critical Thinking

1. Sal Khan's free lectures demonstrate technology's ability to eliminate economic barriers that can prevent educational opportunities. Discuss additional ways Khan Academy creates a more level playing field for access to education, including college test preparation, for the masses.
2. Some teachers using Khan Academy have changed the way their class works. Lectures have been replaced with Khan's videos, which students can watch at home. In class, the focus is on problem solving and discussion. Compare and contrast the merits of a traditional face-to-face approach to teaching with teaching methods using Khan Academy materials. What are the benefits of each?

Sources: Company website, "About" and "Pixar in a Box," http://khanacademy.org, accessed May 18, 2018; Peter High, "Salman Khan, the Most Influential Person in Education Technology," *Forbes*, http://www.forbes.com, accessed May 18, 2018; Brit Cruise, "Pixar in a Box: The Math Behind the Movies," https://www.khanacademy.org, accessed May 18, 2018; Gregory Ferenstein, "Khan Academy Gets Rare Partnership to Close Wealth Gap in College Test Prep," *TechCrunch*, http://techcrunch.com, accessed May 18, 2018; "Khan Academy: The Future of Education?" *CBS News*, http://www.cbsnews.com, accessed May 18, 2018; Robert Montenegro, "Pixar and Khan Academy Join Forces for a Super Cool Learning Collaboration," *BigThink*, http://bigthink.com, accessed May 18, 2018; Stephanie Frances Ward, "Free LSAT Prep, from Khan Academy and the LSAC, Coming in June," *ABA Journal*, www.abajournal.com, accessed May 19, 2018.

Case 14.2 Digital Reality: Multisensory Product Delivery

Over the next decade, one of the hottest trends will be digital reality—a blending of augmented reality (AR), virtual reality (VR), mixed reality, 360°, and immersive technologies. Augmented reality overlays digitally created content into the user's real-world environment while virtual reality creates a fully rendered digital environment (with body and motion tracking capabilities) that replaces a user's real-world environment. Mixed reality blends the user's real-world environment and digitally created content in a way that allows both environments to coexist. The result is an immersive or deeply engaging, multisensory delivery of a digital experience—commonly found in gaming and entertainment.

Across retail, travel, hospitality, leisure, and real estate, companies are using digital reality to bring potential customers closer to their products, service, and experiences. The real estate industry has been transformed by virtual reality—by allowing prospective purchasers to visit a property by attaching a VR headset to your smart phone without attending an open house. This bodes well for properties still under construction. A new condo or office space can begin sales by way of interactive 3-D walk-throughs—and buyers have the ability to personalize the space with their own furniture and touches.

To promote their Outdoor Terex Collection, Adidas created a VR experience allowing users to step into their shoes and take on the granite mountain by following two accomplished climbers through their ascent of the Bavellas mountain range in Corsica. Digital reality will create many more adventures for those of us ready to make the trek.

Questions for Critical Thinking

1. Provide additional examples of how companies, using mixed reality, are integrating their brands into powerful user experiences.
2. Companies like UPS are using digital reality for training purposes to allow new drivers to prove themselves in a virtual environment before getting behind the wheel of a five-ton delivery vehicle. What are some other training-related applications?

Sources: Nav Athwal, "The Rise of Virtual Reality in Real Estate," *Forbes*, http://www.forbes.com, accessed May 22, 2018; Allan V. Cook, Ryan Jones, Ash Raghavan, and Irfan Saif, "Digital Reality: The Focus Shifts from Technology to Opportunity," *Deloitte Tech Trends 2018*, https://www2.deloitte.com, accessed May 22, 2018; Scott Kramer, "Virtual Showrooms: The Future of Homebuying Is Now Reality," *Forbes*, http://www.forbes.com, accessed May 22, 2018; company website, "10 Best Uses of Virtual Reality in Marketing (2018)," http://www.mbryonic.com, accessed May 21, 2018; Sarah Tseggay, "Estee Lauder's Latest Project Uses AR to Find Your Perfect Lipstick," http://www.nextreality.com, *Next Reality*, accessed May 21, 2018.

Case 14.3 Technology Drives Zipcar's Success

As a member of Zipcar, the world's largest car-sharing service, consumers avoid the costs associated with car ownership: gasoline, insurance, maintenance, and parking. Based in Cambridge, Massachusetts, Zipcar was founded by two moms who met when their children were in the same kindergarten class. Prior to its launch, Zipcar raised $75,000, most of which was spent to develop technology. Today, Zipcar is owned by Avis Budget and offers self-service, on-demand cars by the hour or day. The company provides automobile reservations to its more than one million members and offers more than 12,000 cars in urban areas, on college campuses, and at airports worldwide.

With a seamless user experience, it may be difficult for Zipsters (the company's name for its members) to realize the complex technology that goes into making the car-sharing service so user-friendly. Zipcar relies on a number of different technologies, including mobile, web, telematics, radio-frequency identification (RFID), operational information administration systems, and phone and interactive voice response systems for support and customer service. In addition, there are teams responsible for the company's security infrastructure, mobile app development, and auto maintenance to make sure Zipcar's fleet of vehicles is ready for members.

At the heart of Zipcar's technologies is an operational administration system. As a data-driven company, Zipcar relies heavily on information to make company decisions and manage assets. The system enables the company to manage its physical assets—its vehicles—in many locations worldwide. The system provides data about car utilization, when and how people are driving, specific locations, hours used, and miles driven. Using the data, analytics are performed that allow the company to optimize utilization levels. This type of information is valuable for making strategic decisions about supply and demand, including when and where to place cars, the models and types to use, and when to change them.

The technology in the cars provides information that allows the company to understand how its cars are being used. Zipcar has created a telematics board for each vehicle with GPS and RFID, which supplies geographic, customer, and utilization information. Using transponders, the RFID technology works with a card reader physically placed on the car's windshield. After the customer makes a reservation either on the web or via mobile device, the RFID card is used to enter and exit any Zipcar. This technology identifies the user and his or her car reservation. Once the car is unlocked, the key is in the car attached to a tether on the steering column. The user will also find a toll pass (members pay for tolls) and a gas card (price of gas is included in the rental fee).

Because of Zipcar's technology, the keys can be left in the car without concern of theft. When a user enters or exits a car, hours, usage, and mileage are uploaded to a central computer via a wireless data link. However, for privacy purposes, the location of the vehicle is not tracked. In addition, all cars are equipped with a "kill" function, which allows the company to prevent theft. For security purposes, the car opens only to the designated user. With a mobile device, a user is able to unlock and lock the car and honk its horn, which helps determine a car's location.

Because 98% of Zipcar users have smart phones, mobile and web applications are integral to interfacing with customers. At the heart of Zipcar's car sharing is a self-serve transaction that allows a user to find, reserve, and access a specific car at a specific location at a specific time. The information is then sent wirelessly to the car, and Zipcar members use their Zipcard to open the car door. Once the car is returned and locked, billing is finalized and information is made available to the member.

It is rare that Zipsters interact directly with someone from the company because reservations happen via a mobile device or online. Providing top-notch customer service when something goes wrong requires constant attention to innovative technology solutions. Dedicated phone systems and customer support systems are crucial for things like on-the-road issues. The Zipcar phone system identifies users who are calling, their reservations, and the cars they are driving, so that timely support and problem solving can happen quickly. Technology also supplies information about the vehicle's service history, which helps with troubleshooting and service.

As transportation needs continue to change, Zipcar is working to improve its technology base. The company remains committed to assessing consumer transportation and parking needs for business and personal use. Zipcar is focused on understanding and assessing trip-type needs, whether it is an errand for a few hours, an afternoon at the beach, or a business meeting. Using various technologies, the company has created a seamless experience for consumers who desire alternatives to car ownership. So, the next time you decide to reserve a Zipcar and drive to the beach for the day, thanks to the company's focus on technology, you will have a strong support system without much sand in your face.

Questions for Critical Thinking

1. What type of data does Zipcar use to make decisions on behalf of its customers? Its operations? How do the data used to make customer decisions differ from the data used to make decisions related to operations? Discuss.
2. Discuss how Zipcar manages and deals with information security. What are some of the issues the company faces with regard to security?
3. What information does Zipcar use to manage its fleet? What information is utilized to decide which types of cars to purchase, how they will be used, and where they will be located? How might weather patterns or seasonality impact the types and number of cars the company purchases?
4. Discuss how Zipcar leverages technology to acquire new members. Based upon its segmentation of consumers, businesses, and college students, discuss the various technologies utilized to identify the relevant target audiences and the types of messages conveyed to each of them.

Sources: Company website, "Rates and Plans," http://www.zipcar.com, accessed May 17, 2018; company website, "Is Zipcar for Me?" http://www.zipcar.com, accessed May 17, 2018; company website, "Zipcar Overview," http://zipcar.com, accessed May 17, 2018; company website, "The Zipcar Grant Program," http://zipcar.com, accessed May 17, 2018; company website, "Just Landed from a JetBlue Flight?" http://zipcar.com, accessed May 17, 2018; Chris Ready, "Zipcar Rolls Out One-Way Service with Guaranteed Parking," *Boston Globe*, http://www.bostonglobe.com, accessed May 17, 2018; Mark Rogowsky, "Zipcar, Uber, and the Beginning of Trouble for the Auto Industry," *Forbes*, http://www.forbes.com, accessed May 17, 2018; Carol Hymowitz, "Zipcar Founder Robin Chase on Starting Buzzcar and a Portugal Venture," *Bloomberg Business*, http://www.bloomberg.com, accessed May 17, 2018; Natalie Zmuda, "Marketers Hitting Campus Harder than Ever," *AdAge*, http://adage.com, accessed May 17, 2018.

CHAPTER 15

Understanding Accounting and Financial Statements

LEARNING OBJECTIVES

1. Discuss the users of accounting information.
2. Describe accounting professionals.
3. Identify the foundation of the accounting system.
4. Outline the steps in the accounting cycle.
5. Explain financial statements.
6. Discuss financial ratio analysis.
7. Describe the role of budgeting.
8. Outline international accounting practices.

Changemaker

Chris Goodney/Bloomberg/Getty Images

Cathy Engelbert, Chief Executive Officer

Company: Deloitte LLP

Industry: Financial Services

Website: http://www.deloitte.com

With company headquarters in New York, CEO Cathy Engelbert (see photo) leads the largest professional services firm in the world, Deloitte LLP. She is the first U.S. female CEO of a Big Four accounting firm, which refers to the four largest international professional services firms of Deloitte LLP, PwC (PricewaterhouseCoopers), EY (Ernst & Young), and KPMG. Deloitte, with more than 88,000 professionals, has four subsidiaries providing audit, tax, consulting, and financial advisory services. Engelbert, a certified public accountant and former college basketball player, earned a bachelor's degree in accounting in college.

A 30-year company veteran, Engelbert previously served as chair and CEO of Deloitte's audit group. In this role, she was charged with providing independent financial statement and internal control audits (FS&ICA) to a variety of clients. Deloitte's FS&ICA team evaluates a company's financial statements and internal controls—things like employee benefits plans and other services related to financial reporting.

As the accounting profession continues to experience exponential change, Engelbert is charged with leading Deloitte into the next decade—which includes leveraging technology to drive value for her firm and her clients. Engelbert sees the future as a wide set of forces, including technological innovation such as robotics, artificial intelligence, sensors, blockchain and cloud computing, as well as huge demographic shifts including longer lives, multiple generations working together, increased diversity, and increased customer empowerment. As a result, this requires hiring different people than before, including more data scientists.

Named one of *Fortune* magazine's Most Powerful Women in Business, Engelbert has placed a priority on women in corporate America. As a board chair of Catalyst, a nonprofit focused on advancing women in the workplace, Engelbert has created and developed mentorship programs. "No one is thinking about your career as much as you are," says Engelbert. "If you don't go find those mentors and sponsors . . . you're going to end up leaving."[1]

Overview

Accounting professionals who work for firms like Deloitte prepare the financial information that organizations present in their annual reports. Whether you begin your career by working for a company or by starting your own company, understanding the importance of the work of accountants and what they do is crucial in today's global business environment.

Accounting is the process of measuring, interpreting, and communicating financial information to enable people inside and outside a company to make informed decisions. In many ways, accounting is the language of business. Accountants gather, record, report, and interpret financial information in a way that describes the status and operation of an organization and aids in decision making.

Millions of men and women throughout the world describe their occupation as an accountant. In the United States alone, almost 1.4 million people work as accountants. According to the Bureau of Labor Statistics, the number of accounting-related jobs, tied closely to the health of an economy, is expected to increase by around 10% between now and 2026.[2] Accounting is one of the most in-demand majors on college campuses, and corresponding salaries are projected to grow almost 5% in the coming year. Accounting professionals with technical proficiency in cloud-based systems, information security, big data analysis, and database management software, and with experience in risk, compliance, the regulatory environment, and internal audits are in demand.[3] In a small and midsize business environment, professionals with advanced Excel expertise and QuickBooks competence are in demand.[3]

This chapter begins by describing who uses accounting information. It discusses business activities involving accounting statements: financing, investing, and operations. It explains the accounting process, defines double-entry bookkeeping, and presents the accounting equation. We then discuss the development of financial statements from information about financial transactions, the methods of interpreting these statements, and the roles of budgeting in planning and controlling a business. The chapter concludes with a discussion of the development and implementation schedule of a uniform set of accounting rules for global business.

1 Users of Accounting Information

accounting process of measuring, interpreting, and communicating financial information to enable people inside and outside the company to make informed decisions.

People both inside and outside an organization rely on **accounting** information to make business decisions. **Figure 15.1** lists the users of accounting information and the applications they find for that information. Firms such as Deloitte provide such information and help their customers make the best use of it.

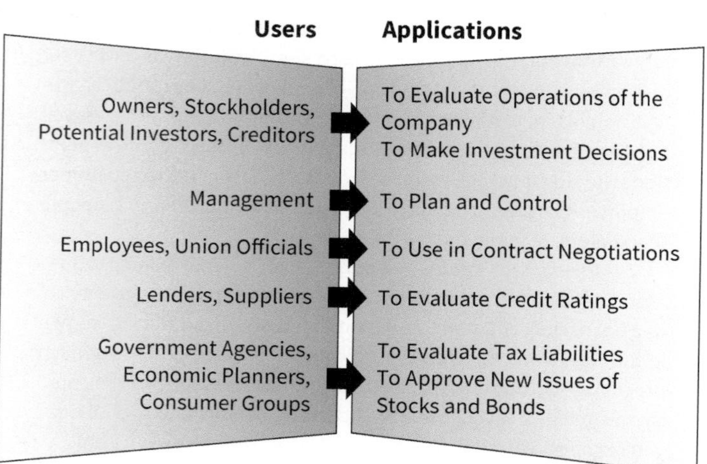

FIGURE 15.1 Users of Accounting Information

Managers with a business, government agency, or not-for-profit organization are the major users of accounting information because it helps them plan and control daily and long-range operations. Business owners and boards of directors of not-for-profit groups also rely on accounting data to determine how well managers are operating the organizations. Union officials use accounting data in contract negotiations, and employees refer to it as they monitor their company's productivity and profitability performance.

Known as *open book management*, many companies share financial information with employees as partners so they become more business literate and understand financial statements. This empowers them to use the information in cost cutting and quality improvement, and some companies even reward employees for their success. Proponents believe that viewing financial information helps employees better understand how their work contributes to the company's success.

Outside a company, potential investors evaluate accounting information to help them decide whether to buy a company's stock. As we'll discuss in more detail later in the chapter, any company whose stock is traded publicly must file reports with the Securities Exchange Commission (SEC) to keep shareholders informed on a regular basis and in a transparent manner. Bankers and other lenders use accounting information to evaluate a potential borrower's creditworthiness. The Internal Revenue Service (IRS) and state tax officials use it to determine a company's tax liability. Citizens' groups and government agencies use such information in assessing the efficiency of operations such as Massachusetts General Hospital; the Topeka, Kansas, school system; Community College of Denver; and the Art Institute of Chicago.

Accountants are in a strategically important position that allows them to contribute to the development and growth of a company, the economy, and ultimately society. Within a constantly changing environment, their responsibilities range from business analysis to strategy to legal compliance and reporting. In addition, thousands of individuals volunteer each year to help people with their taxes. One of the largest organized programs is Tax-Aide, sponsored by AARP (formally known as the American Association of Retired Persons). For more than 40 years this volunteer program has assisted about 50 million low- and middle-income Americans—especially people 60 and older—with their income tax preparation at more than 5,000 locations nationwide.[4]

Business Activities Involving Accounting

The natural progression of a business begins with financing. Subsequent steps, including investing, lead to operating the business. All organizations, profit oriented and not-for-profit, perform these three basic activities, and accounting plays a key role in each one:

1. Financing activities provide necessary funds from investors to start a business and expand it after it begins operating.
2. Investing activities provide valuable assets required to run a business.
3. Operating activities focus on selling goods and services, but they also consider expenses as important elements of sound financial management.

Assessment Check

1. Define *accounting*.
2. Who uses accounting information?
3. What are the three business activities that involve accounting?

2 Accounting Professionals

Accounting professionals work in a variety of areas in and for businesses, government agencies, and not-for-profit organizations. They can be classified as public, management, government, and not-for-profit accountants. **Table 15.1** lists the diverse roles accountants play in the private and public sectors, in academia, and in society.

Public Accountants

A **public accountant** provides accounting services to individuals or companies for a fee. Most public accounting firms provide three basic services to clients: (1) auditing, or examining, financial records; (2) tax preparation, planning, and related services; and (3) management consulting.

public accountant accountant who provides accounting services to individuals or business firms for a fee.

TABLE 15.1 The Diverse Roles of Professional Accountants

In Business	• Ensure quality and safeguard integrity of financial reporting at the source where the numbers and figures are produced • Provide a pragmatic and objective approach to solving issues • Assist with corporate strategy, provide advice, and help businesses reduce costs, increase revenues, and reduce risks
In Society	• Contribute to the overall stability and progress of society
As Board Director	• Represent the interests of company owners (i.e., private individuals who own a business or shareholders in a public company) • Govern the organization (such as approving annual budgets and being accountable to stakeholders for the company's performance) • Help appoint the company's chief executive; determine management's compensation
As Chief Financial Officer	• Oversee all matters relating to a company's financial health • Create and drive the strategic direction of the business • Analyze, create, and communicate financial information
As Internal Auditor	• Provide independent assurance to management that the organization's risk management, governance, and internal control processes are operating effectively
In the Public Sector	• Shape governmental fiscal policies that have a far-reaching impact on the lives of many
In Academia	• Impart the knowledge, skills, and ethical standards of the accounting profession to the next generation of students and professionals

Sources: Len Jui and Jessie Wong, "Professional Accountants in Business—A Varied Profession," *Chinese Accounting Journal,* https://www.ifac.org, accessed May 24, 2018; organization website, "The Future of Learning," http://futureoflearning.aicpa.org, accessed May 24, 2018; Susan S. Davis, "What Role Does an Account Play in Business Operations?" *Houston Chronicle,* http://smallbusiness.chron.com, accessed May 24, 2018.

Because public accountants are not employees of a client firm, they can provide unbiased advice about the firm's financial condition.

Although there are hundreds of public accounting firms in the United States, a handful dominate the industry. The four largest public accounting firms—Deloitte, PwC (PricewaterhouseCoopers), EY (Ernst & Young), and KPMG, referred to as the "Big Four," earned nearly $134 billion in a recent fiscal year. With hundreds of thousands of employees, the Big Four have the highest-profile clients and control about 80% of the market share of all public company clients. Deloitte and PwC alternate as global leaders on a revenue basis. Currently Deloitte occupies the top spot with recent global revenues of more than $38.8 billion.[5]

Hiring and finding the right talent is a top challenge and a growing concern faced by public accounting firms. Next is downward price pressure because of increased competition and automation. Because the services offered by firms are similar in nature, as firms struggle to differentiate themselves in the throes of increased involvement in the RFP (request for proposal) process by procurement and purchasing departments, commoditization has become an issue. Last, an increasing concern is keeping up with changing technology—or being replaced by technology. The "Business & Technology" feature discusses how accounting firms like EY have used social media and technology to help solve the issue of talent recruitment in a highly competitive job market.[6]

As the U.S. economy has improved, the search for top talent has become a challenge as job candidates have become more discriminating when evaluating offers and career opportunities. After completing internships, top accounting graduates are often recruited and enticed with, among other perks, signing bonuses.

As public accounting firms continue to promote themselves as "one-stop shops," many have tapped lucrative growth areas in nonaccounting services like consulting—sometimes at

Business & Technology

Talent Wars: Using Social Media to Build a Brand

Ernst & Young, known as EY, is one of the "Big Four" professional services and accounting firms. Contending with a competitive market, these companies remain focused on recruitment and retention efforts. Not only has EY recently made *Fortune's* "100 Best Companies to Work For" list for the 20th consecutive year, the company is a pioneer in developing an effective social media strategy to recruit talent.

Inviting students to meet on Facebook, EY is well known for its ability to build relationships with students and graduates early on. The company is focused on using social media to provide exceptional recruiting experiences for interns, gig workers, and full-time hires. To simplify and speed up the hiring process, EY has started to use digital interviewing, which has reduced the time of its overall hiring process by 40%.

To capitalize on the "gig economy" and people seeking shorter term assignments and greater work flexibility, EY has launched an innovative technology platform that allows gig workers to directly access contract opportunities. The company boasts one of the largest employee referral programs, and in a recent year, paid more than $4 million employee referral bonuses. Over half of the firm's experienced hires were found through referrals.

All stories and advice on its social media sites are generated by EY employees who speak about actual experiences. The company's branding leader believes that shifting the balance to user-generated content from created "corporate" content is more authentic. Videos, sent in from employees, are linked to EY's various social media accounts, which include Facebook, Twitter, and LinkedIn. The hope: To give recruits an honest and unscripted "peek behind the doors" at EY.

Questions for Critical Thinking

1. In your opinion, how important is a company's social media strategy when it comes to recruitment? Have you ever looked at a prospective employer's use of social media when exploring job or career opportunities? Discuss.
2. Describe ways companies are utilizing social media for recruitment efforts. After evaluating EY's social media channels, do you think the company's use of social media is effective in a highly competitive market? Why or why not?

Sources: "How EY Uses Social Media to Recruit," *Link Humans*, http://linkhumans.com, accessed May 25, 2018; Peter Yewell, "Social Recruiting: How Ernst & Young Paved the Way," *Smart Recruiters*, https://www.smartrecruiters.com; accessed May 25, 2018; company website, "EY Named to FORTUNE's '100 Best Companies to Work For' List for 18th Year," http://www.goodcall.com, http://www.ey.com, accessed May 25, 2018; "When a Little Girl Dreams about Becoming an Accountant," *Daily Beast*, http://www.thedailybeast.com, accessed May 25, 2018; Melissa Suzuno, "How EY Uses Content Marketing to Create an Exceptional Candidate Experience," *After College*, http://employer.aftercollege.com, accessed May 25, 2018; Kailyn Smigelski, "EY announces new global talent programs to prepare its people and its business for the future of work," https://www.ey.com, accessed May 25, 2018.

the expense of auditor quality and independence. This has resulted in inevitable conflicts of interest as the balance of services has shifted from auditing to more lucrative offerings, including everything from legal services and insolvency procedures to capital markets advisory work and consulting work on cybersecurity. Now, under the AICPA's recently issued cybersecurity reporting framework, CPAs have an opportunity to expand the services they offer to help clients manage and understand cyber risks. Regulators continue to warn accounting firms about the potential conflicts of interest between their core auditing business and the growing demand for more lucrative consulting services.[7]

Certified public accountants (CPAs), consistently in high demand, must meet requirements that vary by state. Generally, requirements include a minimum of a bachelor's degree (with the equivalent of 24 semester hours in business, including at least 12 semester hours in accounting); 150 hours of education and experience; and the completion of a number of rigorous tests in accounting theory and practice, auditing, law, and taxes. Other accountants who meet specified educational and experience requirements and pass certification exams carry the title *certified management accountant, certified fraud examiner,* or *certified internal auditor*.

Management Accountants

An accountant employed by a business other than a public accounting firm (public companies, private businesses, and government agencies) is called a *management accountant*, who typically collects and records financial transactions and prepares financial statements used by the company's managers in decision making. Management accountants, also called corporate accountants, provide timely, relevant, accurate, and concise information that executives can use to operate their companies more effectively and more profitably than they could without this input. A management accountant plays a major role in both preparing and interpreting financial statements. A management accountant should provide answers to many important questions:

- Where is the company going?
- What opportunities await it?
- Do certain situations expose the company to excessive risk?
- Does the company's technology provide detailed and timely information to all levels of management?

Management accountants frequently specialize in different aspects of accounting. A cost accountant, for example, determines the cost of goods and services and helps set their prices. An internal auditor examines the company's financial practices to ensure that its records include accurate data and that its operations comply with federal, state, and local laws and regulations. A tax accountant works to minimize a company's tax bill and assumes responsibility for its federal, state, county, and city tax returns. Some management accountants achieve a *certified management accountant (CMA)* designation. A CMA designation is a credential similar to CPA, but with greater focus on cost accounting, financial planning, and management issues.

Changing federal regulations affecting accounting and public reporting have increased the demand for management accountants in recent years. As a result, salaries for these professionals are rising.

Government and Not-for-Profit Accountants

Federal, state, and local governments also require accounting services. Government accountants and those who work for not-for-profit organizations perform professional services similar to those of management accountants. Government accountants at the federal level manage public funds, investigate white-collar crime, perform audits for government agencies, and stay up-to-date on emerging accounting and regulatory issues. At state and local levels, they manage use of local revenues; investigate fraud; perform financial, performance, and compliance audits; and recommend corrective action where needed. Government accountants work closely on the budget and financial reporting process.[8]

Not-for-profit organizations, such as churches, labor unions, charities, schools, hospitals, and universities, also hire accountants. In fact, the not-for-profit sector is one of the fastest growing segments of accounting practice. An increasing number of not-for-profits publish financial information because contributors want more accountability from these organizations and are interested in knowing how the groups spend the money that they raise.

Assessment Check

1. List the three services offered by public accounting firms.
2. What tasks do management accountants perform?

3 The Foundation of the Accounting System

generally accepted accounting principles (GAAP) principles that encompass the conventions, rules, and procedures for determining acceptable accounting and financial reporting practices at a particular time.

To provide reliable, consistent, and unbiased information to decision makers, accountants follow guidelines, or standards, known as **generally accepted accounting principles (GAAP)**. These principles encompass the conventions, rules, and procedures for determining acceptable accounting and financial reporting practices at a particular time.

All GAAP standards are based on four basic principles: consistency, relevance, reliability, and comparability. Consistency means that all data should be collected and presented in the same manner across all periods. Any change in the way in which specific data are collected or presented must be noted and explained. Relevance states that all information being reported should be appropriate and assist users in evaluating that information. Reliability implies that the accounting data presented in financial statements are reliable and can be verified by an independent party such as an outside auditor. Finally, comparability ensures that one company's financial statements can be compared with those of similar businesses.

In the United States, the **Financial Accounting Standards Board (FASB)** is primarily responsible for evaluating, setting, or modifying GAAP. The U.S. Securities and Exchange Commission (SEC), the chief federal regulator of the financial markets and accounting industry, actually has the statutory authority to establish financial accounting and reporting standards for publicly held companies. (A publicly held company is one whose stock is publicly traded in a market such as the New York Stock Exchange.) However, the SEC's policy has been to rely on the accounting industry for this function, as long as the SEC believes the private sector is operating in the public interest. Consequently, the Financial Accounting Foundation—an organization made up of members of many different professional groups—actually appoints the members (currently seven) of the FASB, although the SEC does have some input. Board members are all experienced accounting professionals and serve five-year terms. They may be reappointed for a second five-year term. Board members must sever all connections with the companies they served prior to joining the board. The board is supported by a professional staff of more than 60 individuals.[9]

Financial Accounting Standards Board (FASB) an organization responsible for evaluating, setting, or modifying GAAP in the United States.

The FASB carefully monitors changing business conditions, enacting new rules and modifying existing rules when necessary. It also considers input and requests from all segments of its diverse constituency, including corporations and the SEC. Recent updates by the Financial Accounting Standards Board (FASB) to U.S. Generally Accepted Accounting Principles (GAAP) include an updated revenue recognition standard that requires companies to recognize revenue from contracts at the time the promised goods and services are delivered to a customer. This has positively impacted DISH Network's net income by $27 million, while reducing income tax for the period by $116 million. This is due mainly to recently passed U.S. tax legislation, which lowered the corporate tax rate from 35% to 21%.[10]

In response to well-known cases of accounting fraud, and questions about the independence of auditors, the Sarbanes-Oxley Act of 2002—commonly known as SOX—created the Public Accounting mentioned In the "Judgment Call" feature. The five-member board has the power to set audit standards and to investigate and sanction accounting firms that certify the books of publicly traded companies. Members of the Public Accounting Oversight Board are appointed by the SEC. No more than two of the five members of the board can be certified public accountants.

In addition to creating the Public Accounting Oversight Board, SOX also increased the reporting requirements for publicly traded companies. Senior executives including the chief executive officer (CEO) and chief financial officer (CFO), for example, must personally certify that the financial information reported by the company is correct. More than a decade after its enactment, the message behind SOX is that behavior in the boardroom and corporate governance in general were in need of a fundamental overhaul in the form of increased corporate compliance, fiduciary duty to shareholders, and ethical behavior.

It is expensive for companies to adhere to GAAP standards and SOX requirements. Audits, for instance, can cost millions of dollars each year. Still, there are some who contend that SOX was an unnecessary and costly government intrusion into corporate management that places U.S. corporations at a competitive disadvantage with foreign firms, thus driving businesses out of the United States. These expenses can be especially burdensome for small businesses. Consequently, some have proposed modifications to GAAP and SOX for smaller companies, arguing that some accounting rules were really designed for larger companies. Others disagree.

Judgment Call

Should Company Audits Name Names?

To promote greater audit reliability, new disclosures about audits of U.S. public companies are being made available to investors. In response to investor demand, the new disclosures allow investors to evaluate the quality of an audit, and, as shareholders, to vote on both audit committee members and the auditor firm.

In a new rule adopted by the Public Company Accounting Oversight Board (PCAOB), U.S. audit firms will be required to publicly disclose the name of the engagement partner in charge of each company audit, along with the names of any other firms that contributed 5% or more of the total hours spent on the audit. While audit partners fear legal backlash, the hotly debated change has been put in place as audit firms face an overall requirement for greater transparency and accountability within the accounting profession.

Backers of this measure support the claim that naming auditors will increase accountability among auditors, create a higher level of detail, and provide an incentive for an auditor not to fall to a client's pressure of bending accounting rules. Additionally, a name will provide more information about the person behind the audit of a company whose shares of stock he or she happens to hold—or may be considering buying.

The policy will allow investors to check an audit partner's track record and any previous issues of prior company audits. Opponents say this request will slow down the auditing process, delaying deadlines as permission from the individuals whose names are to be disclosed is sought.

The chairman of the PCAOB believes that investors have the right to know the name of the person in charge of the audit, whose role is of singular importance to the reliability of the audit. Still others ponder what kind of assurance, if any, a name will provide.

Questions for Critical Thinking

1. **Some argue that when a company falls apart, it is due primarily to insider collusion that may not have been detected by an auditor. Do you agree? Why or why not?**
2. **Discuss both concerns of critics and why supporters are in favor of new disclosures.**

Sources: Samantha Ross, "Audit Transparency Disclosures Give Investors New Tools," *Pensions & Investments,* http://www.pionline.com, accessed May 25, 2018; Michael Rapoport, "Regulator Approves Naming of Audit-Firm Partners in Charge of Corporate Audits," *The Wall Street Journal*, http://www.wsj.com, accessed May 25, 2018; Adrienne Gonzales, "SEC Tired of Telling PCAOB How to Do Their Job," *Going Concern*, http://goingconcern.com, accessed May 25, 2018; organization website, "Standard Setting Agenda," http://pcaobus.org, accessed May 25, 2018.

Assessment Check

1. Define *GAAP*.
2. What are the four basic requirements to which all accounting rules must adhere?
3. What is the role played by the FASB?

4 The Accounting Cycle

Accounting involves financial transactions between a company and its employees, customers, suppliers, and owners; bankers; and various government agencies. For example, payroll checks result in a cash outflow to compensate employees. A payment to a vendor results in receipt of needed materials for the production process. Cash, check, and credit purchases by customers generate funds to cover the costs of operations and to earn a profit. Prompt payment of bills preserves a company's credit rating and its future ability to earn a profit. The procedure by which accountants convert data about individual transactions to financial statements is called the **accounting cycle**.

accounting cycle set of activities involved in converting information and individual transactions into financial statements.

Figure 15.2 illustrates the activities involved in the accounting cycle: recording, classifying, and summarizing transactions. Initially, any transaction that has a financial impact on the business, such as wages or payments to suppliers, should be documented. All these transactions are recorded in journals, which list transactions in chronological order. Journal listings are then posted to ledgers. A ledger shows increases or decreases in specific accounts such as cash or wages. Ledgers are used to prepare the financial statements, which summarize financial transactions.

Basic Data

Transactions
Receipts, invoices, and other source documents related to each transaction are assembled to justify making an entry in the company's accounting records.

Processing

Record
Transactions are recorded, usually electronically, in chronological order in books called journals, along with a brief explanation for each entry.

Classify
Journal entries are transferred, or posted, usually electronically, to individual accounts kept in a ledger. All entries involving cash are brought together in the ledger's cash account; all entries involving sales are recorded in the ledger's sales account.

Summarize
All accounts in the ledger are summarized at the end of the accounting period, and financial statements are prepared from these account summaries.

Financial Statements

- **Balance Sheet**
- **Income Statement**
- **Statement of Owners' Equity**
- **Statement of Cash Flows**

FIGURE 15.2 **The Accounting Cycle**

asset anything of value owned or leased by a business.

liability anything owed to creditors—the claims of a company's creditors.

owners' equity the owner's initial investment in the business plus profits that were not paid out to owners over time in the form of cash dividends.

accounting equation formula that states that assets must equal liabilities plus owners' equity.

The Accounting Equation

Three fundamental terms appear in the accounting equation: assets, liabilities, and owners' equity. An **asset** is anything of value owned or leased by a business. Assets include land, buildings, supplies, cash, accounts receivable (amounts owed to the business as payment for sales when credit is extended), and marketable securities.

Although most assets are tangible assets, such as equipment, buildings, and inventories, intangible possessions such as copyrights, research and development, patents, and trademarks are often a company's most important assets. This kind of asset is essential for many companies, especially those in the software, biotechnology, and pharmaceutical industries. For example, Johnson & Johnson (see photo)—which has both biotechnology and pharmaceutical operations—reported more than $53 billion in intangible assets, including goodwill, in a recent year, out of a total of $157 billion in total assets. The value of intangible assets of in-process research and development is for technology programs for unapproved products.[11]

Courtesy of JLABS

Johnson & Johnson opened JLABS, a 34,000-square-foot innovation life sciences incubator next door to Texas Medical Center in Houston. It will provide entrepreneurs the opportunity for further research and development and new patents—intangible assets.

Two groups have claims against the assets of a company: creditors and owners. A **liability** of a business is anything owed to creditors—that is, the claims of a company's creditors. When a company borrows money to purchase inventory, land, or machinery, the claims of creditors are shown as accounts payable, notes payable, or long-term debt. Wages and salaries owed to employees also are liabilities (known as *wages payable* or *accrued wages*).

Owners' equity is the owner's initial investment in the business plus profits that were not paid out to owners over time in the form of cash dividends. A strong owners' equity position often is used as evidence of a company's financial strength and stability.

The **accounting equation** (also referred to as the *accounting identity*) states that assets must equal liabilities plus owners' equity. This equation reflects the financial position of a company at any point in time:

$$\text{Assets} = \text{Liabilities} + \text{Owners' equity}$$

Because financing comes from either creditors or owners, the right side of the accounting equation also represents the business's financial structure.

double-entry bookkeeping process by which accounting transactions are recorded; each transaction must have an offsetting transaction.

The accounting equation also illustrates **double-entry bookkeeping**—the process by which accounting transactions are recorded. Because assets must always equal liabilities plus equity, each transaction must have an offsetting transaction. For example, if a company increases an asset, either another asset must decrease, a liability must increase, or owners' equity must increase. So if a company uses cash to purchase inventory, one asset (inventory) is increased while another (cash) is decreased by the same amount. Similarly, a decrease in an asset must be offset by either an increase in another asset, a decrease in a liability, or a decrease in owners' equity. If a company uses cash to repay a bank loan, both an asset (cash) and a liability (bank loans) decrease, and by the same amount.

Two simple numerical examples will help illustrate the accounting equation and double-entry bookkeeping. First, assume the owner of a photo studio purchases a new camera system for $5,000 using her personal funds. The accounting transaction would look as follows:

Increase plant, property, and equipment (an asset) by $5,000

Increase owners' equity by $5,000

So, the left side of the accounting equation would increase by $5,000 and be offset by a $5,000 increase on the right side.

Second, assume a company has a $100,000 loan from a bank and decides to pay it off using some of its cash. The transaction would be recorded as:

Decrease bank loan (liability) by $100,000

Decrease cash (asset) by $100,000

In this second example, the left side and right side of the accounting equation would both decrease by $100,000.

The relationship expressed by the accounting equation underlies development of the company's financial statements. Three financial statements form the foundation: the balance sheet, the income statement, and the statement of owners' equity. The information found in these statements is calculated using the double-entry bookkeeping system and reflects the basic accounting equation. A fourth statement, the statement of cash flows, is also prepared to focus specifically on the sources and uses of cash for a company from its operating, investing, and financing activities.

The Impact of Computers and Technology on the Accounting Process

For hundreds of years, bookkeepers recorded, or posted, accounting transactions as manual entries in journals. They then transferred the information, or posted it, to individual accounts listed in ledgers. The accounting industry was one of the first to be impacted by an increase in advanced data technology with the adoption tax software. A potential disruption to the accounting industry is Artificial Intelligence, or AI. Poised to play an important role in years to come, it will alter the profession and help accountants become more strategic advisors. With AI, accountants can more easily make financial decisions and recommendations to their clients by sifting through tons of data quickly and accurately. Artificial intelligence should improve compliance work and free up time so accountants can focus more on revenue-generating, client-facing tasks. Tax preparation firm H&R Block is using IBM Watson's cognitive computing power to help ensure every deduction and credit is found.

Accounting software programs are used widely today in both large and small businesses. They allow a do-it-once approach, in which a single input leads to automatic conversion of a sale into a journal entry, which then is stored until needed. Decision makers can then access up-to-date financial statements and financial ratios instantly. Improvements in technology,

Clean & Green Business

Hershey Accounts for Sustainability

When you bite into that Reese's Peanut Butter Cup, you and your taste buds will now know that the Hershey Company is part of a broad effort to define and develop sustainable accounting practices within the consumer products industry.

Based in Hershey, Pennsylvania, the candy maker is part of the Sustainability Accounting Standards Board (SASB), a nonprofit organization created to develop and disseminate industry-specific accounting standards to publicly held U.S. companies by industry.

Hershey believes that, although rigorous, SASB's efforts to define, develop, and promote sustainability accounting standards are a key step in enabling the company to disclose decision-useful information to its investors. Disclosure topics include food safety, labeling and marketing integrity, climate change adaptation, and supply-chain management. Because consumption businesses like Hershey require resources to produce food products, SASB standards help companies in these industries manage water scarcity, packaging, and climate impacts like crop yield (for cacao beans) and commodity prices.

To date, the Hershey Company, as part of its sustainability accounting reporting, plans to reduce greenhouse gas emissions in its U.S. distribution and transportation operations by 10% over the next several years, achieve zero-waste-to-landfill at two additional plants, and achieve a recycling rate of 90%. The company's environmental stewardship focus plays an important role not only in its business operations but also in its accounting standards, which, for stakeholders, may be equally as sweet as chocolate and peanut butter combined.

Questions for Critical Thinking

1. How can the company educate customers about its efforts? How might consumers of Hershey's products perceive efforts to develop more sustainable accounting practices?
2. What are some of the challenges faced by the SASB in its efforts to develop and disseminate sustainability accounting standards or integrated reporting?

Sources: Company website, "Appendix: Progress Toward Our Goals," http://thehersheycompany.com, accessed May 25, 2018; organization website, "For Companies: What Others Are Doing" and "Welcome to the Sustainability Accounting Standards Board," http://www.sasb.org, accessed May 25, 2018; Baker & McKenzie, "What Is the Sustainability Accounting Standards Board and How Does Its Work Affect Your Company?" *Lexology*, http://www.lexology.com, accessed May 25, 2018; Jill Metzger, "SASB Issues Provisional Sustainability Accounting Standards for Consumption Industries," *PR Newswire*, http://www.prnewswire.com, accessed May 25, 2018.

access to data, and accounting software continue to make the process even faster and easier. In addition, accounting firms have begun to use mobile computing to better serve their clients. Smart phones provide connections between employees and their company's network, which means they can access current, vital information from anywhere. Accounting firms may also provide mobile computing to clients with branded applications allowing clients to access their financial information and services via their smart phones.[12]

Because the accounting needs of entrepreneurs and small businesses differ from those of larger firms, companies like Intuit have developed software solutions that meet specific user needs. Some examples of accounting software designed for entrepreneurs and small businesses, and designed to run on personal computers, include QuickBooks, and Sage50. Software designed for larger companies, often requiring more sophisticated computer systems, include products from NetSuite, Oracle, and SAP.

For companies that conduct business worldwide, software producers have introduced new accounting programs that handle all of a company's accounting information for every country in which it operates. The software handles different languages and currencies, as well as the financial, legal, and tax requirements of each nation in which the company conducts business.

Designed for small and medium-size businesses, several cloud-based accounting applications are available. Among other benefits, these products allow users in other departments, remote, or branch offices to access the same data with the same version of the software from anywhere using a standard web browser. The "Clean & Green Business" feature explains how the Hershey Company is reporting on sustainability to measure its impact on the environment, using standards set through the Sustainability Accounting Standards Board.

Assessment Check

1. List the steps in the accounting cycle.
2. What is the accounting equation?
3. Briefly explain double entry bookkeeping.

5 Financial Statements

Financial statements provide managers with essential information needed to evaluate the liquidity position of an organization—its ability to meet current obligations and needs by converting assets into cash; the company's profitability; and its overall financial health. The balance sheet, income statement, statement of owners' equity, and statement of cash flows provide a foundation on which managers can base their decisions. By interpreting the data provided in these statements, managers can communicate the appropriate information to internal decision makers and to interested parties outside the organization.

Of the four financial statements, only the balance sheet is considered to be a permanent statement; its amounts are carried over from year to year. The income statement, statement of owners' equity, and statement of cash flows are considered temporary because they are closed out at the end of each fiscal year.

Public companies are required to report their financial statements at the end of each three-month period, or quarter, as well as at the end of each fiscal year. Annual statements must be examined and verified by the company's outside auditors. These financial statements are public information available to anyone.

Sometimes companies choose their fiscal year in order to match income and expenses for the reportable tax year. For example, a company that must buy inventory during the winter months probably won't want to report its earnings during this time because the higher-than-normal purchases will decrease its earnings for this period and create a less-than-favorable image of the company's financial standing for that period of time. A traditional January through December calendar year would split these into two different years. For example, Nike's fiscal year consists of the 12 months between June 1 and May 31.

The Balance Sheet

balance sheet statement of a company's financial position on a particular date.

A company's **balance sheet** shows its financial position on a particular date. It is similar to a photograph of the company's assets together with its liabilities and owners' equity at a specific moment in time. Balance sheets must be prepared at regular intervals, because a company's managers and other internal parties often request this information daily, weekly, or at least monthly. On the other hand, external users, such as stockholders or industry analysts, may use this information less frequently, perhaps every quarter or once a year.

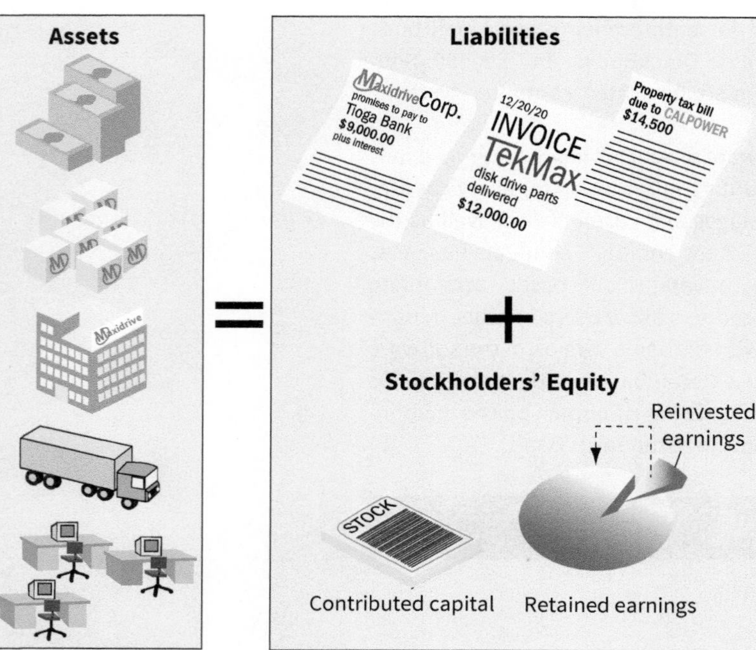

FIGURE 15.3 The Accounting Equation

The balance sheet follows the accounting equation. As shown in **Figure 15.3**, on the left side of the balance sheet are the company's assets—what it owns. These assets, shown in descending order of liquidity (in other words, convertibility to cash), represent the uses that management has made of available funds. Cash is always listed first on the asset side of the balance sheet.

On the right side of the equation are the claims against the company's assets. Liabilities and owners' equity indicate the sources of the company's assets and are listed in the order in which they are due. Liabilities reflect the claims of creditors—financial institutions or bondholders that have loaned the company money; suppliers that have provided goods and services on credit; and others to be paid, such as federal, state, and local tax authorities. Owners' equity represents the owners' claims (those of stockholders, in the case of a corporation) against the company's assets. It also amounts to the excess of all assets over liabilities.

1 **Current Assets:** Cash and other liquid assets that can or will be converted to cash within one year.

2 **Plant, Property, and Equipment (net):** Physical assets expected to last for more than one year; shown net of accumulated depreciation—the cumulative value that plant, property, and equipment have been expensed (depreciated).

3 Value of assets such as patents and trademarks.

4 **Current Liabilities:** Claims of creditors that are to be repaid within one year; accruals are expenses, such as wages, that have been incurred but not yet paid.

5 **Long-Term Debt:** Debts that come due one year or longer after the date on the balance sheet.

6 **Owners' (or shareholders') Equity:** Claims of the owners against the assets of the company; the difference between total assets and total liabilities.

Belle's Fine Coffees

Balance Sheet

	($ thousands)	**2021**	**2020**
	Assets		
1	Current Assets		
	Cash	$ 800	$ 600
	Short-term investments	1,250	940
	Accounts receivable	990	775
	Inventory	2,200	1,850
	Total current assets	5,240	4,165
2	Plant, property, and equipment (net)	3,300	2,890
3	Goodwill and other intangible assets	250	250
	Total Assets	8,790	7,305
	Liabilities and Shareholders' Equity		
4	Current Liabilities		
	Accruals	$ 350	$ 450
	Accounts payable	980	900
	Notes payable	700	500
	Total current liabilities	2,030	1,850
5	Long-term debt	1,100	1,000
	Total liabilities	3,130	2,850
6	Shareholders' equity	5,660	4,455
	Total Liabilities and Equity	8,790	7,305

FIGURE 15.4 **Belle's Fine Coffees Balance Sheet (Fiscal Year Ending December 31)**

Figure 15.4 shows the balance sheet for Belle's Fine Coffees, a small Texas-based coffee wholesaler. The accounting equation is illustrated by the three classifications of assets, liabilities, and owners' equity on the company's balance sheet. Remember, total assets must always equal the sum of liabilities and owners' equity. In other words, the balance sheet must always balance.

The Income Statement

income statement financial record summarizing a company's financial performance in terms of revenues, expenses, and profits over a given time period, say, a quarter or a year.

Whereas the balance sheet reflects a company's financial situation at a specific point in time, the **income statement** indicates the flow of resources that reveals the performance of the organization over a specific time period. Resembling a video rather than a photograph, the income statement is a financial record summarizing a company's financial performance in terms of revenues, expenses, and profits over a given time period, say, a quarter or a year.

In addition to reporting a company's profit or loss results, the income statement helps decision makers focus on overall revenues and the costs involved in generating these revenues. Managers of a not-for-profit organization use this statement to determine whether its revenues from contributions, grants, and investments will cover its operating costs. Finally, the income statement provides much of the basic data needed to calculate the financial ratios managers use in planning and controlling activities. **Figure 15.5** shows the income statement for Belle's Fine Coffees.

An income statement (sometimes called *a profit and loss,* or *P&L, statement*) begins with total sales or revenues generated during a year, quarter, or month. The costs, related to producing the revenues, are deducted. They are often individual entries on subsequent lines after revenue. Typical categories of costs include those involved in producing the company's goods or services, operating expenses, interest, and taxes. After all of them have been subtracted, the remaining net income may be distributed to the company's owners (stockholders, proprietors, or partners) or reinvested in the company as retained earnings. The final figure on the income statement—net income after taxes—is literally the *bottom line.*

FIGURE 15.5 Belle's Fine Coffees Income Statement (Fiscal Year Ending December 31)

1 **Sales:** Funds received from the sale of goods and services over a specified period of time.

2 **Cost of Goods Sold:** Cost of merchandise or services that generate the company's sales.

3 **Operating Expenses:** Salaries and other operational expenses not directly related to the acquisition, production, or sale of the company's output.

4 **Depreciation:** Noncash expenses that reflect the systematic reduction in the value of the company's plant, property, and equipment.

5 **Net Income:** Sales minus total expenses; profit after taxes.

Belle's Fine Coffees

Income Statement

	($ thousands)	**2021**	**2020**
1	Sales	$17,300	$14,200
2	Cost of goods sold	10,380	8,804
	Gross profit	6,920	5,396
3	Operating expenses	3,550	2,950
	Operating profit	3,370	2,446
4	Depreciation	350	300
	Interest expense (net)	98	75
	Earnings before taxes	2,922	2,071
	Income taxes	1,005	650
5	Net income	1,917	1,421

Controlling costs is an important focus of running a business. Too often, however, companies lose sight when the focus is on increasing revenue above and beyond controlling costs. Regardless of how much money a company collects in revenues, it won't stay in business for long unless it eventually earns a profit.

Statement of Owners' Equity

The **statement of owners', or shareholders', equity** is designed to show the components of the change in equity from the end of one fiscal year to the end of the next. It uses information from both the balance sheet and income statement. A somewhat simplified example is shown in **Figure 15.6** for Belle's Fine Coffees.

statement of owners' equity record of the change in owners' equity from the end of one fiscal period to the end of the next.

Note that the statement begins with the amount of equity shown on the balance sheet at the end of the prior year. Net income is added, and cash dividends paid to owners are subtracted (both are found on the income statement for the current year). If owners contributed any additional capital—say, through the sale of new shares—this amount is added to equity. On the other hand, if owners withdrew capital—for example, through the repurchase of existing shares—equity declines. All of the additions and subtractions, taken together, equal the change in owners' equity from the end of the last fiscal year to the end of the current one. The new amount of owners' equity is then reported on the balance sheet for the current year.

Statement of Cash Flows

In addition to the statement of owners' equity, the income statement, and the balance sheet, most companies prepare a fourth accounting statement—the **statement of cash flows**. Public companies are required to prepare and publish a statement of cash flows. In addition, commercial lenders often require a borrower to submit a statement of cash flows. The statement of cash flows provides investors and creditors with relevant information about a company's cash receipts and cash payments for its operations, investments,

statement of cash flows statement showing the sources and uses of cash during a period of time.

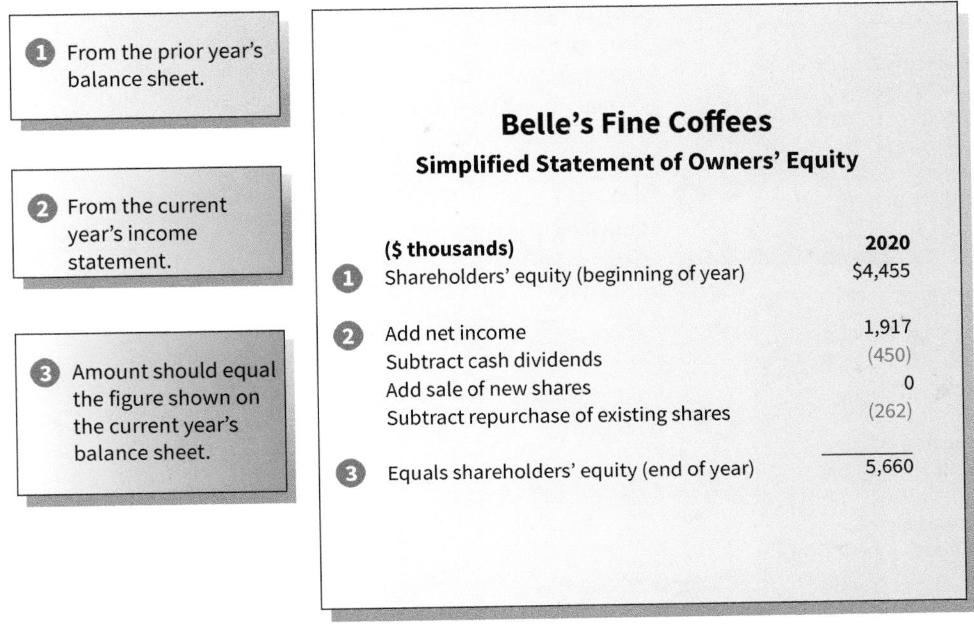

1 From the prior year's balance sheet.
2 From the current year's income statement.
3 Amount should equal the figure shown on the current year's balance sheet.
Belle's Fine Coffees
Simplified Statement of Owners' Equity

($ thousands)	2020
1 Shareholders' equity (beginning of year)	$4,455
2 Add net income	1,917
Subtract cash dividends	(450)
Add sale of new shares	0
Subtract repurchase of existing shares	(262)
3 Equals shareholders' equity (end of year)	5,660

FIGURE 15.6 **Belle's Fine Coffees Simplified Statement of Owners' Equity (Fiscal Year Ending December 31)**

and financing during an accounting period. **Figure 15.7** shows the statement of cash flows for Belle's Fine Coffees.

accrual accounting accounting method that records revenues and expenses when they occur, not necessarily when cash actually changes hands.

Companies prepare a statement of cash flows due to the widespread use of accrual accounting. **Accrual accounting** recognizes revenues and costs when they occur, not when actual cash changes hands. As a result, there can be differences between what is reported as sales, expenses, and profits, and the amount of cash that actually flows into and out of the business

1 Operating Activities: The nuts and bolts of day-to-day activities of a company carrying out its regular business; increases in accounts receivable and inventory are uses of cash, while increases in accruals and accounts payables are sources of cash; in financially healthy companies, net cash flow from operating activities should be positive.

2 Investing Activities: Transactions to accumulate or use cash in ways that affect operating activities in the future; often a use of cash.

3 Financing Activities: Ways to transfer cash to or from creditors and to or from owners; can be either positive or negative.

4 Net Cash Flow: The sum of cash flow from operating, investing, and financing activities, a reconcilement of cash from the beginning to the end of the accounting period (one year in this example).

Belle's Fine Coffees

Statement of Cash Flows

	($ thousands)	**2020**
	Cash Flow from Operating Activities	
1	Net income	$1,917
	Depreciation	350
	Change in accounts receivable	(215)
	Change in inventory	(350)
	Change in accruals	(100)
	Change in accounts payable	80
	Total cash flow from operating activities	1,682
2	Cash Flow from Investing Activities	
	Capital expenditures	(760)
	Change in short-term investments	(310)
	Total cash flow from investing activities	(1,070)
3	Cash Flow from Financing Activities	
	Cash dividends	(450)
	Sale/repurchase of shares	(262)
	Change in notes payable	200
	Change in long-term debt	100
	Total cash flow from financing activities	(412)
4	Net Cash Flow	200
	Cash (beginning of year)	600
	Cash (end of year)	800

FIGURE 15.7 Belle's Fine Coffees Statement of Cash Flows (Fiscal Year Ending December 31)

during a period of time. An example is depreciation. Companies depreciate fixed assets—such as machinery and buildings—over a specified period of time, which means that they systematically reduce the value of the asset. Depreciation is reported as an expense on the company's income statement (see Figure 15.5) but does not involve any actual cash. The fact that depreciation is a noncash expense means that what a company reports as net income (profits after tax) for a particular period actually understates the amount of cash the company took in, less expenses, during that period of time. Consequently, depreciation is added back to net income when calculating cash flow.

The fact that *cash flow* is the lifeblood of every organization is evidenced by the business failure rate. Many former owners of failed companies blame inadequate cash flow for their company's demise. Those who value the statement of cash flow maintain that its preparation and scrutiny by various parties can prevent financial distress for otherwise profitable firms, too many of which are forced into bankruptcy due to a lack of cash needed to continue day-to-day operations.

Even for companies for which bankruptcy is not an issue, the statement of cash flows can provide investors and other interested parties with vital information. For instance, assume that a company's income statement reports rising earnings. At the same time, however, the statement of cash flows shows that the company's inventory is rising faster than sales—often a signal that demand for the company's products is softening, which may in turn be a sign of impending financial trouble.

Assessment Check

1. List the four financial statements.
2. How is the balance sheet organized?
3. Define *accrual accounting.*

6 Financial Ratio Analysis

Accounting professionals fulfill important responsibilities beyond preparing financial statements. In a more critical role, they help managers interpret the statements by comparing data about the company's current activities to those for previous periods and to results posted by other companies in the industry. *Ratio analysis* is one of the most commonly used tools for measuring a company's liquidity, profitability, and reliance on debt financing as well as the effectiveness of management's resource utilization. This analysis also allows comparisons with other companies and against the company's own past performance.

Comparisons with ratios of similar companies help managers understand their company's performance relative to competitors' results. These industry standards are important metrics and help pinpoint problem areas as well as areas of excellence. Ratios for the current accounting period also may be compared with similar calculations for previous periods to spot developing trends. Ratios can be classified according to their specific purposes.

Liquidity Ratios

A company's ability to meet its short-term obligations when they must be paid is measured by *liquidity ratios.* Increasing liquidity reduces the likelihood that a company will face emergencies caused by the need to raise funds to repay loans. On the other hand, companies with low liquidity may be forced to choose between default or borrowing from high-cost lending sources to meet their maturing obligations.

Two commonly used liquidity ratios are the current ratio and the acid-test or quick ratio. The current ratio compares current assets to current liabilities, giving executives information about the company's ability to pay its current debts as they mature. The current ratio of Belle's Fine Coffees can be computed as follows (unless indicated, all amounts from the balance sheet or income statement are in thousands of dollars):

$$\text{Liquidity ratio} = \frac{\text{Current assests}}{\text{Current liabilities}} = \frac{5{,}240}{2{,}030} = 2.58$$

In other words, Belle's Fine Coffees has $2.58 of current assets for every $1.00 of current liabilities. In general, a current ratio of 2:1 is considered satisfactory liquidity. This rule of thumb must be considered along with other factors, such as the nature of the business, its seasonality, and the quality of the company's management team. Belle's Fine Coffees' management and other interested parties are likely to evaluate this ratio of 2.58:1 by comparing it with ratios for previous operating periods and with industry averages.

The acid-test (or quick) ratio measures the ability of a company to meet its debt payments on short notice. This ratio compares quick assets—the most liquid current assets—against current liabilities. Quick assets generally consist of cash and equivalents, short-term investments, and accounts receivable. So, generally quick assets equal total current assets minus inventory.

Belle's Fine Coffees' current balance sheet lists total current assets of $5.24 million and inventory of $2.2 million. Therefore, its quick ratio is as follows:

$$\text{Acid-test ratio} = \frac{\text{Current assets} - \text{Inventory}}{\text{Current liabilities}} = \frac{(5{,}240 - 2{,}200)}{2{,}030} = 1.50$$

Because the traditional rule of thumb for an adequate acid-test ratio is around 1:1, Belle's Fine Coffees appears to have a strong level of liquidity. However, the same cautions apply here as for the current ratio. The ratio should be compared with industry averages and data from previous operating periods to determine whether it is adequate for the company.

Activity Ratios

Activity ratios measure the effectiveness of management's use of the company's resources. One of the most frequently used activity ratios, the inventory turnover ratio, indicates the number of times merchandise moves through a business:

$$\text{Inventory turnover} = \frac{\text{Cost of goods sold}}{\text{Average inventory}} = \frac{10{,}380}{[(2{,}200 + 1{,}850)/2]} = 5.13$$

Average inventory for Belle's Fine Coffees is determined by adding the inventory as of December 31, 2021 ($2.2 million) with the inventory as of December 31, 2020 ($1.85 million) and dividing it by 2. Comparing the 5.13 inventory turnover ratio with industry standards gives a measure of efficiency. It is important to note, however, that inventory turnover can vary substantially, depending on the products a company sells and the industry in which it operates.

If a company makes a substantial portion of its sales on credit, measuring receivables turnover can provide useful information. Receivables turnover can be calculated as follows:

$$\text{Receivables turnover} = \frac{\text{Credit sales}}{\text{Average accounts receivable}}$$

Because Belle's Fine Coffees is a wholesaler, let's assume that all of its sales are credit sales. Average receivables equals the simple average of 2021's receivables and 2020's receivables. The ratio for the company is:

$$\text{Receivables turnover} = \frac{17{,}300}{[(990 + 775)/2]} = 19.60$$

Dividing 365 by the figure for receivables turnover, 19.6, equals the average age of receivables, 18.62 days. Assume Belle's Fine Coffees expects its retail customers to pay outstanding bills within 30 days of the date of purchase. Given that the average age of its receivables is less than 30 days, Belle's Fine Coffees appears to be successful at collecting its credit sales.

Another measure of efficiency is total asset turnover. It measures how much in sales each dollar invested in assets generates:

$$\text{Total asset turnover} = \frac{\text{Sales}}{\text{Average total assets}}$$

$$= \frac{17{,}300}{[(8{,}790 + 7{,}305)/2]} = 2.15$$

Average total assets for Belle's Fine Coffees equals total assets as of December 31, 2021 ($8.79 million) plus total assets as of December 31, 2020 ($7.305 million) divided by 2.

Belle's Fine Coffees generates about $2.15 in sales for each dollar invested in assets. Although a higher ratio generally indicates that a company is operating more efficiently, care must be taken when comparing companies that operate in different industries. Some industries simply require higher investment in assets than do other industries.

Profitability Ratios

Some ratios measure the organization's overall financial performance by evaluating its ability to generate revenues in excess of operating costs and other expenses. These measures are called *profitability ratios*. To compute these ratios, accountants compare the company's earnings with total sales or investments. Over a period of time, profitability ratios may reveal the effectiveness of management in operating the business. Three important profitability ratios are gross profit margin, net profit margin, and return on equity (see photo):

$$\text{Gross profit margin} = \frac{\text{Gross profit}}{\text{Sales}} = \frac{6{,}920}{17{,}300} = 40.0\%$$

$$\text{Net profit margin} = \frac{\text{Net income}}{\text{Sales}} = \frac{1{,}917}{17{,}300} = 11.1\%$$

$$\text{Return on equity} = \frac{\text{Net income}}{\text{Average equity}} = \frac{1{,}917}{[(5{,}660 + 4{,}455)/2]} = 37.9\%$$

All of these ratios indicate positive results of the current operations of Belle's Fine Coffees. For example, the net profit margin indicates that the company realizes a profit of slightly more than 11 cents on each dollar of merchandise it sells. Although this ratio varies widely among businesses, Belle's Fine Coffees compares favorably with wholesalers in general, which have an average net profit margin of around 5%. However, this ratio, like the other profitability ratios, should be evaluated in relation to profit forecasts, past performance, or more specific industry averages to enhance the interpretation of results. Similarly, although the company's return on equity of almost 38% appears outstanding, the degree of risk in the industry also must be considered.

Spencer Platt/Getty Images

Kenneth Frazier is CEO and a member of the board of directors for pharmaceutical company Merck & Co. Frazier is the first African-American to lead a major pharmaceutical company and he has encouraged the company to take financial risks in developing new treatments.

Leverage Ratios

Leverage ratios measure the extent to which a company relies on debt financing. They provide important information to potential investors and lenders. If management has assumed too much debt in financing the company's operations, problems may arise in meeting future interest payments and repaying outstanding loans. As we discuss in Chapter 17, borrowing money does have advantages. However, relying too heavily on debt financing may lead to a reduced credit rating, or even to bankruptcy. More generally, both investors and lenders may prefer to deal with companies whose owners have invested enough of their own money to avoid overreliance on borrowing. The debt ratio and long-term debt to equity ratio help interested parties evaluate a company's leverage:

$$\text{Debt ratio} = \frac{\text{Total liabilities}}{\text{Total assets}} = \frac{3{,}130}{8{,}790} = 35.6\%$$

$$\text{Long-term debt to equity} = \frac{\text{Long-term debt}}{\text{Owners' equity}} = \frac{1{,}100}{5{,}660} = 19.43\%$$

A total liabilities to total assets ratio greater than 50% indicates that a company is relying more on borrowed money than owners' equity. Because Belle's Fine Coffees' total liabilities to total assets ratio is 35.6%, the company's owners have invested considerably more than the total amount of liabilities shown on the company's balance sheet. Moreover, the company's long-term debt to equity ratio is only 19.43%, indicating that Belle's Fine Coffees has only about 19.4 cents in long-term debt to every dollar in equity. The long-term debt to equity ratio also indicates that Belle's Fine Coffees hasn't relied very heavily on borrowed money.

The four categories of financial ratios relate balance sheet and income statement data to one another, help management pinpoint a company's strengths and weaknesses, and indicate areas in need of further investigation. Large, multiproduct companies that operate in diverse markets use their information systems to update their financial ratios, often in real time. Each company's management must decide on an appropriate review schedule to avoid the costly and time-consuming mistake of overmonitoring.

In addition to calculating financial ratios, managers, investors, and lenders should pay close attention to how accountants apply a number of accounting rules when preparing financial statements. GAAP gives accountants leeway in reporting certain revenues and expenses. Public companies are required to disclose, in footnotes to the financial statements, how the various accounting rules were applied.

Assessment Check

1. List the four categories of financial ratios.
2. Define the following ratios: *current ratio, inventory turnover, net profit margin,* and *debt ratio*.

7 Budgeting

budget a planning and controlling tool that reflects the company's expected sales revenues, operating expenses, and cash receipts and outlays.

Although the financial statements discussed in this chapter focus on past business activities, they also provide the basis for planning in the future. A **budget** is a planning and controlling tool that reflects the company's expected sales revenues, operating expenses, and cash receipts and outlays. It quantifies the company's plans for a specified future period. Because it reflects management estimates of expected sales, cash inflows and outflows, and costs, the budget is a financial blueprint and can be thought of as a short-term financial plan. It becomes the standard for comparison against actual performance.

Budget preparation is frequently a time-consuming task that involves many people from various departments within the organization. The budgeting process varies with the size and complexity of the organization. Large corporations such as Marvel, Verizon, and Activision Blizzard maintain complex and sophisticated budgeting systems. Besides serving as planning

Job Description

Accountants and Auditors

Overview Accountants and auditors prepare, examine, analyze, and communicate financial information for various entities, such as companies, individual clients, and federal, state, and local governments. They help to ensure that public records are accurately kept and that taxes are paid on time. When preparing and examining financial records, their goal is to assess financial operations to ensure that organizations are run efficiently.

Responsibilities Accountants and auditors typically organize and maintain financial records and examine financial statements to ensure that they are accurate and comply with laws and regulations. They compute taxes owed, prepare tax returns, and ensure that taxes are paid on schedule. Books and systems are inspected for efficiency and accuracy of accounting principles. Best practice recommendations are made to management so that financial operations can run smoothly, and recommendations are made to reduce costs, enhance revenues, and improve company profits. Findings must be articulated and explained to clients and managers, which often involves written reports and face-to-face meetings.

Requirements Most jobs require at least a bachelor's degree in accounting or a related field. Job opportunities are favorable, especially for certified public accountants (CPAs) or those with certification within a specific field of accounting. Accountants are often "numbers" people who do well with being organized and detailed. They must also possess a high degree of ethics and integrity because they are often dealing with conveying important and impactful financial results. Accountants who possess effective and strong communications skills will set themselves apart when interacting with clients to communicate important information.

Outlook The outlook for careers in accounting and auditing looks very favorable. According to the U.S. Bureau of Labor Statistics, employment opportunity for accountants is expected to grow by 10% through 2026, a significantly more rapid rate than the average for all other occupations. This likely lucrative future for accountants and auditors is due to an increased emphasis on accountability, transparency, and controls in financial reporting and overall increased scrutiny of company finances and accounting procedures.

Sources: Government website, "Accountants and Auditors," *Occupational Outlook Handbook*, 2017–2018 Edition, http://www.bls.gov, accessed May 25, 2018; organization website, "CPA Careers," http://www.aicpa.org, accessed May 25, 2018; company website, "Accountant," *U.S. News and World Report*, http://money.usnews.com, accessed May 25, 2018.

and controlling tools, their budgets help managers integrate across numerous divisions. However, budgeting in both large and small companies is similar to household budgeting in its purpose: to match income and expenses in a way that accomplishes objectives while projecting the timing and amount of cash inflows and outflows.

An accounting department provides financial support and accounting services to the organization to which it belongs. The overall master, or operating, budget is actually a composite of many individual budgets for separate units of the company. These individual budgets typically include the production budget, cash budget, capital expenditures budget, advertising budget, sales budget, and travel budget. However, being an accountant involves more than just creating budgets. The "Job Description" feature describes more fully the responsibilities, job outlook, and requirements for accountants and auditors today.

Technology has revolutionized and made the budgeting process easier and far more efficient. The accounting software products discussed earlier—such as QuickBooks—all include budgeting features. Many banks now offer their customers personal financial management tools (PFMs). Mint.com is a PFM leader and online tool for managing personal finances. Developed by Aaron Patzer, who was frustrated with available online tools for managing his finances, Mint.com was later sold to Intuit. What makes Mint.com unique is a patent-pending categorization technology that automatically identifies and organizes transactions made in most bank, credit, investment, brokerage, or retirement accounts.[13]

One of the most important budgets prepared by companies is the *cash budget*. The cash budget, usually prepared monthly, tracks the company's cash inflows and outflows. **Figure 15.8** illustrates a sample cash budget for Birchwood Paper, a small Maine-based paper products company. The company has set a $150,000 target cash balance. The cash budget indicates months in which the company will need temporary loans—May, June, and July—and how much it will need (close to $3 million). The document also indicates that Birchwood will generate a cash surplus in August and can begin repaying the short-term loan. Finally, the cash budget produces a tangible standard against which to compare actual cash inflows and outflows.

Birchwood Paper Company
Four-Month Cash Budget

($ thousands)	May	June	July	August
Gross sales	*$ 1,200.0*	*$ 3,200.0*	*$ 5,500.0*	*$ 4,500.0*
Cash sales	300.0	800.0	1,375.0	1,125.0
One month prior	600.0	600.0	1,600.0	2,750.0
Two months prior	300.0	300.0	300.0	800.0
Total cash inflows	1,200.0	1,700.0	3,275.0	4,675.0
Purchases				
Cash purchases	1,040.0	1,787.5	1,462.5	390.0
One month prior	390.0	1,040.0	1,787.5	1,462.5
Wages and salaries	250.0	250.0	250.0	250.0
Office rent	75.0	75.0	75.0	75.0
Marketing and other expenses	150.0	150.0	150.0	150.0
Taxes		300.0		
Total cash outflows	1,905.0	3,602.5	3,725.0	2,327.5
Net cash flow				
(Inflows – Outflows)	(705.0)	(1,902.5)	(450.0)	2,347.5
Beginnning cash balance	250.0	150.0	150.0	150.0
Net cash flow	*(705.0)*	*(1,902.5)*	*(450.0)*	*2,347.5*
Ending cash balance	(455.0)	(1,752.5)	(300.0)	2,497.5
Target cash balance	150.0	150.0	150.0	150.0
Surplus (deficit)	(605.0)	(1,902.5)	(450.0)	2,347.5
Cumulative surplus (deficit)	(605.0)	(2,507.5)	(2,957.5)	610.0

FIGURE 15.8 **Four-Month Cash Budget for Birchwood Paper Company**

Assessment Check

1. What is a budget?
2. How is a cash budget organized?

8 International Accounting

As more companies conduct international operations with workforces from multiple countries, accountants who understand diverse cultures, business perspectives, international laws, and regulations will be in demand. Today, accounting procedures and practices must be adapted to accommodate an international business environment. The Coca-Cola Company and McDonald's both generate more than half their annual revenues from sales outside the United States. Nestlé, the giant chocolate and food products company, operates throughout the world. It derives the majority of its revenues from outside Switzerland, its home country. International accounting practices for global companies, must reliably translate the financial statements of the company's international affiliates, branches, and subsidiaries and convert data about foreign currency transactions to dollars. Also, foreign currencies and exchange rates influence the accounting and financial reporting processes of companies operating internationally.

The "Business Model" feature describes the impact of recent tax law—and the money being brought back to the United States from overseas.

Business Model

Tax Changes Free Up Overseas Cash

With a recent reduction of the statutory corporate tax rate from 35% to 21%, many American corporations realized a bottom line increase. Previously, multinational companies were reluctant to bring cash back to the United States because of heavy tax burdens. The recently signed tax bill offers companies a one-off lower tax rate on funds brought back to the United States. Technology companies, who hold more cash offshore than any other industry, mostly in tax haven subsidiaries, supported the law because of the one-time discounted rate of as much as 15.5% on overseas holdings.

Supporters of the tax change argue that an incentive to bring the money home could boost the U.S. economy with increased hiring and investment. Still, others argue that the only ones who stand to win are the wealthy, along with shareholders who will receive dividend and stock buybacks. In fact, computer networking company Cisco announced plans to pass along a good proportion of its $67 billion windfall to shareholders through share buybacks and increased dividend payments. A share buyback is a program by which a company buys back its own shares from the marketplace, usually because management thinks the shares are undervalued, reducing the number of outstanding shares. On the day of this announcement, Cisco's stock increased 7%.

Apple announced that it would make a $38 billion one-time tax payment on its offshore cash holdings, bring most of the money home, and boost U.S. spending to include the creation of 20,000 new jobs. Other companies are planning acquisitions, stock share buybacks, new production plants, and worker bonuses. However, it remains to be seen when more cash will be "brought home," and if so, who stands to benefit from this new tax law.

Questions for Critical Thinking

1. It isn't clear how much of Apple's investment was triggered by tax considerations and whether the company would have done so anyway. Some firms are clear that investments are made only when a company sees an opportunity—rather than a result of tax reform—and that spending plans remain unchanged. What are your thoughts?
2. The new rules also mean companies can no longer avoid paying taxes on past international profits by holding the cash outside the United States. They must pay tax on the money whether they bring it back to the country or not. What strategies do you think companies will employ? Discuss.

Sources: Doug Mac Millan and Jay Greene, "Tech Giants are in No Rush to Spend Overseas Cash," *The Wall Street Journal*, www.wsj.com, accessed May 26, 2018; Stratfor, "How Tax Overhaul Will Net The U.S. Big Returns," *Forbes*, www.forbes.com, accessed May 26, 2018; Daniel Shane, "Cisco: We're Moving Our $67 Billion Cash Pile to the U.S.," Forbes, www.forbes.com, accessed May 26, 2018; Jesse Drucker and Alan Rappeport, "The Tax Bill's Winners and Losers," *The New York Times*, www.nytimes.com, accessed May 28, 2018.

Exchange Rates

As defined in Chapter 4, an exchange rate is the ratio at which a country's currency can be exchanged for other currencies. Currencies can be treated as goods to be bought and sold. Like the price of any product, currency prices change daily according to supply and demand. So exchange rate fluctuations complicate accounting entries and accounting practices.

Accountants who deal with international transactions must appropriately record their company's foreign sales and purchases. Accounting software helps companies handle all of their international transactions within a single program. An international company's consolidated financial statements must reflect any gains or losses due to changes in exchange rates during specific periods of time—for example, Nestlé's Nescafé (see photo). Financial statements that cover operations in two or more countries also need to treat fluctuations consistently to allow for comparison.

In the United States, GAAP requires companies to make adjustments to their earnings that reflect changes in exchange rates. A strong dollar hurts American companies like McDonald's, impacted by foreign currency exchange rates. If McDonald's sells a hamburger in Japan, it collects Japanese yen for that burger. The company now must exchange the yen for dollars when it brings those proceeds back to the

Nelson Ching/Bloomberg/Getty Images, Inc.

Nestlé's Nescafé' coffee is packaged for shipment at a Chinese production plant. Because this Swiss corporation operates around the world, its profits and its financial statements are affected by foreign exchange rates.

United States. If the dollar gains in value against the yen, when McDonald's exchanges the currency, it takes a hit on that revenue it earned from the sale of the hamburger. Because the dollar appreciated against the yen, it now takes more yen to equal one dollar than it did before. To compensate for this, management reviews and analyzes business results excluding the effect of foreign currency translation—with the belief that this better represents underlying business trends.[14]

International Accounting Standards

International Accounting Standards Board (IASB) organization established in 1973 to promote worldwide consistency in financial reporting practices.

International Financial Reporting Standards (IFRS) standards and interpretations adopted by the IASB.

The International Accounting Standards Committee (IASC) was established in 1973 to promote worldwide consistency in financial reporting practices and soon developed its first set of accounting standards and interpretations. In 2001, the IASC became the **International Accounting Standards Board (IASB)**. **International Financial Reporting Standards (IFRS)** are the standards and interpretations adopted by the IASB. The IASB operates in much the same manner as the FASB does in the United States, interpreting and modifying IFRS.

Because of increased global trade, there is a real need for comparability of and uniformity in international accounting rules. Despite a global world economy and the support of world leaders for the worldwide standardization of accounting practices, the United States has not yet adopted IFRS. Some cite GAAP as a superior standard, while others point to a potentially costly and complex conversion. In addition, synthesizing differing cultural, legal, regulatory, and economic priorities among nations is no small task.

Nearly 100 other countries currently require, permit the use of, or have a policy of convergence with IFRS. These nations and other entities include members of the European Union, India, Australia, Canada, and Hong Kong. At first, the United States was skeptical of IFRS, even though major American accounting organizations have been involved with the IASB since its inception. In fact, the SEC used to require all companies whose shares were publicly traded in the United States to report financial results using GAAP. This rule applied regardless of where companies were located.

This requirement started to change some years back, when the FASB and the IASB met and committed to the eventual convergence of IFRS with GAAP. Around the same time, the SEC began to loosen its rules on the use of IFRS by foreign companies whose shares trade in the United States. Today, many foreign companies can report results using IFRS as long as they reconcile these results to GAAP in a footnote. Some large U.S. companies were allowed to use international accounting standards beginning in 2009. Thus far, U.S. and international accounting standards have not been unified. However, FASB, responsible for setting U.S. accounting standards, and IASB, responsible for setting foreign standards, do work together closely, and the progress toward a single global financial-reporting standard continues.[15]

How does IFRS differ from GAAP? Although many similarities between IFRS and GAAP exist, there are some important differences. For example, under GAAP, plant, property, and equipment are reported on the balance sheet at the historical cost minus depreciation. Under IFRS, plant, property, and equipment are shown on the balance sheet at current market value. A major difference between GAAP and IFRS is that GAAP is rules-based, whereas IFRS is principles-based. This gives a better picture of the real value of a company's assets. Many accounting experts believe that IFRS is overall less complicated than GAAP and more transparent.[16]

Assessment Check

1. How are financial statements adjusted for exchange rates?
2. What is the purpose of the IASB?

What's Ahead

This chapter describes the role of accounting in an organization. Accounting is the process of measuring, interpreting, and communicating financial information to interested parties both inside and outside the company. The next two chapters discuss the finance function of an organization. Finance deals with planning, obtaining, and managing the organization's funds to accomplish its objectives in the most efficient and effective manner possible. Chapter 16 outlines the financial system, the system by which funds are transferred from savers to borrowers. Organizations rely on the financial system to raise funds for expansion or operations. The chapter includes a description of financial institutions, such as banks; financial markets, such as the New York Stock Exchange; financial instruments, such as stocks and bonds; and the role of the Federal Reserve System. Chapter 17 discusses the role of finance and the financial manager in an organization.

Chapter in Review

Summary of Learning Objectives

LEARNING OBJECTIVE 1 Discuss the users of accounting information.

Accountants measure, interpret, and communicate financial information to parties inside and outside the company to support improved decision making. Accountants gather, record, and interpret financial information for management. They also provide financial information on the status and operations of the company for evaluation by outside parties, such as government agencies, stockholders, potential investors, and lenders. Accounting plays key roles in financing activities, which help start and expand an organization; investing activities, which provide the assets it needs to continue operating; and operating activities, which focus on selling goods and services and paying expenses incurred in regular operations.

Assessment Check Answers

1.1 **Define *accounting*.** Accounting is the process of measuring, interpreting, and communicating financial information to enable people inside and outside the company to make informed decisions.

1.2 **Who uses accounting information?** Managers of all types of organizations use accounting information to help them plan, assess performance, and control daily and long-term operations. Outside users of accounting information include government officials, investors, creditors, and donors.

1.3 **What are the three business activities that involve accounting?** The three activities involving accounting are financing, investing, and operating activities.

LEARNING OBJECTIVE 2 Describe accounting professionals.

Public accountants provide accounting services to other companies or individuals for a fee. They are involved in such activities as auditing, tax return preparation, management consulting, and accounting system design. Management accountants collect and record financial transactions, prepare financial statements, and interpret them for managers in their own companies. Government and not-for-profit accountants perform many of the same functions as management accountants, but they analyze how effectively the organization or agency is operating, rather than its profits and losses.

Assessment Check Answers

2.1 **List the three services offered by public accounting firms.** The three services offered by public accounting firms are auditing, tax services, and management consulting.

2.2 **What tasks do management accountants perform?** Management accountants work for the organization and are responsible for collecting and recording financial transactions and for preparing and interpreting financial statements.

LEARNING OBJECTIVE 3 Identify the foundation of the accounting system.

The foundation of the accounting system in the United States is GAAP (generally accepted accounting principles), a set of guidelines or standards that accountants follow. There are four basic requirements to which all accounting rules should adhere: consistency, relevance, reliability, and comparability. The Financial Accounting Standards Board (FASB), an independent body made up of accounting professionals, is primarily responsible for evaluating, setting, and modifying GAAP. The U.S. Securities and Exchange Commission (SEC) also plays a role in establishing and modifying accounting standards for public companies—companies whose shares are traded in financial markets.

Assessment Check Answers

3.1 **Define *GAAP*.** GAAP stands for generally accepted accounting principles and is a set of standards or guidelines that accountants follow in recording and reporting financial transactions.

3.2 **What are the four basic requirements to which all accounting rules must adhere?** The four basic requirements to which all accounting rules must adhere are consistency, relevance, reliability, and comparability.

3.3 **What is the role played by the FASB?** The Financial Accounting Standards Board (FASB) is an independent body made up of accounting professionals and is primarily responsible for evaluating, setting, and modifying GAAP.

LEARNING OBJECTIVE 4 Outline the steps in the accounting cycle.

The accounting process involves recording, classifying, and summarizing data about transactions and then using this information to produce financial statements for the company's managers and other interested parties. Transactions are recorded chronologically in journals, posted in ledgers, and then summarized in accounting statements. Today, much of this activity takes place electronically. The basic accounting equation states that assets (what a company owns) must always equal liabilities (what a company owes creditors) plus owners' equity. This equation also illustrates double-entry bookkeeping, the process by which accounting transactions are recorded. Under double-entry bookkeeping, each individual transaction must have an offsetting transaction.

Assessment Check Answers

4.1 **List the steps in the accounting cycle.** The accounting cycle involves the following steps: recording transactions, classifying the transactions, summarizing transactions, and using the summaries to produce financial statements.

4.2 **What is the accounting equation?** The accounting equation states that assets (what a company owns) must always equal liabilities (what a company owes) plus owners' equity. Therefore, if assets increase or decrease, there must be an offsetting increase or decrease in liabilities, owners' equity, or both.

4.3 **Briefly explain double-entry bookkeeping.** Double-entry bookkeeping is a process by which accounting transactions are recorded. Each transaction must have an offsetting transaction.

LEARNING OBJECTIVE 5 Explain financial statements.

The balance sheet shows the financial position of a company on a particular date. The three major classifications of balance sheet data are the components of the accounting equation: assets, liabilities, and owners' equity. The income statement shows the results of a company's operations over a specific period. It focuses on the company's activities—its revenues and expenditures—and the resulting profit or loss during the period. The major components of the income statement are revenues, cost of goods sold, expenses, and profit or loss. The statement of owners' equity shows the components of the change in owners' equity from the end of the prior year to the end of the current year. Finally, the statement of cash flows records a company's cash receipts and cash payments during an accounting period. It outlines the sources and uses of cash in the basic business activities of operating, investing, and financing.

Assessment Check Answers

5.1 **List the four financial statements.** The four financial statements are the balance sheet, the income statement, the statement of owners' equity, and the statement of cash flows.

5.2 **How is the balance sheet organized?** Assets (what a company owns) are shown on one side of the balance sheet and are listed in order of convertibility into cash. On the other side of the balance sheet are claims to assets, liabilities (what a company owes), and owners' equity. Claims are listed in the order in which they are due, so liabilities are listed before owners' equity. Assets always equal liabilities plus owners' equity.

5.3 **Define *accrual accounting*.** Accrual accounting recognizes revenues and expenses when they occur, not when cash actually changes hands. Most companies use accrual accounting to prepare their financial statements.

LEARNING OBJECTIVE 6 Discuss financial ratio analysis.

Liquidity ratios measure a company's ability to meet short-term obligations. Examples are the current ratio and the quick, or acid-test, ratio. Activity ratios—such as the inventory turnover ratio, accounts receivable turnover ratio, and the total asset turnover ratio—measure how effectively a company uses its resources. Profitability ratios assess the overall financial performance of the business. The gross profit margin, net profit margin, and return on owners' equity are examples of profitability ratios. Leverage ratios, such as the total liabilities to total assets ratio and the long-term debt to equity ratio, measure the extent to which the company relies on debt to finance its operations. Financial ratios help managers and outside evaluators compare a company's current financial information with that of previous years and with results for other companies in the same industry.

Assessment Check Answers

6.1 **List the four categories of financial ratios.** The four categories of ratios are liquidity, activity, profitability, and leverage.

6.2 **Define the following ratios: *current ratio, inventory turnover, net profit margin*, and *debt ratio*.** The current ratio equals current assets divided by current liabilities. Inventory turnover equals cost of goods sold divided by average inventory. Net profit margin equals net income divided by sales. The debt ratio equals total liabilities divided by total assets.

LEARNING OBJECTIVE 7 Describe the role of budgeting.

Budgets are financial guidelines for future periods and reflect expected sales revenues, operating expenses, and cash receipts and outlays. They reflect management expectations for future occurrences and are based on plans that have been made. Budgets are important planning and controlling tools because they provide standards against which actual performance can be measured. One important type of budget is the cash budget, which estimates cash inflows and outflows over a period of time.

Assessment Check Answers

7.1 **What is a budget?** A budget is a planning and control tool that reflects the company's expected sales revenues, operating expenses, cash receipts, and cash outlays.

7.2 **How is a cash budget organized?** Cash budgets are generally prepared monthly. Cash receipts are listed first. They include cash sales as well as the collection of past credit sales. Cash outlays are listed next. These include cash purchases, payment of past credit purchases, and operating expenses. The difference between cash receipts and cash outlays is net cash flow.

LEARNING OBJECTIVE 8 Outline international accounting practices.

One accounting issue that affects global business is exchange rates. An exchange rate is the ratio at which a country's currency can be exchanged for other currencies. Daily changes in exchange rates affect the accounting entries for sales and purchases of companies involved in international markets. These fluctuations create either losses or gains for particular companies. The International Accounting Standards Board (IASB) was established to provide worldwide consistency in financial reporting practices and comparability of and uniformity in international accounting standards. It has developed International Financial Reporting Standards (IFRS). Many countries have already adopted IFRS, and the United States is in the process of making the transition to it.

Assessment Check Answers

8.1 **How are financial statements adjusted for exchange rates?** An exchange rate is the ratio at which a country's currency can be exchanged for other currencies. Fluctuations of exchange rates create either gains or losses for particular companies because data about international financial transactions must be translated into the currency of the country in which the parent company is based.

8.2 **What is the purpose of the IASB?** The International Accounting Standards Board (IASB) was established to provide worldwide consistency in financial reporting practices and comparability and uniformity of international accounting rules. The IASB has developed the International Financial Reporting Standards (IFRS).

Business Terms You Need to Know

Review Questions

1. Define *accounting*. Who are the major users of accounting information?
2. What are the three major business activities in which accountants play a major role? Give an example of each.
3. What does the term *GAAP* mean? Briefly explain the roles of the Financial Accounting Standards Board and the Securities and Exchange Commission.
4. What is double-entry bookkeeping? Give a brief example.
5. List the four major financial statements. Which financial statements are permanent, and which are temporary?
6. What is the difference between a current asset and a long-term asset? Why is cash typically listed first on a balance sheet?
7. List and explain the major items found on an income statement.
8. What is accrual accounting? Give an example of how accrual accounting affects a company's financial statement.
9. List the four categories of financial ratios and give an example of each. What is the purpose of ratio analysis?
10. What is a cash budget? Briefly outline what a simple cash budget might look like.

Projects and Teamwork Applications

1. Using LinkedIn or your personal or professional network, make contact with someone who works as an accountant at either a public accounting firm, government, or nonprofit to set up an interview. Ask the individual what his or her educational background is, what attracted the individual to the accounting profession, and what he or she does during a typical day. Prepare a brief report on your interview. Do you now want to learn more about the accounting profession? Are you more interested in possibly pursuing a career in accounting?

2. Using open book management, companies make it a practice to share financial and company information with employees. The risk–reward relationship is that sharing what might be sensitive information creates transparency, which encourages employees to understand financial matters and think and act like owners. Do you agree? What are the risks to using this strategy? What are the rewards?

3. Identify two public companies operating in different industries. Collect at least two years' worth of financial statements for the firms. Calculate the financial ratios discussed in the chapter. Prepare an oral report summarizing, comparing, and contrasting your findings.

4. Human asset accounting, also referred to as human resource accounting, considers the value and role of people within an organization. This includes their replacement cost. How would you apply the concept of human asset accounting to Amazon and the role founder Jeff Bezos plays in the organization? You may choose another company with an individual who plays a defining role. Discuss your findings.

5. Adapting the format of Figure 15.8, prepare on a sheet of paper your personal cash budget for next month. Keep in mind the following suggestions as you prepare your budget:

a. *Cash inflows*. Your sources of cash would include your payroll earnings, if any; gifts; scholarship monies; tax refunds; dividends and interest; and income from self-employment.

b. *Cash outflows*. When estimating next month's cash outflows, include any of the following that may apply to your situation:

i. Household expenses (rent or mortgage, utilities, maintenance, home furnishings, telephone/cell phone, cable TV, household supplies, groceries)

ii. Education (tuition, fees, textbooks, supplies)

iii. Work (lunches, clothing)

iv. Clothing (purchases, cleaning, laundry)

v. Automobile (auto payments, repairs) or other transportation (bus, bicycle, ride sharing apps, train)

vi. Gasoline expenses

vii. Insurance premiums

- Renter's (or homeowner's)
- Auto
- Health
- Life

viii. Taxes (income, Social Security, Medicare, real estate)

ix. Savings and investments

x. Entertainment/recreation (dining, movies, health club, vacation/travel)

xi. Debt (credit cards, installment loans)

xii. Miscellaneous (charitable contributions, child care, gifts, medical expenses)

c. *Beginning cash balance*. This amount could be based on a minimum cash balance you keep in your checking account and should include only the cash available for your use; therefore, money such as that invested in retirement plans should not be included.

Web Assignments

1. **Letter to Shareholders.** Berkshire Hathaway's annual letter to shareholders, written by CEO Warren Buffett, happens to be one of the most interesting, down-to-earth, folksy, and unique communications for a corporation of this size. Conduct a search for Berkshire Hathaway's most recent annual report and read the letter from Mr. Buffett. What are your impressions?

2. **Apple's balance sheet.** Go to Apple's website to review the company's most recent annual report. Find the balance sheet and the corresponding discussion. Using concepts from the chapter, review and calculate some of the company's key ratios. Based upon this information, what unique and unusual things have you found, and how would you evaluate Apple's current financial situation? Discuss your findings. **www.apple.com**

3. **Preparing a personal balance sheet.** Go online to find a template for a personal balance sheet. Fill in as many items as you can, and create your own asset categories if needed. Upon evaluating your results, how would you assess your liquidity, debt, and debt-to-equity ratios? What sort of change would you recommend to modify your current situation?

Note: Internet web addresses change frequently. If you don't find the exact sites listed, you may need to access the organization's home page and search from there or use a search engine such as Google or Bing.

Cases

Case 15.1 Forensic Accountants Search for Fraud

A crime fighter might not immediately come to mind when most people think about the role an accountant plays in everyday business. Yet the rapidly growing field of forensic accounting involves investigating white-collar crimes such as business fraud, improper financial reporting, and illegal investment schemes.

Forensic accounting is performed in preparation for legal review. Forensic accountants investigate an organization's accounting system to reconstruct suspicious transactions to find evidence about what actually happened. They also testify as expert witnesses if a case goes to trial. The job requires a bachelor's degree in accounting and CPA certification, with further training in investigative techniques for certification as a certified fraud examiner (CFE) or a certified forensic accountant (CrFA).

When energy giant Enron Corporation collapsed, forensic accounting investigations revealed that for several years the company had issued false financial statements, which exaggerated company earnings, thereby increasing the company's stock prices. The statements painted a picture of steady and rising profits that met earnings targets and expectations. However, in reality, Enron's own investments were performing poorly, and the company was actually losing money. Even after the truth leaked out and the company's stock prices tumbled, top management kept issuing false financial statements, hoping to camouflage the truth. In a federal trial, two former executives were convicted of conspiracy, wire fraud, and securities fraud.

Increased regulations have helped the forensic accounting services industry grow, particularly over the past decade. Forensic accountants who are able to use newer software and technology tools to identify fraudulent business practices will bring the most benefits to clients. The tools in the forensic accountant's toolkit have become much sharper.

Questions for Critical Thinking

1. Demand for forensic accountants has grown over the past decade since the economic slowdown, and following a notorious series of scandals such as those involving Enron and Bernard Madoff. Based upon the past, what would you say the industry can predict for the future?
2. How is the role of a forensic accountant different from that of an auditor? How might forensic accounting change the world of business?

Sources: Michael Cohn, "Demand Growing for Forensic Accountants," *Accounting Today*, http://www.accountingtoday.com, accessed May 25, 2018; Jesse Chiang, "Accountants Uncover Opportunities in Forensics," *Ibis World*, http://www.ibisworld.com, accessed May 25, 2018; Caleb Newquist, "What Are Your Questions for a Forensic Accounting Partner?" *Going Concern*, http://goingconcern.com, accessed May 25, 2018; company website, "Risk Management," http://www.pwc.com/nz, accessed May 25, 2018; Tracy Coenen, "Enron: The Good, the Bad, and the Ugly," *Wisconsin Law Journal*, http://wislawjournal.com, accessed May 25, 2018; James A. DiGabriele, "Applying Forensic Skepticism to Lost Profits Valuations," *Journal of Accountancy*, http://www.journalofaccountancy.com; accessed May 25, 2018, Ralph Heibutzki, "What Are the Issues Facing Forensic Accounting?" *eHow*, http://www.ehow.com, accessed May 25, 2018.

Case 15.2 Taxing Issues for the Internet of Things

The Internet of Things (IoT), as discussed in Chapter 14, has blurred the line between products and services—and, as a result, taxes. The issue is how companies are taxed, because products are taxed differently than services. To add to the confusion, if what a company sells is classified as "telecommunications," then it is taxed as a regulated utility. It is estimated that in the next year, there will be 50 billion connected devices with close to $9 trillion in revenue affected by this designation.

As cloud computing, mobile computing, and big data continue to spur the growth of the Internet of Things, businesses have capitalized on creating value from traditional products by adding Internet connectivity, sensors, and other IoT capabilities. As a result, the question persists about what is classified as a product and what is classified as a service. Take for example, refrigerators, ovens, thermostats, cars, and medical devices. The issue of taxes has become increasingly complex due mainly to recurring (and changing) revenue models.

Manufacturers of automakers, medical device makers, and appliances are adding value to their product offerings by providing connectivity services and sometimes by offering ongoing subscriptions. Is a former product company that offers a smart product with sensors now considered a service business? These are the very decisions regulatory and taxing authorities will be forced to make when evaluating companies that generate revenue streams that now include service and communication offerings delivered over the Internet.

Generally, when a service like dry cleaning or a haircut is provided, it is taxed. However, sometimes services are consumed over an ongoing period of time—for example, Netflix, iTunes, or Hulu. Utilities, for another example, are billed on a "pay for what you use" or consumption-based model.

The question of what constitutes a product, a service, or a high-tech bundled service has become increasingly complex. To make sure they collect the appropriate amount of tax revenues, taxing authorities are particularly interested in answering this question. Even trying to figure out what the service offering entails can be far less straightforward than in the past. For now, tax authorities will continue to rethink and figure out tax rules to make sure they receive their fair share of taxes from additional services provided via the Internet of Things.

Questions for Critical Thinking

1. Why do you think services are taxed differently than products? Is this fair? Why or why not?
2. What tax planning should a business consider if it is involved in the Internet of Things?

Sources: "Tax Implications of the Internet of Things," *Wall Street Journal*, http://deloitte.wsj.com, accessed May 25, 2018; Jonathan Marashlian, "Internet of Things: Quick Guide to Tax and Regulatory Considerations," *LinkedIn*, https://www.linkedin.com, accessed May 25, 2018; government website, "Internet of Things: Privacy and Security in a Connected World," http://www.ftc.gov, accessed May 25, 2018; Eileen Bernardo, "Billing and Taxation in an IoT World—Today and in the Future," *Aria*, https://www.ariasystems.com, accessed May 25, 2018.

Case 15.3 Mei Mei's Secret Recipe: Attention to Accounting Details

The success of the Mei Mei Group, which includes its Street Kitchen food truck and its new restaurant, can be credited to three siblings from the Boston area. Andy, Irene, and Margaret Li's award-winning food truck serves up creative Chinese American cuisine made with sustainably raised meats and locally sourced produce from small family farms. Using a repurposed shipping container kiosk, Mei Mei Group recently opened a third location, Mei Mei Design, at the Boston Design Center. "Mei Mei" is Mandarin for "little sister," and the secret to Mei Mei's staying power can be partly attributed to one of the "little sisters" in the group, Margaret, or Mei for short. She uses accounting information to make important strategic decisions about labor and food.

A key component of the company's success is its proactive approach and keen attention to recording, summarizing, and analyzing financial data. The food truck has been a great way to test and experiment with different dishes, while spending less money than running a full-service restaurant. After evaluating the results of its operation on a daily basis, the owners decided to expand operations by adding a restaurant to its business.

The Li siblings balance choices that make good financial sense with their business values and practices. The siblings believe cooking and serving food that reflects the humane treatment of animals can make a difference in the local food system, and balancing these values against costs is integral to their budgeting, financial planning, and overall operations. Keeping track of costs on a daily basis actually allows Mei to make decisions to maintain and grow the businesses profitably. Mei uses accounting information to make decisions about food costs, which are maintained at a targeted percentage of sales. For all new product development, including new menu items, decisions are made with a focus on the numbers and metrics, or food costs as a percentage of the selling price.

While costs to source locally can be considerably higher, creativity and experience certainly help. For example, Mei purchases whole pigs from suppliers, which lowers the price per pound for pork. In addition, Mei keeps a watchful eye on fixed costs like rent and labor to be sure they remain at a targeted percentage of sales. With 40 employees, tracking labor costs and allocating staff have become increasingly important for the company.

Two business activities, financing and investing, involve accounting, and for the Mei Mei Group and most small businesses, both can be a challenge. For the funds required to get its Street Kitchen rolling, the Li siblings used a lot of their own personal savings, along with loans from other family members. For the Mei Mei restaurant, partial financing of $35,000 came through Kickstarter, an online crowdfunding site.

A wall in the restaurant will be dedicated to Kickstarter donors who believed that adding a restaurant to the Mei Mei business portfolio made good financial sense. The siblings agree that making the right investment decisions early on can make or break any small business. Their perseverance has paid off. The restaurant was named Eater Boston's Restaurant of the Year and made *Boston* magazine's list of 50 Best Restaurants.

Because employees and suppliers need to be paid on time, Mei makes it a point to check the books every day to be sure there is sufficient money coming in against the money being paid out. With regularly scheduled owner meetings the siblings communicate business results with one another on an ongoing basis. Information is also shared with managers and employees so accurate decisions can be made regarding food purchases, labor, and other business components. When Mei Mei managers understand the impact of a decision and its effects on company's finances, it proves to be an appetizing combination of continued growth and profitability.

Questions for Critical Thinking

1. In Mei Mei Street Kitchen's accounting equation, what are some of the firm's assets and liabilities? Based upon this data, what assumptions would you make about its owners' equity?
2. Identify the types of expenses that Mei Mei Street Kitchen might list on its income statement. How might these expenses vary?
3. Why is it important for a small company like the Mei Mei Group to prepare a regular budget? Discuss what you believe the budgeting process might look like at Mei Mei Street Kitchen as compared to the company's restaurant.
4. Discuss some of the financial challenges the Li siblings face in balancing local sourcing and doing business for a sustainable future. If the siblings did not have this value system, how might company financial statements differ, and what trade-offs might exist?

Sources: Company website, "Container" and "Pantry," http://meimeiboston.com, accessed May 25, 2018; Kara Baskin, "Awesome Bowls in a Repurposed Seaport Shipping Container," *Boston Globe,* http://www.bostonglobe.com, accessed May 25, 2018; company website, "2015 Best Dumplings," http://www.bestofboston.com, accessed May 25, 2018; Kate Krader, "The New Originals," *Food and Wine*, http://www.foodandwine.com, accessed May 25, 2018; Mei Mei Street Kitchen Facebook page, https://www.facebook.com/meimeiboston, accessed May 25, 2018; "Meet Young Guns Semi-Finalists Irene Li and Max Hull of Boston's Mei Mei," *Eater.com*, http://www.eater.com, accessed May 25, 2018; Sascha Garey, "Lunch Anyone? Mei Mei," *BU Today*, http://www.bu.edu, accessed May 25, 2018; Rachel Leah Blumenthal, "Changing the Way the World Eats: Mei Mei Street Kitchen at TED," *YouTube*, http://www.youtube.com, accessed May 25, 2018; Christopher Hughes, "Five Reasons You Should Be Eating at Mei Mei Street Kitchen," *Boston*, http://www.bostonmagazine.com, accessed May 25, 2018; Devya First, "Mei Mei Crew Inventively Spins Off Its Truck Menu," *Boston Globe*, http://www.bostonglobe.com; accessed May 25, 2018, Jon Giardiello, "Mei Mei Street Kitchen Opens New Location," http://www.boston.com, accessed May 25, 2018; Morgan Rousseau, "Cray Cray for Mei Mei: Boston Food Truck to Open Green Eatery," *Metro US Magazine*, http://www.metro.us, accessed May 25, 2018; Rachel Travers, "Rolling with the Mei Mei Street Kitchen," *Boston.com*, http://www.boston.com; accessed May 25, 2018, Brian Samuels, "Serving Local on the Road: Mei Mei Street Kitchen," *Edible Boston*, http://edibleboston.com, accessed May 25, 2018.

CHAPTER 16

The Financial System

LEARNING OBJECTIVES

1. Understand the financial system.
2. List the various types of securities.
3. Discuss financial markets.
4. Understand the stock markets.
5. Describe financial institutions and the growth of financial technology (FinTech).
6. Explain the role of the Federal Reserve System.
7. Describe the regulation of the financial system.
8. Discuss the global perspective of the financial system.

Changemaker

Fabrizio Costantini/The New York Times/Redux Pictures

Dan Gilbert, CEO and Founder

Company: Quicken Loans

Industry: Mortgage Lending/Financial Services

Website: http://www.quickenloans.com

In addition to owning the National Basketball Association's Cleveland Cavaliers, Dan Gilbert leads one of the nation's largest online mortgage lenders. As founder and chairman of privately held Quicken Loans, Gilbert is helping millions of borrowers live the increasingly challenging dream of home ownership. This chapter covers financial institutions, the largest of which are commercial banks. Commercial banks offer the most services of any financial institution, one of which is a mortgage loan made to a borrower to purchase a home. Detroit, Michigan—based Quicken Loans has recently surpassed traditional lending institution Wells Fargo to become the nation's largest mortgage lender. Known as a leader in FinTech (financial technology), convenience, and customer service, Quicken Loans has earned J.D. Power's top spot for customer service for four consecutive years.

While in college and during law school, Gilbert sold real estate part time, and that is when he realized there was far greater potential in originating loans for buyers than selling them homes. In early 1990, with his brother and another friend, Gilbert started what was then called Rock Financial. Sales catapulted, and soon after, Gilbert positioned his company as one of the first direct-to-consumer online mortgage lending platforms.

Gilbert figured he could disrupt the traditional mortgage lending industry by making the process for borrowers more streamlined, less stressful, quicker, and more efficient. The online process of obtaining a home mortgage, while convenient, is not for everyone. Some still prefer to work face-to-face with a traditional bank mortgage lender. Others, responding well to sharing credit scores and finances online, prefer the 24/7 electronic communication and the ability to check the status of a loan application at any time.

Recently, Gilbert's efforts have moved beyond company headquarters in downtown Detroit, and into the classroom. The company is making computer science literacy a central part of the K–12 educational experience by ensuring 15,000 Detroit students receive computer science training over the next five years.[1]

Overview

Businesses, governments, and individuals often need to raise capital. Assume the owner of a small business either forecasts a sharp increase or drop in sales; one might require more inventory and the other reduced production in order to survive. The owner might turn to a major bank or a nontraditional lender for a loan that would provide the needed cash. On the other hand, some individuals and businesses have incomes that are greater than their current expenditures and wish to earn a rate of return on the excess funds. For instance, say your income this month is $3,000 but your expenditures are only $2,500. You can take the extra $500 and deposit it in your bank savings account, which pays you a minimal rate of interest.

The two transactions just described are examples of what is known as the financial system, the process by which money flows from savers to users—or between lenders, investors, and borrowers. Virtually all businesses, governments, and individuals participate in the financial system, and a well-functioning one is vital to a nation's economic well-being.

We begin by describing the financial system and its components in more detail. Then, the major types of financial instruments, such as stocks and bonds, are outlined. Next we discuss financial markets, where financial instruments are bought and sold. We then describe the world's major stock markets, such as the New York Stock Exchange.

Next, banks and other financial institutions are described in depth. The structure and responsibilities of the U.S. Federal Reserve System (the Fed), along with the tools it uses to control the supply of money and credit, are detailed. The chapter concludes with an overview of the major laws and regulations affecting the financial system and a discussion of today's global financial system and the rise of financial technology, known as FinTech.

1 Understanding the Financial System

financial system process by which money flows from savers to users.

Households, businesses, government, financial institutions, and financial markets together form what is known as the **financial system**. A simple diagram of the financial system is shown in **Figure 16.1**.

On the left are savers—those with excess funds. For a variety of reasons, savers choose not to spend all of their current income, so they have a surplus of funds. Users are the opposite of

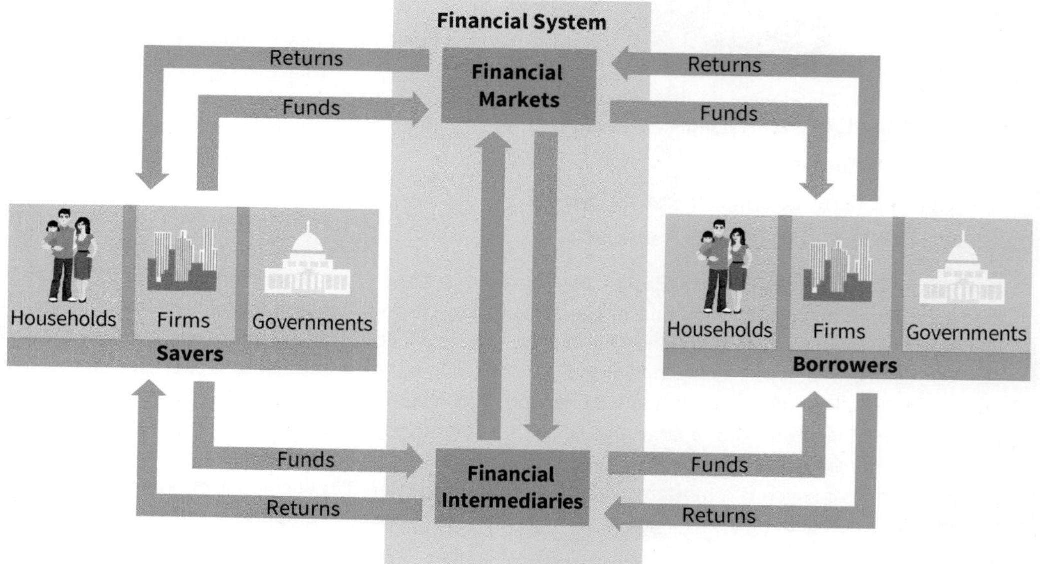

FIGURE 16.1 Overview of the Financial Systems and Its Components

savers; their spending needs exceed their current income, so they have a deficit. They need to obtain additional funds to make up the difference. Savings are provided by some households, businesses, and the government; but other households, businesses, and the government are borrowers. Households may need money to buy automobiles or homes. Businesses may need money to purchase inventory or build new production facilities. Governments may need money to build highways and courthouses.

Generally, in the United States, households are net savers—meaning that as a whole they save more funds than they use—whereas businesses and governments are net users—meaning that they use more funds than they save. The fact that most of the net savings in the U.S. financial system are provided by households may be a bit of a surprise initially, because Americans do not have a reputation for being savers. Yet even though the savings rate of American households is low compared with those of other countries, American households still save hundreds of billions of dollars each year.

How much an individual saves is a function of many variables. One of the most important is the person's age. People often transition from net borrowers to net savers as they get older. When you graduate from college and begin a career, you likely have little in the way of savings. In fact, you may be deeply in debt. In the early years of your career, you may spend more than you make as you acquire major assets, such as a home. So in these early years your *net worth*—the difference between the value of what you own and what you currently owe—is very low and may even be negative. However, as your career progresses and your income rises, you will begin to build a financial nest egg to fund retirement and other needs. Your net worth is also likely to increase. It will continue to increase until you retire and begin drawing on your retirement savings.

Funds can be transferred between savers and users in two ways: directly and indirectly. A direct transfer means that the user raises the needed funds directly from savers. While direct transfers occur, the vast majority of funds flow through either financial markets or financial institutions. For example, assume a local school district needs to build a new high school. The district doesn't have enough cash on hand to pay for the school construction costs, so it sells bonds to investors (savers) in the financial market. The district uses the proceeds from the sale to pay for the new school and in return pays bond investors interest each year for the use of their money.

Clean & Green Business

New Resource Bank Lends to Change Makers

New Resource Bank, which recently merged with New York–based Amalgamated Bank, is a popular green-bank alternative, designed to encourage sustainability among its many customers. The bank's stability and growth are in part due to its philosophy of serving mission-oriented customers, nonprofits, and traditional businesses wanting to incorporate sustainability practices. Combined, the two banks have footholds in four key communities where changemaking organizations are concentrated—New York City, Washington, D.C., San Francisco, and Boulder, Colorado. They will build a platform for a nationwide, values-based, socially responsible bank that can serve the interests of changemakers working to make a positive difference in climate and social inequities.

Both banks earn much of their appeal from a focus on sustainability and a strong commitment to the triple bottom line of people, planet, and prosperity. Both are Certified B Corporation banks that approach lending to businesses and nonprofits with green goods and services that include natural and organic products, clean energy, green real estate, and sustainable companies and nonprofits.

By using banking to promote people and planet well-being, the focus is on four key areas: environmental protection, health and wellness, education and community empowerment, and sustainable commerce. In addition, 84% of current loan commitments are invested in organizations that benefit the community and help preserve the planet.

Questions for Critical Thinking

1. **Banking industry insiders call the popularity of green banks "a broader cultural shift in what people expect from their bank." Do you agree? Why or why not?**
2. **How important to customers is a bank's involvement in the local community and other nonprofit organizations? Discuss the additional types of consumer banking and business customers New Resource Bank might target.**

Sources: Lucas High, "New Resource Bank Merges with Amalgamated Bank," *Daily Camera*, http://www.dailycamera.com, accessed May 29, 2018; company website, "About Us" and "New Resource Bank Receives A+ Rating for Financial Health," http://www.newresourcebank.com, accessed May 28, 2018; organization website, "What Is a Green Bank?" *Coalition for Green Capital*, http://www.coalitionforgreencapital.com, accessed May 28, 2018; Constance Gustke, "5 Green Banking Tips to Save the Planet," *Bank Rate*, http://www.bankrate.com, accessed May 29, 2018; Kevin Roose, "Amid Wall Street Protests, Smaller Banks Gain Favor," *New York Times*, http://www.nytimes.com, accessed May 29, 2018.

The other way in which funds can be transferred indirectly is through financial institutions. The bank pools customer deposits and uses the funds to make loans to businesses and households. These borrowers pay the bank interest, and it, in turn, pays depositors interest for the use of their money. This will be discussed further in the section on financial institutions.

The "Clean & Green Business" feature describes the growing appeal of "green" banking.

Assessment Check

1. What is the financial system?
2. In the financial system, who are the borrowers and who are the savers?
3. List the two most common ways in which funds are transferred between borrowers and savers.

2 Types of Securities

securities financial instruments that represent obligations on the part of the issuers to provide the purchasers with expected stated returns on the funds invested or loaned.

For the funds they borrow from savers, businesses and governments provide different types of guarantees for repayment. **Securities**, also called financial instruments, represent obligations on the part of the issuers—businesses and governments—to provide the purchasers with expected or stated returns on the funds invested or loaned. Securities can be grouped into three categories: money market instruments, bonds, and stock. Money market instruments and bonds are both debt securities, which represent money that is borrowed and must be repaid. Stocks or equities are units of ownership (called shares) held by shareholders in corporations like Sony, Ralph Lauren, Target, and Apple.

Money Market Instruments

Money market instruments are short-term debt securities issued by governments, financial institutions, and corporations. All money market instruments mature within one year from the date of issue. The issuer pays interest to the investors for the use of their funds. Money market instruments are generally low-risk securities and are purchased by investors when they have surplus cash. Examples of money market instruments include U.S. Treasury bills, commercial paper, and bank certificates of deposit.

Treasury bills are short-term securities issued by the U.S. Treasury and backed by the full faith and credit of the U.S. government. Treasury bills are sold with a maturity of 30, 90, 180, or 360 days and have a minimum denomination of $1,000. They are considered virtually risk free and easy to resell. Commercial paper is securities sold by corporations, such as Raytheon, that mature in 1 to 270 days from the date of issue. Although slightly riskier than Treasury bills, commercial paper is still generally considered a very low-risk security.

A certificate of deposit (CD) is a time deposit at a financial institution, such as a commercial bank, savings bank, or credit union. The sizes and maturity dates of CDs vary considerably and can often be tailored to meet the needs of purchasers. CDs in denominations of $250,000 or less per depositor are federally insured. CDs in larger denominations are not federally insured but can be sold more easily before they mature.

Bonds

Bondholders are creditors (an entity to whom a debt is owed) of a corporation or government body. In much the same way as people need money, so do governments. By selling bonds, a company obtains long-term debt capital. Federal, state, and local governments also acquire funds through the sale of bonds. Bonds are issued in various denominations, or face values, usually between $1,000 and $25,000. Each issue indicates a rate of interest to be paid to the bondholder—stated as a percentage of the bond's face value—as well as a maturity date on which the bondholder is paid the bond's full face value. Because bondholders are creditors, they have a claim on the company's assets that must be satisfied before any claims of stockholders in the event of the company's bankruptcy, reorganization, or liquidation.

Types of Bonds A prospective bond investor can choose among a variety of bonds. The major types of bonds are summarized in **Table 16.1**. *Government bonds* are bonds sold by the U.S. Department of the Treasury. Because government bonds are backed by the full faith and credit of the U.S. government, they are considered the least risky of all bonds. The Treasury sells bonds that mature in 2, 3, 5, 7, or 10 years from the date of issue.

Municipal bonds are bonds issued by state or local governments. Two types of municipal bonds are available. A *revenue bond* is a bond issue whose proceeds will be used to pay for a project that will produce revenue, such as a toll road or bridge. The Niagara Falls Bridge Commission, for example, has issued such bonds. A *general obligation bond* is a bond whose proceeds are to be used to pay for a project that will not produce any revenue, such as a new Indiana State Police post. General obligation bonds can be sold only by states or local governmental units—such as Grand Rapids, Michigan, or Bergen County, New Jersey—that have the power to levy taxes. An important feature of municipal bonds is that their interest payments are

TABLE 16.1 Types of Bonds

Issuer	Types of Securities	Risk	Special Features
U.S. Treasury (government bonds)	Notes: Mature in 2, 3, 5, 7, or 10 years from date of issue.	Treasury bonds and notes carry virtually no risk.	Interest is exempt from state income taxes.
	Bonds: Mature in 30 years from date of issue.		
State and local governments (municipal bonds)	General obligation: Issued by state or local governmental units with taxing authority; backed by the full faith and credit of the state where issued.	Risk varies, depending on the financial health of the issuer.	Interest is exempt from federal income taxes and may be exempt from state income taxes.
	Revenue: Issued to pay for projects that generate revenue, such as water systems or toll roads; revenue from project used to pay principal and interest.	Most large municipal bond issues are rated in terms of credit risk (AAA or Aaa is the highest rating).	
Corporations	Secured bonds: Bonds are backed by specific assets.	Risk varies depending on the financial health of the issuer.	A few corporate bonds are convertible into shares of common stock of the issuing company.
	Unsecured bonds (debentures): Backed by the financial health and reputation of the issuer.	Most corporate bond issues are rated in terms of credit risk (AAA or Aaa is the highest rating).	
Financial institutions	Mortgage pass-through securities.	Generally very low risk.	They pay monthly income consisting of both interest and principal.

exempt from federal income tax. Because of this attractive feature, municipal bonds generally carry lower interest rates than either corporate or government bonds.

Corporate bonds are a diverse group and often vary based on the collateral—the property pledged by the borrower—that backs the bond. For example, a *secured bond* is backed by a specific pledge of company assets. These assets are collateral, just like a home is collateral for a mortgage. However, many companies also issue unsecured bonds, called *debentures*. These bonds are backed only by the financial reputation of the issuing corporation.

Another popular type of bond is the *mortgage pass-through security*. These securities are backed by a pool of mortgage loans purchased from lenders, such as savings banks. As borrowers make their monthly mortgage payments, these payments are "passed through" to the holders of the securities. Most mortgage pass-through securities are relatively safe because all mortgages in the pool are insured.

Wiping out trillions of dollars and impacting world financial markets, mortgage-backed securities, or so-called *subprime mortgages*, played a critical role in the monetary crisis that began in 2007. The steady demand for these repackaged mortgages, along with low interest rates and a strong housing market encouraged more and more lending by banks. Turning mortgages into securities and selling to investors allowed a bank to move a mortgage off its books—thus freeing up more lending capital. Many of these securities turned out to be quite risky and, in part, triggered what became known as the credit crisis. The extent of the crisis forced the federal government to undertake a massive bailout of the financial system. The Office of Financial Stability—part of the U.S. Department of the Treasury—was created to purchase poor-quality mortgage-backed and other securities from financial institutions.

Quality Ratings for Bonds Two factors determine the price of a bond: its risk and its interest rate. Bonds vary considerably in terms of risk. One tool bond investors use to assess the risk of a bond is its *bond rating*. Several investment firms rate corporate and municipal bonds, the best known of which are Standard & Poor's (S&P), Moody's, and Fitch. **Table 16.2**

TABLE 16.2 Standard & Poor's Bond Ratings

Grade	Rating	Description
Investment Grade ↑	**AAA**	Extremely strong capacity to meet financial commitments; highest rating
	AA	Very strong capacity to meet financial commitments
	A	Strong capacity to meet financial commitments but somewhat susceptible to adverse economic conditions and changes in circumstances
	BBB	Adequate capacity to meet financial commitments but more subject to adverse economic conditions
	BBB–	*Considered lowest investment grade by market participants*
Speculative Grade ↓	**BB+**	*Considered highest speculative grade by market participants*
	BB	Less vulnerable in the near term but faces major ongoing uncertainties related to adverse business, financial, and economic conditions
	B	More vulnerable to adverse business, financial, and economic conditions but currently has capacity to meet financial commitments
	CCC	Currently vulnerable and dependent on favorable business, financial, and economic conditions to meet financial commitments
	CC	Currently highly vulnerable
	C	A bankruptcy petition has been filed or similar action taken, but payments of financial commitments are continued
	D	Payment default on financial commitments

Note: Standard & Poor's assigns a plus or minus following a letter rating to show relative standing within the major rating categories. For instance, AA+ means that the bond is higher quality than most AA bonds but hasn't quite met AAA standards.

lists the S&P bond ratings. Moody's and Fitch use similar rating systems. Bonds with the lowest level of risk are rated AAA. As ratings drop, risk increases. Bonds with ratings of BBB and above are classified as *investment-grade bonds*. By contrast, bonds with ratings of BB and below are classified as *speculative* or *junk bonds*. Junk bonds attract investors by offering high interest rates in exchange for greater risk. Junk bonds pay a higher yield to bondholders because the borrower's options are limited due to their less than desirable credit ratings. Historically, average yields on junk bonds have been 4 to 6% higher than those for comparable U.S. Treasuries.

The second factor affecting the price of a bond is its interest rate. Other things being equal, the higher the interest rate, the higher the price of a bond. However, the bonds may not be equally risky, or one may have a longer maturity. Investors must evaluate the trade-offs involved.

Another important influence on bond prices is the *market interest rate*. Because bonds pay fixed rates of interest, as market interest rates rise, bond prices fall, and vice versa. For instance, the price of a 10-year bond, paying 5% per year, would fall by about 8% if market interest rates rose from 5% to 6%.

Most corporate and municipal bonds, and some government bonds, are callable. A *call provision* allows the issuer to redeem the bond before its maturity at a specified price. Not surprisingly, issuers tend to call bonds when market interest rates are declining.

Stock

The basic form of corporate ownership is embodied in **common stock**. Purchasers of common stock represent the owners of a corporation. Holders of common stock have rights pertaining to their investment, one of which is the right to vote on corporate matters such as elections for the board of directors and proposed changes in corporate strategies, goals, or structure. In addition, shareholders have the right to vote on matters pertaining to stock ownership, a company's merger or acquisition, and executive compensation packages. The nature of stockholders' rights, along with the specific issues on which they are entitled to vote, vary from one company to another. Some companies grant stockholders one vote for each share owned, while others give those with a greater investment greater say.

common stock basic form of corporate ownership.

Companies issue shares of common stock, also called *equity financing*, to raise capital. The advantage of this strategy is that no repayment is required for money raised. Companies that are incorporated and without a track record can sell stock as an alternative to borrowing money. A rising stock value can increase a company's credit rating and make it easier to borrow in the future. Companies that sell shares of stock attract investors on the basis of potential for growth and profits.

The disadvantages of issuing shares of stock include the increased scrutiny and the constant need to explain and justify actions to shareholders—considered owners. In addition, the requirement to reveal information about assets, expenses, and results on an ongoing basis, along with granting voting rights on issues impacting a company, can be complex. Agreeing to pay dividends and being under pressure to maintain or increase share price can have its own price.

In return for the money they invest, most shareholders hope for a return. This return can come in the form of cash dividend payments, expected price appreciation (the price per share increases), or both. When the sales price exceeds the purchase price, a *capital gain* is the profit that results from the sale of the stock.

Although dividends vary widely from company to company, a company is under no legal obligation to pay a dividend. Generally, faster-growing companies pay less in dividends because they need to preserve funds to finance their growth. Consequently, investors expect stocks paying little or no cash dividends to show greater price appreciation compared with stocks paying more generous cash dividends. Dividends can be issued as cash payments, shares of stock, or other property. Along with a stock's appreciation, many shareholders prefer the regular income of cash dividends on their investment.

Figure 16.2 outlines the typical items found in a **stock quote**, the price of a specific stock and performance information.

stock quote price of a specific stock and performance information.

American Express Co. (NYSE: AXP)

Last Trade:	98.25	Day's Range:	98.27–99.34
Trade Time:	2:48PM ET	52wk Range High/Low:	$103.24/$76.65
Change:	−0.050 (0.051%)	Volume:	2,710,229
Prev. Close:	98.30	Avg. Vol (3m):	3,763,299
Open:	99.34	Market Cap:	$94.53B
Bid:	N/A	P/E:	28.73
Ask:	N/A	EPS:	3.42
1y Target Est.:	111	Div. & Yield:	1.42%

Ticker Symbol	Each stock has a unique identifier of letters (or numbers).
Last Trade	This reflects the last price at which a single share of this particular stock sold. It can change in an instant: it's set by buyers and sellers trading the stock for whatever they think it's worth right now.
Trade Time	The trade time tells you whether you should really rely on that last trade price—at the time that the last trade took place—or you should go out and get an update.
Change	Change indicates the difference between the last trade price and what the price before that was.
Previous Close	The previous close is the price at which the last share of stock sold yesterday (or the last day of trading). It's only one sale in a 24-hour period, limiting how big a picture it can provide you.
Open	The open is today's price of the first share of stock sold.
Bid & Ask	It's common to see both the bid and ask sections of a stock quote blank or listed as "N/A". A bid is the highest price that a principal brokerage firm has announced it's willing to pay for a share of a specific stock at a specific time. The ask is the opposite: it's the lowest price at which a firm has said it's willing to sell a particular stock.
1y Target Estimate	This is an estimate of a stock's future price based upon an earnings forecast and assumed valuation multiples.
Day's Range	The day's range gives you the range that a stock's price has varied by over the course of the day.
52-Week Range	The range of prices a stock has sold for over the course of the last year (52 weeks).
Volume	Trading volume shows the number of shares traded for the day. If a stock is particularly active, it is worth researching.
Avg. Volume (3m)	The average volume of the stock over the past three months.
Market Cap	Total value of the company calculated by multiplying the outstanding shares by the current market value (or last trade) of the stock price.
P/E (Price Earnings)	Calculated by dividing the current stock price by earnings per share over the last year.
EPS (Earnings Per Share)	The portion of a company's profit that is allocated to each outstanding share of common stock. It is the portion of a company's net income that would be earned per share if all the profits were paid out to its shareholders.
Div. & Yield	*Dividend* is the payment the company pays to shareholders based on its profits. The *yield* is the dividend expressed as a percentage of the price per share.

FIGURE 16.2 Stock Quotation

stock split occurs when a company decides to divide its existing shares of stock into multiple shares.

A **stock split**, the most common of which is 2-for-1 or 3-for-1, occurs when a corporation decides to divide its existing shares of stock into multiple shares. For example, when a company decides to split its stock 2-for-1, if it has 20 million shares outstanding and trading at a price of $100 per share, it will double the shares to 40 million, with an adjusted share price of $50. Each shareholder now owns double the number of shares previously owned at half the price. The value remains unchanged, but the lower price per share might interest new investors.

In a 2012 annual report, Warren Buffett, legendary investor and CEO of Berkshire Hathaway, wrote: "We relish the dividends we receive from most of the stocks that Berkshire owns, but pay nothing ourselves." Buffett believes that investing back into his business provides more long-term value to shareholders than paying them directly (with dividends). In essence, the company's financial success rewards shareholders with higher stock values.[2]

Common stockholders benefit from company success, and they risk the loss of their investment if the company declines. If a company dissolves, claims of creditors must be satisfied before stockholders receive anything. Because creditors have the first (or senior) claim to assets, holders of common stock are said to have a residual claim on company assets.

The market value of a stock is the price at which the stock is currently selling—and market value can quickly change. When online game developer Zynga missed second quarter earnings targets in 2012, its stock fell over 40 percent in a single day.[3] A stock's market value can be a function of supply and demand or of market forces. What investors feel a company is worth will also impact its stock price. However, one of the most important factors is a company's earnings.

Preferred Stock In addition to common stock, a few companies also issue preferred stock—stock whose holders receive preference in the payment of dividends. General Electric and Ford are examples of companies with preferred stock outstanding. Also, if a company is dissolved, holders of preferred stock have claims on the company's assets that are ahead of the claims of common stockholders. On the other hand, preferred stockholders rarely have any voting rights, and the dividend they are paid is fixed, regardless of how profitable the company becomes.

Convertible Securities Companies may issue bonds or preferred stock that contains a conversion feature. Such bonds or stock are called *convertible securities*. This feature gives the bondholder or preferred stockholder the right to exchange the bond or preferred stock for a fixed number of shares of common stock.

Assessment Check

1. What are the major types of securities?
2. What is a government bond? A municipal bond?
3. Why do investors purchase common stock?

3 Financial Markets

Securities are issued and traded in **financial markets**. While there are many different types of financial markets, one of the most important distinctions is between primary and secondary markets. In **primary markets**, corporations and governments issue securities and sell them initially to the general public. When a company needs capital to purchase inventory, expand a plant, make major investments, acquire another firm, or pursue other business goals, it may sell a bond or stock issue to the investing public. Drug store chain CVS Health recently sold $40 billion of bonds in advance to take advantage of low interest rates and to help finance its $69 billion acquisition of health insurer Aetna.[4]

financial markets markets in which securities are issued and traded.

primary markets financial markets in which corporations and governments issue securities and sell them initially to the general public.

A stock offering gives investors the opportunity to purchase ownership shares in a firm and to participate in its future growth, in exchange for providing current capital. When a company offers stock for sale to the general public for the first time, it is called an *initial public offering (IPO)*. IPOs in a recent year include DocuSign, Dropbox, and Spotify.[5]

Profit seeking corporations and government agencies also rely on primary markets to raise funds by issuing bonds. For example, the federal government sells Treasury bonds to finance part of federal outlays such as interest on outstanding federal debt.

Securities are sold to the investing public in two ways: in open auctions and through investment bankers. Virtually all securities sold through open auctions consist of U.S. Treasury securities. A week before an upcoming auction, the Department of the Treasury announces the type and number of securities it will be auctioning. Sales of most corporate and municipal securities are made via financial institutions such as Morgan Stanley. These institutions purchase the issue from the company or government and then resell the issue to investors. This process is known as *underwriting*.

Financial institutions underwrite stock and bond issues at a discount, meaning that they pay the issuing company or government less than the price the financial institutions charge investors. This discount is compensation for services rendered, including the risk financial institutions incur whenever they underwrite a new security issue. Although the size of the discount is often negotiable, it usually averages around 5% for all types of securities. The size of the underwriting discount, however, is generally higher for stock issues than it is for bond issues. For instance, underwriting discounts for IPOs are generally between 3 and 7%.

investment banker assist companies in raising capital and provide merger and acquisition services.

Investment bankers are typically involved in helping corporations and governments raise capital. In the case of issuing securities, investment bankers create the documentation (a process called underwriting) for the Securities and Exchange Commission (SEC) to enable a company to go public. They also assist corporations considering acquisitions, mergers, reorganizations, spin-offs, or a sale. Typically, they work in the division of a large bank involved in these activities or at an investment bank such as Goldman Sachs, Morgan Stanley, or JPMorgan Chase.[6] The "Job Description" feature in this chapter describes the skill set and career of an investment banker.

Corporations and governments are willing to pay for the services provided by financial institutions and investment banks because of their expertise in financial markets. In addition to locating buyers for a public offering of stock, they typically advise the issuer on such details as the pricing of the stock and the timing of the offering. It is common for several financial institutions or investment banks to participate in the underwriting process.

secondary market collection of financial markets in which previously issued securities are traded among investors.

News reports of stock and bond trading are most likely to refer to trading in the **secondary market**, a collection of financial markets in which previously issued securities are traded among investors. The corporations or governments that originally issued the securities being traded are not directly involved in the secondary market. They make no payments when securities are sold nor receive any of the proceeds when securities are purchased. The New York Stock Exchange (NYSE), for example, is a secondary market. In terms of the dollar value of securities bought and sold, the secondary market is four to five times as large as the primary market. In a recent quarter, an average of 1.46 billion shares ranging in value between $38 billion and $115 billion were traded on the NYSE.[7] The characteristics of the world's major stock exchanges are discussed in the next section.

Assessment Check

1. What is a financial market?
2. Distinguish between a primary and a secondary financial market.
3. Briefly explain the role of financial institutions in the sale of securities.

4 Understanding Stock Markets

stock markets companies that list stocks for public investors to buy and sell.

exchanges infrastructure that facilitates the trading of equity securities and stocks.

Stock markets represent companies that list stocks for public investors to buy and sell, and **exchanges** consist of the infrastructure that facilitates the trading of those equity securities, or stocks. The two largest stock markets in the world, the NYSE and the NASDAQ stock market, are located in the United States. The Dow Jones Industrial Average (often referred to as the Dow) is a price-weighted average of the 30 most significant stocks traded on the NYSE and the NASDAQ (see **Table 16.3**).

The New York Stock Exchange

The New York Stock Exchange (NYSE)—sometimes referred to as the Big Board—is the most famous and one of the oldest stock markets in the world, having been founded in 1792. Today,

TABLE 16.3 Companies and Symbols of the Dow Jones Industrial Average

Symbol	Company Name	Symbol	Company Name
AXP	American Express	MCD	McDonald's Corp
AAPL	Apple	MMM	3M
BA	Boeing	MRK	Merck & Co
CAT	Caterpillar	MSFT	Microsoft Corp
CSCO	Cisco Systems	NKE	Nike Inc
CVX	Chevron Corp	PFE	Pfizer Inc
DD	Dow DuPont	PG	Procter & Gamble
XOM	Exxon Mobil Corp	TRV	Travelers Companies
GS	Goldman Sachs Group	UNH	UnitedHealth Group
HD	Home Depot	UTX	United Technologies
IBM	International Business Machines	VZ	Verizon Communications
INTC	Intel Corp	V	Visa
JNJ	Johnson & Johnson	WBA	Walgreens Boots Alliance Inc
KO	Coca-Cola Co	WMT	Wal-Mart Stores
JPM	JPMorgan Chase and Co	DIS	Walt Disney Co

the stocks of about 2,800 companies (ranging from well-established and financially sound blue-chip companies to high-growth companies) are listed on the NYSE. These stocks represent most of the largest, best-known companies in the United States. In terms of the total value of stock traded, the NYSE is the world's largest stock market.

For a company's stock to be traded on the NYSE, size and liquidity requirements must be met. While it varies by exchange, a company listed on the NYSE must have at least 1.1 million publicly traded shares outstanding valued at a minimum of $100 million.[8]

Trading on the NYSE takes place face-to-face on a trading floor. Buy and sell orders are transmitted to a specific post on the floor of the exchange. Buyers and sellers then bid against one another in an open auction. Only investment firms that are designated members of the NYSE and that own at least one trading license are allowed to trade on the floor of the exchange. The NYSE issues up to 1,366 one-year trading licenses at a cost of about $40,000 each.[9]

In 2005, NYSE purchased a fully electronic exchange, now called NYSE Arca. The NYSE also purchased the American Stock Exchange, now called NYSE American. Today, all three national stock exchanges—NYSE, NYSE Arca, and NYSE American—are owned by Intercontinental Exchange (ICE), a global markets operator. Today, most trading is done electronically but floor traders remain to set pricing and deal in high-volume institutional trading.[10] As described in the "Business Model" feature, the New York Stock Exchange recently appointed its first-ever female president.

The NASDAQ Stock Market

The world's second-largest stock market, NASDAQ—National Association of Securities Dealers Automated Quotation—is a global electronic marketplace where securities are bought and sold. The electronic trading system, which began almost 50 years ago as a more efficient alternative to trading, attracted growing technology companies in the 1980s and 1990s.

Business Model

First in 227 Years: Female President of the New York Stock Exchange

In 1792, 24 stockbrokers signed the Buttonwood Agreement to trade securities on commission on Wall Street in New York City, and what was born would later be named the New York Stock Exchange (NYSE). Members initially sat in 553 chairs to trade, thus the term "seats" was coined. Holding a seat allowed the owner to directly trade on the exchange. In 2005, the New York Stock Exchange became a for-profit, publicly traded company, and at that time, seat owners received compensation and shares of the newly formed corporation. Despite its well-known brand, the New York Stock Exchange, once a 1990s duopoly with NASDAQ, and a floor with thousands of brokers, clerks and traders, has seen its volume fall as a result of new rivals, technology, and electronic trading.

Much has changed at the NYSE in 227 years—most notably, the recent appointment of its first-ever female President, Stacey Cunningham. Cunningham, the exchange's former Chief Operating Officer, began her career in 1994 as an intern while still in college. Soon after graduating, she became a trader on the floor of the exchange—as one of 40 women among 1,300 men. "I loved the place right out of the gate and now I'm excited to be running it," she said in an interview.

Today, two of the best known stock exchanges—the NYSE Group and NASDAQ, Inc.—are run by women. NASDAQ appointed Adena Friedman as its President and CEO in 2017. Both women hope for more diversity in the finance sector—and believe in the importance of spreading and modeling messages and behavior to young girls and women by showcasing Wall Street as a more inclusive place for women to spend an entire career.

Questions for Critical Thinking

1. The term "Glass Cliff" refers to an observation that women are promoted into top positions during challenging times and, sometimes, upheaval. Research some of the current challenges of the NYSE today, and comment on your thoughts and opinions.
2. The people running many of the most valuable companies in the world, known as "unicorns," such as Airbnb and SpaceX, are choosing not to go public. What are some of the issues behind this decision? How does this impact the New York Stock Exchange?

Sources: Nicole Bullock, "NYSE Plan to Expand Floor-Traded Stocks Hits Snag," *Financial Times*, http://www.ft.com, accessed May 30, 2018; Bob Pisani, "NYSE's New President Takes on Challenges As Exchanges Compete for IPOs, Fees," *CNBC*, http://www.cnbc.com, accessed May 30, 2018; Bradley Hope and Alexander Osipovich, "The New York Stock Exchange Is Set to Get Its First Female Leader in Its 226-Year History," *The Wall Street Journal*, http://www.wsj.com, accessed May 30, 2018; Jennifer Pagliara, "Will Women Leading NYSE, NASDAQ Exchanges Bring More Diversity in Finance World?" *Tennessean*, http://www.tennessean.com, accessed May 30, 2018; Vauhini Vara, "The New York Stock Exchange Has Its First Woman President. Is She on a Glass Cliff?" *Atlantic*, http://www.atlantic.com, accessed May 30, 2018.

The NASDAQ Composite, a reference to NASDAQ, is an index of more than 3,000 stocks listed on the exchange, including well-known iconic brands such as Apple, Google, Facebook, Microsoft, Oracle, Amazon, and Intel. These companies could easily meet the listing requirements for the NYSE but have decided to stay on the NASDAQ. Generally, NASDAQ-listed corporations tend to be smaller and less well-known than those listed on the NYSE.

Other U.S. Stock Markets

In addition to the NYSE and NASDAQ, several other stock markets operate in the United States. The American Stock Exchange, or AMEX, focuses on the stocks of smaller companies, as well as other financial instruments, such as options. In comparison with the NYSE and NASDAQ, the AMEX is tiny.

The Securities and Exchange Commission (SEC) recently approved Investor's Exchange (IEX), an Alternative Trading System (ATS), to operate as a public stock exchange. IEX was created in order to operate in a transparent and fair manner in response to controversial, widely used, high-frequency trading practices (HFT). NASDAQ remains in competition with the NYSE for IPOs. Two newer technology-savvy companies, IEX, made famous by Michael Lewis's book *Flash Boys*, and Bats Global Markets, are also in search of increased stock trading.

Foreign Stock Markets

Stock markets exist throughout the world. It is relatively easy to purchase foreign stocks listed on foreign exchanges, and conversely, foreign investors can also invest in U.S. securities listed on U.S. stock exchanges. In addition to their domestic exchanges, international stocks are cross-listed and trade on one or more foreign stock exchanges. Virtually all developed countries and many developing countries have stock exchanges. Examples include Mumbai, Helsinki, Hong Kong, Mexico City, Paris, and Toronto.

ECNs and the Future of Stock Markets

For years a so-called *fourth market* has existed—the direct trading of exchange-listed stocks off the floor of the exchange (in the case of NYSE-listed stocks) or outside the network (in the case of NASDAQ-listed stocks). Originally, trading in the fourth market was limited to institutional investors buying or selling large blocks of stock.

Now, however, the fourth market is open to smaller, individual investors through markets called *electronic communications networks (ECNs)*, an automated system that matches buy and sell orders for securities without an intermediary. An ECN connects major brokerages and individual traders virtually using the Internet, so that trades can be made directly without going through an intermediary. Most trading on ECNs are NASDAQ-listed stocks. More than a dozen ECNs operate in the U.S. markets, and a fee is charged for each transaction.[11]

Investor Participation in the Stock Markets

Because most investors aren't members of the NYSE or any other stock market, they need to use the services of a brokerage firm authorized to trade securities and to buy or sell stocks. Examples of brokerage firms include Interactive Brokers and TD Ameritrade. Investors establish an account with the brokerage firm and then enter orders to trade stocks. The brokerage firm executes the trade on behalf of the investor, charging the investor a fee for the service. While some investors still prefer to phone in orders or visit the brokerage firm in person, many today use their PCs or mobile devices to trade stocks online. The requirements for setting up an account vary from broker to broker. Selecting the right brokerage firm is one of the most important decisions investors make.

There are many different investment goals and strategies, which often change over a person's lifetime. A person nearing retirement, intent on preserving funds and potentially living on a fixed income, is more likely to be risk averse than a younger person who can afford, given the luxury of time, to recover from potential losses—and thus take more risk. *Risk tolerance* simply refers to how much risk an investor is willing to tolerate, and many times it is the underlying premise of an investment strategy. There are numerous considerations when investing, which include *risk*, *yield* (return on an investment), *duration* (length of time a commitment is made), *liquidity* (how quickly invested funds can be converted to cash), and *tax* implications. Before making investment decisions, investors should consider *diversification*, which refers to investing in a mix of assets in order to reduce risk exposure to an individual asset category. Other strategies include buy and hold, investing for income, investing for growth, and value investing. A smart phone app, Robinhood, started by two entrepreneurs who had previously built high-frequency trading platforms in New York, allows individuals to invest in publicly traded companies without paying a commission.[12]

The most common type of order is called a *market order*. It instructs the broker to obtain the best possible price—the highest price when selling and the lowest price when buying. If the stock market is open, market orders are filled within seconds. Another popular type of order is called a *limit order*. It sets a price ceiling when buying or a price floor when selling. If the order cannot be executed when it is placed, the order is left with the exchange's market maker. It may be filled later if the price limits are met.

Assessment Check

1. What are the world's two largest stock markets?
2. What is an electronic communications network (ECN)?
3. Explain the difference between a market order and a limit order.

5 Financial Institutions

financial institutions intermediary between savers and borrowers, collecting funds from savers and then lending the funds to individuals, businesses, and governments.

One of the most important components of the financial system is **financial institutions**. They are an intermediary between savers and borrowers, collecting funds from savers and then lending the funds to individuals, businesses, and governments. Financial institutions greatly increase the efficiency and effectiveness of the transfer of funds from savers to users. For many, traditional financial institutions provide safety, convenience, security, and the opportunity to obtain a loan or financing for a business, new car, or home. Picture prospective borrowers identifying and negotiating terms with each saver individually. Traditionally, financial institutions have been classified into depository institutions—institutions that accept deposits that customers can withdraw on demand—and non-depository institutions.

Commercial Banks

Commercial banks are the largest and probably most important financial institution in the United States, and in most other countries as well. In the United States, the approximately 4,852 commercial banks hold total assets of more than $16.6 trillion. Commercial banks offer the most services of any financial institution. These services include a wide range of checking and savings deposit accounts, consumer loans, credit cards, home mortgage loans, business loans, and trust services. Commercial banks also sell other financial products, including securities and insurance.[13]

Although 4,852 may sound like a lot of banks, the number of banks has actually declined dramatically in recent years; just 20 years ago there were 8,962 commercial banks. A new law will lift regulations for banks with less than $250 billion in assets, which frees them to make loans to small businesses, return capital to shareholders, and evaluate growth opportunities through mergers and acquisitions. When stock prices and bank profits rise, the purchasing power makes smaller banks, historically not in the target asset range for mergers and acquisitions, more attractive. The top five largest commercial banks include JPMorgan Chase, Wells Fargo, Bank of America, Citibank, and USBank.[14]

Community banks typically serve a single city or county and focus on the local needs of the businesses and families that live within the community where they have branches and offices. Many consumers and small-business owners prefer smaller banks because they believe they offer a higher level of personal service and often charge lower fees. A recent bill opens the door to further consolidation, which should create market opportunities for new and existing community banks.

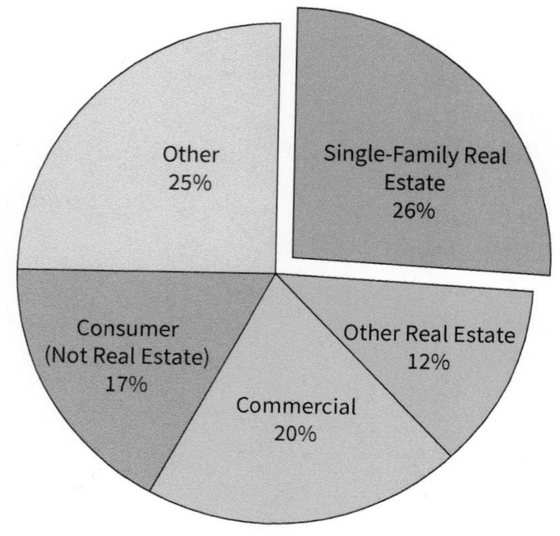

Source: Government website, "FDIC—Statistics on Depository Institutions Report," https://www5.fdic.gov, accessed May 31, 2018.

FIGURE 16.3 Distribution of Outstanding Commercial Bank Loans

How Banks Operate

Banks raise funds by offering a variety of checking and savings deposits to customers. The banks then pool these deposits and lend most of them out in the form of consumer and business loans. Recently, banks held over $12.2 trillion in deposits and had about $9.2 trillion in outstanding loans.[15] The distribution of outstanding loans is shown in **Figure 16.3**. As the figure shows, banks lend a great deal of money to both households and businesses for a variety of purposes. Commercial banks are an especially important source of funds for small businesses. When evaluating loan applications, banks consider the borrower's ability and willingness to repay the loan.

Banks make money based on the interest rate spread, or the difference between the interest rate charged to borrowers and the rate of interest paid to depositors. Banks also make money from other sources, such as fees they charge customers for checking accounts, using ATMs, or for overdrawing an account.

A different type of banker than the one found in most commercial banks is called an investment banker, described further in the "Job Description" feature.

Job Description

Investment Banker

Overview An investment banker structures financial deals and serves as a consultant for a corporation, government, or nonprofit, usually in a fast-paced and competitive environment. An investment banker helps underwrite equity and debt (bond) offerings and helps devise and implement financial strategies. Some investment bankers specialize in mergers and acquisitions. Many investment banks divide their corporate finance departments into industry subgroups such as healthcare, pharmaceuticals, and financial institutions.

Responsibilities Investment bankers serve as a facilitator for a company or business that wants to issue stocks or bonds. They help private companies go public and do so by structuring the offering, pricing the stock to maximize financial revenues, and adhering to strict financial regulations and requirements of the Securities and Exchange Commission. An investment bank will often buy all or most of a company's pre-IPO (initial public offering) shares and later sell them at a markup from the price it initially paid.

When companies wish to merge or be acquired, an investment banker who is an expert in a specific industry provides advisory services regarding structuring such a deal, analyzing gains or losses, and developing contracts or agreements. Other responsibilities include conducting research, reviewing and analyzing data, creating reports, and making recommendations.

Requirements Investment bankers typically have an educational background in accounting, finance, or economics as well as industry certifications such as CFA (chartered financial analyst). Competition is fierce, and large firms such as JP Morgan, Goldman Sachs, and Morgan Stanley often very recruit from top-ranked schools for very few job openings.

While still in college, many students vie for competitive internships, which increase the chances of a full-time job offer after graduation. Those with a minimum of an undergraduate degree typically begin first as an analyst. The hierarchy of positions at an investment bank, beginning with the most junior, typically includes analyst, associate, vice president, senior vice president, and managing director.

Investment bankers have an aptitude for numbers, analytics, and deal making and typically thrive in a fast-paced and hyper-competitive environment. Analytical skills will help an investment banker to spot market trends and future industry-related challenges. However, it is important to remember that while investment bankers are very well paid, they typically work very long, grueling hours.

Outlook Prior to the financial crisis that began in 2008, investment banks were adding jobs at an annual peak rate of 17%. More recently, job growth is forecasted at about 11% over the next several years.

Sources: "Investment Banker Career and Salary Profile," *Florida Tech*, http://www.floridatechonline.com, accessed May 30, 2018; "Career Overview: Investment Banking," *Wet Feet*, https://wetfeet.com, accessed May 30, 2018; "A 2015 Outlook for Investment Banking Jobs," *Trades and Tombstones*, http://investmentbanking.jobsearchdigest.com, accessed May 30, 2018; "Ask a Banker: What do Investment Bankers Really Do?" *NPR*, http://www.npr.org, accessed May 30, 2018; "Investment Banker," *Investopedia*, http://www.investopedia.com, accessed May 30, 2018.

Electronic Banking More and more funds each year move through electronic funds transfer systems (EFTSs) over secure electronic networks for bill payments, purchases, and pay processes—leading to a paper-free banking system. Most employers, for example, directly deposit employee paychecks in their bank accounts rather than issuing employees paper checks. Today nearly all Social Security checks and other federal payments made each year arrive as electronic data rather than paper documents.

The automated teller machine (ATM), an original form of electronic banking, allows users worldwide access to bank accounts through networked systems. *Debit cards*—also called check cards—allow customers to pay for purchases directly from their checking or savings account.

Recently the rise of *financial technology* or *FinTech* has created an emerging financial services sector that includes new forms of financing (crowdfunding), loan alternatives, and payment systems. Companies using technology to make financial services more efficient fall into the FinTech industry. FinTech start-ups disrupting traditional financial systems include peer-to-peer lending sites like Lending Club; mobile banking and mobile trading and investing technologies; robo-advisor services (automated, algorithm-based online portfolio and wealth management services without humans); cryptocurrency (digital currency that uses encryption techniques); mobile payment processing systems such as Square and Stripe; and personal financial planning and money management tools such as WealthFront and Mint.com. Start-ups eager to offer innovative financial service solutions are providing newer and more agile business models to meet customer preferences, including increased flexibility and lower costs, than traditional financial institutions. The growth of FinTech poses both an opportunity and a risk for traditional financial institutions. One survey reveals that in a few years, 23% of a bank's business could be at risk due to FinTech innovation. To respond, banks are partnering with FinTech companies.Kabbage, a U.S.-based leading online lender, has partnered with large players such as Scotiabank, for streamlining online lending; MasterCard, for business loans through MasterCard's network of acquirers; ING, to provide capital to small businesses; and Santander Bank, for loans to small and medium enterprises. JPMorgan Chase recently partnered with On Deck Capital to team up on small business loans. **Table 16.4** lists a number of FinTech categories and companies disrupting investing, banking, insurance, personal finance, and payments.[16]

TABLE 16.4 FinTech Categories and Companies

FinTech Category	Description	Companies
Payments FinTech has changed the way small (and large) businesses and digital marketplaces can take payments.	Digital payments—both from consumers to businesses and between businesses—allow money to be sent quickly and cost effectively via mobile app or Internet, and some companies accept payments from major credit and debit cards.	Square Stripe ApplePay Venmo PayPal Adyen Veem
Lending The lending process has changed with FinTech—with less of a need to turn to banks or credit unions to borrow money. With quick online approval, FinTech companies are now lending directly to consumers and small businesses.	FinTech lenders offer a range of services including debt refinancing; lending platforms that go beyond the traditional FICO score to finance people; peer-to-peer lending; and online lending exchanges to connect consumers with multiple lenders, banks, and credit partners competing for business. They also offer loans for everything from mortgages to home improvement projects to education to business loans.	Upstart Kabbage SoFi Greensky Prosper Lending Tree Lending Club OnDeck Funding Circle Quicken Loans Rocket Mortgage
Personal Finance In the past, people needed to talk to financial advisors at banks to get personal finance advice.	There are many apps that can offer advice and help with budgeting, saving, and investing. There are also FinTech companies providing credit scores and tracking, along with retirement or investment advice. Robinhood offers commission-free stock, bond, and ETF trading.	Wealthfront Mint Lending Club Credit Karma Robinhood Motif NerdWallet
Blockchain and Bitcoin Bitcoin is digital money used worldwide for secure and instant transfer of value. It is not controlled or issued by any bank or government; instead it is an open network managed by its users, and processing payments is more cost effective than with banks.	As a digital currency wallet and platform, Coinbase enables merchants and consumers to complete transactions using new digital currencies. Bitcoin is the most well-known, but the company also facilitates the use of Ethereum and Litecoin.	Ripple Coinbase
Insurance (InsurTech) Simplifying and improving the process of insurance with the integration of artificial intelligence, blockchain, and drones.	Insurtech is exploring avenues that large insurance firms have less incentive to exploit, such as offering ultra-customized policies (renter's insurance and car insurance only when driving a friend's car), government-sponsored insurance, and healthcare. Premiums are dynamically priced according to observed behavior using new streams of data from Internet-enabled devices.	Metromile Lemonade Cuvva Clover Health MetroMile
Digital Banks Digital banking is the move away from physical branches to online banking where banking services are delivered over the internet or through intuitive mobile apps.	Digital-only providers place an emphasis on mobile and digital engagement over more traditional channels such as the branch.	Ally Chime Moven Simple

Sources: Angela Scott-Briggs, "Top Ten FinTech Payment Companies," *Tech Bullion*, https://www.techbullion.com, accessed June 3, 2018; Maggie McGrath, "Forbes FinTech 50 2018: The Future of Payments," *Forbes*, https://www.forbes.com, accessed June 3, 2018; Angela Scott-Briggs, "Top 10 FinTech Lending Companies and Their Worth," https://www.techbullion.com, accessed June 3, 2018; Samantha Sharf, "Forbes FinTech 50 2018: The Future of Lending," *Forbes*, https://www.forbes.com, accessed June 3, 2018; Ben Deda, "Most Disruptive Insurtech Startups to Watch in 2017," *Vertafore*, https://www.vertafore.com, accessed June 3, 2018; Jeffrey Pilcher, "25 Online Only Digital Banks to Watch," *The Financial Brand*, https://thefinancialbrand.com, accessed June 3, 2018; Courtney Gakman, "Understanding FinTech Categories," *Ian Martin*, https://ianmartin.com, accessed June 4, 2018; Ian Dillon, "How FinTech Is Changing the World (and How Blockchain Is a Part of This)," *Entrepreneur*, https://www.entrepreneur.com, accessed June 4, 2018; Ryan Brown, "Insurance Firms Face Major Disruption from Digital Start-Ups in Most Sectors, Report Says," *CNBC*, https://www.cnbc.com, accessed June 5, 2018.

Online and Mobile Banking Two-thirds of Americans use online and mobile banking. Meanwhile, 18% of Americans said they still use bank branches most often. Nearly half of Americans ages 18 to 29 use mobile banking the most. Along with traditional bricks-and-mortar banks with online sites, there are Internet-only banks such as Ally Bank. With banking transactions, payments, and shopping increasingly taking place on mobile devices, it is difficult for traditional financial institutions to ignore mobile and digital trends—and the changing relationship and interactions with consumers. Using a mobile device, consumers can deposit checks, pay bills, transfer funds, and even pay for purchases—a substitute for a debit or credit card.[17]

Federal Deposit Insurance Most commercial bank deposits are insured by the **Federal Deposit Insurance Corporation (FDIC)**, a federal agency. Deposit insurance means that, in the event the bank fails, insured depositors are paid in full by the FDIC, up to $250,000. Federal deposit insurance was enacted by the Banking Act of 1933 as one of the measures designed to restore public confidence in the banking system. Before deposit insurance, so-called *runs* were common as people rushed to withdraw their money from a bank, often just on a rumor that the bank was in a troubled financial condition. With more and more withdrawals in a short period, the bank was eventually unable to meet customer demands and closed its doors. Remaining depositors often lost most of the money they had in the bank. Deposit insurance shifts the risk of bank failures from individual depositors to the FDIC. Although banks still fail today, no insured depositor has ever lost any money.

Federal Deposit Insurance Corporation (FDIC) federal agency that insures deposits at commercial and savings banks.

Savings Banks and Credit Unions

Commercial banks are by far the largest depository financial institution in the United States, but savings banks and credit unions also serve a significant segment of the financial community. Today savings banks and credit unions offer many of the same services as commercial banks.

Savings banks used to be called *savings and loan associations* or *thrift institutions*. They were originally established in the early 1800s to make home mortgage loans. Savings and loans originally raised funds by accepting only savings deposits and then lent these funds to consumers to buy homes. Savings banks still exist today, offering many of the same services as commercial banks, including checking accounts, yet they are not major lenders to businesses. As Internet banking, also called direct banking, has increased in popularity, savings banks commonly provide higher levels of interest in return for clients doing banking solely over the Internet.[18] Deposits in savings banks are FDIC insured.

Credit unions are cooperative financial institutions that are owned by their depositors, all of whom are members. Around 111 million Americans belong to one of the nation's approximately 5,573 federally insured credit unions, which have seen their share of consolidations. Combined, credit unions have more than $1.38 trillion in assets. By law, credit union members must share similar occupations, employers, or membership in certain organizations. This law effectively caps the size of credit unions.[19]

Credit unions are designed to serve consumers, not businesses. Credit unions raise funds by offering members a number of demand and saving deposits—checking accounts at credit unions are referred to asthare draft accounts—and then, in turn, lend these funds to members. Because credit unions are not-for-profit institutions, they often pay savers higher rates of interest, charge lower rates of interest on loans, and have fewer fees than other financial institutions.

Nondepository Financial Institutions

Nondepository financial institutions accept funds from businesses and households, much of which they then invest. Generally, these institutions do not offer checking accounts (demand deposits). Three examples of nondepository financial institutions are insurance companies, pension funds, and finance companies (see photo).

Insurance Companies Households and businesses buy insurance to transfer risk from themselves to the insurance company. The insurance company accepts the risk in return for a series of payments, called *premiums*. Underwriting is the process insurance companies use to determine whom to insure and what to charge. During a typical year, insurance companies collect more in premiums than they pay in claims. After they pay operating expenses, they invest this difference. Insurance companies are a major source of short- and long-term financing for businesses. Life insurance companies alone have total assets of more than $6.3 trillion invested in everything from bonds and stocks to real estate.[20] Examples of life insurers include Prudential and New York Life. See Appendix B for more about insurance and risk management.

Pension Funds Pension funds provide retirement benefits to workers and their families. They are set up by employers and are funded by regular contributions made by employers and employees. Because pension funds have predictable long-term cash inflows and very predictable cash outflows, they invest heavily in assets, such as common stocks and real estate. Pension funds are typically managed by a third party for most businesses; however, sometimes larger corporations operate their own pension funds in house. Pension funds make up some of the largest institutional investors. For example, almost 61% of Apple Inc.'s shares of stock are owned by institutional investors.[21]

Finance Companies Consumer and commercial finance companies, such as Ford Motor Credit and John Deere Capital Corporation, offer short-term loans to borrowers. A commercial finance company supplies short-term funds to businesses that pledge tangible assets such as inventory, accounts receivable, machinery, or property as collateral for the loan. A consumer finance company plays a similar role for consumers. Finance companies raise funds by selling securities or borrowing funds from commercial banks.

The *shadow banking system* refers to nonbank financial intermediaries that resemble banks and provide financial services (and credit) similar to that of commercial banks. Because they cannot legally accept deposits, their regulations are less stringent. A *hedge fund*, a nondepository financial institution, can provide higher returns, albeit with greater risk. After the subprime market meltdown occurred about a decade ago, the shadow banking system came under increased scrutiny and regulations.

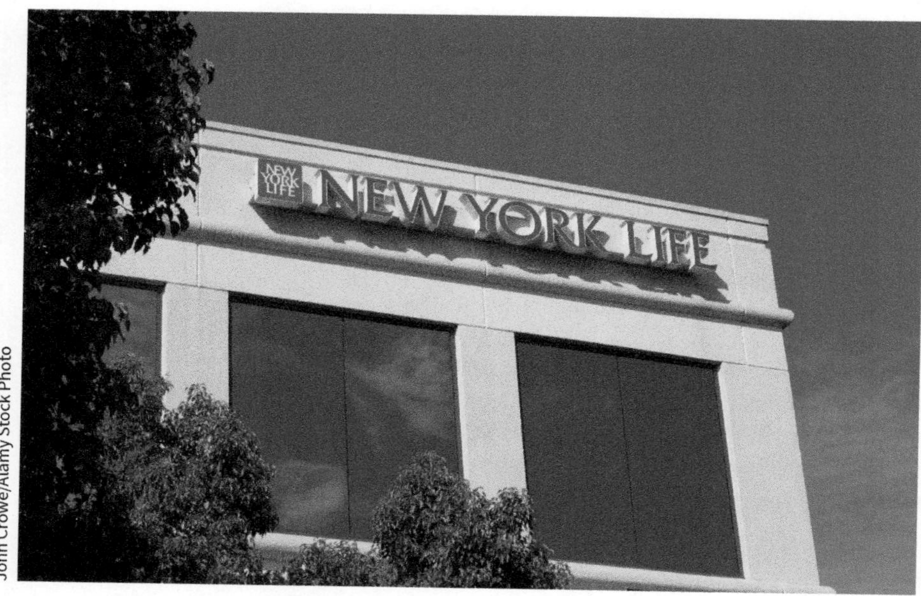

John Crowe/Alamy Stock Photo

Life insurance companies such as New York Life are a major source of financing for businesses. Considered a *nondepository financial institution*, insurance companies obtain funds from consumers and businesses and invest most of the money.

Mutual Funds and Exchange Traded Funds

Mutual funds are financial intermediaries that raise money or a pool of funds, from many investors with the purpose of selling shares in those securities—stocks, bonds, or money market instruments—to the general public. Mutual funds have various objectives ranging from industry type to company size to level of risk. With a minimal investment, mutual funds provide investors with professionally managed diverse portfolios.

Business & Technology

Robo Advisors Use Software to Select Investments

Financial and investment advisers may have served a purpose in the past, but today younger people with smaller amounts to invest are embracing robo advisors, a type of automated, digital, or online financial service—with little or no human intervention. A robo advisor uses software with algorithms and formulas to manage portfolios of low-cost investments. Part of the FinTech (financial technology) industry, robo advisors are gaining traction among asset managers and financial services providers who are selling their products and services to the masses at a fraction of the fees charged by traditional investment advisors.

Many companies, from start-ups to fund giants, are using automation to select investments to match a client's goals. Most of the low-cost, passive portfolios are made up of exchange-traded funds (ETFs) and index funds. Questionnaires are designed to customize a portfolio according to a customer's goals and risk tolerance. Rebalancing allows for allocations of investments in different asset classes to be kept in line with a client's risk tolerance.

Charles Schwab, who revolutionized the industry with a discount brokerage, has introduced Schwab Intelligent Portfolios, a free tool that provides low-cost personalized investment advice to the public with very little money to invest.

Schwab advertises no advisory fees, account service fees, and commissions. Wealthfront and Betterment are two other companies popularizing robo-advising, which continues to swell. Recent acquisitions of robo advisor start-ups by Northwestern Mutual Life Insurance Co. (LearnVest) and BlackRock Inc. (FutureAdvisor) further reinforce the notion that more first-time investors may very well entrust their small sum to a robo advisor at a fraction of the cost charged by an "old-school" human advisor.

Questions for Critical Thinking

1. **What are the pros and cons of robo advisors? Do you agree that this type of advisor appeals mainly to a younger demographic with less money to invest? Would you use a robo advisor?**
2. **Some accuse robo advisors of providing second-rate portfolio solutions, suitable only for small investors who cannot afford a traditional advisor. Others argue that young people are being educated on less-expensive and more-efficient ways to invest. What are your thoughts?**

Sources: Nathaniel Popper, "The Robots Are Coming for Wall Street," *New York Times,* http://www.nytimes.com, accessed May 31, 2018; Tara Siegel Bernard, "Robo-Advisers for Investors Are Not One-Size-Fits-All," *New York Times,* http://www.nytimes.com, accessed May 31, 2018; organization website, "Everyone Wants a Robo-Advisor, Right?" *SWFI,* http://www.swfinstitute.org, accessed May 31, 2018; Tara Siegel Bernard, "Schwab's Service for Investors Seeking Thrifty Advice Raises Eyebrows," *New York Times,* http://www.nytimes.com, accessed May 31, 2018; Burton Malkiel, "The Pros and Cons of Robo Advising," *The Wall Street Journal,* http://blogs.wsj.com, accessed May 31, 2018; Arielle O'Shea and Anna Louise Jackson, "Best Robo-Advisors 2018 Top Picks," *Nerdwallet,* http://www.nerdwallet.com, accessed May 31, 2018.

Mutual funds can be typically categorized as small-, mid- or large-cap, or by market capitalization. Mid-cap stocks are typically companies between $2 billion and $10 billion and are riskier than large-cap stocks but less risky than small-cap stocks, companies between $300 million to $2 billion. Large-cap stocks are companies $10 billion or above. Today, there are over 10,000 mutual funds with over $18.7 trillion in assets. Top mutual fund companies include the Vanguard Group, Fidelity Investments, and American Funds.[22]

Another type of mutual fund is called an *index fund,* also called a passively managed fund (because there is no fund manager) and tied to a broad stock market index, such as the S&P 500. An index fund will always earn a return identical to the market that it is tracking.

Exchange traded funds or ETFs combine characteristics of mutual funds and stocks. ETFs, which provide diversification, are composed of a group of securities and trade in a way similar to common stock on an exchange. Typically, ETFs seek to match a market index like the S&P 500. Many robo advisers select low-cost exchange-traded funds for investors, as discussed in the "Business & Technology" feature.

Assessment Check

1. What are the two main types of financial institutions?
2. What are the primary differences between commercial banks and savings banks?
3. What is a mutual fund?

6 The Role of the Federal Reserve System

Federal Reserve System (Fed) central bank of the United States.

Created in 1913, the **Federal Reserve System, or Fed**, is the central bank of the United States and is an important part of the nation's financial system. The Fed has four basic responsibilities: regulating commercial banks, performing banking-related activities for the U.S. Department of the Treasury, providing services for banks, and setting monetary policy. Not all banks belong to the Fed. Banks with federal charters are required to belong to the Fed, but membership is optional for state-chartered banks. Because the largest banks in the country are all federally chartered, the bulk of banking assets is controlled by Fed members. The Fed acts as the bankers' bank for members. It provides wire transfer facilities, clears checks, replaces worn-out currency, and lends banks money.

Organization of the Federal Reserve System

The nation is divided into 12 federal reserve districts, each with its own federal reserve bank. District banks are run by a nine-member board of directors, headed by a president.

The governing body of the Fed is the board of governors. The board consists of seven members, including a chair and vice chair, appointed by the president and confirmed by the Senate. A full term for a Fed governor is 14 years. If a governor serves a full term, he or she cannot be reappointed. A governor can be reappointed if he or she was initially appointed to an unexpired term. The chair and vice chair serve in those capacities for four years and can be reappointed. The chair of the board of governors is a very important position.

The Fed is designed to be politically independent. Terms for Fed governors are staggered in such a way that a president cannot appoint a majority of members, assuming that all members serve their entire terms. The Fed also has its own sources of revenue and does not depend on congressional appropriations.

An integral part of the Fed is the *Federal Open Market Committee (FOMC)*. The FOMC sets most policies concerning monetary policy and interest rates. It consists of 12 members—the seven Fed board governors, plus five representatives of the district banks who serve on a rotating basis. The Fed chair is also chair of the FOMC.

Check Clearing and the Fed

One of the Fed's responsibilities is to help facilitate the clearing of checks. Despite the fact that no stamp or envelope is needed, and electronic fund transfer is cheaper, faster, and more efficient, about 20% of people still write checks. Up until a decade ago, behind cash, a check was the most popular form of payment.In a recent year, people wrote 38 checks on average.[23] When a check is cleared, funds are transferred from the check writer to the recipient. As a "bank for banks," the Federal Reserve provides a variety of financial services to depository institutions, credit unions, and savings and loans in much the same way that depository institutions provide services to their customers. These services include collecting checks, electronically transferring funds, and distributing and receiving cash and coin.

Monetary Policy

The Fed's most important function is controlling the supply of money and credit, or monetary policy. The Fed's job is to make sure that the money supply grows at an appropriate rate, allowing the economy to expand and inflation to remain in check. If the money supply grows too slowly, economic growth will slow, unemployment will increase, and the risk of a recession will increase. If the money supply grows too rapidly, inflationary pressures will build. The Fed uses its policy tools to push interest rates up or down. If the Fed pushes interest rates up, the growth rate in the money supply will slow, economic growth will slow, and inflationary pressures will ease. If the Fed pushes interest rates down, the growth

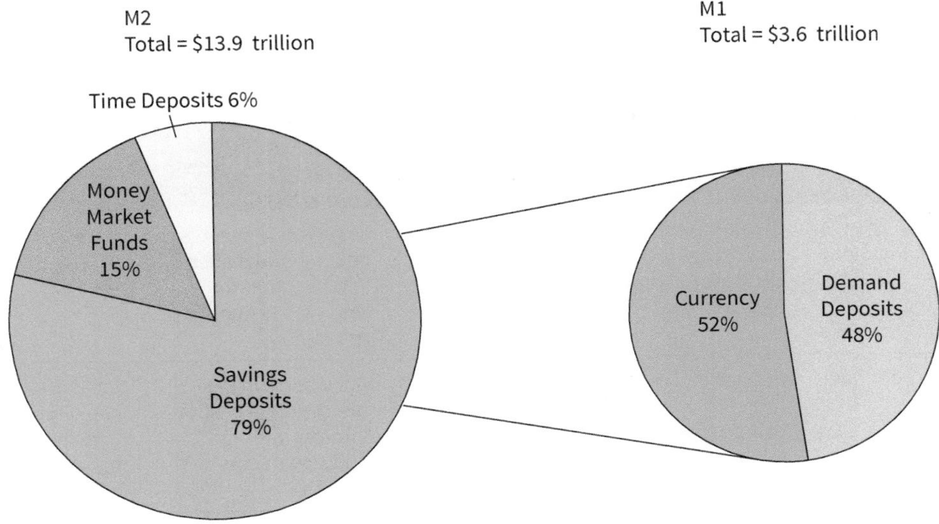

Source: Board of Governors of the Federal Reserve System, "H.6 (508) Money Stock Measures" and "Money Stock Measures: H.6," May 31, 2018, http://www.federalreserve.gov, accessed May 31, 2018.

FIGURE 16.4 Breakdown of M1 and M2

rate in the money supply will increase, economic growth will pick up, and unemployment will fall.

The two common measures of the money supply are called M1 and M2. M1 consists of currency in circulation and balances in bank checking accounts. M2 equals M1 plus balances in some savings accounts and money market mutual funds. **Figure 16.4** shows the approximate breakdowns of M1 and M2. The Fed has three major policy tools for controlling the growth in the supply of money and credit: reserve requirements, the discount rate, and open market operations.

The Fed requires banks to maintain reserves—defined as cash in their vaults plus deposits at district Federal Reserve banks or other banks—equal to a certain percentage of what the banks hold in deposits. For example, if the Fed sets the reserve requirement at 5%, a bank that receives a $500 deposit must keep on reserve $25, so it has only $475 to invest or lend to individuals or businesses. By changing the reserve requirement, the Fed can affect the amount of money available for making loans. The higher the reserve requirement, the less banks can lend out to consumers and businesses. The lower the reserve requirement, the more banks can lend out. Because any change in the reserve requirement can have a sudden and dramatic impact on the money supply, the Fed rarely uses this tool. Reserve requirements range from 0 to 10%, depending on the type of account.

Another policy tool is the so-called *discount rate,* the interest rate at which Federal Reserve banks make short-term loans to member banks. A bank might need a short-term loan if transactions leave it short of reserves. If the Fed wants to slow the growth rate in the money supply, it increases the discount rate. This increase makes it more expensive for banks to borrow funds. Banks, in turn, raise the interest rates they charge on loans to consumers and businesses. The end result is a slowdown in economic activity. Lowering the discount rate has the opposite effect.

The third policy tool, and the one used most often, is *open market operations,* the technique of controlling the money supply growth rate by buying or selling U.S. Treasury securities. If the Fed buys Treasury securities, the money it pays enters circulation, increasing the money supply and lowering interest rates. When the Fed sells Treasury securities, money is taken out of circulation and interest rates rise. When the Fed uses open market operations it employs the so-called *federal funds rate*—the rate at which banks lend money to each other overnight—as its benchmark.

Table 16.5 illustrates how the tools used by the Federal Reserve can stimulate or slow the economy.

The Federal Reserve has the authority to exercise selective credit controls when it thinks the economy is growing too rapidly or too slowly. These credit controls include the power to

TABLE 16.5 Tools Used by the Federal Reserve to Regulate the Growth in the Money Supply

Tool	Brief Description	Impact on the Growth Rate of the Money Supply	Impact on Interest Rates and the Economy	Frequency of Use
Reserve requirements	Change in the percentage of deposits held as reserves	Increases in reserve requirements slow the growth rate in the money supply.	Increases in reserve requirements push interest rates up and slow economic growth.	Rarely used
Discount rate	Change in the rate the Fed charges banks for loans	An increase in the discount rate slows the growth rate in the money supply.	An increase in the discount rate pushes interest rates up and slows economic growth.	Used only in conjunction with open market operations
Open market operations	Buying and selling government securities to increase or decrease bank reserves	Selling government securities reduces bank reserves and slows the growth rate in the money supply.	Selling government securities pushes interest rates up and slows economic growth.	Used frequently

set margin requirements—the percentage of the purchase price of a security that an investor must pay in cash on credit purchases of stocks or bonds. The Fed can also inject capital into the financial system in response to a financial crisis.

Transactions in the foreign exchange markets also affect the U.S. money supply and interest rates. The Fed can lower the exchange value of the dollar by selling dollars and buying foreign currencies, and it can raise the dollar's exchange value by doing the opposite—buying dollars and selling foreign currencies. When the Fed buys foreign currencies, the effect is the same as buying securities because it increases the U.S. banking system's reserves. Selling foreign currencies, on the other hand, is like selling securities, in that it reduces bank reserves.

Assessment Check

1. What is the Federal Reserve System?
2. How is the Fed organized?
3. List the three tools the Fed uses to control the supply of money and credit.

7 Regulation of the Financial System

It is not surprising that many components of the financial system are subject to government regulation and oversight. Although the financial crisis occurred over a decade ago, the resulting threat to the stability of the nation's financial system has created ongoing financial regulation, reform, oversight, and scrutiny. To provide some context, let's first attempt to understand the causes of the financial crisis.

How the Financial Crisis Unfolded

The precursor to the financial crisis of 2007–2008 was a flood of irresponsible mortgage (home) lending.[24] There isn't a simple answer to the cause of the crisis, which threatened the fall of large financial institutions and resulted in an approved government bailout, known as Troubled Asset Relief Program (TARP), in excess of $700 billion.[25] According to a U.S. Senate report, it was concluded that the crisis, which could have been avoided, was the result of "high risk, complex financial products; undisclosed conflicts of interest; and the failure of regulators, credit rating agencies, and the market itself to rein in the excesses of Wall Street."[26]

A flood of liquidity in the economy and policies encouraging home ownership provided further incentives for banks to provide easy money loans to borrowers with poor credit who were already at high financial risk. The loans were subsequently passed on to financial people at big banks who bundled large numbers of these loans for sale to hungry investors (other banks and hedge funds) worldwide as alleged low-risk securities. Investors, eager for higher rates of return in a low-interest economy, purchased the pooled mortgages (known as collateralized debt obligations or CDOs). The CDOs came with triple-A credit ratings assigned by credible credit rating agencies such as Moody's, which were paid by the very banks creating the CDOs. To most, the investments felt safe—on paper, the loans were backed by homes that continued to increase in value as the frenzied demand for home loans and mortgage lending reached epic proportions.[27]

But when the housing bubble burst in late 2007, the value of investments tied to housing and real estate also plummeted. This not only caused a chain reaction of damage to financial institutions (who owned the mortgages on the home loans and had put too little money aside to absorb these exorbitant losses) but also to borrowers—resulting in foreclosures, evictions, prolonged unemployment, and a global recession. The solvency of banks came into question as credit tightened, consumer confidence disappeared, and international trade declined. Global stock markets suffered, and consumers lost trillions of dollars of wealth. *The American Recovery and Reinvestment Act of 2009,* referred to as the *Stimulus*, was signed into law to save and create jobs and to provide financial assistance to those most affected by the financial crisis.[28]

Who is to blame? While certainly not an easy question to answer, some point to the credit rating agencies for a lack of transparency. Others point to the greed of the big banks that, from the sale of the risky CDOs, prioritized short-term deal flow and mega-profits. Still, some blame the Federal Reserve for failing in its regulatory duties and oversight of financial institutions while continuing to lower interest rates to near zero. Borrowers have also been blamed for taking on debt they knew might be difficult to repay.[29]

Fast forward a decade later, and to date banks have paid over $321 billion in fines for their questionable behavior and role in the crisis. In addition, regulatory reforms (discussed in the next section), including monetary and fiscal policies and required liquidity standards, were enacted to reduce the chance of a financial crisis of this magnitude ever happening again.[30]

Bank Regulation

The main purpose of bank regulation is to ensure public confidence in the safety and security of the banking system. Banks are critical to the overall functioning of the economy, and a collapse of the banking system can have disastrous results. Changes made to capital and liquidity requirements in the United States and globally have created a more resilient and robust banking system. Today, U.S. banks have more capital and larger liquidity buffers than prior to the crisis.

All banks, whether commercial or savings, and credit unions have either state or federal charters. Most commercial banks are state chartered; however, federally chartered banks control more than half of all banking assets. State-chartered banks are regulated by the appropriate state banking authorities; federally chartered commercial banks are regulated by the Federal Reserve, the Federal Deposit Insurance Corporation, and the Comptroller of the Currency. Furthermore, state-chartered commercial banks that are federally insured—and virtually all are—are also subject to FDIC regulation.

At the federal level, savings banks are regulated by the Office of Thrift Supervision and the FDIC. Federal credit unions are subject to NCUA regulation. State-chartered savings banks and credit unions are also regulated by state authorities. Banks and credit unions are subject to periodic examination by state or federal regulators.

Government Regulation of the Financial Markets

Regulation of U.S. financial markets is primarily a function of the federal government, although states also regulate them. Federal regulation grew out of various trading abuses during the 1920s. To restore confidence and stability in the financial markets after the 1929 stock market crash, Congress passed a series of landmark legislative acts that have formed the basis of federal securities regulation ever since. Many other regulations have followed.

In response to the financial crisis, the *Dodd-Frank Wall Street Reform and Consumer Protection Act* was passed in 2010. The major aim of this sweeping financial reform is twofold: Wall Street reform and consumer protection. New government agencies monitor corporations deemed "too big to fail" and assist with the needed liquidation or restructuring of weak or threatened banks or other financial companies. Insurance companies posing a risk are also identified, and consumer protections are focused on preventing predatory mortgage lending (approved mortgage loans for too much money for consumers to repay based on their financial status and monthly cash flow). In addition, new registration and reporting requirements have been implemented for hedge funds.[31] The "too big to fail" theory asserts that corporations and financial institutions are so important (and interconnected) to the economy that their failure would result in a disastrous effect on the overall economic system. Recently, the U.S. Senate passed a modification to the Dodd-Frank Act—the Economic Growth, Regulatory Relief, and Consumer Protection Act (Economic Growth Act)—to relieve some of the regulatory burdens imposed on community and midsize banks.[32]

As noted in Chapter 15, the U.S. Securities and Exchange Commission, created in 1934, is the principal federal regulatory overseer of the securities markets. The SEC's mission is to administer securities laws and protect investors in public securities transactions (see photo). The SEC has broad enforcement power. It can pursue civil actions against individuals and corporations, but actions requiring criminal proceedings are referred to the U.S. Justice Department.

insider trading use of material nonpublic information about a company to make investment profits.

The SEC requires virtually all new public issues of corporate securities to be registered. As part of the registration process for a new security issue, the issuer must prepare a prospectus. The typical prospectus gives a detailed description of the company issuing the securities, including financial data, products, research and development projects, and pending litigation. It also describes the stock or bond issue and underwriting agreement in detail. The registration process seeks to guarantee full and fair disclosure.

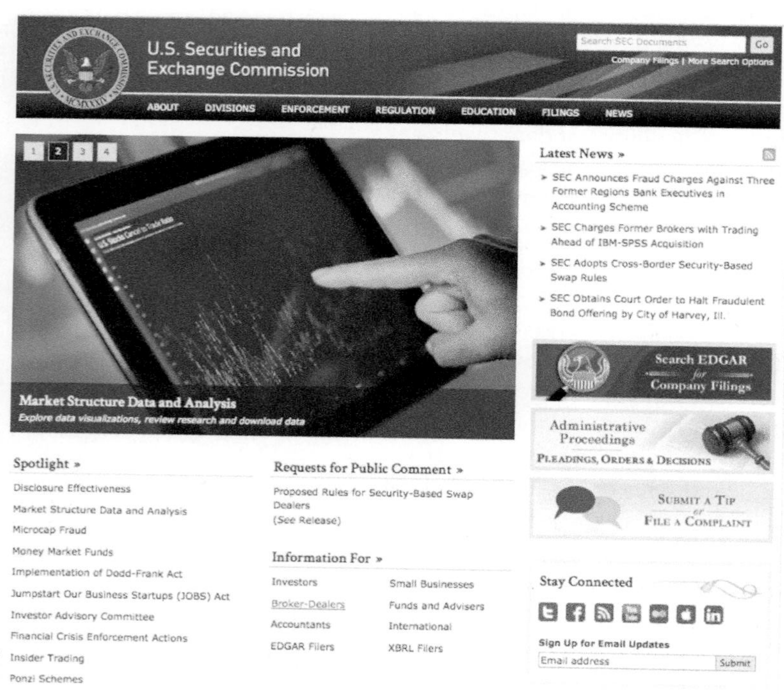

Courtesy of SEC

The Securities and Exchange Commission is charged with regulating financial markets. Its website, featured here, is a good source of information for would-be investors.

Besides primary market registration requirements, SEC regulation extends to the secondary markets as well, keeping tabs on trading activity to make sure it is fair to all participants. Every securities exchange must by law follow a set of trading rules that have been approved by the SEC. In addition, the Market Reform Act of 1990 gave the SEC emergency authority to halt trading and restrict practices such as program trading—whereby computer systems are programmed to buy or sell securities if certain conditions arise—during periods of extreme volatility.

Insider trading is defined as the use of material nonpublic information about a company to make investment profits. Examples of material nonpublic information include a pending merger or a major oil discovery, which could affect the company's stock price. The SEC's definition of insider trading goes beyond corporate insiders—people such as the company's officers and directors. It includes lawyers, accountants, investment bankers, and even reporters—anyone who uses nonpublic information to profit in the stock market at the expense of ordinary investors. Although some actions or communications are clearly

Judgment Call

The Rise of Stock Buybacks: Who Profits?

The debate over corporations racing to buy back shares of their own stock has drawn criticism among industry insiders whose concern is that companies have invested too much money in buybacks and not enough in future plans for growth. Fueled by a new tax law that is freeing up cash and encouraging money to be brought back to the United States, the trend of stock repurchases recently reached its highest level over the last two decades, the year prior to the financial crisis. Spending billions of dollars, companies such as Apple, Mondelez International (Oreo Cookies), Amgen, eBay, Boeing, JPMorgan Chase, and PepsiCo have repurchased shares of their stock.

When a publicly traded company buys back or repurchases shares of its own stock, the number of available shares in the market is reduced. As a result, stock prices typically rise—based on the theory of supply and demand. Even if total earnings remain unchanged, stock buybacks typically boost earnings per share by the reduction in the number of shares available for purchase. Even in a market with uncertainty around global trade, interest rates, and regulation around the technology industry, buybacks seem to be effective.

As activist investors encourage buybacks as a way to return more capital to shareholders, some have pushed for increased transparency and more disclosure. In fact, after the buyback of $100 billion of its stock, Apple recently saw its stock surge 4.4% the next day and 13% for the full week. Critics remain concerned that underinvesting in innovation, skilled employees, or essential capital expenditures to sustain long-term growth is a consequence of the instant gratification felt by a company buying back its own stock. For some, buybacks are perceived as an artificial and short-term way to boost profits, and typically when CEO and executive compensation is tied to stock awards, the initiation of buybacks occurs with even greater frequency. With extra cash on companies' balance sheets, buybacks may or may not be just a trend.

Questions for Critical Thinking

1. **Companies usually argue that a stock buyback is the best use of capital at a particular time and that there is no better investment than in the company itself. Do you agree? Why or why not?**
2. **What other ways might a company go about increasing shareholder value? Are buybacks simply a trend of a few companies with extra cash on their balance sheets?**

Sources: Ben Eisen and Akane Otani, "Record Buybacks Help Steady Wobbly Market," *The Wall Street Journal*, http://www.wsj.com, accessed May 31, 2018; James Brumley, "10 Companies Making Huge Stock Buybacks in 2018," *Kiplinger*, http://www.kiplinger.com, accessed May 31, 2018; Joe Nocera, "Sorry, Warren Buffett, Stock Buybacks Aren't That Simple," *Bloomberg*, http://www.bloomberg.com, accessed May 31, 2018; E. S. Browning, "Is the Surge in Stock Buybacks Good or Evil?" *The Wall Street Journal*, http://www.wsj.com, accessed May 31, 2018; Gretchen Morgenson, "Stock Buyback Plans, Seen as Shareholder Boon, Can Backfire," *The New York Times*, http://www.nytimes.com, accessed May 31, 2018; Lu Wang, "There's Only One Buyer Keeping S&P 500's Bull Market Alive," *Bloomberg*, http://www.bloomberg.com, accessed May 31, 2018; Cory Jansen, "Stock Buybacks: Breakdown," *Investopedia*, http://www.investopedia.com, accessed May 31, 2018.

insider trading, others are more ambiguous. When it comes to stocks, since the financial crisis, companies have recently purchased back the highest number of their own shares, as the "Judgment Call" feature describes.

Securities laws also require every public corporation to file several reports each year with the SEC; the contents of these reports become public information. The best known, of course, is the annual report. Public corporations prepare annual reports for their shareholders, and they file another report containing essentially the same information, Form 10-K, with the SEC. The SEC requires additional reports each time certain company officers and directors buy or sell a company's stock for their own accounts (Form 4) or anytime an investor accumulates more than 5% of a company's outstanding stock (Form 13-d). All of these reports are available for viewing and download at the EDGAR Online website (http://www.edgar-online.com).

Industry Self-Regulation

The securities markets are also heavily self-regulated by professional associations and the major financial markets. The securities industry recognizes that rules and regulations designed to ensure fair and orderly markets promote investor confidence and benefit all participants. Two examples of self-regulation are the rules of conduct established by the various professional organizations and the market surveillance techniques used by the major securities markets.

Professional Rules of Conduct Prodded initially by federal legislation, the National Association of Securities Dealers (NASD) established and periodically updates rules of conduct for members—both individuals and companies. These rules are intended to ensure that brokers perform their basic functions honestly and fairly, under constant supervision. Failure to adhere to rules of conduct can result in disciplinary action.

Market Surveillance All securities markets use a variety of methods to spot possible violations of trading rules or securities laws. For example, the NYSE continuously monitors trading activity throughout the trading day. A key technical tool used by the NYSE is called Stock Watch, an electronic monitoring system that flags unusual price and volume activity. The NYSE then seeks explanations for unusual activity from the member firms and companies involved. In addition, all market participants must keep detailed records of every aspect of every trade (called an *audit trail*). The NYSE's enforcement division may impose a variety of penalties on members for rule violations. In addition, the exchange turns over evidence to the SEC for further action if it believes that violations of federal securities laws may have occurred.

Although self-regulation by the financial industry has been an important component of securities market regulation, some contend that the industry can never truly regulate itself effectively in today's market environment.

Assessment Check

1. Who regulates banks?
2. Define *insider trading*.
3. List two ways in which the securities markets are self-regulated.

8 The Financial System: A Global Perspective

Alex Grimm/Reuters/Newscom

A sculpture of the euro in Frankfurt, Germany—the symbol for the European Union's currency—shows 12 yellow stars, which represents the initial EU member countries— including the United Kingdom.

Not surprisingly, the global financial system is becoming more and more intertwined each year. Shares of U.S. companies trade in other countries, and shares of international companies trade in the United States. In fact, investors in China and Japan own more U.S. Treasury securities than do domestic investors.

Financial institutions have also become a global industry. Major U.S. banks—such as Citibank, JPMorgan Chase, and Bank of America—have extensive international operations. They have offices, lend money, and accept deposits from customers throughout the world.

Although most Americans recognize large U.S. banks such as Citibank among the global financial giants, only three of the world's 20 largest banks (measured by total assets) are U.S. institutions: JPMorgan Chase (ranked 6th); Bank of America (ranked 12th); and Wells Fargo (ranked 13th). The other 17 are based in continental Europe, Great Britain, and Asia. The world's largest bank is Industrial & Commercial Bank of China Limited, with over $4 trillion in assets. These international banks operate worldwide, including locations in the United States.[33]

Virtually all nations have some sort of a central bank, similar to the U.S. Federal Reserve. Examples include the Banks of Canada, England, and Japan and the European Central Bank. These central banks (see photo) play roles much like that of the Fed, such as controlling the money supply and regulating banks. Policymakers at other nations' central banks often respond to changes in the U.S. financial system by making similar changes in their own systems. For example, if the Fed pushes U.S. interest rates lower, central banks in Japan and Europe may also push their interest rates lower. These changes can influence events in countries around the world. Lower U.S. and European interest rates not only decrease the cost of borrowing for U.S. and

European companies but also increase the amount of money available for loans to borrowers in other countries.

Assessment Check Answers

1. Where do U.S. banks rank compared with international banks?
2. Do other countries have organizations that play roles similar to those played by the Federal Reserve?

What's Ahead

This chapter explored the financial system, a key component of the U.S. economy and something that affects many aspects of contemporary business. The financial system is the process by which funds are transferred between savers and borrowers and includes securities, financial markets, and financial institutions. The chapter also described the role of the Federal Reserve and discussed the global financial system. In the next chapter, we discuss the finance function of a business including the role of the financial managers, financial planning, asset management, and sources of short- and long-term funds.

Chapter in Review

Summary of Learning Objectives

LEARNING OBJECTIVE 1 Understand the financial system.

The financial system is the process by which funds are transferred between those having excess funds (savers) and those needing additional funds (users). Savers and users are individuals, businesses, and governments. Savers expect to earn a rate of return in exchange for the use of their funds. Financial markets, financial institutions, and financial instruments (securities) make up the financial system. Although direct transfers are possible, most funds flow from savers to users through the financial markets or financial institutions, such as commercial banks. A well-functioning financial system is critical to the overall health of a nation's economy.

Assessment Check Answers

1.1 **What is the financial system?** The financial system is the process by which funds are transferred between those having excess funds (savers) and those needing additional funds (users).

1.2 **In the financial system, who are the borrowers and who are the savers?** Savers and borrowers are individuals, businesses, and governments. Generally, individuals are net savers, meaning they spend less than they make, whereas businesses and governments are net borrowers.

1.3 **List the two most common ways in which funds are transferred between borrowers and savers.** The two most common ways funds are transferred are through the financial markets and through financial institutions.

LEARNING OBJECTIVE 2 List the various types of securities.

Securities, also called *financial instruments,* represent obligations on the part of issuers—businesses and governments—to provide purchasers with expected or stated returns on the funds invested or loaned. Securities can be classified into three categories: money market instruments, bonds, and stock. Money market instruments and bonds are debt instruments. Money market instruments are short-term debt securities and tend to be low-risk securities. Bonds are longer-term debt securities and pay a fixed amount of interest each year. Bonds are sold by the U.S. Department of the Treasury (government bonds), state and local governments (municipal bonds), and corporations. Mortgage pass-through securities are bonds backed by a pool of mortgage loans. Most municipal and corporate bonds have risk ratings. Common stock represents ownership in corporations. Common stockholders have voting rights and a residual claim on the company's assets.

Assessment Check Answers

2.1 **What are the major types of securities?** The major types of securities are money market instruments, bonds, and stock.

2.2 **What is a government bond? A municipal bond?** A government bond is one issued by the U.S. Treasury. Municipal bonds are issued by state and local governments.

2.3 **Why do investors purchase common stock?** There are two primary motives for purchasing common stock. One is to receive dividends, cash payments to shareholders by the company. The other is potential price appreciation of the shares.

LEARNING OBJECTIVE 3 Discuss financial markets.

A financial market is a market where securities are bought and sold. The primary market for securities serves businesses and governments that want to sell new security issues to raise funds. Securities are sold in the primary market either through an open auction or via a process called *underwriting*. The secondary market handles transactions of previously issued securities between investors. The New York Stock Exchange is a secondary market. The business or government that issued the security is not directly involved in secondary market transactions. In terms of the dollar value of trading volume, the secondary market is about four to five times larger than the primary market.

Assessment Check Answers

3.1 **What is a financial market?** A financial market is a market in which securities are issued and traded.

3.2 **Distinguish between a primary and a secondary financial market.** The primary market for securities serves businesses and governments that want to sell new security issues to raise funds. The secondary market handles transactions of previously issued securities between investors.

3.3 **Briefly explain the role of financial institutions in the sale of securities.** Financial institutions purchase new securities issues from corporations or state and local governments and then resell the securities to investors. The institutions charge a fee for their services.

LEARNING OBJECTIVE 4 Understand the stock markets.

The best-known financial markets are the stock exchanges. They exist throughout the world. The two largest—the New York Stock Exchange and NASDAQ—are located in the United States. The NYSE is bigger, measured in terms of the total value of stock traded. Larger and better-known companies dominate the NYSE. Buy and sell orders are transmitted to the trading floor for execution. The NASDAQ stock market is an electronic market in which buy and sell orders are entered into a computerized communication system for execution. Most of the world's major stock markets today use similar electronic trading systems.

Assessment Check Answers

4.1 **What are the world's two largest stock markets?** The world's two largest stock markets are the New York Stock Exchange (NYSE) and the NASDAQ.

4.2 **What is an electronic communications network (ECN)?** An ECN connects major brokerages and individual traders virtually using the Internet, so that trades can be made directly without going through an intermediary.

4.3 **Explain the difference between a market order and a limit order.** A market order instructs the investor's broker to obtain the best possible price when buying or selling securities. A limit order sets a maximum price (if the investor wants to buy) or a minimum price (if the investor wants to sell).

LEARNING OBJECTIVE 5 Describe financial institutions and the growth of financial technology (FinTech).

Financial institutions act as intermediaries between savers and users of funds. Depository institutions—commercial banks, savings banks, and credit unions—accept deposits from customers that can be redeemed on demand. Commercial banks are the largest and most important of the depository institutions and offer the widest range of services. Savings banks are a major source of home mortgage loans. Credit unions are not-for-profit institutions offering financial services to consumers. Government agencies, most notably the Federal Deposit Insurance Corporation, insure deposits at these institutions. Nondepository institutions include pension funds and insurance companies. Nondepository institutions invest a large portion of their funds in stocks, bonds, and real estate. Mutual funds are another important financial institution. These companies sell shares to investors and, in turn, invest the proceeds in securities. Many individuals today invest a large portion of their retirement savings in mutual fund shares.

The rise of *financial technology* or FinTech has created an emerging financial services sector, which includes new forms of financing (such as crowdfunding), loan alternatives, payment systems, and even wealth management tools.

Assessment Check Answers

5.1 **What are the two main types of financial institutions?** The two major types of financial institutions are depository institutions (those that accept deposits that customers can draw on demand) and nondepository institutions.

5.2 **What are the primary differences between commercial banks and savings banks?** Today commercial and savings banks offer many of the same services. However, commercial banks lend money to businesses as well as to individuals. Savings banks lend money primarily to individuals, principally in the form of home mortgage loans.

5.3 **What is a mutual fund?** A mutual fund is an intermediary that raises money by selling shares to investors. It then pools investor funds and purchases securities that are consistent with the fund's objectives.

LEARNING OBJECTIVE 6 Explain the role of the Federal Reserve System.

The Federal Reserve System is the central bank of the United States. The Federal Reserve regulates banks, performs banking functions for the U.S. Department of the Treasury, and acts as the bankers' bank (clearing checks, lending money to banks, and replacing worn-out currency). It controls the supply of credit and money in the economy to promote growth and control inflation. The Federal Reserve's tools include reserve requirements, the discount rate, and open market operations. Selective credit controls and purchases and sales of foreign currencies also help the Federal Reserve manage the economy.

Assessment Check Answers

6.1 **What is the Federal Reserve System?** The Federal Reserve System is the U.S. central bank. It is responsible for regulating commercial banks, providing banking-related services for the federal government, providing services for banks, and setting monetary policy.

6.2 **How is the Fed organized?** The country is divided into 12 districts, each of which has a Federal Reserve Bank. The Fed is run by a seven-member board of governors headed by a chair and vice chair. An important part of the Fed is the Federal Open Markets Committee, which sets monetary and interest rate policy. The Fed is designed to be politically independent.

6.3 **List the three tools the Fed uses to control the supply of money and credit.** The three tools are reserve requirements, the discount rate, and open market operations.

LEARNING OBJECTIVE 7 Describe the regulation of the financial system.

A flood of liquidity in the economy and policies encouraging home ownership provided incentives for banks to provide easy-money loans to high-risk borrowers with poor credit. These irresponsible mortgage loans were a precursor to the financial crisis of 2007–2008, which ultimately led to a government bailout and subsequently, stricter regulatory requirements.

Commercial banks, savings banks, and credit unions in the United States are heavily regulated by federal or state banking authorities. Banking regulators require institutions to follow sound banking practices and have the power to close noncompliant ones. In the United States, financial markets are regulated at both the federal and state levels. Markets are also heavily self-regulated by the financial markets and professional organizations. The chief regulatory body is the Securities and Exchange Commission. It sets the requirements for both primary and secondary market activity, prohibiting a number of practices, including insider trading. The SEC also requires public companies to disclose financial information regularly. Professional organizations and the securities markets also have rules and procedures that all members must follow.

Assessment Check Answers

7.1 **Who regulates banks?** All banks have either state or federal charters. Federally chartered banks are regulated by the Federal Reserve, the FDIC, and the Comptroller of the Currency. State-chartered banks are regulated by state banking authorities and the FDIC.

7.2 **Define *insider trading*.** Insider trading is defined as the use of material nonpublic information to make an investment profit.

7.3 **List two ways in which the securities markets are self-regulated.** Professional organizations such as the National Association of Securities Dealers have codes of conduct that members are expected to follow. Major financial markets have trading rules and procedures to identify suspicious trading activity.

LEARNING OBJECTIVE 8 Discuss the global perspective of the financial system.

Financial markets exist throughout the world and are increasingly interconnected. Investors in other countries purchase U.S. securities, and U.S. investors purchase foreign securities. Large U.S. banks and other financial institutions have a global presence. They accept deposits, make loans, and have branches throughout the world. Foreign banks also operate worldwide. The average European or Japanese bank is much larger than the average American bank. Virtually all nations have central banks that perform the same roles as the U.S. Federal Reserve System. Central bankers often act together, raising and lowering interest rates as economic conditions warrant.

Assessment Check Answers

8.1 **Where do U.S. banks rank compared with international banks?** Banks in Asia and Europe are generally much larger than U.S. banks. In fact, only 4 out of the world's 20 largest banks are based in the United States.

8.2 **Do other countries have organizations that play roles similar to those played by the Federal Reserve?** Yes, virtually all nations have central banks that perform many of the same functions that the U.S. Federal Reserve System does.

Business Terms You Need to Know

financial system 432
securities 434
common stock 437
stock quote 437
stock split 438
financial markets 439
primary markets 439
investment banker 440
secondary market 440
stock markets 440
exchanges 440
financial institutions 444
Federal Deposit Insurance Corporation (FDIC) 447
Federal Reserve System (Fed) 450
insider trading 454

Review Questions

1. What is the financial system? Why is the direct transfer of funds from savers to users rare?
2. What is a security? Give several examples.
3. List the major types of bonds. Explain a mortgage pass-through.
4. What are the differences between common stock and preferred stock?
5. Explain the difference between a primary financial market and a secondary financial market.
6. Why are commercial banks, savings banks, and credit unions classified as depository financial institutions? How do the three differ?
7. Why are life insurance companies, pension funds, and mutual funds considered financial institutions?
8. Briefly explain the role of the Federal Reserve and list the tools it uses to control the supply of money and credit.
9. What methods are used to regulate banks? Why are state-chartered banks also regulated by the FDIC?
10. Explain how the Federal Reserve, acting in conjunction with other central banks, could affect exchange rates.

Projects and Teamwork Applications

1. Day trading refers to buying and selling securities (stocks and bonds, for example) in the same day, with hopes of an upward price movement. What information does a day trader need to make accurate decisions? Do you consider day trading gambling? Why or why not?

2. You've probably heard of U.S. savings bonds—you may even have received some bonds as a gift. What you may not know is that two different types of savings bonds exist. Do some research and compare and contrast the two types of savings bonds. What are their features? Their pros and cons? Assuming you were interested in buying savings bonds, which of the two do you find more attractive?

3. Working with a partner, assume you are considering buying shares of Lowe's or Home Depot. Describe how you would go about analyzing the two companies' stocks and deciding which, if either, you would buy.

4. Discuss investment strategies with regard to diversification and asset allocation for someone in their 20s versus someone in their 40s. How does risk tolerance change with age? Discuss in pairs or small groups.

5. How would you decide whether to use an investment advisor or stockbroker at a full-service brokerage firm such as Charles Schwab or to open a brokerage account and try your hand at do-it-yourself online investing? Would you consider a robo advisor? What services does each provide, and what are some of the advantages and disadvantages of each?

Web Assignments

1. **Virtual stock trading.** The website listed below is a virtual stock contest and training ground of sorts for students and investors alike. Go to the site, read "Getting Started" as well as the frequently asked questions, and create a stock portfolio. With $10,000 in virtual dollars, pick three to five stocks and track the results over a period of time. What did you learn? If you had invested in those same stocks six months earlier, what would your portfolio's gain or loss have been? Are you ready to invest with real money? Discuss.
www.howthemarketworks.com

2. **Researching and managing investments.** Go to the website listed below this paragraph, sponsored by the U.S. Securities and Exchange Commission. Under "Researching & Managing Investments," read more about "Investing on Your Own." Make a brief presentation to the class or a small group about the different ways to invest on your own and the steps involved. Take the quiz to test your money smarts and discuss what you have learned.
www.investor.gov

3. **IPOs.** A number of different sources are available for finding recently filed IPOs, or initial public offerings. Research companies that have recently filed IPOs. What industries are these companies in? Now research companies that have recently gone public. How has the stock performed during the first week of its IPO?

Note: Internet web addresses change frequently. If you don't find the exact sites listed, you may need to access the organization's home page and search from there or use a search engine such as Google or Bing.

Cases

Case 16.1 Shareholder Meetings Go Virtual

For the first time ever, Hewlett-Packard has abandoned its annual convention-style shareholder meeting in favor of a virtual one. Another format, a hybrid meeting, is where companies hold both virtual and in-person meetings. Annual shareholder meetings, generally required of all public corporations, have traditionally allowed for shareholders of all types to meet face-to-face with top company executives in a question-and-answer format—in order to learn more about the company's plans for the future.

Hewlett-Packard will not be the first company to host its annual event online, but to date it is the largest to do so. Review-site Yelp and El Pollo Loco, a chain of chicken restaurants, have moved their annual meeting to virtual as well. Less than a decade ago, 21 companies hosted virtual shareholder meetings, as compared to 300 in a recent year. While a virtual event allows for a greater number of attendees, critics argue that questions from shareholders can be prescreened. Face-time, relationship building, networking, and spontaneity become diminished, along with the all-important shareholder–company bond. Companies in favor of the virtual move argue that online meetings save money, particularly when past attendance at the annual meetings has been sparse.

At one point, consumer products giant Procter & Gamble amended its bylaws to allow for a virtual-only shareholder's meeting, only later to be met with such shareholder resistance that it reverted back to a traditional face-to-face event. Intel and Microsoft have hosted what is known as a hybrid meeting, during which a physical event is held and shareholders can "show up" online.

Companies such as Walmart and Berkshire Hathaway are well-known for their "extravaganza and family-style" shareholder meetings—weekend events that include celebrity entertainment and a variety of other activities. For the 40,000 attendees at Berkshire Hathaway's annual "Woodstock for Capitalists" event, a virtual meeting would be like holding a virtual party.

Questions for Critical Thinking

1. Those who are not fans of online-only meetings argue that investors should have the opportunity to look a CEO or board member in the eye. Others argue that technology can largely replicate the

experience of a shareholder's meeting and that online meetings could actually expand the all-important Q&A session. Do you agree? Why or why not?

2. Some argue that using technology for shareholder meetings broadens access, while others argue that it shuts out shareholders. Which side do you agree with? Explain.

Sources: Jena McGregor, "More Companies Are Going Virtual for Their Annual Shareholder Meetings," *Washington Post*, http://www.washingtonpost.com, accessed May 31, 2018; company website, "Virtual Shareholder Meeting," http://www.broadridge.com, accessed May 31, 2018; Tom Braithwaite, "U.S. Companies Embrace Virtual Annual Meetings," *Financial Times*, http://www.ft.com, accessed May 31, 2018; Fredrikson & Byron PA, "Virtual Shareholder Meetings in 2018: Facts, Figures and Best Practices," *Lexology*, https://www.lexology.com, accessed May 31, 2018; Emily Chasan, "Investors Opposing Virtual Shareholder Meetings Notch Wins," *Bloomberg*, http://www.bloomberg.com, accessed May 31, 2018.

Case 16.2 SoFi Takes a Radical Approach to Financing

Financial technology firms continue to make headway by taking away loan and mortgage business from traditional banks. One of the most valued fintech companies today is SoFi, short for "social finance." The company, which considers its approach to banking as radical, deems itself "a modern finance company that's fueling the shift to a bankless world." Started by four students who met in business school, SoFi's original lending model connected students and recent graduates from specific schools with alumni and institutional investors. It became a win–win: investors received a financial return, and borrowers were able to borrow at lower than federal government rates.

SoFi soon expanded its product range to include online-only student loan refinancing, mortgages, wealth management services, credit cards, and personal loans. What makes the company unique is its nontraditional underwriting model, which focuses on a person's overall financial well-being instead of a consumer credit score. Intent on lending to financially responsible individuals, SoFi analyzes "forward-looking" factors to determine a prospective borrower's future potential. Many start-ups are betting that more progressive and predictive lending models like this will work well in challenging business environments and allow them to lend, on average, to 10% more applicants.

SoFi believes that traditional credit scores are "backward-looking" and do not capture borrowers' current income or ability to repay loans. Most important for SoFi is a borrower's current income, history of paying off debt, and remaining monthly cash after expenses are paid. A borrower's education and employment background are also considered to be important. A high credit score may help secure traditional loans, but without a healthy cash flow, a loan simply doesn't make sense, according to the company's CEO.

In addition to competitive interest rates, SoFi offers "community benefits" to borrowers such as social events, career services, and mentoring for those who are interested in starting a business. Traditional banks are taking notice of SoFi, who hopes to soon have its members invest in cryptocurrency.Backed by venture capital firms, including PayPal founder Peter Thiel, SoFi's 500,000 members may someday see their favorite nontraditional lender as a public company.

Questions for Critical Thinking

1. SoFi has gone to a place where traditional banks have not—refinancing student loans. SoFi takes into consideration the reputation of a borrower's university when evaluating an applicant for refinancing. Discuss the pros and cons of this approach, along with SoFi's nontraditional credit evaluation techniques.
2. Discuss how SoFi has caused disruption in the financial services sector, and whether, in your opinion, traditional financial institutions are struggling to adapt to the way consumers and businesses want to use SoFi's services.

Sources: Company website, "Who We Are" and "In the News," https://www.sofi.com, accessed May 31, 2018; Peter Rudegeair, "Silicon Valley: We Don't Trust FICO Scores," *Wall Street Journal*, http://www.wsj.com, accessed May 31, 2018; Peter Rudegeair, Telis Demos, and Rolfe Winkler, "Online Lender Social Finance's Latest Fundraising Implies $4 Billion Valuation," *Wall Street Journal*, http://www.wsj.com, accessed May 31, 2018; Anya Martin, "The Online Mortgage Has Finally Arrived," *Wall Street Journal*, http://www.wsj.com, accessed May 31, 2018; Chloe Aiello, "SoFi Will Get Crypto Investing by 2019, Says CEO Anthony Noto," *CNBC*, http://www.cnbc.com, accessed May 31, 2018; "50. SoFi," *CNBC*, http://www.cnbc.com, accessed May 31, 2018.

Case 16.3 New Harvest Coffee Goes Beyond Fair Trade

"Fair Trade has always been part of my legacy in coffee," says Rik Kleinfeldt, president and co-founder of Rhode Island-based New Harvest Coffee Roasters. "That's where I started with New Harvest." But in less than a decade, New Harvest's business model has evolved beyond Fair Trade to something different.

New Harvest is a small-batch coffee roaster specializing in certified organic coffee that is grown and harvested by farms with sustainable practices. Rik Kleinfeldt notes that he built his company on two pillars: 1) the highest quality coffee, and 2) sustainable sourcing practices. "But these two weren't really gelling at first," he admits. At the beginning, Kleinfeldt tried to source from Fair Trade cooperatives, but this wasn't really fulfilling his objective. "Fair Trade is based on the commodity system," Kleinfeldt explains, "which creates a floor price at which coffee can't drop below. But it doesn't really address the issue of quality." The groups that work with Fair Trade are large cooperatives, sometimes encompassing several thousand small farms. All the coffee is blended together as a commodity, so it is impossible for a roaster like New Harvest to deal directly with each farm, selecting the specific harvest that it wants to buy.

Kleinfeldt is quick to point out that when Fair Trade began over a decade ago, it was a lifeline to small farmers because coffee prices were at an all-time low—these growers were selling their crops for less than it cost to produce them. Without Fair Trade, many of these farms would have gone out of business. With the coffee market somewhat stabilized though, commodity pricing brings its own set of problems. "The commodity pricing usually has nothing to do with the coffee itself," says Kleinfeldt. Prices are set at the New York Stock Exchange, not in the growing fields of Costa Rica or Colombia. He notes that roasters, retailers, and consumers may end up paying way too much or way too little for a particular year's crop.

So Kleinfeldt has become part of what he calls the Artisan Coffee movement—growers, roasters, and retailers who prefer to deal directly with each other as individual businesses. "We connect directly with our growers and determine price based on quality," he explains. Kleinfeldt and his staff, along with some of his retailers such as the owner of Blue State Coffee and the owner of Pejamajo Café, travel to the farms in Costa Rica and Colombia where they actually taste the coffee before purchasing a crop. Kleinfeldt believes this is the only way to get the best coffee on the market. These visits help develop strong relationships, find solutions to problems, and develop strategies for surviving and thriving as businesses. Through visiting, he says, "we can understand their challenges." One farm in particular is located in Colombia. The farmer decided he didn't want to participate in a large Fair Trade cooperative—instead, he wanted to develop a market for his own coffee. So he approached New Harvest with the idea, and the match was ideal. He is now one of New Harvest's premier growers.

Sourcing the coffee beans directly from individual farms also helps New Harvest keep close track of organic and sustainability practices. Gerra Harrigan, director of business development for New Harvest Coffee Roasters, notes that this is an important part of the firm's business. The owners of local coffee shops—and their customers—like the reassurance that New Harvest stands behind all of its claims.

Kleinfeldt wants consumers to know they are getting a great deal when they ask for New Harvest at their local shop. He points out that the price differentiation isn't as much as people might think. A visit to the supermarket reveals that Starbucks and Green Mountain sell for about the same price as New Harvest Coffee—between $13 to $15 per lb. Because of the richness of New Harvest, most customers actually get more cups of coffee from a pound of New Harvest than they do from the other premium brands.

Kleinfeldt hopes that the Artisan Coffee movement, as he refers to his company's practices, will flourish and grow. He believes that if you're going to drink a cup of coffee, it should be really fresh and of the highest quality—with beans preferably roasted by New Harvest.

Questions for Critical Thinking

1. What are the benefits and drawbacks of treating coffee as a commodity in the marketplace? What do you predict will be the future of Fair Trade?
2. Should the entire coffee market be regulated in any way? Why or why not? If so, how?
3. How would New Harvest change as a business if it made an initial public offering (IPO)?
4. What is your opinion of the so-called Artisan Coffee movement as a business model? Do you think it will be successful in the long run? Why or why not?

Sources: Company website, www.newharvestcoffee.com, accessed May 31, 2018; "New Harvest Coffee Roasters," *Green People*, http://www.greenpeople.org, accessed May 31, 2018; Richard Garcia, "Pejamajo Cafe & New Harvest Roasters," Chefs Daily Food Bank, http://www.chefsdailyfoodbank.com, accessed May 31, 2018; Amanda Milkovitz, "Java 101: Learn to Brew Like a Pro at Pawtucket's New Harvest Coffee Roasters", *Providence Journal*, http://www.providencejournal.com. accessed May 31, 2018.

CHAPTER **17**

Financial Management

LEARNING OBJECTIVES

1. Define the role of the financial manager.
2. Describe financial planning.
3. Outline how organizations manage their assets.
4. Discuss the sources of funds and capital structure.
5. Identify short-term funding options.
6. Discuss sources of long-term financing.
7. Describe mergers, acquisitions, buyouts, and divestitures.

Changemaker

Tribune Content Agency LLC/ Alamy Stock Photo

Jess Lee, Partner

Company: Sequoia Capital

Industry: Venture Capital /Financial Services

Website: https://www.sequoiacap.com

In 2016, at the age of 33, Jess Lee joined Sequoia Capital as its first female partner in the venture capital firm's history. As a child in Hong Kong, Lee dreamed of becoming a comic book artist. However, her parents were not in agreement and instead, she attended Stanford University—which is where she first fell in love with the field of computer science. Recruited by Google, Lee's first boss, and subsequent mentor, was Marissa Mayer (Mayer had worked at Google before becoming CEO of Yahoo). Alongside Mayer, Lee worked on My Maps, which allowed users to create maps of their own.

One of Silicon Valley's biggest venture capital firms, Sequoia Capital invests primarily in early and seed-stage privately held technology companies. Seed-stage financings, used to develop a new product or service, are often the first stage of venture capital funding, and they're usually modest amounts compared to later venture rounds. The firm has funneled millions of dollars to include the likes of Dropbox, Google, Airbnb, LinkedIn, Robinhood, 23andMe, and Eventbrite, to name a few.

While at Google, Lee became an "obsessive user" of fashion, design hub, and social commerce website Polyvore, and she began making recommendations to improve the site to its founder, Pasha Sadri. It wasn't long before Lee found herself working as a product manager at Polyvore, where she spent eight years doing everything from writing code, selling ads, hiring and firing—to eventually becoming the company's CEO.

Today, with $8 billion under management and as one of Sequoia Capital's youngest partners, Lee represents a new breed of women breaking into the male-dominated tech investing arena. Only 9% of partners at U.S. venture capital firms are female. Lee along with other female venture partners recently launched "Female Founder Office Hours," a networking initiative for female company founders. Concerning this initiative—a series of events at which investors talk with, mentor, and advise women entrepreneurs—Lee says, "We want to extend our group and kick-start this virtuous cycle of women helping women."[1]

Overview

Previous chapters discuss two essential functions that a business must perform. First, the company must produce a good or service or contract with suppliers to produce it. Second, the company must market its good or service to prospective customers. This chapter introduces a third, equally important, function: a company's managers must ensure that it has enough money to operate successfully, in both the present and the future, and that these funds are invested properly. Adequate funds must be available to purchase materials, equipment, and other assets; pay bills; and compensate employees. This third business function is finance—planning, obtaining, and managing the company's funds in order to accomplish its objectives as effectively and efficiently as possible. When it comes to financing, that's where Jess Lee of Sequoia Partners comes in.

An organization's financial objectives include not only meeting expenses and investing in assets but also maximizing its overall worth, often determined by the value of the company's common stock. Financial managers are responsible for meeting expenses, investing in assets, and increasing profits to shareholders. Solid financial management is critical to the success of a business.

This chapter focuses on the finance function of organizations. It begins by describing the role of financial managers, their place in the organizational hierarchy, and the increasing importance of finance. Next, the financial planning process and the components of a financial plan are outlined. Then the discussion focuses on how organizations manage assets as efficiently and effectively as possible. The two major sources of funds—debt and equity—are then compared, and the concept of leverage is introduced. The major sources of short-term and long-term funding are described in the following sections. A description of mergers, acquisitions, buyouts, and divestitures concludes the chapter.

1 The Role of the Financial Manager

finance planning, obtaining, and managing a company's funds to accomplish its objectives as effectively and efficiently as possible.

financial managers executives who develop and implement the firm's financial plan and determine the most appropriate sources and uses of funds.

Because of the intense pressures they face today, organizations are increasingly measuring and attempting to control or reduce the costs of business operations, in an effort to maximize revenues and profits. This business function is called **finance**. As a result, **financial managers**—executives who develop and implement their company's financial plan and determine the most appropriate sources and uses of funds—are among the most vital people within an organization.

Figure 17.1 shows what the finance function of a typical company might look like. At the top is the chief financial officer (CFO). The CFO usually reports directly to the company's chief executive officer (CEO) or chief operating officer (COO). In some companies, the CFO is also a member of the board of directors. One study found that companies with CFOs on their own company boards had more effective internal controls over financial reporting and a lower likelihood of restatements.[2] Richard A. Galanti, CFO of Costco Wholesale, also serves on his

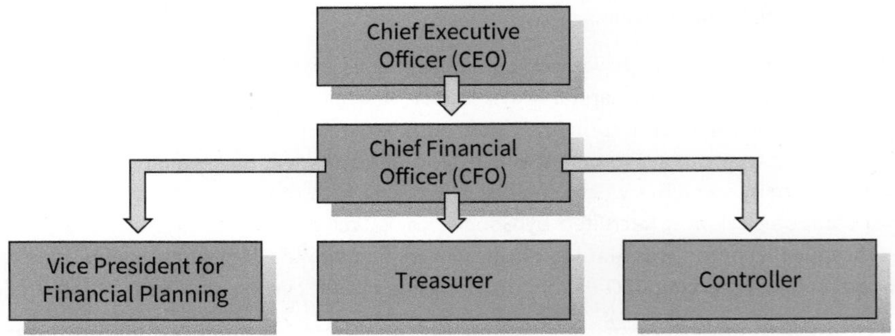

FIGURE 17.1 What the Finance Organization at a Typical Company Looks Like

company's board of directors.[3] It is also not uncommon for current and retired CFOs to serve on the boards of other corporations, government entities, and nonprofits. As noted in Chapter 15, the CFO, along with the company's CEO, must certify the accuracy of the company's financial statements.

Often reporting directly to the CFO are three senior managers. Although titles can vary, these three executives are commonly called the *vice president for financial management* (or *planning*), the *treasurer,* and the *controller*. The vice president for financial management or planning is responsible for preparing financial forecasts and analyzing major investment decisions, such as new products, new production facilities, and acquisitions. The treasurer is responsible for all of the company's financing activities, including cash management, tax planning and preparation, and shareholder relations. The treasurer also works on the sale of new security issues to investors. The controller is the chief accounting manager. The controller's functions include keeping the company's books, preparing financial statements, and conducting internal audits. The "Business Model" feature (and photo) highlights the appointment of a new chief financial officer at entertainment conglomerate The Walt Disney Company.

The growing importance of financial professionals is reflected in the growing number of CEOs who have been promoted from financial positions. Indra Nooyi, CEO of PepsiCo, and John Watson, CEO of Chevron, both served as their company's CFO prior to assuming the top job. The importance of finance professionals is also reflected in how much CFOs earn today. While the median annual salary for CFOs depends largely on the size of the company, in a recent year, the average salary of a CFO in the United States is $313,541, according to Salary.com. One of the highest paid CFOs on record, Ruth Porat, CFO of Alphabet (Google's parent company), recently earned a compensation package that includes a salary of $650,000 and stock valued at $38 million.[4]

In performing their jobs, financial professionals continually seek to balance risks with expected financial returns. Risk is the uncertainty of gain or loss; return is the gain or loss

Business Model

Disney Taps Its First Female CFO

When Disney recently named Christine M. McCarthy as its new chief financial officer (CFO), she wasn't only Disney's first female CFO, but she also happens to be the company's highest-ranking female ever. Serving as Disney's treasurer for the past 18 years, McCarthy will be at the helm of an entertainment conglomerate—part of the almost 13% of female CFOs at Fortune 500 companies. Like their male counterparts, most women ascend to the CFO position through various fields, including accounting, corporate cash management, or investment banking.

McCarthy's four-year employment contract with Disney lands her an annual base salary of $1.25 million, with the potential for an additional bonus of $2.5 million. Stock awards and other benefits can also dramatically increase her total compensation package. In the previous year, Disney's outgoing CFO, with a base salary of $1.75 million, collected a total of $16.2 million, including salary and other add-ons.

McCarthy most recently worked as VP of corporate real estate and alliances and company treasurer. Her team was involved in corporate finance, capital markets, financial risk, international treasury and investments, credit, and risk management. McCarthy is credited with producing strong results in the company's studio entertainment and parks and resorts segments. Additionally, the recent purchase of assets of 21st Century Fox, launch of streaming video, and ESPN+ streaming service can also be attributed to McCarthy's strong financial leadership. In a statement, McCarthy expressed that she was "humbled and honored to be entrusted with the role of CFO of this incredibly dynamic company."

Questions for Critical Thinking

1. **One recruitment firm executive suggests that companies are still hesitant to take a risk on promoting a woman to a senior position because she doesn't "fit" their standard leadership profile. Explain why you think Disney is beginning to deviate from its standard leadership profile and promoting women to top jobs.**
2. **The head of an executive search firm that focuses on CFOs notes only 7.5% of both male and female CFOs move up to the chief executive position. Why do you think this percentage is so low? How can this percentage be increased?**

Sources: Danny Vena, "Disney Executives Talk Marvel, Streaming, and Fox," *The Motley Fool*, http://www.fool.com, accessed June 5, 2018; Michael Cohn, "Women and Minorities Increasingly Attain CFO Position," *Accounting Today*, http://accountingtoday.com, accessed June 5, 2018; James Rainey, "Christine McCarthy Named New Disney Chief Financial Officer," *Variety*, http://variety.com, accessed March 28, 2016; Daniel Roberts, "Disney's New CFO Is Its Highest-Ranking Woman Ever," *Fortune*, http://fortune.com, accessed March 28, 2016.

Courtesy of The Walt Disney Company

The Walt Disney Company appointed Christine M. McCarthy, its first-ever female CFO, and highest ranking female executive in its history.

risk–return trade-off process of maximizing the wealth of a company's shareholders by striking the optimal balance between risk and return.

that results from an investment over a specified period of time. Financial managers strive to maximize the wealth of their company's shareholders by striking the optimal balance between risk and return. This balance is called the **risk–return trade-off**. For example, relying heavily on borrowed funds may increase the return (in the form of cash) to shareholders, but the more money a company borrows, the greater the risks to shareholders. An increase in a company's cash on hand reduces the risk of being unable to meet unexpected cash needs. However, because cash in and of itself does not earn much, if any, return, failure to invest surplus funds in an income-earning asset—such as in securities—reduces a company's potential return or profitability. Many examples of the risk–return trade-off are provided throughout this chapter.

Every financial manager is faced with evaluating a company's risk–return trade-off. However, many times entrepreneurs—risk takers also responsible for managing their finances—may see the risk–return trade-off through a different lens. Many, like Elon Musk, are willing to make a high-risk, high-reward financial decision. At the height of the most recent economic recession almost a decade ago, and with the economy at its lowest, Elon Musk took a financial risk. Feeling the financial strain of many companies during that time, Musk invested $35 million to create Tesla. Today, Tesla's market capitalization has reached over $49 billion.[5]

Directly accountable for the performance of their organization, CFOs have assumed increasingly complex strategic roles as shareholder expectations and scrutiny over corporate conduct and compliance increase. In addition to preserving profit margins, managing working capital, earnings performance, growth strategies, cybersecurity risks, strategic planning, and efficiency of forecasting and budgeting, the biggest concerns for CFOs of large companies include managing technology disruption and technological change in the face of political upheaval, policy uncertainty, and changing geopolitics.[6]

Assessment Check

1. What is the structure of the finance function at a typical firm?
2. Explain the risk–return trade-off.

2 Financial Planning

Financial managers develop their organization's **financial plan**, a document that specifies the funds needed by a company for a given period of time, the timing of inflows and outflows, and the most appropriate sources and uses of funds. Some financial plans, often called *operating plans,* are short-term in nature, focusing on projections no more than a year or two in the future. Other financial plans, sometimes referred to as *strategic plans,* have a much longer time horizon, perhaps up to 5 or 10 years. For small businesses, the time frame generally required for working capital loans is short term, as described in the "Business & Technology" feature.

financial plan document that specifies the funds needed by a company for a period of time, the timing of inflows and outflows, and the most appropriate sources and uses of funds.

Regardless of the time period, a financial plan is based on forecasts of production costs, required purchases, plant and equipment expenditures, and expected sales activities for the period covered. Financial managers use forecasts to determine the specific amounts and timing of expenditures and receipts. They build a financial plan based on the answers to three questions:

1. What funds will the company require during the planning period?
2. When will it need additional funds?
3. Where will it obtain the necessary funds?

While funds flow into a company when it sells its goods and services, funding needs, depending upon the type of business, will vary. The financial plan must reflect both the amounts and timing of inflows and outflows of funds. Even a profitable company may face a financial squeeze as a result of its need for funds when sales lag, when the volume of its credit sales increases, or when customers are slow in making payments.

In general, preparing a financial plan consists of three steps. The first is a forecast of sales or revenue over some future time period. This projection is, in fact, the key variable in any financial plan because without an accurate sales forecast, the company will have difficulty

Business & Technology

PayPal Makes Small Business Loans

As loans to large companies continue to increase, filling the gap for small business loans are a number of technology companies, including PayPal, a well-known electronic payments company. With transaction data from small business customers, and part of a strategy to expand its service offerings, PayPal Working Capital is providing loans to its customers who run small businesses.

PayPal's working capital business loan allows a company to pay back the loan on a daily rather than monthly basis—as the small business gets paid. Repayment is based on a fixed percentage of the company's daily sales. No credit check is required, and no periodic interest rate is charged. A fixed fee is paid in advance, and the loan is paid back daily by determining the percentage of each day's PayPal transactions. Although payment is easier, it is difficult to calculate an annual interest rate for PayPal's loan product. A PayPal spokesman said the company is looking for ways to help customers make an "apples to apples comparison" with other types of financing, and currently the company claims that interest rates run about 10%.

Upon approval, the funds are transferred within minutes and available immediately for use. With a loan limit of as much as 30% of their annual PayPal sales, up to a maximum of $97,000 for the first loan, credit decisions are made against a company's future revenue stream, which is well documented through PayPal's payment system. Merchants repay more when sales volume is high and less when sales are low. Payments are a percentage of sales agreed upon beforehand.

PayPal acknowledges that data drives its decisions to lend wisely, and because payments are made on a daily rather than monthly basis, risk and delinquency rates are reduced. PayPal, part of the financial technology or fintech industry, is using technology to make financial services more plentiful and efficient.

Questions for Critical Thinking

1. From a strategy standpoint, do you think it is smart for PayPal not to perform credit checks on possible borrowers? Why or why not?
2. Is this approach a good alternative to small business lending from traditional banks? Discuss the pros and cons of alternative lenders like PayPal.

Sources: Ruth Simon, "Tech Firms Venture into New Territory: Lending," *Wall Street Journal*, http://www.wsj.com, accessed June 5, 2018; Harriet Taylor, "PayPal Has Lent More Than $1 Billion to Small Biz," *CNBC*, http://www.cnbc.com, accessed June 5, 2018; company website, "Take Your Business Further with PayPal Working Capital," https://www.paypal.com, accessed June 5, 2018; company website, "Is Alternative Business Lending Going Mainstream?" https://www.corecard.com, accessed June 5, 2018; company website, "What Is PayPal Working Capital?" http://www.fundera.com, accessed June 5, 2018.

accurately estimating other variables, such as production costs and purchasing needs. The best method of forecasting sales depends on the nature of the business. For instance, a retailer's CFO might begin with the current sales-per-store figure. Then he or she would look toward the near future, factoring in expected same-store sales growth, along with any planned store openings or closings, to come up with a forecast of sales for the next period. If the company sells merchandise through other channels, such as online, the forecast is adjusted to reflect those additional channels. Same-store sales is a calculation that determines the difference in revenue of a retailer's existing stores over a certain period of time, usually quarterly, compared to the identical period of time in a prior year.

Next, the CFO uses the sales forecast to determine the expected level of profits for future periods. This longer-term projection involves estimating expenses such as purchases, employee compensation, and taxes. Many expenses vary with a company's sales. For example, the more a company sells, generally the greater its purchases and its expenses. Along with estimating future profits, the CFO should also determine what portion of these profits will likely be paid to shareholders in the form of cash dividends.

After coming up with the sales and profit forecast, the CFO needs to estimate how many additional assets the company will need to support projected sales. Increased sales, for example, might mean the company needs additional inventory, stepped-up collections for accounts receivable, or even new plant and equipment. Depending on the nature of the industry, some businesses need more assets than others to support the same amount of sales. The technical term for this requirement is *asset intensity*. For instance, the chemical manufacturer DuPont has approximately \$2.40 in assets for every dollar in sales. So for every \$100 increase in sales, the company would need about \$240 of additional assets. The warehouse retailer Costco (see photo), by contrast, has only roughly \$0.28 in assets for every dollar in sales. It would require an additional \$28 of assets for every \$100 of additional sales.[7] This difference is not surprising; manufacturing is a more asset-intensive business than retailing.

A simplified financial plan illustrates these steps. Assume a growing company is forecasting that sales next year will increase by \$40 million to \$140 million. After estimating expenses, the CFO believes that after-tax profits next year will be \$12 million and the company will not pay dividends. The projected increase in sales next year will require the company to invest another \$20 million in assets, and because increases in assets are uses of funds, the company will need an additional \$20 million in funds. The company's after-tax earnings will contribute \$12 million,

Justin Sullivan/Getty Images, Inc.

Costco has a lower *asset intensity* than a typical manufacturing business might have.

meaning that the other $8 million must come from outside sources. So the financial plan allows the CFO to determine how much money will be needed and when it will be needed. Armed with this knowledge, and given that the company has decided to borrow the needed funds, the CFO can then begin negotiations with banks and other lenders.

The cash inflows and outflows of a business are similar to those of a household. The members of a household depend on weekly or monthly income, mainly in the form of a paycheck, for funds, but their expenditures may vary greatly from one pay period to the next. The financial plan should indicate when the flows of funds entering and leaving the organization will occur and in what amounts. One of the most significant business expenses, as outlined in Chapter 8, is employee compensation.

A good financial plan also includes financial control, a process of comparing actual revenues, costs, and expenses with forecasts. This comparison may reveal significant differences between projected and actual figures, so it is important to discover them early to take quick action.

To support decision making, over 70% of finance executives plan to increase the use of data analytics in the next few years. Using techniques from data mining, statistics, modeling, machine learning, and artificial intelligence, predictive analytics allows an organization to analyze current data to make better predictions about unknown future events. For example, Amazon uses predictive analytics as part of its patented anticipatory shipping model to predict what products a customer is likely to purchase, and when and where they might be needed. A local distribution center or warehouse receives the products in anticipation of an order, and its subsequent shipment. To help decide programs of interest to subscribers, Netflix uses the massive data of its 100 million users as part of its recommendation system. This influences over 80% of the content watched while increasing retention and maintaining profitability. Businesses of all types and sizes are using predictive business analytics to improve customer engagement, and the result is increased revenues and profits.[8]

Assessment Check

1. What three questions does a financial plan address?
2. Explain the steps involved in preparing a financial plan.

3 Managing Assets

As noted in Chapter 15, assets consist of what a company owns. But assets also represent uses of funds. To grow and prosper, companies need to obtain additional assets. Sound financial management requires assets to be acquired and managed as effectively and efficiently as possible. As the "Job Description" feature describes, financial managers are responsible for overseeing finances of a company, along with directing investment activities, which includes acquiring and managing assets of a company.

Short-Term Assets

Short-term, or current, assets consist of cash and assets that can be, or are expected to be, converted into cash within a year. The major current assets are cash, marketable securities, accounts receivable, and inventory.

Cash and Marketable Securities The major purpose of cash is to pay day-to-day expenses, much in the same way individuals maintain balances in checking accounts to pay bills or buy food and clothing. In addition, most organizations strive to maintain a minimum

Job Description

Financial Manager

Overview Financial managers oversee the finances of government organizations, public companies, and private firms in a variety of industries, including banks and insurance companies. They are responsible for directing investment activities and producing financial reports, cash flow statements, and profit forecasts. In addition, they develop short- and long-term plans and strategies with a focus on the company's goals and overall financial health. Financial managers act as advisors throughout an organization by providing context and helping others understand the complexities of financial reports and the impact of decisions on financial results. CFOs, controllers, and treasurers are types of finance managers.

Responsibilities Financial managers prepare financial statements, business activity reports, and forecasts. They monitor details to meet compliance for legal requirements and supervise employees who typically perform budgeting and financial reporting. They review financial data and reports and make recommendations about cost and expense reduction. Market and competitive trends are analyzed so that profits can be maximized and opportunities for growth can be explored and evaluated. Financial managers perform advisory services and data analysis.

Financial managers monitor funds to be sure sufficient money is available for operations and capital investments. They monitor cash flow and evaluate borrowing needs, returns on investment, and cost of funds, including interest rates. They arrange for debt and equity financing, invest funds, and recommend dividend issuance, when applicable.

Requirements A minimum of a bachelor's degree in finance, accounting, economics, or business administration and, on average, five or more years of experience are required. Preference is often given to candidates with a master's degree in business administration (MBA). Certifications including certified public accountant (CPA), certified management accountant (CMA), and chartered financial analyst (CFA) are common. Financial managers typically have work experience in accounting, auditing, securities, or financial analysis.

Analytical skills and abilities, with an aptitude for math, are required to make impactful decisions. Communication skills are essential to work with a variety of people both inside and outside of an organization and to explain complex financial data, transactions, and information. Experience managing others is beneficial, as financial managers often oversee a staff. Attention to detail is required when preparing and analyzing financial reports. With immense data and information to evaluate and analyze, staying organized is important. In a global environment, understanding international accounting and financial transactions is also crucial.

Outlook By 2026, it is expected that the job growth for financial managers will be about 19%. Those with specialized backgrounds in international finance, securities, derivatives, accounting, and finance will be in a particularly favorable and more marketable position.

Sources: Government website, "Financial Manager," *Occupational Outlook Handbook*, 2017–2018 Edition, http://www.bls.gov, accessed June 5, 2018; company website, "Financial Managers," http://money.usnews.com, accessed June 5, 2018; "Finance Manager Job Description," *Accounting Tools*, http://www.accountingtools.com, accessed June 5, 2018.

cash balance in order to have funds available in the event of unexpected expenses. As noted, because cash earns little, if any, return, most companies invest excess cash in so-called *marketable securities*—low-risk securities that either have short maturities or can be easily sold in secondary markets. Money market instruments—described in Chapter 16—are popular choices for companies with excess cash. The cash budget, discussed in Chapter 15, is one tool for managing cash and marketable securities because it shows expected cash inflows and outflows for a period of time. The cash budget indicates months when the company will have surplus cash and can invest in marketable securities and months when it will need additional cash.

Critics of some companies' budgeting practices contend that cash on hand has been rising for companies since the recession. The top cash-rich companies, primarily technology related, include Apple, Microsoft, Alphabet, Cisco, Oracle, General Electric, Amgen, Qualcomm, Gilead Sciences, and Coca-Cola. These firms collectively possess more than $800 billion in cash reserves.[9] The ability to grow organically through research and development activities, make acquisitions, and pay dividends are a few of the advantages for companies that hold large amounts of cash.

Accounts Receivable Accounts receivable are yet-to-be-collected credit sales and can represent a significant percentage of a company's assets. The financial manager's job is to collect the funds owed to the company as quickly as possible while still offering sufficient credit to customers to generate increased sales. In general, a more liberal credit policy means higher sales but also increased collection expenses, higher levels of bad debt, and a higher investment in accounts receivable.

Management of accounts receivable is composed of two functions: determining an overall credit policy and deciding which customers will be offered credit. Formulating a credit policy involves deciding whether the company will offer credit and, if so, on what terms. Will a discount be offered to customers who pay in cash? Often, the overall credit policy is dictated by competitive pressures or general industry practices. If all your competitors offer customers credit, your company will likely have to as well. The other aspect of a credit policy is deciding which customers will be offered credit. Managers must consider the importance, financial health, and repayment history of the customer.

One simple tool for assessing how well receivables are being managed is calculating accounts receivable turnover, as shown in Chapter 15, over successive time periods. If receivables turnover shows signs of slowing, it means that the average credit customer is paying later. This trend warrants further investigation.

Inventory Management For many companies, such as retailers, inventory represents the largest single asset. At the home furnishings retailer Bed Bath & Beyond (see photo), inventory makes up about 40% of total assets. Even for nonretailers, inventory is an important asset. At the heavy-equipment manufacturer Caterpillar, inventory is almost 12% of total assets.[10] On the other hand, some types of companies, such as electric utilities and transportation companies, have no inventory. For the majority of companies, which do carry inventory, proper management of it is vital.

Inventory control is more than just managing items going in and out of a company. It involves managing working capital (current assets minus current liabilities) and making sure that too much cash is not tied up in operations. The cost of inventory includes more than just the acquisition cost. It also includes the cost of ordering, storing, insuring, and financing, as well as the cost of stockouts, which are lost sales due to insufficient inventory. Financial managers try to minimize the cost of inventory. But production, marketing, and logistics also play important roles in determining proper inventory levels. Optimizing inventory management involves inventory tracking technology and the use of big data and analytics. Leading to better insights, trends can be identified using machine-learning and artificial intelligence (AI) by combing through mounds of data to identify patterns and changes in inventory movements. This can also add up to significant company savings. With omnichannel shopping through mobile devices, desktop computers, bricks-and-mortar stores, and apps, technology must function seamlessly across multiple shopping channels—and this will most certainly impact inventory management.

Trends in the inventory turnover ratio—described in Chapter 15—can be early warning signs of impending trouble. For example, if inventory turnover has been slowing for several consecutive quarters, it indicates that inventory is increasing faster than sales. In turn, this may suggest that customer demand is softening and the company needs to take action, such as reducing production or increasing promotional efforts.

Keith Bedford/Reuters/Newscom

At Bed Bath & Beyond, inventory is the company's most valuable asset. Managing inventory can be a costly and highly complex undertaking, particularly for retailers that carry thousands of unique products.

Capital Investment Analysis

In addition to current assets, companies also invest in long-lived assets. Unlike current assets, long-lived assets are expected to produce economic benefits for more than one year. These investments often involve substantial amounts of money on fixed assets such as a new plant, machinery, equipment, or real estate. A downturn in capital spending typically suggests a sentiment of economic uncertainty or potential weakness. A five-year high of capital expenditures will come from investments from information technology companies rather than industrial companies. As the corporate tax rate has recently been cut from 35% to 21%, the additional capital seems to have gone the way of stock buybacks and dividends paid to shareholders. With plans to increase capital expenditures, cruise operator Royal Caribbean plans to spend $1.7 billion on the purchase of a few new ships.[11]

The process by which decisions are made regarding investments in long-lived assets is called *capital investment analysis*. Companies make two basic types of capital investment decisions: expansion and replacement. BMW's South Carolina plant investments are examples of expansion decisions. Replacement decisions involve upgrading assets by acquiring new ones.

Financial managers must estimate all of the costs and benefits of a proposed investment, which can be quite difficult, especially for very long-lived investments. Only those investments that offer an acceptable return—measured by the difference between benefits and costs—should be undertaken. BMW's financial managers believe that the benefits of continuing to expand its Spartanburg, South Carolina, production facility outweigh the significant cost. Since opening the facility in 1994, BMW Group has invested $8 billion and produced almost 4 million vehicles. Over the next three years, the company plans to add 1,000 more jobs by investing an additional $600 million in its manufacturing infrastructure for its BMW X models. To stay ahead of rivals Audi and Mercedes-Benz, BMW's capital expenditures, 5.7% of revenue in a recent year, also included investment in new models and new self-driving car technologies. Spartanburg, South Carolina is BMW's largest plant worldwide, and approximately 70% of the vehicles produced are exported to 140 countries worldwide.[12]

Managing International Assets

Today, companies often have assets worldwide. Chevron Corporation, Procter & Gamble, and Hewlett-Packard generate more than half of their annual sales outside the United States. The vast majority of sales for Unilever and Nestlé occur outside their home countries (the Netherlands and Switzerland, respectively). Managing international assets creates several challenges for the financial manager, one of the most important of which is the issue of exchange rates.

As we discussed in several other chapters, an exchange rate is the rate at which one currency can be exchanged for another. Exchange rates can vary substantially from year to year, creating a problem for any company with international assets. For example, assume a U.S. firm has a major subsidiary in the United Kingdom. Assume that the U.K. subsidiary earns an annual profit of £750 million (stated in British pounds). Over the past five years, the exchange rate between the U.S. dollar and the British pound has fluctuated between a low of 1.2 and a high of 1.7 (dollars per pound). This means the dollar value of U.K. profits ranged from $902 million to $1.28 billion.

Consequently, many global companies engage in activities that reduce the risks associated with exchange rate fluctuations. Some are quite complicated. However, one of the simplest and most widely used is called a *balance sheet hedge*. Essentially, a balance sheet hedge creates an offsetting liability to the non–dollar-denominated asset, one that is denominated in the same currency as the asset. In our example, the U.K. subsidiary is a pound-denominated asset. To create an offsetting liability, the company could take out a loan, denominated in British pounds, creating a pound-denominated liability. If done correctly, this hedge will reduce or even eliminate the risk associated with changes in the value of the dollar relative to the pound. This will improve the financial performance of the company, which can have a positive impact on its stock price.

Assessment Check

1. Why do companies often choose to invest excess cash in marketable securities?
2. What are the two aspects of accounts receivable management?
3. Explain the difference between an expansion decision and a replacement decision.

4 Sources of Funds and Capital Structure

The use of debt for financing can increase the potential for return but also increase loss potential. Recall the accounting equation introduced in Chapter 15:

$$\text{Assets} = \text{Liabilities} + \text{Owner's equity}$$

If you view this equation from a financial management perspective, it reveals that there are only two types of funding: debt and equity. *Debt capital* consists of funds obtained through borrowing. *Equity capital* consists of funds provided by the company's owners when they reinvest earnings, make additional contributions, liquidate assets, issue stock to the general public, or raise capital from outside investors. The mix of a company's debt and equity capital is known as its **capital structure**.

capital structure mix of a company's debt and equity capital.

Companies often take very different approaches to choosing a capital structure. As more debt is used, the risk to the company increases since the company is now obligated to make the interest payments on the money borrowed, regardless of the cash flows coming into or going out of the company. Choosing more debt increases the fixed costs a company must pay, which in turn makes a company more sensitive to sales revenues. Debt is frequently the least costly method of raising additional financing dollars, one of the reasons it is so frequently used.

Companies choose varying amounts of debt and equity to use when financing, and this will vary by industry. Since the automobile industry is capital intensive (requiring large amounts of money to produce goods and services) and requires far more borrowing than other industries, companies within this industry typically have higher debt-to-equity (D/E) ratios. The D/E ratio indicates how much debt a company is using to finance its assets relative to the amount of value represented by shareholders' equity. In a recent year, the aerospace industry had a debt-to-equity ratio of almost 17%. In comparison, Ford's D/E ratio was 2.89, and Cheesecake Factory's D/E ratio was 0.5.[14]

leverage increasing the rate of return on funds invested by borrowing funds.

Leverage and Capital Structure Decisions

Raising needed cash by borrowing allows a company to benefit from the principle of **leverage**, increasing the rate of return on funds invested by borrowing funds. The key to managing leverage is to ensure that a company's earnings remain larger than its interest payments, which increases the leverage on the rate of return on shareholders' investment. Of course, if the company earns less than its interest payments, shareholders lose money on their original investments.

Figure 17.2 shows the relationship between earnings and shareholder returns for two identical hypothetical companies that choose to raise funds in different ways. Leverage Company obtains 50% of its funds from lenders who purchase company bonds. Leverage Company pays 10% interest on its bonds. Equity Company raises all of its funds through sales of company stock.

Notice that if earnings double, from, say, $10 million to $20 million, returns to shareholders of Equity Company also double—from 10% to 20%. But returns to shareholders of Leverage Company more than double—from 10% to 30%. However, leverage works in the opposite direction as well. If earnings fall from $10 million to $5 million, a decline of 50%, returns to shareholders of Equity Company also fall by 50%—from 10% to 5%. By contrast, returns to shareholders of Leverage Company

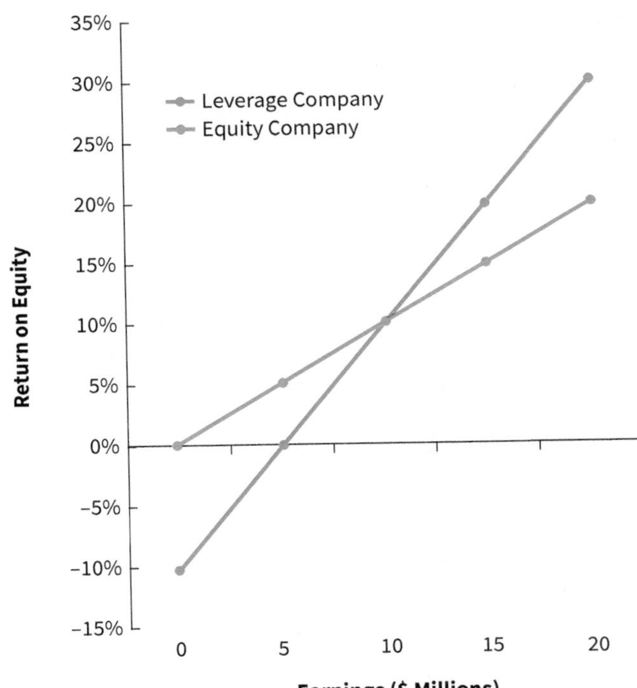

FIGURE 17.2 How Leverage Works

Note: The example assumes that both companies have $100 million in capital. Leverage Company consists of $50 million in equity and $50 million in bonds (with an interest rate of 10%). Equity Company consists of $100 million in equity and no bonds. This example also assumes no corporate taxes.

fall from 10% to zero. Thus, leverage increases potential returns to shareholders but also increases risk.

Another concern with borrowing money is that an overreliance on borrowed funds may reduce management's flexibility in future financing decisions. If a company raises equity capital this year and needs to raise funds next year, it will probably be able to raise either debt or equity capital. But if it raises debt capital this year, it may be forced to raise equity capital next year.

Equity capital has drawbacks as well. Because shareholders are owners of the company, they usually have the right to vote on major company issues and elect the board of directors. Whenever new equity is sold, the control of existing shareholders is diluted, and the outcome of these votes could potentially change. One contentious subject today between companies and shareholders is whether shareholders should be able to vote on executive pay packages.

Another disadvantage of equity capital is that it is more expensive than debt capital. First, creditors have a senior claim to the assets of a company relative to shareholders. Because of this advantage, creditors are willing to accept a lower rate of return than shareholders are. Second, the company can deduct interest payments on debt, reducing its taxable income and tax bill. Dividends paid to shareholders, on the other hand, are not tax deductible. A key component of the financial manager's job is to weigh the advantages and disadvantages of debt capital and equity capital, creating the most appropriate capital structure for his or her company.

Mixing Short-Term and Long-Term Funds

Another decision financial managers face is determining the appropriate mix of short-and long-term funds. Short-term funds consist of current liabilities, and long-term funds consist of long-term debt and equity. Short-term funds are generally less expensive than long-term funds, but they also expose the company to more risk. This is because short-term funds have to be renewed, or rolled over, frequently. Short-term interest rates can be volatile. During a recent 12-month period, for example, rates on commercial paper, a popular short-term financing option, ranged from a high of 2.23% (for 90-day loans) to a low of 1.69% (for 1-day loans).[15]

Because short-term rates move up and down frequently, interest expense on short-term funds can change substantially from year to year. For instance, if a company borrows $50 million for 10 years at 4% interest, its annual interest expense is fixed at $2 million for the entire 10 years. On the other hand, if it borrows $50 million for 1 year at a rate of 3%, its annual interest expense of $1.5 million is only fixed for that year. If interest rates increase the following year from 3% to 5%, the interest expense increases to $2.5 million, or an additional $1 million. Another potential risk of relying on short-term funds is availability. Even financially healthy companies can occasionally find it difficult to borrow money.

Because of the added risk of short-term funding, most companies choose to finance all of their long-term assets, and even a portion of their short-term assets, with long-term funds. Johnson & Johnson is typical of this choice. **Figure 17.3** shows a recent balance sheet broken down between short- and long-term assets, and short- and long-term funds.

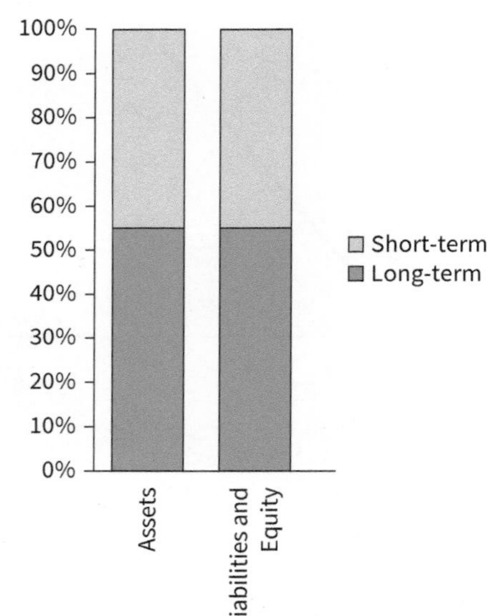

Source: Johnson & Johnson balance sheet, Yahoo! Finance, http://finance.yahoo.com, accessed June 5, 2018.

FIGURE 17.3 Johnson & Johnson's Mix of Short- and Long-Term Funds

Dividend Policy

Along with decisions regarding capital structure and the mix of short- and long-term funds, financial managers also make decisions regarding a company's dividend policy. *Dividends* are periodic cash payments to shareholders. The most common type of dividend is paid quarterly and is often labeled as a *regular dividend*. Occasionally, companies make one-time special or extra dividend payments.

Nordstrom (see photo) announced a special dividend of $4.85 per share for a total payout of $900 million after completing the sale of its credit-card business to Toronto-Dominion (TD) Bank.[16] Earnings that are paid in dividends are not reinvested in the firm and don't contribute additional equity capital.

Companies are under no legal obligation to pay dividends to shareholders. Although some companies pay generous dividends, others pay nothing. Until 2010, Starbucks never paid a dividend to its shareholders, and recently, the parent of Hawaiian Airlines offered its first-ever dividend. A company's decision about dividends can sometimes reflect the company's financial health. Known for its Post-it Notes, 3M has paid dividends for over 30 consecutive years.[17] Companies that pay dividends try to increase them or at the very least hold them steady from year to year. However, in rare cases, companies must cut or eliminate dividends, as discussed in the "Judgment Call" feature.

Many factors determine a company's dividend policy, one of which is its investment opportunities. If a company has numerous investment opportunities and wishes to finance some or all of them with equity funding, it will likely pay little, if any, of its earnings in dividends. Shareholders may actually want the company to retain earnings, because if they are reinvested, the company's future profits, and the value of its shares, will increase faster. By contrast, a firm with more limited investment opportunities generally pays more of its earnings in dividends.

Bob Bert/Moment Mobile/Getty Images

Companies are under no legal obligation to pay dividends to their shareholders. Nordstrom paid shareholders a special dividend after completing the sale of its credit-card business to TD bank.

Judgment Call

The Dividend Dilemma

What do Wells Fargo, The Coca-Cola Company, IBM, Procter & Gamble, Walmart, and Verizon have in common? All pay dividends to their shareholders. In contrast, some companies maintain a strict "no dividends" policy. Warren Buffett's Berkshire Hathaway has paid only one dividend, in 1967, and Buffett jokes that he "must have been in the bathroom" when the decision was made. He agrees that his shareholders are better served when the company's immense riches are "plowed back into the business."

Rising dividends often go hand-in-hand with strong company results, and many investors prefer dividend payments now rather than waiting for the stock to appreciate. Similarly, when the stock market begins to slide downward, a dividend can show shareholders that a company is confident in the market's rebound—and can prop up its stock price. But what happens when a company decides to dramatically cut its dividend?

In the energy sector, as crude prices fluctuated dramatically between 2014 and 2016, oil and gas companies were forced to reconsider their dividend policies. During that time, Chevron, which had paid uninterrupted dividends since 2002, paid out more in dividends than its actual stock's earnings. Another oil giant, ConocoPhillips, whose share price hit a 5-year low, cut its dividend for the first time in 25 years. Moreover, British Petroleum (BP), which plunged more than 45% during that time, continued to pay dividends, despite reporting a loss. Fast forward to higher commodity prices and increased production, and the result is a spike in Chevron's stock, resulting in what happens also to be one of the best dividend stocks to date. While dividend decisions can be complex, external factors related to commodity prices can create an even greater dilemma for both companies and investors. The dividend dilemma continues, especially in the energy and commodities sector. Dividend seekers stand to benefit most when there is great upside to oil prices.

Questions for Critical Thinking

1. How understanding are shareholders when a company cuts its dividend? When this decision is made, discuss the pros and cons for shareholders and the company.
2. If you decided to purchase a portfolio of stocks, would you choose stocks that pay dividends or those with appreciation potential? Explain your reasoning.

Sources: Brian Bollinger, "5 High-Yield Stocks with Safe Dividends," *The Street*, http://www.thestreet.com, accessed June 5, 2018; Brett Owens, "1 Stock to Settle the Dividend vs. Buyback Debate," *Forbes*, http://www.forbes.com, accessed June 5, 2018; Marthe Fourcade, "Glaxo's Generous Dividend Policy May End after Witty's Exit," *Bloomberg Business*, http://www.bloomberg.com, accessed June 7, 2018; Jimmy Atkinson, "4 Reasons Why Dividend Stocks Outperform," *Dividend Reference*, http://dividendreference.com, accessed June 7, 2018; Siddhi Bajaj, "3 Oil Companies Likely to Cut Dividends as Crude Prices Continue Freefall," *The Street*, http://www.thestreet.com, accessed June 7, 2018; Anna Driver and Swetha Gopinath, "Conoco Cuts Dividend for First Time in 25 Years on Crude Crash," *Reuters*, http://www.reuters.com, accessed June 5, 2018; Tip Ranks, "Buy These 4 Strong Energy Stocks to Ride Oil's Rally Successfully," *The Street*, http://www.thestreet.com, accessed June 5, 2018.

Assessment Check

1. Explain the concept of leverage.
2. Why do companies generally rely more on long-term funds than short-term funds?
3. What is an important determinant of a company's dividend policy?

5 Short-Term Funding Options

Many times throughout a year, an organization may discover that its cash needs are seasonal and exceed its available funds. Retailers generate surplus cash for most of the year, but they need to build up inventory during the late summer and fall to get ready for the holiday shopping season. Consequently, they often need funds to pay for merchandise until holiday sales generate revenue. Then they use the incoming funds to repay the amount they borrowed. In these instances, financial managers evaluate short-term sources of funds. By definition, short-term sources of funds are repaid within one year. Three major sources of short-term funds exist: trade credit, short-term loans, and commercial paper. Large companies often rely on a combination of all three sources of short-term financing.

Trade Credit

Trade credit is extended by suppliers when a company receives goods or services and agrees to pay for them at a later date. Trade credit is common in many industries such as retailing and manufacturing. Suppliers routinely ship billions of dollars of merchandise to retailers each day and are paid at a later date. Without trade credit, the retailing sector would probably look much different—with fewer selections. Under this system, the supplier records the transactions as an account receivable, and the retailer records it as an account payable. Accounts receivable typically represent 40% of a company's assets. Although available, and still relatively unknown, very few businesses purchase costly trade credit insurance, which protects a seller against losses from non-payment of a commercial trade debt.[18] The main advantage of trade credit is its easy availability because credit sales are common in many industries. The main drawback to trade credit is that the amount a company can borrow is limited to the amount it purchases.

What is the cost of trade credit? If suppliers do not offer a cash discount, trade credit is effectively free. For example, assume a supplier offers trade credit under the terms net 30—meaning that the buyer has 30 days to pay. This is similar to borrowing $100 and repaying $100 in 30 days. The effective rate of interest is zero. Interest fees and late payment fees can be a way to increase revenues for creditors extending trade credit. In addition, some suppliers offer a discount if they are paid in cash. If a 2% discount is offered to cash buyers for payment in 10 days, and instead they choose to pay in 30 days, they are essentially borrowing $98 today and repaying $100 30 days from today. The annual interest rate on such a loan exceeds 24%. Companies must be mindful of the downside to trade credit.

Short-Term Loans

Loans from commercial banks are a significant source of short-term financing for businesses. Often businesses whose sales fluctuate on a seasonal basis use these loans to finance inventory and accounts receivable. For example, late fall through early winter is the period of highest sales for a small manufacturer of ski equipment. To meet this demand, it has to begin building inventory during the summer. The manufacturer also has to finance accounts receivable (credit sales to customers) during the fall and winter. So it may take out a bank loan during the summer. As the inventory is sold and accounts receivable collected, the company repays the loan.

There are two types of short-term bank loans: lines of credit and revolving credit agreements. A line of credit specifies the maximum amount the company can borrow over a period of time, usually a year. The bank is under no obligation to actually lend the money, however. It does so only if funds are available. Most lines of credit require the borrower to repay the original amount, plus interest, within one year. By contrast, a revolving credit agreement is essentially a guaranteed line of credit—the bank guarantees that the funds will be available when needed. Banks typically charge a fee, on top of interest, for revolving credit agreements.

The cash budget is an important tool for determining the size of a line of credit because it shows the months when additional financing will be needed or when borrowed funds can be repaid. For instance, assume the ski manufacturer's cash budget indicates that it will need \$2.5 million for the June through November period. The financial manager might set up a line of credit with the bank for \$2.8 million. The extra \$300,000 is a cushion for any unexpected cash outflows.

In addition to commercial banks, commercial finance companies also make short-term loans to businesses. Although most bank loans are unsecured, meaning that no specific assets are pledged as collateral, loans from commercial finance companies are often secured with accounts receivable or inventory.

Another form of short-term financing backed by accounts receivable is called *factoring*. The business sells its accounts receivable to either a bank or finance company—called a *factor*—at a discount. The size of the discount determines the cost of the transaction. Factoring allows the company to convert its receivables into cash quickly without worrying about collections. A discussion of using receivables, or supply chain financing, can be found in Case 17.2 at the end of this chapter.

The cost of short-term loans depends not only on the interest rate but also on the fees charged by the lender. In addition to fees, some lenders require the borrower to keep so-called *compensating balances*—5% to 20% of the outstanding loan amount—in a checking account. Compensating balances increase the effective cost of a loan because the borrower doesn't have full use of the amount borrowed.

Say, for example, that a company borrows \$100,000 for one year at 5% interest. The borrower will pay \$5,000 in interest (5% × \$100,000). If the lender requires that 10% of the loan amount be kept as a compensating balance, the company has use of only \$90,000. However, because it still will pay \$5,000 in interest, the effective rate on the loan is actually 5.56% (\$5,000 divided by \$90,000).

Commercial Paper

Commercial paper is a short-term IOU sold by a company; this concept was briefly described in Chapter 16. Commercial paper is typically sold in multiples of \$100,000 to \$1 million and has a maturity that ranges from 1 to 270 days. Most commercial paper is unsecured. It is an attractive source of financing because large amounts of money can be raised at rates that are typically 1% to 2% less that those charged by banks. A significant benefit of commercial paper, which makes it cost effective is that it does not need to be registered with the Securities and Exchange Commission (SEC) as long as it matures before nine months, or 270 days.[19] Although commercial paper is an attractive short-term financing alternative, only a small percentage of businesses can issue it. That is because access to the commercial paper market has traditionally been restricted to large, financially strong corporations.

Assessment Check

1. What are the three sources of short-term funding?
2. Explain trade credit.
3. Why is commercial paper an attractive short-term financing option?

6 Sources of Long-Term Financing

Funds from short-term sources can help a company meet current needs for cash or inventory. A larger project or plan, however, such as acquiring another company or making a major investment in real estate or equipment, usually requires funds for a much longer period of time. Unlike short-term sources, long-term sources are repaid over many years.

Organizations acquire long-term funds from three sources. One is long-term loans obtained from financial institutions such as commercial banks, life insurance companies, and pension funds. A second source is bonds—certificates of indebtedness—sold to investors. A third source is equity financing that is acquired by selling stock in the company or reinvesting company profits.

Public Sale of Stocks and Bonds

Public sales of securities such as stocks and bonds are a major source of funds for corporations. Such sales provide cash inflows for the issuing firm and either a share in its ownership (for a stock purchaser) or a specified rate of interest and repayment at a stated time (for a bond purchaser). Because stock and bond issues of many corporations are traded in the secondary markets, stockholders and bondholders can easily sell these securities. A recent panel of bond managers at a well-known investment firm agrees that with low interest rates and the possibility of an increase, there will not be a significant return from bond holdings. However, bonds do remain a key diversification strategy (relative to stocks) for some investors. Although returns are expected to be fairly modest, bonds do serve a key role in generating income and preserving wealth. Continued concerns about global growth have also subdued bond yields.[20]

In Chapter 16, we discussed the process by which most companies sell securities publicly—through investment bankers via a process called *underwriting*. Investment bankers purchase the securities from the issuer and then resell them to investors. The issuer pays a fee to the investment banker, called an *underwriting discount*.

Private Placements

Some new stock or bond issues are not sold publicly but instead to a small group of major investors such as pension funds and insurance companies. These sales, or non-public offerings, are referred to as *private placements*. An alternative to debt financing, most private placements involve corporate debt securities.

It is often less expensive for a company to sell a security privately than publicly, and there is less government regulation because it is not required that private placements be registered with the Securities and Exchange Commission. Institutional investors such as insurance companies and pension funds buy private placements because they typically carry slightly higher interest rates than publicly issued bonds. In addition, the terms of the issue can be tailored to meet the specific needs of both the issuer and the institutional investors. Of course, the institutional investor gives up liquidity because privately placed securities do not trade in secondary markets.[21]

Venture Capitalists

venture capitalists business firms or groups of individuals that invest in new and growing firms in exchange for an ownership share.

Venture capitalists are an important source of private equity financing, especially to small, early-stage emerging firms with high growth potential. Venture capitalists raise money from wealthy individuals and institutional investors. In exchange for the risk taken by investing in early-stage companies, venture capitalists become owners, offering strategic advice—and often, assuming control over decisions. In a recent year, venture capital funding flowed into technology companies at the highest rate since the dot-com boom of 1995–2001.

"Seed funding" is followed by subsequent rounds of Series A, B, and C funding. Each letter refers to a company's stage of development when raising capital, and may eventually lead to an "exit" whereby shares are sold to the public for the first time in an initial public offering or IPO. Sam Altman (see photo), President of Y Combinator, whose motto is "Make Something People Want," is an American Seed Accelerator. To date, Y Combinator has funded close to 2,000 start-ups from bi-annual groups of carefully chosen companies who receive seed money, advice, and connections in exchange for 7% equity.[22]

David Paul Morris/Bloomberg via Getty Images

Sam Altman is President of Y Combinator, a program that helps company founders further refine and develop their product, team, and market.

Private Equity Funds

Similar to venture capitalists, *private equity funds* are investment companies that raise funds from wealthy individuals and institutional investors and use those funds to make large investments in both public and privately held companies. Unlike venture capital funds, which tend to focus on small, start-up companies, private equity funds invest in all types of businesses, including mature ones. For example, 3G Capital, a Brazilian private equity firm, is best known for its acquisition of consumer and retail brands such as Burger King. Recently, in conjunction with Berkshire Hathaway, 3G paid nearly $40 billion to create a merger between H.J. Heinz and the Kraft Foods Group, as discussed further in Case 17.2 at the end of this chapter.[23] A variety of different funds, including money market funds and exchange-traded funds, have become increasingly important for socially responsible investors. See the "Clean & Green Business" feature to learn more. Often private equity funds invest in transactions to take public companies private or conduct leveraged buyouts (LBOs). In these transactions, discussed in more detail in the next section, a public company reverts to private status.

A variation of the private equity fund is the so-called *sovereign wealth fund*. These companies are owned by governments and invest in a variety of financial and real assets, such as real estate. Although sovereign wealth funds generally make investments based on the best risk–return trade-off, political, social, and strategic considerations also play roles in their investment decisions.

Norway's Government Pension Fund—Global—is the world's largest sovereign wealth fund. Recently, the fund exceeded $1 trillion in value for the first time, a thirteen-fold increase since 2002. The fund invests in international securities, and it is the largest stock owner in Europe.[24] The assets of the 10 largest sovereign wealth funds are shown in **Figure 17.4**. Together, these 10 funds have more than $5.7 trillion in assets.

Clean & Green Business

Socially Responsible Investing on Campus

Colleges and universities control billions of dollars in endowment funds—money or other assets donated to them. Some schools, including Yale University, are giving students hands-on investment experience with money from these endowments.

Almost a decade ago, the Dwight Hall organization at Yale University launched the first socially responsible investment fund run by undergraduates. Initially started with $50,000 of the organization's endowment, the Dwight Hall Socially Responsible Investment Fund (DHSRI) is managed by a team of 20 college students.

DHSRI uses traditional methods of investing but avoids investing in companies that sell or produce tobacco and alcohol or businesses associated with gambling. Instead, the fund seeks out companies engaged in environmental sustainability and clean energy efforts. It invests in mutual funds, exchange-traded funds, real estate investment trusts, and local community development banks.

Providing students with this experience gives them an opportunity to experience hands-on investing and to understand the connections between business and society. Students are given the chance to apply financial theory to hands-on decision making and invest in companies that are responsible corporate citizens.

Questions for Critical Thinking

1. What are the costs and benefits of a socially responsible approach to investing?
2. As a socially responsible investor, what type of investments would you choose? What type would you avoid?

Sources: Organization website, http://dwighthall.org, accessed June 5, 2018; organization website, "About Us," http://www.dwighthallsri.org, accessed June 5, 2018; university website, Cara Masset, "Socially Responsible Investment Club at University of Pittsburgh to Begin Managing $100,000 Portfolio," http://www.news.pitt.edu, accessed June 5, 2018; Janet Brown, "Sustainable, Responsible Investing Can Be Profitable, Here's How," *Forbes*, http://www.forbes.com, accessed June 5, 2018.

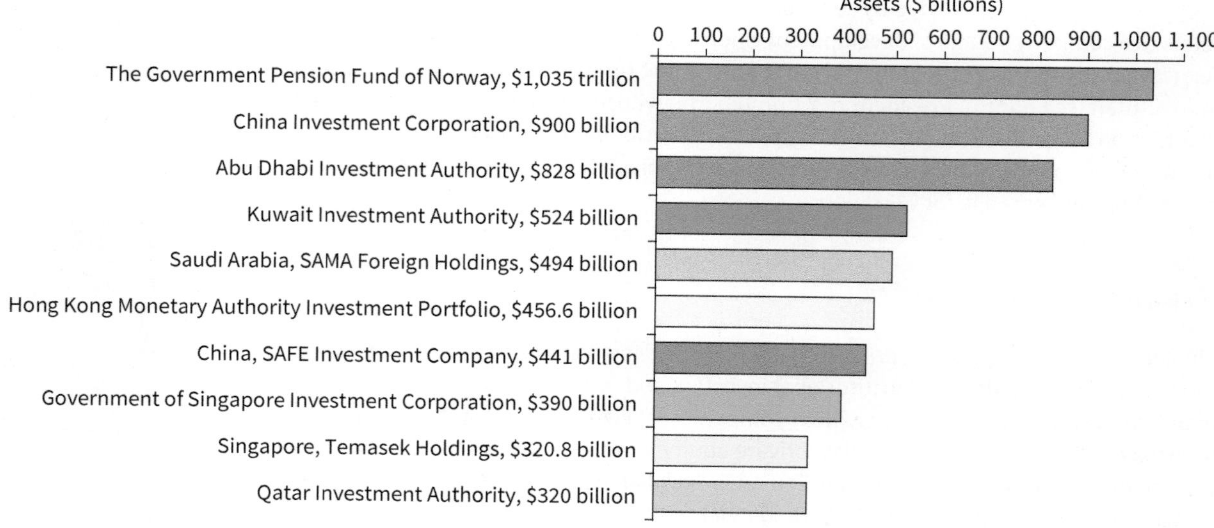

Source: Sovereign Wealth Fund Institute, "Sovereign Wealth Fund Rankings," http://www.swfinstitute.org, accessed June 5, 2018.

FIGURE 17.4 The World's Ten Largest Sovereign Wealth Funds

Hedge Funds

Hedge funds are private investment companies open only to qualified large investors. In recent years, hedge funds have become a significant presence in U.S. financial markets. Before the economic downturn that began in 2007, some analysts estimated that hedge funds accounted for about 60% of all secondary bond market trading and around one-third of all activity on stock exchanges.[25] The world's largest hedge fund, Bridgewater Associates, founded by billionaire investor Ray Dalio, manages about $160 billion for some of the largest global institutional clients including public and corporate pension funds, university endowments, charitable foundations, supranational agencies, sovereign wealth funds, and central banks. One of the biggest trends in the hedge fund industry is the evolution of decision making and traditional investment processes as a result of new technologies such as quantitative analytics, alternative data sources and artificial intelligence. Due mainly to stock investments, a cautious optimism has returned to the global hedge fund industry, which recently had its best returns since 2013.[26]

Assessment Check

1. What is the most common type of security sold privately?
2. Describe venture capitalists.
3. What is a sovereign wealth fund?

7 Mergers, Acquisitions, Buyouts, and Divestitures

Chapter 5 briefly described mergers and acquisitions. A merger is a transaction in which two or more companies combine into one. In an acquisition, one company buys the assets and assumes the obligations of another company. Chapter 5 also listed some well-known mergers and acquisitions (Figure 5.3) and the classifications of mergers and acquisitions—vertical, horizontal, and conglomerate—and corporate deal making by publicly traded companies seeking growth will continue to dominate the news media. Technology acquisition, a trend driving M&A activity, also brings with it an in-place and well-versed employee base.[27] In this section, we focus on the financial implications of not only mergers and acquisitions but also buyouts and divestitures.

Note that even in a merger, there is a buyer and seller. The seller is often referred to as the *target*. Financial managers evaluate a proposed merger or acquisition in much the same way they would evaluate any large investment—by comparing the costs and benefits. To acquire another company, a company typically offers a higher price than the current market price for the target's shares. The action usually triggers a fluctuation in the stock prices of both companies. When The Walt Disney Company purchased Marvel Entertainment for $4.6 billion, the deal was priced to include a mix of cash and stock. Marvel shareholders received a 29% per share premium that included $30 per share in cash plus approximately three-quarters of a Disney share for each share of Marvel. The value of the deal was affected by the fluctuating closing price of Disney stock on the day of the acquisition.[28]

When the buyer makes what is known as a **tender offer** for the target's shares, it specifies a price and the form of payment. The buyer can offer cash, securities, or a combination of the two, as Disney did when it purchased Marvel. The tender offer can be friendly, meaning it is endorsed by the target company's board of directors, or unfriendly. Shareholders of both the buyer and target must vote to approve a merger.

tender offer offer made by a company to the target company's shareholders specifying a price and the form of payment.

Justifying such a premium requires the financial manager also to estimate the benefits of a proposed merger. These benefits could take the form of cost savings from economies of scale or reduced workforces or the buyer getting a bargain price for the target's assets. Sometimes, a buyer finds that the most cost-effective method of entering a new market is simply to buy an existing company that serves the market. Johnson & Johnson has a long history of making such acquisitions. When it decided to enter the contact lens market, Johnson & Johnson bought Vistakon, the company that invented disposable contact lenses under the brand name Acuvue. The term used to describe the benefits produced by a merger or acquisition is *synergy*—the notion that the combined company is worth more than the buyer and the target are individually.

Leveraged buyouts, or LBOs, were briefly introduced in the preceding section. In an LBO, public shareholders are bought out, and the company reverts to private status. The term *leverage* comes from the fact that many of these transactions are financed with high degrees of debt—often in excess of 75%. Private equity companies and hedge funds provide equity and debt financing for many LBOs. The company's incumbent senior management is often part of the buyout group. Tightening borrowing will impact LBO activity, but as the economy recovers LBO activity will increase. Some highly leveraged deals are being refinanced or renegotiated. Toys 'R' Us recently shut down over 800 retail stores and terminated employment with over 30,000 employees. Protesting a lack of severance pay, an amount paid to an employee upon termination, angered employees cite that the company's troubles began when a 2005 leverage buyout burdened the toy retailer with over $5 billion in debt.[29]

leveraged buyouts (LBO) transaction in which public shareholders are bought out and the company reverts to private status.

Why do so many LBOs occur? One reason is that private companies enjoy benefits that public companies do not. Private companies are not required to publish financial results, are subject to less SEC oversight, and are not pressured to produce the short-term profits often demanded by Wall Street. Some argue that LBOs, because of the high degree of debt, enforce more discipline on management to control costs. Although LBOs do have advantages, history has shown that many companies that go private reemerge as public companies several years later.

In a sense, a **divestiture** is the reverse of a merger. That is, a company sells assets such as subsidiaries, product lines, or production facilities. Two types of divestitures exist: sell-offs and spin-offs. In a *sell-off,* assets are sold by one company to another. As part of a plan to raise $10 billion through divestiture, Newell Brands, known for many products including Sharpie pens, Crock-Pot cookware, and Elmer's Glue, recently sold its Rawlings Sporting goods brand (producer of the official ball and helmet of Major League Baseball) to Seidler Equity partners for $395 million.[30]

divestiture sale of assets by a company.

The other type of divestiture is a *spin-off*. In this transaction, the assets sold form a new company. Shareholders of the divesting company become shareholders of the new company as well. Henry Schein, a health-care products distributor, is spinning off its animal health business and merging it with Vets First Choice to form a new company. The new deal will combine Henry

Schein's veterinary supplies, software for practices, and distribution network with Vets First Choice's prescription management platform.[31]

Companies divest assets for several reasons. Sometimes divestitures result from prior acquisitions that didn't work out as well as expected. In early 2001, America Online and Time Warner merged to create AOL Time Warner, Inc. Nine years later, Time Warner announced it would spin off AOL. The merger—now considered one of the worst mistakes in corporate history—failed to generate the much-heralded synergies between the two companies.

In other cases, a company makes a strategic decision to concentrate on its core businesses and decides to divest anything that falls outside this core. Consumer products giant Procter & Gamble made the decision to divest 100 underperforming and noncore brands. The company's focus will be on 70 brands in 10 business categories, which account for over 90% of the company's revenues. Duracell batteries was sold to Berkshire Hathaway, and Camay and Zest soap brands were sold to competitor Unilever, while beauty brands Cover Girl and Max Factor were sold to Coty, Inc.[32]

Assessment Check

1. Define *synergy*.
2. What is an LBO?
3. What are the two types of divestitures?

What's Ahead

Contemporary Business concludes with Chapter 18: Trends in E-Commerce and six appendixes. Appendix A, "Business Law," outlines the main legal issues encountered in business. It reviews the types of laws, the regulatory environment of business, and the core of business law, including discussions of contract law and property law. Appendix B examines risk management and insurance. It describes the concept of risk, alternative ways of dealing with risk, and the various kinds of insurance available to business and individuals. Appendix C discusses some of the important components of personal financial planning, such as budgeting, credit, and retirement planning. Appendix D describes how to write an effective business plan, and Appendix E discusses career searches and options to help you prepare for your future in business.

Chapter in Review

Summary of Learning Objectives

LEARNING OBJECTIVE 1 Define the role of the financial manager.

Finance deals with planning, obtaining, and managing a company's funds to accomplish its objectives efficiently and effectively. The major responsibilities of financial managers are to develop and implement financial plans and determine the most appropriate sources and uses of funds. The chief financial officer (CFO) heads a company's finance organization. Three senior executives reporting to the CFO are the vice president for financial management, the treasurer, and the controller. When making decisions, financial professionals continually seek to balance risks with expected financial returns.

Assessment Check Answers

1.1 **What is the structure of the finance function at a typical company?** The person in charge of the finance function of a company has the title of chief financial officer (CFO) and generally reports directly to the company's chief executive officer. Reporting to the CFO are the treasurer, the controller, and the vice president for financial management.

1.2 **Explain the risk-return trade-off.** Financial managers strive to maximize the wealth of their company's shareholders by striking the optimal balance between risk and return.

LEARNING OBJECTIVE 2 Describe financial planning.

A financial plan is a document that specifies the funds needed by a company for a given period of time, the timing of inflows and outflows, and the most appropriate sources and uses of funds. The financial plan addresses three questions: What funds will be required during the planning period? When will funds be needed? Where will funds be obtained? Three steps are involved in the financial planning process: forecasting sales over a future period of time, estimating the expected level of profits over the planning period, and determining the additional assets needed to support additional sales.

Assessment Check Answers

2.1 **What three questions does a financial plan address?** The financial plan addresses three questions: What funds will be required during the planning period? When will funds be needed? Where will the necessary funds be obtained?

2.2 **Explain the steps involved in preparing a financial plan.** The first step is to forecast sales over a future period of time. Second, the financial manager must estimate the expected level of profits over the planning period. The final step is to determine the additional assets needed to support additional sales.

LEARNING OBJECTIVE 3 Outline how organizations manage their assets.

Assets consist of what a company owns and also comprise the uses of its funds. Sound financial management requires assets to be acquired and managed as effectively and efficiently as possible. The major current assets are cash, marketable securities, accounts receivable, and inventory. The goal of cash management is to have sufficient funds on hand to meet day-to-day transactions and pay any unexpected expenses. Excess cash should be invested in marketable securities, which are low-risk securities with short maturities. Managing accounts receivable, which are uncollected credit sales, involves securing funds owed the company as quickly as possible while offering sufficient credit to customers to generate increased sales. The main goal of inventory management is to minimize the overall cost of inventory. Production, marketing, and logistics also play roles in determining proper inventory levels. Capital investment analysis is the process by which financial managers make decisions on long-lived assets. This involves comparing the benefits and costs of a proposed investment. Managing international assets poses additional challenges for the financial manager, including the problem of fluctuating exchange rates.

Assessment Check Answers

3.1 **Why do companies often choose to invest excess cash in marketable securities?** Cash earns no rate of return, which is why excess cash should be invested in marketable securities. These are low-risk securities that have short maturities and can be sold easily in the secondary markets. As a result, they are easily converted back into cash, when needed.

3.2 **What are the two aspects of accounts receivable management?** The two aspects of accounts receivable management are determining an overall credit policy (whether to offer credit and, if so, on what terms) and deciding which customers will be offered credit.

3.3 **Explain the difference between an expansion decision and a replacement decision.** An expansion decision involves choosing between offering new products or building or acquiring new production facilities. A replacement decision is one that considers whether to replace an existing asset with a new one.

LEARNING OBJECTIVE 4 Discuss the sources of funds and capital structure.

Businesses have two sources of funds: debt capital and equity capital. Debt capital consists of funds obtained through borrowing, and equity capital consists of funds provided by the company's owners. The mix of debt and equity capital is known as the company's capital structure, and the financial manager's job is to find the proper mix. Leverage is a technique of increasing the rate of return on funds invested by borrowing. However, leverage increases risk. Also, overreliance on borrowed funds may reduce management's flexibility in future financing decisions. Equity capital also has drawbacks. When additional equity capital is sold, the control of existing shareholders is diluted. In addition, equity capital is more expensive than debt capital. Financial managers are also faced with decisions concerning the appropriate mix of short- and long-term funds. Short-term funds are generally less expensive than long-term funds but expose companies to more risk. Another decision involving financial managers is determining the company's dividend policy.

Assessment Check Answers

4.1 **Explain the concept of leverage.** Leverage is a technique of increasing the rate of return on funds invested by borrowing funds. However, leverage also increases risk.

4.2 **Why do companies generally rely more on long-term funds rather than short-term funds?** Although short-term funds are generally less expensive than long-term funds, short-term funds expose the company to more risk. Thus, most companies choose to finance their long-term assets with long-term funds.

4.3 **What is an important determinant of a company's dividend policy?** An important determinant of a company's dividend policy is its investment opportunities. Companies with more profitable investment opportunities often pay less in dividends than do companies with fewer such opportunities.

LEARNING OBJECTIVE 5 Identify short-term funding options.

The three major short-term funding options are trade credit, short-term loans from banks and other financial institutions, and commercial paper. Trade credit is extended by suppliers when a company receives goods or services, agreeing to pay for them at a later date. Trade credit is relatively easy to obtain and costs nothing unless a supplier offers a cash discount. Loans from commercial banks are a significant source of short-term financing and are often used to finance accounts receivable and inventory. Loans can be either unsecured or secured, with accounts receivable or inventory pledged as collateral. Commercial paper is a short-term IOU sold by a company. Although large amounts of money can be raised through the sale of commercial paper, usually at rates below those charged by banks, access to the commercial-paper market is limited to large, financially strong corporations.

Assessment Check Answers

5.1 **What are the three sources of short-term funding?** The three sources of short-term funding are trade credit, short-term loans, and commercial paper.

5.2 Explain trade credit. Trade credit is extended by suppliers when a buyer agrees to pay for goods and services at a later date. Trade credit is relatively easy to obtain and costs nothing unless a cash discount is offered.

5.3 Why is commercial paper an attractive short-term financing option? Commercial paper is an attractive financing option because companies can raise large amounts of money by selling commercial paper at rates that are generally lower than those charged by banks.

LEARNING OBJECTIVE 6 Discuss sources of long-term financing.

Long-term funds are repaid over many years. There are three sources: long-term loans obtained from financial institutions, bonds sold to investors, and equity financing. Public sales of securities represent a major source of funds for corporations. These securities can generally be traded in secondary markets. Public sales can vary substantially from year to year depending on the conditions in the financial markets. Private placements are securities sold to a small number of institutional investors. Most private placements involve debt securities. Venture capitalists are an important source of financing for new companies. If the business succeeds, venture capitalists stand to earn large profits. Private equity funds are investment companies that raise funds from wealthy individuals and institutional investors and use the funds to make investments in both public and private companies. Unlike venture capitalists, private equity funds invest in all types of businesses. Sovereign wealth funds are investment companies owned by governments.

Assessment Check Answers

6.1 What is the most common type of security sold privately? Corporate debt securities are the most common type of security sold privately.

6.2 Describe venture capitalists. Venture capitalists raise money from wealthy individuals and institutional investors and invest the funds in promising companies. If the business succeeds, venture capitalists can earn substantial profits.

6.3 What is a sovereign wealth fund? A sovereign wealth fund is a government-owned investment company. These companies make investments in a variety of financial and real assets, such as real estate. Although most investments are based on the best risk–return trade-off, political, social, and strategic considerations play roles as well.

LEARNING OBJECTIVE 7 Describe mergers, acquisitions, buyouts, and divestitures.

A merger is a combination of two or more companies into one company. An acquisition is a transaction in which one company buys another. Even in a merger, there is a buyer and a seller (called the *target*). The buyer offers cash, securities, or a combination of the two in return for the target's shares. Mergers and acquisitions should be evaluated as any large investment is: by comparing the costs with the benefits. *Synergy* is the term used to describe the benefits a merger or acquisition is expected to produce. A leveraged buyout (LBO) is a transaction in which shares are purchased from public shareholders, and the company reverts to private status. Usually LBOs are financed with substantial amounts of borrowed funds. Private equity companies are often major financers of LBOs. Divestitures are the opposite of mergers, in which companies sell assets such as subsidiaries, product lines, or production facilities. A sell-off is a divestiture in which assets are sold to another company. In a spin-off, a new company is created from the assets divested. Shareholders of the divesting company become shareholders of the new company as well.

Assessment Check Answers

7.1 Define *synergy*. *Synergy* is the term used to describe the benefits produced by a merger or acquisition. It is the notion that the combined company is worth more than the buyer and the target are individually.

7.2 What is an LBO? An LBO—a leveraged buyout—is a transaction in which public shareholders are bought out, and the company reverts to private status. LBOs are usually financed with large amounts of borrowed money.

7.3 What are the two types of divestitures? A sell-off is a divestiture in which assets are sold to another company. In a spin-off, a new company is created from the assets divested. Shareholders of the divesting company become shareholders of the new company as well.

Business Terms You Need to Know

Review Questions

1. Explain the risk–return trade-off and give two examples.
2. Describe the financial planning process. How does asset intensity affect a financial plan?
3. What are the principal considerations in determining an overall credit policy? How do the actions of competitors affect a company's credit policy?
4. Why do exchange rates pose a challenge for financial managers of companies with international operations?
5. Discuss the concept of leverage. Use a numerical example to illustrate the effect of leverage.
6. What are the advantages and disadvantages of both debt and equity financing?

7. Compare and contrast the three sources of short-term financing.

8. Define *venture capitalist, private equity fund, sovereign wealth fund,* and *hedge fund*. Which of these four sources of funds invests the most money in start-up companies?

9. Briefly describe the mechanics of a merger or acquisition.

10. Why do companies divest assets?

Projects and Teamwork Applications

1. Using qualitative and quantitative measures, lenders utilize a review process called the "five C's of credit" to evaluate a borrower. They include an evaluation of the borrower's **character** (trustworthiness or reputation); **capacity** (borrowing history and repayment track record); **capital** (the level of capitalization and how much money is invested); **collateral** (while cash flow is very important, a lender will evaluate a secondary source of repayment or the value of an individual's or company's assets); and **conditions** (what are current economic conditions, and how is the company or individual doing?). In small teams or in pairs, compare and contrast each of the five C's, and discuss whether you believe each is an accurate assessment of a borrower's ability to pay. What additional criteria, if any, would you include?

2. Working with a partner, assume that a company needs $10 million in additional long-term capital. It currently has no debt and $40 million in equity. The options are issuing a 10-year bond (with an interest rate of 7%) or selling $10 million in new equity. You expect next year's earnings before interest and taxes to be $5 million. (The company's tax rate is 21%.) Prepare a memo outlining the advantages and disadvantages of debt and equity financing. Using the numbers provided, prepare a numerical illustration of leverage similar to the one shown in Figure 17.2.

3. Your new small business has really grown, but now it needs a substantial infusion of capital. A venture capital company has agreed to invest the money you need. In return, the venture capital company will own 75% of the business, and you will be replaced as CEO by someone chosen by the venture capital firm. You will retain the titles of founder and chairman of the board. Would you be willing to take the money but lose control over your business? Why or why not?

4. Working in a small team, select three publicly traded companies. Visit each company's website. Most have a section devoted to information for investors. Review each company's dividend policy. Does the company pay dividends? If so, when did it begin paying dividends? Have dividends increased each year? Or have they fluctuated from year to year? Is the company currently repurchasing shares? Has it done so in the past? Prepare a report summarizing your findings.

5. In small groups or in pairs, and based upon the current economic environment, research and discuss top CFO priorities.

Web Assignments

1. **Peer-to-peer lending.** Technology has played an integral role in helping entrepreneurs or anyone with a cause to raise funds. The concept of peer-to-peer (P2P) lending took off during the Great Recession of 2007, when traditional banks and other institutions tightened the money they were willing to lend. Peer-to-peer lending is a new method of debt financing that allows people to borrow and lend money faster and less expensively than a financial institution. Using technology and big data, P2P platforms connect borrowers to investors. Go to any of the peer-to-peer lending sites (two links are listed below) and discuss the pros and cons of this type of financing. Is this something you might participate in as a lender or borrower? Explain your reasoning.

www.prosper.com

www.lendingclub.com

2. **Code of Conduct.** Companies have codes of conduct, and with recent financial scandals, there are a few that have specific codes of conducts spelled out for their CFOs. Research three companies with specific codes of conducts for their CFOs, officers, and/or top-level financial executives. Discuss whether a company's CFO and top-level financial executives should be held to a higher code of conduct or standard than the rest of the company's employees.

3. **Mergers and acquisitions.** Using any news source, search for a recent merger or acquisition announcement. Discuss the nature of the merger or acquisition, its terms, and, to date, its current results.

Note: Internet web addresses change frequently. If you don't find the exact sites listed, you may need to access the organization's home page and search from there or use a search engine such as Google or Bing.

Cases

Case 17.1 How Ketchup Merged with Mac and Cheese

The continued acceleration of merger and acquisition (M&A) activity remains strong. As companies find it more challenging to increase revenue growth from within their organizations, big mergers across a wide range of industries have become a common growth strategy. In addition, available debt financing has provided another incentive for companies to snap up or merge with competitors. Today, companies are viewing mergers and acquisitions as a substitute for previous traditional growth strategies that involved capital expenditures and expansion.

The $40 billion cash and stock merger of H.J. Heinz Co. and Kraft Foods Group is the brainchild of two investors, 3G Capital and Berkshire Hathaway, run by legendary investor Warren Buffett. Together, the two companies represent the third-largest food and beverage company in North America, and the fifth largest in the world. H.J. Heinz Company, best known for its iconic ketchup brand, also produces sauces, meals, soups, snacks, and infant nutrition. Kraft Foods Group is best known for its Macaroni and Cheese, Capri Sun, Jell-O, Kool-Aid, Oscar Mayer, and Maxwell House, to name a few brands. The newly formed company, with dual headquarters in Pittsburgh, Pennsylvania, and Chicago, Illinois, will assign leaders from both organizations.

With this merger, investors benefit from the potential of a $1.5 billion annual savings, mainly a result of economies of scale in the North American market. In a struggling foods industry with well-known companies like PepsiCo, General Mills, and Campbell's, some predict that next Buffett will build a food conglomerate in much the same way he has done with Berkshire Hathaway, owning a variety of companies in unrelated businesses from Geico Insurance to NetJets to Dairy Queen.

Questions for Critical Thinking

1. Heinz derives 60% of its sales from outside the United States while Kraft derives 98% of its sales within the country. Based on this data, discuss the opportunities for this combined entity. Was this a consideration in the merger? Discuss.
2. Discuss the opportunity for the combined entity given the fact that Kraft's credit rating is far superior to that of Heinz. What might the combined entity do to create efficiencies, and what potential impact might these have on overall financial results?

Sources: Company website, "The Kraft Heinz Company Announces Successful Completion of the Merger between Kraft Foods Group and H.J. Heinz Holding Corporation," http://news.heinz.com, accessed June 7, 2018; John Reid Blackwell, "Big Merger and Acquisition Deals Seen Continuing in 2016," *Richmond-Times Dispatch*, http:// www.richmond.com, accessed June 7, 2018; Antoine Gara, "The Record Merger Boom Won't Stop in 2016, Because Money Is Still Cheap," *Forbes*, http:// www.forbes.com, accessed June 7, 2018; Antoine Gara, "Why the Heinz-Kraft Foods Merger Is a Rare Kind of Warren Buffett Deal," *Forbes*, http:// www.forbes.com, accessed June 7, 2018; Trefis Team, "Analysis of the Kraft-Heinz Merger," *Forbes*, http:// www.forbes.com, accessed June 7, 2018.

Case 17.2 Supply-Chain Financing Helps Cash Flow

With small business loans accounting for a small percentage of a bank's lending business, some banks are providing alternative funding to small businesses. It's called supply-chain financing, and it allows small businesses to extend payment terms with their suppliers. Supply-chain financing, also called reverse factoring, provides for short-term credit while creating a collaboration between buyer and seller.

Typically a buyer attempts to delay payment for as long as possible, whereas a seller seeks to receive payment as quickly as possible. When the buyer of products has a better credit rating than the seller, the buyer can typically access capital at a lower cost. Often, better terms can be negotiated, which means payment terms can be extended, allowing a company to preserve cash longer and to pay for expenses related to other business activities. In addition, a buying company's bank can step in and pay a supplier early (including a discount for early payment) and later request payment from its customer, the buying firm. The seller benefits by having access to less-expensive capital with the option to sell its receivables (the money the company is owed) to a bank in exchange for immediate payment. The supplier might receive its payment in 30 days, for example, for bills due in 60 days.

Home improvement company Lowe's has enjoyed 15 additional days in its payment cycle over the last decade, mainly as a result of suppliers willing to charge less in exchange for more beneficial payment terms. Because of its scale and size, Lowe's is typically able to dictate the terms of its payments to vendors, many of whom are willing to offer merchandise discounts to get paid faster or for more consistent payments and cash flow. Lowe's benefits by hanging on to cash longer without having to squeeze its suppliers.

Similarly, consumer products giant Procter & Gamble has also enjoyed the benefits of supply-chain financing as pressure on its cash flow has grown in recent years. The company has extended the time it takes to pay suppliers to 75 days from 45 days, and by doing so up to $2.3 billion in cash has been freed up. When buyers use a bank's capital to pay invoices, suppliers realize the benefit of quicker cash and access to funds. The benefit for buyers is the use of the funds for other projects. Supply-chain financing, when used correctly, can simultaneously optimize cash flow for both buyer and seller.

Questions for Critical Thinking

1. Supply-chain financing typically works well for a company like Lowe's that has power over its suppliers. What situation might occur when a company has less, if any, power over its suppliers?
2. Do the advantages of supply-chain financing outweigh its disadvantages? Does this financing strategy favor buyer, seller, or both?

Sources: "Banks Offer Small Companies an Indirect Route to Raising Cash," *Wall Street Journal*, http://www.wsj.com, accessed June 7, 2018; Maxwell Murphy, "Lowes Continues to Focus on Supply Chain Financing," *Wall Street Journal*, http://blogs.wsj.com, accessed June 7, 2018; company website, "What Is Supply Chain Finance?" *Investopedia*, http://www.investopedia.com, accessed June 7, 2018; Robert Murphy, "How Supply Chain Finance Is Offering Companies a New Cash Source," *Forbes*, http://forbes.com, accessed June 8, 2018.

Case 17.3 Seed + Mill Investors Keen on Sesame Seed–Based Artisanal Food Products

While on vacation in the Middle East, entrepreneur Lisa Mendelson witnessed a group of American tourists sampling halvah at an outdoor marketplace. The experience immediately brought back childhood memories of this confection made from sesame seeds, nuts, and sugar, with the flakiness found inside a Butterfinger candy bar.

Mendelson returned to New York with a vision to take a couple of ancient Middle East food products and modernize them in the United States. The result is Seed + Mill, an artisanal food stall in New York City's famous Chelsea Market that sells tahini, much like a rich and creamy nut spread, and halvah, both of which are made from sesame seeds.

Mendelson did not execute her vision of healthy and artisanal sesame food products without first thinking about how she would finance her venture selling popular Middle Eastern and Mediterranean food staples in the United States. Whether a business is large or small, financial management and identifying short-term and longer-term funding options can be a challenge. It requires long-range thinking and planning—and diligence, creativity, and discipline.

Mendelson knew that executing her vision would require money. She and her two partners decided to seek individual investors—often called angel investors—who shared their vision and passion. After sending out Seed + Mill's business plan and many rejections later, two investors who shared the same passion for tahini and halvah became a part of Seed + Mill, the only store in the United States solely dedicated to sesame seed products. To date, there are a total of five investors, including the three active partners.

Lisa Mendelson is a serial entrepreneur, and Rachel Simons was previously a human resources lawyer. However, at the heart and soul of Seed + Mill's finance operation is Monica Molenaar, who possesses a graduate degree in business from Stanford University. Monica built the company's financial model and continues to come up with and evaluate ideas for financing options. The partners agreed to avoid any sources of traditional bank or venture capital funding, choosing instead personal investors more closely connected with their mission of on-site milling of tahini with the highest-quality Ethiopian sesame seeds.

The company's financial plan, like most, is a document that specifies the funds needed by the company for a given period of time, the timing of inflows and outflows, and the most appropriate sources and uses of funds. Monica admits that building a financial plan was a challenge at the beginning. Because Seed + Mill imports halvah from Israel, stores it in nearby Brooklyn, and then transports it to the company's food stall, each of the stages of the supply chain is not only costly, but also time consuming. Monica visits the financial plan on an ongoing basis—which is critical to making sure that Seed + Mill is on target and close to plan.

The most interesting challenge for Seed + Mill has been managing cash flow—due mainly to the amount of time it takes to actually produce the products and have them sent by sea from Israel to New York. All in all, it takes about eight weeks from start to finish, so while Seed + Mill generates cash from daily operations through the sale of its goods in Chelsea Market, advance payment is required to purchase goods that will arrive eight weeks later. The timing of cash inflows and outflows is an integral part of Seed + Mill's financial management efforts. Built into the company's financial plan is a buffer—extra money for unforeseen emergencies or expenses—which, Monica admits, has been exercised.

As Seed + Mill's financial manager, Monica manages funds to make sure that sufficient money is available for daily operations and capital investments. Cash flow and borrowing needs are evaluated on an ongoing basis—and close attention is paid to return on investment, cost of funds, and interest rates.

To date, Seed + Mill has shown a profit, and with continued growth into wholesale operations and its products available on Amazon.com, the partners remain optimistic. Their current location in New York's Chelsea Market, which attracts more than 6 million visitors annually, is a big plus. Growth requires financing, and the initial goal of Seed + Mill was to "walk before we run" by getting the food stall up and running—and to determine whether people liked the products. "We're going to start running," says Monica, "and there's a lot of work that needs to go into it to get ourselves conditioned for that sprint." Whether or not the partners decide to sell out, merge with a larger company, or grow by franchising, one thing remains true: the potential growth of Seed + Mill is "Open Sesame."

Questions for Critical Thinking

1. In five years, Mendelson hopes to see tahini on every kitchen table. What would be the most appropriate source of large-scale funding if Mendelson's vision becomes a reality? Might the newfound passion for the flavors of the Middle East help the company in its funding efforts?
2. Seed + Mill chose to pursue individual investors rather than venture capital firms or banks. Discuss why you believe this decision was made and its impact upon future expansion plans.
3. The mix of debt and equity capital is known as a company's capital structure. Based on what you know, evaluate Seed + Mill's current capital structure. What changes might occur to its capital structure as tahini and halvah are modernized and become more well-known in the United States?
4. What types of companies or suppliers might have an interest in either merging or acquiring Seed + Mill? What would be the benefit to Seed + Mill of a merger or acquisition? Discuss both options as they apply to Seed + Mill in terms of the company's growth.

Sources: Company website, "About," http://www.seedandmill.com/about, accessed June 7, 2018; Emma Christensen, "Open Sesame: What to Do with a Jar of Tahini," *Kitchn*, http://www.thekitchn.com, accessed June 7, 2018; Julia Moskin, "Sesame Extends Its Sweet Reach Beyond the Middle East," *New York Times*, http://nytimes.com, accessed June 7, 2018; Tejal Rao, "SPEND: A Spectacular Take on a Beloved Middle-Eastern Sweet," *Bloomberg*, http://www.bloomberg.com, accessed June 7, 2018; "From Chelsea Market: A Seed, Without a Doubt," *Kitchen Kvell*, http://www. kitchenkvell.com, accessed June 7, 2018; company website, "Things I Love," http://ruthreichl.com, accessed June 8, 2018.

CHAPTER **18**

Trends in E-Commerce

LEARNING OBJECTIVES

1. Discuss the function of e-commerce.
2. List the major functions of B2B e-commerce.
3. Explain B2C e-commerce.
4. Describe the challenges associated with e-commerce.
5. Discuss how organizations use the web to communicate.
6. Describe the global environment for e-commerce.
7. Discuss building and managing a website.
8. Identify current trends in e-commerce.

Changemaker

Ben Baker/Redux Pictures

Jake Nickell, Founder and Chief Executive Officer

Company: Threadless, Inc.

Industry: e-commerce/apparel/retail

Website: http://www.threadless.com

Chances are you've probably seen someone wearing a quirky, originally designed T-shirt from Threadless, an e-commerce company. The company is an online community of artists that creates crowdsourced T-shirt designs and allows the crowd to vote on designers who submit their creations. Each week, the 10 best designs are selected and printed and sold through the website. The designer gets notoriety, a commission, and a cash bonus if the design is reprinted. In fact, its "Cookie Loves Milk" T-shirt, submitted over a decade ago and designed by Jess Finkelstein, has printed over 5.4 million of the cartoonlike happy couple—a milk carton and chocolate chip cookie, both with arms and legs, holding hands with the cookie adoringly proclaiming "I Love You."

In 2000, while living in Chicago, Jake Nickell got the idea for Threadless when he submitted a T-shirt design and won an online contest held by a small London-based web design festival. Today, the Threadless community has more than 3.2 million members, with an alumni club for those who have had their designs picked and printed, and more recently an annual "Family Reunion" so that Threadless community members can meet in person. In addition, there are Threadless meetups nationwide. Thermos sells water bottles and lunch coolers with Threadless designs, and Apple and Dell both sell phone covers, laptop covers, and laptop sleeves with Threadless designs. Recently, the company purchased Bucketfeet, which also offers printed custom designs on sneakers submitted by its own network of artists.

Nickell likes the idea of spreading his brand's appeal more naturally and organically, mainly through word of mouth. Threadless doesn't advertise, and Nickell prefers that someone hear about his company by reading an article or seeing the product on someone else rather than through an advertisement. To date, the company boasts over 260,000 Instagram followers—primarily the result of Threadless's values as a community-driven business.[1]

Overview

During the few months that elapse while you are taking this course, new technologies, goods, and services will be introduced. Some will help businesses reach customers in revolutionary ways; others will offer consumers convenience, speed, customization, and choices. Few developments in the way companies conduct business have been as significant as the Internet and its related technologies.

E-commerce refers to conducting business via the Internet. These activities include business-to-consumer transactions, business-to-business transactions, electronic data interchange, gathering and distributing information, and communication through e-mail, texting, social media, and other Internet outlets. The size and scope of e-commerce continue to expand at a rapid pace, even as markets are saturated with specific products. The United States ranks third behind China and India in Internet users, with more than 312 million, representing 95% of the population.[2] E-commerce accounts for 57% of the value of all manufacturing shipments, sales, and revenues, totaling more than $3.4 trillion.[3] Although it still represents a little more than 13% of all retail spending in the United States, e-commerce has transformed the way companies do business.[4] As technology changes become more pervasive, so do offerings and expectations. In a recent year, U.S. online retail grew faster than it has in more than a decade. E-commerce represented retail sales growth of 49%, and much of this growth can be attributed to Amazon.[5]

In addition to buying and selling transactions, the web is now a popular medium for new-product introduction, as well as an effective medium for the exchange of information and opinion. Government agencies, schools, and not-for-profit organizations use the Internet to raise awareness and funds, promote events or causes, and reduce the paperwork and time involved in registration for everything from courses to autos.

This chapter examines trends in e-commerce. We begin by discussing the capabilities and benefits of e-commerce and the ways organizations use the web within the context of a larger global environment. Next, we focus on B2B transactions that make up the vast majority of e-commerce activity today. Then we explore B2C e-commerce, including online retail and the evolving ways that information and access to goods and services are available. We discuss the widespread use of social media as well as web hosting services. We then outline how to create and manage an effective business website and conclude with a discussion of current trends in e-commerce.

1 The Capabilities of E-Commerce

The Internet levels the playing field, allowing entrepreneurs to reach a global market far beyond their garages and local storefronts. On example is Kasasa, an online banking platform, which allows small community banks to offer big-bank perks such as rewards checking, ATM fee reimbursements, and even smart phone apps.[6]

At the other end of the spectrum, large corporations use **e-commerce (or e-business)** strategies to expand their product and service offerings in new markets. The Internet has enabled American Express to introduce OPEN, its services tailored to small businesses. The Internet has increased the capabilities of not-for-profit organizations as well. Teach for America, an organization that recruits college graduates to give two years of full-time service in low-income communities, uses its website to accept donations and online applications, promote upcoming events, publicize news, publish testimonials, and provide in-depth information about the program.[7]

e-commerce (or e-business) conducting business via the Internet.

E-commerce offers a wide variety of capabilities and benefits to businesspeople and consumers:

- *Global reach.* The web allows goods and services to be marketed and sold to customers regardless of geographic location. Suppose you live in Michigan and want to rent an

Jeremy Liebman/Getty Images, Inc.

E-commerce offers a wide variety of benefits to consumers. The Vacation Rentals by Owner website provides global reach to its consumers. You can search for a dream vacation spot and soon be enjoying the warm sunshine on your balcony, or list your own rental property regardless of geographic location.

apartment in Miami Beach: just visit the website for Vacation Rentals by Owner (VRBO) to search for and reserve your accommodations such as the one shown in the photo. You can also list your home through VRBO, take direct bookings, and pay no commission.[8]

- *Customization*. Download your favorite songs from the iTunes store and create your own playlist.
- *Interactivity*. Buyers and sellers can communicate, negotiate, and complete transactions directly online. Gagan Biyani founded Udemy in order to connect people who want to learn something with people who want to teach it online. Currently Udemy offers more than 80,000 online courses ranging from Thai cooking to calculus. Many Udemy courses are offered at no cost, and most can be taken for around $50.[9]
- *Right-time and integrated marketing*. Online retailers can provide products when and where customers want them. Moreover, the Internet enables the coordination of all promotional activities and communication to create a unified, customer-oriented promotional message. Viewers of home shopping channel QVC can order any product they want through their smart phone or tablet by downloading a free app from the company website.[10]
- *Cost savings*. E-commerce can reduce the costs associated with starting and operating a business. Intuit's QuickBooks Online helps small businesses execute their accounting functions at a much lower cost than hiring an outside accountant or accounting firm. QuickBooks online software allows entrepreneurs to create invoices, pay bills, and monitor expenses at a minimal cost—only $30 per month, with no contract required.[11]

In addition to the benefits listed here, increasing evidence shows that an effective online presence improves the performance of traditional brick-and-mortar operations. As noted, many consumers now use the web as their primary source of product information, even if they make an actual purchase at the local Toyota dealer or Target. In a recent survey of smart phone users, 62% have used their phone in the past year to look up information about a health condition, 57% to do online banking, 44% to look up real estate listings or other information about a place to live, 43% to look up information about a job, 40% to look up government services or information, 30% to take a class or get educational content, and 18% to submit a job application.[12]

As smart phone screens increase in size, mobile is now the first point of contact for an increasing number of consumers—which makes shopping even more accessible and convenient. In a recent year, smartphones were used in over one-third—or more than $1 trillion—of total U.S. retail sales, including research, price comparisons, and purchases; and over 40 percent of online transactions were made on mobile devices.[13]

Business Websites

Most businesses—large or small—have websites. These may offer information about the company and its general products; provide links to other sites including social media; offer online promotions and shopping; and provide opportunities for customer contact through blogs, online chats, e-mail, or phone numbers.

corporate website website designed to increase a company's visibility, promote and showcase products, and provide other information about a company.

There are two main types of company websites. The **corporate website** is designed to increase visibility, promote and showcase products, publicize socially responsible actions or programs, and provide information such as store locations. Rather than selling products directly, these sites attempt to build customer goodwill and assist retailers and other resellers in their marketing efforts. At the website for Cannondale bicycles, consumers can find detailed information about the products, which retail for as much as $13,000. But because bikes are

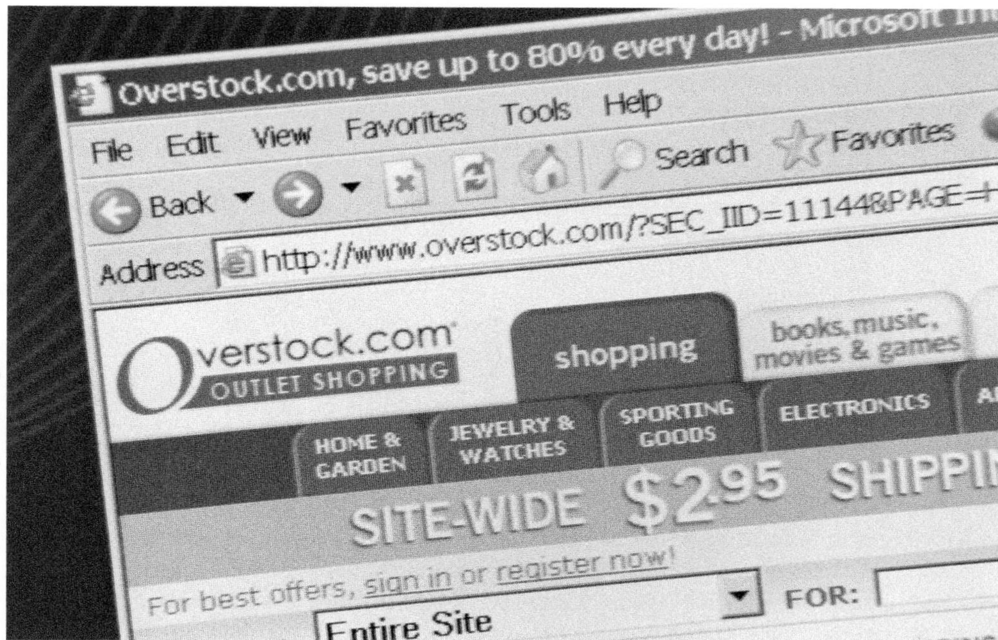

Daniel Acker/Bloomberg/Getty Images Inc.

Overstock.com is a technology-based outlet shopping experience offering customers a wide variety of high-quality products, at great value, with superior customer service.

expensive, and riders generally want to try them before buying, the site directs customers to dealers near them.[14] Corporate websites also may distribute financial information to investors, post job openings and applications, and provide opportunities for customer feedback.

Marketing websites often include information about company history, products, employment opportunities, and financial information, but their primary goal is to sell goods or services and build relationships with customers. To find information about company history or career opportunities at the Overstock.com website (see photo), you have to scroll all the way to the bottom of the home page. But you can purchase just about anything you can think of—from a pair of suede boots to a closet system—from the site.[15] Websites have become increasingly complex, loaded with graphics and video, games and contests, coupons and frequent-buyer rewards, links to social media, and more.

marketing websites website whose main purpose is to sell goods and services, and build relationships with customers.

Assessment Check

1. Define *e-commerce.*
2. What is the difference between a corporate website and a marketing website?

2 B2B E-Commerce

Business-to-business (B2B) e-commerce is the use of the Internet for business transactions between organizations. Although we hear more about e-commerce that affects us as consumers, B2B e-commerce is about three times larger than B2C ecommerce sales, and expected to hit over $7 trillion in an upcoming year.[16]

business-to-business (B2B) e-commerce electronic business transactions between organizations using the Internet.

In addition to generating sales revenue, B2B e-commerce also provides detailed product descriptions whenever they are needed, and payments and other information are transferred on the web. Moreover, B2B e-commerce can slash order-processing expenses. Business-to-business transactions, which typically involve more steps than consumer purchases, are more efficient on the Internet. B2B activity over the Internet spans a wide range of companies, goods, and services. Companies may also use such tools as electronic data interchanges, extranets, private exchanges, and e-procurement. Health care insurance provider Aetna offers online services to large and small firms, including enrollment and premium payment, tax credit estimation, forms and documents, and information to help companies manage their employees' benefits.[17]

In the "Business Model" feature, learn how e-commerce companies like Dollar Shave Club are creating buzz with humorous YouTube videos that have gone viral.

Electronic Data Interchanges, Extranets, and Private Exchanges

One of the oldest applications of technology to business transactions is electronic data interchange (EDI), computer-to-computer exchanges of invoices, purchase orders, price quotations, and other sales information between buyers and sellers. Use of EDI cuts paper flow, speeds the order cycle, and reduces errors. In addition, by receiving daily inventory status reports from vendors, companies can set production schedules to match demand.

Internet commerce also offers an efficient way for businesses to collaborate with vendors, partners, and customers through extranets and to secure networks used for e-commerce accessible through the company's website by external customers, suppliers, or other authorized users. Extranets go beyond ordering and fulfillment processes by giving selected outsiders access to valuable internal information for better decision making. As with other forms of e-commerce, extranets provide additional benefits such as enhanced relationships with business partners. For example, your college probably has an extranet for current students, parents, and alumni.

Security and access authorization have become increasingly crucial, and most companies create virtual private networks (VPNs) that protect information traveling over public communications media. As discussed in Chapter 14, these networks control who uses a company's resources and the information users can access. Also, they cost considerably less than leasing dedicated lines.

Business Model

Dollar Shave Club Offers Cutting Edge E-Commerce

Dollar Shave Club was founded a little over five years ago by Mark Levine and Michael Dubin, who met at a party and began discussing their frustration with the cost of razors. Competing against the likes of razor giant Gillette, Dollar Shave Club, a Venice, California–based e-commerce company, has successfully managed to satisfy an unmet customer need. Using a subscription-based business model, Dollar Shave Club sends its mostly male user base of more than 2 million a razor, shaving cream, and wipes for as little as $1 to $9 monthly.

Changing consumer shopping habits has given rise to subscription-based consumer products such as razors, creating a hassle-free shopping experience and cutting out the local drugstore or big-box retailer. With ample supplies kept on hand, subscribers don't have to worry about reordering and running out. To date, the company's humorous YouTube video, which has gone viral, garnered over 25 million views, selling 12,000 razors in just two days. While Dubin's social media prowess is cutting edge, Unilever, a large consumer products company, has taken notice of Dubin's cutting edge social media prowess by purchasing Dollar Shave Club for $1 billion in cash.

Questions for Critical Thinking

1. **Shaving subscriptions seem to be a winning proposition, but can Dollar Shave Club win out against behemoth Gillette and smaller player Harry's? Evaluate the websites of each to determine how Dollar Shave Club differentiates itself from the competition.**
2. **Birchbox is a company that delivers beauty products on a monthly subscription basis. Discuss the growth of the subscription business model and its potential impact on the traditional department store or drugstore. What are its benefits? Drawbacks?**

Sources: David Pierson, "Why Silicon Valley Venture Capital Firms Are Funding Online Retailers Like Dollar Shave Club," *Los Angeles Times*, http://www.latimes.com, accessed July 12, 2018; Adam Lashinsky, "The Cutting Edge of Care," *Fortune*, http://fortune.com, accessed July 12, 2018; Darren Dahl, "Riding the Momentum Created by a Cheeky Video," *New York Times*, http://www.nytimes.com, accessed July 12, 2018; Neal Ungerleider, "Dollar Shave Club Is Now Worth $615 Million," *Fast Company*, http://www.fastcompany.com, accessed July 12, 2018; Elizabeth Segran, "From Socks to Sex Toys: Inside America's Subscription-Box Obsession," *Fast Company*, http://www.fastcompany.com, accessed July 12, 2018; Don Primack, "Unilever Buys Dollar Shave Club for $1 Billion," *Fortune*, http://fortune.com, accessed July 12, 2018.

The next generation of extranets is the *private exchange*, a secure website at which a company and its suppliers share all types of data related to e-commerce, from product design through order delivery. A private exchange is more collaborative than a typical extranet. The participants can use it to collaborate on product ideas, production scheduling, distribution, order tracking, and any other functions a business wants to include. Partners in a private exchange often form strategic alliances. Another variant of extranets is an intranet, which provides similar capabilities but limits users to an organization's employees or members.

Electronic Exchanges and E-Procurement

The earliest types of B2B e-commerce usually consisted of a company setting up a website offering information and products to any buyer willing to make online purchases. Then entrepreneurs created electronic exchanges, online marketplaces that bring buyers and sellers together and cater to a specific industry's needs. Under its C2 program, the Chicago Board Options Exchange (CBOE) offers all-electronic options trading among some of Wall Street's largest banks.[18]

E-procurement uses web-based systems to enable all types of organizations to improve the efficiency of their procurement processes. E-procurement benefits the public and not-for-profit sectors. For instance, states such as Kentucky and North Carolina have e-procurement systems that combine Internet technology with traditional procurement practices to streamline the purchasing process and reduce costs. State and local governmental agencies, public schools, and state-supported colleges can use the system to purchase products from state-approved vendors.

Assessment Check

1. How do extranets and private exchanges work?
2. What is an electronic exchange?

3 B2C E-Commerce

When was the last time you shopped online? Known as **business-to-consumer (B2C) e-commerce**, this technology involves selling directly to consumers over the web. Online retail sales, sometimes called e-*tailing*, is driven by convenience, time and cost savings, fast delivery, large selections, no crowds, and ease in sending gifts. Mobile devices are a key driver in the growth of e-tailing.[19] **Figure 18.1** shows the steady growth in online retail sales over the past several years.

business-to-consumer (B2C) e-commerce selling directly to consumers over the web.

There are basically two types of B2C websites: shopping sites and informational sites. Nordstrom (http://www.nordstrom.com) is a shopping site. Customers can view product information and place orders online. By contrast, Honda's website (http://automobiles.honda.com) is informational only. Consumers can view detailed product information, "build" their ideal Honda, compare financing alternatives, and even request a price quote from a local dealer. They cannot, however, buy a new Honda online. Still, a car buyer who wants to purchase a used Honda might very well find one online at Craigslist (http://www.craigslist.org).

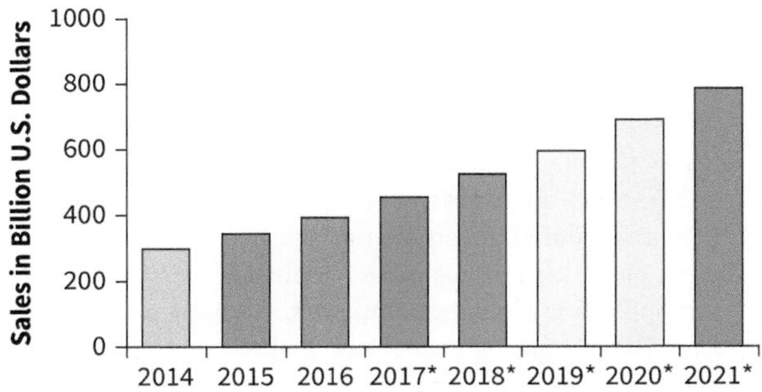

*Data for these years is estimated.

Source: "Retail e-Commerce Sales in the United States from 2014 to 2021 (in billion U.S. dollars)," Statista, http://www.statista.com, accessed July 13, 2018.

FIGURE 18.1 Online Retail Sales Through 2021

Technology has allowed e-tailing to expand into new markets and offer new goods and services to consumers. Whereas online shopping once began with a few goods such as electronics, CDs, and books, consumers now have a wide range of choices. They can buy everything from groceries to airline tickets. They can even buy a new home, along with all the furnishings. And they can purchase just about any service, ranging from banking to insurance. One product that has burgeoned online is print information, from online newspapers to e-books. As print subscribers for newspapers slowly disappear, traditional newspapers struggle to survive in the face of digital-only news outlets without paywalls—like BuzzFeed, whose CEO believes that paywalls are bad for democracy. Without a paid subscription, a paywall system prevents users from accessing news content.[20]

Electronic Storefronts

electronic storefronts website that sells products to customers.

Retailers large and small have set up **electronic storefronts**, websites that sell items to consumers. Some retailers, such as Walmart and L.L. Bean, started out as bricks-and-mortar stores long before the existence of the web, then later adapted to include e-tailing. Others, like Overstock.com, exist entirely on the web. The Internet has provided vast opportunities for young entrepreneurs like Amanda Thomas, the creative founder of Luv Aj. Thomas has built a global empire with her jewelry line that has created buzz among celebrities like Beyoncé, Gigi Hadid, and Emily Ratajkowski. Because setting up an Internet business costs far less than starting a traditional retail store—and because the reach of the Internet is so wide—small businesses have an increased chance at success. Similarly, for an omni-channel retail experience, beauty giant L'Oréal recently created a virtual makeup app to leverage the power of mobile commerce and to drive traffic to its website and to retail stores, as described in the "Business & Technology" feature.

One of the biggest trends in e-commerce will be the blending of e-commerce with mobile messaging apps such as Facebook Messenger and Snapchat. In China, shopping using mobile messaging app WeChat is common, and in the United States, Facebook intends to use "conversational commerce" through its Messenger app. Snapchat has invested in an e-commerce platform to integrate products and shopping into their app. Conversational

Business & Technology

L'Oréal's Virtual Cosmetic Counter

French cosmetics giant L'Oréal has solved one of the biggest problems known to women who want to look good in selfies. The cosmetics counter is now not only virtual but also mobile. To millions of makeup connoisseurs, the testing of thousands of colors and what looks right (or not) can be expensive, cumbersome, and tedious. To further add to the challenge, not all retailers make product testers readily available.

The solution: L'Oréal has built an app that allows consumers using their smart phone's front-facing camera to apply and test makeup based upon a real- time reflection. It's called Makeup Genius, and L'Oréal hopes that its virtual makeup counter will lead to more purchases through its e-commerce platform or at local retail stores.

Downloaded more than 2 million times, the virtual makeup tester is available for free from the iTunes store in the United States and France. Prior to assembling a technology team to build its app, L'Oréal evaluated the problems they were trying to solve as a company, along with its customers' problems. Prior to the creation of this app, a few cosmetic companies, requiring picture uploads, offered virtual makeup counters on their websites and at drugstores, allowing users to photoshop (or paint) different colors of lipstick and eye shadow onto the image.

With its app, L'Oréal has created a more immersive experience for its customers. Here's how it works: turn to either side, smile, frown, pucker up, and the digital "application" also moves along—allowing different combinations of foundation, lip liner, lipstick, and eye shadow. Seeing the end result helps consumers believe that technology really does work at the cosmetics counter.

Questions for Critical Thinking

1. **In comparison to competitors, discuss how L'Oréal's strategy of an experiential and immersive customer experience might translate to deeper connections and increased customer loyalty.**
2. **With mobile as the fastest-growing part of Internet advertising, combined with the amount of time people spend on their smart phones, companies like L'Oréal have revamped their brand experience. Can you think of other companies like L'Oréal that have researched customer wants and needs to create an immersive and experiential experience?**

Sources: Company website, "Makeup Genius," http://www.lorealparisusa.com, accessed July 13, 2018; company website, "Makeup Genius Changes Makeup Application Forever," http://www.lorealparisusa.com, accessed July 13, 2018; Charlie Sorrel, "L'Oréal Makeup Sales Jump Because People Want to Look Good in Selfies," *Fast Company*, http://www.fastcoexist.com, accessed July 13, 2018; "Don't Let Mobile Pass You By," *Tech Crunch*, http://techcrunch.com, accessed July 13, 2018; Elisa Mala, "Most Innovative Companies 2015," *Fast Company*, http://www.fastcompany.com, accessed July 13, 2018; Caroline Winter, "L'Oréal's Makeup Genius App: The Cosmetics Counter Goes Digital," *Bloomberg*, www.bloomberg.com, accessed July 13, 2018.

commerce involves building deeper relationships by communicating to and buying from retail merchants.[21]

Mobile Commerce

Mobile commerce is similar to having "a retailer in a customer's pocket." Commonly referred to as the next generation of e-commerce, mobile commerce involves any monetary transaction completed using a mobile device or tablet—and sometimes through apps such as Snapchat, as shown in the photo.[22] With mobile commerce, shopping can occur whenever and wherever, and consumers don't need a tablet or desktop computer. It is projected that by 2021, mobile e-commerce could represent 73% of e-commerce sales. Research firm Forrester anticipates that smart phone purchases will represent $175.4 billion by 2022.[23] New mobile commerce applications that will enhance the customer experience are being implemented by top retailers like Ikea and Sephora, who are using augmented reality apps to complement their mobile commerce business. Chatbots and messenger apps are also making it easier to service customers and increase sales. In fact, the average mobile commerce order recently increased from $18.37 to $32.81.[24]

Who Are the Online Buyers and Sellers?

Although one might assume online shopping trends are driven by teens and Millennials, many middle-aged people have fully embraced the convenience of online shopping. Conventional wisdom also suggests that women are driving shopping trends; however, when it comes to online shopping, men spend almost as much as women online.[25]

Online shoppers vary by age, gender, income, and education. Making up 18% of the total population, approximately 23% of online shoppers are between the ages of 35 and 44. With less than 20% of the total population, 24% of online shoppers are between the ages of 45 and 54.[26] Despite lower income than older adults, Millennials, the dominant online shopping demographic, spend more money than any other age group—an average of $2,000 annually. Despite higher incomes, adults between the ages of 35 and 44 spend about $1,930 annually. With more consumers purchasing through a mobile device, Boomers and seniors have also adapted to mobile commerce. The increased frequency of purchases and higher dollar value per purchase continue to be online trends.[27]

As technology becomes pervasive worldwide, more consumers are going online and the e-commerce industry is growing. Leading the pack are e-commerce subsidiaries of the Alibaba group, namely Taobao, Alibaba.com, Tmall, and others. With 35% of annual growth, China is also one of the fastest growing e-commerce markets. Other top e-commerce markets by sales include the United States, led by Amazon and eBay. The United Kingdom, led by Amazon UK, Argos, and Play.com, has the highest e-commerce sales as a percentage of retail sales. Rakuten of Japan is a leading global m-commerce player. Rakuten has recently acquired a number of e-commerce websites worldwide. Germany is Europe's second largest e-commerce market after the UK, and like the UK, Amazon has a stronghold in Germany's market with online retailer Otto.[28]

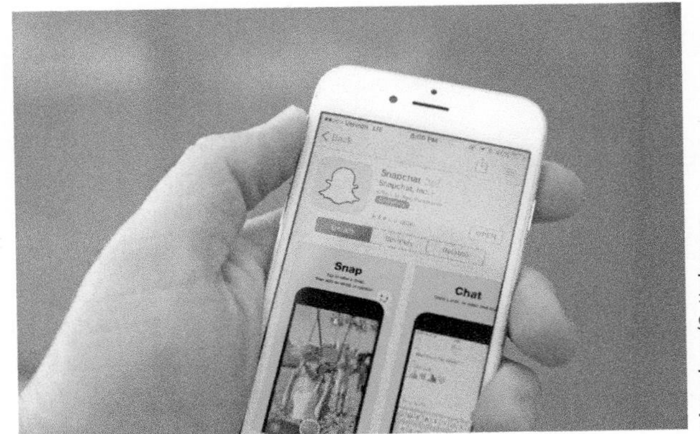

Bloomberg/Getty Images

In an effort to attract a wider range or brands, social platform and video message app Snapchat is monetizing its services with e-commerce to include shopping sections.

Benefits of B2C E-Commerce

Why do consumers shop online? Three main reasons are most often cited in consumer surveys: convenience, lower prices, and personalization.

Convenience and time-saving are probably the greatest benefits to online shopping for consumers. You can order anything, any time, from anywhere. And a well-designed, user-friendly website will make the transaction quick and easy. In addition, you can readily compare prices from one site to another using comparison shopping engines like Google Shopping, NexTag, Shopzilla, and PriceGrabber.

Many products actually cost less online than they do at traditional retail stores because e-tailers—particularly those that operate exclusively online—have lower overhead expenses than do brick-and-mortar stores. Some retailers that operate both bricks-and-mortar locations and websites (click and mortar) offer online specials or exclusives at lower prices in order to offset the fact that they must offer the same regular prices for items online as they do in their stores. Urban Outfitters is one such company; shoppers can find such price breaks as web exclusives and free shipping on its site.

Successful B2C e-commerce companies know how important personalization is to the quality of the shopping experience. Understanding customer preferences and personalization will continue to be a focus. Artificial Intelligence, which goes hand-in-hand with personalization, is key to building customer relationships. Online clothing and fashion retailers like ASOS are using machine learning to focus on innovative shopping. For example, customers can try on items using a "selfie-mode" without ever having to visit a store or think about returns. With endless opportunities, there's also an option to search for items seen on people in the street. Users snap a photo of a garment or fashion accessory with their device camera or pull in an existing outfit shot or Instagram screengrab (say) from their camera roll and have the app show clothes items that are at least in the general fashion ballpark of whatever it is they're trying to find. From virtual shoppers to personal recommendation technology powered by AI software, e-commerce will become more personalized. Customer satisfaction is greatly affected by the company's ability to offer service tailored to many customers. But different people expect different levels of customer service. Consequently, most online retailers provide consumers with convenience, chatbot and messenger apps, extensive product selection, quick returns, and the ability to purchase and send gifts with ease. In addition, fewer in-person crowds remain a big benefit.

With the importance of customization, marketers for shopping sites focus on one-to-one marketing, creating loyal customers who are likely to make repeat purchases. Sites such as Amazon.com welcome past shoppers by name and make suggestions for purchases based on past buying history. A shopper who elects to view a specific pair of boots at Anthropologie.com is also shown alternative styles as a sidebar in the margin of the web page. Many sites offer the opportunity to receive targeted e-mails, updates, and newsletters.

Assessment Check

1. What are the two different types of B2C websites?
2. Describe the various types of people who shop online.

4 E-Commerce Challenges

Not surprisingly, e-commerce has had its problems and challenges. Safe online payment, privacy, and security are the biggest areas of concern for both consumers and businesses. E-commerce merchants remain concerned about product returns, customer acquisition and loyalty, same-day delivery and free shipping, the necessity to optimize e-commerce for mobile sales, onsite and marketing personalization and customization, market competition (namely, Amazon), and multi- or omni-channel shopping experiences.[29]

Developing Safe Online Payment Systems

Companies continually try to update and improve their payment systems for e-commerce. While credit card payment is the most common with 90% of B2C transactions, electronic cash via sites like PayPal and electronic wallets like Apple Pay are also used.

Web browsers contain sophisticated encryption systems designed to protect the data that are entered at the site by customers. **Encryption** is the process of encoding data for security purposes. When such a system is active, users see a special icon indicating that they are at a protected website. To increase consumer security, most companies involved in e-commerce use *Secure Sockets Layer (SSL)* technology to encrypt information and verify the identity of senders and receivers (called authentication). SSL—software that encrypts and decrypts information—consists of a public key and a private key. The public key is used to encrypt information, and the private key is used to decipher it. When a browser points to a domain with an SSL certificate, the technology authenticates (verifies the identity of) the server and the visitor and establishes an encryption method and a unique session key. Both parties can then begin a secure session that guarantees a message's privacy and integrity. VeriSign (shown in the photo), a Symantec business, is a leading provider of the SSL technology employed by nearly 9 of 10 Internet users. In addition to securing payment data, VeriSign offers a wide range of other services, such as Internet domain name registry and intelligence research.[30]

VeriSign uses SSL encryption technology to protect businesses and their customers against online cyber attacks. The company also manages the registry of .com and .net domain names.

Used by both businesses and consumers, PayPal is a worldwide encrypted online payment processor that supports online money transfers and serves as an electronic alternative to traditional paper methods. PayPal stores shoppers' credit card numbers in its own "bank" so that the numbers are never revealed. When consumers review their credit card statements, they see the words "PayPal" and then the merchant's name or a code number. In addition to making purchases (consumers) and receiving payments (businesses) through PayPal, members can transfer money within the United States and abroad.[31]

Other payment options include the use of electronic wallets and mobile payment companies (part of the financial technology or fintech industry) such as Square and Venmo. An electronic wallet isan encrypted storage medium holding a customer's credit card and other financial information that can be used to complete e-transactions without reentering the stored data for each new transaction. To complete a purchase, regular shoppers at a site can click on a walletlike icon to retrieve saved information. Square, a mobile payment company founded by Twitter's Jack Dorsey, was designed for merchants to accept payments with (or without) a card reader that plugs into the audio jack of a smart phone. Square also provides a service for merchants to accept online payments, and the company has recently expanded into small business financing and payroll services. Venmo, part of PayPal, was started by two friends while in college. Venmo is a free mobile payment service that allows users to transfer money to each other for items such as rent, car rides, and restaurant bills. Businesses are also realizing the benefits of Venmo.[32]

encryption the process of encoding data for security purposes.

Other Security and Privacy Issues

Despite the continuing growth of e-commerce, due to widespread media attention on data breaches consumers worry about identity theft and other breaches of security online. It's not just credit card numbers—it's personal information that could include home address, phone number, health information, bank account numbers, employment data, and Social Security numbers. When a company's online security is compromised, many people are usually affected, and the company's reputation is compromised.

Because consumers want assurances that any information they provide won't be leaked or sold to others without their permission, online merchants have adopted policies to protect consumer information. For example, many Internet companies have signed on with Internet privacy organizations such as TRUSTe. By displaying the TRUSTe logo on their websites, they indicate that they have promised to disclose how they collect personal data, what they do with the information, and how they follow the industry's best practices. Prominently displaying a privacy policy is an effective way to build customers' trust, but identity thieves can be very adept at developing new ways to access information. With widespread attention surrounding consumer privacy, Visa recently implemented a program asking credit card customers to opt in to use their cell phone location to help verify credit card transactions by location. This is described in further detail in the "Judgment Call" feature.

Sometimes a data breach occurs in a seemingly unlikely place—not a bank or store but a service provider. Recently, an "unauthorized party" gained access to customer data on the Adidas U.S. website, and customers who shopped and purchased items on the site may have been impacted by the data breach. Estimated at a few million customers, at risk is customer contact information, like login information, email addresses, and physical addresses.[33]

Medical and health care information is another area of concern. Despite laws requiring providers to be more and more restrictive about the information that they gather and store about their patients, theft of this information does occur. Of course, security issues offer continuing opportunities for firms that provide software and other solutions for maintaining and protecting online security. A few months after a security breach on the Anthem Blue Cross website, Oracle introduced a new program, called Security Governor for Healthcare. The program offers complete identity management for fraud prevention and regulation compliance.[34] Businesses must also protect their own information. To prevent intrusions, companies install firewalls to keep unauthorized Internet users from tapping into private corporate data.

Judgment Call

Using Location-Based Anti-Fraud Systems

Would you be willing to allow a credit card company to match your phone's location with your computer's IP address? Furthermore, if you knew that your chances of credit card fraud would be reduced dramatically, how might you feel about allowing the use of unique biometrics like facial and voice recognition? With the increase in online e-commerce transactions, real-time geolocation technology provides a geographic location by IP address of the computer from which the e-commerce purchase is being made, which can be a further deterrent to fraudsters. Ultimately, these strategies help companies like Visa prevent credit card fraud EMV (Europay, Mastercard and Visa) is a global standard for cards equipped with computer chips and the technology used to authenticate chip-card transactions. To combat large-scale data breaches and increasing rates of counterfeit card fraud, U.S. card issuers have migrated to this new technology to protect consumers and reduce the costs of fraud.

Credit card issuer Visa has asked cardholders to opt in to a new service called Visa Mobile Location Confirmation, which tracks a smart phone's physical location whenever a retail purchase is made. When a user's mobile device is in the same location as the payment transaction, say a retail store, the bank can be more confident about the authenticity of the transaction.

Visa is committed to responsible data practices. At stake is transparency and the choice that many believe should be given to consumers to "opt in" to have their location data used. In addition, transparency around how the data are being used gives consumers a better understanding of what they are consenting to. However, the question remains whether consumers are willing to trade off privacy for greater security in financial transactions—and, ultimately how the data they consent to share will be used.

Banks are considering more invasive types of requests, including facial recognition and fingerprint authentication, which could ultimately eliminate the need for plastic credit cards. While many welcome such legitimate authentication measures, others with privacy concerns, question the subsequent use of the information and its potential sale to other companies for marketing purposes.

Questions for Critical Thinking

1. For consumers making purchases from a personal computer, the transaction would need a way to confirm that the computer and the phone are located near each other. Discuss the issues associated with this type of location information.
2. Visa offers location-based anti-fraud services, but other banks have been reluctant to request that customers opt in to this type of service because of privacy concerns. Would you opt in to a service such as this if you knew fraud would be significantly reduced?

Sources: John Zorabedian, "Visa Asks to Track Your Smartphone to Help Sniff Out Credit Card Fraud," *Naked Security*, https://nakedsecurity.sophos.com, accessed July 14, 2018; Robin Sidel, "Why Your Bank Wants to Track Your Phone," *Wall Street Journal*, http://www.wsj.com, accessed July 14, 2018; company website, "10 Measures to Reduce Credit Card Fraud for Internet Merchants," https://www.fraudlabs.com, accessed July 14, 2018; Siena Kossman, "8 FAQs about EMV Credit Cards," creditcard.com, http://creditcard.com, accessed July 14, 2018.

A *firewall* is an electronic barrier between a company's internal network and the Internet that limits access into and out of the network. However, an impenetrable firewall is difficult to find, as skilled hackers are always developing new ways to gain access. So it is important for firms to test their websites and networks for vulnerabilities regularly and to back up critical data in case an intruder breaches security measures.

Another issue facing businesses is whether or not they are responsible for monitoring the information their users and customers are posting online on their sites. Craigslist periodically comes under fire for permitting inappropriate ads on its site.[35]

Internet Fraud

Fraud is another barrier to e-commerce. The Internet Crime Complaint Center (http://www.ic3.gov), run by the FBI and the National White Collar Crime Center, compiles complaints concerning Internet fraud. Intellectual Property Rights (IPR) matters, computer intrusions (hacking), economic espionage (theft of trade secrets), online extortion, international money laundering, identity theft, and a growing list of Internet-facilitated crimes make up major categories of Internet-related complaints referred to law enforcement agencies. The website also reports on and offers tips for avoiding every kind of Internet scam imaginable, ranging from fraudulent work-at-home offers to lottery schemes.[36]

Fraud is a serious issue both for online customers and for trustworthy online businesses. One common type of Internet fraud, **phishing** (also discussed in Chapter 14), is a high-tech scam to acquire sensitive information using e-mail or pop-up messages claiming to be from familiar businesses or organizations, such as banks, Internet service providers, or even government agencies.

phishing high-tech scam that uses e-mail or pop-up messages to get unsuspecting victims to reveal personal information.

Payment fraud is another problem for many e-tailers. Orders are placed online and paid for with a credit card, and the merchandise is shipped. Then, the cardholder asks the credit card issuer for a chargeback to the e-tailer. The cardholder claims that he or she never made the purchase or never received the merchandise. Some claims are legitimate, but others involve fraud. Because an online purchase doesn't require a customer's signature or credit card imprint, the merchant, not the credit card issuer, bears the liability in most fraud cases. E-tailers are trying to reduce payment fraud by employing software that spots fraud before it happens, using payment verification services offered by credit card companies such as Visa, and even hiring companies that specialize in fighting credit card chargebacks.

Channel Conflicts

Companies invest time and money to nurture relationships with their partners. But when a manufacturer sells online directly to customers, it can compete with its usual partners. Retailers often have their own websites and don't want their suppliers competing with them for sales. As e-commerce broadens its reach, producers must decide whether these relationships are more important than the potential of selling directly on the web. A dispute among producers, wholesalers, and retailers is called a **channel conflict**.

channel conflict conflict between two or more members of a supply chain, such as a manufacturer, wholesaler, or retailer.

Pricing is another potential area of conflict. In their eagerness to establish themselves as online leaders, some companies sell merchandise at discount prices. However, while Vermont-based athletic footwear manufacturer Merrell does sell its products online, as well as at retail stores, the online store's prices are never lower than a customer would find at a local retail outlet. This policy helps minimize potential channel conflict. Bicycle and parts manufacturer Specialized Bicycle Components takes a slightly different approach. Prices on its online store are often slightly higher than they are at retail dealers. Specialized does this to provide a small incentive for shoppers to purchase items from one of its retailer dealers rather than the online store.

One online firm taking items out of landfills is Hipcycle. See the "Clean & Green Business" feature to learn more about the practice of upcycling.

Clean & Green Business

Hipcycle Lessens the Load on Landfills

You are certainly familiar with the concept of recycling, but what about upcycling? Recycling requires energy, and it takes paper, plastic, metal, and glass and breaks them down so their components can be remade into new, often lesser-quality products. According to green e-commerce seller Hipcycle, its upcycling business model converts old or discarded materials, which would otherwise end up in landfills, into something useful and often beautiful.

Hipcycle is the latest breed of upcycling companies, and through its e-commerce site you can purchase housewares, furniture, garden supplies, apparel, and office supplies. If you're looking for a jigsaw puzzle made from a vinyl record, or a tote bag made from a tire tube, you're in the right place—and believe it or not, you can shop by type of material on the website. Hipcycle sells unique items made from railroad parts, skateboards, vinyl records, wine barrels, fire hoses, and more.

The concept of upcycling, or reusing found or useful objects and artifacts to create other products, is here to stay. It's unique, it's green, and Hipcycle has created an e-commerce enterprise by selling attractive, durable, and well-priced goods.

Questions for Critical Thinking

1. **The process of remanufacturing or refurbishing secondhand electronics products can be viewed as upcycling because of the reduced energy and material consumption used as compared to new manufacturing. What are some examples of companies participating in this trend?**
2. **Provide examples of how you might upcycle in your daily life.**

Sources: Company website, http://hipcycle.com, accessed July 13, 2018; Sindhu Kashyap, "A Basic Concept Design: Your Trash Is This Designer's Treasure," *Your Story,* http://yourstory.com, accessed July 13, 2018; company website, "Social Enterprise Company Spotlight: Hipcycle," http://givetogetjobs.com, accessed July 13, 2018; Chris Rickert, "Upcycling the Meadowood Neighborhood Part of a Golden Opportunity," *Wisconsin State Journal,* http://host.madison.com, accessed July 13, 2018; Steven Kurutz, "Hipcycle, a Place for Repurposed Goods," *New York Times,* http://www.nytimes.com, accessed July 13, 2018.

Assessment Check

1. What is encryption, and why is it important?
2. How does a business protect its own information?
3. Describe a potential channel conflict for a company conducting e-commerce.

5 Using the Web to Communicate

The Internet has four main functions: e-commerce, entertainment, information, and communication. More and more, these functions are blending together as businesses discover new ways to reach customers. For example, a company might send location-based text messages or e-mails to customers with sales promotions and coupons. Visitors to a company's website might find a game or contest there. And many companies use social media to communicate with customers and provide product updates and information about events and promotions.

Online Communities

In addition to e-mail, many companies use Internet forums, newsgroups, and web communities that appeal to people who share common interests. All of these virtual communities take advantage of the communication power of the Internet, which as noted earlier in the chapter, is still a main reason people go online. Members congregate online and exchange views and information on topics of interest. These communities may be organized for commercial or noncommercial purposes.

Online communities can take several forms, including social networking sites, chat rooms, forums, e-mail lists, and discussion boards. People may also join online communities through video games, blogs, and virtual worlds. All offer specific advantages to diverse users and organizations alike. Companies often use forums to ask questions and exchange information with customers. Adobe, which designs such software as Acrobat and Photoshop, operates a user-to-user forum on its website as a support community for its customers. Customers who share common personal and professional interests can congregate, exchange industry news and practical product tips, share ideas, and—equally important—create publicity for Adobe products.

Blogs and Publishing Platforms

blog a web page that serves as a publicly accessible personal journal for an individual or organization.

Another type of online communication method that has grown significantly is the **blog**. Short for *web log*, a blog is a series of discrete entries or posts that serve as a publicly accessible personal journal for an individual or organization. An effective blog posted by a large company helps put a local "face" on the company, whereas a blog posted by a small business owner can help broaden that firm's reach and potentially build brand trust. Honda uses blogs to connect with customers about its various car models, while Susan Koger of ModCloth uses bloggers to help develop her online vintage clothing business.[37]

While a blog is still a place for a writer to write, it's no longer *the* primary online publishing platform. Popular sites such as WordPress, Medium, LinkedIn Publisher, Tumblr, Facebook, and even *Harvard Business Review* attract a wide variety of audiences. Writers can now publish directly on multiple publishing platforms to target different audiences and vary their distribution platform.

When blogging first began, technology didn't empower writers to upload immediate videos or to stream online podcasts. Soon, social media platforms like Facebook and Twitter (for smaller forms of text-based publishing) cropped up, and conversational long-form articles became less frequent. The result was more of a "stream of consciousness" style of writing.[38]

An effective publishing platform can boost a company's visibility and reputation, and help build brand loyalty. One that is poorly conceived and written can result in a poor image, and sometimes even negative publicity. Sometimes readers' responses on publishing platforms can be offensive or inappropriate. Consider an employee who criticizes specific individuals within the organization or the organization itself. To avoid this situation, some publishing platforms have an approval process for postings before they appear online. Still others provide a way to report inappropriate content. When something negative or inappropriate is posted, it's best to respond professionally and address the comment or engage the reader by asking how the problem can be fixed. Arguing an issue online in front of thousands of readers can often backfire.

Effective blogging and publishing require planning, thoughtfulness, skill, time, and effort. **Table 18.1** lists five tips for attracting more comments, including posting consistently and asking readers for topic ideas.

Web-Based Promotions

Using augmented reality (AR), Facebook is letting users "try on" clothes, makeup, jewelry, and furniture before purchasing. Appearing in the same way as other ads in the News Feed,

TABLE 18.1 Five Tips for Effective Blogging

1. Write on a theme and deliver value. Your content will draw readers and comments to your blog. Writing informative and engaging content will give readers something to talk about.
2. Be consistent. Post new blogs on a regular basis so your readers will know when to check back for new entries. Consistent content quality is also important.
3. Don't write only about yourself—write about your readers as well. Each post should include something that will give your readers a reason to keep reading.
4. Give your blog a story that readers will want to follow. If you continue to tell a story throughout your blog posts, it will give readers something to comment on as well as follow from post to post.
5. Ask readers for topic ideas. Posting information that readers have asked about will continue the conversation between the blogger and the reader.

Sources: Nelson Antony, "Simple Tips to Make a Successful Blog," http://www.bukisa.com, accessed July 14, 2018; Neil Patel, "8 Must-Have Ingredients of a Successful Blog Post," *Entrepreneur,* http://www.entrepreneur.com, accessed July 14, 2018.

a new "Tap to try on" option in the photo allows access to the phone's camera and allows users to see how the item would look on them. Video ads, many of which are uploaded to YouTube, will continue to dominate Internet advertising. A video ad is similar to a cut-down version of a TV ad, which is shown before, during, and/or after a video stream on the Internet. Video advertising is often seen on social channels such as YouTube (owned by Google), which is dedicated to hosting billions of videos (as shown in photo). In addition, social media platforms such as Facebook and Snapchat are already offering video advertising options. In response to queries by searchers, Google uses in-SERP (search engine results page) video advertising or pop-up videos in unexpected places. Studies have shown that video advertisements engage users at a higher rate and that visitors will stay on a site for an average of two minutes longer.[39]

Companies will continue to use native advertisements over the traditional banner ads of the past. While many Internet users have employed ad blockers, the effectiveness of banner ads, though not entirely gone, has faded somewhat. A native ad looks like part of the content of a web page and can be a sponsored article, blog post, tweet, Facebook post, Instagram photo, or any other recommended content. A paid-for native advertisement generates engagement and traffic, and the idea is to sell a product or build awareness without trying too hard to resemble an advertisement.[40]

search engine optimization (SEO) process used by a company to increase the number of visitors to its website via a search engine such as Google or Bing.

Another type of online advertising is called **search engine optimization or SEO**. It is the process used by a company to increase the number of visitors to its website by providing a search ranking and results via a search engine such as Google or Bing. When a user enters certain keywords for a search, companies pay online search engines to have their websites listed in the search engine results pages. Google and other search engines include "sponsored links" on the right side of the search results page. When users click on a sponsored link, they are taken to that site, and the company pays the search engine a small fee. A survey shows that 90% of users find sites through search engines, therefore 65% of retailers and e-tailers agree that SEO will remain a crucial strategic initiative.

More recently, SEO has evolved into what some might call "content marketing," a result of more sophisticated and advanced search engine algorithms able to filter what content is genuinely useful for the end user. Digital assistants like Siri (Apple), Alexa (Amazon), Google Now (Google), and Cortana (Microsoft) utilize traditional search engines to find important information for consumers.[41]

Companies like Procter & Gamble and PetSmart also use online coupons to promote their products via the web. Consumers can go to a company's website to download coupons, and today, more frequently, coupons are received directly on a smart phone through a company's app.

Nicholas Kamm/Getty Images

In addition to ads that run alongside Internet content, video advertisements are growing in popularity. Advertisements can also be in the form of videos, directly uploaded to YouTube.

Social Media

Chances are you have a Facebook account. In fact, an estimated 2.19 billion people use Facebook worldwide, with 214 million in the United States alone; that's almost half the total U.S. population.[42] While Facebook, Twitter, and LinkedIn are currently the most widely visited social networking sites, others like YouTube are growing rapidly.[43] Examples of other social sites include Snapchat, Instagram, Pinterest, and Tumblr. Worldwide, social networks and blogs account for the most time spent online.

Estimates show that people spend an average of 12 hours a day with some sort of media. No longer the dominant media type, television accounts for almost 4 hours a day. Time spent with digital media (which includes desktop/laptop, nonvoice mobile, and other connected devices) accounted for 5 hours, 53 minutes in a recent year—or 48.9% of U.S. adults' average daily time with media. Nonvoice mobile time will be responsible for 3 hours, 17 minutes, while desktop/laptop will contribute 2 hours, 3 minutes, and other connected devices, 33 minutes.[44]

It would be difficult for marketers to ignore the proliferation and influence of **social networking sites**. Most businesses utilize social media—namely Facebook, Instagram, and Twitter, with links from their own websites. There, customers can communicate with each other and the companies, learning about products, promotions, community involvement, and more. Walk by your local bakery or hardware store and you may see the little blue Facebook icon in the window with an invitation to "Find us on Facebook." Since so many people are online at social sites, and since tech experts predict that Millennials will make a lifelong habit of visiting these sites, it makes sense for marketers to continue expanding their strategies using social media.

social networking sites websites that provide a virtual community for people to socialize about a particular subject or any topic in general.

However, just creating a social media site is not sufficient. A business needs to monitor the site daily in order to manage its activity. While most feedback, even if it is critical, will be constructive and informative, overly negative or inappropriate postings can damage a company's reputation.

LinkedIn is a career and business-related social networking site intended specifically to link businesses and businesspeople with each other. LinkedIn was launched in the living room of co-founder Reid Hoffman. Early on, he understood the coming shift of the Internet from a framework for data to a framework for people. LinkedIn currently has more than 500 million members, of which 40% use the site daily to post résumés, look for jobs, and connect with colleagues around the world. Available in 20 languages, LinkedIn makes its money by selling ads and licensing its software product, LinkedIn Recruiter. LinkedIn features an activity feed (similar to the one on Facebook) that continually updates job changes, new connections, and the sharing of content through its publishing platform.[45]

Assessment Check

1. Describe the benefits of online communities.
2. What is the major drawback of blogging?
3. What is search engine optimization or SEO?

6 The Global Environment for E-Commerce

By its very nature, e-commerce has global implications for every company. For many companies, future growth is directly linked to a global e-commerce strategy. Online sales are growing in emerging regions such as Asia-Pacific. In addition, the BRIC countries, Brazil, Russia, India, and China, will surpass the U.S. e-commerce market. While cross-border shopping isn't as prevalent in the United States, due mainly to supply, consumers in many markets can't get the

Job Description

E-Commerce Professional

Overview With opportunities available as a result of a growing industry, a career in e-commerce allows for a blend of business, marketing, merchandising, and electronic retailing with digital marketing. E-commerce companies have a high demand for talented tech-savvy individuals who possess an understanding of both retail and the Internet. As an e-commerce professional, the roles are varied. There is the option to set up your own e-commerce site as a scrappy start-up or to seek employment with an already established industry player.

Responsibilities Roles may include developing presentation and marketing strategies, evaluating and analyzing customer feedback and behavior, managing distributors and partners, and ensuring online security. Since customers are never seen face-to-face, a customer centric approach, along with problem-solving skills, is a crucial element to online purchasing and e-commerce. While e-commerce allows for lots of testing, the real-time feedback, mainly in the form of sales revenues, accelerates the marketing learning curve. Keeping up to date with the latest trends, what competitors are doing, and how your product or service offering is different will be a crucial element for all e-commerce professionals. A career in e-commerce requires "soft skills," along with a deep appreciation for the value of brand and customer experience.

Requirements Gaining knowledge and insight about how e-commerce works for different product and service categories within various industries will prove beneficial. Individuals who can promote online brands offline will do well in e-commerce. There are academic degrees offered in e-commerce and marketing that will help with a career in e-commerce. Traditionally, e-commerce professionals have marketing or retail experience and an interest in online business. A business degree may combine coursework in economics, management, marketing, entrepreneurship, and software applications. Within any e-commerce venture, there are opportunities for marketing, finance, management, procurement, advertising, and distribution specialists. E-commerce provides exposure to product marketing, supply chain, pricing and profit management, customer acquisition, cross-selling, up-selling, customer service, and more. If you're hoping to launch your own e-commerce site, as an entrepreneur you will need self-discipline, planning skills, and determination.

Outlook As established companies have realized new marketing and sales growth opportunities through e-commerce, and customers have found online shopping to be less expensive, efficient, and time saving, the industry is positioned for further growth. Online selling opportunities continue to grow overseas in China, India, Brazil, Russia, and Southeast Asia. As smart phones continue to prevail over desktops and laptops, mobile commerce is positioned for additional growth.

Sources: William Frierson, "Skills You Need for a Career in Ecommerce Store," *College Recruiter,* https://www.collegerecruiter.com, accessed July 13, 2018; Brian Fetherstonhaugh, "5 Reasons Why a Career in E-commerce Is Hot Right Now," *LinkedIn,* https://www.linkedin.com, accessed July 13, 2018; company website, "What Does It Mean to Study e-Commerce?" *World Wide Learn,* http://www.worldwidelearn.com, accessed July 13, 2018; Leon Bailey Green, "An Insider's Guide to Working in e-Commerce," *The Guardian,* http://www.theguardian.com, accessed July 13, 2018.

things they want. This represents a significant opportunity for U.S. e-commerce companies.[46] To learn more about careers in e-commerce, see the "Job Description" feature. U.S. companies, no matter how small, will at some point be affected by this global reality. **Figure 18.2** shows the number of Internet users by world region.

What does this mean for businesses considering going online? With so many users and so much buying power, the Internet creates an enormous pool of potential customers. Companies can market their goods and services internationally and locate distribution sources and trading partners abroad. Customers can search for products at their convenience, browsing through online catalogs that always show current information. Many companies deliver content internationally, based upon a user's location. For example, when you visit software company Symantec's website, you are first asked your country of origin; after entering the information, you are automatically taken to that country-specific portion of the website. A list of the products available for your country is shown, along with local distributors and service centers. And the information on the site is presented in the local language.

One practical implication of this global marketplace is the different languages that buyers and sellers speak. Reflecting the Internet's origins, slightly more than one-fourth of Internet users communicate in English. However, the remainder speak or write other languages, led by Chinese, Spanish, Japanese, Portuguese, German, and Arabic. So far, the majority of web pages are still in English, slowing the adoption of the Internet in non–English-speaking countries.[47]

E-commerce can heighten competition. In the virtual global marketplace, many manufacturers use the Internet to search online catalogs for the lowest-priced parts. No longer can local suppliers assume that they have locked up the business of neighboring companies.

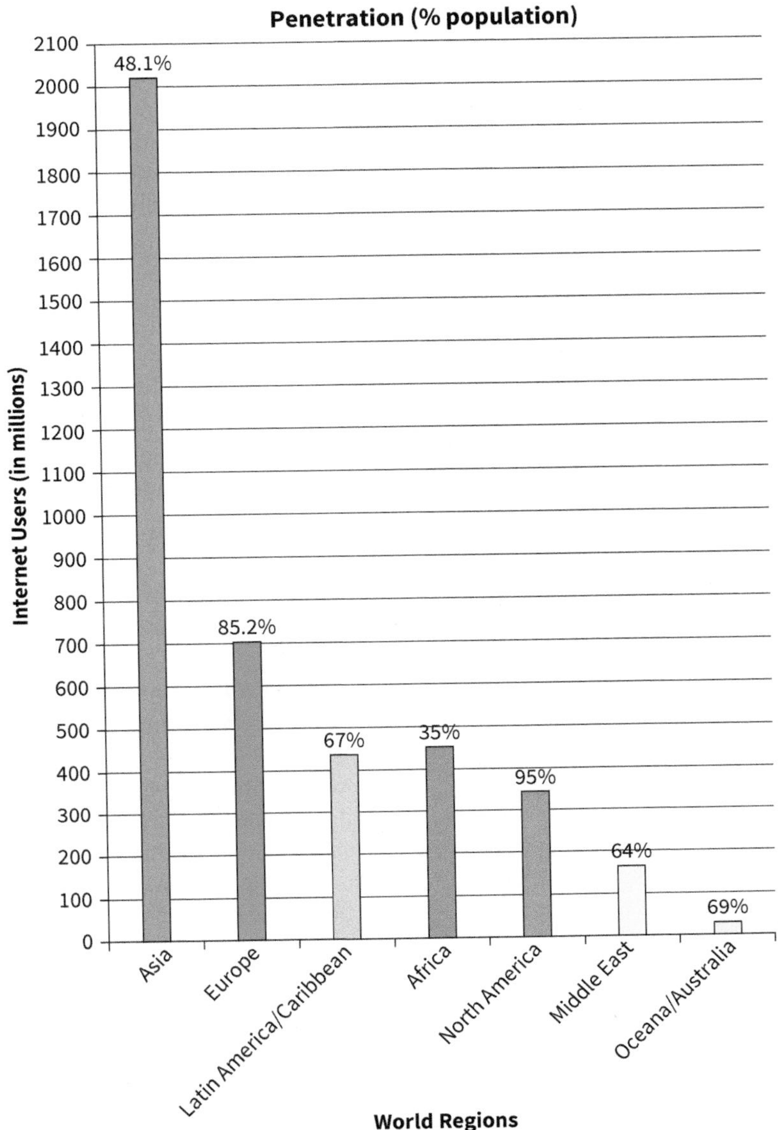

Source: "Internet Usage Statistics," *Internet World Stats,* http://www.internetworldstats.com, accessed July 14, 2018.

FIGURE 18.2 **World Internet Usage Statistics**

Furthermore, the Internet is a valuable way to expand a company's reach, especially for small businesses that would otherwise have difficulty finding customers overseas.

One issue that has proven challenging at times is adhering to local laws and customs. Obviously, U.S. companies should be sensitive to cultural differences, and they must respect local laws. The question, however, is how far they should go. Should they, for instance, allow their websites to be censored? How much should they cooperate with local law enforcement?

Assessment Check

1. On which continent is the greatest number of Internet users located?
2. Identify three challenges in the global marketplace for e-businesses.

7 Building and Managing a Website

Because a company's website may be its most wide reaching and important tool of communication with the marketplace, it is important to plan, design, and build the site carefully—then manage it diligently. How a company uses its site to achieve organizational goals will go a long way toward determining the site's success. **Table 18.2** describes some of the most popular websites in the United States.

Developing a Website

A successful website means different things to different organizations. One company might feel satisfied by maintaining a site that conveys company information or reinforces name recognition—just as a billboard or magazine ad does—without requiring any immediate sales activity. Another might want to broaden its reach to the global marketplace, while still another might simply want to generate as many sales transactions as possible.

Planning and Preparation What is the company's goal for its website? Answering this question is the first step in the website development process. For discount brokerage firm Charles Schwab, the primary objective is to sign up new customers. So the website designers put a link called "Open an Account" prominently on the site's home page. In addition, to reinforce Schwab's image as a respectable and trustworthy investment firm, the site uses a streamlined format that provides helpful information.

Objectives for the website also determine the scope of the project. If the company's goal is to sell goods or services online, the site must include a user-friendly method for customers to find the items they want, ask questions, place orders, and track shipping. Deciding upon a domain name is another important early step in the planning process. A domain name should reflect the company and its products, and it should be easy to remember. Overstock.com states

TABLE 18.2 Popular Websites in the United States

Website	Description
Google	Enables users to search the world's information, including web pages, images, and videos.
Facebook	A social media website that connects people to keep up with friends and family, upload photos, share links and videos.
YouTube	Upload, tag, and share videos worldwide.
Amazon	Seeks to be the most customer centric website, where customers can find and discover anything they want.
Reddit	Social news aggregate and discussion forum
Wikipedia	A free encyclopedia built collaboratively using wiki software.
Twitter	Social networking and microblogging service utilizing instant messaging, SMS, or a web interface.
Yahoo	A major Internet portal and service provider offering search results, customizable content, and financial news.
Instagram	A photo- and video-sharing social networking service owned by Facebook
eBay	International person-to-person auction site

Sources: Lily Feinn, "The Most Popular Websites in the United States Reveal a Lot About Our Online Habits," *Bustle*, https://www.bustle.com, accessed July 14, 2018; "Top Sites in the United States," *Alexa*, https://www.alexa.com/, accessed July 14, 2018.

exactly what the site sells. Although Zappos.com does not, the name is so unusual and easy to remember—and the site has gained such popularity—that the firm's identity remains strong.

Other key decisions include whether to create and maintain a site in-house or to contract with an outside company. Some companies prefer to retain control over content and design by developing their own sites. But planning and building a site require specific skills, and many companies discover they will save money and get better results by hiring a professional.

Finally, determining how customers are most likely to access the site—from a laptop, tablet, or mobile device—will play an important role in the site's design. Companies redesigning their websites want to keep up to date with technological changes. In order to do so, new websites will continue to be built responsively. Responsive websites will adjust to fit the width of a browser, making the viewing experience optimal for any device on which it is loaded.[48]

Content and Connections People obviously are more inclined to visit a site that interests them. Many e-commerce websites try to distinguish themselves by offering information or online communities along with a chance to buy. Stop & Shop's website offers recipes, health information, the opportunity to earn points toward gas rewards, a mobile phone app, a link to Peapod delivery, and more.[49]

New e-commerce platforms and hybrid integration strategies are creating more interesting and varied shopping experiences for engaged, socially connected consumers. This means that e-commerce sites will veer away from the traditional product grid with more engaging content, more fluid layouts, and rich media (including augmented reality) to increase social interaction and potential sales.[50]

Costs As with any technological investment, website costs are an important consideration. Developing and managing a website can range from a few hundred dollars to many thousands, depending on size and complexity. There is the initial investment plus the expense of maintaining the site, whether this is done in-house or through a third party. A website must remain current in order to be useful; updating design and content is another expense to consider.

Measuring Website Effectiveness

Measuring the effectiveness of a website is tricky, and it often depends on the purpose of the website. Profitability is relatively easy to measure in companies that generate revenues directly from online product orders, advertising, or subscription sales. Moreover, and as noted, evidence shows that web-to-store shoppers—a group that favors the Internet primarily as a research tool and time-saving device for retail purchases made in stores—are a significant consumer niche. For companies whose websites primarily or exclusively provide information—rather than generate immediate online sales—success is measured by increased brand awareness and brand loyalty, which presumably translates into greater profitability through offline transactions. Trader Joe's is one such site. Consumers will find everything from product information to recipes, but the store locator directs them to bricks-and-mortar retail outlets.

Advertisers typically measure the success of their ads in terms of *click-through rate*, which is a percentage of users who click on an ad. Another measurement is the *conversion rate*, the percentage of website visitors who actually make purchases. A company can use its advertising cost, site traffic, and conversion rate data to calculate the cost to win each customer. E-commerce companies try to boost their conversion rates by ensuring that their sites download quickly, are easy to use, and deliver on their promises.

Besides measuring click-through and conversion rates, companies can study samples of consumers. Research firms such as comScore and RelevantKnowledge recruit panels of computer users to track Internet site performance and evaluate web activity; this service monitors web audiences in much the same way that television audience viewing habits are rated. Webtrends provides information on website visitors, including where they come from, what they see, and the number of visits to the site, during different times of the day. Other surveys of web users reveal their brand awareness and their attitudes toward websites and brands.

Artificial intelligence (AI)-powered personalization is creating a web experience for consumers that includes specific push notifications to deliver the right message at the right time. By analyzing user data points such as location, demographics, device, and interaction with the website, AI can deliver the best fitting offers and content for increased conversion rates.[51]

It wasn't long ago that product ideas and recommendations were limited to media outlets and product review sites. New types of Internet advertising continue to develop, as do new ways of delivering content. Influencer marketing has skyrocketed over the last few years as companies, big and small, hoping to build their brand credibility, are aligning with social media influencers. Influencers can range from a well-liked and respected celebrity to a blogger, but the one thing they have in common is their content, credibility, following, and, usually, a growing niche and audience. They collaborate with businesses to create campaigns targeted to their social audience (followers), designed to create awareness and, ultimately, sales, in a genuine and authentic way. They're compensated with money or samples and basically are online product promoters. However, choosing an influencer is important, as they should match the brand's tone, style, and mission, as well as, of course, the audience the brand is trying to reach.[52] Sperry, a well-known boat shoe brand, works with over 100 micro-influencers (high influencers with smaller numbers of followers) on Instagram who were previously sharing high-quality images of its products. The company invited these users to begin sharing images and developing visual content on its official Instagram account.[53]

E-commerce is experiencing a shift from transaction-based commerce, focused on price and efficiency, to experiential commerce, a more immersive experience with the intention of understanding a shopper through his or her journey while inspiring, informing, and developing an emotional connection.[54]

Assessment Check

1. What is the first question a company must ask when planning a website?
2. Identify the two conventional methods for measuring the success of online ads.

8 Continuing Trends in E-Commerce

E-commerce is experiencing a shift from transaction-based commerce, focused on price and efficiency, to experiential commerce, a more immersive experience with the intention of understanding a shopper through his or her journey while inspiring, informing, and developing an emotional connection. With value-based pricing and flexible delivery options, savvy digital customers, in search of a seamless experience, wish to shop anywhere at any time and from any location.[54]

Other e-commerce trends include faster shipping and better delivery logistics, greater integration of artificial intelligence and machine learning, the use of augmented reality technologies, explosive growth in mobile checkout and the Internet of Things (see Chapter 14), voice search as a leading driver of innovation in the e-commerce space, the rise of ROPO (research online, purchase offline), and an increase in the number of storefront apps to accommodate mobile device shopping.[55]

An undisputable e-commerce leader, Amazon has set a high bar for fast delivery with its one-hour Prime delivery service. To date, its fastest deliveries include a forehead thermometer in 8 minutes and 5 pints of ice cream in 9 minutes.[56]

Augmented and virtual reality options will soon become standard. Ikea offers an AR app that lets you place true-to-scale 3D products in your home. As voice-activated devices grow in popularity, voice search may ultimately become the preferred method of search. Walmart has made it possible for consumers to order any of their items by voice on the Google Express. ROPO (research online, purchase offline) combines information from social media, mobile tracking/

geolocation, mobile payments, in-store inventory, analytics tools, CRM systems, and more to figure out which ads and site pages led consumers to in-store purchases. Using machine learning, Netflix makes recommendations on movies through its 1,300 "taste communities" rather than dividing viewers by age, location, or gender. Last, the continued rise of mobile, specifically mobile checkout and payment systems and Internet-connected devices, will remain a focus for e-commerce companies.[57]

Assessment Check

1. What are the benefits to both consumers and e-commerce companies of an omni-channel or multi-channel retail experience?
2. Discuss mobile or m-commerce.

What's Ahead

The one certainty about e-commerce is that it will continue to evolve with technology. So far, B2B transactions are leading the way online. B2C e-commerce is growing and attracting new buyers every year. Companies continue to harness the communication power of the web to help achieve higher levels of customer satisfaction and loyalty. In spite of the challenges, there is no doubt that the future of e-commerce will include innovation, entrepreneurship, and interactivity between businesses and their customers.

Chapter in Review

Summary of Learning Objectives

LEARNING OBJECTIVE 1 Discuss the functions of e-commerce.

E-commerce offers companies a global reach, customization, interactivity between a business (or its products) and its customers, right-time and integrated marketing, and cost savings.

Assessment Check Answers

1.1 **Define e-commerce.** E-commerce refers to conducting business via the Internet.

1.2 **What is the difference between a corporate website and a marketing website?** Corporate websites are designed to increase visibility and to provide information about the company. Marketing websites are intended to sell goods or services and to build relationships with customers.

LEARNING OBJECTIVE 2 List the major functions of B2B e-commerce

Business-to-business (B2B) e-commerce generates sales revenue, provides detailed product descriptions and other information, handles payment options over the Internet, and helps firms slash costs. Electronic data interchange (EDI), extranets, and private exchanges allow companies to exchange data accurately, rapidly, and collaboratively without paper flow. Electronic exchanges are online B2B marketplaces, while e-procurement allows firms to improve the efficiency of their procurement processes.

Assessment Check Answers

2.1 **How do extranets and private exchanges work?** An extranet is a secure network used for e-business and accessible through a firm's website to external customers, suppliers, or other authorized users. A private exchange is a secure website at which a company and its suppliers share their data with each other.

2.2 **What is an electronic exchange?** An electronic exchange is an online marketplace that brings buyers and sellers together and is tailored to a specific industry's needs.

LEARNING OBJECTIVE 3 Explain B2C e-commerce.

Business-to-consumer (B2C) e-commerce connects companies with consumers through shopping sites and informational sites. Electronic storefronts allow consumers to make online purchases, while informational sites provide information about products, the company, store location, community involvement, and the like. Benefits of B2C e-commerce include convenience, time and cost savings, fast delivery, and large selections.

Assessment Check Answers

3.1 **What are the two different types of B2C websites?** B2C occurs through shopping sites and informational sites. Shopping sites allow consumers to make direct purchases, whereas informational sites provide information that is intended to lead to purchases offline.

3.2 **Describe the various types of people who shop online.** Online shoppers vary by age, gender, income, and education. Online shopping trends are driven by teens and Millennials, the dominant online shopping demographic. In addition, middle-aged people have embraced its convenience, and men spend almost as much money online as women.

LEARNING OBJECTIVE 4 Describe the challenges associated with e-commerce.

Challenges confronting e-business firms include developing safe online payment systems, battling security breaches and Internet fraud, overcoming consumer fears about identity theft, and dealing with potential channel conflicts.

Assessment Check Answers

4.1 **What is encryption, and why is it important?** Encryption is the process of encoding data for security purposes. Successful encryption keeps consumer information secure from unauthorized access.

4.2 **How does a business protect its own information?** A company protects its own information through the use of a firewall, which is an electronic barrier between the company's internal network and the Internet.

4.3 **Describe a potential channel conflict for a firm conducting e-commerce.** A channel conflict might occur when a producer sells its goods for less online than it does through a retailer.

LEARNING OBJECTIVE 5 Discuss how organizations use the web to communicate.

Companies communicate with each other, customers, suppliers, and the general public via online communities, blogs and other publishing platforms, web-based promotions, and social networking. Doing so allows them to gain more knowledge about the marketplace, adapt to consumer preferences, and create a wide-ranging positive image.

Assessment Check Answers

5.1 **Describe the benefits of online communities.** Online communities offer information exchange, facilitate marketing, and build relationships among participants.

5.2 **What is the major drawback of blogging?** A poorly conceived and written blog can result in bad publicity, as can a negative blog written by someone outside the organization.

5.3 **What is search engine optimization or SEO?** SEO is a crucial strategic initiative employed by businesses because so many users find sites through search engines. It is a way companies increase visitors to their websites by paying a fee to online search engines such as Google to have their websites listed in the search engine results pages as "sponsored links" on the right side of the search results page.

LEARNING OBJECTIVE 6 Describe the global environment for e-commerce.

Although 87% of North Americans are online as compared to 40% of Asians, the actual number of Internet users in Asia (1.6 billion) dwarfs the number in North America (314 million). These statistics present many global opportunities for companies that do business via the Internet. The global nature of e-commerce can also heighten competition. Challenges include language barriers and adhering to local laws and customs.

Assessment Check Answers

6.1 **On which continent is the greatest number of Internet users located?** Asia has the greatest number of Internet users (1.6 billion).

6.2 **Identify three challenges in the global marketplace for e-businesses.** One challenge is language barriers; a second is heightened competition; third is adhering to local laws and customs.

LEARNING OBJECTIVE 7 Discuss building and managing a website.

A successful website requires careful planning and preparation, decisions about content and Internet connections, and cost. A website must be updated continually in order to remain useful. Measuring the effectiveness of a website depends on the purpose of the website—is it intended to dispense information and develop brand loyalty or to generate sales?

Assessment Check Answers

7.1 **What is the first question a company must ask when planning a website?** The first question is "What is the goal for this website?"

7.2 **Identify the two conventional methods for measuring the success of online ads.** The two methods are click-through rate and conversion rate. Click-through rate calculates a percentage of users who click on an ad; conversion rate calculates the percentage of website visitors who actually make purchases.

LEARNING OBJECTIVE 8 Identify current trends in e-commerce.

With value-based pricing and flexible delivery options, savvy digital customers, in search of a seamless experience, wish to shop anywhere at any time and from any location.

Assessment Check Answers

8.1 **What are the benefits to both consumers and e-commerce companies of an omni-channel or multichannel retail experience?** Consumers will increasingly leverage a variety of online and in-store options including retail stores, online stores, mobile stores, and mobile app stores. A mobile strategy will be important as consumers transition between multiple touchpoints. A result of such a multichannel experience will be increased company revenues and, ultimately, customer loyalty.

8.2 **Discuss mobile or m-commerce.** The new world of mobile or m-commerce means that e-businesses interested in capturing consumers who make purchases on their mobile devices will need a mobile strategy in place. Mobile commerce will reach 20% of overall e-commerce in the coming year.

Business Terms You Need to Know

e-commerce (or e-business) 489
corporate website 490
marketing website 491
business-to-business (B2B) e-commerce 491
business-to-consumer (B2C) e-commerce 493
electronic storefronts 494
encryption 497
phishing 499
channel conflicts 499
blog 501
search engine optimization (SEO) 502
social networking sites 503

Review Questions

1. How does a small business specifically benefit from e-commerce? A large business?

2. Health insurance is one industry in which B2B e-commerce is prevalent. Name another industry that you think is suitable for B2B e-business and explain why.

3. What is e-tailing? How does it work?

4. What are the benefits of B2C e-commerce, to both consumers and companies?

5. What are consumers' greatest concerns about e-commerce? How are businesses addressing these concerns?

6. Do you predict that businesses will continue to use social networking as part of their e-commerce strategy over the next decade? Why or why not?

7. Most of the world's Internet users live in Asia. Identify two implications that you believe this fact will have on e-commerce over the next few years.

8. If a business is planning to develop its website for use by mobile phone devices, what factors should it keep in mind when designing the site?

9. Do you agree with the decision by some firms to abandon their websites and rely on social networking sites and blogging sites instead? Why or why not?

10. Discuss current e-commerce trends. As an online shopper, can you identify additional trends?

Projects and Teamwork Applications

1. Visit your local market, hardware store, casual restaurant, or clothing store. How might the business benefit from engaging in e-commerce? What kinds of challenges might it face? If it is already online, how effective is its presence in your eyes as a consumer?

2. Visit the website http://medium.com, a blog publishing platform. Evaluate how it works, and read some of the blogs posted. Choose one blog post that you think is effective and one that is not. Explain your choices.

3. Conduct research to learn more about companies that have successfully utilized social media to build their brands. Consider a consumer products company, an electronics company, an automobile company, or an airline. Discuss the various ways companies use social media, and include examples. Visit at least three social media sites to assess the company's approach on each site.

4. As e-commerce companies make the shift to the large and growing mobile commerce (m-commerce) market of consumers accessing and shopping on their smart phones, benefits to consumers include different and better deals—and discounts. However, the smaller screen size of smart phones can be one of the challenges when navigating and selecting from among many items. Discuss and evaluate the advantages and disadvantages of the growing m-commerce phenomenon. Do the benefits outweigh the drawbacks? What is your experience with m-commerce?

5. There is a widely held belief that native apps, an application program that has been developed for use on a particular platform or device, will one day replace a company's website. Therefore, many developers are recreating their company's web content into an app environment. Discuss when it makes sense to use an app and when it makes sense to use a browser to access a company's website. Do you agree that apps will one day replace some of the over 1.5 billion websites in existence?

Web Assignments

1. **Research Internet use.** Some of the top e-commerce trends include lower prices, vast product selections, and free and faster shipping, to name a few. Research some of the other trends and bring your list of the top 10 trends to class.

2. ***Fortune's* fastest-growing companies.** Pick a B2B company and evaluate its use of social media. By visiting its social media sites, including Facebook, LinkedIn, Twitter, and Instagram, how does the company use social media to communicate with its employees, customers, investors, and suppliers?

3. How are service companies jumping on the e-commerce or m-commerce bandwagon? Provide examples of service companies engaged in e-commerce or m-commerce.

4. Research, using the link below, what it would take to place an advertisement on YouTube. Outline the steps and options for the class. How are companies using video advertising? What are the benefits and drawbacks? **https://www.youtube.com/yt/advertise**

Note: Internet web addresses change frequently. If you don't find the exact sites listed, you may need to access the organization's home page and search from there.

Cases

Case 18.1 Fashion Retailers Haul in Sales via YouTube

Combining enthusiasm, retail shopping, and technology, a *hauler* is commonly a female in her teens who creates a homemade video. The video is posted on YouTube to brag about the virtues of recent "shopping hauls" or purchases. Haul videos began to gain traction on YouTube about a decade ago and made their mark a little over five years ago when National Public Radio (NPR) covered this emerging genre.

Fashion retailers like Forever 21 are fueling the fire of this online marketing phenomenon, with deals and incentives for their young haulers. These shoppers can earn in excess of six figures and become quick celebrities, but most do it for the fun, online exposure, and the love of fashion.

Rising stars and prolific YouTube haulers include Zoella, Bethany Mota, and Carli Bybel—each with her own channel, and each garnering millions of views. The stars laugh, cajole, gush, and provide advice while holding up their fashion finds from Forever 21, Zara, American Apparel, and TopShop, to name just a few. All are driving sales for the brands with whom they partner, and each is an integral part of a retail partner's social media and marketing strategy.

There are close to 1 million haul videos on YouTube to date, with many promoting not only fashion finds but also home products, beauty, fitness, health, and wellness. The homemade videos are authentic and objective product testimonies without a hard-sell edge. Bethany Mota, who goes beyond YouTube to promote, has 5.4 million Instagram followers, which has made the 21-year-old online star a sought-after ambassador for companies such as Aeropostale.

More recently, the haulternative movement features videos of well-known haulers such as Connie Glynn as Nooderella, a vlogger (video blogger) who advocates purchasing items at vintage and thrift stores and swapping with friends for a more eco-conscious approach to shopping.

Questions for Critical Thinking

1. Do haulers as brand ambassadors actually seem more genuine than the brands promoting the products themselves?
2. What is your opinion of retailers like Aeropostale and Forever 21 that actually pay haulers to promote their goods?

Sources: Kristen Bousquet, "43 Best Fashion YouTube Vloggers To Follow in 2018," *Stylecaster*, http://stylecaster.com, accessed July 14, 2018; company website, http://www.forever21.com, accessed July 14, 2018; Armando Roggio, "3 Ways to Use 'Haul' Videos in E-commerce Marketing," *Practical E-commerce*, http://practicale-commerce.com, accessed July 14, 2018; Tasmin Blachard, "YouTube 'Haulers' Get Ethical with a New haulternative Campaign for Fashion Revolution Day," *Telegraph Fashion*, http://fashion.telegraph.co.uk, accessed July 14, 2018; Rebecca Deczynski and Shalayne Pulia, "Want to Go Shopping Without Spending a Dime? Allow Us to Introduce You to Haul Videos," *InStyle*, http://www.instyle.com, accessed July 14, 2018; "Deck the Hauls," *Pymnts.com*, http://www.pymnts.com, accessed July 14, 2018; Sapna Maheshwari, "YouTube Shopper Haul Videos Have More Combined Views Than 'Gangnam Style,'" *BuzzFeed*, http://www.buzzfeed.com, accessed July 14, 2018.

Case 18.2 ModCloth Offers Vintage Clothing Online and Offline

Susan Gregg's closet was stuffed with vintage clothing and shoes. She couldn't possibly wear them all, and she didn't have space for new purchases. So she did the only thing a budding entrepreneur could do: start her own business. Gregg and her then-boyfriend (now husband), Eric Koger, launched a quirky, retro online vintage clothing boutique called ModCloth.com, selling fashion from independent designers and their own ModCloth-branded lines. Within two years, the site netted 60,000 visitors a month, and in a recent year revenue growth of 50%. After graduation, the couple married and grew the business by hiring designers to create an all-new, indie, retro-style line.

Recently ModCloth launched a wedding collection, ranging from boho-chic to beach bride. ModCloth plans to expand product lines to include intimates, athletic wear, accessories, and even home goods.

In addition, a temporary West Coast shop was launched as a "fit shop" to provide women, mainly in their 20s and 30s, a place where they can try on more than 100 items of clothing prior to placing an order online for two-day shipment. In addition to pop-up shops, the company recently hired a vice president of stores and retail operations to expand its bricks-and-mortar presence to become a clicks-and-mortar phenomenon offering quirky vintage appeal.

In a recent year, ModCloth was acquired by Walmart for close to $75 million, which came as a shock to the brand's fans. Subsequently the brand has struggled, due mainly to increased online competition. When Walmart, in its strategy to build its fashion brands, included the acquisition of ModCloth, the company assured its longtime customers that Walmart's deep pockets would allow for a better and continued shopping experience for the unique brand.

Questions for Critical Thinking

1. Can you think of other e-commerce companies that have added retail stores? How do the two business models differ?
2. What kind of e-business could you run from your current residence? What tips might you take from the founders of ModCloth?

Sources: Elizabeth Segran, "This Is ModCloth's Plan to Win Over Customers After the Walmart Acquisition," *Fast Company*, http://fastcompany.com, accessed July 15, 2018; company website, http://www.modcloth.com, accessed July 14, 2018; Adele Chapin, "ModCloth's Affordable Wedding Collection Launches Today," *Racked*, http://racked.com, accessed July 14, 2018; Sarah Perez, "ModCloth Co-Founder Eric Koger Exits Role As CEO; Urban Outfitters' Matthew Kaness Joins," *Tech Crunch*, http://techcrunch.com, accessed July 14, 2018; Kim Bhasin, "ModCloth Plans Huge Expansion Under New CEO," *Bloomberg Business*, http://www.bloomberg.com, accessed July 14, 2018; Jennifer Wang, "Out of Her Closet, a $50 Million Business," *Entrepreneur*, http://www.entrepreneur.com, accessed July 14, 2018; Deborah Belgum, "ModCloth Ramping Up to Add Stores," *California Apparel News*, https://www.apparelnews.net, accessed July 14, 2018.

Appendix A

Business Law

No More Playing Around: RIP Toys "R" Us

Toys "R" Us, an American toy, clothing, video game, and baby product retailer founded in New Jersey over 70 years ago, announced that it would close all its U.S. stores. However, just a few months prior, its CEO had mapped out a goal of upgrading online sales, renovating stores, and introducing augmented reality into the toy shopping experience. To achieve those goals, the company planned to close a few hundred stores so that the remaining stores could become healthier. The turn of events came as a surprise to those who thought that the retailer would simply reorganize in order to survive.

A few missteps point to the toy retailer's demise—the first of which happened to be its heavy debt load. Saddled with heavy debt when purchased by private equity firms Bain Capital and Kohlberg Kravis Roberts in 2005, not much had changed by 2017. The debt load stood at about $5 billion. Filing for Chapter 11 bankruptcy protection (which provides for reorganization to keep a business alive and pay creditors over time) before the holiday season further added to the company's demise. During the peak selling months of the holiday season, a period which the company needed to focus for achieving strong results, the distraction of bankruptcy persisted. In addition, once word got out of the struggles faced by the much-beloved retailer, Amazon, Walmart, and Target ratcheted up discounts and suppliers temporarily tightened up product terms for fear of suffering losses.[1]

Overview

As the opening story points out, legal issues (such as bankruptcy law) affect every aspect of business. Despite the best efforts of most businesspeople, legal issues do arise. A dispute may arise over a contract, an employee may file a lawsuit for wrongful termination, or a town may challenge the environmental impact of a new gas station. Unfortunately, the United States has the dubious distinction of being the world's most litigious society. Lawsuits are as common as business deals. Consider Walmart, which is involved in ongoing lawsuits from customers and employees for issues ranging from unsafe shopping environments to religious, sex, and pay discrimination.

Even if you are never involved in a lawsuit, the cost still affects you. The average U.S. family pays a hidden "litigation tax" of 5% each year because of the costs of lawsuits that force businesses to increase their prices. Small businesses, such as dentists' offices, doctors' offices, and daycare providers are often the hardest hit and may cut back on their services or close. One example of a frivolous lawsuit occurred when an animal rights group filed a lawsuit on behalf of a female monkey asserting that the monkey should enjoy copyright protection on a "selfie" she took when she swiped a photographer's camera out of his hands. The photographer claims to own the picture.[2] Rule 11 of the Federal Rules of Civil Procedure was designed in 1993 to prevent frivolous lawsuits, but has been weakened by loopholes.

There are ongoing proposals for new laws intended to protect businesses, consumers, and the general public—but somehow they fall short. In addition, laws that no longer serve a purpose are still on the books. For instance, in Alaska, it's illegal to wake a bear to take its picture, but it is perfectly legal to shoot a bear while it is sleeping. In Hawaii, it is against the law to insert pennies in your ear. In Louisiana, it is illegal to gargle in public. In Montana, it is against the law to operate a vehicle with ice picks attached to the wheels. In North Carolina, it is illegal to use elephants to plow cotton fields. And in Arizona, it's illegal to hunt camels.[3] The origins of these laws raise about as many questions as the laws themselves.

Legislation that specifically affects how business functions is analyzed in each chapter of this book. Chapter 2 presents an overview of the legal environment, and legislation affecting international operations is covered in Chapter 4. Chapter 5 discusses laws related to small businesses. Laws regarding human resource management and labor unions are examined in Chapter 8. Laws affecting other business operations, such as environmental regulations and product safety, are one of the topics in Chapter 12, and marketing-related legislation is examined in Chapter 13. Finally, legislation pertaining to banking and the securities markets is discussed in Chapters 16 and 17.

In this appendix, we provide a general perspective of legislation at the federal, state, and local levels, and point out that, although business executives may not be legal experts, they do need to be knowledgeable and aware of laws in their specific area of responsibility. A good amount of common sense also helps avoid potential legal problems. This appendix looks at the general nature of business law, the court system, basic legal concepts, and the changing regulatory environment for U.S. business. Let's start with some initial definitions and related examples.

Legal System and Administrative Agencies

judiciary court system, or branch of government that is responsible for settling disputes by applying laws.

The **judiciary**, or court system, is the branch of government responsible for settling disputes among parties by applying laws. This branch consists of several types and levels of courts, each with a specific jurisdiction. Court systems are organized at the federal, state, and local levels. Administrative agencies also perform some limited judicial functions, but these agencies are more properly regarded as belonging to the executive or legislative branches of government.

At both the federal and state levels, *trial courts*—courts of general jurisdiction—hear a wide range of cases. Unless a case is assigned by law to another court or to an administrative agency, a court of general jurisdiction will hear it. The majority of cases, both criminal and civil, pass through these courts. Within the federal system, trial courts are known as U.S. district courts, and at least one such court operates in each state. In state court systems, the general jurisdiction courts are often called circuit courts, and states typically provide one for each county. Other names for general jurisdiction courts are superior courts, common pleas courts, or district courts.

State judiciary systems also include many courts with lower, or more specific, jurisdictions. In most states, parties can appeal the decisions of the lower courts to the general jurisdiction courts. Examples of lower courts are probate courts—which settle the estates of people who have died—and small-claims courts—where people can represent themselves in suits involving limited amounts of money. For example, a landlord might go to small-claims court to settle a dispute with a tenant over a security deposit.

Decisions made at the general trial court level may be appealed in *appellate courts*. Both the federal and state systems have appellate courts. For instance, the U.S. Court of Appeals for the Fourth Circuit, which is based in Richmond, Virginia, covers the states of Maryland, Virginia, West Virginia, North Carolina, and South Carolina.[4] The appeals process allows a higher court to review the case and correct any lower court error indicated by the appellant, the party making the appeal.

Appeals from decisions of the U.S. circuit courts of appeals can go all the way to the nation's highest court, the U.S. Supreme Court. Appeals from state courts of appeal are heard by the highest court in each state, usually called the state supreme court. In a state without intermediate appellate courts, the state supreme court hears appeals directly from the trial courts. Parties who are not satisfied by the verdict of a state supreme court can appeal to the U.S. Supreme Court and may be granted a hearing if they can cite grounds for such an appeal, and if the Supreme Court considers the case significant enough to be heard. The Supreme Court typically has 7,000 to 8,000 cases on the docket per year. However, only about 100 are granted review with oral arguments by attorneys. Formal written decisions are delivered for about 80 of those cases.[5]

While most cases are resolved by the system of courts described here, certain highly specialized cases require particular expertise. Examples of specialized federal courts are the U.S. Tax Court for tax cases and the U.S. Court of Claims, which hears claims against the U.S. government itself. Similar specialized courts operate at the state level.

Administrative agencies, also known as bureaus, commissions, or boards, decide a variety of cases at all levels of government. These agencies usually derive their powers and responsibilities from state or federal statutes. Technically, they conduct hearings or inquiries rather than trials. Examples of federal administrative agencies are the Federal Trade Commission (FTC), the National Labor Relations Board (NLRB), and the Federal Energy Regulatory Commission (FERC). The FTC has the broadest power of any of the federal regulatory agencies. It enforces laws regulating unfair business practices, and it can stop false and deceptive advertising practices. Examples at the state level include public utility commissions and boards that govern the licensing of various trades and professions. Zoning boards, planning commissions, and boards of appeal operate at the city or county level.

Types of Law

Law consists of the standards set by government and society in the form of either legislation or custom. This broad body of principles, regulations, rules, and customs that govern the actions of all members of society, including businesspeople, is derived from several sources. **Common law** refers to the body of law arising out of judicial decisions, some of which can be traced back to early England.

Statutory law, or written law, includes state and federal constitutions, legislative enactments, treaties of the federal government, and ordinances of local governments. Statutes must be drawn precisely and reasonably to be constitutional, and thus enforceable. Still, courts frequently must interpret their intentions and meanings.

With the growth of the global economy, knowledge of international law has become crucial. **International law** refers to the numerous regulations that govern companies conducting global business. Companies must be aware of the domestic laws of trading partners, trade agreements such as NAFTA, and the rulings of such organizations as the World Trade Organization. International law affects trade in all kinds of industries. When a range of defective or tainted products manufactured in China—but sold in the United States—was recalled, companies discovered that although the goods came from China, the liability for their defects lay squarely within the United States. Tainted or defective toothpaste, pet food, toys, tires, and shrimp all fell under the scrutiny of the Food and Drug Administration (FDA), the Consumer Product Safety Commission (CPSC), and other agencies, which hold U.S. manufacturers responsible for the quality of their foreign-made products. A few years ago, the United States, the

law standards set by government and society in the form of either legislation or custom.

common law body of law arising out of judicial decisions, some of which can be traced back to early England.

statutory law written law, including state and federal constitutions, legislative enactments, treaties of the federal government, and ordinances of local governments.

international law the numerous regulations that govern international commerce.

© Keith Bedford/Bloomberg via Getty Images

Expertise in international law has become very important as the global economy continues to expand. In one case, the United States, Japan, and the WTO joined forces to bring a case against China for its restrictions on exports of rare metals used to make various electronic goods. The WTO ruled against China's export restrictions.

World Trade Organization (WTO), and Japan joined forces to bring a lawsuit against China for its restrictions on exports of rare-earth metals, which are used in making electronic goods such as smart phones, renewable energy, flat-screen TVs, compact fluorescent light bulbs, and electric cars. Currently, China mines 95 to 97% of these metals, which include scandium, lanthanum, and fifteen other elements. The WTO ruled against China's export restrictions on the rare minerals. China has increased efforts to restrict illegal mining and exporting of its rare-earth minerals with a new system in place to certify the origin of supplies of the in-demand minerals.[6]

In a broad sense, all law is business law because all firms are subject to the entire body of law, just as individuals are. In a narrower sense, however, **business law** consists of those aspects of law that most directly influence and regulate the management of various types of business activity. Specific laws vary widely in their intent from business to business and from industry to industry. The legal interests of airlines, for example, differ from those of oil companies.

business law aspects of law that most directly influence and regulate the management of business activity.

State and local statutes also have varying applications. Some state laws affect all businesses that operate in a particular state. Workers' compensation laws, which govern payments to workers for injuries incurred on the job, are an example. Other state laws apply only to certain firms or business activities. States have specific licensing requirements for businesses, such as law firms, funeral homes, and hair salons. Many local ordinances also deal with specific business activities. Local regulations on the sizes and types of business signs are commonplace. Some communities even restrict the sizes of stores, including height and square footage.

Regulatory Environment for Business

Government regulation of business has changed over time. Depending on public sentiment, the economy, and the political climate, we see the pendulum swing back and forth between increased regulation and deregulation. But the goal of both types of legislation is protection of healthy competition. One industry that has experienced some deregulation in the past is still subject to relatively tight regulations: banking. Despite the relaxation of banking regulations across state lines and the advent of online banking, laws governing everything from stock trading to retirement investing remain strict. In response to a crisis in which lending institutions granted mortgages to home buyers who were then unable to meet payments that later increased—precipitating record numbers of foreclosures—a new bill was introduced in Congress. The Mortgage Reform and Anti-Predatory Lending Act of 2007 modifies the Truth in Lending Act. The intent of this legislation is to protect consumers by establishing fair lending practices. In addition, after the near-collapse of Wall Street, the Dodd-Frank Act was signed into law in 2010. This law created the Bureau of Consumer Financial Protection and tightened regulations on all firms involved in the financial industry. Under the Dodd-Frank Act, taxpayers can no longer be asked to bail out failing financial firms. The Securities and Exchange Commission, along with the FBI, announced it would investigate high-frequency stock traders to determine whether they have an unfair speed advantage, sometimes less than a fraction of a second, when executing trades. In a recent study, it was found that high-frequency trading firms have a 500-microsecond advantage over a firm that doesn't use a direct feed from the exchanges to quote prices. System engineers at NASDAQ, the New York-based stock exchange, recently built a prototype and began testing an algorithm and software that they hope can synchronize a giant network of computers with nanosecond precision.[7]

Let's look at the issues surrounding regulation and deregulation and the legislation that has characterized them.

Antitrust and Business Regulation

John D. Rockefeller's Standard Oil monopoly launched antitrust legislation. Breaking up monopolies and restraints of trade was a popular issue in the late 1800s and early 1900s. In fact, President Theodore Roosevelt always promoted himself as a "trust-buster." The highly publicized Microsoft case of the 1990s is another example of antitrust litigation. Microsoft was accused of abusing monopoly-type power on Intel-based personal computers with regard to operating system and web browser sales. The issue was whether Microsoft should have been allowed to bundle its Internet Explorer (IE) web browser software with its Microsoft Windows operating system. Because every Windows user had a copy of IE, the argument was made that the market for competing web browsers such as Netscape was restricted.[8]

During the 1930s, several laws designed to regulate business were passed. The basis for many of these laws was protecting employment. The world was in the midst of the Great Depression, so the government focused on keeping its citizens employed. Recently, government officials became concerned with the security aspects of international business transactions, Internet usage, the sources of funds, and their effects on U.S. business practices. New regulatory legislation in the form of the USA Patriot Act was enacted in response to the attacks of September 11, 2001. Congress has voted to reauthorize this law several times. The law includes a provision that allows the federal government, with approval from a federal judge, to seize business records in investigations involving national security.[9]

The major federal antitrust and business regulation legislation includes the following:

Law	What It Did
Sherman Act (1890)	Set a competitive business system as a national policy goal. The act specifically banned monopolies and restraints of trade.
Clayton Act (1914)	Put restrictions on price discrimination, exclusive dealing, tying contracts, and interlocking boards of directors that lessened competition or might lead to a monopoly.
Federal Trade Commission Act (1914)	Established the FTC with the authority to investigate business practices. The act also prohibited unfair methods of competition.
Robinson-Patman Act (1936)	Outlawed price discrimination in sales to wholesalers, retailers, or other producers. The act also banned pricing designed to eliminate competition.
Wheeler-Lea Act (1938)	Banned deceptive advertising. The act gave the FTC jurisdiction in such cases.
USA Patriot Act (2001)	Limited interactions between U.S. and foreign banks to those with "know your customer" policies; allowed the U.S. Treasury Department to freeze assets and bar a country, government, or institution from doing business in the United States; gave federal authorities broad powers to monitor Internet usage and expanded the way data are shared among different agencies. Reauthorization (2005) created a new Assistant Attorney General for Security, enhanced penalties for terrorism financing, and provided clear standards and penalties for attacks on mass transit systems.

The protection of fair competition remains an issue in industries today. The Federal Communications Commission (FCC) announced plans to enact a net-neutrality regulation, whose goal would be to advocate for a neutral Internet and open platform in which all websites would be treated equally and not subject to additional fees to use Internet "fast lanes." Net neutrality advocates for the idea that all traffic on the Internet (in terms of speed) should be treated equally. In other words, there is no paid prioritization. Under this law, an Internet service provider cannot accept fees for favored treatment or create fast lanes that allow content companies such as Netflix to deliver their content to customers faster. However, recently the FCC voted to repeal net neutrality rules, freeing broadband providers (AT&T, Comcast, and Verizon) to block or throttle content as they see fit unless Congress or the courts block the agency's decision.[10]

Business Deregulation

Deregulation was a concept that began in the 1970s and whose influence continues today. Within a particular industry, deregulation, designed to create more competition, is the reduction or elimination of government power. Many formerly regulated industries were freed to pick the markets they wanted to serve. The deregulated industries, such as utilities and airlines, were also allowed to price their products without the guidance of federal regulations. For the most part, deregulation led to lower consumer prices. In some cases, it also led to a loss of service. Many smaller cities and airports lost airline service because of deregulation.

Following are several major laws related to deregulation:

Law	What It Did
Airline Deregulation Act (1978)	Allowed airlines to set fares and pick their routes.
Motor Carrier Act and Staggers Rail Act (1980)	Permitted the trucking and railroad industries to negotiate rates and services.
Telecommunications Act (1996)	Cut barriers to competition in local and long-distance phone, cable, and television markets.
Gramm-Leach-Bliley Act (1999)	Permitted banks, securities firms, and insurance companies to affiliate within a new financial organizational structure; required them to disclose to customers their policies and practices for protecting the privacy of personal information.

Consumer Protection

There are numerous laws designed to protect consumers. In many ways, business itself has evolved to reflect this focus on consumer safety and satisfaction. Recently, Congress passed the broadest changes in the country's consumer protection system in decades, including stricter regulations governing toy manufacturing, public access to complaints about products, and a major overhaul of the Consumer Product Safety Commission (CPSC) designed to improve communication and efficiency. One provision includes stricter limits on the amount of lead in children's toys, and another requires mandatory safety standards for nursery items such as cribs and playpens. The Dodd-Frank Act covers consumer financial protection.[11] The Food and Drug Administration Amendments Act (FDAA) of 2007 reauthorizes existing laws and includes new provisions designed to enhance drug safety, encourage the development of pediatric medical devices, and enhance food safety.[12] The FDA recently issued warning letters to 13 sellers of nicotine-containing e-liquids that look like kid-friendly juice boxes, candy, or cookies. One of the companies receiving a warning letter was also cited for illegally selling the product to a minor.[13]

The major federal laws related to consumer protection include the following:

Law	What It Did
Federal Food and Drug Act (1906)	Banned adulteration and misbranding of foods and drugs involved in interstate commerce.
Consumer Credit Protection Act (1968)	Required disclosure of annual interest rates on loans and credit purchases.
National Environmental Policy Act (1970)	Established the Environmental Protection Agency to deal with various types of pollution and organizations that create pollution.
Public Health Cigarette Smoking Act (1970)	Prohibited tobacco advertising on radio and television.
Consumer Product Safety Act (1972)	Established the Consumer Product Safety Commission with authority to specify safety standards for most products.
Nutrition Labeling and Education Act (1990)	Stipulated detailed information on the labeling of most foods.
Dietary Supplement Health and Education Act (1994)	Established standards with respect to dietary supplements including vitamins, minerals, herbs, amino acids, and the like.
Food and Drug Administration Amendments Act of 2007	Reauthorized several laws dealing with prescription drugs and added new ones enhancing food safety, drug safety, development of pediatric medical devices, and clinical trial registries.
Credit Card Accountability, Responsibility and Disclosure Act of 2009 (CARD Act)	Limits fees and penalties charged by credit card companies as well as when they may increase interest rates and by how much.

Employee Protection

Chapters 2 and 8 cover many of the issues employers face in protecting their employees from injury and harm while on the job. But employees must also be protected from unfair practices by employers. In 2009, Congress passed the Lilly Ledbetter Fair Pay Act. This law helps protect workers from wage discrimination. Companies such as Starbucks, Apple, Salesforce, Intel, and Adobe have recently taken matters into their own hands with payroll audits. The result is full pay parity for women and underrepresented minorities in the United States.[14]

Some of the relevant laws related to employee protection include the following:

Law	What It Did
Fair Labor Standards Act (1938)	For hourly workers, provided payment of the minimum wage, required overtime pay for time worked over 40 hours in a workweek, restricted the employment of children, and required employers to keep records of wages and hours.
OSHA Act (1970)	Required employers to provide workers with workplaces free of recognized hazards that could cause serious injury or death and required employees to abide by all safety and health standards that apply to their jobs.
Americans with Disabilities Act (1991)	Banned discrimination against the disabled in public accommodations, transportation, and telecommunications.
Family and Medical Leave Act (1993)	Required covered employers to grant eligible employees up to 12 workweeks of unpaid leave during any 12-month period for the birth and care of a newborn child of the employee, placement with the employee of a son or daughter for adoption or foster care, care of an immediate family member with a serious health condition, or medical leave for the employee if unable to work because of a serious health condition.
Uniformed Services Employment and Reemployment Rights Act (1994)	Protects the job rights of individuals who voluntarily or involuntarily leave their jobs to perform military service. Also prohibits employment discrimination in such cases.
American Jobs Creation Act (2004)	Reduced taxes for manufacturing in the United States, provided temporary tax breaks for income repatriated to the United States, and encouraged domestic job growth.
Pension Protection Act (2006)	Required companies with underfunded pension plans to pay extra premiums; made it easier for companies to automatically enroll employees in defined contribution plans; provided greater access to professional advice about investing.
Lilly Ledbetter Fair Pay Act (2009)	Reinstated protection against pay discrimination; made it clear that pay discrimination claims based on sex, race, national origin, age, religion, and disability "accrue" whenever an employee receives a discriminatory paycheck as well as when a discriminatory pay decision or practice is adopted.
Patient Protection and Affordable Care Act (2010) and the Health Care and Education Reconciliation Act (2010)	Health-related provisions to expand Medicaid eligibility, subsidize insurance premiums, provide businesses with incentives to provide health care benefits, prohibit claims denied for preexisting conditions.

Investor Protection

Chapters 15, 16, and 17 describe the institutions subject to investor protection laws and some of the events that brought the Sarbanes-Oxley law into being. (See the entry in the following table for specific provisions of Sarbanes-Oxley.) Following is a summary of legislation to protect investors:

Law	What It Did
Securities Exchange Act (1934)	Created the Securities and Exchange Commission with the authority to register, regulate, and oversee brokerage firms, transfer agents, clearing agencies, and stock exchanges; the SEC also has the power to enforce securities laws and protect investors in public transactions.
Bank Secrecy Act (1970)	Deterred laundering and use of secret foreign bank accounts; created an investigative paper trail for large currency transactions; imposed civil and criminal penalties for noncompliance with reporting requirements; improved detection and investigation of criminal, tax, and regulatory violations.
Sarbanes-Oxley Act (2002)	Required top corporate executives to attest to the validity of the company's financial statements; increased the documentation and monitoring of internal controls; prohibited CPA firms from providing certain types of consulting services for their clients; established a five-member accounting oversight board.
Dodd-Frank Wall Street Reform and Consumer Protection Act (2010)	Established the Bureau of Consumer Financial Protection and the Financial Stability Oversight Council; instituted stringent new regulations for transparency and accountability, designed to protect investors. Congress recently approved the first Dodd-Frank rollback, which relaxes federal oversight of banks with assets of less than $250 billion.

Cyberspace and Telecommunications Protection

Computers and widespread use of the Internet and telecommunications have dramatically expanded the reach of businesses. They have also raised some thorny issues such as computer fraud and abuse, online privacy, cyberbullying, and cyberterrorism. Under a Supreme Court ruling, Internet file-sharing services are now held accountable if their intention is for consumers to use software to exchange songs and videos illegally. This ruling helps protect copyrights, which are covered later in this appendix.

As part of YouTube's Content ID program, copyright holders can upload works to the online video channel, and the system scans for content that might infringe on someone else's material. If a video includes even a small trace of content that may infringe, they are placed under the control of the copyright holder who has the ability to collect advertising revenue from the video if they deem it is appropriate to remain online. The copyright holders evaluate complaints of copyright infringement. On the other hand, the Digital Millennium Copyright Act (DMCA) for sites like YouTube that host third-party content makes sure that they can't be sued for anything their users do. To avoid being sued, Google simply must inform users of their infringement, take down and inform the user, and terminate the rights of those who repeatedly infringe.[15]

Following are some of the major laws enacted to regulate cyberspace and telecommunications:

Law	What It Did
Computer Fraud and Abuse Act (1986)	Clarified definitions of criminal fraud and abuse for federal computer crimes and removed legal ambiguities and obstacles to prosecuting these crimes; established felony offenses for unauthorized access of "federal interest" computers and made it a misdemeanor to engage in unauthorized trafficking in computer passwords.
Children's Online Privacy Protection Act (1998)	Authorized the FTC to set rules regarding how and when firms must obtain parental permission before asking children marketing research questions.
Identity Theft and Assumption Deterrence Act (1998)	Made it a federal crime to knowingly transfer or use, without lawful authority, a means of identification of another person with intent to commit, aid, or abet any violation of federal, state, or local law.
Anticybersquatting Consumer Protection Act (1999)	Prohibited people from registering Internet domain names similar to company or celebrity names and then offering them for sale to these same parties.
Homeland Security Act (2002)	Established the Department of Homeland Security; gave government wide new powers to collect and mine data on individuals and groups, including databases that combine personal, governmental, and corporate records including e-mails and websites viewed; limited information citizens can obtain under the Freedom of Information Act; gave government committees more latitude for meeting in secret.
Amendments to the Telemarketing Sales Rule (2003), extended by the Do-Not-Call Improvement Act of 2007 and the Do-Not-Call Fee Extension Act of 2007	Created a national do-not-call registry, which prohibits telemarketing calls to registered telephone numbers; restricted the number and duration of telemarketing calls generating dead air space with use of automatic dialers; cracked down on unauthorized billing; and required telemarketers to transmit their caller ID information. Telemarketers must check the do-not-call list quarterly, and violators could be fined for each occurrence. Excluded from the registry's restrictions are charities, opinion pollsters, and political candidates. The 2007 DNC Improvement Act allowed registered numbers to remain on the list permanently, unless consumers call to remove them themselves; the FTC will remove disconnected and reassigned numbers from the list. The Fee Extension Act of 2007 set annual fees telemarketers must pay to access the registry.
Check Clearing for the 21st Century Act (2003)	Created the substitute check, allowing banks to process check information electronically and to deliver substitute checks to banks that want to continue receiving paper checks. A substitute check is the legal equivalent of the original check.

The Core of Business Law

Contract law and the law of agency; the Uniform Commercial Code, sales law, and negotiable instruments law; property law and the law of bailment; trademark, patent, and copyright law; tort law; bankruptcy law; and tax law are the cornerstones of U.S. business law. The sections that follow set out the key provisions of each of these legal concepts.

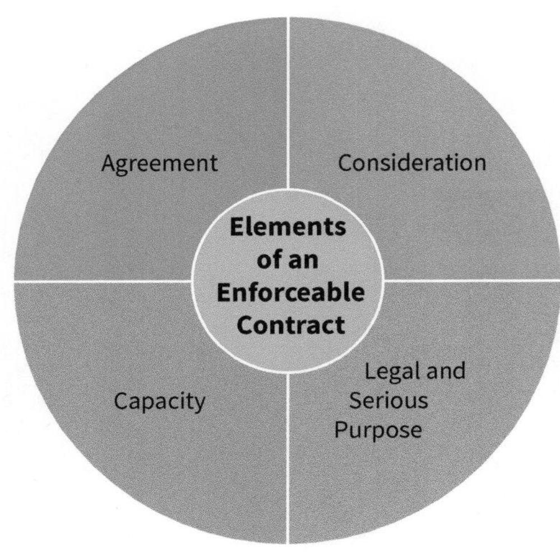

FIGURE A.1 Four Elements of an Enforceable Contract

contract legally enforceable agreement between two or more parties regarding a specified act or thing.

Contract Law and Law of Agency

Contract law is important because it is the legal foundation on which business dealings are conducted. A **contract** is a legally enforceable agreement between two or more parties regarding a specified act or thing.

Contract Requirements

As **Figure A.1** points out, the four elements of an enforceable contract are agreement, consideration, legal and serious purpose, and capacity. The parties must reach agreement about the act or thing specified. For such an agreement, or contract, to be valid and legally enforceable, each party must furnish consideration—the value or benefit that a party provides to the others with whom the contract is made. Assume that a builder hires an electrician to install wiring in a new house. The wiring job and the resulting payment are the considerations in this instance. In addition to consideration, an enforceable contract must involve a legal and serious purpose. Agreements made as a joke or involving the commission of crimes are not enforceable as legal contracts. An agreement between two competitors to fix the prices for their products is not enforceable as a contract because the subject matter is illegal.

The last element of a legally enforceable contract is capacity, the legal ability of a party to enter into agreements. The law does not permit certain people, such as those determined to lack mental capacity, to enter into legally enforceable contracts. Contracts govern almost all types of business activities. You might sign a contract to purchase a car or cell phone service, or to lease an apartment.

Breach of Contract

A violation of a valid contract is called a *breach of contract*. The injured party can go to court to enforce the contract provisions and, in some cases, collect *damages*—financial payments to compensate for a loss and related suffering.

Law of Agency

Many companies conduct business affairs through a variety of agents, such as partners, directors, corporate officers, and sales personnel. An agency relationship exists when one party, called the principal, appoints another party, called the agent, to enter into contracts with third parties on the principal's behalf.

The law of agency is based on common-law principles and case law decisions of state and federal courts. Relatively little agency law has been enacted into statute. The law of agency is important because the principal is generally bound by the actions of the agent.

The legal basis for holding the principal liable for acts of the agent is the Latin maxim *respondeat superior* ("let the master answer"). In a case involving agency law, the court must decide the rights and obligations of the various parties. Generally, the principal is held liable if an agency relationship exists and the agent has some type of authority to do the wrongful act. The agent in such cases is liable to the principal for any damages.

Uniform Commercial Code

Most U.S. business law is based on the *Uniform Commercial Code*—usually referred to simply as the UCC. The UCC covers topics such as sales law, warranties, and negotiable instruments. All 50 states have adopted the UCC, although Louisiana also relies on elements of civil law based on French, German, and Spanish codes, in addition to Roman law. While the other U.S. states rely on the tenets of English common law, which is also known as judge-based law, Louisiana's civil law system is found in most European nations. The UCC is actually a "model law" first written by the National Conference of Commissioners on Uniform State Laws, which states can then review and adopt, adopt with amendments, or replace with their own laws. The idea of the UCC is to create at least some degree of uniformity among the states.[16]

sales law law governing the sale of goods or services for money or on credit.

Sales law governs sales of goods or services for money or on credit. Article 2 of the UCC specifies the circumstances under which a buyer and a seller enter into a sales contract. Such agreements are based on the express conduct of the parties. The UCC generally requires written agreements for enforceable sales contracts for products worth more than $500. The formation of a sales contract is quite flexible because certain missing terms in a written contract or other ambiguities do not prevent the contract from being legally enforceable. A court will look to past dealings, commercial customs, and other standards of reasonableness to evaluate whether a legal contract exists.

Courts also consider these variables when either the buyer or the seller seeks to enforce his or her rights in cases in which the other party fails to perform as specified in the contract, performs only partially, or performs in a defective or unsatisfactory way. The UCC's remedies in such cases usually involve the award of monetary damages to injured parties. The UCC defines the rights of the parties to have the contract performed, to have it terminated, and to reclaim the goods or place a lien—a legal claim—against them.

Warranties Article 2 of the UCC also sets forth the law of warranties for sales transactions. Products carry two basic types of warranties: An express warranty is a specific representation made by the seller regarding the product, and an implied warranty is only legally imposed on the seller. Generally, unless implied warranties are disclaimed by the seller in writing, they are automatically in effect. Other provisions govern the rights of acceptance, rejection, and inspection of products by the buyer; the rights of the parties during manufacture, shipment, delivery, and passing of title to products; the legal significance of sales documents; and the placement of the risk of loss in the event of destruction or damage to the products during manufacture, shipment, or delivery.

Negotiable Instruments A *negotiable instrument* is commercial paper that is transferable among individuals and businesses. The most common example of a negotiable instrument is a check. Drafts, certificates of deposit (CDs), and notes are also sometimes considered negotiable instruments.

Article 3 of the UCC specifies that a negotiable instrument must be written and must meet the following conditions:

1. It must be signed by the maker or drawer.
2. It must contain an unconditional promise or order to pay a certain sum of money.
3. It must be payable on demand or at a definite time.
4. It must be payable to order or to bearer.

Checks and other forms of commercial paper are transferred when the payee signs the back of the instrument, a procedure known as endorsement.

Property Law and Law of Bailment

Property law is a key feature of the private enterprise system. *Property* is something for which a person or firm has the unrestricted right of possession or use. Property rights are guaranteed and protected by the U.S. Constitution. However, under certain circumstances property may be legally seized under the law of eminent domain. In a U.S. Supreme Court ruling, the city of New London, Connecticut, was granted permission to seize a distressed area of real estate—owned by individual citizens—for future economic development by private business. In fact, this development was never completed. In response, 44 states have since passed legislation limiting the use of eminent domain. Although an appellate court in New York ruled that the state could not seize a tract of land by eminent domain in order for Columbia University to expand its campus, the higher court of appeals overturned the ruling, paving the way for the university's $6.3 billion expansion.[17] Eminent domain procedures were recently initiated in Omaha, Nebraska, to acquire a building from a private owner in order to build a juvenile detention center on the site. The owner, who cites money as a non-issue, says the 98-year-old structure is a big part of Omaha's history—and plans to repeal.[18]

As **Figure A.2** shows, property can be divided into three basic categories. Tangible personal property consists of physical items such as equipment, supplies, and delivery vehicles.

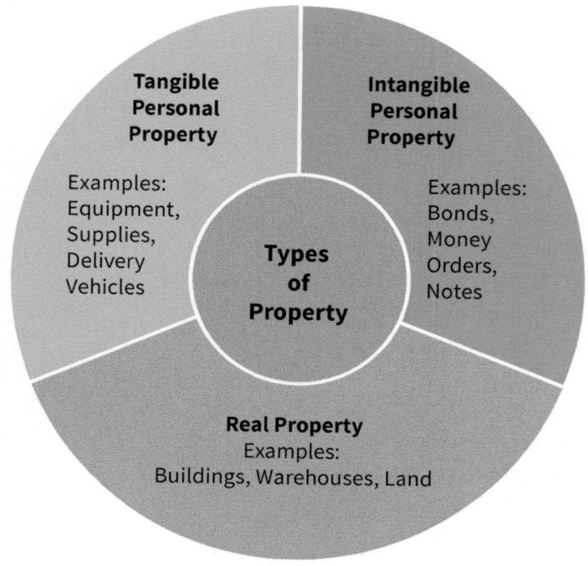

FIGURE A.2 **Three Basic Types of Property**

Intangible personal property is nonphysical property such as mortgages, stocks, and checks that are most often represented by a document or other written instrument, although it may be as vague and remote as a computer entry. You are probably familiar with certain types of intangible personal property such as checks or money orders. But other examples include bonds, notes, letters of credit, and receipts.

A third category of property is real property, or real estate. Most companies have some interaction with real estate law because of the need to buy or lease the space in which they operate. Some companies are created to serve these real estate needs. Real estate developers, builders, contractors, brokers, appraisers, mortgage companies, escrow companies, title companies, and architects all deal with various aspects of real property law.

The law of bailment deals with the surrender of personal property by one person to another when the property is to be returned at a later date. The person delivering the property is known as the bailor, and the person receiving the property is the bailee. Some bailments benefit bailees, others benefit bailors, and still others provide mutual benefits. Most courts now require that all parties practice reasonable care in all bailment situations. The degree of benefit received from the bailment is a factor in court decisions about whether parties have met the reasonable-care standards.

Bailment disputes are most likely to arise in business settings such as hotels, restaurants, banks, and parking lots. A series of rules have been established to govern settlement of these disagreements. The law focuses on actual delivery of an item. For instance, a restaurant owner is not liable if a customer's coat or purse is stolen from the back of his or her chair. This is because the customer has not given the item to the restaurant for safekeeping. However, if the customer delivers the coat or purse to the restaurant checkroom, receives a claim check, and the item is stolen, then the restaurant is liable.

Trademarks, Patents, and Copyrights

trademark words, symbols, or other designations used by firms to identify their offerings.

Trademarks, patents, and copyrights provide legal protection for key business assets by giving a firm the exclusive right to use these assets. A **trademark** consists of words, symbols, or other designations used by firms to identify their offerings. The Lanham Act (1946) provides for federal registration of trademarks. Trademarks are a valuable commercial property. Coca-Cola and McDonald's are two of the world's most widely recognized trademarks, so they are very valuable to the companies that own them.

If a product becomes too well-known, its fame can create issues. Once a trademark becomes a part of everyday usage, it loses its protection as a legal trademark. Consider the words *aspirin, cola, nylon, kerosene,* and *linoleum*. All these product names were once the exclusive property of their manufacturers, but they have passed into common language, and now anyone can use them. More recent examples are *Xerox, Kleenex,* and *Velcro*. Although legally these are trademarked names, people often use them in everyday language instead of the correct generic terms *photocopy, facial tissue, and hook-and-loop.*

Companies understand the value of their trademarks and fight hard to protect them. A small, family-run pharmaceutical company, Apollo Generics, recently defeated global drug giant GlaxoSmithKline in a trademark dispute over the name of an over-the-counter pain-relieving drug and nutritional supplement. Apollo Generics registered its brand Zanamol, which was opposed by GlaxoSmithKline on the basis that consumers would confuse the drug with one of its biggest selling pain relief brands, Panadol. The ruling was in favor of Apollo Generics, whereby the judge stated that neither pharmaceutical and healthcare professionals, nor members of the public, would be confused by the marks.[19]

patent legal protection that guarantees an inventor exclusive rights to an invention for 17 years.

By law, a **patent** guarantees an inventor exclusive rights to an invention for 17 years. Copyrights and patents have a constitutional basis; the U.S. Constitution specifies that the federal government has the power "to promote the progress of science and useful arts, by securing for limited times to authors and inventors the exclusive rights to their respective writings or discoveries." Patent process and laws have been under scrutiny, and the Patent Reform Act was introduced in 2011. Under the act, which is supported by the information technology industry, it is now more difficult for firms to sue for patent infringement. Instead of filing for a patent on a first-to-invent basis, companies will receive patents on a first-to-file basis, which is more common around the world.[20]

A **copyright** protects written or printed material such as books, designs, cartoon illustrations, photos, computer software, music, and videos. This class of business property is referred to as *intellectual property*. Copyrights are filed with the Library of Congress. Congress has extended copyright protection for creative material by an additional 20 years, covering artistic works for the lifetime of the creator plus 70 years; for companies, the time is 95 years. Not surprisingly, the Internet has opened up a whole new realm of copyright infringement, ranging from downloading music files to illegally sharing video footage.

copyright legal protection of written or printed material such as books, designs, cartoons, photos, computer software, music, and videos.

A judge recently ruled that all of the "Happy Birthday to You" song copyright claims are invalid. For many decades, Warner/Chappel had been enforcing the copyright claims on one of the songs most sung worldwide when it bought a company that was a successor to Clayton F. Summy Co., which claimed the original disputed copyright. In a reversal of decades of copyright claims, the judge recently ruled that Warner/Chappel never had the right to charge for use of the "Happy Birthday to You" song and that the original copyright filed by the Summy Co. in 1935 only pertained to the piano arrangements of the music rather than the actual song. "Happy Birthday is free after eighty years," says the attorney for a group of filmmakers producing a documentary about the history of the song.[21]

Despite publicity about Internet copyright infringement, many people engage in this practice unintentionally. Some schools are now making an effort to educate students about the practice so they can make better and more informed choices about downloading material from the Internet.

Law of Torts

A **tort** (French for "wrong") refers to a civil wrong inflicted on another person or the person's property. The law of torts is closely related to the law of agency because a business entity, or principal, can be held liable for torts committed by its agents in the course of business dealings. Tort law differs from both criminal and contract law. While criminal law is concerned with crimes against the state or society, tort law deals with compensation for injured people who are the victims of noncriminal wrongs.

tort civil wrong inflicted on one person or the person's property by another person.

Tort cases are often extremely complex and may result in large monetary awards. Because these awards have skyrocketed, some states have taken steps to limit them. Wisconsin limits the amount of any compensatory damages recovered by a plaintiff in a tort litigation dealing with injury or health problems resulting from exposure to toxins to $200,000.[22]

Types of Torts A tort may be intentional, or it may be caused by negligence. Assault, slander, libel, and fraud are all examples of intentional torts. Businesses can become involved in such cases through the actions of both owners and employees. A security guard who uses excessive force to apprehend an alleged shoplifter may have committed a tort. Under agency law, the guard's employers, such as a shopping mall or retailer, can be also held liable for any damages or injury caused by the security guard.

The other major group of torts results from negligence. This type of tort is based on carelessness rather than intentional behavior that causes injury to another person. Under agency law, businesses can also be held liable for the negligence of their employees or agents. A delivery truck driver who injures a pedestrian while transporting goods creates a tort liability for his or her employer if the accident results from negligence.

Product Liability An area of tort law known as *product liability* has been developed by both statutory and case law to hold businesses liable for negligence in the design, manufacture, sale, or use of products. Some states have extended the theory of tort law to cover injuries caused by products, regardless of whether the manufacturer is proven negligent. This legal concept is known as strict product liability.

The business response to product liability has been mixed. To avoid lawsuits and fines, some recall defective products voluntarily; others decide to fight recall mandates if they believe the recall is not justified. On the Consumer Product Safety Commission website, the following are categories of common product recalls: clothing and accessories, electronics, fuel lighters and fireworks, babies and kids, containers and packaging, sports and recreation, toys, yard and garden, personal care, and home appliances. Toy recalls are common, due mainly to the risk of a choking hazard.[23]

Class-Action Fairness

A *class-action suit* groups a number of individual plaintiffs, such as consumers with adverse reactions to medications, to allow for efficient processing under one lawsuit. Congress passed the Class-Action Fairness Act of 2005, which imposes certain restrictions on class-action lawsuits. First, it automatically moves most large, multistate class actions—those with potential damages exceeding $5 million and in which more than two-thirds of the plaintiffs are geographically dispersed—from state courts into federal courts. This restriction prevents "shopping around" for sympathetic locations but lets cases that belong within a particular state remain there. Second, judges must consider the actual monetary value of any damage done so that plaintiffs receive true compensation for injury instead of large, arbitrary awards. Third, attorneys now receive payment differently. Under the old system, attorneys would receive a percentage of the gross settlement amount, regardless of whether all plaintiffs collected. Now judges can require uncollected awards to go to charity or government agencies, instead of into the pockets of lawyers. If the attorneys' fees are not based on a percentage, then they must charge based on the time they spent on the case.

Effects of the act are already being felt. In many states, the tide has already begun to turn away from huge, long, expensive lawsuits. A Minnesota judge recently denied over 100 former National Hockey League (NHL) players class-action status against the league for "not making them aware of the dangers of head injuries while promoting a culture of violence." The judge cited difficulties in administering the state-by-state medical monitoring that players, some diagnosed with brain trauma, are seeking.[24]

Bankruptcy Law

bankruptcy legal nonpayment of financial obligations.

Bankruptcy, legal nonpayment of financial obligations, is a common occurrence in today's economic environment. Federal legislation passed in 1918 and revised several times since then provides a system for handling bankruptcies. Bankruptcy has two purposes. One is to protect creditors by providing a way to obtain compensation through debtors' assets. The second goal, which is almost unique to the United States, is to also protect debtors, allowing them to get a fresh financial start.

Federal law recognizes two types of bankruptcy. Under voluntary bankruptcy, a person or firm asks to be judged bankrupt because of inability to repay creditors. Under involuntary bankruptcy, creditors may request that a party be judged bankrupt.

Personal Bankruptcies

With a growing number of individuals amassing large personal debt—often through credit cards—Congress recently revised personal bankruptcy law to make it more difficult for people to erase their debt instead of being held accountable for it. Under the Bankruptcy Abuse Prevention and Consumer Protection Act of 2005, it is more difficult for individuals to file Chapter 7 bankruptcy, which traditionally has wiped out most debt. If their earnings exceed their state's median income, they will instead be required to file Chapter 13 bankruptcy, which sets up a repayment plan as designed by the court. A few years after the law's passage, personal bankruptcies still hovered at the high mark, likely because of a slow economy. Reports revealed that more homeowners were walking away from large mortgages that they were unable to pay instead of reorganizing their debt and trying to hang onto their homes. As the economy rebounds, the rate of personal bankruptcies has declined. Driven mainly by stable unemployment levels, increased consumer confidence, and continued housing market growth, personal bankruptcy filings recently fell for the eighth consecutive year, declining approximately 6% to 8%. Many personal bankruptcies are related to outstanding medical conditions, injuries, or illnesses where medical expenses not covered by insurance or losing weeks of work can cause financial hardship.[25]

Business Bankruptcies

Businesses can also go bankrupt for a variety of reasons—mismanagement, plunging sales, an inability to keep up with competitors, or changes in the marketplace. Under Chapter 11 of the U.S. Bankruptcy Code, a firm may reorganize and develop a plan to repay its debts. Chapter 11 also permits prepackaged bankruptcies, in which companies enter bankruptcy proceedings after obtaining approval of most—but not necessarily all—of their creditors. Often companies can emerge from prepackaged bankruptcies sooner than those that opt for conventional Chapter 11 filings. Airlines have managed to accomplish this, as well as some large retailers. For example, automobile giant General Motors emerged from Chapter 11 bankruptcy, the fourth-largest bankruptcy reorganization in the history of the United States.[26]

Tax Law

A branch of law that affects every business, employee, and consumer in the United States is tax law. A **tax** is an assessment by a governmental unit. Federal, state, and local governments and special taxing authorities all levy taxes. Appendix C, "Personal Financial Planning," also covers tax law.

tax assessment by a governmental unit.

Some taxes are paid by individuals and some by businesses. Both have a decided impact on contemporary business. Business taxes reduce profits, and personal taxes cut the disposable incomes that individuals can spend on the products of industry. Governments spend the revenue from taxes to buy goods and services produced by businesses. Governments also act as transfer agents, moving tax revenue to other consumers and transferring Social Security taxes from the working population to retired or disabled people.

Governments can levy taxes on several different bases: income, sales, business receipts, property, and assets. The type of tax varies from one taxing authority to the other. The individual income tax is the biggest source of revenue for the federal government. Many states also rely heavily on income taxes as well as sales taxes, which vary widely. Cities and towns may collect property taxes in order to operate schools and improve roads. So-called luxury taxes are levied on items such as yachts and expensive sports cars, while so-called sin taxes are levied on items such as cigarettes and alcohol. In addition, the issue of whether to tax different types of Internet services and use has been hotly debated.

Business Terms You Need to Know

Projects and Teamwork Applications

1. In light of the pervasiveness of technology in everyday life, why not consider resolving a dispute online using a technology platform like Modria? Cyber-mediation or online dispute resolution (ODR) is gaining traction as a low-cost and efficient way to mediate and resolve disputes. With increasing online purchases, transactions, and exchanges of many kinds, the number of disputes is on the rise. Settling such disputes can be time consuming and costly. Explore www.modria.com and discuss how ODR works and the specifics of how users and e-commerce benefit. What are its drawbacks?

2. Ever wonder about what life as a consumer was like before the creation of the Federal Trade Commission (FTC) in 1914? The FTC has the power to define unfair competition and to issue cease and desist orders so that companies halt unfair business practices. Go to the FTC website at www.ftc.gov and explore the "Tips & Advice" link and then "for consumers," to gain additional insight as to how consumers are protected. Present your findings in class. What did you find particularly useful?

3. The business world is filled with tort cases, particularly those involving product liability. One of the most famous cases is probably the one in which a customer sued McDonald's because a cup of hot McDonald's coffee spilled in her lap, causing burns and scalding. A jury awarded her $2.7 million in punitive damages, an amount that was later reduced by a judge to less than $500,000. On your own or with a classmate, go online to research other famous product liability cases. Choose a case and learn as much as you can about it, including the effect the outcome had on the firm or firms involved. Present your findings in class.

4. Go online and research more about the Bankruptcy Abuse Prevention and Consumer Protection Act of 2005, and the implications it has in today's economy. Do you think the law is fair? Why or why not? How does filing for personal bankruptcy affect a person's standing in the marketplace? Present your thoughts to the class.

Appendix B

Insurance and Risk Management

The Connected Car and the Insurance Industry

Connected car trends will create monumental changes in the automobile insurance industry. One of the biggest innovations in automobile history, connected cars will park themselves, help drivers avoid traffic, and automatically find the closest gas station. The connected car is designed to improve risk factors and accidents while offering drivers a more connected digital lifestyle and a safer, smarter driving experience.

For insurance companies, leveraging the enormous volume of data (big data analytics, discussed in Chapter 14) that comes from connected cars will be a challenge. A typical connected car offers telematics, which provides insurers with information about how and where a driver drives. This data can be used to monitor and gain valuable customer insights, patterns, and driving trends to help with product innovation and better insurance solutions.

If connected cars do serve their purpose to decrease accidents and reduce driving risks, claims will also be reduced, which may result in greater profits for insurance companies. On the other hand, if driverless cars do become the norm, even in the event of an accident, replacing costly sensors, radars, and cameras may impact premiums and profits in ways difficult to predict.

Insurance companies must plan now to invest in the resources needed to navigate the evolving landscape of an industry driven by data. If they don't, there will be third-party competitors able to better understand big data and analytics, and to potentially produce pricing models and products that more aptly suit the needs of connected and driverless car owners. BMW, for example, has discussed the option to not share the data of their drivers and instead to bundle their own automobile insurance policies with their vehicles.

Connected cars are causing insurance companies to rethink traditional policies, claims processing, and overall business models. In addition, with the continued growth of car-sharing services like Lyft and Uber, car ownership is being challenged, and those who do own cars may begin to demand pay-as-you-drive automobile insurance rates. Insurers have reason to be concerned about the prospect of fewer automobile owners and lower overall premiums. In addition, if accidents are reduced when human error is removed from the driving equation, claims also drop—leading to lower premiums.

A pattern is evolving in the insurance industry. Technology-led companies called "InsurTechs" are entering the sector and taking advantage of new technologies to provide more personalized coverage to a more digitally savvy customer base. The road is clear for insurers who embrace the upcoming change and those who utilize speed to embrace a smart and connected automobile industry.[1]

Overview

Risk is a daily fact of life for both individuals and businesses. Sometimes it presents itself in the form of a serious illness or injury. In other instances, it takes the form of property loss, such as the extensive damage to homes and businesses due to the tornadoes that have swept across midwestern and southern states. Risk can also occur as the result of the actions of others—such as a driver who is texting while driving and runs a stop sign. In still other cases, risk may occur as a result of our own actions—we might venture out in a boat during a thunderstorm or fail to heed warnings about high blood pressure.

Businesspeople must understand the types of risk they face and develop methods for dealing with them. One approach to risk is to shift it to the specialized expertise of insurance companies. This appendix discusses the concept of insurance in a business setting. It begins with a definition of risk. We then describe the various ways in which risk can be managed. Next, we list some of the major insurance concepts, such as what constitutes an insurable risk. The appendix concludes with an overview of the major types of insurance.

The Concept of Risk

risk uncertainty about loss or injury.

Risk is uncertainty about loss or injury. Consider the risks faced by a typical business. A factory or warehouse faces the risk of fire and smoke, burglary, and storm damage. Data loss, injuries to workers, and loss of facilities are some of the risks faced by businesses. Risks can be divided into two major categories: speculative risk and pure risk.

Speculative risk gives the firm or individual the chance of either a profit or a loss. A firm that expands operations into a new market may experience higher profits or the loss of invested funds. A contractor who builds a house without a specific buyer may sell the house at a profit or lose money if the house sits unsold for months.

Pure risk, on the other hand, involves only the chance of loss. Motorists, for example, always face the risk of accidents. If they occur, both financial and physical losses may result. If they do not occur, however, drivers do not profit. Insurance often helps individuals and businesses protect against financial loss resulting from some types of pure risk.

Risk Management

risk management calculations and actions a firm takes to recognize and deal with real or potential risks to its survival.

Because risk is an unavoidable part of business, managers must find ways to deal with it. The first step in any **risk management** plan is to recognize what's at risk and why it's at risk. After that, the manager must decide how to handle the risk. In general, businesses have four alternatives in handling risk: avoid it, minimize it, assume it, or transfer it.

Executives must consider many factors when evaluating risks, both at home and abroad. These factors include a nation's economic stability; social and cultural factors, such as language; available technologies; distribution systems; and government regulations. International businesses are typically exposed to less risk in countries with stable economic, social and cultural, and political and legal environments.

© Clint Spencer/iStockphoto

Businesses can reduce some of the pure risks they encounter. For example, a company could locate a new production facility away from areas that are prone to tornadoes.

Avoiding Risk

Some of the pure risks facing people can be avoided by leading a healthy lifestyle. Not smoking and maintaining a good diet and exercise are ways of avoiding health risks. By the same token, businesses can also avoid some of the pure risks they face. A manufacturer can implement safety programs and locate a new production facility away from an area that is prone to floods tornadoes, hurricanes, or earthquakes.

Reducing Risk

Managers can reduce or even eliminate many types of risk by removing hazards or taking preventive measures. Many companies develop safety programs to educate employees about potential hazards and the proper methods of performing certain dangerous tasks. Any employee who works at a hazardous waste site is required to have training and medical monitoring that meet the federal Occupational Safety and Health Administration (OSHA) standards. The training and monitoring not only reduce risk but pay off on the bottom line. Aside from the human tragedy, accidents cost companies time and money.

Although many preventative measures can reduce the risk involved in business operations, they cannot eliminate risk entirely. Most major insurers help their clients avoid or minimize risk by offering the services of loss-prevention experts to conduct thorough reviews of their operations. These health and safety professionals evaluate customers' work environments and recommend procedures and equipment to help firms minimize worker injuries and property losses.

By the same token, people can take actions to reduce risk. For instance, obeying the rules of the road and doing regular maintenance on a car can reduce the risks associated with driving. Boarding up windows in preparation for a hurricane can reduce the risk of wind damage. However, such actions cannot entirely eliminate risk.

Self-Insuring Against Risk

Instead of purchasing insurance against certain types of pure risk, some companies accumulate funds to cover potential losses. These self-insurance funds are special funds created by periodically setting aside cash reserves that the firm can draw on in the event of a financial loss resulting from a pure risk. A firm makes regular payments to the fund, and it charges losses to the fund. Such a fund typically accompanies a risk-reduction program aimed at minimizing losses.

One of the most common forms of self-insurance is employee health insurance. Most employers provide health insurance coverage to employees as a component of their benefit programs. Some, especially larger ones, find it more economical to create a self-insurance fund covering projected employee health care expenses, as opposed to purchasing a health insurance policy from a health insurance company. Self-insured employers, however, almost always contract with a health insurer to administer their employee health plans.

Shifting Risk to an Insurance Company

Although organizations and individuals can take steps to avoid or reduce risk, the most common method of dealing with it is to shift it to others in the form of **insurance**—a contract by which an insurer, for a fee, agrees to reimburse another firm or individual a sum of money if a loss occurs. The insured party's fee to the insurance company for coverage against losses is called a *premium*. Insurance substitutes a small, known loss—the insurance premium—for a larger, unknown loss that may or may not occur. In the case of life insurance, the loss—death—is a certainty; the main uncertainty is the date when it will occur.

insurance contract by which the insurer, for a fee, agrees to reimburse the insured a sum of money if a loss occurs.

It is important for the insurer to understand the customer's business, risk exposure, and insurance needs. Firms that operate worldwide usually do business with insurance companies that maintain global networks of offices.

Basic Insurance Concepts

Figure B.1 illustrates how an insurance company operates. The insurer collects premiums from policyholders in exchange for insurance coverage. The insurance company uses some of these funds to pay current

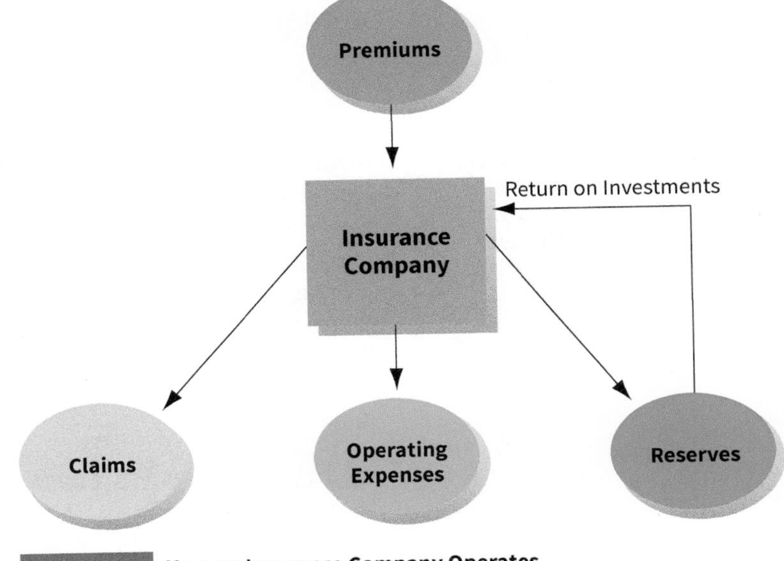

FIGURE B.1 **How an Insurance Company Operates**

claims and operating expenses. What's left over is held in the form of reserves, which in turn are invested. Reserves can be used to pay for unexpected losses. The returns from insurance company reserves may allow the insurer to reduce premiums, generate profits, or both. By investing reserves, the insurance industry represents a major source of long-term financing for other businesses, as discussed in Chapter 16.

An insurance company is a professional risk taker. For a fee, it accepts risks of loss or damage to businesses and individuals. Four basic principles underlie insurance: the concept of insurable interest, the concept of insurable risk, the rule of indemnity, and the law of large numbers.

Insurable Interest

To purchase insurance, an applicant must demonstrate an *insurable interest* in the property or life of the insured. In other words, the policyholder must stand to suffer a loss, financial or otherwise, due to fire, storm damage, accident, theft, illness, death, or lawsuit. A homeowner has an insurable interest in his or her home and its contents. In the case of life insurance coverage purchased for the main income provider in a household, the policyholder's spouse and children have a clear insurable interest.

A company can purchase property and liability insurance on physical assets—such as an office or warehouse—to cover losses due to such hazards as fire and theft because the company can demonstrate an obvious insurable interest. Because top executives are important assets to a company, a business often purchases key-person life insurance, which compensates the business should an important individual die.

Insurable Risk

Insurable risk refers to the requirements that a risk must meet in order for the insurer to provide protection. Only some pure risks, and no speculative ones, are insurable. There are four basic requirements for a pure risk to be considered an insurable risk:

1. The likelihood of loss should be reasonably predictable. If an insurance company cannot reasonably predict losses, it has no basis for setting affordable premiums.
2. The loss should be financially measurable.
3. The loss should be accidental, or unexpected.
4. The risk should be spread over a certain geographic area.

The insurance company has the right to set standards for accepting risk. This process of setting these standards, and deciding what to charge, is known as *underwriting*.

Rule of Indemnity

rule of indemnity requirement that the insured cannot collect more than the amount of the loss and cannot collect for the same loss more than once.

The **rule of indemnity** states that the insured cannot collect more than the amount of the loss. Nor can the insured collect for that loss more than once. Assume that a florist's delivery van is damaged in an accident. If the total damage amounts to $2,500, then that is the maximum amount the business can collect from the insurance company.

Occasionally a loss may be covered by more than one policy. For instance, assume that a $5,000 loss is covered by two different policies. The rule of indemnity means that the insured individual or business can only collect a total of $5,000 from both insurance companies. It is up to the insurers to decide which pays how much based on policy specifics.

The Law of Large Numbers

Insurance is based on the law of averages, or statistical probability. Insurance companies simply cannot afford to sell insurance policies unless they can reasonably predict losses. As a result, insurance companies have studied the chances of occurrences of deaths, injuries, property damage, lawsuits, and other types of hazards. From their investigations, insurance companies have developed *actuarial tables*, which predict the number of fires, automobile accidents, or deaths that will occur in a given year. Premiums charged for insurance coverage are based on these tables. Actuarial tables are based on the law of large numbers. In essence, the **law of large numbers** states that seemingly random events will follow a predictable pattern if enough events are observed. An actuary is a professional who uses math, statistics, and financial theory to study the impact of risk and uncertainty, primarily related to insurance and pension programs.

law of large numbers concept that seemingly random events will follow predictable patterns if enough events are observed.

An example can demonstrate how insurers use the law of large numbers to calculate premiums. Previously collected statistical data on a city with 50,000 homes indicates that the city will experience an average of 500 fires a year, with damages averaging $30,000 per occurrence. What is the minimum annual premium an insurance company would charge to insure one residence?

To simplify the calculations, assume that the premiums would not produce profits or cover any of the insurance company's operating expenses—they would just produce enough income to pay policyholders for their losses. In total, fires in the city would generate claims of $15 million (500 homes damaged × $30,000). If these losses were spread over all 50,000 homes, each home-owner would be charged an annual premium of $300 ($15 million × 50,000 homes). In reality, though, the insurer would set the premium at a higher figure to cover operating expenses, build reserves, and earn a reasonable profit. About one in 40 insured homes have a property damage claim each year related to wind and hail, and about one in 50 insured homes has a property damage claim caused by water damage or freezing each year. Theft property damage claims average about one in 250 insured homes each year. The least common claim, about one in 750 homes, is related to liability and the cost of lawsuits for bodily injury or property damage that the policyholder or family members cause to others. Changes in the percentage of each type of homeowners' loss from year to year are partially influenced by large fluctuations in the frequency and severity of weather-related events such as hurricanes and winter storms.[2]

Some losses are easier for insurance companies to predict than others. Life insurance companies can predict with high accuracy the number of policyholders who will die within a specified period of time. Life insurance companies classify applicants according to their risk of death, which is estimated from the history of disease and the presence of any risk factors. Mortality tables and algorithms for assessment of risk are based primarily on medical literature. Proposals to include genetic information, which would enhance risk assessment and underwriting, are currently being debated. To date, the Genetic Information Nondiscrimination Act passed in 2008 keeps health insurance companies and employers from discriminating on the basis of information that might be found in a genetic screening.[3]

Sources of Insurance Coverage

The insurance industry includes both for-profit companies—such as Prudential, State Farm, and Liberty Mutual—and a number of public agencies that provide insurance coverage for business firms, not-for-profit organizations, and individuals. In addition, there is a new breed of insurance companies, ripe for innovation and disruption. Part of the InsurTech industry, these companies are using technology innovations to create savings and efficiency from the current insurance industry model.

Public Insurance Agencies

A *public insurance agency* is a state or federal government unit established to provide specialized insurance protection for individuals and organizations. It provides protection in such areas as job loss (unemployment insurance) and work-related injuries (workers' compensation). Public insurance agencies also sponsor specialized programs, such as deposit, flood, and crop insurance.

Unemployment Insurance Every state in the United States has an unemployment insurance program that assists unemployed workers by providing financial benefits, job counseling, and placement services. Compensation amounts vary depending on workers' previous earnings and the states in which they file claims. These insurance programs are funded by payroll taxes paid by employers.

Workers' Compensation Under state laws, employers must provide workers' compensation insurance to guarantee payment of wages and salaries, medical care costs, and such rehabilitation services as retraining, job placement, and vocational rehabilitation to employees who are injured on the job. In addition, workers' compensation provides benefits in the form of weekly payments or single, lump-sum payments to survivors of workers whose work-related injuries result in death. Premiums are based on the company's payroll, the on-the-job hazards to which it exposes workers, and its safety record.

Social Security The federal government is the nation's largest insurer. The Social Security program, established in 1935, provides retirement, survivor, and disability benefits to millions of Americans. *Medicare* was added to the Social Security program in 1965 to provide health insurance for people age 65 and older and certain other Social Security recipients. More than 9 out of 10 workers in the United States and their dependents are eligible for Social Security program benefits. The program is funded through a payroll tax, half of which is paid by employers and half by workers. Self-employed people pay the full tax.

Private Insurance Companies

Much of the insurance in effect is provided by private firms. These companies provide protection in exchange for the payment of premiums. Some private insurers are stockholder owned, and therefore they are run like any other business; others are so-called mutual associations. Most, though not all, mutual insurance companies specialize in life insurance. Technically, mutual insurance companies are owned by their policyholders, who may receive premium rebates in the form of dividends. In spite of this, however, there is no evidence that an insurance policy from a mutual company costs any less than a comparable policy from a stockholder-owned insurer. In recent years some mutual insurance companies have reorganized as stockholder-owned companies, including Prudential, one of the nation's largest insurers.

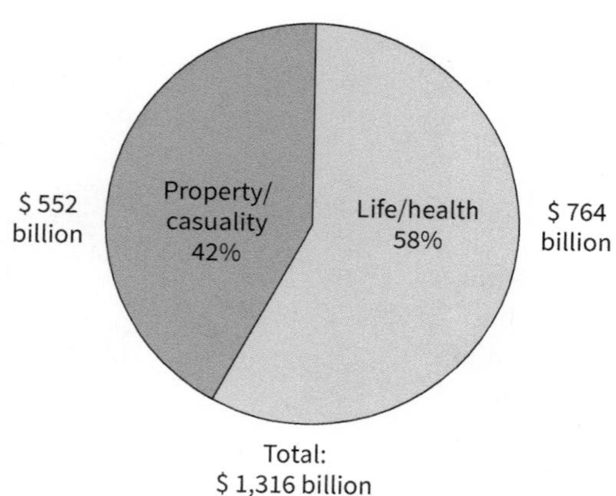

Note: Property/casualty is defined as net premiums written, excluding state funds. Life/health includes premiums, annuity considerations (fees for annuity contracts), and deposit-type funds.

Source: Insurance Information Institute, "Insurance Industry at a Glance," http://www.iii.org, accessed July 18, 2018.

FIGURE B.2 U.S. Property/Casualty and Life/Health Insurance Premiums

InsurTech Companies

A portmanteau of "insurance" and "technology," InsurTech was inspired by the term finTech (see Chapter 16). Exploring avenues that large insurance companies have less incentive to exploit, InsurTech offers ultra-customized policies such as social insurance. New streams of data are being used from Internet-enabled devices to dynamically price premiums according to observed behavior. To find the right mix of policies for an individual, InsurTech startups are using artificial intelligence (AI) to handle tasks previously handled by brokers. Apps are also being used to pull disparate policies into a single platform for management and monitoring, creating on-demand insurance for micro-events such as borrowing a friend's car, and the adoption of a peer-to-peer model to both create customized group coverage and incentivize positive choices through group rebates.

Types of Insurance

Individuals and businesses spend hundreds of billions of dollars each year on insurance coverage. **Figure B.2** shows how much insurance companies collected in premiums in a recent year. Unfortunately, both business firms and consumers make poor decisions when buying insurance. Here are four tips to remember when buying insurance:

1. Insure against large losses, not small ones. It is generally much more cost effective to self-insure against small losses.
2. Buy insurance with broad coverage, not narrow coverage. For example, it is much less expensive generally to buy a homeowners' policy that protects you from multiple events (perils such as fire and theft) than to buy several policies that cover individual events.
3. Shop around. Premiums for similar policies can vary widely from company to company.
4. Buy insurance only from financially strong companies. Insurance companies occasionally go bankrupt. If that happens, the insured is left with no coverage and little hope of getting premiums back.

Although insurers offer hundreds of different policies, they all fall into three broad categories: property and liability insurance, health and disability insurance, and life insurance.

Property and Liability Insurance

Insurance that protects against fire, accident, theft, or other destructive events or perils, is called **property and liability insurance**. Examples of this insurance category include homeowners' insurance, auto insurance, business or commercial insurance, and liability insurance. Most property and liability policies are subject to deductibles. A deductible is the amount of the loss the insured pays out of pocket.

property and liability insurance general category of insurance that protects against losses due to a number of perils.

Homeowners' Insurance Homeowners' insurance protects homeowners from damage to their residences due to various perils. If a home is destroyed by fire, for example, the homeowners' policy will pay to replace the home and its contents. Virtually all homeowners carry coverage of this nature.

Homeowners' insurance premiums have risen sharply in recent years. Moreover, homeowners in coastal areas are finding it increasingly difficult to obtain insurance because of the rising number of claims related to erosion, hurricanes, and floods. If homeowners can obtain private coverage, those plans may be very expensive. In some cases they may be able to purchase insurance through a state-run program instead. States with the most costly homeowners insurance include Florida, Texas, Louisiana, Oklahoma, and Mississippi.[4]

Although standard policies cover a wide range of perils, most do not cover damage from widespread catastrophes such as floods and earthquakes. Homeowners must purchase separate policies to protect against damage caused by these perils. Flood insurance is available through the National Flood Insurance Program. Earthquake coverage is offered in several earthquake-prone states such as California and Washington but is very expensive.

Auto Insurance Automobile insurance is the country's largest category of property and liability insurance. Automobile insurance policies cover losses due to automobile accidents or theft, including personal and property claims. Almost all states require drivers to have a minimum amount of auto insurance coverage. The average cost of automobile insurance premiums in a recent year amounted to a little over $900 annually.[5]

Commercial and Business Insurance Commercial and business insurance protects firms from financial losses resulting from the suspension of business operations (*business interruption insurance*) or physical damage to property as a result of destructive events. These policies may also protect employers from employee dishonesty or losses resulting from nonperformance of contracts.

Liability Insurance *Liability insurance* protects an individual or business against financial losses to others for which the individual or business was responsible. If a business sells a defective product, the firm's liability insurance would pay for financial losses sustained by customers. A standard amount of liability coverage is usually attached to auto, homeowners', and commercial insurance policies. Additional amounts of liability insurance can be purchased if needed. Adequate liability insurance is critically important today for both businesses and individuals. Walmart, for example, requires its suppliers to have at least $2 million in liability coverage for their products; some products considered to be high risk, such as chain saws, tires, and barbecues, can require a minimum of $10 million.[6]

Health and Disability Insurance

health insurance category of insurance that pays for losses due to illness or injury.

Each of us faces the risk of getting sick or being injured in some way. Even a relatively minor illness can result in substantial health care bills. To guard against this risk, most Americans have some form of **health insurance**—insurance that provides coverage for expenses due to sickness or accidents. With soaring costs in health care, this type of insurance has become an important consideration for both businesses and individuals.

Sources of health insurance include private individual policies, private group policies, and the federal government, through Medicare and Medicaid (health insurance for lower-income people). More than 60% of Americans are covered by private group health insurance provided by their employer as an employee benefit. Four of every five U.S. employees work for businesses and not-for-profits that offer some form of group health insurance. Group policies resemble individual health insurance policies but are offered at lower premiums. Health insurance costs have soared in recent years, and employers have responded by cutting back on benefits, requiring employees to pay more of the premium, charging higher deductibles, or even dropping coverage altogether. In response to the growing cost and increasing numbers of individuals without adequate coverage, Congress passed a pair of health care reform bills entitled the Patient Protection and Affordable Care Act and the Health Care and Education Reconciliation Act. Although the bills were the subject of heated debate among legislators, businesspeople, and consumers, they were signed into law. More recently, Congress repealed the mandate with the Tax Cuts and Jobs Act.[7]

Private health insurance plans fall into one of two general categories: fee-for-service plans and managed care plans. In a *fee-for-service plan*, the insured picks his or her doctor and has almost unlimited access to specialists. Fee-for-service plans charge an annual deductible and copayments. By contrast, a *managed care plan* pays most of the insured's health care bills. In return, the program has a great deal of say over the conditions of health care provided for the insured. Most managed care plans, for example, restrict the use of specialists and may specify which hospitals and pharmacies can be used. Some employers offer employees a choice between a fee-for-service and a managed care plan. Multiple managed care plans are sometimes available.

Managed care plans have become extremely popular in recent years. More than 160 million Americans are enrolled in some form of managed care plan, and many fee-for-service plans have adopted some elements of managed care. A primary reason for the popularity of managed care is simply cost: Managed care plans generally cost employers and employees less than fee-for-service plans. Managed care, however, is not without its critics. The effort to control costs has caused a backlash because of restrictions placed on doctors and patients. Legislation at both the federal and state levels has forced managed care plans to give patients and physicians more control over medical decisions.

Types of Managed Care Plans Two types of managed care plans can be found in the United States: health maintenance organizations and preferred provider organizations. Although both manage health care, important differences exist between the two.

Health maintenance organizations (HMOs) do not provide health insurance; they provide health care. An HMO supplies all of the individual's health care needs, including prescription drugs and hospitalization. The individual must use the HMO's own doctors and approved treatment facilities in order to receive benefits. Doctors and other health care professionals are actually employees of the HMO. Individuals pick a primary care physician and cannot see a specialist without a referral. An HMO charges no deductibles and only a fixed-dollar copayment for some services.

The second type of managed care plan is the preferred provider organization (PPO). In the United States, more individuals are covered by PPOs than by HMOs. In a PPO, an employer negotiates a contract between local health care providers (physicians, hospitals, and pharmacies) to provide medical care to its employees at a discount. These plans have fixed-dollar copayments. They are generally much more flexible than HMOs. Members can choose their primary care physician from a list of doctors. If a referral is given or hospitalization is required, the member again chooses from a list of approved health care providers. A member who obtains treatment from a health care provider outside the PPO network may be reimbursed at a lower rate. In a recent year, UnitedHealth Group was the largest health insurance provider in the United States, with annual sales of more than $201 billion.[8]

Disability Income Insurance Not only is *disability income insurance* one of the most overlooked forms of insurance, but many workers also don't have enough coverage. The odds that a person will develop a disability are considerably higher than most people realize. Take a group of five randomly selected 45-year-olds. There is approximately a 95% chance that one of the five will develop some form of disability during the next 20 years. Disability income insurance is designed to replace lost income when a wage earner cannot work due to an accident or illness.

Two sources of disability income insurance exist: Social Security and private disability insurance policies. Social Security disability benefits are available to virtually all workers, but they have very strict requirements. Private disability insurance is available on either an individual or group basis. As with health insurance, a group policy is less expensive than an individual policy. Many employers provide at least some disability coverage as an employee benefit. Employees often have the option of obtaining additional coverage by paying more.

Life Insurance

Life insurance protects people against the financial losses that occur with premature death. Three of every four Americans have some form of life insurance. The main reason people buy life insurance is to provide financial security for their families in the event of their death. With assets totaling $6.8 trillion, the life insurance industry is one of the nation's largest businesses.[9]

life insurance protects people against the financial losses that occur with premature death.

Types of Life Insurance As with health and disability insurance, both individual and group life insurance policies are available. Many employers offer life insurance to employees as a component of the firm's benefit program. However, unlike health and disability insurance, an individual life insurance policy is usually cheaper than a group policy for younger people.

The different types of life insurance fall neatly into two categories: term policies and cash value policies. Term policies provide a death benefit if the policyholder dies within a specified period of time. It has no value at the end of that period. Cash value policies—sometimes called whole life and universal life—combine life insurance protection with a savings or investment feature. The cash value represents the amount of the savings or investment portion of the policy. Although there are arguments in favor of cash value policies, many experts believe that term life insurance is a better choice for most consumers. For one thing, a term policy is less expensive than a cash value policy.

Do you need life insurance? The general rule is that a person should have life insurance if he or she has family members who depend financially on that individual. For example, a young parent could easily need $500,000 or more of life insurance. A single person with no dependents may see little or no need for life insurance coverage.

How Much Life Insurance Should You Have? People can purchase life insurance policies for almost any amount. Life insurance purchases are limited only by the amount of premiums people can afford and their ability to meet medical qualifications. The amount of life insurance a person needs, however, is a very personal decision. The general rule of thumb is that a person needs life insurance if he or she has family members who financially depend on that individual. A young parent with three small children could easily need $500,000 or more of life insurance. A single person with no dependents would reasonably see little or no need for a life insurance policy.

Businesses, as well as individual consumers, buy life insurance. The death of a partner or a key executive is likely to result in a financial loss to an organization. Key person insurance reimburses the organization for the loss of the services of an essential senior executive and covers the executive search expenses needed to find a replacement. In addition, life insurance policies may be purchased for each member of a partnership to be able to repay the deceased partner's survivors for his or her share of the firm and permit the business to continue.

Business Terms You Need to Know

Projects and Teamwork Applications

1. Choose one of the following companies, or select another one that interests you. Research the company online, learning what you can about the firm's goods and services, work processes, and facilities. Then create a chart identifying risks you believe the company faces—and ways the firm can avoid those risks or reduce the risks. Suggested firms:
   a. Carnival Cruises
   b. Los Angeles Dodgers
   c. Whole Food Markets
   d. The Hershey Company

2. Assess your own personal insurance needs. What types of coverage, if any, do you currently have? How do you see your insurance needs changing in the next 5 to 10 years? Go to www.lifehappens.org to assess your insurance needs by using some of the online calculators.

3. Sometimes an insured consumer, knowing that risk is transferred to the insurer, has a tendency to act carelessly or with a false sense of security. This behavior is sometimes termed a "moral hazard." Research how companies deal with the obligation to provide coverage when the insured consumer behaves in such a way as to increase the company's risk or liability. What impact does this phenomenon have on the insurance company?

4. Insurance fraud is pervasive and occurs when an insured individual receives money from an insurance company through deception over an insurance matter. Go to the website for the Coalition Against Insurance Fraud at www.insurancefraud.org. Click on "Info," and research common forms of insurance fraud. Discuss your findings with the class.

Personal Financial Planning

Personal Savings Strategies for Millennials

Do you know how to have $90,000 in the bank in just 30 years? By saving only $250 a month, beginning now. That's about what most workers today spend on coffee and lunch each month.

Unfortunately, saving isn't as easy as it sounds. Burdened with student loan and credit-card debt, many young people view saving for retirement as a job for someone else, despite their declining faith in Social Security. And in the wake of the recent economic slowdown, many U.S. consumers are focusing on paying down personal debt rather than on saving for the long term.

At the same time, however, many financial advisors believe younger workers need to save for retirement even more carefully than earlier generations, because they'll need much more money in reserve than today's retirees to see them through their later years. Most advisors agree that because nothing is certain, including the future of the Social Security system, today's younger workers should be aiming to set aside between $2 and $3 million for themselves and their families for retirement. Financial advisors often recommend an 80% income replacement rate as a common benchmark. If an investor makes $100,000 annually, a portfolio that generates $80,000 in income each year plus adjustments for inflation should be a target. Other financial advisors recommend having enough for 25 years of expenses in retirement.

That's a daunting number for most people when viewed as a lump sum. The only way to approach it realistically is to save as much as possible on a regular basis, beginning as early as you can. For example, back to that $250 a month: some advisors suggest simple strategies such as eating breakfast at home and packing a lunch, including a container of home-brewed coffee, instead of stopping at Starbucks on the way to work.

Other advice includes acknowledging that you'll have competing financial priorities, and that their relative importance will change as you get older. Also try thinking of your financial health as being just as important as your physical health. You exercise, so why not save too? If you find it easier to stick with an exercise program when you have a buddy, include your spouse or a friend in your savings plan. A little reinforcement can go a long way.

Finally, even if you start small, be sure you start. As one financial advisor says, "It's the pennies that add up."[1]

Overview

You are studying business, but much of what you learn in this course can also be applied to your personal life. For example, you learn about each of the important functions of a business—from accounting to marketing, from finance to management. Learning about each business function will help you choose a career, and a career choice may be one of the most important personal financial decisions you will make. You will learn why firms prepare budgets and financial statements. But budgets and financial statements are also important tools for individuals and households.

Everyone, regardless of age or income, can probably do a more effective job of managing finances. As a group, Americans are much better at making money than they are at

personal financial management study of the economic factors and personal decisions that affect a person's financial well-being.

managing money. This appendix introduces you to personal financial management. **Personal financial management** deals with a variety of issues and decisions that affect a person's financial well-being. It includes basic money management, credit, tax planning, major consumer purchases, insurance, investing, and retirement planning.

The appendix will draw from many of the topics you will learn while studying business, but it introduces you to some new concepts as well. It is hoped that after completing the appendix, you will be a better-informed financial consumer and personal money manager and that you will be motivated to learn more about personal finance. The rewards, in both monetary and nonmonetary terms, can be tremendous.

The Meaning and Importance of Personal Finance

Personal finance affects, and is affected by, many things we do and many decisions we make throughout our lives. Having a plan will make a significant difference.

On one level, personal finance involves money know-how. It is essential to know how to earn money as well as how to save, spend, invest, and control it in order to achieve goals. The reward of sound money management is an improvement in a person's standard of living. **Standard of living** consists of the necessities, comforts, or luxuries a person seeks to attain or maintain.

standard of living necessities, comforts, and luxuries one seeks to obtain or to maintain.

On another level, personal finance directly impacts each person's lifestyle—the way we live our daily lives. Our choice of careers, friends, hobbies, communities, and possessions is determined by personal finances, and yet our personal finances can also be determined by our lifestyles. If you're a college student living on a shoestring budget, you may have to make serious financial sacrifices to achieve your educational goals. Where you live is determined by the school you attend and how much you can afford to pay for room and board; your vacation is set by your academic schedule and your savings account; your clothing depends on the climate and your budget. All these lifestyle decisions are largely determined by your personal finances.

© Ryan McVay/Photodisc/Getty Images

If you're on a budget, skiing at expensive resorts won't leave much money in your savings account.

The Importance of Personal Finance Today

Good money management has always been important, but ongoing changes in the economic environment have made personal finance even more important today. And this is true whether you're a 20-year-old college student with hefty tuition bills, a 40-year-old parent with a mortgage to pay, or a 60-year-old thinking about retirement. Let's look at three reasons personal financial planning is so important in today's environment.

Sluggish Growth in Personal Income Personal income in the United States grew, on average, a rate of 4.4% a year over the last two years. States with the highest growth rates include California, Oregon, Nevada, Utah, Colorado, Tennessee, North Carolina, South Carolina, Georgia, and Florida. The percentage change in net earnings in a recent year ranged from −1.9% in North Dakota to 5.3% in Idaho. Earnings in farming fell 6.6% and, more than any industry, took away the growth in personal income in three of the slowest-growing states: Kansas, Nebraska, and South Dakota.[2]

The sometimes unpredictable growth in personal income makes sound money management even more important. You cannot count on rising personal income alone to improve your standard of living. Rather, you need to save and invest more money, stick to a budget, and make major purchases wisely.

Changes in the Labor Market Job security and the notion of work have changed in recent years. People rarely work for the same company throughout an entire career; The average person changes jobs 10 to 15 times (with an average of 12 job changes) during their career. On average, five years or less is spent in every job. One poll revealed that nearly half of Americans age 50 and older say they plan to postpone retirement due to an uncertain economy, inadequate finances, lack of confidence in Social Security, and a higher-than-expected cost of living.[3]

The fact is that you and your classmates will likely change jobs and even employers several times during your careers. Some will end up working part-time or on a contract basis, with little job security and fewer benefits. Others will take time off to care for small children or elderly parents. And a goal many people have today is to start their own business and work for themselves.

Furthermore, it is estimated that one in four workers today will be unemployed at some point during their working lives. You never know when your employer will downsize, taking your job with it, or outsource your job elsewhere. Just read today's headlines and you will see that while unemployment rates have improved announcements of well-known companies downsizing and outsourcing are still common.

These changes make personal financial management even more important. It is crucial to keep your career skills up-to-date and accumulate sufficient financial resources to weather an unexpected crisis.

More Options The number of choices today in such areas as banking, credit, investments, and retirement planning can be bewildering. Today you can do most of your banking with a brokerage firm and then buy mutual fund shares online. Even a simple checking account has become more complicated. The typical bank offers several different types of checking accounts, each with its own features and fees. Choosing the wrong account could easily cost you hundreds of dollars in unnecessary fees each year.

Twenty years ago, few college students carried credit cards, and those who did typically had cards tied to their parents' accounts. Banks and other credit card issuers didn't consider college students to be reasonable risks. Then the situation changed, resulting in a credit card debt crisis among students. The Credit Card Accountability Responsibility and Disclosure Act of 2009 (the CARD Act), however, contains reforms aimed at reversing this trend so that students will become more educated about their use of money. Credit card issuers must now include minimum payment disclosures in statements that show a snapshot comparison of how long it will take to pay off a credit card balance if only minimum payments are made versus the payment each month to pay off the balance in three years.

One of the first things you'll do when you start a full-time job is make decisions about employee benefits. The typical employer may offer lots of choices in such areas as health insurance, disability insurance, group life insurance, and retirement plans. Selecting the right health insurance plan can save you thousands of dollars each year; by the same token, choosing the right retirement plan will enhance your economic security many years from now.

Personal Financial Planning—A Lifelong Activity

Personal financial planning is an equally important activity whether you're 20, 40, or 60; whether you're single or married with children; and whether your annual income is $40,000 or $200,000. Many experts say that if you can't stick to a budget and control your spending when you're making $40,000 a year, you'll find it difficult to live within your means even if your income doubles or triples.

The fact that sound planning is a lifelong activity, of course, doesn't mean your financial goals and plans remain the same throughout your life—they won't. The major goal when you're young may be to buy your first car or pay off your college loans. For older people, the major goal is to pay off their home mortgage and have as much money as possible for retirement.

A Personal Financial Management Model

financial plan guide to help a person reach desired financial goals.

A **financial plan** is a guide to help you reach targeted goals in the future, closing the gap between your current situation and where you'd like to be in the future. Goals might include buying a home, starting your own business, traveling extensively, sending children to college, or retiring early. Developing a personal financial plan consists of several steps, as illustrated in **Figure C.1**.

The first step in the process is to establish a clear picture of where you currently stand financially. Next, develop a series of short- and long-term goals. These goals should be influenced by your values as well as an assessment of your current financial situation. The next step is to establish a set of financial strategies—in each of the personal planning areas—designed to help close the gap between where you are now and where you want to be in the future. Next, put your plan into action and closely monitor its performance. Periodically evaluate the effectiveness of your financial plan and make adjustments when necessary.

Financial plans cannot be developed in a vacuum. They should reflect your available resources—especially salary and fringe benefits, such as health insurance and retirement plans. For example, your goals and financial strategies should be based on a realistic estimate of your future income. If you cannot reach your financial goals through your current career path, you will have to scale back your goals or consider switching careers.

In addition, external factors—such as economic conditions and employment prospects—will influence your financial plan and decisions. For instance, assume you currently rent an apartment but have a goal of buying a duplex. While you can afford to buy right now, you believe there is a good chance you'll be offered a much better job in a new city within the next year. Depending on the real estate market, a wise financial move might be to postpone buying until your employment future becomes clearer.

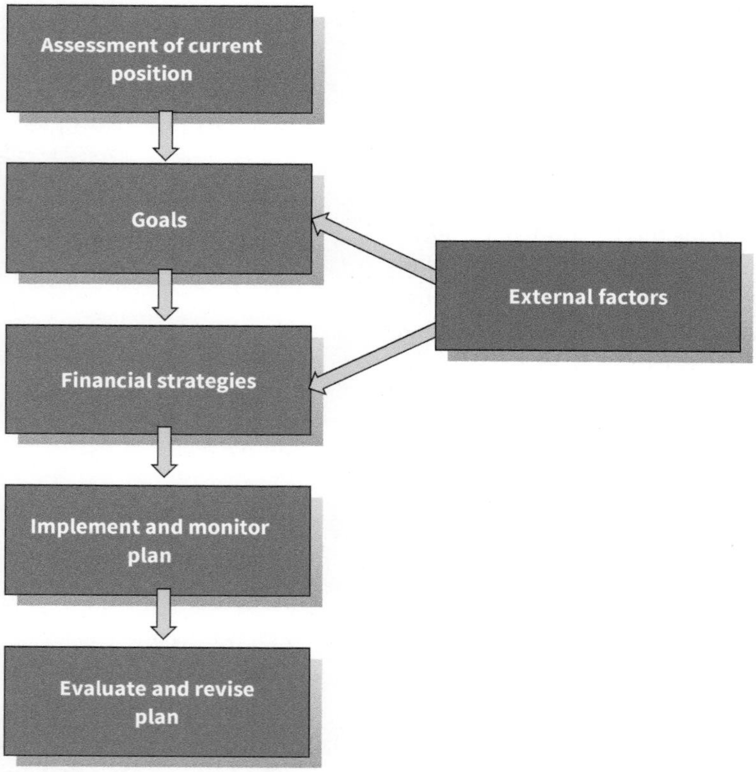

FIGURE C.1 **A Model of Personal Financial Management**

General Themes Common to All Financial Plans

Regardless of the specifics, all financial plans revolve around three general themes: (1) maximizing income and wealth, (2) using money more effectively, and (3) monitoring expenditures.

Maximizing Income and Wealth Maximizing your income and wealth means to increase something as much as possible. Work smarter; seek retraining or additional education for a better, higher-paying job; take career risks that may pay off in the long run; make sound investment decisions—all these are examples of the implementation of the first step. The amount of money you earn is a vital part of any financial plan, and it is up to you to make the most of your opportunities.

Using Money More Effectively Money has two basic uses: consumption and savings. Even if you are a regular saver, you'll still spend most of your income, probably more than 90%. You must try to spend every dollar wisely and make every major buying decision part of your overall financial plan. Avoid impulsive spending or giving in to a hard sell. Learn to assess the difference between a "want" and a "need."

And it's not just big expenditures you need to watch. Cutting back your spending on small items can make a difference. Little purchases do add up. Packing your own lunch a few times a week rather than buying your sandwiches at the local deli could save at least $100 to $200 a month, or $1,200 to $2,400 a year. Invest that savings of $200 a month at 3% interest (per year) and you'll have almost $117,092 in 30 years.

Small expenses really add up. Bringing your own lunch to the office instead of eating out can really enhance your bank account.

Monitoring Expenditures Budgeting is the key to controlling expenditures. A budget provides a view of where the money is going and whether a person's goals are being met. It also suggests appropriate times for reevaluating priorities. If your budget doesn't reflect what you want from life both now and in the future, change it.

Information and knowledge also help you keep your expenditures under control. The more you know about real estate, consumer loans, credit-card rates and laws, insurance, taxes, and major purchases, the more likely you are to spend your money wisely.

The Pitfalls of Poor Financial Planning

Unfortunately, too many people fail to plan effectively for their financial future. Not only do many find it difficult to improve their standard of living, but quite a few also find themselves with mounting debts and a general inability to make ends meet. According to the American Bankruptcy Institute, the number of personal bankruptcy filings has reached historic lows, but may rise as consumer households take on more debt.[4] Related to previous bankruptcies is foreclosure, which results when homeowners are unable to pay their mortgage loans.

Although there are laws in effect that generally favor consumers who run into difficulty, and although there are credit consolidation and counseling bureaus that help people organize and pay their debt, foreclosure and bankruptcy are generally actions of last resort, and it's best to avoid taking these steps.

net worth difference between an individual or household's assets and liabilities.

Setting Personal Goals

Whatever your personal financial goals, they are more easily accomplished if they reflect your personal values. Values are a set of fundamental beliefs of what is important, desirable, and worthwhile in your life. Your values will influence how you spend your money and, therefore, might be the foundation of your financial plan. Each person's financial goals will be determined by the individual's values because every individual considers some things more desirable or important than others. Start by asking yourself some questions about your values, the things that are most important to you, and what you would like to accomplish in your life.

Your goals are also influenced by your current financial situation. Prepare a set of current financial statements for yourself and update them at least once a year. Just like a business, a personal income statement reflects income and expenditures during a year. A balance sheet is a statement of what you own (assets) and what you owe (liabilities) at a specific point in time. For an individual or household, the difference between assets and liabilities is called **net worth**. As shown in **Figure C.2**, as you accumulate assets over your life, your net worth increases.

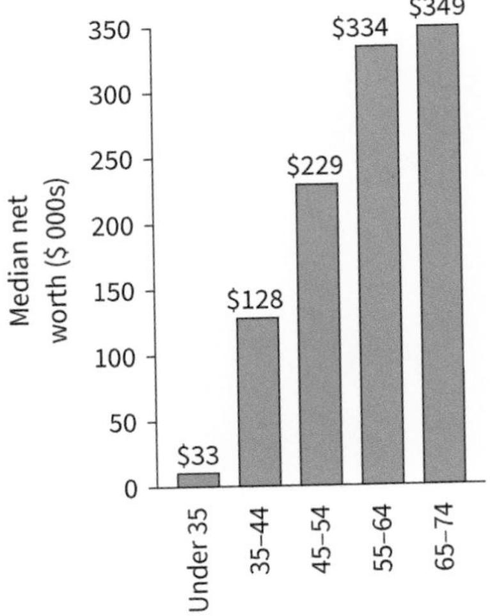

Source: Brian Stoffel, "The Typical American's Net Worth by Age: Here's Where You Stand," *Motley Fool*, http://www.fool.com, accessed July 23, 2018. Data from U.S. Census Bureau.

FIGURE C.2 Relationships Between Age and Household Net Worth

After reviewing your current financial statements, you should prepare a budget. It is an excellent tool for monitoring your expenditures and cash flow and permits you to track past and current expenditures and plan future ones. Budgets are usually prepared on a monthly basis, but you can make a weekly budget if that works better for you. Most budgets divide expenditures into fixed expenses (those that don't change much from month to month) and variable expenses (those that vary). Your monthly apartment rent or your meal plan at school is probably a fixed expense, but the amount you spend on transportation, gas for your car (unless you have an electric vehicle), or entertainment is a variable expense. One key to effective budgeting is to make sure that the budgeted amounts are realistic.

Next, establish a series of financial goals based on your values and current financial situation. Separate your goals into short-term goals (those you want to achieve within the next six months or year) and long-term goals (those you plan to achieve over the next 5 or 10 years). A short-term goal might be to pay off your credit-card balances by the end of this year, or to save enough money to take a vacation next summer. A long-term goal might be to buy a house by age 30. Your goals are reinforced if they support each other—if you pay off your credit cards, you'll likely have enough money saved to take that vacation or eventually buy your house. Some goals are monetary—such as paying off your credit cards. Others are nonmonetary, such as planning to retire by age 55. Whether short-term or long-term, monetary or nonmonetary, the best financial goals are defined specifically and focused on results. Goals also need to be realistic. You might not be able to pay off all of your credit cards by the end of this year, but you might pay off one. You might not buy the house by age 30, but maybe by 35 or even later. So be sure to set goals that you can actually attain. Keep in mind also that your financial goals will change over your lifetime. It's a good idea to review them periodically and adjust them when necessary, such as when you lose or get a job, relocate to another area, or have children.

Your Personal Financial Decisions

You can use financial strategies in such areas as career choice, credit management, and tax planning to help you chart your economic future. These strategies should reflect your goals and be designed to close the gap between where you are and where you want to be.

Career Choice

No factor exerts as strong an influence on your personal finances as your career choice. Virtually all of your income, especially when you're just starting out, will come from wages and salaries. It is through work that all of us acquire the income needed to build a lifestyle; to buy goods and services, including insurance protection; to save and invest; and to plan for retirement. Your job also has many important fringe benefits, such as health insurance and retirement savings plans, that are important components of your financial future. Throughout *Contemporary Business*, we've discussed ways to select a career that fits your skills and interests, find a job, and perform in that job. In addition, the *Occupational Outlook Handbook* published by the Bureau of Labor Statistics is an excellent resource for careers, growth rates, and average salaries.

Basic Money Management

Basic money management involves managing checking and savings accounts. Properly managing these relatively simple financial assets is an important first step toward managing more complicated financial assets such as investment and retirement accounts. You must choose a bank or other financial institution and then select the right checking account. Banks today offer several different types of checking accounts, each with its own set of features and fees.

TABLE C.1 Some Tips for Choosing and Managing a Checking Account

• Shop around. There are lots of financial institutions that offer checking accounts. Fees and services vary considerably.
• Learn about the various ways to get a free checking account. Some banks require a minimum deposit, while others require a minimum balance, companion savings account, or certificate of deposit.
• Choose the best account for the way you bank. Consider how often you write checks, if at all; how often you use ATMs; when and where you use your debit card; and your average monthly balance.
• Keep good records and balance your account regularly. If there is no fee, sign up for online banking to monitor your account and pay bills electronically.
• Watch how you use your ATM card. Know which ATMs are owned by your bank and how much you're charged to use another bank's ATM.
• Notify your bank immediately if your ATM card is lost or stolen.
• Sign up for overdraft protection.
• Understand how your bank calculates minimum monthly balance.
• Read the fine print in your monthly statement.

Table C.1 lists several tips for selecting and managing a checking/debit account. Managing a savings account involves understanding the importance of savings, setting savings goals, and picking the best savings option.

Credit Management

Credit is the area of personal finance that gets more people into financial difficulties than any other area. And Americans love credit. According to recent data from the Federal Reserve, Americans now owe in excess of $3.9 trillion, excluding home mortgage loans. This amount has increased by 30% over the last five years.[5]

Credit allows a person to purchase goods and services by borrowing the necessary funds from a lender, such as a bank. The borrower agrees to repay the loan over a specified period of time, paying a specified rate of interest. The **finance charge** is the difference between the amount borrowed and the amount repaid. Credit is available from many sources today, but rates vary, so it pays to shop around.

credit receiving money, goods, or services on the basis of an agreement between the lender and the borrower that the loan is for a specified period of time with a specified rate of interest.

finance charge difference between the amount borrowed and the amount repaid on a loan.

There are two broad types of consumer credit: revolving (or open-end) credit and installment credit. Revolving credit is a type of credit arrangement that enables consumers to make a number of different purchases up to a credit limit, specified by the lender. The consumer has the option of repaying some or all of the outstanding balance each month. If the consumer carries a balance from month to month, finance charges (interest) are levied. An example of revolving credit is a credit card, such as Visa or MasterCard.

An installment loan is a credit arrangement in which the borrower takes out a loan for a specified amount, agreeing to repay the loan in regular installments over a specified period of time. Part of each payment is interest and part goes to repay principal (the amount borrowed). Generally, installment loan payments are made monthly and are for the same amount. Most student loans, auto loans, and home mortgage loans are examples of installment loans.

People have good reasons for borrowing money. They include purchasing large, important goods and services (cars, homes, or a college education), dealing with financial emergencies, taking advantage of opportunities, and establishing or improving your credit rating. All of these reasons are appropriate uses of credit if you can repay the loans in a timely manner.

However, a wrong reason for borrowing money is using credit to live beyond your means. For instance, you may want to go to Cancun for a vacation but really cannot afford to, so you charge the trip. Using credit to live beyond your means often leads to credit problems. Watch for these warning signs of potential credit problems:

- You use credit to meet basic living expenses.
- You use credit to make impulse purchases.
- You take a cash advance on one credit card to repay another.
- The unpaid balance on your credit cards increases month after month.

Consumers who think of credit purchases as a series of small monthly payments should be well aware that this can be risky. As noted earlier, most college students today have at least one credit card, and more than half carry balances from month to month. On average, Americans between the ages of 18 and 65 have $5,700 of credit card debt. Although the CARD Act is aimed at curbing this debt, college students—and consumers in general—must also curb their credit spending.[6] How long would it take you to become debt free if you had $3,000 on your credit card, if you paid only $50 each month? The answer is more than 18 years—and you would have paid more than $7,600 in interest.

If you feel as though you have a problem with credit, or may be developing one, you should seek help as soon as possible. Your college or university may offer credit counseling services. If not, contact a local not-for-profit credit counseling service or the National Foundation for Credit Counseling (http://www.nfcc.org). According to the experts, one of the keys to the wise use of credit is education. Learning about the pros and cons of borrowing money, as well as learning about responsible spending, can help people avoid problems with credit.

Tax Planning

Everyone pays a variety of taxes to federal, state, and local governments. The major taxes paid by individuals include federal and state income taxes, Social Security and Medicare taxes, real estate taxes, and sales taxes. The bottom line is that excluding sales tax, the average American household paid $14,210 in various taxes in a recent year—which translates to an effective tax rate of about 24% for the average household.[7] Think about your own situation and the taxes you pay. You have federal income taxes withheld from each paycheck. In addition, if you live in one of the 41 states with a state income tax, you have state income tax withheld also. The following nine states do not have an income tax: Alaska, Florida, Nevada, New Hampshire, South Dakota, Tennessee, Texas, Washington, and Wyoming.[8] Social Security and Medicare taxes amount to a percentage of your wages split between you and your employer (you pay the entire amount if you're self-employed). If you rent an apartment, part of your monthly rent goes to pay the landlord's real estate tax bill. In most states, every time you buy something, you pay sales tax to your state or local government.

By law, you must pay your taxes. You can use some of the popular software such as TurboTax to calculate your federal and state income taxes or have a professional handle them—these two options are likely to find you any legal deductions you can take. If you do the tax return yourself—even with the aid of software—you will learn more about your personal finances. The Internal Revenue Service (IRS) has several excellent publications to help you prepare a federal income tax return. One of the best is IRS Publication #17 (*Your Federal Income Tax*). This and all other IRS publications are available free of charge from local IRS offices or the IRS website (http://www.irs.gov).

Major Purchases

Even if you follow a strict budget and manage to save money regularly, you may still spend most of your income each year. Effective buying is an important part of your financial plan. Within personal budget limits, an individual exercises his or her rights as a consumer to select or reject the wide range of goods and services that are available. As you purchase an auto-mobile, a home, or any other major item, you need to carefully evaluate alternatives, separate needs from wants, and determine how you are going to finance the purchase. Your goal is to make every dollar you spend count.

Americans spend an average of more than $9,000 annually on transportation, most of which goes to gasoline at $3,000 per year. Given that new vehicles average more than $36,270 today, and even good used cars can cost in excess of $20,000, buying an automobile is a significant purchase.[9] On top of that, most car purchases are financed. Buying a car involves weighing many factors, including whether you want a new or used car, what makes and models appeal to you, and how much you can afford to pay. Many consumers today choose not to buy a new car but rather to lease one. While leasing has advantages, it also has drawbacks and, overall, is often more expensive than buying. Some consumers in urban areas choose not to purchase a car, and instead take advantage of ride- and car-sharing services such as Zipcar, Lyft, and Uber.

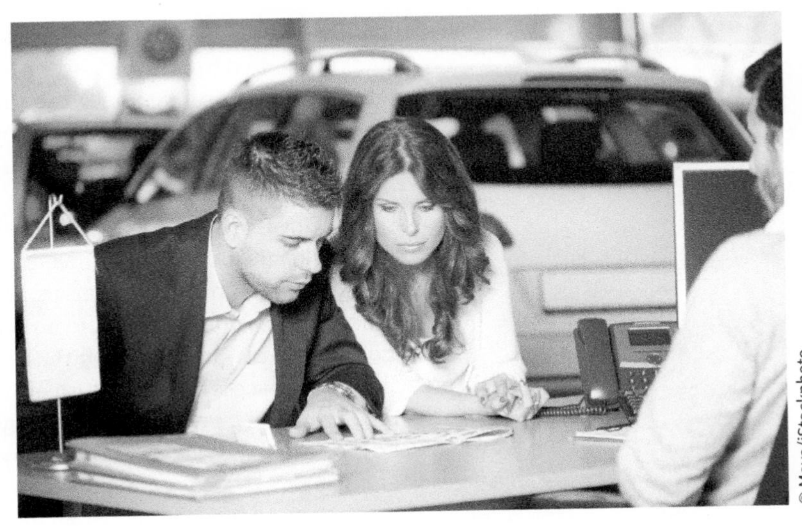

© Maya/iStockphoto

When purchasing a car, there are pros and cons to both leasing and buying.

For most people, housing consumes a large share of their monthly budgets, whether in rent or mortgage payments. Home ownership is a goal of most people. Owning a home has a number of advantages, both financial and nonfinancial. Some of the financial benefits include tax savings (home mortgage interest and property taxes are both tax deductible) and the potential increase in the home's value called appreciation. Nonfinancial benefits include pride of ownership and the freedom to improve or change the home however you want. The major barrier to home ownership is the money required for a down payment, along with the income required to obtain a mortgage loan.

The other major housing option is renting. Renting also offers a number of advantages, including cost savings (the landlord takes care of maintenance and repairs) and mobility. It is much easier to move if you rent than if you own a home. People who plan on staying in an area for a short period of time are usually better off renting even if they can afford to buy a home. The choice between buying and renting is obviously a major financial decision that needs to be approached rationally, not emotionally.[10]

Insurance

Another important personal planning area is insurance. Insurance is an admittedly expensive but necessary purchase. From age 16 to 78, the average person spends a total of $94,000 on car insurance.[11] Some of the basic principles and the various types of insurance are described in Appendix B. Although the focus of that appendix is business insurance, much of what is discussed applies to personal insurance needs as well.

Your goal is to have adequate and appropriate coverage in each of the major insurance types—life, health, disability, and property and liability. Insurance needs can vary substantially from individual to individual. As noted earlier in *Contemporary Business*, some types of insurance are provided to employees as fringe benefits. They typically include health insurance, disability insurance, and life insurance. In the standard arrangement, employers pay a portion of the premium. A few employers contract with insurance companies to offer employees auto and homeowners' insurance at discounts.

Investment Planning

Investing is a process by which money acquired through work, inheritance, or other sources is preserved and increased. Sound investment management is an important component of the financial plan and can make it easier to attain other personal goals, such as buying a home, sending children to college, starting a business, or retiring comfortably. Furthermore, it is very difficult today to substantially increase wealth without investing. And, given the changes to the external environment—such as the economy, health care costs, and employer-sponsored retirement plans—it is likely that you will have to make investment decisions at some point during your life.

The investment process consists of four steps. The first step is to complete some preliminary tasks, including setting overall personal goals, having a regular savings program, and managing credit properly. The second step is to establish a set of investment goals—why you want to invest, what you want to accomplish, and what kind of time frame you have. Obviously, your investment goals should be closely related to your overall personal goals and values. Next, you need to assess risk and return. You invest because you expect to earn some future rate of return. At the same time, however, all investing exposes you to a variety of risks. You need to find the proper balance between risk and return because investments offering the highest potential returns also expose you to more risk. Your age, income, and short- and long-term investment time frames all have an impact on the risk–return trade-off.

The final step is to select the appropriate investments. As discussed in Chapter 16 of *Contemporary Business*, there are three general types of investments: money market instruments, bonds, and common stock. The proper mix of these three investments depends on such factors as your investment goals and investment time horizon. For example, a 25-year-old investing for retirement should have close to 100% of his or her funds invested in common stocks because growth in capital is the overriding investment objective. Stocks have generally outperformed all other investment alternatives over longer periods of time. On the other hand, if the 25-year-old is investing to have sufficient funds for a down payment on a house within the next couple of years, the investor should have a proportion of his or her funds invested in money market instruments or bonds, given the short time horizon. Even after selecting the appropriate investments, investors must monitor their performance and be prepared to make changes when necessary.

Financial Planning for Tomorrow

The last major aspect of personal planning deals with future financial needs, such as sending children to college and retirement and estate planning. College is expensive, and college costs are rising at a rate that exceeds the overall rate of inflation. By beginning a college savings program early, parents will have a better chance of offering their children a choice of colleges when the time comes. While they may not have enough to cover tuition entirely, they (and their children) will likely have to borrow less and accrue less debt for a college education. A variety of college savings programs exist, some of which provide parents with tax benefits.

Most people want to retire with sufficient funds to ensure a degree of financial security. Social Security will provide only a fraction of what you will need; you will be responsible for the rest. Depending on the standard of living you hope to maintain, you will probably need a savings nest egg of at least $2 million by the time you retire. Four important principles apply when it comes to saving for retirement: start early, save as much as you can each month, take advantage of all tax-deferred retirement savings plans to which you are entitled, and invest your retirement savings appropriately.

Two major sources of retirement income exist: employer-sponsored retirement plans and individual retirement plans. Most employers offer their workers a retirement plan; some offer more than one plan. For most people, employer-sponsored retirement plans will likely provide the bulk of their retirement income. Essentially, two types of employer-sponsored retirement plans exist. A defined benefit plan guarantees a worker a certain retirement benefit each year. The size depends on a number of factors, including the worker's income and the length of time he or she worked for the employer. Pension plans are classified as defined benefit plans.

The other type of employer-sponsored retirement plan is the defined contribution plan. In this type of retirement plan, you contribute to your retirement account and so does your employer. You are given some choice of where your retirement funds can be invested. Often you are given a list of mutual funds in which to invest your money. A so-called 401(k) is an example of a defined contribution plan. Defined contribution plans are widely used and are in many cases replacing defined benefit plans.

Millions of Americans have some sort of individual retirement plan not tied to any employer. These workers may be self-employed or may merely want to supplement their employer-sponsored retirement savings. Examples of individual retirement plans include regular IRAs (individual retirement accounts), Roth IRAs, and simplified employee pension (SEP) plans. To set up one of these retirement plans, you must meet certain eligibility requirements.

Another element of financial planning for the future is estate planning. Of all the personal planning areas, estate planning is probably the least relevant for young people, although your parents and grandparents probably face some estate-planning issues. However, all adults, regardless of age, need to have two documents: a valid will (naming a guardian if you have any minor children) and a durable power of attorney (the name varies from state to state, but it is a document that gives someone else the power to make financial and medical decisions if you are incapacitated).

This appendix has just scratched the surface of personal financial planning. We hope it has encouraged you to learn more. Consider taking a class in personal financial planning if your institution offers one. It may be one of the most helpful classes you take while you're in college.

Business Terms You Need to Know

Projects and Teamwork Applications

1. Prepare a chart outlining your current standard of living, the standard of living you had while growing up, and the standard of living you expect or hope to achieve once you have completed your education.

2. The "comparison complex" is a phenomenon that makes it difficult for people to feel content with what they have. "Keeping up with the Joneses" is an expression that refers to the comparison to one's friends, co-workers, relatives, or neighbors with regard to accumulating goods as a means of social identification and social standing. Research and discuss the social and financial impact of this phenomenon.

3. Create a weekly budget and a monthly budget. Keep a daily journal of your expenses for the next month to see how well you stick to the budget. Compare your results in class. In what areas did you do well? In what areas do you need improvement?

4. Even though you are still in school, you face a number of important financial issues, everything from paying college expenses to dealing with credit cards. Go to the booklet entitled "30 Days to Financial Fitness" to read over this proposal. http://www.bplonline.org/virtual/databases/tutorials/doc/30DaysToFinancialFitness.pdf Is this program realistic? Evaluate each of the 30 days and provide feedback about what might be challenging for you.

5. Evaluate your current credit situation. What are your existing debts? How much are you paying each month? Assess the reason you used credit. Did you borrow for the right reasons? List some steps you think you should take to improve your management of credit. Go to the websites www.feedthepig.org or http://creditkarma.com to learn more.

Appendix D

Developing a Business Plan

Business Plan Competitions: More Than Just Prizes

If you have ever considered entering a business plan competition, there are many different types, including local competitions, university and college competitions, and corporate and social entrepreneurship contests, and each has unique benefits.

Aside from the honor of winning the competition, the obvious benefit is the cash prize, which varies in dollar amounts. For the last 30 years, at one of the largest and best-known annual business plan competitions in the world, the Massachusetts Institute of Technology (MIT) Entrepreneurship Competition, the contest winner comes away with a generous prize of $100,000, which can easily be used as seed money to fund a business. The competition includes a series of distinct, increasingly intensive contests: Pitch, Accelerate, and Launch.

Entering a competition focused on a particular industry provides targeted feedback from investors and seasoned professionals in your specific field. This may help prepare you for the rigors of talking to venture capitalists and angel investors and generally becoming comfortable with pitching your business idea to others.

Regardless of whether you make the short list or not, entering a business plan competition can offer entrants invaluable advice, mentoring, exposure, and support. In addition, entrants learn to articulate ideas and strategies, hone financial projections, and talk to potential investors. And there's no limit to the number of competitions a group can enter.

Many schools grant prize money that typically ranges from $5,000 to $10,000. A few of the big-money contests require winners to agree to sign over a percentage of equity in the new business, which might be a difficult decision for a would-be entrepreneur. Even the entrants who do not walk away with the prize money agree that the competition provides a sounding board and unparalleled networking—all well worth the pressure and competitive environment of such a competition. With or without a win, introductions are made to a network of judges, some of whom may be willing to finance a business start-up or introduce you to other industry experts. While there can only be one winner of the competition, the networking possibilities and connections can be a winning combination.[1]

Overview

Many entrepreneurs and small-business owners have written business plans to help them organize their businesses, get them up and running, and raise money for expansion. In this appendix, we cover the basics of business planning: what business plans are, why they're important, and who needs them. We also explain the steps involved in writing a good plan and the major elements it should contain. Finally, we cover additional resources to get you started with your own business plan—to help you bring your unique ideas to reality with a business of your own.

What Is a Business Plan?

You may wonder how the millions of different businesses operating in the United States and throughout the world today got their start. Often it involves a formal business plan. A *business plan* is a written document that defines what a company's objectives are, how those objectives will be achieved, how the business will be financed, and how much money the company expects to bring in. In short, it describes where a company is, where it wants to go, and how it intends to get there.

Why a Business Plan Is So Important

A well-written business plan serves two key functions:

1. It organizes the business and validates its central idea.
2. It summarizes the business and its strategy to obtain funding from lenders and investors.

First, a business plan gives a business formal direction, whether it is just starting, going through a phase of growth, or struggling. The business plan forces the principals—the owners—through rigorous planning and analysis, to think through the realities of running and financing a business. In their planning, they consider many variables. How will inventory be controlled and accounted for? Where should the business be located? How will the business use the Internet as part of its overall strategy? And most important, how will the business make enough money to make it all worthwhile?

A business plan also gives the owners a well-reasoned blueprint to refer to when daily challenges arise, and it acts as a benchmark by which successes and disappointments can be measured. In addition, a solid business plan will sell the potential owner on the validity of the idea. In some cases, the by-product of developing the plan is demonstrating to a starry-eyed person that he or she is trying to start a business that may not be viable. In other words, the process of writing a plan benefits a would-be businessperson as much as the final plan benefits potential investors.

Finally, a business plan articulates the business's strategy to financiers who may fund the business, and it is usually required to obtain a bank loan. Lenders and venture capitalists need to see that the business owner has thought through the critical issues and presented a promising idea before they will consider investing in it. They are, after all, interested in whether it will bring them significant returns.

Who Needs a Business Plan?

Every business owner who expects to be successful needs a business plan. Some people mistakenly believe that they need a business plan only if it will land in the hands of a venture capitalist or a business lender at a bank. Others think that writing a plan is unnecessary if their bank or lending institution doesn't require it. Such assumptions miss the point of planning, because a business plan acts as a road map to guide the way through the often tangled roads of running a business. Every small-business owner should develop a business plan because it empowers that person to take control.

How Do I Write a Business Plan?

Developing a business plan should mean something different to everyone. Think of a business plan as a clear statement of a business's identity. A construction company has a different identity from a newly launched online news magazine, which has yet a different identity from a restaurant hoping to expand its share of the market. Each business has unique objectives and processes, and each faces different obstacles.

At the same time, good business plans contain similar elements no matter who the business owner or entrepreneur is, what he or she sells, or how far the owner is into the venture. Through a business plan, a savvy business owner or entrepreneur creates a professional and personal representation of the company's needs and goals. The plan should also realistically assess the risks and obstacles specific to the business and present solutions for overcoming them.

Because the document is important, it takes time to perform research and to collect needed information and organize it. Don't be misled into believing that you will simply sit down and begin writing. Before any writing begins, the business owner or entrepreneur must become an expert in his or her field. Researching important information about the company, the market, and the overall industry will make the writing easier and faster. Some critical pieces of information to have on hand are the following items:

- The company's name, legal form of organization, location, financial highlights, and owners or shareholders (if any)
- Organization charts, list of top managers, consultants or directors, and employee agreements
- Marketing research, customer surveys, and information about the company's major competitors
- Product information, including goods and services offered; brochures; patents, licenses, and trademarks; and research and development plans
- Marketing plans and materials
- Financial statements (both current and forecasted)

The business owner also must do a lot of soul searching and brainstorming to answer important questions necessary to build the backbone of a healthy business. **Figure D.1** lists some critical questions worth asking.

Once these questions have been answered, you can begin writing the document, which can range between 10 and 50 pages long. The length of the plan depends on the complexity of

**Take a few minutes to read and answer these questions.
Don't worry about answering in too much detail at this point.
The questions are preliminary and
intended to help you think through your venture.**

1. In general terms, how would you explain your idea to a friend?
2. What is the purpose or objective of your venture?
3. What service are you going to provide, or what goods are you going to produce?
4. Is there any significant difference between what you are planning and what already exists?
5. How will the quality of your product compare with competitive offerings?
6. What is the overview of the industry or service sector you are going to enter?
7. What is the history, current status, and future of the industry?
8. Who is your target customer or client base?
9. Where and by whom will your good or service be marketed?
10. How will your product or service be priced?
11. Where is the financing going to come from to initiate your venture?
12. What training and experience do you have that qualifies you (and your team) for this venture?
13. Does such training or experience give you a significant edge?
14. If you lack specific experience, how do you plan to gain it?

FIGURE D.1 **Questions to Ask When Starting a Business**

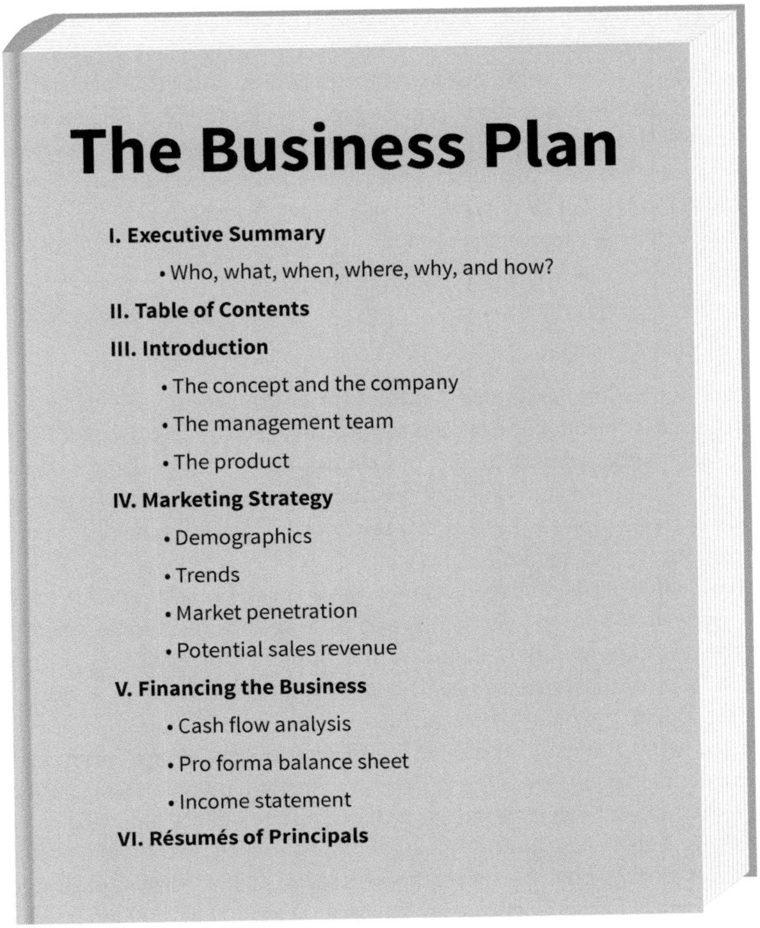

The Business Plan

I. Executive Summary

- Who, what, when, where, why, and how?

II. Table of Contents

III. Introduction

- The concept and the company
- The management team
- The product

IV. Marketing Strategy

- Demographics
- Trends
- Market penetration
- Potential sales revenue

V. Financing the Business

- Cash flow analysis
- Pro forma balance sheet
- Income statement

VI. Résumés of Principals

FIGURE D.2 **Outline of a Business Plan**

the company, whether the company is a start-up (established companies have longer histories to detail), and how the plan will be used. Regardless of size, the business plan should be well organized and easy to use, especially if the business plan is intended for external uses, such as to secure financing. Number all pages, include a table of contents, and make sure the format is attractive and professional. Include illustrative charts or graphs and highlight the sections and important points with headings and bulleted lists. **Figure D.2** outlines the major sections of a business plan.

As discussed briefly in Chapter 5, the following paragraphs discuss the most common elements of an effective business plan. If you need additional instruction or information as you write, refer to the "Resources" section at the end of the appendix.

Executive Summary

The primary purpose of an executive summary is to entice readers to read more about the business. An *executive summary* is a one- to two-page snapshot of what the overall business plan explains in detail. Consider it a business plan within a business plan. Through its enthusiasm and quick description, the summary should capture the reader's imagination. Describe your strategy for succeeding in a positive, intriguing, and realistic way and briefly yet thoroughly answer the first questions anyone would have about your business: who, what, why, when, where, and how. Lenders and investors always read the executive summary first. If it isn't presented professionally, or lacks the proper information, they will quickly move on to the next business plan. The executive summary is just as important to people funding the business with personal resources, however, because it channels their motivations into an articulate mission statement. It is a good idea to write the summary last, because it will inevitably be revised once the business plan is finalized.

To write an effective executive summary, focus on the issues that are most important to your business's success and save the supporting matters for the text. The executive summary should describe the firm's mission, vision, strategy, and goals, the good or service it is selling, and the advantages it has over the competition. It should also give a snapshot and brief overview of how much money will be required to launch the business, how it will be used, and how the lenders or investors will recoup their funds.

Introduction

The introduction follows the executive summary. After the executive summary has offered a thorough synopsis, the introduction should begin to discuss the fine details of the business. It should include any material the upcoming marketing and financing sections do not cover. The introduction should describe the company, the management team, and the product or service in detail. If one of these topics is particularly noteworthy for your business, you may want to present that topic as its own section.

Include basic information about the company—its past, present, and future. What are the company's origins, what is its current status, and what actions need to be taken to achieve its goals? If you are starting a company, include a description of the evolution of the concept and idea. Be sure to tie all of the business's goals and plans to the industry in which it will operate, and describe the industry and its recent and historic trends.

A business doesn't run itself, of course. People are the heart of a business, so include a compelling and detailed overview of the business's management team. Who are the key players and how does their experience resonate with the company's goals? Describe their—or your, if you are a sole proprietor—education, training, and experience, and highlight and refer to résumés included later in the plan. Be honest, however—not all businesses are started by experts. If you lack demonstrated experience in a certain area, explain how you plan to get it.

Also describe the product, the driving force behind the venture. What are you offering, and how will you differentiate your product or service? What are the costs of the service or price tag on the good? Analyze the features of the offering and the effect these features have on the overall cost.

Marketing Strategy

Next comes the marketing strategy section. The *marketing strategy* describes the market's (and, ultimately, the customer's) need for the good or service and the way the business will fulfill it. Marketing strategies are not based on informal projections or observations. They are the result of careful market research and analysis, as discussed in Chapter 11. So formulating a marketing strategy allows the business owner to become familiar with every aspect of the specific market. If done properly, it will allow you to define your target market and position your business within that sector to get its share of sales.

The marketing strategy includes a discussion of the size (in both revenues and customers) of the customer base or market that will want to purchase your good or service and the projected rate of growth for the product or category. *Demographics* are statistical characteristics of the segment of the market, such as income, gender, and age. What types of people will purchase your product? How old are they, and where do they live? What is their lifestyle like? For example, someone starting an interior design business will want to report how many homeowners live within a certain radius as well as their median income. Of course, this section of the marketing analysis will be quite different for an e-commerce company that conducts all of its business online. In that case, you will want to know the types of people who might shop online for your particular product or service, but your discussion won't be limited to one geographic area. It is also a good idea to describe the trends in your product category. Trends are consumer and business tendencies or patterns that business owners can capitalize on to gain market share in an industry.

The marketing strategy should also detail your distribution, pricing, and promotional goals. Discuss the average price of your offering and the reasons behind the price you have chosen. How do you intend to let your potential customers know that you have a product to sell? How will you sell it—through a catalog, in a retail location, online, or perhaps a combination of all three? The effectiveness of your distribution, pricing, and promotional goals determines the extent to which you will be able to gain market share.

Knowledge of competitors is another important part of your marketing strategy. What companies are already selling products similar to yours? Include and thoroughly research your competitors to show that you know exactly who they are and what you are up against. Describe what you think are their major strengths, weaknesses, opportunities, and threats and how successful they have been within your market.

Also include the *market penetration*, which is the percentage of total customers who have purchased a company's product. If there are 10,000 people in your market, and 5,000 have purchased your product, your market penetration is 50%. The *potential sales revenue*, also an important figure to include, is the total revenue of a company if it captured 100% market penetration. In other words, this figure represents the total dollar value of sales you would bring in if everyone who is a potential customer purchased your product.

Financing the Business

The goal of a business is to make a profit. The business plan provides the foundation for the *financing section*. Business owners should not skip this section even if they are not seeking outside money. While it is crucial to have an accurate financial analysis to get financing, it also is a necessary exercise for business owners funding the venture themselves. The financing section provides information related to the cost of the product, operating expenses, expected sales revenue and profit, and the amount of the business owner's personal funds or startup expenses that will be invested to get the business up and running. The financial projections should be compelling but accurate and based on realistic assumptions. The owner should be able to defend them.

Any assumptions made in the body of the business plan should be tied into the financial section. For example, if you think you will need a staff of five, your cash flow analysis should include salary information and how the employees will be paid. A cash flow analysis, a mandatory component of a financial analysis, shows how much money will flow in and out of your business throughout the year. It helps you plan for staggered purchasing, high-volume months, and slow periods. Your business may be cyclical or seasonal, so the cash flow projection lets you know if you need to arrange a line of credit to cover periodic shortfalls. In addition, an income statement is a critical component. The income statement is a statement of income and expenses your company has accrued over a period of time.

Remember that including as many details as possible with complete transparency is a wise approach. The plan must include your assumptions about the conditions under which your business will operate. It should cover details such as market strength; date of start-up; sales buildup; gross profit margin; equipment, furniture, and fixtures required; and payroll and other key expenses that will affect the financial plan. In addition, a banker will want a pro forma balance sheet, which provides an estimate of what the business owns (assets), what it owes (liabilities), and what it is worth (owner's equity). Refer to Chapters 15, 16, and 17 of *Contemporary Business* for additional details on accounting, financial statements, and financial management.

Résumés of Principals

The final element of the business plan is the inclusion of the résumés of the principals behind the business: the management team. Each résumé should include detailed employment information and accomplishments. If applicable to your business, consider expanding on the traditional résumé by including business affiliations, professional memberships, hobbies, and leisure activities.

However you choose to develop a business plan, make sure that *you* develop the plan. It should sound as though it was written by the entrepreneur, not by some outside "expert."

Resources

A tremendous amount of material is available to help business owners—whether existing or prospective—write effective business plans. The biggest task is narrowing down which resources are right for you. The Internet delivers an abundance of sound business-planning tools and advice, much of which is free. It allows you to seek diverse examples and opinions, which is important because no one source will match your situation exactly. Your library and career center also have a wealth of resources. Following are some helpful resources for business planning.

Books

Dozens of books exist on how to write a business plan. Examples include the following:

- Richie Banksy, *Business Plan Writing Guide*, 12th ed. (Amazon Business Services, 2016).
- Tim Berry, *Lean Business Planning: Get What You Want from Your Business* (Carlsbad, CA: Motivational Press, 2015).
- Veechi Curtis, *Creating a Business Plan for Dummies* (Hoboken, NJ: Wiley, 2014).
- Alex Genadinik, *How to Write a Business Plan* (CreateSpace: Independent Publishing Platform, 2016).
- Mike McKeever, *How to Write a Business Plan*, 12th ed. (Berkeley, CA: Nolo Press, 2014).
- John W. Mullins, *The New Business Road Test: What Entrepreneurs and Executives Should Do Before Writing a Business Plan*, 3rd ed. (Harlow Essex, UK: Financial Times/Prentice Hall, 2012).
- Hal Shelton, *The Secrets to Writing a Successful Business Plan: A Pro Shares a Step-by-Step Guide to Creating a Plan That Gets Results* (Rockville, MD: Summit Valley Press, 2014).

Websites

Useful websites include the following:

- *Entrepreneur, Inc.*, and *Bloomberg Businessweek* magazines offer knowledgeable guides to writing a business plan. *Entrepreneur*'s website also contains sample business plans.
  http://www.entrepreneur.com
  http://www.inc.com
  http://www.businessweek.com
- If you are hoping to obtain funding with your business plan, you should familiarize yourself with what investors are looking for. Three professional associations for the venture capital industry are the following:
  http://www.nvca.org (National Venture Capital Association)
  http://www.nasbic.org (Small Business Investor Alliance—formerly the National Association of Small Business Investment Companies)
  http://fundingpost.com (Bringing together entrepreneurs and investors)

Software

Business-planning software can give an initial shape to your business plan. The most widely used business plan software is Business Plan Pro from Palo Alto software. However, a word of caution is in order if you write a business plan using a template from software. Bankers and potential investors, such as venture capitalists, read so many business plans that those based on templates may seem less original or authentic. Also, if you are not seeking financing, using software can eliminate the main purpose of writing a plan—learning about, through research and analysis, your unique idea and its viability. Remember, software is a tool. It can help you get started, stay organized, and build a professional-looking business plan, but it won't actually write the plan for you.

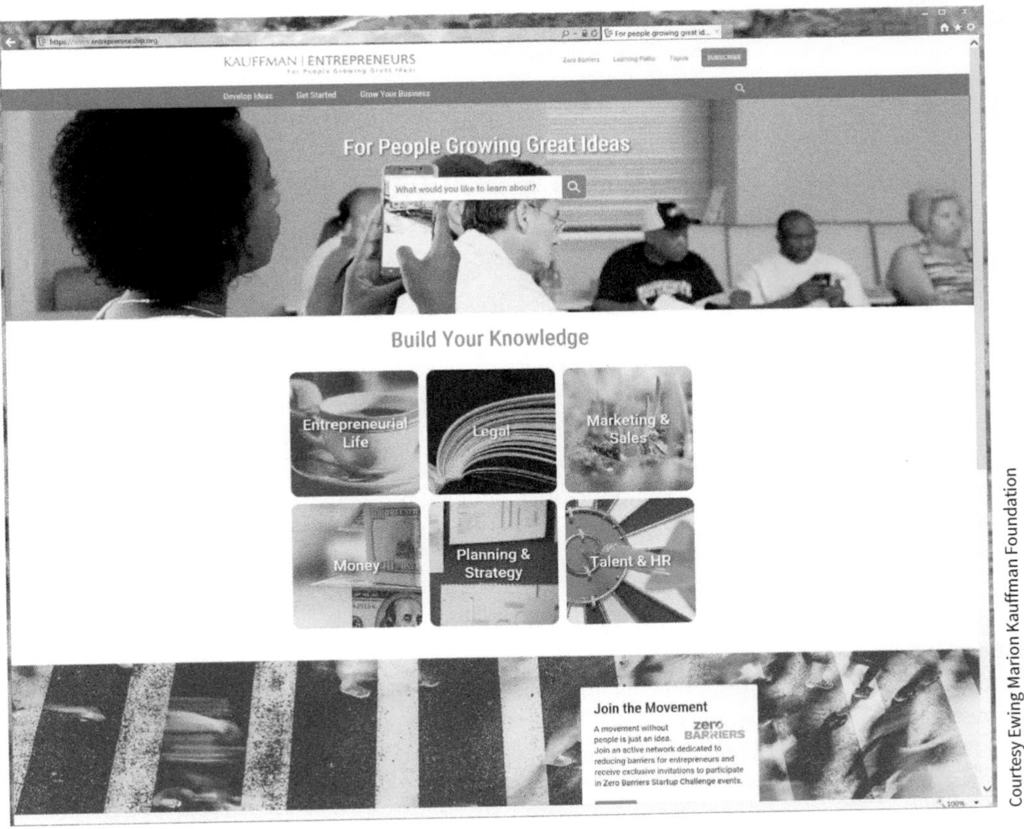

Courtesy Ewing Marion Kauffman Foundation

The Ewing Marion Kauffman Foundation's website, www.kauffman.org, offers a wealth of information about starting, managing, and expanding small businesses.

Associations and Organizations

Many government and professional organizations provide assistance to would-be business owners. Here is a partial list:

- The U.S. Small Business Administration offers planning materials, along with other resources.
  http://www.sba.gov
- Women's Business Centers represent a national network, sponsored by the SBA, that helps female entrepreneurs.
  http://www.sba.gov/tools/local-assistance/wbc
- One of the missions of the Ewing Marion Kauffman Foundation is to encourage entrepreneurship across the United States. The foundation's websites offer online resources for new and growing businesses.
  http://www.kauffman.org

Projects and Teamwork Applications

1. Visit the website below and review the various types of business plan competitions, along with the requirements of each. Discuss which would be the most appropriate for you.

www.businessplancompetition.com

2. Do you dream of starting your own business? Take your idea and answer as many of the self-evaluation questions in Figure D.1 as you can. Share your answers with the class. Then file away your answers to read at a future date—either when you have graduated from college or when you think you are ready to pursue your own business.

3. Write the executive summary portion of the business plan for your potential business. You may use the answers to the questions in Figure D.1 as a springboard.

Appendix E

Careers in Business Today

If you're not already in the job market, you may, in the near future, be considering your career options. Regardless of what industry you want to work in—financial services, advertising, travel, construction, hospitality, manufacturing, wireless communications—an education certainly helps. Attending college and taking a business course like this one give you an edge because business skills and knowledge are needed in many different fields. But education comes in many forms. In addition to taking classes, you may want to gain related real-life experience. A summer job, an internship, or even a volunteer opportunity can give you excellent experience that you can build on once you graduate. Cooperative education programs and work-study programs can also give you hands-on experience while you pursue your education. While many students will be doing the same thing, you can set yourself apart through your work ethic and initiative.

You may be responsible for earning a living once you leave school—if you aren't already doing so. Your level of education will probably influence your earnings. As reported by the U.S. Census Bureau, not only is there a wide discrepancy between earnings for high-school graduates and college graduates, and while the gender pay gap between men and women has narrowed, in a recent year, women earned 82% of what men earned.[1]

Keep in mind that while a degree may help you get in the door for certain job interviews and may put you on a path for advancement, it doesn't guarantee success; you have to achieve that yourself.

Companies plan their hiring strategies carefully in order to attract and retain the most productive, creative employees and avoid the cost of rehiring. So, soon-to-be graduates still need to be proactive and prepared. But creativity has never been in short supply among business students, and by the time you finish this class—and college—you will be well equipped to take on the challenge. You'll be able to think of your search for employment as a course in itself, at the end of which you will have a job. And you will be on your way toward a rewarding business career.

During this course, you are exposed to all the functional areas of business. You learn how companies operate and how they are organized. You find out who does what in a company. Gradually, you identify industries and disciplines—such as sales, finance, or product design—that interest you. And you learn about many organizations, large and small—who founded them, what products and services they offer, how they serve their customers, and what types of decisions they make. In short, you gain knowledge about business that you can apply to your career search and life.

Choosing a career is an important life decision. It sets you on a path that will influence where you live, how much money you earn, what type of people you meet, and what you do every day. And whether your goal is to operate an organic farm or to rise within the ranks of a major corporation, you'll need to understand the principles of business. Even if you think you're headed down a different path, business skills may prove to be important. In addition, many fields are beginning to recognize the importance of a broader base of knowledge than specialized technical skills, and business knowledge is part of that base.

For example, some careers, like engineering, used to rely almost solely on a foundation of technical skill and expertise. But experts in the industry now report a desired trend toward a more well-rounded education. While engineers still need a strong technical foundation, they need additional skills as well. Engineers who survived the economic downturn without being laid off claim that having knowledge across several areas made them more valuable to their employer than, say, a colleague whose knowledge was concentrated in one or two areas. That's why this appendix discusses the best way to approach career decisions and to prepare for an *entry-level job*—your first permanent employment after leaving school. We then look at a range of business careers and discuss employment opportunities in a variety of fields.

It's important to remember that you'll be looking for a job regardless of the state of the overall economy. You'll read about job cuts and unemployment rates, hiring freezes and wage increases. But if you remain flexible and diligent about being ready to work—just about anytime and anywhere—you'll succeed.

Internships—A Great Way to Acquire Real-World Experience

Many business students complete one or more *internships* prior to completing their academic careers. Some arrange internships during the summer, while others work at them during a semester away from college. An internship gives you hands-on experience in a real business environment, whether it's in banking, hospitality, or retail. Not only does an internship teach you how a business runs, but it can also help you decide whether you want to pursue a career in a particular industry. You might spend a summer interning in the admissions department of a hospital and then graduate with your job search focused on hospital administration. Or you might decide you'd much rather work for a magazine publisher or a retailer.

When you apply for an internship, don't expect to be paid much, if at all. The true value of an internship lies in its hands-on experience. An internship bridges the theory–practice educational gap. It will help carry you from your academic experience to your professional future. One career advisor suggests trying to gain experiences that will help you down the road by taking an educated guess on where you want to be in three to five years (or more). Also keep in mind that, as an intern, you will not be running a department. People may not ask for your input or ideas. You may work in the warehouse or copy center. You might be answering phones or entering data. But it is important to make the most of your internship. Because many companies make permanent job offers—or offers to enter paid training programs—to the best interns, you'll want to stand out.

Internships can serve as critical networking and job-hunting tools. In many instances, they lead to future employment opportunities, allowing students to demonstrate technical proficiency while providing cost-effective employee training for the company. Even if you don't end up being hired by the company for which you interned, the experience is extremely valuable to your job hunt because you include it on your résumé. All of the Big Four accounting firms offer internships to college juniors and seniors—many of whom receive offers for full-time work upon completion. Typically between 90% and 93% of new employees at KPMG get offers to join the firm full-time after graduation, and the acceptance rate hovers around 95%.[2]

With this information in mind, start thinking the way a professional does now. Here are some tips for a successful internship experience. These guidelines are also helpful for your first job.

- **Dress like a professional.** Dress appropriately for your future career. During an interview visit, look around to see what the dress code is like. If you have any questions, ask your supervisor.
- **Act like a professional.** Arrive on time to work. Be punctual for any meetings or assignments. Ask questions and listen carefully to the answers. Complete your work thoroughly and meet deadlines. Maintain good etiquette on the phone, in meetings, in e-mails, and in all interactions with other people.
- **Stand out.** Work hard and take initiative, but remain humble and behave appropriately. Show that you are curious, open, and willing to learn.
- **Be evaluated.** Even if your internship does not include a formal evaluation, ask your employer for feedback to learn how you can improve.

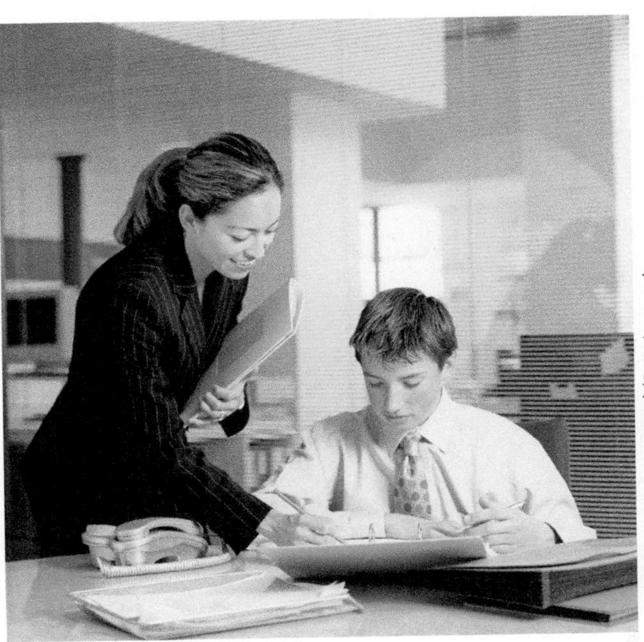

An internship at a Big Four accounting firm means that a student has the opportunity to gain hands-on business experience and enter the world of professional accounting while still in college. Over half of entry-level hires at KPMG are previous interns with the company.

- **Keep in touch.** Once you complete your internship, stay in touch periodically with the company so that people know what you are currently doing.

An excellent source of information about outstanding internships can be found on various websites, such as Indeed.com, aftercollege.com, and internmatch.com.

In addition to an internship, you can build your résumé with work and life experience through volunteer opportunities, extracurricular activities, and summer or off-campus study programs. *Cooperative education* also provides valuable experience. Cooperative education programs are similar to internships, combining classroom-based education with practical work experience. Commonly referred to as a "co-op," cooperative education provides academic credit for structured job experience.[3]

Self-Assessment for Career Development

You are going to spend a lot of time during your life working, so why not find a job—or at least an industry—that interests you? To choose the line of work that suits you best, you must first understand yourself. Self-assessment involves looking in the mirror and seeing the real you—with all your strengths and weaknesses. It means answering some tough questions. But being honest with yourself pays off because it will help you find a career that is challenging, rewarding, and meaningful to you. You may realize that to feel secure you need to earn enough to put away substantial savings. Or you might learn that you are drawn to risks and the unknown, characteristics that might point you toward owning your own business someday. Each of these discoveries provides you with valuable information in choosing a career.

Many resources are available to help you in selecting a career. They include school libraries, career guidance and placement offices, counseling centers, and online career and job search services. They include alumni from your college, as well as friends, family, and neighbors. Don't forget the contacts you make during an internship—they can help you in many ways. Ask questions of anyone you know—a local accountant, banker, or restaurant owner. Many people will be happy to share knowledge with you or arrange a time to do so.

If you are interested in a particular industry or company, you might be able to arrange an informational interview—an appointment with someone who can provide you with more knowledge about an industry or career path. This type of interview is different from one that follows your application for a specific job, although it may ultimately lead to that. The informational interview can help you decide whether you want to pursue a particular avenue of employment. It also gives you some added experience in the interview process—without the pressure. To arrange an interview, tap anyone you know—friends of your parents, local businesspeople, or coordinators of not-for-profit organizations. Using LinkedIn, it is easy to reach out to graduates and alums of your college who are working in various fields and are willing to speak with students on an informational basis.

To help you get started asking and answering the questions that will help you begin looking in the right direction, you can visit a number of websites that offer online career assessment tests. Career Explorer at http://www.careerexplorer.net is one such site. These and other sites, such as Quintcareers.com and O*NET OnLine at https://www.onetonline.org, help you identify your interests, strengths, and weaknesses—including some that may surprise you.[4] In addition, follow the self-assessment process outlined in the next section to learn more about yourself.

The Self-Assessment Process

For a thorough assessment of your goals and interests, follow these steps:

1. **Outline your career interests.** What field or work activities interest you? What rewards do you want to gain from work?
2. **Outline your career goals.** What do you want to achieve through your career? What type of job can you see yourself doing? Where do you see yourself in a year? In five years? Do you

have an ultimate dream job? How long are you willing to work to reach it? Write your goals down so that you can refer to them later.

3. **Make plans to reach your goal.** Do you need more education? Additional training? Does the career require work experience or a certain number of years on the job? Outline the requirements you'll need to meet in order to reach your goal.
4. **List your skills and specific talents.** Write down your strengths—job skills you already have as well as skills you have developed in life. For instance, you might know how to use financial software, and you might have strong interpersonal skills. In addition, your school's career development office probably has resources that can help determine your aptitude for specific careers. However, take these only as a guideline. If you really want to pursue a certain career, go for it.
5. **List your weaknesses.** This can be tough, but it can also be fun. If you are shy about meeting new people, put shyness on your list. If you are quick to argue, admit it. If you aren't the best business-letter writer or think you're terrible at math, confess to yourself. This list gives you an opportunity to see where you need improvement—and then you can take steps to turn weaknesses into strengths.
6. **Briefly sketch out your educational background.** Write down the schools, colleges, and special training programs you have attended, along with any courses you plan to complete before starting full-time employment. Make a candid assessment of how your background matches the current job market. Then make plans to complete any further education you may need.
7. **List the jobs you have held.** Include paid jobs, internships, and volunteer opportunities. They all gave you valuable experience. As you make your list, think about what you liked and disliked about each. Maybe you liked working with the general public as a supermarket cashier. Perhaps you enjoyed caring for animals at a local shelter.
8. **Consider your hobbies and personal interests.** Many people have turned hobbies and personal pursuits into rewarding careers. Mick Jagger, lead singer of the Rolling Stones, has a master's degree from the London School of Economics. This fact probably helped him manage his rock group's vast business dealings. Jake Burton Carpenter earned a bachelor's degree in economics, but he loved winter sports. So he started a snowboard manufacturing company—and revolutionized the way people get from the top of a snowy mountain to the bottom. Over 25 years ago, Michele Hoskins capitalized on a recipe handed down by her great-great grandmother. With a fond memory of pancakes smothered in butter crème syrup on Sundays with her grandmother, Hoskins took the secret syrup recipe and made it a national success. Today Hoskins sells her products in over 8,000 retail grocery stores.[5] Turning a hobby into a career doesn't happen overnight, though—nor is it easy. It requires the same amount of research and hard work as any other business. But for many people, it is a labor of love—and ultimately it succeeds because they refuse to give up.

Job Search Guidelines

Once you have narrowed your choice of career possibilities to a few that seem to be a fit for you, you are ready to begin your exploration and search. The characteristics that made these career choices attractive to you are also likely to catch the attention of other job seekers, so you must prepare for a competitive environment. Locate available positions that interest you; then be resourceful! Your success depends on being as creative as possible, and gathering as much information as possible.

Use Your Career Center

If one is available, visit your school's career center. Most placement offices list new jobs online, so check frequently. Find out how the career center arranges interviews with company representatives who might visit campus. If your school holds career events or sponsors industry speakers, be sure to attend. The career centers of most schools assist students and alumni with a full range of services, from internships to employment opportunities, and even guidance for long-term and lifelong career success. In fact, as an alumnus, your school's career center and job listings can be an invaluable resource.

Creating an Online Profile Using Social Media

Creating a comprehensive online profile using a site like LinkedIn should include the following:

- A comprehensive profile that includes a summary, your educational background, and detailed descriptions of all of your work (and volunteer) experiences and skills
- Examples of your work in the form of videos, slideshows, or other multimedia files worth having prospective employers view
- An updated and professional profile picture

Studies show that sharing or commenting in an insightful way on various topics at least weekly will increase the chances of your online profile being viewed by the hiring manager. Pay close attention to shared acquaintances and mutual connections on the profiles of those you wish to meet.[6]

Letters of recommendation are very important because they give prospective employers both personal and professional insights about you. They can influence a hiring decision. So, make a careful list of people who might be willing to write letters of reference. LinkedIn allows for online recommendations and endorsements—a powerful addition to a résumé is a LinkedIn profile. Your references should not be family members or close friends. Instead, choose a coach, an instructor, a former employer, or someone else whose knowledge could contribute to your job application. A soccer coach could vouch for your hard work and determination both on and off the field. An instructor might be able to detail how well you participate and contribute in class. A former employer might describe your solid work ethic and ability to get along with others. If possible, include one or more references from your school's business faculty.

Always ask people personally for letters of reference. Be prepared to give them brief outlines of your academic preparation, along with information about your job interests and career goals. This information will help them prepare their letters quickly and efficiently. It also shows that you are serious about the task and respect their time. Remember, however, that these people are very busy. Allow them at least a couple of weeks to prepare their reference letters; then follow up politely on missing ones. Always call or write to thank them for writing the letters and keep them updated on your progress, especially if you land a great job.

General Sites

Craigslist.org
CareerBuilder.com
Glassdoor.com
Indeed.com
LinkedIn.com
Monster.com
SimplyHired.com
Snagajob.com
Vault.com

Government Sites

USAJobs.gov

Industry and Specialized Sites

Business and Finance

Accounting.com
Efinancialcareers.com

Communication

iABC.com

Healthcare

jobs.cdc.gov
jobs.nih.gov
healthecareers.com/

Marketing

Marketingjobs.com
ama.org

Nonprofits/Social Entrepreneurship

Idealist.org
bridgespan.org
ynpn.org

Sales

Salesjobs.com

Technology

Dice.com

Women/Minorities

womenforhire.com
iHispano.com
Womensjoblist.com

FIGURE E.1 Helpful Internet Job Sites

Finding Employment Online

The Internet plays a crucial role in connecting employers and job seekers. Companies of all sizes post their job opportunities on the web, on their own sites, on LinkedIn, and on job sites such as Indeed.com, Vault.com, Craigslist.org, Glassdoor.com, SimplyHired.com, and Monster.com. Specialized or niche sites such as Dice.com and Techcareers.com are also gaining popularity among tech workers, and USAjobs.gov has appeal among those interested in government jobs. Some sites are free to applicants, while others charge a subscription fee. **Figure E.1** provides a sampling of general, nonprofit, and industry-focused career sites.

Career websites typically offer job postings, tips on creating an effective résumé, a place to post your résumé, and advice on interviews and careers. If this sounds easy, keep in mind that these sites may receive hundreds of thousands of hits each day from job hunters, which means you have plenty of competition. This doesn't mean you shouldn't use one of these sites as part of your job search; just don't make it your sole source. Savvy job seekers often find that their time is better spent zeroing in on niche boards offering more focused listings. Naturally, if a particular company interests you, go to that firm's website, where available positions will be posted. For example, if you are interested in working at the accounting firm Ernst & Young, visit the Ernst & Young website, http://www.ey.com. If you are looking for a job with Whole Foods Market, visit http://www.wholefoodsmarket.com. And if you fancy yourself working for an outdoor retailer, go to Bass Pro Shops at http://www.basspro.com.

Newspapers, previously the source for traditional classified want ads, also post their ads on the web. Job seekers can even visit sites that merge ads from many different newspapers into one searchable database, such as CareerBuilder (http://www.careerbuilder.com). Some sites go a step further and create separate sections for each career area. For example, entire sections may be devoted to accounting, marketing, and other business professions. Searches can then be narrowed according to geographic location, entry level, company name, job title, job description, and other categories.

As mentioned, you can connect with potential employers by creating a profile on a social media site like LinkedIn or even, with 140 characters, on Twitter, or by posting your résumé on job sites. Employers search LinkedIn's site or other job sites for prospects with the right qualifications. One commonly used approach is for an employer to list one or more *keywords* to select candidates for personal interviews—for example, "retail sales experience," "network architecture," or "spa management"—and then browse the résumés that contain all the required keywords. Employers also scan résumés into their human resource database, and then when a manager requests, say, 10 candidates, the database is searched by keywords that have been specified as part of the request. Job seekers are responding to this computer screening of applicants by making sure that relevant keywords appear on their résumés.

Online résumé social media website LinkedIn recently announced a new app to assist college graduates in their job search. As students contemplate the types of jobs available with specific majors, LinkedIn saw this as an opportunity to develop LinkedIn Students, an app that gives students at the exploratory stage a way to highlight companies and job titles that might be a good fit based upon their school and major. The app lists alumni, by school, who work at each recommended company.[7]

The *Contemporary Business* companion website hosts a comprehensive job and career assistance section. The site is updated frequently to include the best job and career sites for identifying and landing the career you want, as well as current strategies for getting the best results from your web-based career-search activities.

Finding Employment through Other Sources

You may also want to contact private and public employment services available in your location or in the area where you would like to live. A discussion of each follows here.

Private Employment Agencies These firms often specialize in certain types of jobs—such as marketing, finance, sales, or engineering—offering services for both employers and job candidates that are not available elsewhere. Many private agencies interview, test, and screen job applicants so that potential employers do not have to do so. Job candidates benefit from the service by being accepted by the agency and because the agency makes the first contact with the potential employer.

A private employment agency usually charges the prospective employer a fee for finding a suitable employee. Other firms charge job seekers a fee for helping find them a job. Be sure that you understand the terms of any agreement you sign with a private employment agency.

State Employment Offices Don't forget to check the employment office of your state government. Remember that in many states these public agencies process unemployment compensation applications along with other related work. Because of the mix of duties, some people view state employment agencies as providing services for semiskilled or unskilled workers.

However, these agencies *do* list jobs in many professional categories and are often intimately involved with identifying job finalists for major new facilities moving to your state. In addition, many of the jobs listed at state employment offices may be with state or federal agencies and may include professionals such as accountants, attorneys, health care professionals, and scientists.

Learning More About Job Opportunities

Carefully study the various employment opportunities you have identified. Obviously, you will like some more than others, but you can examine a variety of factors when assessing each job possibility:

- actual job responsibilities
- industry characteristics
- reputation of the company
- geographic location
- salary and opportunities for advancement
- how the job fits into your long-range career goals and objectives

Too many job applicants consider only the most positive features of a job, perhaps its location, industry or title, employee perks, or the salary offer. However, a comprehensive review of job openings will provide a balanced perspective of the overall employment opportunity, including both long-run and short-run factors.

Building a Résumé

Regardless of how you locate job openings, you must learn how to prepare and submit a *résumé,* a written summary of your personal, educational, and professional achievements. The résumé is a personal document covering your educational background, work experience, career preferences and goals, and major interests that may be relevant. It also includes such basic contact information as your home and e-mail addresses, as well as your phone number. It should *not* include information on your age, marital status, race, or ethnic background.

Your résumé is usually your formal introduction to an employer, so it should present you in the best light, accentuating your strengths and potential to contribute to a firm as an employee. However, it should *never* contain embellishments or inaccuracies. You don't want to begin your career behaving unethically, and an employer is bound to discover any discrepancies in fact—either immediately or during the months following your employment. Either event is very risky, and typically results in short-circuiting your career path.

Some argue that the LinkedIn profile has surpassed the résumé in terms of importance and popularity for job seekers. While résumés are often updated and dusted off for a job search, a LinkedIn profile, on the other hand, is dynamic and can be updated on an ongoing basis, including various forms of media. Many argue that the purpose of the LinkedIn profile is networking. Still, some argue that the traditional résumé has its merits for a more in-depth conversation with a candidate and to create a framework for an interview. Some recruiters (and candidates) use a LinkedIn profile as a supplement to a résumé, including a view into a candidate's personal recommendations and connections as well.[8]

Organizing Your Résumé

The primary purpose of a résumé is to highlight your qualifications for a job, usually on a single page. An attractive layout facilitates the employer's review of your qualifications. You can prepare your résumé in several ways. You may use narrative sentences to explain job duties and career goals, or you may present information in outline form. A résumé included as part of your credentials file at the career center on campus should be quite short. Remember to design it around your specific career objectives.

Figures E.2, **E.3**, and **E.4** illustrate different ways to organize your résumé—by *reverse chronology,* or time; by *function;* and by *results*. Regardless of which format you select, you will want to include the following: a career "snapshot" highlighting some of your key skills; your work or professional experience; your education; your personal interests such as sports or music; and your volunteer work. While all three formats are acceptable, recruiters and prospective employers generally prefer the reverse chronological format—with the most recent experience listed first—because it is easiest to follow.[9]

Tips for Creating a Strong Résumé

Your résumé should help you stand out from the crowd, just as your college admissions application did. Many companies use recruiting and applicant tracking system software, which also includes cognitive technology. In some cases, applicants will submit a resume and cover letter

FELICIA SMITH-WHITEHEAD
4265 Popular Lane
Cleveland, Ohio 44120
216-555-3296
FeliciaSW@gmail.com

Experienced office manager with excellent organizational and interpersonal skills.
Conscientious team player; creative problem solver.

WORK EXPERIENCE

ADM Distribution Enterprises, Cleveland, Ohio 2019–Present
Office Manager of leading regional soft-drink bottler. Coordinate all bookkeeping, correspondence, scheduling of 12-truck fleet to serve 300 customers, promotional mailings, and personnel records, including payroll. Install computerized systems.

Merriweather, Hicks & Bradshaw Attorneys, Columbus, Ohio 2017–2019
Office Supervisor and Executive Assistant for Douglas H. Bradshaw, Managing Partner. Supervised four clerical workers and two paraprofessionals, automated legal research and correspondence functions, and assisted in coordinating outside services and relations with other firms and agencies. Promoted three times from Secretary to Office Supervisor.

Conner & Sons Custom Coverings, Cleveland, Ohio 2013–2015
Administrative Assistant in family's upholstery and awning company. Performed all office functions over the years, running the office when the owner was on vacation.

EDUCATION
McBundy Community College, Associate's Degree in Business 2015
Mill Valley High School, Honors 2011

COMPUTER SKILLS
Familiar with Microsoft Office and Adobe Acrobat

LANGUAGE SKILLS
Fluent in Spanish (speaking and writing)
Adequate speaking and writing skills in Portuguese

PERSONAL
Member of various community associations; avid reader; enjoy sports such as camping and cycling; enjoy volunteering in community projects.

FIGURE E.2 **Chronological Résumé**

Enrique Garcia
5 Oceanside Drive, Apt. 6B
Los Angeles, CA 90026
215-555-7092
egarcia@gmail.com

Experienced merchandiser with strong skills in category management, planning, and problem solving. Solid background in retailing and knowledge of vendor management programs.

Professional Experience

Administration
Management responsibilities in a major retailing buying office, coordinated vendor-relation efforts. Supervised assistant buyers.

Category Management
Experience in buying home improvement and sport and recreation categories.

Planning
Chaired a team charged with reviewing the company's annual vendor evaluation program.

Problem Solving
Successfully developed a program to improve margins in the tennis, golf, and fishing lines.

Work Experience

Senior Buyer for Southern California Department Stores 2019–Present

Merchandiser for Pacific Discount Stores, a division of Southern California Department Stores 2014–2019

Education

Bachelor's Degree
California State University–San Bernardino 2012–2014

Associate's Degree
Los Angeles City College 2008–2012

FIGURE E.3 Functional Résumé

(if requested) via email. A company may receive hundreds or even thousands of résumés, so you want yours to get noticed. Here are some do's and don'ts:

Do:

- Begin the résumé with a few descriptive phrases that give the reader an immediate "snapshot" of who you are and help set the tone for the reader to review your-document.
- Use terms related to your field, so that a human resource manager can locate them quickly. If you are submitting your résumé online, use words that will create an automatic "match" with a job description or field. If you are applying for an entry-level job in marketing, the phrase "communication skills" is likely to generate a match. You can identify such words and phrases by reading job descriptions online.
- Provide facts about previous jobs, internships, cooperative education programs, or volunteer work, including results or specific achievements. Include any projects or tasks you undertook through your own initiative.
- Emphasize your education if you are a recent graduate. Place it closer to the top of your résumé instead of the bottom.
- Highlight your strengths and skills, such as research, writing, or analytics.
- Write clearly and concisely.

ANTONIO PETTWAY
101 Beverly Road
Upper Montclair, NJ 07043
820-555-1234
apettway@yahoo.com

Highly motivated construction supervisor with knowledge in all aspects of the construction industry. Affirming leader and team player; experienced in introducing new processes that increase productivity.

PROFESSIONAL EXPERIENCE

DAL Construction Company, Orange, NJ 2019–Present

Established automated, on-site recordkeeping system improving communications and morale between field and office personnel, saving 400 work hours per year, and reducing the number of accounting errors by 20 percent. Developed a crew selected as "first choice crew" by most workers wanting transfers. Completed five housing projects ahead of deadline and under budget.

NJ State Housing Authority, Trenton, NJ 2015–2019

Created friendly, productive atmosphere among workers enabling first on-time job completion in 4 years and one-half of usual materials waste. Initiated pilot materials delivery program with potential savings of 3.5 percent of yearly maintenance budget.

Essex County Housing Authority, Montclair, NJ 2015

Produced information pamphlets increasing applications for county housing by 22 percent. Introduced labor-management discussion techniques saving jobs and over $29,000 in lost time.

Payton, Durnbell & Associates Architects, Glen Ridge, NJ 2012–2015

Developed and monitored productivity improvements, saving 60 percent on information transfer costs for firm's 12 largest jobs.

EDUCATION

Montclair State University, Bachelor's Degree in Business 2008–2012

COMPUTER SKILLS

Familiar with Microsoft Office and Adobe Acrobat

PERSONAL

Highly self-motivated. Willing to relocate. Enjoy tennis and hiking.

FIGURE E.4 **Results-Oriented Résumé**

- Proofread your résumé carefully for grammar, usage, and typographical errors. Refer to a dictionary or style manual.
- Keep your résumé to a single page.
- Avoid including personal information unless it is directly related to the job for which you're applying (for example, playing intramural basketball and volleyball during school might be relevant details if you were applying for a job as a recreation director at a community center).

Don't:

- Offer any misleading or inaccurate information.
- Make broad-based statements, such as "I work well with others" or "I want a position in business."
- State your objective as "to run this company," "to find a job that matches my skill set," or "to advance as quickly as possible."
- Include a salary request.
- Make demands about vacation time, work hours, or excessive benefits.

- Highlight your weaknesses.
- Submit a résumé with typos or grammatical errors.
- Use slang or other inappropriate phrases or comments.
- Include pictures or graphics, or use fancy type fonts.[10]

Take your time creating your résumé; it is one of the most important tools you will use during your career. If you need help, go to your school's career center, if one is available.

Keep in mind that you will probably have to modify your résumé at times to tailor it to a particular company or job. Again, take the time to do this; it may mean the difference between standing out and being lost in a sea of other applicants.

Preparing Your Cover Letter

In most cases, your résumé will be accompanied by a *cover letter*. This letter should introduce you, explain why you are submitting a résumé (cite the specific job opening and where you learned about it, if possible), call out some specific point in your résumé that qualifies you for the position, and ask for an interview. An effective cover letter will make the recipient want to take the next step and read your résumé. Here are a few tips for preparing an outstanding letter:

- Write the letter to a specific person, if possible. A letter addressed to "To whom it may concern" may never reach the right person. Check the company's website for the name of the person to whom you should send your letter. It might be someone in human resources or a person in the department where you'd actually be working. Be sure to obtain the person's title if possible (such as general manager or director), and spell the person's name correctly.
- Introduce yourself and explain the purpose of your letter—to apply for a job.
- Describe briefly an example of your best work or most ambitious project.
- Keep it short—a page is acceptable, half a page even better.
- Request an interview.
- Thank the person for his or her time and consideration.
- Make sure all your contact information is in the letter—name, address, home phone number, cell phone number, and e-mail address.
- Proofread your letter carefully.[11]

Recently, some argue that the cover letter is dead. In a recent survey, two-thirds of recruiters polled reported that they do not read cover letters, due primarily to speed, technology, and volume of applicants. Many prefer to skip the cover letter and dive into the essence of the résumé. In addition, since many companies recruit online today, there isn't always a section for a cover letter. Some suggestions for creating a cover letter of sorts include adding a summary of what makes you different; highlighting personal information and hobbies; spotlighting awards and accomplishments; and listing your social media profile addresses.[12]

Submitting Your Online Résumé

You may write a sparkling cover letter and stellar résumé, but if your online submission is blocked or tossed aside by an automated processing system, it won't have a chance to impress the person for whom it was intended. Thanks to social media recruitment, which uses social media profiles, blogs, and other sites to find information on candidates, attracting and engaging a broad range of candidates with desired skills is a more efficient and accurate process. Recruitment has become a digital experience, as candidates come to expect convenience, speed, and mobile contact. Savvy recruiters will use fast-response new talent acquisition technologies, some of which include cognitive and robotic technologies—such as machine learning, artificial intelligence (AI), and robotic process automation (RPA). Here are a few tips for making certain your letter and résumé reach their mark.

- Review the formatting of your résumé to make sure it will appear the same to the recipient as it does to you. Delete any unusual symbols or fonts.
- Use keywords that create a match and allow your résumé through the company's filter. This applies to the subject line of your e-mail as well, which should be specific and contain keywords such as "application for sales trainee job."
- Include your cover letter in the e-mail.
- Send your résumé in the body of the e-mail—not as an attachment. This is more convenient for the recipient, and it also avoids the disaster of having your attachment automatically deleted by an antivirus system.
- Do not send graphics, because they may be blocked.
- If you are answering an ad, read the instructions for application and follow them exactly.[13]

The Job Interview

Congratulations! You've prepared an effective résumé, and you've been contacted for an interview. An interview is more than a casual conversation, and an initial, prescreening interview can take place over the phone or via FaceTime or Skype. During an interview, at least one manager will learn about you, and you'll learn more about the company and the job. Although you may feel nervous about the interview, you can control some of its outcome by doing your homework: planning and preparing for this important encounter with your potential employer. Before you meet with an interviewer, learn everything you can about the company. The simplest way to do this is to visit the company's website. You can also check with your school's career center. If you know anyone who works for the company, you may ask the person about the firm. There are also many online resources like Glassdoor.com, which provide actual reviews by current employees of a company. Try to do as much research about a company as possible to learn the answers to the following questions:

- What does the company do—manufacture clothing, market snack foods, produce films, sell cars? If you are applying for a job at a large corporation, zero in on the division for which you would like to be working.
- What is the company's mission? Many firms include a statement about their purpose in the business world—to supply affordable energy to communities, to serve fresh food, to make communication easier. Understanding why the company exists will help you grasp where it is headed and why.
- Where, when, and by whom was the company founded? Learn a little about the history of the company.
- What is its position in the marketplace? Is it a leader, or is it trying to gain a competitive advantage? Who are its main competitors?
- Where is the company based? Does it have facilities located around the country and the world, or is it purely local?
- How is the company organized? Are there multiple divisions and products?
- Learning about the company indicates to the interviewer that you have initiative and motivation as well as an interest in the company's culture and history. You have taken the time and effort to find out more about the organization, and your enthusiasm shows.

Tips for Successful Interviewing

An interview is your personal introduction to the company. You want to make a good impression, but you also want to find out whether you and the company are a good fit. Although the interviewer will be asking most of the questions, you will want to appear curious and ask some as well. People who conduct interviews say that the most important qualities candidates can exhibit are self-confidence, curiosity, preparedness, and an ability to communicate clearly.

When you are contacted for an interview, find out the name(s) of the person or people who will be interviewing you. It's also appropriate to ask whether the initial interview will be with a human resource manager or with the person to whom you would be reporting on the job, or both. Many people who conduct initial job interviews work in their firms' human resource divisions. These interviewers act as gatekeepers and can make recommendations to managers and supervisors about which individuals to interview further or hire. Managers who head the units in which an applicant will be employed may get involved later in the hiring process. Some hiring decisions come from human resource personnel together with the immediate supervisor of the prospective employee. In other cases, immediate supervisors make the decision alone. If your interview is face to face, keep in mind the following tips.

Do:

- **Dress appropriately.** Dress as if it is your first day of work at the company.
- **Arrive a few minutes early.** This gives you time to relax and take in the surroundings. It also shows that you are punctual and care about other people's time.
- **Introduce yourself with a smile and a handshake.** Be friendly but not overly familiar.
- **Be yourself—at your best.** Don't suddenly adopt a new personality, but try to be confident, polite, respectful, and interested in the people who are spending time with you. Be sure to thank each person who interviews you.
- **Listen.** Pay attention to what the interviewer is saying. If something is unclear to you, ask for clarification. Turn off your cell phone and put it away. Your full attention should be on the conversation you are having in the interview.
- **Use appropriate language.** As in your résumé and cover letter, be sure to use correct English. You don't need to be stiff or formal, but avoid slang or phrases that you know are inappropriate for the situation.
- **Be positive in your outlook.** Be enthusiastic about the company and the job, but don't go overboard.

Don't:

- **Talk too much.** Avoid telling the interviewer a lot about your personal life, or negative aspects of why you left a particular job. Answer questions honestly and thoroughly, but don't dip into irrelevant details.
- **Be arrogant or aggressive.** Self-confidence is a good trait, but don't miss the mark by behaving in an arrogant or condescending manner. Certainly don't become aggressive, demanding that the interviewer offer you the job or even another interview.
- **Act indifferent or bored.** This may not be the job you ultimately want, but treat the interview and the interviewer with respect and attention. If you make a good impression, the interviewer is likely to keep you in mind should another job come up.
- **Don't get ahead of yourself.** This is not the time to discuss salary, vacation, or benefits.[14]

Answering and Asking Questions

In a typical format, the interviewer gives you ample opportunity to talk about yourself and your goals. Prepare in advance for this opportunity. You want to present your thoughts clearly and concisely, in an organized fashion, without rambling or bringing up unrelated topics. The interviewer may wait until you are finished or prompt you to talk about certain subjects by asking questions. Be as specific as possible when answering questions. The questions that interviewers ask often include the following:

- "Why do you want this job?"
- "Why are you a good fit for this position?"

- "Why do you want to work in this field?"
- "What are your short-term goals? Long-term objectives?"
- "Where do you see yourself in five years? In ten years?"
- "What are your strengths? What are your weaknesses?"
- "What motivates you?"
- "Describe a situation in which you made a tough decision or solved a problem."
- "What did you like best about your last job? What did you like least?"
- "Why did you leave your last job?"
- "Why should my company hire you?"
- "Are you considering other jobs or companies?"

Some of these questions may seem tougher than others, but you can reduce your anxiety by preparing for them. First, figure out which questions you fear the most. Then think about possible answers that are both truthful and positive. Videotaping yourself and watching later can be difficult, yet helpful. Rehearse your delivery in front of a mirror or with a friend.[15]

At some point, the interviewer will probably ask you whether you have any questions of your own. It's a good idea to come prepared with some questions, but others may arise during the interview. Try to keep your list concise, say, three or four of your most important questions. The questions you ask reflect just as much about you as the answers you give to the interviewer's questions. Here is a sample of appropriate questions for the initial interview:

- "Could you clarify a certain aspect of the job responsibilities for me?"
- "Do people who start in entry-level jobs at this company tend to develop their careers here?"
- "In what ways could I perform above and beyond the job requirements?"

At some point during your conversation, the interviewer may give you an idea of the salary range for the job. If not, they will do so during a subsequent interview. You may ask about the range, but do not ask exactly how much you will be paid if you get the job. Keep in mind that usually there is little or no negotiation of an entry-level salary. However, you may ask if there is a probationary period with a review at the end of the period. Here are a few other questions *not* to ask:

- "When will I be promoted?"
- "How much time off do I get?"
- "When will I get my first raise?"
- "How many people are applying for this job?"
- "What are my chances of getting this job?"

At the end of the interview, be sure to thank the interviewer with a smile and a handshake, and leave on a positive, upbeat note. Even if you know the job isn't the best fit, another opportunity may come along in the future, and you want to leave the door open. Be sure to ask for a business card or contact information from each person who interviewed you. Within 24 hours, write a note or e-mail to each person separately, thanking him or her for the opportunity to speak further about the job opportunity. Thank-you notes really do make a lasting impression on a person, and it gives you another chance to differentiate yourself and reinforce your interest.

A successful first interview often leads to a second. The purpose of a second interview is to better determine your specific qualifications and fit with the company. You may be introduced to more people—potential co-workers, people in other divisions, or sales staff. You may have another meeting with human resource staff members in which you'll learn more about salary, employee benefits, the firm's code of ethics, and the like. Depending on the type of job, you might be asked to take some job-related skills tests. If you are interviewing for an accounting position, you might be required to take some accounting-type tests. If you are going to work for a publisher, you might be asked to take an editing test or do some proofreading. If you are applying for a job as a sales

© Goodluz/iStock/Getty Image Plus

Congratulations! You've accepted an offer for your first job. You are now a member of the workforce.

representative, you may be given a test that assesses your personality traits. Don't be intimidated by these tests; you are not expected to know everything or be perfect. They are really just a trial run to give the employer a sense of whether you can think fast on your feet and perform under pressure.

Making the Employment Decision

After receiving your résumé, conducting one or two interviews, and administering a skills test, a potential employer knows a bit more about you. You should also know a lot about the company. If the experience has been positive on both sides, you may be offered a job. If you have interviewed at several companies and are offered more than one job, congratulations! Often, an employer will phone you to make the job offer, saying that the formal offer will follow via e-mail or through the mail. Whether you receive one offer or several, thank the person making the offer. If you choose to accept immediately, feel free to do so. However, employers commonly expect that the candidate will want to review the offer letter before formally accepting. If you have doubts about the job or need to decide between two, it is appropriate to ask for a short period of time to respond. If you must decline an offer, do so promptly and politely. After all, you may end up working for that firm sometime in the future. If you get a few rejections before you receive an offer, don't give up. Every application and interview adds to your experience.

As you think about an offer, consider the aspects that are most important. You'll want to choose a job that comes closest to your career interests and objectives. But don't rule out the element of surprise—you might wind up with a job you like in an industry you'd never considered before. Don't worry too much about the salary. The point of an entry-level job is to set you on a forward path, commonly known as a "stepping stone." And keep in mind that your first job won't be your last. Once you have accepted an offer, you'll be given a start date as well as the name of the person to whom you should report on arrival.

Nontraditional Students

Take a quick glance around your class. You'll likely see classmates of all ages. Some will fall into the traditional college age group of 18 to 24, but many don't. Perhaps you are a veteran returning from military duty overseas. Maybe you have been engaged in a full-time career but want to broaden your education. Students who fall outside the 18- to 24-year-old age group are often referred to as *nontraditional students,* but these students have become the norm on many campuses. Stay-at-home parents returning to school to retool and add skills to their résumés before returning to the workforce and workers who have been laid off due to an economic downturn are other examples of nontraditional students. As diverse as this group is, they share one thing in common: They are older than traditional students, typically 25 and older. This means that they face different challenges—but they also enjoy some advantages over their younger classmates.

One major challenge faced by nontraditional students is scheduling. Often they are juggling the responsibilities of work, school, and family. They may have to study at odd times—during meals, while commuting, or after putting the kids to bed. If they are switching careers, they may be learning an entirely new set of skills as well. But nontraditional students have an important advantage: experience. Even experience in an unrelated field is a plus. Older students know how organizations operate. Often, they have developed useful skills in human relations, management, budgeting, and communications. Even a former stay-at-home parent has skills in all of these areas. Through observing other people's successes and failures—as well as living through their own—they have developed an inventory of what to do and what not to do. So, in some ways these students have a head start on their younger counterparts. But they also face the reality that they have fewer years in which to develop a career.

The Job Market: Where Do You Fit In?

The industry you choose, and the career you follow within it, are part of a bigger picture. They reflect the needs of society, changing populations, developing technology, and the overall economy. For instance, the U.S. population is expected to increase at a slower rate of growth for the foreseeable future than during the previous two decades. The U.S. labor force will reach 168 million by 2024. In addition, the U.S. workforce will continue to become more diverse, with Hispanics accounting for both the largest share of jobs, projected at 23% over the next two decades, as compared to 16% in a recent year.[16]

The number of women in the workforce is growing at a slightly faster rate than that of men. As a result, the share of women in the labor force is projected to increase to 47.2% in 2024. The men's share of the labor force is expected to decrease to 52.8% in 2024.[17]

All of these facts combine to shape a picture of the needs of U.S. society and the workforce available to serve it. As the Baby Boom generation ages, the age group between 55 and 64 will increase by more than one-third. Thus, the United States will need more health care services as well as other services for an aging population, such as assisted living facilities and leisure and hospitality. The group between the ages 25 and 54 will rise a mere 0.4%, while the youth population between 16 and 24 will decline by 1.4%. But today's younger workers are receiving more education and training to fill the need for professional and business service workers. These projections affect both the workforce and the types of goods and services needed to satisfy consumers. So jobs in health care are estimated to increase by more than 5.6 million and in professional and business services by 3.8 million.[18]

Careers in service-providing industries (see chapter 1 for a list) continue a long-term rise. Service jobs in educational services will increase, while manufacturing jobs will continue to shrink. But industries that produce certain types of goods, such as those related to the needs of an aging population and those related to green technologies or products, will probably increase.[19]

The good news is that even in a weaker job market, employers are looking to hire recent college graduates. Continuing to hire entry-level employees makes good business sense. The National Association of Colleges and Employers (NACE) reports that college hiring is actually on the rise as employers plan to hire 4% more new college graduates this year than last.[20] Some of the hot jobs can be found in accounting, sales, management training, engineering, and business services. So celebrate your graduation, and keep your résumé and LinkedIn profile current and your outlook positive: a job is out there for you.

A Long-Range View of Your Career

Choosing a career is an important life decision. A career is a professional journey—regardless of whether you want to run a small restaurant or a bank branch, whether you are fascinated by language or math, or whether you prefer to work with animals or people. In the end, you hope to contribute something good to society while enjoying what you do—and make a reasonable living at it.

Throughout your career, it is important to stay flexible and continue learning. Challenging new skills will be required of managers and other businesspeople, particularly during a time when technology is creating change at lightning speed. Remain open to unexpected changes and opportunities that can help you learn and develop new skills. Keep in mind that your first job will not be your last. But tackle that first job with the same enthusiasm you'd have if someone asked you to run the company itself, because everything you learn on that job will be valuable at some point during your career—and someday you may actually run the company.

Finally, if you haven't already started your career search, begin now. Do this by utilizing your contacts and network, lining up an internship, looking for a part-time job on or off campus, or volunteering for an organization. Register with the campus career center long before you graduate. Then, when you reach your final semester, you'll be well on your way to finding the job you want.

This textbook presents a panorama of career options for you. Whatever you decide, be sure it is right for you—not your friends, your instructors, or your parents. As the old saying goes, "You pass this way just once." Enjoy the journey!

More Career Information available in WileyPLUS Learning Space

More career information is available to students using *Contemporary Business* at WileyPlus. The careers section on the website enables you to learn more about business careers along with additional resources for job opportunities. The site provides a vast number of career resources such as links to job sites, career guidance sites, and the like. Also, many links include extensive career information and guidance, such as interviewing techniques and tips for résumé writing.

Projects and Teamwork Applications

1. Visit one of the job websites, such as Indeed or Glassdoor, and research an industry in which you think you might be interested. Prepare a report on what you learned about the field. Was the site helpful? What types of jobs were available in the field? Based on your report, do you plan to pursue this industry or select another field?
2. Prepare your résumé following the procedures outlined in this section. Exchange your résumé with a classmate so you can critique each other's work. Then revise and proofread your résumé.
3. Go online to the website for a specific company for which you might be interested in working. Click on the "Careers" or "Job Opportunities" section of the site, and read carefully the job descriptions for any entry-level positions and the procedure for applying for them. Also review any general information about career development at the firm. Write a cover letter as if you were actually applying for one of the jobs.
4. With a classmate, practice interviewing for the job you selected in question 3. Prepare commonly asked questions for each other and take turns interviewing and being interviewed. What parts of the interview did you handle well? What could you improve?
5. Think about where you would like to be in your career in five years and write about your plans. Share your plans with the class, then either write and save them in an email or seal them in an envelope. Keep the email or envelope and open it in five years to see how close you came to your predictions.

Appendix F

Launching Your Career

Global Business and Economics

Business has always been an exciting career field, whether you choose to start your own company, work at a local business, or set your sights on working for a multinational corporation. But today's environment is especially attractive because businesses have expanded their horizons to compete in a global economy—and they need dedicated and talented people to help them accomplish their goals. In fact, professional and business service jobs are found in some of the fastest-growing industries in the U.S. economy and are projected to grow during this decade.[1] So now is the time to explore several different career options that can lead you to your dream job. This text profiles a few of the many opportunities available in business.

If you're good at math and are interested in how societies and companies function, then maybe a career as an *economist* is in your future. Economists study how resources are allocated, conduct research by collecting and analyzing data, monitor economic trends, and develop forecasts. They look into such vital areas as the cost of energy, foreign trade and exchange between countries, the effect of taxes, and employment levels—both from a big-picture national or global viewpoint and from the perspective of individual businesses. Economists work for corporations to help them run more efficiently, for consulting companies to offer special expertise, or for government agencies to oversee economic decision making. Typically, advanced degrees are needed to climb to top-level positions. Economists typically earn about $102,490 per year.[2]

Or perhaps you are interested in global business. Companies increasingly search the world for the best employees, supplies, and markets. You could work in the United States for a foreign-based company such as Siemens or Toyota; abroad in Australia, Asia, Europe, or Latin America for a U.S.-based company such as Microsoft; or with overseas co-workers via computer networks to develop new products for a company such as General Electric. With technology and telecommunications, distance is no longer a barrier to conducting business. Global business careers exist in all the areas presented in this text—business ownership, management, marketing, technology, and finance.

Global business leaders are not born but made—so how can you start on that career path? Here are the three areas that businesses consider when selecting employees for overseas assignment:

- *competence*—including technical knowledge, language skills, leadership ability, experience, and past performance
- *adaptability*—including interest in overseas work, communication and other personal skills, empathy for other cultures, and appreciation for varied management styles and work environments
- *personal characteristics*—level of education, experience, and social compatibility with the host country[3]

Solid experience in your field or within a company ranks at the top of the list of required skills. Companies want to send employees who have expertise in their business and loyalty to the company to represent them overseas. Companies are reluctant to send new graduates abroad immediately. Instead, they invest in training to onboard employees to the new assignment.

Knowledge of and interest in other languages and cultures is the second-highest priority. Businesspeople need to function smoothly in another society, so they are selected based on their familiarity with other languages and cultures. Because many companies are doing business in China, some people have become fluent in Mandarin Chinese to increase their career prospects. Also, many school systems are offering Chinese language classes in addition to their standard offerings of Spanish, French, German, and Russian.

Finally, employees are evaluated on their personal characteristics to be certain that they will fit well in their new country. A person's talent is still foremost in making assignments, but executives with cross-cultural skills are in high demand.

Career Assessment Exercises in Economics and Global Business

1. With the ups and downs in the U.S. economy, economists have been highlighted in the news. The head of the Federal Reserve, Jerome Powell, is charged with managing the nation's currency, money supply, and interest rates. To get an idea of the role economists play in a federal government agency, research Powell's background and qualifications. Now make a list of your own skills. Looking at Powell's background, how can you improve your skill set?
2. To see the effect of the global economy in your community, go to any major retailer. Look at the number of different countries represented in the products on the shelves. Compare your list with those of your classmates to see who found the most countries and what goods those countries provided. Go online to research the career opportunities at the retailer's website.
3. To learn more about other countries, do research online for a country in which you are interested. Here are some sources that may be useful:
   - *The World Factbook*, published by the Central Intelligence Agency, https://www.cia.gov/library/publications/the-world-factbook. This publication, updated yearly, contains a wealth of information about countries—geography and climate, population statistics, cultural and political information, transportation and communications methods, and economic data.
   - *Bloomberg Businessweek* magazine, www.bloomberg.com. The website has a direct link to global technology news (www.bloomberg.com/technology), where you can explore breaking news or information on global technology companies.
   - Online news sites Yahoo! News and Google News, http://news.yahoo.com and http://news.google.com. Both of these online news sites have links to global business news.

Write a one-page summary of what you found. Make a list of abilities you would need to function well as a businessperson in that country. Concentrate on the areas of competence, adaptability, and personal characteristics. How might you formulate a plan to gain those skills?

Entrepreneurial

You've been introduced to a wide variety of entrepreneurial or small businesses; the forms they can take—sole proprietorship, partnership, or corporation—and the reasons that some new ventures succeed and others fail. You learned that entrepreneurs are visionaries who build companies that create wealth and that they share traits such as vision and creativity, high energy, optimism, a strong need to achieve, and a tolerance for failure. By now you might be wondering how you can make all this information work for you. Here are some career ideas and opportunities in the small-business and e-business areas.

First, whatever field attracts you as a future business owner, try to acquire experience by working for someone else in the industry initially. The information and skills you pick up will be invaluable when you start out on your own. Lack of experience is often cited as a leading reason for small-business failure.[4]

Next, look for a good fit between your own skills, abilities, and characteristics and a market need or niche. For example, the U.S. Department of Labor reports that opportunities in many health care fields are rising with the nation's increased demand for health services. Employment of medical and health services managers is projected to grow 20 percent until 2026.[5]

As the population of older people rises, and as young families find themselves increasingly pressed for time, the need for childcare and elder services will also increase—and so will the opportunities for new businesses in those areas. So read as many business publications as possible, and keep your eyes on trends to find ideas that you can use or adapt.

Another way to look for market needs is to talk to current customers or business associates. When the owner of Michigan-based Moon Valley Rustic Furniture wanted to retire, he went to see Rick Detkowski, who was in the real estate business. The owner intended to offer the buildings to Detkowski and close down the business. But the real estate agent, who owned several pieces of Moon Valley furniture himself, instead decided to buy, not just the buildings, but the furniture business, too. Before the sale was completed—and to determine whether he could run Moon Valley profitably—Detkowski talked with existing customers and furniture dealers, who had been hoping for years that the company would expand its line of sturdy cedar and pine items from the traditional summer lawn furniture into more innovative designs. Further research showed that the general environmental trend among consumers was boosting demand for rustic furniture. So Detkowski took the plunge and is now in the furniture manufacturing business. He has expanded the company's product lines and reorganized the factory floor for more efficiency—and cost savings.[6]

Are you intrigued by the idea of being your own boss but worried about risking your savings to get a completely new and untried business off the ground? Then owning a franchise, such as Planet Fitness or Dunkin' Donuts, might be for you. The Small Business Administration advises aspiring entrepreneurs that while franchising can be less risky than starting a new business from scratch, it still requires hard work and sacrifice. In addition, you need to completely understand both the resources to which you will be entitled and the responsibilities you will assume under the franchise agreement. Again, filling a market need is important for success. To find more information about franchising, access the Federal Trade Commission's consumer guide to buying a franchise at https://www.ftc.gov/tips-advice/business-center/guidance/consumers-guide-buying-franchise.

Are you skilled in a particular area of business, technology, or science? The consulting industry will be a rapidly growing area for several years, according to the Bureau of Labor Statistics.[7] Consulting companies offer their expertise to clients in private, government, not-for-profit, and even foreign business operations. Business consultants influence clients' decisions in marketing, finance, manufacturing, information systems, e-business, human resources, and many other areas including corporate strategy and organization. Technology consultants support businesses in all fields, with services ranging from setting up a secure website or training employees in the use of new software to managing an off-site help desk or planning for disaster recovery. Science consulting companies find plenty of work in the field of environmental consulting, helping businesses deal with pollution cleanup and control, habitat protection, and compliance with government's environmental regulations and standards.

But perhaps none of these areas appeals to you quite so much as tinkering with gears and machinery or with computer graphics and code. If you think you have the insight and creativity to invent something completely new, you need to make sure you're informed about patents, trademarks, and copyright laws to protect your ideas. Each area offers different protections for your work, and none will guarantee success. Here again, hard work, persistence, and a little bit of luck will help you succeed.

Career Assessment Exercises in Entrepreneurship and Business Ownership

1. Go online and search for "Entrepreneur Quiz." You should be able to find a variety of different ways to determine what it takes to become an entrepreneur. Take a few of the quizzes. Are you ready to strike out on your own? What did your results reveal? What can you do to increase the likelihood of your success?
2. Find an independent business or franchise in your area, and make an appointment to talk to the owner about his or her start-up experience. Prepare a list of questions for a 10- to

15-minute interview, and remember to ask about details such as the number of hours worked per week, approximate start-up costs, goals of the business, available resources, lessons learned since opening, and rewards of owning the business. How different are the owner's answers from what you expected?

3. Search online for information about how to file for a patent, trademark, or copyright. A good starting point is http://www.uspto.gov. Assume you have an invention you want to protect. Find out which forms are required, the necessary fees, how much time is typically needed to complete the legal steps, and what rights and protections you may gain.

Management

Now you've learned about top executives and company founders who not only direct their companies' strategy but lead others in their day-to-day tasks to keep them on track, middle managers who devise plans to turn the strategies into realities, and supervisors who work directly with employees to create strong teams that satisfy customers. An incredible variety of jobs is available to those choosing management careers. And the demand for managers will continue to grow. The U.S. Department of Labor estimates that managerial jobs will grow by about 8% over the next decade.[8]

So what kinds of jobs might you be able to choose from if you launch a management career? As you learned, three levels of management jobs exist: supervisory managers, middle managers, and top managers. Supervisory management, or first-line management, includes positions such as supervisor, office manager, department manager, section chief, and team leader. Managers at this level work directly with the employees who produce and sell a company's goods and services.

Middle management includes positions such as general managers, plant managers, division managers, and regional or branch managers. They are responsible for setting objectives consistent with top management's goals and planning and implementing strategies for achieving those objectives.

Top managers include such positions as chief executive officer (CEO), chief operating officer (COO), chief financial officer (CFO), chief information officer (CIO), and executive vice president. Top managers devote most of their time to developing long-range plans, setting a direction for their organization, and inspiring a company's executives and employees to achieve their vision for the company's future. Top managers travel frequently between local, national, and global offices as they meet and work with customers, vendors, and company managers and employees.

Most managers start their careers in areas such as sales, production, or finance, so you likely will start in a similar entry-level job. If you do that job and other jobs well, you may be considered for a supervisory position. Then, if you are interested and have the technical, human, and conceptual skills to succeed, you'll begin your management career path. But what kinds of supervisory management jobs are typically available? Let's review the exciting possibilities.[9]

Administrative services managers manage basic services—such as clerical work, payroll, travel, printing and copying, data records, telecommunications, security, parking, and supplies—without which no organization could operate. On average, administrative service managers earn $94,020 a year.

Construction managers plan, schedule, and coordinate the building of homes, commercial buildings such as offices and stores, and industrial facilities such as manufacturing plants and distribution centers. Unlike administrative service managers, who work in offices, construction managers typically work on building sites with architects, engineers, construction workers, and suppliers. On average, construction managers earn $91,370 a year.

Food service managers run restaurants and services that prepare and offer meals to customers. They coordinate workers and suppliers in kitchens, dining areas, and banquet operations; are responsible for those who order and purchase food inventories; maintain kitchen equipment; and recruit, hire, and train new workers. Food service managers can work for chains such as Ruby Tuesday or Olive Garden, for local restaurants, and for corporate food service departments in organizations. On average, food service managers earn more than $52,030 a year.

Human resource managers help organizations follow federal and local labor laws; effectively recruit, hire, train, and retain talented workers; administer corporate pay and benefits plans; develop and administer organizational human resource policies; and, when necessary, participate in contract negotiations or handle disputes. Human resource management jobs vary widely, depending on how specialized the requirements are. On average, human resource managers earn $110,120 a year.

Lodging managers work in hotels and motels but also help run camps, ranches, and recreational resorts. They may oversee guest services, front desk, kitchen, restaurant, banquet, house cleaning, and maintenance workers. Because they are expected to help satisfy customers around the clock, they often work long hours and may be on call when not at work. On average, lodging managers earn about $51,800 a year.

Medical and health services managers work in hospitals, nursing homes, doctors' offices, and corporate and university settings. They run departments that offer clinical services; ensure that state and federal laws are followed; and handle decisions related to the management of patient care, nursing, surgery, therapy, medical records, and financial payments. On average, medical and health service managers earn $98,350 a year.

Sales managers direct organizations' sales teams. They set sales goals, analyze data, and develop training programs for organizations' sales representatives. On average, sales managers earn roughly $121,060 a year. Industrial production managers oversee the daily operations of manufacturing and related plants. They coordinate, plan, and direct the activities used to create a wide range of goods, such as cars, computer equipment, or paper products. On average, industrial production managers earn almost $100,580 a year.

Career Assessment Exercises in Management

1. The American Management Association is a global, not-for-profit professional organization that provides a range of management development and educational services to individuals, companies, and government agencies. Access the AMA's web site at http://www.amanet.org. Explore under "Articles and White Papers." Pick an article or research area that interests you. Provide a one-page summary of the management issues discussed in the feature.
2. Go online to a business news website like *Wall Street Journal, Forbes,* or *Fortune.* Find a news release about a first-line supervisor, middle manager, or top executive. Summarize that person's responsibilities. What decisions does that person make, and how do those decisions impact his or her organization?
3. Pick a supervisory management position that interests you from the descriptions provided here. Research the career field. What skills do you possess that would make you a good candidate for a management position in that field? What work and other experience do you need to help you get started? Create a list of both your strengths and weaknesses and formulate a plan to add to your strengths.

Marketing

The text has emphasized the central role of customer satisfaction in defining value and developing a marketing strategy in traditional and nontraditional marketing settings. You learned about the role of marketing research and the need for relationship marketing in today's competitive environment. You discovered how new products are developed and how they evolve through the four stages of the product life cycle, from introduction through growth and maturity to decline. You also learned about the role of different channels in creating effective distribution strategies. Finally, you saw the impact of integrated marketing communications on the company's promotional strategy, the role of advertising, and the way pricing influences consumer behavior. Perhaps you came across some marketing tasks and functions that sounded especially appealing to you. Here are a few ideas about careers in marketing that you may want to pursue.

One career path in marketing is sales. Do you work well with others and read their feelings accurately? Are you a self-starter? Being a *sales representative* might be for you. Selling jobs exist in every industry, and because many use a combination of salary and performance-based commissions, they can pay handsomely. Sales jobs are often part of a career trajectory to upper-management positions as well. Sales representatives work for wholesalers and manufacturing companies (and even for publishers such as the one that produces this book). They sell automobiles, computer cybersecurity systems and technology, pharmaceuticals, advertising, insurance, real estate, commodities and financial services, and all kinds of consumer goods and services.

If you're interested in mass communications, note that print and online magazines, newspapers, and broadcast companies generate most of their revenue from advertising, so sales representatives who sell space and time slots in the media contribute a great deal to the success of these companies.[10] See the "Job Description" feature in chapter 13 to learn more about a career as an advertising sales representative. And if you like to travel, consider that many sales jobs involve travel.

Advertising, marketing management, and *public relations* are other categories of marketing. In large companies, marketing managers, product managers, promotion managers, and public relations managers often work long hours under pressure; they may travel frequently or transfer between jobs at headquarters and positions in regional offices. Their responsibilities include directing promotional programs, overseeing advertising campaigns and budgets, and creating communications such as press releases for the company's customers. Thousands of new positions for public relations managers and specialists are expected to open up in the next several years; the field is expected to grow 9% over the next decade. Growth of the Internet and social media has especially increased demand for advertising and public relations specialists.[11]

Advertising and public relations companies together employed about 495,000 people in a recent year.[12] About 25% of U.S. advertising employees work in California, and another 20% work in New York. Most advertising agencies develop specialties; many of the largest are international in scope and earn a major proportion of their revenue abroad. Online and social media advertising is just one area in which new jobs will be opening in the future, as more and more client companies have expanded their online sales operations.

Career Assessment Exercises in Marketing

1. Choose an industry that interests you. Go online to research types of sales positions within that industry. Locate a few entry-level job openings and evaluate the career steps that the positions can lead to. (You might start with a popular job-posting site such as Indeed.com.) Note the job requirements, the starting salary, and the form of compensation—straight salary? salary plus commission?—and write a one-page summary of your findings.
2. Go online to identify and investigate two or three of the leading advertising agencies in the United States, such as Weiden + Kennedy, BBDO, Digitas, or Omnicom Group. What are some of their recent ad campaigns, or who are their best-known clients? Where do the agencies have offices? What job openings are currently listed, and what qualifications should applicants for these positions have? Write a brief report comparing the agencies you selected, decide which one you would prefer to work for, and give your reasons.
3. Test your research skills. Choose an ordinary product, such as toothpaste or soft drinks, and conduct a survey to find out why people chose the brand they most recently purchased. For example, suppose you wanted to find out how people choose their shampoo. List as many decision criteria as you can think of, such as availability, scent, price, packaging, benefits from use (conditioning, dandruff reducing, and so on), brand name, and ad or social media campaign. Ask 8 to 10 friends (or use SurveyMonkey.com) to rank these decision factors, and note some simple demographics about your research subjects such as their age, gender, and occupation. Tabulate your results. What did you find out about how your subjects made their purchase decision? Did any of your findings surprise you? Can you think of any ways in which you might have improved your survey?

Information Technology

We have discussed well-known technology companies such as Google as well as smaller organizations that use computer technology to manage information. These examples illustrate that all organizations need to manage technology and information. And with the complexity and scope of technology and information (including big data) likely to increase in the years ahead, the demand for information systems professionals is expected to grow.

According to the U.S. Department of Labor, employment in such information technology occupations as computer systems design, the manufacture of computers, electronic components and peripheral equipment, and information services is expected to grow 12% in the next decade, faster than the average for all occupations. This is due in part to cloud computing, the Internet of Things, and a continued demand for mobile computing.[13]

What types of jobs are available in information systems? What are the working conditions like? What are the career paths? Information technology is a fairly broad occupation and encompasses a wide variety of jobs. In some cases you'll work in the IT department of a business such as Procter & Gamble or Shell. In other cases, you'll work for a specialized information systems company, such as IBM, which provides services to governments, not-for-profit organizations, and businesses.

Information technology and information systems are popular business majors, and many entry-level positions are available each year. Many IT graduates spend their entire careers in the field, while others move into other areas. People who began their careers in information systems are well represented in the ranks of senior management today. Let's look briefly at some of the specific jobs you might find after earning an IT degree.

Computer systems analysts are goal focused and process oriented. Computer systems analysts must understand computer hardware, software, and networks and how they work together so they can make recommendations to organizations for the best operations systems to use. See the "Job Description" feature in Chapter 14 to learn more detail about this career. In a recent *U.S. News & World Report* study on "Best Technology Jobs," software developer landed the number-one spot. Software developers are in high demand, and they are employed in a range of industries, including computer systems design, manufacturing, and finance. Because businesses are increasingly reliant on information technology, jobs in this field should continue to grow by 21% over the next decade.[14]

Information security analysts plan and monitor security of computer networks. This occupation will grow by more than 28% in the next decade.

Database administrators set up databases to fit a company's need and then maintain those systems as part of the company's day-to-day operations.

IT managers are the go-to-personnel when your e-mail won't send or your word processor won't work. As the head of the IT department, they triage the operations of an organization's technical network, and they are part of a growing profession.

Computer systems administrators keep your e-mails moving and your web pages loading, plus they lend their tech-savvy skills to managing various telecommunication networks.

Career Assessment Exercises in Information Systems

1. Assume you're interested in a career as a systems analyst. Go to the career website http://www.indeed.com. After reviewing a number of jobs that interest you, prepare a brief report outlining the responsibilities of a systems analyst, who hires for these positions, and what kind of educational background is required.
2. Identify a person working in your local area in information technology and arrange an interview with that person (your college career center may be able to help you). Ask that person about his or her job responsibilities, educational background, and the best and worst aspects of his or her job.

Finance

Finance deals with planning, obtaining, and managing an organization's funds to accomplish its objectives in the most effective way possible. We covered accounting principles and various financial statements. We also discussed the financial system, including the various types of securities, financial markets and institutions, the Federal Reserve System, financial regulators, and global financial markets. We examined the role financial managers play in an organization; financial planning; short- and long-term financing options; and mergers, acquisitions, buyouts, and divestitures. We described the finance functions of a variety of businesses, governments, and not-for-profit organizations. As the text illustrates, finance is a very diverse profession and encompasses many different occupations. According to the U.S. Department of Labor, over the next decade most finance-related occupations are expected to experience 10% employment growth. Employment in the financial investment industry should be strong because of the number of Baby Boomers in their peak earning years with funds to invest and the globalization of securities markets.[15]

In most business schools, finance is one of the most popular majors among undergraduates. Combining finance with accounting is a common double major. Those with degrees in finance also enjoy relatively high starting salaries. A recent survey found that the average starting salary for a person with an undergraduate degree in finance was nearly $84,300 per year.[16]

All organizations need to obtain and manage funds, so they employ finance professionals. To learn more about the role of a financial manager, see the "Job Description" feature in chapter 17. Financial institutions and other financial services companies employ a large percentage of finance graduates. These businesses provide important finance-related services to businesses, governments, and not-for-profit organizations. Some graduates with finance degrees take jobs with financial services companies such as Bank of America and JPMorgan Chase, while others begin their careers working in the finance departments of businesses in other industries such as construction and mining, transportation, governments, or not-for-profit organizations. You may begin your career evaluating commercial loan applications for a bank, analyzing capital investments for a business, or helping a not-for-profit organization decide how to invest its endowment. Often finance professionals work as members of a team, advising top management. Some individuals spend their entire careers working in finance-related occupations; others use their finance experience to move into other areas of the company. Today, the chief financial officer—the senior finance executive—holds one of the most critical jobs in any organization. In addition, the number of CEOs who began their careers in finance is growing.

Finance is a diverse, exciting profession. Here are a few of the specific occupations you might find after earning a degree in finance.

Financial analysts provide guidance to businesses and individuals making investment decisions. They are responsible for assessing the performance of a variety of securities, including stocks, bonds, and other types of investments. Financial analysts work in a variety of settings, including banks, pension funds, mutual funds, securities companies, insurance companies, and other businesses. They evaluate data, study economic and business trends, examine and analyze a company's financial statements, meet with company managers to gain insight into the company's strategies and operations, and prepare written reports. They are often referred to as *securities analysts* or *investment analysts.*[17]

Most *loan officers* work for commercial banks and other financial institutions. They find potential clients and help them apply for loans. Loan officers typically specialize in commercial, consumer, or mortgage loans. In many cases, loan officers act in a sales capacity, contacting individuals and organizations about their need for funds and trying to persuade them to borrow the funds from the loan officer's institution. Thus, loan officers often need marketing as well as finance skills.

Security analysts generally work for financial services companies such as Fidelity or Raymond James & Associates. Security analysts review economic data, financial statements, and other information to determine the outlook for securities such as common stocks and bonds. They make investment recommendations to individual and institutional investors.

Many senior security analysts hold a chartered financial analyst (CFA) designation. Obtaining a CFA requires a specific educational background, several years of related experience, and a passing grade on a comprehensive, three-stage examination.

Portfolio managers manage money for an individual or institutional client. Many portfolio managers work for pension funds or mutual funds for which they make investment decisions to benefit the funds' beneficiaries. Portfolio managers generally have extensive experience as financial managers or security analysts, and many are CFAs.

Personal financial planners help individuals make decisions in areas such as insurance, investments, and retirement planning. Personal financial planners meet with their clients, assess their needs and goals, and make recommendations. Approximately 30% of personal financial planners are self-employed, and many hold certified financial planner (CFP) designations. Like the CFA, obtaining a CFP requires a specific educational background, related experience, and passing a comprehensive examination.

Career Assessment Exercises in Finance

1. Assume you're interested in pursuing a career as a security analyst. You've heard that the CFA is an important designation and can help enhance your career. Visit the CFA's website (http://www.cfainstitute.org) to learn more about the CFA. Specifically, what are the requirements to obtain a CFA, and what are the professional benefits of having a CFA?
2. Arrange for an interview with a commercial loan officer at a local bank. Ask the loan officer about his or her educational background, what a typical day is like, and what the loan officer likes and doesn't like about his or her job.
3. Ameriprise Financial offers financial planning services to individuals and organizations. Visit the company's careers website (https://www.joinameriprise.com). Review the site, and write a brief summary of what you learned about being a personal financial planner. Does such a career interest you? Why or why not?

Company Index

D

E

F

Glossary

360-degree performance review employee performance review that gathers feedback from co-workers, supervisors, managers, and sometimes customers.

3D printing etching of plastic layers into different shapes by laying down successive layers of material to form a 3D solid.

401(k) plan retirement savings plan to which employees can make pretax contributions; employers often make additional contributions to the plan.

accounting process of measuring, interpreting, and communicating financial information to support internal and external business decision making.

accounting cycle set of activities involved in converting information and individual transactions into financial statements.

accounting equation formula that states that assets must always equal the sum of liabilities and owners' equity.

accrual accounting accounting method that records revenues and expenses when they occur, not necessarily when cash actually changes hands.

acquisition agreement in which one company purchases another.

activity ratios measures of how efficiently a firm utilizes its assets.

actuarial table probability of the number of events that are expected to occur within a given year.

advertising paid nonpersonal communication usually targeted at large numbers of potential buyers.

affective conflict disagreement that focuses on individuals or personal issues.

affinity program marketing effort sponsored by an organization that solicits involvement by individuals who share common interests and activities.

affirmative action programs programs designed by employers to increase job opportunities for women, minorities, disabled people, and other protected groups.

alien corporation firm incorporated in one nation and operating in another nation.

angel investors wealthy individuals who invest directly in a new venture in exchange for an equity stake.

appellate courts courts that hear appeals of decisions made at the general trial court level; both the federal and state systems have appellate courts.

application service provider (ASP) outside supplier that provides both the computers and the application support for managing an information system.

arbitration bringing in an impartial third party called an arbitrator to render a binding decision in a dispute.

assembly line manufacturing technique that carries the product on a conveyor system past several workstations where workers perform specialized tasks.

asset anything of value owned by a company.

asset intensity amount of assets needed to generate a given level of sales.

autocratic leadership management approach whereby leaders make decisions on their own without consulting employees.

balance of payments overall money flows into and out of a country.

balance of trade difference between a nation's exports and imports.

balance sheet statement of a company's financial position—what it owns and claims against its assets—at a particular point in time.

balanced budget situation in which total revenues raised by taxes and fees equal total proposed government spending for the year.

bankruptcy legal nonpayment of financial obligations.

banner ad advertisement placed by an organization on another organization's website; interested parties click on the ad for more information.

benchmarking process of determining how well other companies perform business functions or tasks.

benefit corporation type of for-profit entity that includes a positive impact on society and the environment as part of its defined goals.

big data information collected in massive amounts and at unprecedented speed from both traditional and digital sources that is used in business decision making; complex structured or unstructured sets of information that traditional processing applications are unable to analyze.

blog a web page that serves as a publicly accessible personal journal for an individual or organization.

board of directors governing body of a corporation.

bot short for robot—a program that allows online shoppers to compare prices for a specific product at several e-tailers.

botnet a network of PCs that have been infected with one or more data-stealing viruses.

boycott effort to prevent people from purchasing a firm's goods or services.

brand name, term, sign, symbol, design, or some combination that identifies the products of one company and differentiates them from competitors' offerings.

brand equity added value that a respected and successful name gives to a product.

brand name part of a brand consisting of words or letters that form a name that identifies and distinguishes an offering from those of competitors.

branding process of creating an identity in consumers' minds for a good, service, or company; a major marketing tool in contemporary business.

breach of contract violation of a valid contract.

breakeven analysis pricing-related technique used to determine the minimum sales volume a product must generate at a certain price level to cover all costs.

broadband the most used form of Internet access. With its high access speeds, it is offered in four different forms: DSL (or Digital Subscriber Line), fiber-optic, cable, and satellite.

budget company's plan for how it will raise and spend money during a given period of time.

budget deficit situation in which the government spends more than the amount of money it raises through taxes.

budget surplus excess funding that occurs when government spends less than the amount of funds raised through taxes and fees.

business all profit-seeking activities and enterprises that provide goods and services necessary to an economic system.

business (B2B) product good or service purchased to be used, either directly or indirectly, in the production of other goods for resale.

business ethics standards of conduct and moral values regarding right and wrong actions in the work environment.

business incubator local programs designed to provide low-cost shared business facilities to small start-up ventures.

business intelligence activities and technologies for gathering, storing, and analyzing data to make better competitive decisions.

business interruption insurance type of insurance that protects firms from financial losses resulting from the suspension of business operations.

business law aspects of law that most directly influence and regulate the management of business activity.

business plan written document that provides an orderly statement of a company's goals, methods, and standards.

business-to-business (B2B) e-commerce electronic business transactions between organizations using the Internet.

business-to-consumer (B2C) e-commerce selling directly to consumers over the Internet.

call provision right of the issuer to buy a bond back from the investor before maturity at a specified price.

capital production inputs consisting of technology, tools, information, and physical facilities.

capital investment analysis process of comparing the costs and benefits of a long-term asset investment.

capital structure mix of a company's debt and equity capital.

capitalism economic system that rewards companies for their ability to perceive and serve the needs and demands of consumers; also called the private enterprise system.

cash budget budget that shows cash inflows and outflows during a period of time.

cash flow sources of cash minus uses of cash during a specified period of time.

cash value policy type of life insurance that combines insurance protection with a savings feature.

category advisor vendor that is designated by the business customer as the major supplier to assume responsibility for dealing with all the other vendors for a project and presenting the entire package to the business buyer.

category manager person who oversees an entire group of products and assumes profit responsibility for the product group.

cause advertising form of institutional advertising that promotes a specific viewpoint on a public issue as a way to influence public opinion and the legislative process.

cause marketing marketing that promotes a cause or social issue, such as preventing child abuse, anti-littering efforts, and stop-smoking campaigns.

Central America–Dominican Republic Free Trade Agreement (CAFTA-DR) agreement among the United States, Costa Rica, El Salvador, Guatemala, Honduras, Nicaragua, and the Dominican Republic to reduce tariffs and trade restrictions.

centralization decision making based at the top of the management hierarchy.

certified management accountant (CMA) management accountant who meets specified educational and experience requirements and has passed an examination covering management accounting topics.

certified public accountant (CPA) public accountant who meets specified educational and experiential requirements and has passed a comprehensive examination on accounting theory and practice, auditing, law, and taxes.

chain of command set of relationships that indicates who directs which activities and who reports to whom.

channel conflict conflict between two or more members of a supply chain, such as a manufacturer, wholesaler, or retailer.

chief information officer (CIO) executive responsible for managing a firm's information system and related computer technologies.

Class-Action Fairness Act of 2005 law that moves most large, multistate class-action lawsuits to federal courts, ensures judicial oversight of plaintiffs' compensation, bases lawyers' compensation on awards actually distributed or actual time spent, and ensures plaintiffs' interests are protected equally with those of their lawyers.

classic entrepreneur person who identifies a business opportunity and allocates available resources to tap that market.

click-through rate number of visitors who click on a web banner ad.

cloud computing powerful servers store applications software and databases for users to access the software and databases via the web using anything from a PC to a smart phone.

cobranding cooperative arrangement in which two or more businesses team up to closely link their names on a single product.

code of conduct formal statement that defines how an organization expects its employees to resolve ethical issues.

cognitive ability tests tests that measure job candidates' abilities in perceptual speed, verbal comprehension, numerical aptitude, general reasoning, and spatial aptitude.

cognitive conflict disagreement that focuses on problem- and issue-related differences of opinion.

collective bargaining process of negotiation between management and union representatives.

comarketing cooperative arrangement in which two businesses jointly market each other's products.

committee organization organizational structure that places authority and responsibility jointly in the hands of a group of individuals rather than a single manager.

common law body of law arising out of judicial decisions, some of which can be traced back to early England.

common stock shares that give owners voting rights but only residual claims to the firm's assets and income distributions.

communication meaningful exchange of information through messages.

communism economic system in which all property would be shared equally by the people of a community under the direction of a strong central government.

compensation amount employees are paid in money and benefits.

competition battle among businesses for consumer acceptance.

competitive differentiation unique combination of organizational abilities, products, and approaches that sets a company apart from competitors in the minds of customers.

competitive pricing strategy that tries to reduce the emphasis on price competition by matching other companies' prices and concentrating their own marketing efforts on the product, distribution, and promotional elements of the marketing mix.

compressed workweek scheduling option that allows employees to work the regular number of hours per week in fewer than the typical five days.

computer-aided design (CAD) process that allows engineers to design components as well as entire products on computer screens faster and with fewer mistakes than they could achieve working with traditional drafting systems.

computer-aided manufacturing (CAM) computer tools to analyze CAD output and enable a manufacturer to analyze the steps that a machine must take to produce a needed product or part.

computer-based information systems information systems that rely on computer and related technologies to store information electronically in an organized, accessible manner.

computer-integrated manufacturing (CIM) production system in which computers help workers design products, control machines, handle materials, and control the production function in an integrated fashion.

conceptual skills ability to see the organization as a unified whole and to understand how each part interacts with others.

conflict situation in which one person or group's needs do not match those of another, and attempts may be made to block the opposing side's intentions or goals.

conflict of interest situation in which an employee must choose between a business's welfare and personal gain.

conglomerate merger merger that combines unrelated firms, usually with the goal of diversification, spurring sales growth, or spending a cash surplus in order to avoid a takeover attempt.

consumer (B2C) product good or service that is purchased by end users.

consumer behavior actions of ultimate consumers directly involved in obtaining, consuming, and disposing of products and the decision processes that precede and follow these actions.

consumer orientation business philosophy that focuses first on determining unmet consumer wants and needs and then designing products to satisfy those needs.

Consumer Price Index (CPI) measurement of the monthly average change in prices of goods and services.

consumerism public demand that a business consider the wants and needs of its customers in making decisions.

contingency planning plans that allow a firm to resume operations as quickly and as smoothly as possible after a crisis while openly communicating with the public about what happened.

contract legally enforceable agreement between two or more parties regarding a specified act or thing.

controlling function of evaluating an organization's performance against its objectives.

convenience product item the consumer seeks to purchase frequently, immediately, and with little effort.

conversion rate percentage of visitors to a website who actually make a purchase.

convertible securities bonds or preferred stock issues that are convertible into a set number of shares of the issuing company's common stock.

cooperative organization whose owners join forces to collectively operate all or part of the functions in their business.

cooperative advertising allowances provided by marketers in which they share the cost of local advertising of their company's product or product line with channel partners.

copyright protection of written material such as books, designs, cartoon illustrations, photos, and computer software.

core inflation rate inflation rate of an economy after energy and food prices are removed.

corporate charter legal document that formally establishes a corporation.

corporate culture organization's system of principles, beliefs, and values.

corporate philanthropy effort of an organization to make a contribution to the communities in which it earns profits.

corporate website website designed to increase a company's visibility, promote its offerings, and provide information to interested parties.

corporation legal organization with assets and liabilities separate from those of its owner(s).

cost-based pricing formulas that calculate total costs per unit and then add markups to cover overhead costs and generate profits.

countertrade barter agreement whereby trade between two or more nations involves payment made in the form of local products instead of currency.

creative selling persuasive type of promotional presentation.

creativity capacity to develop novel solutions to perceived organizational problems.

credit receiving money, goods, or services on the basis of an agreement between the lender and the borrower that the loan is for a specified period of time with a specified rate of interest.

critical path sequence of operations that requires the longest time for completion.

critical thinking ability to analyze and assess information to pinpoint problems or opportunities.

cross-functional team a team made up of members from different functions, such as production, marketing, and finance.

crowdsourcing enlisting the collective talent of a number of people to get work done.

cyclical unemployment people who are out of work because of a cyclical contraction in the economy.

damages financial payments to compensate for a loss and related suffering.

data raw facts and figures that may or may not be relevant to a business decision.

data mining computer searches of customer data to detect patterns and relationships.

data warehouse customer database that allows managers to combine data from several different organizational functions.

database centralized integrated collection of data resources.

debenture unsecured corporate bond.

debt capital funds obtained from borrowing.

debt financing borrowed funds that entrepreneurs must repay.

decentralization decision makeup based at lower levels of the organization.

decision making process of recognizing a problem or opportunity, evaluating alternative solutions, selecting and implementing an alternative, and assessing the results.

decision support system (DSS) gives direct support to businesspeople during the decision-making process.

deflation opposite of inflation, occurs when prices continue to fall.

delegation managerial process of assigning work to employees.

demand willingness and ability of buyers to purchase goods and services.

demand curve graph of the amount of a product that buyers will purchase at different prices.

democratic leadership management approach whereby leaders delegate assignments, ask employees for suggestions, and encourage their participation.

demographic segmentation dividing markets on the basis of various demographic or socioeconomic characteristics such as gender, age, income, occupation, household size, stage in family life cycle, education, or ethnic group.

demographics statistical characteristics of the segment of the market that might purchase a product.

departmentalization process of dividing work activities into units within the organization.

deregulation regulatory trend toward elimination of legal restraints on competition in industries previously served by a single firm in an attempt to improve customer service and lower prices through increased competition.

devaluation reduction in a currency's value relative to other currencies or to a fixed standard.

digital marketing marketing of products or services using digital channels to reach consumers through promotion of brands through various forms of digital media.

direct distribution channel marketing channel that moves goods directly from producer to ultimate user.

directing guiding and motivating employees to accomplish organizational objectives.

disability income insurance type of insurance that pays benefits to those who cannot work due to some sort of disability.

discrimination biased treatment of a job candidate or employee.

dispatching phase of production control in which the manager instructs each department on what work to do and the time allowed for its completion.

display ad glossy-looking online ad often targeted at a specific user.

disruptive innovations less expensive and simpler versions of existing products and services that target an entirely new group of customers.

distribution channel path through which products—and legal ownership of them—flow from producer to consumers or business users.

distribution strategy deals with the marketing activities and institutions involved in getting the right good or service to the company's customers.

diversity blending individuals of different genders, ethnic backgrounds, cultures, religions, ages , and physical and mental abilities to enhance a company's chances of success.

divestiture sale of assets by a company.

domestic corporation company that operates in the state where it is incorporated.

double-entry bookkeeping process by which accounting transactions are entered; each individual transaction always has an offsetting transaction.

downsizing process of reducing the number of employees within a company by eliminating jobs.

dumping selling products abroad at prices below production costs or below typical prices in the home market to capture market share from domestic competitors.

e-commerce (or e-business) conducting business via the Internet.

e-procurement use of the Internet by business and government agencies to solicit bids and purchase goods and services from suppliers.

economic model one in which businesses believe strongly that their sole role is to maximize profits and increase value to shareholders.

economics social science that analyzes the choices people and governments make in allocating scarce resources.

electronic data interchange (EDI) computer-to-computer exchanges of invoices, purchase orders, price quotations, and other information between buyers and sellers.

electronic exchange online marketplace that caters to an industry's specific needs.

electronic shopping cart file that holds items that the online shopper has chosen to buy.

electronic storefront company website that sells products to customers.

electronic wallet secure computer data file set up by an online shopper at an e-business site that contains credit card and personal identification information.

embargo total ban on importing specific products or a total halt to trading with a particular country.

employee benefits additional compensation such as vacation, retirement plans, profit-sharing, health insurance, gym membership, child and elder care, and tuition reimbursement, paid entirely or in part by the company.

employee ownership business ownership in which workers own shares of stock in the company that employs them.

employee separation broad term covering the loss of an employee for any reason, voluntary or involuntary.

employee stock-ownership plan (ESOP) plan that benefits employees by giving them ownership stakes in the companies for which they work.

empowerment giving employees authority and responsibility to make decisions about their work.

encryption process of encoding data for security purposes, using software that encodes and scrambles messages.

end-use segmentation marketing strategy that focuses on the precise way a B2B purchaser will use a product.

enterprise zones specific geographic areas designated for economic revitalization.

entrepreneur risk taker in the private enterprise system, a person who seeks a profitable opportunity and takes the necessary risks to set up and operate a business.

enterprise computing many different types of hardware networked together to create a seamless data flow between organizations.

entrepreneurship willingness to take risks to create and operate a business.

environmental impact study analyzes how a proposed plant would affect the quality of life in the surrounding area.

environmental scanning analysis of external environmental factors by marketers to understand how they impact business and marketing decisions.

Equal Employment Opportunity Commission (EEOC) commission created to increase job opportunities for women and minorities and to help end discrimination based on race, color, religion, disability, gender, or national origin in any personnel action.

equilibrium price prevailing market price at which you can buy an item.

equity capital funds obtained from owners.

equity financing funds invested in new ventures in exchange for part ownership.

equity theory an individual's perception of fair and equitable treatment.

European Union (EU) 28-nation European economic alliance.

event marketing marketing or sponsoring short-term events such as athletic competitions and cultural and charitable performances.

everyday low pricing (EDLP) is a strategy devoted to maintaining continuous low prices rather than relying on short-term price cuts such as cents-off coupons, rebates, and special sales.

exchange control restriction on importation of certain products or against certain companies to reduce trade and expenditures of foreign currency.

exchange process activity in which two or more parties give something of value to each other to satisfy perceived needs.

exchange rate value of one nation's currency relative to the currencies of other countries.

exchanges infrastructure that facilitates the trading of equity securities and stocks.

exclusive distribution distribution strategy involving limited market coverage by a single retailer or wholesaler in a specific geographical territory.

executive summary one- to two-page snapshot of what the overall business plan explains in detail.

executive support system (ESS) lets senior executives access the company's primary databases, often by touching the computer screen, pointing and clicking a mouse, or using voice recognition.

expansionary monetary policy government actions to increase the money supply in an effort to cut the cost of borrowing, which encourages business decision makers to make new investments, in turn stimulating employment and economic growth.

expectancy theory the process people use to evaluate the likelihood that their efforts will yield the results they want, along with the degree to which they want those results.

expert system computer program that imitates human thinking through complicated sets of "if-then" rules.

exports domestically produced goods and services sold in other countries.

external communication meaningful exchange of information through messages transmitted between an organization and its major audiences.

extranet secure network used for e-business and accessible through an organization's website; available to external customers, suppliers, and other authorized users.

factoring selling receivables to another party, called a factor, for cash.

factors of production four basic inputs for effective operation: land, labor, capital, and entrepreneurship.

fair trade a market-based approach to pay higher prices to producers on exports from developing countries to developed countries in order for the developing countries to obtain better trading conditions and promote sustainability.

family brand brand name used to identify several different, but related, products.

family leave the Family and Medical Leave Act of 1993 states that employers with 50 or more employees must provide unpaid leave up to 12 weeks annually for any employee who wants time off for the birth or adoption of a child, to become a foster parent, or to care for a seriously ill relative, spouse, or self.

Federal Deposit Insurance Corporation (FDIC) federal agency that insures deposits at commercial and savings banks.

Federal Open Markets Committee Fed body that has primary responsibility for money policy.

Federal Reserve System (Fed) central bank of the United States.

fee-for-service plan traditional form of health insurance in which the insured chooses his or her health care provider, pays for treatment, and is reimbursed by the insurance company; also called an indemnity plan.

finance planning, obtaining, and managing a company's funds to accomplish its objectives as effectively and efficiently as possible.

finance charge the difference between the amount borrowed and the amount repaid on a loan.

Financial Accounting Standards Board (FASB) organization responsible for evaluating, setting, or modifying GAAP in the United States.

financial institutions intermediary between savers and borrowers, collecting funds from savers and then lending the funds to individuals, businesses, and governments.

financial managers executives who develop and implement the firm's financial plan and determine the most appropriate sources and uses of funds.

financial markets markets in which securities are bought and sold.

financial plan document that specifies the funds needed by a company for a period of time, the timing of inflows and outflows, and the most appropriate sources and uses of funds.

financial system process by which money flows from savers to users.

financing section section of a business plan that demonstrates the cost of the product, operating expenses, expected sales revenue and profit, and the amount of the business owner's own funds that will be invested to get the business up and running.

firewall limits data transfers to certain locations and log system use so that managers can identify attempts to log on with invalid passwords and other threats to a system's security.

fiscal policy government spending and taxation decisions designed to control inflation, reduce unemployment, improve the general welfare of citizens, and encourage economic growth.

flexible benefit plan benefit system that offers employees a range of options from which they may choose the types of benefits they receive.

flexible manufacturing system (FMS) production facility that can be quickly modified to manufacture different products.

flexible work plan employment that allows employees to adjust their working hours and places of work to accommodate their personal needs.

flextime scheduling system that allows employees to set their own work hours within constraints specified by the firm.

follow-up phase of production control in which employees and their supervisors spot problems in the production process and determine needed adjustments.

foreign corporation firm that operates in states where it is not incorporated.

Foreign Corrupt Practices Act federal law that prohibits U.S. citizens and companies from bribing foreign officials to win or continue business.

foreign licensing agreement international agreement in which one company allows another to produce or sell its product, or use its trademark, patent, or manufacturing processes, in a specific geographical area in return for royalties or other compensation.

formal communication channel messages that flow within the chain of command defined by an organization.

form utility conversion of raw materials, component parts, and other inputs into finished goods and services.

franchise contractual agreement in which a franchisee gains the right to produce and/or sell the franchisor's products under that company's brand name if they agree to certain operating requirements.

franchisee individual or business firm purchasing a franchise.

franchising contractual business arrangement between a manufacturer or other supplier, and a dealer such as a restaurant operator or retailer.

franchisor firm whose products are sold to customers by the franchisee.

free-rein leadership management style of leaders who believe in minimal supervision and leave most decisions to their subordinates.

frequency marketing marketing initiative that rewards frequent purchases with cash, rebates, merchandise, or other premiums.

frictional unemployment applies to members of the workforce who are temporarily not working but are looking for jobs.

General Agreement on Tariffs and Trade (GATT) international trade accord that substantially reduced worldwide tariffs and other trade barriers.

generally accepted accounting principles (GAAP) principles that encompass the conventions, rules, and procedures for determining acceptable accounting practices at a particular time.

geographical segmentation dividing an overall market into homogeneous groups on the basis of their locations.

global business strategy offering a standardized, worldwide product and selling it in essentially the same manner throughout a firm's domestic and foreign markets.

goal target, objective, or result that someone tries to accomplish.

goal-setting theory says that people will be motivated to the extent to which they accept specific, challenging goals and receive feedback that indicates their progress toward goal achievement.

government bonds bonds issued by the U.S. Department of the Treasury.

grapevine internal information channel that transmits information from unofficial sources.

green marketing a marketing strategy that promotes environmentally safe products and production methods.

grievance formal complaint filed by an employee or a union that management is violating some provision of a union contract.

gross domestic product (GDP) sum of all goods and services produced within a country's boundaries during a specific time period, such as a year.

guerrilla marketing innovative, low-cost marketing effort designed to get consumers' attention in unusual ways.

hardware all tangible elements of a computer system.

health insurance category of insurance that pays for losses due to illness or injury.

high-context culture society in which communication depends not only on the message itself but also on nonverbal cues, past and present experiences, and personal relationships between the parties.

home-based businesses firm operated from the residence of the business owner.

horizontal merger merger that joins firms in the same industry for the purpose of diversification, increasing customer bases, cutting costs, or expanding product lines.

human resource inventory also called a skills inventory, contains employee data such as age, gender, education, experience, training, and specialized skills.

human resource management function of attracting, developing, and retaining employees who can perform the activities necessary to accomplish organizational objectives.

human skills interpersonal skills that enable a manager to work effectively with and through people; the ability to communicate with, motivate, and lead employees to accomplish assigned activities.

hygiene factors factors that if present are essential to job satisfaction, although they cannot motivate an employee.

hyperinflation economic situation characterized by soaring prices.

imports foreign goods and services purchased by domestic customers.

income statement financial record of a company's revenues, expenses, and profits over a period of time.

individual brand different brand names given to each product within a line.

inflation economic situation characterized by rising prices caused by a combination of excess consumer demand and increases in the costs of raw materials, component parts, human resources, and other factors of production.

infomercial form of broadcast direct marketing; 30-minute programs that resemble regular TV programs but are devoted to selling goods or services.

informal communication channel messages outside formally authorized channels within an organization's hierarchy.

information knowledge gained from processing data.

information system organized method for collecting, storing, and communicating past, present, and projected information on internal operations and external intelligence.

infrastructure basic systems of communication, transportation, and energy facilities in a country.

initial public offering (IPO) sale of stock to the public for the first time.

insider trading use of material nonpublic information about a company to make investment profits.

institutional advertising involves messages that promote concepts, ideas, philosophies, or goodwill for industries, companies, organizations, or government entities.

insurable interest demonstration that a direct financial loss will result if some event occurs.

insurable risk requirement that a pure risk must meet for an insurer to agree to provide coverage.

insurance contract by which the insurer for a fee agrees to reimburse the insured a sum of money if a loss occurs.

integrated marketing communications (IMC) coordination of all promotional activities—media advertising, direct mail, personal selling, sales promotion, and public relations—to produce a unified customer-focused message.

integrity adhering to deeply felt ethical principles in business situations.

intensive distribution distribution strategy that involves placing a firm's products in nearly every available outlet.

International Accounting Standards Board (IASB) organization established in 1973 to promote worldwide consistency in financial reporting practices.

International Financial Reporting Standards (IFRS) standards and interpretations adopted by the IASB.

international law regulations that govern international commerce.

International Monetary Fund (IMF) organization created to promote trade, eliminate barriers, and make short-term loans to member nations that are unable to meet their budgets.

International Organization for Standardization (ISO) organization whose mission is to develop and promote international standards for business, government, and society to facilitate global trade and cooperation.

Internet of Things a web-connected ecosystem of everyday objects with network connectivity, including TVs, cars, household appliances, and wearable tech devices.

intranet computer network that is similar to the Internet but limits access to authorized users.

intrapreneurship process of promoting innovation within the structure of an existing organization.

introduction section of a business plan that describes the company, the management team, and the product in detail.

inventory control function requiring production and operations managers to balance the need to keep stock on hand to meet demand against the costs of carrying inventory.

investment bankers assist companies in raising capital and provide merger and acquisition services.

investment-grade bond bond with a rating of BBB or above.

job analysis is a process to identify and determine in detail the particular job duties and requirements and the relative importance of these duties for a given job.

job description includes information such as job title, location, reporting to and of employees, job summary, nature and objectives of a job, and tasks and duties to be performed.

job enlargement job design that expands an employee's responsibilities by increasing the number and variety of tasks assigned to the worker.

job enrichment change in job duties to increase employees' authority in planning their work, deciding how it should be done, and learning new skills.

job rotation systematically moving employees from one job to another.

job sharing program management decision that allows two or more employees to divide the tasks of one job.

job specification is a written statement of educational qualifications, specific qualities, level of experience, physical, emotional, technical, and communication skills required to perform a job.

joint venture partnership between companies formed for a specific undertaking.

judiciary court system, or branch of government that is responsible for settling disputes by applying laws.

just-in-time (JIT) system broad management philosophy that reaches beyond the narrow activity of inventory control to influence the entire system of production and operations management.

labor includes anyone who works, including both the physical labor and the intellectual inputs contributed by workers.

labor union group of workers who have banded together to achieve common goals in the areas of wages, hours, and working conditions.

land is used in the production of a good, and includes all production inputs or natural resources that are useful in their natural states such as oil, gas, minerals, and timber.

law standards set by government and society in the form of either legislation or custom.

law of large numbers concept that seemingly random events will follow predictable patterns if enough events are observed.

leadership ability to direct or inspire people to attain certain goals.

LEED (Leadership in Energy and Environmental Design) voluntary certification program administered by the U.S. Green Building Council, aimed at promoting the most sustainable construction processes available.

leverage increasing the rate of return on funds invested by borrowing funds.

leverage ratios measures of the extent to which a company relies on borrowed funds.

leveraged buyout (LBO) transaction in which public shareholders are bought out and the company reverts to private status.

liability anything owed to creditors—the claims of a company's creditors.

liability insurance a type of insurance that protects people against financial losses to others for acts for which the insured was responsible.

life insurance a type of insurance that protects people against the financial losses that occur with premature death.

lifestyle entrepreneur person who starts a business to reduce work hours and create a more relaxed lifestyle.

lifetime value of a customer revenues and intangible benefits (referrals and customer feedback) from a customer over the life of the relationship, minus the amount the company must spend to acquire and serve that customer.

limit order order that puts a ceiling or floor on a security purchase or sale.

limited-liability company (LLC) secures the corporate advantage of limited liability while avoiding the double taxation characteristic of corporations.

line manager executive involved with the functions of production, financing, or marketing.

line organization organizational structure that establishes a direct flow of authority from the chief executive to subordinates.

line-and-staff organization structure that combines the direct flow of authority of a line organization with staff departments that support the line departments.

liquidity ratios measures of a firm's ability to meet its short-term obligations.

listening receiving a message and interpreting its intended meaning by grasping the facts and feelings it conveys.

local area networks (LANs) computer networks that connect machines within limited areas, such as a building or several nearby buildings.

lockout management decision to put pressure on union members by closing the firm.

logistics process of coordinating flow of goods, services, and information among members of the supply chain.

low-context culture society in which communication tends to rely on explicit written and verbal messages.

macroeconomics study of a nation's overall economic issues, such as how an economy maintains and allocates resources and how a government's policies affect the standards of living of its citizens.

make, buy, or lease decision choosing whether to manufacture a needed product or component in-house, purchase it from an outside supplier, or lease it.

malware any malicious software program designed to infect computer systems.

managed care plan health care plan in which most, if not all, of the insured's health care bills are paid by the insurance company; in exchange, the insured has much less say over his or her treatment.

management process of achieving organizational objectives through people and other resources.

management accountant accountant who works for a firm and provides accounting services to that firm.

management by objectives (MBO) systematic approach that allows managers to focus on attainable goals and to achieve the best results based on the organization's resources.

management development program training designed to improve the skills and broaden the knowledge of current and potential executives.

management information system (MIS) information system designed to produce reports for managers and others within the organization.

management support systems information systems that are designed to provide support for effective decision making.

manufacturer's (national) brand brand offered and promoted by a manufacturer or producer.

market order order that instructs the investor's broker to obtain the best possible price.

market penetration percentage of the market that has purchased your product.

market segmentation process of dividing a total market into several relatively homogeneous groups.

marketable securities low-risk securities with short maturities.

marketing activity, set of institutions, and processes for creating, communicating, delivering, and exchanging offerings that have value for customers, clients, partners, and society at large.

marketing concept companywide consumer orientation to promote long-run success.

marketing mix blending the four elements of marketing strategy—product, distribution, promotion, and pricing—to fit the needs and preferences of a specific target market.

marketing research collecting and evaluating information to support marketing decision making.

marketing strategy section of a business plan that presents information describing the market's need for a product and how the business will satisfy it.

marketing website website whose main purpose is to increase purchases by visitors.

Maslow's hierarchy of needs theory of motivation proposed by Abraham Maslow. According to the theory, people have five levels of needs that they seek to satisfy: physiological, safety, social, esteem, and self-actualization.

mass production system for manufacturing products in large quantities through effective combinations of employees with specialized skills, mechanization, and standardization.

materials requirement planning (MRP) computer-based production planning system that lets a company ensure that it has all the parts and materials it needs to produce its output at the right time and place and in the right amounts.

matrix structure project management structure that links employees from different parts of the organization to work together on specific projects.

mediation dispute resolution process that uses a third party, called a mediator, to make recommendations for settling labor–management differences.

Medicare public health insurance program for those age 65 or older.

merger agreement in which two or more firms combine to form one company.

microeconomics study of small economic units, such as individual consumers, families, and businesses.

microloans small-business loans often used to buy equipment or operate a business.

middle management second tier in the management hierarchy that focuses on specific operations within the organizations.

mission statement written explanation of an organization's business intentions and aims.

missionary selling indirect form of selling in which the representative promotes goodwill for a company or provides technical or operational assistance to the customer.

mixed market economies systems that draw from both types of economies, to different degrees.

monetary policy government actions to increase or decrease the money supply and change banking requirements and interest rates to influence bankers' willingness to make loans.

money market instruments short-term debt securities issued by financial institutions, companies, and governments.

monopolistic competition market structure in which large numbers of buyers and sellers exchange heterogeneous products so each participant has some control over price.

monopoly market situation in which a single seller dominates trade in a good or service for which buyers can find no close substitutes.

morale mental attitude of employees toward their employer and jobs.

motivator factors factors that can produce high levels of motivation when they are present.

multidomestic business strategy developing and marketing products to serve different needs and tastes of separate national markets.

multinational corporation (MNC) firm with significant operations and marketing activities outside its home country.

municipal bonds bonds issued by state and local governments.

mutual fund financial intermediary that pools funds from investors by selling shares of itself and uses the funds to purchase securities.

national debt money owed by government to individuals, businesses, and government agencies who purchase Treasury bills, Treasury notes, and Treasury bonds sold to cover expenditures.

nearshoring outsourcing production or services to locations near a company's home base or closer to customers.

negotiable instrument commercial paper that is transferable among individuals and businesses.

net worth the difference between an individual or household's assets and liabilities.

newsgroup noncommercial online forum.

nonpersonal selling consists of advertising, sales promotion, direct marketing, and public relations.

nonprogrammed decision complex and unique problem or opportunity with important consequences for the organization.

nonverbal communication transmission of messages through actions and behaviors.

North American Free Trade Agreement (NAFTA) (renamed US-Mexico-Canada Agreement, or USMCA), an agreement among the United States, Canada, and Mexico to break down tariffs and trade restrictions.

not-for-profit corporations organizations whose goals do not include pursuing a profit.

not-for-profit organizations organizations that have primary objectives such as public service rather than returning a profit to its owners.

objectives guideposts by which managers define the organization's desired performance in such areas as new-product development, sales, customer service, growth, environmental and social responsibility, and employee satisfaction.

odd pricing pricing method using uneven amounts, which sometimes appear smaller than they really are to consumers.

offshoring relocation of business processes to lower-cost locations overseas.

oligopoly market structure in which relatively few sellers compete and high start-up costs form barriers to keep out new competitors.

on-the-job training training method that teaches an employee to complete new tasks by performing them under the guidance of an experienced employee.

open book management practice of sharing financial information with employees and teaching them how to understand and use financial statements.

open market operations technique in which the Fed buys or sells government bonds to affect the supply of money and credit.

operational planning detailed standards that guide implementation of tactical plans.

operational support systems information systems designed to produce a variety of information on an organization's activities for both internal and external users.

order processing form of selling, mostly at the wholesale and retail levels, that involves identifying customer needs, pointing them out to customers, and completing orders.

organization structured group of people working together to achieve common goals.

organization chart visual representation of a firm's structure that illustrates job positions and functions.

organization marketing marketing strategy that influences consumers to accept the goals of, receive the services of, or contribute in some way to an organization.

organizing process of blending human and material resources through a formal structure of tasks and authority; arranging work, dividing tasks among employees, and coordinating them to ensure implementation of plans and accomplishment of objectives.

outsourcing using outside vendors—contracting work out to another party—for the production of goods or fulfillment of services and functions previously performed in house.

owners' equity funds contributed by owners plus profits not distributed to owners in the form of cash dividends.

ownership utility orderly transfer of goods and services from the seller to the buyer; also called possession utility.

paid time off (PTO) bank of time that employees can use for holidays, vacation, and sick days.

partnership association of two or more persons who operate a business as co-owners by voluntary legal agreement.

patent guarantee to an inventor exclusive rights to an invention for 17 years.

penetration pricing strategy that sets a low price as a major marketing tactic.

performance appraisal evaluation of and feedback on an employee's job performance.

perpetual inventory system that continuously monitors the amount and location of a company's stocks.

person marketing use of efforts designed to attract the attention, interest, and preference of a target market toward a person.

personal financial management study of the economic factors and personal decisions that affect a person's financial well-being.

personal selling the most basic form of promotion: a direct person-to-person promotional presentation to a potential buyer.

PERT (Program Evaluation and Review Technique) chart that seeks to minimize delays by coordinating all aspects of the production process.

phishing high-tech scam that uses authentic looking e-mail or pop-up ads to get unsuspecting victims to reveal personal information.

physical distribution actual movement of products from producer to consumers or business users.

picketing workers marching at a plant entrance to protest some management practice.

place marketing attempt to attract people to a particular area, such as a city, state, or nation.

place utility availability of a product in a location convenient for customers.

planned economy economic system in which government controls determine business ownership, profits, and resource allocation to accomplish government goals rather than those set by individual firms.

planning process of anticipating future events and conditions and determining courses of action for achieving organizational objectives.

podcast audio or video blog.

point-of-purchase (POP) advertising displays or demonstrations that promote products when and where consumers buy them, such as in retail stores.

pollution environmental damage caused by a company's products or operating processes.

pop-up ad Internet ad that pops-up in a new window; interested parties can click on the ad for more information.

positioning form of promotion in which marketers attempt to establish the identity and value of their products in the minds of customers by communicating to buyers meaningful distinctions about the attributes, price, quality, or use of a good or service.

potential sales revenue amount of revenue the business would collect if its market penetration were 100 percent.

preferred stock shares that give owners limited voting rights, and the right to receive dividends or assets before owners of common stock.

premium amount paid by the insured to the insurer to exchange for insurance coverage.

pre-roll video ad a short advertising video clip that begins automatically whenever a user visits a particular website.

prestige pricing strategies that establish relatively high prices to develop and maintain an image of quality and exclusiveness.

price exchange value of a good or service.

primary markets financial markets in which corporations and governments issue securities and sell them initially to the general public.

private enterprise system economic system that rewards firms for their ability to identify and serve the needs and demands of customers.

private equity funds investment companies that raise funds from individuals and institutional investors and use the funds to take large stakes in a wide range of public and private companies.

private exchange secure website at which a company and its suppliers share all types of data related to e-business, from product design through order delivery.

private placements sale of securities to a small number of investors.

private property most basic freedom under the private enterprise system; the right to own, use, buy, sell, and bequeath land, buildings, machinery, equipment, patents, individual possessions, and various intangible kinds of property.

private (store) brand product that is not linked to the manufacturer, but instead carries the label of a retailer or wholesaler.

privatization conversion of government-owned and operated companies into privately held businesses.

problem-solving team temporary or permanent combination of workers who gather to solve a specific problem.

process control systems operational support system to monitor and control physical processes.

Producer Price Index (PPI) measurement of the average change in prices of goods and services received by domestic producers.

product bundle of physical, service, and symbolic attributes designed to satisfy buyers' wants.

product advertising consists of messages designed to sell a particular good or service.

product liability the responsibility of manufacturers for injuries and damages caused by their products.

product life cycle four basic stages—introduction, growth, maturity, and decline—through which a product progresses.

product line group of related products marked by physical similarities or intended for the same market.

product mix the assortment of product lines and individual goods and services that a firm offers to consumers and business users.

product placement form of promotion in which marketers pay fees to have their products showcased in various media, ranging from newspapers and magazines to original online television and movies.

production use of resources, such as people and machinery, to convert materials into finished goods and services.

production and operations management oversee the production process by managing people and machinery in converting materials and resources into finished goods and services.

production control creates a well-defined set of procedures for coordinating people, materials, and machinery to provide maximum production efficiency.

production planning phase of production control that determines the amount of resources (including raw materials and other components) a firm needs in order to produce a certain output.

productivity relationship between the number of units produced and the number of human and other production inputs necessary to produce them.

product-related segmentation dividing consumer markets into groups based on buyers' relationships to the good or service.

profitability objectives common objectives included in the strategic plans of most companies.

profitability ratios measures of a company's overall financial performance by evaluating its ability to generate revenues in excess of expenses.

profits rewards earned by businesspeople who take the risks involved in blending people, technology, and information to create and market want-satisfying goods and services.

programmed decision simple, common, and frequently occurring problem for which a solution has already been determined.

promotion function of informing, persuading, and influencing a purchase decision.

promotional mix combination of personal and nonpersonal selling components designed to meet the needs of a company's target customers and effectively and efficiently communicate its message to them.

property and liability insurance general category of insurance that protects against losses due to a number of perils.

psychographic segmentation dividing consumer markets into groups with similar attitudes, values, and lifestyles.

public accountant accountant who provides accounting services to individuals or business firms for a fee.

public insurance agency public agency that provides certain types of insurance coverage.

public ownership organization owned and operated by a unit or agency of government.

public relations organization's communications and relationships with its various public audiences.

publicity nonpersonal stimulation of demand for a good, service, place, idea, event, person, or organization by unpaid placement of information in print or broadcast media.

pulling strategy promoting a product by generating consumer demand for it, primarily through advertising and sales promotion appeals.

pure competition market structure, in which large numbers of buyers and sellers exchange homogeneous products and no single participant has a significant influence on price.

pure risk type of risk where there is only the possibility of loss.

pushing strategy personal selling to market an item to wholesalers and retailers in a company's distribution channels.

quality control measuring output against established quality standards.

quality good or service that is free of deficiencies.

quota limit set on the amounts of particular products that can be imported.

ratio analysis commonly used tool for measuring the financial strength of a firm.

recession cyclical economic contraction that lasts for six months or longer.

recycling reprocessing of used materials for reuse.

regulated monopolies market situations in which local, state, or federal government grants exclusive rights in a certain market to a single firm.

relationship era business era in which companies seek ways to actively nurture customer loyalty by carefully managing every interaction.

relationship management collection of activities that build and maintain ongoing, mutually beneficial ties with customers and other parties.

relationship marketing developing and maintaining long-term, cost-effective exchange relationships with partners.

restrictive monetary policy government actions to reduce the money supply to curb rising prices, overexpansion, and concerns about overly rapid economic growth.

retailer distribution channel members that sell goods and services to individuals for their own use rather than for resale.

risk uncertainty about loss or injury.

risk management calculations and actions a firm takes to recognize and deal with real or potential risks to its survival.

risk–return trade-off process of maximizing the wealth of a firm's shareholders by striking the optimal balance between risk and return.

robot reprogrammable machine capable of performing numerous tasks that require manipulation of materials and tools.

routing phase of production control that determines the sequence of work throughout the facility and specifies who will perform each aspect of production at what location.

rule of indemnity requirement that the insured cannot collect more than the amount of the loss and cannot collect for the same loss more than once.

S corporation corporations that do not pay corporate taxes on profits; instead, profits are distributed to shareholders, who pay individual income taxes.

salary pay calculated on a periodic basis, such as weekly or monthly.

sales law law governing the sale of goods or services for money or on credit.

sales promotion consists of types of promotion such as coupons, product samples, and rebates that support advertising and personal selling.

Sarbanes-Oxley Act federal legislation designed to deter and punish corporate and accounting fraud and corruption and to protect the interests of workers and shareholders through enhanced financial disclosures, criminal penalties on CEOs and CFOs who defraud investors, safeguards for whistle-blowers, and establishment of a new regulatory body for public accounting firms.

scheduling development of timetables that specify how long each operation in the production process takes and when workers should perform it.

search engine optimization (SEO) process used by companies to increase the number of visitors to its website via a search engine such as Google or Bing.

seasonal unemployment joblessness of workers in a seasonal industry.

secondary market collection of financial markets in which previously issued securities are traded among investors.

Secure Sockets Layer (SSL) technology that secures a website by encrypting information and providing authentication.

securities financial instruments that represent obligations on the part of the issuers to provide the purchasers with expected stated returns in the funds invested or loaned.

seed capital initial funding needed to launch a new venture.

selective distribution distribution strategy in which a manufacturer selects only a limited number of retailers to distribute its product lines.

self-managed team work team that has the authority to decide how its members complete their daily tasks.

sell-off transaction in which assets are sold by one firm to another.

serial entrepreneur person who starts one business, runs it, and then starts and runs additional businesses in succession.

server the heart of a midrange computer network

set-aside program component of a government contract specifying that certain government contracts (or portions of those contracts) are restricted to small businesses and/or to women- or minority-owned companies.

sexism discrimination against members of either sex but primarily affecting women.

sexual harassment unwelcome and inappropriate actions of a sexual nature in the workplace.

shopping product item typically purchased only after the buyer has compared competing products in competing stores.

skimming pricing strategy that sets an intentionally high price relative to the prices of competing products.

skunkworks project initiated by a company employee who conceives the idea, convinces top management of its potential, and then recruits human and other resources from within the firm to turn it into a commercial project.

small business independent business with fewer than 500 employees, not dominant in its market.

Small Business Administration (SBA) principal government agency concerned with helping small U.S. firms.

Small Business Investment Company (SBIC) business licensed by the Small Business Administration to provide loans to small businesses.

social audits formal procedures that identify and evaluate all company activities that relate to social issues such as conservation, employment practices, environmental protection, and philanthropy.

social entrepreneur person who recognizes societal problems and uses business principles to develop innovative solutions.

social era business era in which companies seek ways to connect and interact with customers using technology.

social networking sites websites that provide a virtual community for people to socialize about a particular subject or any topic in general.

social responsibility business's consideration of society's well-being and consumer satisfaction, in addition to profits.

socialism economic system characterized by government ownership and operation of major industries, such as communications.

socioeconomic model the belief that business, as part of its role, owes its existence to improving the society in which it operates.

software all the programs, routines, and computer languages that control a computer and tell it how to operate.

sole proprietorship business ownership in which there is no legal distinction between the sole proprietor's status as an individual and his or her status as a business owner.

sovereign wealth funds government-owned investment companies.

spam popular name for junk e-mail.

span of management number of subordinates a manager can supervise effectively.

specialty advertising promotional items that prominently display a company's name, logo, or business slogan.

specialty product item that a purchaser is willing to make a special effort to obtain.

speculative (junk) bond a bond with a rating below BB.

speculative risk type of risk where the possibility of gain and loss both exist.

spin-off transaction in which divested assets form a new company.

sponsorship involves providing funds for a sporting or cultural event in exchange for a direct association with the event.

spyware software that secretly gathers user information through the user's Internet connections without his or her knowledge, usually for advertising purposes.

staff manager executive who provides information, advice, or technical assistance to aid line managers; does not have the authority to give orders outside his or her own department or to compel line managers to take action.

stakeholders customers, investors, employees, and public affected by or with an interest in a company.

standard of living necessities, comforts, and luxuries one seeks to obtain or to maintain.

statement of cash flows statement showing the sources and uses of cash during a period of time.

statement of owners' equity record of the change in owners' equity from the end of one fiscal period to the end of the next.

statutory law written law, including state and federal constitutions, legislative enactments, treaties of the federal government, and ordinances of local governments.

stock markets companies that list stocks for public investors to buy and sell.

stock options rights to buy a specified amount of company stock at a given price within a given time period.

stock quote price of a specific stock and performance information.

stock split occurs when a company decides to divide its existing shares of stock into multiple shares.

stockholders owners of a corporation due to their purchase of stock in the corporation.

strategic alliance partnership formed to create a competitive advantage for the businesses involved; in international business, a business strategy in which a company finds a partner in the country where it wants to do business.

strategic planning process of determining the primary objectives of an organization and then acting and allocating resources to achieve those objectives.

strike temporary work stoppage by employees until a dispute is settled or a contract signed.

structural unemployment people who remain unemployed for long periods of time, often with little hope of finding new jobs like their old ones.

subcontracting international agreement that involves hiring local companies to produce, distribute, or sell goods or services in a specific country or geographical region.

subprime mortgage loan made to a borrower with a poor credit rating.

supervisory management first-line management; includes positions such as supervisor, line manager, and group leader; responsible for assigning nonmanagerial employees to specific jobs and evaluating their performance every day.

supply willingness and ability of sellers to provide goods and services.

supply chain complete sequence of suppliers that contribute to creating a good or service and delivering it to business users and final consumers.

supply curve graph that shows the relationship between different prices and the quantities that sellers will offer for sale, regardless of demand.

sustainable the capacity to endure in ecology.

SWOT analysis SWOT is an acronym for *strengths*, *weaknesses*, *opportunities*, and *threats*. By systematically evaluating all four of these factors, a firm can then develop the best strategies for gaining a competitive advantage.

synergy notion that a combined firm is worth more than the two firms are individually.

tactical planning implementing the activities specified by strategic plans.

target market group of people toward whom an organization markets its goods, services, or ideas with a strategy designed to satisfy their specific needs and preferences.

tariff tax imposed on imported goods.

tax assessment by a governmental unit.

team group of people with certain skills who are committed to a common purpose, approach, and set of performance goals.

team cohesiveness extent to which team members feel attracted to the team and motivated to remain part of it.

team diversity variances or differences in ability, experience, personality, or any other factor on a team.

team level average level of ability, experience, personality, or any other factor on a team.

team norm standard of conduct shared by team members that guides their behavior.

technical skills manager's ability to understand and use techniques, knowledge, and tools and equipment of a specific discipline or department.

technology business application of knowledge based on scientific discoveries, inventions, and innovations.

telecommuter home-based employee.

telemarketing personal selling conducted entirely by telephone, which provides a company's marketers with a high return on their expenditures, an immediate response, and an opportunity for personalized two-way conversation.

tender offer offer made by a company to the target company's shareholders specifying a price and the form of payment.

term policy pure type of life insurance policy providing only a death benefit.

test marketing introduction of a new product supported by a complete marketing campaign to a selected city or geographic area.

Theory X assumption that employees dislike work and will try to avoid it.

Theory Y assumption that employees enjoy work and seek social, esteem, and self-actualization fulfillment.

Theory Z assumption that employee involvement is key to productivity and quality of work life.

time utility availability of a good or service when customers want to purchase it.

top management managers at the highest level of the management pyramid who devote most of their time to developing long-range plans for their organizations.

tort civil wrong inflicted on another person or the person's property.

trade credit credit extended by suppliers in which the buyer agrees to pay for goods and services received now at a later date.

trade promotion sales promotion geared to marketing intermediaries rather than to final consumers.

trademark brand that has been given a legal protection.

transaction management building and promoting products in the hope that enough customers will buy them to cover costs and earn profits.

transaction processing systems operational support system to record and process data from business transactions.

trends consumer and business tendencies or patterns that firms can exploit to gain market share in an industry.

trial courts federal and state courts of general jurisdiction.

triple bottom line strategic business approach used by companies to evaluate performance by placing equal value on financial, social, and environmental factors.

Trojan horse program that claims to do one thing but in reality does something else, usually something malicious.

underwriting process used by an insurance company to determine who, or what, to insure and how much to charge.

unemployment rate percentage of the total workforce actively seeking work but currently unemployed.

Uniform Commercial Code The basis of U.S. business law; referred to as UCC.

utility power of a good or service to satisfy a want or need.

vendor-managed inventory process in which the producer and the retailer agree that the producer (or the wholesaler) will determine how much of a product a buyer needs and will automatically ship new supplies when needed.

venture capital money invested in a business by another business firm or group of individuals in exchange for an ownership share.

venture capitalists business firms or groups of individuals that invest in new and growing firms in exchange for an ownership share.

vertical merger merger that combines firms operating at different levels in the production and marketing process.

virtual network common type of technology infrastructure, which consists of links that are not wired connections.

virtual private networks (VPNs) secure connections between two points on the Internet.

virtual team group of geographically or organizationally dispersed co-workers who use a combination of telecommunications and information technologies to accomplish an organizational task.

viruses programs that secretly attach themselves to other programs (called *hosts*) and change them or destroy data.

vision ability to perceive marketplace needs and what an organization must do to satisfy them.

volume objectives objects based on pricing decisions on market share, the percentage of a market controlled by a certain company or product.

wages pay based on an hourly rate or the amount of work accomplished.

web-to-store use of the web to aid shoppers at brick-and-mortar retailers.

wheel of retailing theory of retailing in which new retailers gain a competitive foothold by offering low prices and limited services and then add services and raise prices, creating opportunities for new low-price competitors.

whistle-blowing employee's disclosure to company officials, government authorities, or the media of illegal, immoral, or unethical practices committed by an organization.

wholesaler distribution channel member that sells primarily to retailers, other wholesalers, or business users.

wide area networks (WANs) tie larger geographical regions together by using telephone lines and microwave and satellite transmission.

Wi-Fi wireless network that connects various devices and allows them to communicate with one another through radio waves.

wiki web page that can be edited by users.

work team relatively permanent group of employees with complementary skills who perform the day-to-day work of organizations.

World Bank organization established by industrialized nations to lend money to less-developed countries.

World Trade Organization (WTO) 159-member international institution that monitors GATT agreements and mediates international trade disputes.

Notes

Chapter 1

[1] Mark Bergen and Brad Stone, "Everyone Is Mad at Google and Sundar Pichai Has to Fix It," *Bloomberg*, https://bloomberg.com, accessed January 29, 2018; Alanna Petroff, "Google CEO: AI Is 'More Profound than Electricity or Fire', *CNN Money*, http://money.cnn.com, accessed January 29, 2018; Jessi Hempel, "Sundar Pichai, "I Just Inherited the Most High-Pressure Job at Alphabet," *Wired*, http:// www.wired.com, accessed February 1, 2018; company website, "Google Announces Plans for New Operating Structure," https://investor.google.com, accessed February 1, 2018; company website, "G Is for Google," https://abc.xyz, accessed February 1, 2018; Robert McMillan and Rolf Winkler, "For Google's New CEO Sundar Pichai, a Low-Key Style Pays Off," *The Wall Street Journal*, http://www.wsj.com, accessed February 1, 2018; Alistair Barr and Rolfe Winkler, "Sundar Pichai to Lead Google, Now a Subsidiary of Alphabet, After Restructuring," *The Wall Street Journal*, http://blogs.wsj.com, accessed February 5, 2018; Susan Adams, "Who Is Google's New Chief, Sundar Pichai?" *Forbes*, http://www.forbes.com, accessed February 1, 2018; Jillian D'Onfro, "Sundar Pichai Challenge," *Business Insider*, http://www.businessinsider.com, accessed January 29, 2018; Prachi Bhardwaj, "Google's Parent Company Just Announced a New Project to Give the Digital World 'an Immune System'," *Business Insider*, http://www.businessinsider.com, accessed January 31, 2018; Victor Tangermann, "These Are Some of the Biggest Moonshots Alphabet Ever Attempted," https://futurism.com, accessed February 1, 2018.

[2] Organization website, "How Many Nonprofits Are There in the U.S.?", http://grantspace.org, accessed February 2, 2018.

[3] Brice McKeever and Marcus Gaddy, "The Nonprofit Workforce: By the Numbers," https://nonprofitquarterly.org, accessed February 3, 2018.

[4] Organization website, "Facts for Media," https://www.stjude.org, accessed February 2, 2018.

[5] Organization website, "About Us," https://www.aspca.org, accessed February 2, 2018.

[6] Lindsay LaVine, "Lessons from Inside the $800 Million Girl Scout Cookie Selling Empire," *Fast Company*, http://www.fastcompany.com, accessed February 3, 2018; "30 Online Stores that Benefit Nonprofits," *Nonprofit Tech for Good*, http://www.nptechforgood.com, accessed February 3, 2018.

[7] "Timber Industry Report for February 4," *The News Review*, https://www.nrtoday.com, accessed February 4, 2018.

[8] Company website, "Fortune 100 Best Companies to Work For®: Mars Ranks 50th in 2017," http://www.mars.com, accessed February 4, 2018; company website, "History of Mars," and "The Five Principles," http://www.mars.com, accessed February 4, 2018.

[9] Company website, "Journey," https://waymo.com, accessed February 4, 2018.

[10] Company website, "Company Profile," http://www.netflix.com, accessed February 4, 2018.

[11] Jonathan Vanian, "Drones May One Day Buzz Inside a Walmart Near You," *Fortune*, http://fortune.com, accessed February 4, 2018.

[12] Company website, "Frequently Asked Questions," *Bumble*, http://www.bumble.com accessed February 5, 2018.

[13] Yuyu Chen, "How Does Under Armour Differentiate Itself from Nike via Digital Marketing?", https://www.clickz.com, accessed February 5, 2018.

[14] Government website, "Truth in Advertising," https://www.ftc.gov, accessed February 6, 2018; government website, "The Anti-trust Laws," https://www.ftc.gov, accessed February 6, 2018; government website, "Guide to Anti-Trust Laws," https://www.ftc.gov, accessed February 6, 2018.

[15] Government website, "Small Business Administration: FAQs," http://www.sba.gov, accessed February 6, 2018; U.S. Census Bureau, "Statistics About Business Size, Employment Size of Firms, Table 2a," http://www.census.gov, accessed February 6, 2018.

[16] Company website, accessed February 6, 2018, http://goodto-go.com; Aislinn Sarnacki, "Maine's Good To-Go, Gourmet Trail Food, Reaches 600 Stores," *BDN Outdoors*, https://bangordailynews.com, accessed February 6, 2018.

[17] Company website, "Nike SNKRS App," http://www.nike.com, accessed February 6, 2018; Edgar Alvarez, "Nike's SNKRS App Uses AR to Help You Buy Limited-Edition Shoes," *engadget*, https://www.engadget.com, accessed February 6, 2018.

[18] Company website, http://etudeapp.com, accessed February 5, 2018.

[19] "Best Global Brands: 2017," *Interbrand*, http://interbrand.com, accessed February 6, 2018.

[20] Andreas Kaplan and Michael Haenlein, "Users of the World, Unite! The Challenges and Opportunities of Social Media," *Business Horizons* 53:59–68, 2010, http://michaelhaenlein.eu, accessed February 7, 2018.

[21] Allison Enright, "GameStop Will Pilot Geo-Fencing and Beacons in 36 Stores in Q2," *Internet Retailer*, https://www.internetretailer.com, accessed February 7, 2018.

[22] Michael Wayland, "Can Amazon Talk Its Way into Autos?" *Automotive News*, http://www.autonews.com, accessed February 7, 2018; Khari Johnson, "5 CES 2018 Announcements That Put Alexa Inside Cars," *Venture Beat*, https://venturebeat.com, accessed February 7, 2018.

[23] "King & King Architects LLP Receives High-Performance Energy Efficiency Award from NYSERDA," press release, http://www.nyserda.ny.gov, accessed February 7, 2018.

[24] Company website, http://greensulate.com, accessed February 7, 2018.

[25] Company website, http://www.solarcity.com, accessed February 7, 2018; Max Chafkin, "SolarCity's Rooftop Panels Are About to Get Way, Way Better," *Fast Company*, http://www.fastcompany.com, accessed February 7, 2018.

[26] Staff, "AI Is Already Replacing Knowledge Workers," CEB, accessed February 8, 2018, https://www.cebglobal.com; Julie Bort, "39 Ways the American Workforce Is Dramatically Changing in 2015," *Business Insider*, http://www.businessinsider.com, accessed February 7, 2018; Makada Henry-Nickie, "AI Should Worry Skilled Knowledge Workers Too," *Brookings Institute*, https://www.brookings.edu, accessed February 8, 2018.

[27] Government website, "Employment Level—65 yrs. & Over," http://www.bls.gov, accessed February 7, 2018; government website, "Employment Status of the Civilian Noninstitutional Population by Age, Sex, and Race," http://www.bls.gov, accessed February 7, 2018;

government website, "Older Employees in the Workplace," http://www.cdc.gov, accessed February 7, 2018.

[28] Organization website, "Workplace Diversity Practices: How Has Diversity and Inclusion Changed over Time? SHRM Poll," http://www.shrm.org, accessed February 7, 2018; Noor Wazwaz, "It's Official: The U.S. Is Becoming a Minority-Majority Nation," *U.S. News & World Report*, http://www.usnews.com, accessed February 7, 2018.

[29] J. J. McCorvey, "Can Intel Solve Tech's Diversity Problem?" *Fast Company*, http://www.fastcompany.com, accessed February 7, 2018; Barbara Whye, "Intel's 2017 Diversity and Inclusion Midyear Report and the Road Ahead," *Newsroom Intel*, https://newsroom.intel.com, accessed February 7, 2018.

[30] "Leading Countries in Offshore Business Services Worldwide in 2017," https://www.statista.com, accessed February 7, 2018.

[31] Rita Gunther McGrath, "Why 'Nearshoring' Is Replacing 'Outsourcing'," *The Wall Street Journal*, http://blogs.wsj.com, accessed February 7, 2018.

[32] Drew DeSilver, "5 Ways the U.S. Workforce Has Changed, a Decade Since the Great Recession Began," *Pew Research Center*, http://www.pewresearch.org, accessed February 7, 2018; Shelley Kramer, "The Future of Work: How the Workplace Is Changing in 2017," *Digitalist Magazine*, http://www.digitalistmag.com, accessed February 7, 2018.

[33] Society for Human Resource Management, "Five Key Trends from SHRM's Special Expertise Panels," http://www.shrm.org, accessed February 7, 2018.

[34] Julie Bort, "Mark Benioff: I'm Trying to Fill Steve Jobs Shoes As a Visionary," *Business Insider*, http://www.businessinsider.com, accessed February 7, 2018; "Mark Benioff," Crunchbase Profile, *Tech Crunch*, http://techcrunch.com, accessed February 7, 2018.

[35] Tanza Loudenback, "Meet Reed Hastings, the Man Who Built Netflix," *Business Insider*, http://www.businessinsider.com, accessed February 7, 2018; company website, "Company Profile," http://ir.netflix.com, accessed February 7, 2018; Rani Molla, "Netflix Now Has Nearly 118 Million Streaming Subscribers Globally," https://www.recode.net, accessed February 8, 2017.

[36] "World's Most Admired Companies 2018," *Fortune*, http://money.cnn.com, accessed April 7, 2018.

Chapter 2

[1] Organization website, "About Us," "Summer Immersion Program," https://www.girlswhocode.com, accessed February 19, 2018; Scott Behrens, "Man, Computer Science Needs More Women," *USA Today*, http://college.usatoday.com, accessed February 19, 2018; Eliana Dockterman, "Cracking the Girl Code: How to End the Tech Gender Gap," *Time*, http://www.time.com, accessed February 19, 2018; WGU, "Fail First, Fail Hard, and Fail Fast," Western Governors University, https://www.prnewswire.com, accessed February 19, 2018.

[2] Karsten Strauss, "The 10 Companies with the Best CSR Reputations in 2017," *Forbes*, http://www.forbes.com, accessed February 15, 2018; company website, "Starbucks Hiring Efforts for Military, Youth, and Refugees," https://news.starbucks.com, accessed February 15, 2018.

[3] Jeff Fromm, "Panera and Shake Shack Create Sustainability Platform That Wins with Millennials," *Forbes*, http://www.forbes.com, accessed February 15, 2018.

[4] Alex Espenson, "5 Companies Doing Corporate Social Responsibility Right," *Business2Community*, http://www.business2community.com, accessed February 15, 2018; company website, "Ethical Sourcing: Coffee," http://www.starbucks.com, accessed February 15, 2018; company website "About Us," http://www.starbucks.com, accessed February 15, 2018; "Number of Starbucks Stores Worldwide from 2003 to 2017," https://www.statista.com, accessed February 15, 2018.

[5] Company website, "2017 Sustainability Report," http://www.coca-colacompany.com, accessed February 15, 2018.

[6] Organization website, "Global Business Ethics Survey," http://www.ethics.org, accessed February 15, 2018.

[7] Company website, "Ethisphere Institute Announces 135 Companies Honored as World's Most Ethical Companies," https://ethisphere.com, accessed February 15, 2018.

[8] Organization website, "National Business Ethics Survey," http://www.ethics.org, accessed February 16, 2018.

[9] Taylor Armerding, "The 17 Biggest Data Breaches of the 21st Century," *CSO*, https://www.csoonline.com, accessed February 16, 2018; Donna Borak and Kathryn Vasal, "The Equifax Hack Can be Worse Than We Thought," *CNNMoney*, http://www.cnnmoney.com, accessed February 16, 2018; Michael Riley, Anita Sharpe, and Jordan Robertson, "Equifax Suffered a Hack Almost Five Months Earlier Than the Date It Disclosed," *Bloomberg*, https://www.bloomberg.com, accessed February 16, 2018.

[10] Emily Glazer, "Wells Fargo's Sales-Scandal Tally Grows to Around 3.5 Million Accounts," *The Wall Street Journal*, https://www.wsj.com, accessed February 16, 2018; Mark Pastin, "The Surprise Ethics Lesson of Wells Fargo," *Huffington Post*, https://www.huffingtonpost.com, accessed February 16, 2018; Harley Comrie, "Wells Fargo Fake Accounts Scandal," https://sevenpillarsinstitute.org, accessed February 16, 2018.

[11] Jean-Claude Trichet, "How Can We Rebuild Trust in Banks?" *World Economic Forum*, https://agenda.weforum.org, accessed February 16, 2018. Sarah O'Brien, "SEC Wants Advisors to Come Clean About High-Fee Fund Shares," *CNBC*, https://www.cnbc.com, accessed February 16, 2018.

[12] Lindsay Olson, "The Top 10 Lies People Put on Their Résumés," *U.S. News & World Report*, http://money.usnews.com, accessed February 16, 2018; Marielle Segarra, "How to Avoid Résumé Fraud," *CFO.com*, https://ww2.cfo.com, accessed February 16, 2018.

[13] Emmie Martin, "These Are the Top 10 Productivity Killers at Work," *Business Insider*, http://www.businessinsider.com, accessed February 17, 2018.

[14] Neil Weinberg, "JP Morgan Whistle-Blowing Case Resulted in $30 million Award," *Bloomberg*, http://www.bloomberg.com, accessed February 17, 2018.

[15] Company website, "Google Code of Conduct," https://investor.google.com, accessed February 17, 2018.

[16] Company website, "Code of Conduct," http://www.lockheedmartin.com, accessed February 17, 2018.

[17] Company website, "About SAI Global," http://www.saiglobal.com, accessed February 17, 2018.

[18] Company website, "Business Ethics and Compliance: Standards of Business Conduct," http://globalassets.starbucks.com, accessed February 17, 2018.

[19] Natalie Peace, "How Kindness and Generosity Made My Businesses More Profitable," *Forbes*, http://www.forbes.com, accessed February 16, 2018; company website, "Tone at the Top Definition," https://www.ventureline.com, accessed February 16, 2018.

[20] Company website, "CSR Results: FY17," http://csr.cisco.com, accessed February 17, 2018.

[21] "Triple Bottom Line," *The Economist*, http://www.economist.com, accessed February 17, 2018; "Southwest: A Triple Bottom Line Airline," *Conscious Company*, http://www.consciouscompanymagazine.com, accessed February 17, 2018; "People, Planet, Profit: The Rise of Triple-Bottom-Line Businesses," *World Watch*, http://www.worldwatch.org, accessed February 17, 2018.

[22] Abigail Zhu, "The Socioeconomic View vs. the Classical View," *Knoji,* https://operations-management.knoji.com, accessed February 17, 2018.

[23] DeWayne Patterson, "Several States Ban a Person Smoking in a Vehicle with Children Present," *The Daily Sentinel,* http://thedailysentinel.com, accessed February 17, 2018.

[24] Bruce Jaspen, "After CVS Stopped Cigarette Sales, Smokers Stopped Buying Elsewhere, Too," *Forbes*, http://www.forbes.com, accessed February 17, 2018; Bruce Japsen, "CVS Health Kicks Smoking Habit and Still Has Record Sales," *Forbes,* http://www.forbes.com, accessed February 17, 2018; Alexandra Sifferlin, "Has CVS's Cigarette Ban Reduced Smoking?" *TIME,* http://time.com, accessed February 17, 2018; Bruce Japsen, "Why Walgreen Won't Stop Selling Tobacco Like CVS Health," *Forbes*, http://www.forbes.com, accessed February 17, 2018; Matt Egan, "CVS Banned Tobacco. Now Its Sales Are Hurting," *CNN Money,* http://money.cnn.com, accessed February 17, 2018.

[25] Organization website, "Influenza/Flu," https://www.cdc.gov, accessed February 17, 2018; Bill Siwicki, "Here Are the 12 Healthcare Issues That Will Define 2018, According to PwC," *Health Care IT News*, http://www.healthcareitnews.com, accessed February 17, 2018; Chris Weller, "Bill Gates Reveals the Biggest Public Health Threats Over the Next 10 Years," *Business Insider*, http://www.businessinsider.com, accessed February 17, 2018; "CDC: 10 Most Important Public Health Problems and Concerns," *Becker's Hospital Review*, https://www.beckershospitalreview.com, accessed February 17, 2018; Sandra Eskin, "4 Food Safety Issues to Watch in 2018," *Eco Watch*, http://ecowatch.com, accessed February 17, 2018.

[26] Company website, "Assessing the Environmental Impacts of Our Suppliers," http://corporate.ford.com, accessed February 17, 2018; Akhila Vijayaraghavan, "Kaiser Permanente Greens Its Supply Chain by Switching to Safer IV Equipment," *Triple Pundit*, http://www.triplepundit.com, accessed February 17, 2018.

[27] Kate Abnett, "Just Fix It: How Nike Learned to Embrace Sustainability," *Business of Fashion*, https://www.businessoffashion.com, accessed February 17, 2018; company website, "Top Things to Know About Sustainable Innovation at Nike," https://news.nike.com/news/sustainable-innovation, accessed February 17, 2018; Erich Lawson, "9 Companies with Great Environmental Initiatives,"*SmartCitiesDIVE*, https://www.smartcitiesdive.com, accessed February 17, 2018.

[28] Organization website, "Economic Impact Study: U.S. Based Scrap Recycling Industry 2015," www.isri.org, accessed February 17, 2018.

[29] Sharon Guynup, "The Zero Waste Factory," *Scientific American*, http://scientificamerican.com, accessed February 17, 2018.

[30] Anne Marie Mohan, "The FTC Cracks Down on Biodegradable Marketing Claims," *Greener Package,* http://www.greenerpackage.com, accessed February 17, 2018.

[31] Organization website, "Our CleanTech Economy," http://www.researchtrianglecleantech.org, accessed February 17, 2018; company website, "Clean Tech Industry Is on the Rise," http://cleantechnica.com, accessed February 17, 2018.

[32] Government website, "Table 5. Quartiles and Selected Deciles of Usual Weekly Earnings of Full-Time Wage and Salary Workers by Selected Characteristics, Fourth Quarter 2017 Averages, Not Seasonally Adjusted," http://www.bls.gov, accessed February 17, 2018.

[33] Eugene Kim, "Why Amazon Paid for 2,000 Employees to Take Classes in Things Like Airplane Mechanics and Nursing," *Business Insider*, http://www.businessinsider.com, accessed February 17, 2018.

[34] Company website, "The 2017 DiversityInc Top 50 Companies for Diversity," http://www.diversityinc.com, accessed February 17, 2018.

[35] Company website, "The Logistics of Caring: Road Safety," http://sustainability.ups.com, accessed February 17, 2018; company website, "The UPS Foundation Sets Global Goal to Plant 15 Million Trees by the End of 2020," https://www.pressroom.ups.com, accessed February 17, 2018.

[36] Company website, "Corporate Responsibility: Initiatives," American Express, http://www.americanexpress.com, accessed February 19, 2018; Diana O'Brien, "The Science of a Brand Movement, *The Wall Street Journal*, http://www.wsj.com, accessed February 19, 2018.

[37] Company website, "Life at Deloitte," www2.deloitte.com, accessed February 19, 2018.

[38] Jesse Newman and Annie Gasparro, "Blue Bell Ice Cream Returns to Store Shelves in Select Cities," *The Wall Street Journal*, http://www.wsj.com, accessed February 28, 2018.

[39] Chris Moran, "5-Hour Energy to Pay $4.3 Million for Deceptive Ads," *Consumerist*, http://www.consumerist.com, accessed February 19, 2018.

[40] David Lazarus, "Direct-to-Consumer Drug Ads: A Bad Idea That's About to Get Worse," *Los Angeles Times*, http://www.latimes.com, accessed February 19, 2018.

[41] Kimberly Palmer, "The 3 Best Places to Complain About a Company," *US News and World Report*, http://www.usnews.com, accessed February 20, 2018; organization website, "Better Business Bureau," http://www.bbb.org, accessed February 20, 2018; organization website, "Having a Problem with a Financial Product or Service?" https://www.consumerfinance.gov/complaint, accessed February 20, 2018.

[42] Organization website, "Facts for Employers: Safer Jobs for Teens," http://youngworkers.org, accessed February 19, 2018; government website, "Young Workers," http://www.osha.gov, accessed February 19, 2018; government website, "Youth Rules!" http://www.youthrules.dol.gov, accessed February 19, 2018; government website, "Table A-8. Fatal Occupational Injuries by Event of Exposure and Age, All United States, 2015," http://www.bls.gov, accessed February 20, 2018.

[43] Kathryn Dill, "The Best Companies for Work-Life Balance," *Forbes,* http://www.forbes.com, accessed February 19, 2018; company website, "About," http://www.hrblock.com, accessed February 19, 2018.

[44] Craig Bloem, "Netflix and Virgin Both Have Unlimited Vacation Policies. Here's How You Can Make It Work," *Inc.*, http://www.inc.com, accessed February 20, 2018; Amy Elisa Jackson, "Cool Companies Offering Unlimited Vacation & Hiring Now," *Glassdoor.com*, http://www.glassdoor.com, accessed February 20, 2018.

[45] Alex Hickey, "Systematic Gender Discrimination Costing Tech Billions," *CIODive*, http://www.ciodive.com, accessed February 20, 2018.

[46] Government website, http://www.eeoc.gov, accessed February 19, 2018; Russell Cawyer, "Bill to Add Lilly Ledbetter Act Provisions to Texas Labor Code Enrolled," *Texas Employment Law Update*, http://www.texasemploymentlawupdate.com, accessed February 19, 2018.

[47] Mike Sunnucks, "'LA Times' Lawsuit a Warning for Employers Looking to Replace Older, Better Paid Workers," *Phoenix Business Journal*, http://www.bizjournals.com, accessed February 19, 2018.

[48] Ralph Silberman, "Conference Board Job Satisfaction Survey Finds Older Workers as Dissatisfied as Others," *Aging Workforce News*, http://www.agingworkforcenews.com, accessed February 20, 2018.

[49] Government website, Mitra Toossi and Elka Torpey, "Older Workers: Labor Force Trends and Career Options," http://www.bls.gov, accessed February 19, 2018.

[50] Government website, "Charges Alleging Sexual Harassment FY 2010–FY 2017," http://www.eeoc.gov, accessed February 19, 2018.

[51] Sarah Almukhtar, Michael Gold, and Larry Buchanan, "After Weinstein: 71 Men Accused of Sexual Misconduct and Their Fall From Power," accessed February 20, 2018, *New York Times,* http://www.nytimes.com, accessed February 20, 2018.

[52] Government website, "Model EEO Programs Must Have an Effective Anti-Harassment Program," http://www.eeoc.gov, accessed February 19, 2018; Matthew Goldstein, Tiffany Hsu, and Kenneth P. Vogel, "Stephen Wynn, Casino Mogul, Accused of Decades of Sexual Misconduct," *New York Times*, http://www.nytimes.com, accessed February 21, 2018.

[53] Government website, "Equal Pay Act of 1963 and Lilly Ledbetter Fair Pay Act of 2009," http://www.eeoc.gov, accessed February 19, 2018.

[54] Government website, "Did You Know that Women Are Still Paid Less Than Men?" http://www.whitehouse.gov, accessed February 19, 2018; organization website, "The Simple Truth About the Gender Pay Gap," http://www.aauw.org, accessed February 19, 2018.

Chapter 3

[1] Company website, "About Us" and "Airbnb Economic Impact," http://www.airbnb.com, accessed February 21, 2018; Kerry Close, "4 Things Airbnb's Brian Chesky Thinks All Young Entrepreneurs Need to Know," *Inc.*, http://www.inc.com, accessed February 21, 2018; "Joe Gebbia: How Airbnb Stayed on Mission During Tough Times (video)," *Inc.*, http://www.inc.com, accessed February 21, 2018; Craig Karmin, "Airbnb Crimps Hotels' Power on Pricing," *The Wall Street Journal*, http://www.wsj.com, accessed February 21, 2018; Jonathan Tuason, "Airbnb's Lesson on Supply and Demand," *Elegran*, http://www.elegran.com, accessed February 21, 2018; Chris Hemmeter, "Airbnb Could Disrupt Supply–Demand Equation," *Hotel News Now*, http://www.hotelnewsnow.com, accessed February 21, 2018; "Room for All, For Now," *Economist*, http://www.economist.com, accessed February 21, 2018; Jean Folger, "The Pros and Cons of Using Airbnb," *Investopedia*, http://www.investopedia.com, accessed February 21, 2018; Dara Kerr, "Vexed in the City: The 'Sharing' Economy's Hidden Toll on San Francisco," *CNET*, http://www.cnet.com, accessed February 21, 2018; Rolfe Winkler and Douglas MacMillan, "The Secret Math of Airbnb's $24 Billion Valuation," *The Wall Street Journal*, http://www.wsj.com, accessed February 21, 2018; Derek Thompson, "Airbnb and the Unintended Consequences of 'Disruption'," *The Atlantic*, http://www.theatlantic.com, accessed February 21, 2018.

[2] He Wei, "Growth of Middle Class Means Major Changes for China," *China Daily*, http://www.chinadaily.com, accessed February 22, 2018; Andrew Ross Sorkin, "While Other U.S. Companies Flee China, Starbucks Doubles Down," *New York Times*, http://www.nytimes.com, accessed February 22, 2018.

[3] Jemima Webber, "Demand for Vegan and Vegetarian Food Increased by 987% in 2017," *LIVEKINDLY*, https://www.livekindly.co, accessed February 22, 2018; "'Going Vegan' Is Predicted to Be the Biggest Food Trend of 2018," *Rise of the Vegan*, https://www.riseofthevegan.com, accessed February 22, 2018.

[4] "Airline Pricing Secrets: How Carriers Come up with Fares," *CNN*, http://www.cnn.com, accessed February 27, 2018.

[5] Company website, "About Zume Pizza," http://www.zume.com, accessed February 27, 2018.

[6] Maria Aspan, "The Latest Moves in the Battle to Become the Next PayPal," *Inc.*, http://www.inc.com, accessed February 21, 2018; Dan Blystone, "Search Engines That Compete with Google," *Investopedia*, http://www.investopedia.com, accessed February 21, 2018; Jordan Kahn, "Apple Reportedly Considering 'Dramatic Overhaul' of iTunes to Help Fight Rising Competition," *9to5Mac*, http://9to5mac.com, accessed February 21, 2018; Larissa MacFarquhar, "When Giants Fail," *The New Yorker*, http://www.newyorker.com, accessed February 21, 2018.

[7] Grant Gross, "Net Neutrality Rules Go into Effect: What Happens Now," *PCWorld*, http://www.pcworld.com, accessed February 21, 2018.

[8] Bart Jansen, "Airline Executives Urge Privatization of Air-Traffic Control," *USA Today*, http://www.usatoday.com, accessed February 21, 2018; Bart Jansen, "Trump Budget Continues to Support Air-Traffic Control Privatization," *USA Today*, https://www.usatoday.com, accessed February 24, 2018.

[9] Brian Alexander, "Privatization Is Changing America's Relationship with Its Physical Stuff," *The Atlantic*, http://www.theatlantic.com, accessed February 24, 2018.

[10] Ron Sommer, "Don't Be Fooled by Dollar Tree's Revenue Growth," *Seeking Alpha*, http://www.seekingalpha.com, accessed February 24, 2018; Tae Kim, "JP Morgan: Buy Dollar Tree Because Lower-Income Earners to Get Boost from Tax Cuts, Wage Hikes," *CNBC*, https://www.cnbc.com, accessed February 26, 2018; Christopher Matthews, "Will Dollar Stores Rule the Retail World?" *Time*, http://business.time.com, accessed February 21, 2018.

[11] Government website, "National Economic Accounts," http://www.bea.gov, accessed February 21, 2018; Mark Skousen, "Beyond GDP: Get Ready for a New Way to Measure the Economy," *Forbes*, http://www.forbes.com, accessed February 21, 2018; government website, *The World Factbook*," http://www.cia.gov, accessed February 21, 2018.

[12] Paul Toscano, "The Worst Hyperinflation Situations of All Time," *CNBC*, http://www.cnbc.com, accessed February 21, 2018.

[13] Lisa Smith, "How to Profit from Inflation," *Investopedia*, https://www.investopedia.com, accessed February 25, 2018.

[14] "How Does Inflation Impact Consumers?" *Investopedia*, http://www.investopedia.com, accessed February 25, 2018.

[15] Government website, "Consumer Price Index January 2018," http://www.bls.gov, accessed February 21, 2018.

[16] Government website, "Current Employment Statistics Highlights BLS January 2018," http://www.bls.gov, accessed February 21, 2018.

[17] Government website, "How the Government Measures Unemployment," http://www.bls.gov, accessed February 21, 2018.

[18] Organization website, "World Bank Supports Sierra Leone's Efforts in Landside Recovery," http://www.worldbank.org, accessed February 21, 2018.

[19] Organization website, "U.S. Debt Clock," www.usdebtclock.org, accessed February 25, 2018; government website, "U.S. and World Population Clock," https://www.census.gov, accessed February 26, 2018.

[20] Organization website, "World Economic Forum: Global Risks 2015, 10th Edition," http://www3.weforum.org, accessed February 21, 2018.

[21] Organization website, "World Economic Forum: Global Risks 2015, 10th Edition," http://www3.weforum.org, accessed February 21, 2018.

[22] Government website, "U.S. and World Population Clock," http://www.census.gov, accessed February 21, 2018.

[23] Government website, "Lithium-Ion Battery Safety Standards for Consumer Product Import into the United States," http://www.cpsc.gov, accessed February 21, 2018.

[24] Carolyn Heneghan, "RTD Tea Is Ready to Guzzle a Larger Beverage Market Share," *Food Dive*, http://www.fooddive.com, accessed February 21, 2018; Rachel Arthur, "Energy Drinks May Hog the Limelight, But Watch Out for RTD Teas," *Beverage Daily*, http://www.beveragedaily.com, accessed February 21, 2018; "Asian Soft Drinks Consumption Continues to Drive Future Closure Demand," *Market Publishers*, http://marketpublishers.com, accessed February 21, 2018.

Chapter 4

[1] Jennifer Reingold, "What the Heck Is Angela Ahrendts Doing at Apple?" *Fortune*, http://fortune.com, accessed March 1, 2018; Austin Carr, "Apple's Angela Ahrendts on Where the Company Is Taking Retail Next," *Fast Company*, http://www.fastcompany.com, accessed

March 1, 2018; Ana Swanson, "How the Apple Store Took Over the World," *The Washington Post*, https://www.washingtonpost.com, accessed March 1, 2018; Rex Crum, "Apple's Retail Strategy Is Still Paying Off in a Big Way," *The Street*, http://www.thestreet.com, accessed March 1, 2018; Clare O'Connor, "Apple's China iPhone Coup Shows Angela Ahrendts Is Worth Every Penny," *Forbes*, http://www.forbes.com, accessed March 1, 2018; "Angela Ahrendts' Plan for the Future of Apple Retail: China Emphasis, Mobile Payments, Revamped Experience," *9to5 Mac*, http://www.9to5mac.com, accessed March 1, 2018; Kathy Gordon, "A Flair for Tech as Well as 'Burberry Check,'" *The Wall Street Journal*, http://www.wsj.com, accessed March 1, 2018; Jon Russell, "iPhone 8 Launch Propels Apple to Growth in China After 18 Months of Sales Dips," *TechCrunch*, http://www.techcrunch.com, accessed March 1, 2018; Adrianne Pasquarelli, "Power Players 2017: Apple's Angela Ahrendts Says Retail Is the Product," *AdAge*, http://www.adage.com, accessed March 1, 2018; Chance Miller, "Apple Again Found to Be the World's Top Retailer in Sales per Square Foot," *9to5mac*, https://9to5mac.com, accessed March 1, 2018; Don Reisinger, "Here's the Latest on How Apple Is Expanding in China," *Fortune*, http://www.fortune.com, accessed March 1, 2018.

[2] Government website, "United States," *World Factbook*, http://www.cia.gov, accessed March 1, 2018.

[3] Alwyn Scott, "Boeing Signs Deal to Sell 300 Planes Worth $37 Billion to China," *Reuters*, https://www.reuters.com, accessed March 1, 2018.

[4] Don Reisinger, "Here's the Latest on How Apple Is Expanding in China," *Fortune*, http://www.fortune.com, accessed March 1, 2018; Jon Russell, "iPhone 8 Launch Propels Apple to Growth in China After 18 Months of Sales Dips," *TechCrunch*, http://www.techcrunch.com, accessed March 1, 2018.

[5] Organization website, "World Population Prospects: The 2017 Revision," http://www.esa.un.org, accessed March 1, 2018.

[6] Organization website, "GDP Growth (Annual %)," http://data.worldbank.org, accessed March 1, 2018.

[7] Holden Wilen, "Medifast to Begin Selling in Hong Kong and Singapore Next Year," *Baltimore Business Journal*, https://www.bizjournals.com, accessed March 1, 2018.

[8] Government website, "Top Trading Partners—December 2017—Year-to-Date Total Trade," http://www.census.gov, accessed March 1, 2018; government website, "State Exports from Texas," http://www.census.gov, accessed March 1, 2018; government website, "State Exports from California," http://www.census.gov, accessed March 1, 2018; Daniel Workman, "United States Top 10 Exports," *World's Top Exports*, http://www.worldstopexports.com, accessed March 1, 2018; Matthew Speiser, "The Top Export and Import in Every U.S. State," *Business Insider*, http://www.businessinsider.com, accessed March 1, 2018.

[9] "Iran Accounts for 94% of World Saffron Production," *The Iran Project*, http://theiranproject.com, accessed March 1, 2018; Marryam H. Reshii, "What Makes Saffron the Most Expensive Spice in the World?" *NDTV Food*, https://food.ndtv.com, accessed March 1, 2018.

[10] Tracey E. Schelmetic, "The U.S. Contact Center Industry Is Growing, and With It, the Need for a Multichannel, Multi-Skilled Platform," *TMCnet.com*, http://www.tmcnet.com, accessed March 1, 2018.

[11] Daniel Workman, "United States Top 10 Exports," http://www.worldstopexports.com, accessed March 2, 2018; Daniel Workman, "United States Top 10 Imports," http://www.worldstopexports.com, accessed March 2, 2018; government website, "U.S. Trade in Goods and Services—Balance of Payments (BOP) Basis, 1960–2014," http://www.census.gov, accessed March 1, 2018; government website, "U.S. International Trade in Goods and Services—December 2017," press release, http://www.bea.gov, accessed March 1, 2018.

[12] Robert Vaux, "Disney Theme Parks Around the World," *USA Today*, http://traveltips.usatoday.com, accessed March 1, 2018; company website, "Disney Unveils New Magic in Shanghai: Resort Filled with Innovative Attractions and Entertainment Especially for Chinese Guests," https://www.shanghaidisneyresort.com.cn, accessed March 1, 2018.

[13] "25 Most Traded Currencies," https://www.countries-ofthe-world.com/most-traded-currencies.html, accessed March 2, 2018; "Most Traded Currencies in 2018," https://www.invest.com, accessed March 2, 2018.

[14] Julie Jargon, "Yum to Split Off China Business," *The Wall Street Journal*, http://www.wsj.com, accessed March 1, 2018.

[15] Company website, "Chinese Taboo," *About.com*, http://chineseculture.about.com, accessed March 1, 2018.

[16] Kent Miller, "Global Fintech Investment Remains Robust on Back of Strong VC Funding: KPMG Pulse of Fintech Report," https://home.kpmg.com, accessed March 3, 2018.

[17] Sophia Yan, "Thailand Political Unrest Unleashes Market Turmoil," *CNN Money*, http://money.cnn.com, accessed March 1, 2018.

[18] W. S. Blackmer, "GDPR: Getting Ready for the New EU General Data Protection Regulation," *Information Law Group*, http://www.infolawgroup.com, accessed March 3, 2018.

[19] Luca Solca, "The 'Made In' Dilemma: To Label, or Not to Label," *Business of Fashion*, http://www.businessoffashion.com, accessed March 1, 2018; Joe Ayling, "'Made in Italy' Thrives Without EU Label Law," *Just Style*, http://www.just-style.com, accessed March 1, 2018.

[20] Ana Swanson, "Trump to Impose Sweeping Steel and Aluminum Tariffs," *New York Times*, https://www.nytimes.com, accessed March 3, 2018.

[21] Organization website, "U.S. Sugar Policy," http://sugarcane.org, accessed March 1, 2018; government website, "Sugar Import Program," http://www.fas.usda.gov, accessed March 1, 2018.

[22] Associated Press, "China Imposes Anti-Dumping Measure Amid Trade Tensions," *US News and World Report*, http://www.usnews.com, accessed March 3, 2018.

[23] Associated Press, "U.S. May Accept UN Condemning Trade Embargo Against Cuba for First Time," *The Guardian*, http://www.theguardian.com, accessed March 1, 2018; "Cuba and US to Restore Postal Service After 52 Years," *BBC News*, http://www.bbc.com, accessed March 1, 2018.

[24] Organization website, "The Doha Round," https://www.wto.org, accessed March 1, 2018.

[25] Noah Feldman, "Yuan Move Is Good for China's Politics," *Bloomberg Business*, http://www.bloomberg.com, accessed March 1, 2018; Josh Boak, "IMF Adds China's Yuan to Basket of Top Currencies," *Associated Press*, http://bigstory.ap.org, accessed March 1, 2018.

[26] Government website, "North America," *World Factbook*, http://www.cia.gov, accessed March 1, 2018; government website, "North American Free Trade Agreement," http://www.ustr.gov, accessed March 1, 2018; "GDP as Share of World GDP at PPP by Country," https://www.quandl.com, accessed March 1, 2018; government website, "Gross Domestic Output," http://www.bea.gov, accessed March 1, 2018; M. Angeles Villarreal and Ian F. Fergusson, "The North American Free Trade Agreement," *Congressional Research Service*, https://www.fas.org, accessed March 1, 2018.

[27] Ibid.

[28] Ibid.

[29] Government website, "Trade in Goods with CAFTA-DR," http://www.census.gov, accessed March 1, 2018; government website, "CAFTA-DR (Dominican Republic-Central America FTA)," https://ustr.gov, accessed March 5, 2018.

[30] Organization website, "Countries," http://europa.eu, accessed March 1, 2018; government website, *World Factbook*, http://www.cia.gov,

accessed March 1, 2018; Alex Hunt and Brian Wheeler, "Brexit: All You Need to Know About the UK Leaving the EU," *BBC News*, http://www.bbcnews.com, accessed March 5, 2018.

[31] Anna Hensel, "Here Are the 10 Fastest-Growing Companies in Los Angeles," *Inc.*, http://www.inc.com, accessed March 1, 2018; company website, "Franchise" and "Sky Zone Becomes First US-Based Trampoline Park to Go Global," http://www.skyzone.com, accessed March 1, 2018.

[32] Company website, "Our History" and "Under Armour Global Office Locations," http://www.underarmour.com, accessed March 1, 2018.

[33] Company website, "Domino's Locations," https://www.dominos.com, accessed March 1, 2018; company website, "Domino's 101 Basic Facts," https://biz.dominos.com, accessed March 1, 2018; company website, "What Types of Pizza Toppings Does Domino's Use?" http://www.biz.dominos.com, accessed March 3, 2018.

[34] Reuters, "Alibaba Signs Deal to Offer Disney Shows on Video Platforms," *Reuters*, http://www.reuters.com, accessed March 3, 2018.

[35] "2017 Top 100 Outsourcing Destinations Rankings," *Tholons*, http://tholons.com, accessed March 1, 2018; company website, "China vs. Mexico: A Breakdown for U.S. Businesses," https://www.chase.com, accessed March 1, 2018.

[36] "Countries with the Most FDI in 2018," *Global Finance*, https://www.gfmag.com, accessed March 5, 2018.

[37] Chris Isidore, "Toyota and Mazda to Build $1.6 Billion Joint Plant in Alabama," *CNN Money*, http://www.cnn.com, accessed March 5, 2018.

[38] Richard Feloni, "7 Brilliant Strategies Coca-Cola Used to Become One of the World's Most Recognizable Brands," *Business Insider*, http://www.businessinsider.com, accessed March 1, 2018; Crystal Vogt, "What Is Global Standardization in Marketing?" *Chron*, http://smallbusiness.chron.com, accessed March 1, 2018.

[39] Shilpa Kannan, "How McDonald's Conquered India," *BBC News*, http://www.bbc.com, accessed March 1, 2018; Colin Shaw, "Successful Globalization: If McDonalds Can Do It, Any Company Can!" *Beyond Philosophy*, http://beyondphilosophy.com, accessed March 1, 2018; Elizabeth Entenmen, "10 McDonald's International Menu Items You Can Eat in Other Countries," *Complex*, http://www.complex.com, accessed March 3, 2018.

Chapter 5

[1] Company website, "About Us," Zume Pizza, http://www.zume.com, accessed March 7, 2018.

[2] Government website, "Office of Advocacy—Frequently Asked Questions August 2017," http://web.sba.gov, accessed March 7, 2018.

[3] Ibid.

[4] Georgia McIntyre, "What Is the SBA's Definition of Small Business (and Why)?" *Fundera*, http://www.fundera.com, accessed March 7, 2018; government website, "U.S. Small Business Administration Table of Small Business Size Standards Matched to North American Industry Classification Codes," http://sba.gov, accessed March 7, 2018; government website, "Summary of Size Standards by Industry Sector," http://www.sba.gov, accessed March 7, 2018.

[5] Company website, "History," http://www.riflepaperco.com, accessed March 7, 2018; Aileen Kwun, "How One Designer Built a $22M Company—Selling Paper," *Fast Company*, http://www.fastcompany.com, accessed March 7, 2018.

[6] Government website, "Structure and Finances of U.S. Farms: Family Farm Report," http://www.ers.usda.gov, accessed March 7, 2018.

[7] Company website, "About Cider Hill Farm," http://ciderhill.com, accessed March 7, 2018.

[8] Government website, "Frequently Asked Questions About Small Business," https://www.sba.gov, accessed March 8, 2018.

[9] Company website, "The Fat Brain Toys Story," https://www.fatbraintoys.com, accessed March 7, 2018; Bill Briggs, "Fat Brain Toys Chooses a 'Fat' Screen for Its Site Redesign," *Internet Retailer*, https://www.internetretailer.com, accessed March 7, 2018; PR Newswire, "Fat Brain Toys® Showcasing Kid-Invented 'Door Pong' as the Highlight of Its Product Introductions at 2018 Toy Fair," *Cision PR Newswire*, http://www.prnewswire.com, accessed March 8, 2018; Solomon Thimoth, "How Small Businesses Can Embrace Technology to Grow Their Company Using Digital Marketing," *Forbes*, http://www.forbes.com, accessed March 8, 2018; Tim Day, "Technology Is Essential to Future of Small Businesses Across America," *The Hill*, http://www.thehill.com, accessed March 8, 2018.

[10] Government website, "Frequently Asked Questions About Small Business," https://www.sba.gov, accessed March 8, 2018.

[11] Rhea Gaur, "Small Businesses Readying Themselves to Compete in Global Markets," *Small Biz Technology*, http://www.smallbiztechnology.com, accessed March 7, 2018.

[12] Government website, "Frequently Asked Questions," http://archive.sba.gov, accessed March 7, 2018.

[13] Organization website, "The Importance of Young Firms for Economic Growth," *Kauffman Foundation*, http://www.kauffman.org, accessed March 11, 2018.

[14] Company website, "Nordstrom Company History," http://shop.nordstrom.com, accessed March 7, 2018.

[15] Katie Chang, "Here's What You Need to Know about Manscaping in 2015," *Details*, http://details.com, accessed March 7, 2018; company website, "FAQs," http://dollarshaveclub.com, accessed March 7, 2018.

[16] Government website, "Frequently Asked Questions," https://www.sba.gov, accessed March 7, 2018.

[17] Government website, "Frequently Asked Questions: Advocacy Small Business Statistics and Research," https://www.sba.gov/advocacy, accessed March 7, 2018.

[18] Company website, "Krispy Kreme to Be Acquired by JAC Beech for $21 Per Share in Cash," http://hotnews.krispykreme.com, accessed March 8, 2018.

[19] Patricia Schaefer, "The Seven Pitfalls of Business Failure and How to Avoid Them," *Business Know-How*, http://www.businessknowhow.com, accessed March 7, 2018.

[20] Jayson Demers, "5 Common Pitfalls That Ruin Businesses—and How to Avoid Them," *Entrepreneur*, http://www.entrepreneur.com, accessed March 7, 2018.

[21] Government website, "Advocacy Small Business Statistics and Research—Small Business Finance," http://web.sba.gov, accessed March 7, 2018.

[22] Company website, "About Us—TN Moonshine Cakes," http://www.tnmoonshinecakes.com, accessed March 7, 2018; "Local Love: Chattanooga Moonshine Cakes," *News Channel 9*, http://www.newschannel9.com, accessed March 7, 2018.

[23] Christopher M. Matthews, "Compliance More Costly for Small Firms, Survey Finds," *The Wall Street Journal*, http://blogs.wsj.com, accessed March 7, 2018; William Dunkelberg, "The Hidden Costs of Regulations," *Forbes*, http://www.forbes.com, accessed March 9, 2018.

[24] Government website, "U.S. Department of Labor: e-Laws, Family and Medical Leave Act Advisor," http://www.dol.gov, accessed March 7, 2018; government website, "The Affordable Care Act Increases Choice and Saving Money for Small Businesses," *The White House*, http://www.whitehouse.gov, accessed March 7, 2018.

[25] Government website, "Business Tax Credits," http://www.irs.gov, accessed March 7, 2018; government website, "HUBZone Program," http://www.sba.gov, accessed March 7, 2018.

[26] Company website, "The Whole Story Begins with You," http://www.warbyparker.com, accessed March 7, 2018; Michael Fitzgerald, "For

Warby Parker, Free Glasses Equals Clear Company Vision," *Entrepreneur,* http://www.entrepreneur.com, accessed March 7, 2018.

[27] "Expert Advice: 10 Tips to Craft a Strong Business Plan," *Entrepreneur,* http://www.entrepreneur.com, accessed March 7, 2018.

[28] Government website, "What We Do" and "Mission Statement," https://www.sba.gov, accessed March 7, 2018.

[29] Government website, "Loans and Grants" and "SBA Loan Programs," https://www.sba.gov, accessed March 7, 2018.

[30] Government website, "Microloan Program," https://www.sba.gov, accessed March 7, 2018.

[31] Government website, "Government Contracting 101—Part 1: Overview of Small Business Programs," https://www.sba.gov, accessed March 7, 2018.

[32] Government website, "Local Assistance" and "SBA Learning Center," https://www.sba.gov, accessed March 7, 2018.

[33] Thurston County Economic Development Council, "Mission," http://www.thurstonedc.com, accessed March 7, 2018.

[34] Organization website, "About Us," http://www2.nbia.org, accessed March 7, 2018; Jeff Schmitt, "The Top University Business Incubators," http://poetsandquants.com, accessed March 7, 2018; "12 Business Incubators Changing the World," *Forbes,* http://www.forbes.com, accessed March 7, 2018; organization website, "Business Incubation FAQs," http://www.inbia.org, accessed March 7, 2018; Andre Bourque, "7 Incubators That Can Help Your Startup," *Entrepreneur,* accessed March 9, 2018, http://www.entrepreneur.com; organization website, "Northwestern Opens Door to Innovation Incubator," https://news.northwestern.edu, accessed March 9, 2018.

[35] Organization website, "About NVCA," http://www.nvca.org, accessed March 7, 2018; Peter Delevett, "Venture Capital Looks to Be in Full-Blown Recovery—But Is It Too Much Too Soon?" *San Jose Mercury News,* http://www.mercurynews.com, accessed March 7, 2018; "Greatest Concentration of Venture Capital? Not Where You Think," http://vcwithme.com, accessed March 7, 2018; Tanya Benedicto Klich, "VC 100: The Top Investors in Early-Stage Startups," *Entrepreneur,* http://www.entrepreneur.com, accessed March 7, 2018; Richard Florida, "Venture Capital Remains Highly Concentrated in Just a Few Cities," *City Lab,* http://www.citylab.com, accessed March 9, 2018; "Venture Capital Funding Report 2017," *CB Insights,* https://www.cbinsights.com, accessed March 9, 2018; Neil Petch, "What Venture Capitalists Look for When Investing in a Startup," *Entrepreneur,* http://www.entrepreneur.com, accessed March 9, 2018.

[36] Government website, "Survey of Business Owners and Self-Employed Persons (SBO)," http://www.uscensus.gov, accessed March 9, 2018.

[37] Company website, "About Us," http://www.michelesfoods.com, accessed March 9, 2018.

[38] Government website, "Mentor-Protégé Program" and "Minority Owned Businesses," http://www.sba.gov, accessed March 7, 2018; Kavita Sahai, "Female Millennials: Why They're Leaving Corporate Life," *Forbes,* http://www.forbes.com, accessed March 9, 2018.

[39] Organization website, "The Economic Impact of Franchised Businesses," http://www.franchise.org, accessed March 7, 2018.

[40] Julie Jargon and Maria Armental, "Yum Brands Cuts Profit Outlook on China Woes," *The Wall Street Journal,* http://www.wsj.com, accessed March 7, 2018; "Yum's China Lesson," *The Wall Street Journal,* http://www.wsj.com, accessed March 7, 2018; "2017 Top Global Franchises," *Entrepreneur,* http://www.entrepreneur.com, accessed March 7, 2018; company website, "Baskin-Robbins: About Us," http://www.baskinrobbins.com, accessed March 7, 2018.

[41] Company website, "Territories and Investment," http://www.greatclips.com, accessed March 7, 2018; "Great Clips at a Glance," *Entrepreneur,* http://www.entrepreneur.com, accessed March 7, 2018.

[42] Edward N. Levitt, "What's So Great About Franchising?" *Franchise Know How,* http://www.franchiseknowhow.com, accessed March 7, 2018.

[43] Ibid.

[44] "Franchise 101: Why People Are Drawn to Franchising," *Business Franchise World,* http://www.businessfranchiseworld.com, accessed March 7, 2018.

[45] Edward N. Levitt, "What's So Great About Franchising?" *Franchise Know How,* http://www.franchiseknowhow.com, accessed March 7, 2018.

[46] "How Much Does a Franchise Cost?" *All Business,* http://www.allbusiness.com, accessed March 7, 2018.

[47] Company website, "Own a Heaven's Best Franchise," http://www.heavensbest.com, accessed March 7, 2018.

[48] Jonathan Chew, "McDonald's Franchisees Are Really Depressed About the Future," *Fortune,* http://fortune.com, accessed March 7, 2018; Bryan Gruley and Leslie Patton, "McRevolt: The Frustrating Life of the McDonald's Franchisee," *Bloomberg Business,* http://www.bloomberg.com, accessed March 11, 2018; Kate Taylor, "Furious Franchisees Slam McDonald's for Costly Demands and 'Wasteful' Changes," *Business Insider,* http://www.businessinsider.com, accessed March 9, 2018.

[49] Whitney Bauck, "Ulta Just Got Hit with Another Huge Lawsuit," *Fashionista,* http://www.fashionista.com, accessed March 9, 2018.

[50] Nellie Akalp, "10 Things to Know about the Upcoming S Corporation Deadline," *Small Business Trends,* http://smallbiztrends.com, accessed March 7, 2018; government website, "IRS Launches Study of S Corporation Reporting Compliance," http://www.irs.gov, accessed March 7, 2018.

[51] Organization website, "Benefit Corporation Information Center," http://benefitcorp.net, accessed March 7, 2018.

[52] Organization website, "National Center for Employee Ownership—A Statistical Profile of Employee Ownership—Updated November 2017," https://www.nceo.org, accessed March 10, 2018.

[53] Organizational website, "The Employee Ownership 100: America's Largest Majority Employee-Owned Companies," https://www.nceo.org, accessed March 7, 2018; organization website, "ESOP Companies Report Continued Economic Growth," http://www.employeeownershipfoundation.org, accessed March 7, 2018.

[54] Company website, "2014 Family Business Survey," http://www.pwc.com, accessed March 7, 2018.

[55] Company website, "About Us," www.nhsoda.com, accessed March 7, 2018; Jesse Scardina, "An Old Time Treat," *Seacoastonline,* http://www.seacoastonline.com, accessed March 7, 2018.

[56] Organization website, "National Center for Charitable Statistics," http://nccs.urban.org, accessed March 10, 2018.

[57] Company website, "Company Directory by Business Classification," *Hoover's,* http://www.hoovers.com, accessed March 7, 2018.

[58] Company website, "National Fact Sheet: FY2016-2017," http://www.amtrak.com, accessed March 10, 2018.

[59] Organization website, "Co-operative Facts and Figures," http://ica.coop, accessed March 7, 2018.

[60] Organization website, "We're Cabot," http://www.cabotcheese.coop, accessed March 7, 2018.

[61] Company website, "Definition of Incorporator," http://smallbusiness.chron.com, accessed March 7, 2018.

[62] Luke Graham, "The 5 Biggest M&A Deals of the Year (So Far)," *CNBC,* http://www.cnbc.com, accessed March 7, 2018.

[63] Lin Grossman, "What the Amazon Effect Means for Retailers," *Forbes,* http://www.forbes.com, accessed March 10, 2018; Laura Stevens, "Amazon to Deliver Whole Foods Groceries," *Wall Street Journal,* http://www.wsj.com, accessed March 10, 2018.

[64] Ben Fritz, Amol Sharma, and Sarah Rabil, "Disney Agrees to Buy Key Parts of 21st Century Fox in $52.4 Billion Deal," *The Wall Street Journal*, http://www.wsj.com, accessed March 10, 2018.

[65] Michael Martinez, "FCA to Invest $280M in India Joint Venture," *Detroit News*, http://www.detroitnews.com, accessed March 7, 2018.

[66] Company website, "Share Your Cause with the World," https://www.google.com, accessed March 12, 2018.

Chapter 6

[1] Chanelle Bessette, "10 Questions: Jennifer Hyman, Co-Founder and CEO, Rent the Runway," *Fortune*, accessed March 12, 2018, http://fortune.com; company website, "FAQs," http://renttherunway.com, accessed March 12, 2018; Caroline Howard, "The 12 Most Disruptive Names in Business: The Full List," *Forbes*, http://www.forbes.com, accessed March 12, 2018; Teri Agins, "Rent a Dress? There's Risk, But the Rewards Are Big," *The Wall Street Journal*, http://www.wsj.com, accessed March 12, 2018; company website, "Stores," http://www.renttherunway, accessed March 12, 2018; Megan Rose Dicki, "Alibaba's Jack Ma and Joe Tsai Invest $20 Million in Rent the Runway," *TechCrunch*, http://www.techcrunch.com, accessed March 12, 2018.

[2] Company website, "2017 Annual Report," http://stock.walmart.com, accessed March 12, 2018.

[3] Company website, "About Annie's," http://www.annies.com, accessed March 12, 2018; William Alden, "General Mills to Buy Annie's for $820 Million in Cash," *The New York Times*, http://dealbook.nytimes.com, accessed March 12, 2018; Monica Watrous, "General Mills Partners with Small Farmers to Launch Limited-Edition Annie's Products," *Baking Business*, http://www.bakingbusiness.com, accessed March 12, 2018.

[4] Karsten Strauss, "The Rise, Fall and Resurgence of the Pond Guy: Aquascape," *Forbes*, http://www.forbes.com, accessed March 12, 2018; company website, "The Aquascape Team," http://www.aquascapeinc.com, accessed March 12, 2018.

[5] Dan Schawbe, "How to Win at the Sport of Business: If I Can Do It, You Can Do It," *Forbes*, http://www.forbes.com, accessed March 12, 2018; Jillian D'Onfro, "Mark Cuban Dishes the Dirt on the Success Rate of His 'Shark Tank' Investments," *Business Insider*, http://www.businessinsider.com, accessed March 12, 2018; Sarah Field, "Shark Tank Advice: Be Nice, Cultivate Optimism, and Get Your Head Out of the Clouds," *Inquisitr*, http://www.inquisitr.com, accessed March 12, 2018; Kim Lachance Shandrow, "Billionaire Entrepreneur Mark Cuban: 'Failure Is Part of the Success Equation'," *Entrepreneur*, http://www.entrepreneur.com, accessed March 12, 2018.

[6] Company website, "About Us," http://www.revolutionfoods.com, accessed March 12, 2018; Ainsley O'Connell, "Most Innovative Companies 2015: Revolution Foods for Selling Good, Cheap Food to Children Who Need It Most," *Fast Company*, http://www.fastcompany.com, accessed March 12, 2018; company website, "Our Products," http://revolutionfoods.com, accessed March 12, 2018.

[7] Leigh Buchanan, "The U.S. Now Has 27 Million Entrepreneurs," *Inc.*, http://www.inc.com, accessed March 12, 2018.

[8] Company website, "Play to Give," "Energy Access," and "M.O.R.E. Inside," http://unchartedplay.com, accessed March 12, 2018; Claire Groden, "Meet Fortune's 2015 Most Promising Women Entrepreneurs," *Fortune*, http://fortune.com, accessed March 12, 2018; "Toyota Mothers of Invention," *The New York Times*, http://paidpost.nytimes.com, accessed March 12, 2018.

[9] Company website, "Planet Fitness Announces Pricing of Initial Public Offering," http://investor.planetfitness.com, accessed March 12, 2018; "Planet Fitness Returns as 'The Biggest Loser' National Gym Partner for Fifth Year in a Row," *PR Newswire*, http://www.prnewswire.com, accessed March 12, 2018; David Trainer, "Planet Fitness Not As Financially Fit As It Appears," *Forbes*, http://www.forbes.com, accessed March 12, 2018; Mallory Schlossberg, "The Fastest-Growing Gym in America Has $10 Memberships and Gives Out Free Pizza, Bagels, and Candy," *Business Insider*, http://www.businessinsider.com, accessed March 12, 2018.

[10] Company website, "About Zappos," http://www.zappos.com, accessed March 12, 2018.

[11] Office of Advocacy, U.S. Small Business Administration, "The Small Business Advocate—November 2017," http://www.sba.gov, accessed March 12, 2018.

[12] Rohit Bagaria, "Entrepreneurship Is Essentially About Problem Solving," *Entrepreneur*, http://www.entrepreneur.com, accessed March 17, 2018.

[13] Christina Farr, "How Tim Ferriss Has Turned His Body Into a Research Lab," *KQED*, http://ww2.kqed.org, accessed March 12, 2018; company website, "Tim Ferriss Bio," http://fourhourworkweek.com, accessed March 12, 2018; Tom Foster, "Tim Ferris' 4-Hour Reality Check," *Inc.*, http://www.inc.com, accessed March 12, 2018; Joseph Yi, "Examples of Three Successful Lifestyle Entrepreneurs," *Ecommerce Rules*, http://ecommercerules.com, accessed March 12, 2018.

[14] Organization Laura Begley Bloom, "The 10 Most (and 10 Least) Innovative States in the U.S.," *Forbes*, http://www.forbes.com, accessed March 13, 2018.

[15] Barb Darrow, "LinkedIn Claims Half a Billion Users," *Fortune*, http://www.fortune.com, accessed March 17, 2018; Craig Smith, "By the Numbers: 125+ Amazing LinkedIn Statistics," *Expanded Ramblings*, http://expandedramblings.com, accessed March 12, 2018; "LinkedIn Has Over 30 Million Users in India; Grew 50 Percent in 2 Years," *Gadgets 360*, http://gadgets.ndtv.com, accessed March 12, 2018; "Linkedin by the Numbers: Stats, Demographics & Fun Facts," https://www.omnicoreagency.com, accessed March 13, 2018.

[16] Organizational website, "Global Entrepreneurship Monitor 2016/2017 Global Report," http://www.gemconsortium.org/report, accessed March 12, 2018.

[17] Organization website, "Global Facts," http://uk.gew.co, accessed March 12, 2018.

[18] Educational website, "Faculty and Research Entrepreneurship and Innovation, Northeastern University," http://www.damore-mckim.northeastern.edu, accessed March 12, 2018.

[19] Organization website, "Our Story," http://enactus.org, accessed March 12, 2018; organization site, "About Us," https://www.kauffman.org, accessed March 17, 2018.

[20] Abigail Hess, "10 Ultra-Successful Millionaire and Billionaire College Dropouts," *CNBC*, http://www.cnbc.com, accessed March 13, 2018.

[21] Madeline Berg, "The World's Highest-Paid YouTube Stars," *Forbes*, http://www.forbes.com, accessed March 12, 2018; company website, "Smosh," *YouTube*, https://www.youtube.com, accessed March 12, 2018; Brian Crescente, "Smosh Co-Founder Leaves YouTube Channel Over Lack of Creative Freedom," *Polygon*, https://www.polygon.com, accessed March 13, 2018.

[22] Organization website, Robert W. Fairlie, Arnobio Morelix, E. J. Reedy, and Joshua Russell, "The Kauffman Index Startup Activity National Trends 2015," http://www.kauffman.org, accessed March 12, 2018.

[23] Company website, "Our Story," https://insomniacookies.com, accessed March 12, 2018; Elizabeth Hoyt, "20 of the Coolest College Start-Ups Ever," *Fast Web*, http://www.fastweb.com, accessed March 12, 2018.

[24] Fitz Tepper, "Feather Raises $3.5M to Rent Furniture to Millennials," *TechCrunch*, http://www.techcrunch.com, accessed March 13, 2018; company website, "About Us," https://www.rentfeather.com, accessed

March 13, 2018; Madeline Gressel, "For the Startups Disrupting Home Décor, Less Is More," *New York Post*, http://www.nypost.com, accessed March 13, 2018.

[25] Company website, "Google and HTC Announce US$1.1 Billion Cooperation Agreement," http://www.htc.com, accessed March 14, 2018; Neal Ungerleider, "Most Influential Women in Technology 2011—Cher Wang," *Fast Company*, http://www.fastcompany.com, accessed March 14, 2018.

[26] "Whoops! The 10 Greatest (Accidental) Inventions of All Time," *Popular Science*, http://www.popsci.com, accessed March 12, 2018.

[27] John Rampton, "How Many Hours Should You Work Each Week?" *Inc.*, http://www.inc.com, accessed March 12, 2018; "A Day in the Life of an Entrepreneur," *Princeton Review*, http://www.princetonreview.com, accessed March 12, 2018.

[28] Company website, "The Entrepreneur I Most Admire," http://www.virgin.com, accessed March 12, 2018.

[29] Mark Stone, "What We Can Learn from Elon Musk's Unbalanced Ratio of Failures to Successes," *Forbes*, http://www.forbes.com, accessed March 14, 2018.

[30] Company website, "Bobbi's History," http://www.bobbibrown cosmetics.com, accessed March 12, 2018; Nancy Giles, "How Bobbi Brown Put a New Face on the Makeup Industry," *CBS News*, http://www.cbsnews.com, accessed March 12, 2018; Bobbi Brown and Athena Schindelheim, "How I Did It," *Inc.*, http://www.inc.com, accessed March 12, 2018; Karin Eldor, "Beauty Icon Bobbi Brown's Newest Project: Meet The World's Most Beautiful Bar," *Forbes*, http://www.forbes.com, accessed March 14, 2018.

[31] Company website, "A Look at Our History," http://www.gogoair.com, accessed March 12, 2018; company website, "InFlight Systems," http://concourse.gogoair.com, accessed March 12, 2018; company website, "Empowering Your Fleet for Connected Skies," http://commercial.gogoair.com, accessed March 12, 2018; Andrew Hawkins, "Wi-Fi on Some International Flights Is About to Get Much Better," *The Verge*, http://www.theverge.com, accessed March 14, 2018.

[32] Teresa Novellino, "Talkspace Raises $9.5M to Let Users Text Their Therapists," *New York Business Journal*, http://www.bizjournals.com, accessed March 14, 2018; Jessica Caldwell, "The Anti-Anxiety App," *The Wall Street Journal*, http://www.wsj.com, accessed March 14, 2018; company website, "How Therapy Works on Talkspace," http://www.talkspace.com, accessed March 14, 2018.

[33] Jacqueline Ronson, "Netflix Isn't Giving Up on DVDs Anytime Soon," *Motherboard*, http://motherboard.vice.com, accessed March 12, 2018; Logan Hill, "The Business of Being Netflix," *The Wall Street Journal*, http://online.wsj.com, accessed March 12, 2018; McKinley Noble, "Netflix Still Has Millions of DVD Subscribers Because Rural US Broadband Is Terrible," *Quartz*, http://www.qz.com, accessed March 14, 2018.

[34] Company website, "About Us," http://www.braunability.com, accessed March 12, 2018; Kasey Wehrum, "How I Did It: Ralph Braun of BraunAbility," *Inc.*, http://www.inc.com, accessed March 12, 2018.

[35] Organization website, "Jeffrey P. Bezos Interview," http://www.achievement.org, accessed March 12, 2018.

[36] Martin Zwilling, "7 Seed-Stage Funding Sources That Might Finance Your Startup," *Entrepreneur*, http://www.entrepreneur.com, accessed March 12, 2018; company website, "The 106 Most Active Seed Venture Capital Firms," *CB Insights*, www.cbinsights.com, accessed March 12, 2018; "Cumulative Amount of Funding Pledged to Kickstarter Projects As of January 2018 (in Million U.S. Dollars)," *Statista*, http://www.statista.com, accessed March 14, 2018.

[37] Ruth Simon, "Big Banks Cut Back on Loans to Small Business," *The Wall Street Journal*, http://www.wsj.com, accessed March 12, 2018.

[38] Lauren Thomas, "Warby Parker Raises $75 Million in Latest Round of Funding," *CNBC*, http://www.cnbc.com, accessed March 17, 2018; Zoë Corbyn, "Take One Start-Up, Add Expertise and Grow with Care," *The Financial Times*, http://www.ft.com, accessed March 18, 2018.

[39] Shahram Safai and Ronnie Dabbasi, "Making Monetary Sense: How to Understand Your VC Term Sheet," *Entrepreneur*, http://www.entrepreneur.com, accessed March 12, 2018.

[40] Organization website, "Florida Enterprise Zone Program," http://floridajobs.org, accessed March 12, 2018.

[41] George Deeb, "Big Companies That Embrace Entrepreneurship Will Thrive," *Entrepreneur*, http://www.entrepreneur.com, accessed March 12, 2018; Jennifer Alsever, "Startups . . . Inside Giant Companies," *Fortune*, http://fortune.com, accessed March 12, 2018.

[42] Company website, "All 3M Products," http://www.3m.com, accessed March 12, 2018; Catherine Clifford, "Keep Your Employees Loyal by Encouraging Them to Pursue Their Own Projects and Passions," *Entrepreneur*, http://www.entrepreneur.com, accessed March 12, 2018.

[43] "10 Inspiring Examples of Successful Intrapreneurship," *Vocoli*, http://www.vocoli.com, accessed March 12, 2018; Jennifer Alsever, "Startups . . . Inside Giant Companies." *Forbes*, http://forbes.com, accessed March 12, 2018.

Chapter 7

[1] Karl Taro, "How Mark Parker Keeps Nike in the Lead," *The Wall Street Journal*, http://www.wsj.com, accessed March 17, 2018; Barbara Farfan, "Nike Mission Statement and Maxims," *The Balance*, http://www.thebalance.com, accessed March 17, 2018; company website, "Nike, Inc. Reports Fiscal 2017 Fourth Quarter and Full-Year Results," http://www.news.nike.com, accessed March 18, 2018; Jill Bernstein, "Why Nike Sees Social Responsibility as an Opportunity to Innovate," *Fast Company*, http://www.fastcompany.com, accessed March 17, 2018; Kurt Blazek, "A Participatory Leadership Style: Nike's CEO Mark Parker," *The Booth Company*, http://www.boothco.com, accessed March 18, 2018; Shana Leibowitz, "Here's the Leadership Strategy Nike's CEO Uses to Make Employees Smarter," *Business Insider*, http://www.businessinsider.com, accessed March 18, 2018.

[2] Company website, "Working at McDonald's Restaurants," https://www.mcdonalds.com, accessed March 18, 2018; John Dudoyskiy, "McDonald's Leadership and McDonalds Organizational Structure," *Research Methodology*, https://research-methodology.net, accessed March 18, 2018; Andrew Thompson, "McDonald's Organizational Structure Analysis," *Panmore Institute*, http://panmore.com, accessed March 18, 2018; Trefis Team, "McDonald's Dependence on High Growth Markets Will Be Increasing," *Forbes*, http://www.forbes.com, accessed March 18, 2018.

[3] "Chipotle: Rise and Fall of a Wall Street Darling," *Investopedia*, http://www.investopedia.com, accessed March 18, 2018; James Peltz, "Can Taco Bell's Former Chief Restore Chipotle's Once-Sizzling Growth?" *Los Angeles Times*, http://www.latimes.com, accessed March 10, 2018.

[4] Bridgett Weaver, "David Novak Wants to Train the Next Generation of Business Leaders: Here's How," *Louisville Business First*, http://www.bizjournals.com, accessed March 18, 2018; company website, "newsroom," http://ogolead.com/news, accessed March 18, 2018.

[5] Lorri Freifeld, "Training Magazine Ranks 2018 Training Top 125 Organizations," *Training*, https://trainingmag.com, accessed March 19, 2018.

[6] Lydia Ramsey, "The First Female Big Pharma CEO Had the Perfect Response to a Question About Women in Leadership," *Business Insider*, http://www.businessinsider.com, accessed March 19, 2018; Denise

Roland, "Glaxo's New CEO Is a Steady Hand in Pharmaceuticals' Rolling Seas," *The Wall Street Journal*, http://www.wsj.com, accessed March 19, 2018.

7 Roy Maurer, "2015: Succession Planning Will Be Crucial," *Society for Human Resource Management*, http://www.shrm.org, accessed March 18, 2018; Forbes Coaches Council, "Roadmap Succession Planning at All Levels Is the Key to Success," *Forbes*, http://www.forbes.com, accessed March 19, 2018.

8 Tim Mullaney, "Warren Buffett Turns 85: What He Wants in a Successor," *The Street*, http://www.thestreet.com, accessed March 18, 2018; Stephen Gandel, "Warren Buffett on His Successor: We Have Our Man," *Fortune*, http://fortune.com, accessed March 18, 2018; Adam Shell, "Warren Buffett Successor? Berkshire Hathaway CEO Elevates Two Potential Contenders," *USA Today*, http://www.usatoday.com, accessed March 19, 2018.

9 Graham Winfrey, "How Steve Jobs Used Masterful Storytelling to Motivate Employees," *Inc.*, http://www.inc.com, accessed March 19, 2018.

10 Company website, "Our Workplace Culture," http://www.eileenfisher.com, accessed March 18, 2018.

11 Anne Shields, "Creative Cloud Subscriptions Continue to Boost Adobe's Growth," *Yahoo Finance*, http://finance.yahoo.com, accessed March 18, 2018; Chuck Cohn, "5 Visionary CEOs and Their Key Traits That Every Leader Should Master," *Entrepreneur*, http://www.entrepreneur.com, accessed March 18, 2018; Trefis Team, "Adobe Stock Hits Record Highs Driven by Creative Cloud, Marketing Cloud," *Forbes*, http://www.forbes.com, accessed March 19, 2018.

12 Luz Lazo, "After United Dragging Incident, 3 Major Airlines Change Policies Affecting Bumped Passengers," *Washington Post*, https://www.washingtonpost.com, accessed March 19, 2018; Julia Horowitz and Jon Ostrower, "The Often-Overlooked Reason United Can Kick You off Your Flight," *MoneyCNN*, http://www.money.cnn.com, accessed March 19, 2018.

13 Company website, "World's Most Ethical Companies—Honorees," http://ethisphere.com, accessed March 18, 2018; Tania Soussan, "Winning by Doing the Right Thing," *Albuquerque Journal*, https://www.abqjournal.com, accessed March 19, 2018.

14 "Doing the Right Thing Can Cost You Everything," *Daily Stoic*, http://www.dailystoic.com, accessed March 19, 2018; Erin Griffin, "Theranos and Silicon Valley's 'Fake It Till You Make It' Culture," *Wired*, http://www.wired.com, accessed March 19, 2018.

15 Kate Taylor, "Coca-Cola Wants to Dominate a $7 Billion Industry with a New Type of Beverage That's Taking Over the World," *Business Insider*, http://www.businessinsider.com, accessed March 19, 2018; Journey Staff, company website, "7 Coca-Cola Stories That Made Headlines in 2017," http://www.coca-colacompany.com, accessed March 19, 2018.

16 Dan Berthiaume, "Home Depot Builds Physical Omnichannel Infrastructure," *Retailing Today*, http://retailingtoday.com, accessed March 18, 2018; Josh Bond, "Home Depot Builds an Omni-Channel Supply Chain," *SupplyChain247*, www.supplychain247.com, accessed March 18, 2018; Stuart Lauchlan, "Home Depot—Building Interconnected Retail for Digital DIY," *Diginomica*, http://www.diginomica.com, accessed March 19, 2018.

17 Brent Robinson, "Omnichannel Retailing and the Mobile Solution to Showroom Shoppers," *Bazaar Voice*, http://blog.bazaarvoice.com, accessed March 18, 2018.

18 Jack Stewart, "Tesla Delays Its Model 3 Production Goals—Again," *Wired*, http://www.wired.com, accessed March 19, 2018.

19 Kate Taylor, "Starbucks Needs to Fix Its Biggest Problem," *Business Insider*, http://www.businessinsider.com, accessed March 19, 2018; company website, "Starbucks Named Fifth Most Admired Company Worldwide" and "Starbucks Food Strategy and La Boulange Update," https://news.starbucks.com, accessed March 18, 2018; Leo Sun, "SWOT Analysis of Starbucks Corporation," *Motley Fool*, http://www.fool.com, accessed March 18, 2018; Jessica Lombardo, "Starbucks Coffee SWOT Analysis," *Panmore Institute*, http://panmore.com, accessed March 18, 2018.

20 Company website, "Starbucks Details Five-Year Plan to Accelerate Profitable Growth" and "Complete Recap of Starbucks 2017 Meeting of Annual Shareholders," https://news.starbucks.com, accessed March 22, 2018; Leo Sun, "SWOT Analysis of Starbucks Corporation," *Motley Fool*, http://www.fool.com, accessed March 18, 2018; Jessica Lombardo, "Starbucks Coffee SWOT Analysis," *Panamore Institute*, accessed March 18, 2018, http://panamore.com; Associated Press, "Online Shopping Turning Starbucks Sales Tepid," *Denver Post*, http://www.denverpost.com, accessed March 18, 2018.

21 "Why Is Gucci on the Up? Because of Millennials (and Elton John)," *The Guardian*, http://www.guardian.com, accessed March 19, 2018; Sam Reed, "Gucci and Yeezy Are the Hottest Brands in the World According to New Hot Brand Index," *Hollywood Reporter*, http://www.hollywoodreporter.com, accessed March 19, 2018.

22 Scott Peterson, "Slack Working to Keep Rivals at Bay to Remain Killer Collaboration App," *eweek.com*, http://www.eweeks.com, accessed March 19, 2018; Jeff Bercovici, "Slack Is Our Company of the Year. Here's Why Everybody's Talking About It," *Inc.*, http://www.inc.com, accessed March 18, 2018; Harry McCracken, "Slack: For Slaying Interoffice Email," *Fast Company*, http://www.fastcompany.com, accessed March 18, 2018; Jordan Novet, "Google's Slack Competitor Is Now Available to Any Company," *CNBC*, https://www.cnbc.com, accessed March 20, 2019.

23 Timothy Bednarz, "Seven Key Benefits of an Empowered Workplace," *Examiner.com*, http://www.examiner.com, accessed March 18, 2018.

24 Julie Bort, "LinkedIn Is Giving Its Employees 'Unlimited' Vacation Plus 17 Paid Holidays," *Business Insider*, http://www.businessinsider.com, accessed March 18, 2018; Thomas C. Frohlich, "7 Companies with Unlimited Vacation," *USA Today*, http://www.usatoday.com, accessed March 18, 2018.

25 Anna Wilde Mathews, Emily Glazer, and Laura Stevens, "Triple Threat: Amazon, Berkshire, JPMorgan Rattle Health-Care Firms," *The Wall Street Journal*, http://www.wsj.com, accessed April 4, 2018.

26 Company website, "CRO's 100 Best Corporation Citizens 2017," http://www.thecro.com, accessed March 18, 2018.

27 Paul Morello, "11 Leadership Lessons We Can Learn From Tim Cook," *Life Hack*, http://www.lifehack.org, accessed March 19, 2018; "What Is Tim Cook's Leadership Style?" *Investopedia*, http://www.investopedia.com, accessed March 19, 2018.

28 Andrea Huspeni, "Google's 20 Percent Rule Actually Helps Employees Fight Back Against Unreasonable Managers," *Entrepreneur*, http://www.entrepreneur.com, accessed March 19, 2018.

29 Dana Mattioli and Jeffrey A. Trachtenberg, "Martha Stewart Nears Deal to Sell Fading Empire," *The Wall Street Journal*, http://www.wsj.com, accessed March 18, 2018; Mary Teresa Bitti, "Martha Stewart on Leadership and Her Success: 'Hardship Does Not Make You Better. I Was Good to Start with,'" *Financial Post*, http://business.financialpost.com, accessed March 18, 2018; company website, "Autocratic Leadership," http://www.money-zine.com, accessed March 18, 2018; company website, "Examples of Companies with Autocratic Leadership," http://www.brighthubpm.com, accessed March 18, 2018.

30 Company website, "Our Culture," http://https://www.google.com, accessed March 18, 2018; "Is Google Still Competitive with Microsoft and Facebook in the War for Talent?" *Good & Co. Career Insights*, http://good.co, accessed March 18, 2018.

[31] "Former Executive Shares the Secrets to How Disney Runs Its Empire," *Fast Company*, http://www.fastcompany.com, accessed March 18, 2018; Bruce I. Jones, "People Management Lessons from Disney," *Training Industry,* http://www.trainingindustry.com, accessed March 18, 2018; "Leadership Lessons from Walt Disney: Perfecting the Customer Experience," *Inc.*, http://www.inc.com, accessed March 18, 2018.

[32] Company website, "Company Overview," http://investor.activision.com, accessed March 18, 2018.

[33] Company website, "Global Workplaces," http://www.levistrauss.com, accessed March 18, 2018.

[34] Company website, "PG at a Glance," http://www.pginvestor.com, accessed March 18, 2018; company website, "Corporate Structure," http://us.pg.com, accessed March 18, 2018.

[35] Company website, "Empowering Employees at Zappos," https://www.accenture.com, accessed March 18, 2018; Brandon Gutman, "Zappos' Marketing Chief: 'Customer Service Is the New Marketing!'" *Fast Company*, http://www.fastcompany.com, accessed March 18, 2018.

[36] Company website, "Management Structure," http://www.olympus-global.com, accessed March 18, 2018.

Chapter 8

[1] Company website, "Cars," https://www.ford.com, accessed March 23, 2018; company website, "Our Company," https://www.ford.com, accessed March 23, 2018; company website, "People," https://corporate.ford.com, accessed March 23, 2018; company website, "Ford Appoints Kiersten Robinson as Chief Human Resources Officer," https://media.ford.com, accessed March 24, 2018; Brett Walsh and Erica Volini, "Rewriting the Rules for the Digital Age," https://www2.deloitte.com, accessed March 24, 2018.

[2] Jeff Maggioncalda, "Coursera Teams Up with Google to Bridge the IT Experience Gap," *Coursera Blog,* https://blog.coursera.org, accessed March 21, 2018; Kathryn Moody, Ryan Golden, and Kate Torone, "10 Trends That Will Shape HR in 2018," *HRDive*, https://www.hrdive.com, accessed March 21, 2018.

[3] Alice Williams, "10 Ways HR Tech Has Changed Recruiting Forever," *The Undercover Recruiter*, http://www.undercoverrecruiter.com, accessed March 21, 2018; Patrick Lynch, "Will Your LinkedIn Profile Ever Replace the Traditional Resume?" *LinkedIn*, http://www.linkedin.com, accessed March 21, 2018.

[4] Josh Millet, "The 2018 Human Resources Trends to Keep on Your Radar," *Forbes*, http://www.forbes.com, accessed March 21, 2018.

[5] Government website, "Fact Sheet on Employment Tests and Selection Procedures," http://www.eeoc.gov, accessed March 25, 2018.

[6] Kathryn Moody, Ryan Golden, and Kate Torone, "10 Trends That Will Shape HR in 2018," *HRDive*, https://www.hrdive.com, accessed March 21, 2018; government website, "What You Should Know About EEOC and the Enforcement Protections for LGBT Workers," http://www.eeoc.gov, accessed March 21, 2018.

[7] Roy Maurer, "4 Trends That Will Shape Recruiting in 2018," http://www.shrm.org, accessed March 24, 2018; Kate Davidson, "Employers Find 'Soft Skills' Like Critical Thinking in Short Supply," *Wall Street Journal*, http://www.wsj.com, accessed March 24, 2018.

[8] Mariah Deleon, "What Really Happens When You Hire the Wrong Candidate," *Entrepreneur,* http://www.entrepreneur.com, accessed March 25, 2018.

[9] Organization website, "4 Trends That Will Shape Recruiting in 2018," http://www.shrm.org, accessed March 24, 2018; Alice Williams, "10 Ways HR Tech Has Changed Recruiting Forever," *The Undercover Recruiter*, http://www.undercoverrecruiter.com, accessed March 21, 2018; Brett Walsh and Erica Volini, "Rewriting the Rules for the Digital Age," https://www2.deloitte.com, accessed March 24, 2018.

[10] Education website, "Technical Scholars Program" and "BMW Scholars Program," http://www.sccsc.edu, accessed March 25, 2018.

[11] Company website, "Welcome to EYU," http://www.ey.com, accessed March 25, 2018; company website, "Explore," http://exceptionaley.com, accessed March 25, 2018.

[12] Company website, "Leadership Programs," http://careers.geico.com, accessed March 25, 2018.

[13] Elena Kvochko, "Why There Are Still Few Women Leaders in Tech," *Forbes*, http://www.forbes.com, accessed March 25, 2018; Dana Swanson Switzer, Jasmin Jacks, and Jessie Reese, "Uncovering the Gap: Why the Old-School Numbers for Women Leaders in Tech?" *HR Times Blog*, http://www.hrtimesblog.com, accessed March 25, 2018; Kathryn Moody, Ryan Golden, and Kate Torone, "10 Trends That Will Shape HR in 2018," *HRDive*, https://www.hrdive.com, accessed March 21, 2018.

[14] Company website, "Power Up Performance Reviews," http://www.paylocity.com, accessed March 25, 2018; "Turn Your Performance Review System into One That Works," *Quality Digest Magazine,* http://www.qualitydigest.com, accessed March 25, 2018; Beth Jones and David Rock, "Why the Typical Performance Review Is Overwhelmingly Biased," *Quartz*, https://work.qz.com, accessed March 25, 2018.

[15] Kris Duggan, "Why the Annual Performance Review Is Going Extinct," *Fast Company*, http://www.fastcompany.com, accessed March 25, 2018; company blog, "Reinventing the Wheel: How Companies Like GE, Adobe, and Deloitte Get Rid of the Performance Review with One on Ones," *Lighthouse*, https://getlighthouse.com, accessed March 25, 2018.

[16] Organization website, "S.181 Lilly Ledbetter Fair Pay Act of 2009," http://www.opencongress.org, accessed March 25, 2018.

[17] Company website, "Action on Equal Pay," https://www.salesforce.com, accessed March 25, 2018; Heather Kelly and Poppy Harlow, "Salesforce CEO Marc Benioff's Push for Equality," *CNNTech*, http://www.money.cnn.com, accessed March 25, 2018; Todd Zenger, "The Downside of Full Pay Transparency," *Wall Street Journal,* http://www.wsj.com, accessed March 25, 2018.

[18] Government website, "Employer Costs for Employee Compensation, December 2017," press release, http://www.bls.gov, accessed March 25, 2018.

[19] Rebecca Greenfield, "These Employers Give Moms and Dads Equal Baby Leave," *Bloomberg Business*, http://www.bloomberg.com, accessed March 25, 2018.

[20] Lindsay Rothfield, "7 Companies with Amazingly Unique Wellness Programs," *Mashable*, http://www.mashable.com, accessed March 25, 2018.

[21] Company website, "Boeing VIP Ranked Top Five 401(K) Plan in U.S.," http://www.boeing.com, accessed March 25, 2018; "How Good Is Your Company's 401K?" *Bloomberg Business*, http://www.bloomberg.com, accessed March 25, 2018.

[22] Company website, "Flexibility Makes a Difference," http://www.ey.com, accessed March 25, 2018.

[23] Company website, http://www.shiftboard.com, accessed March 25, 2018.

[24] Jeanne Sahadi, "The 4-Day Workweek Is Real ... for Employees at These Companies," *CNN Money*, http://money.cnn.com, accessed March 25, 2018; Stephanie Vozza, "How These Companies Have Made Four-Day Work Weeks Feasible, *Fast Company*, http://www.fastcompany.com, accessed March 25, 2018; Leslie Belknap, "The Five Day Workweek Is Bad for Business. Here's Why," *Ethos3*, http://www.ethos3.com, accessed March 25, 2018.

[25] Brie Weiler Reynolds, "4 Remote Work Trends Professionals Should Know for 2018," *FlexJobs*, http://www.flexjobs.com, accessed March 25, 2018.

[26] Nicole Kobie, "What Is the Gig Economy and Why Is It So Controversial?" *Wired*, http://www.wired.com, accessed March 25, 2018; "HR in 2018: Gig Economy the New Norm," *HR Gazette*, https://hr-gazette.com, accessed March 25, 2018.

[27] Laura Hemphill, "Amid Layoffs—A Financial Analyst's Survivor Guilt," *Bloomberg Business*, http://www.businessweek.com, accessed March 25, 2018; Ken Eisold, "The American Way of Unemployment," *Psychology Today*, http://www.psychologytoday.com, accessed March 25, 2018.

[28] Eric Mandel, "More Layoffs: Coca-Cola Cutting 250–350 Management Positions as Part of Reorganization," *Atlanta Business Chronicle*, https://www.bizjournals.com, accessed March 25, 2018.

[29] Harold Sirkin, "Reshoring Is More Than Just a Buzzword," *Forbes*, http://www.forbes.com, accessed March 25, 2018; Stephanie Overby, "10 Outsourcing Trends to Watch in 2016," *CIO.com*, http://cio.com, accessed March 25, 2018.

[30] Company website, "Maslow's Hierarchy of Needs," *Accel-Team.com*, http://www.accel-team.com, accessed March 25, 2018.

[31] Sarah N. Lynch, "U.S. SEC Adopts Rules Mandating Disclosure of CEO–Worker Pay Ratios," Reuters, http://www.reuters.com, accessed January 29, 2018; Vanessa Fuhrmans and Theo Francis, "How Does the Boss's Pay Compare to the Rank and File?" *Wall Street Journal*, http://www.wsj.com, accessed March 26, 2018; government website, "The CEO Pay Ratio Rule: A Workable Solution for Both Issuers and Investors," http://www.sec.gov, accessed March 25, 2018.

[32] Company website, "Our Company," http://www.pamperedchef.com, accessed March 25, 2018; Doris Christopher, *The Pampered Chef: The Story of One of America's Most Beloved Companies* (New York: Crown Business, 2005).

[33] Company website, "Development Programs: Unleash the Power of Your Potential," http://www.emc.com, accessed March 25, 2018.

[34] Government website, "Union Members—2017," http://www.bls.gov, accessed February 8, 2015.

[35] Organization websites: http://www.nea.org; http://www.afscme.org; http://www.seiu.org; http://www.teamster.org; http://www.ufcw.org; http://www.uaw.org, accessed March 25, 2018.

[36] Government website, "Work Stoppages," http://www.bls.gov, accessed March 25, 2018.

[37] "Verizon Workers Picket over Stalled Contract Talks," *WGRZ*, http://www.wgrz.com, accessed March 25, 2018.

[38] Terence P. Jeffrey, "48.9% of Union Members Worked for Government in 2015," *CNS News*, http://www.cnsnews.com, accessed March 25, 2018.

Chapter 9

[1] Carmine Gallo, "Seven Customer Service Lessons I Learned in One Day with Richard Branson," *Forbes*, http://www.forbes.com, accessed March 28, 2018; company website, "Three Customer Service Lessons from Beloved Virgin America Airlines," http://blog.selfstorage.com, accessed March 28, 2018; Efrat Ravid, "Enterprises That Have Truly Mastered Customer Experience," *Business2Community*, www.business2community.com, accessed March 28, 2018; Lucy Handley, "Richard Branson: Planes, Trains, and Space Mobiles," *CNBC*, http://www.cnbc.com, accessed March 28, 2018; Ruth Umoh, "3 Traits Billionaire Richard Branson Looks for When Promoting Employees," *CNBC*, http://www.cnbc.com, accessed March 28, 2018.

[2] Company website, "About KIND," http://www.kindsnacks.com, accessed March 28, 2018; Daniel Lubetzky, *Do the KIND Thing: Think Boundlessly, Work Purposefully, Live Passionately* (New York: Ballantine Books, 2015); Marc Gunther, "A Snack Bar Aims to Change the World," *Strategy + Business*, http://www.strategy-business.com, accessed March 28, 2018; Jacquelyn Smith, "How to Create an Authentic and Transparent Work Environment," *Forbes*, http://www.forbes.com, accessed February 9, 2018.

[3] Company website, "Toyota Production System," http://www.setpointusa.com, accessed March 28, 2018.

[4] Company website, "Lebanon Valley Brethren Home" and "Green Houses," http://www.lvbh.org, accessed March 28, 2018; Becka Livesay, "The Culture Change Way: Empowering Direct Care Workers to Improve Care," *Direct Care Alliance*, http://blog.directcarealliance.org, accessed March 28, 2018.

[5] Organization website, "ESOP (Employee Stock Ownership Plan) Facts," updated 2017, http://www.nceo.org, accessed March 28, 2018.

[6] Organization website, "Flying as a Team Gives Our ESOP Wings—Employee Stock Ownership Month 2017 Press Event and Planning Kit," http://www.esopassociation.org, accessed March 28, 2018.

[7] Organization website, "A Statistical Profile of Employee Ownership," updated 2017, http://www.nceo.org, accessed March 28, 2018.

[8] Organization website, "Are ESOPs Good Retirement Plans?" http://www.nceo.org, accessed March 28, 2018.

[9] Organization website, "Employee Stock Options Fact Sheet," http://www.nceo.org, accessed March 28, 2018.

[10] Organization website, "Employee Stock Options Fact Sheet," http://www.nceo.org, accessed March 28, 2018; Gretchen Morgensen, "Safety Suffers as Stock Options Propel Executive Pay Packages," *The New York Times*, http://www.nytimes.com, accessed March 28, 2018.

[11] Kaite Hafner, "Google Options Make Masseuse a Multi-Millionaire," *The New York Times*, http://www.nytimes.com, accessed March 28, 2018.

[12] Ananya Bhattacharya, "Apple Extends Stock Grants to All Employees," *CNN Money*, http://money.cnn.com, accessed March 28, 2018; Mark Gurman, "Tim Cook Memo: Apple Launches RSU Shares Program for All Employees to Retain Talent," *9 to 5 Mac*, http://9to5mac.com, accessed March 28, 2018; company website, "Restricted Stock Units (RSUs)," https://scs.fidelity.com, accessed March 28, 2018; Chaim Gartenberg, "Apple Is Giving Employees $2,500 Bonuses in Restricted Stock Units After New Tax Law," *The Verge*, http://www.verge.com, accessed March 28, 2018.

[13] Mallory Schlossberg, "Lululemon Is Changing the Way It Sells Pants to Solve an Annoying Problem," *Business Insider*, http://www.businessinsider.com, accessed March 29, 2018; company website, "women's bottoms," https://shop.lululemon.com, accessed March 29, 2018; Alyssa Vingan Klein, "Lululemon introduces new pant styles," *Fashionista*, http://www.fashionista.com, accessed March 29, 2018.

[14] Company website, "Whole Foods Market's Core Values," http://www.wholefoodsmarket.com, accessed March 28, 2018; company website, "Whole Foods—A Disciplined Democracy," http://freibergs.com, accessed March 28, 2018; Matthew Sturdevant, "Top Large Employer: Whole Foods Teamwork Is a Natural," *Hartford Courant*, http://www.courant.com, accessed March 28, 2018.

[15] "3M's Cross-Functional Teams," *YouSigma*, http://www.yousigma.com, accessed March 29, 2018.

[16] Rachel Gillett, "Productivity Hack of the Week: The Two Pizza Approach to Productive Teamwork," *Fast Company*, http://www.fastcompany.com, accessed March 28, 2018.

[17] Jessica Guynn, "Google Opens Howard University West to Train Black Coders," *USA Today*, http://www.usatoday.com, accessed March 29, 2018; Brittney Olvier, "Top Companies Are Missing Talent from Historically Black Colleges," *Fast Company*, http://www.fastcompany.com, accessed March 29, 2018; Megan Rose Dickey, "A Conversation with Google's Director of Diversity and Inclusion," *Tech Crunch*, http://techcrunch.com, accessed March 28, 2018; Vauhini Vara, "Why

Doesn't Silicon Valley Hire Black Coders?" *Bloomberg Businessweek*, http://www.bloomberg.com, accessed March 28, 2018; Joel Lyons, "Google 'Embeds' Engineers at HBCUs to Boost Diversity in Tech," *Black Enterprise*, http://www.blackenterprise.com, accessed March 28, 2018.

[18] Company website, "Team Building Programs," http://www.teambonding.com, accessed March 28, 2018; Paul E. Kandarian, "Stoughton Company Offers Programs to Help Your Employees Bond," *Boston Globe*, http://www.bostonglobe.com, accessed March 28, 2018.

[19] Company website, "A Career at The Container Store," and "Our Employee First Culture," http://www.containerstore.com, accessed March 28, 2018.

[20] Michiel Kruyt, Judy Malan, and Rachel Tuffield, "Three Steps to Building a Better Top Team," *Forbes*, http://www.forbes.com, accessed March 28, 2018; Tara Duggan, "Leadership vs. Conflict Resolution," *Houston Chronicle*, http://smallbusiness.chron.com, accessed March 28, 2018.

[21] Jessica Dineen, "Why Brooks Brothers and Other Apparel Companies Are Moving Manufacturing Back Home," *Forbes*, http://www.forbes.com, accessed March 28, 2018.

[22] Max Nisen, "Four Ways McDonald's Almost Ruined Chipotle," *Quartz*, http://qz.com, accessed March 28, 2018; Kyle Stock and Vanessa Wong, "Chipotle: The Definitive Oral History," *Bloomberg Business*, http://www.bloomberg.com, accessed March 28, 2018.

[23] Company website, "The Ritz Carlton: A Tradition of Storytelling," http://ritzcarltonleadershipcenter.com, accessed March 28, 2018; "Managing Mystique: How Ritz-Carlton Delivers Amazing Customer Service" (blog), http://ryanestis.com, accessed March 28, 2018.

[24] Elizabeth Bernstein, "How Active Listening Makes Both Participants in a Conversation Feel Better," *The Wall Street Journal*, http://www.wsj.com, accessed March 28, 2018; Glenn Llopsis, "6 Ways Effective Listening Can Make You a Better Leader," *Forbes*, http://www.forbes.com, accessed March 28, 2018.

[25] Company website, "About," http://www.sanebox.com, accessed March 28, 2018.

[26] Kayla Matthews, "10 Things People with Effective Communication Skills Have in Common," *Lifehack*, http://lifehack.org, accessed March 28, 2018; company website, "Expand Trust in Your Organization," and "8 Steps to Stronger Organizational Communication," *Peter Stark.com*, http://www.peterstark.com, accessed March 28, 2018.

[27] Rachel Weingarten, "Four Ways to Stop Gossip in the Workplace," *Forbes*, http://www.forbes.com, accessed March 28, 2018; Jitendra Mishra, "Managing the Grapevine," *Analytic Tech*, http://www.analytictech.com, accessed March 28, 2018.

[28] John Boe, "How to Read Your Prospect Like a Book!" *John Boe International*, http://johnboe.com, accessed March 28, 2018.

[29] Lily Hay Newman, "Equifax Officially Has No Excuse," *Wired*, http://www.wired.com, accessed March 29, 2018; Lucinda Chen, "The 10 Biggest Business Scandals of 2017," *Fortune*, http://www.fortune.com, accessed March 29, 2018.

[30] Jonathan Bernstein, "The Ten Steps of Crisis Communications," *Bernstein Crisis Management*, http://www.bernsteincrisismanagement.com, accessed March 28, 2018.

[31] Lily Hay Newman, "All the Ways Equifax Epically Bungled Its Breach Response," *Wired*, http://www.wired.com, accessed March 29, 2018; Quora, "The Many Problems With Equifax's Response to the Privacy Breach Crisis," *Forbes*, http://www.forbes.com, accessed March 29, 2018.

Chapter 10

[1] Company website, "Tesla Fourth Quarter & Full Year 2017 Update," "Tesla Motors 2017 Q4 Shareholder Letter," and "Factory Upgrade," http://tesla.com, accessed April 1, 2018; company website, "Tesla Motors (TSLA) Earnings Report: Q4 2017 Conference Call Transcript," http://www.thestreet.com, accessed April 1, 2018; Daniel Sparks, "Tesla Motors, Inc. to Roll Out Mobile Stores," *Motley Fool*, https://www.fool.com, accessed April 1, 2018; Ashlee Vance, *Elon Musk: Tesla, SpaceX, and the Quest for a Fantastic Future* (New York: Harper Collins, 2015); Nathan Bomey, "This Machine Could Help Musk Whisk You from NY to DC in 29 Minutes," *USA Today*, http://www.usatoday.com, accessed April 1, 2018; Marco della Cava, "Tesla Producing Far Fewer Model 3s Than Elon Musk Promised, Extending Wait Time," *USA Today*, http://www.usatoday.com, accessed April 1, 2018; Tim Higgins, "Tesla Begins Taking Model 3 Orders From First-Time Reservation Holders," *The Wall Street Journal*, http://www.wsj.com, accessed April 1, 2018; Daniel Terdiman, "How Elon Musk and Jeff Bezos Are Trying to Upend Space Exploration," *Fast Company*, http://www.fastcompany.com, accessed April 1, 2018.

[2] Richard Lacayo, "Suburban Legend William Levitt," *Time*, http://content.time.com, accessed April 1, 2018.

[3] Company website, "Manufacturing," http://www.hondainamerica.com, accessed April 1, 2018; company website, "Major U.S. Facilities List," http://corporate.honda.com, accessed April 1, 2018; company website, "Honda's East Liberty Plant Builds 5 Millionth Vehicle with Production Startup of Refreshed 2016 Acura RDX," http://ohio.honda.com, accessed April 1, 2018.

[4] Timothy W. Martin and Tripp Mickle, "Samsung, Apple Intensify Battle for Smartphone Users," *The Wall Street Journal*, http://www.wsj.com, accessed April 1, 2018; Martin, "Product-Driven vs. Customer-Driven Businesses," *Cleverism*, http://www.cleverism.com, accessed April 1, 2018.

[5] Patrick McGroarty, "McDonald's Puts Fresh Beef on the Menu," *The Wall Street Journal*, www.wsj.com, accessed April 1, 2018; Aamer Madhani, "McDonald's to Start All-Day Breakfast Nationally on Oct. 6," *USA Today*, http://www.usatoday.com, accessed April 1, 2018.

[6] Sophie Chapman, "Gap Announces Sustainable Manufacturing Targets to Save 10 Billion Litres of Water by 2020," *Global Manufacturing*, http://www.manufacturingglobal.com, accessed April 1, 2018.

[7] Organization website, http://www.usgbc.org, accessed April 1, 2018.

[8] Katie Johns, "How Is Artificial Intelligence Changing the Manufacturing Industry in 2018?" *Ishir*, http://www.ishir.com, accessed April 1, 2018; Alex Beall, "IFR Report: 1.7m New Industrial Robots to Be Installed by 2020," *The Robot Report*, https://www.therobotreport.com, accessed April 1, 2018; Jason Bellini and Matt McDonald, "The New Robot Revolution in Manufacturing," *The Wall Street Journal*, http://www.wsj.com, accessed April 1, 2018.

[9] "Types of Robots," *All On Robots*, http://www.allonrobots.com, accessed April 1, 2018; company website, http://www.ni.com, accessed April 1, 2018.

[10] Allison DiMatteo, "Shaping Dentistry with CAD/CAM Technology," *Consumer Guide to Dentistry*, http://www.yourdentistryguide.com, accessed April 1, 2018.

[11] Susan Haigney, "Getting Flexible with Manufacturing," *Pharmaceutical Technology*, http://www.bptc.com, accessed April 1, 2018.

[12] "Vistaprint to Accelerate New Product Introductions with Stibo Systems' MDM," *Yahoo Finance*, http://finance.yahoo.com, accessed April 1, 2018; "On the Open Road to CIM with JDF: An EFI White Paper on Computer Integrated Manufacturing," *Office Product News*, http://www.officeproductnews.net, accessed April 1, 2018.

[13] Jeff Bennett and Cameron McWhirter, "Volvo Car to Build First U.S. Car Plant in South Carolina," *The Wall Street Journal*, http://www.wsj.com, accessed April 1, 2018.

[14] Bruce Smith, "Volvo Breaks Ground on $500 Million South Carolina Plant," *The Washington Times*, http://www.washingtontimes.com,

accessed April 1, 2018; Cassie Cope, "How South Carolina Won Volvo," *The State*, http://www.thestate.com, accessed April 1, 2018; Douglas A. Bolduc, "How BMW Helped Volvo Choose Its U.S. Plant Location," *Automotive News*, http://www.autonews.com, accessed April 1, 2018.

15 Company website, "Mondelez International to Invest $190 Million in Largest Plant in Asia Pacific," http://ir.mondelezinternational.com, accessed April 1, 2018; Ivana Kottasova, "Investors Pull $1 Trillion from Emerging Markets in a Year," *CNN Money*, http://money.cnn.com, accessed April 1, 2018; Lorene Yue, "Mondelez Gets a Lesson in Global Economics," *Crain's Chicago Business*, http://www.chicagobusiness.com, accessed April 1, 2018; Joe Cahill, "Irene Rosenfeld's 2016 Challenge at Mondelez," *Crain's Chicago Business*, http://www.chicagobusiness.com, accessed April 5, 2018.

16 Linette Lopez, "Tesla Model 3 Production Is Being Killed by Robots Say Bernstein Co. Analysts," *Financial Review*, http://www.afr.com, accessed April 1, 2018.

17 "Most Innovative Companies: #38: American Giant," *Fast Company*, http://www.fastcompany.com, accessed April 1, 2018.

18 Company website, "FAQs," http://www.ariba.com, accessed April 1, 2018; "Ariba Network Gets Bigger, More Global," *Yahoo Finance*, http://finance.yahoo.com, accessed April 1, 2018.

19 Sharon Bailey, "Nordstrom's Capital Expenditure for New Stores, Technology," *Yahoo Finance*, http://finance.yahoo.com, accessed April 1, 2018; Christopher Mulrooney, "Nordstrom President Announces Aggressive Mobile Enhancement Strategy," *Retail Info Systems News*, http://risnews.edgl.com, accessed April 1, 2018.

20 Company website, "Vendor Managed Inventory," http://www.dow.com, accessed April 1, 2018.

21 Organization website, Patricia Moody, "Lean Factor: Seattle Children's Hospital," http://www.ame.org, accessed April 1, 2018; Sabriya Rice, "Learning to Be Lean," *Modern Health Care*, http://www.modernhealthcare.com, accessed April 1, 2018; organization website, "Continuous Performance Improvement," http://www.seattlechildrens.org, accessed April 1, 2018.

22 Company website, "SYSPRO ERP Software Choice of Nutritional Bar Manufacturer," https://www.syspro.com, accessed April 1, 2018.

23 Jessica Golden, "Inside the Football Factory That Powers the Super Bowl," *CNBC*, http://www.cnbc.com, accessed April 1, 2018; company website, "Wilson Football in the NFL," http://www.wilson.com, accessed April 1, 2018.

24 Company website, http://www.jetcam.com, accessed April 1, 2018.

25 Company website, "About Us" and "History," http://www.turnerbikes.com, accessed April 1, 2018; company website, "Turner Bicycles," http://usersolutions.com, accessed April 1, 2018.

26 Multiple authors, "Massive Takata Airbag Recall: Everything You Need to Know, Including Full List of Affected Vehicles," *Car and Driver*, http://www.caranddriver.com, accessed April 2, 2018; "Takata Airbag Recall—Everything You Need to Know," *Consumer Reports*, http://www.consumerreports.com, accessed April 2, 2018.

27 Sarah Shelton, "Teardown Reveals BMW i3 Is "Most Advanced Vehicle on the Planet," *Hybrid Cars*, http://www.hybridcars.com, accessed April 1, 2018.

28 Lee Campe, "Lean and Six Sigma: Solving Problems Rather Than Improving Processes," *Savannah Morning News*, http://savannahnow.com, accessed April 1, 2018; organization website, "What Is Six Sigma?" http://www.isixsigma.com, accessed April 1, 2018; "IT Optimization Brings Lean Six Sigma to IT Service Management," *Press Release Rocket*, http://www.pressreleaserocket.net, accessed April 1, 2018.

29 Organization website, http://www.iso.org, accessed April 1, 2018.

Chapter 11

1 Company website, "About," http://www.forever21.com, accessed April 6, 2018; Enrique Soriano, "Husband and Wife Behind Forever 21's Global Success," *Asian Journal*, http://asianjournal.com, accessed April 6, 2018; "America's Largest Private Companies: #95. Forever 21," *Forbes*, http://www.forbes.com, accessed April 6, 2018; Christina Binkley, "Millennial Fashion Grows Up," *The Wall Street Journal*, http://www.wsj.com, accessed April 6, 2018; Chavie Lieber, "Forever 21 Has an Identity Crisis—and It Works," *Racked*, http://www.racked.com, accessed April 6, 2018; Suzanne Kapner, "Cavernous Stores Wear on Forever 21," *The Wall Street Journal*, http://www.wsj.com, accessed April 6, 2018.

2 Organization website, "Definition of Marketing," https://www.ama.org, accessed April 6, 2018.

3 Organization website, "Heart Attack Risk Assessment," http://www.heart.org, accessed April 6, 2018.

4 Lindsay Kolowich, "12 Truly Inspiring Company Vision and Mission Statement Examples," *HubSpot*, http://blog.hubspot.com, accessed April 6, 2018.

5 Company website, "Minute Clinic," http://www.cvs.com, accessed April 6, 2018; company website, "Overview/Programs," https://www.netjets.com, accessed April 6, 2018; company website, "About," http://airbnb.com, accessed April 6, 2018; Lindsay Harrison, "50 Most Innovative Companies—Airbnb," *Fast Company*, http://www.fastcompany.com, accessed April 6, 2018.

6 Neil Kokemuller, "Five Different Types of Utility in Marketing," *CareerTrend*, http://www.careertrend.com, accessed April 7, 2018; "Harley Davidson Launches 2018 Model Year With Largest Product Development Project," *BizTimes*, http://www.biztimes.com, accessed April 7, 2018; Joseph Hincks, "Harley-Davidson Rolls Out a New Range to Target Younger Riders," *Fortune*, http://www.fortune.com, accessed April 7, 2018.

7 Justin, "Customer Experience Lessons from Amazon," *Covalent Marketing*, http://www.covalentmarketing.com, accessed April 6, 2018; Kevin Baldacci, "7 Customer Service Lessons from Amazon CEO Jeff Bezos," *Salesforce Blog*, http://www.salesforce.com, accessed April 6, 2018; Tim Mullaney, "5 Key Business Lessons From Amazon's Jeff Bezos," *CNBC*, http://www.cnbc.com, accessed April 6, 2018.

8 Laura Lake, "What Is Nonprofit Marketing?" *The Balance*, https://www.thebalance.com, accessed April 6, 2018.

9 Organization website, "10 Supersize Charities," https://www.charitynavigator.org, accessed April 7, 2018.

10 Company website, "Fact Sheet," http://give.uncf.org, accessed April 6, 2018; Erdin Beshimov, "Trends to Watch: Non-Profit and Business Partnerships," *Experience by Simplicity*, https://www.experience.com, accessed April 6, 2018; Organization website, "2017 UNCF Merck Manufacturing Leadership Development" https://scholarships.uncf.org, accessed April 7, 2018.

11 Bianca Stitch, "The 5 Most Generous Celebrity Givers," *Young Hollywood*, http://www.younghollywood.com, accessed April 6, 2018; Mila Pantovich, "11 Celebrity-Founded Charities & Nonprofits to Discover During This Season of Giving," *Just Luxe*, http://www.justluxe.com, accessed April 6, 2018; "15 of the Most Charitable Celebs," *Day Styles*, http:/www.daystyles.com, accessed April 6, 2018; Gil Kaufman, "Taylor Swift Makes 'Generous' Donation to Joyful Heart Foundation for Survivors of Sexual Assault," *Billboard*, http://www.billboard.com, accessed April 7, 2018; Emily Vang, "Taylor Swift Made a "Generous Donation" to Rape, Abuse & Incest National Network," *TeenVogue*, http://www.teenvogue.com, accessed April 7, 2018.

[12] Kurt Badenhausen, "Michael Jordan Leads the NBA's Biggest Shoe Deals at $110 Million This Year," *Forbes*, http://www.forbes.com, accessed April 7, 2018.

[13] Company website, "Super Bowl 50," http://www.nfl.com, accessed April 6, 2018.

[14] Organization website, "American Diabetes Association Tour de Cure," http://tour.diabetes.org, accessed April 6, 2018.

[15] Organization website, "State Farm," http://www.madd.org/, accessed April 6, 2018.

[16] Company website, "Community Donations," https://www.wholefoodsmarket.com, accessed April 6, 2018.

[17] Maurice Peebles, "It's Good! How the NBA Is Winning at Social Media," *Complex Sports*, http://complex.com, accessed April 6, 2018.

[18] Company website, "2017 Annual Report," http://investors.cvshealth.com, accessed April 8, 2018; Jay Green, "In Era of Health Reform, Retail Clinics Become Part of the Health Care Delivery System," *Detroit Business*, http://www.crainsdetroit.com, accessed April 6, 2018; Christopher Cheney, "CVS Ramps Up Retail Clinics with Provider Affiliations," *Health Leaders Media*, http://healthleadersmedia.com, accessed April 6, 2018; organization website, "Growing Retail Clinic Industry Employs, Empowers Nurse Practitioners," http://www.rwjf.org, accessed April 6, 2018; organization website, "About CCA," http://www.ccaclinics.org, accessed April 6, 2018; Bruce Jaspen, "CVS Drives Retail Clinic Growth As Obamacare Launches," *Forbes*, http://www.forbes.com, accessed April 6, 2018; Heidi Godman, "Retail Health Clinics: The Pros and Cons," *Harvard Health Publications*, http://www.health.harvard.edu, accessed April 6, 2018; company website, "About," http://www.takecarehealth.com, accessed April 6, 2018.

[19] Lexi Nickens, "The 20 Dunkin' Donuts Items You Won't Find in America," *Spoon University*, http://www.spoonuniversity.com, accessed April 8, 2018; company website, "Naughty Lucy Veg," http://www.dunkinindia.com, accessed April 8, 2018; Osama Jolali, "The Story in Between," *The Hindu*, http://www.thehindu.com, accessed April 6, 2018; Preetika Rana, "Dipping Into India, Dunkin Donuts Changes Menu," *The Wall Street Journal*, http://www.wsj.com, accessed April 6, 2018; company website, "Burgers," http://www.dunkinindia.com, accessed April 8, 2018.

[20] Robert Weisman, "Boomers Are Going Bionic, and They Want Joint Replacements to Let Them Do It All," *Boston Globe*, http://www.bostonglobe.com, accessed April 8, 2018.

[21] Colin Sebastian, "Big Data Market Research Myths and Missteps," *Data Informed*, http://data-informed.com, accessed April 6, 2018; company website, "What Is Big Data?" http://www-01.ibm.com, accessed April 6, 2018; Lisa Arthur, "What Is Big Data?" *Forbes*, http://www.forbes.com, accessed April 6, 2018; Naomi Eide, "The Rise of Big Data and Why Companies Are Amassing Information to Drive Insights," *CIO Dive*, http://wwwciodive.com, accessed April 8, 2018.

[22] Company website, "Mobile Commerce," *Mobile Marketing Association*, http://www.mmaglobal.com, accessed April 6, 2018; Danyl Bosomworth, "Mobile Marketing Statistics Compilation," *Smart Insights*, http://www.smartinsights.com, accessed April 6, 2018; "Smartphones and Tablets Drive Nearly 7 Percent of Total U.S. Digital Traffic" (press release), *comScore*, http://www.comscore.com, accessed April 6, 2018.

[23] Company website, "How Herschel Supply Used Hootsuite to Boost Customer Satisfaction by 60%," https://hootsuite.com, accessed April 9, 2018; Moryt Milo, "Great Businesses Lean Forward, Respond Fast," *Silicon Valley Business Journal*, http://www.bizjournals.com, accessed April 9, 2018; dataSpring editors, "Six Trends in the Market Research Industry for 2018," http://www.d8aspring.com, accessed April 9, 2018; organization website, "Agile Marketing Techniques to Expect in 2018," http://www.greenbookblog.org, accessed April 9, 2018.

[24] Vicki Wright, "Observational Techniques in Market Research," *Houston Chronicle*, http://smallbusiness.chron.com, accessed April 6, 2018.

[25] "Pitch Brief: Campbell's Soup and Millennials? *Well Yes!*," *Business Wire*, https://www.businesswire.com, accessed April 9, 2018; Jeff Gelsky, "Campbell Soup Shifts Marketing Strategy," *Meat and Poultry*, http://www.meatpoultry.com, accessed April 9, 2018; Jim Walsh, "Emerging Firm in Camden: Campbell Snack Co.," *Courier Post*, http://www.courierpost.com, accessed April 9, 2018; Associated Press, "Can Campbell Soup Win Back Millennials?" *Christian Science Monitor*, http://www.csmonitor.com, accessed April 6, 2018; company website, "Brands," http://snyderslance.com/brands, accessed April 9, 2018; Lauren Hirsch, "Campbell Soup to Buy Snacks Company Snyder's-Lance for $4.87 Billion," *CNBC*, http://www.cnbc.com, accessed April 9, 2018.

[26] Harriet Baskas, "Alaska Airlines' Iconic Eskimo Gets a Makeover," *USA Today*, http://www.usatoday.com, accessed April 6, 2018; David Shadpour, "How Social Media Can Serve As the New Focus Group for Your Brand," *Forbes*, http://www.forbes.com, accessed April 9, 2018.

[27] Company website, "Challenges and Wants," http://www.unilever.com, accessed April 6, 2018; company website, "Unilever Launches Crowdsourcing Initiative to Drive Sustainable Growth Ambition," https://www.unilever.com, accessed April 6, 2018; company website, "Open Innovation," https://www.unilever.com, accessed April 9, 2018.

[28] Company website, "About Blue Chip," http://bluechipmarketing-worldwide.com, accessed April 6, 2018; Natasha Singer, "Sharing Data, But Not Happily," *The New York Times*, http://www.nytimes.com, accessed April 6, 2018.

[29] Kashmir Hill, "How Target Figured Out a Teenage Girl was Pregnant Before Her Father Did," *Forbes*, http://www.forbes.com, accessed April 9, 2018; "5 Real Life Applications of Data Mining and Business Intelligence," *Matillion*, http://www.matillion.com, accessed April 9, 2018.

[30] Rick Armstrong, "Unity's Future of VR Ads and How Cinemachine and Timeline Will Change Storytelling As We Know It," *Unity3D*, https://blogs.unity3d.com, accessed April 12, 2018; company website, "Analytics," http://unity3d.com, accessed April 6, 2018.

[31] Aaron Smith and Monica Anderson, "Social Media Use in 2018," *Pew Research*, http://www.pewinternet.org, accessed April 10, 2018.

[32] Christopher Groskopf, Nikhil Sonnad, and Youyou Zhou, "Amazon Buying Whole Foods Puts It Right Next to One-Third of America's Richest Households," *Quartz*, http://www.quartz.com, accessed April 10, 2018; Daniel Keyes, "Whole Foods Still Tied to Affluent Shoppers," *Business Insider*, http://www.businessinsider.com, accessed April 10, 2018.

[33] Alexandra Whittaker, "Target Adds a Gender Neutral Kids Collection After Dropping Mossimo and Merona," *InStyle*, http://www.instyle.com, accessed April 12, 2018; Rachel Hosie, "John Lewis Gets Rid of 'Boys' and 'Girls' Labels in Clothing," *Independent*, https://www.independent.co.uk, accessed April 12, 2018; J'na Jefferson, "H&M Is Defying Gender Norms With Their New Unisex Denim Line," *Vibe*, http://www.vibe.com, accessed April 12, 2018; Sarah Steiner, "Do Consumers Want Gendered Products?" *American Marketing Association*, http://www.ama.org, accessed April 10, 2018; Ashleigh Austen, "The Rise of Genderless Beauty," *New York Post*, http://www.

nypost.com, accessed April 10, 2018; Mi-Anne Chan, "CoverGirl Just Announced Its First Male Face—& He Couldn't Be More Deserving," *Refinery29*, http://www.refinery29.com, accessed April 13, 2018; Lucy Whitehouse, "L'Oreal Uses First Ever Male Model in a Cosmetics Campaign," *Cosmetics Design Europe*, https://www.cosmeticsdesign-europe.com, accessed April 13, 2018; WITW Staff, "Maybelline Reveals Its First Ever Male Makeup Model," *Women in the World*, https://womenintheworld.com, accessed April 13, 2018; Emine Saner, "Joy of Unisex: the Rise of Gender-Neutral Clothing," *The Guardian*, https://www.theguardian.com, accessed April 14, 2018.

[34] Company website, https://www.diaperdude.com, accessed April 6, 2018; company website, "Products" and "Get Started," http://www.justformen.com, accessed April 6, 2018.

[35] Michelle King, "Want a Piece of the 18 Trillion Dollar Female Economy? Start With Gender Bias," *Forbes*, http://www.forbes.com, accessed April 12, 2018; company website, "Research Brief: Women Control $20 Trillion in Annual Consumer Spending," http://www.pmda.com, accessed April 6, 2018; Bridget Brennan, "Top 10 Things Everyone Should Know About Women Consumers," *Forbes*, http://www.forbes.com, accessed April 6, 2018.

[36] Rob Bates, "Pandora, Alex and Ani, and the Ongoing Charm Wars," *JCKOnline.com*, http://jckonline.com, accessed April 6, 2018.

[37] Organization website, "Population Distribution by Age," https://www.kff.org, accessed April 12, 2018; "United States Population 2018," http://worldpopulationreview.com, accessed April 12, 2018.

[38] Gail Marks Jarvis, "Baby Boomers, Planning to Work Past Retirement? Here's Why That Idea Could Be a Bust," *Chicago Tribune*, http://www.chicagotribune.com, accessed April 12, 2018; company website, "Marketing to Women: Quick Facts," http://she-conomy.com, accessed April 6, 2018; Emily Brandon, "The Recession's Impact on Baby Boomer Retirement," *US News Money*, http://money.usnews.com, accessed April 6, 2018.

[39] "Which Brand Attributes Matter Most to Millennials?" http://marketingcharts.com, accessed April 6, 2018; Sujan Patel, "3 Essential Tips for Marketing to Millennials," *Entrepreneur*, http://www.entrepreneur.com, accessed April 6, 2018; Andrew Swinand, "Corporate Social Responsibility Is Millennials' New Religion," *Crain's Chicago Business*, http://www.chicagobusiness.com, accessed April 6, 2018; Dione Searsey, "Marketers Are Sizing Up the Millennials," *The New York Times*, http://www.nytimes.com, accessed April 6, 2018.

[40] Michelle Castillo, "Why Would Univision Hook Up with The Onion?" *CNBC*, http://www.cnbc.com, accessed April 6, 2018; "Telemundo Redesigns Digital Platforms," *Advanced Television*, http://advanced-television.com, accessed April 6, 2018; "Telemundo Novelas for iPhone," *CNET*, http://download.cnet.com, accessed April 6, 2018; Leila Cobo, "Univision Launches Radio App for iPhone," *Billboard Business*, http://www.billboardbiz.com, accessed April 6, 2018; Antonio Florez, "How the U.S. Hispanic Population Is Changing," *Pew Research*, http://www.pewresearch.org, accessed April 14, 2018.

[41] Corr S. Pondent, "The Stages of Family Life Cycle Marketing," *Bizfluent*, http://www.bizfluent.com, accessed April 12, 2018.

[42] Erin Brodwin, "Here's the Personality Test Cambridge Analytica Had Facebook Users Take," *Business Insider*, http://www.businessinsider.com, accessed April 13, 2018; Kevin Granville, "Facebook and Cambridge Analytica: What You Need to Know as Fallout Widens," *New York Times*, http://www.nytimes.com, accessed April 13, 2018; Antonio Garcia Martinez, "The Noisy Fallacies of Psychographic Targeting," *Wired*, http://www.wired.com, accessed April 13, 2018.

[43] Organization website, "Annual Sales Data U.S. Domestic Markets," http://www.toyassociation.org, accessed April 6, 2018; Erica Loop, "This Is How Much Parents Spent on Toys on Amazon Last Year (It Was . . . a LOT)," *Red Tricycle*, http://www.redtricycle.com, accessed April 12, 2018.

[44] "Electric Car Benefits Most Loved by Buyers," *EVObsession.com*, http://evobsession.com, accessed April 6, 2018; company website, "Seed Your Sole," http://mamachia.com.

[45] Company website, http://www.sodexousa.com, accessed April 6, 2018; "Sodexo to Open Loyola Marymount University Food Truck," *Mobile-Cuisine*, http://mobile-cuisine.com, accessed April 6, 2018; Mike Buzalka, "Sodexo's Food Truck Concept Rolls into Rock Hill Schools," *Food Management*, http://food-management.com, accessed April 6, 2018.

[46] Rick Romwell, "Inside Amazon's Amazing Prime Now Two-Hour Delivery Operation," *USA Today*, http://www.usatoday.com, accessed April 13, 2018; company website, "Same Day Delivery on Everything You Love," https://www.google.com/express, accessed April 6, 2018; Sarah Perez, "Amazon Brings Its One-Hour Delivery Service, Prime Now, to the San Francisco Bay Area," *Tech Crunch*, http://techcrunch, accessed April 6, 2018.

[47] Courtney Reagan, "How the Recession Changed the Ways Americans Spend Money," *CNBC*, http://www.cnbc.com, accessed April 14, 2018; Joshua Brustein, "Walgreen's Beth Stiller on Customer Behavior and the Recession," *Bloomberg Business*, http://www.bloomberg.com, accessed April 6, 2018.

[48] Company website, "Corporate Social Responsibility," http://www.timberland.com, accessed April 10, 2018.

[49] Scott McCartney, "Hotel Rewards Programs: The Best and the Rest," *The Wall Street Journal*, http://www.wsj.com, accessed April 10, 2018; "Marriot Rewards: #1 in Best Hotel Rewards Programs," *US News and World Report*, https://travel.usnews.com, accessed April 12, 2018.

[50] Deena Crawley and Steve McKee, "Twenty Co-Branding Examples," *Bloomberg Business*, http://www.bloomberg.com, accessed April 10, 2018; company website, "New Treats from Betty Crocker and Hershey's," http://www.blog.generalmills.com, accessed April 10, 2018.

[51] Company website, "Salesforce Essentials CRM," http://www.salesforce.com, accessed April 10, 2018; company website, "Top CRM Software," http://www.capterra.com, accessed April 10, 2018.

[52] Company website, "About VALS," http://www.strategicbusinessinsights.com, accessed April 10, 2018.

Chapter 12

[1] Organization website, "Jodi Goodman, President Northern California, Live Nation Entertainment," http://thejgsi.org, accessed April 15, 2018; company website, "Jodi Goodman Tapped," *Hits Daily Double*, http://hitsdailydouble.com, accessed April 15, 2018; Christine Ryan, "Hot 20: The Music Woman: Jodi Goodman," *7 x 7 Magazine*, http://www.7x7.com, accessed April 15, 2018; company website, "Live Nation Entertainment Reports Fourth Quarter and Full Year 2017 Results," http://investors.livenationentertainment.com, accessed April 15, 2018; Ethan Smith, "Boards Move Close to Live Nation Deal," *The Wall Street Journal*, https://www.wsj.com, accessed April 15, 2018.

[2] Kirsten Korosec, "Lamborghini's New $200,000 SUV is here," *Fortune*, http://www.fortune.com, accessed April 15, 2018.

[3] Company website, "Gorilla Products," http://www.gorillatough.com, accessed April 15, 2018.

[4] Company website, "Brands," http://www.coca-colacompany.com, accessed April 15, 2018.

[5] Alex Davis, "Heat Seeking Cameras Could Help Keep Self-Driving Cars Safe," *Wired*, http://www.wired.com, accessed April 21, 2018; Jason

Karaman, "The Four Stages of Product Life Cycle with Examples," *ExpertCaller.com*, http://www.expertcaller.com, accessed April 21, 2018.

[6] Stephen Lacy, "Everyone Is Revising Their Electric Vehicle Forecasts Upward—Except Automakers," *GTM*, http://greentechmedia.com, accessed April 21, 2018; organization website, "Global EV Outlook 2017 Two million and counting," https://www.iea.org, accessed April 21, 2018; company website, "Electric Vehicle Market Forecasts," http://www.navigantresearch.com, accessed April 15, 2018; Jess Shankleman, "The Electric Car Revolution Is Accelerating," *Bloomberg*, http://www.bloomberg.com, accessed April 21, 2018; "Global Electric Vehicles Market to Grow at a CAGR of 28.3% (in Volume) From 2017 to 2026," *BIS Research,* www.prnewswire.com, accessed April 21, 2018.

[7] Sara Salinas, "Global Smartphone Sales Fall for the First Time in More Than a Decade," *CNBC*, http://www.cnbc.com, accessed April 21, 2018; Davey Alba, "Smartphone Growth Is Slowing. That's Great News for Apple," *Wired*, http://www.wired.com, accessed April 15, 2018; Daisuke Wakabayashi, "Apple iPhone Sales Grow at Slowest Rate Ever," *The Wall Street Journal*, http://www.wsj.com, accessed April 15, 2018.

[8] Danielle Wiener-Bronner, "Why Coke Is Winning the Cola War over Pepsi," *CNN*, http://www.cnn.com, accessed April 21, 2018; Phil Wahba, "PepsiCo's Snacks Help It Overcome Weak Soda Sales," *Fortune*, http://www.fortune.com, accessed April 21, 2018.

[9] Jessica Bruso, "Two Week Kellogg's Weight Loss Plan," *Live Strong*, http://www.livestrong.com, accessed April 15, 2018; Toby Amidor, "3 Diets That Aren't What You Think They Are," *U.S. News and World Report,* http://health.usnews.com, accessed April 15, 2018.

[10] Company website, "Barbie(R) Honors Global Role Models on International Women's Day," https://news.mattel.com, accessed April 15, 2018; "Twenty-Eight Uses for Everyday Items," *Real Simple*, http://www.realsimple.com, accessed April 15, 2018; Paul Ziobro, "Mattel to Add Curvy, Petite, Tall Barbies," *The Wall Street Journal*, http://www.wsj.com, accessed April 15, 2018; Eliana Dockterman, "Barbie's Got a New Body," *TIME*, http://time.com, accessed April 15, 2018.

[11] Company website, "$5 Starter Sets," https://www.dollarshaveclub.com, accessed April 15, 2018; Paul Ziobro and Anne Steele, "P&G's Gillette Sues Dollar Shave Club," *The Wall Street Journal*, http://www.wsj.com, accessed April 15, 2018; company website, "About," http://try.dollarshaveclub.com, accessed April 15, 2018.

[12] Monique Randolph, "Corps Reaches Final Stages of Tropical Boots, Uniform Testing," *Marine Corps Systems Command*, http://www.marcorsyscom.marines.mil, accessed April 15, 2018; James K. Sanborn, "Tropical Uniform Prototypes Fail to Deliver," *Marine Times*, http://www.marinecorpstimes.com, accessed April 15, 2018; company website, "RFI—Tropical Combat Uniform," http://www.marinecorpstimes.com, accessed April 15, 2018; government website, https://govtribe.com, accessed April 15, 2018.

[13] Simon Hattenstone, "The Rise of eSports: Are Addiction and Corruption the Price of Its Success?" *The Guardian*, http://www.theguardian.com, accessed April 16, 2018; Janet Stilson, "Pro Video Gaming Is Exploding in Popularity," "Activision Created an Overwatch League to Cash In," and "Basing Teams in Cities, Like the NFL and MLB Do," *AdWeek*, http://www.adweek.com, accessed April 16, 2018; Kinsey Grant, "Overwatch League: Can It Boost Activision Blizzard As Much As First Thought?" *The Street,* http://www.thestreet.com, accessed April 16, 2018; Tony Owusu, "3 Great eSports Investments for the Technology Savvy Retiree," *The Street*, http://www.thestreet.com, accessed April 16, 2018.

[14] Stuart Miles, "Wear a Fuel Band? Nike Says Take It Off," *Pocket Lint*, http://www.pocket-lint.com, accessed April 15, 2018; Nick Statt, "Exclusive: Nike Fires Majority of FuelBand Team, Will Stop Making Wearable Hardware," *CNET*, http://cnet.com, accessed April 15, 2018.

[15] Leander Kahney, "Steve Jobs Finally Reveals Where The Name 'Apple' Came From," *Cult of Mac*, https://www.cultofmac.com, accessed April 15, 2017; company website, "How to Choose a Great Brand Name," http://www.marketingmo.com, accessed April 15, 2018; Steven Benna and Skye Gould, "How 17 Famous Companies Got Their Quirky Names," *Business Insider*, http://www.businessinsider.com, accessed April 15, 2018.

[16] Company website, http://www.ikea.com, accessed April 15, 2018.

[17] Brett Casella, "21 Recognizable Brand Logos with Strong Brand Identities," *Impact Bound,* http://www.impactbnd.com, accessed April 15, 2018; company website, "Top 100 Global Brands," http://interbrand.com, accessed April 15, 2018.

[18] Cara Lombardo, "Coca-Cola, Criticized for Plastic Bottles, Sets Recycling Goals," *The Wall Street Journal*, http://www.wsj.com, accessed April 17, 2018; company website, "Unpacking Coke's Bold New Sustainable Packaging Vision," http://www.coca-colacompany.com, accessed April 17, 2018; Jennifer McKevitt, "Foam No More: McDonald's Sets Goals for Sustainable, Recycled Packaging," *Supply Chain Dive,* http://www.supplychaindive.com, accessed April 17, 2018; Adele Peters, "McDonald's Says It Will Cut Its Carbon Footprint Enough To Actually Make A Difference," *Fast Company*, http://www.fastcompany.com, accessed April 17, 2018; Benjamin Kentish, "Coca-Cola 'Increases Production of Plastic Bottles by a Billion'," *Independent*, http://www.independent.com, accessed April 17, 2018.

[19] Government website, "Proposed Changes to the Nutrition Facts Label" and "Changes to the Nutrition Facts Label," http://www.fda.gov, accessed April 15, 2018; Alexandra Sifferlin, "FDA Revising Food Nutrition Labels," *Time,* http://healthland.time.com, accessed April 15, 2018.

[20] Jonathan Ratner, "Smartphone Distribution Disruption: The Winners and Losers," *Financial Post,* http://business.financialpost.com, accessed April 15, 2018; Mark Spoonauer, "Smartphones: Best Phones of 2017," *Tom's Guide*, http://www.tomsguide.com, accessed April 15, 2018; Matt Hamblen, "U.S. Businesses Jump on Trend to Buy Unlocked Smartphones," *ComputerWorld,* http://www.computerworld.com, accessed April 17, 2018.

[21] Abha Bhattarai, "Everlane Is Opening Its First Stores, After Years of Swearing It Wouldn't," *Washington Post,* https://www.washingtonpost.com, accessed April 18, 2018; company website, "About," http://www.everlane.com, accessed April 15, 2018; Ryan Caldbeck, "The 25 Most Innovative Consumer and Retail Brands," *Entrepreneur*, http://www.entrepreneur.com, accessed April 15, 2018.

[22] Government website, "Wholesale Trade: NAICS 42," *Occupational Outlook Handbook,* 2017–2018 Edition, http://www.bls.gov, accessed April 15, 2018; government website, "County Business Patterns—Wholesale Trade," http://www.census.gov, accessed April 15, 2018.

[23] Company website, http://www.acehardware.com, accessed April 15, 2018.

[24] Marianne Wilson, "eMarketer: E-Commerce to Grab 10% of U.S. Retail Sales in 2018," *Chain Store Age*, http://www.chainstoreage.com, accessed April 19, 2018; Robert Klara, "Bad News, Brick-and-Mortar Stores: The Internet Finally Has You Beat," *Ad Week*, http://www.adweek.com, accessed April 19, 2018; Lin Grossman, "What the Amazon Effect Means for Retailers," *Forbes*, http://www.forbes.com, accessed April 19, 2018.

[25] Company website, "About," http://www.wegobabies.com, accessed April 15, 2018; Emily Jed, "WeGoBabies Vends Essentials for Parents on the Go, Makes OneShow Debut," *Vending Times*,

http://vendingtimes.com, accessed April 15, 2018; Lisa Horten, "We're Having a 'Why Didn't We Think of This?' Moment," *Pop Sugar*, http://www.popsugar.com, accessed April 15, 2018.

26 James Haskett, "Can Amazon Do What Walmart Couldn't, Stop the 'Wheel of Retailing'?" *Harvard Business Review*, http://www.hbr.com, accessed April 19, 2018; company website, http://saksfifthavenue.com, accessed April 15, 2018.

27 Company website, "About," https://www.skullshaver.com, accessed April 18, 2018, organization website, "Men's Hair Loss," http://www.americanhairloss.org, accessed April 19, 2018.

28 Neil Boudette, "Toyota Brass Sees More Strong U.S. Sales, But Must Adapt Product Mix," *Automotive News,* http://www.autonews.com, accessed April 15, 2018; Joann Muller, "The World's Most Popular Vehicles of 2017: Cars Still Rule, But SUVs Coming on Strong," *Forbes*, http://www.forbes.com, accessed April 19, 2018.

29 Company website, http://www.traderjoes.com, accessed April 15, 2018.

30 Jeff Hardwick, "The Mall Is Dead. Americans Shop at 'Lifestyle Centers'," *New Republic*, https://newrepublic.com, accessed April 15, 2018.

31 Katie Richards, "The North Face's New Campaign Aims to Focus More on Women in Advertising," *AdWeek*, http://www.adweek.com, accessed April 19, 2018.

32 Kathleen Burke, "This Is How Rivals Are Trying to Compete with Amazon," *Market Watch*, http://www.marketwatch.com, accessed April 15, 2018; Lisa R. Melsted, "Retailers Turn to Omnichannel Strategies to Remain Competitive," *Forbes*, http://www.forbes.com, accessed April 15, 2018; Dave Blanchard, "Top 25 Supply Chains of 2015," *Industry Week*, http://www.industryweek.com, accessed April 15, 2018; Greg Bensinger, "Amazon Plans Hundreds of Brick-and-Mortar Bookstores, Mall CEO Says," *The Wall Street Journal*, http://www.wsj.com, accessed April 15, 2018.

33 Company website, "23andMe Granted First FDA Authorization for Direct-to-Consumer Genetic Test on Cancer Risk," https://mediacenter.23andme.com, accessed April 20, 2018; "How CEO Anne Wojcicki Turned 23andMe Around After Falling Out with the FDA," *Fast Company,* http://www.fastcompany.com, accessed April 15, 2018; Elizabeth Murphy, "Inside 23andMe Founder Anne Wojcicki's $99 DNA Revolution," *Fast Company*, http://www.fastcompany.com, accessed April 15, 2018.

34 Company website, http://topshop.com, accessed April 15, 2018; company website, http://www.nordstrom.com, accessed April 15, 2018.

35 Company website, "About Chicago Premium Outlets," http://www.premiumoutlets.com, accessed April 15, 2018.

36 Company website, http://www.verayo.com, accessed April 15, 2018; company website, "Metro Group Future Store Initiative," press release, http://www.metrogroup.com, accessed April 15, 2018.

37 Organization website, "Reports, Trends, and Statistics," http://www.trucking.org, accessed April 15, 2018; Svetlana Guineva, "Five Awesome Infographics About the Trucking Industry," http://cerasis.com, accessed April 15, 2018.

38 Organization website, "U.S. Freight Railroad Industry Snapshot," http://www.aar.org, accessed April 15, 2018; organization website, "Railroads and States," https://www.aar.org/d, accessed April 21, 2018.

Chapter 13

1 Organization website, "About," http://fohta.org, accessed May 6, 2018; company website, "Perfect Marketing: Kanye West and Pharrell Boost Adidas Sales," http://www.sneakerwatch.com, accessed May 6, 2018; Alex Rynne, "Intelligent Risk and Intention: 5 Creativity Lessons from Pharrell Williams," *LinkedIn* Marketing Solutions Blog, https://businesslinkedin.com, accessed May 6, 2018; Mike Gabaly, "Pharrell Williams Is a Digital Marketing Genius, *The Hub,* http://www.thehubcomms.com, accessed May 6, 2018; Mary Kaye Schilling, "Get Busy: Pharrell's Productivity Secrets," *Fast Company*, http://www.fastcompany.com; accessed May 6, 2018; Suzanne Labarre, "Not a Joke: Pharrell Builds a Stunning, $35M Afterschool Space for Kids," *Co.Design,* http://www.fastcodesign.com, accessed May 6, 2018; Joelle Diderich, "Chanel and Pharrell Williams Drop World's Most Exclusive Sneakers," *WWD*, http://www.wwd.com, accessed May 12, 2018; Nerisha Penrose, "Pharrell Williams to Open His First Restaurant & Cocktail Lounge in Miami," *Billboard*, http://www.billboard.com, accessed May 12, 2018; Riley Jones, "You Can Buy Pharrell's New Friends and Family NMDs for $5,000," *Sole Collector,* http://www.solecollector.com, accessed May 12, 2018.

2 Company website, "Fresh California Avocados," http://www.californiaavocado.com, accessed May 6, 2018; Issie Lapowsky, "4 Takeaways from the Iconic 'Got Milk?' Ad Campaign," *Inc.,* http://www.inc.com, accessed May 6, 2018; company website, "About Us," http://www.beefusa.org, accessed May 6, 2018; company website, "Who We Are," http://www.wmmb.com, accessed May 6, 2018.

3 Forbes Agency Council, "12 Most Memorable Marketing Campaigns of 2017," *Forbes*, http://www.forbes.com, accessed May 1, 2018.

4 Alexis Samuely, "McDonald's Builds Free Breakfast Delivery Promotion Around Mobile Nominations," *Retail Dive*, https://www.retaildive.com, accessed May 1, 2018; Suzanne Vranica, "McDonald's to Review Its $2 Billion Global Media Buying Account," *The Wall Street Journal,* http://www.wsj.com, accessed May 1, 2018; Jessica Wohl, "McDonald's Tweaks Value Marketing After Visits Fall," *AdAge*, http://www.adage.com, accessed May 1, 2018; Great Speculations, "Mobile Payment Options Should Drive Growth for McDonald's, Burger King," *Forbes*, http://www.forbes.com, accessed May 2, 2018.

5 Mediakix Team, "What the 19th Coachella Music Festival 2018 Holds for Brands and Advertisers," *Media Kix,* accessed May 1, 2018, http://mediakix.com; George Kuruvill, "Portugal. The Man Lead Singer Creates Designs for BMW i Models for Coachella," *The Drive*, http://www.thedrive.com, accessed May 2, 2018; Gabriel Nica, "BMW i Continues Partnership with Coachella in 2018," *BMW Blog*, http://www.bmwblog.com, accessed May 2, 2018.

6 Company website, "FAQs," https://www.johndeereclassic.com, accessed May 2, 2018; company website, "Form 10Q," https://investor.deere.com, accessed May 2, 2018; company website "Strategy and Core Values," https://www.deere.com, accessed May 2, 2018; Neha Chamaria, "Better Buy Now: Caterpillar Inc. vs. Deere & Company," *Motley Fool*, http://www.motleyfool.com, accessed May 2, 2018.

7 Reuters, "US Prescription Drug Spending as High as $610 Billion by 2021: Report," *CNBC*, http://www.cnbc.com, accessed May 2, 2018; Larry Husten, "Entresto Maker in Deep Water over Terrifying TV Advertisement," *CardioBrief,* http://cardiobrief.org, accessed May 6, 2018; "Persuading the Prescribers: Pharmaceutical Industry Marketing and Its Influence on Physicians and Patients," *Pew Health Research,* http://www.pewhealth.org, accessed May 6, 2018; Adam Fein, "New CMS Forecast: Drug Spending Grows Along with Impossible Hospital and Doctor Spending," *Drug Channels*, http://www.drugchannels.net, accessed May 6, 2018.

8 Marci Medina, "H&M Taps Moschino for 2018 Designer Collaboration," *WWD*, http://www.wwd.com, accessed May 2, 2018; Lucy Hutchings, "H&M Confirms Moschino as Its Next Designer Collaboration," *Harper Bazaar*, http://www.harpersbazaar.com, accessed

May 2, 2018; Ana Colon, "All The Times Balmain X H&M Was Already Worn on the Red Carpet," *Refinery29*, http://www.refinery29.com, accessed May 6, 2018; Marketing Team, "Why Should Luxury Brands Collaborate with Fast Fashion Retailers?" *Optimy*, http://blog.optimy.com, accessed May 6, 2018.

[9] Damien O'Carroll, "A-Class Is Another New Beginning for Mercedes-Benz," *Stuff*, https://www.stuff.co.nz, accessed May 2, 2019; Christoph Rauwald, "Mercedes Plans Electric S-Class to Challenge Tesla's Flagship," *Bloomberg*, http://www.bloomberg.com, accessed May 2, 2018.

[10] Brian Steinberg, "Apple Polishing: iPhone Giant Can't Keep Mum About Behind-the-Scenes TV Role," *Variety*, http://www.variety.com, accessed May 3, 2018; Anthony D'Alessandro, "'Spider-Man: Homecoming' Delivers Franchise's Biggest Promotional Campaign At $140M+," *Deadline*, http://deadline.com, accessed May 4, 2018.

[11] "Genius Guerrilla Marketing Campaign: Zappos Schools Google, Y'all," *The American Genius*, http://theamericangenius.com, accessed May 6, 2018.

[12] Jessica Wohl, "Pizza Hut's New Shoes Let You Order and Pause the Game," *AdAge*, http://www.adage.com, accessed May 4, 2018; company website, "Pizza Hut" https://play.google.com, accessed May 4, 2018, company website, "Definition of Digital Marketing," *Financial Times*, http://lexicon.ft.com, accessed May 4, 2018.

[13] David Lamoureux, "How Many Marketing Messages Do We See in a Day?" *Fluid Drive Media*, http://www.fluiddrivemedia.com, accessed May 6, 2018.

[14] Kantar Media, "Global Advertising Expenditure Q1 2017 vs. Q1 2016," *Kantar Media*, http://www.kantarmedia.com, accessed May 4, 2018; Dani Jordan, "Global Ad Spend to Hit $563.4 Billion in 2017 with Digital Driving Growth," *Dentsu Aegis Network*, http://www.dentsuaegisnetwork.com, accessed May 4, 2018; Jack Loechner, "Digital Ads Overtake TV," *MediaPost*, http://www.mediapost.com, accessed May 4, 2018.

[15] Bradley Johnson, "World's Largest Advertisers: Spending Is Growing (and Surging in China), *AdAge*, http://www.adage.com, accessed May 4, 2018.

[16] Brian Faust, "5 Top Advertising Trends in 2018: The Future Is Digital," *MarTech* Advisor, http://www.martech.com, accessed May 4, 2018; Tiffany Li, "After the Cambridge Analytica Facebook Scandal, Here's What Mark Zuckerberg Must Do to Save His Company," *NBC News*, http://www.nbcnews.com, accessed May 4, 2018.

[17] Organization website, http://keepachildalive.org, accessed May 6, 2018.

[18] Mike Shields, "The Future of Ad Agencies Has Never Been More in Doubt," *Business Insider*, http://www.businessinsider.com, accessed May 4, 2018; Sarah Vizard, "How Marketing Is Changing and How Agencies Are Not Keeping Pace," *Marketing Week*, http://www.marketingweek.com, accessed May 4, 2018.

[19] Company website, "Advertising Expenditure Forecasts March 2018," http://www.zenithmediacorp.com, accessed May 5, 2018; Global Advertising Industry 2012–2017: Trends, Profits and Forecast Analysis, accessed May 5, 2018; Marcel Oedi, "Global Trends in the Advertising Industry Part I: Follow the Money," *Medium*, http://www.medium.com, accessed May 5, 2018; Varsha Jain and Subhadip Roy, "The Emerging Trends in Global Advertising," *TandFOnline*, http://www.tandfonline.com, accessed May 5, 2018.

[20] Company website, "TV Systems," *Althos*, www.althos.com, accessed May 5, 2018; company website, "Leading Ad Supported Broadcast and Cable Networks in the United States in 2017, by Average Number of Viewers," http://www.statista.com, accessed May 5, 2018; Jeanine Poggi, "Dear TV: We Love You. You're Perfect. Now Change. (But Not Too Much)." *AdAge*, http://www.adage.com, accessed May 5, 2018; John Martin, "John Martin, Chairman and CEO of Turner: The Future of Television Is Happening Now," *Recode*, http://www.recode.com, accessed May 5, 2018; Todd Spangler, "Cord-Cutting Explodes: 22 Million U.S. Adults Will Have Canceled Cable, Satellite TV by End of 2017," *Variety*, http://www.variety.com, accessed May 5, 2018; company website, "Internet/Broadband Fact Sheet," *Pew Research*, http://www.pewresearch.com, accessed May 5, 2018.

[21] Shalini Ramachandran and Imani Moise, "Netflix Subscriber Growth Tops Expectations," *The Wall Street Journal*, http://www.wsj.com, accessed May 5, 2018; James Wilcox, "Guide to Streaming Video Services," *Consumer Reports*, http://www.consumerreports.org, accessed May 5, 2018; Conor Cawley, "10 Most Popular Streaming Services in the US," *Tech.Co*, https://tech.co, accessed May 5, 2018; Jeff Prince and Shane Greenstein, "Does Original Content Help Streaming Services Attract More Subscribers?" *Harvard Business Review*, http://www.hbr.org, accessed May 5, 2018; Jason Cross, "Apple's Original TV Shows and Series: Are You Sleeping, Starring Octavia Spencer, Gets 10-Episode Season Order," *MacWorld*, http://www.macworld.com, accessed May 5, 2018.

[22] Company website, "Superbowl 2018 Advertisers," *iSpotTv*, http://www.ispottv.com, accessed May 5, 2018; Mary Hanbury, "This Year's Super Bowl Commercials Are More Expensive Than Ever—Here's Your Complete Guide to All the Ads That Will Air," *Business Insider*, http://www.businessinsider.com, accessed May 5, 2018; Darren Rovell, "Eagles-Patriots Super Bowl Watched by Fewer People," *ESPN*, http://www.espn.com, accessed May 5, 2018.

[23] Patrick Kelly, "10 Most Followed Brands on Instagram," *Smart Insights*, http://www.smartinsights.com, accessed May 6, 2018; Alex York, "21 Instagram Accounts to Follow for Brand Inspiration," *Sprout Social*, http://www.sproutsocial.com, accessed May 6, 2018; company website, "Advertising Expenditure Forecasts March 2018," http://www.zenithmediacorp.com, accessed May 5, 2018; "Global Advertising Industry 2012–2017: Trends, Profits and Forecast Analysis," accessed May 5, 2018; Marcel Oedi, "Global Trends in the Advertising Industry Part I: Follow the Money," *Medium*, http://www.medium.com, accessed May 5, 2018; Varsha Jain and Subhadip Roy, "The Emerging Trends in Global Advertising," *TandFOnline*, http://www.tandfonline.com, accessed May 5, 2018.

[24] John Ebbert, "Define It—What Is Programmatic Buying?" *Ad Exchanger*, http://adexchanger.com, accessed May 6, 2018.

[25] Olivia Petter, "Kylie Jenner's Instagram Posts Are Now Worth $1 Million Each, New Report Finds," *Independent*, www.independent.co.uk, accessed May 6, 2018; Meghan Keaney Anderson, "7 of the Best Promotional Product Videos Ever Produced," *HubSpot*, http://www.hubspot.com,accessedMay6,2018;DollarShaveClub,"OurBladesAre F***ing Great," https://www.youtube.com/watch?v=ZUG9qYTJMsI, accessed May 6, 2018; Kristin Tauer, "A$AP Ferg Launches Tiffany Paper Flowers Campaign with Elle Fanning," *Women's Wear Daily*, http://www.wwd.com, accessed May 6, 2018.

[26] Company website, "Advantages of Newspaper Advertising," http://www.mansimedia.com, accessed May 5, 2018; Michael Barthel, "Newspapers: Fact Sheet," *Pew Research Center*, http://www.pewresearch.org, accessed May 6, 2018; organization website; "Newspapers by the Numbers," *State of the Media*, http://stateofthemedia.org, accessed May 6, 2018.

[27] Company website, "Top 4 Radio Advertising Trends for 2018," https://www.adsforcarts.com, accessed May 5, 2018; Symon Edmonds, "How You Can Tackle the Three Largest Digital Trends for Radio in 2018," *SoCast*, http://www.socast.com, accessed May 5, 2018.

[28] Company website, "What Could 2017 Magazine Publishing Trends Mean for 2018?" *Sheridan*, http://www.sheridan.com, accessed May 5, 2018.

29 Colleen D'Alessandro, "Top 15 Direct Mail Marketing Trends for 2018," *Postalytics*, http://www.postalytics.com, accessed May 6, 2018; company website, "What Is Direct Mail?" http://www.wisegeek.org, accessed May 6, 2018; Mark Pageau, "Direct Mail Trends from the DMA Conference," *Darwill*, http://www.darwill.com, accessed May 6, 2018; Denise Yee Yohn, "Why the Print Catalog Is Back in Style," *Harvard Business Review*, https://hbr.org, accessed May 6, 2018; organization website, "Trends and Future of Direct Mail through 2020," http://www.cmocouncil.org, accessed May 6, 2018.

30 Michelle Peel, "The Evolution of Credit Card Direct Mail Offers," *IWCO Direct*, http://www.iwco.com, accessed May 6, 2018.

31 Organization website, "Out of Home Advertising up 1.2% to $7.7 Billion in 2017," http://www.ooaa.org, accessed May 6, 2018.

32 Organization website, "Out of Home Advertising up 1.2% to $7.7 Billion in 2017," http://www.ooaa.org, accessed May 6, 2018; Larry Malloy, "4 Hot Trends in Digital Billboards," *InterMap*, http://www.intermap.com, accessed May 6, 2018; Ben Davis, "Six Clever Examples of What Dynamic Outdoor Advertising Can Do," econsultancy.com, http://www.econsultancy.com, accessed May 8, 2018; Wade Rifkin, "Clear Channel Outdoor on How Location Data Helps Brands with OOH and the Future of OOH Measurement," *Viant*, http://www.viantinc.com, accessed May 8, 2018.

33 Florence Broderick, "The Biggest Data Trends in Outdoor Advertising in 2017," *Carto*, http://www.carto.com, accessed May 8, 2018; organization website, "Out of Home Advertising up 1.2% to $7.7 Billion in 2017," http://www.ooaa.org, accessed May 10, 2018; Larry Malloy, "4 Hot Trends in Digital Billboards," *InterMap*, http://www.intermap.com, accessed May 6, 2018; company website, "Billboards," http://www.outfrontmedia.com, accessed May 6, 2018; company website, "What Is Digital Outdoor?" http://www.watchfiredigitaloutdoor.com, accessed May 6, 2018; company website, "Electronic Advertising," http://www.cbsoutdoor.com, accessed May 6, 2018.

34 Florence Broderick, "The Biggest Data Trends in Outdoor Advertising in 2017," *Carto*, http://www.carto.com, accessed May 8, 2018.

35 Company website, "Sponsorship Spending Report—Signs Point to Healthy Sponsorship Spending in 2018," http://www.sponsorship.com, accessed May 6, 2018.

36 Chris Smith, "Nascar's Most Valuable Teams," *Forbes*, http://www.forbes.com, accessed May 6, 2018; company website, "Hendrick MotorSports," http://www.hendrickmotorsports.com, accessed May 8, 2018; company website, "Player of the Year," http://www.gatorade.com, accessed May 6, 2018; Bob Pockrass, "Monster Energy 'Highly Unlikely' to Sponsor Cup Series after 2019," *ESPN*, http://www.espn.com, accessed May 8, 2018.

37 Jennifer Wood, "10 Best Selling Infomercial Products," *Mental Floss*, http://mentalfloss.com, accessed May 6, 2018.

38 Company website, "About Us," http://www.adsticks.com, accessed May 6, 2018; company website, "About Us," http://cartvertising.com, accessed May 6, 2018.

39 Yohap News Agency, "Samsung's Sales Promotion Costs Top Ad Spending Through September," *Global Post*, http://www.globalpost.com, accessed May 6, 2018; Ken Wysocky, "Huge Promotion Floats Customers' Boats," *Autonews*, http://www.autonews.com, accessed May 8, 2018.

40 Alexandra Bruell, "Netflix Plans 54% Boost in Ad Spending to Promote Shows," *AdAge*, http://www.adage.com, accessed May 8, 2018.

41 Christine Birkner, "How Bobbleheads Became Baseball's Secret Weapon to Boost Attendance," *AdWeek*, http://www.adweek.com, accessed May 8, 2018; Brad Tuttle, "The History of Coupons," *Time*, http://www.time.com, accessed May 8, 2018; company website, "Facts on Coupon Market Trends in the United States," http://www.statista.com, accessed May 6, 2018; Phillip Redmond, "Retail Transitions to Target Mobile Customers as Sales Channel Changes," *CIO*, http://www.cio.com, accessed May 6, 2018; company website, "Market-Level Data and Analysis of Redemption Drivers," *NCH Marketing*, http://www.nchmarketing.com, accessed May 8, 2018; company website, "Modern Shoppers and Their Quest for Savings." 2K18 Valassis Coupon Intelligence Report, http://www.valassis.com, accessed May 8, 2018; Jill Cataldo, "Super Couponing Tips: New Statistics On Coupon Shoppers," *Orlando Sentinel*, http://www.orlandosentinal.com, accessed May 8, 2018; Khalid Saleh, "Digital Coupon Marketing—Statistics and Trends," Invespcro, https://www.invespcro.com, accessed May 8, 2018.

42 Kevin Danaher, "Are Mail-In Rebates Dead (Or Just Genetically Modified)," *Sales Promotions*, https://salespromotions.org, accessed May 8, 2018.

43 Organization website, "Avocado Oreos?—Crowdsourcing in the CPG World," *Harvard Business Review*, https://digit.hbs.org, accessed May 9, 2018; Maya Salam, "When Just Vanilla Won't Do, How About a Blueberry Pie Oreo?" *The New York Times*, http://www.nytimes.com, accessed May 9, 2018; Matthew Sedacca, "The Business Strategy Behind Oreo's Constant, Weird New Flavors," *GQ*, http://www.gq.com, accessed May 9, 2018; Joe McGauley, "Oreo Is Unleashing These Three New Flavors Created by Fans," *Thrillist*, http://www.thrillist.com, accessed May 9, 2018.

44 Company website, "About," http://www.popai.com, accessed May 6, 2018; "Point-of-Purchase Advertising Trends," *Storify*, https://storify.com, accessed May 6, 2018; company website, "Point-of-Purchase Promotions," *Boundless Marketing*, https://www.boundless.com, accessed May 6, 2018; company website, "Point-of-Purchase Advertising," http://www.allbusiness.com, accessed May 6, 2018.

45 Company website, "CES by the Numbers," https://www.ces.tech, accessed May 8, 2018.

46 Government website, "U.S. Department of Labor. Table 1.1 Employment by Major Occupational Group, 2016 and Projected 2026 (Numbers in Thousands), 2016 and Projected 2026," http://www.dol.gov, accessed May 6, 2018; government website, "Sales Occupations," http://www.bls.gov, accessed May 6, 2018.

47 Company website, "Porsche 918 Spyder," http://www.porsche.com, accessed May 6, 2018; Doug Murray, "10 Ridiculously Luxurious Services for the Super Rich," *Splice*, http://www.splice.ca.com, accessed May 9, 2018; company website, "About," http://www.boesendorfer.com, accessed May 6, 2018; "$1,200,000 Piano: The Kuhn Bösendorfer," *YouTube*, http://www.youtube.com, accessed May 6, 2018.

48 "Dynamic Pricing: What Retailers Need to Know About Competing in Real Time," *eMarketer*, http://www.emarketer.com, accessed May 6, 2018.

49 Company website, "FAQ," https://saleshero.ai/faq, accessed May 9, 2018; David Keane, "Can AI Improve Sales Productivity in Pharma?" *PharmExec.com*, http://www.pharmexec.com, accessed May 9, 2018; company website, "The Rebirth of the Pharmaceutical Sales Force," https://www.accenture.com, accessed May 9, 2018; Beth Snyder Bulik, "Sales Reps Need to Bone Up on Tech Skills as Drug Launches Move Digital," *Fierce Pharma Marketing*, http://www.fiercepharmamarketing.com, accessed May 9, 2018; Jeanne Whalen, "Drug Makers Replace Reps with Digital Tools," *The Wall Street Journal*, http://www.wsj.com, accessed May 9, 2018.

50 Tara Siegel Bernard, "Yes, It's Bad. Robocalls, and Their Scams, Are Surging," *The New York Times*, http://www.nytimes.com, accessed May 9, 2018; John Egan, "What's the Future of Robots in Telemarketing?" *DMA Nonprofit Federation*, https://chi.nonprofitfederation.org, accessed May 9, 2018; government website, "Telemarketing Sales Rule,"

https://www.ftc.gov, accessed May 9, 2018; Robert Cordray, "What Jobs Will Robots Take from Humans in the Future?" *Wired*, http://www.wired.com, accessed May 9, 2018; government website, "Q&A for Telemarketers and Sellers About the Do Not Call Provisions of the FTC's Telemarketing Sales Rule," http://www.business.ftc.gov, accessed May 9, 2018.

51 Mark Wayshack, "6 Must-Have Tech Tools to Close More Sales," *Forbes*, http://www.forbes.com, accessed May 9, 2018; Forbes Technology Council, "10 Ways Sales Teams Can Use Technology," *Forbes*, http://www.forbes.com, accessed May 8, 2018; Barbara Weaver Smith, "Ten Tactics to Drive B2B Sales with Social Media," *Blog World*, http://www.blogworld.com, accessed May 9, 2018.

52 Nat Robinson, "SlideRocket Presentation Tip—4 Ways for Using Multimedia Strategically," *SlideRocket*, http://www.sliderocket.com, accessed May 9, 2018.

53 Sandeep Chandrasekhar, "The NFL: Bad Publicity Is Better Than No Publicity," *Sports Media Business,* http://www.sportsmediabusiness.com, accessed May 9, 2018; Harris Poll, "Harris Poll: NFL Remains King Among U.S. Adults, But Gap with Baseball Closer," *Sports Business Daily,* http://www.sportsbusinessdaily.com, accessed May 9, 2018; Ben Volin, "NFL Offseason Is off to a Bad Start," *Boston Globe,* http://www.bostonglobe.com, accessed May 9, 2018; Joe Giglio, "NFL Won't Allow Players with Domestic Violence, Sexual Assault Convictions at Combine or Draft," *NJ.com*, http://www.nj.com, accessed May 9, 2018.

54 Ira Boudway and Josh Eidelson, "NFL's New Cheerleader Scandal May Expose League to Legal Risk," *Bloomberg*, http://www.bloomberg.com, accessed May 9, 2018; Chris Yuscavage, "How Many Scandals Can the NFL Possibly Fit into 1 Season?" *Complex*, http://www.complex.com, accessed May 9, 2018.

55 Lisa Black, "Toy Creator Unwraps Story of Success," *Chicago Tribune*, http://articles.chicagotribune.com, accessed May 9, 2018.

56 Phil Rosenthal, "Peet's, Subway, Haagen-Dazs—Less Is More Isn't Always Easy to Digest," *Chicago Tribune,* http://www.chicagotribune.com, accessed May 9, 2018.

57 Brian Blackstone and Julie Jargon, "Starbucks Sells Nestlé the Rights to Offer Its Coffee in Stores," *The Wall Street Journal*, http://www.wsj.com, accessed May 9, 2018; Sejuti Banerjea, "Nestle-Starbucks Distribution Deal: Win-Win," *NASDAQ*, https://www.nasdaq.com, accessed May 9, 2018.

58 Company website, "Chris McMillan," http://www.chrismcmillanthesalon.com, accessed May 9, 2018; Merle Ginsberg, "This Is Where Reese Witherspoon and Beyoncé Get Their Hair Done," *Hollywood Reporter,* http://www.hollywoodreporter.com, accessed May 9, 2018.

Chapter 14

1 Company website, "Leadership Team," https://www.easysol.net, accessed May 22, 2018; Nancy Dahlberg, "Tech Company Easy Solutions Out to Stop Financial Fraudsters in Their Tracks," *Miami Herald*, http://www.miamiherald.com, accessed May 21, 2018; Kevin Granville, "9 Recent Cyberattacks Against Big Businesses," *The New York Times*, http://www.nytimes.com, accessed May 21, 2018; Gaurav Pendse, "Why the Cyber Security Industry Is Poised for Growth," *Pure Funds*, http://www.pureetfs.com, accessed May 22, 2018; Joe Philip, "Easy Solutions: Providing Effective Solutions for the Fraud of Today and Tomorrow," *CIO Review*, http://www.cioreview.com, accessed May 21, 2018; Kaja Whitehouse, "Regulator Warns of 'Armageddon' Cyber Attack on Banks," *USA Today*, http://www.usatoday.com, accessed May 22, 2018; Jessica Silver-Greenberg and Matthew Goldstein, "After JPMorgan Chase Breach, Push to Close Wall St. Security Gaps," *The New York Times*, http://www.nytimes.com, accessed May 21, 2018; company website, "Cybersecurity 500," http://cybersecurityventures.com, accessed May 21, 2018; Maria Korolov, "Banks Get Attacked Four Times More Than Other Industries," *CSO*, http://www.csoonline.com, accessed May 21, 2018.

2 Cornelius Baur and Dominik Wee, "Manufacturing's Next Act," https://www.mckinsey.com, accessed May 23, 2018; Company website, "50 Things Your Smart Phone Replaced [Or Will Replace in the Future]," http://www.geckoandfly.com, accessed May 22, 2018; company website, "Tech Trends 2018," https://www2.deloitte.com, accessed May 17, 2018; Gavyn Davies, "The Greatest Unknown—The Impact of Technology on the Economy," *Financial Times*, http://ft.com, accessed May 17, 2018; Amanda C. Kooser, "What Is Business Technology?" *Houston Chronicle*, http://smallbusiness.chron.com, accessed May 17, 2018; Cyril Paciullo, "Business and Technology: A Love-Hate Relationship," *Neowin*, http://www.neowin.net, accessed May 17, 2018; "How Is Technology Changing Business?" *The Wall Street Journal*, http://wsj.com, accessed May 17, 2018.

3 Company website, "Disruptive Innovation," http://www.claytonchristensen.com, accessed May 17, 2018; "What Disruptive Innovation Means," *The Economist*, http://www.economist.com, accessed May 17, 2018.

4 Scott Austin, Chris Canipe, and Sarah Slobin, "The Billion Dollar Startup Club," *The Wall Street Journal*, http://www.wsj.com, accessed May 22, 2018; company website, "The Unicorn List 2018," *Fortune*, http://fortune.com, accessed May 17, 2018; company website, Clayton M. Christensen, "Disruptive Innovation," http://www.claytonchristensen.com, accessed May 22, 2018; Michael E. Raynor and Rory McDonald, "What Is Disruptive Innovation?" *Harvard Business Review*, http://hbr.org, accessed May 17, 2018.

5 John Shinal, "The Ten Biggest US Tech Companies Will Top $1 Trillion in Sales This Year," *CNBC*, http://www.cnbc.com, accessed May 17, 2018; company website, "The Unicorn List 2018," *Fortune*, http://fortune.com, accessed May 17, 2018; Erin Griffith, "The Top Technology Companies of the Fortune 500," *Fortune*, http://fortune.com, accessed May 17, 2018.

6 Rob Preston, "The Top 10 Strategic CIO Priorities of 2018," *Forbes*, http://www.forbes.com, accessed May 18, 2018; Ernest Von Simpson, "The New Role of the CIO," *Bloomberg Business*, http://www.bloomberg.com, accessed May 17, 2018; David Moschella, Doug Neal, John Taylor, and Piet Opperman, "Consumerization of Information Technology," *Leading Edge Forum*, http://lef.csc.com, accessed May 17, 2018.

7 Yves Mulkers, "5 Companies Using Big Data to Disrupt Healthcare," *Medium*, https://medium.com, accessed May 18, 2018; Rachel Emma Silverman, "Bosses Tap Outside Firms to Predict Which Workers Might Get Sick," *The Wall Street Journal*, http://www.wsj.com, accessed May 17, 2018; Jonah Comstock, "Ginger.io Relaunches as Full-Stack Online Mental Healthcare Service," *Mobile Health News*, http://www.mobilehealthnews.com, accessed May 18, 2018.

8 Government website, "Quick Facts," http://quickfacts.census.gov, accessed May 17, 2018.

9 Museum website, "Timeline of Computer History," http://www.computerhistory.org, accessed May 17, 2018.

10 Tom Brant, "The Best Cheap Laptops of 2018," *PC Magazine*, http://www.pcmag.com, accessed May 17, 2018; company website, "Choose Your Macbook Pro," https://www.apple.com/shop/buy-mac/macbook-pro/15-inch, accessed May 17, 2018.

11 Jon Russell, "Apple Continues to Dominate the Tablet Market as Sales Decline Once Again," *TechCrunch*, http://www.techcrunch.com, accessed May 18, 2018.

12 Mike Elgan, "With Smartphones Like These, Why Do We Need Laptops?" *ComputerWorld*, http://www.computerworld.com, accessed May 18, 2018; company website, "Forecast for Global Shipments of Tablets, Laptops and Desktop PCs from 2010 to 2019 (in Million Units)," *Statista*, http://www.statista.com, accessed May 17, 2018.

13 Roger Cheng, "Notch Appeal? Smartphone Sales Set to Bounce Back This Year," *CNET*, www.cnet.com, accessed May 18, 2018; Dom Galeon, "AI Smartphones Will Soon Be Standard, Thanks to Machine Learning Chip," *Futurism*, http://www.futurism.com, accessed May 18, 2018; Mike Elgan, "With Smartphones Like These, Why Do We Need Laptops?" *ComputerWorld*, http://www.computerworld.com, accessed May 18, 2018.

14 David Pierce, "5 Wi-Fi Hotspot Finders to Find Free Wi-Fi Spots Near You," *Make Use of*, http://www.makeuseof.com, accessed May 17, 2018; Linda Poon, "Cities Want Super-Fast Wireless Internet, But on Their Terms," *City Lab*, http://www.citylab.com, accessed May 18, 2018.

15 Lisa Quast, "Why Knowledge Management Is Important to the Success of Your Company," *Forbes*, http://www.forbes.com, accessed May 17, 2018.

16 Company website, "So, Who Really Did Invent the Internet?" http://www.nethistory.info, accessed May 17, 2018; organization website, "Brief History of the Internet," http://www.internetsociety.org, accessed May 17, 2018.

17 Organization website, "Bylaws for Internet Corporation for Assigned Names and Numbers," https://www.icann.org, accessed May 17, 2018.

18 Company website, "What Is Sharepoint?" https://support.office.com, accessed May 19, 2018.

19 Louis Columbus, "Forrester's 10 Cloud Computing Predictions for 2018," *Forbes*, http://www.forbes.com, accessed May 19, 2018; Marty Puranik, "5 Cloud Computing Trends to Prepare for in 2018," *Network World*, http://www.networkworld.com, accessed May 19, 2018; James Bourne, "The State of the Cloud in 2018: *DevOps*, Docker Momentum Grows As Hybrid Hits Its Stride," *CloudTech*, http://www.cloudcomputing-news.net, accessed May 17, 2018.

20 Bob Evans, "The Top 5 Cloud-Computing Vendors: #1 Microsoft, #2 Amazon, #3 IBM, #4 Salesforce, #5 SAP," *Forbes*, http://www.forbes.com, accessed May 19, 2018; Eric Knorr, "2018: The Year We See the Real Cloud Leaders Emerge," *InfoWorld*, http://www.infoworld.com, accessed May 17, 2018.

21 Company website, "Definition of SaaS," *PC Magazine*, http://www.pcmag.com, accessed May 17, 2018; R. Kelly Rainer and Brad Prince, *Introduction to Information Systems*, 7th Edition (Hoboken, NJ: Wiley, 2018); company website, "Public Cloud," https://searchcloudcomputing.techtarget.com, accessed May 19, 2018.

22 Paul Laudicina, "This Is the Future of the Internet," *World Economic Forum*, http://www.weforum.com, accessed May 19, 2018; NCTA, "Here's What the Internet Will Look Like in 5, 10, and 15 Years," *Business Insider*, http://www.businessinsider.com, accessed May 17, 2018.

23 Taylor Armerding, "17 Biggest Data Breaches of the 21st Century," *CSO*, http://www.csoonline.com, accessed May 19, 2018.

24 Zusha Elinson and Shira Ovide, "Kill Switch Is No Dead Certainty to Stop Phone Theft," *The Wall Street Journal*, http://www.wsj.com, accessed May 17, 2018.

25 Charlie Osborne, "How Criminals Clear Your Stolen iPhone for Resale," *ZDNet*, http://www.zdnet.com, accessed May 19, 2018; CBS Local, "Despite Anti-Theft Features, Thieves Still Seek out iPhones," *CBS Local*, http://www.cbslocal.com, accessed May 19, 2018; Martyn Williams, "Smartphone Thefts Plummet After Kill-Switch Introduction," *PC World*, http://www.pcworld.com, accessed May 17, 2018; Zusha Elinson and Shira Ovide, "Kill Switch Is No Dead Certainty to Stop Phone Theft," *The Wall Street Journal*, http://www.wsj.com, accessed May 17, 2018.

26 A. Ellison, "The Effectiveness and Growth of Spear Phishing Attacks," *Accumen Innovations*, https://www.acumen-innovations.com, accessed May 17, 2018.

27 Company website, "About Us," http://www.magnoliahealthcorp.com, accessed May 17, 2018; Steve Ragan, "Multiple Organizations Report Phishing Attacks Targeting Employee Data," *CSO*, http://www.csoonline.com, accessed May 17, 2018.

28 Lisa Vaas, "IRS Reports 400% Increase in Phishing & Malware in the Past 12 Months," *Naked Security*, https://nakedsecurity.sophos.com, accessed May 17, 2018; Maria Korolov, "Phishing Is a $37 Million Annual Cost for Average Large Company," *CSO*, http://www.csoonline.com, accessed May 17, 2018.

29 Jonathan Matusitz, "Cyberterrorism," *American Foreign Policy Interests* 2:137–147, 2005.

30 Government website, "What Is a Denial-Of-Service Attack?" https://www.us-cert.gov, accessed May 23, 2018; Lily Hay Newman, "Github Survived the Biggest DDOS Attack Ever Recorded," *Wired*, http://www.wired.com, accessed May 19, 2018.

31 Jim Norman, "North Korea, Cyberterrorism Top Threats to U.S.," *Gallup*, http://www.gallup.com, accessed May 19, 2018; Bob Haring, "How Can an Organization Prevent Cyberterrorism?" *Houston Chronicle*, http://smallbusiness.chron.com, accessed May 17, 2018.

32 Dan Goodin, "Here's Why the Epidemic of Malicious Ads Grew So Much Worse Last Year," *Arstechnica*, https://arstechnica.com, accessed May 17, 2018; Charlie Osborne, "Brutal Cryptocurrency Mining Malware Crashes Your PC When Discovered," *ZDNet*, www.zdnet.com, accessed May 19, 2018.

33 Ericka Chickowski, "7 Ways Banking Botnets Are Keeping with the Times," *DarkREADING*, http://www.darkreading.com, accessed May 17, 2018.

34 Organization website, "Workplace Privacy and Employee Monitoring," https://www.privacyrights.org, accessed May 17, 2018; organization website, "Privacy in America: Electronic Monitoring," https://www.aclu.org, accessed May 17, 2018; R. Kelly Rainer and Brad Prince, *Introduction to Information Systems*, 7th Edition (Hoboken, NJ: Wiley, 2018).

35 Molly Montag, "Surveillance Cameras Raise Privacy Concerns," *Washington Times*, http://www.washingtontimes.com, accessed May 17, 2018; R. Kelly Rainer and Brad Prince, *Introduction to Information Systems*, 7th Edition (Hoboken, NJ: Wiley, 2018).

36 Alvin Chang, "The Facebook and Cambridge Analytica Scandal, Explained with a Simple Diagram," *Vox*, http://www.vox.com, accessed May 19, 2018; John Brodkin, "Verizon Accused of Violating Net Neutrality Rules by Throttling Video," *Ars Technica*, https://arstechnica.com, accessed May 22, 2018.

37 Company website, http://www.falconstor.com, accessed May 21, 2018.

38 Paul Daugherty, Marc Carrel-Billiard, and Michael Biltz, "Intelligent Enterprise Unleashed: Five Technology Trends Shaping the Future of Business," *Accenture*, https://www.accenture.com, accessed May 22, 2018; Kasey Panetta, "Gartner Top 10 Strategic Technology Trends for 2018," http://www.cio.com, accessed May 22, 2018.

39 Anthony Abbatiello, Tim Boehm, Jeff Schwartz, and Sharon Chand, "No-Collar Workforce: Humans and Machines in One Loop—Collaborating in Roles and New Talent Models," *Tech Trends 2018*, https://www2.deloitte.com, accessed May 22, 2018.

40 Paul Helzel, "12 Technologies That Will Disrupt Business in 2018," *CIO*, www.cio.com, accessed May 22, 2018; Bernard Marr, "Google's

Nest: Big Data and the Internet of Things in the Connected Home," *Forbes*, http://www.forbes.com, accessed May 17, 2018.

41 Company website, "Tech Trends 2018," https://www2.deloitte.com, accessed May 17, 2018.

Chapter 15

1 Zack Friedman, "Deloitte CEO Cathy Engelbert: Lessons on Leadership," *Forbes*, http://www.forbes.com, accessed May 24, 2018; Vicky Valet, "'Your Career Is Not Linear': "Deloitte CEO Cathy Engelbert on Her Rise to the Top," *Forbes*, http://www.forbes.com, accessed May 24, 2018; Belinda Luscombe, "How Deloitte CEO Cathy Engelbert Rose to the Top," *TIME*, http://www.time.com, accessed May 24, 2018; company website, "Meet Cathy Engelbert, Chief Executive Officer, Deloitte LLP," http://www2.deloitte.com, accessed May 23, 2018; Paul Vigna, "Deloitte CEO Engelbert Sees 'Great Opportunity to Step Up,'" *The Wall Street Journal*, http://www.wsj.com, accessed May 23, 2018; "Fortune's Most Powerful Women in Business," *Fortune*, http://fortune.com, accessed May 23, 2018.

2 Government website, "Accountants and Auditors," *Occupational Outlook Handbook,* 2017–18 Edition, http://www.bls.gov, accessed May 23, 2018.

3 Cheri O'Neil, "Accounting Salaries, Job Opportunities Projected to Keep Growing," *Robert Half International*, https://www.roberthalf.com, accessed May 23, 2018; Donna Fuscaldo, "Positive Career Outlook for Tech and Business Grads, According to NACE," *Education News*, http://www.goodcall.com, accessed May 23, 2018; Cheri O'Neil, "The Rise of the Accounting Salary and 10 Top Accounting Jobs," Robert Half International, https://www.roberthalf.com, accessed May 24, 2018.

4 Organization website, "AARP Foundation Tax-Aide," http://www.aarp.org, accessed May 23, 2018; Chinweike, "Duties, Roles, and Responsibilities of an Accountant in Modern Society," *Accountant Next Door,* http://www.accountantnextdoor.com, accessed May 23, 2018.

5 Company website, "Revenue of the Big Four Accounting/Audit Firms Worldwide in 2018 (in Billion U.S. Dollars)," *Statista*, https://www.statista.com, accessed May 23, 2018; company website, "The Top Accounting Firms of the World's Biggest Corporations," *Motley Fool*, http://fool.com, accessed May 23, 2018; Sarah Butcher, "Working for PWC, Deloitte, EY and KPMG. What's the Difference?" *efinancial Careers*, http://news.efinancialcareers.com, accessed May 23, 2018; Lee Frederiksen, "The Top 5 Business Challenges for Accounting & Financial Services Firms," *Hinge*, http://www.hinge.com, accessed May 25, 2018.

6 Lee Frederiksen, "The Top 5 Business Challenges for Accounting & Financial Services Firms," *Hinge*, http://www.hinge.com, accessed May 25, 2018; "New Survey Reveals Top Concerns for Accountants in 2018," *Accounting Web*, http://accountingweb.com, accessed May 23, 2018.

7 Russ Banham, "Cybersecurity: A New Engagement Opportunity," *Journal of Accountancy*, https://www.journalofaccountancy.com, accessed May 28, 2018; Nicholas Sinclair, "Big Four Accounting Firms Risk Conflict of Interest," *The Outsourced Accountant*, http://theoutsourcedaccountant.com, accessed May 25, 2018; Neil Amato, "Recruiting Remains a Challenge for Finance Decision Makers," *Journal of Accountancy,* https://www.journalofaccountancy.com, accessed May 28, 2018; Courtney Vien, "Hiring at Public Accounting Firms Hits All-Time High," *Journal of Accountancy,* https://www.journalofaccountancy.com, accessed May 28, 2018; Harriet Agnew, "Professional Services: Accounting for Change," *Financial Times,* http://ft.com, accessed May 23, 2018; Kadhim Shubber, "PwC Tops Deloitte to Lead Big Four Auditors," *Financial Times*, http://ft.com, accessed May 23, 2018.

8 Organization website, "Government Accountant," http://www.acfe.com, accessed March 2, 2018; organization website, "What Does a Government Accountant Do?" http://www.topaccountingdegrees.org, accessed May 23, 2018.

9 Organization website, http://www.fasb.org, accessed May 23, 2018.

10 Organization website, "Accounting Standards Updated Issued," http://fasb.org, accessed May 25, 2018; Ezequiel Minaya, "Dish Network Profit Boosted By New Accounting Rules," *Wall Street Journal,* http://www.wsj.com, accessed May 25, 2018.

11 Company website, "Johnson & Johnson Annual Report 2017: Consolidated Balance Sheets," http://www.investor.jnj.com, accessed May 23, 2018; company website, "The Mobile Tax and Accounting Office of the Future," https://cs.thomsonreuters.com, accessed May 23, 2018.

12 Company website, "H&R Block with IBM Watson Reinventing Tax Preparation," http://www.hrblock.com, accessed May 28, 2018; Matt Jagst, "Mobile Computing Takes Accountants to a New Level of Productivity," *Accounting Web,* http://www.accounting web.com, accessed May 23, 2018.

13 Company website, "Back in the Day," http://mint.com, accessed May 23, 2018; Willy Staley, "Which Are the Best Personal Financial Management (PFM) Tools?" *MyBankTracker.com,* http://www.mybanktracker.com, accessed May 23, 2018.

14 Company website, "McDonald's Reports First Quarter 2018 Results," http://www.mcdonalds.com, accessed May 26, 2018; Associated Press, "Why a Stronger Dollar Hurts Corporate Earnings," CBSNews, www.cbsnews.com, accessed May 28, 2018; Nicholas Rossolillo, "How a Strong Dollar Hurts McDonald's," http://www.fool.com, *Motley Fool*.

15 Jason Bramwell, "Fitch: IFRS Adoption in the US Unlikely," *Accounting Web*, http://www.accountingweb.com, accessed May 23, 2018; Tatyana Shumsky, "SEC Nods to Multinationals," *The Wall Street Journal*, http://www.wsj.com, accessed May 23, 2018; Caleb Newquist, "Accounting News Roundup: Valeant's Probably Restating; SEC Warming Up to IFRS," *Going Concern*, http://goingconcern.com, accessed May 23, 2018.

16 Rosemary Peavler, "IFRS and FASB—What Are Financial Reporting Standards?" *The Balance*, http://thebalancesb.com, accessed May 26, 2018; "What Are the Differences Between IFRS and U.S. GAAP for Revenue Recognition?" *Motley Fool,* http://fool.com, accessed May 23, 2018.

Chapter 16

1 Company website, "Quicken Loans Ranked Highest in the Nation for Client Satisfaction Among Mortgage Servicers by J. D. Power for 4th Consecutive Year," http://www.quickenloans.com, accessed May 29, 2018; Candace Williams, "Quicken Loans Becomes the Nation's Largest U.S. Mortgage Lender," *Detroit News*, http://www.detroitnews.com, accessed May 29, 2018; PR Newswire, "Quicken Loans Partners with Grand Circus, CSforALL to Train 5,000 Detroit Students the Basics of Computer Coding," *PR Newswire*, http://www.prnewswire.com, accessed May 29, 2018; company website, "About Us," http://www.quickenloans.com, accessed May 29, 2018; Jody Shenn and Laura J. Keller, "The Owner of the Cleveland Cavaliers Gets a $1 Billion Payday from Cheap Bonds," *Bloomberg Business*, http://www.bloomberg.com, accessed May 28, 2018; Joe Light, "New Mortgage Rules May Spark Delays, Frustration," *The Wall Street Journal*, http://www.wsj.com, accessed May 28, 2018; Daniel Kurt, "Mortgage Choice: Quicken Loans Vs. Your Local Bank," *Investopedia*, http://www.investopedia.com, accessed May 28, 2018.

2 Joseph Lisanti, "When It Comes to Dividends, Warren Buffett Believes It's Better to Receive Than Give," *Financial Planning BIC*, http://bic.

financial-planning.com, accessed May 29, 2018; Rupert Hargreaves, "Why Berkshire Hathaway Won't Pay a Dividend," *NASDAQ*, http://www.nasdaq.com, accessed June 3, 2018.

[3] Owen Thomas, "The Complete Timeline of Zynga's Disastrous 2012," *Business Insider*, http://www.businessinsider.com, accessed May 29, 2018.

[4] Matthew Wirz, "CVS Bets Big With $40 Billion Bond Sale," *The Wall Street Journal*, http://www.wsj.com, accessed May 30, 2018.

[5] Theodore Schleifer, "There Have Been Twice as Many Tech IPOs in 2018 as There Were at This Point in 2017," *Recode*, http://www.recode.com, accessed May 30, 2018.

[6] Company website, "What Is an Investment Banker?" *Investopedia*, http://www.investopedia.com, accessed May 28, 2018.

[7] Company website, "Daily NYSE Group Volume in NYSE Listed, 2017," http://www.nyxdata.com, accessed May 28, 2018.

[8] Company website, "Listing Requirements," http://www.investopedia.com, accessed May 28, 2018.

[9] Organization website, "Rule 300. Trading Licenses," http://rules.nyse.com, accessed May 28, 2018.

[10] Company website, "Electronic Trading: The Exchanges," *Investopedia*, http://www.investopedia.com, accessed May 30, 2018; Michael Hiltzik, "End of an Era: The NYSE Floor Isn't Even Good for PR Photos," *Los Angeles Times*, www.latimes.com, accessed May 28, 2018; Bob Pisani, "Here's What's Really Surprising About Today's Shutdown of the NYSE Floor," *CNBC*, http://www.cnbc.com, accessed May 28, 2018.

[11] Government website, "Electronic Communication Network," http://www.sec.gov, accessed May 30, 2018.

[12] Company website, "About," https://robinhood.com, accessed May 28, 2018; Halah Touryalai, "Forget $10 Trades, Meet Robinhood: New Brokerage Targets Millennials with Little Cash," *Forbes*, http://www.forbes.com, accessed May 28, 2018.

[13] Government website, "Commercial Banks in the U.S." and "Total Assets, All Commercial Banks," http://research.stlouisfed.org, accessed May 28, 2018.

[14] Government website, "Large Commercial Banks," http://www.federalreserve.gov, accessed May 31, 2018; Ben Walsh, "Expect More Mergers After Dodd-Frank Rollback," *Barrons*, http://www.barrons.com, accessed May 30, 2018; Theresa Rivas, "More Bank Mergers are on the Way . . . Finally," *Barrons*, http://www.barrons.com, accessed May 30, 2018; Newswire, "Bank M&A Transactions Remain Brisk in First Quarter of 2018 According to New Research from Integrated Legacy Solutions," *Newswire*, http://www.businesswire.com, accessed May 30, 2018.

[15] Government website, "Loans and Leases in Bank Credit, All Commercial Banks," http://research.stlouisfed.org, accessed May 28, 2018; government website, "FDIC—Statistics on Depository Institutions Report as of March 31, 2018," http://www5.fdic.gov, accessed May 28, 2018.

[16] René Lacerte, "Is 2017 the Year Bank-Fintech Partnerships Hit Product/Market Fit?" *Forbes*, http://www.forbes.com, accessed May 31, 2018; educational website, "Banks and FinTech: Adversaries or Partners?" http://knowledge.wharton.upenn.edu, accessed May 31, 2018; company website, "What Is FinTech?" *Investopedia*, http://www.investopedia.com, accessed May 28, 2018; Sebastian Meyen, "APIs in Banking Are the Key to the Future—The FinTech Way," *JAXenter*, https://jaxenter.com, accessed May 28, 2018; Jim Neckopulos, "Fintechs: Friends or Foes?" *CB Insight*, http://www.cbinsight.com, accessed May 28, 2018.

[17] "ABA Survey: Two-Thirds of Americans Use Digital Banking Channels Most Often," *ABA Banking Journal*, http://bankingjournal.aba.com, accessed May 31, 2018; "Best Online Bank: Ally," *TIME*, http://time.com, accessed May 28, 2018.

[18] Government website, "Safe Internet Banking," http://www.fdic.gov, accessed May 28, 2018.

[19] Association website, "Industry at a Glance December 31, 2017," http://www.ncua.gov, accessed May 28, 2018; company website, "Credit Union Trends Report," http://www.cunamutual.com, accessed May 28, 2018; government website, "Fed Survey: Mobile Banking a 'Standard' Service for Consumers," http://www.nafcu.org, accessed May 31, 2018.

[20] Government website, "Z.1 Financial Accounts of the United States," http://www.federalreserve.gov, accessed May 28, 2018.

[21] Company website, "U.S. Pension Fund Assets Remain Stable," http://www.willistowerswatson.com, accessed May 28, 2018; company website, "Apple, Inc. Institutional Ownership," http://www.nasdaq.com, accessed May 28, 2018.

[22] Keith Thune, "7 of the Best Mutual Funds to Buy," *Investor Place*, accessed May 31, 2018, http://www.investorplace.com; organization website, "2018 Investment Company Factbook," http://www.ici.org, accessed May 28, 2018; "The 25 Largest Mutual Funds," *MarketWatch*, http://www.marketwatch.com, accessed May 28, 2018.

[23] Desiree Stennett, "This Is Why the Average American Still Uses a Shocking 38 Checks a Year," *The Penny Hoarder*, http://www.pennyhoarder.com, accessed June 2, 2018; Katie Robertson, "Why Can't Americans Give Up Paper Checks?" *Bloomberg*, http://www.bloomberg.com, accessed May 31, 2018.

[24] "Three Top Economists Agree 2009 Worst Financial Crisis Since Great Depression; Risks Increase If Right Steps Are Not Taken," *Reuters*, http://www.businesswire.com, accessed May 28, 2018.

[25] Government website, "TARP Programs," http://www.treasury.gov, accessed May 28, 2018.

[26] Government website, "Senate Financial Crisis Report: Wall Street and the Financial Crisis: Anatomy of a Collapse," http://www.hsgac.senate.gov, accessed May 28, 2018.

[27] "Crash Course," *The Economist*, http://www.economist.com, accessed May 28, 2018.

[28] "Crash Course," *The Economist*, http://www.economist.com, accessed May 28, 2018; government website, "The Recovery Act," http://www.whitehouse.gov, accessed May 28, 2018.

[29] John Maxfield, "Crash Course" and "25 Major Factors That Caused or Contributed to the Financial Crisis," *Motley Fool*, http://www.fool.com, accessed May 28, 2018.

[30] Damian Paletta and Aaron Lucchetti, "Senate Passes Sweeping Finance Overhaul," *The Wall Street Journal*, http://www.wsj.com, accessed May 28, 2018; Jeff Cox, "Misbehaving Banks Have Now Paid $204B in Fines," *CNBC*, http://www.cnbc.com, accessed May 28, 2018.

[31] Government website, "Financial Regulatory Reform," https://www.treasury.gov, accessed May 28, 2018; company website, "How Does Dodd-Frank Affect Hedge Funds?" http://www.investmentlawgroup.com, accessed May 28, 2018; educational website, "Dodd-Frank Principles and Provisions," https://corpgov.law.harvard.edu, accessed May 28, 2018; company website, "Too Big to Fail," and "Dodd-Frank Wall Street Reform and Consumer Protection Act," *Investopedia*, http://www.investopedia.com, accessed May 28, 2018.

[32] Richard M. Alexander, Christopher L. Allen, Robert C. Azarow, Christopher J. Dodd, A. Patrick Doyle, David F. Freeman, Jr., Paul A. Howard, Howard L. Hyde, L. Charles Landgraf, Michael A. Mancusi, Brian C. McCormally, Henry G. Morriello, and Kevin M. Toomey, "Senate Passes Bill Modifying the Dodd-Frank Act and Providing Other Regulatory Relief; House Action Next," *Arnold and Porter*, http://www.arnoldporter.com, accessed May 31, 2018.

[33] "Bank Ratings—Top Banks in the World," *Accuity*, http://www.accuity.com, accessed May 28, 2018.

Chapter 17

[1] Tracey Lien, "How I Made It: Jess Lee's Unlikely Path to Running Polyvore," *Los Angeles Times,* http://latimes.com, accessed June 7, 2018; Daniel Roberts, "How Polyvore CEO Jess Lee Got Started," *Fortune*, http://fortune.com, accessed June 7, 2018; Claire Zillman, "Top Women Investors Are Answering the VC Boys' Club With One of Their Own," *Fortune*, http://fortune.com, accessed June 7, 2018; Ryan Tate, "How One Startup Found Success by Making an Obsessive User Its CEO," *Wired*, https://www.wired.com/accessed, June 7, 2018; company website, "People," https://www.sequoiacap.com/people/jess-lee, accessed June 7, 2018; Jonathan Shieber, "Some of the Top Female Founders in the U.S. Are Backing the Latest Female Founders Fund," *TechCrunch*, https://techcrunch.com, accessed June 7, 2018; Zoe Bernard, "30 Women in Venture Capital to Watch in 2018," *Business Insider*, http://www.businessinsider.com, accessed June 6, 2018; company website, "We Help the Daring Build Legendary Companies," http://sequoiacap.com, accessed June 7, 2018; Alex Konrad and Biz Carson, "The 36 Women Secretly Breaking Up Silicon Valley's Old Boys' Club," *Forbes*, http://forbes.com, accessed June 7, 2018.

[2] Alix Stuart, "Should CFOs Serve on Their Own Boards?" *CFO*, http://ww2.cfo.com, accessed June 3, 2018.

[3] Company website, "Costco Wholesale Corp (COST.O)," http://www.reuters.com, accessed June 3, 2018; Maxwell Murphy, "A Waste of a Board Seat?" *Wall Street Journal*, http://www.wsj.com, accessed June 3, 2018.

[4] Julia Cooper, "50 Highest-Paid CFOs in the Bay Area," *San Francisco Business Times,* https://www.bizjournals.com, accessed June 5, 2018; company website, "What's the Average Salary of a Chief Financial Officer (CFO)?" https://www.investopedia.com, accessed June 5, 2018.

[5] Larry Alton, "5 Iconic Entrepreneurs and Their Business Gambles That Paid Off," *Entrepreneur*, http://www.entrepreneur.com, accessed June 3, 2018; company website, "Tesla Motors, Inc.," http://finance.yahoo.com, accessed June 5, 2018.

[6] Bertil E. Chappuis, Aimee Kim, and Paul J. Roche, "Starting Up as CFO," *McKinsey and Company*, http://www.mckinsey.com, accessed June 5, 2018; Greg Dickinson, "Technology and Talent Are Among CFOs' Top Concerns: CFO Signals," *The Wall Street Journal*, http://deloitte.wsj.com, accessed June 5, 2018.

[7] Company website, "DowDuPont Reports Fourth Quarter and Full Year 2017 Results," http://www.dow-dupont.com, accessed June 3, 2018; company website, "Financial Reports," http://phx.corporate-ir.net, accessed June 3, 2018.

[8] Editorial Team, "How Netflix Uses Big Data to Drive Success," *Inside Big Data*, http://insidebigdata.com, accessed June 5, 2018; John Markman, "Amazon Using AI, Big Data to Accelerate Profits," *Forbes*, http://forbes.com, accessed June 5, 2018; Jennifer Wills, "7 Ways Amazon Uses Big Data to Stalk You (AMZN)," *Investopedia*, http://investopedia.com, accessed June 5, 2018; Larry Maisel, "Five Keys for Financial Planning & Analysis When Applying Predictive Analytics," *CFO Innovation,* http://www.cfoinnovation.com, accessed June 5, 2018; Sarah Morris, "CFO Tips to Improve Financial Planning and Analysis," *Smarter with Gartner*, http://www.gartner.com, accessed June 5, 2018.

[9] Anaele Pelisson and Graham Rapier, "CHART: The 17 US Companies with the Biggest Piles of Cash," *Business Insider*, http://businessinsider.com, accessed June 3, 2018.

[10] Company website, "Financial Reports," http://phx.corporate-ir.net, accessed June 3, 2018; company website, "Caterpillar Reports 2017 Fourth-Quarter and Full-Year Financial Results; Provides Outlook for 2018," http://www.caterpillar.com, accessed June 3, 2018.

[11] Evelyn Chang, "Technology Companies Are Driving a Capital Spending Surge," *CNBC*, http://cnbc.com, accessed June 5, 2018.

[12] Elisabeth Behrmann, "BMW Tempers Growth Forecast as Spending Remains High," *Bloomberg Business*, http://www.bloomberg.com, accessed June 3, 2018; Trevor Anderson, "SC Expects BMW Expansion to Create More Supplier Jobs," *The State,* http://www.thestate.com, accessed June 3, 2018; Chris Isidore, "South Carolina Plant to Become BMW's Largest," *CNN Money*, http://money.cnn.com, accessed June 3, 2018; Saskia Essbauer, "Success Story: BMW Group Plant Spartanburg in the US Becomes Largest Production Location Within 25 Years," *BMW Group*, http://www.press.bmwgroup.com, accessed June 5, 2018.

[13] Company website, "U.S. Dollar per 1 British Pound Graph," http://www.x-rates.com, accessed June 3, 2018.

[14] Company website, "Ford Debt to Equity Ratio" and "Cheesecake Factory Debt to Equity Ratio," http://ycharts.com, accessed June 3, 2018.

[15] Government website, "Federal Reserve Board, Commercial Paper Rates and Outstanding Summary," http://www.federalreserve.gov, accessed June 3, 2018.

[16] Josh Beckerman, "Nordstrom Declares Special Dividend, Completes Sale of Credit-Card Business," *The Wall Street Journal*, http://www.wsj.com, accessed June 3, 2018.

[17] Company website, "3M Company Dividend Date & History," http://www.nasdaq.com, accessed June 3, 2018; Dave Segal, "Hawaiian Airlines' Parent to Offer First-Ever Dividend," *Star Advertiser*, http://www.staradvertiser.com, accessed June 5, 2018; Hibah Yousuf, "Starbucks to Start Pouring Dividends," *CNNMoney*, http://money.cnn.com, accessed June 5, 2018.

[18] Gregory DL Morris, "Trade Credit Insurance Blossoms at Last in the U.S.," *Risk and Insurance*, http://riskandinsurance.com, accessed June 5, 2018.

[19] Government website, "Commercial Paper Rates and Outstanding Summary," http://www.federalreserve.gov, accessed June 3, 2018.

[20] Kate Trafecante, "Why Investors are Stressed About the Bond Market," *CNNMoneyInvest*, http://cnnmoney.com, accessed June 5, 2018.

[21] Organization website, "Private Placements, Explained," http://www.finra.org, accessed June 5, 2018.

[22] Company website, "About," http://ycombinator.com, accessed June 7, 2018; company website, "The New Deal," https://blog.ycombinator.com, accessed June 7, 2018; Seung Lee, "Venture Capital Investing Hits $84 Billion, Highest Since Dot-Com Boom," *Mercury News*, https://www.mercurynews.com, accessed June 7, 2018.

[23] Company website, "The Kraft Heinz Company Announces Successful Completion of the Merger Between Kraft Foods Group and H.J. Heinz Holding Corporation," http://news.heinz.com, accessed June 3, 2018.

[24] Richard Milne, "Norway's Oil Fund Tops $1tn in Assets for First Time," *Financial Times*, http://ft.com, accessed June 5, 2018; government website, "The Fund," http://www.nbim.no, accessed June 3, 2018.

[25] Kelly Bit, "Hedge Funds Trail Stocks for 5th Year with a 7.4% Return," *Bloomberg News,* http://www.bloomberg.com, accessed June 3, 2018.

[26] Company website, "What We Do," https://www.bridgewater.com, accessed June 8, 2018; Lindsay Fortado, "Hedge Funds Produce Best Returns in 4 Years," *Financial Times,* http://ft.com, accessed June 6, 2018; Michael Selby-Green, "Ranked: The 10-Biggest Hedge Funds in the US," *Business Insider*, http://businessinsider.com, accessed June 6, 2018; Michael Fischer, "6 Hedge Fund Trends to Watch in 2018," *ThinkAdvisor*, http://thinkadvisor.com, accessed June 6, 2018.

[27] Company website, "The State of the Deal: M&A Trends 2018," https://www2.deloitte.com, accessed June 6, 2018.

[28] Rory Maher, "Disney to Acquire Marvel in $4 Billion Deal," *Business Insider*, http://www.businessinsider.com, accessed March 28, 2018.

[29] Abha Bhattarai, "How Can They Walk Away with Millions and Leave Workers with Zero? Toys R Us Workers Say They Deserve Severance," *Washington Post*, http://washingtonpost.com, accessed June 6, 2018.

[30] Maria Armental, "MLB Buys Rawlings from Newell Brands for $395 Million," *The Wall Street Journal*, http://wsj.com, accessed June 6, 2018; company website, "About," https://www.newellbrands.com/our-company, accessed June 6, 2018.

[31] Angelica LaVito, "Henry Schein to Spin Off, Merge Its Animal Health Business with Start-up," *CNBC*, http://www.cnbc.com, accessed June 6, 2018.

[32] Ravi Vij, "How Procter & Gamble Makes Money? Understanding P&G Business Strategy," *Revenues & Profits,* http://revenuesandprofits.com, accessed June 3, 2018; company website, "P&G Expects Brand Consolidation to Be Over by Summer," http://www.trefis.com, accessed June 3, 2018.

Chapter 18

[1] Company website, "Big News: Threadless and Bucketfeet Are Fusing Forces!" http://threadless.com, accessed July 16, 2018; Tracey E. Roby, "What Happened to the Internet's Favorite T-Shirt Company?" *Racked*, http://racked.com, accessed July 12, 2018; Viskan Veerasamy, "10 Successful E-Commerce Founders, 21 Great Interviews, A Whole Lotta Wisdom," *Referral Candy*, http://www.referralcandy.com, accessed July 12, 2018; Oliver Lindberg, "The Secrets Behind Threadless' Success," *TechRadar*, http://www.techradar.com, accessed July 12, 2018; company website, "Participate" and "Top 20 of all Time," https://www.threadless.com, accessed July 12, 2018; Andy Hur, "The Accidental Business: Threadless, 10 Years Later," *Fast Company*, http://www.fastcompany.com, accessed July 12, 2018.

[2] "Top 20 Countries with the Highest Number of Internet Users," *Internet World Stats*, https://www.internetworldstats.com, accessed July 12, 2018.

[3] U.S. Census Bureau, "E-Stats," www.census.gov, accessed July 12, 2018, Stefany Zaroban, "U.S. E-Commerce Sales Grow 16.0% in 2017," *Internet Retailer,* https://www.digitalcommerce360.com, accessed July 12, 2018.

[4] Government website, "Estimated Quarterly U.S. Retail E-Commerce Sales as a Percent of Total Quarterly Retail Sales: 1st Quarter 2008 – 1st Quarter 2018," https://www.census.gov, accessed July 12, 2018.

[5] Stefany Zaroban, "U.S. E-Commerce Sales Grow 16.0% in 2017," *Internet Retailer,* https://www.digitalcommerce360.com, accessed July 12, 2018

[6] Company website, http://www.kasasa.com, accessed July 12, 2018.

[7] Company website, http://www262.americanexpress.com, accessed July 12, 2018; organization website, "About Us," http://www.teachforamerica.org, accessed July 12, 2018.

[8] Company website, http://www.vrbo.com, accessed July 12, 2018.

[9] Company website, "FAQ," http://www.udemy.com, accessed July 12, 2018.

[10] Company website, http://www.qvc.com, accessed July 12, 2018.

[11] Company website, "Choose Your Quickbooks Online Plan," http://search2.quickbooksonline.com, accessed July 12, 2018.

[12] Aaron Smith, "U.S. Smart Phone Use," *Pew Research Center,* http://www.pewinternet.org, accessed July 12, 2018.

[13] Company website, "E-Commerce Industry Outlook," http://www.criteo.com, accessed July 12, 2018. Lisa Lacy, "Mobile Shopping Is on the Rise, But Remains Split Between the Mobile Web and Apps," *AdWeek*, http://www.adweek.com, accessed July 13, 2018.

[14] Company website, http://www.cannondale.com, accessed July 12, 2018.

[15] Company website, http://www.overstock.com, accessed July 12, 2018.

[16] Aaron Orendorff, "Global E-Commerce: Statistics and International Growth Trends [Infographic]," *Shopify*, https://www.shopify.com, accessed July 13, 2018; U.S. Census Bureau, "E-Stats," http://www.census.gov, accessed July 12, 2018; Marcia Kaplan, "B2B Ecommerce Growing; Becoming More Like B2C," http://practicalecommerce.com, accessed July 12, 2018.

[17] Company website, http://www.aetna.com, accessed July 12, 2018.

[18] Company website, https://www.c2exchange.com, accessed July 13, 2018.

[19] Janko Roettgers, "Buzzfeed's CEO, Jonah Peretti: Paywalls are Bad for Democracy," *Variety*, http://variety.com, accessed July 13, 2018; company website, "US E-Commerce Sales as Percent of Retail Sales Chart," http://ycharts.com, accessed July 12, 2018; "US Retail Sales Forecast to Grow by 3.1% This Year," *Marketing Charts*, http://www.marketingcharts.com, accessed July 12, 2018; company website, "e-retailers," *Internet Retailer*, http://internetretailer.com, accessed July 12, 2018; Stefany Zaroban, "U.S. E-Commerce Grows 14.6% in 2015," *Internet Retailer*, http://internetretailer.com, accessed July 12, 2018.

[20] Gerry Smith and Edmund Lee, "The Fading Newspaper," *Bloomberg QuickTake,* http://bloombergview.com, July 13, 2018.

[21] Robert Locascio, "Interfaces of the Future: The Importance of Conversational Commerce," Forbes, http://forbes.com, accessed July 13, 2018; Craig Miller, "The 3 Big Trends Shaping Online Commerce," *Forbes*, http://forbes.com, accessed July 13, 2018; Erica Perry, "Snapchat Is Focusing More On E-Commerce, Likely Through Its Discover Channels," *Social Media Week,* http://socialmediaweek.org, accessed July 13, 2018; Leonie Roderick, "Why Snapchat Is Moving into Ecommerce," *Marketing Week*, http://marketingweek.com, accessed July 13, 2018.

[22] Tim Merel, "Six Drivers Of The $700B Mobile Internet," *TechCrunch*, http://techcrunch.com, accessed July 14, 2018.

[23] Nabeena Mali, "Your M-Commerce Deep Dive: Data, Trends and What's Next in the Mobile Retail Revenue World," *BigCommerce*, https://www.bigcommerce.com, accessed July 14, 2018; Lisa Lacy, "Mobile Shopping Is on the Rise, But Remains Split Between the Mobile Web and Apps," *AdWeek*, http://adweek.com, accessed July 14, 2018; Dyfed Loesche, "Mobile E-Commerce Is Up and Poised for Future Growth," *Statista*, http://statista.com, accessed July 14, 2018.

[24] Cy Khormaee, "2017 Mobile Commerce Insights to Improve Your Mobile Checkout Experience," *Moovweb*, https://www.moovweb.com, accessed July 14, 2018.

[25] Cooper Smith, "The Surprising Facts About Who Shops Online and on Mobile," *BusinessInsider*, http://businessinsider.com, accessed July 13, 2018.

[26] Cooper Smith, "The Surprising Facts About Who Shops Online and on Mobile," *BusinessInsider*, http://businessinsider.com, accessed July 14, 2018.

[27] Cooper Smith, "Gen X and Baby Boomers Present a Huge Opportunity for Online Retailers," *BusinessInsider*, http://www.businessinsider.com, accessed July 14, 2018.

[28] Richie Edquid, "10 of the Largest E-Commerce Markets in the World by Country," *Business.com*, http://www.business.com, accessed July 14, 2018.

[29] Inge Keizer, "The Top 8 E-Commerce Challenges of 2018," http://www.linkedin.com, accessed July 14, 2018.

[30] Company website, http://www.verisign.com, accessed July 12, 2018.

[31] Company website, http://www.paypal.com, accessed July 18, 2018.

[32] Company website, "Build Your Business with a Free Online Store," and "Payments, Receipts, and Refunds," http://squareup.com, accessed July 14, 2018.

[33] Patrick Howell O'Neill, "Adidas Warns U.S. Customers of New Data Breach," cyberscoop.com, http://www.cyberscoop.com, accessed July 14, 2018.

[34] Company website, "Oracle Security Governor," http://www.oracle.com, accessed July 14, 2018.

[35] Ric Romero, "Craigslist Illegal Drug Trade Exposed," *ABC News,* http://abclocal.go.com, accessed July 14, 2018.

[36] Organization website, "About," http://www.ic3.gov, accessed July 12, 2018.

[37] "By the Numbers: 25 Amazing WordPress Statistics," http://expandedramblings.com, accessed July 14, 2018; Owen Williams, "The 18 Best Blogging Sites and Publishing Platforms on the Internet Today," *NextWeb*, http://thenextweb.com, accessed July 14, 2018; company website, "Bloggers," http://www.modcloth.com, accessed July 14, 2018; company website, "Planet Honda," http://www.planethonda.com, accessed July 14, 2018.

[38] Megan McArdle, "Goodbye to the Dish and Blogging, Too," *Bloomberg View,* http://www.bloombergview.com, accessed July 14, 2018; Michael Stelzner, "Is Blogging Dead? Building Your Content Home on Rented Land," *Social Media Examiner,* http://www.socialmediaexaminer.com, accessed July 14, 2018; Virginia Heffernan, "The Old Internet Neighborhoods," *New York Times,* http://nytimes.com, accessed July 14, 2018.

[39] Sean Keane, "Facebook Lets You 'Try On' Clothes and Makeup with AR Ads," *Cnet*, http://cnet.com, accessed July 14, 2018; Scott Bagguley, "What Is Video Advertising? 4 Video Ad Examples," *ExactDrive*, http://www.exactdrive.com, accessed July 14, 2018.

[40] Danielle Gibson, "Shaping the Future of Native Advertising, *The Drum*, http://thedrum.com, accessed July 14, 2018.

[41] Nancy Rothman, "Every Digital Assistant You Need to Know & Understand," *Search Engine Journal,* http://www.searchenginejournal.com, accessed July 16, 2018.

[42] Cristof Baron, "Number of Facebook Users by Age in the U.S. As of January 2018 (in Millions)," *Statista*, http://statista.com, accessed July 14, 2018; "Number of Monthly Active Facebook Users Worldwide As of 1st Quarter 2018 (in Millions)," *Statista*, http://statista.com, accessed July 14, 2018.

[43] Kevin Murnane, "Which Social Media Platform Is The Most Popular In The US?," *Forbes*, http://forbes.com, accessed July 14, 2018; Anthony Maina, "20 Popular Social Media Sites Right Now," *Small Business Trends,* accessed July 14, 2018, http://smallbusinesstrends.com.

[44] eMarketer Report, "US Time Spent with Media: eMarketer's Updated Estimates for 2017," *eMarketer*, http://emarketer.com, accessed July 14, 2018.

[45] Paul Sawers, "LinkedIn Passes 500 Million Member Milestone," *Venture Beat,* http://venturebeat.com, accessed July 14, 2018; Salman Aslam, "Linkedin by the Numbers: Stats, Demographics & Fun Facts," *Omnicore*, http://www.omnicoreagency.com, accessed July 14, 2018; company website, "Recruiter," http://business.linkedin.com, accessed July 14, 2018; company website, "LinkedIn Pulse," http://www.linkedin.com, accessed July 14, 2018.

[46] Mike Moriarty, Jodie Kassak, and Eric Peterson, "Emerging Market Retailing in 2030: Future Scenarios and the $5.5 Trillion Swing," *ATKearney*, http://www.atkearney.com, accessed July 16, 2018.

[47] "Internet World Users by Language," *Internet World Stats*, http://www.worldinternetstats.com, accessed July 14, 2018.

[48] Jess Kirkwood, "11 Powerful Examples of Responsive Web Design," *inBlog*, http://www.invisionapp.com, accessed July 14, 2018.

[49] Company website, www.stopandshop.com, accessed July 14, 2018.

[50] Brian Rigney, "E-Commerce Innovation Through Content That Converts," *TotalRetail*, http://www.mytotalretail.com, accessed July 14, 2018.

[51] Karola Karlson, "8 Ways Intelligent Marketers Use Artificial Intelligence," *Content Marketing Institute,* http://contentmarketinginstitute.com, accessed July 16, 2018.

[52] Laura Forer, "The Lowdown on Social Media Influencers," *MarketingProf*, http://marketingprof.com, accessed July 14, 2018; Ellevate, "Why Influencer Marketing Is Essential for Any Brand to Grow," *Forbes*, http://www.forbes.com, accessed July 14, 2018.

[53] Karla Cook, "10 Influencer Marketing Campaigns to Inspire and Get You Started with Your Own," *HubSpot Blog*, http://blog.hubspot.com, accessed July 14, 2018.

[54] Sunny Dhillon, "The Rise of Experiential Commerce," *TechCrunch*, http://techcrunch.com, accessed July 16, 2018.

[55] Dan Shewan, "7 Ecommerce Trends You Can't Ignore in 2018," *The WorldStream Blog*, http://www.wordstream.com, accessed July 16, 2018; John Hall, "7 E-Commerce Trends to Pay Attention to in 2018," *Forbes*, http://forbes.com, accessed July 16, 2018; Caroline Forsey, "10 E-Commerce Trends to Expect in 2018," *HubSpot*, http://hubspot.com, accessed July 16, 2018.

[56] Ibid.

[57] Ibid.

Appendix A

[1] Nathan Bomey, "5 Reasons Toys R Us Failed to Survive Bankruptcy," *USA Today*, http://usatoday.com, accessed July 17, 2018; Michael Corkery, "At Toys 'R' Us, a $200 Million Debt Problem Could Lead to $348 Million in Fees," *New York Times,* http://nytimes.com, accessed July 17, 2018; Susan Berfield, Eliza Ronalds-Hannon, Matthew Townsend, and Lauren Coleman-Lochner, "Tears 'R' Us: The World's Biggest Toy Store Didn't Have to Die," *Bloomberg*, http://bloomberg.com, accessed July 17, 2018.

[2] Joe Patrice, "Top 10 Frivolous Lawsuits List Is . . . Frivolous, But Funny," *Above the Law*, http://abovethelaw.com, accessed July 17, 2018.

[3] Organization website, "All States Have Silly Laws," http://foodstamp.aphsa.org, accessed July 17, 2018.

[4] Government website, "United States Court of Appeals for the Fourth Circuit," http://www.ca4.uscourts.gov, accessed July 17, 2018.

[5] Government website, "The Justices' Caseload," Supreme Court of the United States, http://www.supremecourt.gov, accessed July 17, 2018.

[6] David Ferris, "5 Years after Crisis, U.S. Remains Dependent on China's Rare Earth Elements," *E&E Publishing,* http://www.eenews.net, accessed July 17, 2018; Robin Bromby, "China Rare Earth Minerals Exports on the Rise," *Investor Intel,* http://investorintel.com, accessed July 17, 2018; Cecilia Jamasmie, "China Gets Tougher on Illegal Mining, Exporting of Rare Earths," *Mining.com,* http://mining.com, accessed July 17, 2018; Matthew Dalton and William Mauldin, "WTO Confirms China Loses Rare-Earths Case," *The Wall Street Journal*, http://www.wsj.com, accessed July 17, 2018; Shawn Donnan, "WTO Rules Against China on 'Rare Earths' Export Restrictions," *Financial Times,* http://www.ft.com, accessed July 17, 2018; Keith Bradsher, "Trade Issues with China Flare Anew," *The New York Times*, http://www.nytimes.com, accessed July 17, 2018; Stephanie Ginter,

"WTO Lawsuit over China's Rare Earth," *Energy & Capital,* http://www.energyandcapital.com, accessed July 17, 2018.

[7] Peter J. Henning, "High-Frequency Trading Falls in the Cracks of Criminal Law," *The New York Times,* http://www.nytimes.com, accessed July 17, 2018; "FBI to Probe High-Frequency Stock Trading," *CBS News*, http://www.cbsnews.com, accessed July 17, 2018; John Markoff, "Time Split to the Nanosecond Is Precisely What Wall Street Wants," *New York Times*, http://nytimes.com, accessed July 17, 2018.

[8] "U.S. v. Microsoft: Timeline," *Wired,* http://www.wired.com, accessed July 17, 2018.

[9] Government website, "U.S.A. Patriot Act: Preserving Life and Liberty," https://www.justice.gov, accessed July 17, 2018; Charlie Savage, "Deal Reached on Extension of Patriot Act," *The New York Times,* http://www.nytimes.com, accessed July 17, 2018; Gail Russell Chaddock, "Patriot Act: Three Controversial Provisions That Congress Voted to Keep," *Christian Science Monitor,* http://www.csmonitor.com, accessed July 17, 2018.

[10] Keith Collins, "Net Neutrality Has Officially Been Repealed. Here's How That Could Affect You," *New York Times*, http://nytimes.com, accessed July 17, 2018; Clint Finley, "The Wired Guide to Net Neutrality," *Wired*, http://wired.com, accessed July 17, 2018; Marguerite Reardon, "13 Things You Need to Know about the FCC's Net Neutrality Regulation," *CNET*, http://www.cnet.com, accessed July 17, 2018; Brendan Sasso, "FCC Moves to Revive Net-Neutrality Rules," *National Journal*, http://www.nationaljournal.com, accessed July 17, 2018; Rob Pegoraro, "Court Cuts FCC's Net-Neutrality Power; Now What?" *The Washington Post,* http://voices.washingtonpost.com, accessed July 17, 2018.

[11] Government website, "U.S. Senate Committee on Banking, House, and Urban Affairs, Brief Summary of the Dodd-Frank Wall Street Reform and Consumer Protection Act," http://www.cpsc.gov, accessed July 17, 2018.

[12] Government website, "Food and Drug Administration Amendments Act (FDAAA) of 2007," http://www.fda.gov, accessed July 17, 2018.

[13] Government website, "FDA Warns More Companies to Stop Misleading Kids with E-Liquids That Resemble Kid-Friendly Foods As Part of Youth Tobacco Prevention Plan," http://fda.gov, accessed July 17, 2018; Lydia Zuraw, "FDA Seeks Input on Reportable Food Registry Amendments," *Food Safety News,* http://www.foodsafetynews.com, accessed July 17, 2018.

[14] Jennifer Calfas, "How These Major Companies Are Getting Equal Pay Right," *Fortune*, accessed July 17, 2018, http://fortune.com; government website, "Notice Concerning the Lilly Ledbetter Fair Pay Act of 2009," U.S. Equal Employment Opportunity Commission, http://www.eeoc.gov, accessed July 17, 2018.

[15] "Google Supports YouTube for Copyright Battles—Daly City Tech Part," *Daily Star Albany*, http://www.albanydailystar.com, accessed July 17, 2018; Callum Borchers, "7 Takeaways from Mark Zuckerberg's Marathon Congressional Testimony," *Washington Post*, http://washingtonpost.com, accessed July 17, 2018.

[16] Kelly Kunsch, "Commercial Law and the Uniform Code," Seattle University School of Law, http://lawlibguides.seattleu.edu, accessed July 17, 2018.

[17] Scott Streater and Charles V. Bagli, "Court Upholds Columbia Campus Expansion Plan," *The New York Times*, http://www.nytimes.com, accessed July 17, 2018.

[18] "Owner Says He'll Fight to Save Historic Building After Eminent Domain Vote," *WOWT News*, http://wowt.com, accessed July 17, 2018.

[19] Toby Melville, "Small Pharma Defeats Big Pharma in Trademark Dispute," *The Times*, https://www.thetimes.co.uk, accessed July 17, 2018.

[20] Company website, "Patent Reform Act of 2011: An Overview," *Patently-O,* http://www.patentlyo.com, accessed July 17, 2018.

[21] Christine Mai-Duc, "All the 'Happy Birthday' Song Copyright Claims Are Invalid, Federal Judge Rules," *Los Angeles Times,* http://www.latimes.com, accessed July 17, 2018.

[22] Melissa J. Lauritch, "New Wisconsin Law in Toxic Tort Litigation," *Martindale.com,* http://www.martindale.com, accessed July 17, 2018.

[23] Government website, "Recalls by Product," http://www.cpsc.gov, accessed July 17, 2018.

[24] Evan Grossman, "Judge Denies Class-Action Status for NHL Concussion Lawsuit," *New York Daily News,* http://www.nydailynews.com, accessed July 17, 2018.

[25] Government website, "Total Bankruptcy Filings Decline in Calendar Year 2017," https://www.acainternational.org, accessed July 17, 2018.

[26] Barbara Farfan, "General Motors Chapter 11 Bankruptcy: U.S. Business History's 4th Largest," *Retail Industry*, http://retailindustry.about.com, accessed July 17, 2018.

Appendix B

Driverless Cars Will Change Auto Insurance. Here's How Insurers Can Adapt

[1] John Cusano and Michael Costonis, "Driverless Cars Will Change Auto Insurance. Here's How Insurers Can Adapt," *Harvard Business Review*, http://hbr.org, accessed July 17, 2018; Alyssa Pei, Shamik Lala, Neeti Bhardwaj, Joseph Reifel, and Mike Hales, "The Connected Car: From Threat to Opportunity," *Property Casualty 360,* http://www.propertycasualty360.com, accessed July 17, 2018; Mahbubul Alam, "The Top Five Trends for the Connected Car in 2016," *Tech Crunch*, http://techcrunch.com, accessed July 17, 2018; Nigel Walsh, "Connected Cars Drive Insurers to Rethink Coverage Issues," *Property Casualty 360,* http://www.propertycasualty360.com, accessed July 17, 2018; Tanguy Catlin, Johannes-Tobias Lorenz, Björn Münstermann, Braad Olesen, and Valentino Ricciardi, "Insurtech—The Threat That Inspires," *McKinsey & Company Financial Services*, https://www.mckinsey.com, accessed July 22, 2018.

[2] Organization website, "Facts + Statistics: Homeowners and Renters Insurance," *Insurance Information Institute*, https://www.iii.org, accessed July 17, 2018.

[3] Colin Lalley, "How Genetic Testing Can Affect Your Life Insurance Rates," *Policy Genius*, http://policygenius.com, accessed July 18, 2018; Christina Farr, "If You Want Life Insurance, Think Twice Before Getting a Genetic Test," *Fast Company*, http://fastcompany.com, accessed July 18, 2018.

[4] "Home Buyers Insurance Checklist," *Insurance Information Institute,* http://www.iii.org, accessed July 17, 2018; Les Masterson, "Average Homeowners Insurance Rates by State," *Value Penguin*, https://www.insurance.com, accessed July 18, 2018.

[5] Organization website, "Average Car Insurance Rates," http://www.dmv.org, accessed July 17, 2018.

[6] Company website, "Insurance Requirements," http://cdn.corporate.walmart.com, accessed July 17, 2018.

[7] Amy Goldstein and Juliet Eilperin, "Affordable Care Act," http://www.dol.gov, accessed July 17, 2018; government website, "About the Law," http://www.hhs.gov, accessed July 17, 2018; Kimberly Amadeo, "2010 Patient Protection & Affordable Care Act Summary," *The Balance,* https://www.thebalance.com, accessed July 22, 2018.

[8] Shelby Livingston, "United Health Revenue Cracks $200 Billion Mark," *Modern Healthcare*, http://www.modernhealthcare.com, accessed July 18, 2018.

[9] *ACLI Life Insurers Fact Book 2017,* "Assets," http://www.acli.com, accessed July 17, 2018.

Appendix C

[1] Tom Anderson, "How Much Do You Really Need for Retirement?" *CNBC*, http://www.cnbc.com, accessed July 22, 2018; Alexandra Mondalek, "Millennials Are Outpacing Everyone in Retirement Savings," *Money*, http://time.com, accessed July 22, 2018; Jeff Rose, "30 Financial Rules That Every 30 Year-Old Should Know (or Risk Going Broke)," *Good Financial Cents,* http://www.goodfinancialcents.com, accessed July 22, 2018; Jinnie Regli, "Retirement Planning: 12 Practical Tips for Millennials," *Milliman Insights,* http://www.milliman.com, accessed July 22, 2018.

[2] Government website, "State Personal Income 2017," http://www.bea.gov, accessed July 22, 2018.

[3] Alison Doyle, "How Often Do People Change Jobs?" *The Balance Careers*, https://www.thebalancecareers.com, accessed July 23, 2018; Stephen Miller, "More Workers Plan to Postpone Retirement, If They Can," *Society for Human Resource Management*, https://www.shrm.org, accessed July 22, 2018.

[4] American Bankruptcy Institute, "Quarterly Non-Business Filings by Chapter," http://news.abi.org, accessed July 22, 2018; Diane Davis, "Bankruptcy Filings at Historic Lows But Expected to Rise," *Bloomberg Law,* https://www.bna.com, accessed July 23, 2018.

[5] "Consumer Credit," *Federal Reserve Statistical Release G.19,* May 2018, http://federalreserve.gov, accessed July 22, 2018.

[6] "The Average American Is in Credit Card Debt, No Matter the Economy," *Money*, http://time.com, accessed July 22, 2018.

[7] Matthew Frankel, "How Much Does the Average American Pay in Taxes?" *The Motley Fool,* http://motleyfool.org, accessed July 22, 2018.

[8] Sandra Block, "9 States with No Income Tax," *Kiplinger*, http://kiplinger.com, accessed July 23, 2018.

[9] "Average New-Car Prices Rise Nearly 4 Percent For January 2018 On Shifting Sales Mix, According to Kelley Blue Book," *Kelley Blue Book*, https://mediaroom.kbb.com, accessed July 23, 2018.

[10] Tara Siegal Bernard, "To Buy or Rent a Home? Weighing Which Is Better?" *The New York Times*, http://www.nytimes.com, accessed July 22, 2018; Heather Long, "Not Buying a Home Was My Smartest Financial Move," *CNN Money,* http://money.cnn.com, accessed July 22, 2018.

[11] "How Much Will You Spend Over Your Lifetime on Car Insurance?" *TCI Insurance,* https://www.tciteam.com, accessed July 22, 2018.

Appendix D

[1] Organization website, "MIT $100K Overview," http://www.mit100k.org, accessed April 18, 2018; company website, http://www.bizplancompetitions.com, accessed July 31, 2018, organization website, "5 Reasons to Enter a Business Plan Competition," http://www.bizplancompetitions.com, accessed July 31, 2018; Michelle Goodman, "Crash Course in Business Plan Competitions," *Inc.,* http://www.inc.com, accessed July 31, 2018.

Appendix E

[1] U.S. Census Bureau, "Table P-32. Educational Attainment—Full-Time, Year-Round Workers 18 Years Old and Over by Mean Earnings, Age, and Sex: 1991 to 2017," *Current Population Reports,* http://www.census.gov, accessed July 10, 2018; Nikki Graf, Anna Brown and Eileen Patten, "The Narrowing, but Persistent, Gender Gap in Pay," *PewResearch*, http://www.pewresearch.org, accessed July 10, 2018.

[2] Dan Butcher, "Everything You Need to Know to Land a Coveted KPMG Internship in the U.S.," *eFinancial Careers*, https://news.efinancialcareers.com, accessed July 10, 2018.

[3] Organization website, "The Cooperative Education Model," http://www.co-op.edu, accessed July 10, 2018; organization website, "Welcome to CEIA," http://www.ceiainc.org, accessed July 10, 2018.

[4] "Take Our Career Aptitude Test!" *Career Explorer*, http://www.careerexplorer.net, accessed July 10, 2018; "Free Career Test!" *Live Career,* www.livecareer.com, accessed July 10, 2018; "Assessing Your Skills," *Monster,* http://career-advice.monster.com, accessed July 10, 2018; organization site, https://www.onetonline.org, accessed July 10, 2018.

[5] Company website, "About," http://www.michelefoods.com, accessed July 10, 2018.

[6] Liz Ryan, "Ten Ways to Use LinkedIn in Your Job Search," *Forbes*, http://www.forbes.com, accessed July 10, 2018.

[7] Ken Yeung, "LinkedIn's Newest App Helps College Grads Find Jobs," *Venture Beat*, http://venturebeat.com, accessed July 10, 2018.

[8] Matt Kapko, "Is LinkedIn Killing the Traditional Resume?" *CIO*, http://www.cio.com, accessed July 10, 2018; Jessica Holbrook Hernandez, "Does Your LinkedIn Profile Serve as a Good Resume Supplement?" *Career Realism*, http://www.careerealism.com, accessed July 10, 2018.

[9] "Chronological Resume: The Preferred Resume Layout," *Top Sales Jobs*, http://www.topsalesjobs.com, accessed July 10, 2018.

[10] Kim Isaacs, "Five Resume Tips for College Students," *Monster.com*, http://www.monster.com, accessed July 10, 2018; Michael Murray, "Five Resume Tips for College Students," *The Student Development Company*, http://www.thestudentdevelopment.com, accessed July 10, 2018.

[11] Eugene Volokh, "How to Write a Great Cover Letter: Top 7 Tips," *Opposing Views*, http://www.opposingviews.com, accessed July 10, 2018; "Here's an Example of a Great Cover Letter," *Ask a Manager*, http://www.askamanager.com, accessed July 10, 2018.

[12] Stephanie Vozza, "Cover Letters Are Dead: Do This Instead," *Fast Company*, http://www.fastcompany.com, accessed July 10, 2018; Catey Hill, "The Cover Letter is Dead," *New York Post*, https://nypost.com, accessed July 10, 2018.

[13] Debra Wheatman, "5 Tricks to Get Noticed When Submitting a Resume Online," *GlassDoor.com*, http://www.glassdoor.com, accessed July 10, 2018; Pattie Hunt Sinacole, "Tips on Sending a Resume via Email," *Boston.com*, http://www.boston.com, accessed July 10, 2018.

[14] Carole Martin, "Ten Tips to Boost Your Interview Skills," *Monster.com*, http://career-advice.monster.com, accessed July 10, 2018.

[15] Rob Taub, "How to Answer Tough Interview Questions Correctly," *Career Realism*, http://www.careerrealism.com, accessed July 10, 2018.

[16] U.S. Bureau of Labor Statistics, "Labor Force Projections to 2024: The Labor Force Is Growing, But Slowly," *Monthly Labor Review*, http://www.bls.gov, accessed July 10, 2018; Nick Timiraos, "Hispanics Could Account for 40% of U.S. Job Growth by 2020," *The Wall Street Journal*, http://blogs.wsj.com, accessed July 10, 2018.

[17] Ibid.

[18] Ibid.

[19] Ibid.

[20] Organization website, "College Hiring Projected to Increase by 4 Percent in Strengthening Market," National Association of Colleges and Employers, http://www.naceweb.org, accessed July 10, 2018.

Appendix F

After Chapter 4

End of Part 1: Launching Your Global Business and Economics Career

[1] Government website, "Professional and Business Services," *Occupational Outlook Handbook 2018–2019*, http://www.bls.gov, accessed July 8, 2018; Emily Richards, "Occupational Employment Projections to 2022," *Monthly Labor Review Online,* http://www.bls.gov, accessed July 8, 2018.

[2] Government website, "Economists," *Occupational Outlook Handbook 2018–2019,* http://www.bls.gov, accessed July 8, 2018.

[3] "Character Traits of an Excellent Expat," *Defining Moves,* http://www.definingmoves.com, accessed July 8, 2018.

After Chapter 6

[End of Part 2: Launching Your Entrepreneurial Career—Notes]

[4] Small Business Association website, http://www.sba.gov, accessed July 8, 2018.

[5] U.S. Bureau of Labor Statistics, "Employment Projections: 2010–2020 Summary," press release, http://www.bls.gov, accessed July 8, 2018; U.S. Bureau of Labor Statistics, "Medical and Health Services Managers," http://www.bls.gov, accessed June 12, 2018.

[6] Alex Salkever, "The Furniture Company Wanted to Sell Him Its Buildings—and Close Down. Should He Buy the Company, Too?" *Inc.,* http://www.inc.com, accessed July 8, 2018.

[7] U.S. Bureau of Labor Statistics, "Industries with the Fastest Growing and Most Rapidly Declining Wage and Salary Employment," http://data.bls.gov, accessed July 8, 2018.

After Chapter 10

Part 3 Launching Your Management Career

[8] Government website, "Management Occupations, http://www.bls.gov, accessed July 9, 2018.

[9] Salary data in this section is taken from U.S. Bureau of Labor Statistics, "Occupational Employment Statistics—Management Occupations," *Occupational Outlook Handbook,* 2018–19 Edition, http://www.bls.gov, accessed July 9, 2018.

After Chapter 13

Part 4: Launching Your Marketing Career

[10] Government website, "Sales Occupations," *Occupational Outlook Handbook,* 2018–19 Edition, http://www.bls.gov, accessed July 9, 2018.

[11] Government website, "Public Relations Specialists," *Occupational Outlook Handbook,* 2018–19 Edition, http://www.bls.gov, accessed July 9, 2018.

[12] Government website, "NAICS 541800—Advertising, Public Relations, and Related Services," http://www.bls.gov, accessed July 9, 2018.

After Chapter 14

Part 5: Launching Your Information Technology Career

[13] Government website, "Computer and Information Technology Occupations," and "Computer and Information Systems Managers," *Occupational Outlook Handbook,* 2018–19 Edition, http://www.bls.gov, accessed July 9, 2018.

[14] Susannah Snider, "The Best Jobs of 2018," *U.S. News and World Report,* http://www.money.usnews.com, accessed July 9, 2018.

Part 6 Launching Your Finance Career

[15] Government website, "Business and Finance Occupations," *Occupational Outlook Handbook,* 2018–19 Edition, http://www.bls.gov, accessed July 9, 2018.

[16] Government website, "Business and Finance: Financial Analysts," *Occupational Outlook Handbook,* 2018–19 Edition, http://www.bls.gov, accessed July 9, 2018.

[17] Government website, "Financial Managers," *Occupational Outlook Handbook,* 2018–2019 Edition, http://www.bls.gov, accessed July 9, 2018.

Name Index

Subject Index

*Entries in **bold** refer to the "Business Terms You Need to Know," which are listed at the end of each chapter.*

C

D

F

G